The Growing Child

The Growing Child
An Applied Approach

Second Edition

Helen Bee

LONGMAN

An imprint of Addison Wesley Longman, Inc.

New York • Reading, Massachusetts • Menlo Park, California • Harlow, England
Don Mills, Ontario • Sydney • Mexico City • Madrid • Amsterdam

Editor-in-Chief: **Priscilla McGeehon**
Executive Editor: **Becky Dudley**
Development Editor: **Becky Kohn**
Supplements Editor: **Cyndy Taylor**
Marketing Manager: **Anne Wise**
Project Manager: **Bob Ginsberg**
Design Manager and Text and Cover Designer: **John Callahan**
Cover Photo: **Camille Takerud, Tony Stone Images**
Art Studio: **ElectraGraphics**
Photo Researcher: **Rosemary Hunter**
Prepress Services Supervisor: **Valerie A. Vargas**
Electronic Production Specialist: **Joanne Del Ben**
Print Buyer: **Denise Sandler**
Printer and Binder: **World Color Book Services**
Cover Printer: **Lehigh Press, Inc.**

For permission to use copyrighted material, grateful acknowledgment is made to the copyright holders on page 582, which is hereby made part of this copyright page.

Library of Congress Cataloging-in-Publication Data

Bee, Helen L., date,
    The growing child, an applied approach / Helen Bee.—2nd ed.
        p.   cm.
    Previous ed. published in 1995.
    Includes bibliographical references and index.
    ISBN 0-321-01346-8
    1. Child development.   I. Title.
    HQ767.9.B43 1998
    305.231—dc21   97-45180
        CIP

Please visit our website at http://longman.awl.com

ISBN 0-321-01346-8

12345678910—RNV—01009998

To my sister Carol,
whose journey through childhood and adulthood
has been so different from my own

Brief Contents

Contents

4
Physical Development and Health in Infancy and Toddlerhood   *112*

5 Perceptual and Cognitive Development in Infancy and Toddlerhood   *144*

6 **Social and Personality Development in Infancy and Toddlerhood**   *178*

Interlude Two: **Summing Up Preschool Development**

10 Physical Development and Health at School Age   *326*

14 Cognitive Development in Adolescence   *452*

Interlude Four: **Summing Up Development in Adolescence**

A Summary of Boxes

Social Policy Debates

Cultures and Contexts

Psychology in Action

To the Instructor

Those of you who choose a chronological rather than a topical organization for your child development classes do so for many different reasons. For some of you, the key argument is that only a chronological approach can make clear the interlocking aspects of the child's development. For others, the most convincing reason for selecting a chronological organization is that many of your students are planning careers working with children of some particular age—infants, toddlers, or school-age. These students are not going to have careers studying some aspect of children's development; rather, they will be working with the whole child, and they will need information about all aspects of children of particular ages. For such students, a chronological approach—especially one with a strong applied slant—is clearly the most valuable. This text is designed quite specifically to satisfy these several reasons for choosing a chronological organization. It addresses the integration of information about each age not only through a basic chronological organization, but through the summarizing "interludes" at the end of each age section. At the same time, it addresses the practical needs of your students through extensive use of applied examples. This, then, is not just a topical text with the furniture rearranged; it is a genuinely chronological text, designed to meet the special needs of those who choose that organization.

In planning this second edition, I was guided by five major objectives: (1) to **actively engage the student** in as many ways as possible; (2) to make it clear that child development research is **relevant to the real world**; (3) to provide a **strong founda-tion of biological coverage,** including discussions of children's health; (4) to **forge connections among biological, cognitive, and social aspects of development;** and (5) to continue to provide **solid coverage of classic and current theory and research.**

Actively Engaging the Student

If a text is scientifically sound but does not engage the student, you've lost half the battle. I have made every effort to catch and maintain the student's interest through a variety of means:

- *An informal, personal narrative style.* This edition, like all my texts, is written in the first person, as if it were a conversation with the student. Students report that they enjoy reading the text—surely the first hurdle.
- *Opening Chapter 1 with practical questions.* In an effort to capture the student's interest from the very first word, I have opened the first chapter of this edition with a series of practical questions, to illustrate the kind of real-life questions that can be or have been answered by research on human development.
- *Preview Questions.* Each chapter begins with a set of preview questions designed specifically to catch the student's interest. Sometimes these questions relate to practical applications of the chapter topic; sometimes they are deliberately intended to catch the student out, by asking a question the student may think has an obvious

answer, but where the answer turns out to be more complex or exactly the opposite of what he or she might think.

- *Critical Thinking Questions.* As in the first edition, this edition includes **critical thinking questions** in every chapter that are designed to encourage the students to ponder, analyze, and think more creatively. These questions ask the student to pause and consider a particular point before going on. Often they ask the reader to consider how the material may apply to his or her own life. In other cases, they ask the student to think about how one could design a piece of research to answer a particular question. Sometimes they ask theoretical questions, or ask the student to analyze her or his own point of view or feelings on the subject at issue. These questions may be useful for provoking class discussion; it is also my hope that they will make the reading process more active and thus make learning deeper. They may also help the student to gain greater skill in the important process of critical thinking—learning how to think about and evaluate his or her own feelings, thoughts, and behavior so as to clarify and improve them.

- *Psychology in Action boxes.* A set of 11 *Psychology in Action* boxes give instructions for various projects in which students can observe or test children directly or investigate some aspect of children's environments. Four of the 11 boxes in this group describe projects that students could carry out without your needing to go through a Human Subjects review; the other seven would all need to be cleared with your school's review committee. All these projects will involve students in observing children or testing hypotheses; all will introduce your students to some aspect of the scientific process.

- *Social Policy Debate boxes.* Sprinkled through the book are seven *Social Policy Debate* boxes, each exploring some highly practical—but complex and difficult—question facing policymakers for which human development research is relevant. For example: Should the government play an active role in increasing the intake of folic acid by pregnant women (in Chapter 3)? What kind of school feeding programs most benefit children's intellectual and physical development (Chapter 10)? In each of these boxes I have tried to raise both sides of the various

controversies so that students can see just how difficult it can be to create widely acceptable and scientifically backed social policy about children.

Child Development in the Real World

Because practical, real-world applications of basic knowledge are inherently interesting to most students, this goal obviously overlaps with the aim of engaging the student. But there are several features of this edition that are focused specifically on this theme, including:

- *Parenting and Teaching boxes.* Each chapter includes at least one box in which the various research findings are translated into quite specific advice to parents or teachers. For example, a new box in Chapter 5, "What Can You Do to Give a Baby the Best Intellectual Start?", gives four specific pieces of advice to a parent or day-care worker. Similarly, a *Parenting* box in Chapter 9, "Rearing Helpful and Altruistic Children," lists (and explains) six strategies for fostering helpful, generous behavior in children. A second box in the same chapter provides advice on how to soften the effects of divorce. These boxes are designed not only to be immediately helpful to those of your students who are, or soon will be, working directly with children; they are also intended to illustrate the ways in which basic information can be translated into practical action.

- *Cultures and Contexts boxes.* Because the real world contains children from myriad cultures (and because many of your students will be caring for and teaching children from a rich array of ethnic and cultural backgrounds), it is important to keep emphasizing all the ways in which development is independent of culture, and the ways in which it is shaped by culture. Discussion of such cultural commonalities and variations is included in the main body of the text throughout; specific examples are highlighted in 19 *Cultures and Contexts* boxes.

- *Applied examples throughout.* In this edition, I have tried always to address the question "Why is this important?" by giving a great many practical examples, making clear how specific theories or research is useful or applicable to the tasks of a day-care worker, a parent, a nurse, or a teacher. For example, how are children affected by the type of discipline they receive? What are the consequences of spanking children? Is this ever a good practice? Answers to all such questions are naturally of interest to psychologists and psychology majors as well as to those who will have careers working with children, but the latter groups are especially in need of information of this kind.

Strong Foundation of Biological Coverage

Students who are planning careers working with children need to have extensive information about children's physical development as well as their emotional and cognitive development. They need to be able to spot possible illnesses or physical problems, to be knowledgeable about such things as recommended immunization schedules, optimum diets, or when to begin solid food in infancy, so as to be able to provide appropriate physical care or advise parents about such care. In addition, of course, any student of human development needs to explore our new and growing knowledge about the genetic, neurological, and hormonal foundations of behavior. This edition addresses these needs in several ways:

- *Two new chapters on physical development.* Each set of age-related chapters now includes a full chapter on physical development and health, and the two previously existing chapters on this topic have been expanded, collectively extending the coverage of these topics by 50 or more pages in this edition. Among the topics added are sleeping arrangements in infancy and their effects, as well as sleep problems in preschool (Chapters 4 and 7); significant chronic childhood illnesses, such as otitis media and asthma (Chapters 4 and 7); cross-cultural comparisons of infant and childhood mortality rates and health patterns (Chapters 4 and 7); good and bad health habits at each

age, including discussion of how to promote better health habits among children (Chapters 4, 7, 10, and 13); children's dietary needs and the effects of poor diets (Chapters 7, 10); physical fitness and exercise (Chapter 10); child abuse and neglect and its effects, both physical and psychological (Chapter 7); the relationship between poverty and health (Chapter 10); sexually transmitted diseases (Chapter 13); risky behavior among adolescents (Chapter 13).

- *Added coverage of new, basic research on genetics and neurological development.* I have strengthened and expanded discussions of the biological aspects of development throughout, since this is a burgeoning and highly fruitful current area of research and theorizing. You will see this new emphasis in a considerably expanded discussion of behavior genetics in Chapter 1, in an expanded discussion of synaptogenesis, dendrite formation, and pruning in the development of the nervous system (Chapters 3 and 4), as well as in the new chapters on physical development.

Integration of Biological, Cognitive, and Social Development

Even in a chronologically organized text, it is often difficult to trace the many ways in which the child's biological, cognitive, and social development are linked to one another. Because our research is typically organized around specific aspects of development (rather than around children of specific ages), we tend to describe the research the same way. So we lecture on language development in infancy, and then object permanence in infancy, and then attachment—struggling always to find ways to link up the several threads. Naturally, I have tried to create such linkages in every chapter whenever that seemed possible. I have also addressed this problem directly with a series of *Interludes*, capping each set of age-linked chapters. In each interlude I have quite specifically asked how all the different threads weave together, and what internal and external factors appear to be the most critical causal elements in shaping the child's development in that age period.

Solid Coverage of Research and Theory

You may well think that by adding all those applications, along with the extra chapters on physical development and health, I must necessarily have sacrificed basic discussions of theory and research. Not true. I have *added* applications and coverage of physical development, but I have not omitted any of the discussions of basic research or theory. Even if most of the students in your courses are unlikely to go on for graduate study in child development or even to major in psychology, they still need a strong grounding in the research on which practical applications are based; they need a grasp of theory as an aid in organizing information and their own thinking. My goal, in this book as in all of my texts, is to make the basic research and theory both interesting and comprehensible.

- *Research Report boxes.* Research findings are not only described and discussed in the main body of the text, they are also highlighted in a series of 36 *Research Report* boxes—the most common type of box in the text. Every chapter has at least one, most have two or more. Each of these boxes discusses either a single research study or a body of research on a specific topic. They are designed to illustrate the ways in which social scientists go about trying to answer basic or applied questions.
- *Updating.* Naturally, the research discussions and references cited have also been updated throughout. I have sometimes chosen to continue to include discussion of an older study when it has become a classic, or when it is still the best example to be found, but in most cases I have searched for the most current examples I can find, not only in the text but in the tables and figures. Forty-two of the figures are either totally new or updated with recent data.

What's New in This Edition

Some of what is new in this edition will be obvious from what I've already said, but let me highlight a few of the new features briefly.

New Chapters on Physical Development and Health

Two entirely new chapters have been added, bringing to four the number of chapters covering physical development and health. Particular new emphasis has been given to gross and fine motor skill development in the preschool and early elementary school years, to patterns of normal physical growth at each age, and to health—both disease and positive health habits.

Stronger Applications for Parents, Child-Care Workers, and Teachers

This change is evident not only in the new *Parenting/Teaching* boxes, but in the text of every chapter.

Strengthened Emphasis on Culture

In the first edition, one of my primary goals was to infuse the entire book with a multicultural or cross-cultural flavor—to search for those basic developmental processes that are the same across cultures, and to try to understand the ways in which culture and subculture shape an individual child's development. In this edition I have tried to add to this process, such as by introducing the contrast between cultural *individualism* and *collectivism*. I have introduced this distinction in Chapter 1, in an expanded introduction to the concept of culture, and have then carried the concepts through the book. The list of *Cultures and Contexts* boxes has also been expanded to a total of 19 in this edition. An example of a new box in this group is "Sleeping Arrangements for Infants" (Chapter 4), which compares the typical individualist-cultural practice of separate sleeping with the common collectivist-cultural system of cosleeping with parents. Another example: A box on "China's One-Child Policy," in Chapter 9, describes this policy and its several consequences.

Ethnic Group Labels. Throughout the discussions of cultural similarities and differences, I also struggled, as do all social scientists, with the problem of terminology and labels for various cultural and ethnic groups. Should one use *black* or *African-American*? Should one say *Hispanic* or *Latino*? And how should one label the dominant white cultural group: *white*, *Caucasian*, *Anglo*, or *Euro-American*? Some authors have resolved the dilemma by choosing one label from each set and then using those labels consistently. I have rejected that solution because there just seems to me to be still too much flux, too much variability of usage by members of these groups as well as by social scientists and other writers. I have opted instead for a less elegant solution that I think better reflects current usage: I have used all of the alternative terms at various times, as the occasion seemed to demand. For example, when I report results from the Census Bureau's wide-ranging surveys, I typically use the terms *white* and *black*, because these are the labels the Census Bureau uses; when I talk about studies of Hispanic children, I have generally used the word *Anglo* to refer to the contrasting white culture, because this is the term most often used by Hispanics themselves. And when I need to emphasize the European origin of the dominant white culture in the United States, I have used the term *Euro-American*, especially in contrast to other hyphenated American groups, such as African-American or Asian-American. Sometimes, I confess, I have used the briefer terms simply because the repeated use of hyphenated labels becomes cumbersome.

New Topics and Themes

New topics have also been added, the coverage of other topics expanded, primarily in response to requests from those of you who used the first edition and asked for specific additions. Some illustrations:

Vygotsky's Theory. At the urging of a variety of reviewers, I have added Vygotsky's theory to Chapter 2 and have included some of his ideas in later chapters, particularly Chapter 11. Application of his theory to teaching is also covered in a new *Teaching* box in that chapter.

Siegler's Model of Variability in Thinking. Robert Siegler's new model of cognitive development is given prominent space in Chapter 11, replacing the discussion of Siegler's earlier work on rule development.

Current Research on Day-Care Effects. The results of the Early Child Care Research Network study—

the very best current information, based on a nationwide collaborative study—is now included in Chapter 6.

Expanded Discussion of Sibling Relationships. A new *Research Report* on sibling relationships in middle childhood has been added to the coverage of this topic.

Relational Aggression. New work by Crick and others on relational aggression in elementary school children is now included in Chapter 12.

Increased Coverage of Emotion. The discussion of emotion has been expanded in a number of chapters:

- Discrimination of others' emotions in infancy: Chapter 5
- The emergence of the infant's own repertoire of emotional expressions: Chapter 6
- An expanded discussion of "reading" others' emotions, exploring the link between such an ability and the emerging theory of mind: Chapter 8. In this same chapter I have also added a discussion of the child's emerging ability to regulate her own emotions.
- A new discussion of emotion regulation: Chapter 7
- An expanded discussion of the child's own expression of emotion: Chapter 10
- A discussion of both the universality and cultural variations in emotional expression: Chapter 12

Expanded Photo Program. For this edition, we have also considerably expanded the number of photos and replaced many of the photos used in the first edition. Over 100 of the photos are new for this book, including a number of photo displays to illustrate important points such as infant reflexes and motor skills in the preschool years.

Pedagogy

This edition maintains many of the same pedagogical features present in the first edition, including **end-of-chapter summaries, boldfaced key terms** defined in the glossary, **critical thinking questions,** an **annotated list of suggested readings,** the **interludes,** and several types of **boxes** (*Research Reports, Cultures and Contexts*). New pedagogical features include:

- *Preview Questions* at the beginning of each chapter
- *Three new kinds of boxes*: Parenting/Teaching, Social Policy Debate, and *Psychology in Action* boxes.

Supplements

Naturally, there are also a variety of supplements available to the instructor and the student.

Instructor's Manual (ISBN 0-321-03476-7). The IM for this edition, prepared by Diane Martin is an expansion and updating of the extensive manual prepared for the first edition. Features include chapter outlines, tips on lecture organization, lecture material, text references, and chapter resources.

Test Bank (ISBN 0-321-03477-5). Written by Rita Curl, the test bank contains approximately 2000 questions. Each of these multiple-choice, true-false and essay questions is referenced to page number, topic, and skill.

Study Guide (ISBN 0-321-03478-3). Written by Peggy Skinner, each chapter of the comprehensive study guide contains a brief chapter outline, chapter summaries, a definition of key terms, lists of key concepts and individuals, and three practice tests containing multiple-choice, matching, and fill-in-the-blank questions with their answers.

StudyWizard Tutorial (ISBN 0-321-03923-8 for Windows and ISBN 0-321-03488-0 for the Macintosh). Pam Griesler has written this interactive computerized tutorial for IBM, Macintosh, and IBM-compatible computers. In addition to chapter outlines and glossary terms, StudyWizard provides immediate correct answers to multiple-choice, true-false, and short-answer questions. All of the material is referenced to the text page. The tutorial contains material not found in the study guide and provides a running score for students. A new feature provides reasons for correct and incorrect answers.

Computerized Test Bank. TestGen Computerized Testing System is a flexible, easy-to-master computerized test bank that includes all the test items in the printed test bank. The TestGen software allows instructors to edit existing questions and add their own items. It is available in IBM (ISBN 0-321-03479-1) or Macintosh (ISBN 0-321-03483-X) formats.

QuizMaster is a new software program, available to instructors, that allows students to take TestGen-produced tests on computer. QuizMaster gives the students their scores right away as well as a diagnostic report at the end of the test. This report lets the students know what topics or objectives they may need to study to improve their scores. Test scores can be saved on disk, allowing instructors to keep track of scores for individual students, class sections, or whole courses.

Video (ISBN 0-321-02059-6). We have created a custom video to accompany this edition of *The Growing Child*. It consists of a wide variety of brief segments to illustrate developmental concepts. These "lecture launchers" (each two to eight minutes long) cover topics such as the Apgar test, the Kohlberg dilemma, language development, and fetal alcohol syndrome.

Transparencies (ISBN 0-321-04043-0). A set of 100 full-color transparencies includes images from the text and beyond. It is available to adopters of the text.

Website. This text is supported by a website that contains a variety of resources for professors and students. It includes practice tests, illustrations for downloading, research links, and fun activities. Please visit this site at: <http://longman.awl.com /psychzone>

Bouquets

My work on this edition, as with every edition, has been greatly aided by faculty reviewers, who take the time out of busy schedules to provide criticism and suggestions. In this instance, I am especially indebted to the many colleagues who commented on the first edition—comments I took fully to heart, as evidenced by the major expansions in this edition. Another group of colleagues read the new draft as it emerged from my computer, letting me know where I had strayed off the course I had set myself, and where I was on target. My thanks to the following: Lynn Haller Augsbach, Morehead State University; Rebecca Bigler, University of Texas at Austin; Mick Coleman, University of Georgia; Rita M. Curl, Minot State University; Nancy Darling, The Pennsylvania State University; Olivia Eisenhauer, Palo Alto College; William R. Fisk, Clemson University; James E. Hart, Edison Community College; Bert Hayslip, Jr., University of North Texas; Paul E. Jose, Loyola University, Chicago; Gary Levy, University of Wyoming; Kathryn Markell, Cardinal Stritch University; Cynthia Marshall, Skyline College; Rich Metzger, University of Tennessee at Chattanooga; Martha Meyer, Butler University; R. Robert Orr, University of Windsor; Charles Overstreet, Tarrant County Junior College; Ligaya P. Paguio, University of Georgia; Roger Phillips, Pinebrook Services for Children and Youth; Nicolas R. Santilli, John Carroll University; Harry Saterfield, Foothill College; Penelope Skoglund, Northeastern Junior College; Daniel E. Williams, Montclair State University.

My work is also made enormously easier because of the terrific team of people at Addison Wesley Longman—the same team I have now worked with on several books. By now, we know each other's strengths and weaknesses and the process has become remarkably smooth. Becky Dudley, the acquisitions editor, is extremely energetic, full of new ideas, always willing to listen, and blessed with that most delightful of traits: she answers her mail immediately! Becky Kohn is certainly the best development editor on the face of the earth. She reads every chapter and makes helpful comments; she answers all my technical questions; sometimes she calls just to hear how things are going, which gives me a rare opportunity to agonize over whatever current dilemma is facing me. Not many people have the patience to listen to a writer's dilemmas! For this edition, her critical acumen was particularly important in helping me analyze the many reviews and plan the appropriate

changes. Becky also keeps the paperwork flowing and acts as a capable liaison with all the many departments at Addison Wesley Longman. I couldn't get along without her.

The third member of this *team extraordinaire* is photo researcher Rosemary Hunter, who provides me with heaps of wonderful photos to choose from and searches out special pictures when we need them. Rosemary and I have now worked together so many times that we hardly need to talk to one another anymore; she knows just what I need and sends it to me even before I ask. Even more important, her meticulousness and her aesthetic sense are unerring. Rosemary's work was especially important in this revision because we knew from the beginning that we wanted to increase the number of photos substantially, and we wanted a somewhat different "look" to the book. To all three of these special women, my deepest thanks.

Last but never least, there is my personal "convoy," who truck along with me through each book. My computer-science-professor husband, Carl de Boor, solves computer puzzles and sometimes keeps me from tearing out my hair in clumps when deadlines become too tight or chapter structures defy solution. In this case his computer skills were particularly vital because I upgraded to a faster, fancier computer about two-thirds of the way through the book. Without his help I don't know how I would ever have figured out how to transfer my gigantic file of references, which has grown too large to hold on a single disk. I simply don't know what other people do without this kind of resident helper.

My local friends, especially Sarah Brooks, Diane Edie, and Deb Harville, drop in regularly just to say Hi or to give me a hug or to sing—a welcome break from the solitary exercise of writing. Sarah has also taken on the thankless task of organizing my files so that I can actually find my copy of that 1992 paper from the *New England Journal of Medicine* I need at some specific moment. Quite literally, I could not live without these laughing and loving people. Thank you.

HELEN BEE

To the Student

To my admittedly prejudiced view, the study of human development is one of the most fascinating of all subjects. Because humans are astonishingly complex, understanding comes slowly and with great effort. But the process of trying to achieve understanding is full of wonderful puzzles and questions, blind alleys, theoretical leaps forward. There is an added element of intrigue because it is *ourselves* we are studying. One of my great hopes in writing this book is that I can draw you into the excitement and fascination.

I have used every strategy I know to lure you. I have written the book in the first person so that it sounds like a live person talking to you. In the process, I have told you my opinions, shared some of my concerns, and said clearly when we do not know or cannot answer some question. I have also talked about how to apply the research and theory to your work with children, both in extended discussions in boxes called *Parenting* and *Social Policy Debate*, and in the text itself.

I have also tried to entice you into thinking more deeply and critically about what you are reading by the use of "critical thinking questions." Each time you encounter such a question I hope you will pause and consider, mull over the dilemma posed, think about your feelings on the issue under discussion, or try to figure out some way of testing a specific hypothesis. Critical thinking is a skill that can be practiced and learned. It involves active processes, such as analyzing data for value and content, synthesizing information, resisting overgeneralization, being open minded about divergent views, distinguishing fact from opinion, and applying knowledge to new situations. It also involves observing your own thinking process, or going back later and trying to figure out how you reached a particular conclusion. In your adult life, you will find the ability to think critically to be a vital skill. Here's a chance to practice it.

Finally, I naturally also want you to come away from reading this book with a firm grounding of knowledge in the field. Although there is much that we do not yet know or understand, we do now have a great deal of excellent research and helpful theories. These theoretical perspectives and research findings will be of help to you professionally if you are planning (or are already in) a career with children—such as teaching, nursing, social work, medicine, or psychology; the facts and ideas should also be useful to you as parents, now or in the future. You will have much to learn, including both facts and theories. I hope you enjoy the learning as much as I have enjoyed the writing.

H.B.

The Growing Child

CHAPTER 1

Basic Questions

Preview Questions

1 Why do we need scientific research on children's development?

2 What are the key concepts and terms in the nature/nurture debate?

3 What are the major techniques used in the study of behavior genetics?

4 How do individualist and collectivist cultures differ?

5 What are the advantages and disadvantages of the several major research designs in the study of development?

Chapter Outline

Let me begin with the most basic of questions: Why should you study child development at all? You might argue that vast numbers of children around the world have successfully moved through childhood despite the fact that their parents have never read a text like this one or taken a course on human development. Children's development appears to be so normal, so natural a process; why do we need to bother with scientific research, and why do you need to know about the results of such research? I think there are several compelling reasons.

In the first place, nearly all of you will be (or already are) parents. It is certainly true that a great many parents do a competent job without ever studying the subject of child development. You should, however, be able to do an even better job if you have more knowledge. I will not always be able to give you clear answers about what is best for your children because the research is not always complete or definitive. Still, a great many parental questions *can* be answered, based on careful research. A few examples:

- What is the right diet during pregnancy? New research on the role of folic acid in preventing neural tube defects (such as in the disorder called *spina bi da*) tells us that specific nutrients may be vital for normal development. Accumulating data also make the detrimental effects of smoking, alcohol, and other drugs during pregnancy even more clear. (I'll discuss all this in Chapter 3.)

- Will placing your child in day care during infancy mean that the baby is not going to be strongly or securely attached to you? The answer seems to be no, based on a major new collaborative study by psychologists all over the United States—a study prompted by inconsistent results from a number of earlier, smaller studies on this question (Chapter 6).

- How important is it for you to be involved with your child's school? Should you make a serious effort to get to parent-teacher conferences and school events, or is that pretty unimportant? The answer is clear: Children whose parents are more involved with the school do better—and this is as true of poverty-level, inner-city children as of middle-class, suburban children (Chapter 11).

Psychological research tells us that children benefit when their parents participate in school activities like parent-teacher conferences—only one example of the many useful bits of knowledge to be gleaned from research on children's development.

[?] *Critical Thinking*

Can you think of other questions you may have about children or child rearing for which you would want or need good scientific research to help you be a better parent?

For those of you who plan careers working with children, as teachers, day-care workers, recreation workers, social workers, counselors, nurses, or doctors, there are equally compelling practical reasons to study both the research and the theory. Understanding the basic theories of human development will allow you to put both new and old information into a framework that will help you make sense out of it; understanding our current knowledge will enable you to do your job better. Again, some examples:

- A number of studies show that when day-care workers have had at least one basic course in human development, the infants and young children in their care do better intellectually and socially (Chapter 6).

- An extensive and growing body of research tells us that a critical quality of adult-infant or adult–young child interaction is something usually called "responsiveness" or "contingent responsiveness." Children whose caregivers interact with them in this way are more likely to be securely attached and to show a more optimal intellectual development (Chapter 6). Child-care workers can learn to behave in this way.

- A somewhat controversial, but important, set of studies points to the importance of teachers' expectations on children's achievement in school. When a teacher expects a particular child to do well, the teacher's behavior with that child is subtly different than the behavior of the same teacher toward a child he or she expects to do less well. A subset of those higher/lower expectations have to do with teachers' differing expectations for, and thus differing behavior toward, boys and girls. As one example, girls' lower rate of participation in mathematics in high school seems to have its root in part in differential teacher behavior in elementary school (Chapter 11).

The scientific study of human development can also help to provide answers to *societal* questions about children and their growth—questions that touch all of us, as parents, as child-care professionals, or as citizens. For instance:

- Why is the rate of low birth weight roughly twice as high among African-American infants as among Euro-American or Hispanic infants? (Chapter 3)
- What steps should we take to increase the health of pregnant women and their infants, so as to reduce the rate of infant disease or disability? (Chapter 3)

- Do programs like Head Start really help poor children? Should such programs be available to all children? (Chapter 8)
- What are the positive and negative effects of television viewing on children? Do violent programs make children more aggressive? Do educational programs really educate? What public policies follow from our findings? (Chapter 12)
- Which teenagers become delinquents and why? How can we prevent delinquency? (Chapter 15)

Scientists who study children's development—psychologists, sociologists, epidemiologists, biologists, physicians—do not yet have clear answers to all these important practical questions. Nonetheless, I think it is vital to *ask* the questions and to ask what we know and don't yet know in each case. It is also important to understand why such questions are so very hard to answer clearly. Good research on human development is not only important and fascinating, it is extremely difficult to do well. You need to understand the problems so that you can appreciate the limits of our knowledge.

Because all the examples I have given so far are real-life or "applied" questions, you may think that what I am advocating here is primarily the study of issues of practical science and applications. Not true. Such applied questions are important, but answering them rests on our understanding of *basic* developmental patterns as much as or more than it rests on research specifically targeted to an applied issue. For example, our understanding of the impact of day care on children's attachment rests fundamentally on our more basic understanding of the attachment process and how to measure it. Only when we have such a fundamental understanding

---

Table 1.1

Four Reasons for the Scientific Study of Human Development

- *As parents,* you will want to have information that will help you to make important practical decisions about and for your children and do the best possible job of parenting;
- *As child-care professionals,* you can use up-to-date research information to improve your skills and widen your knowledge base;
- *As a society,* we need first-rate research to answer important questions about children and their optimal development; and
- *As students,* we can all enter into the fascination of the research process.

can we ask what effect different early experiences—such as day care versus full-time home rearing—may have on the attachment. Similarly, being able to answer questions about delinquency depends on basic understanding of children's personality and social development, including peer relationships, temperamental differences, and family interaction patterns. Thus, while you may be (initially) more interested in the applied questions, you need a firm grounding in the underlying theory and research in order to frame and answer the real-life questions.

What I want to do in the remainder of this chapter is to give you a preliminary framework for looking at the basic processes of development. What are the key questions we need to be able to answer? What central concepts have proven most helpful? What are the methods we have devised to try to answer both the basic and the applied questions?

Enduring Questions

In our effort to reach a basic understanding of children's development, psychologists have wrestled with a series of fundamental, somewhat overlapping, questions:

• **Nature and nurture:** Is each child's development primarily governed by a pattern built in at birth, or is it shaped primarily by experiences after birth? This may seem to be an entirely theoretical question, but it has direct practical relevance. For example, the Head Start program, which provides enriched educational experiences for children living in poverty, rests on a fundamental assumption that children's intellectual development is substantially shaped by their environment and can thus be enhanced by exposure to a more stimulating environment. If that assumption is not valid, or is only partially valid, then we would have to rethink this kind of program.

For an even more personal example, think for a minute about your own qualities—your physical characteristics, your personality traits, your skills. Which of those qualities do you think are built in and which are the result of specific experiences?

Do you have certain temperamental qualities, such as shyness or gregariousness, that have been fairly consistent from early childhood to today? Did you experience particular upheavals, such as your parents' divorce, that had a lasting effect on your behavior? Did you have special rivalries with your siblings that shaped you, or did you have a particularly terrific teacher in first grade who got you off to a good academic start? If you are a member of a minority group, has this affected you in lasting ways?

The task for psychologists is to try to sort out these myriad potential influences and to understand how they do or do not interact with one another to shape each child similarly or uniquely.

• **Developmental universals and individual variations:** An equally central basic issue has to do with common versus individual patterns of development. In what ways is development the same in every child, in every culture? Do all children learn language at the same ages and at essentially the same rate? Does every child come to understand the differences between males and females at the same age, or through the same process? Conversely, in what ways is development unique for each child, or identifiably different for subgroups of children, such as children with similar temperaments or children that share a common culture or a similar family configuration?

Answering these questions is not always as easy as it might seem. Sometimes a pattern that looks like it is universal—perhaps biologically based—turns out to vary as a function of quite specific cultural experiences. For example, you probably know that in the first weeks after they are born, babies do not sleep through the night; they wake roughly every two hours to be fed. By about 6 weeks of age, though, most babies are able to string several two-hour stretches together, and begin to show something approximating a day/night sleeping pattern (Bamford, Bannister, Benjamin et al., 1990). That certainly sounds like a basic biological change, one that would occur in pretty much the same way regardless of the child's environment. Yet, according to one study (Super & Harkness, 1982), babies in rural Kenya who are carried about by their mothers in a sling all day and fed on demand at night do not show any shift toward a nighttime sleep pattern over the first eight months of life. So what looked like a universal, biological

In traditional Kenyan culture, still seen in some rural areas, babies are carried in slings all day and allowed to nurse on demand at night. This cultural pattern, quite different from what we see in most Western societies, seems to have an effect on the baby's sleep/wake cycle.

Stating the question more generally, we need to ask what changes and what stays the same over the years of childhood. Children clearly change in systematic ways. They grow bigger and stronger; they learn to walk and talk, to read and write; they figure out whether they are boys or girls and the implications of their own gender; and so on and on. The very word *development* implies such changes. At the same time, we also need to understand the ways in which children remain consistent over time—in style, personality, or physical traits.

• **The nature of developmental change:** A fourth enduring question concerns the nature of developmental change itself. For example, a 2-year-old is likely to have no individual friends among her playmates, while an 8-year-old is likely to have several. We could think of this as a *quantitative* change (a change in amount) from zero friends to some friends, or we could think of it as a *qualitative* change (a change in kind or type) from disinterest to interest in peers or from one type of peer relationship to another.

For another example, think again about yourself for a moment. Do you think that the way you analyze a problem or the way you go about making a decision is essentially the same as was true of you at age 7 or 8—maybe a bit faster or more efficient, but pretty much the same process—or do you think that you approach tasks and problems now in really different ways? Developmental psychologists have disagreed strongly on this question of qualitative versus quantitative change.

We have also disagreed on the related question of whether development occurs in *stages*. If development consists only of additions (quantitative changes), then the concept of stages is not needed. But if development involves reorganization or the emergence of wholly new strategies, skills, or behaviors (qualitative changes), then the concept of stages may become attractive. Certainly we hear a lot of "stagelike" language in everyday conversation about children: "He's just in the terrible twos," or "It's only a stage she's going through."

The idea of stages clearly goes a step beyond the assertion that development involves changes in quality as well as quantity; it implies some kind of reorganization, some new structure or understanding in each stage. Stage models of development are appealing (and I have been greatly drawn to them) because of the clarity and orderliness they

process may turn out not to be universal at all. It may be affected by culture—by attitudes and values expressed through variations in care and handling.

• **Continuity and change:** Among the children I know well, sweet-tempered young Malcolm and ebullient Crystal always give me many hugs; Malcolm's older brother Elliot, far shyer, always begins by gazing at me silently from some measured distance. He warms up eventually, but his behavior is quite different from his brother's and remains noticeably constant from year to year, just as 16-year-old Stacey has been a bit dreamy and a little slow-moving since toddlerhood. Each of these children has a particular style, a particular set of skills, a particular temperament or personality, and these qualities appear to be at least somewhat consistent from year to year, very likely even into adult life. Where do these consistencies come from? Are they built in genetically, or might they be a product of very early experience? Are they truly unchangeable?

Table 1.2

Four Enduring Questions in the Study of Human Development

Nature and nurture To what extent is a child's development determined by patterns built in at birth; to what extent is it influenced by the specific environment in which the child is reared? How do nature and nurture interact?

Developmental universals and individual variations What aspects of development are the same for all children, no matter their culture, gender, or circumstances? What aspects vary from child to child or from culture to culture?

Continuity and change Are there any areas in which children remain the same over time, such as perhaps in temperament or degree of physical coordination? Where do we see major changes?

The nature of developmental change When change occurs over the years of childhood, does it involve simply additions or expansions of skills, or does it involve real qualitative change—changes in the way a child approaches problems or relationships?

Many people, including some psychologists, would explain this boy's behavior by saying he is in a "stage"—the so-called terrible twos—in which tantrums are common. But many psychologists think that the concept of stages is not necessary to explain development.

offer. Yet, as you will see as we go along, in many areas the evidence doesn't lend a great deal of support for stage models of development. Still, many influential stage theories remain, and the whole issue of the existence of stages is still very much an open question.

Each of these enduring questions will appear again and again throughout this book, in various guises. Of the four, the most pervasive—and arguably the most practically relevant—is the issue

of nature and nurture. So let me introduce you to some of the special terminology and concepts that have been part of this debate.

Nature and Nurture: An Ancient Debate

Historically, discussions of nature and nurture have very often been phrased in either/or language, as nature *versus* nurture, heredity *versus* environment, or "nativism" *versus* "empiricism." Within philosophy historically, the nativist/nature side of the controversy was represented principally by Plato and (in the more modern era) René Descartes, both of whom believed that at least some ideas are innate. On the other side of the philosophical argument was ranged a group of British philosophers called "empiricists," such as John Locke, who insisted that at birth the mind is a blank slate—in Latin a *tabula rasa*. All knowledge, the empiricists argued, is created by experience.

No developmental psychologist today would cast this issue in such black-and-white terms. We agree that essentially every facet of a child's development is a product of some pattern of interaction between nature and nurture. Even clearly physical developments have some environmental component. For example, in every culture, puberty occurs sometime between approximately age 9 and age

16, but the timing is affected by environmental factors such as diet. Similarly, some temperamental patterns may be inherited, but they can be and are modified by the parents' style of caregiving. No aspect of development is entirely one or the other. Nonetheless, psychologists have always had lively disagreements about the relative importance of these two factors.

[?] Critical Thinking

Think about your own patterns of behavior for a moment. Which ones do you think are the *most* governed by basic human biology (nature)? Which ones seem to be most a product of your environment, including your upbringing?

Until fairly recently, the theoretical pendulum was well over toward the environmental end of the continuum. Most developmental research—and the majority of the theorizing by developmental psychologists—focused on environmental effects of one type or another. In the last decade or so, though, we have seen a strong and growing emphasis on the biological roots of behavior and of development itself. In part, this shift has grown out of new technology that allows physiologists and psychologists to study the functioning of the brain in much greater detail, as well as from the development of new statistical techniques that make it possible to study genetic influences in new ways. The shift may also have occurred because it became clear that we needed more balance in our explanations of development. Whatever the reasons, a significant resurgence of interest in the biological roots of behavior has occurred.

Inborn Biases and Constraints

One example of this resurgence is an increasing popularity of the concepts of "inborn biases" or "constraints" on development. The argument, which is in some ways a modern descendent of Descartes's notion of inborn ideas, is that children are born with tendencies to respond in certain ways. In computer language we could say that infants are born with certain "default options"; the system is *already* programmed or "biased."

Many such inborn biases appear to be shared by virtually all children. For instance, from the earliest days of life babies seem to listen more to the beginnings and ends of sentences than to the middles (Slobin, 1985a), and they respond visually to motion and to shifts from dark to light (Haith, 1980). Babies also come equipped with inborn patterns of social behavior. For example, they have a set of apparently instinctive behaviors that entice others to care for them, including crying, snuggling, and—very soon after birth—smiling.

Whether these inborn patterns are coded in the genes in some fashion, are created by variations in the prenatal environment, or are brought about by some combination of the two, the basic point is that the baby is not a blank slate at birth. She starts out life already prepared to seek out and react to particular kinds of experiences in particular ways. These biases constrain the number of developmental pathways that are possible (Campbell & Bickhard, 1992).

Maturation

Nature can shape processes after birth in other ways as well, most clearly through genetic programming that may determine whole sequences of later development. This is not a new idea; Arnold Gesell (Gesell, 1925; Thelen & Adolph, 1992) proposed such an idea 70 years ago. He used the term **maturation** to describe such genetically programmed sequential patterns of change, and this term is still uniformly used today. Changes in body size and shape, changes in hormones at puberty, changes in muscles and bones, and changes in the nervous system all may be programmed in this way. You can probably remember your own physical changes during adolescence. The timing of these pubertal changes differs from one teenager to the next, but the basic sequence is essentially the same for all children. Such sequences, which begin at conception and continue until death, are shared by all members of our species.

Any maturational pattern is marked by three qualities: It is *universal*, appearing in all children, across cultural boundaries; it is *sequential*, involving some pattern of unfolding skill or characteristics; and it is *relatively impervious to environmental in uence.*

In its purest form, a maturationally determined developmental sequence occurs regardless of practice or training. You don't have to practice growing pubic hair; you don't have to be taught how to walk. In fact, it would take almost Herculean efforts to *prevent* such sequences from unfolding. Yet even confirmed maturational theorists agree that experience has some effect. These powerful, apparently automatic maturational patterns require at least some minimal environmental support, such as adequate diet and opportunity for movement and experimentation.

Modern research also tells us that specific experience interacts with maturational patterns in intricate ways. For example, Greenough (1991) notes that one of the proteins required for the development of the visual system is controlled by a gene whose action is triggered only by visual experience. So *some* visual experience is needed for the genetic program to operate. In normal development,

of course, every (nonblind) child will have some such experience. Yet examples like this one tell us that maturational sequences do not simply "unfold" automatically. The system appears to be "ready" to develop along particular pathways, but it requires experience to trigger the movement.

I should point out that the term *maturation* does not mean quite the same thing as the term *growth*, although the two words are sometimes used as if they were synonyms. *Growth* refers to some kind of step-by-step change in quantity, as in size, and it can occur either with or without an underlying maturational process. A child's body could grow because her diet has significantly improved, or it could grow because she is getting older. The first of these has no maturational component, while the second does. To put it another way, the term *growth* is a *description* of change, while the concept of maturation is one *explanation* of change.

The shift from crawling to walking is a classic example of a maturationally based unversal development change: It follows the same basic pattern in boys and in girls, in Asians, blacks, Hispanics, Caucasians.

Behavior Genetics

The concept of maturation and the idea of inborn biases are both primarily useful in explaining patterns and sequences of development that are the *same* for all children. Nature can also contribute to *variations* from one individual to the next, since genetic inheritance is individual as well as collective. The study of genetic contributions to individual behavior, called **behavior genetics,** has become a particularly vibrant and influential research area in recent years and has contributed greatly to the renewed interest in the biological roots of behavior.

Using two primary research techniques, the study of identical and fraternal twins, and the study of adopted children (described more fully in the *Research Report* box on p. 12), behavior geneticists have shown that specific heredity affects a remarkably broad range of behaviors. Included in the list are not only obvious physical differences such as height, body shape, or a tendency to skinniness or obesity, but also cognitive abilities such as general intelligence (about which I will have a great deal more to say in Chapter 9), and more specific cognitive skills or problems such as spatial visualization ability or reading disability (Rose, 1995). Newer research is also showing that many aspects of pathological behavior are genetically influenced, including alcoholism, schizophrenia, excessive aggressiveness or antisocial behavior, even anorexia (Gottesman & Goldsmith, 1994; McGue, 1994). Finally, and importantly, behavior geneticists have found a significant genetic influence on children's temperament, including such dimensions as emotionality (the tendency to get distressed or upset easily), activity (the tendency toward vigorous, rapid behavior), and sociability (the tendency to prefer the presence of others to being alone) (Plomin, Emde, Braungart et al., 1993). All this means that some of the personal qualities you see in your own children, or in children you deal with professionally, are likely to have at least some genetic base. Such qualities can be changed, but the way you approach the task of changing a child's behavior will likely differ, depending on whether that behavior is strongly genetically influenced versus primarily environmentally controlled. For instance, if a child has *learned* to behave in an aggressive or emotional way toward other kids, then your task

as a teacher is to teach (reinforce) an alternative behavior. If, instead, a child has a temperamental tendency toward "difficult" behavior, then your task is not only to teach alternative behaviors, but also to focus on helping the child gain greater self-control.

Paradoxically, a child's genetic heritage may also affect his environment (Plomin, 1995), a phenomenon that could occur via either or both of two routes. First, each child inherits his genes from his parents, who *also* create the environment in which he is growing up. So knowing something about the child's genetic heritage may allow us to predict something about his environment as well. For example, parents who themselves have higher IQ scores are not only likely to pass their "good IQ" genes on to their children, they are also likely to create a richer, more stimulating environment for their child.

Second, each child creates her own environmental influences. Because children begin life with varying genetically patterned qualities, they *elicit* different behavior from parents and others. Cranky or temperamentally difficult children are likely to have different kinds of encounters with parents than will babies with more sunny dispositions; genetically brighter children demand a different kind of attention and interact differently with their toys (Saudino & Plomin, 1997). Large and robust children elicit different kinds of caregiving than do frail children. Furthermore, children's interpretations of their experiences are affected by all their inherited tendencies, including not only intelligence but temperament or pathologies. For example, in one recent study of twins and stepsiblings, Robert Plomin and his colleagues (Plomin, Reiss, Hetherington, & Howe, 1994) found that identical twin adolescents described their parents in more similar terms than did fraternal twins. Full siblings in this same study described their parents more similarly than did genetically unrelated stepsiblings. It appears that identical twins are *experiencing* their parents, and their family environment, in more similar ways. This does *not* mean that there is somehow an "experiencing the environment" gene. Rather, the full genetic pattern of each child or adult affects the way he or she experiences and interprets. Because identical twins have the same genetic makeup, they experience and interpret more similarly.

Research Report

How Do Behavior Geneticists Identify Genetic Effects?

Investigators can search for a genetic influence on a trait in either of two primary ways: by studying identical and fraternal twins or by studying adopted children. Identical twins share exactly the same genetic patterning because they develop from the same fertilized ovum. Fraternal twins each develop from a separate ovum, separately fertilized. They are therefore no more alike than are any other pair of siblings, except that they have shared the same prenatal environment and grow up in the same sequential niche within the family. If identical twins turn out to be more like one another on any given trait than do fraternal twins, that would be evidence for the influence of heredity on that trait.

A powerful variant of the twin strategy is to study twins who have been reared apart. If identical twins are still more like one another on some dimension than are fraternal twins, despite having grown up apart from one another, we have even clearer evidence of a genetic contribution for that trait.

In the case of adopted children, the strategy is to compare the degree of similarity between the adopted child and his birth parents (with whom he shares genes but not environment) with the degree of similarity between the adopted child and his adoptive parents (with whom he shares environment but not genes). If the child should turn out to be more similar to his birth parents than to his adoptive parents, or if his behavior or skill is better predicted by the characteristics of his birth parents than by characteristics of his adoptive parents, that would again demonstrate the influence of heredity.

Let me give you two examples, both from studies of intelligence, measured with standard IQ tests. Bouchard and McGue (1981, p. 1056, Figure 1) have combined the results of dozens of twin studies on the heritability of IQ scores, with the following results:

Identical twins reared together	.85
Identical twins reared apart	.67
Fraternal twins reared together	.58
Siblings (including fraternal twins) reared apart	.24

The numbers here are correlations—a statistic I'll explain more fully later in this chapter. For now you need to know only that a correlation can range from 0 to +1.00 or −1.00. The closer it is to 1.00, the stronger the relationship it describes. In this case, the number reflects how similar the IQ scores are for the two members of a twin pair. You can see that identical twins reared together have IQ scores that are highly similar, much more similar than what occurs for fraternal twins reared together. You can also see, though, that environment plays a role, since identical twins reared apart are less similar than are those reared together.

The same conclusion comes from two well-known studies of adopted children, the Texas Adoption Project (Loehlin, Horn, & Willerman, 1994) and the Minnesota Transracial Adoption Study (Scarr, Weinberg, & Waldman, 1993). In both studies the adopted children were recently given IQ tests at approximately age 18. Their scores on this test were then correlated with the earlier-measured IQ scores of their natural mothers and of their adoptive mothers and fathers:

Correlation:	Texas	Minnesota
With the natural mother's IQ score	.44	.29
With the adoptive mother's IQ score	.03	.14
With the adoptive father's IQ score	.06	.08

In both cases the children's IQ scores were at least somewhat predicted by their natural mothers' IQs but *not* by the IQs of their adoptive parents, with whom they had spent their entire childhood. Thus the adoption studies, like the twin studies of IQ, tell us that there is indeed a substantial genetic component in what we measure with an IQ test.

The study of identical twins, like these two boys, is one of the classic methods of behavior genetics research. Whenever pairs of identical twins are more like one another in some behavior or quality than are pairs of fraternal twins, it indicates the presence of a genetic influence.

Research of this kind has forced developmental psychologists to rethink some long-held assumptions about the effects of environment. At the same time, I want to emphasize that no behavior geneticist is saying that heredity is the *only* cause of behavior, or even the most central one in many cases. Indeed, as Robert Plomin points out, behavior genetics research has been as important in showing the significant effect of environment as in proving the centrality of heredity (1995). Certainly, genetic influences are almost totally dominant for some characteristics, such as inherited diseases. For most aspects of development, however, such as variations in personality or intellectual abilities, the effect of a particular genetic pattern is more a matter of probability than certainty. We know there is *some* genetic effect because identical twins are a lot more alike in personality, intelligence, or many specific behavior patterns than are fraternal twins. Yet even identical twins are not identical in these characteristics. For example, studies of adult criminals done in the United States, Germany, Japan, Norway, and Denmark show that if one of a pair of identical twins has been jailed for some criminal act, the probability that the other twin has also been jailed is about 50 percent. Among fraternal twins, this "concordance rate" is only 23 percent. This shows a clear genetic effect, but the role of environment is also obvious. In virtually every case specific outcomes for a given child depend on the interaction of that child's genetic patterning with the particular environment the child encounters and creates.

Aslin's Models of Environmental Influence

Everything I've said so far should underline the fact that theories and models of the role of nature in development have become more subtle and complex, with much more attention paid to the ways in which nurture interacts with nature. On the nurture side of the theoretical issue we see the same increased subtlety and complexity. One particularly good example is a set of models of environmental influence proposed by Richard Aslin (1981), shown schematically in Figure 1.1. In each drawing, the dashed line represents the path of development of some skill or behavior that would occur without a particular experience; the solid line represents the path of development if the experience were added.

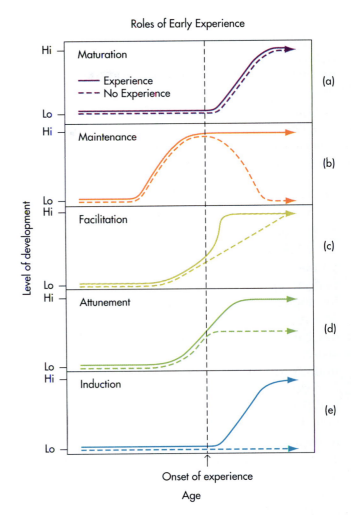

Figure 1.1

Five models of possible relationships between maturation and environment, as proposed by Aslin. The top model shows a purely maturational effect; the bottom model (induction) shows a purely environmental effect. The other three show interactive combinations: **maintenance,** *in which experience prevents the deterioration of a maturationally developed skill;* **facilitation,** *in which experience speeds up the development of some maturational process; and* **attunement,** *in which experience increases the ultimate level of some skill or behavior above the "normal" maturational level. (Source: Aslin, 1981, p. 50.)*

For comparison purposes, the first of the five models actually shows a maturational pattern with *no* environmental effect. The second model, which Aslin calls *maintenance,* describes a pattern in which some environmental input is necessary to sustain a skill or behavior that has already developed maturationally. For example, kittens are born with full binocular vision, but if you cover one of their eyes for a period of time, binocular skill declines. Similarly, muscles will atrophy if not used.

The third model shows a *facilitation* effect of the environment, a paradigm in which a skill or behavior develops earlier than it normally would because of some experience. For example, children whose parents talk to them more often in the first 18 to 24 months of life, using more complex sentences, appear to develop two-word sentences and other early grammatical forms somewhat earlier than do children who are talked to less. However, less-talked-to children do eventually learn to create complex sentences and to use most grammatical forms correctly, so there is no permanent gain.

When a particular experience does lead to a permanent gain or to an enduringly higher level of performance, Aslin would call it *attunement*, which is his fourth model. For example, children born to poverty-level families who attend special enriched day care in infancy and early childhood have consistently higher IQ scores throughout childhood than do children from the same kinds of families who do not have such enriched experience (Campbell & Ramey, 1994; Ramey, 1993; Ramey & Campbell, 1987). Similarly, children whose parents talk to them a lot, using a wide-ranging vocabulary, appear to have a permanent advantage in total vocabulary size over children whose parents talk to them less (Hart & Risley, 1995). Thus a rich early language environment seems to have a facilitation effect on basic grammatical development but an attunement effect on vocabulary.

Critical Thinking

The preschool program Head Start is designed to improve the school preparation of children growing up in poor families. Which of Aslin's models do you think best describes what the designers of Head Start thought (or hoped) would be the result of the program?

Aslin's final model, *induction*, describes a pure environmental effect: a pattern in which a particular behavior would not develop at all, without a particular experience. Giving a child tennis lessons or exposing the child to a second language would fall into this category.

Helpful as they are, Aslin's models still don't take us far enough. At least three other aspects of the environmental side of the equation are also significant in current thinking about development: the timing of experience, the child's own interpretation of experience, and the total ecological/cultural system in which experiences occur.

The Timing of Experience

Just as the importance of nature may vary from one time in development to another, so the timing of specific experiences may matter as well. The impact of day care on an infant may be quite different when he is 6 months old than when he is 16 months old; moving from one school to another may have a different effect when it coincides with puberty than when it does not, and so forth.

Our thinking about the importance of timing was stimulated, in part, by research on other species which showed that specific experiences had different or stronger effects at some points in development than at others. The most famous example is that baby ducks will become *imprinted* on (become attached to and follow) any duck or any other quacking, moving object that happens to be around them 15 hours after they hatch. If nothing is moving or quacking at that critical point, they don't become imprinted at all (Hess, 1972). So the period just around 15 hours after hatching is a **critical period** for the duck's development of a proper following response.

We can see similar critical periods in the action of various teratogens in prenatal development. A **teratogen** is some outside agent, such as a disease organism or chemical, which if present during prenatal development, adversely affects the process of that development. While some teratogens can have negative consequences at any time in gestation, most have effects only during some critical period. For example, if a mother contracts the disease rubella (commonly called German measles) during a narrow range of days in the first three months of pregnancy, some damage or deformity occurs in the fetus. Infection with the same virus after the third month of pregnancy has no such effect.

In the months after birth, too, there seem to be critical periods in brain development—specific weeks or months during which the child needs to encounter certain types of stimulation or experience for the nervous system to develop normally and fully (Hirsch & Tieman, 1987).

Psychologists also use a broader and somewhat looser concept, the **sensitive period,** which is a span of months or years during which a child may be particularly responsive to specific forms of experience or particularly influenced by their absence. For example, the period from 6 to 12 months of age may be a sensitive period for the formation of a core attachment to the parents; other periods may be particularly significant for intellectual development or language.

Internal Models of Experience

Another more subtle and complex way of thinking about environmental effects is with the concept of an internal model of experience. The key idea is that the effect of some experience lies in an individual's *interpretation* of it, the *meaning* the individual attaches to it, rather than in the objective properties of the experience. You can easily come up with everyday examples from your own life. For instance, if a friend says something to you that he thinks is innocuous but that you take as a criticism, what matters for your experience is how you interpreted the comment, not how he meant it. If you regularly hear criticism in other people's comments, we would say that you have an internal model of yourself and oth-

ers that includes a basic expectation that might be something like this: "I usually do things wrong, so other people criticize me," or "No matter how hard I try, people are always critical of me."

Some theorists argue that each child creates several significant internal models, through which all subsequent experience is filtered (Epstein, 1991). John Bowlby expressed this idea when he talked about the child's "internal working model" of attachment (1969; 1980). A child with a "secure" model of attachment assumes that affection and attention are reliably available. A child with a less secure model may assume that affection is contingent on "being good" or that adults are generally angry and hostile and not reliable sources of support. Of course, these expectations are based at least partially on actual experiences, but once formed into an internal model, they generalize beyond the original experience and affect the way the child interprets future experiences. A child who expects adults to be reliable and affectionate will be more likely to interpret the behavior of new adults in this way and will re-create friendly and affectionate relationships with others outside the family; a child who expects hostility will read hostility into otherwise fairly neutral encounters.

A child's self-concept seems to operate in much the same way, as an internal working model of "who I am" (Bretherton, 1991). This "self model" is based on experience, but it also shapes future experience.

If the first year of life is a sensitive period for the establishment of a secure attachment (as some contend), then is it risky for a child of this age to be separated from her parents every day in day care? There is a hot debate among psychologists on this point.

To be sure, these internal models of experience may well have some "nature" component to them. In particular, children with different temperaments may have an initial bias toward one or another type of internal model. For example, an extraverted baby with a generally positive mood may be more likely to create a secure working model of attachment than will a crankier, more difficult infant. But whatever factors contribute to the creation of such an internal model—be they nature or nurture or some combination of the two—once formed, the internal model affects the way the child interprets future experience.

The Ecological Perspective

A third facet of current thinking about environmental effects is a growing emphasis on casting a wider environmental net. Until quite recently, most research on environmental influences focused on a child's family (frequently only the child's mother), perhaps on playmates, or perhaps on some proximate inanimate stimulation, such as toys. If we looked at a larger family context at all, it was usually in terms of the general wealth or poverty of the family.

In the past 10 or 15 years, however, we have tried to widen our scope, to consider the *ecology* or *context* in which each child develops. Urie Bronfenbrenner, one of the key figures in this area (1979; 1989), emphasizes that each child grows up in a complex social environment (a social ecology) with a distinct cast of characters: brothers, sisters, one or both parents, grandparents, baby-sitters, pets, schoolteachers, and friends. And this cast is itself embedded within a larger social and cultural system. The parents have jobs that they may like or dislike; they may have close and supportive friends or they may be quite isolated; they may be living in a safe neighborhood or one full of dangers; the local school may be excellent or poor; and the parents may have good or poor relationships with the school. Bronfenbrenner's argument is that we must not only include descriptions of these more extended aspects of the environment in our research, we must also understand the ways in which all the components of this complex system interact with one another to affect a child's development.

[?] Critical Thinking

How would you describe the "ecology" of your own childhood? What sort of family was yours? What sort of neighborhood and school? What other significant people were in your life? What significant events affected your parents' lives?

A particularly nice example of research that examines such a larger system of influences is Gerald Patterson's work on the origins of antisocial behavior in children (Patterson, 1996; Patterson, DeBarsyshe, & Ramsey, 1989). His studies show that parents who use poor discipline techniques and poor monitoring of the child are more likely to have noncompliant or antisocial children. Once the child has established such an antisocial behavior pattern, this pattern has repercussions in other areas of his life, leading to both peer rejection and academic difficulty. These problems, in turn, are likely to push the young person toward a deviant peer group and still further delinquency (Dishion, Patterson, Stoolmiller, & Skinner, 1991; Vuchinich, Bank, & Patterson, 1992). So a pattern that began in the family is maintained and exacerbated by interactions with peers and with the school system.

Patterson also argues that the family's good or poor disciplinary techniques are not random events but are themselves shaped by the larger context in which the family exists, as shown schematically in Figure 1.2. He finds that those parents who were raised by parents who used poor disciplinary practices are more likely to use those same poor strategies with their own children. He also finds that even parents who possess good basic child-management skills can fall into poor patterns when the stresses in their own lives are increased. A recent divorce or period of unemployment increases the likelihood that parents will use poor disciplinary practices and thus increases the likelihood that the child will develop a pattern of antisocial behavior.

Cultural Influences.   One aspect of such a larger ecology, not emphasized in Patterson's model but clearly part of Bronfenbrenner's thinking, is the still-broader concept of **culture.** There is no commonly agreed-upon definition for this term, but in

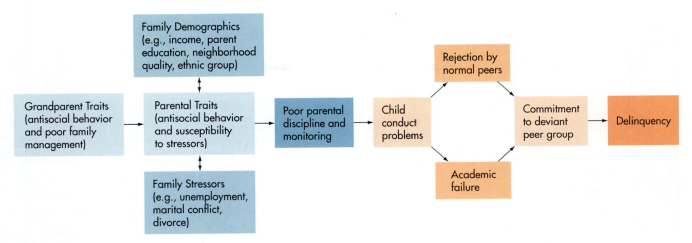

Figure 1.2

Patterson's model describes the many factors that influence the development of delinquency. The core of the process, in this model, is the interaction between the child and the parent. One might argue that the origin of delinquency lies in that relationship. But Patterson argues that there are larger ecological or contextual forces that are also "causes" of the delinquency. (Source: Patterson, 1989, Figures 1 and 2, pp. 331 & 333.)

essence it describes *a system of meanings and customs,* including values, attitudes, goals, laws, beliefs, morals, and physical artifacts of various kinds, such as tools, forms of dwellings, and the like. The majority culture in the United States, for example, is strongly shaped by the values expressed in the Constitution and the Bill of Rights. Other key elements include an emphasis on "can do" attitudes and on competition as well as a belief in the goal of a separate house for each family—a belief that contributes to a more spread-out pattern of housing in the United States than what exists in Europe.

For such a system of meanings to be called a culture, it must be *shared by some identifiable group,* whether that group is a subsection of some population or a larger unit; it must then be *transmitted from one generation of that group to the next* (Betancourt & Lopez, 1993; Cole, 1992). Families and children are clearly embedded in culture, just as they are located within an ecological niche in the culture.

Anthropologists point out that a key dimension on which cultural worlds differ from one another is that of **individualism** versus **collectivism** (e.g., Kim, Triandis, Kâgitçibasi, Choi, & Yoon, 1994). Cultures with an individualistic emphasis assume that the world is made up of independent individuals whose achievement and responsibility is individual rather than collective. Most European cultures are based on such individualistic assumptions, as is the Euro-American culture (the dominant U.S. culture, created primarily by whites who came to the United States from Europe). In contrast, most of the remainder of the world's cultures—roughly seventy percent of the world's population (Greenfield, 1994)—operate with a collectivist belief system in which the emphasis is on collective rather than individual identity, on group solidarity, sharing, duties and obligations, and group decision making. A person living in such a system is integrated into a strong, cohesive group that protects and nourishes that individual throughout his or her life. Collectivism is the dominant theme in most Asian countries as well as in many African and South American cultures.

This distinction between individualism and collectivism can give us a useful conceptual framework for understanding cultural differences and cultural effects. The more basic point is that we must be very careful not to assume that patterns of development we see in white, middle-class American children are necessarily going to occur in other

In the Hispanic-American subculture, families like the Limons, shown here at their annual reunion, are tightly knit, with frequent contact and support. Such a cultural pattern may have wide repercussions.

subcultures within our own society or in other, widely different cultures of the world.

Subcultures and Ethnic Differences. Within any broad culture, we may also find subcultures of various types, often linked to membership in one or another **ethnic group,** defined as "a subgroup whose members are perceived by themselves and others to have a common origin and culture, and shared activities in which the common origin or culture is an essential ingredient" (Porter & Washington, 1993, p. 140). There are myriad such subgroups and subcultures in the United States; the school systems in Los Angeles, New York, and Chicago, for example, include children who speak more than 100 separate languages—languages that are but one aspect of cultures brought to the United States by immigrant families. Among this richness and diversity, the most prominent subcultures are the African-American, the Hispanic-American, and the Asian-American, described in the *Cultures and Contexts* box, all of which have a

more collectivist flavor than does the dominant Euro-American culture.

Note, by the way, that *race* and *ethnicity* are not the same. Ethnicity refers primarily to social and cultural characteristics, while race normally designates a group with specific physical characteristics. Thus the designations Hispanic, African, and Asian American are sometimes viewed as a reference to both ethnic and racial categories, while the designation Polish American or Italian American is generally considered only as an ethnic group reference.

Most of us are aware of the powerful impact of culture or subculture only when we find ourselves outside our own cultural milieu or when we are in a situation in which we must interact consistently with others of another subculture. My own awareness was greatly enhanced by a year I spent living in Germany. I found that small cultural differences often left me feeling dislocated and uncertain. One fairly trivial example: As an American, I quite naturally smiled at strangers I might pass while out walking on one of the many special paths crisscrossing the country. Yet those I met rarely made eye contact, and never smiled at me. Indeed, they often seemed quite put off by my friendliness. I experienced their behavior as coldness and felt quite isolated, even when my logical mind told me that I was merely encountering a different cultural pattern. Experiences like this convinced me that Sapir was right when he said: "The worlds in which different societies live are distinct worlds, not merely the same world with different words attached" (1929, p. 209).

Critical Thinking

Can you think of equivalent examples in your own life?

For teachers, this issue is likely to be highly relevant: Most of you will have children in your classes who come from subcultures with varying values, behavior patterns, and attitudes. An adult example comes from an acquaintance who began teaching classes in a community college that included many Asian and Indian women. It took her a long time to grasp the fact that her expectation of open class participation was inappropriate for

Cultures and Contexts

Basic Values of Major Ethnic Groups in the United States

Subcultural as well as overall cultural values may be significant for any given child's development. As an illustration, consider the different sets of values that characterize several minority ethnic cultures in the United States. Any brief depiction of such values is inevitably an oversimplification, but here is one listing of key values, proposed by the American Psychological Association's Commission on Violence and Youth (1993, pp. 38–40):

African Americans

- *Harmony and interrelatedness with nature;*
- *Spirituality and strong religious orientation;*
- *Communalism rather than individualism;*
- *Child-centeredness, emphasizing the importance of the child to ensure the continuity of the family; and*
- *Flexibility of roles.*

Hispanic Americans

- *Preference for participating in groups (allocentrism);*
- *Strong adherence to family (familism);*
- *Avoidance of interpersonal conflict (simpatia); and*
- *Deference and respect for authority systems (respeto).*

Asian and Pacific Island Americans

- *Pacifism, self-control, and self-discipline linked to Confucianism, especially among Chinese, Korean, Vietnamese, and Japanese cultural groups;*

- *A social order in which there is a hierarchy of interpersonal relations (i.e., parents are superior to children, men to women, and ruler to subject) and in which respect and "saving face" are highly valued;*
- *Strong family ties, a link to ancestors, and expected obedience of the young to their elders;*
- *Strong cultural affiliation and bonding; and*
- *A strong work ethic and achievement motivation.*

Native Americans

- *Harmony with and respect for nature;*
- *Emphasis on family and tradition; and*
- *Emphasis on group cooperation rather than on individual achievement.*

If you were to make an equivalent list to describe the Anglo or Euro-American culture, what items would you list? What effects do you think these different sets of cultural values are likely to have on children growing up in a given subcultural group? How would a Hispanic-American child's experience differ from that of an Asian-American child, for example? We understand these effects only imperfectly as yet. Still, psychologists have increasingly realized that cultural variations such as these form a significant backdrop for all of development.

these women. They had been brought up to believe that women did not behave in that way. Similarly, a teacher in a preschool, elementary, or high school classroom needs to be aware of the different cultural beliefs the children bring with them to school. Children from strongly collectivist subcultures, for example, are not likely to have the same attitudes about individual achievement as do classmates from the dominant individualist culture; they may not respond to the same kinds of motivations; they

may work better in cooperative than in competitive systems.

Aside from these obvious practical and personal applications, studying culture and subculture is important for our theories and basic research on child development for at least two key reasons. First, if we are to understand "nurture," surely we must understand culture as part of the environment in which the child is growing up. How are developmental patterns changed by cultural variations, as in the example of sleeping through the night I have already mentioned? How do different cultural values affect the way children experience their childhood and adolescence? For instance, might it be, as some have argued, that one consequence of the individualist American culture is a much higher level of tolerance of aggression and violence than is true in other cultures (Lore & Schultz, 1993)? Such tolerance, in turn, might be manifested in a variety of ways, including the astonishingly high percentage of teenagers who carry weapons.

A second basic reason for studying cultural variations is, paradoxically, to uncover those developmental patterns or processes that are truly universal. If research with white, middle-class U.S. children points to the existence of some basic developmental sequence or process, we need to observe or test children from a variety of subcultural or cultural groups, from as wide an array of cultures as possible, to check on the universality of the developmental pattern.

As part of this task, we also need to discover whether the *relationship* between some environmental event and the outcome for the child is the same in all cultures. For example, in a study in Egypt, Ted Wachs and his colleagues (Wachs, Bishry, Sobhy et al., 1993) found that babies reared in families in which the parents talked to the infants a lot were later rated as more competent, a result that closely parallels the relationship between these two variables found in studies in the United States.

In other cases, however, the same relationships may *not* hold across cultures or subcultures. For example, poverty is *not* associated with high rates of infant mortality among Mexican Americans, while among African Americans it is (Lambert, 1993). Such a difference obviously has huge practical implications. To design an appropriate intervention to reduce infant mortality we would need to figure out just why this subcultural difference exists—a fascinating question that epidemiologists and physicians have only begun to answer.

Fortunately, our store of cross-cultural research is growing steadily. In a few areas, such as the study of language, moral development, and attachment, we already have a fair amount of information about developmental patterns in myriad cultures. In many other areas our research is still highly

In individualist Euro-American culture, physical aggression tends to be at its peak at about age 2 to 3, as we see here between Laura and Megan, both age 2. But we see little such rise among children from collectivist cultures or subcultures, such as Asian-American children (Farver, Kim, & Lee, 1995).

Eurocentric, but I will bring in cross-cultural or subcultural research wherever I can find it.

Interactions of Nature and Nurture

Nature and nurture do not act independently in shaping each child's development; they interact in complex and fascinating ways. I've suggested several such interactions as I've gone along, such as the need for certain specific types of environmental experience to trigger some maturational development or the fact that children with different genetically influenced temperaments choose different types of environments.

It is also possible that the interactions between nature and nurture *vary* from one child to another. In particular, the same environment may have quite different effects on children who are born with different characteristics. One influential approach of this type is the study of *vulnerable* and *resilient* children.

Vulnerability and Resilience

In her long-term study of a group of children born on the island of Kauai, Hawaii, in 1955 (a study described more fully in the *Research Report* box), Emmy Werner (Werner, Werner & Smith, 1992; 1993; 1995) found that only about two-thirds of the children who grew up in poverty-level, chaotic families

Research Report

Resilience Among Children Growing Up in Poverty

On average, children who grow up in chronic poverty turn out less well than do children reared in more stable and economically well-off families. At the same time, some children reared in poverty nonetheless do very well as adults. How are these *resilient* children different from equally disadvantaged peers? Several fascinating studies begin to give us some answers.

Emmy Werner and Ruth Smith, in their famous study of a group of 505 children born on the Hawaiian island of Kauai in 1955, found that certain specific risk factors predicted serious problems for children later in development: chronic poverty, a low level of education in the mother, family instability (particularly the absence of one parent), and significant physical problems in the infant, prenatally or at birth. Yet among the children in their sample who had experienced high levels of these kinds of risks, roughly one-third managed to avoid various problems of adolescence and young adulthood, including delinquency, learning problems, teenage pregnancy, or mental health problems.

Werner found that these resilient young people had certain protective factors in common:

- *As infants and toddlers, they had been affectionate, good-natured, and easy to deal with.*

- *As infants, they had had an opportunity to form a positive bond with at least one loving caregiver.*

- *In elementary school and high school, they got along well with classmates and had better language and reasoning skills. They had many interests and hobbies, often participating in organized groups such as 4-H or the YMCA or YWCA.*

A study by Janis Long and George Vaillant (1984) of 456 boys who grew up in inner-city neighborhoods in Boston in the 1930s and 1940s points to similar protective factors. They found that the majority of men who had spent their youth in poverty nonetheless became effective adults. These men earned adequate incomes, married, reared their children. But some had been much more successful than others and these more resilient men shared two protective factors: higher IQ scores and good "coping skills" as children. They had had good relationships with parents, teachers, and peers.

Thus an engaging, easy temperament, an ability to get along with others, adequate or good intellectual skills, and access to supportive adults all seem to be protective factors for children growing up in poverty. These results have obvious practical relevance as we think about designing programs for inner-city children. They also have theoretical importance because they underline the fact that the same or similar environments (poverty and chaotic family life, in this case) have different effects on children, depending on the qualities and skills the child brings to the interaction. Environments don't just "happen" to children, willy-nilly. Children interact with their environment, and the outcome depends on both.

turned out to have serious problems themselves as adults. Roughly one-third of these youngsters, despite their poor environmental support, nonetheless turned out to be "competent, confident, and caring adults" (1995, p. 82). Thus similar environments were linked to quite different outcomes.

Theorists such as Norman Garmezy, Michael Rutter, Ann Masten, and others (Garmezy, 1993; Garmezy & Rutter, 1983; Masten & Coatsworth, 1995; Rutter, 1987) argue that the best way to make sense out of results like Werner's is to think of each child as born with certain vulnerabilities, such as a difficult temperament, a physical abnormality, allergies, a genetic tendency toward alcoholism, or whatever. Each child is also born with some *protec-*

tive factors, such as high intelligence, good coordination, an easy temperament, or a lovely smile, that tend to make her more resilient in the face of stress. These vulnerabilities and protective factors then interact with the child's environment so that the *same* environment can have quite different effects, depending on the qualities the child brings to the interaction.

A more general model describing an interaction between the child's qualities and the environmental quality comes from Fran Horowitz, who proposes that the key ingredients are each child's vulnerability or resilience, plus the "facilitativeness" of the environment (1987; 1990). A highly facilitative environment is one in which the child has loving and responsive parents and is provided with a rich array of stimulation. If the relationship between vulnerability and facilitativeness were merely additive, we would find that the best outcomes occurred for resilient infants reared in optimum environments, the worst outcomes for vulnerable infants in poor environments, with the two mixed combinations falling halfway between. But that is not what Horowitz proposes, as you can see schematically in Figure 1.3. Instead, she is suggesting that a resilient child in a poor environment may do quite well, since such a child can take advantage of all the stimulation and opportunities available. Similarly, she suggests that a vulnerable child may do quite well in a highly facilitative environment. According to this model, it is only the double whammy—the vulnerable child in a poor environment—that leads to really poor outcomes for the child.

As you will see throughout this book, a growing body of research shows precisely this pattern. For example, among children born with very low birth weights, the lowest IQ scores are found for those who are *also* reared in poverty-level families. Equivalently low-birth-weight children reared in middle-

class families have essentially normal IQ scores, as do normal-weight infants reared in poverty-level families (Werner, 1986). Other researchers find that even among low-birth-weight children reared in poverty-level families, those whose families show "protective" factors (such as greater residential stability, less crowded living conditions, more acceptance of the child, more stimulation, and more learning materials) turn out better than do equivalently low-birth-weight children reared in the least optimum poverty conditions (Bradley, Whiteside, Mundfrom et al., 1994). The key point here is that neither the quality of the environment nor the child's inborn vulnerabilities alone cause specific outcomes; outcomes result from the unique combination of the two.

[?] *Critical Thinking*

Another possible variation of this same idea: Do you think it is possible that girls and boys, beginning in infancy, respond differently to their environments? If true, what would be the ramifications of such a pattern?

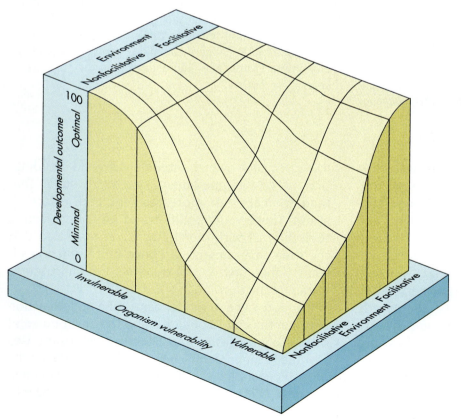

Figure 1.3

Horowitz's model describes one possible type of interaction between the vulnerability of the child and the quality of the environment. The height of the surface is the goodness of the developmental outcome (such as IQ or skill in social relationships). In this model, only the combination of a vulnerable infant and a nonfacilitative environment will result in really poor outcomes. (Source: Horowitz, 1987, Figure 1.1, p. 23.)

Finding the Answers: Research on Development

I've asked an enormous number of questions already in this chapter. Before you can understand the answers—before I can get to the really interesting stuff you are probably most curious about—you need one more tool, namely, at least a modicum of familiarity with the methods researchers use when they explore questions about development. You'll need such a familiarity to make sense out of the research I'll be talking about throughout this book. Those of you who do not make a career in some child-care field but who expect to be parents will also need such a skill if you are going to be intelligent consumers of research information provided through newspapers and magazines. Those of you who plan a career in teaching or child care will need such information even more, in order to glean useful information from the huge array of research findings that will come your way through professional journals, newsletters, and conferences.

Let me walk you through the various alternative methods by using a concrete example with clear practical ramifications. Imagine that you are a social scientist. One day you get a call from your local state representative. She has become seriously concerned about the apparently rising levels of crime and lawlessness among teenagers and wants to propose new legislation to respond to this problem. First, though, she wants to have some answers to a series of basic questions:

1. Does the same problem exist everywhere in the world, or only in the United States? If the latter, then what is it about our culture that promotes or supports such behavior?

2. At what age does the problem begin to be visible?

3. Which kids are most at risk for such delinquent behavior, and why?

How would you, could you, design one or more studies that might answer such questions? Where would you begin? You would face a number of decisions:

- To answer the question about the age at which delinquent acts begin, should you compare groups of children and teenagers of different

How would you go about trying to answer basic questions about the patterns and causes of delinquency in teenagers? The questions are easy to ask, but good answers require very careful research.

ages, or should you select a group of younger children and follow them over time, as they move into adolescence? And should you study young people in many settings or cultures, or in only one setting, such as inner-city youth in the United States? These are questions of *research design*.

- How will you measure delinquent behavior? Can you observe it? Can you ask about it? Can you rely on official records? What other things about each young person might you want to know to begin to answer the "why" question? Family history and relationships? Relationships with peers? Self-esteem? These are questions of *research methodology*.

- How will you analyze the data you collect and how will you interpret your findings? Suppose you find that young people whose families live in poverty are considerably more likely to be delinquent. Would you be satisfied to stop there, or would you want to analyze the results separately for each of several ethnic groups, for children growing up with single mothers, or in other ways that might clarify the meaning of your results? These are questions of *research analysis*.

Research Design

Choosing a research design is crucial for any research, but especially so when the subject matter you are trying to study is change (or continuity) with age. You have basically three choices: (1) You can study different groups of people of different ages, called a **cross-sectional design.** (2) You can study the *same* people over a period of time, called a **longitudinal design.** (3) Or you can combine the two in some fashion, using what is called a **sequential design** (Schaie, 1983; 1994). And if you want to know whether the same patterns hold across different cultures or contexts, you will need to do some kind of **cross-cultural research,** in which equivalent or parallel methods are used in more than one context.

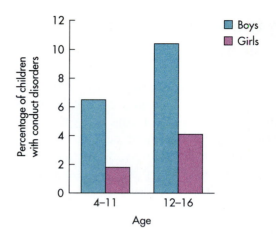

Figure 1.4

In this cross-sectional comparison from the Ontario study of conduct disorders, boys and teenagers showed higher rates of problem behavior. (Source: Offord, Boyle, & Racine, 1991, from Table I 2.4, p. 40.)

Cross-Sectional Designs

The key feature of a cross-sectional design is that the researcher studies groups of children (or adults) drawn from a series of separate age groups, with each subject tested only once. To study delinquency cross-sectionally you might select a group of subjects at each of a series of ages, such as 8, 10, 12, 14, and 16. You would then measure each child or teen's delinquent behavior along with whatever other characteristics you had decided were important. Figure 1.4 gives you the results from just such a study. It shows the rate of "conduct disorders" in a large random sample of all children between the ages of 4 and 16 in the province of Ontario, Canada (Offord, Boyle, & Racine, 1991). (A conduct disorder is akin to what is often called delinquency in everyday language.) The total sample is divided into two age groups, 4- to 11-year-olds and 12- to 16-year-olds, giving us a cross-sectional comparison of preadolescents versus adolescents. As a further division, the researchers report the results separately for boys and girls in each group. Clearly, conduct disorders in this sample were far more common among adolescents and in boys. Such a pattern of results is typical of studies in the United States and other Western countries as well as in Canada.

Cross-sectional research is often enormously useful. It is relatively quick to do, and when age differences are indeed found, it may suggest hypotheses about developmental processes. When the investigators collect a rich array of additional information about each subject, it can also yield highly interesting results. In the Ontario study, for example, Offord and his colleagues found that the probability of a conduct disorder was four times as high in low-income families, nearly three times as high in "dysfunctional" families (those in which the parents reported serious difficulty in communicating, planning, or organizing normal family activities), three times as high in families with domestic violence, and so forth. Thus a research design of this type can begin to tell us *which* children are at risk and give us some hints about the whys.

At the same time, cross-sectional designs have three major problems or limitations. The first of these is the "cohort problem."

The Cohort Problem. Social scientists use the term **cohort** to describe a group of individuals born within some fairly narrow band of years who share the same cultural/historical experiences at the same times in their lives. Within any given culture, successive cohorts may have quite different life experiences. For example, the 4-year-olds in the Offord study were born in 1979; the 16-year-olds were born in 1967. In that span of 12 years, in the United States, the percentage of children whose mothers were working rose about fourteen points; the proportion of children living in single-parent families increased from about eleven percent to about nineteen percent (Hernandez, 1994). Assuming that similar trends (albeit probably less extreme) were also true in Canada, then the two age groups in Figure 1.4 differ not just in age, but also in family experiences. Is the higher level of delinquency in the older group linked to age *per se* or to changes in culture? When we compare different age groups in a single study, as we do in any cross-sectional design, we are also inevitably comparing cohorts to some degree. Thus *cohort* and *age* are totally confounded, and we cannot tell whether some apparent age difference is really attributable to age or only to cohort differences. When the age groups we are comparing are close in age, as is true in most studies of children, this is not usually a major problem since we can assume roughly similar life circumstances. Over age ranges of as much as ten years, however, the cohort differences may be significant.

[?] *Critical Thinking*

Make a list of all the differences you can think of between the likely childhood experiences of the cohort born (in your country) in 1960 and the cohort born in 1980. How might those differences affect the behavior of the children in each group?

The Time-of-Measurement Problem.   A related difficulty is that any study is done at some specific historical time and the results may simply not generalize to other time periods. The Ontario study was done in 1982 and 1983. Would we find the same results if we were to repeat the study today? Might all the problem rates be higher? Would the same family characteristics predict conduct disorders now as predicted them then? This problem of generalizing across time periods is especially acute in any society or culture undergoing rapid change, as is the case in many Western cultures today.

Origins, Sequences, and Consistency.   Finally, and perhaps most important, cross-sectional research cannot tell us much about *sequences* of development or about the cumulative development of some pattern over time. The Ontario study doesn't tell us what factors contribute to the sharp increase in rates of conduct disorders in adolescence. It also doesn't tell us whether there is some typical sequence through which a child passes, such as from minor misbehavior to more serious lawlessness. To give you another example, a cross-sectional study of children's gender concepts might show that 2-year-olds have a different idea of gender than do 4-year-olds. But this won't tell us whether there are steps in between or whether every child acquires this concept in the same sequence.

Similarly, cross-sectional studies will not tell us anything about the consistency of individual behavior over time. For example, it won't tell us whether the children who show conduct disorders at 6 or 7 or 8 are likely to show the same kind of problem in adolescence.

Longitudinal Designs

Two of these three problems can be addressed with longitudinal designs, in which the *same* individuals are studied over a period of time. Such designs allow us to look at sequences of change and individual consistency or inconsistency over time. And because they compare performances by the same people at different ages, they avoid the cohort problem.

Because of these advantages, longitudinal research has become increasingly common. As just one example, research on the origins of aggression and delinquency includes a number of well-known longitudinal studies: Leonard Eron followed a group of 632 children from third grade to age 30, looking specifically at the links between childhood aggression and adult antisocial or criminal behavior (Eron, Huesmann, & Zelli, 1991). Gerald Patterson and his colleagues, as part of their research testing the model you've seen in Figure 1.2 (p. 17), have followed groups of boys thought to be at high risk for later delinquency from fourth grade through junior high school (Patterson, Capaldi, & Bank, 1991; Vuchinich et al., 1992). Terrie Moffitt (Caspi, Lynam, Moffitt, & Silva, 1993; Moffitt, 1990) has looked at the origins of delinquency in a group of more than 1000 children born in the town of Dunedin, New Zealand, in 1972 and 1973. Collectively, such longitudinal research adds enormously to our understanding of the origins of delinquency or aggression.

Longitudinal designs obviously have enormous advantages, but they are not a panacea. Because they are time consuming and expensive, researchers often study quite small samples, making it hard to generalize the findings to broader groups. This design also does not solve the time-of-measurement problem, because each study involves only one group, growing up in a particular

Only by studying the same children over time, such as this boy at three ages, can we identify consistencies (or changes) in behavior across age.

historical context. For example, both the longitudinal studies I described in the *Research Report* box on resilience on page 21 were begun many decades ago—one in the 1940s and one in the 1950s. Can we assume that we would find the same results if we repeated the same study today?

Sequential Designs

One solution to this problem is to repeat a longitudinal study several times, each time with a new cohort. This particular strategy, called a *cohort-sequential design*, is one of a family of research designs, called sequential designs, that involve combinations of cross-sectional or combinations of longitudinal designs, or both. Patterson's study, for example, involves two adjacent cohorts of fourth graders, one year apart, each followed through seventh grade. This makes it possible to check results found on the first group, and increases our confidence that a given pattern is not unique to some special set of children.

Another sequential design is the **time-lag design,** in which you look specifically at historical changes by studying groups at the same age in different cohorts. For example, if you want to know whether rates of teenage drug use are rising or falling, you could collect data on the same age group—perhaps 12- to 16-year-olds—every few years. This is exactly what the Centers for Disease Control do in their repeated studies of this question.

The most complex sequential design is called a **cross-sequential design,** which involves selecting a set of cross-sectional groups and then following *each* group longitudinally. For example, Rolf Loeber and his colleagues, in their Pittsburgh Youth Study (Loeber, Stouthamer-Loeber, Van Kammen, & Farrington, 1991; Lynam, Moffitt, & Stouthamer-Loeber, 1993; Maguin, Loeber, & LeMahieu, 1993), have been studying three groups of boys longitudinally, ages 7, 10, and 13 at the beginning of the study. Each group has so far been followed for four years, which gives the research design shown schematically in Figure 1.5. Such a design gives you an approximation of a longitudinal study covering the ages of 7 to 16, but it only takes four years to complete. And by overlapping the age groups, Loeber now has multiple sets of information on some ages.

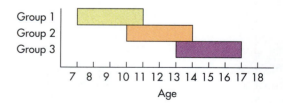

Figure 1.5

An example of a form of sequential research design called a cross-sequential *design. In this study, Rolf Loeber began with three groups of boys, initially aged 7, 10, and 13, and then followed* each *group for four years. This allows both cross-sectional and longitudinal comparisons with the same set of data.*

Table 1.3
Strengths and Weaknesses of the Major Developmental Research Designs

Design	Definition	Strengths	Weaknesses
Cross-sectional	Comparisons of separate groups at each of several ages	• Data can be collected fairly quickly • May suggest hypotheses about age differences or age changes	• Cohort and age groups are always confounded • Cannot tell us anything about individual consistency or sequences of development
Longitudinal	The same subjects studied repeatedly over a period of years	• Allows the study of consistency or inconsistency over time • Allows the study of sequences of development • Avoids the cohort problem	• Time consuming and expensive; hard to keep track of every subject • "Time of measurement" is still a problem
Sequential	Any combination of longitudinal and cross-sectional designs	• Can help avoid the time-of-measurement problem • May allow essentially longitudinal study of a broad range of years in a shorter time	• Complex; requires quite substantial numbers of subjects
Cross-cultural	Intensive study of a single culture; comparison of children or families in several cultures on the same measures	• Essential if we are to discover what aspects of development are truly universal • Enriches our knowledge and suggests new hypotheses	• Extremely difficult to do well • Problem of comparability of measurement across cultures
Experimental	Intentional manipulation of some variable thought to be important; random assignment of subjects to experimental and control groups	• Allows testing of specific causal hypotheses • Can frequently be done relatively quickly, with small numbers of subjects	• Many variables of interest to developmental psychologists cannot be intentionally manipulated

Complex sequential designs like these are becoming much more prevalent as researchers struggle to find ways to uncover basic developmental patterns.

Cross-Cultural or Cross-Context Designs

Also increasingly common are studies specifically designed to compare cultures or contexts, a task that researchers have approached in several ways.

One strategy involves what anthropologists call an **ethnography**—a detailed description of a single culture or context, based on extensive observation. Often the observer lives within the culture for a period of time, perhaps as long as several years. Each such ethnography is intended to stand alone, although it is sometimes possible to combine information from several different ethnographies to see whether similar developmental patterns exist in varying contexts (Whiting & Edwards, 1988). For example, are girls and boys given distinctly different tasks in every culture? Are such segregated gender assignments similar from one culture to the next?

Alternatively, investigators may attempt to compare two or more cultures directly, by studying or testing samples of children in each of several cultures or contexts, using the same or comparable instruments or measures. Sometimes this involves comparing across different countries, as in the example of research described in the *Cultures and Contexts* box on page 28. Sometimes the comparisons

Cultures and Contexts

An Example of a Cross-Cultural Comparison Study

Ann Fernald and Hiromi Morikawa's research on Japanese and American mothers' speech to their infants shows both strong cross-cultural similarities and interesting cultural variations (Fernald & Morikawa, 1993). They took video and audio recordings of 30 Japanese and 30 American mothers with their infants, in the family's own home, playing with the infant's own toys. Ten of the infants in each cultural group were 6 months old, 10 were a year old, and 10 were about 19 months old. So in each culture, Fernald and Morikawa have a cross-sectional study.

There are striking similarities in the ways these two groups of mothers speak to their infants—patterns that have been found in studies of mothers in many cultures (e.g., Fernald, Taeschner, Dunn et al., 1989). In both groups mothers simplify their speech, repeat themselves frequently, use intriguing sounds to attract the child's attention, and speak in a higher-pitched voice. Collectively this pattern is often labeled *motherese* or *infant-directed speech.*

Yet the mothers from these two cultural groups also differed, particularly in the kinds of things they said. One such difference was in the mothers' tendency to label toys or parts of toys for their infants. American mothers did this more often than did Japanese mothers, as you can see in the accompanying figure. The Japanese mothers, in contrast, used many more social routines—greetings such as *hello* and *bye-bye* (Kon-

nichiwa or *O'genki desu ka* in Japanese), or exchange routines involving offering and accepting things politely, such as *here you are* or *thank you* (*Dozo* [please help yourself], *Choodai* [give me], and *Arigatoo* [thank you] in Japanese). One consequence of these differences in the content of mothers' speech appears to be that American children learn more object words sooner. The American 19-month-olds in this study knew significantly more such words than did their Japanese counterparts.

Thus this cross-cultural study not only tells us something about how these two cultures differ, it also gives us important new insights about the whole process of language development during infancy and toddlerhood.

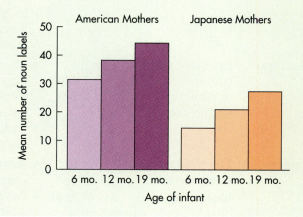

are between subcultures within the same country, as with the increasingly common research in the United States involving comparisons of children living in different ethnic groups or communities, such as African Americans, Hispanic Americans, Asian Americans, and European Americans. You'll see many examples of this kind of work as we go along.

Such cross-cultural or cross-context comparisons are immensely difficult to do well. One of the most troublesome difficulties is the problem of equivalence of measurement. Is it enough just to translate a particular test into another language? Will the same measure or assessment technique be equally valid in all cultures? Do behaviors have the same *meaning* in other contexts, other cultures? For example, Anne-Marie Ambert (1994) makes the point that when Western researchers study parent behavior, they begin with the assumption that the mother

is the most central figure in a child's upbringing. However, in many cultures in the world multiple mothering is the rule, and the biological mother may do relatively little nurturing. If we then try to measure the "quality" of the mother's caregiving behavior by counting the number of her nurturing acts or the frequency of her smiles or verbal interactions, we may come to quite erroneous conclusions.

[?] Critical Thinking

What other problems can you think of that would make it hard to do good cross-cultural research?

Despite these difficulties, cross-cultural research is vitally important if we are to uncover universal patterns of development and if we are to understand the ways in which environmental variation (cultural variation) affects children's development, a point evident in the Fernald and Morikawa study described in the *Cultures and Contexts* box.

Experimental Designs

Most of the research designs I have described so far are alternative ways to look at changes with age. If we are interested in examining a basic process—for example, learning or memory—or in *explaining* any observed phenomena, we may do an **experiment.**

An experiment is normally designed to test a specific hypothesis, a particular causal explanation. For example, Patterson hypothesized that the beginning of the chain of causal events implicated in aggressive and delinquent behavior lies in family discipline patterns. To test this, he might devise an intervention experiment, in which some families of aggressive children are given training in better discipline techniques; other families, with similar children, are given no training. At the end of the training, and perhaps some months or years later, he could check the effectiveness of the training by measuring the dependent variable, in this case the aggressiveness or delinquency of the children in the two groups.

A key feature of an experiment is that subjects are assigned *randomly* to participate in one of several groups. Subjects in the **experimental group** receive the treatment the experimenter thinks will produce an identified effect (such as training in disciplinary strategies), while those in the **control group** receive either no special treatment or a neutral treatment. The presumed causal element in the experiment is called the **independent variable** (in this case the training), and any behavior on which the independent variable is expected to have an effect is called a **dependent variable** (in this case aggression or delinquency).

You can see how all these pieces fit together in a description of a real experiment, on a highly applied problem, in the *Research Report* box on page 30.

Problems with Experiments in Studying Development. Experiments are essential for our understanding of many aspects of development. However, two special problems in studying child development limit the use of experimental designs.

First, many of the questions we want to answer have to do with the effects of particular unpleasant or stressful experiences on the child—for example, abuse, prenatal influences such as the mother's drinking, family poverty, or parental unemployment. For obvious ethical reasons, we cannot manipulate these variables. We cannot ask one set of pregnant women to have two alcoholic drinks a day and others to have none just so that we can see if the alcohol affects the child; we cannot randomly assign adults to become unemployed in order to see the effects of such unemployment on their children. To study the effects of such experiences we must rely on nonexperimental designs, including longitudinal and sequential studies.

Second, the independent variable in which we are often most interested is age itself, and *we cannot assign subjects randomly to age groups.* We can compare 4-year-olds and 6-year-olds in their approach to some particular task, such as searching for a lost object, but the children differ in their general experience in addition to their ages: Older children have obviously had more and different experiences. Thus, unlike psychologists studying other aspects of behavior, developmental psychologists *cannot* systematically manipulate many of the variables we are most interested in analyzing.

To skirt this problem, we can use any one of a series of strategies, sometimes called *quasi experiments*, in which we compare groups without assigning the subjects randomly. Cross-sectional comparisons are a form of quasi experiment. So are studies in which we select naturally occurring groups that differ in some dimension of interest, such as children whose parents choose to place them in day care programs compared with children whose parents rear them at home, or children in single-parent families versus those in two-parent families.

Such comparisons have built-in problems, because groups that differ in one way are likely to be different in other ways as well. Families who place their children in day care, compared with those who rear them at home, are likely to be poorer, may more often be single-parent families, and may have different values or religious backgrounds. If we find that the two groups of children differ in some fashion, is it because they have spent their daytime hours in different places or because of these other differences in their families? We can make such comparisons a bit cleaner if we select our comparison groups initially so that they are matched on those variables we think might matter, such as income or

Research Report

An Example of an Experimental Study with Practical Implications

In many parts of the world, particularly in the Third World, mothers carry their babies with them most of the time, using some kind of sling or wrap that keeps the child against the mother's body. In the United States, in recent years, variations on such a system have become a fairly common sight as well. Moms or dads are seen with a young infant snuggled against them, held by some kind of soft baby carrier. This not only allows moms or dads to have their hands free to work or move while keeping the baby nearby, it also seems to foster a more secure attachment. Mary Ainsworth observed such a link in her studies in Uganda (1967). Now we have experimental data from the United States demonstrating such a link.

Elizabeth Anisfeld and her colleagues (Anisfeld, Casper, Nozyce, & Cunningham, 1990) gave each of a group of low-income mothers a gift right after the birth of her baby. Half the mothers (those in the experimental group) were given a soft baby carrier; the other half (those in the comparison group, or control group) re-ceived a plastic infant seat. Both groups were encouraged to use the item daily, and most did use the item at least some of the time.

The dependent variable in this experiment is the security of the child's attachment later in infancy, measured at 13 months of age, using a standard method, Ainsworth's Strange Situation. When Anisfeld then compared the two groups on this dependent variable, she found that 87% of the experimental-group children but only 38% of the control-group children were securely attached. These experimental results confirm the observational evidence and, therefore, strengthen the argument that there is a causal link between security of attachment and regular physical contact between infant and parent. These results also have potential practical implications—possibly for you when/if you have an infant to carry and care for, and possibly for society as a whole.

Shown schematically, this experimental design looks like this:

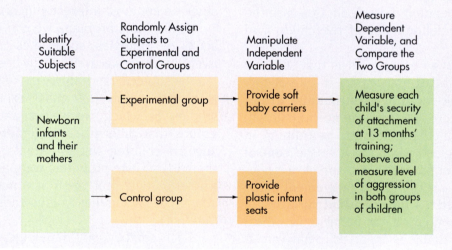

marital status or religion. Still, quasi experiments, by their very nature, will always yield more ambiguous results than will a fully controlled experiment.

Research Methods

Choosing a research design is only the first crucial decision an investigator must make. Equally important is to decide what subjects to study and how to study them.

Choosing the Subjects.   Because we would like to uncover basic developmental patterns that are true for all children or adolescents, the ideal strategy would be to select a random sample of all people in the world to study. This is clearly impractical, so some kind of compromise is necessary. One compromise, becoming more and more common in today's research, is to select large samples that are representative of some subgroup or population—such as the Ontario study I've already described (Figure 1.4, p. 24). This is a widely used strategy in sociology and epidemiology, and it can be very fruitful in psychology as well. But because it is difficult to collect highly detailed information from or about large numbers of subjects, we frequently trade depth for breadth.

The other alternative, very common in psychological research on children, is to focus on studying a smaller group of subjects in greater depth and detail in an attempt to uncover very basic processes. For instance, Alan Sroufe and his colleagues (Sroufe, 1989; Sroufe, Egeland, & Kreutzer, 1990) have studied a group of 267 children and families, beginning before the birth of the child. Families were deliberately chosen from among those thought to be at high risk for later caregiving problems, such as low-education single mothers with unplanned pregnancies. The children have now been repeatedly studied, each time in considerable detail. The sample is not representative of the population as a whole, but the results are enormously informative nonetheless and may tell us more about the process of emotional and social development than we could possibly glean from larger samples studied more broadly. Neither strategy is better than the other; both are useful. In either case, we need to remember that the conclusions we can draw will be limited by the sample we studied and by the type of information we could obtain.

Collecting the Information from Your Subjects: Observations and Questionnaires.

Having chosen your basic design and the subjects you want to study, you then need to decide how to assess them—how to *describe* their behavior, attitudes, or values in some way. How does a 2-year-old or a 4-year-old react to the presence of a strange adult? How often does a teenager show delinquent behavior? The two time-honored ways of trying to answer questions like these are observing people and asking them questions. Because infants and young children are not particularly good at answering questions, observation has been an especially prominent research strategy among developmental psychologists.

Careful observation, though, is not as easy as it may seem. Any researcher planning to use observation to collect information about children or their environments will have to make at least three further decisions: What shall I observe? Where shall I observe? How shall I record the observations?

The decision about what to observe can be divided still further: Should I try to observe everything a child does, or should I focus only on selected behaviors? Should I observe only the child, or should I also observe the immediate environment, such as the responses of the people around the child, or the quality of the home? Which I choose will depend largely on the basic question I am trying to address. If I am interested in the child's first words, I would not need to pay much attention to how close the child was sitting to an adult or whether the child exchanged mutual gazes with the adults in his vicinity. But I might want to make note of what the child was playing with, whether other people were present, and what they said to the child. On the other hand, if I were interested in the development of attachment, I would want to make note of mutual gazes as well as how close or far away from the parent the child might be standing or sitting.

It is also no simple matter to decide *where* we will observe. We can observe in a natural setting, such as a child's home or school, in which case we are introducing an enormous amount of variability into our measurements and increasing the complexity of the observation immensely. Alternatively, we can choose a controlled setting, keeping it the same for each child we observe. For example, the most commonly used measure of the security of a child's attachment to an adult is obtained in what is called the Strange Situation: The child is observed in a series of episodes in a laboratory setting, including periods with the mother, with the mother and a stranger, alone with a stranger, and reunited with the mother. By standardizing the situation, we gain the enormous advantage of having comparable information for each child, but we may lose some ecological validity. We cannot be sure that what we observe in this strange laboratory is representative of the child's behavior in more accustomed settings.

For researchers studying older children, questionnaires and interviews provide an excellent alternative to observation, such as in studies of children's moral development, which you'll read about in Chapter 14, or studies of peer relationships among elementary-school- and high-school-age children. Assessments of parent-child relationships are also often done with questionnaires.

Careful observations of children's behavior, such as those recorded by this psychology student in a day care center, have provided one essential source of information about early development.

Each of these alternatives has costs and benefits. Structured laboratory tests give the experimenter excellent control over the situation, ensuring that each subject is confronted with the same task. Yet, because they are artificial, such tests may not give us an accurate portrayal of how individuals behave in the more complex natural environment. Interviews, especially very open-ended ones in which the subject is only guided toward general topics, may give a rich picture of an individual's thoughts and feelings, but how do you reduce the answers to a set of scores that would allow you to compare groups or individuals with one another? Questionnaires solve some of this problem, but the trade-off may be the richness and individuality of replies. Often the best strategy—although one not always possible because of cost in time or money—is to collect many different kinds of information from or about each subject.

Research Analysis

Finally, you need to analyze the results of your research. In studies of development, researchers use two broad forms of analysis.

First, they can compare different age groups by simply calculating the average score of each group on some measure, just as the Ontario researchers did in comparing rates of conduct disorders for each age or gender group in the results shown in Figure 1.4.

A second strategy allows us to look at relationships between two separate variables, most often using a statistic called a **correlation.** A correlation is simply a number ranging from −1.00 to +1.00 that describes the strength of a relationship between two variables. A zero correlation indicates that there is no linear relationship between those variables. For instance, you might expect to find a zero or near-zero correlation between the length of big toes and IQ scores. People with toes of all sizes have high IQ scores, and those with toes of all sizes have low IQs. The closer a correlation comes to −1.00 or +1.00, the stronger the relationship being described. If the correlation is positive, it indicates that high scores on the two dimensions tend to go together—as do low scores—such as length of big toes and shoe size, for example. Height and weight are also strongly positively correlated.

If the correlation is negative, it describes a relationship in which high scores on one variable are associated with low scores on the other. There is a negative correlation between the amount of disorder and chaos in a family and the child's later IQ score (high chaos is associated with lower IQ, and low chaos with higher IQ).

Correlational relationships can also be shown in something called a **scatter plot,** in which the paired pieces of information are laid out in a two-dimensional grid, such as the ones in Figure 1.6 (p. 34). Figure 1.6(a) shows a high correlation of .74. In this case, the numbers represent IQ scores for 39 pairs of identical twins reared apart from each other, drawn by Susan Farber from a number of classic studies of this type (1981). If the correlation were perfect (+1.00), all the score-pairs would fall along the diagonal line. Clearly, many pairs of twins did not have identical IQ scores; equally clearly, there is a strong tendency for high scores to go together and

Research Report

Ethical Issues in Research on Development

Anytime we try to understand human behavior by observing, testing, asking questions, we are probing into personal lives. If we go into homes to observe the way parents interact with their children, we are invading their privacy. We may even inadvertently give the impression that there must be something wrong with the way they are raising their family. If we give adults or children laboratory tests, some subjects will do very well, others will not. How will the less-successful subject interpret this experience? What is the risk that some subject will become depressed over what he perceives as a poor performance?

Any research on human behavior involves some risks and raises some ethical questions. Because of this, psychologists and other social and biological scientists have established clear procedures and guidelines that researchers must follow before they make any observation or give any test. In every school or college—the settings in which most such research is done—there is a committee of peers who must approve any research plan involving human subjects. The most basic guideline is that subjects must always be protected from any potential mental or physical harm. More specific principles include the following.

Informed Consent. Each adult subject must give written consent to participate. In the case of research on children, the investigator must ask the parent or guardian for informed consent. In every case, the researcher must explain the procedure and its possible consequences in detail, describing as fully as possible any potential risks. For example, if you were studying patterns of communication between teenagers and their parents, you might want to observe each family while they talked about some unresolved issue between them. As part of your informed consent request, you would have to explain to each family that while such discussions often lead to greater clarity, they also occasionally increase tension. And you would need to provide support and debriefing at the end of the procedure to assist any family who found the task stressful or destabilizing.

Right of Privacy. Researchers must make sure that any highly personal information about individual subjects will be kept entirely private, including information about income, attitudes, or illegal behavior like drug taking. Researchers can use the information *collectively,* but they cannot report it individually in any way that will associate a subject's name with some piece of data—unless the subject has specifically given permission for such use.

In virtually all cases, it is also unethical for investigators to observe subjects through a one-way mirror without the subject's knowledge or to secretly record behavior.

Testing Children. These principles are important for any research, but particularly so for research on children. Any child who balks at being tested or observed must *not* be tested or observed; any child who becomes distressed must be comforted; any risk to the child's self-esteem must be avoided.

---

for low scores to go together, which is what the correlation of .74 expresses.

Figure 1.6(b) shows a somewhat weaker relationship, a correlation of .56 between the heights of fathers and of sons in a sample of 192 father-son pairs (McNemar, 1955). You can see that, on average, tall fathers have taller sons, but there is more variability than is apparent in the first scatter plot, hence the lower correlation.

Perfect correlations (−1.00 or +1.00) do not happen in the real world, but correlations of .60 to .80 clearly do occur and are interpreted as reflecting strong relationships. As one further example, the correlation between grades in freshman and sophomore years of college are usually in the range of .75. Correlations between .30 and .60, such as the one in Figure 1.6(b), are more common in psychological research, describing relationships that may suggest important hypotheses or allow helpful predictions. For instance, in the Patterson study I have mentioned several times, the correlation between fourth grade ratings of antisocial behavior and eighth grade delinquency was .46—a moderate relationship, well above chance but still with a fair amount of variation.

Correlations are an enormously useful descriptive tool. They can tell us about consistency over time, or about links between two environmental

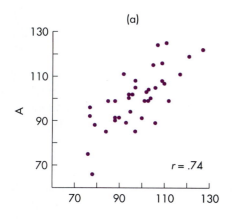

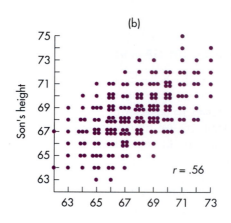

Figure 1.6

Two examples of scatter plots to illustrate high and moderate correlations. Figure 1.6(a) shows a correlation of .74 between IQ scores of pairs of identical twins reared apart. Figure 1.6(b) shows a correlation of .56 between the heights of fathers and sons for a sample of 192 pairs. (Sources: Data for (a) from Farber, 1981, Table 7.1, pp. 171–179; data for (b) from McNemar, 1955, Table 11, p. 123.)

variables, or about links between the child's behavior and some experience he may have had. Useful as they are, though, correlations have a major limitation: They do not tell us about *causal* relationships. For example, several researchers have found a moderate positive correlation between the "difficultness" of a child's temperament and the amount of punishment the child receives from his parents: The more difficult the temperament, the more punishment the child experiences. The problem is to figure out which way the causality runs. Do difficult children *elicit* more punishment? Or does a greater rate of punishment lead to a more difficult temperament? Or is there some third factor that may cause both, such as perhaps some genetic contribution both to the child's difficultness and to the parent's personality? The correlation alone does not allow us to choose among these alternatives. Stating the point more generally: No correlation, standing alone, can prove causality. A correlation may point in a particular direction or suggest possible causal links, but to discover the causes we must then explore such possibilities with other techniques, including experiments.

The Practical Value of Research Sophistication

Even after my best attempts to persuade you that information on research methods is important for your future role as parent or child-care professional, it may still seem to you that these details about research design are of interest and value only to professional researchers. So let me try one

more time to convince you of the many practical, daily applications for knowledge of this kind.

An example: An issue of *Time* magazine several years ago included an article about a system for providing stimulation for the unborn baby. The pregnant woman is supposed to wear a belt full of audio equipment on which tapes of various complex patterns of heartbeat sounds are played. The article reported that the maker of this gadget had done some "research" to demonstrate that this procedure produces smarter, faster-developing babies. To quote *Time:* "Last year 50 of the youngsters [whose mothers had worn the belt], ranging in age from six months to 34 months, were given standardized language, social and motor-skills tests. Their overall score was 25% above the national norm" (September 30, 1991, p. 76).

I hope you would not go out and buy this apparatus on the basis of that finding! After reading what I've said about research design you should be able to see immediately that self-selection is a major problem here. What kind of mothers will buy such a gadget? How are they likely to differ from mothers who would not buy it? In fact, this reported "research" tells us nothing. It isn't even a quasi experiment because there is no comparison group.

[?] *Critical Thinking*

See if you can design a really good study to test the manufacturer's claim that this gadget will make babies smarter.

On the other side of the coin, good research is also often reported in newspapers or magazines—

Psychology in Action

Analysis of Research Presented in Popular Sources

Find at least five separate mentions of research on children or adolescents in newspapers and magazines. For each item, describe the research design that appears to have been used. Is that design appropriate for the question being asked? Are there any flaws you can detect? Does the report in the magazine or newspaper give you enough detail to decide whether the research was any good? What other information would you want to have to decide on the quality of the research?

Some sources you might try for suitable articles:

1. The *New York Times* has a science section every Tuesday that includes articles about behavior and development fairly regularly. The *Times* also has a column titled "Personal Health" each week that often covers relevant material, as well as another weekly column on children's behavior or on parenting.
2. *Time* and *Newsweek* have sections on "behavior" that may be relevant.
3. Most so-called women's magazines (*Ladies Home Journal, Redbook, Family Circle,* etc.) have columns on child rearing or children's development.

although you have to read carefully to figure out what is good and what is not. For example, in February 1996, the *New York Times* published an article with the headline "Lead in Kids' Bones May Be Tied to Crime." The article reported briefly on a study comparing levels of aggression and delinquency in two groups of boys, those with high and those with low concentrations of lead in their blood, finding a link between the two: Kids with higher lead levels in their blood were more likely to be delinquent. The newspaper article says, "The researchers concluded that limiting children's exposure to lead could help prevent them from becoming criminals as adults." What's the problem here? The difficulty, as I'm sure most of you saw immediately, is that this is essentially correlational evidence. The article tells us that high blood lead and aggression tend to go together, but I can think of several other possible explanations of such a link, other than the conclusion that high blood lead levels *cause* aggression, or even contribute to aggressiveness. In particular, I know that children growing up in poverty are more likely to be exposed to high levels of lead *and* are more likely to be high in aggression and delinquency. The newspaper article didn't tell me whether the researchers had somehow controlled for this factor. So I went to the library, copied the original research paper on which the newspaper article was based (Needleman, Riess, Tobin, Biesecker, & Greenhouse, 1996), and read the details for myself. In this case, I found that the au-

thors had indeed been very careful to make sure that the high and low lead groups were statistically matched in poverty, mother's level of education, and other factors that we might guess would contribute to aggression or delinquency. And they still found a link between lead levels and aggression. The basic data are still correlational; it is possible that there is some other explanation. But this careful research makes it considerably more plausible that there may be some kind of causal link between blood lead and aggression.

Equivalent reports of research on children and adolescents appear in newspapers and popular magazines every day. Obviously, I want you to be critical analysts of the research I'll talk about in this book. Even more basically, I want you to become very critical consumers of popularly presented research information. Some of it is very good. Some of it is bunk or, at the very least, inconclusive. I hope you are now in a better position to tell the difference.

Summary

1. Studying human development scientifically has direct importance for you as a parent, as a child-care professional, and as a member of a society faced with myriad problems related to children's welfare.
2. To understand the process of human development we must address a set of fundamental, enduring

questions: the role of nature and nurture; developmental universals and individual variations; continuity and change; the nature of development itself.

3. Both nature and nurture, biology and culture, are involved in all aspects of development, although there has been long-standing disagreement on the relative importance of these factors.

4. Current thinking about the nature side of the equation emphasizes not only the role of maturation but also points to potential inborn strategies of perceiving or responding to the environment.

5. Modern behavior genetics research has also shown clearly that there is some genetic component in nearly every dimension of behavior and development, including cognitive skills, physical characteristics, personality patterns, and deviant behaviors.

6. Current thinking about the nurture side of the equation emphasizes not only the potential importance of the timing of some experience and the significance of a child's interpretation of some experience but also the importance of examining the entire ecological system in which development occurs, including culture.

7. We need to understand those aspects of development that are the same across cultures, as well as the ways in which cultural variations shape children's development in distinct ways.

8. Nature and nurture may not interact in precisely the same way for each child. Children with different inborn qualities (such as vulnerability or resilience) may be affected differently by the same environment.

9. A first major question in planning research is the basic research design. Cross-sectional studies compare different children of different ages; longitudinal studies observe the same children as they develop over time; sequential studies combine some of these features; and cross-cultural studies compare children, their rearing, or nature/nurture relationships in differing cultures or subcultures. Each of these designs has particular strengths and drawbacks.

10. One way to test for causal connections is with an experimental design. In an experiment the researcher controls (manipulates) one or more relevant variables and assigns subjects randomly to different treatment and control groups.

11. In a quasi experiment, subjects are not randomly assigned to separate groups; rather, existing groups are compared. Quasi experiments are needed in developmental research because subjects cannot be randomly assigned either to age groups or to groups that experience such negative treatments as poverty, abuse, or poor attachment.

12. Decisions about research methods include the choice of subjects to be studied and the methods to be used to observe or assess them.

13. When research results are analyzed, the two most common methods are comparing average scores between groups and describing relationships among variables with the statistic called a correlation. A correlation can range from +1.00 to −1.00, and describes the strength of relationship. Correlations may suggest possible causal connections, but correlations cannot prove a causal link.

14. You need some knowledge of research strategies and design to become an informed consumer of research information contained in the popular press. You should not believe everything you read!

Key Terms

behavior genetics   The study of the genetic basis of behavior, such as intelligence or personality. **(p. 11)**

cohort   A group of persons of approximately the same age who have shared similar major life experiences, such as cultural training, historical events, or general economic conditions. **(p. 24)**

collectivism   A cultural perspective or belief system, contrasted with individualism, in which the emphasis is on collective rather than individual identity and on group solidarity, decision making, duties, and obligations. Characteristic of most Asian, Hispanic, and African cultures. **(p. 17)**

control group   The group of subjects in an experiment that receives either no special treatment or some neutral treatment. **(p. 29)**

correlation   A statistic used to describe the degree or strength of a relationship between two variables. It can range from +1.00 to −1.00. The closer it is to ±1.00, the stronger the relationship being described. **(p. 32)**

critical period   Any time period during development when the organism is especially responsive to and learns from a specific type of stimulation. The same stimulation at other points in development has little or no effect. **(p. 14)**

cross-cultural research   Research involving in-depth study of another culture or comparisons of several cultures or subcultures. **(p. 24)**

cross-sectional design   A form of research in which samples of subjects from several different age groups are studied at the same time. **(p. 24)**

cross-sequential design   A complex combination of cross-sectional and longitudinal research designs in which groups of subjects of several different ages are initially selected and compared, and then all groups are followed longitudinally. **(p. 26)**

culture   A system of meanings and customs, shared by some identifiable group or subgroup, and transmitted from one generation of that group to the next. **(p. 16)**

dependent variable   The variable in an experiment that is expected to show the impact of manipulations of the independent variable; also called the outcome variable. **(p. 29)**

ethnic group   "A subgroup whose members are perceived by themselves and others to have a common origin and culture, and shared activities in which the common origin or culture is an essential ingredient" (Porter & Washington, 1993, p. 140). **(p. 18)**

ethnography   A detailed description of a single culture or context, based on extensive observation by a resident observer. **(p. 27)**

experiment   A research strategy in which subjects are assigned randomly to experimental and control groups. The experimental group is then provided with some designated experience that is expected to alter behavior in some fashion. **(p. 29)**

experimental group   The group (or groups) of subjects in an experiment given a special treatment intended to produce some specific consequence. **(p. 29)**

independent variable   A condition or event an experimenter varies in some systematic way in order to observe the impact of that variation on the subjects' behavior. **(p. 29)**

individualism   A cultural perspective or belief system, contrasted with collectivism, in which the emphasis is placed on the separateness and independence of individual development and behavior. Characteristic of most Western cultures. **(p. 17)**

longitudinal design   A research design in which the same subjects are observed or assessed repeatedly over a period of months or years. **(p. 24)**

maturation   The sequential unfolding of physical characteristics, governed by instructions contained in the genetic code and shared by all members of a species. **(p. 9)**

scatter plot   A way to display the type of data on which a correlation is based. **(p. 32)**

sensitive period   Similar to a critical period, except broader and less specific. A time in development when a particular type of stimulation is particularly important or effective. **(p. 15)**

sequential design   A family of research designs involving multiple cross-sectional or multiple longitudinal studies, or a combination of the two. **(p. 24)**

teratogen   Any outside agent, such as a disease or a chemical, the presence of which significantly increases the risk of deviations or abnormalities in prenatal development. **(p. 14)**

time-lag design   A comparison of groups of subjects of the *same* age in different cohorts, such as studying drug use in a separate sample of 15-year-olds each year for 20 years; allows a direct examination of cohort changes in some behavior. **(p. 26)**

Suggested Readings

Bornstein, M. H. (Ed.). (1987). *Sensitive periods in development. Interdisciplinary perspectives*. Hillsdale, NJ: Erlbaum. Bornstein's own paper in this collection of reports is an excellent introduction to the concept of sensitive periods, but the book also contains a number of reports of research exploring potential sensitive periods both in humans and in other animals.

Cole, M. (1992). Culture in development. In M. H. Bornstein & M. E. Lamb (Eds.), *Developmental psychology: An advanced textbook* (3rd ed.) (pp. 731–789). Hillsdale, NJ: Erlbaum. Cole's paper is not at all easy reading, but it offers the best analysis I have yet seen on this very complicated subject.

Greenfield, P. M., & Cocking, R. R. (Eds.). (1994). *Cross-cultural roots of minority child development*. Hillsdale, NJ: Erlbaum. One of the central themes in this excellent collection of papers is the impact of individualism and collectivism on the lives of children in different cultural contexts.

Plomin, R., & McClearn, G. E. (Eds.). (1993). *Nature, nurture & psychology*. Washington, DC: American Psychological Association. If you think the "great debate" about nature and nurture is an old issue, this book will quickly persuade you otherwise. The controversy is alive and well, although the papers in this book reflect the efforts of many people to recast it in more useful terms.

Rowe, D. C. (1994). *The limits of family in uence: Genes, experience, and behavior*. New York: Guilford Press. A clear, well-reasoned book arguing that developmental psychologists have greatly exaggerated the effects of "nurture" on variations in personality, intelligence, and other characteristics and greatly underestimated the effects of heredity. A good introduction to some current thinking on the nature/nurture controversy.

Seitz, V. (1988). Methodology. In M. H. Bornstein & M. E. Lamb (Eds.), *Developmental psychology: An advanced textbook* (2nd ed.) (pp. 51–84). Hillsdale, NJ: Erlbaum. A very good source for a further exploration of various methods of research. Well organized and clearly written.

CHAPTER 2

Theories of Development

Preview Questions

1 How do different theories about child development lead to different behavior by parents or teachers?

2 What are the three "grand schemes" in developmental psychology, and how do they differ?

3 How can we apply basic learning concepts like positive reinforcement, negative reinforcement, and modeling to the study of child development?

4 What basic questions about children's development are central to biological, ecological, and developmental psychopathology models?

Chapter Outline

Two teachers are arguing. The first one says:

> "I want my kids to have time to *explore*, to figure things out for themselves. If I have everything scheduled down to a gnat's eyelash, they don't have any time to play with objects or ideas."

The second teacher replies:

> "I don't want my kids to 'explore' on their own. I want them to stay focused on the tasks I think are important. I want to have control over the classroom so that I can emphasize the important things, reward the kids for good behavior, and restrain their wildness."

These two teachers are probably both very good at their jobs but they go about their task very differently; they have different goals because they are operating with different *theories* of children's development or children's learning. The first teacher is basing her argument on the assumption that children are necessarily active participants in their own development, that they reach understanding by their own explorations and experiments—an argument central to cognitive-developmental theory. The second teacher is basing her argument on the assumption that children are shaped by their environment, so for learning to occur she must control that environment—an argument central to learning theories of development.

This disagreement is an example of just how powerful theories can be. Because they assume different things about children and their development—assumptions they might not even be aware of or be able to articulate clearly—these two teachers behave differently with the children in their classes.

Let me give you another example of how theories can affect our day-to-day behavior. Imagine yourself as a brand-new teacher or day-care worker with your first class of preschoolers. A week or so into the school year you notice that several of the children seem to pull back whenever you try to touch them. Sometimes these youngsters even turn their back on you or step backward when you approach. These are accurate observations; they are "facts." But how do you *interpret* those facts? What theory do you have to explain the behavior of these children? If you think about it for a minute, you'll realize that the theory or explanation you apply to this set of circumstances will make a huge

difference in the way you react to the children. If you are a person who has experienced significant rejection in your own life, you may interpret the children's behavior as being rejection of you, which may lead you to avoid those children in the future. Another possible theory would be to conclude that you must not be a very good teacher, since children can't even bear to be near you. This may lead to a loss of confidence, with general repercussions for your teaching. A third theory would be that these children are temperamentally shy and require a different kind of handling from the more boisterous, approachable kids in the class. Thus the explanation you give yourself—your theory, if you will—for the children's behavior affects your thinking and your behavior.

Scientists operate this way too. Naturally, we try to collect facts. But both the collection of the facts and the interpretation of them are guided by theory. For example, here's a fact: Virtually all children show some negative effects when their parents divorce, but boys show a greater increase than do girls in aggression and other behavior problems, and their school performance deteriorates more than is true for girls (e.g., Hetherington, 1989; Kline, Tschann, Johnston, & Wallerstein, 1989).

When parents divorce, boys are more likely to show disturbed behavior or poorer school performance than are girls. But why? We need theories to help us explain facts like this.

This fact is extremely interesting in and of itself, but the fact itself doesn't provide an explanation. Do mothers treat their sons and daughters differently after a divorce? Do boys suffer more from the absence of the father? Or perhaps boys are somehow inherently less able to handle stress of any kind. Each of these alternative explanations is derived from a different theory; each suggests different types of additional research we might do to check on the validity of the explanation. If differential treatment of sons and daughters is the answer, then we ought to study family interactions in recently divorced families in some detail. If the absence of the father in the son's life is the crucial factor, then we ought to study boys and girls living with their fathers after divorce. If response to stress is involved, we would want to look at other stressful occurrences in family life, such as unexpected parental unemployment, the death of a family member, or a major move, and see whether in these cases, too, boys show more extreme responses.

The key point is that no fact stands alone, without any explanation or framework; instead, we all interpret and create theories about each fact that comes our way, whether in our personal experience or in scientific endeavor. A theory provides a kind of road map. And just as you can get lost if you are trying to make your way in a strange city without a road map, so you can get lost in the minutiae of observation without a theory to guide you. To use another analogy, theories help us to see the size and shape of the forest instead of the individual trees.

In developmental psychology, we have many types or layers of theories. At the broadest level, we have three **grand schemes:** psychoanalytic theory, cognitive-developmental theory, and learning theory—each designed to describe and explain the great sweep of human development and human behavior. These grand schemes have been and continue to be enormously influential, shaping the language we use, the assumptions we make, the kinds of questions we ask. Indeed, the teachers I quoted at the beginning of the chapter are each strongly influenced by one of these grand schemes.

Most psychologists, although still shaped by these grand schemes, work primarily with smaller-scale theories, which we might call **models.** Behavior genetics offers one such model; Bronfenbrenner's ecological approach is another. Neither model is designed to account for all behavior or to explain all development. But each model points us toward important sources of information, toward key questions or hypotheses.

Finally, we have **minitheories,** each designed to explain a narrow range of behavior. For example, Susan Harter proposes a minitheory about the origins of variations in self-esteem, which I'll talk about in Chapter 12; Laurence Steinberg suggests a minitheory to explain the rise in parent-child conflict at the beginning of adolescence (Chapter 15); information processing theorists (of which there are many) have brought concepts from computer simulations of adult intelligence to the problem of explaining children's cognitive development (Chapter 11); and so on. Many such minitheories have their roots in the grand schemes, but the theorists' goals are much more modest. They aren't trying for a theory to explain everything, merely a theory that will handle the data in a narrow area. Ultimately, of course, we hope to be able to add up these minitheories and models into new grand schemes.

My primary goal in this chapter is to introduce you to the three grand schemes and to several of the influential current models. A second goal is to make clear just how real and potentially important the differences among these various theories and models can be, affecting not only the way researchers interpret data, but the way teachers interact with their pupils, the way physicians or nurses act with their patients, or the way we as parents deal with our children. Let's begin with a look at the three grand schemes.

Psychoanalytic Theories

Theorists in the psychoanalytic tradition have been interested in explaining human behavior by understanding the underlying processes of the *psyche,* a Greek term meaning "soul or spirit, mind." Sigmund Freud (1856–1939) (1905; 1920) is usually credited with originating the psychoanalytic approach, and his terminology and many of his concepts have become part of our intellectual culture, even while his explicit influence on developmental psychology has waned. Two other theorists in this tradition, however, remain directly influential: Erik Erikson and John Bowlby.

Some Basic Freudian Concepts

One of Freud's most distinctive theoretical contributions is the idea that behavior is governed not only by conscious but by **unconscious** processes. The most basic of these unconscious processes, according to Freud, is an instinctual sexual drive he called the *libido*, present at birth and forming the motive force behind virtually all our behavior.

Freud also argued that personality has a structure that develops over time. Freud proposed three parts: the **id,** in which the libido is centered; the **ego,** a much more conscious element that serves as the executive of the personality; and the **superego,** the center of conscience and morality, incorporating the norms and moral strictures of the family and society. In Freud's theory, these three parts are not all present at birth. The infant and toddler is all id, all instinct, all desire, without the restraining influence of the ego or the superego. The ego begins to develop in the years from age 2 to about 4, as the child learns to adapt his instant-gratification strategies. Finally, the superego be-

Freud thought that babies put things into their mouths because that is where they have the most pleasurable sensations. If babies don't get enough oral stimulation, he argued, they may become fixated at the oral stage.

gins to develop just before school age, as the child incorporates the parents' values and cultural mores.

Freud also proposed a series of **psychosexual stages** (summarized in Table 2.1) through which the child moves in a fixed sequence that is strongly influenced by maturation. In each stage the libido is invested in that part of the body that is most sensitive at that age. In a newborn the mouth is the most sensitive part of the body, so libidinal energy is focused there. The stage is therefore called the *oral* stage. As neurological development progresses, the infant develops more sensation in the anus (hence the *anal* stage), and later in the genitalia (the *phallic* and eventually the *genital* stages).

Few developmental psychologists today still use Freud's language to describe these several stages; fewer still accept the idea of erogenous zones as a basic explanatory device. But Freud's description of the **Oedipus conflict,** said to occur during the phallic stage, has had a lasting impact. According to Freud, this stage begins at about age 3 or 4, when the genitals increase in sensitivity. He proposed that during this stage, the boy, having discovered his penis, rather naively wishes to use this newfound source of pleasure to please his oldest source of pleasure, his mother. He becomes envious of his father, who has access to the mother's body in a way that the boy does not. The boy also sees his father as a powerful and threatening figure who has the ultimate power—the power to cas-

Many of the specifics of Freud's groundbreaking psychoanalytic theory are no longer widely accepted, but many of his concepts pervade psychology, including the idea of unconscious motivation, and the process of identification.

Table 2.1
Freud's Stages of Psychosexual Development

Stage	Age	Erogenous Zones	Major Developmental Task (potential source of conflict)	Some Adult Characteristics of Children Who Have Been Fixated at This Stage
Oral	0–1	Mouth, lips, tongue	Weaning	Oral behavior, such as smoking, overeating; passivity and gullibility.
Anal	2–3	Anus	Toilet training	Orderliness, parsimoniousness, obstinacy, or the opposite.
Phallic	4–5	Genitalia	Oedipus complex	Vanity, recklessness, and the opposite.
Latency[*]	6–12	No specific area	Development of defense mechanisms	None: Fixation does not normally occur at this stage.
Genital	13–18	Genitalia	Mature sexual intimacy	Adults who have successfully integrated earlier stages should emerge with a sincere interest in others and a mature sexuality.

[*]The latency period, strictly speaking, is not a psychosexual stage because Freud thought that libido was not invested in the body during this period; sexual energy is quiescent in this period.

trate. The boy is caught between desire for his mother and fear of his father's power.

Most of these feelings and the resultant conflict are unconscious. The boy does not have overt sexual feelings or behavior toward his mother. But unconscious or not, the result of this conflict is anxiety. How can the little boy handle this anxiety? In Freud's view, the boy responds with a defensive process called **identification:** The boy "incorporates" his image of his father and attempts to match his own behavior to that image. By trying to make himself as like his father as possible, the boy not only reduces the chance of an attack from the father, he takes on some of the father's power as well. Furthermore, it is the "inner father," with his values and moral judgments, that serves as the core of the child's superego.

[?] *Critical Thinking*

Can you think of any kind of study that would tell us whether Freud was right or not about the Oedipal crisis?

A parallel process is supposed to occur in girls. The girl experiences the same kind of "sexual" attraction to her father as the boy does toward his mother, sees her mother as a rival for her father's sexual attentions, and has some fear of her mother. Like the boy, she resolves the problem by identifying with the same-sexed parent.

Optimum development, according to Freud, requires an environment that will satisfy the unique needs of each period. The baby needs sufficient opportunity for oral stimulation; the 4-year-old boy needs a father present with whom to identify and a mother who is not too seductive. An inadequate early environment will leave a residue of unresolved problems and unmet needs, which are then carried forward to subsequent stages.

[?] *Critical Thinking*

Does this make sense to you—this idea that one carries unresolved issues forward into adulthood? Can you think of any examples from your own experience?

This emphasis on the formative role of early experience, particularly early family experience, is a hallmark of psychoanalytic theories. In this view, the first five or six years of life are a kind of sensitive period for the creation of the individual personality.

Erikson's Theory of Psychosocial Stages

A more contemporary theory in the psychoanalytic mold comes from Erik Erikson (1902–1994) (Erikson, 1950; 1980a; 1980b; 1982; Erikson, Erikson, & Kivnick, 1986; Evans, 1969). Erikson shared most of Freud's basic assumptions but differed from him on several key points. Unlike Freud, who placed central emphasis on inner instincts, Erikson thought development resulted from the interaction between inner instincts and outer cultural and social demands. He therefore labeled his developmental stages **psychosocial stages** rather than psycho*sexual* stages. Furthermore, Erikson thought that development continued through the entire life span, as the child and then the adult developed a sense of ever-changing **identity.** To develop a complete, stable identity, the individual must move through and successfully resolve eight "crises" or "dilemmas" over the course of the lifetime, summarized in Table 2.2. Each dilemma emerges as the

child or adult is challenged by new relationships, tasks, or demands. The fourth stage of "industry versus inferiority," for example, begins when the child starts school and is challenged by the demand to learn to read and write and absorb great chunks of new information.

Each dilemma or stage is defined by a pair of opposing possibilities, such as trust versus mistrust or integrity versus despair. A healthy resolution of each dilemma results in the development of a particular strength, such as the quality of hope that may emerge from the dilemma of trust versus mistrust. A "healthy resolution" of each dilemma, however, does not mean moving totally to the ap-

Table 2.2

Erikson's Stages of Psychosocial Development

Approximate Age	Ego Quality to Be Developed	Potential Strength to Be Gained	Some Tasks and Activities of the Stage
0–1	Basic trust versus mistrust	Hope	Trust in mother or central caregiver and in one's own ability to make things happen. A key element in an early secure attachment.
2–3	Autonomy versus shame, doubt	Will	New physical skills lead to free choice; toilet training occurs; child learns control but may develop shame if not handled properly.
4–5	Initiative versus guilt	Purpose	Organize activities around some goal; become more assertive and aggressive; Oedipus conflict with parent of same sex may lead to guilt.
6–12	Industry versus inferiority	Competence	Absorb all the basic cultural skills and norms, including school skills and tool use.
13–18	Identity versus role confusion	Fidelity	Adapt sense of self to pubertal changes, make occupational choice, achieve adult-like sexual identity, and search for new political and religious values.
19–25	Intimacy versus isolation	Love	Form one or more intimate relationships that go beyond adolescent love; form family groups.
26–65	Generativity versus self-absorption and stagnation	Care	Bear and rear children, focus on occupational achievement or creativity, and train the next generation; turn outward from the self toward others.
65+	Integrity versus despair	Wisdom	Integrate earlier stages and come to terms with basic identity. Accept self.

Erik Erikson, who died only in 1994, continues to have a substantial influence on modern developmental psychologists.

parently positive end of any one of the continua Erikson describes. For example, an infant needs to have experienced some mistrust in order to learn to trust discerningly; too much industriousness can lead to narrow virtuosity; too much identity cohesion in adolescence can result in fanaticism. But healthy development requires a favorable ratio of positive to negative. Let me give you a bit more detail on the five stages in childhood that Erikson described.

Basic Trust Versus Basic Mistrust: Birth–1 Year.
Erikson believed that the behavior of the major caregiver (usually the mother) is critical to the child's establishment of a sense of basic trust. For a successful resolution of this task, the parent must be consistently loving and respond predictably and reliably to the child. Those infants whose early care has been erratic or harsh may develop *mistrust*. In either case, the child carries this

aspect of basic identity through development, affecting the resolution of later tasks.

Autonomy Versus Shame and Doubt: 2–3 Years.
Erikson saw the child's greater mobility during the toddler years as forming the basis for the sense of independence or autonomy. But if the child's efforts at independence are not carefully guided by the parents and she experiences repeated failures or ridicule, then the results of all the new opportunities for exploration may be shame and doubt instead of a basic sense of self-control and self-worth. Once again the ideal is not for the child to have *no* shame or doubt; some doubt is needed for the child to understand which behaviors are acceptable and which are not, which are safe and which are dangerous. But the ideal does lie toward the autonomy end of the continuum.

Initiative Versus Guilt: 4–5 Years.
This phase, roughly equivalent to Freud's phallic stage, is again ushered in by new skills or abilities in the child. The 4-year-old is able to plan a bit, to take initiative in reaching particular goals. With these new cognitive skills, the child attempts to conquer the world around him. He may try to go out into the street on his own; he may take a toy apart, find that he can't put it back together, and then throw it—parts and all—at his mother. It is a time of vigorous action and of behaviors that parents may see as aggressive. The risk is that the child may go too far in his forcefulness or that the parents may restrict and punish too much—either of which can produce guilt. Some guilt is needed, since without it there would be no conscience, no self-control. The ideal interaction between parent and child is certainly not total indulgence. On the other hand, too much guilt can inhibit the child's creativity and free interactions with others.

Industry (Competence) Versus Inferiority: 6–12 Years.
The beginning of schooling is a major force in ushering in this stage. The child is now faced with the need to win approval through specific competence—through learning to read, to do sums, and to develop other school skills. The task of this period is thus simply to develop the repertoire of abilities society demands of the child. If the child is unable to develop the expected skills, he will develop instead a basic sense of inferiority. Yet some failure

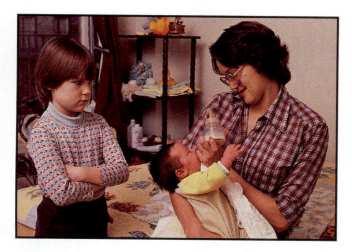

If looks could kill! This child is clearly jealous of the new baby and may well be harboring all sorts of angry and aggressive thoughts. A younger child would probably act out those thoughts and feelings directly. But a child of this age, probably in the period Erikson calls *initiative versus guilt,* feels guilty about her feelings and inhibits the angry actions.

is necessary so that the child can develop some humility; as always, balance is at issue. Ideally, the child must have sufficient success to encourage a sense of competence, but should not place so much emphasis on competence that failure is unacceptable or that she becomes a kind of "workaholic."

Identity Versus Role Confusion: 13–18 Years. Erikson argued that every adolescent, in order to arrive at a mature sexual and occupational identity, must reexamine his identity and arrive at a reasonably mature commitment in four areas: sexual identity, vocational identity, ideological identity (such as political attitudes), and religious (or moral) identity. The risk is that of confusion, arising from the profusion of roles and options opening to the child at this age.

A key idea to take away with you from this very brief presentation of Erikson's theory is that each new task, each dilemma, is thrust upon the developing person because of changes in social demands. Because age marches along, willy-nilly, the developing person is confronted with new tasks whether she has successfully resolved earlier dilemmas or not. You can't stay a 4-year-old until you get it right! You are, instead, pushed forward, carrying the unresolved issues with you as excess baggage. The very earliest tasks are thus especially important because they set the stage for everything that follows.

Other Psychoanalytic Views: Bowlby's Theory of Attachment

Erikson is not the only influential modern theorist whose thinking has been strongly affected by Freud or psychoanalysis. In particular, John Bowlby's theory of the development of attachment, which I mentioned briefly in Chapter 1, is a kind of mini-theory, grounded in part in psychoanalytic thought (1969; 1973; 1980). Like Freud and Erikson, Bowlby assumed that the root of human personality lies in the earliest childhood relationships. Significant failure or trauma in those relationships will permanently shape the child's development. Bowlby focused his attention on the child's first attachment to the mother because it is usually the earliest, and arguably the most central, such relationship.

To describe how that attachment comes about, Bowlby introduced several concepts from *ethological theory*, which brings evolutionary concepts to bear on the study of behavior. Human evolution, Bowlby

John Bowlby (1906–1990) did more than perhaps any other theorist except Freud to "spread the view that the child is the father to the man" (Karen, 1994, p. 25).

Research Report

One Test of Psychoanalytic Theory

Direct empirical tests of Freud's or Erikson's theories are relatively rare, largely because both theories are so general that specific tests are very difficult. One exception has been in the study of the development of early trust versus mistrust, reframed by Bowlby in terms of the security of the child's attachment. I'll be talking about the research on secure and insecure attachments in detail in Chapter 6, but let me give you just one example of the research in this area, since it provides significant support for the basic psychoanalytic hypothesis that the quality of the child's earliest relationship affects the whole course of the child's later development.

Alan Sroufe and his colleagues (Sroufe, 1989; Sroufe, Carlson, & Schulman, 1993; Urban, Carlson, Egeland, & Sroufe, 1991) have followed a group of roughly two hundred families, starting at the birth of a child. The families were selected because all were thought to be at moderately high risk either for child abuse or neglect or for poor developmental outcome in the child. Many of the mothers were teenagers and nearly all were poor, with limited education. The security of the child's attachment to the mother was measured when the children were 12 months old and again when they were 18 months old. These children were then followed through toddlerhood, into elementary school, and finally into adolescence. Those who, despite the poverty of their early environments, became securely attached to their mothers have had much more positive life histories than have the insecurely attached infants.

One specific result to illustrate the point: When the children were preadolescents (age 11–12), 47 of them were observed during a specially designed summer camp. The counselors rated each child on a range of characteristics; observers noted how often children spent time together or with the counselors. Naturally, neither the counselors nor the observers knew what the children's initial attachment classification had been. The findings are clear: Those with histories of secure attachment were rated as more self-confident and as having more social competence. They complied more read-

Research suggests that teens who were securely attached to their mothers as infants form new friendships more easily and quickly than do teens whose earliest attachment was less secure—findings that support one basic proposition of psychoanalytic theory.

ily with counselor requests, expressed more positive emotions, and had a greater sense of their ability to accomplish things—a characteristic Sroufe calls *agency*. They created more friendships, especially with other securely attached youngsters, and engaged in more complex activities when playing in groups. The majority of those with histories of insecure attachment showed some kind of deviant behavior pattern at age 11, such as isolation from peers, bizarre behavior, passivity, hyperactivity, or aggressiveness. Only a few of the originally securely attached children showed any of these behaviors.

These results, along with a large body of other findings, provide good support for the basic Erikson/Bowlby hypothesis that the relationship formed during the earliest stage of psychosocial development seems to create a prototype for later relationships.

suggested, has resulted in the child's being born with a repertoire of instinctive behaviors that elicit caregiving from others—behaviors such as crying, smiling, or making eye contact. Similarly, the mother (or other adult) is equipped with various

instinctive behaviors toward the infant, such as responding to a cry or speaking in a higher voice. Together these instinctive patterns bring mother and infant together in an intricate chain of stimulus and response that causes the child to form a specific attachment to that one adult—a process I'll be talking about in some detail in Chapter 6.

Although Bowlby's theory is not a grand scheme itself, it is nonetheless rooted in one and illustrates the ways in which newer theorists have used psychoanalytic ideas in highly fruitful ways. In particular, Bowlby's ideas have stimulated and profoundly influenced the large body of current research on attachment.

Critique of Psychoanalytic Theories

Psychoanalytic theories like Freud's or Erikson's have several great attractions. Most centrally, they focus our attention on the importance of the emotional quality of the child's earliest relationship with the caregivers. Furthermore, they suggest that the child's needs or "tasks" change with age, so that the parents must constantly adapt to the changing child. One of the implications of this is that we should not think of "good parenting" as if it were a global quality. Some of us may be very good at meeting the needs of an infant but quite awful at dealing with teenagers' identity struggles; others of us may have the opposite pattern. The child's eventual personality, and her overall "health," thus depends on the interactions or transactions that develop in the particular family. This is an extremely attractive element of these theories, supported by a growing body of research that shows the importance of such interactions or transactions. As just one example, new research by Judy Dunn (1994) shows that the differences in the way siblings in the same family are treated by their parents have important effects on each child's emerging personality.

Psychoanalytic theory has also given us a number of helpful concepts, such as the unconscious, defense mechanisms, and identification, that have been so widely adopted that they have become a part of everyday language. The concept of unconscious motivations, in particular, has been a profoundly important idea, whose traces we can certainly see in current theories emphasizing internal models. These strengths have led to a resurgence of influence of both Erikson's theory and the several second-order or third-order psychoanalytic approaches, such as Bowlby's.

The great weakness of all the psychoanalytic approaches is the fuzziness of many of the con-

cepts (Block, 1987). The Oedipal conflict may be an intriguing theoretical notion, but how are we to measure it? How do we measure guilt, or shame, or the degree of a child's identity formation in adolescence? Without more precise operational definitions, it is extremely difficult to test or disconfirm the theory. As a grand scheme, then, psychoanalytic theory has offered a provocative "road map," one that has stimulated a great deal of discussion and argument. But because that road map is so general and imprecise, it has not offered a highly testable theory of development.

Cognitive-Developmental Theories

In contrast, cognitive-developmental theories have been extremely influential, not only because many of the ideas are inherently intriguing but because Piaget and others stated those ideas with precision, making it possible for other researchers to test specific hypotheses derived from the theory. The most central figure in this theoretical approach has been Jean Piaget (1896–1980) (Piaget, 1952; 1970; 1977; Piaget & Inhelder, 1969), a Swiss scientist whose theories have shaped the thinking of several generations of developmental psychologists. In recent years another theorist in the same broad tradition, Lev Vygotsky, has also had a considerable impact on our thinking.

Piaget's Theory

For Piaget the central and only question of interest is, "How does thinking develop?" As he began to try to answer that question, he was struck by the fact that all children seem to go through the same kinds of sequential discoveries about their world, making the same sorts of mistakes and arriving at the same solutions. For example, 3- and 4-year-olds all seem to think that if you pour water from a short, fat glass into a tall, thin one, there is now more water because the water level is higher in the thin glass than it was in the fat glass. But many 7-year-olds and most 8-year-olds realize that the amount of water has not changed.

Piaget's detailed observations of children's thinking led him to several conclusions, the most central of which is that it is the nature of the hu-

Jean Piaget is one of the giants of developmental psychology in the twentieth century. His theory profoundly changed the questions asked and the type of research done by developmental psychologists.

man organism to *adapt* to its environment. This is an active process. Piaget did not think that the environment *shapes* the child, but rather that the child (like the adult) actively seeks to understand her environment. In the process, she explores, manipulates, and examines the objects and people in her world.

The Concept of Scheme.

A pivotal concept in Piaget's model—and one of the hardest to grasp—is that of a **scheme** (sometimes written as *schema*). This term is often used as roughly analogous to the word *concept* or to the phrases "mental category" or "complex of ideas." But Piaget used the term even more broadly to describe mental or physical *actions*. Thus a scheme is not really a category but the *action of categorizing* in some particular fashion. Some purely physical or sensory actions are also schemes. If you pick up and look at a ball, you are using your "looking scheme," your "picking-up scheme," and your "holding scheme." Piaget proposed that each baby begins life with a small repertoire of simple sensory or motor

schemes, such as looking, tasting, touching, hearing, and reaching. For the baby, an object *is* a thing that tastes a certain way, feels a certain way when it is touched, or has a particular color. Later, the toddler and child develops mental schemes as well, such as categorizing or comparing one object to another. Over the course of development, the child gradually adds extremely complex mental schemes, such as deductive analysis or systematic reasoning.

But how does the child get from the simple, built-in sensorimotor schemes to the more internalized, increasingly complex mental schemes we see in later childhood? Piaget proposed three basic processes to account for the emergence of new skills: **assimilation, accommodation,** and **equilibration.**

Assimilation.

Assimilation is the process of *taking in*, of absorbing some event or experience to some scheme. When a baby looks at and then reaches for a mobile above his crib, Piaget would say that the baby had assimilated the mobile to his looking and reaching schemes; when an older child sees a dog and labels it "dog," she is assimilating that animal to her dog category or scheme. When you read this paragraph you are assimilating the information, hooking the concept onto whatever other concept (scheme) you have that may be similar.

The key here is that assimilation is an *active* process. For one thing, we assimilate selectively. We don't take in everything we experience, like a blotter; instead, we pay attention only to those aspects of any experience for which we already have schemes. So when you listen to a professor give a lecture, you may try to write everything down in your notebook or store it in your brain, but in fact you only assimilate ("take in") the thoughts you can connect to some concept or model you already have. Similarly, when I lived in Germany some years ago and struggled to learn German, I could only assimilate a portion of what my German teacher said—the parts for which I already had schemes—and I could only imitate or use the parts that I had assimilated.

Assimilation also changes the information that is assimilated, because each assimilated event or experience takes on some of the characteristics of the scheme to which it was assimilated. If I label your new sweater as green (that is, if I assimilate it

Freud would say that 3-month-old Nellie is sucking on this toy because she is in the oral stage; Piaget would say that Nellie is assimilating the toy to her grasping and sucking schemes.

Through accommodation, we reorganize our thoughts, improve our skills, change our strategies.

[?] Critical Thinking

Think of three or four more examples of assimilation and accommodation in your everyday life.

Equilibration. The third aspect of adaptation is equilibration. Piaget assumed that in the process of adaptation, the child is always striving for coherence, to stay "in balance," to have an understanding of the world that makes overall sense. This is not unlike what a scientist does when she develops a theory—just what I am talking about in this chapter. She wants a theory that will make sense out of every observation and that has internal coherence. When new research findings come along, she assimilates them to her existing theory; if they don't fit perfectly, she might simply set aside the deviant data or she may make minor modifications in her theory. But if enough nonconfirming evidence accumulates, she may need to change some basic theoretical assumptions or she may have to throw out her theory altogether and start over, either of which would be a kind of equilibration.

The road map analogy will also work here. Suppose you are trying to learn your way around in a new city with only a very sketchy and approximate, hand-drawn map, given to you by a friend. As you make your way through this new city, you make corrections in your map, redrawing and writing notes to yourself. Eventually, you will find that your many-times-revised map, although an improvement over the original sketchy version, is both impossible to read and still seriously flawed. So you start over and draw a new map, based on all your information. You carry this around with you, revising it and writing on it, until it, too, is so full of annotations that you need to start over. The annotations you make to your map are analogous to accommodations in Piaget's theory; the process of starting over and drawing a new map is analogous to equilibration.

Piaget thought that a child operated in a similar way, as a "little scientist," creating coherent, more or less internally consistent models or theories. Because the infant starts with a very limited

to my green scheme) even though it is really chartreuse, I will remember it as more green and less yellow than it really is.

Accommodation. The complementary process to assimilation is accommodation, which involves *changing the scheme* as a result of some new information you have taken in by assimilation. As I assimilated new German words and grammar, I gradually changed (accommodated) my concepts and categories, so that I had mental categories for several forms of past tense instead of only one or mental groupings of words with a given prefix. The baby who sees and grasps a square object for the first time will accommodate her grasping scheme, so that next time she reaches for a square object her hand will be more appropriately bent to grasp it. Thus, in Piaget's theory, the process of accommodation is the key to developmental change.

repertoire of schemes (a very primitive initial map), her early "theories" or structures are inevitably primitive and imperfect, which forces her to make periodic major changes in her internal structure.

Piaget saw three particularly significant reorganizations or equilibration points, each ushering in a new stage of development. The first is between roughly ages 18 and 24 months, when the toddler shifts from the dominance of simple sensory and motor schemes to the first really internal representations. The second is at about age 6 or 7, when the child adds a whole new set of powerful schemes Piaget calls **operations.** These are far more abstract and general mental actions, such as mental addition or subtraction.

The third major equilibration is at adolescence, when the child figures out how to "operate on" (to think about, analyze, reorganize, compare) ideas as well as events or objects. These three major equilibrations create four stages:

The **sensorimotor stage,** from birth to about age 2 years

The **preoperational stage,** from 2 years to about age 6

The **concrete operational stage,** from 6 to about age 12

The **formal operational stage,** from age 12 onward

Table 2.3 expands somewhat more fully on these stages, each of which I will describe in greater detail in the appropriate age-based chapters. The key for now is to understand that in Piaget's view, each stage grows out of the one that precedes it; each involves a major restructuring of the child's way of thinking—a substantial redrawing of the road map.

Piaget did not conceive of progress through all these stages as inevitable. He thought the sequence was fixed, so that if the child made cognitive progress, it would be in this order, but that not all children would necessarily reach the same end point or move at the same speed. In other words, the ages are approximate but the sequence is fixed. Piaget thought that virtually all children would move to at least preoperational thought, that the vast majority would achieve concrete operations, but that not all would necessarily achieve formal operations in adolescence or even in adulthood.

Vygotsky's Theory

Russian psychologist Lev Vygotsky (1896–1934) (1978), who was born the same year as Piaget but died at the early age of 38, is normally thought of

---

Table 2.3

Piaget's Stages of Cognitive Development

Approximate Age	Stage	Description
0–2	Sensorimotor	The baby understands the world in terms of her senses and her motor actions. A mobile is how it feels to grasp, how it looks, how it tastes in the mouth.
2–6	Preoperational	By 18 to 24 months, the child can use symbols to represent objects to himself internally; over the preschool years he is increasingly able to take others' perspectives, to classify objects, and to use simple logic.
6–12	Concrete operations	The child's logic takes a great leap forward with the development of powerful new internal mental operations, such as addition, subtraction, and class inclusion. The child is still tied to specific experience but can do mental as well as physical manipulations with known objects.
12+	Formal operations	The child becomes able to manipulate ideas as well as known objects or events. She can imagine and think about things she has never seen or that have not yet happened; she can organize ideas or objects systematically and think deductively.

as belonging to the cognitive-developmental camp because he, too, was primarily concerned with understanding the origins of the child's knowledge. But Vygotsky placed the emphasis somewhat differently than did Piaget (Duncan, 1995). In particular, he was convinced that complex forms of thinking have their origins in *social* interactions more than in the child's private explorations. According to Vygotsky, children's learning of new cognitive skills is guided by an adult (or a more skilled child, such as an older sibling), who models and structures the child's learning experience, a process Jerome Bruner later called **scaffolding** (Wood, Bruner, & Ross, 1976). Such new learning, Vygotsky suggested, is best achieved in what he called the **zone of proximal development**—that range of tasks that are too hard for the child to do alone but that she can manage with guidance. As the child becomes more skilled, the zone of proximal development steadily shifts upward, including ever harder tasks.

Creating an appropriate scaffold for the child's learning is no simple matter for parents or teachers. To be optimally effective, the adult must gain and keep the child's attention, model the best strategy or solution, and adapt the whole process carefully to the child's level of skill and understanding (Landry, Garner, Swank, & Baldwin, 1996; Rogoff, 1990). Vygotsky thought that the key was the language the adult used to describe or frame the task. Later, the child uses this same language to guide her independent attempts to do the same kinds of tasks.

Vygotsky's ideas have some obvious educational applications. Indeed, Vygotsky's theory is as much a theory of education as it is a theory of development (Moll, 1990). Like Piaget's theory, Vygotsky's suggests the importance of opportunities for exploration and active participation. But some form of *assisted discovery* would play a greater role in a Vygotskian than in a Piagetian classroom; the teacher would provide the scaffolding for the children's discovery, through questions, demonstrations, and explanations (Tharp & Gallimore, 1988). To be effective, such assisted discovery processes would have to lie within the zone of proximal development of each child, a condition that would be hard to meet in a classroom of children with many levels of abilities and diverse backgrounds.

Critical Thinking

In most elementary school classrooms children are divided into several different reading groups, based on reading skill. Do you think such a practice fits Vygotsky's model of teaching within each child's zone of proximal development? Why or why not?

Critique of Cognitive-Developmental Theories

It would be difficult to overstate the impact of these theories, especially Piaget's ideas, on the study and understanding of children's development. Piaget's work fundamentally altered the course of developmental psychology by providing what Flavell describes as "an entirely new vision of the nature of children, and of the what, when, and how of their cognitive growth" (1996, p. 200). Piaget's ideas, as well as Vygotsky's, were controversial precisely because they called into question so many earlier, more simplistic views. Piaget also devised a number of remarkably creative techniques for exploring children's thinking—techniques that often showed unexpected and counter-intuitive responses from children, as you can see in the *Research Report* box on page 53. So not only did he offer us a theory that forced us to think about children and their development in a new way, he provided a set of empirical facts that were impossible to ignore and difficult to explain.

By being quite explicit about many hypotheses and predictions, Piaget also enabled others to test his theory. When those tests have been done, Piaget has sometimes turned out to be wrong about the specific ages at which children develop particular skills. As you will see in later chapters, researchers have consistently found evidence of complex concepts at much earlier ages than Piaget proposed, although the *sequences* Piaget described have very often been substantiated. More importantly, Piaget was probably wrong about the breadth and generality of the stages themselves. Most 8-year-olds, for example, show "concrete operational" thinking on some tasks but not on others, and they are much more likely to show complex thinking on a task with which they are very

Research Report

Piaget's Clever Research

Piaget has had an enormous impact on developmental psychologists, not only because he proposed a novel and provocative theory but because of the cleverness of many of the strategies he devised for testing children's understanding. These strategies often showed children doing or saying very unexpected things, results that other theorists found hard to assimilate into their models.

The most famous of all Piaget's clever techniques is probably his method for studying *conservation*. Piaget would begin with two equal balls of clay, show them to the child, and let the child hold and manipulate the clay until she agreed that they had the same amount. Then, in full view of the child, Piaget would squish one of the balls into a pancake or roll it into a sausage. He would then ask the child whether there was still the same amount of clay in each, or whether the pancake or the ball had more. Children ages 4 and 5 consistently said that the ball had more; children of 6 and 7 consistently said that they were still the same.

Or Piaget would start with two equal water glasses, each containing exactly the same amount of liquid. The child would agree that there was the same amount of water or juice in each one. Then, in full view of the child, he'd pour the water from one glass into a shorter, fatter glass, so that the water level in the new glass was lower than the water level in the original. Then he'd ask again whether there was the same amount of water in both. Four- and 5-year-olds thought the amounts were now different, while 7- and 8-year-olds knew that there was still the same amount no matter what size glass the liquid was poured into. Thus the older child has acquired the concept of conservation; she understands that the quantity of water or clay is *conserved* even though it is changed in some other dimension.

In another study, Piaget explored the concept of *class inclusion*—the understanding that a given object can belong simultaneously to more than one category. Fido is *both* a dog and an animal; a high chair is both a chair and furniture. Piaget usually studied this by having children first create their own classes and subclasses of something; he then asked them questions about their groups of things. One $5\frac{1}{2}$-year-old child, for example, had been playing with a set of flowers and had made two heaps, one large group of primroses and a smaller group of other mixed flowers. Piaget then had this conversation with the child:

Piaget: "If I make a bouquet of all the primroses and you make one of all the flowers, which will be bigger?"

Child: "Yours."

Piaget: "If I gather all the primroses in a meadow will any flowers remain?"

Child: "Yes." (Piaget & Inhelder, 1959, p. 108)

The child understood that there are other flowers than primroses, but did *not* yet understand that all primroses are flowers—that the smaller, subordinate class is *included in* the larger class.

In these conversations with children, Piaget was always trying to understand how the child thought, rather than whether the child could come up with the right answer or not. So he used a "clinical method" in which he followed the child's lead, asking probing questions or creating special exploratory tests to try to discover the child's logic. In the early days of Piaget's work, many American researchers were critical of this method, since Piaget did not ask precisely the same questions of each child. Still, the results were so striking, and often so surprising, that they couldn't be ignored. And when stricter research techniques were devised, more often than not the investigators discovered that Piaget's observations were accurate.

familiar than one with which they have little experience. The whole process is a great deal less stage-like and more influenced by specific experience than Piaget had thought.

Nevertheless, a number of aspects of his theory, and Vygotsky's, remain strongly influential, including the following:

- *Constructivism.* The most pervasively influential idea to come from Piaget's theory is that the child is *constructing* her understanding of the world. She is not passive; she actively seeks to understand. A majority of developmentalists have accepted this proposition as a starting point (Flavell, 1996).

- *Qualitative Change.* Piaget's emphasis on qualitative change has also been highly significant. Nearly all developmental psychologists would agree that a 15-year-old approaches problems and tasks in a way that is not just faster but qualitatively different from the way a 3-year-old approaches the same tasks.

- *Social Interaction Effects.* Vygotsky's suggestion that children construct their new understandings not primarily through solitary play but through social interaction with parents and peers is an idea that has gained considerable influence in recent years. Play with peers is now seen as a key source of learning at every age.

- *Other Speci c Concepts and Terms.* Finally, of course, Piaget and Vygotsky provided a legacy of terminology and concepts that are widely used. These include *scheme, assimilation, accommodation, egocentrism, conservation,* and the *object concept* from Piaget, and *scaffolding* and *zone of proximal development* from Vygotsky. In addition, Piaget's division of childhood into four stages has shaped the very way we talk about childhood and the way we organize our textbooks—including this one.

Thus, even though his ideas have not always proven to be correct in their specifics, Piaget's theory truly revolutionized the field of developmental psychology. He changed the way we thought and the questions we asked.

Learning Theories

Learning theories represent a very different theoretical tradition, one in which the emphasis is much more on the way the environment *shapes* the child than on how the child understands his experiences. No learning theorist is arguing that genetics or built-in biases are unimportant. But theorists of this group see human behavior as enormously plastic, shaped by predictable processes of learning. The most central of these processes are classical conditioning and operant conditioning. If you have encountered these concepts in earlier courses, you will be able to skim the next section. But for those of you who lack such a background, a brief description is needed.

Classical Conditioning

This type of learning, made famous by Pavlov's experiments with his salivating dog, involves the acquisition of new signals for existing responses. If you touch a baby on the cheek, he will turn toward the touch and begin to suck. In the technical terminology of **classical conditioning,** the touch on the cheek is the **unconditional stimulus** (UCS); the turning and sucking are **unconditioned responses** (UCR). The baby is already programmed to do all that; these are automatic reflexes. Learning occurs when some *new* stimulus is hooked into the system. The general model is that other stimuli that are present just before or at the same time as the unconditional stimulus will eventually trigger the same responses. In the typical home situation, for example, a number of stimuli occur at about the same time as the touch on the baby's cheek before feeding. There is the sound of the mother's footsteps approaching, the kinesthetic cues of being picked up, and the tactile cues of being held in the mother's arms. Each of these stimuli may eventually become a **conditional stimulus** (CS), which can trigger the infant's response of turning and sucking (called now a **conditioned response** [CR]), even without any touch on the cheek. Figure 2.1 shows the sequence schematically.

   Classical conditioning is of special interest in the study of human development because of the role it plays in the development of emotional responses. For example, things or people present when you feel good will become conditional stimuli for that same sense of goodwill, while those previously associated with some uncomfortable feeling may become conditional stimuli for a sense of unease or anxiety. This is especially important in infancy, since a child's mother or father is present so often when nice things happen—when the child feels warm, comfortable, and cuddled. In this way the mother and father usually come to be a conditional stimulus for pleasant feelings, a fact that makes it possible for the parents' mere presence to reinforce other behaviors as well,

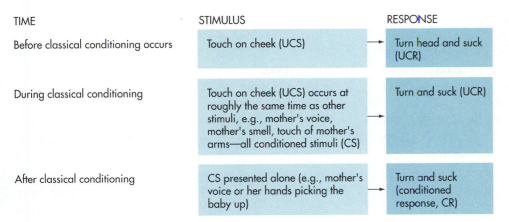

TIME	STIMULUS	RESPONSE
Before classical conditioning occurs	Touch on cheek (UCS) →	Turn head and suck (UCR)
During classical conditioning	Touch on cheek (UCS) occurs at roughly the same time as other stimuli, e.g., mother's voice, mother's smell, touch of mother's arms—all conditioned stimuli (CS) →	Turn and suck (UCR)
After classical conditioning	CS presented alone (e.g., mother's voice or her hands picking the baby up) →	Turn and suck (conditioned response, CR)

Figure 2.1

A schematic representation of the various stages in the establishment of a classically conditioned response.

and that may well lie behind the formation of the child's attachment to the parent. In contrast, a tormenting older sibling might come to be a conditional stimulus for angry feelings, even after the sibling has long since stopped the tormenting.

Operant Conditioning

The second major type of learning is most often called **operant conditioning,** a term coined by B. F. Skinner, the most famous modern proponent of this theory (1953; 1980), whose work is based on the ideas of a still-earlier great, E. L. Thorndike. Unlike classical conditioning, which involves attaching an old response to a new stimulus, operant conditioning involves attaching a new response to an old stimulus, achieved by the application of appropriate principles of reinforcement. Any behavior that is reinforced will be more likely to occur again in the same or a similar situation. There are two types of reinforcements. A **positive reinforcement** is any event that, following some behavior, increases the chances that the behavior will occur again in that situation. Certain classes of pleasant consequences, such as praise, a smile, food, a hug, or attention, serve as reinforcers for most people most of the time. But strictly speaking, a reinforcement is defined by its effect; we don't know something is reinforcing unless we see that its presence increases the probability of some behavior.

The second major type is a **negative reinforcement,** which occurs when something an individual finds *unpleasant* is *stopped* or avoided. Suppose your

| Virtually every child finds a hug reinforcing.

little boy is whining and begging you to pick him up. At first you ignore him, but finally you do pick him up. What happens? He stops whining. So your picking-up behavior has been *negatively reinforced* by the cessation of his whining, and you will be *more* likely to pick him up the next time he whines. At the same time, his whining has probably been *positively reinforced* by your attention, so he will be more likely to whine on similar occasions.

Both positive and negative reinforcements strengthen behavior. **Punishment,** in contrast, is intended to weaken some undesired behavior. Sometimes punishments involve eliminating nice things (like "grounding" a child, taking away television privileges, or sending her to her room); often they involve administering unpleasant things such as a scolding or a spanking. This use of the word *punishment* fits with the common understanding of the term and shouldn't be too confusing. What *is* confusing is the fact that such punishments don't always do what they are intended to do: They do not always suppress the undesired behavior. If your child throws his milk glass at you to get your attention, spanking him may be a positive reinforcement instead of being the punishment you had intended.

[?] *Critical Thinking*

Can you think of examples in your everyday life in which your behavior is affected by classical or operant conditioning, or in which you use these principles to affect others' behavior?

The reverse of reinforcement is **extinction,** which is a decrease in the likelihood of some response after repeated *non*reinforcements. If you stopped reinforcing whining behavior in your child, eventually the child would stop whining, not only on this occasion but on subsequent occasions.

In laboratory settings experimenters can control the situation so that a particular behavior is reinforced every time it occurs or, alternatively, stop reinforcement completely and so cause extinction of the response. But in the real world, consistency of reinforcement is the exception rather than the rule. Much more common is a pattern of **partial reinforcement,** in which some behavior is reinforced on some occasions but not others. Studies of partial reinforcement show that children and adults take longer to learn a new behavior under partial reinforcement conditions, but once established, such behaviors are much more resistant to extinction. If you smile at your daughter only every fifth or sixth time she brings a picture to show you (and if she finds your smile reinforcing), she'll keep on

bringing pictures for a very long stretch, even if you were to quit smiling altogether.

Bandura's Social-Cognitive Theory

Albert Bandura (1977; 1989), whose variation of learning theory is by far the most influential among developmental psychologists today, has built upon the base of these traditional learning concepts, but has added several other key ideas. First, he argues that learning does not always require direct reinforcement. Learning may also occur merely as a result of watching someone else perform some action. Learning of this type, called **observational learning** or **modeling,** is involved in a wide range of behaviors. Children learn ways of hitting from watching other people in real life and on the TV. They learn how to be generous by watching others donate money or goods. Adults learn job skills by observing or being shown by others.

Second, Bandura calls attention to another class of reinforcements called **intrinsic reinforcements** or intrinsic rewards. These are reinforcements internal to the individual, such as the pleasure a child feels when she finally figures out how to draw a star, or the sense of satisfaction you may experience after strenuous exercise. Pride, discovery, that "aha" experience, for example, are powerful intrinsic rewards and have the same power to

Albert Bandura has developed a highly influential modification of basic learning theory, called social-cognitive theory.

Parenting

Learning Principles in Real Family Life

It is a lot harder than you may think to apply basic learning principles consistently and correctly with children at home or in schools. Virtually all parents do try to reinforce some behaviors in their children by praising them or by giving them attention or treats; and most of us do our best to discourage unpleasant behavior through punishment. But it is easy to misapply the principles or to create unintended consequences because we have not fully understood all the mechanisms involved.

For example, suppose your favorite armchair is being systematically ruined by the dirt and pressure of little feet climbing on it. You want the children to *stop* climbing up the chair, so you scold them. After a while you may even stoop to nagging. If you are really conscientious and knowledgeable, you will carefully try to time your scolding so that it operates as a negative reinforcer—you stop your scolding when they stop climbing. But nothing works. They keep on leaving those muddy footprints on your favorite chair. Why? It could be because the children *enjoy* climbing up the chair. That is, the climbing is intrinsically reinforcing to the children, and that effect is clearly stronger than your negative reinforcement or punishment. One way to deal with this might be to provide something *else* for them to climb on.

Another example: Suppose your 3-year-old son repeatedly demands your attention while you are fixing dinner (a common state of affairs, as any parent of a 3-year-old can tell you). Because you don't want to reinforce this behavior, you ignore him the first six or eight times he says "Mommy" or tugs at your clothes. But after the ninth or tenth repetition, with his voice getting louder and whinier each time, you can't stand it any longer and finally say something like, "All right! What do you want?" Since you have ignored most of his demands, you might well be convinced that you have not been reinforcing his demanding behavior. But what you have actually done is to create a partial reinforcement

schedule; you have rewarded only every tenth demand or whine. We know that this pattern of reinforcement helps to create behavior that is *very* hard to extinguish. So your son may continue to be demanding and whining for a very long time, even if you succeed in ignoring his behavior completely.

A third example comes from Patterson's research on aggressive and noncompliant children (recall Figure 1.2 from the last chapter, p. 17). Imagine a child playing in his very messy room. The mother comes into his room and tells the child to clean up the room. The child whines or yells at her that he doesn't want to do it or won't do it. The mother gives in and leaves the room, and the child stops whining or shouting. The mother may believe that she has succeeded in reinforcing non-whining behavior, because the child is no longer misbehaving. But in learning theory terms, this situation is much more complex.

Patterson analyzes this exchange as a pair of negatively reinforced events. When the mother gives in to the child's defiance, her own behavior (giving in) is negatively reinforced by the ending of the child's whining or yelling. This makes it *more likely* that she will give in the next time. She has learned to back down in order to get the child to shut up. At the same time, the child has been negatively reinforced for yelling or whining, since the unpleasant event for him (being told to clean his room) stopped as soon as he whined. So he has learned to whine or yell. Imagine such exchanges occurring over and over, and you begin to understand how a family can create a reinforcement system in which an imperious, demanding, noncompliant child rules the roost.

If any of these situations are familiar to you, it may pay to keep careful records for a while, keeping track of each incident and your response, and then see if you can figure out which principles are really at work and how you might change the pattern.

strengthen behavior as do extrinsic reinforcements such as praise or attention.

Third, and perhaps most important, Bandura has gone far toward bridging the gap between learning theory and cognitive-developmental theory by emphasizing important *cognitive* (mental)

elements in learning. Indeed, he now calls his theory "social cognitive theory" rather than "social learning theory," as it was originally labeled (1986; 1989). For example, Bandura now stresses the fact that modeling can be the vehicle for the learning of abstract as well as concrete skills or

Children learn an enormously wide range of behaviors through modeling—not only physical skills like using chopsticks or cooking, but also attitudes and beliefs. Young Christian, imitating his father while Dad studies, is not only learning about moving a pencil over the paper, he is also undoubtedly learning positive attitudes about books and paper—attitudes that will affect his reaction to school.

information. In this *abstract modeling* the observer extracts a rule that may be the basis of the model's behavior, learning the rule as well as the specific behavior. Hence if a child sees his parents volunteering one day a month at a food bank and taking Christmas baskets to homeless families, he may extract a rule about the importance of "helping others," even if the parents never articulate this rule specifically. In such a fashion a child or adult acquires attitudes, values, ways of solving problems, and even standards of self-evaluation through modeling. Furthermore, what a person learns from observing someone else is influenced by other cognitive processes, such as what we pay attention to, by our ability to make sense out of and remember what we saw, and by our actual capacity to repeat the observed action.

(I will never become an expert tennis player merely by watching Steffi Graf play!) To my ear, all this sounds a great deal like Piaget's concept of assimilation.

[?] *Critical Thinking*

Think about your own upbringing. What values or attitudes do you think you learned through modeling? How were those values and attitudes displayed (modeled) by your parents or others?

Bandura introduces other cognitive components as well. In learning situations children and adults *set goals*, *create expectations* about what kinds of consequences are likely, and *judge* their own perfor-

Children Do What You Do, Not What You Say

One interesting—and very practical—sidelight to the process of modeling has been the repeated research finding that modeling works better than preaching. Thus, if you want children to show a particular behavior—such as generosity, fairness, or diligent work—it is more effective to demonstrate this behavior yourself than it is to simply tell kids that it is good to be generous or fair or hardworking.

In one study, Joan Grusec and her coworkers (Grusec, Saas-Kortsaak, & Simutis, 1978) had elementary school children play a miniature bowling game, ostensibly to test the game. They first observed an adult "test" the game and saw the adult win 20 marbles. Next to the bowling game was a poster that said "Help poor children. Marbles buy gifts." Under the poster was a bowl with some marbles in it. Half the time the adult model donated half his newly won marbles to this bowl; the other half of the time he did not. In addition, the model either "preached" about donating marbles or said nothing. To some of the children, he preached in specific terms, saying that the child should donate half his marbles when he played the game since it would be good to make poor children happy by doing that. To other children, he preached in more general terms, saying that the child should donate half his marbles because it is a good thing to make other people happy by helping them any way one can. The adult model then

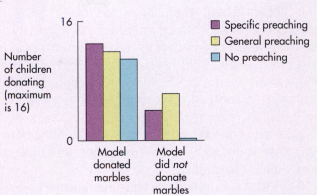

left the room, and the child had an opportunity to play the bowling game and to decide whether to donate any marbles. You can see in the figure above how many children in each group (out of a maximum of 16) donated marbles. Clearly, modeling worked better than preaching.

In general, when there is a conflict between what the model says and what the model does—such as when parents smoke but tell their kids that they should not smoke—children are more likely to follow the behavior rather than the verbal message. So the old adage "Do what I say and not what I do" doesn't seem to work.

mance. Collectively, these additions to traditional learning theory make the system far more flexible and powerful. As one example, Bandura and his coworkers have used his theory as a basis for trying to explain how children come to understand their gender and the behavior that is appropriate to their gender—an approach you'll encounter again in Chapter 9.

Critique of Learning Theories

Several implications of learning theories are worth emphasizing. First of all, learning theorists can handle either consistency or change in a child's behav-

ior. If a child is friendly and smiling both at home and at school, this could be explained by saying that the child was being reinforced for that behavior in both settings rather than by assuming that the child had a "gregarious temperament." But it is equally possible to explain how a child could be friendly and helpful at school and defiant or aggressive at home, simply by assuming that the child is reinforced for helpful behavior at school and for aggression at home. To be sure, each child's behavior will tend to *elicit* similar responses (reinforcements) from others in many settings, which creates a bias toward consistency. But learning theorists have less trouble than do other theorists in accounting for the kind of variations in behavior from one situation to another that we see in almost every child.

Learning theorists, more than most other theorists, also tend to be optimistic about the possibility of change. They would argue that children's behavior can change if the reinforcement system, or their beliefs about themselves, change. That is, "problem behavior" can be modified. An aggressive child can learn other ways of responding to playmates; a clinging child can be reinforced for more independent behavior so that the clinginess will disappear. In contrast, psychoanalytic theorists are more likely to see aggression or clinging behavior as aspects of a well-established personality pattern, rooted in very early experience and much more difficult to change.

The great strength of the learning theorist's view of social behavior is that it seems to give an accurate picture of the way in which many behaviors are learned. It is perfectly clear that children do learn through modeling; it is equally clear that children and adults will continue to perform behaviors that "pay off" for them. The addition of the cognitive elements to Bandura's theory adds further strength, since it offers a beginning integration of learning models and cognitive-developmental approaches.

This theoretical approach does have one important limitation from my view, in that it is really not developmental. That is, it doesn't tell us much about change with age, either in childhood or adulthood. Even Bandura's variation on learning theory does not tell us whether toddlers or preschoolers learn different things from modeling than do school-age children or adolescents. Thus, learning models can help us understand child or human behavior more fully than they can help us understand human development.

Modern Theoretical Models

The term "model" is often used rather loosely to describe almost any kind of theory. As I am using it, it refers to a theoretical *approach* rather than to an entirely explicit theory, to a set of emphases or assumptions about important sources of influence in development as opposed to a grand scheme. In the metaphor I have been using, a model is more like a set of signposts than a detailed road map of development. It points us in a specific direction, aims us at a particular set of questions or issues. Let me describe three such models, each of which is strongly influential in our current thinking.

Biological Models of Development

It is hard to read the science section of a newspaper or magazine these days without coming across new claims about genetic influences on behavior. In the past few years we have heard about the contribution of heredity to various diseases, such as Alzheimer's, heart disease, and cancer; we've read about genetic influences on temperamental traits, such as shyness or aggressiveness, or even on juvenile delinquency. The prominence of this new information is testimony to the growing importance of biological models of development.

You have already encountered many of the key concepts of such models in the discussion of nature and nurture in Chapter 1. The most basic proposition of biological models is that both our common patterns of development and our unique individual behavioral tendencies are at least partially determined by basic physiological processes, including genetic programming or sequences of hormone changes. (Gesell's maturational theory, which you met briefly in the last chapter, is certainly one variation of this view.) But in recent years it has been the behavior geneticists who have most profoundly influenced our thinking. Their work makes it clear that genetic programming is a powerful framework upon which all development is built. Let me give you one example of their work in order to flesh out what I have already said about this approach.

Temperament: An Example of a Biological Model at Work.
It is clear to any observer that babies vary in the way they react to new things, in their typical moods, in their rate of activity, in their preference for social interactions or solitude, in the regularity of their daily rhythms, and in many other ways. These variations in the child's *style* of interacting with those around her, or in the child's level of emotional reactivity, are usually named **temperament.**

As you'll see in Chapter 6, when I discuss the temperament research in much more detail, psychologists who have been interested in these differences have not yet agreed on the key dimensions of variation. Jerome Kagan (Kagan, Reznick, & Snidman, 1990; Kagan, Snidman, & Arcus, 1993), for example, has focused on only a single dimension, which he calls *behavioral inhibition*—an aspect of what most people mean by "shyness." Arnold Buss and Robert Plomin (1984; 1986) propose three dimensions: emotionality, activity, and sociability.

Temperament researchers are in agreement, however, on the assumption that temperamental qualities are *inborn*, carried in the genes. The idea here is not so very different from the notion of "inborn biases" or "constraints" I talked about in Chapter 1, except that here we are talking about *individual* rather than shared behavioral dispositions.

Clear, strong evidence supports such an assumption (Goldsmith, Buss, & Lemery, 1995; Rose, 1995). Studies of twins in many countries show that identical twins are quite a lot more alike in their temperament or personality than are fraternal twins (Rose, 1995). One fairly typical set of results comes from a study by Robert Plomin, Robert Emde, and their many collaborators (Emde, Plomin, Robinson et al., 1992; Plomin et al., 1993). They have studied 100 pairs of identical and 100 pairs of fraternal twins at both 14 and 20 months. At each age, the toddlers' temperament was rated

by their mothers, using the Buss and Plomin categories. In addition, each child's level of behavioral inhibition was measured by observing how he reacted to a strange adult and strange toys in a special laboratory playroom. Did the child approach the novel toys quickly and eagerly, or did he hang back or seem fearful? Did he approach the strange adult, or did he remain close to Mom? You can see in Table 2.4 that the correlations between temperament scores on all four of these dimensions were consistently higher for identical than for fraternal twins, indicating a strong genetic effect.

Many (but not all) temperament theorists take the argument a step further and trace the basic differences in behavior to variations in underlying physiological patterns (e.g., Gunnar, 1994; Rothbart, Derryberry, & Posner, 1994). For example, Jerome Kagan has suggested that differences in behavioral inhibition are based on differing thresholds for arousal in those parts of the brain that control responses to uncertainty, the amygdala and the hypothalamus (Kagan, 1994; Kagan et al., 1990; Kagan et al., 1993). Arousal of these parts of the brain leads to increases in muscle tension and heart rate. Shy or inhibited children are thought to have a *low* threshold for such a reaction. That is, they more readily become tense and alert in the presence of uncertainty, perhaps even interpreting a wider range of situations as uncertain. What we inherit, then, is not "shyness" or some

Table 2.4
Similarity of Identical and Fraternal Twin Toddlers

Temperament Scale	14-Month Correlations		20-Month Correlations	
	Identical	Fraternal	Identical	Fraternal
RATED BY PARENTS				
Emotionality	.35*	−.02	.51*	−.05
Activity	.50*	−.25	.59*	−.24
Sociability	.35*	.03	.51*	.11
OBSERVED				
Behavioral Inhibition	.57*	.26*	.45*	.17

*Indicates that the correlation is statistically significant.

Source: Plomin et al., 1993, from Table 2, p. 1364.

If Kagan is right, this little girl's shyness is the result of the way her brain is organized to respond to novel situations—an example of a biological model of development.

equivalent, but a tendency for the brain to react in particular ways.

Analysis of Biological Models   From my perspective, there are two crucial points to be made about the current status of biological models such as temperament theory.

First, broad-ranging and sophisticated new behavior genetics research has made it clear, beyond any shadow of a doubt, that heredity plays a role in virtually all aspects of behavior and development. Such a statement represents a significant swing of the theoretical pendulum away from the dominance of environmentalism that was a hallmark of developmental psychology in the 1960s and 1970s.

But a second point is equally important: We must be careful not to go too far and assume that all behavior is biologically determined. If behavior genetics research has taught us anything, it is that *both* environment and heredity are important in shaping behavior (Plomin & Rende, 1991).

What we have reached is a deeper awareness of the profound importance of biases and tendencies, both shared and individual, built into the human system. This still leaves us with the task of understanding the ways in which the environment and heredity interact.

Bronfenbrenner's Ecological Model

Bronfenbrenner's ecological model (1979; 1989; 1993), which you also encountered briefly in Chapter 1, is in some ways the flip side of current biological models: Biological theorists are attempting to draw a road map for the effects of nature on development; Bronfenbrenner is trying to provide a similar map of the environmental landscape.

He proposes that we think of the ecological system in which the child develops as having a series of layers or concentric circles. The most central circle is made up of what Bronfenbrenner calls **microsystems,** the collection of all those settings that the child experiences directly. The family is thus a microsystem as is a day care center for a child in such care, school for elementary and high school students, or a job setting for an employed teenager.

The next layer, which Bronfenbrenner calls **exosystems,** includes the whole range of system elements that the child does not experience directly but that influence the child because they affect one of the microsystems, particularly the family. The parents' jobs are one obvious example, as is the parents' network of supportive family or friends. Both these factors influence the child through their effect on the parents, as illustrated in the *Research Report* box on p. 64.

Finally, Bronfenbrenner describes a **macrosystem,** which includes the larger cultural or subcultural setting in which both the micro- and exosystems are embedded. The family's poverty or wealth, their ethnic identity, the neighborhood in which they live, and the larger culture in which the entire system exists are all parts of this macrosystem.

Figure 2.2 (p. 63) gives you a schematic drawing of these three layers for two hypothetical 4-year-old American children, one from the majority Euro-American culture in an intact middle-class family

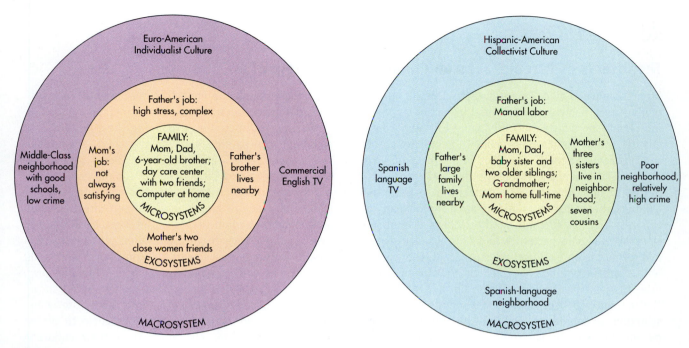

Figure 2.2

Two hypothetical children, in widely different ecological settings, illustrate the layers in Bronfenbrenner's model. To understand how the environment affects a child, we would need to study every aspect of this complex system simultaneously—a tall order.

with parents both employed, the other a Hispanic American living with both parents and a grandmother in a relatively poor, largely Spanish-speaking neighborhood, with the mother at home full-time. If you try to imagine yourself living inside each of these systems you can get a feeling for all the complex ways in which they differ and how all the pieces of the system interact with one another. Bronfenbrenner's point is that until we really understand the ways in which all the elements in such complex systems interact to affect the child, we will not understand development.

[?] *Critical Thinking*

Draw an equivalent set of concentric circles and describe the ecology of your life at age 5 or so. What were the microsystems that affected you? What exosystems had an impact? What larger cultural influences (macrosystems) do you think were significant?

Analysis of Bronfenbrenner's Model. Just as nearly every developmental psychologist would now agree

that biology plays a much larger role than we had assumed 20 years ago, so nearly every one would agree that Bronfenbrenner is also correct—that to understand environment we must go beyond the family microsystem. The problem has been in learning to think in such complex terms. It is hard to keep all the elements of the system in mind at once, let alone to try to study all the relevant parts simultaneously. Perhaps frustrated by that difficulty or perhaps because of the long tradition of examining family and cultural effects in more linear ways, psychologists have continued to design research that explores only small pieces of the total system. Thus much of what we know about family and cultural influences on children is piecemeal rather than systemic. Despite these difficulties, Bronfenbrenner's model has changed the theoretical landscape in profound ways. Whether the specifics of his model, such as the division into micro-, exo- and macro-systems, will turn out to be the most fruitful way to conceptualize these complex interactions remains to be seen. But there is no doubt that this model has permanently altered the questions developmental psychologists ask about children's lives.

Research Report

The Effects of Parents' Jobs on Children: An Example of an Exosystem Process

Bronfenbrenner's model pointed us to a whole new set of questions, namely, the potential impact of a parent's job quality or satisfaction on family life and, consequently, on a child's development. Researchers have tried to come at these questions in a variety of ways.

One way has been to look at the impact of unexpected *un*employment. What happens to parents and children when a parent is laid off from work? Nearly all this research has focused on the father's loss of job; whether the same pattern would hold when a mother lost her job is an empirical question. Still, the existing results are intriguing. They tell us that when a man loses his job, it puts enormous strain on his marriage. Marital conflict rises, and both parents show more symptoms of depression. The resulting effects on family dynamics look much like what we see in divorcing families or in families facing other sorts of stresses: Both parents become less consistent in their behavior toward their children, less affectionate, and less good at monitoring (Conger, Patterson, & Ge, 1995). The children respond to this deterioration in their parents' behavior in the same way children do during a divorce: They show a variety of symptoms, including sometimes depression, aggression, or delinquency. Often their school performance declines (Conger, Conger, Elder et al., 1992; Conger, Ge, Elder, Lorenz, & Simons, 1994; Flanagan & Eccles, 1993). The negative pattern can be softened if the unemployed father receives enough emotional support from his wife, and it is generally cured when the father again finds work. But the whole sequence illustrates nicely how an event outside the family affects the child through the impact on the parents' behavior toward one another and toward the child.

Another set of studies, examining the effects of the quality of the parents' work on the child, point to a similar conclusion. The now classic studies were done by Melvin Kohn and Carmi Schooler (Kohn, 1980; Kohn & Schooler, 1983), who found that men (or women) whose jobs require higher levels of self-direction and autonomy showed increases in intellectual flexibility over time. Routine, highly supervised jobs led to decreases in intellectual flexibility. Kohn's own work and that of several current researchers (Greenberger, O'Neil, & Nagel, 1994; Parcel & Menaghan, 1994) show that these differences spill over into family life. Men and women who work at routine jobs come to place greater emphasis on obedience from their children than is true for parents in more intellectually flexible jobs, a pattern that has been found among African-American parents as well as Euro-American parents (Mason, Cauce, Gonzales, Hiraga, & Grove, 1994). Furthermore, when a mother who has been at home with her children begins work at a job that is low in complexity, the child's home environment deteriorates, becoming less stimulating and supportive than it was before; however, the mother's beginning work at an intellectually complex job is linked to improvements in the child's environment (Menaghan & Parcel, 1995). Thus the character of the parents' job affects their way of thinking, particularly their thinking about authority, and they apply that thinking to their interactions with children.

Developmental Psychopathology

A third important model, called **developmental psychopathology,** has grown primarily out of studies of atypical children or children in atypical families—much as Freud's theorizing originally derived from his analyses of patients with significant psychological problems.

Researchers and theorists in this tradition, such as Norman Garmezy, Michael Rutter, Alan Sroufe, Dante Cicchetti, and others (e.g., Cicchetti & Cohen, 1995; Rutter & Garmezy, 1983), have emphasized several key points:

First, normal and abnormal development are part of a continuum, not separate categories. Both emerge from the same basic processes. To understand either, we must understand both and how they interact. To understand why some adolescents become significantly depressed, for example, we must understand the ways in which self-esteem develops in all children; to understand why some children become highly aggressive or delinquent, we have to understand the basic processes by which most children learn self-control or acquire alternate forms of problem solving. The task of a developmental psychopathologist is to uncover those basic processes—both to see how they work "correctly" for most children and to identify *developmental deviations* and their causes (Sroufe, 1989). Alan Sroufe's studies of the consequences of secure or insecure attachment, described briefly in the *Research Report* box on page 47, is a good example of research based on such assumptions.

Second, the approach is *developmental*. These psychologists are interested in the *pathways* leading to both deviant and normal development, from earliest infancy through childhood and into adult life. What are the sequences of experiences that lead to increased risk of depression in adolescence? Are all depressed adolescents also somewhat depressed earlier in childhood? Have they all experienced some upheaval in family life, or did they create insecure attachments to their parents in infancy? In a similar way, developmental psychopathologists ask what pathways lead to delinquency or other antisocial behavior or to peer rejection. Further, they ask what factors can inhibit or exacerbate an early deviation or turn an initially normal developmental trajectory into a deviant pattern.

One potentially exacerbating factor may be the underlying developmental pathway itself. As Erikson and other psychoanalytic theorists point out, each age has special tasks, special stresses that interact with the child's ongoing patterns and internal models to produce either normal or deviant behavior. For example, it is now very clear that rates of depression among young people rise markedly at adolescence (Compas, Ey, & Grant, 1993; Merikangas & Angst, 1995). A developmental psychopathologist would ask what is unique about adolescence that would contribute to such heightened depression rates.

A third basic proposition of developmental psychopathology is that development is hierarchical. That is, each age or phase builds on what came before. The blackboard is not erased with each new period in the child's life; whatever strengths or weaknesses the child may have—whether those be biological/genetic or environmental in origin—will be carried forward, influencing the child's ability to meet the challenges of the next age period. Early experiences are thus often particularly important because they influence the foundation stones of development, upon which all is later built.

The study of vulnerability and resilience, which I talked about in Chapter 1, is one of the logical outgrowths of this perspective. Children with particular kinds of protective factors, such as a high IQ score or a strong and secure attachment, may be resilient in the face of powerful life stresses precisely because they have such a strong foundation

Developmental psychopathologists argue that this teenager's drug taking is not an isolated phenomenon, appearing suddenly at adolescence, but that it is the culmination of a pathway of development. To understand normal and abnormal development, we have to understand those pathways.

with which to face stress. By the same argument, we may be able to understand children who seem to be unexpectedly vulnerable to life's challenges, despite what appear to be supportive life circumstances; these may be children who carry the seeds of such difficulties from early periods of development or from nonoptimum inborn temperament or neurological patterns.

Analysis of Developmental Psychopathology. This model is a kind of theoretical hybrid, drawing on concepts from both psychoanalytic and cognitive-developmental theories and adding biological themes as well. Like both the biological and ecological models, it is not a grand scheme; it is a way of thinking about development that points us toward a different set of questions, particularly questions about pathways and trajectories of development. And since one cannot study pathways and trajectories cross-sectionally, these new questions have prompted a burst of longitudinal studies of children seen to be at high risk for various kinds of problems, such as Sroufe's study, described in the *Research Report* box on page 47, or some of Patterson's studies of the pathways leading to delinquency that I mentioned in Chapter 1.

Contrasting and Combining the Theories and Models

I wouldn't be surprised if you are a bit bleary-eyed after reading about all these theories. It's hard to make the theoretical issues real to you before you have delved into the data. And at the same time, it is hard for you to assimilate and integrate the data without having some theoretical models to hook them onto. So as a final step, let me try to make all this a bit more concrete by looking at some interesting questions and seeing how each of the several theories and models might answer them. Table 2.5 gives you two such comparisons.

The Effects of Divorce. The first question is one I raised at the beginning of the chapter: How do we explain the observation that, on average, children show an increase in problem behavior immediately following their parents' divorce? You can see that the various theories and models offer different slants on this problem, suggesting different places we might look for the answers.

When we look at the data—as I'll do in more detail in Chapter 9—we find that the basic learning model fits the data quite well. In particular, we now have quite a lot of evidence showing that in the first two years after a divorce, parents do much less well at monitoring their children's behavior and setting clear rules or limits, a pattern that typically persists even if the custodial parent remarries (Hetherington & Clingempeel, 1992). It is this disrupted process within the family that appears to be one of the most critical factors in causing disturbed behavior in the children; in families in which the parent manages to continue good disciplining practices, the children show a smaller increase in disturbed behavior.

At the same time, some of the various hypotheses derived from the three models I've talked about in this chapter have also been supported to at least some degree. For example, temperamentally difficult children show stronger negative reactions to

divorce than do more easygoing children, which points to a role for biology (Tschann, Johnston, Kline, & Wallerstein, 1989). Other hypotheses suggested in the table are yet to be tested, such as the expectation that the negative effects of divorce are larger when the child is facing multiple stresses or that the effects may be larger for children who have a history of an insecure attachment.

The one theory that is not well supported is Freud's: There is little evidence that the negative effects of divorce are greater for preschool-age children.

Preference for Same-Sex Playmates. The second question illustrated in Table 2.5 is why children begin to have such a strong preference for same-sex playmates at about age 5 or 6. Some such preference has been observed in every culture studied by anthropologists or psychologists, which addresses the important question raised by the ecological model. This appears to be a genuinely universal phenomenon. Each of the grand schemes has offered some explanation of it, but (as you'll see in Chapter 9) none of these explanations quite fits the data. In this case, the best theory is a newer minitheory, called *gender schema theory* (Martin, 1991; Martin & Halverson, 1981), that has drawn from both learning and cognitive-developmental theories and added some new elements. The child's understanding of the concept of gender does seem to play some role, but that concept develops more gradually than cognitive-developmental theorists had thought and is more affected by specific experience, including reinforcement.

[?] *Critical Thinking*

Try your hand at comparing these theories: What hypotheses do you think each theory or model would suggest about the potential positive or negative effects on an infant of being in day care starting as early as 6 months of age?

When you look at Table 2.5, you should note another important point: Even the grand schemes do not offer answers to every question. In particular, cognitive-developmental theory is (as the name suggests) aimed at explaining primarily changes in the form and content of the child's thinking; it has little to say about personality or deviant social

Table 2.5

Explanations of Several Interesting Facts by the Three Grand Schemes and Three Models

	Fact to Be Explained	
Theory/Model	Why Do Children Show an Increase in Problem Behavior in the Months Following a Parental Divorce?	Why Do Children Begin to Show Strong Preferences for Playing Only with Same-Sex Children at About Age 5 or 6?
Psychoanalytic theory	Divorce is a trauma because of its effect on the child's central attachment. Freud's theory suggests that the negative effects should be especially strong if the children are in the Oedipal period when the divorce occurs, because the child needs parents of both sex present to complete the process.	The Oedipal crisis ends with the child's identifying with the parent of the same sex; the child is thereafter more interested in knowing how others of the same gender behave.
Cognitive-developmental theory	Has no specific explanation of this phenomenon.	It is only at about age 5 or 6 that the child understands fully that gender is permanent and constant, despite changes in hairstyle or clothing or size. Once that has been understood, the child naturally pays more attention to those of the same gender.
Learning theory	The custodial parent's discipline is likely to become more erratic, so that the children are more often inadvertently reinforced for disruptive behavior. Effects may be worse for boys because they are more likely to lose the male role model.	The preference for same-gender playmates should develop gradually, as a result of higher rates of reinforcement for gender-appropriate play and, specifically, for imitating same-sex models. By age 5 or 6, this gradual shaping has created a strong preference for same-sex playmates.
Biological model	Points out that the effects may vary as a function of the child's genetic/temperamental makeup.	Has nothing special to offer in explaining this phenomenon.
Ecological model	Points out that the shift from two-parent to one-parent family structure changes the microsystem, and any change in the system involves some disruption. Also points out that the degree of negative effect we see in any one child should be a function of the total number of stresses in the system, not just the presence or absence of divorce.	Points out that we should not assume that such same-gender preference exists equally in every culture. We might find variations, depending on the extent to which cultural segregation of boys and girls occurs.
Developmental psychopathology model	Points out that the child's degree of disrupted behavior will be affected by that child's pattern of development, including both inherited patterns and early environmental adaptations, such as attachment.	Has nothing specific to offer on this question.

behaviors and almost nothing to say about family interaction. Thus it offers no insights into questions such as the effects of divorce. In contrast, psychoanalytic theory is focused primarily on personality and social behavior and their origins within the family. It has little to tell us about the growth of thinking. Because of this specialization even in the grand schemes, and because each of these schemes and models offers important ideas and concepts, most psychologists find themselves blending or combining several theories, taking the best or most useful ideas from each.

Nonetheless, at this stage it is useful for you to try to keep the alternatives separate in your mind. As we move into the descriptive chapters, I will be coming back again and again to these basic theories and models, trying to show not only how the data we've collected have been shaped by the theoretical assumptions researchers have made but also how the different theoretical perspectives can help us to understand the information that has accumulated. So hang in there. These ideas will turn out to be useful, helping you (and me) to create some order out of the vast array of facts.

Summary

1. Facts alone will not add up to an explanation of any phenomenon, including development. Theory is also required.

2. Theories can be divided into three rough groupings, depending on their scope: grand schemes, models, and minitheories.

3. Three grand schemes have been influential within developmental psychology: psychoanalytic, cognitive-developmental, and learning theories.

4. Psychoanalytic theorists such as Freud and Erikson have principally studied the development of personality, pointing to the interaction of internal instincts and environmental influences in producing shared stages of development as well as individual differences in personality.

5. Freud emphasized that behavior is governed by unconscious as well as conscious motives and that the personality develops in steps, first the id, then the ego, then the superego.

6. Freud also proposed a set of five psychosexual stages: oral, anal, phallic, latency, and genital. The Oedipal crisis occurs in the phallic stage. This stage system is historically of interest but is not highly influential among modern developmental psychologists.

7. Erikson emphasized social forces more than unconscious drives as motives for development. The key concept is the development of identity, said to occur in eight psychosocial stages over the course of the life span: trust, autonomy, initiative, industry, identity, intimacy, generativity, and ego integrity.

8. Bowlby's theory of the development of attachment, highly influential in current theorizing, has strong roots in psychoanalytic theory.

9. Cognitive-developmental theorists such as Piaget and Vygotsky highlight the child's own active exploration of the environment as a critical ingredient leading to shared stages of development. They strongly emphasize qualitative change.

10. Piaget focused on the development of thinking rather than personality. A key concept is that of adaptation, made up of the subprocesses of assimilation, accommodation, and equilibration.

11. The result of several major equilibrations is a set of four cognitive stages, each of which Piaget thought resulted in a coherent cognitive system: sensorimotor, preoperational, concrete operations, and formal operations.

12. Vygotsky stressed the importance of supportive social interactions, especially interactions with parents, as necessary ingredients in the child's gains in intellectual understanding.

13. Learning theorists generally place strongest emphasis on environmental influences, thought to produce largely quantitative change.

14. Basic learning processes include classical and operant conditioning, with positive, negative, and partial reinforcement principles being especially significant in explaining the acquisition and maintenance of many behaviors.

15. Bandura's influential version of learning theory, called social-cognitive theory, includes more cognitive elements as well as the crucial concept of modeling. It is clear that children learn not only behaviors but also attitudes and values through modeling.

16. Theoretical models are typically less precise than formal theories—signposts rather than detailed

maps. They point us toward significant questions or toward whole categories of important influences.

17. Biological models of development direct us toward the study of important genetic and physiological processes. Behavior genetics studies of infant and child temperament are a good example of research shaped by a biological model.

18. Bronfenbrenner's ecological model points us toward a more elaborate understanding of environmental influences, including microsystem, exosystem, and macrosystem effects.

19. Developmental psychopathology, as a general model of the origin of deviant patterns of development, directs us toward the study of pathways and trajectories of development.

20. No one of these theories or models fully accounts for all the available evidence on human development, but each offers useful concepts, and each may provide a framework within which we can examine bodies of research data.

Key Terms

accommodation   That part of the adaptation process by which a person modifies existing schemes in order to fit new experiences or creates new schemes when old ones no longer handle the data. **(p. 49)**

assimilation   That part of the adaptation process that involves the "taking in" of new experiences or information into existing schemes. Experience is not taken in "as is," however, but is modified (or interpreted) somewhat so as to fit the preexisting schemes. **(p. 49)**

classical conditioning   One of three major types of learning. An automatic unconditioned response, such as an emotion or a reflex, comes to be triggered by a new cue, called the conditioned stimulus (CS), after the CS has been paired several times with the original unconditional stimulus. **(p. 54)**

concrete operational stage   The stage of development between ages 6 and 12, proposed by Piaget, in which mental operations such as subtraction, reversibility, and multiple classification are acquired. **(p. 51)**

conditional stimulus   Term in classical conditioning for the stimulus that, after being paired a number of times with an unconditional stimulus, comes to trigger the unconditioned response. For example, the sound of the mother's footsteps may become a conditional

stimulus for the baby's turning his head as if to suck. **(p. 54)**

conditioned response   Term in classical conditioning for the response to the conditional stimulus. In appearance this behavior may look very much like the unconditioned response, but because it is triggered by a new, learned stimulus it is given a different name. **(p. 54)**

developmental psychopathology   A relatively new approach to the study of deviance that emphasizes that normal and abnormal development are part of a continuum, with common roots, and that pathology can arise from many different pathways or systems. **(p. 64)**

ego   Term in Freudian theory for that portion of the personality that organizes, plans, and keeps the person in touch with reality. Language and thought are both ego functions. **(p. 42)**

equilibration   The third part of the adaptation process as proposed by Piaget, involving a periodic restructuring of schemes into new structures. **(p. 49)**

exosystem   Concept in Bronfenbrenner's ecological model; it is that set of system elements that affects the child indirectly, through its influence on the family or on some other microsystem in which the child exists. For example, the parents' jobs and their network of friends are part of the exosystem for the child. **(p. 62)**

extinction   A decrease in and eventually the elimination of the strength of some response after nonreinforcement. **(p. 56)**

formal operational stage   Piaget's name for the fourth and final major stage of cognitive development, occurring during adolescence, when the child becomes able to manipulate and organize ideas as well as objects. **(p. 51)**

grand schemes   Phrase used in this book to describe the three most comprehensive theories of development: psychoanalytic, cognitive-developmental, and learning theories. **(p. 41)**

id   Term in Freudian theory for the first, primitive portion of the personality; the storehouse of basic energy, continually pushing for immediate gratification. **(p. 42)**

identification   The process of taking into oneself ("incorporating") the qualities and ideas of another person, which Freud thought was the result of the Oedipal crisis between ages 3 and 5. The child attempts to make himself or herself like the parent of the same sex. **(p. 42)**

identity   Term used in Erikson's theory to describe the gradually emerging sense of self, changing through a series of eight stages. **(p. 44)**

intrinsic reinforcements   Concept emphasized in Bandura's theory; those inner sources of pleasure, pride, or satisfaction that serve to increase the likelihood that an individual will repeat the behavior that led to the feeling. **(p. 56)**

libido   Term used by Freud to describe the pool of sexual energy in each individual. **(p. 42)**

macrosystem   Term used by Bronfenbrenner in his ecological model to describe the larger culture or subcultural setting in which both the microsystems and exosystems exist. **(p. 62)**

microsystem   Term used by Bronfenbrenner in his ecological model to describe any setting a child experiences directly, such as the family, the school, or a day care center. **(p. 62)**

minitheories   Term used in this text to describe the narrower, more limited types of theories designed to explain only a particular, somewhat specific phenomenon. **(p. 41)**

modeling   Term used by Bandura and others to describe observational learning. **(p. 56)**

models   Term used in this book to describe the middle level of theories, less comprehensive than a grand scheme but broader than a minitheory; examples are biological and ecological models. **(p. 41)**

negative reinforcement   The strengthening of a behavior because of the removal, cessation, or avoidance of an unpleasant stimulus. **(p. 55)**

observational learning   Learning of motor skills, attitudes, or other behaviors through observing someone else perform them. **(p. 56)**

Oedipus conflict   The pattern of events Freud believed occurred between ages 3 and 5 when the child experiences a "sexual" desire for the parent of the opposite sex; the resulting fear of possible reprisal from the parent of the same sex is resolved when the child "identifies" with the parent of the same sex. **(p. 42)**

operant conditioning   That type of learning in which the probability of a person's performing some behavior is strengthened by positive or negative reinforcements. **(p. 55)**

operations   Piaget's term for the new and powerful class of mental schemes he saw as developing between roughly ages 5 and 7, including reversibility, addition, and subtraction. **(p. 51)**

partial reinforcement   Reinforcement of behavior on some schedule less frequent than every occasion. **(p. 56)**

positive reinforcement   Strengthening of a behavior by the presentation of some pleasurable or positive stimulus. **(p. 55)**

preoperational stage   Piaget's term for the second major stage of cognitive development, generally from ages 2 to 6, marked at the beginning by the ability to use symbols and later by the development of basic classification and logical abilities. **(p. 51)**

psychosexual stages   The stages of personality development suggested by Freud, including the oral, anal, phallic, latency, and genital stages. **(p. 42)**

psychosocial stages   The stages of personality development suggested by Erikson, including trust, autonomy, initiative, industry, identity, intimacy, generativity, and ego integrity. **(p. 44)**

punishment   Unpleasant consequences, administered after some undesired behavior by a child or adult, with the intent of extinguishing the behavior. **(p. 56)**

scaffolding   Term used by Bruner to describe a Vygotskian idea: a teacher (parent, older child, or person in the official role of teacher) structures a learning encounter with a child, so as to lead the child from step to step. **(p. 52)**

scheme   Piaget's word for the basic actions of knowing, including both physical actions (sensorimotor schemes, such as looking or reaching) and mental actions, such as classifying or comparing or reversing. An experience is assimilated to a scheme, and the scheme is modified or created through accommodation. **(p. 49)**

sensorimotor stage   Piaget's term for the first major stage of cognitive development, from birth to about age 2, when the child moves from reflexive to voluntary action. **(p. 51)**

superego   Term in Freudian theory for the "conscience" part of personality, which develops as a result of the identification process. The superego contains the parental and societal values and attitudes incorporated by the child. **(p. 42)**

temperament   Term sometimes used interchangeably with "personality," but best thought of as the emotional substrate of personality; at least partially genetically determined. **(p. 60)**

unconditioned response   Term in classical conditioning for the basic unlearned response that is triggered by the unconditional stimulus. A baby's turning of his head when touched on the cheek is an unconditional response. **(p. 54)**

unconditional stimulus   Term in classical conditioning for the cue or signal that automatically triggers the unconditioned response. A touch on a baby's cheek, triggering head turning, is an unconditional stimulus. **(p. 54)**

zone of proximal development   A concept in Vygotsky's theory describing that range of tasks or problems that are too hard for the child to do alone but that she can manage with guidance. **(p. 52)**

Suggested Readings

Erikson, E. H. (1980a). *Identity and the life cycle*. New York: W. W. Norton (originally published 1959). The middle ·section of this book, "Growth and Crises of the Healthy Personality," is the best description I have found of Erikson's model of the psychosocial stages of development.

Grusec, J. E. (1992). Social learning theory and developmental psychology: The legacies of Robert Sears and Albert Bandura. *Developmental Psychology*, 28, 776–786. One of a series of papers to mark the centennial of the American Psychological Association, describing and celebrating the work of key theorists.

Lerner, R. M. (1986). *Concepts and theories of human development* (2nd ed.). New York: Random House. A very good discussion of most of the major theoretical approaches I have described here.

Thomas, R. M. (Ed.). (1990b). *The encyclopedia of human development and education: Theory, research, and studies*. Oxford, England: Pergamon Press. A very useful volume that includes brief descriptions of virtually all the theories I have described in this chapter as well as a helpful chapter on the concept of stages. Each chapter is quite brief but covers many of the critical issues.

CHAPTER 3

Prenatal Development and Birth

Preview Questions

1 *How do X and Y chromosomes differ? Genotype and phenotype?*

2 *Why is the concept of critical period important in understanding the effects of teratogens in prenatal development?*

3 *What are some of the most significant teratogens, and what effects do they have?*

4 *What preventive measures should any woman take before and during her pregnancy?*

5 *What important decisions do parents have to make about the birth process?*

Chapter Outline

When my daughter-in-law, Jenny, was pregnant with her first child (my grandson Sam, now age 6), I had dinner one night at a restaurant with her and my son Rex. She ordered a glass of wine. After a long pause, during which I tried to calculate whether I thought the research evidence was clear and strong enough for me to risk sounding like a bossy, intrusive mother-in-law, I decided I really needed to say something. I began by asking her what her doctor had advised her about alcohol. His advice, it turned out, was that the occasional glass was okay. More pause for thought on my part. Finally, I said that I thought that perhaps her doctor hadn't seen the most recent information; the occasional glass *might* be okay, but all the evidence suggested that there was no level of alcohol that could be guaranteed completely safe.

This brief encounter gives you a glimpse of some of the complexities—personal as well as medical—involved in making good decisions during pregnancy. The list of "dos" and "don'ts" for pregnant women has become very long indeed, long enough so that it is hard for a conscientious woman (and her partner) to be sure what is okay and what is not. One of my goals in this chapter is to give you the very best information we now have about all those dos and don'ts. To do that, I need to explore what we know about the basic processes of development from conception to birth, as well as what we have learned about the things that can interfere with those basic processes.

Beyond this practical question, it is also essential for any complete understanding of child development that we begin our search at the beginning—at conception and pregnancy. The heredity passed on to the new individual at the moment of conception and the neurological and other physical developments in these first months set the stage for all that is to follow.

Conception

The first step in the development of a single human being is that moment of conception when a single sperm cell from the male pierces the wall of the ovum of the female (shown in the photo in Figure 3.1). Ordinarily, a woman produces one **ovum** (egg cell) per month from one of her two ovaries. This occurs roughly midway between two menstrual periods. If it is not fertilized, the ovum travels from the ovary down the **fallopian tube** toward the **uterus,** where it gradually disintegrates and is expelled as part of the next menstruation.

If a couple has intercourse during the crucial few days when the ovum is in the fallopian tube, one of the millions of sperm ejaculated as part of each male orgasm may travel the full distance through the woman's vagina, cervix, uterus, and fallopian tube, and penetrate the wall of the ovum. A child is conceived. Interestingly, only about half such conceptuses are likely to survive to birth. About a quarter are lost in the first few days after conception, often because of a flaw in the genetic

Figure 3.1

Millions of sperm compete to fertilize a single ovum.

material. Another quarter are aborted spontaneously ("miscarried") at a later point in the pregnancy (Wilcox, Weinberg, O'Connor et al., 1988).

The Basic Genetics of Conception

It is hard to overstate the importance of the genetic events accompanying conception. The combination of genes from the father in the sperm and from the mother in the ovum creates a unique genetic blueprint—the **genotype**—that characterizes that specific individual. To understand how that occurs, I need to back up a few steps.

Except in individuals with particular types of genetic abnormality, the nucleus of each cell in the body contains a set of 46 **chromosomes,** arranged in 23 pairs. These chromosomes include all the genetic information for that individual, governing not only individual characteristics, such as hair color, height, body shape, temperament, and aspects of intelligence, but also all those characteristics shared by all members of our species, such as patterns of physical development or "built-in biases" of various kinds.

The only cells that do *not* contain 46 chromosomes are the sperm and the ovum, collectively called **gametes** or germ cells. In the early stages of development, gametes divide as all other cells do (a process called *mitosis*), with each set of 23 chromosome pairs duplicating itself. But gamete division includes a final step, called *meiosis*, in which each new cell receives only one chromosome from each original pair. Thus each gamete has only 23 chromosomes, instead of 23 *pairs*. When a child is conceived, the 23 chromosomes in the ova and the 23 in the sperm combine to form the 23 *pairs* that will be part of each cell in the newly developing body.

The chromosomes, in turn, are composed of long strings of molecules of a chemical called **deoxyribonucleic acid (DNA)** arranged in the shape of a double helix, a kind of twisted ladder. The remarkable feature of this ladder is that the rungs are made up in such a way that the whole thing can unzip; thus each half can guide or act as a template for the duplication of the missing part, allowing the multiplication of cells so that each new cell contains the full set of genetic information.

The string of DNA that makes up each chromosome can be subdivided further into segments, called **genes,** each of which controls or influences a particular feature or a portion of some developmental pattern. A gene controlling or influencing some specific characteristic, such as your blood type or your hair color, always appears in the same place (the *locus*) on the same chromosome in every individual of the same species. The locus of the gene that determines whether you have type A, B, or O blood is on chromosome 9; the locus of the gene that determines whether you have the Rh factor in your blood is on chromosome 1, and so forth. Geneticists have made remarkable strides in recent years in mapping the loci for a great many features or characteristics, a scientific achievement that has allowed similarly giant strides in our ability to diagnose various genetic defects or inherited diseases before a child is born.

X and Y Chromosomes

A further complexity comes from the fact that there are actually two types of chromosomes. In 22 of the chromosome pairs, called *autosomes*, the members of the pair look alike and contain exactly matching genetic loci. Pair 23, however, operates differently. The chromosomes of this pair, which determine the child's sex and are therefore called the *sex chromosomes*, come in two varieties, referred to by convention as the X and the Y chromosomes. A normal human female has two X chromosomes on this twenty-third pair (an XX pattern), while the normal human male has one X and one Y (an XY pattern). The X chromosome is considerably larger than the Y and contains many genetic loci not matched on the Y.

Note that the sex of the child is determined by the sex chromosome it receives from the sperm. Because the mother has *only* X chromosomes, every ovum carries an X. The father, in contrast, has both X and Y chromosomes. When the father's gametes divide, half the sperm will carry an X, half a Y. If the sperm that fertilizes the ovum carries an X, then the child inherits an XX pattern and will be a girl. If the fertilizing sperm carries a Y, then the combination is XY, and the infant will be a boy.

Geneticists have now discovered that only one very small section of the Y chromosome actually determines maleness—a segment referred to as TDF, or *testis-determining factor* (Page, Mosher, Simpson et al., 1987). Fertilized ova that are genetically XY but that lack the TDF develop physically as female. Several recent studies point to the possibility that there may also be a "femaleness" gene or genes, although this is not yet firmly established (Arn, Chen, Tuck-Muller et al., 1994; Bardoni, Zanaria, Guioli et al., 1994). As in so many areas of science, the more we discover, the more complex we see the process really is.

Patterns of Genetic Inheritance

When the 23 chromosomes from the father and the 23 from the mother come together at conception, they provide a mix of instructions, not always matching. When the two sets of instructions are the same at any given locus (such as genes for blue eyes from both parents), geneticists say they are **homozygous.** When the two sets of instructions differ, the genes are said to be **heterozygous,** such as a gene for blue eyes from one parent and a gene for brown eyes from the other, or a combination of genes contributing to shyness from one parent and for gregariousness from the other. How are these differences resolved? Geneticists are still a long way from having a complete answer to this question, but some patterns are very clear.

Dominant and Recessive Genes

Whenever a given trait is governed by a *single* gene, as is true for some 1000 individual physical characteristics, inheritance patterns follow well-understood rules. In a few such cases, when heterozygosity occurs, the child may express *both* characteristics. For example, type AB blood results from the inheritance of a type A gene from one parent and a type B gene from the other. More typically, one of the two contrasting genes is *dominant* over the other and only the dominant gene is actually expressed. The nondominant gene, called a *recessive* gene, has no visible effect on the individual's behavior, although it continues to be part of the genotype and can be passed on to offspring through meiosis.

Table 3.1

Some Physical Characteristics That Follow a Dominant/Recessive Genetic Pattern

Dominant	Recessive
Curly hair	Straight hair
Dark hair	Blond hair
Dimples in the chin or face	No dimples
Normal vision	Nearsightedness
Farsightedness	Normal vision
Type A blood	Type O blood
Normal blood cells	Sickle-cell anemia
Rh positive blood	Rh negative blood

Note: Eye color does not appear in this list because geneticists now believe that it results from the action of several genes (polygenic). Between blue and brown eye genes, brown is normally dominant, but it *is* possible for two blue-eyed parents to have a brown-eyed child.

Source: McKusick, 1994.

Table 3.1 gives a few examples of physical characteristics that follow these simple dominant/recessive gene rules. You can see from this abbreviated list that this type of inheritance pattern characterizes both ordinary physical characteristics, such as hair color, and many inherited diseases. Figure 3.2 gives you a schematic look at how the dominant/recessive inheritance pattern works, using the illustration of sickle-cell anemia, a disease caused by a *recessive* gene. For an individual to have this disease, she or he must inherit the disease gene from *both* parents. A "carrier" is someone who inherits the disease gene from only one parent. Such a person does not actually have the disease but can pass the disease gene on to his or her children. If two carriers have children together (section III of the figure), or if a carrier and someone with the disease have children (section IV of the figure), their offspring may inherit disease genes from both parents and thus have the disease.

[?] Critical Thinking

Assume for the moment that the inheritance pattern for eye color is that brown is always dominant over blue. Can you figure out what your parents' genotype for eye color would be, based on the color of your eyes, your siblings' eyes, and those of your grandparents?

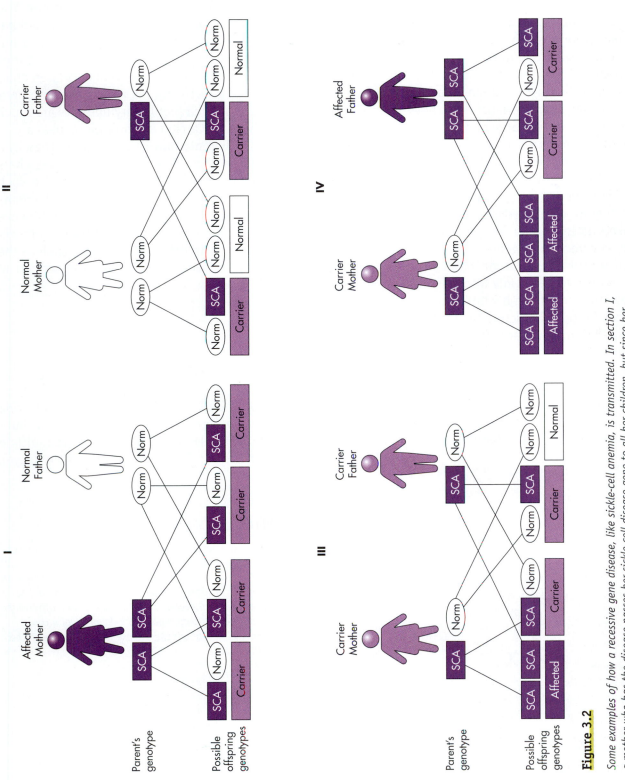

Figure 3.2

Some examples of how a recessive gene disease, like sickle-cell anemia, is transmitted. In section I, a mother who has the disease passes her sickle-cell disease gene to all her children, but since her partner is normal, none of the children actually express the disease. In section II, a normal mother and a carrier father have no children with the disease, but each of their children has a 50/50 chance of carrying the SCA gene. The child can inherit the actual disease either of two ways: with two carrier parents (section III) or with one carrier parent and one affected parent (section IV).

Sex-linked Genetic Transmission

A variation of the dominant/recessive transmission pattern occurs when the locus for some specific gene is on the X chromosome. Because a boy has only one X chromosome, from his mother, he inherits many genes on his X chromosome that are not matched by, or counteracted by, equivalent genetic material on the smaller Y chromosome. Among other things, this means that recessive diseases or other characteristics that have their loci on the nonmatched parts of the X chromosome may be inherited by a boy directly from his mother, a pattern called **sex-linked transmission,** illustrated in Figure 3.3 with the disease hemophilia.

You can see from the figure that, as with other recessive-gene characteristics, a girl can inherit a sex-linked disease such as hemophilia only if she inherits the recessive gene from both parents. A male, in contrast, will inherit the disease by receiving the recessive gene only from his mother. Since his Y chromosome from his father contains no parallel locus for this characteristic, there are no counteracting instructions and the mother's recessive gene dominates. Each of the sons of women who carry such recessive disease genes will have a 50 percent chance of having the disease; the daughters will have a 50 percent chance of being carriers. The sons of those carrier daughters, in turn, will have a 50/50 chance of inheriting the gene for the disease.

Polygenic Inheritance

Characteristics that follow the pattern of dominant and recessive genes are normally either/or characteristics: You either have them or you do not. You may think of this as the most typical pattern of genetic transmission, but in fact the majority of human characteristics aren't like that. Height varies along a continuum, as does intelligence, personality, and rate of growth, among many others. Geneticists argue that such highly varying traits are much more likely to be caused by multiple genes, a pattern called **polygenic inheritance,** rather than by a single dominant or recessive gene. Researchers have not yet discovered all the rules by which such multiple-gene transmission may occur, which means that for complex, polygenetic traits like intelligence or personality, we have to *infer* the presence of a genetic influence from other information, such as the twin studies and adoption studies I described in Chapter 1.

Twins and Siblings

In most cases babies are conceived and born one at a time. However, two to three out of each hundred births in the United States today are multiple births (Centers for Disease Control, 1997c; Guyer,

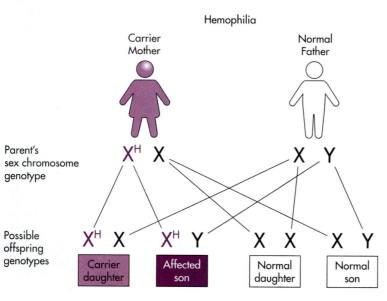

Figure 3.3

Compare the pattern of sex-linked transmission of a recessive disease with the patterns already shown in Figure 3.2 (p. 77). In a sex-linked inheritance, like this example with hemophilia, a carrier mother can pass on the disease to half her sons (on average) because there is no offsetting gene on the Y chromosome. But a daughter of a carrier mother will not inherit the disease itself unless her father has the disease.

You can often see the effects of heredity very clearly in family pictures, like this one of three siblings who have identical smiles and chins.

Strobino, Ventura, MacDorman, & Martin, 1996), a number that has risen dramatically in recent decades in the United States, in large part because widely prescribed new medications given to infertile women frequently stimulate multiple ovulations. The great majority of multiple births are twins; triplets or more occur only about once in every 860 births.

[?] *Critical Thinking*

Speculate for a minute: How do you think our society would differ if one in four of us, or half of us, had a twin? How would family life be different? How might schools differ?

Roughly two-thirds of twins are **fraternal twins,** which occurs when more than one ovum has been produced and both have been fertilized, each by a separate sperm. Such twins, also called **dizygotic twins,** are no more alike genetically than any other pair of siblings and need not even be of the same sex. The remaining one-third are **identical twins** (also called **monozygotic twins**). In such cases a single fertilized ovum apparently initially divides in the normal way, but then for unknown reasons separates into two parts, usually just before implantation, with each part developing into a separate individual. Because identical twins develop from precisely the same original fertilized ovum, they are clones: They have identical genetic heritages. You'll remember from Chapter 1 that comparisons of the degree of similarity of these two types of twins is one of the major research strategies in the important field of behavior genetics.

Genotypes and Phenotypes

Using data from twin and adoption studies, behavior geneticists have made great strides in identifying those skills, characteristics, or traits that are influenced by heredity. At the same time, no geneticist proposes that an inherited combination of genes fully *determines* any outcome for a given individual. Geneticists (and psychologists) make an important distinction between the genotype, which is the specific set of "instructions" contained in a given individual's genes, and the **phenotype,** which is the actual observed characteristics of the individual. The phenotype is a product of three things: the genotype, environmental influences from the time of conception onward, and the interaction between the environment and the genotype. A child might have a genotype associated with high IQ, but if his mother drinks too much alcohol during the pregnancy, there may be damage to the nervous system, resulting in mild retardation. Another child might have a genotype including the mix of genes that contribute to a "difficult" temperament, but have parents who are particularly sensitive and thoughtful, so that the child learns other ways to handle himself.

[?] *Critical Thinking*

Can you think of other examples where the phenotype would be different from the genotype?

The distinction between genotype and phenotype is an important one. Genetic codes are not irrevocable signals for this or that pattern of development or this or that disease. The eventual developmental outcome is also affected by the specific experiences the individual has from conception onward.

Development from Conception to Birth

If we assume that conception takes place two weeks after a menstrual period, when ovulation normally occurs, then the period of gestation of the human infant is 38 weeks (about 265 days). Most physicians calculate gestation as 40 weeks, counting from the last menstrual period. However, all the specifications of weeks of gestation I've given here are based on the 38-week calculation, counting from the presumed time of conception.

Biologists and embryologists divide the weeks of gestation into three subperiods of unequal length. These are: the *germinal* stage, which lasts roughly two weeks; the *embryonic* stage, which continues until about eight weeks after conception; and the *fetal* stage, which makes up the remaining 30 weeks.

The Germinal Stage: From Conception to Implantation

Conception occurs in one of the two fallopian tubes; the fertilized ovum then spends roughly a week floating down the tube to the uterus. Cell division begins 24 to 36 hours after conception; within two to three days there are several dozen cells, and the whole mass is about the size of a pinhead. Approximately four days after conception, the mass of cells, now called a **blastocyst,** begins to subdivide, forming a hollow sphere with two layers of cells around the perimeter. The outermost layer will form the various structures that will support the developing organism, while the inner layer will form the **embryo** itself. When it touches the wall of the uterus, the outer shell of cells breaks down at the point of contact. Small tendrils develop and attach the cell mass to the uterine wall, a process called **implantation.** When implantation is complete, normally ten days to two weeks after conception, the blastocyst has perhaps 150 cells (Tanner, 1990). You can see the sequence schematically in Figure 3.4.

The Embryonic Stage

The embryonic stage begins when implantation is complete and continues until the various support structures are formed fully and all the major organ systems have been laid down in at least rudimentary form, a process that normally takes another six weeks.

Development of Support Structures. The outer layer of cells specializes further into two parts, each of which forms critical support structures. An inner membrane, called the **amnion,** creates a sac or bag, filled with liquid (*amniotic uid*), in which the baby floats. From the outer layer, called the **chorion,** two further organs develop, the **placenta** and the **umbilical cord.** The placenta, which is fully developed by about four weeks of gestation, is a platelike mass of cells that lies against the wall of the uterus. It serves as liver, lungs, and kidneys for the embryo and fetus, and is connected to the embryo's circulatory system via the umbilical cord. Thus the placenta lies between the mother's circulatory system and the embryo's and serves as a sort of filter. Nutrients such as oxygen, proteins, sugars, and vitamins from the maternal blood can pass through to the embryo or fetus, while digestive wastes and carbon dioxide from the infant's blood pass back through to the mother, whose own body can eliminate them (Rosenblith, 1992). At the same time, many (but not all) harmful substances, such as viruses or the mother's hormones, are filtered out because they are too large to pass through the various membranes in the placenta. Most drugs and anesthetics, however, do pass through the placenta, as do some disease organisms.

Development of the Embryo. At the same time, the mass of cells that will form the embryo is itself differentiating further into several types of cells that form the rudiments of skin, sense receptors, nerve cells, muscles, circulatory system, and internal organs. A heartbeat can be detected roughly four weeks after conception; the beginnings of lungs and limbs also are apparent at this time. By the end of the embryonic period, rudimentary fingers and toes, eyes, eyelids, nose, mouth, and external ears are all present, as are the basic parts of the nervous system (Allen, 1996)—a set of changes summarized in Table 3.2 and shown visually in the photo in Figure 3.5 (p. 82). When this *organogenesis* is complete, a new stage, that of the **fetus,** begins.

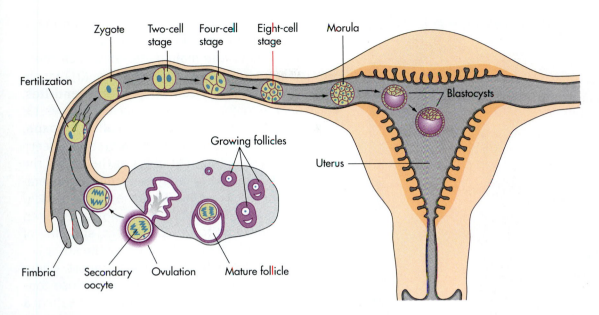

Figure 3.4

In this schematic drawing, you can see the sequence of changes during the germinal stage, with the first cell division and the first differentiation of cell function normally occurring in the fallopian tube.

Table 3.2

Milestones of Early Gestation

Week	Developmental Events
	Germinal Stage
1	Fertilization; beginning differentiation
2	Further differentiation; implantation
	Embryonic Stage
3	First missed menstrual period; urinary pregnancy test first positive; amnion, chorion, and umbilical cord begin to develop; neural tube begins to form.
4	Placenta fully developed; primitive heartbeat begins; neural tube closes (otherwise *spina bifida* occurs); eyes, blood vessels, and lungs begin to develop; total length roughly one-fourth inch.
5	Primitive mouth, arm and leg buds, and fingerlike appendages on hands appear; brain divides into three main sections of forebrain, midbrain, and hindbrain; beginning development of peripheral nerves.
6	Primitive nose and ears develop; facial structures fuse (otherwise facial defects are seen).
7	Eyelids begin; gene that determines maleness "turns on" and begins the chain of events resulting in male genitalia.
8	Ovaries and testes distinguishable; gross structure of the nervous system established; abdominal ultrasound can detect the presence of the embryo; total length now over 1 inch.

Sources: Rosenblith, 1992; Needlman, 1996; Allen, 1996.

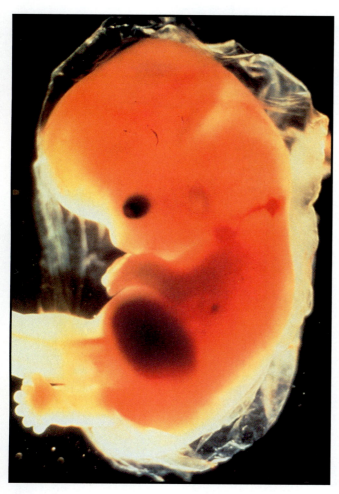

Figure 3.5

A six-week-old embryo.

The Fetal Stage

In the seven months of the fetal stage, all these primitive organ systems are refined, a process outlined in Table 3.3, and shown visually in the photos in Figure 3.6.

Development of the Nervous System.   One particularly vital system that develops almost entirely during the fetal period is the nervous system, which exists in only the most rudimentary form at the end of the embryonic stage. Two basic types of cells are involved, **neurons** and **glial cells.** The glial cells are the glue that holds the whole nervous system together, providing firmness and structure to the brain, helping to remove debris after neuronal death or injury, segregating neurons from one another. It is the neurons that do the job of re-

ceiving and sending messages from one part of the brain or one part of the body to another.

Neurons have four main parts, shown schematically in Figure 3.7 (p. 84): (1) a cell body; (2) branchlike extensions of the cell body called **dendrites,** which are the major receptors of nerve impulses; (3) a tubular extension of the cell body called the **axon,** which can extend as far as one meter (about 3 feet); and (4) branchlike terminal fibers at the end of the axon, which form the primary transmitting apparatus of the nervous system. Because of the branchlike appearance of dendrites, physiologists often use botanical terms to describe them, speaking of the "dendritic arbor" or of "pruning" of the arbor.

The point at which two neurons connect, where the axon's transmitting fibers come into close contact with another neuron's dendrites, is called a **synapse.** Synapses can also be formed between neurons and other kinds of cells, such as muscle cells, and the communication itself is accomplished with chemicals called **neurotransmitters.** The number of such synapses is vast. A single cell in the part of the brain that controls vision, for instance, may have as many as 10,000 to 30,000 synaptic inputs to its dendrites (Greenough, Black, & Wallace, 1987).

Glial cells begin to develop at about thirteen weeks after conception and continue to be added until perhaps two years after birth. The great majority of neurons are formed between 10 and 18 weeks of gestation (Huttenlocher, 1994; Todd, Swarzenski, Rossi, & Visconti, 1995), and—with rare exceptions—these are all the neurons the individual will ever have. Neurons lost later are not replaced.

[?] *Critical Thinking*

Can you think of any practical consequences of the fact that all the neurons one is ever going to have are present in most cases by 28 weeks of gestation?

In these early weeks of the fetal period, neurons are very simple. They consist largely of the cell body with short axons and little dendritic development. It is in the last two months before birth and in the first few years after birth that the lengthening of the axons and the major growth of the "dendritic arbor" occurs. Indeed, as the dendrites first develop in the eighth and ninth months of gestation,

Table 3.3

Milestones of Fetal Development

Weeks	Developmental Events
8–12	Some reflexes visible, such as the startle and sucking reflexes; movement of arms and legs; primitive facial expressions; total length at 12 weeks is about three inches, with the head making up roughly half this length.
13–16	Beginning of second trimester: external genitalia fully differentiated and detectable; skin and true hair; bony skeleton develops; breathing and swallowing motions appear.
17–20	Mother first notices movement ("quickening"); heartbeat audible through stethoscope; 20 weeks is the usual lower limit of viability, with an approximate weight of 460 grams, but the great majority of infants born this small do not survive.
25–28	Eyes open by 28 weeks; subcutaneous fat added; myelinization of spinal cord begins; eyelids and eyebrows fully form; further development of circulatory system; average weight 1300 grams. Good chance of survival if born this early.
28–38	Further subcutaneous fat added; weight added; fine hair that covered the body earlier begins to disappear; myelination of brain cells begins.
38	Birth

Sources: Rosenblith, 1992; Needlman, 1996; Allen, 1996.

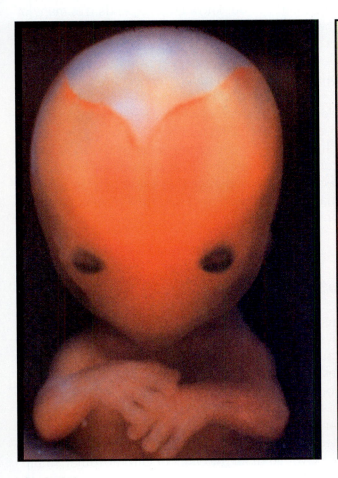
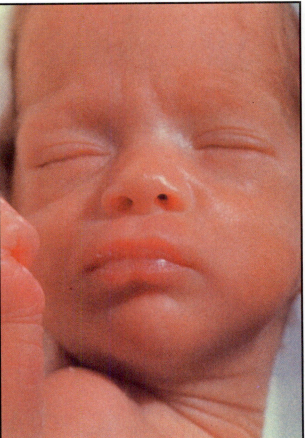

Figure 3.6

On the left is an embryo/fetus of 10–12 weeks' gestation, just at about the point of transition from embryo to fetus. The sex of the child can be determined at this age; eyes, eyelids, and lips are present, as are toes and fingers. The photo on the right shows a fetus of 28–30 weeks, when the nervous system and the circulatory and respiratory systems are all well enough developed to support life, although infants born at this stage are still very tiny.

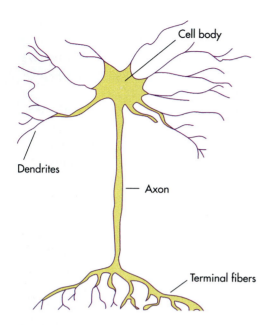

Figure 3.7

The structure of a single developed neuron. The cell bodies develop first, primarily between weeks 12 and 24. Axons and dendrites develop later, especially during the final 12 weeks, and continue to increase in size and complexity for several years after birth.

they appear to be sent out in a kind of exploratory system; many of these early dendrites are later reabsorbed, with only the useful expansions remaining. In these final fetal months, however, synapse formation is much slower; most synapses are formed after birth. For example, in the part of the brain involved in vision, babies have about ten times the number of synapses at 6 months as they had at birth (Huttenlocher, 1994).

Development of Length and Weight.   Similarly, the major growth in fetal size occurs late in the fetal period. The fetus is about half her birth length by about 20 weeks' gestation, but she does not reach half her birth weight until nearly three months later, at about 32 weeks.

An Overview of Prenatal Development

One of the most important points about the child's prenatal development is how remarkably regular and predictable it is. If the embryo has survived the

early, risky period (roughly the first eight to ten weeks) development usually proceeds smoothly, with the various changes occurring in what is apparently a fixed order, at fixed time intervals, following a clear maturational ground plan.

This sequence of development is not immune to modification or outside influence, as you'll soon see in detail. Indeed, as psychologists and biologists have looked more carefully at various kinds of teratogens, it has become clear that the sequence is more vulnerable than we had once thought. Before I begin talking about the various things that can go wrong, though, I want to make sure to state clearly that the maturational system is really quite robust. Normal prenatal development requires an adequate environment, but "adequate" seems to be a fairly broad range. *Most* children are quite normal. The list of things that *can* go wrong is long and getting longer as our knowledge expands. Yet many of these possibilities are quite rare, many are partially or wholly preventable, and many need not have permanent consequences for the child. Keep this in mind as you read through the next few pages.

The potential problems fall into two large classes: genetic errors and those damaging environmental events called teratogens (a term I defined in Chapter 1). Genetic errors occur at the moment of conception and cannot be altered—although new technology may change that eventually; teratogens may affect development any time from conception onward.

Genetic Errors

In perhaps three to eight percent of all fertilized ova, the genetic material itself contains errors caused by imperfect meiosis in the sperm or ovum, resulting in either too many or too few chromosomes. Current estimates are that 90 to 95 percent of these abnormal conceptuses are aborted spontaneously (Tanner, 1990). Only about half of one percent of live newborns have such abnormalities.

Over 50 different types of chromosomal anomaly have been identified, many of them very rare. The most common is **Down syndrome** (also called *trisomy* 21), in which the child has three copies of chromosome 21 rather than the normal two. Roughly one in every 800 or 1000 infants is born with this abnormality (Rogers, Roizen, & Capone, 1996). These children have distinctive facial features, most notably a flattened face and somewhat slanted eyes with an epicanthic fold on the eyelid (as you can see in the photo below), reduced total brain size, and often other physical abnormalities such as heart defects. Typically, they are retarded.

The risk of bearing a child with this deviant pattern is considerably higher for older mothers. For those age 35, the risk is 1 in 385 births; for a woman of 45, it is 1 in 30 (Centers for Disease Control, 1995a).

Sex-Chromosome Anomalies.

A second class of anomalies is associated with an incomplete or incorrect division of either sex chromosome, which occurs in roughly one out of every 400 births (Berch & Bender, 1987). The most common is an XXY pattern, called Klinefelter's syndrome, which occurs in around one out of every 1000 males. Affected boys most often look quite normal, although they have characteristic long arms and legs and underdeveloped testes. Most are not mentally retarded, but language and learning disabilities are common. Somewhat rarer is an XYY pattern. These children also develop as boys and are typically unusually tall with mild retardation. A single-X pattern (XO), called Turner's syndrome, and a triple-X pattern (XXX) may also occur, and in both cases the child develops as a girl. Girls with Turner's syndrome (perhaps one in every 3000 live female births [Tanner, 1990]) show stunted growth and are usually sterile. Without hormone therapy, they do not menstruate or develop breasts at puberty. These girls also show an interesting imbalance in their cognitive skills: They often perform particularly poorly on tests that measure spatial ability but usually perform at or above normal levels on tests of verbal skill (Golombok & Fivush, 1994). Girls with an XXX pattern are of normal size but are slow in physical development. In contrast to Turner's syndrome girls, they have markedly *poor* verbal abilities and an overall low IQ, and they do particularly poorly in school compared with other groups with sex-chromosome anomalies (B. G. Bender, Harmon, Linden, & Robinson, 1995; Rovet & Netley, 1983).

Fragile-X Syndrome.

A quite different type of genetic anomaly is referred to as a "fragile X," which occurs in its full form in about one out of every 1300 males (Adesman, 1996; Rose, 1995). The problem arises not from an improper number of chromosomes but rather from a mutation of a specific gene on the X chromosome. The gene is "fragile" in the sense that the chromosome has a greater tendency to break at that locus when exposed to various kinds of chemicals or other stresses (Adesman, 1996). This is an *inherited* disorder, following the sex-linked inheritance pattern illustrated earlier in Figure 3.3 (p. 78).

The majority of affected children have distinctive facial features, including a long narrow face and a prominent, pointed chin (as in the photo on p. 86); large, prominent ears are also common. Almost all those with fragile-X have at least some degree of mental retardation; very often they show a drop in IQ scores of perhaps 10 points between toddlerhood and adolescence, a decline that frequently shifts them from a level of mild retardation to one of moderate retardation (Adesman, 1996). Current estimates are that among males, 5 to 7

Note the distinctive facial characteristics of this Down syndrome child.

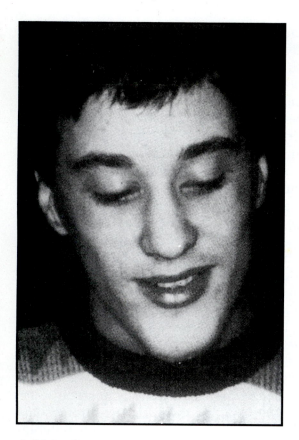

This boy diagnosed with fragile-X syndrome has the long narrow face and prominent chin common in those with this abnormality.

percent of all retardation is caused by this syndrome (Zigler & Hodapp, 1991).

Single Gene Defects. As I mentioned earlier, problems also can occur at conception if the child inherits a gene for a specific disease. The great majority of such diseases are caused by a recessive gene and thus follow the inheritance pattern shown in Figure 3.2 (p. 77). I've listed a few examples in Table 3.4, but this list cannot really convey the diversity of such disorders. Among known causes of mental retardation are 141 diseases or disorders with known genetic loci and 361 more the locus of which has not yet been identified (Wahlström, 1990).

Geneticists estimate that the average adult carries genes for four different recessive diseases or abnormalities (Scarr & Kidd, 1983), but for any one

disease the distribution of genes is not random. For example, sickle-cell genes are more common among blacks; Tay-Sachs is most common among Jews of Eastern European origin.

Teratogens: Diseases, Drugs, and Diet

Deviant prenatal development can also result from variations in the environment in which the embryo and fetus is nurtured. I pointed out in Chapter 1 that the effect of most teratogens seems to depend heavily on their *timing*, an example of *critical periods*. That is, a particular teratogen, such as a drug or a disease in the mother, will result in a defect in the embryo or fetus *only* if it occurs during a particular period of days or weeks of prenatal life. The general rule is that each organ system is most vulnerable to disruption at the time when it is developing most rapidly (Moore & Persaud, 1993). Because most organ systems develop most rapidly during the first eight to ten weeks of gestation, this is the period of greatest risk for most teratogens. Figure 3.8 (p. 89) shows the maximum times of vulnerability for different parts of the body.

Of the many teratogens, the most critical are probably diseases the mother may have and drugs she may take.

Diseases of the Mother

A disease in the mother can affect the embryo or fetus by any one of three mechanisms. Some diseases, particularly viruses, can attack the placenta, reducing the nutrients available to the embryo. Some others have molecules small enough to pass through the placental filters and attack the embryo or fetus directly. Examples of this type include rubella and rubeola (both forms of measles), cytomegalovirus (CMV), syphilis, diphtheria, influenza, typhoid, serum hepatitis, and chicken pox. The third possibility is that disease organisms present in the mucus membranes of the birth canal may infect the infant during birth itself. Genital herpes, for example, is transmitted this way. As far

Table 3.4

Some of the Major Inherited Diseases

Phenylketonuria	A metabolic disorder that prevents metabolism of a common amino acid (phenylalanine). Treatment consists of a special phenylalanine-free diet. The child is not allowed many types of food, including milk. If not placed on the special diet shortly after birth, the child usually becomes very retarded. Affects only 1 in 8000 children. Diagnostic tests for this disorder are now routinely given at birth; cannot be diagnosed prenatally.
Tay-Sachs disease	An invariably fatal degenerative disease of the nervous system; virtually all victims die within the first three to four years. This gene is most common among Jews of Eastern European origin, among whom it occurs in approximately 1 in 3500 births. Can be diagnosed prenatally with amniocentesis or chorionic villus sampling.
Sickle-cell anemia	A sometimes fatal blood disease, with joint pain, increased susceptibility to infection, and other symptoms. The gene for this disease is carried by about 2 million Americans, most often blacks. Can now be diagnosed prenatally through amniocentesis or chorionic villus sampling.
Cystic fibrosis	A fatal disease affecting the lungs and intestinal tract. Many children with CF now live into their twenties. The gene is carried by over 10 million Americans, most often whites. Carriers cannot be identified before pregnancy, and affected children cannot be diagnosed prenatally. If a couple has had one CF child, however, they know that their chances of having another are one in four.
Muscular dystrophy	A fatal muscle-wasting disease, carried on the X chromosome, thus found almost exclusively among boys. The gene for the most common type of MD, Duchenne's, has just been located, so prenatal diagnosis may soon be available.

as researchers now know, AIDS is transmitted both directly through the placenta and during delivery as well as through breast milk after birth (Van de Perre, Simonen, Msellati et al., 1991). Of all these diseases, probably the riskiest for the child are rubella, AIDS, and CMV.

Rubella. The critical period for a negative effect from **rubella** (also called *German measles*) is the first few weeks of gestation. Most infants exposed in the first four to five weeks show some abnormality, while only about ten percent of those exposed in the final six months of the pregnancy are negatively affected (Moore & Persaud, 1993). Deafness, cataracts, and heart defects are the most common abnormalities.

Fortunately, rubella is preventable. Vaccination is available and should be given to all children as part of a regular immunization program. Adult women who were not vaccinated as children can be vaccinated later, but it must be done at least three months before a pregnancy to provide complete immunity.

AIDS. Worldwide, it is estimated that 3 million women are presently infected with HIV, the virus that causes AIDS, and the number of infected women of childbearing age is rising everywhere. In the United States the calculation is that 1.7 out of every 1000 childbearing women is infected (Centers for Disease Control, 1995b). In areas with a high population of drug users, such as inner cities, as many as 3 to 5 percent of all pregnant women are now HIV-infected. In 1993, approximately 6500 infants were born to these infected mothers (Davis, Byers, Lindegren et al., 1995).

These grim numbers are counterbalanced by several bits of good news. First, we now know that only about a quarter of infants born to HIV-infected mothers actually become infected (Abrams, Matheson, Thomas et al., 1995; Newell & Peckham, 1994). Transmission appears to be quite a lot more likely when the mother has developed the full symptoms of AIDS than when she is HIV-positive but is not yet experiencing increased symptoms of the disease (Abrams et al., 1995).

Parenting

Prenatal Diagnosis of Genetic Errors

Not so many years ago, when a child was conceived, that child was born with whatever deformities, diseases, or anomalies happened to come along. The parents had no choices. That is no longer true. Parents today may have access to genetic testing, genetic counseling, and any one of several prenatal diagnostic tests that can detect fetal abnormalities.

Prepregnancy Genetic Testing. Before conceiving, you and your spouse can have blood tests done that will tell you whether you are carriers of genes for those specific diseases for which the loci are known, such as Tay-Sachs or sickle-cell anemia. Because the locations of genes for all genetic diseases have not yet been discovered, carriers of many diseases (such as cystic fibrosis) cannot yet be identified in this way. It may nonetheless be an important step if you and your spouse belong to a subgroup known to be likely to carry particular recessive genes.

Prenatal Diagnosis of the Fetus. Four prenatal diagnostic strategies are now available. Two of these, the **alpha-fetoprotein test** and **ultrasound,** are primarily used to detect problems in the formation of the *neural tube,* the structure that becomes the brain and spinal cord. If the tube fails to close at the bottom end in the fourth week of gestation, a disability called *spina bifida* occurs. Children with this defect (about fifteen hundred of whom are born each year in the United States) are often partially paralyzed, and many (but not all) are retarded.

Alpha-fetoprotein (AFP) is a substance produced by the fetus that is detectable in the mother's blood. If the levels are abnormally high, it suggests that there may be some problem with spinal cord or brain. The blood test is normally not done until the second trimester. If the AFP value is high, it does not mean a problem definitely exists; it means there is a higher *risk* of problems and further tests are usually indicated.

One such further test is ultrasound, which involves the use of sound waves to provide an actual "moving picture" of the fetus. It is frequently possible to detect, or rule out, neural tube defects and some other physical abnormalities with this method. The procedure is not painful and gives parents an often-delightful chance to see their unborn child moving; frequently it can also show whether the fetus is a boy or a girl. What ultrasound cannot provide is any information about the presence of chromosomal anomalies or inherited diseases.

If you want the latter information, you have two choices: **amniocentesis** or **chorionic villus sampling** (CVS). In both cases, a needle is inserted and cells are taken from the developing embryo. In CVS, normally done at 10 to 12 weeks' gestation, the sample is taken from what will become the placenta; in amniocentesis, normally done at 15 to 18 weeks' gestation, the sample is from the amniotic fluid.

Both CVS and amniocentesis will provide information about any of the chromosomal anomalies and about the presence of genes for many of the major genetic diseases. Each technique has advantages and disadvantages. Amniocentesis was developed earlier and is the more widely used of the two. Its major drawback is that, because the amniotic sac must be large enough to allow a sample of fluid to be taken with very little danger to the fetus, the test cannot be done until fairly late in pregnancy, and the results are not typically available for several more weeks. If the test reveals an abnormality, and the parents decide to abort, it is quite late for an abortion to be performed. CVS, in contrast, is done much earlier, so decisions can be made before the pregnancy is so far along. On the other side of the ledger is the fact that CVS is associated with slightly higher rates of miscarriage than is amniocentesis, and with a *slightly* increased risk of missing or abnormal limbs, fingers, or toes (Centers for Disease Control, 1995a). The absolute risk for such abnormalities remains low, even with CVS (current calculations indicate 3.5 cases per 10,000 CVS procedures), but the risk is higher than when no CVS has been done.

Because of the risks associated with either procedure, parents need to think over the options carefully. Most physicians recommend one of the two for women over age 35 (because of the increased risk of Down syndrome) and for women with a known or probable family risk of particular inherited diseases, such as Tay-Sachs or cystic fibrosis.

By the time you are facing such a choice, the decision may have been simplified by the development of new, lower-risk diagnostic techniques using maternal blood samples. Experimental evidence already indicates that such a technique may be suitable for diagnosing Down syndrome or even the sex of the fetus (Lo, Patel, Wainscoat et al., 1989; Wald, Cuckle, Densem et al., 1988). No matter what technique you do or do not select, the moral and ethical choices you may be called upon to make are far from easy.

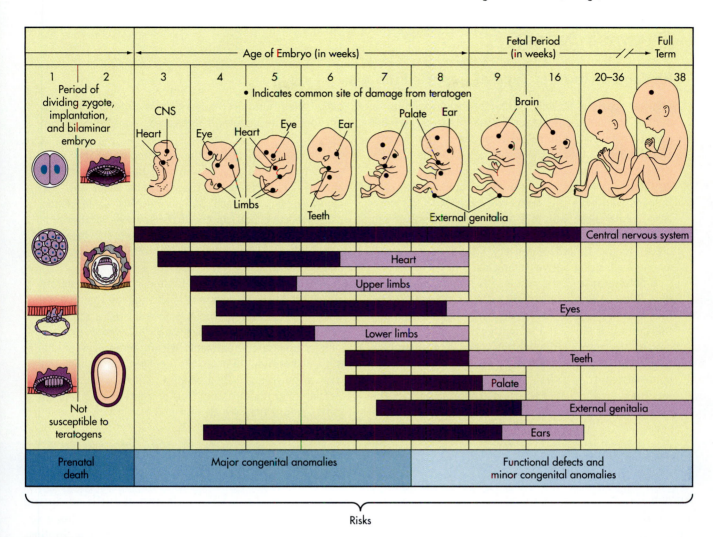

Figure 3.8

Critical periods in the prenatal development of various body parts. The dark purple portion of each line signifies the period during which any teratogen is likely to produce a major structural deformity in that particular body part. The light purple part of each line shows the period in which more minor problems may result. The embryonic period is clearly the time of greatest vulnerability. (Source: Moore & Persaud, 1993, Figure 8-13, p. 156.)

Even more encouraging is the finding that infected women who are treated with the drug AZT during their pregnancy have a markedly lowered risk of transmitting the disease to their children— as low as 8 percent (Centers for Disease Control, 1994a; Fiscus, Adimora, Schoenbach et al., 1996). Because most HIV-positive women are asymptomatic and are unaware they are infected, the Centers for Disease Control recommend routine HIV counseling and voluntary testing for all pregnant women early in their pregnancies, so that they can begin on a course of AZT.

[?] *Critical Thinking*

Do you think the information about the beneficial effects of AZT on the rate of transmission of HIV infection to infants would justify *requiring* HIV testing for all pregnant women? Medical ethicists have offered strong arguments on both sides of this question. What do you think?

CMV. A much less well known but remarkably widespread and potentially serious disease is cytomegalovirus (CMV), a virus in the herpes group.

Rh Factor: Another Type of Genetic Problem

Another possible problem, Rh factor incompatibility, is neither a genetic defect nor an inherited disease, but rather an incompatibility between the mother's genes and the baby's. One of the many factors in the blood is the presence or absence of a red cell antigen, called the Rh factor (so named because rhesus monkeys have it). Humans who have this factor are called Rh+ (Rh positive), while those who lack it are Rh− (Rh negative). Only about fifteen percent of whites and five percent of blacks in the United States are Rh−; it is quite rare among Asians and Native Americans.

Problems arise if the mother is Rh− and the baby is Rh+. Because Rh+ is dominant, a baby with an Rh+ father could inherit an Rh+ gene from him, even though the mother is Rh−. If the mother's and fetus's blood mix in the uterus, the mother's body considers the baby's Rh+ factor to be a foreign substance, and her immune system tries to fight it off by producing antibodies. These antibodies cross the placenta and attack the baby's blood, producing a chemical substance in the baby called bilirubin. Babies with high levels of bilirubin look quite yellow; if untreated, brain damage can occur.

The risk of damage to the fetus increases with each succeeding pregnancy in which an Rh− mother carries an Rh+ baby. Normally, the placenta keeps the two blood systems separate, but during birth some mixing usually occurs. So after the first baby, the mother produces some antibodies. With a second incompatible baby, these antibodies attack the infant's blood, producing negative effects.

This problem used to be treated with rather heroic measures, such as complete exchange of the infant's blood shortly after birth, to remove all the antibodies. Fortunately, scientists have now discovered a much simpler and safer treatment. Within three days of the birth of her first child, an Rh− mother can be injected with a substance called *rhogam*, which prevents the buildup of antibodies, and thus protects subsequent infants, even if they are also Rh+.

It is now thought to be the single most important known infectious cause of both congenital mental retardation and deafness. CMV typically has few, if any, symptoms in an adult. In most cases an affected person doesn't even know she carries this virus, although in an active phase it sometimes has mononucleosis-like symptoms, including swollen glands and low fever. In infants who are infected prenatally or during birth, however, the virus can sometimes produce crippling disabilities.

Roughly half of *all* women of childbearing age have antibodies to CMV (Spector, 1996), indicating that they have been infected at some time. One to 2 percent of babies whose mothers have CMV antibodies become infected prenatally. When the mother becomes newly infected during her pregnancy, the transmission rate is much higher—perhaps as high as 30 to 50 percent (Hagay, Biran, Ornoy, & Reece, 1996; Hanshaw, 1995). In the United States these two patterns add up to close to 40,000 infants born each year who test positive for this virus (Istas, Demmler, Dobbins, Stewart, & Group, 1995). Of these 40,000, 10 to 20 percent exhibit congenital CMV syndrome at birth or during the first year of life, a syndrome that includes a variety of symptoms of neurological damage, including mental retardation, small head size, and calcifications in the brain. Deafness, impaired vision, and dental problems are also common. As many as 30 percent of infants who show this syndrome die in infancy (Hagay et al., 1996).

Transmission appears to follow the same three pathways we see with HIV: prenatally, during delivery, and through breast milk. Unlike HIV infection, however, researchers have not yet found any effective treatment for CMV in pregnancy; no general screening for this virus is presently recommended for pregnant women.

Taken together, this information about CMV is pretty scary for a woman to read, whether she is now pregnant or planning to become pregnant. Here is a common disease that may have massive negative effects on your child, and there is really nothing you can do about it. However, keep the statistics correctly in mind: If the mother's disease is not active, only 1 to 2 percent of babies become infected. Of this number, only at most a fifth show symptoms of the disease—which means that at most 4 out of every 1000 infants whose mothers carry an inactive antibody will show any effect. Until someone discovers a treatment or a vaccine, that's the most optimism I can offer.

Drugs Taken by the Mother

There is now a huge literature on the effects of prenatal drugs, involving everything from aspirin to antibiotics to alcohol and cocaine. Sorting out their effects has proven to be an immensely challenging task, not only because it is clearly not possible to assign women randomly to various drug groups, but also because in the real world many women take multiple drugs during their pregnancy. For example, women who drink alcohol are also more likely to smoke; those who use cocaine are also likely to take other illegal drugs or to smoke or drink to excess. What's more, the effects of drugs may be subtle, visible only many years after birth in the form of minor learning disabilities or increased risk of behavior problems. Still, we are creeping toward some fairly clear conclusions in several areas. Let me give you some examples.

Smoking. One consistent result stands out from the large body of research: Infants of mothers who smoke are on average about half a pound lighter at birth than are infants of nonsmoking mothers (Floyd, Rimer, Giovino, Mullen, & Sullivan, 1993), and they are nearly twice as likely to be born with weights below 2500 grams (5 lb. 8 oz.), the common definition of low birth weight (U.S. Bureau of the Census, 1996). The more the mother smokes, the greater the negative impact on the infant's weight (Nordentoft, Lou, Hansen et al., 1996), and the older the mother, the more likely it is that her smoking will be linked to low birth weight (U.S. Bureau of the Census, 1996). The primary causal mechanism seems to be that nicotine constricts the blood vessels, reducing blood flow and nutri-

tion to the placenta. The resulting lowered birth weight has a variety of potential negative consequences I'll talk about later.

The moral seems clear: The safest plan is to refrain from smoking during pregnancy. If you are a smoker, quit as soon as you learn you are pregnant: Smokers who quit smoking early in their pregnancy have the same rates of low-birth-weight infants as do those who did not smoke at all (Ahlsten, Cnattingius, & Lindmark, 1993). The research also shows a relationship between the "dose" (the amount of nicotine you are taking in) and the severity of consequences for the child. So if you cannot quit entirely, at least cut back.

Drinking. Recent work on the effects of maternal drinking on prenatal and postnatal development also carries a clear message—the very message I tried to convey to my daughter-in-law: To be safe, don't drink during pregnancy.

The effects of alcohol on the developing fetus range from mild to severe. At the extreme end of the continuum are children who exhibit a syndrome called **fetal alcohol syndrome (FAS).** These children, whose mothers were usually heavy drinkers or alcoholics, are generally smaller in stature than normal. Their brains are also smaller, often with distinct anomalies or deformities (Swayze, Johnson, Hanson et al., 1997). They frequently have heart defects, and their faces have certain common features (visible in the two photos in Figure 3.9 p. 92), with a somewhat flattened nose and nose bridge and often an unusually long space between nose and mouth. As children, adolescents, and adults, they continue to be shorter than normal, have smaller heads, and have IQ scores in the range of mild mental retardation. Indeed, FAS is the leading known cause of retardation in the United States, exceeding even Down syndrome (Streissguth, Aase, Clarren et al., 1991).

Recent evidence also points to milder effects of moderate or "social" drinking, such as two glasses of wine a day. Children of mothers who drink at this level during pregnancy are more likely to have IQ scores below 85 and to show poorer attention span. I've given some details about one of the best studies in the *Research Report* box on page 93, so you

 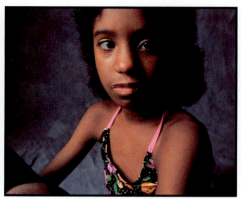

Figure 3.9

These two children, from different countries and racial backgrounds, have been diagnosed with fetal alcohol syndrome (FAS). Both are mentally retarded and have relatively small heads. Note also the short nose and the low nasal bridge typical of FAS children. (Copyright George Steinmetz.)

can get some feeling for how investigators have gone about studying this problem.

We do not yet know if there is any safe level of alcohol consumption during pregnancy, although most researchers in this field are convinced that there is a linear relationship between the amount of alcohol ingested and the risk for the infant. This means that even infrequent drinking at low dosage carries *some* increased risk. Occasional bouts of heavy drinking, such as five or more drinks on one occasion (called binge drinking), carry even greater risk (Olson, Sampson, Barr, Streissguth, & Bookstein, 1992; Streissguth, Barr, & Sampson, 1990). In the face of our remaining ignorance, the *safest* course is not to drink at all.

Cocaine. Significant numbers of pregnant women in the United States (and presumably elsewhere in the world) also take various illegal drugs, most notably cocaine. The best current estimates are that roughly three percent of all babies born in the United States have been exposed prenatally to cocaine. Among babies born to poor, inner-city mothers, the rate may be as high as 20 or 30 percent (Hawley & Disney, 1992).

Cocaine appears to cross the placental barrier quite readily. About a third of all cocaine-exposed babies are born prematurely, and among those born after a normal gestation period, many are lower than normal in birth weight. In addition, cocaine-exposed infants are three times as likely to have a very small head circumference (Needlman, Frank, Augustyn, & Zuckerman, 1995). Some (but not all) also show significant drug withdrawal symptoms after birth, such as irritability, restlessness, shrill crying, and tremors. What is not yet

clear is whether any long-term consequences can be ascribed clearly to prenatal cocaine exposure. Some studies show long-term effects (e.g., S. L. Bender, Word, DiClemente et al., 1995); others do not (Griffith, Azuma, & Chasnoff, 1994; Richardson & Day, 1994). We may eventually find, as with alcohol exposure, that prenatal cocaine exposure does indeed have lasting effects on the child but that the effects are fairly subtle and thus hard to pin down. As of this moment, we simply don't know (Lester, Freier, & LaGasse, 1995).

[?] *Critical Thinking*

Another question of medical ethics for you to ponder: There are now several cases of pregnant women being held in custody to prevent them from excessive drinking or drug taking, on the grounds that the court has the responsibility to prevent harm to the fetus. What do you think about this?

Diet

Another significant factor for prenatal development is the mother's diet. Both the general adequacy of the diet, measured in terms of calories, and the presence of certain key nutrients are critical.

Malnutrition. At a minimum a mother needs sufficient overall calories and protein to prevent malnutrition. When a woman experiences severe malnutrition during pregnancy, particularly during the final three months, she has a greatly increased risk of stillbirths, low infant birth weight, or infant

Streissguth's Study of Prenatal Alcohol Exposure

The best single study of the consequences of prenatal alcohol exposure has been done by Ann Streissguth and her colleagues (Olson et al., 1992; Streissguth, Barr, & Sampson, 1990; Streissguth, Barr, Sampson et al., 1989; Streissguth, Bookstein, Sampson, & Barr, 1995; Streissguth, Landesman-Dwyer, Martin, & Smith, 1980; Streissguth, Martin, Barr et al., 1984; Streissguth, Martin, Martin et al., 1981), who have followed a group of over 500 women and children beginning in early pregnancy. Because the study was begun before there were widespread warnings about the possible impact of alcohol during pregnancy, the sample includes many well-educated, middle-class women with good diets who did not use many other recreational drugs but who did drink alcohol in moderate or even fairly heavy amounts while pregnant—a set of conditions that would be impossible to duplicate today, at least in the United States or other countries in which the risks of alcohol in pregnancy are well advertised.

Streissguth tested the children repeatedly, beginning immediately after birth, again later in infancy, at age 4, at school age, and again at ages 11 and 14. She found that the mother's alcohol consumption in pregnancy was associated with sluggishness and weaker sucking in infancy, lower scores on a test of infant intelligence at 8 months, lower IQ scores at 4 and 7 years, and problems with attention and vigilance at 4, 7, 11, and 14. Teachers also rated the 11-year-olds on overall school performance and on various behavior problems, and on both measures those whose mothers had consumed the most alcohol during pregnancy were rated significantly worse.

Streissguth also was careful to obtain information about other drug use in pregnancy, including smoking, and asked mothers about their diet, education, and life habits. She found that the links between alcohol consumption and poor outcomes for the child held up, even when all these other variables were controlled statistically.

Setting aside those cases in which the child was diagnosed with full fetal alcohol syndrome, the effects of moderate levels of alcohol use during pregnancy are not large in absolute terms, but they have significant practical consequences. For example, the difference in IQ scores at age 7 between children of abstainers and children of women who drank 1 ounce or more of alcohol per day during their pregnancy (roughly equivalent to 2 ounces of hard liquor or one 8-ounce glass of wine) was only about 6 points in Streissguth's sample (Streissguth et al., 1990). Still, this relatively small absolute difference means that three times as many alcohol-exposed children have IQs below 85 than is true among children of abstainers. Alcohol-exposed children are thus greatly overrepresented in special classes in schools and probably also appear in overlarge numbers among high school dropouts and the underemployed in adulthood—although those links remain for longer-term longitudinal studies to confirm.

death during the first year of life (Stein, Susser, Saenger, & Morolla, 1975). The impact appears to be greatest on the developing nervous system, a pattern found in studies of both humans and other mammals. For example, rats whose caloric intake has been substantially restricted during the fetal and early postnatal periods show a condition described as *brain stunting*, characterized by lighter brains with less dendritic development and less rich synaptic formation (Pollitt & Gorman, 1994).

In human studies of cases in which prenatal malnutrition has been severe enough to cause the death of the fetus or newborn, effects very similar to the rat studies have been observed. These infants have smaller brains with fewer and smaller brain cells (Georgieff, 1994).

What is far less clear is whether similarly lasting effects on brain development occur in cases of prenatal *subnutrition*, such as the chronic protein-energy malnutrition common in many populations around the world. One factor that makes it difficult to identify clear prenatal effects is that the same children who are malnourished prenatally are highly likely to encounter mal- or subnutrition after birth as well, frequently accompanied by lower levels of stimulation in the home. This makes it extremely difficult to sort out the effects of the *prenatal* nutrition from the effects of *postnatal* insufficiencies. At the moment, most experts in this area have abandoned the idea that typical levels of prenatal subnutrition have some direct, irremediable, negative effect on the developing brain (Pollitt, Golub, Gorman et al., 1996; Ricciuti, 1993). Instead, what seems to happen is some variation of the interaction pattern I described in Chapter 1 (recall Figure 1.3, p. 22): Prenatal subnutrition may make the infant more "vulnerable," perhaps because it makes him less energetic or responsive or less able to learn from his experiences. In a nonstimulating environment such a vulnerable child is likely to do poorly, yet a stimulating environment may be able to overcome the vulnerability.

Folic Acid. A vital specific nutrient, whose importance during pregnancy has only recently become clear, is folic acid, a B vitamin found primarily in liver, beans, leafy green vegetables, broccoli, orange juice, fortified breakfast cereals, and grain products, especially wheat germ. Inadequate amounts of this nutrient have been clearly linked to the risk of neural tube defects such as *spina bi da*, a deformity in which the lower part of the spine does not close (e.g., Butterworth & Bendich, 1996). Many (but not all) such children are retarded; most have some lower-body paralysis. Because the neural tube develops primarily during the very earliest weeks of pregnancy, before a woman may even know she is pregnant, it is important for women who plan a pregnancy to achieve and maintain at least the minimum level of folic acid (400 micrograms daily).

[?] *Critical Thinking*

What kind of study would you have to do to figure out whether it is okay for pregnant women to maintain high levels of exercise, such as running 30 miles a week?

Weight Gain. A woman's caloric needs go up 10 to 20 percent during a pregnancy in order to support the needed weight gain. As recently as the late 1960s in the United States, physicians routinely advised pregnant women to limit their weight gain to 15–20 pounds; greater gains were thought to increase the risk of labor abnormalities and other problems. In the 1970s, however, new data accumulated showing that weight gains in that low range were associated with increased risk of bearing a low-birth-weight infant and with neurological impairment in the infant. This information led to significant increases in the recommended weight gain. The most recent guidelines, published in 1990 by the National Institute of Medicine, base the recommended gain on a woman's prepregnancy weight for height, as shown in Table 3.5 (p. 96).

Unfortunately, the very women who are otherwise at highest risk for various kinds of problems are also most likely to gain too little weight: those who are lightweight for their height before pregnancy, women older than 35, those with low education, and African-American women, for whom higher levels of weight gain during pregnancy seem optimal (Abrams, 1994; Centers for Disease Control, 1992).

At the same time, there are also risks associated with gaining too much. In particular, women who gain more than the amounts recommended in the table are more likely to have cesarean section delivery (Abrams, 1994); they are also prone to postpartum obesity, which carries a whole set of other health risks, including heart disease and diabetes (Johnson & Yancey, 1996). Gains within the recommended ranges appear optimal, although there is wide variability from one woman to the next.

Finally, women who are obese before they become pregnant have some additional risks, regardless of the amount of weight they gain. Such women are about twice as likely to have infants with neural tube defects, regardless of their intake of folic acid (Shaw, Velie, & Schaffer, 1996; Werler, Louik, Shapiro, & Mitchell, 1996)—a finding that argues in favor of weight loss *before* pregnancy for women who are classed as obese.

Other Teratogens

Other known teratogens include excess amounts of vitamin A, diethylstilbestrol, methylmercury, and

Social Policy Debate

Should the Government Play a Role in Increasing Intake of Folic Acid by Pregnant Women?

There is a special social policy dilemma associated with the issue of increasing intake of folic acid by pregnant women. The critical period for the formation of the neural tube is the first four weeks of pregnancy. To prevent neural tube defects, the woman has to take in at least 400 micrograms of folic acid daily during all these early weeks, before most women even know they are pregnant. As a practical matter, what kind of public health policy is likely to lead to the desired behavior?

We have two basic choices: (1) persuade all women of childbearing age, as a voluntary matter, to change their diets to increase their intake of folic acid or, alternatively, to take folic acid supplements; (2) add folic acid supplements to the basic food supply by fortifying certain foods.

Policymakers in the United States began with the first strategy. In 1992 the Centers for Disease Control recommended that all women of childbearing age increase folic acid intake, an announcement followed by articles in various public sources. For various reasons, however, the information campaign has not been a great success. A Gallup poll of more than 2000 women of childbearing age in 1995 showed that only half had heard anything about folic acid; fewer still understood the link between this nutrient and birth defects. Only about a quarter of these women achieved the minimum daily dosage (Hine, 1996).

In February 1996, having concluded that it would be essentially impossible to reach all childbearing women solely through education, the Food and Drug Administration adopted the second strategy. They announced a program to require fortification of enriched flour with folic acid with 140 micrograms per 100 grams of flour, a requirement that took full effect in January 1998. This step was strongly urged by many researchers convinced that the link between folic acid and neural tube defects had been strongly established by high quality scientific studies. Advocates also contend that there are few possible negative side effects of *too much* folic acid intake—a possible risk of food fortification (e.g., Oakley, Adams, & Dickinson, 1996).

Yet not all scientists agree with the FDA's step. Opponents make two kinds of arguments (e.g., Gaull, Testa, Thomas, & Weinreich, 1996). First, they suggest that the scientific base is not totally firm. While it is clear that folic acid has some causal connection to neural tube defects, other chemicals are also involved, as are genetic patterns that appear to affect crucial metabolic processes. Folic acid supplements are thus not likely to eliminate all neural tube defects. Second, opponents argue that fortification can increase the health risks for another group of individuals, those with pernicious anemia—a disease found primarily among elderly whites. Increased intake of folic acid by these adults might mask the symptoms of the anemia, but the underlying neurological damage associated with the disease would progress nonetheless. There is dispute among scientists about just how large a problem this may be (e.g., Oakley et al., 1996).

This entire argument is a wonderful example of just how hard it is to translate scientific information—even very high quality scientific information—into widely accepted public policy. How do you weigh the various pros and cons? How do you weigh alternate risks against one another? If you were the commissioner of the Food and Drug Administration, do you think you would have made the decision to fortify? What additional information would you want to have before making such a decision?

lead. Many other drugs or chemicals are suspected of being teratogens, but we have too little information to be sure. The latter category includes anticonvulsant medication taken by epileptics, polychlorinated biphenyls (PCBs, compounds widely used in electrical transformers and paint), radiation at high doses, aspirin, some antidepressants, some artificial hormones, and some pesticides (Vorhees & Mollnow, 1987). I don't have room to go into detail about what we know (or don't know) in each case, but let me say just a word about several items that have clear practical significance.

Table 3.5

Currently Recommended Weight Gains During Pregnancy

Prepregnant Weight Category	Recommended Weight Gain
Below normal (90% or less of recommended weight for height)	28 to 40 lb.
Normal	25 to 35 lb.
Overweight (120% to 135% of recommended weight for height)	15 to 25 lb.
Obese (135% or more of recommended weight for height)	15 lb. or more

Source: Taffel, Keppel, & Jones, 1993.

Diethylstilbestrol (DES). DES is a synthetic estrogen that at one time was commonly given to pregnant women to prevent miscarriages. The daughters of these women have been found to have higher rates of some kinds of cancers; sons have higher rates of congenital malformations of the genitalia. Some—but not all—research suggests that the sons also have higher rates of infertility (Rosenblith, 1992; Wilcox, Baird, Weinberg, Hornsby, & Herbst, 1995).

Vitamin A. Vitamin A in small doses is essential for the development of the embryo, but when taken in very large doses (10,000 international units [IU] or more per day) during the first two months of pregnancy, it is linked to significantly increased risk of birth defects, particularly malformations of the head, face, heart, and nervous system (e.g., Rothman, Moore, Singer et al., 1995). The recommended daily allowance of vitamin A is 2700 IU. Most multivitamin pills contain 4000 to 5000 units, but some brands contain as much as 10,000, and straight vitamin A capsules can contain as much as 25,000 units. If you are pregnant, or planning a pregnancy, check your intake of this vitamin.

Aspirin. One of the most widely used drugs, aspirin, is teratogenic in animals when given in high doses. Humans rarely take high enough doses to produce such effects directly, but aspirin in moderate amounts can have negative effects on the human fetus if it is ingested along with benzoic acid, a chemical widely used as a food preservative in foods and condiments such as ketchup. This combination, especially in the first trimester, seems to increase the risk of physical malformations in the embryo/fetus.

Lead. In most industrialized countries adults are exposed to fairly high dosages of lead, although the introduction of unleaded gasoline has helped to lower dosages significantly as has the elimination of lead-based paint. Children may be exposed to lead prenatally (through the mother's blood lead levels) or postnatally, through contact with lead paint, from car exhaust, or from living near a factory that emits high levels of lead. Because most children who are exposed to high levels of lead prenatally are *also* exposed to high levels postnatally, it is extremely difficult to sort out the unique impact of prenatal lead. The best information comes from several excellent longitudinal studies following children from birth through early childhood (e.g., Baghurst, McMichael, Tong et al., 1995; Baghurst, McMichael, Wigg et al., 1992; Dietrich, Berger, Succop, Hammond, & Bornschein, 1993). These researchers find a small link between elevated blood lead levels in newborns and lower IQ scores later in childhood. Exposure to high levels of lead during childhood appears to have a further, even larger, negative effect, not only on IQ scores but also on distractibility and (perhaps) aggressiveness—a finding I talked about in Chapter 1. Even at quite low levels—levels previously classified as "safe" by U.S. federal guidelines and found in children who live in houses without lead-based paint—we see negative effects. Until recently, for example, a level of 20 micrograms per deciliter was thought to be acceptable; newer research shows that children with this level of lead have IQ scores that average

2.6 points lower than do those with only 10 micrograms of blood lead (Schwartz, 1994). Because of such evidence the Centers for Disease Control have changed their guidelines, now listing 10 micrograms as the desirable upper limit. By current estimates, 3 to 6 percent of U.S. infants and young children have blood lead levels that exceed this amount (Centers for Disease Control, 1997d), the greatest percentage of them black or Hispanic children living in inner-city neighborhoods. Lead exposure may therefore be one of the many small factors contributing to the lower average IQ scores of children living in poverty.

As the study of teratogens expands, psychologists have realized that prenatal development is less insulated, less fully protected than we had first thought. In particular, many chemicals associated with modern industrial societies may have unforeseen effects on the fetus.

Other Influences on Prenatal Development

The Mother's Age

One of the particularly intriguing trends in modern family life in the United States and many other industrialized countries is the increasing likelihood

The switch to unleaded gasoline clearly has not solved all the problems of air pollution. Still, it has greatly benefited children by reducing their exposure to lead.

that women will postpone their first pregnancy into their late twenties or early thirties. In 1994, 22.1 percent of first births in the United States were to women over 30, more than double the rate in 1970 (U.S. Bureau of the Census, 1996). Of course, women have many reasons for such delayed childbearing, chief among them the increased need for second incomes in families and the desire of many young women to complete job training and early career steps before bearing children. I'm not going to debate all the pros and cons of such a choice. What I do want to explore, though, is the question that is relevant for the subject of this chapter, namely, the impact of maternal age on the mother's experience of pregnancy and on the developing fetus.

Current research suggests that the optimum time for childbearing is in a woman's early twenties. Mothers over 30 (particularly those over 35) are at increased risk for several kinds of problems, including miscarriage, stillbirth, complications of pregnancy such as high blood pressure or bleeding, cesarean-section delivery, and death during pregnancy or delivery (Berkowitz, Skovron, Lapinski, & Berkowitz, 1990; Hoyert, 1996; McFalls, 1990; Peipert & Bracken, 1993).

The infants born to these older mothers also appear to have higher risk of some kinds of problems. In particular, a number of large studies in several different industrialized countries show that the risk of fetal death—from any of a variety of causes—is higher for mothers of 35 and older, even when the mothers in every age group have received good prenatal care (Cnattingius, Berendes, & Forman, 1993; Fretts, Schmittdiel, McLean, Usher, & Goldman, 1995). Other than the well-established risk of Down syndrome, older mothers do not seem to be at higher risk for bearing children with congenital anomalies, but delayed childbearing clearly does continue to carry some added risk for both mother and child, despite improvements in prenatal and neonatal care.

Risks for mother and child are also higher at the other end of the age continuum, among very young mothers. Because teen mothers are also more likely to be poor and less likely to receive adequate prenatal care, it has been very hard to sort out the causal factors. Fortunately, an unusually well designed new study makes the link quite clear.

Older mothers, like this one, are becoming much more common in the United States and in other industrialized countries. Mothers over 30 (especially those over 35) and their infants have somewhat increased risks of problems during pregnancy and delivery, a point to bear in mind if you choose to delay childbearing.

Alison Fraser and her colleagues studied 135,088 white girls and women, ages 13 to 24, who gave birth in the state of Utah between 1970 and 1990 (Fraser, Brockert, & Ward, 1995). This is an unusual sample for studies on this subject: Almost two-thirds of the teenage mothers in this group were married and most had adequate prenatal care; 95 percent remained in school. These special conditions have enabled Fraser to disentangle the effects of ethnicity, poverty, marital status, and the mother's age—all of which are normally confounded in studies of teenage childbearing. Overall, Fraser found higher rates of adverse pregnancy outcomes among mothers age 17 and younger than among the mothers aged 20 to 24. The rate of preterm births was twice as high; the incidence of low birth weight was almost twice as high. And these differences were found even when Fraser looked only at teenage mothers who were married, attended school, and had adequate prenatal care.

Outcomes were riskier still among teenage mothers who lacked adequate prenatal care, but good care alone did not eliminate the heightened risk of problems linked to teenage birth.

Just why such a heightened risk should exist for teen mothers is not entirely clear. The most likely possibility is that there is some negative biological consequence of pregnancy in a girl whose own growth is not complete.

Stress, Exertion, and Emotional State

The idea that emotional or physical stress is linked to poor pregnancy outcomes is firmly established in folklore, but "its foundation in science is much less secure" (Grimes, 1996). Results from infrahuman studies are clear: Exposure of the pregnant female to stressors such as heat, light, noise, shock, or crowding significantly increases the risk of low-birth-weight offspring as well as later problems in the offspring (Schneider, 1992). Studies of humans are harder to interpret because they necessarily involve quasi-experimental designs rather than random assignment of subjects. Women who experience high levels of stress are quite likely to be different in other ways from those who do not, so it is harder to uncover clear causal connections. Nonetheless, a number of more careful recent studies do show that stressful life events, emotional distress, and physical stress are all linked to slight increases in problems of pregnancy, such as low birth weight, heightened maternal blood pressure, and certain physical problems in the infants, such as cleft palate or respiratory problems (e.g., Hedegaard, Henriksen, Secher, Hatch, & Sabroe, 1996; Henriksen, Hedegaard, Secher, & Wilcox, 1995). The effect appears to be small, but my own conclusion from reading this literature is that stress does have a deleterious effect, at least for some women.

Controlling or Avoiding the Risks of Pregnancy

I've given you a very long list of problems and lots of advice about things to do or not do. To help you keep all these things in mind, and to give you a

Table 3.6

Advice for Pregnant Women and Those Who Expect to Become Pregnant

Things To Do Before You Get Pregnant

- Stop smoking.
- Increase your intake of folic acid to 400 micrograms per day by changing your diet or taking supplements.
- Get a rubella vaccination if you have not already had one.
- Get tested for the HIV virus; if you are positive, begin a program of AZT before you even think about getting pregnant.
- If you and/or your partner belong to subgroups who are known to be at high risk for certain inherited diseases or if you know that certain genetic disorders run in your family, confer with a genetic counselor and have the appropriate blood tests.
- If you are significantly obese (135% or more above the recommended weight for your height), try to lose weight before you become pregnant in order to reduce further your risk of having an infant with a neural tube defect.

Things to Do After You Find Out You Are Pregnant

- Stop drinking.
- Stop smoking if you didn't already do so; if you can't quit entirely, cut back as much as you can.
- Abstain from other drugs, such as cocaine.
- Get good prenatal care.
- Follow the recommended guidelines on weight gain; worry less about your figure and more about the baby's getting enough nutrients.
- Increase your calcium intake and avoid excessive vitamin A.
- If you haven't already done so, get tested for the HIV virus; if you are positive, take AZT under a doctor's supervision.
- Watch out for aspirin; if possible, use a nonaspirin pain medication.
- If you are 35 or older, consider having an amniocentesis or CVS test to discover if your fetus has Down syndrome.

checklist you can use to prepare for your own pregnancy (or that of a partner), I've summarized the key advice in Table 3.6. There is obviously a lot we don't know, but in many cases we can convert the results of large numbers of scientific studies into direct, practical advice for you as a parent.

Sex Differences in Prenatal Development

Because nearly all prenatal development is controlled by maturational codes that are the same for all members of our species—male and female alike—there aren't very many sex differences in prenatal development. Still, there are a few, and

they set the stage for some of the physical differences we'll see at later ages.

- Sometime between four and eight weeks after conception, the male embryo begins to secrete the male hormone *testosterone* from the rudimentary testes. If this hormone is not secreted or is secreted in inadequate amounts, the embryo will be "demasculinized," even to the extent of developing female genitalia. Female embryos do not appear to secrete any equivalent hormone prenatally. However, the accidental presence of male hormone at the critical time (such as from some drug the mother may take or from a genetic disease called *congenital adrenal hyperplasia* acts to "defeminize" or masculinize the female fetus, sometimes resulting in malelike genitalia, frequently resulting in masculinization of later behavior, such as more rough-and-tumble play (Collaer & Hines, 1995).

- The several hormones that affect the development of genitalia prenatally (particularly testosterone in males) also appear to affect the pattern of brain development, resulting in subtle brain differences between males and females affecting patterns of growth-hormone secretions in adolescence, levels of physical aggression, and the relative dominance of the right and left hemispheres of the brain (Todd et al., 1995). The research evidence in this area is still fairly sketchy; it is clear that whatever role such prenatal hormones play in brain architecture and functioning is highly complex. Still, this early research has raised some very intriguing questions.

- Girls are a bit faster in some aspects of prenatal development, particularly skeletal development. They are four to six weeks ahead in bone development at birth (Tanner, 1990).

- Despite the more rapid development of girls, boys are slightly heavier and longer at birth, with more muscle tissue and fewer fat cells. U.S. data, for example, show the 50th percentile birth-length and -weight for boys at 20 inches and $7\frac{1}{4}$ pounds, compared with $19\frac{1}{4}$ inches and 7 pounds for girls (Needlman, 1996).

- Boys are considerably more vulnerable to all kinds of prenatal problems. Many more boys than girls are conceived—on the order of about 120 to 150 male embryos to every 100 female— but more of the males are spontaneously aborted. At birth, there are about 105 boys for every 100 girls. Boys are also more likely to experience injuries at birth (perhaps because they are larger), and they have more congenital malformations (Zaslow & Hayes, 1986).

The striking sex difference in vulnerability is particularly intriguing, especially since it seems to persist throughout the life span. Males have shorter life expectancy, higher rates of behavior problems, more learning disabilities, and usually more negative responses to major stresses, such as divorce. One possible explanation for at least some of this sex difference may lie in the basic genetic difference. The XX combination affords the girl more protection against the fragile-X syndrome and against any "bad" genes that may be carried on the X chromosome. For instance, geneticists have found that a gene affecting susceptibility to infectious disease is carried on the X chromosome (Brooks-Gunn & Matthews, 1979). Because boys have only one X chromosome, such a gene is much more likely to be expressed phenotypically in a boy.

Birth

Once the 38 weeks of gestation are over, the fetus must be born into the world—an event that holds some pain as well as a good deal of joy for most parents. In the normal process, labor progresses through three stages of unequal length.

The First Stage of Labor. Stage 1 covers the period during which two important processes occur: dilation and effacement. The cervix (the opening at the bottom of the uterus) must open up like the lens of a camera (*dilation*) and also flatten out (*effacement*). At the time of actual delivery, the cervix must normally be dilated to about 10 centimeters (about 4 inches). This part of labor has been likened to putting on a sweater with a neck that is too tight. You have to pull and stretch the neck of the sweater with your head in order to get it on. Eventually, the neck is stretched wide enough so that the widest part of your head can pass through.

Customarily, stage 1 is itself divided into phases. In the *early* (or *latent*) phase, contractions are relatively far apart. In the *active* phase, which begins when the cervix is 3 to 4 cm dilated and continues until dilation has reached 8 cm, contractions are closer together and more intense. The last 2 centimeters of dilation are achieved during a period usually called *transition*. It is this period, when contractions are closely spaced and strong, that women typically find the most painful. Fortunately, transition is also ordinarily the shortest phase.

Stage 1 lasts an average of approximately 12 hours for a first birth and perhaps 7 hours for a woman having a second or later child (Moore & Persaud, 1993). Figure 3.10 shows the duration of the several subphases, although neither the figure nor the average numbers convey the wide individual variability that exists. Among women delivering

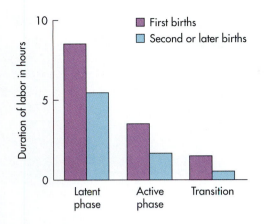

Figure 3.10

Typical pattern of timing of the phases of stage 1 of labor for first births and for second or later births. (Source: Based on Biswas & Craigo, 1994, from Figures 10-16, p. 216, and 10-17, p. 217.)

a first child, stage 1 can last as little as 3 hours or as long as 20 (Biswas & Craigo, 1994; Kilpatrick & Laros, 1989).

The Second Stage of Labor.   At the end of the transition phase the mother will normally have the urge to help the infant out by "pushing." When the birth attendant (physician or midwife) is sure the cervix is fully dilated, she or he will encourage this pushing and the second stage of labor—the actual delivery—begins. The baby's head moves past the stretched cervix, into the birth canal, and finally out of the mother's body. Most women find this part of labor markedly less distressing than the transition phase because it is here that they can assist the delivery process by pushing. The average length is 50 minutes for first infants and 20 minutes for later deliveries (Moore & Persaud, 1993). It rarely takes longer than two hours.

Most infants are delivered head first, facing toward the mother's spine. Three to 4 percent, however, are oriented differently, either feet first or bottom first (called *breech* presentations) (Brown, Karrison, & Cibils, 1994). Several decades ago most breech deliveries were accomplished with the aid of medical instruments such as forceps; today nearly four-fifths of breech presentations are delivered by cesarean section, a procedure I'll discuss more fully in a moment.

In most delivery situations in the United States, once the baby has emerged, he is placed immediately on the mother's abdomen or, after the cord has been cut and the baby is cleaned up a bit—a matter of a few minutes—given to the mother (and the father) to hold. For most parents, this first greeting of the baby is a time for remarkable delight, as they stroke the baby's skin, count the fingers, look at the baby's eyes, talk to the infant.

The Third Stage of Labor.   Stage 3, typically quite brief, is the delivery of the placenta (also called the "afterbirth") and other material from the uterus. You can see all three stages schematically in Figure 3.11.

Birth Choices

What I am going to say here about birth choices is necessarily specific to options and experiences in industrialized countries. In many other cultures there are no decisions to be made about such questions as where the delivery will occur, whether the father should be present or not, or whether the mother should be given drugs to ease her pain. Custom dictates the answers. In many Western industrialized countries, however, patterns and customs in this area continue to change rapidly, which leaves individual parents with decisions to make—decisions that may affect the child's health or the mother's satisfaction with the delivery. Because many of you will face these choices at some point in the future, I want to give you the best current information I have.

Drugs During Delivery.   One key decision concerns the use of drugs during delivery. Three types of drugs are commonly used: (1) *analgesics* (such as the common drug Demerol) that are given during stage 1 of labor to reduce pain; (2) *sedatives* or *tranquilizers* (such as Nembutol, Valium, or Thorazine) given during stage 1 labor to reduce anxiety; and (3) *anesthesia*, given during transition or the second stage of labor to block pain either totally (general anesthesia) or in portions of the body (local anesthesia). Of the three, anesthesia is least often used in the United States, although the use of one form of local anesthesia, the epidural block, has been increasing in frequency, with a current rate of up to 16 percent of all labors (Fields & Wall, 1993).

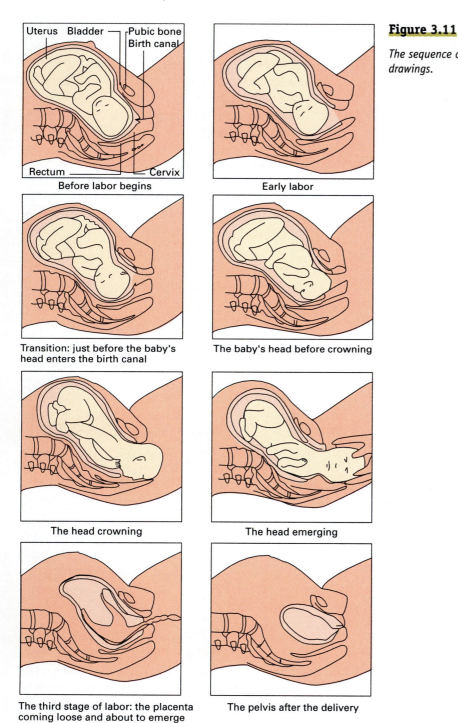

Before labor begins

Early labor

Transition: just before the baby's head enters the birth canal

The baby's head before crowning

The head crowning

The head emerging

The third stage of labor: the placenta coming loose and about to emerge

The pelvis after the delivery

Figure 3.11

The sequence of steps during delivery is shown clearly in these drawings.

Studying the causal links between such drug use and the baby's later behavior or development has proven to be monumentally difficult. Controlled experiments are obviously not possible, and drugs are given in myriad different combinations. Nonetheless, a few reasonably clear conclusions are emerging.

First, nearly all drugs given during labor pass through the placenta, enter the fetal bloodstream, and can remain there for several days. Not surprisingly, then, infants whose mothers have received any type of drug are typically slightly more sluggish, gain a little less weight, and spend more time sleeping in the first few weeks than do infants of mothers who received no drugs during delivery (Maurer & Maurer, 1988). These differences are quite small, but have been observed repeatedly.

Second, beyond the first few days there are no consistently observed effects from analgesics and tranquilizers and only hints from a few studies of long-term effects of anesthesia (Rosenblith, 1992). Given such findings, only one specific piece of advice seems warranted: If you have received medication you need to bear in mind that your baby is also drugged, and that this will affect her behavior in the first few days. If you allow for this effect and realize that it will wear off, your long-term relationship with your child is likely to be unaffected.

The Location of Birth.

A second choice parents must make is *where* the baby is to be born. Today in the United States there are usually four alternatives: (1) a traditional hospital maternity unit; (2) a hospital-based birth center or birthing room, located within a hospital but providing a more home-like setting, with labor and delivery both completed in the same room and family members often present throughout; (3) a freestanding birth center, like a hospital birth center except located apart from the hospital, with delivery typically attended by a midwife rather than (or in addition to) a physician; and (4) home delivery.

At the turn of the century, only about 5 percent of babies in the United States were born in hospitals; today the figure is 99 percent (U.S. Bureau of the Census, 1996). The small fraction remaining are born at home or in birthing centers. Because home deliveries are so uncommon in the United States, much of what we know about them comes from research in Europe, where such deliveries are thought to be both more natural and less expensive for the medical care system. For example, in the Netherlands, a third of all deliveries are at home (Eskes, 1992). Such deliveries are encouraged in uncomplicated pregnancies in which the woman has received good prenatal care. When these conditions are met and when a trained birth attendant is present at delivery, the rate of delivery complications or infant problems is no higher than in hospital deliveries (Rooks, Weatherby, Ernst et al., 1989; Tew, 1985). In contrast, infant mortality rates are significantly higher in *unplanned* home deliveries, in those without trained attendants, or in those in which the mother had experienced some complication of pregnancy (Schramm, Barnes, & Bakewell, 1987). Assuming appropriate safety precautions are in place, then, the choice should be based on what is most comfortable for the individual woman or couple.

[?] *Critical Thinking*

Which birthing location do you think you would choose, and why?

The Presence of Fathers at Delivery.

A third issue is whether the father should be present at delivery. In the United States today this hardly seems like a "decision." As recently as 1972, only about a quarter of U.S. hospitals permitted the father to be present in the delivery room; by 1980, four-fifths of them did (Parke & Tinsley, 1984), and today the father's presence has become absolutely the norm, as it is in all Western countries.

There have been several compelling arguments offered in favor of such a norm. To begin with, when fathers are present during labor and delivery, mothers report lower levels of pain and receive less medication (Henneborn & Cogan, 1975). And when the mother has a coach (the father or someone else), the incidence of problems of labor and delivery goes down and the duration of labor decreases (Nichols, 1993). Furthermore, at least one study shows that women are more likely to report that the birth was a "peak" experience if the father was present (Entwisle & Doering, 1981). Yet, contrary to common belief, the father's presence at the delivery does not seem to have any magical effect on his emotional bond to the baby (Palkovitz, 1985). A father who sees his child for the first time in the newborn nursery, or days later at home, may nonetheless become as strongly attached to the infant as are those fathers who were present at the birth.

This statement is not in any way intended as an argument against fathers' participation in the delivery process. The fact that the father's presence seems to help the mother control pain, promotes a reduction in medication and labor duration, and may enhance the husband-wife relationship all seem to me to be compelling reasons for encouraging continued high levels of paternal participation.

Psychology in Action

Investigation of Birth Options

Warning: This investigative project, like others I have suggested in the book, should be undertaken—with directions from your instructor—either by a *single* student in a class or by a small group of students working collaboratively. It is neither reasonable nor fair to flood local agencies or for-profit companies with calls from dozens of students inquiring about services or programs.

Basic Questions to Answer

- *How many of the four main choices of birth options (regular hospital, hospital-based birth center or birthing room, freestanding birthing center, or home delivery) are available in your area? How recently did nonhospital delivery become available in your area?*

- *How are local births distributed among the available options?*

- *What is the relative cost of the several options?*

- *Who sponsors or runs each program? Are the deliveries in the birth center or at home done by midwives? Do midwives deliver babies at hospitals as well?*

Sources of Information

The yellow pages may be your best first source. If that does not yield information, you might make inquiries of several local obstetricians' offices. You will then need to call hospitals, birthing centers, and midwives for further information, or visit each site to get a firsthand look and to obtain brochures and so forth. At all times you should represent yourself accurately as a student working on a project for a class on human development. Do *not* present yourself as a pregnant woman looking for a place to deliver. Remember always that your questions may be seen as an intrusion on busy workdays of your respondents, so be sensitive to the demands you are placing on them.

Reporting

Your instructor may want you to report back to the class on your findings, either orally or in writing. In any case, you should prepare a written report of what you did, to whom you spoke, and what you found out.

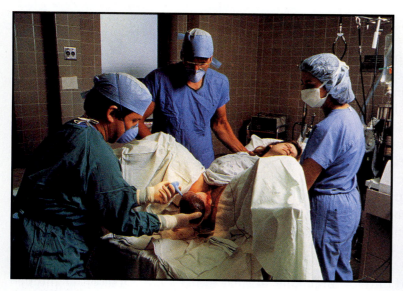

In the United States, the most common delivery setting is still in a hospital, assisted by a physician, as shown in the upper photo (with the father in the background); in Europe, home deliveries assisted by a midwife are much more common, as in the French birth shown in the photo on the right—again with the father present.

In addition, of course, most fathers report powerful feelings of delight at being present at the birth of their children. Reason enough.

Problems at Birth

As with prenatal development, there are some things that can alter the normal pattern I have been describing. One of the most common problems is that the delivery itself may not proceed normally, leading to a surgical delivery through an abdominal incision, called a **cesarean section** (usually abbreviated C-section). A second common problem is that the infant may be born too early.

Cesarean-section Delivery. C-section deliveries occur for a variety of reasons, of which the most common are a previous cesarean delivery, a failure to progress in labor, a breech position of the fetus, or some sign of fetal distress (Cunningham, MacDonald, Leveno, Gant, & Gilstrap, 1993). C-section deliveries are also more common among older mothers in the United States—a group that makes up an increasingly large proportion of all pregnancies (Adashek, Peaceman, Lopez-Zeno, Minogue, & Socol, 1993).

The frequency of C-sections has risen rapidly in many industrialized countries in the past few decades, including Australia, Canada, Britain, Norway, and other European countries (e.g., Notzon, Cnattingius, Pergsjø et al., 1994). In the United States the increase has been particularly striking, more than quadrupling between 1970 and 1985 to a rate of roughly one in every four births (U.S. Bureau of the Census, 1994). This rapid rise created considerable discussion and controversy, with many obstetricians concluding that a rate of nearly 25 percent was a good deal higher than medically necessary. Evidence from a number of European countries, such as Sweden, as well as studies in the United States, suggests that the rate of C-sections could be reduced to a range of 10 to 15 percent without any increase in maternal or infant mortality (e.g., Lagrew & Morgan, 1996; Notzon et al., 1994). In light of this information, the Centers for Disease Control have suggested a goal of lowering the U.S. C-section rate to 12 percent by the year 2000 (Centers for Disease Control, 1993a). The first

steps toward this goal are reflected in a modest drop in the rate of C-sections in recent years, reaching 21.2 percent in 1994 (Guyer et al., 1996).

Low Birth Weight. In talking about various teratogens, I have often mentioned low birth weight as one of the clearest negative outcomes. But how low is too low? The optimum weight range for infants—the weight that is associated with the lowest risk of later death or disability—is between 3000 and 5000 grams (6.6 to 11 pounds) (Rees, Lederman, & Kiely, 1996). Several different labels are used to describe infants whose weight falls below this optimum range. All babies below 2500 grams (about 5.5 pounds) are described with the most general term of **low birth weight (LBW).** Those below 1500 grams (about 3.3 pounds) are usually called **very low birth weight,** while those below 1000 grams are called **extremely low birth weight.**

The incidence of low birth weight has declined in the United States in the past decade, but it is still high: In 1995, 7.3 percent of all newborns were below 2500 grams, a total of about 290,000 infants each year (Guyer et al., 1996). Approximately 18 percent of those small babies weighed less than 1500 grams. Low birth weight is considerably more common among blacks than among either whites or Hispanics in the United States. In 1995 the respective rates were 13.0 percent, 6.2 percent, and 6.2 percent (Guyer et al., 1996). (Interestingly, this black/white difference in low birth weight does *not* exist in Cuba (Hogue & Hargraves, 1993).

Low birth weight occurs for a variety of reasons, of which the most obvious and common is that the infant is born before the full 38 weeks of gestation. Any baby born before 38 weeks of gestation is labeled **preterm.** It is also possible for an infant to have completed the full 38-week gestational period but still weigh less than 2500 grams or to weigh less than would be expected for the number of weeks of gestation completed, however long that may have been. Such an infant is called **small for date.** Infants in this group appear to have suffered from prenatal malnutrition, such as might occur with constriction of blood flow caused by the mother's smoking, or from other significant problems prenatally. These infants generally have

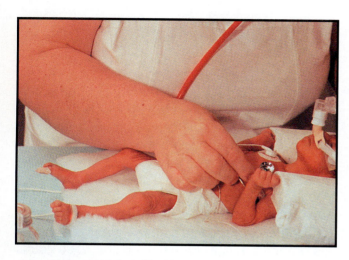

Low-birth-weight infants like this one are not only small, they are also more wrinkled and skinny because the layer of fat under the skin has not fully developed. They are also more likely to have significant breathing difficulties because their lungs lack surfactant.

poorer prognoses than do equivalent-weight infants who weigh an appropriate amount for their gestational age, especially if the small-for-date infant is also preterm (Korkman, Liikanen, & Fellman, 1996; Ott, 1995).

All low-birth-weight infants share some characteristics, including markedly lower levels of responsiveness at birth and in the early months of life. Those born more than six weeks before term also often suffer from **respiratory distress syndrome.** Their poorly developed lungs lack an important chemical, called *surfactant*, that enables the air sacs to remain inflated; some of the sacs collapse, resulting in serious breathing difficulties. Beginning in 1990, neonatologists began treating this problem by administering a synthetic or animal-derived

version of surfactant, a therapy that has reduced the rate of death among very-low-birth-weight infants by about 30 percent (Corbet, Long, Schumacher, Gerdes, & Cotton, 1995; Hamvas, Wise, Yang et al., 1996; Schwartz, Anastasia, Scanlon, & Kellogg, 1994).

About 80 percent of all low-birth-weight infants now survive long enough to leave the hospital, but the lower the birth weight, the greater the risk of neonatal death. This pattern is especially clear in the results in Figure 3.12, which come from a study of a group of 1765 very-low-birth-weight infants born in seven different hospitals around the United States. The limit of viability is about 500–600 grams or about 23 weeks' gestation. Babies born before 23 weeks rarely survive, even with aggressive neonatal care; those born at 23 weeks have at least a small chance of survival, while those born at 24 weeks have better than a 50 percent survival rate (e.g., Allen, Donohue, & Dusman, 1993; La Pine, Jackson, & Bennett, 1995).

Some of these very tiny babies who do survive will have major, continuing, developmental problems; some will not. We do not yet know all the factors that predict such long-term problems among low-birth-weight infants, but a few elements are clear, including the infant's weight at birth, the quality of care available to the infant, and what kind of family he or she grows up in (Bendersky & Lewis, 1994). Because medical advances in the care of LBW infants have been enormous in the past few decades, the more recently such a baby was born, the better the long-term prognosis seems to be (Perlman, Claris, Hao et al., 1995).

The great majority of those above 1500 grams who are not small for date catch up to their normal

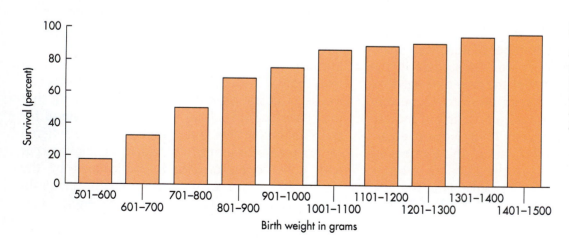

Figure 3.12

Among very-low-birth-weight infants, survival is clearly correlated with birth weight. (Source: Hack et al., 1991, Figure 2, p. 590.)

peers within the first few years of life. Those below 1500 grams, especially those below 1000, have significantly higher rates of long-term problems, including neurological impairment, lower IQ scores, smaller size, and greater problems in school (Breslau, DelDotto, Brown et al., 1994; Hack, Taylor, Klein et al., 1994; Koller, Lawson, Rose, Wallace, & McCarton, 1997; Saigal, Szatmari, Rosenbaum, Campbell, & King, 1991). You can get a better sense of both the type and incidence of such problems from the data in Table 3.7, which lists the results for two studies, one from the United States and the other from Australia.

Two points are worth making about the findings from follow-up studies like those shown in the table. First, some problems do not appear until school age, when the child is challenged by a new level of cognitive task. Many surviving LBW children who appear to be developing normally at age 1 or 2 later show significant problems in school. More optimistically, even in the extremely low-birth-weight group, some children seem to be fine. So it is not the case that *all* LBW children are *somewhat* affected; rather, *some* LBW children are significantly affected while others develop normally. Unfortunately, physicians and researchers have not yet found reliable ways to predict which babies are likely to have later difficulties, beyond the general

correlation with birth weight itself. Our ignorance means that parents of LBW infants may be left in suspense for many years.

A Final Word: A More Balanced View of Risks and Long-Term Consequences of Prenatal and Birth Problems

Each time I write this chapter I am aware that the list of things that can go wrong seems to get longer and longer and scarier and scarier. Physicians, biologists, and psychologists keep learning more about prenatal and birth risks, so the number of warnings to pregnant women seems to increase yearly, if not monthly. All that is true, but I do not want to leave you with the impression that pregnancy is a time to be constantly fearful of potential pitfalls. So before you begin worrying too much, let me try to put this information into perspective.

First, remember again that *most* pregnancies are normal and largely uneventful, and most babies are healthy and normal at birth. Second, there are specific preventive steps that any woman can take to reduce the risks for herself and her unborn

Table 3.7
Two Examples of Long-Term Outcomes for Very-Low-Birth-Weight Infants

	Australian Study[*]	United States Study[**]	
	500–999 g	<750 g	750–1500 g
Number of babies followed	89	68	65
Age at testing	8 years	7 years	7 years
Percent with severe problems of some type (IQ scores below 70, deaf, blind, cerebral-palsied, etc.)	21.3	37.5	17.5
Additional percent with significant learning problem or IQ scores between 70 and 85	19.1	29	20

[*]Victorian Infant Collaborative Study Group, 1991. The study included all surviving children of 500–999 grams born in a single state (Victoria) in Australia between 1979 and 1980. A total of 351 infants were born in this weight range, so only a quarter survived. With today's medical techniques, survival rates might be higher.

[**]Hack et al., 1994. The study includes the 68 survivors of a group of 243 children born in an area in Ohio from 1982 to 1986 with birth weights below 750 grams, plus a comparison group born in the same period who were between 750 and 1500 grams at birth.

child—steps I already summarized in Table 3.6 (p. 99). In particular, she should be sure to get good prenatal care. Many studies show that mothers who receive adequate prenatal care reduce the risks to themselves and their infants (e.g., Hoyert, 1996). Unfortunately, inadequate care remains common in the United States. In 1993, 21 percent of all mothers did not begin their prenatal care until at least the second trimester, and 5 percent had either no care at all or saw a health care provider only in the final few months (Guyer, Strobino, Ventura, & Singh, 1995). Inadequate care was twice as common among black mothers as among whites (9.9 and 4.2 percent, respectively), and in both groups inadequate care was more common among mothers living in poverty and among teenage mothers.

A third point to be made about prenatal problems is that if something does go wrong, the negative consequences are not always long-lasting. Naturally, some negative outcomes *are* permanent, with enduring consequences for the child. Chromosomal anomalies are clearly permanent and nearly always associated with lasting mental retardation or school difficulties. Some teratogens also have permanent effects, such as fetal alcohol syndrome, deafness resulting from rubella, or AIDS. And a significant fraction of very-low-birth-weight infants experience lasting problems.

However, many of the negative outcomes I have talked about in this chapter may be detectable only for the first few years of the child's life and then only in some families. In fact, the relationship between prenatal or birth problems and long-term outcomes illustrates the very pattern of interaction between nature and nurture I talked about in Chapter 1: A biological problem may be amplified by an unstimulating environment but greatly reduced by a supportive one. For example, there are numerous studies showing that LBW infants, infants with poor prenatal nutrition, and infants with equivalent difficulties are likely to show persisting problems if they are reared in unstimulating or unsupportive environments but develop much more normally if reared in more intellectually and emotionally nurturing families (Beckwith & Rodning, 1991; Breitmayer & Ramey, 1986; Kopp, 1990). So it is not the prenatal or birth problem *alone* that is the cause of the child's later problem; rather a nonoptimal prenatal environment may make the infant more vulnerable to later environmental inadequacy. Such children may require a better family

environment to develop normally, and in many cases such normal development *is* possible. So don't despair when you read the long list of cautions and potential problems. The story isn't as gloomy as it first seems.

Summary

1. At conception the 23 chromosomes from the sperm join with the 23 from the ovum to make up the set of 46 that will be reproduced in each cell of the new child's body. Each chromosome consists of a long string of deoxyribonucleic acid (DNA), divisible into specific segments, called genes.

2. The child's sex is determined by the twenty-third pair of chromosomes, a pattern of XX for a girl and XY for a boy.

3. Geneticists distinguish between the genotype, which is the pattern of inherited characteristics, and the phenotype, which is the result of the interaction of genotype and environment.

4. During the first days after conception, called the germinal stage of development, the initial cell divides, travels down the fallopian tube, and is implanted in the wall of the uterus.

5. The second stage, the period of the embryo, which lasts until eight weeks after fertilization, includes the development of the various structures that support fetal development, such as the placenta, as well as primitive forms of all organ systems.

6. The final 30 weeks of gestation, called the fetal period, is devoted primarily to enlargement and refinements in all the organ systems.

7. All the neurons an individual will ever have are developed between 10 and 20 weeks' gestation, but the development of the axon and dendrites on each neuron occurs primarily in the final two months of gestation and in the first few years after birth.

8. Normal prenatal development seems heavily determined by maturation—a "road map" contained in the genes. Disruptions in this sequence can occur; the timing of the disruption determines the nature and severity of the effect, illustrating the principle of critical periods.

9. Deviations from the normal pattern can be caused at conception by any of a variety of chromosomal anomalies, such as Down syndrome, or by the transmission of genes for specific diseases.

10. Prior to conception, it is possible to test parents for the presence of genes for many inherited diseases. After conception, several diagnostic techniques ex-

ist to identify neural tube defects, chromosomal anomalies, or recessive-gene diseases in the fetus.

11. Some diseases contracted by the mother may affect the child, including rubella, AIDS, and CMV. Any of these may result in disease or physical abnormalities in the child.

12. Drugs such as alcohol and nicotine appear to have significantly harmful effects on the developing fetus; the greater the dose, the larger the potential effect appears to be.

13. The mother's diet is also important. If she is severely malnourished, there are increased risks of stillbirth, low birth weight, and infant death during the first year of life. Long-term consequences of milder subnutrition, however, have been more difficult to establish.

14. Older mothers and very young mothers also run increased risks, as do their infants.

15. High levels of anxiety or stress in the mother can also increase the risk of complications of pregnancy or difficulties in the infant, although the research findings here are mixed.

16. During the embryonic period, the XY embryo secretes the hormone testosterone, which stimulates the growth of male genitalia and shifts the brain into a "male" pattern. Without that hormone, the embryo develops as a girl, as do normal XX embryos.

17. Other sex differences in prenatal development are few in number. Boys are slower to develop, bigger at birth, and more vulnerable to most forms of prenatal stress.

18. The normal birth process has three parts: dilation, delivery, and placental delivery.

19. Most drugs given to the mother during delivery pass through to the infant's bloodstream and have short-term effects on infant responsiveness and feeding patterns. There may be some longer-term effects, but this is in dispute.

20. In uncomplicated, low-risk pregnancies, delivery at home or in a birthing center is as safe as hospital delivery.

21. The presence of the father during delivery has a variety of positive consequences, including reduced pain experience for the mother, but does not appear to affect the father's attachment to the infant.

22. Roughly one in five deliveries in the United States is now by cesarean section, a statistic that has been the cause of considerable debate.

23. Infants born weighing less than 2500 grams are designated as low birth weight; those below 1500 are very low birth weight; those below 1000 are ex-

tremely low birth weight. The lower the weight, the greater the risk of neonatal death or of significant lasting problems, such as low IQ scores or learning disabilities.

24. Some prenatal or birth difficulties can produce permanent disabilities or deformities, but many disorders associated with prenatal life or with birth can be overcome if the child is reared in a supportive and stimulating environment.

Key Terms

alpha-fetoprotein test   A prenatal diagnostic test frequently used to screen for the risk of neural tube defects. May also be used in combination with other tests to diagnose Down syndrome and other chromosomal anomalies. **(p. 88)**

amniocentesis   A medical test for genetic abnormalities in the embryo/fetus that may be done at 15–18 weeks of gestation. **(p. 88)**

amnion   The sac or bag, filled with liquid, in which the embryo and fetus floats during prenatal life. **(p. 80)**

axon   The long appendage-like part of a neuron; the terminal fibers of the axon serve as transmitters in the synaptic connection with the dendrites of other neurons. **(p. 82)**

blastocyst   Name for the mass of cells from roughly four to ten days after fertilization. **(p. 80)**

cesarean section   Delivery of the child through an incision in the mother's abdomen rather than vaginally. **(p. 105)**

chorion   The outer layer of cells during the blastocyst stage of prenatal development, from which both the placenta and the umbilical cord are formed. **(p. 80)**

chorionic villus sampling   A technique for prenatal genetic diagnosis that involves taking a sample of cells from the placenta. Can be performed earlier in the pregnancy than amniocentesis but carries slightly higher risks. **(p. 88)**

chromosomes   The structures—arrayed in 23 pairs and contained in each cell in the body—that carry genetic information. Each chromosome is made up of many segments, called genes. **(p. 75)**

dendrites   The branchlike parts of a neuron that form one-half of the synaptic connection to other nerves. Dendrites develop rapidly in the final three prenatal months and the first year after birth. **(p. 82)**

deoxyribonucleic acid (DNA)   The chemical of which genes are composed. **(p. 75)**

dizygotic twins   See *fraternal twins*. **(p. 79)**

Down syndrome A genetic anomaly in which every cell contains three copies of chromosome 21 rather than two. Children born with this genetic pattern are usually mentally retarded and have characteristic physical features. **(p. 84)**

embryo The name given to the organism during the period of prenatal development from about two to eight weeks after conception, beginning with implantation of the blastocyst into the uterine wall. **(p. 80)**

extremely low birth weight Any birth weight below 1000 grams. **(p. 105)**

fallopian tube The tube between the ovary and the uterus down which the ovum travels to the uterus and in which conception usually occurs. **(p. 74)**

fetal alcohol syndrome (FAS) A pattern of physical and mental abnormalities, including mental retardation and minor physical anomalies, found often in children born to alcoholic mothers. **(p. 91)**

fetus The name given to the developing organism from about eight weeks after conception until birth. **(p. 80)**

fraternal twins Children carried in the same pregnancy but resulting from two separate fertilized ova; they are no more alike genetically than other pairs of brothers and sisters. Also called dizygotic twins. **(p. 79)**

gametes Sperm and ova. These cells, unlike all other cells of the body, contain only 23 chromosomes rather than 23 pairs. **(p. 75)**

gene A uniquely coded segment of DNA in a chromosome that affects one or more specific body processes or developments. **(p. 75)**

genotype The pattern of characteristics and developmental sequences mapped in the genes of any specific individual. Will be modified by individual experience into the phenotype. **(p. 75)**

glial cells One of two major classes of cells making up the nervous system, glial cells provide the firmness and structure, the "glue," to hold the system together. **(p. 82)**

heterozygous Term describing the genetic pattern when the pair of genes at any given genetic locus carry different instructions, such as a gene for blue eyes from one parent and for brown eyes from the other parent. **(p. 76)**

homozygous Term describing the genetic pattern when the pair of genes at any given genetic locus carry the same instructions. **(p. 76)**

identical twins Children carried in the same pregnancy who come from the *same* originally fertilized ovum; they are genetically identical to one another. Also called monozygotic twins. **(p. 79)**

implantation Process by which the blastocyst attaches itself to the wall of the uterus, generally during the second week after fertilization. **(p. 80)**

low birth weight (LBW) Any baby born with a weight below 2500 grams is given this label, including both those born too early (preterm) and those who are "small for date." **(p. 105)**

monozygotic twins See *identical twins.* **(p. 79)**

neuron The second major class of cells in the nervous system, neurons are responsible for transmission and reception of nerve impulses. **(p. 82)**

neurotransmitters Chemicals at synapses that accomplish the transmission of signals from one neuron to another. **(p. 82)**

ovum The gamete produced by a woman, which, if fertilized by a sperm from a male, forms the basis for the developing organism. **(p. 74)**

phenotype The expression of a particular set of genetic information in a specific environment; the observable result of the joint operation of genetic and environmental influences. **(p. 79)**

placenta An organ that develops during gestation between the fetus and the wall of the uterus. The placenta filters nutrients from the mother's blood, acting as liver, lungs, and kidneys for the fetus. **(p. 80)**

polygenic inheritance Any pattern of genetic transmission in which multiple genes contribute to the outcome, like that presumed to occur for complex behaviors such as intelligence or temperament. **(p. 78)**

preterm infant Descriptive phrase widely used to label infants born before a 38-week gestational age. **(p. 105)**

respiratory distress syndrome A problem frequently found in infants born more than six weeks before term, in which the infant's lungs lack the chemical surfactant needed to keep the air sacs inflated. **(p. 106)**

rubella A form of measles that, if contracted during the first few weeks of a pregnancy, may have severe effects on the developing baby. **(p. 87)**

sex-linked transmission Pattern of genetic transmission that occurs when the critical gene is carried on a portion of the X chromosome that is not matched by genetic material on the Y chromosome. Diseases such as hemophilia follow this genetic pattern. **(p. 78)**

small for date Term for an infant who weighs less than is normal for the number of weeks of gestation completed. **(p. 105)**

synapse The point of communication between two neurons, where nerve impulses are passed from one neuron to another by means of chemicals called neurotransmitters. **(p. 82)**

ultrasound A form of prenatal diagnosis in which high frequency sound waves are used to provide a picture of the moving fetus. Can be used to detect many physical deformities, such as neural tube defects, as well as multiple pregnancies and gestational age. **(p. 88)**

umbilical cord The cord connecting the embryo/fetus to the placenta, containing two arteries and one vein. **(p. 80)**

uterus The female organ in which the blastocyst implants itself and within which the embryo/fetus develops. (Popularly referred to as the womb.) **(p. 74)**

very low birth weight Any birth weight below 1500 grams (3.3 pounds). **(p. 105)**

Suggested Readings

Bérubé, M. (1996). *Life as we know it. A father, a family, and an exceptional child*. New York: Pantheon Books. A forthright book by a father of a Down syndrome child, described by the *New York Times Book Review* as "an astonishingly good book, important, literate and ferociously articulated."

The Boston Women's Health Collective (1992). *The new our bodies, ourselves: A book by and for women*. New York: Simon & Schuster. This recent revision of a popular book is really focused on the adult female's body rather than on prenatal development, but it has an excellent discussion of health during pregnancy. This is a strongly feminist book; some of you may not be entirely in sympathy with all the political views included. It is nonetheless a very good, compact source of information on all facets of pregnancy and childbirth.

Moore, K. L., & Persaud, T. V. N. (1993). *The developing human: Clinically oriented embryology* (5th ed.). Philadelphia: W. B. Saunders. A highly technical book aimed at medical students that may give more detail than you want, but I guarantee it will tell you anything you might want to know about prenatal development.

Nightingale, E. O., & Goodman, M. (1990). *Before birth. Prenatal testing for genetic disease*. Cambridge, MA: Harvard University Press. This is an extremely informative, clearly written, helpful small book.

Nilsson, L. (1990). *A child is born*. New York: Delacorte Press. This is a remarkable book, full of the most stunning photographs of all phases of conception, prenatal development, and birth.

Rosenblith, J. F. (1992). *In the beginning. Development in the rst two years of life* (2nd ed.). Newbury Park, CA: Sage. A first-rate text covering prenatal development and infancy. Much less technical than the Moore and Persaud book listed above, it would be an excellent next step in your reading if you are interested in this area.

Wright, L. (1995, August 7). Double mystery. *The New Yorker*, pp. 45–62. A fascinating look at all aspects of the study of twins.

Physical Development and Health in Infancy and Toddlerhood

Preview Questions

1 What can a newborn see, hear, and do, and how do those skills affect parents?

2 Why is it better for a woman to breast-feed if she can?

3 We think of a tree as being pruned; why do physiologists talk about pruning of the nervous system in infants?

4 What are the major physical milestones in an infant's first two years of life?

5 What six major preventive health practices can parents follow to improve their child's health?

Chapter Outline

Not long ago I talked to a friend whose first baby was then just about 6 months old. When I asked her how it was going, she said three very typical things: "No one told me how much fun it would be," "No one told me how much work it would be," and "I didn't expect it to be this fascinating. She's changing every day. Now she seems like a real person, sitting up, crawling, beginning to make wonderful noises."

I suspect that someone had indeed told her all those things, but she hadn't heard them. Only when you are with a child every day, care for and love the child, does the reality of the whole amazing process come home to you. I'll do my best to convey that amazement to you, but some of what I am going to say may not be "real" to you unless and until you help to rear a child yourself. Let me begin by describing the child's physical development during the first 18–24 months, starting with a snapshot of the newborn.

The Newborn

Assessing the Newborn

It has become customary in most hospitals to evaluate an infant's status immediately after birth and then again five minutes later to detect any problems that may require special care. The most fre-

quently used assessment system is called an **Apgar score,** developed by a physician, Virginia Apgar (1953). The newborn is given a score of 0, 1, or 2 on each of five criteria, listed in Table 4.1. A maximum score of 10 is fairly unusual immediately after birth because most infants are still somewhat blue in the fingers and toes at that stage. At the five-minute assessment, however, 85 to 90 percent of infants are scored as 9 or 10. Any score of 7 or better indicates that the baby is in no danger. A score of 4, 5, or 6 usually means that the baby needs help establishing normal breathing patterns; a score of 3 or below indicates a baby in critical condition, although babies with such low Apgar scores can and often do survive, and given a sufficiently supportive environment, most develop normally (Breitmayer & Ramey, 1986).

Another test used to assess newborns, widely used by researchers, is the *Brazelton Neonatal Behavioral Assessment Scale* (Brazelton, 1984). In this test a skilled examiner checks out the neonate's responses to a variety of stimuli, her reflexes, muscle tone, alertness, and cuddliness, and her ability to quiet or soothe herself after being upset. Scores on this test can be helpful in identifying children who may have significant neurological problems. More interestingly, several investigators have found that teaching *parents* how to administer this scale to their own infant turns out to have beneficial effects on the parent-infant interaction, apparently because it heightens the parent's awareness of all the

Table 4.1

Evaluation Method for Apgar Score

Aspect of Infant Observed	Score Assigned		
	0	**1**	**2**
Heart rate	Absent	<100/min.	>100/min.
Respiratory rate	No breathing	Weak cry and shallow breathing	Good strong cry and regular breathing
Muscle tone	Flaccid	Some flexion of extremities	Well-flexed
Response to stimulation of feet	None	Some motion	Cry
Color	Blue; pale	Body pink, extremities blue	Completely pink

Source: Francis, Self, & Horowitz, 1987, pp. 731–732.

subtle cues the baby provides (Francis, Self, & Horowitz, 1987).

Reflexes

One important part of the infant's repertoire of behaviors is a large collection of **reflexes,** which are physical responses triggered involuntarily by specific stimuli. Some of these persist into adulthood, such as your automatic eyeblink when a puff of air hits your eye or the involuntary narrowing of the pupil of your eye when you're in a bright light. Others, sometimes referred to as *adaptive re exes*, are essential to the infant's survival but gradually disappear in the first year of life. Sucking and swallowing reflexes are prominent in this category, as is the **rooting reflex**—the automatic turn of the head toward any touch on the cheek, a reflex that helps the baby get the nipple into his mouth during nursing. These reflexes are no longer present in older infants or adults, but are clearly highly adaptive for the newborn.

Finally, newborns have a large collection of **primitive reflexes,** so called because they are controlled by the more primitive parts of the brain, the medulla and the midbrain, both of which are close to being fully developed at birth. For example, if you make a loud noise or startle a baby in some other way, you'll see her throw her arms outward and arch her back, a pattern that is part of the **Moro reflex** (also called the startle reflex). Stroke the bottom of her foot and she will splay out her toes, called the **Babinski reflex.**

[?] *Critical Thinking*

What would be different about development, and about adult-baby interactions, if babies were born *without* any reflexes but instead had to learn every behavior?

These various primitive reflexes disappear over the first year of life (see Table 4.2, p. 116), apparently superseded by the action of the cortex, which by this age is much more fully developed. Yet, even though these reflexes represent neurologically primitive patterns, they are nonetheless linked to important later behavior patterns. The tonic neck reflex (described in Table 4.2), for example, forms the foundation for the baby's later ability to reach for objects because it focuses the baby's attention on the hand; the grasp reflex, too, is linked to the later ability to hold objects.

In a similar way, the walking reflex may be linked to later voluntary walking. In an early study, Zelazo and his colleagues (Zelazo, Zelazo, & Kolb, 1972) stimulated the walking reflex repeatedly in some babies every day from the second to the eighth week after birth. By 8 weeks, these stimulated babies showed many more steps per minute when they were held in the walking position than did nonstimulated babies. And at the end of the first year, these stimulated babies learned to walk alone about a month sooner than did comparison babies who had not had their walking reflex stimulated. Esther Thelen, one of the experts on early motor development, argues that to be able to walk, an infant has to have enough muscle strength in his legs to move his legs in a walking movement (1983). Very young infants are light enough to manage such movement, but then they gain weight quickly. Only late in the first year do the child's weight and leg muscle strength again come into the appropriate balance. The babies in Zelazo's experiment, however, gained added muscle strength in the early weeks because their legs were exercised—just as you gain muscle strength if you begin a program of regular exercise. According to Thelen, these babies were then able to reach the right balance of weight and strength a bit sooner than normal.

Thus primitive reflexes are not just curiosities or remnants from our evolutionary past. They can be informative, as when a baby fails to show a reflex that ought to be there or displays a reflex past the point at which it normally disappears. For example, narcotics-exposed infants or those suffering from anoxia (oxygen starvation) at birth may show only very weak reflexes; Down syndrome infants have only very weak Moro reflexes and sometimes have poor sucking reflexes. When a primitive reflex persists past the normal point, it may suggest some neurological damage or disfunction. Reflexes are also the starting point for many important physical skills, including reaching, grasping, and walking.

Table 4.2

Examples of Primitive and Adaptive Reflexes

Reflex	Stimulation	Response	Developmental Pattern
Tonic neck	While baby is on his back and awake, turn his head to one side	Baby assumes a fencing posture, with arm extended on the side toward which the head is turned	Fades by 4 months
Grasping	Stroke the baby's palm with your finger	Baby will make a strong fist around your finger	Fades by 3 to 4 months
Moro	Make a loud sound near the baby, or let the baby "drop" slightly and suddenly	Baby extends legs, arms, and fingers, arches his back, draws back his head	Fades by about 6 months
Walking	Hold baby under arms with feet just touching a floor or other flat surface	Baby will make steplike motions, alternating feet as in walking	Fades by about 8 weeks in most infants
Babinski	Stroke sole of the baby's foot from toes toward heel	Baby will fan out his toes	Fades between 8 and 12 months
Rooting	Stroke baby's cheek with finger or nipple	Baby turns head toward the touch, opens mouth, and makes sucking movements	After 3 weeks, is transformed into a voluntary head-turning response

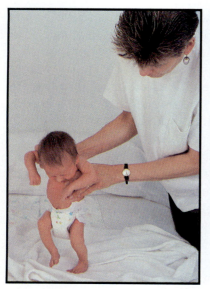

Walking reflex

Moro reflex

Tonic neck reflex

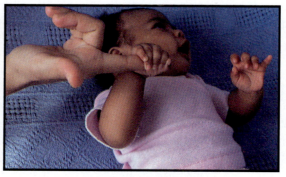

Grasping reflex

Initial Perceptual Skills: What the Newborn Sees, Hears, and Feels

Babies also come equipped with a surprisingly mature set of perceptual skills. I'll be describing the development of those skills in the next chapter; all I want to do here is to give you some sense of the starting point. The newborn can:

- Focus both eyes on the same spot, with 8 to 10 inches being approximately the best focal distance. Within a few weeks the baby can at least roughly follow a moving object with his eyes, and he can discriminate Mom's face from other faces almost immediately.

- Easily hear sounds within the pitch and loudness range of the human voice; roughly locate objects by their sounds; discriminate some individual voices, particularly the mother's voice.

- Taste the four basic tastes (sweet, sour, bitter, and salty) and identify familiar body odors, including discriminating Mom's smell from the smell of a strange woman.

To take just one example, one of the clearest demonstrations of newborn taste perception comes from an elegantly simple set of early studies by Jacob Steiner (Ganchrow, Steiner, & Daher, 1983; Steiner, 1979). Newborn infants who had never been fed were photographed before and after flavored water was put into their mouths. By varying the flavor, Steiner could determine whether the babies reacted differently to different tastes. As you can see in Figure 4.1, babies responded quite differently to sweet, sour, and bitter flavors.

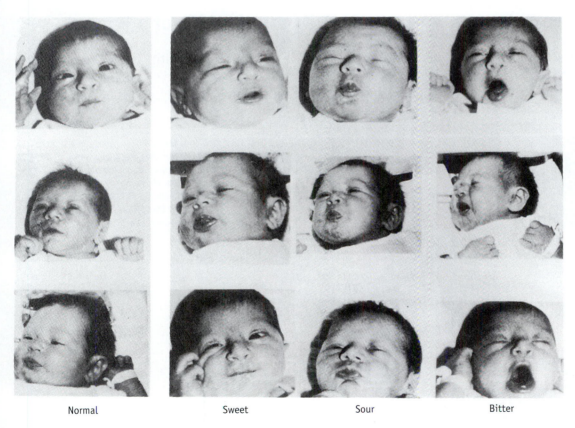

Normal   Sweet   Sour   Bitter

Figure 4.1

These three newborns were part of Steiner's studies of taste response. The left-hand column shows each baby's normal expression; the remaining columns show the change in expression when they were given sweet, sour, and bitter tastes. What is striking is how similar the expressions are for each taste. (Source: J. E. Steiner, 1979, Figure 1, p. 269.)

Brief as this summary is, several points nonetheless stand out. First of all, newborns' perceptual skills are considerably better than most parents believe—better than most psychologists or physicians believed until a few years ago. The better our research techniques have become, the more we have discovered just how skillful the new baby is.

It's also clear from this brief list that the baby's perceptual skills are especially well adapted for interacting with the people in his world. He hears best in the range of the human voice; he can discriminate Mother (or other regular caregiver) from others on the basis of smell, sight, and sound almost immediately; the distance at which he can focus his eyes best is roughly the distance between his eyes and the face of an adult holding him during feeding.

These skills emerge only gradually in the early weeks. By age 1 month, the baby can hold her chin up off the floor or mattress; by 2 months, she can hold her head steady while she's being held, and she's beginning to use her hands to swipe at objects near her. But this progress, notable as it is to moms and dads, can't disguise the fact that babies' motor development begins at a much lower level than is true of perceptual skills, many of which are present at birth.

[?] Critical Thinking

Calves, foals, lambs, and newborns of virtually all mammals besides humans can stand and walk within a few hours after birth. Can you think of any useful evolutionary function for the greater motor helplessness of the human newborn?

Initial Motor Skills: Moving Around

While the new baby's perceptual skills may be unexpectedly impressive, her motor skills certainly are not. She can't reach for things she's looking at; she can't hold up her head, roll over, or sit up.

A Day in the Life of a Baby

What is it like to live with a newborn? How is the infant's day organized? What sort of natural rhythms occur in the daily cycles? What can you

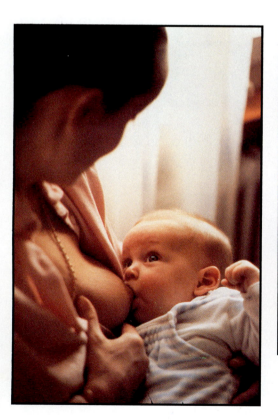

Newborns are pretty nearsighted, but they can focus very well at a distance of about 8 to 10 inches—just about the distance a mother normally holds her baby during nursing, or this father is holding the baby from his face.

expect from the baby, as you struggle to adapt to and care for this new person in your life?

Researchers who have studied newborns have described five different states of sleep and wakefulness in infants, referred to as **states of consciousness,** summarized in Table 4.3. In the newborn the least common of these five states are the two types of awakeness. In the first week of life, babies may be awake and not fussing as little as two to three hours each day.

The five main states tend to occur in cycles, just as your own states occur in a daily rhythm. In the newborn the basic period in the cycle is about $1\frac{1}{2}$ to 2 hours. Most infants move through the states from deep sleep to lighter sleep to fussing and hunger and then to alert wakefulness, after which they become drowsy and drop back into deep sleep. This cycle then repeats itself about every 2 hours: sleep, cry, eat, look; sleep, cry, eat, look. Because the first three parts of this repeating pattern—sleeping, crying, and eating—are so crucial for parents, let me say just a word more about each.

Sleeping

Newborns sleep 70 or 80 percent of the time, some as much as 90 percent. As you can see in Figure 4.2, babies initially sleep as much in the day as at night, but within a few weeks, daytime sleep begins to drop and we see signs of day/night sleep rhythms (called *circadian rhythms*)—at least among infants in Western countries, where regular sleep/wake cycles are more highly valued. Babies this age begin to string two or three 2-hour cycles together without coming to full wakefulness, at

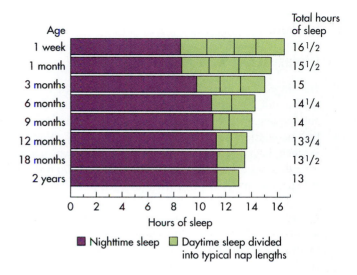

Figure 4.2

The total amount of sleep infants need, and the number of daytime naps they take, typically declines over the first two years of life. (Source: Needlman, 1996, Figure 11-1, p. 42.)

which point we say that the baby can "sleep through the night." Over the first two years, infants shift more and more toward nighttime sleep, with fewer and fewer naps in the day (Needlman, 1996; Whitney & Thoman, 1994).

Figure 4.2 gives the average figures, but of course babies vary a lot around these norms. Of the 6-week-old babies in one study, there was one who slept 22 hours per day and another who slept only 8.8 hours per day (Bamford et al., 1990). (Now *there* must be one tired set of parents!) And some babies, even in Western cultures, do not develop a long, unbroken nighttime sleep period until late in the first year of life.

Table 4.3

The Basic States of Infant Sleep and Wakefulness

State	Characteristics
Deep sleep	Eyes closed, regular breathing, no movement except occasional startles
Active sleep	Eyes closed, irregular breathing, small twitches, no gross body movement
Quiet awake	Eyes open, no major body movement, regular breathing
Active awake	Eyes open, with movements of the head, limbs, and trunk; irregular breathing
Crying and fussing	Eyes may be partly or entirely closed, vigorous diffuse movement with crying or fussing sounds

Sources: Based on the work of Parmelee, Wenner, & Schulz, 1964; Prechtl & Beintema, 1964; Hutt, Lenard, & Prechtl, 1969.

Psychology in Action

Observation in a Newborn Nursery

Warning: This project, like many given in this text, should not be undertaken without explicit permission and guidance from your instructor, who will have to obtain permission from your college or university's Human Subjects Review Committee for any project in which you interview or observe a child or parent directly. **Do not do this project on your own, without such permission.**

You can get a feeling for what newborn babies are like, as well as learn something about observational techniques, by arranging to visit a newborn nursery in a local hospital. Your instructor will have made arrangements with one or more hospitals to allow such observations; you will need to sign up for a specific observation time.

At all times, remember that newborn nurseries are complex, busy places, and they cannot tolerate lots of questions or extra bodies getting in the way. So be unobtrusive and nondemanding, and do what you are told.

Procedure

Position yourself at one side of the window outside the newborn nursery, leaving room at the window for others to see their newborns. From this vantage point, observe one baby for at least 15 minutes. Proceed in the following way:

1. Set up a score sheet that should look something like the one below, continuing the list for thirty 30-second intervals.

2. Reread the material in Table 4.3 (p. 119) until you know the main features of the five states as well as possible. You will need to focus on the eyes (open versus closed and rapid eye movement), the regularity of the baby's breathing, and the amount of body movement.

3. Select one infant in the nursery and observe that infant's state every 30 seconds for 15 minutes. For each 30-second interval, note on your score sheet

the state that best describes the infant over the preceding 30 seconds. Do *not* select an infant to observe who is in deep sleep at the beginning. Pick an infant who seems to be in an in-between state (active sleep or quiet awake), so that you can see some variation over the quarter-hour observation.

4. If you can arrange it, you might do this observation with a partner, each of you scoring the same infant's state independently. When the quarter hour is over, compare notes. How often did you agree on the infant's state? What might have been producing the disagreements?

5. When you discuss or write about the project, consider at least the following issues: Did the infant appear to have cycles of states? What were they? What effect, if any, do you think the nursery environment might have had on the baby's state? If you worked with a partner, how much agreement or disagreement did you have? Why?

You may find yourself approached by family members of babies in the nursery, asking what you are doing, why you have a clipboard and a stopwatch. Be sure to reassure the parents or grandparents that your presence does not in any way suggest that there is anything wrong with any of the babies—that you are doing a school project on observation. You may even want to show them the text describing the various states.

Alternate Project

The same project can be completed in a home setting with any infant under age 1 or 2 months, with appropriate permission obtained from the baby's parents and approval by your instructor. You should observe the infant when he/she is lying in a crib or another sleeping location where it is possible for the child to move fairly freely (thus an infant seat won't do, nor will a baby carrier of any kind).

Baby's State

30-Second Intervals	Deep Sleep	Active Sleep	Quiet Awake	Active Awake	Crying/Fussing
1					
2					
3					
etc.					

Sleeping Arrangements for Infants

When we look at typical infant sleeping arrangements around the world, we find a wonderful example of the contrast between collectivist and individualist cultures as well as a picture of how unaware we often are of our own culture's influence.

In a recent edition of his *Baby and Child Care,* Dr. Spock says:

> I think it is a sensible rule not to take a child into the parents' bed to sleep for any reason (even as a treat when one parent is away on a trip).... Children can sleep in a room by themselves from the time they are born, if convenient, as long as the parents are near enough to hear them when they cry. (Spock & Rothenberg, 1985, pp. 219–220)

Because you are very likely steeped in Euro-American culture, with its strong emphasis on separateness and individuality, you would doubtless agree with Dr. Spock. Most of us see separate sleeping as "right" and "natural" and healthiest for children's psychological development (Morelli, Rogoff, Oppenheim, & Goldsmith, 1992). Yet, in the majority of cultures in the world (and in Western cultures until perhaps 200 years ago), babies sleep in the same bed with their parents, typically until they are weaned, a pattern often called cosleeping. Such an arrangement has many supportive reasons, including, in some cases, lack of alternative space for the infant to sleep. More often, cosleeping seems to reflect a basic collectivist value, one in which contact and interdependence rather than separateness are emphasized (Harkness & Super, 1995). Morelli and her colleagues (Morelli et al., 1992) report that Mayan mothers they interviewed, most of whom practice cosleeping, considered the U.S. practice of separate sleeping as tantamount to child neglect. They are shocked and disbelieving when told that U.S. infants often sleep in a separate room, with no one nearby.

Morelli also reports that bedtime among the Mayan families she studied was rarely a time of discord or difficulty between parent and child, as it so often is in Western families in which infants and toddlers sleep separately. Mayan children also rarely used stuffed animals or other "transitional objects" to comfort themselves as they fell asleep, while this is common among Western infants and toddlers. Thus the cultural assumptions affect not only what we consider as "normal" and "right" for children, they shape the interaction between parent and child, including the nature of their common disputes or struggles.

All these aspects of the baby's sleep pattern have implications for the emerging parent-infant interaction—as does the place the baby sleeps, a point I've explored in the *Cultures and Contexts* box above.

Psychologists have also been interested in sleep patterns because marked irregularity of sleep cycles can be a symptom of some disorder or problem. For example, some babies born to mothers who used cocaine during pregnancy have difficulty establishing a regular pattern of sleeping and waking. Brain-damaged infants often have the same kind of difficulties, so any time an infant fails to develop clear sleep-waking regularity, it *may* be a sign of trouble.

Crying

Newborns actually cry less than you might think. One researcher studying normal newborns found that the figure ranged from 2 to 11 percent of the time (Korner, Hutchinson, Koperski, Kraemer, & Schneider, 1981). This percentage frequently increases over the first few weeks, peaking at two to three hours of crying per day at 6 weeks, and then dropping off to less than one hour a day by 3 months (Needlman, 1996). Such a peak in crying at 6 weeks has been observed in infants from a number of different cultures, including cultures in which mothers have almost constant body contact with the infant (St. James-Roberts, Bowyer, Varghese, & Sawdon, 1994), suggesting that this crying pattern is not unique to the United States or Western cultures. Initially, infants cry most in the evening; later, their most intense crying occurs just before feedings.

The basic function of the child's cry, obviously, is to signal need. Because babies can't move *to* someone, they have to *bring* someone to them, and crying is the main way they have to attract attention. In fact, infants have a whole repertoire of cry sounds, with different cries for pain, anger, or hunger. The basic cry, which often signals hunger, is usually a rhythmical pattern: cry, silence, breath, cry, silence, breath, with a kind of whistling sound often accompanying the in-breath. An anger cry is typically louder and more intense, and the pain cry normally has a very abrupt onset—unlike the more basic kinds of cries, which usually begin with whimpering or moaning. However, not all infants cry in precisely the same way, so each parent must learn the specific sounds of his or her own baby. Alan Wiesenfeld and his colleagues (Wiesenfeld, Malatesta, & DeLoach, 1981) found that mothers (but not fathers) of 5-month-olds could discriminate between taped episodes of anger and pain cries in their own babies, while neither parent could reliably make the same discrimination with the taped cries of another baby.

[?] *Critical Thinking*

The obvious explanation of the mother's greater ability to discriminate among the different cries of her baby is that she spends more time in caregiving than does the father. What kind of study could you design to test this hypothesis?

Colic.   Fifteen to 20 percent of infants develop a pattern called **colic,** which involves intense daily bouts of crying totaling more than three hours a day. The crying is generally worst in late afternoon or early evening—a particularly inopportune time for parents, of course, because that is just the time when they are tired and needing time with one another. Colic typically appears at about age 2 weeks and then disappears spontaneously at 3 or 4 months of age. Neither psychologists nor physicians are sure why colic begins or why it stops without any intervention. Two favorite theories are that colic arises because of (a) a reaction to a specific diet, such as an allergy to cow's milk in formula or to foods eaten by a nursing mother, including cow's milk drunk by the mother; or (b) an anxious new parent with a temperamentally difficult or unadaptable infant.

Neither of these theories seems to explain all cases of colic, although both may contribute in some cases. Diet seems clearly to play a role for some infants, who show improvement when shifted to a formula free of cow's milk, or—among breast-fed infants—when the mother switches to a diet free of milk, wheat, cruciferous vegetables (the cabbage family), and chocolate (e.g., Hill, 1995; Lust, Brown, & Thomas, 1996). Other researchers have found that providing mothers of colicky babies with specific advice on handling the infant is more helpful than merely offering emotional support to the mother (e.g., Wolke, Gray, & Meyer, 1994). Unfortunately, no one of these treatments is effective for every colicky baby, and the underlying cause remains unclear. There is no doubt that colic is a difficult pattern to live with, but the good news is that it *does* go away, even without any specific intervention.

Responding to Infants' Cries.   One of the enduring practical questions for parents about a baby's crying is how they should respond to it. If they pick up the baby right away, every time he cries, will that simply reinforce the baby's crying, so that he will cry more? Or will such an immediate response reassure the child, building the child's expectation that the world is a safe and reliable place?

Ten years ago I was confident that I knew the answer to this question: Always respond immediately. Results from early studies gave no indication that such immediate responding increased the child's crying, and there was a lot of evidence that predictable responding was one ingredient in the development of a secure attachment to the parent. More recent studies, though, make the answer less clear-cut. It now looks as if the parents' response should depend on the type of crying the child is doing. Intense crying, such as when the infant is very hungry, very wet, or very uncomfortable, should be responded to immediately. Whimpering and milder crying, however, such as what a baby may do when she is put down for a nap, is another matter. When a parent responds immediately to all these milder cries, babies seem to learn to cry more often (Hubbard & van IJzendoorn, 1987). Thus both reassurance and reinforcement seem to be involved, and it takes real sensitivity on the part of the parent to sort it out. The best rule of thumb seems to be that if you are not sure, pick up the baby when he cries.

Research Report

Variations in Children's Cries

Parents have always known that some babies have cries that are particularly penetrating or grating; other babies seem to have much less noxious crying sounds. Researchers have confirmed this parental observation in a wide range of studies.

Many groups of babies with known medical abnormalities have different-sounding cries, including those with Down syndrome, encephalitis, meningitis, and those with many types of brain damage. Barry Lester has extended this observation to babies who appear physically normal but who are at risk for later problems because of some perinatal difficulty, such as preterm or small-for-date babies (Lester, 1987; Lester & Dreher, 1989) or those whose mothers were heavy drinkers during pregnancy (Nugent, Lester, Greene, Wieczorek-Deering, & O'Mahony, 1996). Such babies typically make crying sounds that are acoustically distinguishable from what you hear in a normal, low-risk baby. In particular, the cry of higher-risk babies has a more grating, piercing quality. Interestingly, the cries of babies with colic also have some of these same qualities (Lester, Boukydis, Garcia-Coll, Hole, & Peucker, 1992).

On the assumption that the baby's cry may reflect some basic aspect of neurological integrity, Lester also wondered whether one could use the quality of the cry as a *diagnostic* test. Among a group of high-risk babies, for example, could one predict later intellectual functioning from a measure of the gratingness or pitch of the baby's cry? The answer seems to be yes. Lester found that among preterms, those with higher-pitched cries in the first days of life had lower scores on an IQ test at age 5 years (Lester, 1987). The same kind of connection has also been found among both normal babies and those exposed to methadone prenatally. In all these groups, the higher the pitch and more grating the cry, the lower the child's later IQ score or motor development (Huntington, Hans, & Zeskind, 1990).

Eventually, it may be possible for physicians to use the presence of such a grating or piercing cry as a signal that there may be some underlying physical problem with the infant or to make better guesses about the long-term outcomes for individual babies at high risk of later problems—as is the case for many low-birth-weight babies.

Figure 4.3

What to do?

Eating

Eating is not a "state," but it is certainly something that newborn babies do frequently! Given that the baby's natural cycle seems to be about two hours long, a newborn may eat as many as ten times a day. Gradually, the baby takes more and more milk at each feeding and doesn't have to eat so often. By age 2 months, the average number is down to about five-and-a-half feedings each day, dropping to about three by age 8 to 12 months (Barness & Curran, 1996). Both breast-fed and bottle-fed babies eat at about the same frequency, but these two forms of feeding do differ in other important ways.

Breast-Feeding Versus Bottle-Feeding. Several decades of extensive research in many countries make it clear that breast-feeding is nutritionally superior to bottle-feeding. Breast milk provides important antibodies for the infant against many kinds of diseases, so that breast-fed infants are much less likely to suffer from such problems as colds, pneumonia, ear infections, diarrhea, and colic, and less likely to die in infancy (Barness & Curran, 1996; Beaudry, Dufour, & Marcoux, 1995; Cunningham, Jelliffe, & Jelliffe, 1991; Srivastava, Sharma, & Jha, 1994). Breast milk also appears to promote the growth of nerves and intestinal tract, to contribute to more rapid weight and size gain (Prentice, 1994), and may stimulate better immune system function over the long term. On the down side is the fact that some viruses (including both HIV and cytomegalovirus) can be transmitted through breast milk. Because of the obvious benefits, and even taking the added risks into account, the World Health Organization recommends that infants be exclusively breast-fed for the first four months of life. When and if you have a child, I urge you to follow this advice, if at all possible.

Still, I know that for some women, breast-feeding is problematic, if not impossible. Some are physically unable to breast-feed successfully because of inverted or chronically cracked nipples or insufficient milk supply. Many others, working full-time with only a few weeks of maternity leave, find breast-feeding logistically very complicated. (I know one woman who traveled four days a week for her job, but still managed to breast-feed exclusively for the first 6 months of her child's life by us-ing a breast pump and begging space in hotel refrigerators to keep the breast milk while she traveled. After some weeks of this regimen, her son would no longer take breast milk from the breast, but only from a bottle.) For those of you facing such logistical difficulties who nonetheless want to continue breast-feeding as long as possible, one piece of helpful news is that babies appear to derive some of the protections of breast milk with as little as one breast-feeding per day. It may be possible, then, to continue with partial breast-feeding over more months. For those of you who cannot breast-feed at all, it is also reassuring to know that the *social* interactions between mother and child seem to be unaffected by the type of feeding. Bottle-fed babies are held and cuddled in the same ways as are breast-fed babies, and their mothers appear to be just as sensitive and responsive to their babies, just as bonded to their babies, as are mothers of breast-fed infants (Field, 1977).

The bottom line, though, is that although babies can and do thrive on formula, exclusive breast-feeding for at least four months is optimum and at least partial breast-feeding is healthier for the infant than is exclusive bottle-feeding.

[?] Critical Thinking

What specific changes in policies or practices do you think would increase the rate of breast-feeding in your country?

Other Feeding Issues. Some parents begin giving their infants solid food, such as cereal, as early as age 2 months, apparently in the mistaken belief that it will help the baby sleep through the night. It doesn't work; in fact, it interferes with the baby's nutritional needs. Until about age 4 to 6 months, babies need only breast milk or formula. After that, they benefit from a mixture of milk and solid food, with a broader and broader range of solid foods added throughout the first year of life (American Academy of Pediatrics Committee on Nutrition, 1986).

Another poor feeding practice, common with toddlers, is to give a child a bottle of milk or juice at nap time or bedtime. The baby falls asleep with this liquid in his mouth, creating two potential problems. First, the fluid can get trapped in the ear

Cultures and Contexts

Cultural and Social Class Differences in Patterns of Breast-Feeding and Their Consequences

If you look at the incidence of breast-feeding in countries around the world over the past 40 or 50 years, you'll find a common pattern. In each country, artificial feeding was first adopted by that society's elite, followed by the urban poor, and then by the rural dwellers. Then a reversal, back toward breast-feeding, followed the same path, beginning with the educated middle class (World Health Organization, 1982). The United States and most Western countries began this entire cycle earlier than did most developing countries. Today, countries such as Sweden, New Zealand, and the United States are on the rebound toward more breast-feeding, as are fast-developing countries such as Malaysia. For example, in Norway, only 30% of 12-week-old infants were still being breast-fed in 1968; in 1991, the rate was 80% (Endresen & Helsing, 1995). Many developing countries, however, are still in the first phase, with declining rates of breast-feeding (e.g., Amador, Silva, & Valdes-Lazo, 1994; Arnold & Larson, 1993; Perez-Escamilla, 1994).

One contributor to the decline of breast-feeding in less-industrialized countries appears to have been the marketing of infant formula. Manufacturers of formula often gave free samples or free feeding bottles to new mothers, assuring the women that formula is as good or better for babies, while frequently failing to provide adequate instruction on how formula should be used. Some women, knowing no better and faced with extreme economic hardship, diluted their infant's formula with water in order to make it stretch further. Sterilization procedures were also not well explained; for many women, proper sterilization was simply not feasible. Worldwide, the concern aroused by this change in normal feeding practices was sufficient to cause the World Health Organization to issue an "International Code of Marketing of Breast-milk Substitutes" in 1981. Marketing practices have since been modified. Yet the decline in breast-feeding has continued in many parts of the world (Stewart, Popkin, Guilkey et al., 1991).

Such a decline is cause for real concern, because bottle-fed babies in developing or Third World countries are at far higher risk of serious disease or death. In Bangladesh, for example, the risk of death from diarrhea is three times higher among bottle-fed than among breast-fed babies; in Brazil, the risk of death from various kinds of infections ranges from $2\frac{1}{2}$ to 14 times higher among the bottle-fed. In all these studies, the risk associated with bottle-feeding is far higher where the sanitary conditions are poorest (Cunningham et al., 1991). Breast-feeding is thus better for two reasons: It provides the baby with needed antibodies against infection, and it is likely to expose the baby to less infection in the first place.

Patterns in the United States

In view of such findings it is disturbing to learn that in the United States the trend line is again downward. Between 1984 and 1989 the percentage of women beginning breast-feeding dropped from 60 to 52 percent (Ryan, Rush, Krieger, & Lewandowski, 1991). At both time points it was the same subgroups that were more likely to breast-feed: older, well-educated, or higher-income mothers. Whites are also more likely than either blacks or Hispanics to breast-feed. In 1989 the respective rates in the first weeks of the baby's life were 58, 23, and 48 percent (Ryan et al., 1991). In all three groups, however, better-educated mothers are more likely to breast-feed, while the less-educated and the poor are least likely to do so (MacGowan, MacGowan, Serdula et al., 1991). This pattern is of special concern because rates of mortality and illness are already higher among infants born to poor mothers.

A mother's work status also makes some difference in her decision about breast- or bottle-feeding, but it is not the deciding factor in many cases. The majority of women who do not work also do *not* breast-feed, while many working women find creative ways to combine employment (especially part-time work) and breast-feeding (Lindberg, 1996; Ryan et al., 1991).

Overall, it is clear that a large public-health task still remains, not only in the United States but around the world, to educate women still further about the importance of breast-feeding and to create the cultural and practical supports needed to make breast-feeding the norm.

canal, increasing the likelihood of ear infections. Second, the practice promotes a form of tooth decay dentists call **nursing bottle syndrome** (Jones, Berg, & Coody, 1994). The potential long-term consequences for the child's dental health is such that dentists recommend against feeding a child with a bottle after 1 year of age, a recommendation many parents find extremely difficult to follow.

Physical Changes

As my friend with the 6-month-old observed, one of the remarkable things about babies is just how fast they change. If I need any further reminder of this fact, I need only look in my wallet, where I carry several pictures of my new 6-month-old granddaughter, Maggie. The newborn pictures are (of course!) charming, but the 4-months pictures show a remarkably different child. She was beginning to sit up with a little help; she was reaching for things, smiling more often.

Basic Patterns

These very obvious physical changes in the early months follow two broad patterns: Development proceeds from the head downward, called **cephalocaudal,** and from the trunk outward, called **proximodistal**—patterns originally identified by Gesell. We see the operation of these two principles in visible behavior, such as the baby's being able to hold up his head before he can sit and to sit before he can crawl. We can also document the same patterns in the development of the nervous system.

The Nervous System

Figure 4.4 shows the main structures of the brain. At birth the midbrain and the medulla are most fully developed. These two parts, both in the lower part of the skull and connecting to the spinal cord, regulate such basic tasks as attention and habituation, sleeping, waking, elimination, and movement of the head and neck (but not movement of the trunk or limbs)—all tasks a newborn can perform at least moderately well. The least-developed part of

Because motor development is both cephalocaudal and proximodistal, both 7-month-old Helen and 5-month-old Laura are better at reaching and grasping than they are at crawling.

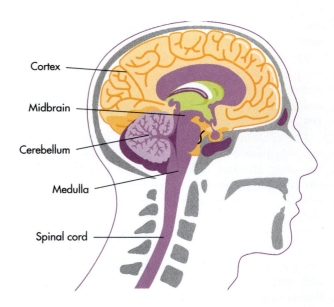

Figure 4.4

The medulla and the midbrain are largely developed at birth. In the first two years after birth it is primarily the cortex that develops, although increases in the dendritic arbor and in synapses also occur throughout the nervous system.

the brain at birth is the **cortex,** the convoluted gray matter that wraps around the midbrain and is involved in perception, body movement, and all complex thinking and language.

Recall from Chapter 3 that all these brain structures are composed of two basic types of cells, *neurons* and *glial cells*. Virtually all of both types of cells are already present at birth. After birth the key developmental process in the brain is the creation of synapses, which involves enormous growth of all parts of the neuron, including the axons and the "dendritic arbor"—that elaborate branching array of dendrites. Most dendritic growth occurs in the cortex, primarily during the first year or two after birth, resulting in a tripling of the overall weight of the brain during those years (Nowakowski, 1987).

This remarkable brain development is not entirely smooth and continuous. Neurophysiologists have identified an initial burst of synapse formation in the first year or so after birth, followed by a "pruning" of synapses in each area of the brain, as redundant pathways and connections are eliminated and the "wiring diagram" is cleaned up (Huttenlocher, 1994).

For example, early in development each skeletal muscle cell seems to develop synaptic connections with several motor neurons in the spinal cord; after the pruning process, each muscle fiber is connected to only one neuron. Some neurophysiologists, such as William Greenough (Greenough et al., 1987), have suggested that the initial surge of development of the dendritic arbor and synaptic formation follows a built-in pattern; the organism is programmed to create certain kinds of neural connections and does so in abundance, creating redundant pathways. According to this argument, the pruning that then takes place in the second year of life is a response to specific experience, resulting in selective retention of the used, or the most efficient, pathways. Putting it briefly, "Experience does not create tracings on a blank tablet; rather experience erases some of them" (Bertenthal & Campos, 1987).

Interestingly, pruning does not occur at the same time in all parts of the brain. For example, the maximum density of synapses in the portions of the brain that have to do with language comprehension and production occurs at about age 3 years, while the part of the cortex devoted to vision is maximally dense at 4 *months* of age, with rapid pruning thereafter (Huttenlocher, 1994).

One of the intriguing points about all this is that the combination of the early surge of synaptic growth and then pruning means that the 1-year-old actually has a *denser* set of dendrites and synapses than an adult does—a piece of information that has surprised many psychologists. Pruning also continues throughout childhood and adolescence. Even at age 4, when the early burst of pruning has

occurred in all areas of the brain, synaptic density is about twice what we see in an adult's brain.

Greenough does not think that all synaptic development is governed by such built-in programming. Parallel with the preprogrammed synaptic development is an equally important process in which genuinely new links are created because of experience. Further, a number of writers have suggested that the richness of the child's environment is a critical ingredient in fostering such experience-generated connections. According to this argument, varied stimulation in the early months of life, such as the infant's being talked to a lot or having things to touch and play with, promotes more brain growth. The evidence to support this proposal comes from several kinds of research, including work with animals. For example, rat infants reared in highly stimulating environments develop a denser network of neurons, dendrites, and synaptic connections (e.g., Escorihuela, Tobena, & Fernández-Teruel, 1994). We also know that in both subhuman primates and humans, infants who experience significant sensory deprivation, such as from being blind in one eye, develop less dense synaptic networks in the part of the brain linked to that particular function (e.g., Gordon, 1995). Finally, we have a growing body of information showing the importance for human babies of being talked to—not from an inanimate source like television but by an attentive, conversational adult. Such conversation appears to help stimulate and organize the infant's brain (e.g., Fifer & Moon, 1994; Kuhl, 1993), so that babies exposed to more such verbal stimulation develop denser and more complex networks of synapses. This denser network, in turn, provides an enduring base for later complex thinking. Thus these early months look like a sensitive period for the development of synapses; neural complexity that is not developed in these early years may not develop later.

We can draw several important implications from all this new information about neurological development. First, we can see that a kind of "programmed plasticity" is built into the human organism. The brain has a remarkable ability to reorganize itself, to make the wiring diagram more efficient, or to find compensatory pathways following some injury. But this plasticity is greater in infancy than it is later. Perhaps paradoxically, the period of greatest plasticity is also the period in which the child may be most vulnerable to major deficits. Just as the time of most rapid growth of any body system prenatally is the time when the fetus is most vulnerable to teratogens (recall Figure 3.8, p. 89), so the young infant needs sufficient stimulation and orderliness in his environment to maximize the early period of rapid growth and plasticity (de Haan, Luciana, Maslone, Matheny, & Richards, 1994). A really inadequate diet or too low a level of verbal or other stimulation in the early months can thus have subtle but long-range effects on the child's cognitive progress (e.g., Pollitt et al., 1996).

An obvious practical implication from the new work on brain development in infancy is that programs like Head Start, which typically begin when children are 3 or 4 years old, may be too little, too late.

[?] Critical Thinking

Someone might argue, based on this information, that supplementary programs designed to alleviate the negative effects of poverty ought to be aimed at infants rather than 3-year-olds. What would be the social effects of a widespread Head-Start-like program for infants?

Paradoxically, the new information about the continuation of the pruning process throughout childhood and adolescence also tells us that brain development is not completed by age 2 or 3, as most of us believed until recently—a fact that reopens many old questions about brain/behavior connections. Does language show a spurt between ages 2 and 3 because that is when the relevant portion of the brain is undergoing significant reorganization? Or is the reverse true? Similarly, are the changes in thinking that we see at age 4, at age 7, or at adolescence, linked in some causal way to further changes in the brain? We do not yet have the data to answer such questions, but the theoretical climate has definitely shifted toward a far greater interest in the neurological underpinnings of development in childhood and adolescence.

Myelination. Another crucial process in neuronal development is the development of sheaths around individual axons, which insulate them from one another and improve the conductivity of the nerve. This sheath is made up of a substance called **myelin**; the process of developing the sheath is called **myelination.**

The sequence with which nerves are myelinized follows both cephalocaudal and proximodistal patterns. Thus nerves serving muscle cells in the arms and hands are myelinated earlier than are those serving the lower trunk and the legs. Myelination is most rapid during the first two years after birth, but it continues at a slower pace throughout childhood and adolescence. For example, the parts of the brain that govern motor movements are not fully

Table 4.4

Summary of Major Changes in the Brain and Nervous System in the First Two Years After Birth

Dendritic growth	Rapid increase occurs in the dendritic arbor of all neurons.
Synapses	Dendritic increase creates a huge number of new synapses—connection points between neurons.
Pruning	Late in the first year and through the second year, dendrites—and thus synapses—are "pruned" to eliminate redundant or unused connections.
Myelination	Axons of individual neurons develop a sheath made up of myelin, which improves conductivity.
Cephalocaudal and proximodistal patterns	Development of the nervous system generally follows the two basic "rules," moving from the head downward (cephalocaudal) and from the trunk outward (proximodistal).

myelinated until perhaps age 6 (Todd, Swarzenski, Rossi, & Visconti, 1995).

To understand the importance of myelin, it may help you to know that *multiple sclerosis* is a disease in which the myelin begins to break down. An individual with this disease gradually loses motor control, with the specific symptoms depending on the portion of the nervous system in which the myelin is affected.

Bones, Muscles, and Teeth

These changes in the nervous system are paralleled by changes in other body structures, including bones, muscles, and teeth, although here the changes occur fairly gradually from infancy through adolescence, rather than in the remarkable early spurt we see in the nervous system.

Bones. The hand, wrist, ankle, and foot all have fewer bones at birth than they will have at full maturity. For example, an adult has nine separate bones in his wrist. A 1-year-old has only three; the remaining six develop during early childhood. Like many aspects of physical development, this process, too, is faster in girls than in boys. The wrist bones are normally fully complete by 51 months in girls but only at 66 months in boys (Needlman, 1996).

One set of bones, though, fuses rather than differentiating. The skull of a newborn is made up of several bones separated by spaces called **fontanels.** Fontanels allow the head to be compressed without injury during the birth process, and they also give the brain room to grow. In most children, the fontanels are filled in by bone by age 12 to 18 months, creating a single, connected skull bone.

All the infant's bones are also softer, with a higher water content, than adults' bones. The process of bone hardening, called **ossification,** occurs steadily from birth through puberty, with bones in different parts of the body hardening in a sequence that follows the typical cephalocaudal and proximodistal patterns. So, for example, bones of the hand and wrist harden before those in the feet.

Bone hardening has some fairly direct practical relevance. Soft bones are clearly needed if the fetus is going to have enough flexibility to fit into the cramped space of the uterus. Yet that very flexibility contributes to a newborn human's relative floppiness and motor immaturity. As the bones stiffen, the baby is able to manipulate his body more surely, which increases the range of exploration he can enjoy and makes him much more independent.

Muscles. In contrast to bones, muscle fibers are virtually all present at birth (Tanner, 1990), although they are initially small and watery, becoming longer, thicker, and firmer at a fairly steady rate until adolescence. The sequence is again both cephalocaudal and proximodistal. So the baby gains muscle strength in the neck fairly early, but does not have enough muscle strength in the legs to support walking until some months later. Similarly, because the sphincter muscles needed for voluntary control over urination or defecation are low in the trunk, the cephalocaudal pattern of muscle (and nerve) development means that they do not develop fully until the second year of life. The practical consequence of this is that there is little point in beginning toilet training until at least that age because the child simply cannot control the process before then. Indeed, most experts suggest waiting until close to age 2 to begin toilet training.

Teeth. Teething—the eruption of teeth through the gums—also occurs in these first two years, as you can see from the information in Table 4.5 (p. 130). These are the **primary teeth** or "baby teeth," all of which will fall out some years later and be replaced by secondary teeth. The first to erupt, and the first to fall out, are the two upper front teeth ("All I want for Christmas is my two front teeth"), followed quickly by the two bottom central teeth. By age 1, most infants have 8 teeth; by age 2, most have 18 to 20 teeth—a fact that makes it clear why dentists begin to be concerned about feeding practices and tooth care at about this age. Although these are "baby teeth" and will eventually be replaced with permanent teeth, these primary teeth can and do decay if they are not treated well. If the

Table 4.5
Sequence of Emergence and Loss of Baby Teeth

Primary or Baby Teeth	Age They First Appear	Age When They Are Lost
Central incisors (central two teeth, top and bottom)	5–8 months	6–8 years
Lateral incisors (two teeth on either side of the central ones, top and bottom)	7–11 months	7–9 years
Canines	16–20 months	9–11 years
First molars	10–16 months	10–12 years
Second molars	20–30 months	10–13 years

Source: Needlman, 1996, adapted from Table 11-6, p. 42.

early teeth have to be extracted because of advanced decay, the child may suffer from longer-term problems with speech, malformations of the secondary (permanent) teeth, and other difficulties.

Pediatric dentists recommend that a child as young as 18 months or 2 years should have his own toothbrush and brush alongside Mom or Dad, using only a tiny amount of fluoride toothpaste (toddlers will swallow most of it). The parents then need to finish the brushing for the toddler (Jones et al., 1994).

[?] Critical Thinking

My guess is that a relatively small proportion of parents actually have their toddlers try to brush their own teeth. How could you find out if my guess is right?

Dentists recommend that children begin to brush their own teeth as early as 18 or 24 months, so that by the time they are preschoolers they will have developed good habits, as these two apparently have.

Size and Shape

All these internal changes obviously affect the baby's size and shape. Babies grow very rapidly in the first months, as you can see in Figure 4.5, which shows the 10th, 50th, and 90th percentiles for height and weight during the first two years for U.S. children, separately for boys and girls. Children at

the 50th percentile are growing at a middle rate: Half of same-gender children are larger, half are smaller. Children at the 10th percentile are growing slower than all but 10 percent of other children of the same gender; those at the 90th percentile are growing faster than all but 10 percent of children.

The rapidity with which babies gain inches and pounds is really quite remarkable. Infants grow an average of a bit more than 6 inches in length in the

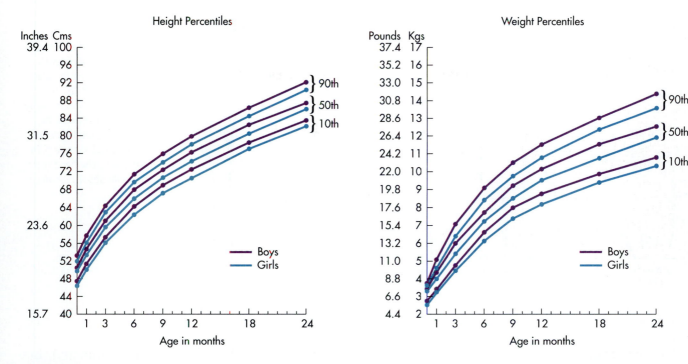

Figure 4.5

Infants gain in both length (height) and weight very rapidly in the first year after birth, somewhat more slowly in the second year. These charts show the 10th, 50th, and 90th percentiles of growth. The boys' curves are in purple, the girls' curves are in blue. Naturally enough, girls are shorter and lighter at every age. But the shape of the curve is virtually identical for both sexes and for small, medium, and large children. (Source: Data from Needlman, 1996, Table 11-2, p. 39, based on information from the National Center for Health Statistics.)

first six months, 10 inches in the first year. In those same months, infants usually triple their body weight. Although the rate of growth drops quite a lot in the second year—to approximately 4½ inches and 5 pounds gained—it is still true that by a little before age 2 for girls, and about age 2½ for boys, the toddler is more than *half as tall as she or he will be as an adult,* a fact I put in italics because it is so surprising to most of us. Look at the figure, though, and you'll see that it's true. At 24 months, the 50th percentile girl is 34 inches tall. If you double that, you have 68 inches, which is 5 feet 8 inches—3 inches taller than the average adult woman in the United States.

Part of the reason that it is so surprising to think of a 2-year-old as half as tall as she or he will eventu-

ally be is that the baby's body proportions are quite different from those of an adult. In particular, babies have proportionately much larger heads than do adults (see Figure 4.6, p. 132)—obviously needed to hold that nearly full-sized brain.

Motor Development

All these physical changes form the substrate on which the child's rapidly improving motor skills are constructed. And, of course, it is precisely those new physical abilities that are so striking and re-markable to parents (and grandparents!).

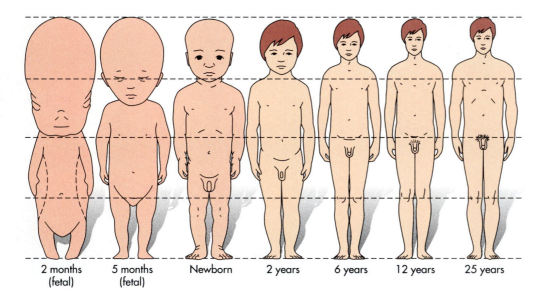

Figure 4.6

Babies and toddlers are proportioned very differently from what we see in older children and adults. One quarter of a newborn's body length is in her head; by age 2, that proportion has dropped to about one fifth. In an adult, the head represents only about one ninth.

2 months (fetal)   5 months (fetal)   Newborn   2 years   6 years   12 years   25 years

Robert Malina (1982) suggests that we divide the wide range of motor skills into three rough groups: *locomotor* patterns, such as walking, running, jumping, hopping, and skipping; *nonlocomotor* patterns, such as pushing, pulling, and bending; and *manipulative* skills, such as grasping, throwing, catching, kicking, and other actions involving receiving and moving objects. Table 4.6 summarizes the developments in each of these three areas over the first 18 months, based primarily on two large studies, one in the United States and one in the Netherlands. The United States study (Capute, Palmer, Shapiro et al., 1984) involved 381 babies tested by their pediatricians at regular visits through the first two years; the Dutch study (Den Ouden, Rijken, Brand, Verloove-Vanhorick, & Ruys, 1991) included 550 babies who had been tested repeatedly for their first five years. The sequence of milestones described in these two studies are highly similar, as were the ages at which babies passed each test.

In these early months of life, babies seem pleased to repeat their limited repertoire of motor skills again and again. They kick, rock, wave, bounce, bang, rub, scratch, or sway repeatedly and rhythmically. Such repeated patterns become particularly prominent at about age 6 or 7 months, although you can see some such behavior even in the first weeks, particularly in finger movements and leg kicking. These repeated movements do not

seem to be totally voluntary or coordinated, but they also do not appear to be random. For instance, Esther Thelen (1981) has observed that kicking movements peak just before the baby begins to crawl, as if the rhythmic kicking were a part of the preparation for crawling.

Thelen's observation reminds us that the baby's new motor skills do not spring forth full blown. Each emerges from the coordination of a wide range of component abilities, perceptual as well as motor (Thelen, 1989; Thelen & Ulrich, 1991). Using a spoon to feed oneself, for example, requires development of muscles in the hand and wrist, bone development in the wrist, eye-hand coordination skills that allow one to readjust the aim of the spoon in moving it toward the mouth, and coordination of all these with properly timed mouth opening (Connolly & Dalgleish, 1989).

Most of us are unaware of this complex of developmental processes when we watch an infant. What we are struck with is the daily change in the baby's behavior and skill. As parents, we are delighted with each new accomplishment, each new milestone—although any parent can tell you that life changes rather dramatically when the baby is able to crawl freely and again when the baby walks. Baby-proofing the house takes on a whole new meaning, as the previously immobile baby now gets into absolutely everything, seemingly the moment your back is turned.

Table 4.6

Milestones of Motor Development

Age	Locomotor Skills	Nonlocomotor Skills	Manipulative Skills
1 mo.	Stepping reflex	Lifts head slightly; slowly follows moving objects with eyes	Grasps object if placed in hand (sometimes called reflexive grasp)
2–3 mo.	Sits with support	Lifts head up to 90 degrees when lying on stomach	Begins to swipe at objects in sight; two-handed grasp with palms
4–6 mo.	Rolls over; sits with self-support by 6 months; moves on hands and knees ("creeps")	Holds head erect in sitting position	Reaches for and grasps objects, using one hand to grasp
7–9 mo.	Sits without support; crawls		Transfers objects from one hand to the other; by 9 months, can grasp with two fingers ("pincer grasp")
10–12 mo.	Pulls himself to standing; walks grasping furniture ("cruising"); then walks without help	Squats and stoops	Some signs of hand preference; grasps a spoon across palm but has poor aim of food to mouth
13–18 mo.	Walks backward and sideways; runs (14–20 mo.)	Rolls ball to adult	Stacks two blocks; puts object into small containers and dumps them

Sources: Capute et al., 1984, and Den Ouden et al., 1991; Gallahue & Ozmun, 1995.

Explaining Early Physical Development

When we search for explanations for the series of physical changes I've been describing, there are some obvious candidates: maturation, heredity, and various environmental factors, including both diet and practice.

Maturation and Heredity

Maturational sequences have to be part of the explanation, especially for such central patterns as neuronal changes and changes in muscles and bones. In all these areas, while the *rate* of development varies from one child to the next, the *sequence* is virtually the same for all children, even those with marked physical or mental disabilities. Mentally retarded children, for example, typically move through the various motor milestones more slowly than do normal children, but they follow the same sequence. Whenever we find such robust sequences, maturation of some kind seems an obvious explanation—although the maturational process itself is immensely complex, involving interlocking changes in muscles, bones, perception, and thinking (Thelen, 1995).

At the same time, our genetic heritage is individual as well as species-specific. In addition to being programmed for many basic sequences of physical development, each of us also receives genetic instructions for unique growth tendencies. Parents and children are similar not only in such obvious characteristics as height but also in hip width, arm length, and short or long trunk. (Some ancestor certainly passed on a gene for long arms to me!)

The rate of the child's growth, as well as her final shape or size, also seems to be an inherited pattern. Parents who were themselves early developers, as measured by such things as bone ossification, tend to have children who are faster developers too (Garn, 1980).

(a)

(b)

(c)

(d)

Milestones of development:
(a) 5 months
(b) 6½ months
(c) 10 months
(d) 12 months

Environmental Effects

Diet.   I mentioned in the last chapter that mothers who are malnourished during pregnancy are more likely to have stillborn infants or infants who die in the first year. It seems logical to assume that the baby's diet after birth would also make a difference in many aspects of physical development, perhaps especially neurological development. But this hypothesis has been very difficult to test clearly, in large part because most babies who are undernourished are also growing up in environments that are also low in other types of stimulation.

What we do know is that poorly nourished children grow more slowly and don't end up as large (Malina, 1982). If their diet later improves, such children may show some catch-up in height or growth rate, but they are typically shorter and slower than their peers.

Practice.   We can also think of environmental influences on physical development in terms of the child's own opportunities to practice various physical activities. Does a baby who spends a lot of time in a toy called an infant walker, which holds up the baby while he moves around, learn independent walking any sooner than a baby who never has that practice? Does a toddler who has many chances to climb stairs learn to climb them sooner or more skillfully than a toddler who is rarely exposed to stairs?

Lots of opportunity to practice basic motor skills like stair climbing probably does not speed up a baby's stair-climbing skill a whole lot, but exercise that strengthens a child's muscles or develops some other basic skill may accelerate some maturational processes.

The answer, as usual, is fairly complicated. Two conclusions are reasonably clear. First, the development of such universal, basic skills as crawling and walking requires some minimum amount of practice just to keep the system working as it should. Children who are deprived of this basic normal practice develop motor skills much more slowly and not in the normal sequence. A classic early study by Wayne Dennis (1960) of children raised in Iranian orphanages is a good illustration. The babies in one of the institutions were routinely placed on their backs in cribs with very lumpy mattresses. They had little or no experience of lying or moving on their stomachs as a normal baby would, and they even had difficulty rolling over because of the hollows in the mattresses. These babies almost never went through the normal sequence of learning to walk, presumably because they didn't have enough opportunity to practice all the on-the-stomach parts of the skill. They did learn to walk eventually, but they were about a year late.

Second, we also know that the development of really smooth, coordinated skill in virtually all complex motor tasks requires practice. The strength and coordination required to throw a basketball high enough to reach the basket may develop in predictable ways over the early years, assuming the environment is sufficiently rich to provide needed maintenance. But to develop the skill needed to get the ball through the hoop with regularity, from different angles and distances, requires endless practice.

Where we are still uncertain is about the role of practice in the acquisition of many basic component skills, such as sitting, walking up stairs, climbing, or catching objects. Early studies seemed to show that extra practice in such basic skills didn't speed up their development at all, perhaps because almost all children have enough opportunity for minimal practice in their ordinary lives. However, some recent studies contradict this conclusion, including one I already mentioned showing that very young infants who are given more practice with the stepping reflex later walk sooner. A more recent study by the same researcher (Zelazo, Zelazo, Cohen, & Zelazo, 1993) similarly shows that very young babies who are given more practice sitting are able to sit upright longer than those without such practice (Zelazo et al., 1993). So it may be that special practice helps to strengthen the muscles or that it affects the neural wiring diagram in some way that speeds up certain aspects of development. In Aslin's terms (recall Figure 1.1, p. 13), practice may have a *facilitating* effect, although the evidence is still pretty mixed.

Health

Illnesses in the First Two Years

Diarrhea.   Worldwide, one of the most common illnesses of infancy and early childhood is diarrhea, which accounts for an estimated 3.5 million infant and child deaths each year. In developing countries, one out of four deaths in children under 5 is due to this illness; in some countries the rate is even higher (Gorter, Sahcnez, Pauw et al., 1995). In the United States diarrhea only rarely leads to death in infants, but virtually every infant or young

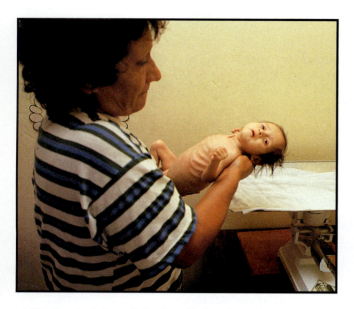

This Peruvian baby, suffering from diarrhea, has a good chance of survival because of being rehydrated in a hospital. Worldwide, more infants and young children die of diarrhea than of any other illness, and most of those deaths are preventable.

child has at least one episode of diarrhea each year; about one in ten cases is severe enough for the child to be taken to a doctor. Nearly ten percent of all hospitalizations in children 5 and younger is due to this illness (Kilgore, Holman, Clarke, & Glass, 1995).

Almost all the deaths from diarrhea could be prevented by prompt treatment, including in particular the giving of fluids to rehydrate the child. In serious cases this rehydration should involve a special solution of salts ("oral rehydration salts," or ORS). The World Health Organization has for some years been involved in a program of training health professionals around the world in the use of ORS, with some success (Muhuri, Anker, & Bryce, 1996). Still, this remains a very serious illness for children in many parts of the world.

Upper Respiratory Infections. A second common disease of infancy is some kind of upper respiratory infection. The average baby in the United States has seven colds in the first year of life. (That's a lot of nose-wipes!) Interestingly, research in a number of countries shows that babies in day care centers have about twice as many infections as do those reared entirely at home, with those in small-group day care falling somewhere in between, presumably because babies in group care

settings are exposed to a wider range of germs and viruses (e.g., Collet, Burtin, Gillet et al., 1994; Hurwitz, Gunn, Pinsky, & Schonberger, 1991; Louhiala, Jaakkola, Ruotsalainen, & Jaakkola, 1995). In general, the more different people a baby is exposed to, the more colds she is likely to get. This is not the unmitigated negative that it may appear to be. First of all, the heightened risk of infection among infants in day care drops after the first few months, while those reared entirely at home have very high rates of illness when they first attend preschool or kindergarten. Attendance at day care simply means that the baby is exposed earlier to the various microorganisms typically carried by children.

Ear Infections. One of the most severe forms of an upper respiratory infection is an ear infection—more properly called **otitis media**—the early childhood illness that in the United States most often leads to a visit to a doctor (Daly, 1997). This kind of infection very often follows a cold or an allergic reaction, either of which can lead to congestion in the eustachian tube—the tube through which middle-ear fluid drains. The fluid thus has nowhere to go and accumulates in the middle ear, creating pressure and pain, often accompanied by fever, headache, and other signs of illness. In the United States as many as 90 percent of all children will have at least one serious ear infection before age 2, with the incidence peaking between ages 6 and 18 months (Daly, 1997; Paradise, Rockette, Colborn et al., 1997). Some children are prone to such infections and have repeated episodes; a few children have none. The earlier a child's first episode, the more likely she is to have repeated infections. A child who has had few or no episodes of otitis media before age 3 is unlikely to have problems later.

The standard treatment is any one of nine antibiotics approved for this disorder, amoxicillin being the most commonly used because it has the least side effects (Klein, 1994), although such treatment is not always effective and increases the likelihood of the emergence of drug-resistant forms of infection (Henderson, 1997). For children with persistent fluid in the ear, which can occur for months at a time without other signs of illness, tubes are sometimes placed in the ear to drain the fluid. This procedure is controversial, requires general anesthesia, and is expensive, so it is normally thought of as a last resort.

Cultures and Contexts

Immunizations

Most of the killer diseases of childhood are entirely preventable when appropriate types of vaccination are given in the first few years of life, and therein lies a wonderfully optimistic tale. (See Table 4.7, p. 138, for the currently recommended schedule of immunizations.) Twenty years ago only about 5 percent of the children in developing countries were fully vaccinated against tetanus, polio, measles, whooping cough, tuberculosis, and diphtheria. By 1987 this figure had risen to 50 percent in developing countries; by 1994 as many as 80 percent of all infants and young children worldwide were being immunized against measles, polio, and diphtheria, with tetanus lagging somewhat behind (Wright, 1995). Astonishingly, many countries—including China, Egypt, Vietnam, Bangladesh, and Algeria—have brought their coverage to over 90 percent (World Health Organization, 1994). In some parts of the world some of these diseases have been eradicated altogether. As just one example, not a single polio case has been reported in all the Americas since 1991.

This enormous change is the result of a massive effort by the World Health Organization and all its member nations, which created an Expanded Programme on Immunization (EPI) in 1987. Some nations reached the goal of 80 percent immunization by mass media campaigns; others have tried to build immunization programs into their primary health care system. Both these strategies have been successful in the short term, although sustained high levels of immunization appear to be more likely when immunization has been made part of an expanded primary care system, as has been done in Burkina Faso, Indonesia, China, and India, to name only a few.

Millions of children have been saved as a result of this effort, as have millions of dollars in health care costs. The Centers for Disease Control estimate that for every dollar spent on the measles-mumps-rubella vaccine, $21 is saved in costs to society. An added benefit, particularly in developing countries, is a decrease in the birthrate. More complete immunizations mean that fewer children die in childhood; parents become more confident that children will survive and be able to take on the roles the family needs filled, so fewer children are conceived and born.

Successful as this WHO effort has been, we should not be too sanguine. There is more to be accomplished. In the United States, as recently as 1992, only 55 percent of children had received the full set of immunizations (Committee on Infectious Diseases, 1996). By 1995, after intensive efforts, this rate was raised to 75 percent (Pear, 1996), an admirable improvement but still short of the goal of 80 percent; more than a million children in the United States are not fully immunized. There is also an object lesson in the experience of the newly independent states of the former USSR, where the incidence of diphtheria skyrocketed during the somewhat chaotic years immediately after the dissolution of the republic when regular immunization programs broke down to some degree. Between 1989 and 1994 the rate of infection went from 0.4 to 26.6 per 100,000 population. Clearly, constant vigilance is needed to reach and maintain a sufficiently high rate of immunizations to prevent the spread of these killer diseases.

The risk of otitis media is unusually high among many Native American peoples, including northern Alaskan and Canadian groups, and higher among Caucasian than among African-American or Hispanic infants; it is more common in boys than in girls, more common in children in day care than those reared at home, more common among children whose parents smoke, and less common among infants who are breast-fed (e.g., Alho, Läärä, & Oja, 1996; Kemper, 1996; Klein, 1994). It is a serious condition, requiring consistent medical treatment—treatment that is not equally available to all children. When it is not treated appropriately, repeated episodes can lead to some permanent hearing loss, which in turn may be linked to language or learning problems, and even some social isolation or withdrawal (Gravel & Nozza, 1997; Roberts & Wallace, 1997; Vernon-Feagans, Manlove, & Volling, 1996).

Infant Mortality

For a small minority of babies, the key health issue is not a few sniffles, or even more serious illnesses like ear infections, but the possibility of death. In the United States in 1995, 7.5 babies out of every 1000 died before age 1 (Guyer et al., 1996). This **infant mortality rate** has been declining steadily for the past few decades (down from 20.0 per 1000 in 1970), but even at this new lower rate, the United States has only the twenty-first lowest infant mortality rate in the world.

Incidentally, the United States looks bad in such comparisons in part because we really do have more high-risk infants, especially those with very low birth weight (disproportionately, African-American infants). At the same time, the traditional comparative statistics are also weighted against the United States because we count every infant who lives even a few minutes as a live birth, whereas many other countries do not. This means that some of the very small infants who die some hours or days after delivery are counted as *infant deaths* in the United States, but are counted as stillbirths or in some other category in other countries (e.g., Sachs, Fretts, Gardner et al., 1995). Yet, even if the U.S. statistics are adjusted by excluding all deaths in the first hour after birth, the U.S. infant mortality rate would still be higher than that of 17 other countries (Wegman, 1996).

Almost two-thirds of infant deaths in the United States occur in the first month of life, and these are most often directly linked either to congenital anomalies or to low birth weight. Only about three deaths per thousand births occur in the remainder of the first year, and nearly half those are cases of **sudden infant death syndrome (SIDS),** in which an apparently healthy in-

fant dies suddenly and unexpectedly. In 1995, 3279 babies in the United States died of SIDS (Guyer et al., 1996).

SIDS is certainly not unique to the United States. It occurs worldwide, although for unexplained reasons the rate varies quite a lot from country to country. For example, SIDS rates are particularly high in Australia and New Zealand and particularly low in Japan and Sweden (Hoffman & Hillman, 1992).

Physicians have not yet uncovered the basic cause of these deaths, although they have learned a fair amount about the factors associated with increased risk, listed in Table 4.8.

Of the items listed in the table, one of the most compelling is the link between prone sleeping position (sleeping on the stomach) and the risk of SIDS. Growing evidence on the role of sleeping position in the risk of SIDS has persuaded pediatricians in many countries to change their standard advice to hospitals and families about the best sleeping position for babies. The American Academy of Pediatrics, for example, has been recommending since 1992 that when healthy infants are put down to sleep, they should be positioned on their sides or backs. Physicians in many other countries have made similar recommendations, a change in advice that has been followed by a significant drop in SIDS cases in every country involved (Willinger, Hoffman, & Hartford, 1994). In the United States, for example, the number of SIDS cases has dropped by nearly thirty percent since 1992. Still, sleeping position cannot be the

Table 4.7

Recommended Childhood Immunization Schedule

Vaccine	Birth	2 mo.	4 mo.	6 mo.	12 mo.	15 mo.	18 mo.	4–6 yr.	11–12 yr.	14–16 yr.
Hepatitis B	HB-1	HB-2		HB-3					catch up	
Diphtheria-tetanus-pertussis (DPT)		1st	2nd	3rd		4th	5th		6th	
Influenza type b		1st	2nd	3rd	4th					
Poliovirus		1st	2nd		3rd		4th			
Measles-mumps-rubella					1st			2nd		
Varicella virus					1st			catch up		

Shaded bars represent the range of acceptable ages for each vaccination.

Source: Centers for Disease Control, 1997a, adapted from Figure 1, p. 36.

Parenting

Six Important Preventive Health Behaviors for Parents of Infants

Parents who follow these six preventive health practices will have the best chance of raising a healthy child (Redman, Booth, Smyth, & Paul, 1992).

1. **Breast-feed until 4 or 6 months.** The optimal pattern is to breast-feed exclusively for the first six months.

2. **No solid food until after 4 months.** Babies do not need and should not have solid food before this age.

3. **Do not smoke during pregnancy or in the infant's home after birth.** Joseph DiFranza and Robert Lew (1996) have estimated the added deaths and diseases for all children (up to age 18) that are linked to parental smoking. The list is quite striking. They calculate that tobacco use by parents (or others living with children) is linked to 284 to 360 deaths each year from lower respiratory illnesses or fires initiated by smoking materials; to more than 300 fire-related injuries; to 354,000 to 2.2 million episodes of otitis media; to

529,000 physician visits for asthma and 1.3 to 2 million visits for coughs; and among children younger than 5, to 260,000 to 436,000 episodes of bronchitis and 115,000 to 190,000 episodes of pneumonia. In addition, parental smoking is linked to increased risk of SIDS, as noted in Table 4.8.

4. **Have the infant fully immunized.** The currently recommended schedule of immunizations is listed in Table 4.7 (p. 138). Keeping to this schedule is, admittedly, often quite difficult, especially for parents living in poverty, who may face long waiting times at public clinics and/or lack reliable transportation; many parents, whether poor or not, find it difficult to schedule appointments around work schedules. Still, this is important!

5. **Use appropriate car seats for the infant for any car trip.**

6. **Take the infant to a physician for regular well-baby checkups.**

full explanation because, of course, *most* babies who sleep on their stomachs do not die of SIDS.

Another important contributor is smoking by the mother during pregnancy or by anyone in the home after the child's birth. Babies exposed to smoking in their environment are about four times as likely to die of SIDS as are babies with no such exposure (Klonoff-Cohen, Edelstein, Lefkowitz et al., 1995; Schoendorf & Kiely, 1992; Taylor & Danderson, 1995). One more powerful reason not to smoke.

Ethnic Differences in Infant Mortality. The higher risk of SIDS for African-American infants is part of a persistent pattern. Infant mortality in general is more than twice as high among black as among white infants in the United States (16.3 and 6.8 per 1000, respectively, in 1992). A somewhat heightened risk also exists for Native-American infants, although *not* for Hispanic-American babies, a set of findings that raises a whole host of questions (Singh & Yu, 1995). The black/white difference has existed at least since recordkeeping began (in

Table 4.8

Factors Linked to Increased Risk of SIDS

Gender	Boys are at higher risk
Birth weight	Low-birth-weight infants are at higher risk
Ethnicity	African Americans are at higher risk
Sleeping position	Babies who sleep on their stomachs are at higher risk
Maternal smoking	Babies whose mothers (or fathers) smoke are at higher risk
Mother's age	Babies with young mothers are at higher risk

Sources: Hoffman & Hillman, 1992; Ponsonby, Dwyer, Gibbons, Cochrane, and Wang, 1993; Malloy & Hoffman, 1995; Taylor, Kreiger, Reay et al., 1996.

1915) and has *not* been declining. It is found even when researchers compare only infants born to college-educated mothers (Schoendorf, Hogue, Kleinman, & Rowley, 1992). Physicians and physiologists do not yet understand all the reasons for this discrepancy, although it is clear that one significant factor is that infants born to African-American mothers are much more likely to be born before the full gestational period is completed and therefore have low birth weight. When only full-term, normal-weight babies are compared, infant mortality is about the same in the two groups. However, saying this only pushes the explanation back one step. We still need to know why African Americans have more preterm, low-birth-weight babies, and the answer to this question is still unclear.

[?] *Critical Thinking*

Can you generate any reasonable hypotheses to explain the finding that infant mortality is not elevated among Hispanic Americans, while it is among African Americans, even though both groups experience significant poverty? What kind of information would you need to check out your hypotheses?

Individual Differences

I've already touched on several kinds of differences among babies that affect their physical development in the first few years: diet, feeding experience, and opportunities for motor practice. Let me sketch several others.

Preterm Babies

Preterm or low-birth-weight babies move more slowly through all the developmental milestones I listed in Table 4.6 (p. 133). You can get some sense of the degree of difference from Table 4.9, which gives several comparisons. The data here are from the same Dutch study I cited in Table 4.6. In addition to studying 555 normal infants, Den Ouden and her colleagues also tested 555 preterm babies—all the otherwise physically normal preterms born at less than 32 weeks' gestation in the Netherlands in 1983. You can see in the table that the preterms are about 10 to 15 weeks behind their full-term peers on most physical skills. This is entirely what we would expect, of course, because the preterm baby is, in fact, maturationally younger than the full-term baby. If you correct for the baby's "gestational age," most (but not all) of the difference in physical development disappears. Parents of preterms need to keep this in mind when they compare their baby's progress with that of a full-term baby. By age 2 or 3, the physically normal preterm will catch up to his peers, but in the early months he is definitely behind.

Boys and Girls

When you hear that a friend or family member has had a new baby, what is your first question? I'll bet it is: "Is it a boy or a girl?" A new child's gender is obviously a highly salient piece of information to all of us. You might assume that such a preoccupa-

Table 4.9

Comparison of Developmental Milestones in Preterm and Normal-Term Babies in the First Two Years

Developmental Milestone	Age at Which 50% of Babies Passed	
	Preterm (<32 weeks)	Normal Term
Lifts head slightly	10 weeks	6 weeks
Transfers object hand to hand	36 weeks	23 weeks
Rolls over	37 weeks	24 weeks
Crawls	51 weeks	36 weeks
Pulls to standing position	51 weeks	42 weeks

Source: Den Ouden et al., 1991, from Table V, p. 402.

Cultures and Contexts

Differences in Early Physical Development

The sequence of physical changes I've been describing in this chapter does seem to hold true for babies in all cultures. Still, there are a few interesting ethnic or racial differences.

Black babies—whether born in Africa or elsewhere—develop somewhat faster, both prenatally and after birth. In fact, the gestational period for the black fetus seems actually to be slightly shorter than for the white fetus (Smith, 1978). Black babies also show somewhat faster development of motor skills, such as walking, and are slightly taller than their white counterparts, with longer legs, more muscle, and heavier bones (Tanner, 1990).

In contrast, Asian infants are somewhat slower to achieve many early motor milestones. This could simply reflect differences in rate of maturation. Alternatively, it could reflect some ethnic differences in the baby's level of activity or placidity—a possibility suggested by research by Daniel Freedman (1979).

Freedman observed newborn babies from four different cultures: Caucasian, Chinese, Navaho, and Japanese. Of the four, he found that the Caucasian babies were the most active and irritable and the hardest to console. Both the Chinese and the Navaho infants he observed were relatively placid, while the Japanese infants responded vigorously but were easier to quiet than the Caucasian infants.

One specific illustration: When Freedman tested each baby for the Moro reflex, he found that the Caucasian babies showed the typical pattern in which they reflexively extended both arms, cried vigorously and persistently, and moved their bodies in an agitated way.

Navaho babies, on the other hand, showed quite a different pattern. Instead of thrusting their limbs outward, they retracted their arms and legs, rarely cried, and showed little or very brief agitation.

Jerome Kagan and his colleagues (1994) have replicated part of these results in their recent comparison of Chinese, Irish, and Euro-American 4-month-olds. They found that the Chinese infants were significantly less active, less irritable, and less vocal than were babies in the other two groups. The white American infants showed the strongest reactions to new sights, sounds, or smells. Similarly, Chisholm has replicated Freedman's findings on Navaho babies, finding them to be significantly less irritable, less excitable, and more able to quiet themselves than Euro-American babies (1989).

Because such differences are visible in newborns, they cannot be the result of systematic shaping by the parents, even though the parents, too, bring their cultural training to the interaction. Freedman and other researchers have observed that both Japanese and Chinese mothers talk less to their young infants than do Caucasian mothers. These differences in mothers' behavior were present from their first encounters with their infants after delivery, so the pattern is not a response to the baby's quieter behavior. Still, such similarity of temperamental pattern between mother and child may strengthen the pattern in the child, which would tend to make the cultural differences larger over time.

One of the key points from this research is that our notions of what is "normal" behavior for an infant may be strongly influenced by our own cultural patterns and assumptions.

tion exists because boy and girl babies are really very different from one another. But in fact they are not. There are remarkably few sex differences in physical development in young infants. As was true at birth, girls continue to be ahead in some aspects of physical maturity, such as the development of bone density, although boys have more muscle tissue and are heavier and taller than girls. Boys continue to be more vulnerable, with higher infant mortality rates. More mixed are the findings on activity level. When researchers observe a difference it is likely to be infant boys who are found to be slightly more active (Campbell & Eaton, 1995), but many investigators report no difference at all (Cossette, Malcuit, & Pomerleau, 1991). There are actually bigger differences between babies from different ethnic groups—described in the *Cultures and Contexts* box above—than there are between boys and girls.

[?] Critical Thinking

Why *do* we all ask immediately whether a new baby is a boy or a girl? Why does this information seem so vital? Think about it.

The physical development of infants is probably more clearly governed by built-in sequences and timetables and more similar from one baby to another than any other aspect of development we'll be looking at. What is striking to the observer is not "boyness" or "girlness," or blackness or whiteness, but "babyness."

Summary

1. Newborns are typically assessed using the Apgar score, which is a rating on five dimensions.

2. Infants have a wide range of reflexes. Some, such as the sucking reflex, are essential for life. Other primitive reflexes are present in the newborn but disappear in the first year as cortical development advances.

3. Even primitive reflexes, however, may be linked to later developmental patterns, such as the stepping reflex and later walking.

4. At birth the baby has a far wider array of perceptual skills than psychologists had earlier supposed. In particular, she can see and hear well enough for most social encounters.

5. In contrast, the newborn has very poor motor skills.

6. Babies move through a series of "states of consciousness," from deep sleep to active sleep to fussing to eating to alert wakefulness, in a cycle that typically lasts $1\frac{1}{2}$ to 2 hours.

7. Newborns sleep an average of 16.5 hours per day; by age 1, this has dropped to 13.75 hours, and more of that sleep is at night.

8. In Western countries babies most often sleep separate from their parents; in many other cultures, babies sleep in the same bed with their parents.

9. Babies cry several hours per day, on average, with the amount of crying peaking at about age 6 weeks. Some infants show more persistent, inconsolable crying (colic), which may last until age 3 or 4 months.

10. Persisting irregularity of sleep patterns or a particularly high pitched or grating cry may be indications of some neurological problem.

11. Breast-feeding is clearly better for the baby nutritionally, providing needed antibodies and reducing the risk of various infections. Mother-infant interactions, however, do not appear to differ, depending on the form of feeding.

12. Solid food should not be given to an infant before 4 months of age.

13. Physical development in the early months follows two basic patterns: from the head downward (cephalocaudal) and from the trunk outward (proximodistal).

14. Changes in the nervous system are extremely rapid in the first two years. In most parts of the brain, dendritic and synaptic development reaches its peak between 12 and 24 months, after which there is a "pruning" of synapses. Myelination of nerve fibers also occurs rapidly in the early years.

15. Bones increase in number and density; muscle fibers become larger and less watery; primary teeth begin to appear at about ages 5 to 6 months.

16. Babies triple their body weight in the first year, and they add 12 to 15 inches in length before age 2.

17. Rapid improvement in locomotor and manipulative skills occurs in the first two years, as the baby moves from creeping to crawling to walking to running and from poor to good ability to grasp objects.

18. It is clear that these virtually universal sequences of development are influenced strongly by common maturational patterns. Individual heredity also makes a difference, as does diet. The role of practice is still in dispute.

19. Common illnesses of childhood include diarrhea (which is linked to many deaths in infants worldwide) and upper respiratory infections. Of the latter, ear infections (otitis media) are often the most serious. All forms of upper respiratory illness are more common among children in day care than in those reared at home.

20. Six good preventive health practices parents can follow to get their infant off to a good start are: breast-feed until 4 to 6 months, don't feed the child solid food until 4 months, get the infant fully immunized, don't smoke, use infant car seats regularly, and take the baby for regular well-child checkups.

21. In the United States and other industrialized countries, most infant deaths in the first weeks are due to congenital anomalies or low birth weight; past the first weeks, sudden infant death syndrome (SIDS) is the most common cause of death in the first year.

22. Infant mortality rates are roughly twice as high among African Americans as among Caucasian Americans, a difference that is not entirely explainable by differences in poverty.

23. Preterm infants are behind their full-term peers in achieving the milestones of development, but they normally catch up within a few years.

24. There are relatively few differences between boys and girls in early physical development. Ethnic dif-

ferences do exist, however. Black infants develop somewhat more rapidly, Asian infants somewhat more slowly.

Key Terms

Apgar score   A rating system for newborns with a maximum of 10 points, based on assessment of heart and respiratory rates, muscle tone, response to stimulation, and color. **(p. 114)**

Babinski reflex   A reflex found in very young infants in which they splay out their toes in response to a stroke on the bottom of the foot. **(p. 115)**

cephalocaudal   One of two basic patterns of physical development in infancy (the other is proximodistal); the term describes development that proceeds from the head downward. **(p. 126)**

colic   A pattern of persistent and often inconsolable crying, totaling more than three hours per day, found in some infants in the first three months of life. **(p. 122)**

cortex   The convoluted gray portion of the brain that governs most complex thought, language, and memory. **(p. 126)**

fontanels   The "soft spots" in the skull present at birth. These disappear when the several bones of the skull grow together. **(p. 129)**

infant mortality rate   Number of deaths in the first year, out of each 1000 live births. **(p. 138)**

Moro reflex   When startled (e.g., by a loud sound or a sensation of being dropped), the infant extends his legs, arms, and fingers, arches his back, and draws back his head. **(p. 115)**

myelin   Material making up a sheath that develops around most axons. This sheath is not completely developed at birth. **(p. 128)**

myelination   The process by which myelin is added. **(p. 128)**

nursing bottle syndrome   Pattern of tooth decay in the primary teeth that can occur when an infant continues to drink from a bottle past about age 1, especially if the child is given a bottle at bedtime or nap time. **(p. 126)**

ossification   The process of hardening by which soft tissue becomes bone. **(p. 129)**

otitis media   The medical name for what most parents call an ear infection: the collection of fluid in the middle ear, often accompanied by other symptoms of acute illness. **(p. 136)**

primary teeth   The "baby teeth" that begin erupting at 5 or 6 months and then are lost, beginning at age 5 or 6, to be replaced by the permanent, or secondary, teeth. **(p. 129)**

primitive reflexes   Collection of reflexes seen in young infants, controlled by the more primitive parts of the brain, that gradually disappear during the first year of life, including the Moro, Babinski, stepping, and others. **(p. 115)**

proximodistal   One of two basic patterns of physical development in infancy (the other is cephalocaudal); the term describes development that proceeds from the center outward, such as from the trunk to the limbs. **(p. 126)**

reflexes   Automatic body reactions to specific stimulation, such as the knee jerk or the Moro reflex. Many reflexes remain among adults, but the newborn also has some "primitive" reflexes that disappear as the cortex is fully developed. **(p. 115)**

rooting reflex   Stroke an infant on the cheek near the mouth and the baby will, reflexively, turn toward the touch, open his mouth, and make sucking movements. **(p. 115)**

states of consciousness   Five main sleep/awake states identified in infants, from deep sleep to active awake states. **(p. 119)**

sudden infant death syndrome (SIDS)   The unexpected death of an infant who otherwise appears healthy; also called crib death. Cause is unknown, but certain risk factors are known. **(p. 138)**

Suggested Readings

Field, T. M. (1990). *Infancy*. Cambridge, MA: Harvard University Press. Field reviews what we know about infancy in an engaging and clear style.

Kemper, K. J. (1996). *The wholistic pediatrician*. New York: HarperCollins. A fine new book that provides advice for parents about the major illnesses of infancy and childhood, including asthma, colds, colic, diarrhea, ear infections, and many others. Kemper reviews what we know about the full range of therapeutic options, from simple things a parent can do at home, through various natural remedies, to traditional medical treatments.

Rosenblith, J. F. (1992). *In the beginning: Development in the first two years of life* (2nd ed.) Newbury Park, CA: Sage. A fine basic text on infant development.

CHAPTER 5

Perceptual and Cognitive Development in Infancy and Toddlerhood

Preview Questions

1 How early can a baby learn?

2 Can a young infant see colors? Recognize his mother's face? Perceive depth? Imitate facial expressions? Understand that objects continue to exist even when they are out of sight?

3 How early do babies really hear differences in the language they are listening to?

4 What does it mean to say that babies "learn the tune before the words"?

5 Is there any way we can predict which babies are likely to have very high, or very low, IQ scores later on?

Chapter Outline

Several years ago, my husband and I lived in Germany for eight months. Because he was born in Germany and has many relatives there who speak no English, it seemed like a good idea for me to learn enough German to be able to speak to his family. So I took intensive German classes and struggled to learn new vocabulary and complex grammar. The entire process turned out to be a lot harder than I had expected, but it certainly gave me a chance to observe the ways I go about learning, remembering, and using new information. I had, throughout, an almost physical sense of my brain at work, struggling to create order and sense out of a bombardment of new information. (Periodically, my brain would simply go on strike and refuse to take in anything more—a sensation I suspect most of you have had at one time or another!)

In our everyday lives each of us faces myriad tasks that call for the same kinds of skills I used in my efforts to learn this new language. We study for exams, try to remember what to buy at the grocery store, balance the checkbook, remember phone numbers, use a map. Not all of us do these things equally well or equally quickly, but all of us perform such activities every day of our lives. Infants, too, perhaps even more than adults, must learn, compare, remember. To be sure, they aren't yet learning how to balance a checkbook or read a map. But for an infant, *everything* is new. He must learn a language, figure out how to recognize familiar objects and what each object is used for; he must compare, contrast, and discriminate objects from one another.

These activities are all part of what psychologists call *cognitive functioning*. What I will be exploring here, and in the parallel chapters on cognition for each age period throughout the book, is how we all acquire and maintain the ability to do all these things. One-year-olds cannot use maps or understand that a piece of clay weighs the same even when you change its shape. How do they come to be able to do so? And how do we explain the fact that not all children learn these things at the same rate or become as skilled?

Theoretical Perspectives

Answering questions like these has been complicated by the fact that psychologists have developed three distinctly different views of cognition, each of which has led to a separate body of research and commentary.

Historically, the first approach to studying cognitive development was focused on individual differences. It is inescapably true that people differ in their intellectual skill, their ability to remember

These babies may look like they are merely "playing," but they are also engaged in important cognitive activities—trying to understand the world around them.

things, the speed with which they solve problems, their ability to analyze complex situations. When we say someone is "bright" or "very intelligent," it is just such skills we mean; one typical psychologist's definition of the term "intelligence," for example, is "the aggregate or global capacity of the individual to act purposefully, to think rationally and to deal effectively with his environment" (Wechsler, 1939, p. 3). When most of us use the word *intelligence*, we also assume that we can rank-order people in their degree of intelligence, an assumption that lies directly behind the development of intelligence tests, which were designed simply to give us a way of measuring individual differences in intellectual *power*.

[?] *Critical Thinking*

When you say someone is "bright" or "intelligent," do you mean they have some kind of overall intellectual "power"? What else do you mean by these terms?

This "power" definition of intelligence, also referred to as a *psychometric* approach, held sway for many years. I'll have a great deal more to say about it in Chapter 8. Yet, despite the obvious appeal of such an approach, it has one great weakness: It does not deal with the compelling fact that intelligence *develops*. As children grow, their thinking becomes more and more abstract and complex. If you give a 5-year-old a list of things to remember to buy at the grocery store, she will have trouble remembering more than a few items, mostly because she doesn't use good strategies to aid her memory, such as rehearsing the list or organizing the items

into groups in her mind. An 8-year-old would remember more things, and probably would rehearse the list under his breath or in his head, as he was walking to the store. Or he might remember that there were three vegetables on the list, a strategy that makes it more likely that he will remember to buy all three.

The fact that intelligence develops in this way forms the foundation of the second great tradition in the study of cognitive development, the cognitive-developmental approach of Jean Piaget and his many followers. Piaget focused on the development of cognitive *structures* rather than intellectual power, on patterns of development that are *common* to all children rather than on individual differences.

These two traditions have lived side by side for some years now, like polite but not very friendly neighbors. In the past few years, though, the two have developed a mutual friend—a third view, called the **information processing** approach, that partially integrates power and structure approaches. Proponents of this third view argue that "Intelligence is not a faculty or trait of the mind. Intelligence is not mental content. *Intelligence is processing*" (Fagan, 1992, p. 82). According to this view, if we are to understand intelligence we need to uncover and find ways to measure the basic processes that make up cognitive activity. Once we have identified such basic processes, we can then ask *both* developmental and individual-differences questions: Do these basic processes change with age? Do people differ in their speed or skill in using the basic processes?

These three themes will appear again and again as we look at cognitive development in childhood and adolescence. But the research in each tradition is not equally distributed across the several age strata. In particular, Piaget's theory has

Table 5.1
Three Contrasting Views of Intelligence

Individual/psychometric	Emphasis on individual differences; intelligence is defined as intellectual power, the ability to perform mental tasks efficiently and well. This view is reflected in the development of IQ tests.
Developmental	Emphasis on changes with age in children's intellectual skills, in the ways they think and solve problems; exemplified by Piaget's and Vygotsky's theories.
Information Processing	Emphasis on the basic building blocks of intellectual activity, the processes we use to learn and solve problems. This approach can be used to analyze both individual differences and developmental patterns.

been the most clearly dominant in research on infant intelligence—perhaps because he was really the first theorist to think of the infant's behavior in terms of intelligence. Thus much of what I will be talking about in this chapter has been cast in a Piagetian framework rather than a cognitive power or information processing frame, although you will see elements of both cognitive power and information processing approaches entering into the overall theoretical fabric.

Piaget's View of the Sensorimotor Period

Recall from Chapter 2 that Piaget assumes the baby is engaged in an *adaptive* process, trying to make sense out of the world around her. She assimilates incoming information to the limited array of schemes she is born with—such as looking, listening, sucking, grasping—and accommodates those schemes based on her experiences. According to Piaget, this is the starting point for the entire process of cognitive development. He called this primitive form of thinking *sensorimotor intelligence,* and the entire stage he called the *sensorimotor period.*

Basic Features of Sensorimotor Intelligence.
In Piaget's view, the baby comes equipped only with reflexes and simple sensory and motor schemes. In the beginning she is entirely tied to the immediate present, responding to whatever stimuli are available. She does not remember events or things from one encounter to the next and does not appear to plan or intend. This gradually changes during the first 18 months as the baby comes to understand that objects continue to exist even when they are out of sight and is able to remember objects, actions, and individuals over periods of time. However, Piaget insisted that the sensorimotor infant is not yet able to *manipulate* these early mental images or memories. Nor does she use symbols to stand for objects or events. It is the new ability to manipulate internal symbols, such as words or images, that marks the beginning of the next stage, *preoperational thought,* usually beginning between 18 and 24 months of age. John Flavell summarizes all this very nicely:

> [The infant] exhibits a wholly practical, perceiving-and-doing, action-bound kind of intellectual functioning; she does not exhibit the more contemplative, reflective, symbol-manipulating kind we

Young Alexandra (4 months old) is using three different sensorimotor schemes here: looking, reaching, and grasping.

usually think of in connection with cognition. The infant "knows" in the sense of recognizing or anticipating familiar, recurring objects and happenings, and "thinks" in the sense of behaving toward them with mouth, hand, eye, and other sensory-motor instruments in predictable, organized, and often adaptive ways. (1985, p. 13)

The change from the limited repertoire of schemes available to the newborn to the ability to use symbols at roughly eighteen months is gradual, although Piaget identified six substages, summarized in Table 5.2.

Each substage represents some specific advance. Substage 2 is marked especially by the beginning of those important coordinations between looking and listening, reaching and looking, and reaching and sucking that are such central features of the 2-month-old's means of exploring the world. The term **primary circular reactions** refers to the many simple repetitive actions we see at this stage, each organized around the infant's own body. The baby accidentally sucks his thumb one day, finds it pleasurable, and repeats the action. **Secondary circular reactions,** in substage 3, differ only in that the baby is now repeating some action in order to trigger a reaction outside his own body. The baby coos and Mom smiles, so the baby coos again, apparently in order to get Mom to smile again; the baby accidentally hits the mobile hanging above his crib, it moves, and he then waves his arm around again, apparently with some intent to make

Table 5.2

Substages of the Sensorimotor Period According to Piaget

Substage	Age	Piaget's Label	Characteristics
1	0–1 mo.	Reflexes	Practice of built-in schemes or reflexes such as sucking or looking. Primitive schemes begin to change through very small steps of accommodation. No imitation; no ability to integrate information from several senses.
2	1–4 mo.	Primary circular reactions	Further accommodation of basic schemes, as baby practices them endlessly—grasping, looking, sucking. Beginning coordination of schemes from different senses, so that baby now looks toward a sound and sucks on anything he can reach and bring to his mouth. But the baby does not yet link his body actions to some result outside his body.
3	4–8 mo.	Secondary circular reactions	Baby becomes much more aware of events outside his own body, and makes them happen again in a kind of trial-and-error learning. Not clear that there is understanding of the causal links yet, however. Imitation may occur, but only of schemes already in the baby's repertoire. Beginning understanding of the "object concept" also detected in this period.
4	8–12 mo.	Coordination of secondary schemes	Clear intentional means-ends behavior. The baby not only goes after what she wants, she may combine two schemes to do so, such as knocking a pillow away to reach a toy. Imitation of novel behaviors occurs, as does transfer of information from one sense to the other (cross-modal transfer).
5	12–18 mo.	Tertiary circular reactions	"Experimentation" begins, in which the infant tries out new ways of playing with or manipulating objects. Very active, very purposeful, trial-and-error exploration.
6	18–24 mo.	Beginning of representational thought	Development of use of symbols to represent objects or events. Child understands that the symbol is separate from the object. Deferred imitation occurs first here, because it requires ability to represent internally the event to be imitated.

it move again. These initial connections between body actions and external consequences are pretty automatic, very like a kind of operant conditioning. Only in substage 4 do we see the beginnings of real understanding of causal connections, and at this point the baby really moves into exploratory high gear.

In substage 5 this becomes even more marked with the emergence of what Piaget calls **tertiary circular reactions.** In this pattern the baby is not content merely to repeat the original behavior but tries out variations. The baby in substage 5 might try out many other sounds or facial expressions to see if they would trigger Mom's smile, or he might

try moving his hand in new ways or directions in order to make the mobile move in new ways. At this stage the baby's behavior has a purposeful, experimental quality. Nonetheless, Piaget thought that even in substage 5 the baby does not have internal *symbols* to stand for objects. The development of such symbols is the mark of substage 6.

Piaget's descriptions of this sequence of development, largely based on remarkably detailed observations of his own three children, have provoked a very rich array of research, some of which confirms the general outlines of his proposals, some of which does not. Let me illustrate the current findings by focusing on several specific lines of re-

Three-month-old Andrea may be showing a secondary circular reaction here, shaking her hand repeatedly to hear the sound of the rattle. In learning theory language, we could say that the pleasure from the sound is reinforcing her hand-shaking behavior.

search: early learning and memory; early perceptual skills, including the ability to combine data from more than one sense; imitation; and the object concept. Not all this research has been done within an explicitly Piagetian framework, but it nonetheless helps us to get a sense of what the baby can do, as well as to evaluate aspects of Piaget's theory.

Learning and Habituation

Most of the work on learning in infancy has been stimulated not by Piaget's theory but by the broader nature/nurture controversy. Those who argue that a child's behaviors and characteristics are a product of experience, rather than being genetically patterned, have attempted to demonstrate that an infant can, indeed, learn from such experience.

The question of whether very young infants learn from experience also has some practical relevance for parents or child-care workers because it touches on the issue of what kind of stimulation is appropriate or helpful for young babies. For example, if a child's perceptual abilities develop largely through maturation rather than learning, it doesn't make much sense to hang mobiles above a baby's crib. But if babies are able to learn from their experience beginning in the earliest days of life, then it would be good to provide various kinds of enrich-

ment, including mobiles or toys of various kinds. What does the evidence tell us?

Classical Conditioning. The bulk of the research suggests that the newborn can be classically conditioned, although it is difficult. It is most likely to be successful when the conditioning relates to feeding in some way, perhaps because these responses are so critical for the infant's survival. As one example, Elliott Blass and his colleagues (Blass, Ganchrow, & Steiner, 1984) gave 1- to 2-day-old infants sugar water in a bottle (the unconditional stimulus), which prompted sucking (the unconditioned response). Then, just before the sugar water was given, the babies' foreheads were stroked (the conditional stimulus). After several such repetitions, the experimenters stroked the infants' foreheads without giving the sugar water, to see if the babies would begin sucking—which they did, thus showing classical conditioning.

Once a baby is 3 or 4 weeks of age, classical conditioning is no longer difficult to establish; it occurs easily with many different responses. In particular, this means that the conditioned emotional responses I talked about in Chapter 2 may begin to develop as early as the first weeks of life. Thus the mere presence of Mom or Dad or other favored person can trigger the sense of "feeling good," a pattern that may contribute to what we see later as the child's attachment to the parent.

[?] *Critical Thinking*

Can you think of other examples of classically conditioned emotional responses that might develop in early infancy? What about negative emotions?

Operant Conditioning. Newborns also clearly learn by operant conditioning. Both the sucking response and head turning have been successfully increased by the use of reinforcements such as sweet-tasting liquids or the sound of the mother's voice or heartbeat (Moon & Fifer, 1990). At the least, the fact that conditioning of this kind can take place means that whatever neurological wiring is needed for learning to occur is present at birth. Results like this also tell us something about the sorts of reinforcements that are effective with very young children; it is surely highly significant for the whole process of mother-infant interaction that the mother's voice is an effective reinforcer for virtually all babies.

Schematic Learning.

The fact that babies can recognize voices and heartbeats in the first days of life is also important because it suggests that another kind of learning is going on as well. This third type of learning, sometimes referred to as **schematic learning,** draws both its name and many of its conceptual roots from Piaget's theory. The basic idea is that from the beginning the baby organizes her experiences into expectancies or "known" combinations. These expectancies, often called *schemas*, are built up over many exposures to particular experiences. Once formed, they help the baby to distinguish between the familiar and the unfamiliar. Carolyn Rovee-Collier (1986) has suggested that we might think of classical conditioning in infants as being a variety of

An obvious example of early operant conditioning: Young Jane, who is 1 month old in this picture, has improved her sucking technique since her birth, presumably in part because her more efficient efforts have been reinforced with a better flow of milk. In Piaget's language, Jane's basic sensorimotor sucking scheme has been accommodated (adapted) as a result of experience.

schematic learning. When a baby begins to move her head as if to search for the nipple as soon as she hears her mom's footsteps coming into the room, in classical-conditioning terms she is indeed displaying a conditioned response, but we could also think of this behavior as the beginning of the development of expectancies. From the earliest weeks, the baby seems to begin to make connections between events in her world, such as the link between the sound of her mother's footsteps and the feeling of being picked up or between the touch of the breast and the feeling of a full stomach. Thus early classical conditioning may be the beginnings of the process of cognitive development.

Habituation.

A related concept is that of **habituation.** Habituation is the automatic reduction in the strength or vigor of a response to a repeated stimulus. For example, suppose you live on a fairly noisy street. The sound of cars going by is repeated over and over during each day. Yet, after a while, you not only don't react to the sound, you quite literally *do not perceive it as being as loud.* The ability to do this—to dampen down the intensity of a physical response to some repeated stimulus—is obviously vital in our everyday lives. If we reacted constantly to every sight and sound and smell that came along, we'd spend all our time responding to these repeated events and not have energy or attention left over for things that are new and deserve attention.

The ability to *dishabituate* is equally important. When a habituated stimulus changes in some way, such as a sudden extra-loud screech of tires on the busy street by your house, you again respond fully. This reemergence of the original response strength is a sign that the perceiver—infant, child, or adult—notices some significant change.

The ability both to habituate and to dishabituate is already present in rudimentary form in a newborn and is well developed by 10 weeks of age. An infant will stop looking at something you keep putting in front of her face; she will stop showing a startle reaction (Moro reflex) to loud sounds after the first few presentations but will again startle if the sound is changed; she will stop turning her head toward a repeating sound (Swain, Zelazo, & Clifton, 1993). Such habituation itself is not a voluntary process; it is entirely automatic. Yet in order for it to work, the newborn must be equipped with the capacity to "recognize" familiar experiences. That is, she must have, or must develop, schemas of some kind.

The existence of these processes in the newborn has an added benefit for researchers: It has enabled them to figure out what an infant responds to as "the same" or "different." If a baby is habituated to some stimulus, such as a sound or a specific photograph, the experimenter can then present slight variations on the original stimulus to see the point at which dishabituation occurs. In this way researchers have begun to get a picture of how the newborn baby or young infant experiences the world around him.

Critical Thinking

Try to imagine a baby who is unable to habituate. What might be the consequences of such a lack?

Results of research of this type tell us that Piaget underestimated the very young infant. Newborns have a good deal to work with besides just primitive schemes applied one at a time. From the earliest weeks of life they can learn connections between their own actions and environmental results, they can create expectancies about which events go together, and they have some ability—however automatic—to store information about previously occurring events so that habituation and dishabituation are possible.

Memory

Such an ability to store information is also obviously part of the baby's emerging memory skills, shown very cleverly in a series of studies by Carolyn Rovee-Collier and her colleagues (Bhatt & Rovee-Collier, 1996; Hartshorn & Rovee-Collier, 1997; Hayne & Rovee-Collier, 1995; Rovee-Collier, 1993). In her most widely used procedure, Rovee-Collier uses an ingenious variation of an operant conditioning procedure to demonstrate that babies as young as age 3 months can remember specific objects, and their own actions with those objects, over periods of as long as a week.

Rovee-Collier first hangs an attractive mobile over the baby's crib and watches to see how the baby responds. In particular, she is interested in how often the baby normally kicks his legs while

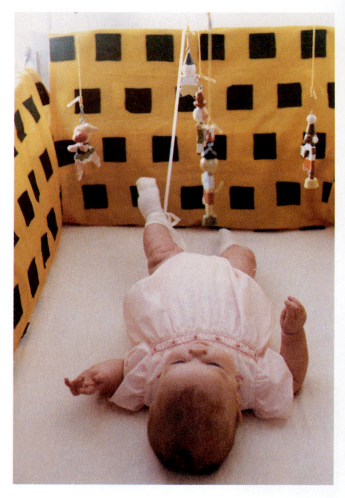

Figure 5.1

This 3-month-old baby in one of Rovee-Collier's memory experiments will quickly learn to kick her foot in order to make the mobile move (an example of a secondary circular reaction). What is striking is that the baby will remember this connection between kicking and the mobile several days later.

looking at the mobile. After three minutes of this "baseline" observation, she attaches a string from the mobile to the baby's leg, as you can see in Figure 5.1, so that each time the baby kicks his leg, the mobile moves. Babies quickly learn to kick repeatedly in order to make this interesting new thing happen (what Piaget would call a secondary circular reaction). Within three to six minutes, 3-month-olds double or triple their kick rates, showing that learning has clearly occurred. Rovee-Collier then tests the baby's memory of this learning by coming back some days later, hanging the same mobile over the crib but *not* attaching the string to his foot. The crucial issue is whether the baby will kick at the mere sight of the mobile. If the baby remembers the previous occasion, he should kick at a higher rate than he did when he first saw the mobile, which is precisely what 3-month-old babies do, even after a delay of as long as a week.

Why is this so interesting? Primarily because it shows us that the young infant is cognitively a whole lot more sophisticated than we (and Piaget) had supposed. At the same time, Rovee-Collier's work also offers some kind of support for Piaget's views, since she observes systematic gains over the months of infancy in the baby's ability to remember. Two-month-olds can remember their kicking action for only one day; 3-month-olds can remember over a week, and by age 6 months the baby can remember over two weeks. At the same time, Rovee-Collier finds that all these early infant memories are *strongly* tied to the specific context in which the original experience occurred. Even 6-month-olds do not recognize or remember the mobile if you make even a very small change, such as hanging a different cloth around the playpen in which the child was originally tested. Thus babies do remember—far more than Piaget believed—but their memories are highly specific. With age, their memories become less and less tied to specific cues or contexts.

Early Perceptual Development

Have you ever seen a toddler trying to feed herself something mushy and messy like chocolate pudding? It is a wonderful and fascinating sight—more charming, of course, if someone else has to clean up the child afterward! In the beginning, most toddlers don't have very good aim, so the pudding goes in the hair, all over the face, and down the front of the shirt. Most babies are not at all bothered by the mess and will look at you with delighted grins in the midst of the goo.

In fact, it is no small task for the toddler to get that spoon reliably into her mouth. It obviously involves motor skills, since she has to be able to grasp the spoon and move her hand and arm toward her mouth. Still, motor skills alone are not enough. She also has to use a wide range of *perceptual* information. She has to see the spoon and/or feel it in her hand, estimate the distance from the mouth, and gauge the appropriate trajectory, all the while coordinating the visual and kinesthetic information as she goes along, so that she can change her aim if she needs to.

Genevieve is doing a pretty good job of getting the food into her mouth—using not just motor skills but also important perceptual skills.

How do these crucial perceptual skills develop? We have a rich body of research information to help us answer this question. To simplify the descriptive task, let me divide the information into two rough groups, which we might call "basic" and "more complex" skills. The distinction I am using here is similar to the distinction between sensation and perception given in most psychology texts. When we study *sensation* we are asking just what information the sensory organs receive. When we study *perception* we are asking what the individual does with the sensory information, how it is interpreted or combined. Let us begin with the basics.

Basic Sensory Skills

The common theme running through all I will say about basic sensory skills is that newborns and young infants have far more sensory capacity than physicians or psychologists thought even as recently as a few decades ago. Perhaps because babies' motor skills are so obviously poor, we assumed that their sensory skills were equally poor. But we were wrong. A newborn does not have all the sensory capacities of a 2-month-old, a 1-year-old, or an adult. Still, most of the basic skills are in place in at least rudimentary form.

Seeing

For example, until 25 or 30 years ago, many medical texts stated that the newborn infant was blind. Now we know that the newborn has quite poor visual **acuity** but is quite definitely not blind. The usual standard for visual acuity in adults is "20/20" vision. This means that you can see and identify something that is 20 feet away that the average person can also see at 20 feet. A person with 20/100 vision, in contrast, has to be as close as 20 feet to see something that the ordinary person can see at 100 feet. In other words, the higher the second number, the poorer the person's visual acuity. At birth the infant's acuity is in the range of 20/200 to 20/400, but it improves rapidly during the first year as a result of all the swift changes occurring in the brain I described in the last chapter, including myelination, dendritic development, and pruning. Most infants reach the level of 20/20 vision by about one year of life (Haith, 1990).

The fact that the newborn sees so poorly is not so negative a thing as it might seem at first. Of course, it does mean that a baby doesn't see faraway things very clearly; he probably can't see well enough to distinguish two people standing nearby. Yet he sees quite well close up, which is all that is necessary for most encounters with the people who care for him or with objects immediately at hand, such as breast, bottle, or mobiles hanging above his crib.

Tracking Objects in the Visual Field. When our young chocolate pudding eater tries to get the spoon in her mouth, one of the things she needs to do is keep her eyes on her hand or the spoon as she moves it toward herself. This process of following a moving object with your eyes is called **tracking,** and you do it every day in a variety of situa-

tions. You track the movement of other cars when you are driving; you track as you watch a friend walk toward you across the room; a baseball outfielder tracks the flight of the ball so that he can catch it. Because a newborn infant can't yet move independently, a lot of her experiences with objects are with things that move toward her or away from her. If she is to have any success in recognizing objects, she has to be able to keep her eyes on them as they move; she must be able to track.

> ### Critical Thinking
> Can you think of examples of professions (other than baseball playing) in which the ability to track well would be especially important?

Studies by Richard Aslin (1987) and others show that tracking is initially fairly inefficient but improves quite rapidly. Infants younger than 2 months show some tracking for brief periods if the target is moving very slowly. Somewhere around ages 6 to 10 weeks, though, a shift occurs, and babies' tracking becomes skillful rather quickly. You can see the change very graphically in Figure 5.2, taken from a study by Aslin.

Color Vision. The tale I can tell about color vision is similar. Researchers in this field have established that the types of cells in the eye (cones)

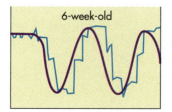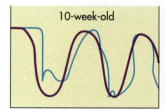

Figure 5.2

The purple line in each figure shows the trajectory of the moving line that each baby tried to follow with its eyes in Aslin's experiment. The blue line represents one baby's eye movements at 6 weeks and again at 10 weeks. At 6 weeks, the baby more or less followed the moving line, but not smoothly. By 10 weeks the same baby's tracking skill was remarkably smooth and accurate. (Sources: Aslin, 1987, p. 87; redrawn from Aslin, 1981.)

necessary for perceiving red and green are clearly present by 1 month, perhaps at birth; those required for perceiving blue are probably present by then as well (Bornstein, Tamis-LeMonda, Tal et al., 1992). Thus infants can and do see and discriminate among various colors.

Taken together, these findings certainly do not support the notion that an infant is blind at birth! While it is true that the infant's acuity is initially poor, it improves rapidly, and other visual capacities are remarkably well developed early on. There are also some interesting hints here that babies shift gears at roughly two months, since a number of skills, including the scanning of objects as well as smooth tracking, improve incrementally at about that age (Bronson, 1994). Whether this shift is the result of neurological changes, such as the rapid proliferation of synapses and the growth of dendrites I described in the last chapter, or of changes in the eye itself, or perhaps of the child's experience, we don't yet know.

Hearing

Although children's hearing improves up to adolescence, newborns' auditory acuity is actually better than their visual acuity. Within the general range of pitch and loudness of the human voice, newborns hear nearly as well as adults do. They have somewhat more difficulty with high-pitched sounds; such a sound needs to be louder before the newborn can hear it than is true for older children or adults (Werner & Gillenwater, 1990).

For parents or day-care workers the key point is that babies can hear language spoken to them without difficulty. And, as you'll see when I talk about the beginnings of the infant's own language, babies make quite remarkably fine discriminations among the language sounds they hear from very early on.

Other Senses

Smelling and Tasting. The senses of smell and taste have been studied much less, but we do have some basic knowledge. As with adults, the two senses are intricately related—that is, if you cannot smell for some reason (like when you have a cold), your taste sensitivity is also significantly reduced. Taste is detected by the taste buds on the tongue, which register four basic tastes: sweet, sour, bitter, and salty. Smell is registered in the mucous membranes of the nose and has nearly unlimited variations.

Newborns appear to respond differentially to all four of the basic flavors (Crook, 1987), as you've already seen in Chapter 4 (recall Figure 4.1, p. 117). Babies as young as a week old can also tell the difference between such complex smells as personal body odors. Specifically, they can discriminate between their mother's and other women's smells, although this seems to be true only for babies who are being breast-fed and who thus spend quite a lot of time with their noses against their mother's bare skin (Cernoch & Porter, 1985).

Touch. The infant's sense of touch may well be the best developed of all. Certainly this sense is sufficiently well developed to get the baby fed. If

---

Table 5.3

Summary of Basic Sensory Skills in Young Infants

Visual acuity	Babies are initially quite nearsighted; achieve adult acuity by age 1.
Tracking of objects	Newborns have primitive ability; big improvement at 2 months.
Color vision	Red and green and probably blue perception are all present by 1 month or earlier.
Hearing acuity	Babies have excellent hearing within the range and loudness of the human voice.
Smelling and tasting	Babies can apparently discriminate among the four major flavors and among some complex smells.
Touch	Infants have a well-developed sense of touch at birth, especially around the mouth and on the hands.

you think back to the list of reflexes in the newborn I gave you in Chapter 4, you'll realize that the rooting reflex relies on a touch stimulus to the cheek and that the sucking reflex relies on touch in the mouth. Babies appear to be especially sensitive to touches on the mouth, the face, the hands, the soles of the feet, and the abdomen, with less sensitivity in other parts of the body (Reisman, 1987).

Putting together all these pieces of information about the basic perceptual skills, Reisman says, "We think of infants as helpless but they are born with some exquisitely tuned sensory abilities" (1987, p. 265).

Complex Perceptual Skills: Preferences, Discriminations, and Patterns

When we turn to studies of more complex perceptual skills, the abilities of very young infants seem even more striking. Very young infants are able to make remarkably fine discriminations among sounds, sights, and feelings, and they pay attention to and respond to *patterns*, not just to individual events. I have room here only to sample this fascinating body of research, but a few examples will give you the flavor.

Depth Perception

One of the complex skills that has been most studied is depth perception. You need this ability any time you reach for something or decide whether you have room to make a left turn before an oncoming car gets to you. In these cases and many, many others, you need to judge distance or depth, just as our young pudding eater does when she tries to aim her spoon toward the bowl of pudding.

An infant needs to be able to judge depth in order to perform all kinds of simple tasks, including judging how far away an object is so that he can reach for it or how far it is to the floor if he has ideas about crawling off the edge of the couch. So it is useful to know just how early an infant can

To reach for this toy, 5-month-old Shina-Mira has to be able to judge depth. How far away is the toy? Is it near enough for her to reach with her hand?

judge depth. This is still an active area of research, so the answer I can give you is not final. The best conclusion at the moment seems to be that babies begin to be able to make this kind of judgment at about age 3 months and are quite skilled by 5 to 7 months—just in time for crawling (Bornstein et al., 1992).

The most famous research on depth perception has been the work of Eleanor Gibson and Richard Walk (1960), who devised an apparatus called a **visual cliff.** You can see from Figure 5.3 that it consists of a large glass table with a sort of runway in the middle. On one side of the runway is a checkerboard pattern immediately below the glass; on the other side—the "cliff" side—the checkerboard is several feet below the glass. If a baby has no depth perception, she should be equally willing to crawl on either side of the runway, but if she can judge

Figure 5.3

In this "visual cliff" apparatus, like the one used by Gibson and Walk, Mom tries to entice her baby out onto the "cliff" side. But because the infant this age (about 6 months) can perceive depth, he thinks he will fall if he comes toward her, so he stays put, looking concerned.

depth, she should be reluctant to crawl out on the "cliff" side.

Since an infant has to be able to crawl in order to be tested in the Gibson and Walk procedure, the original subjects were all 6 months old or older. Most of these infants did *not* crawl out on the cliff side but were quite willing to crawl out on the shallow side. In other words, 6-month-old babies have depth perception.

What about younger infants? One strategy researchers have used is to show a younger infant a film of an object moving toward him, apparently on a collision course. If the infant has some depth perception, he should flinch, move to one side, or blink as the object appears to come very close.

Such flinching has been consistently observed in 3-month-olds (Yonas & Owsley, 1987) but not usually in younger babies. Most experts now agree that this is about the lower age limit of depth perception.

Discriminating Mom from Other People

A complex perceptual skill that is apparent even earlier is the ability to discriminate one face from another. For years I have been telling my friends and relatives that there was clear research showing that babies can't recognize their mothers' faces until at least a month or two of age. None of my friends or relatives believed me; they all said, "I don't care what the research says; I know my baby could recognize my face right away." Well, it looks like they were right and the older research (and I) was wrong.

[?] *Critical Thinking*

Does this mean that researchers ought to believe mothers and fathers more often when they describe what their babies can do? How should scientists weigh anecdotal evidence against research evidence?

We have known for some time that newborns could distinguish between Mom and someone else on the basis of sound. DeCasper and Fifer (1980) found that a newborn could tell his mother's voice from another female voice (but not his father's voice from another male voice) and preferred the mother's, possibly because the baby has become familiar with the mother's voice while still *in utero*. By age 6 months, babies can even match voices with faces. If you put an infant of this age in a situation where she can see both her father and mother and can hear a tape-recorded voice of one of them, she will look toward the parent whose voice she hears (Spelke & Owsley, 1979).

The ability to discriminate between Mom and someone else on the basis of smell also seems to be part of the baby's very early repertoire, as I pointed out a few pages ago. What has been most surprising is the discovery that newborns can also recognize their mothers by sight. Several studies now show this. One of the clearest and cleanest is by Gail Walton (Walton, Bower, & Bower, 1992). Walton videotaped the faces of 12 mothers of newborns and then matched each of these videos with a video of another woman whose hair color, eye color, complexion and hair style were the same as Mom's. Each baby was then shown these two pictures one at a time and could keep the picture turned on by sucking on a pacifier. In this way Walton could count how often the babies sucked in order to keep Mom's picture available, compared with their frequency of sucking for the non-Mom photo. Walton's test babies, who were only a day or two old at the time of the experiment, clearly sucked longer in order to keep the picture of Mom available, as you can see in Figure 5.4. These babies, then, could not only tell the difference between the two faces, they also preferred the mother's face. Walton also has some preliminary

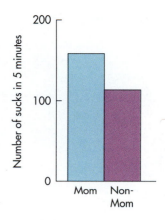

Figure 5.4

The babies in this study were 12 to 36 hours old at the time they were tested. They sucked more to see a picture of Mom than a picture of another woman who looked very much like Mom. (Source: Walton, Bower, & Bower, 1992, p. 267.)

information that babies do *not* discriminate, or do not prefer, their fathers' faces as early as this.

This is a fascinating result. A baby can learn the sound of the mother's voice *in utero* but obviously has to learn the details of the mother's features after birth. Walton's study tells us that babies achieve such learning within hours of birth—an achievement I find remarkable.

Beyond the question of preference, there is also the issue of just what it is that babies are looking at when they scan a face. Before about age 2 months, babies seem to look mostly at the edges of the faces (the hairline and the chin); after 2 months they seem to look more at the internal features, particularly the eyes.

What Babies Look At

This change at about two months in the way babies look at faces is part of a more general shift at about that age in the ways babies look at all objects. From the first days of life, babies scan the world around themselves—not very smoothly or skillfully, to be sure, but nonetheless regularly, even in the dark (Haith, 1980). They will keep moving their eyes until they come to a sharp light/dark contrast, which typically signals the edge of some object. Having found such an edge, the baby stops searching and moves his eyes back and forth across and around the edge. These strategies, which Haith (1980) calls "rules babies look by," seem to change

Research Report

Langlois's Studies of Babies' Preferences for Attractive Faces

So many of the current studies on infant perception seem to point toward the conclusion that many more abilities and preferences are built in than we had supposed. Among all this new work, Judith Langlois's studies of infant preferences for attractive faces rank as some of the most surprising and intriguing. Langlois has found that babies as young as 2 months old will look longer at a face that adults rate as attractive than at one adults judge to be less attractive.

In the first study in this series, Langlois and her colleagues (Langlois, Roggman, Casey et al., 1987) tested 2- to 3-month-olds and 6- to 8-month-olds. Each baby, while seated on Mom's lap, was shown pairs of color slides of 16 adult Caucasian women, half rated by adult judges as attractive, half rated as unattractive. For each trial, the baby saw two slides simultaneously shown on a screen in front of him/her, with each face approximately life-size, while the experimenter peeked through a hole in the screen to count the number of seconds the baby looked at each picture. Each baby saw some attractive/attractive pairs, some unattractive/unattractive pairs, and some mixed pairs. With mixed pairs, even the 2- and 3-month-old babies consistently looked longer at the attractive faces, as you can see below.

One of the nice features of this study is that the researchers used a variety of attractive and unattractive faces. In a later study, Langlois added even more variability by using pictures of men and women, African-American women's faces, and baby faces (Langlois, Ritter, Roggman, & Vaughn, 1991). Again she found that for all these types of face pairs, babies looked longer at the faces that had been rated by adults as more attractive.

In another exploration of this same issue, Langlois observed 1-year-old babies interacting with an adult wearing either an attractive or an unattractive mask

(Langlois, Roggman, & Rieser-Danner, 1990). She found that the toddlers showed more positive affective tone, less withdrawal, and more play involvement with the stranger in the attractive mask. These 1-year-olds also played more with an attractive than with an unattractive doll.

It is hard to imagine what sort of learning experiences could account for such a preference in a 2-month-old. Instead, these findings raise the possibility that there is some inborn template for the "correct" or "most desired" shape and configuration for members of our species, and that we simply prefer those who match this template better. Indeed, in support of this possibility, Langlois has found that the faces babies (and adults) find most attractive and prefer to look at most are those that represent the mathematical average of human faces (Langlois & Roggman, 1990; Langlois, Roggman, & Musselman, 1994)—faces that are highly symmetrical and regular. These preferences have real implications for the ways parents interact with their infants and for the way teachers, other adults, and peers later judge and behave toward attractive and unattractive children. For example, Langlois has found that mothers of infants that judges rate as more attractive show more affection and playfulness toward their newborns than do mothers of infants rated as less attractive (Langlois, Ritter, Casey, & Sawin, 1995). Langlois also finds that, across a variety of studies, attractive children are judged as having greater competence, and as being better-adjusted and more socially appealing. They have fewer negative and more positive interactions with peers and adults and receive more attention and caregiving (Langlois, Kalakanis, Rubenstein, Larson, & Hallam, 1997). All in all, Langlois's results raise a whole host of fascinating, and highly practical, questions.

Average Looking Time (in seconds)

	2–3-month-olds	6–8-month-olds	Male and Female	Black Women	Baby Faces
Attractive faces	9.22*	7.24*	7.82*	7.05*	7.16*
Unattractive faces	8.01	6.59	7.57	6.52	6.62

*Contrast between attractive and unattractive faces is statistically significant.

Sources: Langlois et al., 1987, from Table 1, p. 365; Langlois et al., 1991, Table 1, p. 81.

At age 2 weeks, Rosa can already discriminate Mom's face from the face of another woman, and can also recognize Mom's voice and smell.

at about age 2 months, perhaps because the cortex has developed more fully then, perhaps because of experience, or both. Whatever the cause, at about this time the baby's attention seems to shift from *where* an object is to *what* an object is. Put another way, the baby seems to move from a scanning strategy designed primarily to *nd things* to a strategy designed primarily to *identify* things.

Discriminating Emotional Expressions

At about the same time—2 to 3 months of age— babies begin to respond differently to various emotional expressions as well as to facial features. For example, Haviland and Lelwica (1987) found that when mothers expressed happiness, 10-week-old babies looked happy and interested and gazed at the mother; when the mother expressed sadness,

babies showed increased mouth movements or looked away; when the mother expressed anger, some babies cried vigorously while others showed a kind of still or "frozen" look. These responses did not seem to be merely imitation, but rather responses to the parent's specific emotions.

By 5 or 6 months, babies respond differently to strangers' faces displaying different emotions (Balaban, 1995), as well as to voices speaking with varying emotional tones. They can tell the difference between happy and sad voices and between happy, surprised, and fearful faces (Nelson, 1987; Walker-Andrews & Lennon, 1991). By roughly ten to twelve months, infants may use such emotional cues to help them figure out what to do in novel situations, such as when a stranger comes to visit, when they are in the doctor's office, or even when a new toy is put in front of them. Babies this age will first look at Mom's or Dad's face or listen to their tone of voice to check for the adult's emotional reaction, a process researchers call **social referencing** (Desrochers, Ricard, Décarie, & Allard, 1994; Hirshberg & Svejda, 1990; Mumme, Fernald, & Herrera, 1996; Walden, 1991). If Mom looks and sounds pleased or happy, the baby is likely to explore the new toy with more ease or accept a stranger with less fuss. If Mom looks and sounds concerned or frightened, the baby responds to those cues and reacts to the novel situation with equivalent fear or concern. Indeed, the baby will try to position herself so that she can see the mother's face; if the mother moves, the baby may move to stay in eye-shot. Incidentally, as a parent or teacher, you can use this social referencing process to help a child regulate her emotions. Knowing your child will check your facial expression in a potentially scary situation, you can deliberately keep your expression neutral or interested. In this way, you help the child dampen down the expression of her own anxiety.

Responding to Patterns

To me, the most surprising discovery to come out of the surge of new research on perception is that babies as young as 3 or 4 months old pay attention to *relationships* among objects or among features of objects. For example, suppose you show babies a series of drawings, one at a time, each of which shows a small object above a larger object of the same shape—something like the ones in the top row of

Habituation stimuli

Test stimulus

Figure 5.5

Caron and Caron used pictures like these in a study designed to check whether babies were paying attention to the patterns or the relationships among stimuli. Babies were first habituated to a series of pictures, each of which displayed the same pattern, like those in the upper row. Then they were tested either on more of the same or on one with a reverse pattern, like the one on the bottom. Three- and 4-month old babies show renewed interest in the test stimulus, which indicates that they noticed the pattern and see that it has now changed.

Figure 5.5. After seeing a series of such pictures, babies will habituate; that is, they will look for shorter and shorter periods until they are barely glancing at a new version of the figure before looking away. "Ho hum, another one of those." Once habituation is established, you can then throw in a test picture that illustrates the opposite pattern (in this case, big over small), like the one shown at the bottom of Figure 5.5. What you are likely to find is that babies of 3 and 4 months will show renewed interest in this different pattern. This tells us that the baby's original habituation had not been to the *speci c* stimuli but to a *pattern* (Caron & Caron, 1981).

Cross-Modal Transfer

So far I have talked about seeing, hearing, and smelling as if we experience the world through only one sense at a time. Yet if you think about the way you receive and use perceptual information, you'll realize quickly that you rarely have information

from only one sense at one time. Ordinarily, you have some complex combination of sound, sight, touch, and smell. Psychologists have been interested in knowing how early an infant can combine such information. For example, how early can an infant integrate information from several senses, such as knowing which mouth movements go with which sounds? Even more complex, how early can a baby learn something via one sense and transfer that information to another sense? For example, at what age can a child recognize solely by feel a toy he has seen but never felt before? The first of these two skills is usually called **intersensory integration,** while the latter is called **cross-modal** (or intermodal) **transfer.**

Piaget believed that both these skills were simply not present until quite late in the first year of life, after the infant had accumulated many experiences with specific objects and how they simulta-

Even though 7-month-old Leslie is not looking at this toy while she is chewing on it, she is nonetheless learning something about how it *ought* to look, just based on how it feels in her mouth and in her hands—an example of cross-modal transfer.

Research Report

Babies Even Learn Patterns *in Utero*

The ability to recognize complex patterns is present even before birth. A study by Anthony DeCasper (DeCasper & Spence, 1986) is a particularly striking example. He had pregnant women read a children's story like Dr. Seuss's *The Cat in the Hat* out loud each day for the final six weeks of their pregnancy. After the infants were born, he tested each baby using a procedure based on operant conditioning. He found that these babies would learn to suck on a pacifier in a particular way in order to listen to a recording of the familiar story, but did not increase their sucking in order to listen to an unfamiliar story. That is, the familiar story was reinforcing, while the unfamiliar story was not, showing that the babies preferred the sound of the story they had heard *in utero*. In a more recent study, done in France, DeCasper had pregnant women recite a short children's rhyme out loud each day between weeks 33 and 37 of their pregnancy (DeCasper, Lecaneut, Busnel, Granier-Deferre, & Maugeais, 1994). In week 38 he played a recording of either the same rhyme the mother had

been reading or another, unfamiliar rhyme and then measured the fetal heart rate. DeCasper found that fetal heart rates dropped during the recording of the familiar rhyme but not during the unfamiliar rhyme. So even in the last weeks of gestation the fetus is already paying attention to and discriminating among complex patterns of sounds.

I find these results amazing. I am also struck by the kinds of practical implications they have for the ways parents (or day-care workers) interact with infants. It obviously makes sense to read to your child, beginning in earliest infancy, a point I'll be coming back to in Chapter 8. Similarly, it makes sense to provide babies with a rich visual or auditory environment—mobiles, rattles, pictures on the crib, or whatever—because infants are hard at work extracting information from everything around them. Just as physical practice strengthens the body's muscles, so practice at discovering patterns very likely has a similar "strengthening" effect on babies' intellectual development.

neously looked, sounded, and felt. Other theorists, including James and Eleanor Gibson, have argued that some intersensory integration or even transfer is built in from birth. The baby then builds on that inborn set of skills with specific experience with objects. Research favors the Gibsonian view: Empirical findings show that cross-modal transfer is possible as early as age 1 month and becomes common by 6 months (Rose & Ruff, 1987).

For example, if you attach a nubby sphere to a pacifier and let a baby suck on it, you can test for cross-modal transfer by showing the baby pictures of a nubby sphere and a smooth sphere. If the baby looks longer at the nubby sphere, that would suggest cross-modal transfer. In one recent study of this type, Kaye and Bower demonstrated such transfer in infants 12 *hours* old (1994), a result that provides a strong argument for the "nature" side of the ancient dispute.

In older infants intersensory integration and transfer can be readily demonstrated, not only between touch and sight but between other modalities such as sound and sight. For instance, in one study, Jeffery Pickens (1994) showed 5-month-old babies

two films side by side, each displaying a train moving along a track. Then, out of a loudspeaker, he played recordings of engine sounds of various types. In one recording the engine sounds got gradually louder (as if the engine were coming closer), while in the other the engine sounds got gradually fainter (as if the engine were moving away). The babies in this experiment looked longer at the film of a train whose movement matched the pattern of engine sounds. That is, they appeared to have some understanding of the link between the pattern of sound and the pattern of movement—knowledge that not only demonstrates intersensory integration but also suggests surprisingly sophisticated understanding of the accompaniments of motion.

Equally remarkable is a study in which the researchers showed 7-month-olds pairs of faces displaying happy and angry expressions. Simultaneously, the baby heard a recording of words spoken either in a happy or angry voice. The babies looked longer at the face that matched the *emotion* in the speaking voice—a finding that again points to remarkable sophistication of intermodal integration, and remarkably sophisticated knowledge about emotional expression, by age 7 or 8 months (Soken & Pick, 1992).

I do not want to leave you with the impression that intermodal integration or transfer is a completely automatic process in young infants. It isn't. In 4- and 5-month-olds, it often doesn't occur at all, or only under special circumstances (Lewkowicz, 1994). Still, it is clear that young infants have at least some ability to link simultaneous information from several senses.

All in all, Piaget seems to have been wrong not only about the specific ages at which many of these cognitive and perceptual skills develop but perhaps even in whether they need to "develop" at all. It begins to look as if a great deal of basic understanding about the events in the world is already "built in" at birth—a conclusion further buttressed by recent studies of the object concept.

Development of the Object Concept

One of Piaget's most striking observations of infants was that they seemed not to have a grasp of certain basic properties of objects that adults take completely for granted. You and I know that objects exist outside of our own actions on them. My computer exists independent of my looking at it, and I know that it continues to sit here in my office even if I am somewhere else—an understanding that Piaget called **object permanence.** Piaget thought that babies did not initially know any of these things about objects and acquired this understanding only gradually during the sensorimotor period.

According to his observations, replicated frequently by later researchers, the first sign that the baby is developing object permanence comes at about age 2 months (in substage 2). Suppose you show a toy to a child of this age, then put a screen in front of the toy and remove the toy. When you then remove the screen, the baby shows some indication of surprise, as if she knew that something should still be there. The child thus seems to have a rudimentary schema or expectation about the permanence of an object. At the same time, infants of this age show no signs of searching for a toy they may have dropped over the edge of the crib or that has disappeared beneath a blanket or behind a screen—a pattern of reaction that parents take advantage of when an infant is fussing for some toy or object he can't reach, or when the parent wants an infant to stop fooling with some object. With young infants, the parent can simply put the object out of sight. Out of sight, out of mind.

In substage 3 (at about age 6 or 8 months), however, this begins to change. Babies *will* look over the edge of the crib for the dropped toys or for food that was spilled. (In fact, babies of this age may drive their parents nuts playing "dropsy" in the high chair.) Infants this age will also search for partially hidden objects. If you put a favorite toy under a cloth but leave part of it sticking out, the infant will reach for the toy, indicating that in some sense the infant "recognizes" that the whole object is there even though she can see only part of it. However, if you cover the toy completely with the cloth or put it behind a screen, the infant will stop looking at it and will not reach for it, even if she has seen you put the cloth over it—a pattern shown clearly in the photos in Figure 5.6.

By ages 8 to 12 months, the "out of sight, out of mind" strategy no longer works at all. Infants this age will reach for or search for a toy that has been

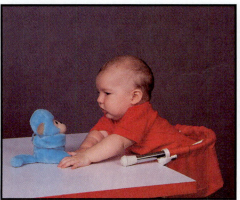 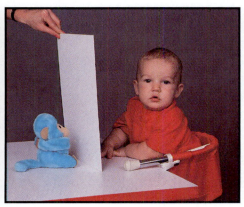

Figure 5.6

A baby in stage 3 of the development of object constancy. The infant stops reaching as soon as the screen is put in front of the toy and shows no sign of knowing that the toy is still there. (As an aside: The type of hook-on-the-table seat shown in these photos is nowadays thought to be dangerous by many pediatricians and is no longer recommended.)

Psychology in Action

Development of the Object Concept

Warning: This project, like many of the *Psychology in Action* suggestions given in this text, should not be undertaken without explicit permission and guidance from your instructor, who will have to obtain permission from your college or university's Human Subjects Review Committee for any project in which you interview or observe a child or parent directly. **Do not do this project on your own, without such permission.**

For this project, you need to locate an infant between 6 and 12 months of age. Obtain permission from the baby's parents, following the procedure your instructor specifies; ask one parent (or both) to be there while you're presenting the materials to the baby.

Procedure

Ask the parents to loan you two of the baby's favorite toys. Place the baby in a sitting position—in a high chair, at a table, or on the parent's lap at a table, or on the floor—in such a way that he can reach for the toy easily. Then perform the following steps:

1. While the baby is watching, place the toy in full view and easy reach. See if the infant reaches for the toy.
2. In full view of the infant, cover part of the toy with a handkerchief, so that only part of it is visible. Does the baby reach for the toy?

3. Take away the handkerchief; wait until the baby is reaching for the toy and then cover it completely with the handkerchief. Does the baby continue reaching? Does the baby try to pull the cloth away or search for the toy in some way?
4. Again, take away the handkerchief. Using a different toy, in full sight of the child (but before the child reaches for the toy), cover the toy completely with the cloth. Does the infant begin reaching for the toy?

Analysis and Report

Jackson, Campos, and Fischer (1978) found that step 2 (continuing to reach for the partly covered toy) is typically "passed" at about age 26 weeks; step 3 (continuing to reach for a fully covered toy) at about 28 or 29 weeks; and the final step (reaching for the toy that was fully covered before the child began to reach) at about 30 or 31 weeks. The closer to these ages your infant is, the more interesting your results are likely to be.

Did your subject's performance conform to those expectations? If not, why do you think it might be different? You might read the Jackson, Campos, and Fischer paper to see some of the reasons they give for differences in results from several studies. Do you think it mattered, for example, that a familiar toy was used? Did it matter that the mother or father was present?

covered completely by a cloth or hidden by a screen. Thus, by 12 months, most infants appear to grasp the basic fact that objects continue to exist even when they are no longer visible.

This sequence of development has been so compelling, so interesting, and so surprising to many psychologists that it has been the subject of reams of research. Until recently, most researchers had concluded that Piaget's description of the sequence of development of the object concept was correct. Certainly, if you follow Piaget's procedures, you will see essentially the same results among children in all cultures.

Newer research, though, points to the possibility that very young babies have far more understanding of the properties of objects, including their permanence, than Piaget supposed. For ex-

ample, Renée Baillargeon (Baillargeon, 1987; 1994; Baillargeon & DeVos, 1991; Baillargeon, Spelke, & Wasserman, 1985), in a series of clever studies, has shown that babies as young as $3\frac{1}{2}$ or 4 months show clear signs of object permanence if you use a *visual* response rather than a reaching response to test it.

More broadly, Elizabeth Spelke (Spelke, 1991; Van de Walle & Spelke, 1996) has shown that young infants respond to objects in a far less transitory and ephemeral way than Piaget thought. For example, 2- and 3-month-olds are remarkably aware of what kinds of movements objects are capable of. They expect objects to continue to move on their initial trajectory and show surprise if the object appears somewhere else, all of which certainly sounds as if quite young infants have some aware-

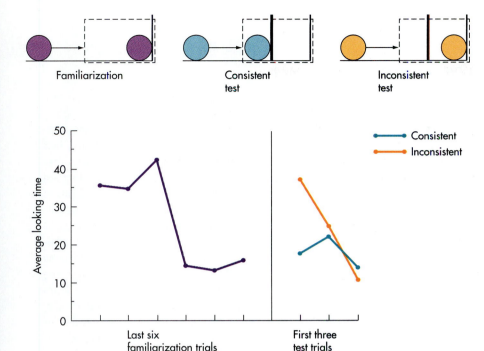

Familiarization

Consistent
test

Inconsistent
test

- Consistent
- Inconsistent

Average looking time

50

40

30

20

10

0

Last six
familiarization trials

First three
test trials

Figure 5.7

The top part of the figure shows a schematic version of the three conditions Spelke used. The bottom half shows the actual results. You can see that the babies stopped looking at the ball and screen after a number of familiarization trials, but showed renewed interest in the inconsistent version—a sign that the babies saw this as somehow different or surprising. The very fact that the babies found the inconsistent trial surprising is itself evidence that infants as young as 2 months have far more knowledge of objects and their behavior than most of us had thought. (Source: Spelke, 1991, Figures 5.3 and 5.4.)

ness that objects continue to exist even when they are out of sight. Infants also seem to have some awareness that solid objects cannot pass through other solid objects.

In one experiment in this series, Spelke used the procedure shown schematically in Figure 5.7. Two-month-old babies were repeatedly shown a series of events like that in the "familiarization" section of the figure: A ball, starting on the left-hand side, was rolled to the right and disappeared behind a screen. The screen was then taken away and the baby could see that the ball had stopped against the wall on the right. After the baby got bored looking at this sequence (habituated), he or she was tested with two variations, one "consistent" and one "inconsistent." In the consistent variation a second wall was placed behind the screen and the sequence run as before, except that now when the screen was removed the ball could be seen resting up against the nearer wall. In the inconsistent variation the ball was surreptitiously placed on the *far* side of the new wall. When the screen was removed the ball was visible in this new and presumably impossible place. Babies in this experiment were quite uninterested in the consistent condition, but showed sharply renewed interest in the inconsistent condition.

[?] Critical Thinking

I find it astonishing that a 2-month-old baby can have enough understanding of the physical world to "know" in some fashion that it is unexpected for the ball to be on the other side of the middle wall in this experiment. Are you also astonished by this result?

Findings like this have reopened the debate about Piaget's description of the development of object permanence. More generally, such results have sparked a new discussion of that old friend, the nature/nurture issue (e.g., Diamond, 1991; Fischer & Bidell, 1991; Karmiloff-Smith, 1991). Just how much is built in at birth? Piaget, of course, never said that *nothing* was built in. He assumed that the baby came equipped with a repertoire of sensorimotor schemes. His most fundamental theoretical proposal, however, was that the child *constructed* his understanding of the world, based on experience. On the other side of this new argument are those who see the baby as being endowed not only with specific knowledge about the world but with built-in constraints in the ways he processes information.

Spelke's own conclusion is that the development of the understanding of objects is more a

Cultures and Contexts

Object Permanence in Zambian Infants

Piaget believed that the emergence of the child's understanding of object permanence followed a universal sequence. One way to test this assumption, of course, is to observe or test children in non-Western societies, particularly infants or children whose early experiences are different from what we see in the United States or Europe. Susan Goldberg's longitudinal study of 38 Zambian infants (1972) gives us one such cross-cultural look.

Goldberg's two years of observations in Zambia made clear that the typical experience of a Zambian baby was quite different in a number of respects from that of most Western infants. From shortly after birth, Zambian babies are carried about in a sling on their mother's back. They spend very little time on the floor or in any position in which they have much chance of independent movement until they are able to sit up at about age 6 months. At that point, they are usually placed on a mat in the yard of the house. From this vantage, the baby can watch all the activity around the house and in the neighborhood, but he has few objects to play with. Goldberg reported that the Zambian mothers did not see it as their task to provide play objects for their infants, nor to structure the child's play in any way. Indeed, Goldberg says she rarely saw the babies playing with objects, even those that might have been available in the yards.

Yet, despite this very limited experience manipulating objects, tests of object permanence showed that the Zambian babies were *ahead* of the American averages on

a measure of the object concept at 6 months of age. At 9 and 12 months of age, the Zambian babies were slightly behind the U.S. norms, but Goldberg believes this difference is due not to any cognitive failure but to the fact that at these ages the Zambian babies were quite unresponsive and passive toward objects, and thus they are very difficult to test. One possible explanation of this is that in Zambian culture, at least as Goldberg observed it, obedience is a highly valued quality in a child. The babies are trained from very early on to be particularly obedient to prohibitions of various kinds. When the baby plays with some object that he is forbidden to touch, the object is taken away. Perhaps, then, the infants learn that when an object is removed, it means "Don't play with that," and he makes no further move to reach for the toy during the object permanence test. This does not necessarily mean that the baby has not understood these later stages of object permanence; it could also mean that our traditional ways of measuring this understanding would need to be modified for these children.

Goldberg's observations thus illustrate both the robustness of some basic developmental patterns *and* the impact of culture on the ways those patterns are displayed by children. Babies in Zambia appear to develop the early steps of the understanding of object permanence even though they have little chance to manipulate objects. At the same time, their response to objects is also affected by their training and experience.

process of elaboration than discovery. Newborn or very young babies may have considerable awareness of objects as separate entities that follow certain rules. Certainly all the research on the perception of patterns suggests that babies pay far more attention to relationships between events than Piaget's model had led us to suppose. Indeed, the research on babies' preferences for attractive faces, which I talked about in the *Research Report* box on page 159, suggests that there may be built-in preferences for particular patterns. Still, even Spelke would not argue that the baby comes equipped with full-fledged knowledge of objects or a well-developed ability to experiment with the world. It remains to be seen just how much of Piaget's view will need to be changed because of work of this type, but it has raised a whole host of fascinating new questions.

Imitation

As a final example of research on infant cognition that has flowed from Piaget's theory, let me say just a word about studies of imitation. If you go back and look again at Table 5.2 (p. 149), you'll see that Piaget thought that the ability to imitate emerged quite gradually over the early months. In broad terms, Piaget's proposed sequence has been supported. For example, imitation of someone else's hand movements or their actions with objects seems to improve steadily during the months of infancy, starting at 1 or 2 months of age; imitation of two-part actions develops only in toddlerhood, perhaps at 15 to 18 months (Poulson, Nunes, & Warren, 1989). In two areas, however, Piaget appears to have been wrong about infants' imitative abilities.

First, although Piaget thought babies could *not* imitate other people's facial gestures until about substage 4 (8–12 months), quite a lot of research now shows that newborns are able to imitate at least some facial gestures. Early studies, particularly those by Andrew Meltzoff and Tiffany Field (Field, Woodson, Greenberg, & Cohen, 1982; Meltzoff & Moore, 1977) indicated that newborns would imitate quite a range of expressions, including tongue protrusion, pursed lips, mouth opening, and even emotional expressions such as happiness or sadness. These initial results were quite controversial, with some researchers raising doubts about whether imitation occurred at all, others arguing that it occurs quite broadly (e.g., Reissland, 1988). The current status of the dispute is that all agree that babies will imitate at least one gesture, tongue protrusion (Anisfeld, 1991), as in the photos in Figure 5.8. So newborns *do* imitate, a striking and surprising fact—although it is entirely consistent with the research I've already described showing that newborns are capable of tactual/visual cross-modal transfer.

Piaget also argued that imitation of any action that wasn't already in the child's repertoire did not occur until about age 1, and that *deferred* imitation, in which a child sees some action and then imitates it at a later point, was possible only at substage 6 (roughly age 18 months), since deferred imitation requires some kind of internal representation. Once again, more recent research points to earlier development of this ability. At least one study (Meltzoff, 1988) shows that babies as young as 9 months can defer their imitation over as long as 24 hours. By 14 months, toddlers can recall and later imitate someone's actions over periods of two days (Hanna & Meltzoff, 1993), a finding that is significant for several reasons. First of all, it makes clear that children of this age can and do learn specific behaviors through modeling, even when they have no chance to imitate the behavior immediately. So the toddlers in a preschool or in day care are busily learning by watching others, playmates as well as teachers.

More broadly, all these results, like so many I have been describing to you in this chapter, suggest that babies may be more skillful than Piaget thought, and that they may have more abilities built in from the beginning than he suggested. At the same time, these results leave open the deeper question of whether the baby is *constructing* his understanding of the world through his experience or whether both his understanding and his experience are *constrained* by powerful built-in biases—issues that arise yet again when we look at the early stages of the development of language in these same months.

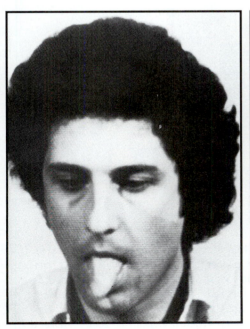 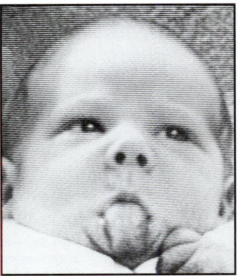

Figure 5.8

Although there is still some disagreement among researchers on just how much newborns will imitate, everyone agrees that they will imitate the gesture of tongue protrusion, demonstrated here by Andrew Meltzoff, in the earliest study of this kind. (Source: Meltzoff & Moore, 1977. Copyright 1977 by the AAAS.)

The Precursors of Language

Most of us think of "language" as beginning when the baby uses her first words, which happens (to the delight of most parents) at about age 12 months. But all sorts of important developments precede the first words.

Perception of Speech Sounds

Let's start with the basic perceptual skills. A baby cannot learn language until he can hear the individual sounds as distinct. Just how early can he do that? If you hadn't just read the rest of this chapter you might be surprised by the answer. But by now you know how this song goes. The answer is "remarkably early."

As early as 1 month, babies can discriminate between speech sounds like *pa* and *ba* (Trehub & Rabinovitch, 1972). By perhaps age 6 months, they can discriminate between two-syllable "words" like *bada* and *baga* and can even respond to a syllable that is hidden inside a string of other syllables, (like ti*ba*ti or ko*ba*ko) (Fernald & Kuhl, 1987; Goodsitt, Morse, Ver Hoeve, & Cowan, 1984; Morse & Cowan, 1982). Even more remarkable, it doesn't even seem to matter what voice quality the sound is said in. By age 2 or 3 months, babies respond to individual sounds as the same, whether they are spoken by male or female voices or child versus adult voices (Marean, Werner, & Kuhl, 1992).

Even more striking is the finding that babies are actually better at discriminating some kinds of speech sounds than adults are. Each language uses only a subset of all possible speech sounds. Japanese, for example, does not use the *l* sound that appears in English; Spanish makes a different distinction between *d* and *t* than occurs in English. It turns out that up to about age 6 months, babies can accurately discriminate all sound contrasts that appear in *any* language, including sounds they do not hear in the language spoken to them. By age 6 months, they begin to lose the ability to distinguish pairs of vowels that do not occur in the language they are hearing; by age 1, the ability to discriminate nonheard consonant contrasts begins to fade (Polka & Werker, 1994).

Some of the best evidence on this point comes from the work of Janet Werker and her colleagues (Werker & Desjardins, 1995; Werker & Tees, 1984).

They have tested 6- and 10-month-old infants on various consonant pairs, including one pair that is meaningful in English (*ba* versus *da*), a pair that occurs in the North American Indian language Salish (*ki* versus *qi*), and one from Hindi, a language from the Indian subcontinent (*ṭa* versus *ta*). Other infants were tested with both English and German vowel contrasts. Figure 5.9 shows the results for babies growing up in English-speaking families on contrasts that do not occur in English. You can see that at age 6 months, these babies could still readily hear the differences between pairs of foreign consonants but were already losing the ability to discriminate foreign vowels. Ten- and 12-month-old infants could not readily hear either type of contrast. Similarly, 12-month-old Hindi infants could easily discriminate a Hindi contrast but not an English contrast. So each group of infants loses only the ability to distinguish pairs that do not appear in the language they are hearing.

It seems to me that these findings are consistent with what we now know about the pattern of rapid, apparently preprogrammed, growth of synapses in the early months of life, followed by synaptic pruning. Many connections are initially created, permitting discriminations along all possible sound continua, but only those pathways that are actually used in the language the child hears are strengthened or retained.

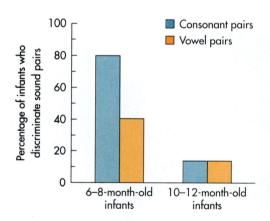

Figure 5.9

These data from Werker's studies are for babies growing up in English-language families, but Werker has similar results from Hindi-language and Salish-language infants. In every case, 6-month-olds can still "hear" the distinctions between consonant pairs that do not occur in their family's language, but by 12 months that ability has largely disappeared. (Source: Werker & Desjardins, 1995, from Figure 2, p. 80.)

Early Sounds and Gestures

The early ability to discriminate among sounds is not matched right away by much skill in producing sounds. For the first month, the most common sound an infant makes is a cry, although you can also hear other fussing, gurgling, and satisfied sounds. This sound repertoire expands at age 1 or 2 months, when we begin to hear some laughing and **cooing** vowel sounds, like *ahhh* or *uuuuuu*. Sounds like these are usually signals of pleasure in babies, and may show quite a lot of variation in tone, running up and down in volume or pitch.

Consonant sounds appear only by age 6 or 7 months, when for the first time the baby has the muscle control needed to combine a consonant sound with a vowel sound. Between 6 and 9 months, we hear a rapid increase in the amount of such vowel-consonant combinations. This type of vocalization, called **babbling,** makes up about half of babies' noncrying sounds between 6 and 12 months of age (Mitchell & Kent, 1990).

Much of the early babbling involves repetitive strings of the same syllables, such as *dadadada* or *nananana* or *yayayaya*. Even in these early months, though, we also hear a form of babbling that is even more like conventional speech, called **jargon** or "variegated babbling," in which the baby strings together sets of different syllables, often with sentencelike inflections (Bloom, 1993).

Adults find babbling delightful to listen to; Lois Bloom also points out that these new sound combinations are much easier for adults to imitate than are the earlier baby sounds, because babbling has more of the rhythm and sounds of adult speech. The imitative game that may then develop between parent and child is not only a pleasure for both, it may also be helpful to the baby in learning language.

Babbling is an important part of the preparation for spoken language in other ways as well. For one thing, we now know that infants' babbling gradually acquires some of what linguists call the *intonational pattern* of the language they are hearing—a process Elizabeth Bates refers to as "learning the tune before the words" (Bates, O'Connell, & Shore, 1987). At the very least, infants do seem to develop at least two such "tunes" in their babbling. When they babble with a rising intonation at the end of a string of sounds, it seems to signal a desire for a response; a falling intonation requires no response.

A second important aspect of babbling is that when babies first start babbling, they typically babble all kinds of sounds, including some that are not part of the language they are hearing. Then, beginning about age 9 or 10 months, their sound repertoire gradually begins to shift toward the set of sounds they are listening to, with the nonheard sounds dropping out (Oller, 1981)—a pattern that clearly parallels the Werker findings you saw in Figure 5.9. Findings like these do not tell us that babbling is *necessary* for language development, but they certainly make it look as if babbling is part of a connected developmental process that begins at birth.

Gestures in the First Year.   Another part of that connected developmental process appears to be a kind of gestural language that develops at around 9 or 10 months. At this age we first see babies "demanding" or "asking" for things using gestures or combinations of gestures and sound. A 10-month-old baby who apparently wants you to hand her a favorite toy may stretch and reach for it, opening and closing her hand, accompanied by whining sounds or other heartrending noises. There is no mistaking the meaning. At about the same age, babies will enter into those gestural games much loved by parents, like "patty-cake", or "soooo-big", or "wave bye-bye." (Bates et al., 1987).

Interestingly, the infant's ability to *understand* the meaning of individual words (which linguists call **receptive language**) also seems to begin at about age 9 or 10 months. Larry Fenson and his colleagues (Fenson, Dale, Reznick et al., 1994) asked hundreds of mothers about their babies' understanding of various words. The mothers of 10-month-olds identified an average of 30 words their infants understood; by 13 months, that number rose to nearly 100 words. Since infants of 9 to 13 months typically speak few (if any) individual words, findings like these make it clear that receptive language comes before **expressive language.** Children understand before they can speak, a highly important point for parents and teachers.

Babies as young as 9 or 10 months are already actively learning the language they are listening to. Not only can they understand some simple instructions, they can benefit from being exposed to a rich array of language.

Adding up these bits of information, we can see that a whole series of changes seems to come together at 9 or 10 months: the beginning of meaningful gestures, the drift of babbling toward the heard language sounds, imitative gestural games, and the first comprehension of individual words. It is as if the child now understands something about the process of communication and is intending to communicate to the adult.

The First Words

Somewhere in the midst of all the babbling, the first words appear, typically at age 12 or 13 months (Fenson et al., 1994). The baby's first word is an event that parents eagerly await, but it's fairly easy to miss. A *word*, as linguists usually define it, is any sound or set of sounds that is used consistently to refer to some thing, action, or quality. It can be *any* sound; it doesn't have to be a sound that matches words the adults are using. As one example, one of my niece Eileen's words was the sound *k*, which she used only to refer to the family cat, a beast named Spook. She would crawl or toddle unsteadily after the cat, reach her hand toward the

critter, and call out K!, K!, K! Neither of her parents realized at first that Eileen was using *k* as a word.

Often, a child's earliest words are used only in one or two specific situations and in the presence of many cues. The child may say "doggie" or "bow-wow" only to such promptings as, "How does the doggie go?" or "What's that?" Generally, this early word learning is very slow, requiring many repetitions for each word. In the first six months of word usage (roughly, between 12 and 18 months of age), children may learn as few as 30 words. Most linguists have concluded that in this earliest word-use phase, the child learns each word as something connected to a set of specific contexts. The toddler has apparently not yet grasped that words are *symbolic*—that they refer to objects or events.

In this early period toddlers often combine a single word with a gesture to create a "two-word meaning" before they actually use two words together in their speech. Elizabeth Bates (Bates et al., 1987) suggests an example: The infant may point to daddy's shoe and say "Daddy," as if to convey "Daddy's shoe." Or she may say "Cookie!" while simultaneously reaching out her hand and opening and closing her fingers, as if to say "Give cookie!" In both cases a sentencelike meaning is conveyed by the use of gesture and body language combined with a word. Linguists call these word-and-gesture combinations **holophrases,** and they are common between the ages of 12 and 18 months.

At 9 months, Alexandra probably hasn't yet spoken her first word, but chances are she already understands quite a few. Receptive language is almost always several months ahead of expressive language.

The Naming Explosion. Somewhere between 16 and 24 months, after the early period of very slow word learning, most children begin to add new words rapidly, as if they had figured out that "things have names," as Vygotsky once noted. According to Fenson's very large cross-sectional study, based on mothers' reports, the average 16-month-old has a speaking vocabulary of about 50 words; by 24 months this has multiplied more than sixfold, to about 320 (Fenson et al., 1994). A parallel study in Italy by Elizabeth Bates and her colleagues (Caselli, Casadio, & Bates, 1997) shows that this rapid rate of vocabulary growth is not unique to children learning English. In this new phase children seem to learn new words with very few repetitions and generalize these new words to many more situations.

For the majority of children this naming explosion is not a steady, gradual process; instead, vocabu-

Research Report

Early Gestural "Language" in the Children of Deaf Parents

Deaf children of deaf parents are a particularly interesting group to study if we want to understand language development. The children do not hear oral language, but they are exposed to *language*—sign language. Do these children show the same early steps in language development as do hearing children, only using gestures?

The answer seems to be yes. Deaf children show a kind of "sign babbling" between 7 and 11 months of age, much as hearing children babble sounds in these same months. Then, at 8 or 9 months of age, deaf children begin using simple gestures, such as pointing, which is just about the same time that we see such gestures in hearing babies of hearing parents. At about age 12 months, deaf babies seem to display their first *referential* signs—that is, signs in which a gesture appears to stand for some object or event, such as signaling that they want a drink by making a motion like a cup being brought to the mouth (Petitto, 1988).

Folven and Bonvillian (1991) have studied an equally interesting group—hearing children of deaf parents. These babies are exposed to sign language from their parents and to spoken language from their contacts with others in their world, including television, teachers, other relatives, and playmates. In a small sample of nine such babies, the first gestures appeared at an average age of 8 months, the first referential sign at 12.6 months, and the first spoken word at 12.2 months. What is striking here is that the first referential signs and the first spoken words appear at such similar times, and that the spoken words appear at such a completely normal time, despite the fact that these children of deaf parents hear comparatively little spoken language.

This marked similarity in the sequence and timing of the steps of early language in the deaf and the hearing child provides strong support for the argument that the baby is somehow primed to learn "language" in some form, be it spoken or gestural.

---

lary "spurts," beginning right about the time that the child has acquired 40 or 50 words. You can see this pattern in Figure 5.10, which shows the vocabulary growth curves of six children studied longitudinally by Goldfield and Reznick (1990)—a pattern found by other researchers as well (e.g., Bloom, 1993).

Not all children show precisely this pattern. In Goldfield and Reznick's study, for example, 13 children showed a vocabulary spurt; 11 other children in the study followed varying growth patterns, including several who showed no spurt at all but only gradual acquisition of vocabulary. Still, a rapid increase over a period of a few months is the most common pattern.

During this early period of rapid vocabulary growth, most observers agree that the bulk of new words are names for things or people, like *ball*, *car*, *milk*, *doggie*, *he*, or *that*. Verblike words tend to develop later, perhaps because they label relationships between objects rather than just a single object (Gleitman & Gleitman, 1992). For example, over half the first 50 words of the eight children Katherine Nelson studied were nounlike words, while only 13 percent were action words (1973). And in Fenson's large cross-sectional study (Fenson et al., 1994), 63 percent of the words mothers said their children knew by age 2 were nouns, while only 8.5

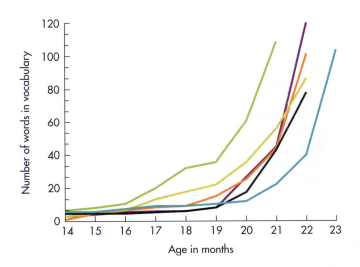

Figure 5.10

Each of the lines in this figure represents the vocabulary growth of one of the children studied by Goldfield and Reznick in their longitudinal study. (Source: Goldfield & Reznick, 1990, Figure 3, p. 177.)

percent were verbs. Studies of children learning other languages show very similar patterns, as you can see in the *Cultures and Contexts* box on page 172.

However, this noun-before-verb pattern does not hold for all children. Katherine Nelson (1973) first noticed that some toddlers use what she

Cultures and Contexts

Early Words by Children in Many Cultures

Cross-cultural studies of children's early language support the generalization that in their earliest word learning, children learn words for people or things before they learn words for actions or other parts of speech.

Here are some (translated) samples from the very early vocabularies of one child from each of four cultures, all studied by Dedre Gentner (1982).

	German Boy	English Girl	Turkish Girl	Chinese Girl
Some of the words for people or things	Mommy	Mommy	Mama	Momma
	Papa	Daddy	Daddy	Papa
	Gaga	Babar	Aba	Grandmother
	baby	baby	baby	horse
	dog	dog	food	chicken
	bird	dolly	apple	uncooked rice
	cat	kitty	banana	cooked rice
	milk	juice	bread	noodles
	ball	book	ball	flower
	nose	eye	pencil	wall clock
	moon	moon	towel	lamp
Some of the nonnaming words	cry	run	cry	go
	come	all gone	come	come
	eat	more	put on	pick up
	sleep	bye-bye	went pooh	not want
	want	want	want	afraid
	no	no	hello	thank you
Total percentage of naming words	67%	69%	57%	59%

It is impressive how very similar these early vocabularies are. Of course, there are some variations, but all these children had names for Mommy and Daddy, for some other relative, for other named and/or live creatures, and for food. All but the Chinese child had words for toys or clothes. All four had also learned more naming words than any other type, with very similar proportions. They don't know the *same* words, but the pattern is remarkably similar.

called an **expressive style.** For them, most early words are linked to social relationships rather than to objects. They often learn pronouns (*you, me*) early, and use many more of what Nelson calls "personal-social" words, such as *no, yes, want,* or *please.* This is in sharp contrast to children who use what Nelson calls a **referential style;** their early vocabulary is made up predominantly of nounlike words. Later researchers have found further signs of such a difference in both grammar and articulation, as you can see in the summary in Table 5.4.

Elizabeth Bates and her colleagues (Bates, Bretherton, & Snyder, 1988; Thal & Bates, 1990) argue that the difference between these two styles

may run fairly deep. Referential-style children are, in some sense, more cognitively oriented. They are drawn to objects, spend more of their time in solitary play with objects, and interact with other people more often around objects. In the very earliest stages of word learning, they use pointing gestures a lot (Dunham & Dunham, 1995); at a later stage, they are much more likely to show a clear spurt in vocabulary development, adding a whole lot of object names in a very short space of time, as if they—more than expressive-style children—had understood the basic principle that things have names. Such children are also advanced in their ability to understand complex adult language.

Table 5.4
Some Differences Between Expressive and Referential Children in Early Language

	Expressive	Referential
Early words	Low proportion of nouns and adjectives	High proportion of nouns and adjectives
Vocabulary growth	Slow, gradual; rarely any spurts	Rapid, with clear spurts at one-word stage
Articulation	Less-clear speech	Clearer speech
Early sentences (described more in Chapter 8)	May have inflections at stage 1, because of high use of "rote strings" (formulas) inserted into sentences (e.g., "What do you want?")	Few rote strings at stage 1 grammar; speech is clearly telegraphic at this stage, with no inflections

Sources: Thal & Bates, 1990; Shore, 1995.

Expressive-style toddlers, on the other hand, are oriented more toward people, toward social interactions. Their early words and sentences include a lot of "formulas," often including strings of words, such as I *want it*, or *don t do that*. Some of these strings are fairly complex grammatically, which makes the expressive child's language sometimes sound more advanced than what we hear in a referential child. But expressive-style toddlers develop vocabulary more slowly, with no obvious spurt.

These observations about children with different styles of early language should remind us that we need to search not just for common developmental pathways but also for individual variations.

[?] *Critical Thinking*

Do you think that referential- and expressive-style babies are likely to differ from each other in other ways as well? What other differences might you hypothesize, and how might you test your hypotheses?

Individual Differences

Discussions of individual differences in cognitive skill are nearly always cast in "cognitive power" terms. We ask whether there are differences in *rate* of development and whether such differences in rate are consistent over time. Questions of this kind about infant development have an important practical implication: If we could accurately measure differences in infants' rate (or pattern) of development in the early months of life, then we might be able to identify infants who are likely to

have problems learning to read or performing in school in other ways. It might then be possible to intervene very early, perhaps thereby averting or at least ameliorating the problem.

Infant IQ Tests. Just such a hope that test scores could be used to help identify infants with current or prospective problems was one of the motivations behind the development of the various infant IQ tests. Most such tests, such as the widely used **Bayley Scales of Infant Development** (Bayley, 1969, revised 1993), have been constructed rather like IQ tests for older children in that they include a series of items of increasing difficulty. However, instead of testing school-like skills—skills an infant does not yet have—infant IQ tests measure primarily sensory and motor skills, such as reaching for a dangling ring (an item for a typical 3-month-old), putting cubes in a cup on request (9 months), or building a tower of three cubes (17 months). Some more clearly cognitive items are also included, such as uncovering a toy hidden by a cloth, an item used with 8-month-old infants to measure an aspect of object permanence.

Bayley's test and others like it have proven to be helpful in identifying infants and toddlers with serious developmental delays. As a more general predictive tool to forecast later IQ scores or school performance, however, such tests have not been nearly as useful as many had hoped. For example, the typical correlation between a 12-month Bayley test score and a 4-year-old IQ score is only about .20 to .30 (e.g., Bee, Barnard, Eyres et al., 1982)—statistically significant but not robust. On the whole, it looks as if what is being measured on typical infant tests is not the same as what is tapped

Alina, at 17 months, would no doubt be able to pass the 17-month-old item on the Bayley Scales of Infant Development that calls for building a tower of three cubes.

by the common childhood or adult intelligence tests (Colombo, 1993). Interestingly, however, recent work emerging from an information processing framework has pointed us in a new direction in our efforts to find links between infant skills and later intellectual abilities.

Recognition Memory.   The most extensive body of such information processing research has dealt with variations in "recognition memory" among infants—the ability to recognize that one has seen or experienced some object or person before. One way to measure this is with a standard habituation test. If we show a baby an object or a picture, over and over, how many exposures does it take before the infant stops showing interest? That is, how quickly does the baby "recognize" the object or picture? The speed with which such habituation/recognition

takes place may tell us something about the efficiency of the perceptual/cognitive system and its neurological underpinnings. And if such efficiency lies behind some of the characteristics we normally call "intelligence," then individual differences in rate of habituation in the early months of life may predict later intelligence test scores.

That is exactly what researchers have found in studies over the past 15 years. Babies who habituate quickly (that is, who rapidly become uninterested when shown the same object repeatedly) when they are 4 or 5 months old are likely to have higher IQs at later ages, while slower infant habituation is associated with lower IQ scores and poorer language at later ages. The average correlation in studies in both the United States and England is in the range of .45 to .50 (Rose & Feldman, 1995; Slater, 1995). This correlation is certainly not perfect, but it is remarkably high, given the difficulties involved in measuring habituation rate in babies.

[?] *Critical Thinking*

Where might such differences in speed of recognition memory come from? Heredity? Richness of experience in the first few months of life? Can you think of any way to study this question?

Certainly these correlations do not prove that intelligence, as we measure it on an IQ test, is *only* a reflection of some kind of "speed of basic processing." Results like these nonetheless underline the potential importance of looking at the basic components of information processing if we want to understand individual differences in cognitive skills in early infancy.

Cognitive Development in Infancy: An Overall Look

In a number of important respects Piaget seems to have underestimated the ability of infants to store, remember, and organize sensory and motor information. Very young babies pay much more attention to patterns, to sequence, to prototypical features than Piaget thought, and can apparently remember them over at least short intervals. Many

Parenting

What Can You Do to Give a Baby the Best Intellectual Start?

Perhaps because I am a researcher myself, I find all the research on early perception, language, and cognition to be utterly fascinating. I hope I have conveyed some of that fascination to you. At the same time, I also need to try to translate all the data and theories into some practical advice for parents, or for others who work with infants and toddlers. The key idea is that babies need to *exercise* all their emerging skills. The more they have things to look at, touch, play with, listen to, or follow with their eyes, the more optimally they develop. In some sense, what you want to do is train the baby's brain. Remember that these are the very months in which the most rapid brain development is occurring. You want to optimize this process by providing as much experience—of many kinds—as the baby can handle. So:

1. **Provide toys or objects for the baby to touch, move, play with.** This might include something interesting hung above the crib, especially something that moves, or that the baby can interact with in some way. Then change it periodically to keep it interesting. Babies need rattles, soft blocks, stuffed animals, things to put in their mouths, things to grasp in the hand. As they get older, they need more complex toys or objects—things that have movement, color, sound.

2. **Respond to the baby's signals.** When the baby makes a sound, imitate that sound or talk back; when the baby smiles, smile back; if the baby signals that he's through eating, stop feeding. Some of a baby's signals may be pretty subtle; some are unmistakable. All the research tells us that "responsiveness" of this kind helps to promote not only a more secure attachment of infant to adult but also better cognitive development.

3. **Talk to the baby or toddler.** Babies pay attention to speech from the first day of life; they begin to notice sound patterns. They don't begin to use words until later, but everything we know says that children's language learning is improved if you talk to your infant from the beginning.

4. **Read to the baby.** Play tapes of poetry, or tapes of you reading a story book, near the baby when you put him to bed; read aloud to the infant, even when he is very small. As soon as the baby is able to sit on your lap, turn the pages of a book in front of the baby and read the words. As the infant gets to be 9 or 10 months old, you can begin to play pointing games with the book and the child.

current theorists have taken this evidence to mean that the baby comes equipped with a wide range of built-in knowledge or inborn constraints on his ways of understanding the world around him.

Arrayed on the other side of the argument, however, is the obvious fact that newborns, despite their remarkable perceptual and cognitive abilities, are *not* as skilled as 6-month-olds or 12-month-olds. Newborns do not use gestures to communicate, they do not talk, they do not show deferred imitation. Six-month-olds do not combine several strategies to achieve some goal and do not seem to experiment with objects in the same way as we see later. Even at 12 months, toddlers do not seem to use symbols to stand for things in any general way. They use a few words but don't yet show pretend play, for example. So, despite all the new and fascinating evidence, it still appears to be correct to describe the infant as *sensorimotor* rather than *symbolic* in her thinking. Over the first 18 to 24 months, the baby seems to be building toward such symbol use, a shift that John Flavell correctly sees as remarkable:

> [A] cognitive system that uses symbols just seems . . . to be radically, drastically, qualitatively different from one that does not and cannot. So great is the difference that the transformation of one system into the other during the first 2 years of life still seems nothing short of miraculous to me, no matter how much we learn about it. (1985, p. 82)

Summary

1. Three distinct theoretical emphases exist in the study of intelligence and cognition: intellectual power, intellectual structure, and information processing.

2. Studies of infant cognition have been most strongly influenced by Piaget's structural view of intelligence.

3. Piaget described the sensorimotor infant as beginning with a small repertoire of basic schemes, from which she moves toward symbolic representation in a series of six substages.

4. Substage 1 is essentially automatic pilot; substage 2 includes coordination of different modalities; in substage 3 the baby focuses more on the outside world; in substage 4 causal connections are understood and the object concept is grasped in a preliminary way; in substage 5 the baby begins to experiment more fully; and in substage 6 we see first signs of symbol usage.

5. Babies are able to learn by both classical and operant conditioning within the first few weeks of life, earlier than Piaget thought.

6. Newborns are also able to habituate to repeated stimuli, indicating that they have the ability to "recognize" that something has been experienced before.

7. Three- and 4-month-old infants show signs of remembering specific experiences over periods of as long as a few days or a week, a sign that they must have some form of internal representation well before Piaget supposed.

8. In examining early perceptual development, it is useful to distinguish between basic sensory capacities and more complex perceptual abilities.

9. Newborns have poor visual acuity, but improve steadily to adult sensory ability by about age 1. Similarly, their ability to track moving objects is poor at first but improves rapidly. Babies also appear to have at least some color vision by at least 1 month, perhaps at birth.

10. Auditory acuity is better than visual acuity at birth. Babies can hear clearly in the range of pitch and loudness of the human voice.

11. Smell, taste, and touch sensation are all present at birth in at least some rudimentary form.

12. Depth perception is among the important complex perceptual skills. It is present in some beginning form by 3 months, and is fairly well developed by 6 months.

13. Newborns can discriminate Mom from other people by sight, sound, and smell. By age 3 months they respond differently to varying emotional expressions.

14. In the first weeks of life, infants appear to be intent on locating objects; after about age 2 months, they seem intent on identifying objects, so their method of scanning changes.

15. From the earliest weeks, babies respond to the patterns of stimuli or to relationships among stimuli, such as "big over small," or to the sound of a particular story. They also prefer to look at attractive rather than at less attractive faces.

16. Babies also show cross-modal transfer as early as a few weeks of age, far earlier than Piaget supposed.

17. In Piaget's experiments, babies began to show real comprehension of object permanence—that objects continue to exist when they are out of sight or not being acted on by the child—only at about age 8 months.

18. Newer research suggests that babies may have far more elaborate understanding of the properties of objects—including their permanence—at much earlier ages than Piaget supposed.

19. Babies are able to imitate some facial expressions in the first days of life, but they do not show deferred imitation until much later.

20. Babies can discriminate among speech sounds in the first weeks and, until about age 12 months, they can make discriminations that adults can no longer make.

21. Babies' earliest sounds are cries, followed at about age 2 months by cooing, then by babbling at about 6 months. At 9 months babies typically use meaningful gestures, and can understand a small vocabulary of spoken words.

22. The first spoken word typically occurs at about age 1 year, after which toddlers add words slowly for a few months and then rapidly. Most have a vocabulary of about 50 words by 18 months.

23. The earliest words are more often names for people or objects than they are words to describe actions.

24. Attempts to measure individual differences in sensorimotor development by constructing IQ-like tests have not been as successful as hoped; such tests are not strongly related to later measures of IQ.

25. Much more predictive are measures of more basic information processing skills in infancy, such as rate of habituation at 4 months, which is correlated with later IQ.

26. On the whole, Piaget seems to have underestimated the infant; it may also be that far more is built in at birth than Piaget supposed. All researchers and theorists would nonetheless agree that progressive development occurs, built upon the base with which the baby begins. This early development culminates in the emergence of the ability to use symbols in play and in thought, at about 18 to 24 months of age.

Key Terms

acuity Sharpness of perceptual ability—how well or how clearly one can see or hear or use other senses. **(p. 154)**

babbling The frequently repetitive vocalizing of consonant-vowel combinations by an infant, typically beginning at about age 6 months. **(p. 169)**

Bayley Scales of Infant Development The best-known and most widely used test of infant "intelligence," revised most recently in 1993. **(p. 173)**

cooing An early stage during the prelinguistic period, typically from 1 to 4 months of age, when vowel sounds are repeated, particularly the *uuu* sound. **(p. 169)**

cross-modal transfer The ability to transfer information gained through one sense to another sense at a later time; for example, identifying visually something you had previously explored only tactually. **(p. 161)**

expressive language The term used to describe the child's skill in speaking and communicating orally. **(p. 169)**

expressive style One of two styles of early language proposed by Nelson, characterized by low rates of noun-like terms, and high use of personal-social words and phrases. **(p. 172)**

habituation An automatic decrease in the intensity of a response to a repeated stimulus, which enables the child or adult to ignore the familiar and focus attention on the novel. **(p. 151)**

holophrases A combination of a gesture with a single word that conveys a sentencelike meaning; often seen/heard in children between 12 and 18 months. **(p. 170)**

information processing Phrase used to refer to a new, third approach to the study of intellectual development that focuses on changes with age and on individual differences in fundamental intellectual skills. **(p. 147)**

intersensory integration The combining of information from two or more senses to form a unified perceptual whole, such as the sight of mouth movements combined with the sound of particular words. **(p. 161)**

jargon A form of babbling in which the infant strings together a series of different vowel-consonant combinations rather than repeating the same combination over and over. **(p. 169)**

object permanence The understanding that an object continues to exist even when it is temporarily out of sight. More generally, the basic understanding that objects exist separate from one's own action on them. **(p. 163)**

primary circular reactions Piaget's phrase to describe the baby's simple repetitive actions in the second substage of the sensorimotor stage, organized around the baby's own body; the baby repeats some action in order to have some desired outcome occur again, such as putting his thumb in his mouth to repeat the good feeling of sucking. **(p. 148)**

receptive language Term used to describe the child's ability to understand (receive) language, in contrast to his ability to express language. **(p. 169)**

referential style Second style of early language proposed by Nelson, characterized by emphasis on objects and their naming and description. **(p. 172)**

schematic learning The development of expectancies of what actions lead to what results or what events tend to go together. Classical conditioning may be thought of as a subset of schematic learning. **(p. 151)**

secondary circular reactions Repetitive actions in the third substage of the sensorimotor period, oriented around external objects; the infant repeats some action in order to have some outside event recur, such as hitting a mobile repeatedly to watch it move. **(p. 148)**

social referencing Using another person's reaction to some situation as a basis for deciding one's own reaction. A baby does this when she checks her parent's facial expression or body language before responding positively or negatively to something new. **(p. 160)**

tertiary circular reactions The deliberate experimentation with variations of previous actions, characteristic of the fifth substage of sensorimotor intelligence, according to Piaget. **(p. 149)**

tracking Also called smooth pursuit. The smooth movements of the eye used to follow the track of some moving object. **(p. 154)**

visual cliff Apparatus designed by Gibson and Walk for their studies of depth perception in infants. **(p. 156)**

Suggested Readings

Baillargeon, R. (1994). How do infants learn about the physical world? *Current Directions in Psychological Science, 3,* 133–140. This is a wonderful, brief paper describing some of Baillargeon's fascinating work on young infants' understanding of objects and the physical world. The paper was written for a general audience of fellow psychologists rather than for experts in perception, so with a little effort it should be comprehensible to an undergraduate student.

Field, T. (1990). *Infancy.* Cambridge, MA: Harvard University Press. One of an excellent series of books on topics in child development, written by experts but intended for lay readers. Field covers many of the topics I have discussed in this chapter and in Chapter 6.

Flavell, J. H., Miller, P. H., & Miller, S. A. (1993). *Cognitive development* (3rd ed.). Englewood Cliffs, NJ: Prentice Hall. This is an update of one of the very best texts in the field, written by one of the major current figures in cognitive-developmental theory (Flavell). The introductory chapter and the chapter on infancy may be especially helpful if you find Piaget's theory somewhat hard to grasp.

Shore, C. M. (1995). *Individual differences in language development.* Thousand Oaks, CA: Sage. A small book summarizing what we know about individual differences in rate and style of language development and the alternative explanations of those differences.

Social and Personality Development in Infancy and Toddlerhood

Preview Questions

1 What mix of emotions is a parent likely to feel when her or his first child is born?

2 Babies smile very early; why is this important for the development of attachment?

3 When do infants start using their parents or caregivers as a "safe base" from which to explore? Why is that behavior so important?

4 What can parents do to foster their baby's secure attachment to them?

5 What are the key aspects of temperament that differentiate one infant from another?

6 Is day care good or bad for children, or something in between?

Chapter Outline

Not long ago, as I had lunch in a restaurant with a friend, we were happily distracted by the sight of an adorable baby at the next table. The infant, perhaps 4 or 5 months old, was sitting on her mom's lap, facing outward, gazing with delight at an older woman sitting across from her—perhaps her grandmother. As the older woman talked to the baby in a high and lilting voice, smiled, and tickled the baby's tummy, the infant responded with one huge smile after another. My friend and I stopped talking as we watched, and could hardly restrain ourselves from trying to join in the whole process. I had my "talking-with-baby voice" all warmed up and ready to go, and found myself smiling as if to try to entice an answering smile from the infant— although the baby didn't look our way at all.

Even as I was personally drawn into this small scene, the psychologist in me was also aware of many aspects of the interaction. In particular, I could see the separate contributions of the baby and the adult to this charming exchange. The infant brought her inborn and emerging physical and cognitive skills, including smiling and a general ability to entice; the adult contributed her own instinctive responses to babies as well as specific knowledge of what would please or attract this particular infant. Just as dance partners need to learn each other's moves in order to dance smoothly, so babies and the adults who care for them adapt to one another's style and rhythm and become more and more skilled at reading one another's cues.

These social interactions between babies and their caregivers are absolutely central to the process of development—as crucial to understand as are the baby's emerging physical or cognitive skills. The baby's ability to entice keeps the parents happily providing care, without which the baby could not survive; the parents' responses to these enticements are critical to the infant's growing attachment to the parent, an attachment that (under optimum circumstances) creates a safe base from which the infant then explores his world. Perhaps most important of all, it is in these social interactions that much of the joy resides—for both the child and the parents.

Adapting to the Newborn

Let me begin by looking at the social and emotional context in which these early interactions occur. The baby is born and Mom, Dad, and infant re-

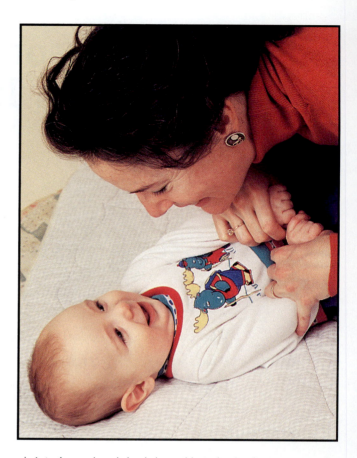

Anton's mom has obviously learned just what it takes to coax a smile or a giggle from her 5-month-old.

turn home and must now adapt to one another and to the massive changes in their lives occasioned by this new member of the family. The baby demands constant care—care that you can't postpone for some more convenient time. Parents get (lots!) less sleep for some months; they can no longer go out whenever they feel like it, but must think about baby-sitters; their sexual relationship doesn't resume immediately because of the residual discomforts from the birth itself, but even after a few months sex may remain infrequent because of fatigue and lack of time. The parents also may feel new financial strains.

Despite these enormous changes, the role of parent brings profound satisfaction for most adults, a greater sense of purpose and self-worth, and a feeling of being grown up. It may also bring a sense of shared joy between husband and wife (Umberson & Gove, 1989). In one large study in the United States, 80 percent of the parents sampled said their lives had been changed for the better by the arrival of children (Hoffman & Manis, 1978).

Parenting

Being a Parent of an Infant

Marc Bornstein offers a particularly clear description of the impact of a new infant on the parents:

> Nothing rivets the attention or stirs the emotions of adults more than the birth of a child. By their very coming into existence, infants forever alter the sleeping, eating, and working habits of their parents; they change who parents are and how parents define themselves. Infants keep parents up late into the night or cause them to abandon late nights to accommodate early waking; they require parents to give up a rewarding career to care for them or take a second job to support them; they lead parents to make new circles of friends with others in similar situations and sometimes cause parents to lose or abandon old friends who are not parents. Yes, parents even seem to take for themselves the names that infants bestow. Parenting an infant is a 168-hour-a-week job, whether by the parents themselves or by a surrogate who is on call, because the human infant is totally dependent on parents for survival. . . . Every day, 11,000 babies are born in the United States—a number equivalent to the population of a small town—and yet every one is unique and special. (1995, pp. 3–4)

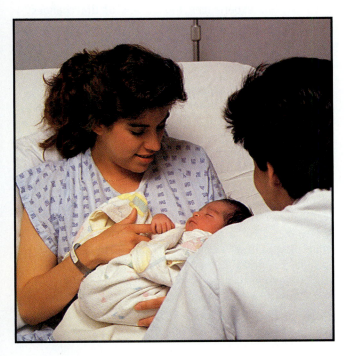

The advent of a new baby—especially a first baby—is one of those richly ambivalent times for many adults: They are delighted and proud, and yet they also typically feel increased strain—the strain of caring for the infant as well as new strains in their relationship.

Nonetheless, it is true that the birth of the first child is often accompanied by real strains.

One sign of that strain, or one consequence of it, is that marital satisfaction typically goes down in the first months and years after a first child is born (Glenn, 1990). Individuals and couples report both fatigue and a feeling that there is too much to cope with. They also describe anxiety about not knowing how best to care for the child and a strong sense of loss of time and intimacy in the marriage relationship itself (Feldman, 1987). In longitudinal studies in which couples have been observed or interviewed during pregnancy and then again in the months after the first child's birth, spouses typically report fewer expressions of love, fewer positive actions intended to maintain or support the relationship, and more expressions of ambivalence after the child's birth than before (Belsky, Lang, & Rovine, 1985). Such strains and reduced satisfaction are less noticeable when the child was planned rather than unplanned and among those couples whose marriage was strong and stable before the birth of the child. Still, virtually all couples experience some strain in the midst of their pleasure and pride. So don't be surprised if this happens to you. It helps to be aware that this is likely to occur; it helps to plan ways for you and your spouse to spend time together. Yet if, despite your best efforts, you still feel less satisfied with your relationship, take heart; this is entirely normal and improves with time.

The Baby's Social Skills

Despite all the early strains, the baby and parents nonetheless form strong emotional bonds, a process that is very definitely a two-way street. The

Parenting

Postpartum Depression

My friend Jane gave birth to her first baby last April, fully expecting to be completely delighted with motherhood, but then unexpectedly found herself weeping at the drop of a hat. She was seriously depressed for several months. I kept assuring her that this was pretty common; at the same time, I urged her to seek professional help.

Jane's problem is indeed quite common. As many as four-fifths of women (at least in Western studies) experience tearfulness or anxiety in the first few days after they give birth, often called the "maternity blues" or "postpartum blues" (Corter & Fleming, 1995). Most women pass through this depression in a few days and then return to a more positive and more stable mood state. Ten to 25 percent of women, though, appear to share Jane's experience of a longer-lasting and more severe postpartum mood disturbance, commonly called a **postpartum depression**—a pattern found in studies in Australia, China, Sweden, Finland, and Scotland as well as in the United States (S. Campbell, Cohn, Flanagan, Popper, & Meyers, 1992; Guo, 1993; Lundh & Gyllang, 1993; Viinamäki, Rastas, Tukeva et al., 1994; Webster, Thompson, Mitchell, & Werry, 1994).

Clinicians use the term *depression* or the phrase *clinical depression* to describe more than just the blues, although sadness or persisting low mood is one of the critical ingredients. The other danger signs include poor appetite, sleep disturbances (inability to sleep or excessive sleep), loss of pleasure in everyday activities, feelings of worthlessness, complaints of trouble thinking or concentrating, or recurrent thoughts of death or suicide. Anyone who shows at least half these symptoms, in addition to a down mood, would be diagnosed as suffering from a clinical depression. Clearly, such a depressive episode is not a trivial experience. So the

fact that as many as two out of every ten women experience such feelings after the birth of a child is striking.

Where do these feelings come from? New research points to the likelihood that hormone patterns play a key role. Specifically, it looks as if women who have unusually high levels of steroid hormones in the late stage of their pregnancies are more likely to experience depression, apparently as a kind of withdrawal symptom from the rapid decline in hormones (Harris, Lovett, Newcombe et al., 1994). Postpartum depression is also more common in women who did not plan their pregnancy, who were high in anxiety during the pregnancy, or whose partner is not supportive of them or is displeased with the arrival of the child (S. Campbell et al., 1992; O'Hara, Schlechte, Lewis, & Varner, 1992). When a woman has experienced high levels of life changes during the pregnancy and immediately after the birth—changes such as moving, the death of someone close, loss of a job, or the like—her risk of depression also rises.

Fortunately, a postpartum depression is normally of briefer duration than other forms of clinical depression, lasting typically six to eight weeks, after which the woman gradually recovers her normal mood. For perhaps one or two percent of women, the depression persists for a year or longer.

I think it is quite common in our society to pass off a woman's postpartum depression as if it were a minor event, "just the blues." And, of course, for many women it is. For a minority, though, the arrival of a child ushers in a much more significant depressive episode, requiring at the very least a sympathetic and supportive environment, if not clinical intervention. If you experience such symptoms after the birth of a child, don't hesitate. Ask for help.

infant's own emerging social skills are an important contributor to the creation of those bonds.

Because they can't yet talk or move around much, young infants make social connections primarily through their expression of emotion—crying, smiling, looking surprised, unhappy, or pleased. Parents use these emotional expressions as clues to adapt their own behavior to the baby's. And as you've already seen in the last chapter, babies rather quickly come to be able to "read" their parents' emotional expressions as well.

The Emergence of Emotional Expression

There is really no way to know just what emotion a baby actually *feels*. The best we can do is to try to judge what emotion a baby appears to *express* through body and face. Researchers have done this by confronting babies with various kinds of events likely to prompt emotions, photographing or videotaping those encounters, and then asking adult judges to say which emotion the baby's face expresses (Izard, Fantauzzo, Castle et al.,

Table 6.1

The Emergence of Emotional Expressions in Infancy and Toddlerhood

Age	Emotion Expressed	Examples of Stimuli That Trigger That Expression
At birth	Interest Distress Disgust Neonatal smile (a "half smile")	Novelty or movement Pain Offensive substances (as in the photos in Figure 4.1) Appears spontaneously for no known reason
3 to 6 weeks	Pleasure/social smile (precursor to joy)	High-pitched human voice; clapping the baby's hands together; hearing a familiar voice; a nodding face
2 to 3 months	Sadness Wariness (precursor of fear) Frustration (precursor to anger) Surprise	In response to a painful medical procedure Response to a stranger's face Response to being restrained; when prevented from performing some established action Jack-in-the-box
7 months	Fear Anger Joy	Extreme novelty; heights (such as in the visual cliff experiment) Failure or interruption of some attempted action, such as reaching for a ball that has rolled under a couch Immediate delighted response to an experience with positive meaning, such as the caregiver's arrival or in peekaboo
12 to 18 months	Shame, guilt	Failure to perform some task, combined with negative self-evaluation of some kind; or hurt inflicted on some other, combined with negative self-evaluation

Sources: Izard & Malatesta, 1987; Mascolo & Fischer, 1995; Sroufe, 1996.

1995; Izard & Harris, 1995; Izard & Malatesta, 1987).

Table 6.1 summarizes the current wisdom about the ages at which various important emotional expressions first appear. As you can see, some rudimentary emotional expressions are visible at birth, including a sort of "half smile" that delights parents, even though they cannot figure out how to elicit it consistently. Within a few weeks, though, babies begin to show a full social smile. Happily, one of the earliest triggers for this wonderful baby smile is the kind of high-pitched voice we all seem to use naturally with infants. So adults seem to be preprogrammed to behave in just the ways that babies will respond to positively. Within a few weeks, babies will also smile in response to a smiling face; and even in these early months, babies will smile more readily to a familiar than an unfamiliar voice or face.

Within a few months, babies' emotional expressions differentiate even further, so that they express sadness, anger, and surprise. Four-month-olds also begin to laugh—and there are few things in life more delightful than the sound of a giggling or laughing baby! Fear only appears as a discrete emotional expression at about seven months, and the "self-conscious" emotions, such as shame or guilt, appear still later, after the child has developed some self-awareness—a development I'll come back to later in the chapter.

Over these early months, babies' emotional expressions become increasingly responsive to the emotions they see their parents express. The baby's social smile, for example, appears more and more often in response to the parent's own smile or pleasure. Similarly, babies whose parents are depressed show more sad and angry facial expression and fewer expressions of interest, a pattern detectable as early as 3 or 4 months of age (Field, 1995). Indeed, Tiffany Field's research suggests that babies of depressed mothers may actually learn *not* to express interest or delight; instead, they learn to display a kind of depressed look, something they show with strangers as well as with their depressed

A baby's laughter is an utter delight for parents; we can also think of it as one of the important social/emotional responses the baby contributes to the emerging parent-child relationship, part of the "glue" that cements them together.

Mom. Thus, even as early as the first year of life, the expression of emotion is a reciprocal process; infants not only respond to adult emotional expression, they seem to adapt their expressions to match or fit with the adult's typical pattern.

Parent-Infant Relationships

It is on the base of such mutually adaptive emotional exchanges that the parent-infant relationship is constructed. Yet that relationship is more than simply the sum of a series of behavioral exchanges. Something else happens in these early months: The infant forms an attachment to the parents, a process described most fully in the work of two important theorists, John Bowlby (whose approach I described briefly in Chapter 2) and Mary Ainsworth (Ainsworth, 1972; 1982; 1989; Ainsworth, Blehar, Waters, & Wall, 1978; Bowlby, 1969; 1973; 1980; 1988a; 1988b). Their work, and the work of those who have followed their lead, has not only given us a rich description of the steps the infant goes through in forming a central attachment, it has made clear just how significant that attachment is in many aspects of the child's development. This is a crucial process, worth exploring in considerable depth.

Bowlby's and Ainsworth's Attachment Model

Bowlby argued that "The propensity to make strong emotional bonds to particular individuals [is] a basic component of human nature, already present in germinal form in the neonate" (1988a, p. 3). Such relationships have *survival* value because they bring nurturance to the infant. They are built and maintained by an interlocking repertoire of instinctive behaviors that create and sustain proximity between parent and child or between other bonded pairs.

Three key concepts in Bowlby's and Ainsworth's writings are affectional bond, attachment, and attachment behaviors.

Ainsworth defines an **affectional bond** as "a relatively long-enduring tie in which the partner is important as a unique individual and is interchangeable with none other. In an affectional bond, there is a desire to maintain closeness to the partner" (1989, p. 711). An **attachment** is a subvariety of emotional bond in which a person's sense of security is bound up in the relationship. When you are attached, you feel (or hope to feel) a special sense of security and comfort in the presence of the other, and you can use the other as a "safe base" from which to explore the rest of the world.

[?] *Critical Thinking*

Think about your own relationships. In Bowlby's and Ainsworth's terms, which are attachments and which are affectional bonds? Can you think of times when you have used someone to whom you are attached as a "safe base"?

In these terms the child's relationship with the parent is an attachment, but the parent's relationship with the child is not. The parent presumably does not feel an enhanced sense of security in the presence of the infant, or use the infant as a safe base. In contrast, your adult relationships with your spouse or partner, with your parents, or with a very close friend, typically are attachments in the sense Ainsworth and Bowlby mean the term.

Because affectional bonds and attachments are internal states, we cannot see them directly. Instead, we deduce their existence by observing **attachment behaviors,** which are all those behaviors that allow a child or adult to achieve and retain proximity to someone else to whom he is attached or with whom he has a strong affectional bond. This could include smiling, making eye contact, calling out to the other person across a room, touching, clinging, or crying.

It is important to make clear that the number of different attachment behaviors a child (or adult) shows on any one occasion is not necessarily a good measure of the quality of that person's underlying attachment or bond toward some other person. An attachment is an enduring underlying state, while attachment behaviors are elicited primarily when the individual feels the need for care, support, or comfort. An infant is in such a needy state much of the time, so he shows attachment behaviors frequently. An older child or an adult will be likely to show attachment behaviors only when frightened, tired, or otherwise under stress. It is the *pattern* of these behaviors, not the frequency, that tells us something about the quality of the attachment or the affectional bond.

[?] *Critical Thinking*

Pick one of your attachment relationships and make a list of all the attachment behaviors you show toward that person. Are any of these the same as the kind of attachment behaviors we see in an infant?

The Parent's Bond to the Infant

To understand the early relationship between the parent and the child, we need to look at both sides of the equation—at the development of the parent's bond to the child and of the child's attachment to the parent.

The Initial Bond.   If you read the popular press, I am sure you have come across articles proclaiming that mothers (or fathers) must have immediate contact with their newborn infant if they are to become properly bonded with the baby. This belief has been based primarily on the work of two pediatricians, Marshall Klaus and John Kennell (1976), who proposed the hypothesis that the first few hours after an infant's birth is a "critical period" for the development of a mother's bond to her infant. Mothers who are denied early contact, Klaus and Kennell thought, are likely to form weaker bonds and thus be at higher risk for a range of disorders of parenting.

Their proposal was one of many factors leading to significant changes in birth practices, including the now-normal presence of fathers at delivery. I would certainly not want to turn back the clock on such changes. However, it now looks as if Klaus and Kennell's hypothesis is essentially incorrect. Immediate contact does not appear to be either necessary or sufficient for the formation of a stable, long-term affectional bond between either mother or father and child (Myers, 1987).

A few studies show some short-term beneficial effects of very early contact. In the first few days after delivery, mothers with such contact may show more tender fondling or more gazing at the baby than is true of mothers who first held their babies some hours after birth (e.g., de Chateau, 1980), but there is little indication of a lasting effect. Two or three months after delivery, mothers who have had immediate contact with their newborns do not smile at them more or hold them differently than do mothers who had delayed contact. Thus neither early nor extended contact appears to be an essential ingredient in forming a strong affectional bond—a comforting conclusion for adoptive parents, among others.

The Development of Synchrony.   What *is* essential in the formation of that bond is the opportunity for the parent and infant to develop a mutual, interlocking pattern of attachment behaviors, a smooth "dance" of interaction. The baby signals his needs by crying or smiling; he responds to being held by quieting or snuggling; he looks at the parents when they look at him. The parents (or grandparents), in their turn, enter into this two-person dance with their own repertoire of caregiving behaviors. They pick the baby up when he cries, wait for and respond to his signals of hunger or other needs, smile at him when he smiles, gaze into his eyes when he looks at them. Some researchers and theorists have described this as the development of *synchrony* (Isabella, Belsky, & von Eye, 1989).

One of the most intriguing things about this process is that we all seem to know how to do this particular dance, and we do it in very similar ways. In the presence of a young infant most adults will automatically display a distinctive pattern of interactive behaviors, including smiling, raised eyebrows, and very wide-open eyes. And we all seem to use our voices in special ways with babies as well. Parents all over the world use a characteristic high-pitched and lilting voice when speaking to an infant, and use similar intonation patterns to signal different meanings. For example, Hanus and Mechthild Papousek (1991) found that Chinese, German, and U.S. mothers all tended to use a rising voice inflection when they wanted their baby to "take a turn" in the interaction and to use a falling intonation when they wanted to soothe their baby.

[?] *Critical Thinking*

Watch yourself next time you interact with a baby. Does your facial expression match the "mock surprise" in the photos below? Do you speak in a higher, lilting voice? Do your intonation patterns match the ones in the Papousek study?

Yet, while we can perform all these attachment *behaviors* with many infants, we do not form a bond with every baby we coo at in a restaurant or the grocery store. For an adult, the critical ingredient for the formation of a bond seems to be the opportunity to develop real synchrony—to practice the dance until the partners follow one another's lead smoothly and pleasurably. This takes time and many rehearsals, and some parents (and infants) become more skillful at it than others. In general, the smoother and more predictable the process becomes, the more satisfying it seems to be to the parents and the stronger their bond to the infant becomes.

Father-Child Bonds.   Most of the research I have talked about so far has involved studies of mothers. Still, many of the same principles seem to hold for fathers. In particular, fathers seem to direct the same repertoire of attachment behaviors toward their infant as do mothers. In the early weeks of the baby's life dads touch, talk to, and cuddle their babies in the same ways that mothers do, and they show the same physiological responses when they interact with their new infant, including increased heart rate and blood pressure (Corter & Fleming, 1995).

Past these earliest weeks, however, we see signs of a kind of specialization of parental behav-

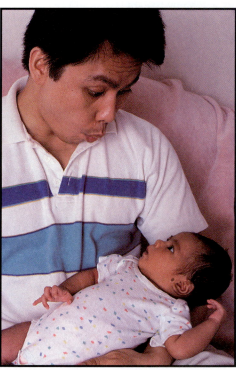

Adults all over the world, both moms and dads, show this same "mock surprise" expression when they are talking to or playing with a baby. The eyebrows are raised, the eyes are wide, and the forehead is wrinkled. A wide-open, smiling mouth, like the mom shows here, is often part of the expression too.

Brandon's dad, like most fathers in U.S. culture, is far more likely to toss the baby in the air or play with him in this vigorous physical way than is his mom. But this sex difference does not exist in every culture.

iors with infants and toddlers. Studies in the United States show that dads spend more time playing with a baby, using more physical rough-housing. Moms spend more time in routine care-giving, and they talk and smile more at the baby (Parke, 1995; Walker, Messinger, Fogel, & Karns, 1992). This does not mean that fathers have a weaker affectional bond with the infant; it does mean that the behaviors they show toward the infant are typically somewhat different from those mothers show.

However, we should not leap to the conclusion that this sex difference is somehow built in; instead, it looks as if it is more likely to be a result of cultural training. Researchers in England and in India have found higher levels of physical play by fathers than by mothers, but researchers in Sweden and Israel have not (Parke, 1995). Findings like this

are a nice illustration of the usefulness of cross-cultural research, which not only tells us something about the universality of a particular pattern but also suggests new hypotheses about patterns we see in our own culture.

The Baby's Attachment to the Parents

Like the parent's bond to the baby, the baby's attachment emerges gradually. Bowlby (1969) suggested three phases in the development of the infant's attachment, sketched schematically in Figure 6.1.

Phase 1: Nonfocused Orienting and Signaling.
Bowlby thought that the baby begins life with a set of innate behavior patterns that orient him toward others and signal his needs. Mary Ainsworth describes these as "proximity promoting" behaviors—they bring people closer. In the newborn's repertoire these behaviors include all the various emotional expressions—crying, making eye contact, clinging, cuddling, and responding to caregiving efforts by being soothed.

At this stage there is little evidence that the baby is attached to the parents. As Ainsworth says, "These attachment behaviors are simply emitted, rather than being directed toward any specific person" (1989, p. 710). Nonetheless, the roots of attachment are to be found in this phase. The baby is building up expectancies and schemas about interaction patterns with the parents, as well as developing the ability to discriminate Mom and Dad from others in many contexts.

Phase 2: Focus on One or More Figure(s).
By age 3 months the baby begins to aim her attachment

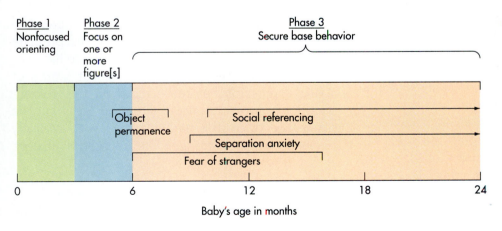

Figure 6.1

This schematic shows how the various threads of development of attachment are woven together.

Cultures and Contexts

Attachment in a Very Different Cultural System

Is the sequence of phases Bowlby and Ainsworth describe universal? Do all babies go through this same sequence, no matter what kind of family or culture they live in? Maybe yes, maybe no. Ainsworth herself observed the same basic three phases in forming a clear attachment among children in Uganda, although they showed a more intense fear of strangers than is usually found in American samples. Note, though, that among the Ganda, as in American and other Western families, the mother is the primary caregiver. What would we find in a culture in which the child's early care is much more communal?

Edward Tronick and his colleagues (Tronick, Morelli, & Ivey, 1992) have studied just such a culture, a pygmy group called the Efe, who forage in the forests of Zaire. They live in small groups of perhaps 20 individuals in camps, each group consisting of several extended families, often brothers and their wives.

Infants in these communities are cared for communally in the early months and years of life. They are car-

ried and held by all the adult women and interact regularly with many different adults. If they have needs, they are tended by whichever adult or older child is nearby; they may even be nursed by women other than the mother, although they normally sleep with the mother.

Tronick and his colleagues report two things of particular interest about early attachment in this group. First, Efe infants seem to use virtually any adult or older child in their world as a safe base, which suggests that they may have no single central attachment. Yet, beginning at about age 6 months, Efe infants nonetheless seem to insist on being with their mother more and to prefer her over other women, although other women continue to help care for the child.

Thus, even in an extremely communal rearing arrangement, we can still see some sign of a central attachment, albeit perhaps less dominant. At the same time, it is clear, as Inge Bretherton says, that "attachment behavior is never purely instinctive, but is heavily overlain with cultural prescriptions" (1992b, p. 150).

behaviors somewhat more narrowly. She may smile more to the people who regularly take care of her and may not smile readily to a stranger. Nevertheless, despite the change, Bowlby and Ainsworth have argued that the infant does not yet have a full-blown attachment. The child still favors a number of people with her "proximity promoting" behaviors, and no one person has yet become the "safe base." Children in this phase show no special anxiety at being separated from their parents and display no fear of strangers.

Phase 3: Secure Base Behavior. Only at 6 months of age or so, according to Bowlby, does the baby form a genuine attachment. For the first time at about this age, the infant uses the "most important person" as a safe base from which to explore the world around her—one of the key signs that an attachment exists. At roughly that same age, the dominant mode of the baby's attachment behavior changes. Because the 6- to 7-month-old begins to be able to move about the world more freely by creeping and crawling, she can move *toward* the caregiver as well as entice the caregiver to come to her. Her attachment behaviors therefore shift from mostly "come here" signals (proximity promoting)

to what Ainsworth calls "proximity seeking," which we might think of as "go there" behaviors.

I should note that not all infants have a *single* attachment figure, even at this stage. Some may show strong attachment to both parents, or to a parent and another caregiver, such as a baby-sitter, a day-care worker, or a grandparent. But even these babies, when under stress, usually show a preference for one of their favored persons over the others.

Once the child has developed a clear attachment, at about 6 to 8 months of age, several related behaviors also appear. One of these is social referencing, which I talked about in the last chapter. The 10-month-old uses his ability to discriminate among various facial expressions to guide his safe-base behavior. He begins to check out Mom's or Dad's expression before deciding whether to venture forth into some novel situation. At about the same age or a little earlier, babies also typically show both fear of strangers and separation anxiety.

Fear of Strangers and Separation Anxiety. Imagine yourself as the parent of 4-month-old James. You find a baby-sitter to take care of the baby one evening, while you and your partner have some much-needed time alone together. You're relieved that James lets the baby-sitter hold him and scarcely gives a whimper when you go out the door. The sitter later reports that James was just fine the whole evening. Four months pass. You hire the same sitter to come for an evening. But this time James screams when you try to hand him to the sitter and screams even more when you go out the door. The sitter reports that she had a hard time calming him down, but that he did eventually do okay. In this second case, James showed both fear of strangers—not wanting to be held by the baby-sitter—and anxiety about your leaving. Both these forms of distress are rare before 5 or 6 months, rise in frequency until about 12 to 16 months, and then decline. The research findings are not altogether consistent, but it looks as though fear of strangers normally appears first, at about the same time that babies show fear emotions about other experiences as well. Anxiety at separation starts a bit later, and it continues to be visible for a longer period, a pattern I've indicated in Figure 6.1 (p. 187).

Researchers have observed the same increase in fear and apparent distress in children from a number of different cultures as well as in both home-reared and day-care-reared children in the United States, all of which makes it look as if some basic cognitive or other age-related developmental timetable underlies this pattern (Kagan, Kearsley, & Zelazo, 1978). If you think about what you've already learned about the object concept, the whole thing makes sense. Prior to about this age, babies seem to lose interest in objects when they are no longer in sight; but between 6 and 8 months, they have figured out that Mom (or Dad or whoever) continues to exist when she is out of sight, but they don't yet have the ability to imagine her returning or to understand her words when she says "I'll be back." So James knows you're gone, but not that you are coming back. Seven or 8 months is also too early for a baby to be able to use social referencing, so it doesn't help to smile or be cheerful. By 12 months, he has made enough cognitive advances that he is better able to understand that Mom or Dad will indeed come back.

Virtually all children show at least mild forms of these two types of distress, although the intensity of the reaction varies widely. Some protest briefly; others are virtually inconsolable. Some of this difference may reflect basic temperamental variations (Kagan, 1994), a subject I'll take up in a moment. Heightened fearfulness may also be a response to some upheaval or stress in the child's life, such as a recent move or a change in the daily schedule. Whatever the origin of such variations in fearfulness, the pattern does eventually diminish in most toddlers, typically by the middle of the second year.

Variations in the Quality of Infants' Attachments

What I have been describing is the normal developmental sequence for a baby's attachment to parent or caregiver. Equally important is the *quality* of the child's attachment. Go to a day care center and watch the way the babies or toddlers greet their parents at the end of the day. Some are calmly pleased to see Mom or Dad, running to be hugged, showing a new toy, or smiling when picked up, showing no distress. Others may run to the parent, crying and clinging to the parent; still others may

A few months ago, this baby probably would have let herself be held by just about anyone without a fuss; now all of a sudden, she clings to Mom in apparent fear when the neighbor reaches for her. Parents are often puzzled by this, but it is absolutely normal.

show little interest, even turning away from the parent when Mom or Dad approaches. These babies may all have formed an attachment to their parents, but the quality of that attachment differs markedly. In Bowlby's terminology, these children have different **internal working models** of their relationships with parents and key others. This internal working model of attachment relationships includes such elements as the child's confidence (or lack of it) that the attachment figure will be available or reliable, the child's expectation of rebuff or affection, and the child's sense of assurance that the other is really a safe base for exploration.

The internal model begins to be formed late in the child's first year of life and becomes increasingly elaborated and firm through the first four or five years. By age 5 most children have clear internal models of the mother (or other caregiver), a self model, and a model of relationships. Once formed, such models shape and explain experiences and affect memory and attention. We notice and remember experiences that fit our models and miss or forget experiences that don't match. Using Piaget's language, we could say that a child more readily assimilates data that fit the model. More importantly, the model affects the child's behavior: The child tends to re-create, in each new relationship, the pattern with which he is familiar. Alan Sroufe gives a nice example that will be especially significant for those of you planning to work with preschool-age children:

What is rejection to one child is benign to another. What is warmth to a second child is confusing or ambiguous to another. For example, a child approaches another and asks to play. Turned down, the child goes off and sulks in a corner. A second child receiving the same negative reaction skips on to another partner and successfully engages him in play. Their experiences of rejection are vastly different. Each receives confirmation of quite different inner working models. (1988, p. 23)

[?] *Critical Thinking*

If internal working models tend to persist—and to affect later relationships—is this the same as saying that the first few years of life are a critical period for the creation of patterns of relationships? How else could we conceptualize it?

Secure and Insecure Attachments

All the theorists in this tradition share the assumption that the first attachment relationship is the most influential ingredient in the creation of the child's working model. Variations in that first attachment relationship are now almost universally described using Mary Ainsworth's category system (Ainsworth et al., 1978). She distinguishes between **secure attachment** and two types of **insecure attachment,** a classification system I'm going to talk about at some length because it is has proven extremely helpful in predicting a remarkably wide range of later behaviors in children, as toddlers and in later childhood—and even in adulthood.

To measure the security of the child's attachment, Ainsworth devised a procedure called the **Strange Situation.** It consists of a series of eight episodes in a laboratory setting, typically used when the child is between 12 and 18 months of age. The child is first with the mother, then with the mother and a stranger, alone with the stranger, completely alone for a few minutes, reunited with the mother, left alone again, and then reunited first with the stranger and then the mother. Ainsworth suggested that children's reactions to this situation—particularly to the reunion episodes—could be classified into three types: *securely attached, insecure/avoidant* (also sometimes called detached), and *insecure/ambivalent* (also sometimes called resistant). Mary Main (Main & Solomon, 1990) has suggested a fourth group, which she calls *insecure/disorganized/ disoriented,* all described in Table 6.2. As you read the descriptions, note that whether the child cries when he is separated from his mother is *not* a helpful indicator of the security of his attachment. Some securely attached infants cry then, others do not, as is true of insecurely attached infants as well. It is the entire pattern of the child's response to the Strange Situation that is critical, not any one response.

These attachment types have been observed in studies in many different countries, and in every country secure attachment is the most common pattern—as you can see from the information in the *Cultures and Contexts* box (p. 192).

Origins of Secure and Insecure Attachments.
Where do these differences in attachment pattern come from? We know that insecurely attached infants are more likely to be found in poverty-level families, in families with a history of abuse or parental

Table 6.2

Categorization of Secure and Insecure Attachment in Ainsworth's Strange Situation

Securely attached	Child readily separates from the caregiver and easily becomes absorbed in exploration; when threatened or frightened, child actively seeks contact and is readily consoled, and does not avoid or resist contact if mother initiates it. When reunited with mother after absence, child greets her positively, or is easily soothed if upset. Clearly prefers mother to stranger.
Insecurely attached: detached/avoidant	Child avoids contact with mother, especially at reunion after an absence. Does not resist mother's efforts to make contact, but does not seek much contact. Shows no preference for mother over the stranger.
Insecurely attached: resistant/ambivalent	Child shows little exploration and is wary of the stranger. Greatly upset when separated from mother, but not reassured by mother's return or her efforts at comforting. Child both seeks and avoids contact at different times. May show anger toward mother at reunion, and resists both comfort from and contact with stranger.
Insecurely attached: disorganized/disoriented	Dazed behavior, confusion, or apprehension. Child may show contradictory behavior patterns simultaneously, such as moving toward mother while keeping gaze averted.

Sources: Ainsworth et al., 1978; Main & Solomon, 1990; Carlson & Sroufe, 1995.

alcohol use, or in families in which the mother is diagnosed as seriously depressed (Cicchetti & Barnett, 1991; Das Eiden & Leonard, 1996; Spieker & Booth, 1988). Securely attached infants are more likely to have parents with satisfying marriages or other sources of good emotional support (e.g., Belsky, 1996; Belsky, Rosenberger, & Crnic, 1995). None of these findings is likely to be at all surprising, but this list still doesn't tell us what is actually happening between parents and children that may foster secure or insecure attachments. Studies of actual parent-child interactions suggest that the crucial ingredients for a secure attachment are acceptance of the infant by the parents and *contingent responsiveness* from the parents toward the infant (Isabella, 1995; Pederson & Moran, 1995; Pederson, Moran, Sitko et al., 1990; Seifer, Schiller, Sameroff, Resnick, & Riordan, 1996). Contingent responsiveness does not just mean that the parents love the baby or take care of the baby well, but rather that in their caregiving and other behavior toward the child they are *sensitive* to the child's own cues and respond appropriately. They smile when the baby smiles, talk to the baby when he vocalizes, pick him up when he cries, and so on (Ainsworth & Marvin, 1995; Sroufe, 1996).

Our certainty that this type of responsiveness is a key ingredient in a secure attachment has been greatly strengthened by an experimental demonstration of the effect by Dymphna van den Boom (1994). For this study, van den Boom identified 100 lower-class Dutch mothers whose infants had all been rated as high in irritability shortly after birth. Half the mothers were then assigned randomly to participate in a set of three relatively brief training sessions aimed at helping them improve their responsiveness to their infant. The other half of the mothers received no such help. When the babies were 12 months old, van den Boom observed the mothers interacting with their infants at home and in the standard Strange Situation. The effects were quite clear: The trained mothers had indeed become more responsive to their babies, and their babies were more likely to be securely attached, as you can see from the results in Table 6.3 (p. 193). In a follow-up study, van den Boom found that these same differences persisted to at least age 18 months (1995).

A low level of responsiveness thus appears to be an ingredient in any type of insecure attachment. Beyond this common factor, each of the several subvarieties of insecure attachment has additional distinct antecedents. For example, a disorganized/disoriented pattern seems especially likely when the child has been abused or is in a family in which either parent had some unresolved trauma in their own childhood, such as abuse or the early death of a parent (Cassidy & Berlin, 1994;

Cultures and Contexts

Secure and Insecure Attachments in Different Cultures

Studies in a variety of countries support Mary Ainsworth's contention that some form of "secure base behavior" occurs in every child, in every culture (e.g., Posada, Gao, Wu et al., 1995). At the same time, we have some evidence suggesting that secure attachments may be more likely in certain cultures than in others. The most thorough analyses have come from a Dutch psychologist, Marinus van IJzendoorn, who has examined the results of 32 separate studies in eight different countries. You can see the percentage of babies classified in each category for each country in the table below (van IJzendoorn & Kroonenberg, 1988).

Cross-Cultural Comparisons of Secure and Insecure Attachments

Country	Number of Studies	Percentage of Each Attachment Type		
		Secure	Avoidant	Ambivalent
West Germany	3	56.6	35.3	8.1
Great Britain	1	75.0	22.2	2.8
Netherlands	4	67.3	26.3	6.4
Sweden	1	74.5	21.6	3.9
Israel	2	64.4	6.8	28.8
Japan	2	67.7	5.2	25.0
China	1	50.0	25.0	25.0
United States	18	64.8	21.1	14.1
Overall Average		65.0	21.3	13.7

Source: Based on Table 1 of van IJzendoorn & Kroonenberg, 1988, pp. 150–151.

We need to be cautious about overinterpreting the information in this table because, in most cases, we have only one or two studies from a given country, normally with quite small samples. The single study from China, for example, included only 36 babies. Still, the findings are thought-provoking.

The most striking thing about these data is actually their consistency. In each of the eight countries, a secure attachment is the most common pattern, found in more than half of all babies studied; in six of the eight, an avoidant pattern is the more common of the two forms of insecure attachment. Only in Israel and Japan is this pattern significantly reversed. How might we explain such differences?

One possibility is that the Strange Situation is simply not an appropriate measure of attachment security in all cultures. For example, because Japanese babies are rarely separated from their mothers in the first year of life, being left totally alone in the midst of the Strange Situation may be far more stressful for them, which might result in more intense, inconsolable crying and hence a classification of ambivalent attachment. Yet, when we look directly at the toddlers' actual behavior in the Strange Situation, we see few cultural differences in such things as proximity seeking or avoidance of Mom, all of which gives us more confidence that the Strange Situation is tapping similar processes among children in many cultures (Sagi, van IJzendoorn, & Koren-Karie, 1991).

Another possibility is that the *meaning* of a "secure" or "avoidant" pattern is different in different cultures, even if the percentages of each category are similar. German researchers, for example, have suggested that an insecure/avoidant classification in their culture may reflect not indifference by mothers, but explicit training toward greater independence in the baby (Grossmann, Grossmann, Spangler, Suess, & Unzner, 1985). Alternatively, because different cultures value quite different behaviors in their children, a secure attachment might simply not look the same in every culture. As one example, Robin Harwood and her colleagues (Harwood, Miller, & Irizarry, 1995) asked Puerto Rican mothers (both island and mainland) and Anglo mothers to evaluate the behaviors toddlers show in the Strange Situation. The Puerto Rican mothers, who live in a more collectivist culture, placed high value on proper demeanor,

Cultures and Contexts

Secure and Insecure Attachments in Different Cultures (*Continued*)

respect, obedience, and politeness. The Anglo mothers, in contrast, liked to see toddlers behaving with independence and self-reliance, a pattern Harwood calls "self-maximization." This finding raises the possibility that behaviors that Anglo researchers see as optimal—as reflecting a secure attachment—may predict good outcomes for Anglo children but not necessarily for those growing up in a more collectivist culture. We need new research to tell us whether those same behaviors would be linked to good outcomes for Hispanic children.

I know of no research of this type comparing Hispanic and Anglo children, but there is one relevant study in Israel. Sagi (1990) found that the Strange Situation attachment classification predicted Israeli children's later social skills in much the same way as is found in United States samples, which suggests that the classification system is valid in both these cultures.

At the moment, the most plausible hypothesis is that the same factors in mother-infant interaction contribute to secure and insecure attachments in all cultures, and that these patterns reflect similar internal models. We need more research like the Israeli work in which the long-term outcomes of the various categories are studied in differing cultures before we can be sure if this is correct.

Table 6.3

The Effect of Mothers' Responsiveness Training on Infants' Attachment Security

	Attachment Classification at 12 Months	
	Number Secure	Number Insecure
Training	31	19
No training	11	39

Source: van den Boom, 1994, from Table 5, p. 1472.

Main & Hesse, 1990). An ambivalent pattern is more common when the mother is inconsistently or unreliably available to the child. Mothers may show such unavailability or periodic neglect for a variety of reasons, but a common ingredient is depression in the mother (Teti, Gelfand, Messinger, & Isabella, 1995).

If the mother regularly rejects or withdraws from contact with the baby, the infant is more likely to develop an avoidant pattern of attachment, although avoidance also seems to occur when the mother is overly intrusive or overly stimulating of the infant (Isabella, 1995).

Stability of Attachment Classification. Do these variations in the quality of the child's early attachment persist over time? Does a 1-year-old who is securely or insecurely attached to his mother still show the same quality of attachment when he's 2,

or 3, or 6? This question is a particularly important one for those researchers and therapists who are concerned about the possible permanence of effects of early abuse or neglect or other sources of insecure attachment. Can children recover from such unfortunate early treatment? Conversely, is a child who is securely attached at 1 year of age forever buffered from the effects of later difficult life circumstances?

The answer, perhaps not surprisingly, is that both consistency and inconsistency occur, depending on the circumstances. When the child's family environment or life circumstances are reasonably consistent, the security or insecurity of his attachment also seems to remain consistent, even over many years. For example, Claire Hamilton assessed current attachment security/insecurity, using a special form of interview with a small group of adolescents whose security had also been assessed in the Strange Situation when they were infants (Hamilton, 1995). Sixteen of the 18 adolescents who had been rated as insecurely attached at 12 months of age were still rated as insecurely attached at age 17, while 7 of the 11 teens who had been classed as securely attached as infants were still rated as securely attached at 17. Similarly, in a shorter-term study in Germany (Wartner, Grossman, Fremmer-Bombik, & Suess, 1994), 82 percent of a group of youngsters from stable, middle-class families were rated in the same category of attachment security at age 6 as they had been at age 1.

When the child's circumstances change in some major way, however, such as when she starts going to day care or nursery school, when grandma comes to live with the family, or when the parents divorce or move, the security of the child's attachment may change as well, either from secure to insecure or the reverse. For example, Everett Waters and his colleagues (Waters, Treboux, Crowell, Merrick, & Albersheim, 1995) followed one group of white, middle-class children from age 1 to age 21, measuring their adult attachment, using the same method Hamilton used in her adolescent study—an interview called the Adult Attachment Interview. Those whose attachment classification changed over this long interval had nearly all experienced some major upheaval, such as the death of a parent, physical or sexual abuse, or a serious illness.

The very fact that a child's attachment security can change from one time to the next does not refute the notion of attachment as an internal working model. Bowlby suggested that for the first two or three years, the particular pattern of attachment a child shows is in some sense a property of each specific *relationship*. For example, studies of toddlers' attachments to mothers and fathers show that about 30 percent of the time the child is securely attached to one parent and insecurely attached to the other, with both possible combinations equally represented (Fox, Kimmerly, & Schafer, 1991). It is the quality of each relationship that determines the child's security with that specific adult. If that relationship changes markedly, the security of the baby's attachment to that person may change too. By age 4 or 5, however, Bowlby argued that the internal working model becomes more a property of the *child*, more generalized across relationships, and thus more resistant to change. At that point, the child tends to impose it upon new relationships, including relationships with teachers or peers.

Thus a child may "recover" from an initially insecure attachment or lose a secure one. Still, consistency over time is somewhat more typical, both because children's relationships tend to be reasonably stable for the first few years and because once the internal model is firmly established, it tends to perpetuate itself.

Long-Term Consequences of Secure and Insecure Attachment. Ainsworth's classification system

has proven to be extremely helpful in predicting a remarkably wide range of other behaviors in children, both as toddlers and in later childhood and adolescence. Dozens of studies show that children rated as securely attached to their mothers in infancy are later more sociable, more positive in their behavior toward friends and siblings, less clinging and dependent on teachers, less aggressive and disruptive, more empathetic, and more emotionally mature in their approach to school and other nonhome settings (e.g., Carlson & Sroufe, 1995; Leve & Fagot, 1995).

At adolescence, those who were rated as securely attached in infancy, or who are classed as secure on the basis of interviews in adolescence, have more intimate friendships, are more likely to be rated as leaders, and have higher self-esteem (Black & McCartney, 1995; Lieberman, Doyle, & Markiewicz, 1995; Ostoja, McCrone, Lehn, Reed, & Sroufe, 1995). Those with insecure attachments—particularly those with avoidant attachments—not only have less positive and supportive friendships in adolescence, they are also more likely to become sexually active early and practice riskier sex (O'Beirne & Moore, 1995).

One particularly clear demonstration of some of these links comes from a longitudinal study by Alan Sroufe and his coworkers (Sroufe, Carlson, & Schulman, 1993; Urban, Carlson, Egeland, & Sroufe, 1991), who have followed a group of youngsters from infancy through early adolescence—a study described in the *Research Report* on page 47. Recall that when the children were ages 11 to 12, some of them attended a special summer camp. Counselors at the camp, and special observers who watched the camp activities, rated each child on a wide range of characteristics and behaviors. The researchers could then look at possible connections between these ratings and the child's initial attachment classification. They found that those children who had been rated as securely attached in infancy behaved much more positively with their peers at age 11, most often forming friendships with other securely attached peers. They also had much more self-confidence; they believed in their own ability to accomplish whatever goal they chose—a highly important quality Albert Bandura calls *self efficacy* and that Sroufe labels *agency*. Those rated as insecurely attached in infancy, in contrast, had more difficulty establishing friendships and were much more likely to show deviant behavior of some kind. In some cases the deviance manifested itself as excessive aggressiveness or hyperactivity, in other cases as isolation or passivity.

Collectively, the findings point to potentially long-term consequences of attachment patterns or internal working models of relationships constructed in the first year or two of life. At the same time, fluidity and change also occur, and we need to know much more about the factors that tend to maintain, or alter, the earliest models.

[?] *Critical Thinking*

Here's a dilemma worth some thought for those of you who will be teachers: You will probably *like* the kids in your classes with early secure attachments better than you will like the insecurely attached kids. Such a perfectly natural bias on your part has the effect of giving the securely attached students yet another advantage. Can you think of any specific things you could do to try to counteract this natural bias?

The Development of the Sense of Self

Eight-month-old James, who cried when you tried to leave him with a baby-sitter, probably would *not* cry if you left him in a room with another 8-month-old. Why? According to psychologist Michael Lewis, such a difference in the baby's reaction suggests that the 8-month-old is just beginning to develop a sense of self, which includes the sense of who is "like me" or "different from me." When this aspect of the sense of self is more fully developed, by about 18 to 24 months, we see toddlers choosing to play more with other toddlers they see as like themselves, such as boys choosing boys and girls choosing girls as playmates. A sense of self is also a critical part of the child's emerging sense that she can influence the world around her—that she is an actor in the great drama.

The baby's sense of self is emerging during the same months that she is developing an attachment to Mom or Dad. If we think of the sense of self as another internal working model—a model of "who I am"—then we see that the infant is already creating two such models: a model of attachment and a model of self.

The Separate Self

The sense of self has two parts to it, which seem to emerge in sequence (Lewis, 1990; 1991; Lewis, Sullivan, Stanger, & Weiss, 1989; Mascolo & Fischer, 1995). First, the baby has to figure out that he is separate from everyone else. Babies seem to begin to develop this feeling of separateness in the early months through the simple process of seeing themselves having an effect on things. When the child touches the mobile, it moves; when he cries, someone responds; when he smiles, his mother smiles back. By this process the baby begins to have a very preliminary feeling that I am doing things.

In these early months, this is still a pretty primitive sense of self. Piaget argued that the next crucial step is the child's understanding of object permanence, at about 8 months of age. Just as the baby is figuring out that Mom and Dad continue to exist when they are out of sight, he is beginning to understand that he, too, exists separately and has some permanence.

Self-Awareness

This isn't the end of the story, though. To have a complete sense of self the baby or toddler has to know more than merely that he is separate from others; he also has to realize that he is an *object* in the world, with properties and qualities. Just as a ball has properties—roundness, the ability to roll, a certain feel in the hand—so the "self" also has qualities or properties, such as gender, size, a name, or qualities like shyness or boldness, coordination or clumsiness. To be able to perceive oneself as having properties, a child (or adult) has to be aware of himself in a quite different way, to be able to see himself as if from the outside. Michael Lewis, one of the key figures in research in this area, sometimes refers to this next step as the development of the **categorical self,** because once the child achieves self-awareness, she begins to place herself in a whole series of categories.

Links to Adult Attachments

Researchers who study attachment have begun to ask a new set of questions about the long-term consequences of early attachment patterns: Do adults' internal models of attachment—presumably a product of their own early history—affect the way they behave with their children and thus shape the child's emerging attachment patterns? That is, is there some kind of intergenerational transmission of secure, or insecure, attachment?

Mary Main and her colleagues have devised an interview that allows them to classify the security or insecurity of an adult's attachment to his or her own parents (Main & Hesse, 1990; Main, Kaplan, & Cassidy, 1985), so we are now able to explore this question. In this interview, adults (or sometimes teenagers) are asked about their childhood experiences and their current relationship with their parents. In one question, interviewees are asked to choose five adjectives to describe their relationship with each parent and to say why they chose each adjective. They are also asked whether they ever felt rejected in childhood and how they feel about their parents currently. On the basis of the interview, the adult's internal working model of attachment is classified as being one of three types:

- Secure/autonomous/balanced. *These individuals value attachment relations and see their early experiences as influential, but they are objective in describing both good and bad qualities. These subjects speak coherently about early experiences and have thoughts about what motivated their parents' behavior.*

- Dismissing or detached. *These adults minimize the importance or the effects of early family experience. They may idealize their parents, perhaps even denying the existence of any negative childhood experiences. They emphasize their own personal strengths.*

- Preoccupied or enmeshed. *These adults often talk about inconsistent or role-reversed parenting. They remain engrossed with their relationship with their parents, still actively struggling to please them or being very angry at them. They are confused and ambivalent, but still engaged.*

When these adult models are linked to the security of attachment displayed by the *children* of those adults, the expected pattern emerges strongly: Adults with se-

cure models of attachment to their own parents are much more likely to have infants or toddlers with secure attachments. Those with dismissing models are more likely to have infants with avoidant attachments, while adults with preoccupied attachments are more likely to have infants with ambivalent attachments. Across 20 studies, the typical finding is that three-fourths of the mother-infant pairs share the same attachment category (van IJzendoorn, 1995). Diane Benoit (Benoit & Parker, 1994) has even found marked consistency across *three* generations: grandmothers, young mothers, and infants.

This is not a genetic transmission—at least not directly. Rather, the link across generations appears to lie in the mother's own behavior toward her child, which varies as a function of her own internal working model of attachment. Mothers who are themselves securely attached are more responsive and sensitive in their behavior toward their infants or young children (van IJzendoorn, 1995). For example, Judith Crowell and Shirley Feldman (1988) observed moms with their preschoolers in a free-play setting. In the middle of the play period, the mother left the child alone for several minutes and then returned. Mothers who were themselves classed as secure in their attachment model were more likely to prepare the child ahead of time for the impending separation, had less difficulty themselves with the separation, and were most physically responsive to the child during reunion. Preoccupied moms were themselves more anxious about separating from the child and prepared the child less. Dismissing mothers also prepared the child very little but left without difficulty and remained physically distant from the child after returning to the playroom.

Crowell and Feldman also noted that mothers with dismissing or preoccupied internal models interpreted the child's behavior very differently than did the secure moms.

> One mother observed her crying child through the observation window and said, "See, she isn't upset about being left." At reunion, she said to the child, "Why are you crying? I didn't leave." (1991, p. 604)

Thus not only does the mother's own internal model affect her actual behavior, it also affects the meaning she ascribes to the child's behavior, both of which will affect the child's developing model of attachment.

When does a child first have such self-awareness? This has been a very hard question to answer, but Lewis devised a clever strategy. He first puts a baby in front of a mirror, just to see how she behaves. Most infants between 9 and 12 months will look at their own images, make faces, or try to interact with the baby-in-the-mirror in some way. After allowing this free exploration for a time, Lewis pretends to wipe the baby's face with a cloth and surreptitiously puts a spot of rouge on the baby's nose. Then he lets the baby look in the mirror again. The crucial test of self-recognition, and thus of awareness of the self, is whether the baby reaches for the spot on her *own* nose, rather than the nose on the face in the mirror.

Figure 6.2 shows you the results from one of Lewis's studies using this procedure. As you can see, none of the 9- to 12-month-old children in this study touched their noses, but by 21 months three-fourths of the children showed that level of self-recognition, a result confirmed in a variety of other research, including studies in Europe (e.g., Asendorpf, Warkentin, & Baudonnière, 1996). The figure also shows the rate at which children refer to themselves by name when they are shown a picture of themselves, which is another commonly used measure of self-awareness. You can see that this development occurs at almost exactly the same time as self-recognition in a mirror. Both are present by about the middle of the second year of life.

Once the toddler achieves such self-awareness, his behavior is affected in a whole range of ways. Self-aware toddlers now begin to insist on doing things for themselves and show a newly proprietary attitude toward toys ("Mine!") or other treasured objects. Looked at this way, much of the legendary "terrible twos," in which toddlers seem to become

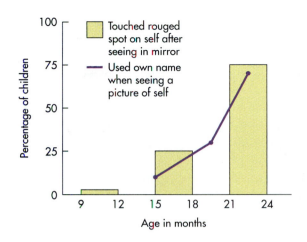

Figure 6.2

Mirror recognition and self-naming develop at almost exactly the same time, both signs of self-awareness. (Source: M. Lewis & Brooks, 1978, pp. 214–215.)

suddenly self-willed and negative, can be understood as an outgrowth of self-awareness. In a quite literal sense they *are* self-willed for the first time. It is an entirely normal process, one that is easier to deal with when you understand what is going on.

For example, it is good to give toddlers choices, even very simple ones, rather than giving commands: "Would you like to wear this shirt, or this one?" "Would you like to go now, or in a few minutes?" It is also good to give warnings ("We're going to start cleaning up in ten minutes"), and to avoid interrupting the child when she is in the midst of some intensely interesting activity. All these strategies recognize the child's newfound power rather than negating it.

Defining "Who I Am." The toddler and early preschooler also begins to define "who I am" by

Four-month-old Lucy seems delighted to look at this interesting face in the mirror, but has no idea that this is herself in the mirror. In contrast, 20-month-old Zahra realizes that this is herself she sees—one of many signs of an emerging sense of self.

learning about her own qualities and her social roles. One of the earliest dimensions of such self-definition is gender. Two-year-olds already can label themselves accurately as boys or girls, and their behavior begins to diverge in clear ways at about this age. For example, if you observe children while they play in a room stocked with a wide range of attractive toys, 2- and 3-year-old girls are likely to play with dolls or at various housekeeping games, including sewing, stringing beads, or cooking. Boys the same age will more often choose to play with guns, toy trucks, fire engines, or carpentry tools (O'Brien, 1992). By age 3, children begin to show a preference for same-sex playmates and are much more sociable with playmates of the same sex (Maccoby, 1988; 1990; Maccoby & Jacklin, 1987)—a pattern that gets progressively stronger through the preschool and early elementary school years.

Toddlers also categorize themselves on other simple dichotomous dimensions, such as big versus little, smart versus dumb, good or bad. At this early stage, they see themselves as one or the other, not both at different times.

In Bowlby's language, the child is creating an internal working model of self. He first learns that he exists separately, that he has effects on the world. Then he begins to understand that he is also an object in the world, with properties, including size and gender. The internal model of self, or the self scheme as it is often labeled, is not developed fully at this early age. Still, the toddler is already building up an image of himself, his qualities, his abilities. Like the internal model of attachment, this self model or self scheme affects the choices the toddler makes, such as choosing to play with other children of the same gender, and it influences the way the toddler will interpret experiences. In this way the internal model is not only strengthened but tends to carry forward.

Individual Differences: Personality and Temperament

In developing both their self scheme and their internal model of attachment, babies do not begin with a blank slate. Each baby starts life with certain built-in qualities, patterns of response, styles of interacting. These built-in patterns affect the way

others respond to each infant as well as shape the way each baby is likely to understand or interpret her experiences.

Psychologists normally use the word **personality** to describe these differences in the way children and adults go about relating to the people and objects in the world around themselves. Like the concept of intelligence, the concept of personality is designed to describe *enduring individual differences* in behavior. Whether we are gregarious or shy, independent or dependent, confident or uncertain, whether we plunge into new things or hold back—all these (and many more) are usually thought of as elements of personality.

Personality differences appear to rest on a very basic emotional *substrate*, usually referred to as **temperament.** These core qualities or response patterns are visible in infancy, reflected in such things as typical activity level, irritability or emotionality, soothability, fearfulness, and sociability (Hartup & van Lieshout, 1995). According to this way of thinking, temperament is "the matrix from which later child and adult personality develops" (Ahadi & Rothbart, 1994, p. 190).

This distinction between temperament and personality is a little like the difference between a genotype and a phenotype. The genotype sets the basic pattern but the eventual outcome is the result of that basic pattern affected by specific experience. Thus temperament may represent the basic pattern; what we measure as personality later in childhood or adulthood reflects the basic pattern affected by myriad life experiences. When we study infants, then, we are looking at variations in temperament—those inborn qualities that each infant brings to the interactions he has with objects and people.

Key Dimensions of Temperament

The psychologists who have studied infant temperament have not yet agreed on a basic set of temperament dimensions. One influential early theory, proposed by Thomas and Chess (1977), included a list of nine dimensions: activity level, rhythmicity, approach/withdrawal, adaptability to new experience, threshold of responsiveness, intensity of reaction, quality of mood (positive or negative), distractibility, and persistence. Thomas and Chess further proposed that variations in these nine qualities tend to cluster into three types,

Table 6.4

Thomas and Chess's Typology of Temperament

The Easy Child	The easy child is regular in biological functioning, with good sleeping and eating cycles, is usually happy, and adjusts easily to change or new experiences.
The Difficult Child	The difficult child is less regular in body functioning and is slow to develop regular sleeping and eating cycles. He reacts vigorously and negatively to new things, is more irritable, and cries more. His cries also have a more "spoiled," grating sound than do the cries of "easy" babies (Boukydis & Burgess, 1982).
The Slow-to-warm-up Child	The slow-to-warm-up infant shows few intense reactions, either positive or negative. To new experiences, he may show a kind of passive resistance, such as drooling out unwanted new foods rather than spitting them or crying. Once he has adapted to something new, however, his reaction is usually fairly positive.

Source: Thomas & Chess, 1977.

which they called the **easy child,** the **difficult child,** and the **slow-to-warm-up child,** described in Table 6.4. The concept of "difficultness" has been especially influential in early research on infant temperament.

In contrast, Buss and Plomin (Buss, 1989; Buss & Plomin, 1984; 1986) have argued for three basic dimensions: activity level, emotionality, and sociability, as I mentioned in Chapter 2. The questionnaire they devised to measure these three qualities has been widely used by researchers studying infants, children, and adults (such as shown in Table 2.4, p. 61).

Neither of these two models has quite won the day. Temperament researchers are still struggling to define the key dimensions and have not reached a clear agreement. However, a few key dimensions are now appearing in the lists of dimensions described by many of the primary researchers (Ahadi & Rothbart, 1994; Belsky, Hsieh, & Crnic, 1996; Kagan, 1997; R. Martin, Wisenbaker, & Huttunen, 1994), so agreement may be close at hand. The most often mentioned temperament dimensions are the following:

- *Activity Level.* A tendency to move often and vigorously, rather than to remain passive or immobile.

- *Approach/Positive Emotionality.* A tendency to move toward rather than away from people, new things, or objects, usually accompanied by positive emotion. This is similar to what Buss and Plomin call sociability.

- *Inhibition.* The flip side of approach; a tendency to respond with fear or withdrawal to new people, new situations, new objects. This dimen-

sion has been intensely studied by Jerome Kagan and his colleagues (e.g., Kagan, 1994; 1997; Kagan, Reznick, & Snidman, 1990), who see this as the precursor to what is called "shyness" in everyday language.

- *Negative Emotionality.* A tendency to respond with anger, fussing, loudness, or irritability; a low threshold of frustration. This appears to be what Thomas and Chess are tapping with their concept of the "difficult" child, and what Buss and Plomin call emotionality.

- *Effortful Control/Task Persistence.* An ability to stay focused, to manage attention and effort.

This is obviously not a final list; temperament researchers are still working their way toward common ground. Still, this set of traits or qualities is probably fairly close to the list we will all eventually agree on.

As I pointed out in Chapter 2, virtually everyone already agrees that these qualities are significantly influenced by heredity. Identical twin infants and toddlers are a lot more alike in their temperament than are fraternal twin infants and toddlers. Clearly, babies are born into the world with important differences in the way they react and interact—a fact that virtually any parent of two or more children can attest to. With a first child you may think the baby behaves as he does because of something you have done (or not done). When you have a second child, especially if that second child is very different in inborn temperament, you realize that each child is different from the very beginning.

For parents—and for researchers—an equally important issue is whether these early patterns

Of course, we can't judge this toddler's temperament from one picture, but if this kind of behavior is typical, we would rate her as high in "negative emotionality."

necessarily persist. Does a baby with a "difficult" or "negative" temperament inevitably remain difficult throughout childhood? Does a highly inhibited child inevitably become an extremely shy toddler or adolescent?

Consistency of Temperament over Time

Most of those who study temperament assume that the early temperamental patterns can indeed be modified under some circumstances, but that they create a kind of "bias" in the system toward particular behaviors. If this is true, then we ought to see a fair amount of stability of temperament over time, reflected in positive correlations between measures of a given temperamental dimension from one age to another. On the whole, that's what investigators have found.

For example, Australian researchers studying a group of 450 children found that mothers' reports

of children's irritability, cooperation/manageability, inflexibility, rhythmicity, persistence, and tendency to approach (rather than avoid) contact were all quite consistent from infancy through age 8 (Pedlow, Sanson, Prior, & Oberklaid, 1993). Similarly, in an American longitudinal study covering the years from age 1 to age 12, Diana Guerin and Allen Gottfried (1994a; 1994b) have found strong consistency in parent reports of their children's overall "difficultness" as well as approach versus withdrawal, positive versus negative mood, and activity level.

Kagan has also found considerable consistency over the same age range in his measure of inhibition, which is based on direct observation of the child's behavior rather than on the parents' ratings of the child's temperament. He reports that half the children in his longitudinal study who had shown high levels of crying and motor activity in response to a novel situation when they were 4 months old were still classified as highly inhibited at age 8, while three-fourths of those rated as *uninhibited* at 4 months remained in that category eight years later (Kagan, Snidman, & Arcus, 1993). Furthermore, the inhibited toddlers in Kagan's sample were *less* likely than their more uninhibited peers to be rated as highly aggressive or delinquent at age 11 (Schwartz, Snidman, & Kagan, 1996).

Thus babies who approach the world around them with some eagerness and with a positive attitude continue to be more positive as young teenagers, while babies who show a high level of behavioral inhibition are quite likely to continue to show such "shyness" at later ages. Similarly, cranky, temperamentally difficult babies continue to show many of the same temperamental qualities ten years later.

Temperament and Environment

Clearly, however, temperament does not inevitably determine personality. The child's experiences play a crucial role as well.

A number of temperament/environment interactions tend to strengthen built-in qualities. For one thing, each of us—including young children—*chooses* our own experiences, a process Sandra Scarr refers to as *niche-picking* (Scarr & McCartney, 1983). Highly sociable children seek out contact with others; children low on the activity dimension are more likely to choose sedentary activities like puzzles or board games rather than baseball. Similarly, temperament may affect the way in which a child *interprets* a given experience—a factor that helps to account for the fact that two children in the same family may experience the family pattern of interaction quite differently.

Imagine, for example, a family that moves often, such as a military family. If one child in this family has a strong built-in pattern of behavioral inhibition, the myriad changes and new experiences will trigger fear responses over and over. This child comes to anticipate each new move with dread and is likely to interpret his family life as highly stressful. A second child in the same family, with a more strongly approach-oriented temperament, finds the many moves stimulating and energizing and is likely to think of his childhood in a much more positive light.

A third environmental factor that tends to reinforce built-in temperamental patterns is the tendency of parents (and others in the child's world) to respond quite differently to children with varying temperaments. The sociable child, who may smile often, is likely to elicit more smiles and more positive interactions with parents simply because she has reinforced their behavior by her positive temperament. Buss and Plomin (1984) have proposed the general argument that children in the middle range on temperament dimensions typically adapt *to* their environment, while those children whose temperament is extreme—like extremely difficult children—force their environment to adapt to them. Parents of difficult children, for example, adapt to the children's negativity by punishing them more and providing them with less support and stimulation than do parents of more adaptable children (Luster, Boger, & Hannan, 1993; M. Rutter, 1978).

[?] *Critical Thinking*

The statement that difficult babies are more often punished is open to several possible interpretations. What are they?

Accurate and helpful as it is, Buss and Plomin's proposal doesn't convey the additional complexities of the process. First of all, sensitive and responsive parents can moderate the more extreme

forms of infant or child temperament. A particularly nice example comes from the work of Megan Gunnar and her colleagues (Gunnar, 1994), who have studied a group of highly inhibited toddlers who differed in the security of their attachment to their mothers. In a series of studies (Colton, Buss, Mangelsdorf et al., 1992; Nachmias, 1993), they have found that *insecurely* attached inhibited toddlers showed the pattern of physiological responses to challenging or novel situations typical of highly inhibited children; *securely* attached temperamentally inhibited toddlers showed no such indications of physiological arousal in the face of novelty or challenge. Thus the secure attachment appears to have modified a basic physiological/temperamental response. Over time, this may shift the child's personality pattern away from extreme inhibition or shyness.

Therefore, while many forces within the environment tend to reinforce the child's basic temperament and thus create stability and consistency of temperament/personality over time, environmental forces can also push a child toward new patterns or aid a child in controlling extreme forms of basic physiological reactions.

Beyond the Family: The Effects of Day Care

In virtually every industrialized country in the world, women have gone into the workforce in great numbers in the past two decades. In the United States the change has been particularly rapid and massive: In 1970, only 18 percent of married women with children under age 6 were in the labor force; by 1995, this number had risen to 63.5 percent. More than half of women with children under age 1 are now working outside the home at least part-time, a rate that appears to be higher than in any other country in the world (Cherlin, 1992b; U.S. Bureau of the Census, 1996). It is now typical for infants as well as school-age children to spend a significant amount of time being cared for by someone other than a parent. One recent study, based on a carefully selected sample of over 1300 families from throughout the United States, indicated that by age 1, 80 percent of infants had experienced some regular nonmaternal child care; the majority entered such care before 6 months of age (NICHD Early Child Care Research Network, 1997b). Although similar changes have occurred in other countries to a lesser degree, raising the same kinds of fundamental questions, in the discussion to follow I'm going to be talking almost exclusively about day care as it exists in the United States.

The key question for psychologists—as well as for teachers or other child-care professionals—is what effect such nonparental care may have on infants and young children. As you can easily imagine, this is *not* a simple question to answer, for a whole host of reasons:

- An enormous variety of different care arrangements are all lumped under the general title of "day care" or "child care."

- Children enter these care arrangements at different ages and remain in them for varying lengths of time.

- Some children have the same alternate caregiver over many years; others shift often from one care setting to another.

- Day care varies hugely in quality.

- Families who place their children in day care are undoubtedly different in a whole host of ways from those who care for their children primarily at home. How can we be sure that effects attributed to day care are not the result of these other family differences instead?

- Mothers also differ in their attitudes toward the care arrangements they have made. Among mothers with children in day care are some who would much rather be at home taking care of their children and others who are happy to be working; similarly, among mothers who are at home full-time are some who would rather be working and some who are delighted to be at home. Research tells us that children show more positive effects when the mother is satisfied with her situation, whether she is working or at home (e.g., DeMeis, Hock, & McBride, 1986; Greenberger & Goldberg, 1989), but in most studies of the effects of day care, we have no information at all about the mother's satisfaction or dissatisfaction.

Much of the research we have to draw on does not really take these complexities into account. Early studies typically compared children "in day care" with those "reared at home," and ascribed any differences between the two groups to the day-care experience. Recent studies are much better, so we are moving toward clearer answers, although many uncertainties remain. Nonetheless, because the question is so critical, you need to be aware of what we know, as well as what we do not yet know.

Who Is Taking Care of the Children?

Let me begin at the descriptive level. Just who is taking care of all those children while their parents work? In some countries, such as France or Belgium, child care is organized and subsidized by the government and free to all parents (though, of course, paid for by higher taxes) (Bergmann, 1996). In the United States we have no such governmental system, and each family must make its own arrangements as best it can.

Figure 6.3 summarizes the solutions working parents have found, based on 1993 Census Bureau data (Hofferth, 1996). These numbers may contain some surprises. When most people think of "day care," they think of a day care center or perhaps someone caring for a group of other people's children in her own home (an arrangement called **family day care**). Yet Figure 6.3 shows that half of preschool children with employed parents are cared for by a family member rather than in a center or in family day care. Most such children are cared for in their own homes rather than in someone else's home.

The data in Figure 6.3 can only begin to convey the enormous variety of solutions parents arrive at in seeking alternative care for their children. For example, in one recent national survey, almost a third of employed mothers reported that their children were in some type of *combined* care, such as family day care some of the time and care by a relative part of the time (Folk & Yi, 1994).

High-quality care is possible in any of these settings, although they do differ from one another in systematic ways. For example, center care typically provides the most cognitive enrichment, including a variety of toys to play with, a high rate of verbal exchange with caregivers, and being read to regularly. Family day care homes typically provide the lowest levels of such enrichment. In contrast, both center care and family day care give the child an opportunity to play with same-age peers, while at-home care normally does not. Such variations

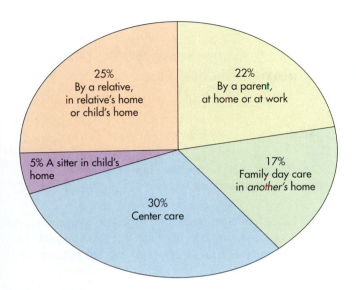

Figure 6.3

Child-care arrangements of working mothers for children age 5 and under in the United States in 1993. (Source: Hofferth, 1996, Figure 2, p. 46, drawing on U.S. Census Bureau data.)

make it very difficult to talk about global effects of day care. Furthermore, many researchers have studied children only in center care, and we cannot be sure that these findings will generalize to children in family day care or with at-home care by someone other than a parent (let alone to some other culture altogether!). Still, let me tell you what the current evidence suggests.

Effects on Cognitive Development

We have a good deal of evidence that good-quality, cognitively enriched day care has beneficial effects on many children's overall cognitive development. In the most recent large investigation, the NICHD Early Child Care Research Network study, 1997),

the researchers found a small but significant positive effect of high-quality care on children's overall cognitive skills and on their language. Such an effect appears to be even larger among infants and children from poor families, who show significant and lasting gains in IQ scores and later school performance after attending highly enriched day care throughout infancy and early childhood (Campbell & Ramey, 1994; Ramey, 1993; Ramey & Campbell, 1987). Even middle-class children show some cognitive benefit when they are in good care (e.g., Peisner-Feinberg, 1995). For example, Alison Clarke-Stewart (Clarke-Stewart, Gruber, & Fitzgerald, 1994) found that regardless of the economic situation of the child's parents, the more cognitively enriched the child's daytime experience the higher the child's later cognitive performance. Children who are read to, talked to, and explicitly taught show greater cognitive gains than do children who spend their days in less stimulating environments—and this was true whether they were cared for entirely at home or in some other care setting. Several longitudinal studies in Sweden confirm such a positive effect of high-quality day care: Those children who had spent the most time in Sweden's very good quality day care centers had better school performance throughout elementary school or better intellectual test scores than did children who had been totally home-reared or those who had been in family day care (Andersson, 1992; Broberg, Wessels, Lamb, & Hwang, 1997). A few studies suggest a less rosy picture, perhaps particularly for middle-class children. For example, in one large study of over 1000 3- and 4-year-olds, Baydar and Brooks-Gunn (1991) found that white children—but *not* black children—who began some kind of alternative care in the first year of life had the lowest vocabulary scores later in preschool, whether they were from advantaged or poverty-

The majority of children in the United States have at least some experience with nonparental care, although group care of the kind shown in both these pictures is not the most common form.

Social Policy Debate

The Pros and Cons of Government-Sponsored and Subsidized Child Care

A panel convened by the National Academy of Sciences to study U.S. child care raised concerns about the quality of child care available in the United States. Their basic conclusions include:

1. *Existing child care services in the United States are inadequate to meet current and likely future needs of children, parents, and society as a whole. . . . The general accessibility of high-quality, affordable child care has immediate and long-term implications for the health and well-being of children, parents, and society as a whole. . . .*

2. *Of greatest concern is the large number of children who are presently cared for in settings that do not protect their health and safety and do not provide appropriate developmental stimulation.* (Hayes, Palmer, & Zaslow, 1990, p. xii)

Since this was written, Congress has passed a parental leave bill allowing time for parents to care for a newborn or for a sick child. Despite this change, however, the United States remains one of the few Western industrialized countries without widespread, government-sponsored and subsidized child care, although most states in the United States do set standards for state-licensed child care.

The arguments in favor of state or federally subsidized child care (e.g., Bergmann, 1996; Liebowitz, 1996) include the following:

- *National standards for child care, including infant care, could be set and enforced.*

- *Subsidized care would enable children from poor families to have good quality, stable care—something often impossible at present.*

- *Good-quality care for all poor children would help to narrow the school-performance gap between poor and middle-class children at older ages.*

The arguments against such state-sponsored subsidized child and infant care include:

- *Subsidized care must be paid for by higher taxes paid by businesses and individuals; every European country with such subsidized child care has substantially higher tax rates than in the United States.*

- *One possible result of such higher taxes, according to some economists, is higher unemployment, which has negative consequences for children. Thus a benefit for children is offset by a disadvantage.*

What do you think? My own feeling is that each society has to make choices about its priorities. In the United States, for example, we grew concerned in the 1970s about the level of poverty among our elders and so raised Social Security benefits substantially. As a result, the rate of poverty among those over 65 dropped from 24.6% in 1970 to 11.7% today. During the same years, the rate of poverty among children age 18 and younger rose from 14.9% to 21.2% (U.S. Bureau of the Census, 1996). I do not argue that we should choose children *instead* of older adults. I do argue that it is time to invest in our children. Programs that help children will also help society in a great many ways over the long run. Still, I am mindful of the economic arguments. Money is not unlimited; if we provide subsidized child care we must stop paying for something else. What form of government programs would you be willing to give up, if any, in order to provide universal, good-quality child care? What other solutions can you think of?

level families. No negative effects were found for those who entered day care after age 1. In a similar large study of 5- and 6-year-olds (Caughy, DiPietro, & Strobino, 1994), researchers found that children from poor families who began day care before age 1 year had *higher* reading or math scores at the start of school, while those from middle-class families who entered day care in infancy had *poorer* scores.

How can we reconcile these conflicting findings? One fairly straightforward possibility is that the critical factor is the discrepancy between the level of stimulation the child would receive at home and the quality of the child care. When the particular day-care setting for a given child provides *more* enrichment than the child would have received at home, then we see some beneficial cognitive effects of day-care attendance; when day care is less stimulating than full-time home care would have been for that child, then day care has negative effects. Most (but not all) of the results I've described are consistent with this hypothesis, but we don't yet have enough good, large studies to be confident that this is the right way to conceptualize the process.

[?] Critical Thinking

Do you buy this argument? What other explanation(s) can you come up with?

Effects on Personality

When we look at the impact of day care on children's personality, we find yet another somewhat confusing story. A number of investigators have found that children in day care are more sociable, more popular, and have better peer-play skills than do those reared primarily at home. Andersson found this in his longitudinal study in Sweden (1989; 1992), as have researchers in the United States (Scarr & Eisenberg, 1993). However, this is by no means the universal finding. Many other researchers find day-care attendance linked to subsequently heightened aggression with peers and lower compliance with teachers and parents.

For example, in one very well designed large study, John Bates and his colleagues (Bates, Marvinney, Kelly et al., 1994) found that kindergarten children who had spent the most time in day care—in infancy, toddlerhood, or preschool years—were more aggressive and less popular with their peers at school age than were children who had been reared entirely at home or who had spent fewer years in day care. Bates did not find that those who had entered day care early in infancy were worse off; the critical variable was the total length of time in nonhome care, not the timing of that care. These negative effects are fairly small. A child's level of aggressiveness in elementary school is influenced by a whole variety of things, including temperament and the effectiveness of the parents' disciplinary techniques. Yet the fact that day care is implicated in this equation certainly raises a cautionary note.

Confusing, isn't it? By some measures day-care children seem to be *more* socially competent; by other measures, they seem less so. One possible resolution is again to look at the relative quality of care at home or in day care. Consistent with this argument is a finding by Tiffany Field (1991) that the beneficial effects of day-care experience on the child's social competence holds only for *good-quality* care. Similarly, Alison Clarke-Stewart, in a study

comparing various types of day care with home care (Clarke-Stewart et al., 1994), finds that what is critical for the child's level of aggression is whether the child was spending his daytime hours in an organized, well-structured situation versus a messy, unstimulating one—whether the unstructured and messy setting was at home or in day care. If this argument holds, then it is not day care *per se* that is at issue but the child's actual experiences on a day-to-day basis. Yet, even if this turns out to be the best explanation of the observed negative effects, it is hardly cause for cheering. The children in Bates's study, for example, were in ordinary, everyday types of day-care situations. And if such run-of-the-mill care is of such poor quality that it has even small negative effects on children's later behavior, we need to be concerned.

Effects on Children's Attachments to Parents

Another vital question is whether an infant or toddler could develop a secure attachment to her mother or father if she is repeatedly separated from them. We know that the majority of infants develop secure attachments to their fathers, even though the father typically goes away every day to work, so it is clear that such regular separations do not *preclude* secure attachment. Still, the early research created enough concern that psychologist Jay Belsky, in a series of papers and in testimony before a congressional committee, sounded an alarm (Belsky, 1985; 1992; Belsky & Rovine, 1988). Combining data from several studies, he concluded that there was a slightly heightened risk of an insecure attachment among infants who enter day care before their first birthday compared with those cared for at home throughout the first year. Subsequent analyses supported Belsky's conclusion. For example, summing across the findings from 13 different studies involving 897 infants, Michael Lamb (Lamb, Sternberg, & Prodromidis, 1992) noted that 35 percent of infants who had experienced at least five hours per week of nonmaternal care were insecurely attached, compared with 29 percent of the infants with exclusively maternal care.

What did such results mean? Psychologists disagreed strongly and vocally, in person and in print (e.g., Clarke-Stewart, 1990; Roggman, Langlois, Hubbs-Tait, & Rieser-Danner, 1994; Sroufe, 1990). Some concluded that these findings meant that day care itself increased the chances of an insecure attachment. Others pointed out that most of the existing research included so many confounding variables that it was impossible to draw any clear conclusion. For example, perhaps the problem was not day care itself but poor-quality care. The self-selection problem was also troubling. Mothers who work are different in other ways from mothers who do not. More are single mothers, more prefer to work or find child care onerous. So how can we be sure that any heightened probability of insecure attachment is due to the day-care experience and not to other factors?

In a wonderful example of the way dispute and disagreement can often lead to very good science, twenty-five researchers at 14 different universities—including all the main protagonists in the debate—got together in 1991 to design and carry out a very large study (the NICHD Early Child Care project) that would address all these questions (NICHD Early Child Care Research Network, 1996a). They enrolled over 1300 infants and their families in the study, including African-American and Hispanic families, mothers with little education as well as those with college or more, and both single mothers and two-parent families.

The basic design of the study is summarized in Table 6.5. As you can see, researchers first visited each home when the baby was 1 month old. During that visit they obtained information about the family organization and income, about the mother's temperament, her level of depression, and her attitude toward working. They also asked her to rate the baby's temperament, using a standard questionnaire.

When the babies were 6 months old, the researchers returned to each home, asking the mother again about her level of depression and her view of her child's temperament. During this visit, they also observed the mother's interactions with her infant during a play session and evaluated the quality of the overall caregiving environment in the home, using a standard instrument. In these observations the researchers were looking particularly at the level of the mother's sensitivity/responsiveness toward the infant—a quality we know is linked to security of attachment.

At 15 months, they made one more home visit, repeating their evaluation of the home environment and their direct observation of the mother and child during play. Each child-mother pair was also brought to a laboratory where they were put

---

Table 6.5

Design of the National Institute of Child Health and Human Development Study of Early Child Care

Age of Infant at Each Contact	Measures Used at That Age
1 month	• Mother's personality • Mother's level of depression • Mother's attitude toward employment • Mother's rating of the infant's temperament • Household composition and family income
6 months	• Mother's rating of the infant's temperament • Mother's level of depression • Observation of the quality of the home caregiving environment • Observation of mother and infant during play • Rating of the quality of any nonhome care setting
15 months	• Mother's level of depression • Observation of mother and child during play • Observation of the quality of the home caregiving environment • Rating of the quality of any nonhome care setting • Child's security of attachment in the Strange Situation

Source: NICHD Early Child Care Research Network, 1996a, from Table 3.

Psychology in Action

Investigation of Day Care Options

Warning: This investigative project, like others I have suggested in the book, should be undertaken—with directions from your instructor—either by a *single* student in a class, or by a small group of students working collaboratively. It is neither reasonable nor fair to flood local agencies or for-profit companies with calls from dozens of students inquiring about services or programs.

Any parent can tell you that it is not easy to obtain good information about available day care options. The purpose of this investigative project is therefore not only to discover as much as possible about the options in your community but to identify good sources and good strategies for obtaining such information.

Basic Questions to Answer

- *What day care center settings are available?*
- *Who runs the centers? For-profit companies? Churches? Schools? Others?*
- *How many and what ages of children do these centers accommodate? What are the costs of such center care?*
- *What is the best way for someone to find out about these care options?*
- *What family day care options are available, and how does one locate them? Is there a registry? A licensing process? Are all family day care providers listed in such registries or licensed?*

- *Are after-school care settings available as well? Who runs them? How much do they cost?*
- *Is care available for children in the evenings and at night (as might be needed by a parent who works evenings or a night shift)?*

Sources

Much of the information you'll need can be gleaned on the phone or from the phone book. The yellow pages will list day care centers, usually under "Child care." Data on family day care is much more difficult to come by (both for you and for parents). For information on licensing, especially licensing of home care or family day care providers, you will want to talk to local or state government agencies. To locate individual care providers, bulletin boards are often the best data source—those located in places parents are likely to be, such as at colleges or universities, on grocery store bulletin boards, in laundromats, and so on. A person or group doing this project will need to sample such sources in some systematic fashion and then call the providers whose names they find in this way to find out how many children are cared for, what ages, for what hours, and what fee is charged.

Analysis and Report

Your instructor may want you to prepare an oral or a written report to present to your class. In any case, you should prepare a written description of the steps you followed and the answers to the questions listed above.

through the series of episodes of the Strange Situation. For those children who were in day care at 6 months and 15 months, the researchers also visited the care setting and rated its quality.

Given the complexity of the study, the results are surprisingly clear: Child care, of itself, was unrelated to the security of the child's attachment. Only among those infants whose mothers were relatively insensitive to the infant's needs at home did day care or other child care have some negative effects. For these children, low-quality care, more than ten hours of care per week, or many shifts from one care arrangement to another were linked to less secure attachment. Thus it is true that day care increases the risk of an insecure attachment

for *some* infants, but not for all. Only the infants who experience the combination of two poor conditions (an insensitive mother and poor care) have a higher risk of being insecurely attached. Infants with insensitive mothers whose day care is of *good* quality or more stable are just as likely as any other child to be securely attached.

Here too, though, there are a few small cautionary flags. The NICHD study researchers also found that the mothers of children in day care showed a very slightly (but statistically significant) increased tendency to behave less sensitively toward their children compared with mothers who reared their children entirely at home. Note that this effect was not sufficient to affect the likelihood

---

Table 6.6

Ideal Characteristics of a Day-Care Setting

- **A low teacher-child ratio.** For children younger than 2, the best ratios appear to be 3:1 or 4:1; for 2- to 3-year-olds, ratios between 4:1 and 10:1 appear to be O.K. To protect against the possibility of child abuse, many good centers require at least two teachers in each room or with each group of infants or children.

- **A small group size.** The smaller the number of children cared for together—whether in one room in a day care center or in a home—the better for the child. This factor appears to be *in addition* to the effect of ratio. So large groups with many adults are less optimal than smaller groups with the same adult-child ratios. For infants, a maximum of 6 to 8 per group appears best; for 1- to 2-year-olds, between 6 and 12 per group; for older children, groups as large as 15 or 20 appear to be O.K.

- **A clean, colorful space, adapted to child play.** Lots of expensive toys are not critical, but there must be a variety of activities that children will find engaging, organized in a way that encourages play.

- **A daily plan with at least some structure,** some specific teaching, some supervised activities. Too much regimentation is not ideal, but children are better off with *some* structure.

- **A caregiver who is positive, involved, and responsive to the child, not merely custodial.**

- **A caregiver with some knowledge of child development.**

Sources: Clarke-Stewart, 1992; Howes, Phillips, & Whitebook, 1992; Scarr & Eisenberg, 1993; NICHD Early Child Care Research Network, 1996b.

---

that the child would be securely attached to the mother. Children in day care were just as likely as those reared entirely at home to be securely attached to Mom. Still, we can see a small potential negative effect.

Combining these findings with what I've already said about the impact of day care on intellectual development and other aspects of personality, you can see that the quality of the alternative care is one critical factor. Good-quality care is generally linked with positive or neutral outcomes, while inconsistent or poor-quality custodial care can be actively detrimental to the child, especially for children from families who are otherwise troubled.

If you are facing a decision about your own child's care, how do you judge what is good quality and what is not? Table 6.6, which lists the characteristics of good-quality programs, gives you a starting point.

Summary

1. Social interactions between infant and parent(s) are a critical part of the child's development, particularly for the development of the child's attachment and concept of self.

2. Parents experience both joys and stresses in their first months with the new infant.

3. A key element in the infant's half of the early social interaction is a range of emotional expressions, some present at birth, some that develop in the early months. A true social smile appears at about one month.

4. Bowlby and Ainsworth distinguish between an affectional bond (an enduring tie to a uniquely viewed partner) and an attachment, which involves the element of security and a safe base. An attachment is deduced from the existence of attachment behaviors.

5. For the parent(s) to form a strong bond to the infant, what is most crucial is the learning and repetition of mutually reinforcing and interlocking attachment behaviors, and not immediate contact at birth.

6. Fathers as well as mothers form strong bonds to their infants, but fathers in most Western cultures show more physically playful behaviors with their children than do mothers.

7. Bowlby proposed that the child's attachment to the caregiver develops through a series of steps, beginning with rather indiscriminate aiming of attachment behaviors toward anyone within reach, through a focus on one or more figures, and finally "secure base behavior," beginning or at about 6 months of age, which signals the presence of a clear attachment.

8. In the second half of the first year babies also typically show fear of strangers and anxiety at separation from their favored person.

9. Children differ in the security of their first attachments, and thus in the internal working model of at-

tachment they develop. The secure infant uses the parent as a safe base for exploration and can be readily consoled by the parent.

10. Studies in many countries suggest that a secure attachment is the most common pattern everywhere, but cultures differ in the frequency of different types of insecure attachment.

11. The security of the initial attachment is reasonably stable and is fostered by contingent responsiveness and acceptance by the parent.

12. Securely attached children appear to be more socially skillful, more curious and persistent in approaching new tasks, and more mature.

13. In the same early months the infant is also beginning to develop a sense of self, first understanding that she is separate from others and then achieving a kind of self-awareness that includes understanding herself as an object with properties. The former is present by age 8 or 9 months; the latter by 18 months or so.

14. Researchers studying individual differences in infants' style of responding have focused on the study of temperament, which is best thought of as the built-in patterns that form the emotional substrate of personality.

15. There remain sizeable differences among temperament theorists on just how best to characterize the basic dimensions of temperament among children, but reasonable agreement exists on the following: activity level, approach/positive emotionality, inhibition, negative emotionality, and effortful control/task persistence.

16. Other formulations that remain influential are Thomas and Chess's easy, difficult, and slow-to-warm-up temperaments, and Buss and Plomin's three-way category system of emotionality, activity, and sociability.

17. There is strong evidence that temperamental differences have a genetic component and that they are at least somewhat stable over infancy and childhood.

18. Temperament is not totally determined by heredity or ongoing physiological processes, although the child's built-in temperament does shape the child's interactions with the world and does affect others' responses to the child.

19. The majority of children in the United States now spend some part of their infancy or preschool years in some form of nonparental care. The most common forms of such care in the United States are care in the child's own home by someone other than the mother, and family day care.

20. Day care often has positive effects on the cognitive development of less-advantaged children, but it may have negative effects on advantaged children if the discrepancy between the home environment and the level of stimulation in day care is large.

21. The impact of day care on children's personality is unclear. Some studies show children with a history of day care to be more aggressive; others show them to be more socially skillful.

22. A major new study shows no overall negative effect of day care on the security of a child's attachment to his parents.

23. The quality of care appears to be a highly significant element. Good-quality care involves small groups of children, in clean spaces designed for children's play, with responsive caregivers trained in child development.

Key Terms

affectional bond A "relatively long-enduring tie in which the partner is important as a unique individual and is interchangeable with none other." **(p. 184)**

attachment An especially intense and central type of affectional bond in which the presence of the partner adds a special sense of security, a "safe base," for the individual. Characteristic of the child's bond with the parent. **(p. 184)**

attachment behaviors The collection of (probably) instinctive behaviors of one person toward another that bring about or maintain proximity and caregiving, such as the smile of the young infant; behaviors that reflect an attachment. **(p. 185)**

categorical self Term used by Michael Lewis to describe the aspect of the self-concept that develops in the second year of life and later, when the child categorizes himself along important dimensions, such as gender, size, or ability. **(p. 195)**

difficult child One of three temperamental patterns described by Chess and Thomas; a child who is irregular in pattern, relatively inflexible, and generally negative in emotional tone. **(p. 199)**

easy child One of three temperamental patterns described by Chess and Thomas; an adaptable child, with regular patterns and a generally positive emotional quality. **(p. 199)**

family day care Nonparental care in which the child is cared for in someone else's home, usually with a small group of other children. **(p. 202)**

insecure attachment Internal working model of relationships in which the child does not as readily use the parent as a safe base and is not readily consoled by the parent if upset. Includes three subtypes of attachment: ambivalent, avoidant, and disorganized/disoriented. **(p. 190)**

internal working model (of social relationships) Cognitive construction, for which the earliest relationships may form the template, of the workings of relationships, such as expectations of support or affection, trustworthiness, and so on. **(p. 190)**

personality The collection of individual, relatively enduring patterns of reacting to and interacting with others that distinguishes each child or adult; temperament is thought of as the emotional substrate of personality. **(p. 198)**

postpartum depression A severe form of the common experience of postpartum blues. Affecting perhaps 10 percent of women, this form of clinical depression typically lasts six to eight weeks. **(p. 182)**

secure attachment Demonstrated by the child's ability to use the parent as a safe base and to be consoled after separation, when fearful, or when otherwise stressed. **(p. 190)**

slow-to-warm-up child One of three temperament patterns described by Chess and Thomas; a child who has moderate emotional reactions but who is relatively inflexible in the face of novelty. **(p. 199)**

Strange Situation A series of eight episodes used by Mary Ainsworth and others in studies of attachment. The child is observed with the mother, with a stranger, when left alone, and when reunited with both stranger and mother. **(p. 190)**

temperament Term sometimes used interchangeably with "personality," but best thought of as the emotional substrate of personality; at least partially genetically determined. **(p. 198)**

Suggested Readings

Bowlby, J. (1988b). *A secure base*. New York: Basic Books. This splendid small book, Bowlby's last before his death, includes a number of his most important early papers as well as new chapters that bring his theory up to date. See particularly Chapters 7 and 9.

Bretherton, I. (1992a). The origins of attachment theory: John Bowlby and Mary Ainsworth. *Developmental Psychology, 28*, 759–775. A clear, current, thoughtful review of both Bowlby's and Ainsworth's ideas, including new data from anthropology and other cross-cultural analyses.

Kagan, J. (1994). *Galen s prophecy*. New York: Basic Books. A detailed presentation, for the lay reader, of Kagan's ideas about the biological bases of temperament, particularly the aspect of temperament he calls behavioral inhibition.

Karen, R. (1994). *Becoming attached*. New York: Warner Books. In this fine book, Robert Karen, who is both a psychologist and a journalist, tells the story of the early research on attachment, focusing on the central players in the scientific drama, including Bowlby and Ainsworth. Written for the lay reader, this book will tell you a lot not only about attachment but also about the process of science.

Interlude One

Summing Up Infant and Toddler Development

WHY INTERLUDES?

This is the first of these "interludes," so let me say a word about their purpose. Because this book is organized chronologically, with a set of chapters describing each age period, you might think that you will automatically gain a sense of the basic characteristics of each era. The difficulty is that psychological research—and our discussion of that research—tends to focus on only one system at a time, such as attachment, perceptual skills, or language, and my descriptions tend to follow the same pattern. In these interludes, I want to try to put the baby or child back together, to look at all the threads at once.

A second purpose is to examine, albeit briefly, some of the external influences on the basic processes. In particular, I want to be sure that we keep coming back to the effects of the larger social system in which the child is developing.

A Summary of the Threads of Infant Development

Aspect of Development	Age in Months											
	0	2	4	6	8	10	12	14	16	18	20	22
Physical development		Increase in cortical involvement	Reaches for objects	Sits	Stands; crawls		Walks alone			Dendritic and synaptic "pruning"		
Perceptual development	Many perceptual skills present at birth; visually discriminates Mom from stranger	Scans to identify object; depth perception	Discriminates patterns of sounds and sights; cross-modal transfer	Discriminates facial expressions								
Cognitive development	Possibly imitation of some facial gestures		Beginning of object permanence; specific memories over 1 week		Object permanence quite well established; coordinates actions to solve problems			Deferred imitation; finds *new* solutions to problems			Beginning internal manipulation of symbols	
Language development		Coos		Babbles	Meaningful gestures; understands a few words		First word				Vocabulary of 30–50 words	
Social/ personality development	Spontaneous social smiling; interest, distress, disgust shown	Sadness, anger, and surprise shown	Early signs of attachment; self/other differentiation		Clear attachment	Stranger fear and separation anxiety			Plays with peers	Clear evidence of self-awareness		
					Fear shown			Shame and guilt shown				

In each interlude, then, I will ask the same three questions: What are the *basic characteristics* of development in that period? What are the *central processes* that seem to be shaping those developmental patterns? What other forces affect or *influence* those processes?

BASIC CHARACTERISTICS OF INFANCY

The table on page 211 summarizes the various developmental patterns I've described in the past three chapters. The rows in the figure correspond to the various threads of development; what we need to do now is read up and down the figure in addition to looking across the rows.

The overriding impression one gets of the newborn—despite her remarkable skills and capacities—is that she is very much on automatic pilot. There seem to be built-in rules or schemas that govern the way the infant looks, listens, explores the world, and relates to others.

One of the really remarkable things about these rules is how well designed they are to lead both the child and the caregivers into the "dance" of interaction and attachment. Think of an infant being breast-fed. The baby has the needed rooting, sucking, and swallowing reflexes to take in the milk; in this position, the mother's face is at just about the optimum distance from the baby's eyes for the infant's best focusing; the mother's facial features, particularly her eyes and mouth, are just the sort of visual stimuli that the baby is most likely to look at; the baby is particularly sensitive to the range of sounds of the human voice, particularly the upper register, so the higher-pitched, lilting voice most mothers use is easily heard by the infant. And during breast-feeding the release of a hormone called *cortisol* in the mother has the effect of relaxing her and making her more alert to the baby's signals. Both the adult and the infant are thus primed to interact with one another.

Sometime between 6 and 8 weeks there seems to be a change, with these automatic, reflexive responses giving way to behavior that looks more volitional. The child now looks at objects differently, apparently trying to identify what an object is rather than merely where it is; at this age she also shows a genuine social smile for the first time, sleeps through the night, and generally becomes a more responsive creature.

Because of these changes in the baby, and also because it takes most mothers six to eight weeks to recover physically from the delivery (and for the mother and father jointly to begin to adjust to the immense

change in their routine), we also see big changes in mother-infant interaction patterns at this time. The need for routine caretaking continues, of course (ah, the joys of diapers!), but as the child stays awake for longer periods, smiles, and makes eye contact more, exchanges between parent and child become more playful and smoother-paced.

Once this transition has occurred, there seems to be a brief period of consolidation lasting perhaps five or six months. Of course, change continues during this consolidation period. Neurological change, in particular, is rapid, with the motor and perceptual areas of the cortex continuing to develop. The child's perceptual skills also show major changes in these months, with depth perception, clear cross-modal transfer, and identification of patterns of sounds and sights all emerging. Nonetheless, despite all these changes, a kind of equilibrium exists in this period—an equilibrium that is altered by a series of changes that occur typically between 7 and 9 months, when: (1) the baby forms a strong central attachment, followed a few months later by separation anxiety and fear of strangers; (2) the infant begins to move around independently (albeit very slowly and haltingly at first); (3) communication between infant and parents changes substantially, as the baby begins to use meaningful gestures and to comprehend individual words; (4) object permanence is grasped at a new level; the baby now understands that objects and people can continue to exist even when they are out of sight. At the very least, these changes profoundly alter the parent-child interactive system, requiring the establishment of a new equilibrium, a new consolidation, a new system.

The baby continues to build gradually on this set of new skills—learning a few spoken words, learning to walk, consolidating the basic attachment—until 18 or 20 months of age, at which point the child's language and cognitive development appear to take another major leap forward—a set of changes I'll be talking about in chapters yet to come.

CENTRAL PROCESSES

What is causing all these changes? Any short list of such causes is inevitably going to be a gross oversimplification. Still, undaunted, let me suggest four key processes that seem to me to be shaping the patterns shown in the summary table.

Physical Maturation. First and most obviously, the biological clock is ticking very loudly indeed during these early few months. Only at adolescence do we again see such an obvious maturational pattern at work. In infancy, it is the pre-patterned growth of neural dendrites and synapses that appears to be the key. The shift in behavior we see at 2 months, for example, seems to be governed by just such built-in changes, as synapses in the cortex develop sufficiently to control behavior more fully.

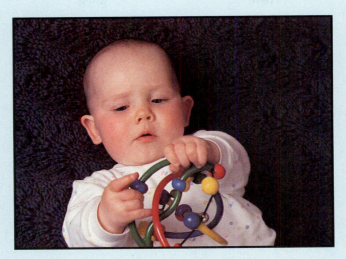

Important as this built-in program is, it nonetheless *depends on* the presence of a minimum "expectable" environment (Greenough, Black, & Wallace, 1987). The brain may be wired to create certain synapses, but the process has to be triggered by exposure to particular kinds of experience. Because such a minimum environment exists for virtually all infants, the perceptual, motor, and cognitive developments we see are virtually identical from one baby to the next. But that does not mean that the environment is unimportant.

The Child's Explorations. A second key process is the child's own exploration of the world around her. She is born *ready* to explore, to learn from her experience, but she still has to learn the specific connections between seeing and hearing, to tell the differences between Mom's face and someone else's, to pay attention to the sounds emphasized in the language she is hearing, to discover that her actions have consequences, and so on and on.

Clearly, physiological maturation and the child's own exploration are intimately linked in a kind of perpetual feedback loop. The rapid changes in the nervous system, bones, and muscles permit more and more exploration, which in turn affects the child's perceptual and cognitive skills, which in turn affects the architecture of the brain. For example, we now have a good deal of evidence that the ability to crawl—a skill that rests on a whole host of maturationally based physical changes—profoundly affects the baby's understanding of the world. Before the baby can move independently, he seems to locate objects only in relation to his own body; after he can crawl, he begins to locate objects with reference to fixed landmarks (Bertenthal, Campos, &

Kermoian, 1994). This shift, in turn, probably contributes to the infant's growing understanding of himself as an object in space.

Attachment. A third key process seems obviously to be the relationship between the infant and the caregiver(s). I am convinced that Bowlby is right about the built-in *readiness* of all infants to create an attachment. But in this domain, the quality of the specific experience the child encounters seems to have a more formative effect than is true for other aspects of development. A wide range of environments are "good enough" to support physical, perceptual, and cognitive growth in these early months. For the establishment of a secure central attachment, however, the acceptable range seems to be narrower.

Still, attachment does not develop along an independent track. Its emergence is linked both to maturational change and to the child's own exploration. For example, the child's understanding of object permanence may be a necessary precondition for the development of a basic attachment. As John Flavell puts it, "how ever could a child persistently yearn and search for a specific other person if the child were still cognitively incapable of mentally representing that person in the person's absence?" (1985, p. 135).

We might also turn this hypothesis on its head and argue that the process of establishing a clear attachment may cause, or at least affect, the child's cognitive development. For example, securely attached youngsters appear to persist longer in their play and develop the object concept more rapidly (e.g., Bates, Bretherton, Beeghly-Smith, & McNew, 1982). Such a connection might exist because the securely attached child is simply more comfortable exploring the world around him from the safe base of his secure person. He thus has a richer and more varied set of experiences, which may stimulate more rapid cognitive (and neurological) development.

Internal Working Models. We could also think of attachment as being a subcategory of a broader process, namely the creation of internal working models. Seymour Epstein (1991) proposes that what the baby is doing is nothing less than beginning to create a "theory of reality." In Epstein's view, such a theory includes at least four elements:

- A belief about the degree to which the world is a place of pleasure or pain;
- A belief about the extent to which the world is meaningful—predictable, controllable, and just versus capricious, chaotic, or uncontrollable;
- A belief about whether people are desirable to relate to or threatening; and
- A belief about the worthiness or unworthiness of the self.

The roots of this theory of reality, so Epstein and others argue (e.g., Bretherton, 1991), lie in the experiences of infancy, particularly the experiences with caregivers and other humans. Indeed, Epstein suggests that the beliefs created in infancy are likely to be the most basic and therefore the most durable and resistant to change at later ages. Not all psychologists would agree with Epstein about the broadness of the infant's "theory" of reality. However, virtually all would now agree that the baby begins to create at least two significant internal models: one of the self and one of relationships with others (attachment). Of the two, the attachment model seems to be the most fully developed at 18 or 24 months; the model of the self undergoes many elaborations in the years that follow. For example, it is only at about age 6 or 7 that the child seems to have a sense of his *global* worth—a characteristic we usually call self-esteem (Harter, 1987; 1990).

INFLUENCES ON THE BASIC PROCESSES

These four basic processes are quite robust (Masten, Best, & Garmezy, 1990). Nonetheless, infants can be deflected from the common trajectory by several kinds of influences.

Organic Damage.   The most obvious potential influence is some kind of damage to the physical organism, either from genetic anomalies, inherited disease, or teratogenic effects *in utero*. Yet even here, we see an interaction between nature and nurture. Recall from Chapter 3 that the long-term consequences of such damage may

be more or less severe, depending on the richness and supportiveness of the environment the baby grows up in.

Family Environment.   The specific family environment in which the child is reared also affects the trajectory. On one end of the continuum we can see beneficial effects from an optimal environment that includes a variety of objects for the baby to investigate, at least some free opportunity to explore, and loving, responsive, and sensitive adults who talk to the infant often and respond to the infant's cues (Bradley, Caldwell, Rock et al., 1989). On the other end of the continuum some environments can be so poor that they fall outside the "good enough" range and thus fail to support the child's most basic development. Severe neglect or abuse would fall into this category, as might deep or lasting depression in a parent, or persisting upheaval or stress in family life. In between these extremes are many variations in enrichment, in responsiveness, in loving support, all of which seem to have at least some impact on the child's pattern of attachment, his motivation, the content of his self-concept, his willingness to explore, as well as his specific knowledge. We see the consequences of such differences further down the developmental road, when the child is facing the challenging tasks of school and the demands of relating to other children.

Influences on the Family.   I've made the point before, but let me make it again: The baby is embedded in the family, but the family is part of a larger economic, social, and cultural system, all of which can have both direct and indirect effects on the infant. Let me give you just two examples.

The most obvious point is that the parents' overall economic circumstances may have a very wide-ranging impact on the baby's life experience. Poor families are less able to provide a safe and secure environment. Their infants are more likely to be exposed to environmental toxins such as lead, less likely to have regular health care, including immunizations, and more likely to have nutritionally inadequate diets. If they place the infant in day care, they may be unable to afford good-quality care, and they are more likely to have to shift the baby from one care arrangement to another. Collectively, these are large differences. We do not see the effects immediately; babies reared in poverty-level families do not look much different from babies reared in more affluent circumstances. By age 2, 3, or 4, though, the differences begin to be obvious.

Another example, one that cuts across all social classes, is the effect of the parents' own social support on the infant's development. Parents who have access to adequate emotional and physical support— from each other or from friends and family—are able to respond to their children more warmly, more consistently, and with better control (Crnic, Greenberg, Ragozin, Robinson, & Basham, 1983; Taylor, Casten, & Flickinger, 1993). Their children, in turn, look better on a variety of measures (Melson, Ladd, & Hsu, 1993). For example, children whose parents have access to more assistance from friends complete more years of school than do children whose parents have less support of this type (Hofferth, Boisjoly, & Duncan, 1995).

The effect of social support on parents is particularly evident when they are experiencing stress of some kind, such as job loss, chronic poverty, teenage childbirth, a temperamentally difficult or handicapped infant, divorce, or even just fatigue. One example comes from a study by Susan Crockenberg (1981), who found that temperamentally irritable infants were likely to end up with an insecure attachment to their mothers *only* when the mother *lacked* adequate social support. When the mother felt that she had enough support, similarly irritable children were later securely attached.

This "buffering" effect of social support can even be demonstrated experimentally. Jacobson and Frye (1991) randomly assigned 46 poverty-level mothers either to a control group or to participate in an experimental support group that met both prenatally and for the first year after delivery. When Jacobson and Frye evaluated the infants' attachment at 14 months, they found that the babies whose moms had been in the support group were more securely attached than those whose moms had had no such special help.

One Last Word. One of the strongest impressions one gets from so much of the current research on babies is that they are far more capable than we had thought. They appear to be born with many more skills, many more templates for handling their experiences. Still, they are not 6-year-olds, and we need to be careful not to get too carried away with our statements about how much the baby can do. As you will see in the next three chapters, the preschooler makes huge strides in every area.

Physical Development and Health in the Preschool Years

Preview Questions

1 What are some of the likely characteristics of left-handed children (or adults), compared to right-handers?

2 What important new physical skills does a child develop in the preschool years?

3 What is the most common serious disease of early childhood?

4 What specific constructive steps can a parent or teacher take to reduce a young child's risk of disease or accident?

5 Why do some parents abuse their children and how might we prevent it from occurring?

Chapter Outline

During one of my recent visits with my son and his family I was able to watch while my then not-quite-5-year-old grandson Sam rode a bike for the first time without training wheels. His father and I stood by the side of the road, hearts in our mouths but grins on our faces, as Sam wobbled down the road, tried a turn, and crashed. To Sam, this was about as big a deal as landing on the moon. It didn't matter that he crashed. It mattered that he'd ridden 50 feet. "Hey Dad! Did you see that? I did it! Grandma Helen, I did it!!!!" For the next hour, he tried again and again, crashing often but riding farther and farther, with growing confidence and always with complete delight.

I tell you this story not only because I am a proud grandmother, but to illustrate an important point about physical development in these preschool years: The skill milestones may not be as obvious or striking as what we see with crawling and walking in infancy, but from the preschool child's perspective, each new increment of physical control and skill brings big gains in independence and confidence as well as intrinsic pleasure.

Certainly it is true that the rate of physical changes slows down in these years. Yet, though the changes may be slower and less striking, a very great deal is happening physically in these years that is important to the child and to those who care for him.

Basic Patterns of Growth

Let's begin with the basics: Just how is the child's body changing in the years from age 2 to age 5 or 6?

Size and Shape

The simplest statement is that preschoolers grow more slowly than do infants. In the first three months of life, a baby gains about 2 pounds a month; in the preschool years, this rate has dropped to something more like 7 ounces a month—still pretty rapid, but not so strikingly fast as in infancy.

Figure 7.1 (p. 220) shows the changes graphically. As in the equivalent figure for infancy (Figure

4.5, p. 131), I've shown the 10th, 50th, and 90th percentile growth lines for boys and girls. At least three things should jump out at you from this figure. First, although kids vary in their starting point, the trajectories are virtually identical, especially for changes in height—a sure sign of the operation of some kind of powerful maturational pattern. Second, preschool-age boys continue to be taller and heavier than girls, but at this age, the sex differences in size are quite small. At age 6, the difference in height between a boy and a girl at the 90th percentile is less than a half an inch. What is far more striking is the variation *within* each gender. By age 6, the tallest boys and girls are about 6 inches taller than the shortest boys and girls the same age, a difference that only increases through school age and adolescence. These differences between big and small children are far larger than the differences between boys and girls. They are probably also more significant psychologically, because both children and adults associate tallness with greater maturity. So taller children are treated differently from small children, perhaps being given more responsibilities, or being chosen as a leader by their peers (Lerner, 1985).

Critical Thinking

Think about the way you react to preschool children. Do you treat bigger ones differently from smaller ones, even when they are all the same age? What effect do you think such differences might have on the children?

What Affects the Child's Size?   What makes one child relatively large and another relatively small? The simple answer, of course, is "both nature and nurture." Heredity has a clear role here, with multiple genes apparently involved. Indeed, when children are physically healthy and are being reared in a sufficiently supportive environment, heredity explains virtually all the variation among their heights. For example, at age 4, the correlation between the heights of identical twins reared together is about .95—about as close to a perfect correlation as we are likely to find in psychological research (Tanner, 1990). In contrast, the correlation between the heights of fraternal twins reared to-

These children may all be the same age, but they won't be treated exactly alike: The taller children are likely to have certain advantages simply because other kids—and adults—think of bigger kids as "older" or "better" or "more mature."

gether is closer to .60. What this means, of course, is that tall parents are likely to have taller children, short parents will have shorter children, although the genetics of height is complex enough that quite a lot of variation may nonetheless exist among brothers and sisters in a given family.

Still, heredity is not everything. Table 7.1 (p. 220) lists some of the other factors we know are linked to children's size. When children are reared in less supportive environments, such as when they suffer regular or periodic mal- or subnutrition or are chronically abused, their growth rate drops. Chronically or frequently ill children, such as those with asthma, also grow less rapidly. The *trajectory* stays essentially the same, but the child's rate of growth falls to a lower line on the graph. This effect is especially clear in several studies done in developing countries in which children and mothers living at a subsistence level in small villages, where chronic subnutrition is the norm, have been given supplementary nutrition to increase both protein and total caloric intake. Children given such supplemental food grow faster in the early months and years of life than do equivalent children given more limited vitamin and caloric supplements. In one of the best of these studies, done in Guatemala, the difference in eventual height between the children given the protein-rich supplement and those given the vitamins-plus-calories supplement was about 1 inch at age 7 (Schroeder, Martorell, Rivera, Ruel, & Habicht, 1995).

The various factors listed in the table act cumulatively and interactively. For example, among children who have experienced episodes of mal- or subnutrition, those who also have episodes of serious illness, particularly diarrhea, are more likely to show reduced growth rates and smaller eventual stature.

Predicting Final Height from Preschool Information.   The growth charts like the ones in Figure 7.1 (p. 220) can be used not only to compare one child with another but also to compare each child with herself over time. The growth trajectories are remarkably regular; a child who is at the 90th percentile in height at age 2, for example, is likely to remain near the 90th percentile through childhood. Indeed, the correlation between height at age 2 and adult height is .78 (Tanner, 1990). (In contrast, the correlation between length at birth and adult height is only .30, because the newborn's size is affected by fetal conditions more than by heredity.) Because the 2-year-old correlation is so strong, it is possible to make reasonably accurate predictions of a child's

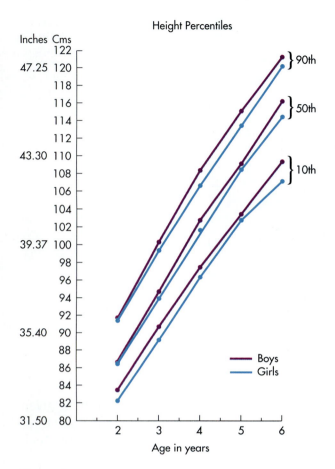

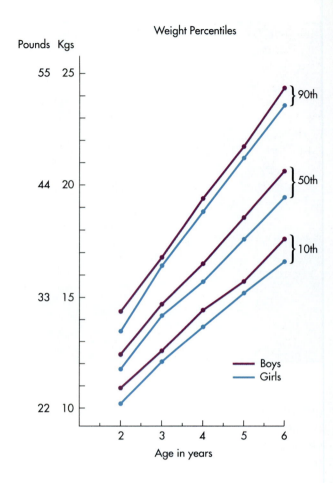

Figure 7.1

Gains in height and weight during the preschool years. The three lines for each sex show the 10th, 50th, and 90th percentile trajectories. (Source: Needlman, 1996, data from Table 13-1, pp. 50–51.)

Table 7.1

Some Factors Related to Children's Height

Children are taller if	Children are shorter if
they live in urban areas;	they live in rural areas;
their family is well-off;	their family is poor;
mother did not smoke in pregnancy;	mother smoked in pregnancy;
they are well nourished in infancy and toddlerhood;	they are poorly nourished;
they have not had repeated illnesses;	they have had multiple illnesses or one chronic illness;
they are the firstborn child in family.	they are later-born child in family.

Source: Tanner, 1990.

final height from her height in the preschool years. I mentioned in Chapter 4 that a 2-year-old girl is roughly half as tall as she will be when she is fully grown. Garn (1966) has given more precise formulas, given in Table 7.2. (The calculation is simple: Multiply the child's height at any of the specified birthdays by the appropriate multiplier given in the table.) These formulas will work well for children whose parents are of average height; when the parents are much taller or shorter than average, you need to take their height into account as well. Judith Hall and her colleagues (Hall, Froster-Iskenius, & Allanson, 1989) suggest the following formulas:

Boys = 0.545 height at 2 years
  + 0.544 average parental height
  + 14.85 inches

Girls = 0.545 height at 2 years
  + 0.544 average parental height
  + 10.09 inches

Precise as they are, even these formulas are not perfect (Hall et al., 1989). Among other things, as you'll see when we get to Chapter 13, the timing of puberty is an added factor influencing final height: Those who go through puberty early tend to be shorter as adults than you would have predicted using the formulas, while those who go through puberty late tend to be taller as adults. Still, both the simple multipliers shown in Table 7.2 and the more precise formulas that include parental height should give you a close approximation.

Table 7.2

Predicting an Individual Child's Height from Height in the Preschool Years

Age	Multiplier for Boys	Multiplier for Girls
1	2.46	2.30
2	2.06	2.01
3	1.86	1.76
4	1.73	1.62
5	1.62	1.51
6	1.54	1.43

Source: Garn, 1966, p. 536.

Brain Development

You'll remember from Chapter 4 that the infant's brain develops rapidly, adding huge numbers of new dendrites and synapses and then pruning them, as well as beginning the process of myelination. These processes continue in the preschool years. The pace of change is less rapid, but the significance of the continuing changes is substantial. For example, the myelination of the neurons in the basic motor and sensory areas of the brain is not complete until about age 6 (Todd, Swarzenski, Rossi, & Visconti, 1995), a fact that has a lot to do with the relatively poor eye-hand coordination and comparative motor clumsiness of the preschooler.

Hemispheric Lateralization. Another change in the brain that begins prenatally and continues through the preschool years is the specialization of the two halves of the brain, called hemispheres. Although the two hemispheres look superficially much alike, in fact they are organized somewhat differently, with each responsible for somewhat different tasks, a process usually referred to as **hemispheric lateralization.**

In general, the left hemisphere of the brain (which controls sensory input from and movement of the *right* side of the body) is much more involved in processing language, while the right hemisphere (which controls the *left* side of the body) deals with spatial information, nonspeech sounds, and emotion. The right side uses visual or auditory images to code incoming information; the left side uses words. Tanner makes the point clearly:

As Levy puts it, "The right hemisphere may know that 'cat' means a furry small pet with claws, but it does not know that 'cat' rhymes with 'rat.'" That association is made in the left hemisphere. (Tanner, 1990, p. 114)

Early researchers thought that the specialization of these two hemispheres didn't really begin until about age 2, that infant brains were highly plastic and could adjust fairly readily if injured. Current evidence shows that infant brains are indeed more plastic than the brains of older children or adults but not nearly so flexible as the early scientists thought. Some brain lateralization has already occurred at birth. For example, EEG (electroencephalograph or brain wave) recordings of newborns show more neurological response to speech in the left hemisphere than in the right and more response to nonspeech stimuli such as flashing lights in the right hemisphere than in the left (Hahn, 1987; Molfese & Molfese, 1979).

This tells us that brains have built-in biases from earliest life. Those biases or preferences, however, do not mean that lateralization is complete at birth. Studies of the development of children's hand preferences tell us that hemispheric specialization is still continuing in the preschool years.

Handedness.   Eighty-five or 90 percent of you reading this paragraph would describe yourself as "right-handed." You write with your right hand, eat with that hand, throw a ball with that hand. Another 8 to 10 percent think of yourself as left-handed, and maybe 3 percent would describe yourselves as ambidextrous—percentages that have been found in countries all over the world (Perelle & Ehrman, 1994). What this means is that, for the majority of us right-handers, it is the *left* side of our brain that primarily controls our motor movements as well as language. For a left-handed person, the right side of the brain is more involved in physical actions. Interestingly, language and motor functions are more often *shared* between the two hemispheres in left-handed people. Many more left-handers than right-handers also think of

themselves as at least somewhat ambidextrous; they prefer to use their left hand but can use their right hand with reasonable dexterity if they need to. Thus left-handers seem to have much less strong hemispheric dominance than do right-handers. Left-handers are different in other interesting ways as well, listed in Table 7.3. Some of their special advantages seem to come from their relatively less specialized hemispheres. They recover from brain injury more readily, for example, because both halves of their brain are more involved in a variety of tasks. If one half of the brain is injured, the other half can take over that function to some degree. Their advantage in spatial relations, on the other hand, doubtless comes from the greater dominance of the right hemisphere, which is the part of the brain that normally deals with spatial relationships. It is not accidental that left-handers are overrepresented in the ranks of both architects and mathematicians.

On the other side, though, you can see from Table 7.3 that left-handers are also at higher risk for a variety of problems, some of them significant. At this point, no one has a good theory to explain this mixture of advantages and disadvantages, although several have been proposed (e.g., Geschwind & Galaburda, 1987).

Heredity clearly plays some role in a child's hand preference, since handedness patterns run in families. When one parent is left-handed, the children are about twice as likely to be left-handed than is true if both parents are right-handed, indi-

---

Table 7.3
Other Characteristics of Left-Handed Children and Adults

Left-handers:
- are more often males;
- have a somewhat greater likelihood of suffering from allergies and migraine headaches;
- are somewhat more likely to be learning disabled or be diagnosed with attention deficit disorder (both of which I'll describe in later chapters);
- are somewhat more likely to stutter;
- are likely to be better at spatial tasks and some kinds of advanced mathematics;
- recover more readily from brain injury.

Note: The statements in this table do *not* mean that all left-handed children will be learning disabled, or have allergies, or stutter. It means only that they have a higher probability of having such a problem. In one study reported by Geschwind and Galaburda, for example, about ten percent of left-handers reported significant allergies, compared to roughly five percent of right-handers.

Sources: Benbow, 1986; Geschwind & Galaburda, 1987.

cating the presence of a genetic pattern (McManus, 1991). Yet, although heredity is at work here, full hand preferences are not present at birth. Most young infants will swipe at objects with either hand; by ages 5 to 6 months the majority will use their right hand to reach for an object, and by age 2 some degree of handedness is apparent in virtually all children. These preferences strengthen further in the preschool years. A 3-year-old may kick a ball with either foot or may happily use the nonpreferred hand to reach with when he's holding a cookie in his favored hand. By age 6, though, hand and foot preference is much more firmly established.

In earlier years in the United States and elsewhere, prejudice against left-handers was so strong that left-handed children were routinely forced to learn to write with their right hands when they started school. Fortunately, this is much less often the case today. There is absolutely no reason why a child's hand preference should be altered in any way.

Sleep Patterns

Like changes in the nervous system and the gains in height and weight, changes in children's sleep patterns over these preschool years are less striking than those in infancy. The typical 2-year-old sleeps 13 hours a day, including one daytime nap. By age 6, the typical child sleeps about 10 hours, with no nap (Adair & Bauchner, 1993; Needlman, 1996). Three fewer hours of sleep may seem like a fairly small change, but the practical effects for parents (or preschool teachers) can be substantial. The parent at home with a 2-year-old counts on nap time to get housework done, to do paid work at home, to sit and have a quiet cup of coffee. The parent at home with a nonnapping 4- or 5-year-old, or a teacher with a group of such children, has no such respite.

Many preschool children also have problems with or during sleeping, problems that parents need to manage, including bedtime struggles, nightmares, night terrors, and bed-wetting.

Bedtime Struggles. "Mom, I need a drink of water!" "I have to go to the bathroom." "Leave a light

Judging by this picture, I'd guess that 2-year-old Salma is right-handed because she's holding the pencil in that hand. But she's clearly able to use her left hand with some skill as well. Like most children of this age, she has a hand preference, but her brain will become even more specialized over the next three or four years.

on!" "Let me stay up a little longer!" I remember all these from when my daughter was ages 4 and 5. Virtually any parent of a preschooler could give you an equivalent list of children's bedtime-delaying tactics, comfort needs, or arguments. Struggles between parents and children around bedtimes or sleeping rituals are probably more common in this age range than at any other point.

Part of the child's increased bedtime distress arises from the fact that he probably takes longer to fall asleep now than he did a few years earlier. He's also more aware of being left alone and may experience significant anxiety, exacerbated by the fact that he is now old enough to have heard about and imagine a great many scary events and objects—monsters in the closet, devils, or whatever. (My own scary bedtime thought from this age was of a huge bear that was somehow going to jump out of a dark place and get me.) A great many children handle their anxieties with some kind of self-soothing behavior, including thumb-sucking or the use of a "security blanket" or a cuddly toy (called **transitional objects** by psychologists) as a kind of companion for the time when the child is awake and alone. As many as seventy percent of 4-year-olds use such an object at least occasionally; almost half do so regularly (Klackenberg, 1987). My daughter, at this age, had a favored blanket that she used at any time of anxiety, including bedtime. To extend its life, and also so that we could wash it regularly, we finally cut it into pieces. She was quite happy using any piece of this blanket for comfort. By school age the pieces were mere rags and she finally gave up the habit. In this she was typical: Among 6-year-olds, only about a quarter still regularly use a transitional object at bedtime (Klackenberg, 1987).

Critical Thinking

I could make an argument that the use of "transitional objects" does not end in childhood. Can you think of examples of objects or rituals an adult might use to help make the shift from waking to sleeping or from social interaction to solitude? Do adults simply use more subtle forms of transitional objects?

Bedtime struggles are doubtless more common in this age range also because preschoolers are now able to express their feelings verbally and are newly assertive as part of their growing awareness of their own separate selves. Parents of children this age may also be more eager to establish regular routines, including regular bedtimes, which means that the child must also adapt to a new pattern.

For all these reasons, occasional protest or distress around bedtime is extremely common among preschoolers. For 20 to 30 percent of children, though, the bedtime struggles are prolonged and repeated, lasting an hour or more at least three times a week (Lozoff, Wolf, & Davis, 1985). Some of these children seem to have persisting problems because the parents have been unable

A teddy bear to sleep with—a common sight among preschool children. They use these favored toys to help them deal with the anxiety of being left alone. Most outgrow the habit by school age.

Parenting

How to Deal with Bedtime Struggles

The best way to prevent bedtime struggles from arising, and the best way to deal with them once they have begun, is to establish a regular bedtime ritual and follow it consistently. Here are some of the key ingredients (Ferber, 1987a; Kemper, 1996).

- *Put the child to bed at the same time every night.*

- *Follow the same routine every night, such as a bath (which is soothing if it isn't too filled with play), toothbrushing, toileting, pajamas, storytelling or prayers, hugs, lights out (or night-light on).*

- *Have the child wear special clothes to bed, rather than sleeping in day clothes or underwear.*

- *Read a story or poem every night. You may want to have special books that are only read at bedtime.*

- *Play the same music for the child every night after the story and when the lights are already out. This might be a recording of lullabies, or some other favorite, but it should be soothing music—not Sousa marches or rock music.*

- *Make sure the child has his favorite "transitional object" available—teddy bear, blanket, or equivalent.*

- *Say the same words for goodnight every night.*

- *Hug the child and tell her you love her.*

If problems persist despite your best efforts, specific strategies based on learning theory principles may be helpful. If your struggles with your child are severe, it would be best to consult a behavior modification specialist rather than forging ahead on your own. Such a specialist is likely to recommend very specific regimens. For example, Mindell and Durand (1993) worked successfully with six families who experienced severe bedtime struggles. Although they tailored their recommended strategies individually to each family's pattern, a common system was first to have the family establish a fixed routine. Then, if the child cried or called out repeatedly, the parent was to wait 5 minutes before responding the first time, then provide comfort for no more than 2 minutes. They were to wait 10 minutes before responding to a second cry, and 15 minutes before a third visit. After two nights of this routine, the parents were told to wait 10 minutes before their first response; after six nights, they were to wait 15 minutes before responding to the child's distress. The six children described in this report all showed significant decreases in their distress and in the length of time it took them to fall asleep; they also woke less often in the night, which had a beneficial effect on the parents' sleep patterns.

This method is typical of the various behavior modification strategies used with success by many psychologists (e.g., see Ferber, 1985).

---

to establish and maintain any kind of limits around bedtime (Ferber, 1987b). Sometimes this is a spiraling problem: The child resists going to bed, the parents first try to force the issue and then give up, thus reinforcing the child's protesting behavior, which makes the situation worse. In other families the difficulty arises because the parents simply establish no regular routine at all. In still other children intense bedtime struggles develop after some significant life change or stress: a recent illness or accident in the family, a family move, or a change in the parent's routine, such as a mother's returning to work or school or becoming depressed (Adair & Bauchner, 1993). Any of these experiences can increase a child's overall level of anxiety, making the separation at bedtime even more difficult.

Whatever the origin of the problem, for virtually all children the best way to respond to these bedtime disputes or struggles is to follow a standard routine at bedtime—described in the *Parenting* box.

Nightmares and Night Terrors. A quite different category of sleep problems are episodes of crying or screaming in the night, including both nightmares and night terrors. Both these problems are more common among preschoolers than any other age group. In one very large study (Achenbach & Edelbrock, 1981), 40 percent of the parents of 4- and 5-year-olds reported that their children had nightmares, a number that dropped to about 20 percent by age 8. Other researchers count the incidence between 25 and 50 percent among preschoolers (Adair & Bauchner, 1993).

Nightmares, which are as likely in boys as in girls, are most likely to occur in the second half of the child's nighttime sleep, which means they usually happen in the early morning. The child wakes up, terrified, usually calling for the parent, crying, or screaming. A parent naturally needs to respond to this distress. It is often helpful to ask the child to describe the bad dream as well as to reassure the child both that bad dreams are not real and that the parent is there to protect and care for the child.

While nightmares can be very distressing for the child (and for the parent), they are quite normal and do not usually signify any underlying emotional or psychological problem. If they happen only occasionally, a parent should not be alarmed. Frequent nightmares, however, may be a sign that the child is under more than normal stress. Themes in the child's nightmares may give you a clue to the source of the problem. In any case, you may want to think about ways to reduce strains on the child.

Night terrors are quite different (Adair & Bauchner, 1993). For one thing, they usually occur early in the child's sleep. The child seems to waken abruptly, may sit up in bed and scream, but in fact the child is not fully awake, is not able to talk sensibly to the adult who comes to care for her, is usually easily soothed, returns readily to sleep, and normally does not recall the episode the next morning. Such episodes appear to stem from an unusually rapid transition from very deep sleep to near-awakeness; they may be somewhat more likely when the child has been physically exhausted or under unusual stress, but they do not seem to signal or be linked to any underlying emotional disturbance (Kemper, 1996). Night terrors may thus be more terrifying for the parent than for the child.

Bed-Wetting. A third nighttime problem among preschoolers is bed-wetting (called **enuresis** by physicians). Strictly speaking, this is not a *sleep* disorder; it is not more likely in children who sleep very deeply, for example, and is not linked to any particular pattern of sleep (Kemper, 1996). I've included it here because it does happen during sleep, and because most parents classify it as a sleep-linked problem.

Many parents believe that once a child is out of diapers—at perhaps age 2 or 3—the child is fully "toilet trained" and should not be wet at night. In fact, though, children simply vary a lot in how long it takes them to control their bladders for as long as the 8 to 10 hours of nighttime sleep. Surveys in a number of countries show that about one-fourth of all 4-year-olds wet the bed at least occasionally, a number that drops to about ten percent by age 7 (Wille, 1994). Most pediatricians do not even consider it a significant problem unless it persists past the age of 6—and it is only a problem then because it may cause some social difficulties for the child (Fergusson & Horwood, 1994). Everyone eventually outgrows the problem without any intervention at all.

Enuresis is more common in boys and tends to run in families. When both parents have a history of bed-wetting, their child has a 70 to 80 percent chance of being a bed-wetter; when only one parent was a bed-wetter (especially the father), the child has about a 50 percent chance of enuresis (Kemper, 1996).

One cause of the problem is a smaller-than-normal bladder. A second is a difference in the way the child's brain signals the kidneys to make urine. A hormone called ADH (antidiuretic hormone) signals the kidneys to make *less* urine. In adults—and in children who do not suffer from enuresis—the brain makes more ADH at night, resulting in lower urine production at night. Children who wet the bed, in contrast, secrete the same amount of ADH throughout the day and night, which means they simply have to urinate more often in the night (Kemper, 1996). These children eventually do develop the typical diurnal pattern of ADH secretion; it is just a slower process for them than for the average child.

If your preschooler wets the bed regularly, you should take him (or her) at least once to a pediatrician in order to rule out any other explanations, such as a bladder infection, diabetes, or perhaps some kinds of food allergies. Once assured that your child's bed-wetting is simply a normal developmental process, you have several choices. One is simply to wait for the child's natural development to reach the point where he can be dry through the night. For 3- and 4-year-olds, this makes a good deal of sense. Do not punish the child, do not scold. You may want to provide rewards (such as gold stars) for dry nights, but do not punish for wet nights. You can also aid the child by not letting him drink any fluids for several hours before bedtime.

If enuresis persists to age 5 or 6 (or later), however, you may want to consider any of several behavioral therapies that can help the child learn how to control the process voluntarily—not because bed-wetting at this age is abnormal but because it may cause the child some social embarrassment. The most successful strategy is a bed-wetting alarm, which has a cure rate of 70 to 90 percent—better than any medication. The child sleeps on a moisture-sensitive pad, with an alarm attached. When the first few drops of urine hit the pad, the alarm goes off. The child gets up, goes to the bathroom, resets the alarm, and goes back to bed. When parents stress that this is the *child's* alarm, that he is responsible for setting it up and making sure it is working, and when the parents support and praise the child in this effort, the success rate is excellent.

Motor Development

The many gradual changes I've been describing, such as the changes in size and shape and in brain functioning, combine to enable the child to make steady progress in motor development. The changes are not so dramatic as the beginning of walking, but there is no doubt that a 6-year-old uses his body far more confidently and skillfully than a 2-year-old.

Table 7.4 (p. 228), which parallels Table 4.6, shows the major locomotor, nonlocomotor, and manipulative skills that emerge in these preschool years. What is most striking are the impressive gains the child makes in large muscle skills. By age 5 or 6, children are running, jumping, hopping, galloping, climbing, and skipping. They can ride a trike; some (like my grandson Sam) can ride a two-wheeled bike. They can catch and throw a ball—not with great precision or accuracy, but using nearly mature forms of movement—a pattern you can see in Figure 7.2 (p. 229).

Small-muscle or "fine motor" abilities also improve in these preschool years, but not to the same level of confident skill. Three-year-olds can indeed pick up Cheerios, and by 5 they can thread beads on a string. Yet, even at age 5 or 6, children are not highly skilled at such fine motor tasks as using a pencil or crayon or cutting accurately with scissors. When they use a pencil or scissors, their whole body is still involved—the tongue moving and the whole arm and back involved in the writing or cutting motion—a pattern plain in the photograph of the boy cutting below. They also don't do these fine motor motions terribly quickly, especially repeti-

Preschoolers become confident of their large motor skills—running, kicking, riding trikes, throwing balls. At this age, though, the child's whole body is still involved in fine motor skills like cutting or writing—the tongue is moving, the whole shoulder and back are involved.

Table 7.4

Milestones of Preschool Motor Development

Age	Locomotor Skills	Nonlocomotor Skills	Manipulative Skills
18–24 mo.	Runs stiffly (20 mo.); walks well (24 mo.); climbs stairs with both feet on each step	Pushes and pulls boxes or wheeled toys; unscrews lid on a jar	Shows clear hand preference; stacks 4 to 6 blocks; turns pages one at a time; picks things up without over-balancing
2–3 yr.	Runs easily; climbs up and down furniture unaided; jumps to floor with both feet (28 mo.)	Hauls and shoves big toys around obstacles; throws facing target, using only arm	Picks up small objects (e.g., Cheerios); holds crayon with fingers; throws small ball forward while standing
3–4 yr.	Walks upstairs one foot per step; skips on both feet; walks on tiptoe	Pedals and steers a tricycle; walks in any direction pulling a big toy; rotates body when throwing, but still uses only arm	Begins to button and unbutton; catches large ball between outstretched arms and body; cuts paper with scissors; holds pencil between thumb and first two fingers
4–5 yr.	Walks up- *and* downstairs one foot per step; stands, runs, and walks well on tiptoe	Some boys show mature throwing pattern (using body as well as arm); kicks with more back and forth swing of leg and arm opposition	Strikes ball with bat; catches ball using the hands only; threads beads but not needle; grasps pencil maturely; can copy figure like a triangle with a pencil
5–6 yr.	Skips on alternate feet; walks a thin line; slides, swings; shows mature jumping pattern	Most children show mature throwing pattern; mature kicking pattern (kicks through the ball)	Mature catching pattern; threads needle and sews stitches

Sources: The Diagram Group, 1977; Connolly & Dalgleish, 1989; Fagard & Jacquet, 1989; Mathew & Cook, 1990; Thomas, 1990a; Gallahue & Ozmun, 1995; Needlman, 1996; Hagerman, 1996.

tive motions such as drawing letters, because it takes longer for their muscles to relax between each movement (Lin, Brown, & Walsh, 1996). These are important points for teachers to understand: The same 5- or 6-year-old who confidently rides a bike or throws a ball will approach a task like writing with tense concentration and slow, still imprecise, body movements.

Health and Health Problems

Day-care workers, teachers, and parents also need to be familiar with some of the common health problems of children in this age as well as the various steps you can take to prevent or ameliorate those problems.

Fortunately, the majority of children in industrialized countries, and many children in developing countries, enjoy essentially good health—a few colds a year, an occasional brief bout with diarrhea, a few cuts and bruises, but otherwise no problems. For a significant minority of children, though, the picture is not so bright. They must cope with chronic illness or disability, or with more serious accidents, even with the risk of death.

Mortality

Those of us who live in industrialized countries (which is nearly all of you reading this book) correctly think of the preschool years as a pretty safe time, a time when children are not likely to die. If we broaden our scope, though, and look at the ex-

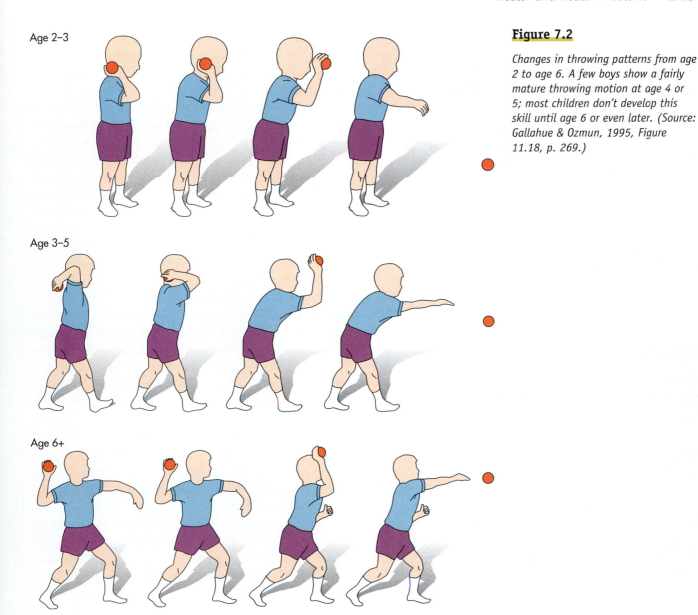

Age 2–3

Age 3–5

Age 6+

Figure 7.2

Changes in throwing patterns from age 2 to age 6. A few boys show a fairly mature throwing motion at age 4 or 5; most children don't develop this skill until age 6 or even later. (Source: Gallahue & Ozmun, 1995, Figure 11.18, p. 269.)

perience of children in less industrialized countries, a different picture emerges, as you can see in Figure 7.3 (p. 230). The figure compares death rates for infants and preschoolers in the United States with the worldwide rates and the rates in several subsets of countries. The United States, by the way, does not have the lowest mortality rates for children in this age range; indeed, as is true of infant mortality, the United States ranks behind most other industrialized countries because of our high rate of accidents and violence. Even so, the U.S. figures are strikingly lower than the worldwide average, or than the average in technologically less developed countries.

[?] *Critical Thinking*

You might think that if the rate of infant and child mortality were greatly reduced in any country, or worldwide, one consequence would be a population explosion. But in fact that's not what happens: When child mortality goes down, the birthrate goes down too. Why do you think that might be true?

As you can see, worldwide about four percent of children die between ages 1 and 5. In less technologically developed countries as a whole, and in Africa in particular, the rate is still higher. The

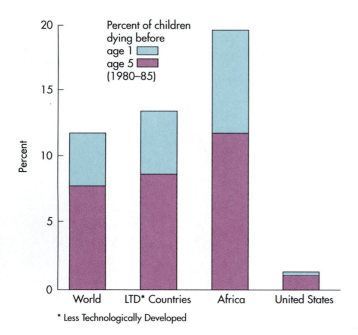

Figure 7.3

I find this a stunning figure, showing so clearly the different prospects for children from technologically developed countries like the United States compared with children in poorer countries. (Source: Mandelbaum, 1992, Figure 1, p. 133.)

causes of these childhood deaths are myriad and complex, but the obvious factors are inadequate nutrition and lack of immunization against common childhood diseases. Lack of appropriate health care, especially for diarrhea, is also a critical element in the equation. The average child in the United States has less than 7 days of diarrhea in one year, but a child in a less technologically devel-

oped country has as many as 20 or 30 days of acute diarrhea each year, with correspondingly increased risk of serious dehydration and death (Mandelbaum, 1992).

In the United States the most common cause of death in a preschool-age child is not diarrhea or preventable diseases, but accidents. Table 7.5 summarizes the most current information, giving you the rate of death for each of the top seven causes for children ages 1 to 4. It also gives the rank order of these same causes separately for blacks, Hispanics, and whites. You can see that the two most common causes of death are the same for all ethnic groups, but that there are some variations beyond that. Death by homicide and HIV infection are more frequent among black preschoolers; fatal diseases of the heart are less common among Hispanics. Not evident in the table is the fact that African-American children have roughly twice the overall death rate—73.2 deaths per 100,000 children compared to 38.1 for whites, 41.7 for Hispanics, and 63.5 for Native Americans (Singh & Yu, 1996). There are also sex differences. Boys in this age range (as in virtually every age range) die at somewhat higher rates: 48 deaths per 100,000 population compared to 39 for girls. When you put these two facts together, you find the highest death rates among young black boys—77.6 per 100,000 children.

To a considerable degree these racial/ethnic differences are really poverty or social class differences in disguise. Children living in poor families have about three times the risk of dying in their

---

Table 7.5

Primary Causes of Death Among Children Ages 1 to 4 in the United States

Cause	Number of Deaths per 100,000 Children	Rank Order of Causes for Each Ethnic/Racial Group		
		White	Black	Hispanic
Accidents	15.9	1	1	1
Congenital anomalies	5.5	2	2	2
Cancer	3.1	3	6	3
Homicide	2.8	4	3	4
Diseases of the heart	1.8	5	5	7
Pneumonia or influenza	1.2	6	7	5
HIV infection	1.0	7	4	6

Source: National Center for Health Statistics, 1996, data from Table 1, pp. 18, 21, 25, 28.

Research Report

Children's Art

A particularly fascinating window on the motor-skill changes of the preschool years is found in children's art, studied in detail by Rhoda Kellogg (1970).

Kellogg, who has looked at more than a million free-hand drawings of children all over the world, finds that children everywhere draw the same kinds of figures at about the same ages, reflecting the basic maturation of the brain over the years of childhood.

The first step is the **scribble,** typically beginning between ages 18 months and 2 years. Kellogg has identified 20 basic scribbles, including dots, horizontal and vertical lines, curved or circular lines, and zigzags. Collectively, these scribble patterns form "the building blocks of art." By age 3, children enter what Kellogg calls the **shape stage,** when they begin to draw particular shapes deliberately (albeit highly imperfectly!), such as circles, squares, or X shapes. This is followed quickly by the **design stage,** in which they mix several basic shapes into more complex designs.

Only at age 4 or 5 does the child begin to draw pictures of objects or events from real life (the **pictorial stage**), including humans and houses—all made up of combinations of the basic scribbles and shapes.

Kellogg argues persuasively that this is an absolutely natural sequence, requiring no intervention or instruction by adults. Whether children scribble with a stick in the dirt or on a piece of paper with a crayon, the patterns they draw are the same everywhere. Kellogg goes further, suggesting that adults frequently succeed in stifling a child's interest in art by providing instruction or by asking the child to copy a specific form. Children quickly learn to please their teachers by drawing the way the adult requests, usually by making the drawing "look like" some specific object in desired ways. In the process they give up the experimentation and exploration that is the essence of children's art. Kellogg says,

> I believe that teachers should accept everything made with good grace and should not try to evaluate its worth. No questions need ever be asked, and comments that teachers make can be restricted to such constructive ones as "very interesting," "nice colors," "I like that," "good work," "a nice scribble," "pretty," etc. (1970, p. 157)

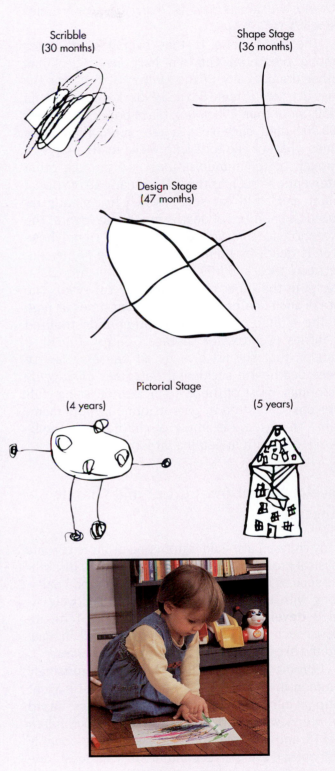

Scribble (30 months)

Shape Stage (36 months)

Design Stage (47 months)

Pictorial Stage

(4 years)

(5 years)

Olivia, at 18 months, is clearly in the stage Kellogg calls *scribbling*.

early years as do children from more affluent families, and this is especially true for children living in neighborhoods with high concentrations of poverty, a characteristic of many U.S. inner cities (Singh & Yu, 1996).

The good news is that overall death rates among preschool children have been declining rather dramatically in the United States over the past decades (Singh & Yu, 1996). For example, in 1950, more than 250 young black boys out of every 100,000 died each year, a rate more than three times what we see today. So we've made progress, through better immunizations and through other interventions such as the widespread use of special infant and child car seats, which has greatly reduced the number of deaths in auto accidents. The exception to this general downward trend, however, is death by homicide, which rose 86 percent between 1968 and 1992, primarily (but not exclusively) in the inner cities (Singh & Yu, 1996). The rate of such deaths is more than four times as high in the United States as in other industrialized countries (Centers for Disease Control, 1997b), a statistic that should give us all pause. A few of these deaths are accidental outcomes of drive-by shootings; most of these homicides of young children are committed by parents or household members—an extreme example of child abuse, a subject I'll deal with in detail a bit later.

Developmental Disabilities and Chronic Illnesses

Many children also suffer from one or more chronic physical problems. By convention, physical disabilities such as blindness, deafness, and cerebral palsy, along with mental retardation, are collectively labeled **developmental disabilities.** Long-term illnesses such as asthma, diabetes, sickle-cell anemia, and the like are referred to as **chronic illnesses.**

Chronic conditions like these are surprisingly common in childhood. The best and most current national information from the United States, based on interviews with parents of over 17,000 children age 18 and younger in 1988, shows that roughly one out of every five children has at least one chronic problem, *not* counting children with some

mental retardation. If you add in such problems as frequent ear infections, headaches, or diarrhea, the rate rises to three children out of ten (Newacheck, 1994; Newacheck & Stoddard, 1994).

Table 7.6 lists some of the most common of these chronic difficulties. Of the items on this list, the most common problem in this age range is some kind of allergy. More severe or potential fatal diseases such as sickle-cell disease (most common among blacks), cancer, diabetes, or anemia are much less frequent—although if it is your child suffering from any of these diseases, it won't be much comfort to have me say that the problem is relatively rare. The one serious disease that is *not* rare among preschoolers is asthma, a disease that has been increasing at a surprising and alarming rate in the United States and elsewhere in the world. Among children in the United States, for example, the rate of asthma more than doubled from approximately three percent in 1980 to the 6.9 percent the Bureau of the Census lists today (Gortmaker, Walker, Weitzman, & Sobol, 1990; U.S. Bureau of the Census, 1995), a figure that is fairly representative of similar increases around the world.

Table 7.6	

Most Common Forms of Chronic Conditions Among Children (Ages 1 to 18) in the United States

Condition	Percent of Children
Deafness and blindness	2.8%
Asthma	6.9%
Hay fever and other respiratory allergies	9.7%
Eczema and other skin allergies	3.7%
Digestive allergies	2.5%
Frequent ear infections	8.3%
Frequent or severe headaches	2.5%
Sickle-cell disease	0.1%
Anemia	0.9%
Diabetes	0.1%

Sources: Newacheck, 1994, information from Table 1, p. 1146; asthma figure from Centers for Disease Control, 1996a.

Asthma.   The symptoms of **asthma** include a dry cough (especially at night), wheezing during exhalation, a feeling of tightness in the chest, and difficulty breathing (Kemper, 1996). Many children have coughs without the other symptoms; some may have a cough and some wheezing during the flu and at no other time. However, when a child has a chronic cough or shows any of the other symptoms, she should be seen by a physician for a full diagnosis.

The immediate cause of the coughing and wheezing is inflammation of the small airways in the lungs, which blocks the airflow to the air sacs. The wheezing sound comes from the air passing through these narrowed airways. Most children (and adults) with asthma do not suffer from breathing problems all the time; instead, they have acute episodes triggered by some allergy or illness, such as an allergy to a particular pollen, to cat hair, or to dust mites. Emotional stress can also trigger an asthmatic episode, as can exercise, especially in cold, dry air. In fact, many top-level athletes (particularly those who regularly exercise in cold air, such as cross-country skiers) develop **exercise-induced asthma,** an entirely treatable disease that need not inhibit athletic competition. Other children may also have allergic reactions to these same stressors or allergens, but their reaction may involve other parts of the body than the lungs, such as the sinuses or skin.

Asthma has a somewhat different developmental pattern in boys than in girls. In boys it commonly begins in late infancy or in the preschool years; in girls it doesn't usually start until school age or later. For both sexes, however, the factors that predict asthma (and predict deaths from asthma) are essentially the same (Centers for Disease Control, 1996a; Kemper, 1996; Weitzman, Gortmaker, & Sobol, 1990):

- It is more common among children living in crowded conditions and/or in poverty; in U.S. inner cities, rates as high as 14% have been reported (Crain, Weiss, Bijur et al., 1994);
- It is more common among children of single mothers;
- It is more common and begins at younger ages among African Americans than among whites;
- It is more common among children who live with someone who smokes and among children whose mother smoked during pregnancy;
- It is more common among children who were classified as low birth weight;
- It is more common among children who live near significant sources of air pollution, such as busy roads, factories, or power stations;
- It is more common among children who live in new, energy-efficient houses, which are so tightly constructed that they trap indoor air pollutants, including dust mites, animal dander, and mold.

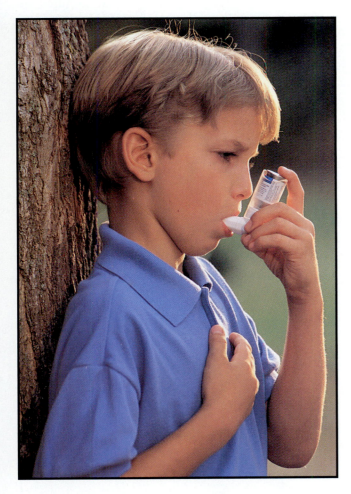

Children with moderate or severe asthma can do virtually anything a nonasthmatic child can do—provided their disease is appropriately treated. The most common treatment involves prescription drugs given through an inhaler, like this one.

[?] **Critical Thinking**

After reading this list of factors linked to higher rates of asthma, can you generate any hypotheses to account for the recent rise in the incidence of this disease?

Asthma is a serious disease. Whether mild, moderate, or severe, it requires regular monitoring and appropriate treatment (Centers for Disease Control, 1996a). At the same time, parents and teachers need to know that a child with asthma, if the asthma is treated appropriately, can do all the same things a nonasthmatic child can do, including participating in vigorous physical activities. These children do not need to be sheltered; they need to be seen regularly by a physician or other health professional. Unfortunately, in inner cities and other poverty areas, such regular health care may be hard for parents to find or afford, so many children go untreated—a state that does indeed interfere with their normal activities.

Acute Illnesses and Accidents

All children also suffer from brief illnesses, such as colds or viruses, called **acute illnesses** by physicians, to differentiate them from chronic illnesses of the kind I've been describing. Preschool children have fewer acute illnesses than infants do, but still contract perhaps six each year (Parmelee, 1986). The average child is sick in bed about five days per year, and has perhaps another four days of lowered activity ("feeling puny" as one of my friends says) (Starfield, 1991).

[?] **Critical Thinking**

Children who are sick a lot early in life have a higher risk of having health problems in adolescence or adulthood. How many different explanations can you think of for such a link between childhood illness and adult health?

At every age, children who are experiencing high levels of stress or family upheaval are more

likely to become ill. For example, a large nationwide U.S. study shows that children living in mother-only families have a generally higher vulnerability to illnesses of many types (including asthma and headaches as well as colds or other acute illnesses) than do those living with both biological parents (Dawson, 1991). Figure 7.4 shows one comparison from this study, using a "health vulnerability score" that is the sum of nine questions answered by parents about their child's health. You can see in the figure that the average score is only about 1.0 out of a possible 9.0, which implies that most children are quite healthy. At the same time, it is clear in the figure that children living in more stressful family structures have higher health vulnerability—and this is true even when such other differences between the families as race, income, and mother's level of education are factored out.

Children experiencing higher levels of short-term personal stress, such as the family moving, a new sibling, some change in the family routine, special challenges at school, or stresses in friend-

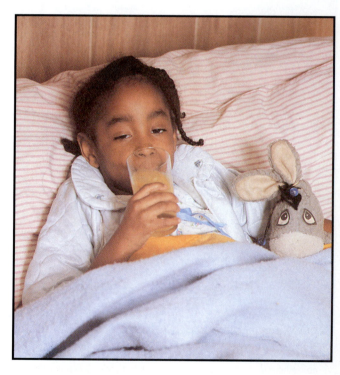

Most kids this age are sick in bed like this with some kind of acute illness, such as a cold or the flu, about six times a year.

ships, are also more likely to catch whatever cold or flu is going around, although the size of this effect is fairly small, just as it is in studies of stress and illness in adults. That is, many children (and adults) experiencing higher levels of stress do *not* get sick (Cohen & Williamson, 1991). One possible explanation, suggested by Thomas Boyce and his colleagues (Boyce, Chesney, Alkon et al., 1995), is that some children may be especially susceptible to the effects of stress, and thus be more likely to become ill when their level of stress rises. Boyce tested this possibility in a group of preschool children, measuring their ordinary stress by asking the preschool teachers to describe the "daily hassles" experienced by each child. He measured the child's susceptibility to stress by looking at changes in heart rate and blood pressure during a challenging series of special tests. The final piece of the puzzle was a measure of the rate of upper respiratory illnesses in the children, based on a nurse's diagnosis. Boyce found that the children who showed stronger physiological reaction to challenging tasks got more colds and flu when they had more stressful everyday experiences. Among the less "reactive" children, on the other hand, levels of personal stress and rates of illness were unconnected.

This work is still very preliminary and needs to be replicated and expanded. Two implications in particular are intriguing and worth further research. Most directly, these results point to the possibility that it may not be accurate to say that *all* children are more likely to become ill when they are under stress; instead, only some children will respond to stress this way. Second, I am struck by the possible link with Kagan's studies of behavioral inhibition (the biological root of shyness), described in Chapter 6. Children who are high in behavioral inhibition show stronger physical reactions to novel or challenging situations. Could this mean that inhibited children are more likely to become ill when their home or school life is stressful?

[?] *Critical Thinking*

See if you can design a study to test this hypothesis.

Nonfatal Accidents.   You already know that accidents are the leading cause of death among U.S. children in this age group. Less serious accidents are also common. In any given year, about a quarter of all children under 5 in the United States have at least one accident that requires some kind of medical attention (Starfield, 1991; U.S. Bureau of the Census, 1996). At every age, accidents are more common among boys than girls, presumably because of boys' more active and daring styles of play. Accidents are also more common among the children of the poor.

The majority of accidents among children in this age range occur at home—falls, cuts, accidental poisonings, and the like (Shanon, Bashaw, Lewis, & Feldman, 1992). Automobile accidents are the second leading source of injuries among preschoolers, although, happily, the rate of serious injury and death from auto accidents has fallen dramatically in recent years because of new laws mandating the use of restraint devices for infants and toddlers traveling in cars (Christophersen, 1989)—although new statistics on young children's risks of death from air bags make it clear that we still have a ways to go to maximize children's safety in automobiles.

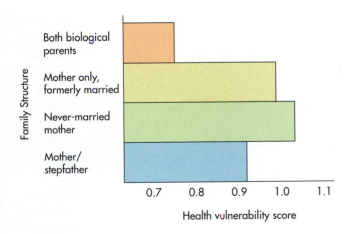

Figure 7.4

Dawson finds that children from single-parent and stepparent families are more likely to be sick, a fact that probably demonstrates the effect of stress on illness. (Source: Dawson, 1991, from Table 3, p. 577.)

Parenting

What Parents and Teachers Can Do to Foster Better Health in Preschoolers

Here are some highly specific things you can do to improve the chances that a preschooler you care for will have good health and avoid accidents:

1. **Provide a smoke-free environment for the child,** even if it means you stop smoking yourself. Among other things, children who live with smokers are more likely to suffer from asthma.

2. **Cut down on allergens in the environment,** especially dust mites, which now appear to be a major culprit for many kinds of allergies (in adults as well as children) (Sporik & Platts-Mills, 1992). Dust mites are microscopic critters, part of what we think of as "house dust." They are particularly likely to live in carpeting; regular vacuuming helps but does not eliminate them. They are also found in bedclothes. To alleviate this particular problem you must wash sheets in hot water and enclose mattresses in plastic or special covers. If you have a child who is prone to allergies or asthma, you may also want to consider eliminating carpets or shifting to area rugs that can be washed or cleaned regularly.

3. **Make sure your child uses car safety seats and seat belts.** Many of us remember to do this when we are on long trips; it is the short trips, when we are in a hurry, when we're most likely to slip up. To avoid problems with air bags, children should sit in the back seat.

4. **Have your child wear a helmet when riding a bike or skateboarding.** If the child *always* wears a helmet for these activities, starting early in preschool, it will become a habit and will considerably reduce the risk of serious head injury later when the child roams more freely (and more speedily) on a bicycle, skateboard, or in-line skates.

5. **Make sure your child completes all immunizations.** Go back and look at Table 4.7 (p. 138). You'll see that the fifth DPT, the fourth polio, and the second measles/mumps/rubella immunizations are all scheduled during the preschool years.

6. **Make sure your child eats a good diet, low in saturated fats and sugar, with enough iron and other nutrients.** To follow this dictum, you'll have to find "treats" that are lower in fat and lower in sugar than many children prefer. Fresh fruit, juice bars, dried fruit such as raisins, or even vegetables such as carrots are possible substitutes.

Health Habits: Good and Bad

For all parents, poor or middle class, the child's preschool years are an important time to try to establish various good health habits and to try to avoid (or break) some of the bad ones. One of the most crucial is a good diet.

A Good Diet for the Preschool Years. Just what, and how much, should a 3-year-old or 5-year-old be eating in order to foster optimum physical (and mental) growth? Table 7.7 (p. 237) gives you a detailed summary. Children obviously need enough pure calories to provide energy for normal activity and for growth. For children in this age range, this means about 90 calories per kilogram of weight per day, which translates to an intake of 1500–1700 calories a day for an average-sized 4-year-old—fewer calories per pound, by the way, than an infant

needs. Many toddlers and preschoolers respond to this decline in caloric need by eating less, a pattern that often worries parents or child-care workers. Some children seem suddenly to become very picky eaters, appearing to eat too little. If this is true of your child or children in your care, it's worth keeping a detailed food diary for a week or so, just to see what the child is eating. Very often, parents and teachers find that the child is actually eating quite enough for growth.

Pure calories are not the whole story, of course. If they were, a child could grow and flourish on a diet of pure sugar. The calories need to be distributed over the various food groups in order to make sure the child gets all the different nutrients, vitamins, and minerals he needs. The current recommendation, from most of the experts, is that the child (like the adult) should get no more than 30% of calories from fat, with another 10–12% of calo-

Table 7.7

Recommended Dietary Allowances (RDAs) for Children Aged 1–10

Nutrient	Recommended Allowance	Intake of Average 3- to 5-year-old Child Today	Good Food Source
Total calories	About 90 calories per kilogram (41 calories per pound) of body weight. For a 2-year-old = about 1300 calories; for a 5-year-old, about 1800.	1591	
Protein	No official RDA for children, but typical recommendation is about 10% of total calories.	67 gm (14–16% of total calories)	Meat, poultry, fish; eggs, milk, cheese; legumes, nuts, grains
Fiber	No official RDA for children, but American Academy of Pediatrics recommends 0.5 gm of fiber per kilogram of weight.	10.72 gm	Fruits, vegetables; grains, breads
Fat	No official RDA; most current groups recommend an upper limit of 30% of total calories; only 10% of total calories should be saturated fat.	59 gm total fat; 23 gm saturated fat (33.3% and 13% of total calories, respectively)	All meat, poultry, fish, dairy products, and vegetable oils
Vitamin A	4000–7000 international units	4275	Liver; egg yolk, whole milk; fortified breakfast cereals; dark-green leafy vegetables, yellow vegetables, fruits
Vitamin E	3–4 mg	5.89	Oil from soybeans, sunflowers, corn, and cottonseed; nuts; fish liver oil
Thiamin (Vitamin B$_1$)	0.7–1.2 mg	1.38	Whole grains, legumes, enriched flour; liver
Riboflavin	0.8–1.4 mg	1.81	Milk and milk products; whole grain products; meat, liver, fish, poultry; dark-green vegetables
Niacin	9–16 mg	16	Meats, poultry, fish; whole grain products, legumes, nuts
Vitamin B$_6$	0.9–1.6 mg	1.42	Meat, poultry, fish; bananas, nuts
Vitamin B$_{12}$	2.0–3.0 micrograms	3.70	All foods of animal origin, including meats, fish, eggs, dairy products; some kelps
Folic acid	100–300 micrograms	227	Liver; dark-green leafy vegetables; dry beans, peanuts, wheat germ
Vitamin C	45 mg	102	Citrus fruits, green leafy vegetables, tomatoes, potatoes; liver
Calcium	800 mg	855	Milk, cheese; broccoli, dark-green leafy vegetables
Iron	ages 1–3: 15 mg ages 4–10: 10 mg	ages 1–3: 9.53 ages 3–5: 11.86	Liver, red meat; whole grain and enriched grain products; beans, nuts; dark-green leafy vegetables

Sources: Committee on Diet and Health, 1989; Subcommittee on the 10th Edition of the RDAs, 1989; American Academy of Pediatrics Committee on Nutrition, 1992; Alaimo et al., 1994; McDowell et al., 1994; Saldanha, 1995.

ries from protein—although the recommendation concerning fat intake is not without critics, as you can see from the *Social Policy* box on page 240. The rest of a child's calories should come from high-fiber foods—cereals, vegetables, and fruits, with low levels of refined sugar. As you can see from Table 7.7 (p. 237), the average diet of U.S. children is not wildly off from this recommended pattern, although it includes too much fat, slightly too much protein, not quite enough fiber, and too little iron. If you want your own child, or children in your care, to develop the kinds of eating habits that will best match the recommended pattern, it is important not only to monitor what the child eats but to *model* healthy eating patterns, including low-fat snacks, vegetables and fruit, and low levels of junk food. As in so many things, children will do what you do, not what you say.

One further word about iron intake: You can see from Table 7.7 that children over the age of 3 are most often getting adequate iron but the average 1- to 3-year-old is getting only about two-thirds of what he needs. The rate of iron-deficiency anemia is high among U.S. preschoolers, especially among the poor. In one study in a poor county in Florida, for example, 21 percent of preschoolers in a Head Start program showed blood iron levels that classed them as anemic (Francis, Williams, & Yarandi, 1993). This type of anemia, the major symptoms of which are listlessness and fatigue, can be cured fairly directly by improving the child's diet, although many 2- and 3-year-olds are not so easily persuaded to eat some of the high-iron foods—such as liver, leafy green vegetables, nuts, or beans—as any of you who has tried to get your toddler to eat spinach can attest! This is one area where day care centers or preschools could focus some attention, making sure that snacks and lunches provided to young children are as rich as possible in iron.

Another flaw in the typical child's diet, at least in the United States, is too many sweets, which cause tooth decay and reduce the child's appetite for more nourishing foods.

Dental Care.   Beyond limiting sweets, good dental care is the best preventative against tooth decay. I mentioned in Chapter 4 that most pediatric dentists recommend that parents begin brushing the child's teeth when the child is still a toddler,

gradually turning over this task to the child. Flossing regularly and using fluoride toothpaste will increase the resistance to cavities (Jones, Berg, & Coody, 1994).

If the child sucks his thumb, dentists strongly recommend that a parent try to break the child of this habit. Thumb-sucking is a normal activity of infancy; it can frequently be seen on ultrasound pictures *in utero*. In infants and toddlers it poses no serious problems. When thumb-sucking (or finger-sucking) persists to age 4 or 5, however, it can have serious repercussions, including malformations of the bones around the mouth and changes in the placement of the teeth that increase the need for orthodontic treatment at a later age—at considerable expense for the parents and discomfort for the child (Rosenberg, 1995). Thumb-sucking can also be a source of infection or accidental poisoning. At a social level, it may also have an impact on a child: A number of studies show that children who are still thumb-sucking when they begin school are less likely to be approved or accepted by their peers (e.g., Friman, McPherson, Warzak, & Evans, 1993).

Strategies for breaking a child's thumb-sucking habit include simple measures like having the child wear mittens or tape on the thumb or painting the thumb with an icky-tasting substance. When these simple strategies don't work, dentists will sometimes install complex appliances in the child's mouth that prevent thumb-sucking. Behavior modification strategies can also work, such as praising the child or providing other reinforcement like stars for increasingly longer periods without thumb-sucking.

Thumb-sucking may also reflect a heightened level of anxiety or stress in the child. If a child you care for is still showing this behavior at age 4 or 5 or 6, it would be wise to begin by looking at the child's habitual stress or anxiety, before jumping immediately into any systematic attempt to eliminate the habit. The most helpful thing you can do may be to eliminate or reduce some of the stresses in the child's life—if you can.

Child Abuse and Neglect

We come, finally, to what may be the most harrowing of all the dangers of childhood—the physical, sexual, or psychological abuse of children. I'm going to talk about it in this chapter on physical development because the most obvious effect of most abuse is some kind of damage to a child's body. Bear in mind, though, that abuse has profound effects on children's minds and hearts as well as their bodies.

Definitions

Let's begin at the beginning. What do we mean by "abuse"? You may think that this is a straightforward question to answer, but it is not. Among other things, culture plays a significant role. To take a simple example, in a society in which any kind of spanking is both legally prohibited and socially disapproved (such as Sweden), a few swats on the behind might be classed as abuse; in another culture in which spanking is widely accepted as normal (such as the United States today), those swats on the rear end would be neither reported nor condemned. Experts also disagree on whether maltreatment or abuse should be defined in terms of the behavior of the adults or in terms of the effects on the child (Cicchetti & Lynch, 1995). The most helpful current definitions come from Douglas Barnett and his colleagues (Barnett, Manly, & Cicchetti, 1993; Rogosch, Cicchetti, Shields, & Toth, 1995), who propose a series of subtypes:

physical abuse involves the nonaccidental infliction of bodily injury on the child. It may range in severity from a black-and-blue mark all the way to injuries so extreme that the child requires hospitalization, or dies.

sexual abuse involves any kind of sexual contact between a child and a responsible adult that is for the purpose of the *adult s* gratification or gain. It may range from exposing the child to inappropriate sexual stimuli to forced intercourse to prostituting the child.

physical neglect includes both the failure to provide adequately for the child's nurturance and basic care and the failure to provide adequate supervision. The latter subtype obviously depends on the child's age. Leaving a 4-year-old alone overnight would be classed as physical neglect, while leaving a teenager alone for the same period of time would not.

emotional maltreatment frequently co-occurs with other forms of abuse, but can occur in isolation as well. It includes such things as deliberate or persistent thwarting of the child's basic emotional needs, such as a sense of safety, acceptance, or self-esteem. A parent who constantly belittles or ridicules a child, or disciplines a child by using intimidation or extreme fear, would be labeled as emotionally maltreating. Locking a child in an enclosed space for protracted periods of time would also belong in this category.

moral-legal-educational maltreatment is the fuzziest and least often discussed of Barnett's categories. Parents who maltreat in this way either fail to provide the child with the needed opportunities to become integrated in society or expose the child to illegal activities. Failing to send a child to school falls in this category, as would using drugs or abusing alcohol in the child's presence.

These types of abuse rarely occur in isolation. In three cases out of four they occur in combination.

Frequency

The next obvious question is how often such abuse occurs. A variety of sources of information tells us that in the United States, about one child out of every seventy is abused in any given year. One source of this estimate comes from cases of suspected abuse or neglect reported to Children's Protective Services each year. Roughly two million are reported, about a million of which are later substantiated (U.S. Bureau of the Census, 1996). This tells us that a minimum of one million children per year are abused or neglected, out of roughly seventy million children 17 and younger in the population. A similar estimate (1.45%) comes from the most recent national survey conducted by the National Center on Child Abuse and Neglect in 1988 (1988). When the survey researchers included a category they called "endangered" children—children at risk for harm but who had not yet been harmed—the rate rose to 2.26%. Children between ages 2 and 9 are most likely to be abused; infants are least likely, although they are the most likely to die of any abuse they receive (National Center on

Social Policy Debate

Childhood Diet and the Prevention of Adult Heart Disease

The average child in the United States eats a diet that includes 33 to 35 percent of calories from fat (McDowell, Briefel, Alaimo et al., 1994). Studies of adults have shown repeatedly that such higher fat diets are associated with higher levels of blood cholesterol, which in turn is linked to higher risk of heart disease. It is for this reason that the current dietary recommendation by virtually all experts is for a diet in which no more than 30% of total calories are from fat. Among adults with evidence of already-existing atherosclerosis (such as partial blockage of arteries), diets with as little as 10% of calories from fat have helped to reduce both cholesterol and atherosclerosis (e.g., Ornish, 1990).

The question that pediatricians and nutritionists have been struggling with is whether they should encourage similarly lower-fat diets for children. Most expert groups, including the American Academy of Pediatrics (American Academy of Pediatrics Committee on Nutrition, 1992) in their most recent pronouncement, have concluded that such a 30%–fat recommendation is justified, on several grounds:

- *A reduction in fat intake to 30% will probably lower the child's risk of heart disease in adulthood;*

- *Food habits are established in childhood and will thus carry over into adulthood; a child used to a lower-fat diet will find it easier to maintain such a diet in adulthood; children who are in the habit of eating raisins as snacks instead of potato chips will carry such a pattern throughout life;*

- *A lower-fat diet for all children would help lower the rapidly rising rate of obesity among children in the United States and most Western countries—a pattern I'll talk about at length in Chapter 10.*

Despite these strong arguments, however, questions remain. Part of the difficulty is that we have no long-term longitudinal studies of children who have been deliberately given fat-restricted diets. Such studies are needed to uncover either beneficial effects or potentially negative side effects. So the present recommendations are based essentially on extrapolations from adult research, as well as on the observation that the process of atherosclerosis is detectable in adults as young as their twenties, thus indicating that the very earliest steps of the disease process may begin in childhood (Harper, 1996; R. Olson, 1995).

Beyond the lack of good follow-up studies, some pediatricians and nutritionists have hesitated to embrace a 30% guideline because they are concerned that the effects may depend a lot on what kind of calories replace the fat in a lower-fat diet. Children need calories, both to sustain basic body functions and to grow. So if all we do is reduce the fat, we are also reducing calories, which may have a negative impact on children's energy or growth. Or a child might replace the fat calo-

Child Abuse and Neglect, 1988; U.S. Bureau of the Census, 1996).

Why Do Parents Abuse Their Children?

This question is perhaps the hardest of all. There is simply no easy answer. We can identify certain risk factors, but abuse does not normally occur unless several of these risks occur in the same family at the same time. One helpful way to conceptualize it is to use Bronfenbrenner's ecological model as a framework. You'll recall from Chapter 2 that he suggests we think of each of us being influenced by elements of the macrosystem, exosystems, and microsystems. If we apply this kind of analysis to abuse, as several psychologists have done (Belsky, 1980; Cicchetti & Lynch, 1995), we end up with a list of risks like the one given in Table 7.8 (p. 243).

One common thread among the various entries in this table is obviously the role of the parents' stress in triggering abuse. The risk of abuse is higher in any family experiencing significant stress, whether that stress arises from unemployment, neighborhood violence, a lack of social support, or an especially difficult or demanding infant. No doubt each of us has some threshold of stress above which we are likely to snap—with a fit of anger, with aggression, or, in some cases, with abuse of a child.

Social Policy Debate

Childhood Diet and the Prevention of Adult Heart Disease (*Continued*)

ries with sugar calories, an exchange that would provide energy but no other benefits. Alternatively, the child might eat more fiber—primarily grains, vegetables, and fruits—to make up the difference. Some physicians have expressed concern that too much fiber might result in suboptimal growth in children (e.g., Lifshitz & Tarim, 1996).

We do not have a great deal of research to draw on relating to this last point, but the early results are reassuring. A study in Australia comparing children whose diet included less than 30% fat calories with those whose normal diet included more than 30% fat shows no difference in height or weight (Boulton & Magarey, 1995). Other studies of vegetarian children (Dwyer, 1995) such as Seventh-Day Adventists, who eat a diet much higher in fiber than normal, suggest no ill effects. Such children grow normally and have excellent health. Even children following a totally nondairy/nonegg diet (called a vegan diet), a diet necessarily very high in fiber and low in fat, show essentially normal growth patterns *if* they have supplemental sources of Vitamin B_{12}, although they tend to be somewhat lighter for their height than is typical. Only when a very low fat/high fiber diet contains inadequate amounts of the various vitamins and minerals listed in Table 7.8 do researchers find significant growth deficits and low energy.

Thus it is quite possible to devise a diet for children that includes 30 percent or fewer calories from fat that is balanced and sufficient for the child's growth. However, parents (and school dieticians) have to be more careful; a number of studies suggest that when adults and children try to reduce their fat intake, they have some difficulty substituting the kind of complex carbohydrates that will provide both the needed calories and nutrients (Nicklas, 1995a; 1995b; Zlotkin, 1996).

Several compromise positions have been proposed. The Canadian Pediatric Society, for example, recommends a slow transition from the naturally high-fat intake of infancy (because breast milk and formula are both very high in fat, needed by the infant), reaching the level of 30% of total calories only at the end of adolescence. In contrast, the European Society of Pediatric Gastroenterology and Nutrition (ESPGAN Committee on Nutrition, 1994) argues that we should focus not on the calories from all forms of fat, but only on saturated fat, which should surely be 10% or less of total calories. Thus olive oil or rapeseed oil are quite okay, even if their consumption raises the total fat intake to a level higher than 30%. Because most fat from animal sources is saturated, this means the ideal diet for the child would include much less meat, poultry, and dairy products than the typical American child eats, more protein from grains and legumes, and reasonable amounts of oil.

The whole discussion is yet another example of how difficult it is to have *enough* really good evidence to allow unequivocal advice.

Still, stress alone, even fairly severe stress, is not enough to make abuse a certainty. Another key ingredient is a parent who lacks the skill to find other ways of dealing with the child and with the stresses of her or his own life. Some parents, who were themselves abused, simply know no other way to deal with frustration and stress or with disobedience in their child, other than striking the child in some way. Others are depressed or unable to form the kind of emotional bond to the child that would help to prevent abuse.

A third key element, apparent in the table, is a lack of social support; or to put it in negative terms, the parent who abuses is likely to be socially isolated.

When several of these key ingredients intersect—a high level of stress, a lack of personal support, a lack of alternative strategies or skills, and the personal inability to deal well with stress—abuse (of a child or a spouse) becomes highly likely.

Long-Term Consequences

Long-term, the outcomes for abused children are pretty negative. Physically abused children are far more likely than are nonabused children to become aggressive or delinquent at school age and in

Research Report

Straus and Gelles's Survey of the Rate of Physical Abuse

The estimate that 1 child out of every 70 in the United States is abused each year, striking as it is, may not capture the entire problem. Murray Straus and Richard Gelles give us a glimpse into a wider world of abuse in a rather different type of national survey (1986). They interviewed one adult in each of a national probability sample of over 6000 households, including in their interview an instrument called the Conflict Tactics Scales. Each respondent is asked to think of several situations in the past year when they had had a disagreement with or were angry at another family member. The interviewer then lists a series of specific acts that a person might use to respond to such a situation, asking in each case how often the respondent had used that act or strategy. Included in the list are a series of violent acts: (1) throwing something at the other person; (2) pushing, grabbing, or shoving; (3) slapping or spanking; (4) kicking, biting, or hitting with a fist; (5) hitting or trying to hit with some object; (6) beating up the other; (7) threatening with a knife or a gun; (8) and using a knife or a gun. Straus and Gelles class the first three of these as minor violence; the last five they class as severe violence.

The figure shows how many parents, out of the 1428 households with a child between the ages of 3 and 17, reported that they had performed the various severely violent acts toward a child: Overall, Straus and Gelles found that 10.7% of the parents they interviewed admitted to one or more of the severe forms of violence, a rate obviously vastly higher than the 1 in 70 others have estimated. Yet the estimates may not be so hugely different after all. Straus and Gelles make the point that in U.S. culture, hitting a child with a belt, a hairbrush, or a stick is within culturally acceptable norms for most subgroups. When they remove these cases from the total, they arrive at an estimate of

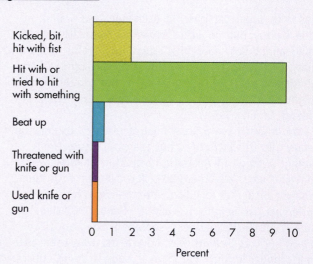

1.9% of families admitting they committed the other severe forms of violence, a group they label as "abusive" according to cultural standards. This final figure, 1.9%, is obviously not much higher than the 1.45% researchers have arrived at by other means. Remember, though, that even if we use the lower number from the Straus and Gelles study (1.9%), they are only counting *physical* abuse, whereas the National Center on Child Abuse and Neglect has attempted to count all forms of abuse. In the survey by the latter group, about half the total abuse was physical abuse. If we thus double the most conservative figure from Straus and Gelles, we arrive at an estimate of 3.8%, or 1 in roughly every 26 children.

Thus Straus and Gelles's study points to the likelihood that the estimate of 1 child out of every 70 is a significant underestimate of actual rates of abuse in the United States.

adolescence or violent as an adult, including such behaviors as date rape or spousal abuse. They are more likely to be substance abusers in adolescence and adulthood, to attempt suicide, to have emotional problems such as anxiety or depression or more serious forms of emotional illness, and to have lower IQs and poorer school performance (Malinosky-Rummell & Hansen, 1993; National Re-

search Council, 1993; Rogosch et al., 1995). They have more difficulty forming intimate friendships at school age and in adolescence (Parker & Herrera, 1996).

Sexually abused children also show a wide variety of disturbances, including fears, behavior problems, sexual promiscuity or sexual offenses in adolescence and adulthood, poor self-esteem, and

Table 7.8

Risk Factors for Child Abuse

Macrosystem (Cultural) Influences	
Social acceptance of violence	Abuse is higher in cultures (such as the United States) in which other forms of violence are widespread and relatively acceptable.
Racism	Overt and subtle racism places extra stress on minority families, and stress is linked to increased rates of abuse.

Exosystem Influences	
Poverty	Abuse occurs in all social class groups, but disproportionately among the poor (of any ethnic group), especially among mothers of young children; those families living in areas of concentrated poverty are still more likely to abuse.
Unemployment	Periods of high job loss in any community or nation are followed by increased rates of child abuse. The effect is strongest for fathers.
Neighborhood qualities	Among poor neighborhoods, abuse is highest in those with few social resources —where families do not lend support to one another.

Microsystem Influences (the Immediate Family Environment)	
Parents' history of abuse	Roughly thirty percent of adults who were themselves maltreated as children will maltreat their own children, a rate that may be far higher among those who have been chronically physically or sexually abused. Among parents who abuse their children, some three-fourths were themselves maltreated.
Parents' personalities	Parents who abuse are more likely to be depressed or to be rated as lacking impulse control. They are "emotionally unstable" and have difficulty coping with stress.
Parents' personal resources	Abusing parents have weaker social networks; they are socially isolated.
Parenting styles	Abusing parents are generally less playful, supportive, affectionate, and responsive to their children; they are inclined toward controlling methods of discipline and rarely use reasoning or affection as methods of control.
Child characteristics	Children born preterm, physically disabled children, and those with difficult temperaments are more likely to be abused than are full-term, able-bodied, or easy-temperament infants.

Sources: Rogosch et al., 1995; Cicchetti & Lynch, 1995; Spieker, Bensley, McMahon, Fung, & Ossiander, 1996.

posttraumatic stress disorder—a pattern of disturbance that includes flashbacks of the traumatic event, nightmares, persistent efforts to avoid thinking about or being reminded of the traumatic event, and signs of heightened arousal such as hypervigilance, exaggerated startle reactions, sleep disturbances, and interferences with concentration and attention (Kendall-Tackett, Williams, & Finkelhor, 1993; National Research Council, 1993; Pynoos, Steinbert, & Wraith, 1995).

Children who suffer either type of abuse do not typically show *all* these symptoms, but they are far more likely than are their nonabused peers to show some form of significant disturbance. The more lasting and severe the abuse, the greater the likelihood of problems of these types.

The picture is not totally bleak. Some abused children are remarkably resilient, showing no measurable symptoms. Others show a decline in symptoms of distress when the abuse is stopped, especially if the child's mother was supportive and protective. Despite these few comforting words, though, let us not lose sight of the fact that long-term problems are common among children who experience this degree of hostility or hurt, nor of the fact that our society has not yet found good ways of reducing the incidence of such abuse.

Prevention and Treatment

In light of the contributing factors listed in Table 7.8 (p. 243), think for a minute about how you might try to prevent child abuse. One obvious possibility is to try to reduce the social isolation and stress experienced by poverty-level families or others we might list as high risk for abuse. How might you go about achieving such a goal?

One way might be to provide general support for poor families and their children, via, for example, such federal programs as Parent-Child Development Centers or Head Start. Many programs for young, poor, or otherwise high-risk mothers include some combination of day care for the infant or child along with support and parenting training for the mothers. Few of these programs have been aimed directly at prevention of child abuse, and we have little information about their effectiveness in reducing maltreatment. Still, programs like these do often help the children more generally, sustaining and supporting both cognitive and emotional development (which I'll talk about more in Chapter 8); good programs of this kind also seem to help mothers stay in school, an outcome that might be expected to have at least an indirect effect on the risk of abuse (Brooks-Gunn, 1995b). All these strategies are promising, but at this point we simply don't have the kind of good research that will tell us what parts or pieces of these programs are especially helpful in reducing maltreatment.

A more direct type of intervention is to assign high-risk families to a home visitor, often a nurse or an educator, who comes to the home regularly, provides the parents with emotional support, and

Programs like Head Start were not designed specifically to reduce child abuse, though they may have that effect, especially if the program for the child is combined with programs for the parents.

may give the parents some instruction or help in learning new ways to handle the child. When programs like these are comprehensive, well designed, and last long enough, like David Olds's program in a very poor rural county in upstate New York (Olds & Henderson, 1989), they do seem to reduce the risk of abuse.

Olds's program focused on young, mostly white, unmarried, poor mothers pregnant with a first child—a group with a relatively high risk of abuse because of the high levels of stress in their lives. The women who enrolled in this study/intervention were assigned at random to one of four treatments, ranging from a no-treatment comparison group to the most complete home-visitor program that involved at least nine visits before the birth of the child and then regular visits until the child was age 2. The visitor not only dealt with health problems in the mother and child, she also provided "parental enhancement" of various kinds, such as encouraging and supporting the mother in her efforts to find work, to return to school, or to prevent subsequent pregnancies. At the end of the two-year period, Olds found that 19% of the non-treated comparison group had abused or neglected their child, compared to only 4% of the nurse-visited group.

This program is clearly not a panacea; a 4% rate of abuse is still three times the rate in the population as a whole. The results are nonetheless encouraging, suggesting what might be possible with really well designed, well targeted programs that begin early and last long enough. Of course, few existing programs meet all these criteria; still, this study points us in a helpful direction.

Intervention After Abuse.   The other half of the social problem, of course, is to decide what to do for a child and for the family after some kind of abuse has occurred. Here the story is quite discouraging, not only because no pattern of treatment for known-abusing families has been consistently effective but because it is virtually impossible to do decent research on this problem, which makes it just that much harder to demonstrate that a given program is—or is not—effective.

For one thing, a researcher cannot randomly assign abusing parents to either some form of treatment or a nontreatment comparison group. All those who are referred for abuse must receive some kind of treatment. Further, among those who might be included in a demonstration project, many will refuse to participate or will not stick with whatever program you may have devised. Then there is the problem of discovering whether each of these families abuses again at a later time.

Because of these problems, most of what we know about the effectiveness of various treatments comes from less-than-perfect studies of complex, multifaceted intervention projects. Given that, perhaps it shouldn't be surprising that Anne Cohn and Deborah Daro, reviewing ten years of government-funded studies of the effectiveness of abuse-treatment programs, concluded:

> Child abuse and neglect continue despite early, thoughtful, and often costly intervention. Treatment programs have been relatively ineffective in initially halting abusive and neglectful behavior or in reducing the future likelihood of maltreatment in the most severe cases of physical abuse, chronic neglect, and emotional maltreatment. One-third or more of the parents served by these intensive demonstration efforts maltreated their children while in treatment, and over one-half of the families served continued to be judged by staff as likely to mistreat their children following termination. (1987, p. 440)

In the midst of the gloom there are a few rays of hope. Cohn and Daro found that programs that provide families with a range of services, including teaching parents new disciplining skills, seem to be somewhat more effective. Longer programs also seem to work better than shorter ones (D. Barnett, 1997). On the whole, however, attempts to change the circumstances and the behavior of actively abusing families have been only marginally successful, despite significant effort.

Let me give you just one example of a particular program, Project 12-Ways, which is interesting because it included virtually all the components that would seem to make sense, given the items listed in Table 7.8 (p. 243). The originators of this intervention project, David Wesch and John Lutzker (1991), customized the program for each parent, utilizing some combination of support groups, behavioral training, parental aides to provide training on such things as nutrition and home safety, job placement, assertiveness training, vocational skills training, and alcoholism treatment. Wesch and Lutzker find that parents in the program do change some of their behavior while they are actually in the program. For example, some learn to provide more nutritious meals; others learn to keep their home cleaner. Yet when Wesch and Lutzker compared the families they worked with to other abusing families who were referred to Child Protective Services but who were not assigned to Project 12-Ways, they found no difference in the incidence of later abuse, foster-home placement, or adoption. This project, one of the better ones around, does not make one confident that this kind of **parental enhancement program** will consistently reduce the rate of re-abuse of children.

The results of a related category of program, referred to as **family preservation programs,** are also equivocal. The aim of these interventions is to prevent the removal of the child from the home while at the same time ensuring the child's safety. They frequently involve intense, brief interventions with the family after an incident of abuse. Some such programs, like the Homebuilders program developed in Washington State and widely replicated, have reported short-term improvements in family functioning; but longer term studies suggest that the effects fade over time (National Research Council, 1993). Nonetheless, programs like this are widespread, in part because we have such a strong cultural commitment to the sanctity of the family and to parental rights. These kinds of programs also recognize the fact that, despite the abuse, most children are attached to their parents and do not want to leave them.

An obvious alternative is **foster care.** Instead of trying to preserve the family unit, the abused child is simply removed from the family altogether, at least for a period of time. Although there are documented cases of children being abused by foster parents, the primary advantage of such placement for most children is that it eliminates the risk of further abuse. The drawbacks, however, are multiple: good, stable foster families are scarce; children are often moved from one foster placement to another, a pattern guaranteed to increase the child's stress and anxiety; foster care is expensive. Because of the difficulties, and because of our societal commitment to the concept of families, government policies in most states favor keeping the child in the family if at all possible.

It would be very helpful to those hardworking, overburdened caseworkers who have to make critical decisions about abused children every day, if we had really good outcome studies comparing the long-term effects of foster care placement versus family preservation. Unfortunately, no such study exists; arguably, no such study could ever be designed or carried out, for both ethical and practical reasons. The lack of such information, and the lack of clearcut success for even well-designed and funded intervention programs, mean that the caseworker has few resources to work with and can only use her or his best judgment in each case—providing assistance to families when that seems most helpful, placing the child in foster care when that seems essential. Sometimes, the caseworker's judgment turns out to be wrong—as happened in several highly publicized cases in New York City in 1995 and 1996 in which a repeatedly abused child who had been left with or returned to the abusing parent died of abuse in ugly circumstances. Doubtless there are many other cases, less publicized, in which children have suffered repeatedly. I am sure other cases exist, equally unpublicized, in which the outcome has been better. The problem for the caseworker is not only that she is likely to be dealing with far too many cases but that *no* solution is without risk for the child, especially in the absence of really effective treatment programs for the families.

Despite the lack of perfect information and a scarcity of good solutions, we must take action to reduce the rate of abuse. Caseworkers need smaller caseloads, which means that cities and states have to provide more resources for children's protective services. And we have to put energy and resources into preventive programs, which in the long run are a better answer than treatment. We know something about the subgroups within our society who are at especially high risk for abusing their children, such as poor, single, young mothers; we know something about how to support those parents in ways that will reduce the risk of later abuse. On both humanitarian and economic grounds, it makes sense to fund such programs, just as it makes sense to continue to fund careful research on methods of treating already-abusing families. I know that scientists are always saying "We need more research on this question." It is nearly always true, but never more so than in this case.

A Last Look at Preschool Physical Development

Despite the many physical risks and problems in this age group, you shouldn't lose sight of one of the most critical things about preschoolers' physical development—the pure *joy* they get from moving their bodies. They climb things, throw things, run, leap, build things. When a child first masters any one of these skills, the utter delight and pride on the child's face is a wonder to behold. When a child is working hard on some physical skill—trying to thread a needle for the first time or trying to build a huge, complex construction out of blocks—she is likely to have a look of intense concentration, often with her tongue sticking out a little bit, and other parts of her body tense as she focuses on the specific movement. Yes, children this age face certain health risks and common physical problems or challenges. But let us not forget that preschoolers are developing new motor skills every month, skills that they practice over and over, delighting in their newfound abilities.

Summary

1. Children grow more slowly during the preschool years than during infancy, but still at a fairly rapid rate. Differences in total size between faster-growing and slower-growing children become very noticeable.

2. The brain and nervous system continue to change, with further dendritic development, further myelination, and some further dendritic pruning. Hemispheric lateralization is also clearly established in these years.

3. Roughly ninety percent of all children show a clear right-handed (or right-sided) preference by age 5 or 6.

4. Preschoolers sleep fewer and fewer hours, and nap less and less. They also exhibit certain typical problems linked with sleep, such as bedtime struggles, nightmares, night terrors, and bed-wetting.

5. Gross motor skills improve substantially through the preschool years. By age 6 or 7 most children show essentially mature patterns of movement for significant gross motor skills, such as running, skipping, jumping, throwing, and catching.

6. Fine motor skills improve as well but more slowly, so that at school age most children are still slow and labored in such tasks as writing.

7. Rates of mortality among preschoolers are very low in industrialized countries; in less technologically developed countries, however, mortality rates are high: 5 to 6 percent in these years.

8. The most frequent causes of death among preschoolers are accidents, congenital anomalies, and cancer.

9. The most common chronic illnesses among preschoolers are allergies and asthma. The rate of asthma, in particular, is rising dramatically in most parts of the world.

10. Asthma is more common among poor children, among those living in crowded conditions or with single mothers, among African Americans, among children living with someone who smokes, and among those who live near significant sources of pollution.

11. The average preschooler is sick in bed with an acute illness (e.g., cold, flu, diarrhea) about five days a year. Illness is more frequent among children experiencing higher levels of stress.

12. About a quarter of all children (in the United States) have at least one nonfatal accident requiring medical attention each year.

13. A recommended good diet for a child includes no more than 30% fat (of which no more than 10% is saturated fat), 10–12% protein, and the remainder from carbohydrates, fruits, and vegetables. The average U.S. child eats somewhat too much fat and protein, and somewhat too little fiber.

14. Among children ages 2 and 3, diets too low in iron are common, increasing the risk of iron deficiency anemia.

15. Regular tooth care is another good habit to be established in these years.

16. A minimum of 1 in 70 children in the United States is abused each year. About half that abuse is physical; the remainder includes sexual and psychological abuse and neglect.

17. Factors that may contribute to abuse include macrosystem influences (such as cultural norms for styles of punishment), exosystem influences (such as poverty, unemployment, or lack of neighborhood supports), and microsystem influences (parents' history of abuse, parents' personalities and personal resources, and child characteristics such as difficult temperament or disability).

18. Of the many programs designed to prevent or treat abuse, the most successful have been prevention programs aimed at providing increased skills and social support to parents in high-risk, high-stress subgroups. Programs for parents who have already abused their children have been difficult to study, but no one treatment plan has been consistently successful.

Key Terms

acute illness   Brief (rather than chronic) illnesses, such as colds, the flu, or diarrhea. **(p. 234)**

asthma   The most common chronic disease of childhood, increasing in frequency in recent decades. Symptoms include chronic cough, wheezing, tightness in the chest, and difficulty breathing. **(p. 233)**

chronic illness   Any illness that persists six months or longer. In children this category includes asthma, cancer, diabetes, sickle-cell disease, and others. **(p. 232)**

design stage   Third stage in the development of children's drawings, as proposed by Kellogg; the mixing of several basic shapes into more complex designs. **(p. 231)**

developmental disabilities   Permanent physical problems, such as blindness, deafness, cerebral palsy, limb deformations, and the like. Mental retardation is also typically classed in this category. Combined with chronic illnesses to create the larger category of "chronic conditions." **(p. 232)**

emotional maltreatment   A form of child abuse involving deliberate thwarting of a child's basic emotional needs. Includes belittling, ridicule, intimidation, and threats. **(p. 239)**

enuresis   The technical medical term for bed-wetting. **(p. 226)**

exercise-induced asthma   A form of asthma triggered by heavy exercise, especially in cold, dry air. Common among top-level athletes, such as Jackie Joyner-Kersee. **(p. 233)**

family preservation program   A type of treatment program for abusing families that focuses on providing intensive, short-term assistance to the family so that the abused child may remain with the family. **(p. 246)**

foster care   A form of treatment for abused children involving removal of the child from the family and placement of him with another family for temporary care. **(p. 246)**

hemispheric lateralization   The specialization of tasks in the two hemispheres of the brain. Verbal tasks are primarily handled in the left brain, spatial tasks and emotional responses in the right. Left-handed individuals are usually somewhat less firmly lateralized. **(p. 221)**

moral-legal-educational maltreatment   A form of child abuse in which the parent fails to provide the child with the needed opportunities to become integrated in society or exposes the child to illegal activities. Failure to ensure the child's attendance at school would be one example. **(p. 239)**

nightmares   Scary, upsetting dreams, occurring normally in the early morning. **(p. 226)**

night terrors   A form of sleep disruption occurring early in a night's sleep for some children. The child may scream but is not fully awake and returns to sleep readily. **(p. 226)**

parental enhancement programs   A form of treatment focused on providing abusing parents with improved parenting skills as well as support in solving other life crises. **(p. 246)**

physical abuse   A form of child abuse involving the nonaccidental inflicting of bodily injury on a child. **(p. 239)**

physical neglect   A form of child abuse that includes both the failure to provide adequately for the child's nurturance and basic care and the failure to provide adequate supervision. **(p. 239)**

pictorial stage   Fourth stage in the development of children's drawings, as proposed by Kellogg; the child draws pictures of real-life objects such as people or houses, using combinations of the basic shapes. **(p. 231)**

scribble   First stage in the development of children's drawings, as proposed by Kellogg; she identifies 20 basic scribbles which form the foundation of the basic shapes. **(p. 231)**

sexual abuse   A form of child abuse that includes any kind of sexual contact between a child and a responsible adult that is for the purpose of the *adult s* gratification or gain. **(p. 239)**

shape stage   Second stage in the development of children's drawings, as proposed by Kellogg; the child begins to draw specific shapes (lines, circles, squares) deliberately. **(p. 231)**

transitional object   An object such as a "security blanket" or a favored toy used by a child to aid the transition from waking to sleeping or from being with people to being alone. **(p. 224)**

Suggested Readings

Kemper, K. J. (1996). *The wholistic pediatrician*. New York: HarperCollins. I recommended this book in Chapter 4, and do so again here. Among other topics, Kemper talks in detail about asthma and sleep problems, including bed-wetting.

National Research Council (1993). *Understanding child abuse and neglect*. Washington, DC: National Academy Press. This excellent book summarizes the work of a panel of experts, brought together to analyze all of what we now know about maltreatment of children.

Cognitive Development in the Preschool Years

Preview Questions

1 What does the language of a 2-year-old sound like?

2 Is it possible that the ability to learn language is, in some important respects, built into the human brain?

3 Why is it important for parents (and teachers) to read to children?

4 What do psychologists mean by a "theory of mind"?

5 How many different ways can we explain the fact that children living in poverty have lower average IQs than do children growing up in more advantaged circumstances?

6 Given what we now know, would it be good social policy to provide intensive preschool programs, beginning perhaps in infancy, for all poor children?

Chapter Outline

Watch an 18-month-old playing near his mom or dad, and you'll notice that he doesn't go too far away. He may also glance at his parent regularly, as if checking to make sure the safe base is still there. Watch the same child a few years later and he is probably playing in a separate room, maybe with a chum. Because his language is so greatly improved, he can stay in touch with Mom or Dad by calling out to them occasionally, perhaps asking them to come and see something he has created. His play is also noticeably different. Instead of simply building things with blocks, for example, he may create elaborate pretend games alone or with his friends. Some of these changes, like the huge explosion in children's language we see in these years, are easily as dramatic as any changes in infancy; others are more subtle, but no less significant for the child. In the years from 2 to 6, the child changes from being a dependent toddler, able to communicate only in very primitive ways, to a remarkably competent, communicative, social creature, ready to begin school.

Talking in Sentences: The Next Steps in Language Development

When we left the infant in Chapter 5, he was just beginning to use a few individual words. This is no small accomplishment, but what happens to language in the following few years is even more remarkable. By age 2½ the average child has a vocabulary of about 600 words; by age 5 or 6 that number has risen to roughly fifteen *thousand* words—an astonishing increase of ten words *a day* (Pinker, 1994). The toddler also moves with amazing rapidity from single words to simple and then complex sentences. By age 3 most children have acquired all the basic tools needed to form sentences and make conversation (Bloom, 1991).

First Sentences: 18 to 27 Months

The first two-word sentences usually appear between 18 and 24 months, beginning only after a child has reached a threshold vocabulary of 100 to 200 words (Fenson, Dale, Reznick et al., 1994). These first sentences have several distinguishing

Katherine, at 16 months, probably uses only a few words, but within a year she is likely to have a vocabulary of over 600 words and to be able to create a variety of simple sentences. Here she is responding to a question from her mother: "Where are Daddy's teeth?"

features: They are *short*—generally two or three words—and they are *simple*. Nouns, verbs, and adjectives are usually included, but virtually all the purely grammatical markers (which linguists call **inflections**) are missing. Roger Brown, one of the most famous American language researchers, once described this early language as **telegraphic speech** because it sounds a bit like a telegram, including only the most critical words (1973). At this early stage, for example, children learning English do not normally use the *s* for plurals or put the *-ed* ending on verbs to make the past tense. Neither do they use the *s* of the possessive or auxiliary verbs like *am* or *do*. So, for example, they might say "I tired" or "me tired" rather than "I am tired," or "I not want it" rather than "I *don't* want it." It is also clear that children create even these earliest sentences following rules. Not adult rules, to be sure, but rules nonetheless. Children focus on certain types of words and put them together in particular orders. They also manage to convey a variety of different meanings with their simple sentences.

For example, young children frequently use a sentence made up of two nouns, such as *Mommy sock* or *sweater chair* (Bloom, 1973). We might conclude from this that a "two noun" form is a basic grammatical characteristic of early child language. But that misses the complexity. For instance, the child in Lois Bloom's classic study who said *Mommy sock* said it on two different occasions. The first time was when she picked up her mother's sock and the second was when the mother put the child's own sock on the child's foot. In the first case, *Mommy sock* seems to mean Mommy's sock (a possessive relationship). In the second instance the child seems to convey "Mommy is putting a sock on me," which is an *agent* (Mommy)–*object* (sock) relationship.

Grammar Explosion: 27 to 36 Months

Just as a vocabulary explosion follows an early, slow beginning, so a grammar explosion follows several months of short, simple sentences. One sign of the change is that children's sentences get longer, as you can see in Figure 8.1, which shows the maximum sentence length reported by parents of toddlers of various ages, drawn from Fenson's large cross-sectional study. Most 18- to 20-month-olds are still using one- and two-word sentences. By 24 months the longest sentences include four and five words; by 30 months sentence length has almost doubled again.

At the same time, children's speech ceases to be telegraphic, as they rather quickly add many of the inflections and function words. Within a few months, they use prepositions, plurals, past

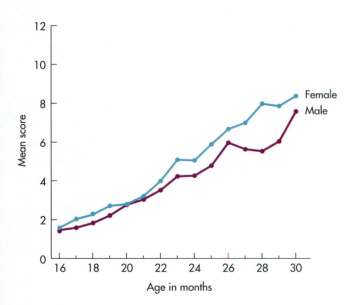

Figure 8.1

In this cross-sectional study Fenson and his colleagues asked 1130 parents of toddlers (ages 16 to 30 months) to describe the longest sentence used by their child. (Source: Fenson et al., 1994, Figure 27, p. 82.)

tenses, and auxiliary verbs such as *is* or *does*. You can get some feeling for the sound of the change from Table 8.1, which lists some of the sentences of a little boy named Daniel, recorded by David Ingram (1981). The left-hand column lists some of Daniel's sentences at about age 21 months, when he was still using the simplest forms; the right-hand column lists some of his sentences only $2\frac{1}{2}$ months later (age 23 to 24 months), when he had just begun to shift into higher gear.

Daniel obviously did not add all the inflections at once. In the sample of his speech shown in the table, he uses only a few, such as the *s* for plural, although the beginning of a negative construction is apparent in "no book," and "where going?" shows the beginning of a question form.

Questions and Negatives.   Daniel's early questions and negatives are typical of early forms of these constructions. Indeed, children move through predictable sequences in their developing use of both questions and negatives. In each case the child seems to go through periods when he creates types of sentences that he has not heard adults use, but that are consistent with the particular set of rules he is using. For example, in the development of questions in English, children first put a *wh* word (who, what, when, where, why) at the front end of a sentence, but don't yet have the auxiliary verb put in the right place, creating sentences such as: *Why it is resting now?* Similarly, in the development of negatives, we hear a stage in which the *not* or *n t* or *no* is put in, but the auxiliary verb is omitted, as in *I not crying*, or *there no squirrels*.

Overregularization.   Another intriguing phenomenon of this second phase of sentence construction is **overregularization** or overgeneralization. No language is perfectly regular; every language includes some irregularly conjugated verbs or unusual forms of plurals. What children this age do is apply the basic rule to all these irregular instances, thus making the language more regular than it really is. In English this is especially clear in children's creation of past tenses like *wented, blowed, sitted* or in plurals like *teeths* or *blockses* (Fenson et al., 1994; Kuczaj, 1977; 1978). Stan Kuczaj has pointed out that young children initially learn a small number of irregular past tenses and use them correctly for a short time. Then, rather suddenly the child

Table 8.1
Examples of Daniel's Early Sentences

Simple Sentences (age 21 months)	More Complex Sentences (age 23 months)	
a bottle	a little boat	cat there
here bottle	doggies here	boat here
horse doggie	give you the book	it's a boy
broke it	it's a robot	it's cat
it a bottle	little box there	no book
kitty cat	oh cars	oh doggie
oh a doggie	sit down	this a bucket
poor Daddy	that flowers	there's a boat
thank you	those little boat	there
that hat?	what's that	what those?
that monkey	where going?	what this?
want a bottle		where the boat?
want that?		

Source: Reprinted by permission of the publisher. D. Ingram, Early patterns of grammatical development, in R. E. Stark (Ed.), *Language behavior in infancy and early childhood,* Tables 6 and 7, pp. 344–345. Copyright © 1981 by Elsevier Science Publishing Co., Inc.

seems to discover the rule of adding *ed* and overgeneralizes this rule to all verbs, after which he must relearn the exceptions one at a time. Even among preschoolers this type of "error" is not hugely common, accounting perhaps for as few as 2 to 3 percent of all past tenses in English (Marcus, Pinker, Ullman et al., 1992). Still, these overregularizations stand out because they are so distinctive, and because they illustrate yet again that children create forms that they have not heard but that are logical within their current grammar.

Complex Sentences: 36 to 48 Months

After children have figured out the inflections and basic sentence forms, like negation and questions, they soon begin to create remarkably complex sentences, using conjunctions like *and* or *but* to combine two ideas or employing embedded clauses. Here are some examples from de Villiers and de Villiers from children ages 30 to 48 months old (1992, p. 379):

I didn't catch it, but Teddy did!
I'm gonna sit on the one you're sitting on.

Where did you say you put my doll?
Those are punk rockers, aren't they?

When you remember that only about eighteen months earlier, the child had been saying little more complex than *see doggie*, you can appreciate how far he has come in a short time.

The Development of Word Meaning

To understand language development, it is not enough to know how children learn to string words together to form sentences. We also have to understand how the words in those sentences come to have meaning. Linguists are still searching for good ways to describe (or explain) children's emerging word meaning. So far, several sets of questions have dominated the research.

Which Comes First, the Meaning or the Word?
The most fundamental question is whether the child learns a word to describe a category or class he has *already* created through his manipulations of the world around him, or whether the existence of a word forces the child to create new cognitive cat-

Parenting

Rearing Bilingual Children

What I've said so far about early language development describes what happens when a child learns a *single* language. What happens to children who are exposed to two or more languages from the beginning? Should parents who speak different native languages try to expose their children to both, or will that only confuse the child and make any kind of language learning harder? What's the best way to do this?

Parents should have no fears about exposing their child to two or more languages from the very beginning. Such simultaneous exposure usually slows the child down a bit in word learning and early sentence construction; your child will probably "mix" words or grammar from the two languages in individual sentences at the beginning too (Genesee, 1993). Bilingual children then catch up rapidly to their monolingual peers and by age 2 or 3 can switch readily from one language to the other.

The experts agree that the best way to help a child learn two languages fluently is to speak both languages to the child from the beginning, *especially* if the two languages come to the child from different sources. For example, if Mom's native language is English and Dad's is Italian, Mom should speak only English to the infant/toddler and Dad should speak only Italian. If both parents speak both languages to the child, or mix them up in their own speech, this is a much more difficult situation for the child, and language learning will be delayed (McLaughlin, 1984). It will also work if one language is always spoken at home and the other in a day care center, or with playmates, or in some other outside situation.

egories. This may seem like a highly abstract argument, but it touches on the fundamental issue of the relationship between language and thought. Does the child learn to represent objects to himself *because* he now has language, or does language simply come along at about this point and make the representations easier?

Not surprisingly, the answer seems to be both (Clark, 1983; Cromer, 1991; Greenberg & Kuczaj, 1982). On the cognitive side of the argument are several pieces of evidence I described in Chapter 5, such as the fact that young babies are able to remember and imitate objects and actions over periods of time, long before they have language to assist them.

The naming explosion may also rest on new cognitive understandings. Vygotsky noted many years ago (1962) that somewhere in the child's second year the child seems to "discover" that objects have names and begins to ask for the names of objects all around her. In part, this new discovery seems to rest on another new cognitive ability, the ability to categorize things. In several studies, Alison Gopnik and Andrew Meltzoff (1987; 1992) have found that the naming explosion typically occurs just after, or at the same time as, children first show spontaneous categorization of mixed sets of objects, such as putting balls into one group and blocks into another. Having discovered "cate-

Does this 18-month-old know the word *doll* because she first had a concept of doll and later learned the word, or did she learn the word first and then create a category or concept to go with the word?

gories," the child may now rapidly learn the names for categories she already knows.

Extending the Class.

Just what kind of categories does the child create? Suppose your 2-year-old, on catching sight of the family tabby, says, *See kitty*. No doubt you will be pleased that the child has the right word applied to the animal. But what does the word *kitty* mean to the child? Does he think it is a name only for that particular fuzzy beast? Or does he think it applies to all furry creatures, or all things with four legs, or things with pointed ears, or what?

One way to figure out the kind of class or category the child has created is to see what other creatures or things he also calls "kitty." That is, we can ask how the class is *extended* in the child's language. If the child has a kitty category based on furriness, then many dogs and perhaps sheep would also be called kitty. Or perhaps the child uses the word *kitty* only for the family cat. This would imply a very narrow category indeed. The general question for researchers has been whether children tend to use words narrowly or broadly, overextending or underextending them.

The research tells us that underextension is most common at the earliest stages, particularly before the naming explosion (Harris, 1992), which suggests that most children initially think of words as belonging to only one thing, not as names for categories. Once the naming explosion starts, however, the child appears to grasp the idea that words go with categories, and overextension becomes more common. At that stage, we're more likely to hear the word *cat* applied to dogs or guinea pigs than we are to hear it used for just one animal (Clark, 1983). All children seem to show overextensions, but the particular classes the child creates are unique to each child. One child Eve Clark observed used the word *ball* to refer to toy balls, to radishes, and to stone spheres at park entrances, while another child used the word *ball* to refer to apples, grapes, eggs, squash, and a bell clapper (Clark, 1975).

Constraints on Word Learning.

Another of the fundamental questions about word meanings, the subject of hot debate among linguists in recent years, is just how a child figures out which part of

some scene a word may refer to. The classic example: A child sees a brown dog running across the grass with a bone in its mouth. An adult points and says "doggie." From such an encounter the toddler is somehow supposed to figure out that the word *doggie* refers to the animal, and not to running, bone, dog-plus-bone, brownness, ears, grass, or any other combination of elements in the whole scene.

Many linguists have proposed that a child could conceivably cope with this monumentally complex task only if she operated with some built-in biases or *constraints* (e.g., Baldwin, 1995; Golinkoff, Mervis, & Hirsh-Pasek, 1994; Markman, 1992; Waxman & Kosowski, 1990). For example, the child may have a built-in assumption that words refer to whole objects and not to their parts or attributes.

Another possible built-in constraint is the *principle of contrast*, which is the assumption that every word has a different meaning, so if a new word is used, it must refer to some different object or a different aspect of an object (Clark, 1990). For example, in a widely quoted early study, Carey and Bartlett (1978) interrupted a play session with 2- and 3-year-old children by pointing to two trays and saying, "Bring me the chromium tray, not the red one, the chromium one." These children already knew the word *red* but did not know the word *chromium*. Nonetheless, most of the children were

If Dad says "goose" while he and his toddler are looking at this scene, how does the boy know that "goose" means the animal and not "white," or "dirt,"or "honk honk," or some other feature? In fact, in this case as in most instances, the child first *points* and then the father labels, which greatly simplifies the problem.

able to follow the instruction by bringing the nonred tray. Furthermore, a week later, about half the children remembered that the word *chromium* referred to some color, and that the color was "not red." Thus they learned the meaning by contrast.

Early proponents of constraints argued that the constraints are innate—built into the brain in some fashion. Another alternative is that the child learns the various principles over time. For example, Carolyn Mervis and Jacquelyn Bertrand (1994) have found that not all children between 16 and 20 months use the principle of contrast to learn the name of a new, unknown object. In their sample, those children who did use this principle also had larger vocabularies and were more likely to be good at sorting objects into sets. Thus the use of the principle of constraint may be a reflection of the child's general level of language or cognitive skill, rather than something that is built-in to all children.

Using Language: Communication and Self-Direction

In the past several decades linguists have also turned their attention to a third aspect of children's language, namely, the way children learn to *use* speech, either to communicate with others (an aspect of language linguists call **pragmatics**) or to regulate their own behavior.

Language Pragmatics. Children seem to learn the pragmatics of language at a remarkably early age. For example, children as young as 18 months show adultlike gaze patterns when they are talking with a parent: They look at the person who is talking, look away at the beginning of their own speaking turn, and then look at the listener again when they are signaling that they are about to stop talking (D. Rutter & Durkin, 1987).

Furthermore, a child as young as 2 years adapts the form of his language to the situation he is in or the person he is talking to. He might say "gimme" to another toddler as he grabs the other child's glass, but might say "more milk" to an adult (Becker, 1982). Among older preschoolers, language is even more clearly adapted to the listener: Four-year-olds use simpler language when they talk

Clare, at 20 months, already follows some of the social rules of conversation, such as taking turns and showing gaze patterns.

to 2-year-olds than when they talk to adults (Tomasello & Mannle, 1985). Thus, from very early—probably from the beginning—the child's language is meant to *communicate*, and the child adapts the form of his language in order to achieve better communication.

Language and Self-Control. Children also use language to help control or monitor their own behavior. Such "private speech," which may consist of fragmentary sentences, muttering, or instructions to the self, is detectable from the earliest use of words and sentences. For example, when 2- or 3-year-olds play by themselves, they give themselves instructions, or stop themselves with words, or describe what they are doing: "No, not there," "I put that there," or "Put it" (Furrow, 1984).

Vygotsky, a theorist you will remember from Chapter 2, argued that this kind of private speech is highly significant in the child's cognitive development. It helps children learn how to plan, it helps them focus their attention on one aspect of a problem at a time, and it helps them control their tendency to act impulsively (Díaz, Neal, & Amaya-Williams, 1990). Such self-regulatory language has largely gone "underground" by age 9 or 10, but we can still hear it in older children—even in adults—when they are working on hard problems and need to help themselves focus their attention on the critical aspects of the task (Bivens & Berk, 1990).

Even this brief foray into the research on the child's use of language points out that a full understanding of language development is going to require understanding of both cognitive development and of the child's social skills and understanding. It reminds us once again that the child is not divided into tidy packages labeled "physical development," "social development," or "language development" but is a coherent, integrated system.

Explaining Language Development

Explaining how a child learns language has proven to be one of the most compelling, and one of the most difficult, challenges within developmental psychology. This may surprise you. I suspect that most of you just take for granted that a child learns to talk by listening to the language she hears. What is magical or complicated about that? Well, the more you think about it, the more amazing and mysterious it becomes. For one thing, as Steven Pinker (1987) points out, there is a veritable chasm between what the child hears as language input and the language the child must eventually speak. The input consists of some set of sentences spoken to the child, with intonation, stress, and timing. They are spoken in the presence of objects and events, and the words are given in a particular order. All that may be helpful, even essential. Yet what the child must learn from such input is nothing less than a set of rules for *creating* sentences. And the rules are not directly given in the sentences she hears. How does the child accomplish this feat? How does she figure out the rules? Theories abound. Let me start on the nurture end of the theoretical continuum.

Imitation and Reinforcement.
The earliest theories of language were based either on learning theory or on the commonsense idea that language is learned by imitation. Imitation obviously has to play some part; children imitate sentences they hear and they learn to speak with the accent of their parents. Further, those toddlers who most readily imitate an adult when the adult speaks a new word are also the ones who show the most rapid vocabulary growth in the first year or two of the language explosion, which tells us that imitation is an important ingredient in the process (Masur, 1995). Still, imitation alone can't explain all language acquisition because it cannot account for the creative quality of the child's language. In particular, children consistently create types of sentences and forms of words that they have never heard—words like *goed* or *footses*.

Reinforcement theories such as Skinner's (1957) fare no better. Skinner argued that, in addition to the role of imitation, parents shape language through systematic reinforcements, gradually rewarding better and better approximations of adult speech. Yet when researchers have listened to parents talking to children, they find that parents don't seem to do anything like what Skinner proposed. Instead, parents are remarkably forgiving of all sorts of peculiar constructions and meaning (R. Brown & Hanlon, 1970; Hirsh-Pasek, Trieman, & Schneiderman, 1984); they reinforce children's sentences based on whether the sentence is true rather than on whether it is grammatically correct. In addition, children learn many grammatical forms, such as plurals in English, with relatively few errors, so some process other than shaping has to be involved.

Newer Environmental Theories: Talking to the Child.
Still, it seems obvious that what is said to the child has to play *some* role in the process. At the simplest level, we know that children whose parents talk to them often, read to them regularly, and use a wide range of words in their speech, begin to talk sooner, develop larger vocabularies, use more complex sentences, and learn to read more readily when they reach school age (Hart & Risley, 1995; Huttenlocher, 1995; Snow, 1997). That is to say, the sheer quantity of language a child hears is a significant factor. Furthermore, the children who are exposed to less (and less varied) language in their earliest years don't seem to catch up later in vocabulary, as you can see in the data shown in Table 8.2. These numbers come from the National Longitudinal Survey of Labor Market Experience of Youth (NLSY), a 12-year longitudinal study of a large sample of young women, begun when they were still teenagers. Table 8.2 shows one piece of information about the preschool-age *children* of these

Table 8.2

Percentage of Children Ages 4 to 7 Scoring Below the 30th Percentile on the Peabody Picture Vocabulary Test as a Function of Family Poverty

Type of Family	Number of Cases	Observed Percentage	Adjusted Percentage[*]
AFDC (welfare)	196	60%	52%
Poor, but not AFDC	116	47%	42%
Nonpoor	659	27%	30%

[*]These percentages have been adjusted statistically to subtract out the effects of differences in parents' education, family structure, family size, and age, sex, and ethnicity of the child.

Source: Zill, Moore, Smith, Stief, & Coiro, 1995, Table 2.3, p. 45.

young women, namely the percentage who had vocabulary scores below the 30th percentile on the most commonly used measure of vocabulary, called the **Peabody Picture Vocabulary Test,** or **PPVT.**

Clearly, by age 4 the difference in vocabulary between poor and better-off children is already substantial, a gap that only widens over the school years. Similarly, Catherine Snow (1997) finds that 4-year-old children reared in poverty use shorter and less complex sentences than do their better-off peers. Many factors no doubt contribute to these differences, but the richness and variety of the language a child hears is obviously one highly significant ingredient. Of all these factors, being read to less often may be one of the most critical, as you can see from the *Research Report* box on page 260.

Beyond the mere quantity of language directed at the child, the quality of the parents' language may also be important in helping the child learn language. In particular, we know that adults talk to children in a special kind of very simple language, originally called **motherese** by many linguists, now more scientifically described as **infant-directed speech.** This simple language is spoken in a higher-pitched voice and at a slower pace than is talk between adults. The sentences are short, with simple, concrete vocabulary, and they are grammatically simple. When speaking to children, parents also repeat a lot, introducing minor variations ("Where is the ball? Can you see the ball? Where is the ball? There is the ball!"). They may also repeat the child's own sentences but in slightly longer, more grammatically correct forms—a pattern referred to as an *expansion* or a *recasting.*

Parents don't talk this way to children in order to teach them language. They do so with the hope that they will communicate better by using simpler language. Infant-directed speech may nonetheless be very useful, even necessary, for the child's language acquisition. We know, for example, that babies as young as a few days old can discriminate between motherese and adult-directed speech and *that they prefer to listen to motherese* (Cooper & Aslin, 1994; Pegg, Werker, & McLeod, 1992; Werker, Pegg, & McLeod, 1994). The quality of motherese that seems to be particularly attractive to babies is its higher pitch. Once the child's attention is drawn by this special tone, the very simplicity and repetitiveness of the adult's speech may help the child to pick out repeating grammatical forms.

Children's attention also seems to be drawn to recast sentences. For example, Farrar (1992) found that a 2-year-old was two or three times as likely to imitate a correct grammatical form after he had heard his mother recast his own sentences than he was when the mother used that same correct grammatical form in her own normal conversation. Experimental studies also show that children who are deliberately exposed to higher rates of specific types of recast sentences seem to learn those grammatical forms more quickly (K. Nelson, 1977).

Sounds good, doesn't it? Still, environmental theories of language acquisition have holes. For one thing, recasts are actually relatively rare in normal parent-toddler conversations. Yet virtually all children nevertheless acquire a complex grammar, which suggests that the kind of feedback provided

Research Report

The Importance of Reading to the Child

A series of studies by G. J. Whitehurst and his colleagues gives us strong evidence for the importance of the child's environment in early language learning. In their first study (Whitehurst, Falco, Lonigan et al., 1988), they trained some parents to read picture books to their toddlers and to interact with them in a special way during the reading, using a style Whitehurst calls *dialogic* reading. Specifically, they were trained to use questions that could not be answered just by pointing. So a mother reading *Winnie the Pooh* might say, "There's Eeyore. What's happening to him?" Similarly, the parent might ask, pointing to an object shown in a book, "What's the name of that?" or ask a question about a character in a story, such as "Do you think the kitty will get into trouble?" Other parents were encouraged to read to the child but were given no special instructions about how to read. After a month, the children in the experimental group showed a larger gain in vocabulary than did the children in the comparison group.

Whitehurst has now replicated this study in day care centers for poor children in both Mexico and New York City (Valdez-Menchaca & Whitehurst, 1992; Whitehurst, Arnold, Epstein et al., 1994) and in a large number of Head Start classrooms (Whitehurst, Fischel, Crone, & Nania, 1995). In the Mexican study, one teacher in a day care center was trained in dialogic reading. She then spent ten minutes each day for six to seven weeks reading with each of ten 2-year-olds. A comparison group of children in the same day care center spent an equivalent amount of time with the same teacher each day, but were given arts and crafts instruction rather than reading. At the end of the intervention, the children who had been read to had higher vocabulary scores on a variety of standardized tests and used more complex grammar when talking with another adult.

In Whitehurst's U.S. day-care and Head Start studies, children were read to in this special way either by their teacher or by both their mother and the teacher, while control group children experienced normal interactions with day-care workers or teachers. In both studies, the children who had participated in dialogic reading gained in vocabulary significantly more than did the control group children, and the effect appears to last.

Similarly, Catherine Crain-Thoreson and Philip Dale (1995) found that they could significantly increase language skills in language-delayed children by teaching either parents or teachers to read to them in this special way.

The fact that we now have evidence of the same types of effects in two different cultures, with two different languages, with both teachers and parents, with both poor and middle-class children, and with language-delayed children greatly strengthens the argument that richer interactive language between adult and child is one important ingredient in fostering the child's language growth.

by recastings is probably not the major source of grammatical information for most children (Morgan, Bonamo, & Travis, 1995). And while motherese does seem to occur in the vast majority of cultures and contexts, it does not occur in *all*. For example, Pye (1986) could find no sign of motherese in one Mayan culture, and studies in the United States show it is greatly reduced among depressed mothers (Bettes, 1988). Children of these mothers nonetheless learn language. Accordingly, while motherese may be helpful, it doesn't appear to be *necessary* for language.

Innateness Theories. On the other side of the theoretical spectrum we have the innateness theorists, who argue that much of what the child needs for learning language is built-in to the organism.

Early innateness theorists like Noam Chomsky (1965; 1975; 1986; 1988) were especially struck by two phenomena: the extreme complexity of the task the child must accomplish and the apparent similarities in the steps and stages of children's early language. Newer cross-language comparisons now make it clear that more variability exists than first appeared—a set of findings I've described in the following *Cultures and Contexts* box. Nonetheless, innateness theories are alive and well and increasingly accepted.

One particularly influential innateness theorist is Dan Slobin (1985a; 1985b), who assumes that every child is born with a basic language-making capacity made up of a set of fundamental *operating principles*. Just as the newborn infant seems to come programmed with "rules to look by," so Slobin is ar-

Cultures and Contexts

Universals and Variations in Early Language

In the beginning years of research on children's language development, linguists and psychologists were strongly impressed by the apparent similarities across languages in children's early language. You've already seen some of the evidence that supports this impression in an earlier *Cultures and Contexts* box in Chapter 5 (p. 172), illustrating large similarities in early vocabularies. Studies in a wide variety of language communities, including Turkish, Serbo-Croatian, Hungarian, Hebrew, Japanese, a New Guinean language called Kaluli, German, and Italian, have revealed other important similarities in early language:

- *The prelinguistic phase seems to be identical in all language communities. All babies coo, then babble; all babies understand language before they can speak it; babies in all cultures begin to use their first words at about one year.*

- *In all language communities studied so far, a one-word phase precedes the two-word phase, with the latter beginning at about a year and a half.*

- *In all languages studied so far, prepositions describing locations are added in essentially the same order. Words for* in, on, under, *and* beside *are learned first. Then the child learns the words* front *and* back *(Slobin, 1985a).*

- *Children seem to pay more attention to the ends of words than the beginnings, so they learn suffixes before they learn prefixes.*

At the same time, cross-linguistic comparisons show that children's beginning sentences are not nearly so similar as the early innateness theorists had supposed. For example:

- *The specific word order a child uses in early sentences is not the same for all children in all languages. In some languages a noun–verb sequence is fairly common, in others a verb–noun sequence may be heard.*

- *Particular inflections are learned in highly varying orders from one language to another. Japanese children, for example, begin very early to use a special kind of marker, called a* pragmatic marker, *that tells something about the feeling or the context. For instance, in Japanese, the word* yo *is used at the end of a sentence when the speaker is experiencing some resistance from the listener; the word* ne *is used when the speaker expects approval or agreement. Japanese children begin to use these markers very early, much earlier than other inflections appear in most languages.*

- *Most strikingly, there are languages in which there seems to be no simple two-word sentence stage in which the sentences contain no inflections. Children learning Turkish, for example, use essentially the full set of noun and verb inflections by age 2 and never go through a stage of using uninflected words. Their language is simple, but it is rarely ungrammatical from the adult's point of view (Aksu-Koc & Slobin, 1985).*

Obviously, any theory of language acquisition must account for both the common ground and the wide variations from one language to the next.

guing that infants and children are programmed with "rules to listen by."

You've already encountered a good deal of evidence in Chapter 5 that is consistent with this proposal. From earliest infancy, babies focus on individual sounds and on syllables in the stream of sounds they hear, pay attention to sound rhythm, and prefer speech of a particular pattern—namely, motherese. Babies also seem to be preprogrammed to pay attention to the beginnings and endings of strings of sounds as well as to stressed sounds (Morgan, 1994). Together, these operating principles would help to explain some of the features of children's early grammars. In English, for example, the stressed words in a sentence are normally the verb and the noun—precisely the words that English-speaking children use in their earliest sentences. In Turkish, on the other hand, prefixes are stressed, and Turkish-speaking children learn prefixes very early. Both these patterns make sense if we assume that what is built in is not "verbness" or "nounness" or "prefixness" but "pay attention to stressed sounds."

The fact that this innateness model is consistent with the growing information about apparently built-in perceptual skills and processing bi-ases is certainly a strong argument in its favor. But other compelling theoretical alternatives have also been proposed. In particular, some theorists argue persuasively that what is important is not the built-in biases but the child's *construction* of language as part of the broader process of cognitive development. In this view, the child is a "little linguist," applying her emerging cognitive understanding to the problem of language, searching for regularities and patterns (e.g., Tomasello & Brooks, in press).

Constructivist Theories of Language. One prominent proponent of this view, Melissa Bowerman, puts the proposition this way: "When language starts to come in, it does not introduce new meanings to the child. Rather, it is used to express only those meanings the child has already formulated independently of language" (1985, p. 372). Even more broadly, Lois Bloom argues that from the beginning of language, the child's intent is to communicate, to share the ideas and concepts in his head. He does this as best he can with the gestures or words he knows, and he learns new words when they help him communicate his thoughts and feelings (Bloom, 1993; 1997).

One type of evidence in support of this argument comes from the observation that it is children and not mothers who initiate the majority of verbal exchanges (Bloom, 1997). Further evidence comes from studies showing links between achievements in language development and the child's broader cognitive development. For example, symbolic play, such as drinking from an empty cup, and imitation of sounds and gestures both appear at about the same time as the child's first words, suggesting some broad "symbolic" understanding that is reflected in a number of behaviors. In children whose language is significantly delayed, both symbolic play and imitation are normally delayed too (Bates, O'Connell, & Shore, 1987; Ungerer & Sigman, 1984).

A second example occurs later: At about the point at which two-word sentences appear, we can also see children begin to combine several gestures into a sequence in their pretend play, such as pouring imaginary liquid, drinking, then wiping the mouth. Those children who are the first to show this sequencing in their play are also the first to show two- or three-word sentences in their speech (e.g., McCune, 1995; Shore, 1986).

My own view is that we need not choose between Slobin's and Bowerman's approaches. Both may be true. The child may begin with built-in operating principles that aim her attention at crucial features of the language input. The child processes that information according to her initial (perhaps built-in) strategies or schemes. Then she modifies those strategies or rules as she receives new information, such as by arriving at some of the constraints about word meanings. The result is a series of rules for understanding and creating language. The strong similarities we see among children in their early language constructions come about both because all children share the same initial processing rules and because most children are exposed to very similar input from the people around them. But because the input is not identical, because languages differ, language development follows less and less common pathways as the child progresses.

As these brief descriptions of theory make clear, linguists and psychologists who have studied language have made progress, but we have not yet cracked the code. The fact that children learn the complex and varied use of their native tongue within a few years remains both miraculous and largely mysterious.

The broader changes in the child's cognitive skills over the same years seem less mysterious, but we continue to learn more about the remarkable cognitive accomplishments of the preschool child, as well as the limitations on her thinking.

Changes in Thinking

Let me begin, as I did in Chapter 5, with a look at Piaget's view of the cognitive changes during these years, because his thinking has formed the framework of so much of our research on this age period.

Piaget's View of the Preoperational Period

According to Piaget, at about two years of age the child begins to use *symbols*—images or words or actions that *stand for* something else. Children this

Table 8.3

A Summary of Theories of Language Development

Theory	Supporting Evidence	Problem Evidence
Imitation	Child clearly learns the language he hears, including regional accents; children who imitate more learn vocabulary more quickly.	Child's sentence construction frequently includes patterns not heard from adults.
Reinforcement	Child gets reinforced when he speaks clearly because he is more likely to get what he wants.	Parents rarely use explicit reinforcement to train language; children learn some grammatical forms with few errors and thus no corrections or reinforcements.
Other environmental theories	Children who are talked to more have larger vocabularies and faster grammar development; children prefer to listen to motherese; children's grammar development is helped by recastings and expansions.	Children who do not hear recastings or motherese nonetheless learn language.
Innateness	From birth, children have biases in what aspects of language they pay attention to; at later ages, children appear to operate with shared word-meaning constraints; the early stages of language development are pretty much the same, regardless of the language being learned.	Early grammar varies more from one language community to another than some innateness theories would imply; some word-meaning constraints appear to be learned rather than built in.
Constructivist	Certain aspects of language development appear only when the child has developed a more general cognitive ability to support them, such as a general ability to "combine" as a precursor to two-word sentences.	Cannot ignore the evidence of built-in "operating principles" in early infancy.

age begin to pretend in their play, for example (a development I've talked about in the *Research Report* box on p. 264). At age 2 or 3 or 4 a broom may become a horsie, or a block may become a train. We can also see such symbol use in the emergence of language or in the preschooler's primitive ability to understand scale models or simple maps (De-Loache, 1995). And we see the child's improving ability to manipulate these symbols internally in such things as her improving memory, or in her ability to search more systematically for lost or hidden objects.

Beyond the accomplishment of symbol use, Piaget focused mostly on all the things the preschool age child still *cannot* do, which gives an oddly negative tone to his description of this period. Even the term he used to describe this stage conveys some of this tone: It is *preoperational*. To Piaget, the preschooler's thinking is rigid, captured by appearances, and insensitive to inconsistencies.

Piaget also described the preoperational child as one who looks at things entirely from her own perspective, her own frame of reference, a characteristic Piaget called **egocentrism** (Piaget, 1954). The child is not being selfish; rather, she simply assumes that everyone sees the world as she does. Figure 8.2 (p. 265) is a photo of a classic experiment illustrating this kind of egocentrism. The child is shown a three-dimensional scene with mountains of different sizes and colors. From a set of drawings, he picks out the one that shows the scene the way he sees it. Most preschoolers can do this without much difficulty. Then the examiner asks the child to pick out the drawing that shows how someone *else* sees the scene, such as the little clay man or the examiner. At this point, preschool children have difficulty. Most often they again pick

Research Report

Young Children's Play

If you watch young children during their unstructured time, you'll see them building towers out of blocks, talking to or feeding their dolls, making "tea" with the tea set, racing toy trucks across the floor, dressing up in grown-up clothes. They are, in a word, *playing*. This is not trivial or empty activity; it is the stuff of which much of cognitive development seems to be built.

The form of this play changes in very obvious ways during the years from 1 to 6, following a sequence that matches Piaget's stages rather well (Rubin, Fein, & Vandenbert, 1983).

Sensorimotor Play. The child of 12 months or so spends most of her playtime exploring and manipulating objects, using all the sensorimotor schemes in her repertoire. She puts things in her mouth, shakes them, moves them along the floor.

Constructive Play. Such simple exploratory play with objects does continue past 12 months, especially with a totally new object, but by age 2 or so children also begin to use objects to build or construct things—creating a block tower, putting together a puzzle, making something out of clay or with Tinkertoys—a form that makes up nearly half the play of children ages 3 to 6.

First Pretend Play. Pretend play also begins during the second year. The first sign of such pretending is usually something like a child using a toy spoon to "feed" himself or a toy comb to comb his hair. The toys are still used for their actual or typical purposes (e.g., spoon for feeding), and the actions are still oriented to the *self*, but some pretending is involved. This shifts between 15 and 21 months: The recipient of the pretend action now becomes another person or a toy, most often a doll. The child is still using objects for their usual purposes (such as drinking from a cup), but now she is using the toy cup with a doll instead of herself. Dolls are especially good toys for this kind of pretending, because it is not a very large leap from doing things to yourself to doing things with a doll. So children feed dolls imaginary food, comb their hair, soothe them.

Substitute Pretend Play. Between 2 and 3 years of age children begin to use objects to stand for something altogether different. They may comb the doll's hair with a baby bottle while saying that it is a comb,

| Constructive play

| First pretend play

or use a broom to be a horsie, or make "trucks" out of blocks. By age 4 or 5, children spend as much as 20 percent of their playtime in this new, complicated kind of pretending (Field, De Stefano, & Koewler, 1982).

Sociodramatic Play. Somewhere in the preschool years, children also begin to play parts or take roles when they play together. This is really still a form of pretending except that now several children create a mutual pretense. They play "daddy and mommy," "cowboys and Indians," "doctor and patient," and the like. At first children simply take up these roles; later, they name the roles to one another and may give each other explicit instructions about the right way to pretend a particular role. You can begin to see this form of play in some 2-year-olds; by age 4 virtually all children engage in some play of this type (Howes & Matheson, 1992). Interestingly, at about the same ages a great many children seem to create imaginary companions (M. Taylor, Cartwright, & Carlson, 1993). For many years psychologists believed that the existence of such an imaginary companion was a sign of disturbance in a child; now it is clear that such a creation is a normal part of the development of pretense in many children.

Children clearly get great delight out of all these often-elaborate fantasies. Equally important, by playing roles, by pretending to be someone else, they also become more and more aware of how things may look or feel to someone else, and their egocentric approach to the world declines.

Figure 8.2

One of the types of experimental arrangements used to study egocentrism in children.

the drawing that shows their *own* view of the mountains (Flavell, Everett, Croft, & Flavell, 1981; Gzesh & Surber, 1985).

[?] *Critical Thinking*

Can you think of any examples of egocentrism in your own behavior? What about buying someone else the gift you were hoping to receive yourself? Other examples?

The preschool child's focus on the appearance of objects is another important theme in Piaget's work, evident in some of the most famous of his studies, those on **conservation,** which I described in a *Research Report* in Chapter 2 (p. 53). Children rarely show any type of conservation before age 5. They think that spreading out a row of pennies means that there are now more pennies or that

pouring water from a fat glass into a taller, thinner glass means there is now more water because the water has risen higher in the thinner glass. Piaget took such responses as a sign that preschoolers were still captured by the *appearance* of change and did not focus on the underlying, unchanging aspect.

Newer Views of the Preoperational Child

These same two themes—egocentrism and the child's ability to understand the distinction between appearance and reality—continue to dominate much of the research on the thinking of the preschool-age child. A rich and intriguing new body of evidence suggests that preschoolers are a great deal less egocentric than Piaget thought, but that they do indeed struggle with the problem of distinguishing between appearance and reality.

Perspective Taking. Research on the child's ability to take others' perspectives shows that children as young as 2 and 3 have at least *some* ability to understand that other people see things or experience things differently than they do. For example, children this age will adapt their speech or their play to the demands of their companion. They play differently with older or younger playmates, and they talk differently to a younger or a disabled child (Brownell, 1990; Guralnick & Paul-Brown, 1984).

Yet such understanding is clearly not perfect at this young age. John Flavell has proposed two levels of perspective-taking ability: At level 1, the child knows *that* some other person experiences something differently. At level 2, the child develops a whole series of complex rules for figuring out precisely *what* the other person sees or experiences (Flavell, Green, & Flavell, 1990). Two- and 3-year-olds have level 1 knowledge but not level 2. We begin to see some level 2 knowledge in 4- and 5-year-olds.

Appearance and Reality. This shift seems to be part of a much broader change in the child's understanding of appearance and reality. Flavell has studied this in a variety of ways; for example, by showing objects under colored lights, which changes their apparent color, or by putting masks on animals to make them look like another animal. He finds that 2- and 3-year-olds consistently judge

things by their appearance; by age 5, however, the child begins to be able to separate the appearance from the underlying reality and knows that some object isn't "really" red even though it looks red under a red-colored light or that a cat with a dog mask is still "really" a cat (Flavell, Green, & Flavell, 1989; Flavell, Green, Wahl, & Flavell, 1987).

In the most famous Flavell procedure, the experimenter shows the child a sponge that has been painted to look like a rock. Three-year-olds, faced with this odd object, will either say that the object looks like a sponge and is a sponge or that it looks like a rock and is a rock. Four- and 5-year-olds can distinguish the two; they realize that it looks like a rock but *is* a sponge (Flavell, 1986). In other words, the older child now understands that the same object can be represented differently, depending on one's point of view.

Using the same type of materials, investigators have also asked if a child can grasp the principle of a **false belief.** For example, after the child has felt the sponge/rock and has answered questions about what it looks like and what it "really" is, you can ask something like this: "Your friend John hasn't touched this, he hasn't squeezed it. If John just sees it over here like this, what will he think it is? Will he think it's a rock or will he think that it's a sponge?" (Gopnik & Astington, 1988, p. 35). By and large, 3-year-olds think that John will believe it is a sponge, while 4- and 5-year-olds realize that because John hasn't felt the sponge, he will have a false belief that it is a rock. Thus the child of 4 or 5 understands that someone else can believe something that isn't true *and will act on that belief.*

Theories of Mind. Evidence like this has led a number of theorists (e.g., Astington & Gopnik, 1991; Gopnik & Wellman, 1994; Harris, 1989) to propose that the 4- or 5-year-old has developed a new and quite sophisticated **theory of mind.** The child this age has begun to understand that you cannot predict what other people will do solely from observing the situation itself; the other person's desires and beliefs also enter into the equation. So the child develops various theories about other people's ideas, beliefs, and desires and about how those ideas or beliefs will affect the other person's behaviors.

The 3-year-old on the right is able to adapt her speech and her play to the needs of her blind friend, which is one sign that preschoolers are less egocentric than Piaget thought.

Cultures and Contexts

Understanding of Appearance and Reality in Other Cultures

A number of studies from widely different cultures suggest that the shift at approximately age 4 in children's understanding of appearance and reality and of false belief may well be a universal developmental pattern.

Jeremy Avis and Paul Harris (1991) adapted the traditional false belief testing procedure for use with a group called the Baka, who live in Cameroon. The Baka are a hunter-gatherer people who live together in camps. Each child was tested in his or her own hut, using materials with which they were completely familiar. They watched one adult, named Mopfana (a member of the tribe), put some mango kernels into a bowl with a lid. Mopfana then left the hut and a second adult (also a tribe member) told the child they were going to play a game with Mopfana: They were going to hide the kernels in a cooking pot. Then he asked the child what Mopfana was going to do when he came back: Would he look for the kernels in the bowl, or in the pot? The second adult also asked the child whether Mopfana's heart would feel good or bad before he lifted the lid of the bowl, and then after he lifted the lid. Younger children—that is, 2-, 3-, and early 4-year-olds—were likely to say that Mopfana would look for the kernels in the pot, or to say that he would be sad before he looked in the bowl, while older 4- and 5-year-olds were nearly always right on all three questions.

Similarly, when Flavell used his sponge/rock task with children in mainland China, he found that Chinese 3-year-olds were just as confused about this task as are American or British 3-year-olds, whereas 5-year-old Chinese children had no difficulty with the problem (Flavell, Zhang, Zou, Dong, & Qi, 1983), a result paralleled by a recent study of Junín Quechua children in the high mountains of Peru (Vinden, 1996).

Using a somewhat different kind of problem, but one that still touches on the difference between appearance and reality, Paul Harris and his colleagues have asked children in several cultures how characters in a story *really* feel, and what emotion *appears* on their faces. For example:

> Diana is playing a game with her friend. At the end of the game Diana wins and her friend loses. Diana tries to hide how she feels because otherwise her friend won't play any more. (Harris, 1989, p. 134)

Four-year-old children in Britain and the United States, faced with such stories, have no trouble saying how the character will really feel but do have trouble saying how the character would look, while, by age 5 or 6, the child grasps the possible difference. Harris has found that the same age shift occurs in Japan (Gardner, Harris, Ohmoto, & Hamasaki, 1988), and Joshi and MacLean (1994) found a similar shift in India, despite the fact that both the Japanese and Indian cultures put far more emphasis on the disguising of emotions than is true in British or American cultures.

In these very different cultures, then, something similar seems to be occurring between age 3 and age 5. In these years all children seem to understand something general about the difference between appearance and reality, seem to develop a certain type of theory of mind.

Such a theory of mind does not spring forth full-blown at age 4. As early as 18 months, toddlers have some beginning understanding of the fact that people (but not inanimate objects) operate with goals and intentions (Meltzoff, 1995). Children this age also understand something about other people's desires. For example, when they see an adult looking happy after eating one food and looking disgusted after eating another, an 18-month-old understands that the adult will choose to eat the pleasing food (Repacholi & Gopnik, 1997). By age 3, children understand some aspects of the links between people's thinking or feeling and their behavior. For example, they know that a person who wants something will try to get it. They also know that a person may still want something even if she can't have it (Lillard & Flavell, 1992). What they do not yet understand is the basic principle that each person's actions are based on his own *representation* of reality, and that a person's representation may differ from what is "really" there. People act on the basis of what they believe or feel, even if what they believe is incorrect or what they feel is unexpected or apparently inconsistent in a given situation. Thus a person who feels sad even though she has succeeded at something will act on that sadness, not on the visible success. It is this new aspect of the theory of mind that seems to be absent in the 3-year-old but that clearly emerges at about 4 or 5.

Still, there is much that the 4- or 5-year-old doesn't yet grasp about other people's thinking. The child of this age understands that other people think, but he does not yet understand that those same other people think about *him*. In the famous infinite regress, the 4-year-old understands "I know that you know," but he does not yet fully understand that this process is reciprocal, that "You know that I know." Such an understanding of the reciprocal nature of thought seems to develop between ages 5 and 7 for most children (Perner & Wimmer, 1985; Sullivan, Zaitchik, & Tager-Flusberg, 1994)—a particularly important development, because it is probably necessary for the creation of genuinely reciprocal friendships, which we see in the elementary school years.

[?] *Critical Thinking*

Consider your own theory of mind. What assumptions do you make about the way other people's behavior is affected by their beliefs or feelings or ideas? You operate on the basis of such a theory all the time, but can you articulate it?

Metacognition and Metamemory. Such an increased awareness of the ways in which thinking operates is also apparent in other areas. For example, between ages 3 and 5, children figure out that in order to tell if a rock painted like a sponge is really a sponge or a rock, a person would need to touch or hold it. Just looking at it doesn't give you enough information (Flavell, 1993; O'Neill, Astington, & Flavell, 1992). In a similar vein, 4-year-olds (but not 3-year-olds) understand that to remember or forget something, one must have known it at a previous time (Lyon & Flavell, 1994). These developments are important because they seem to be the first signs of what psychologists now call **metamemory** and **metacognition**—knowing about the process of memory and the process of thinking. By age 4 or 5 most children seem to have some very elementary grasp of these processes.

All this new work on the child's theory of mind has not only opened up a fascinating new area of research, it has clearly demonstrated that the preschool child is vastly less egocentric than Piaget supposed. By age 4, and in more limited ways at earlier ages, the child has the ability to understand other points of view and can predict other people's behavior on the basis of deductions about their beliefs.

These emerging understandings seem to be aided by at least two things: practice at pretend play, especially shared pretense with other children (Dockett & Smith, 1995), and certain aspects of language skill, especially the learning of words for feelings, desires, and thoughts—words like *want*, *need*, *think*, or *remember* (Astington & Jenkins, 1995). Indeed, some level of language facility may be a necessary condition for the development of a theory of mind. Jennifer Jenkins and Janet Astington (1996) have found that children simply do not succeed at false belief tasks until they have reached a certain threshold of general language skill. Further support for the same point comes from the finding that children as old as 13 who were born deaf and learned no sign language before school age—who thus had no structured language to work with during the preschool year—typically fail false belief tests and other measures of the theory of mind (Peterson & Siegal, 1995).

Understanding and Regulating Emotions. Another necessary skill for the emergence of a representational theory of mind is the child's ability to understand or "read" others' emotions. You already know that by 10 to 12 months, babies can tell the difference between positive or negative facial expressions because at that age they already show *social referencing*. By age 4, children's emotional vocabulary has expanded enough that they can recognize facial expressions and situations that convey the emotions happy, sad, mad, loving, and scared. More than that, though, preschoolers begin to understand the links between other people's emotions and their circumstances. For example, a child this age understands that another person will feel sad if she fails or happy if she succeeds. The preschool child also begins to figure out that particular emotions occur in situations involving specific relationships between desire and reality. Sadness, for example, normally occurs when someone

Psychology in Action

Assessing a Child's Theory of Mind

Warning: This project, like many of the *Psychology in Action* suggestions given in this text, should not be undertaken without explicit permission and guidance from your instructor, who will have to obtain permission from your college or university's Human Subjects Review Committee for any project in which you interview or observe a child or parent directly. *Do not do this project on your own, without such permission.*

For this project, you will need to locate a child between the ages of 3 and 5. You must obtain written permission from the child's parents, following whatever procedure your instructor specifies. The testing should be done in a quiet place in the child's home.

The task that has most often been used to assess the child's theory of mind has been called *the Smarties task,* because it uses a box of a type of candy called "Smarties," common in England and Canada where much of this research has been done. United States children, however, are not going to be familiar with Smarties, so we need to revise the procedure, using a bag of M&Ms filled with a set of small rocks.

Procedure

Find a quiet place where you and the child can sit down at a table or on the floor. Tell the child:

> We're going to play a game where I show you some things and ask you questions about them.

Bring out your M&M bag and ask the child to look at it. Then open the bag and show the child that there are rocks inside. Ask,

> What's inside the bag?

If the child doesn't say "rocks," ask again, *What are they?* When it is clear that the child knows that they

are really rocks, put the rocks back in the bag and close the bag. Now ask the following questions (all adapted from the procedure used by Gopnik & Astington, 1988), and write down the child's answers carefully.

- *Does it look like this bag has rocks in it, or does it look like it has candies in it?*

- *What's really inside the bag? Are there really rocks inside it, or are there really candies inside it?*

- *When you first saw the bag, before we opened it, what did you think was inside it? Did you think there were rocks inside it, or did you think there were candies inside it?*

- *Your Mom hasn't seen inside this bag. If your Mom sees the bag all closed up like this, what will she think is inside it? Will she think there are rocks inside it, or will she think there are candies inside it?*

When you are done, thank the child, tell him/her he answered the questions really well, and stay long enough to play with the child at some game the child chooses.

Analysis and Report

Describe the setting in which you worked with the child, report how the child answered each of these questions, and compare the child's answers with those described in the text. Did your child behave in the way you expected, given her or his age? Does your child understand the difference between appearance and reality? Does she or he understand false belief?

---

fails to acquire some desired object or loses something desired (Harris, 1989).

All this may make it sound as if 4- and 5-year-olds have already understood everything they need to know about others' emotions. In fact, there is a good deal more sophisticated knowledge still to come, such as in understanding more complex or subtle emotions and in grasping the fact that a person can have more than one emotion at the same time, even competing emotions.

For example, 4-year-olds can easily recognize facial expressions and situations that convey the emotions happy, sad, mad, loving, and scared. Expressions of pride or shame, however, are understood only in middle childhood (Harter & Whitesell, 1989). Similarly, by age 6, children understand that a person can switch rather rapidly from sadness to happiness if circumstances change, but it is only at about age 10 that children begin to understand that a person can feel opposite feelings at the same moment (ambivalence) (Harter & Whitesell, 1989).

It is reasonable to ask—as with virtually all the developmental sequences I have given you in this book—whether children in every culture learn about emotions in this same way. In this case, we have a bit of evidence.

The Utka, an Inuit band in northern Canada, have two words for fear, distinguishing between fear of physical disaster and fear of being treated badly. In some African languages, there are no separate words for fear and sorrow. Samoans use the same word for love, sympathy, and liking, and Tahitians have no word at all that conveys the notion of guilt. These examples, drawn by James Russell (1989) from the anthropological literature, remind us that we need to be very careful when we talk about the "normal" process of a child's learning about emotional expression and emotional meaning. From an English-speaking, Western perspective, emotions like fear or anger seem like "basic" emotions that all infants would understand early and easily. But what would be the developmental sequence for a child growing up in a culture in which fear and sorrow are not distinguished?

At the same time, the work of Paul Ekman (1972; 1973; 1989) has given us evidence of a strong cross-cultural similarity in people's facial expressions when conveying certain of these same "basic" emotions, such as fear, happiness, sadness, anger,

and disgust. (Figure 8.3 shows two such common expressions.) In all cultures studied so far, adults understand these facial expressions as having the same core meaning. Cultural variations are laid on top of these basic expressive patterns, and cultures have different rules about which emotions may be expressed and which must be masked. Still, there appears to be some common ground as well. One could argue that infants and toddlers are already quite good at discriminating and understanding these shared patterns. Even 2-year-olds can recognize and categorize happy and sad expressions. The child must then slowly learn all the cultural overlays—the links between emotion and situation that hold for each culture, the specific meanings of emotional language, the scripts that govern the appropriate expression of emotion in a given culture. No small task. What is remarkable is just how much of this information the preschooler already comprehends and reflects in his own behavior.

Conservation.   In contrast to the studies of egocentrism, studies of conservation have generally confirmed Piaget's basic observations. Although younger children can demonstrate some understanding of conservation if the task is made very simple (Gelman, 1972; Wellman, 1982), most children do not begin to solve conservation problems until age 5 or 6 or later (e.g., Sophian, 1995).

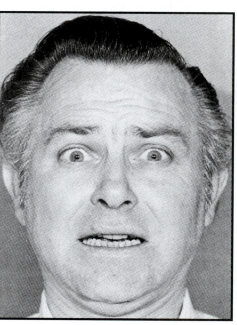

Figure 8.3

What emotion is being expressed in each of these photos? If you said happiness and fear, you agree with virtually all observers, in many countries, who have looked at these pictures. (Source: Copyright Paul Ekman.)

The relatively late development of the child's understanding of conservation makes sense if we think of conservation tasks as a particularly sophisticated form of the problem of appearance and reality. When I pour juice from a short fat glass into a tall thin glass, the amount of juice appears to increase (rises higher in the glass), even though in reality it remains the same. That is, conservation cannot be grasped until after the child has made considerable progress in understanding the distinction between appearance and reality, typically by age 5 or so.

Overview of the Preschool Child's Thinking

How can we add up these bits and pieces of information about the preschool child's thinking? At minimum, we can say that preschool children are capable of forms of logic that Piaget thought impossible at this stage. In particular, by age 4, and certainly by age 5, they not only can take others' perspectives, they understand at least in a preliminary way that other people's behavior rests on inner beliefs and feelings.

Of course, it might be that Piaget was right about the basic sequences but simply got the ages wrong, that the transition he saw at 6 or 7 really happens closer to age 4 or 5. Certainly the various understandings that children seem to come to at about that age—about false belief, about appearance and reality, about other people's physical perspective, and about the meanings of emotional expressions—are remarkably stagelike in that they all tend to appear at about the same time.

Or it might be that the newer research exaggerates the preschooler's abilities to at least some degree. Preschoolers can indeed do some sophisticated-looking things, but their understanding remains specific rather than general. It is still tied heavily to specific situations or can be displayed only with a great deal of support. Studies of both conservation and children's logic show that sophisticated performances can be *elicited* in 2-, 3-, and 4-year-old children, but preschoolers do not typically show such skills spontaneously. In order for the preschool child to demonstrate these relatively advanced forms of thinking, you have to make the task quite simple, eliminate distractions, or give special clues. The fact that children this age can solve these problems at all is striking, but Piaget was clearly correct in pointing out that preschool children think differently from older children. The very fact that they can perform certain tasks *only* when the tasks are made very simple or without distractions is evidence for such a difference.

More broadly, preschoolers do not seem to experience the world or think about it with as general a set of rules or principles as we see in older children, and therefore they do not easily generalize something they have learned in one context to a similar but not identical situation. It is precisely such a switch to general rules that Piaget thought characterized the thinking of the school-age child—a subject I'll take up in Chapter 11.

Finally, all the newer research has helped to confirm a basic proposition of Vygotsky's theory: Children's cognitive development is fostered to a considerable degree by *social* interactions. Piaget saw the child's development as being dependent mostly on independent play with objects. Such play is surely important, but play with other children and interactions with various adults are probably even more so, for it is in these reciprocal interactions that the child learns about others' feelings and reactions—experiences that are necessary for the child's emerging theory of mind. As just one example, Charlie Lewis and his colleagues have shown that among preschool children in Crete and Cyprus, those with many adult kin and many older siblings are more likely to understand false belief than are those with smaller family circles (Lewis, Freeman, Kyriakidou, Maridaki-Kassotaki, & Berridge, 1996). Thus social encounters both support and foster a child's cognitive development.

Individual Differences

The descriptions of the sequences and patterns of language and cognitive development I've given tell you something about the average or normative pattern, but any such average is at least partially misleading. Children vary in important ways, particularly in their relative ability to perform intellectual tasks. We see such differences not only in the speed of the child's language development but in measures of cognitive power, such as IQ tests.

Differences in Rate of Language Development

Some children begin using individual words at 8 months, others not until 18 months; some do not use two-word sentences until 3 years or even later. You can see the range of normal variation in sentence construction very clearly in Figure 8.4, which shows the average sentence length—referred to by linguists as the **mean length of utterance,** or **MLU**—of ten children, each studied longitudinally. Eve, Adam, and Sarah were studied by Roger Brown (1973); Jane, Martin, and Ben (all African-American children), by Ira Blake (1994); and Eric, Gia, Kathryn, and Peter, by Lois Bloom (1991). I have drawn a line at the MLU level that normally accompanies a switch from simple, uninflected two-word sentences to more complex forms. You can see that Eve was the earliest to make this transition, at about 20 months, while Adam and Sarah passed over this point about a year later. These variations are confirmed in Fenson's much larger cross-sectional study of more than 1000 toddlers, whose language was described by their parents. In this group the earliest age at which parents reported more complex than simple sentences was about 22 months, with an average of about 27 months. However, as many as a quarter of the children had not reached this point by 30 months (Fenson et al., 1994).

I should point out that more than half of children who talk late catch up eventually. The subset that does not catch up is primarily made up of children who *also* have poor *receptive* language (Bates, 1993; Thal, Tobias, & Morrison, 1991). This group appears to remain behind in language development and perhaps in cognitive development more generally. In practical terms, this means that if your child, or a child you care for, is significantly delayed in *understanding* as well as speaking language, you should seek professional help to try to diagnose the problem and begin appropriate intervention.

How can we explain these variations in speed of early language development? One obvious possibility is that the rate of language development may be something you inherit—in the same way that intelligence or the rate of physical development may be partially influenced by heredity. Certainly, if we assume that some language-processing patterns are built into the brain, it makes sense to think that some children may inherit a more efficient built-in system than others, just as some babies habituate faster to repeated stimuli.

Twin studies and adoption studies designed to test this possibility have yielded the typical mixture of findings. In the twin studies the common

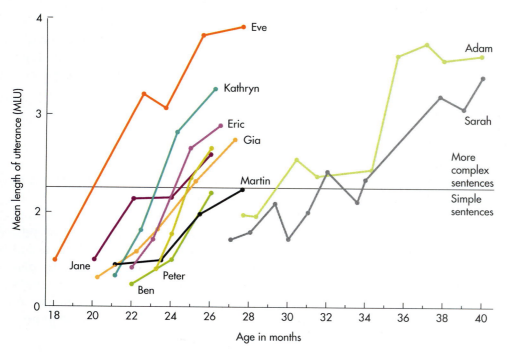

Figure 8.4

The ten children whose language is charted here, studied by three different linguists, moved from simple one- and two-word sentences to more complex sentences at markedly different times. (Sources: R. Brown, 1973, Figure 1, p. 55; Bloom, 1991, Table 3.1, p. 92; Blake, 1994, Table 9.1, p. 169, and Figure 9.1, p. 171.)

finding is that vocabulary size, but *not* grammatical complexity, is more similar in identical than in fraternal twins (Mather & Black, 1984).

Adoption studies show both a genetic and an environmental effect: Adopted 2-year-olds' language skill can be predicted about equally well from the IQs or language skills of either the natural or the adoptive parents (Plomin & DeFries, 1985). Among adoptive families, those who talked the most and provided the most toys had children whose language was more advanced, a finding that fits with the research I've already mentioned that links richness of the language spoken to the child and the rate of the child's language development. As in most areas of development, then, we find that both nature and nurture must be invoked to explain individual differences. A similar story can be told about differences in measured intelligence.

Differences in Intelligence

In Chapter 5 I mentioned that so-called infant IQ tests were not strongly related to later measures of IQ, but I did not give you a full description of such later measures, nor define IQ. It is now time to do both.

Remember from Chapter 5 that the study of intelligence is part of the "cognitive power" tradition. Those who approached the study of thinking in this way were struck by the obvious variations among individuals in their ability to think, analyze, solve problems, or learn new material. These researchers sought ways to measure and to understand those differences.

The First IQ Tests.   The first modern intelligence test was published in 1905 by two Frenchmen, Alfred Binet and Theodore Simon (1905). From the beginning, the test had a practical purpose—namely, to identify children who might have difficulty in school. For this reason, the tests Binet and Simon devised were very much like some school tasks, including measures of vocabulary, comprehension of facts and relationships, and mathematical and verbal reasoning. For example, can the child describe the difference between wood and glass? Can the young child touch his nose? His ear? His head? Can he tell which of two weights is heavier?

Lewis Terman and his associates at Stanford University modified and extended many of Binet and Simon's original tests when they translated and revised the test for use in the United States (Terman, 1916; Terman & Merrill, 1937). The several Terman revisions, called the **Stanford-Binet,** consist of a series of six individual tests for children of each age. A child taking the test is given the age tests beginning below his actual age, then those for his age, then those for each successively older age, until the child reaches a level at which he fails all six tests.

Terman initially described a child's performance in terms of a score called an **intelligence quotient,** later shortened to **IQ.** This score was computed by comparing the child's chronological age (in years and months) with his **mental age,** defined as the level of questions he could answer correctly. For example, a child who could solve the problems for a 6-year-old but not those for a 7-year-old would have a mental age of 6. The formula used to calculate the IQ score was

$$\frac{\text{Mental age}}{\text{Chronological age}} \times 100 = \text{IQ}$$

This formula results in an IQ score above 100 for children whose mental age is higher than their chronological age and an IQ score below 100 for children whose mental age is below their chronological age.

This old system for calculating an IQ score is not used any longer, even in the modern revisions of the Stanford-Binet. IQ score calculations are now based on a direct comparison of a child's performance with the average performance of a large group of other children his own age, with a score of 100 still typically defined as average. Two-thirds of all children achieve scores between 85 and 115; approximately 95 percent of scores fall between 70 and 130.

Mental Retardation.   The extreme ends of the IQ distribution have always been of special interest. Children with scores below 70 or 75 are normally referred to as **mentally retarded,** or in current parlance *intellectually disabled*. More precisely, mental retardation is diagnosed when a child has "consistently subaverage intellectual functioning" (normally operationalized as an IQ score below 70 or

75) *and* has significant problems in *adaptive behavior*—such as an inability to dress or eat alone or a problem getting along with others or adjusting to the demands of a regular school classroom (MacMillan & Reschly, 1997). That is, a low IQ score is a necessary but not sufficient condition for an individual to be classed as retarded. As Thomas Achenbach says, "Children doing well in school are unlikely to be considered retarded no matter what their IQ scores" (1982, p. 214).

Low IQ scores are customarily divided into several ranges, with different labels attached to each, as you can see in Table 8.4. I've given both the labels used by psychologists and those that may be more common in the school system. (There are no school system labels for children with IQs below 35 because schools very rarely deal with children functioning at this level.)

The farther down the IQ scale you go, the fewer children there are. More than 80 percent of all children with IQs below 70 are in the "mild" range; only about two percent of low-IQ youngsters (perhaps 3500 children in the United States) are profoundly retarded (Broman, Nichols, Shaughnessy, & Kennedy, 1987).

Retarded children can be divided into two distinct subgroups, depending on the cause of the retardation. The smaller subset, making up 15 to 25 percent of the total, are children who have some evident physical damage. Included here are those with a genetic anomaly such as Down syndrome or the fragile-X syndrome. Damage resulting in retardation can also be caused by a teratogen, such as prenatal alcohol, disease, or severe prenatal malnutrition, or it can occur during the birth itself, such as from prolonged anoxia. A small subset of these physically damaged retarded children suffer their injury after birth, such as in an auto accident or a fall. Let me hasten to make clear that not all children who are injured in such accidents, or who are affected by teratogens, are necessarily retarded. Instead, what I'm saying is that some children we know to be retarded have been disabled by some purely physical injury, disease, or anomaly.

The remaining three-fourths of retarded children show no obvious signs of brain damage or other physical disorder. In these cases the cause of the retardation is some combination of genetic and environmental conditions. Typically, these children come from families in which the parents have low IQs or mental illness, family life is highly disorganized, or the home life is emotionally or cognitively deprived. To be sure, in these cases, too, the child's intellectual disability may be exacerbated by the effects of teratogens or other hazards, such as moderate amounts of prenatal alcohol or elevated levels of prenatal or postnatal lead.

Large-scale studies have now shown quite conclusively that these several causes of retardation are not distributed evenly across the range of low IQ scores. The lower the IQ, the more likely it is that the cause is physical rather than environmental/genetic (Broman et al., 1987).

The Gifted. When a child's IQ score is above 130 or sometimes 140, she is commonly classed as **gifted**—a group of children that provide another set of challenges for parents and school systems.

Table 8.4

IQ Scores and Labels for Children Classed as Retarded

Approximate IQ Score Range	Label Used by Psychologists	Label Used in Schools
68–83	Borderline retarded	
52–67	Mildly retarded	Mildly intellectually disabled (sometimes called educable mentally retarded [EMR])
36–51	Moderately retarded	Moderately intellectually disabled (sometimes called trainable mentally retarded)
19–35	Severely retarded	
Below 19	Profoundly retarded	

Let me give you an extreme example, a child named Michael described by Halbert Robinson:

> When Michael was 2 years and 3 months old, the family visited our laboratory. At that time, they described a youngster who had begun speaking at age 5 months and by 6 months had exhibited a vocabulary of more than 50 words. He started to read English when he was 13 months old. In our laboratory he spoke five languages and could read in three of them. He understood addition, subtraction, multiplication, division, and square root, and he was fascinated by a broad range of scientific constructs. He loved to make puns, frequently bilingual ones. (1981, p. 63)

Michael's IQ score on the Stanford-Binet was in excess of 180 at age 2; two years later, when Michael was 4½, he performed on the test like a 12-year-old and was listed as having an IQ beyond 220.

We can certainly all agree that Michael should be labeled as gifted. Defining the term precisely is more difficult (Sternberg & Davidson, 1986). Giftedness includes those with exceptional specific talents, such as musical, artistic, mathematical, or spatial ability, as well as those with very high IQ scores. This broadening of the definition of giftedness has been widely accepted among theorists, who agree that there are many kinds of exceptional ability, each of which may reflect unusual speed or efficiency with one or another type of cognitive function. Within school systems, however, giftedness is still most often defined entirely by IQ test scores, usually by all scores above some cutoff, such as 130 or 140.

Robinson suggested that it may be useful to divide the group of high-IQ children into two sets, the "garden variety gifted," with high IQ scores (perhaps 130 to 150) but without extraordinary ability in any one area, and the "highly gifted" (like Michael), with extremely high IQ scores and/or remarkable skill in one or more areas. These two groups of children can have quite different experiences at home and in school.

The "garden variety gifted" appear to be much like their peers in social and emotional development. Most are well adjusted and socially adept (Gottfried, Gottfried, Bathurst, & Guerin, 1994). Children in the highly gifted subgroup, though, sometimes fare less well. These children are *so* different from their peers that they are likely to be seen as strange or disturbing and may have trouble making friends. Dorothy Kennedy (1995) describes her observations of a fifth grader named Joshua, with an IQ score over 200. His school and his teacher worked hard to provide him with adequate intellectual challenges, with limited success. Social relationships proved even more problematic. Two years younger than his classmates, Joshua alienated them by showing off or belittling their efforts, although Kennedy concluded that he attacked in this way because he felt his classmates ignored him. Children like Joshua, unlike the garden variety gifted, do show higher rates of emotional problems than do nongifted children (Janos & Robinson, 1985).

Modern IQ Tests. The two tests used most frequently by psychologists today are the Revised Stanford-Binet and the third revision of the **Wechsler Intelligence Scales for Children,** called the **WISC-III,** a test originally developed by David Wechsler (1974). (Several other well-known tests are listed in Table 8.5, p. 276.) The WISC-III involves ten different types of problems, each ranging from very easy to very hard. The child begins with the easiest problem of each type and continues with that type of item until he cannot go further, then goes on to the next problem type. Five of the tests, called *verbal tests,* rely strongly on verbal skills (e.g., vocabulary, describing similarities between objects, general information); the other half, collectively called *performance tests,* demand less-verbal types of thinking, such as arranging pictures in an order that tells a story or copying a pattern using a set of colored blocks. Many psychologists find this distinction between verbal and performance tests helpful, because significant unevenness in a child's test skill may indicate particular kinds of learning problems.

Stability and Predictive Value of IQ Tests. Because these tests were originally designed to predict a child's ability to perform in school, it is obviously crucial to know whether they do this job well. The research findings on this point are quite consistent: The correlation between a child's test score and her current or future grades in school is typically in the range of .50 to .60 (Brody, 1992; Carver, 1990; Neisser, Boodoo, Bouchard et al.,

Table 8.5

Other Widely Used Tests That May Be Used in Place of the Stanford-Binet and the Wechsler by Researchers or Educators

Peabody Picture Vocabulary Test (PPVT)	Not originally designed as an IQ test, but widely used as a quick measure of intelligence because the scores correlate so highly with Binet or Wechsler scores. Includes 150 pages, each page with four pictures, with the pages arranged in order of increasing difficulty. The examiner names a word and asks the child to point to the appropriate picture, as in the example on the right below. Widely used with preschool children. (This is the test used in the study described in Table 8.2, p. 259.)
Raven's Progressive Matrices	Each of the 36 items shows a pattern on a rectangular space, such as a set of dots covering the space. One section of the rectangle is blanked out, and the subject must choose which of six alternative fill-in options will match the original matrix, like the one on the left below. Designed as a nonverbal measure of intelligence.
Kaufman Assessment Battery for Children (K-ABC)	Kaufman does not call this an intelligence test, although it is often used in this way. Suitable for children ages 2½ to 12; includes three tests of *sequential processing* (such as number recall), seven tests of *simultaneous processing* (including face recognition), combined to provide an overall IQ, based primarily on nonverbal measures. Six achievement subtests can also be given, including vocabulary, riddles, and reading. The test also allows flexible testing procedures, including the use of other languages, alternate wording, gestures, all of which make the test one of the fairest for ethnic minorities and children from poverty-level families.

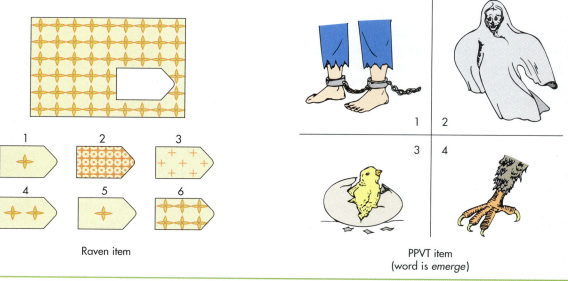

Raven item

PPVT item
(word is *emerge*)

Sources: Jensen, 1980, pp. 157 & 532; Kaufman & Kaufman, 1983a, 1983b.

1996). This is a moderate but by no means perfect correlation. It tells us that, on the whole, children with top IQ scores will also be among the high achievers in school and those who score low will be among the low achievers. At the same time, success in school also depends on many other factors than measured intelligence, including motivation, interest, and persistence. Because of this, many children with high IQ scores don't shine in school while some lower-IQ children do.

It is important to point out that this correlation between school performance and IQ scores holds adolescence, and criminal behavior in adulthood (Baydar, Brooks-Gunn, & Furstenberg, 1993; Stattin & Klackenberg-Larsson, 1993). This is not to say that all lower-IQ individuals are illiterate or criminals. That is clearly not the case. But low intelligence makes a child more vulnerable, just as high intelligence increases the child's resilience.

This second grader is working on one of the subtests of the WISC-III, in which he must use a set of blocks to try to copy the design shown in the book.

[?] *Critical Thinking*

How or why do you think having a higher IQ score makes the child more resilient? For example, in what specific ways might the life of a brighter child living in a slum be different from the life of a less-bright child in the same environment?

IQ scores are also quite stable. If two tests are given a few months or a few years apart, the scores are likely to be very similar. The correlations between adjacent-year IQ scores in middle childhood, for example, are typically in the range of .80 (Honzik, 1986). Yet this high level of predictability masks an interesting fact: Many children show quite wide fluctuations in their scores. Robert McCall, analyzing several longitudinal studies in which children had been given IQ tests repeatedly over many years, concludes that about half of children show noticeable changes from one test to another and over time (1993). Some show steadily rising scores, some declining; some show a peak in middle childhood and then a decline in adolescence. In rare cases, the shifts may cover a range as large as 40 points.

Such wide fluctuations are more common in young children. The general rule of thumb is that the older the child, the more stable the IQ score becomes, although even with older children scores may still show fluctuations in response to major stresses, such as parental divorce, a change of schools, or the birth of a sibling.

within each social class and racial group in the United States as well as in other countries and cultures. Among the poor as well as among the middle class, and among African Americans and Hispanics as well as among Anglos, those children with higher IQ scores are more likely to get good grades, complete high school, and go on to college (Brody, 1992). Such findings have led a number of theorists to argue that intelligence adds to the child's *resilience*—a concept I talked about in Chapter 1. Numerous studies now show that poor children, be they from the majority group or from a minority group, are far more likely to develop the kind of self-confidence and personal competence it takes to move out of poverty if they have greater intelligence (Luthar & Zigler, 1992; Werner & Smith, 1992).

At the other end of the scale, low intelligence is associated with a number of negative long-term outcomes, including adult illiteracy, delinquency in

Limitations of IQ tests. Before I move on to the question of the possible origins of differences in IQ, it is important to emphasize a few key limitations of such tests or the scores derived from them.

IQ tests do not measure underlying competence. An IQ score cannot tell you (or a teacher, or anyone else) that your child has some specific, fixed, underlying capacity. Traditional IQ tests also do not measure a whole host of skills that are likely to be highly significant for getting along in the world. IQ tests were originally designed to measure only the specific range of skills that are needed for success in school. This they do quite well. What they do not tell us is how good a particular person may be at other cognitive tasks requiring skills such as creativity, insight, street smarts, reading social cues, or understanding spatial relationships—a point I've explored in more detail in the *Research Report* on pages 280–281.

[?] *Critical Thinking*

Given what I have said so far about IQ tests, do you think it would be worthwhile to have every preschool child tested? How would you use such scores? What would be the drawbacks of such universal testing?

Explaining Differences in IQ

You will not be surprised to discover that the arguments about the origins of differences in IQ scores nearly always boil down to a dispute about nature versus nurture. When Binet and Simon wrote the first IQ test, they did not assume that intelligence as measured on an IQ test was fixed or inborn. Many of the American psychologists who revised and promoted the use of the tests, however, *did* believe that intellectual capacity is inherited and largely fixed at birth. Those who share this view, and those who believe that the environment is crucial in shaping a child's intellectual performance, have been arguing—often vehemently—for at least 60 years. Both groups can muster research to support their views.

Evidence for the Importance of Heredity. Both twin studies and studies of adopted children show strong hereditary influences on IQ, as you already know from the *Research Report* in Chapter 1 (p. 12). Identical twins are more like one another in IQ scores than are fraternal twins, and the IQs of adopted children are better predicted from the IQs of their natural parents than their adoptive parents (Brody, 1992; Loehlin, Horn, & Willerman, 1994; Scarr, Weinberg, & Waldman, 1993). These

are precisely the findings we would expect if there were a strong genetic element at work.

Evidence for the Importance of Environment. Adoption studies also provide some strong support for an environmental influence on IQ scores because the actual *level* of IQ scores of adopted children is clearly affected by the environment in which they have grown up. The clearest evidence for this comes from a French study by Christiane Capron and Michel Duyme (1989), who studied a group of 38 French children, all adopted in infancy. Roughly half the children had been born to better educated/higher-social-class parents while the other half had been born to working-class or poverty-level parents. Some of the children in each group had then been adopted by higher social-class parents, while the others grew up in poorer families. Table 8.6 shows the children's IQ scores in adolescence. If you compare the two columns in the table, you can see the effect of rearing conditions: The children reared in upper-class homes have IQs that are 11 or 12 points higher than those reared in lower-class families, regardless of the social-class level or education of the birth parents. At the same time, you can see a genetic effect if you compare the two rows in the table: The children *born to* upper-class parents have higher IQs than do those from lower-class families, no matter what kind of rearing environment they encountered.

Combining the Information. Virtually all psychologists would now agree that heredity is a highly important influence on IQ scores. Studies

Table 8.6

IQ Scores at Adolescence for Capron and Duyme's Adopted Children

		Social Class of Adoptive Parents	
		High	**Low**
Social Class of Biological Parents	High	119.60[*]	107.50
	Low	103.60	92.40

[*]*The numbers in each cell represent the average IQ score for that group of children.*

Source: Capron & Duyme, 1989, Table 2, p. 553.

around the world consistently yield estimates that roughly half the variation in IQ scores within the population is due to heredity (Neisser et al., 1996; Plomin & Rende, 1991; Rogers, Rowe, & May, 1994). The remaining half is clearly due to environment or to interactions between environment and heredity.

One useful way to conceptualize this interaction is with the concept of **reaction range.** The basic idea is that genes establish some range of possible reactions, some upper and lower boundary of functioning. Where a child will fall within those boundaries will be determined by environment. Richard Weinberg (1989) estimates that the reaction range for IQ scores is about 20 to 25 points. That is, given some specific genetic heritage, each child's actual IQ test performance may vary as much as 20 or 25 points, depending on the richness or poverty of the environment in which he grows up. When we change the child's environment for the better, the child moves closer to the upper end of his reaction range. When we change the environment for the worse, the child's effective intellectual performance falls toward the lower end of his reaction range. Thus, even though intelligence as measured on an IQ test is highly heritable, the absolute score within the reaction range is determined by environment. Just what is it about family environments that seems to make a difference?

Specific Family Characteristics and IQ.
When we watch the ways individual families interact with their infants or young children and then follow the children over time to see which ones later have high or low IQs, we can begin to get some sense of the kinds of specific family interactions that foster higher scores. The research tells us that families with higher-IQ children tend to do the following:

- They provide an *interesting and complex physical environment* for the child, including play materials that are appropriate for the child's age and developmental level (Bradley et al., 1989; Pianta & Egeland, 1994).

- They are *emotionally responsive* to and *involved* with their child. They respond warmly and contingently to the child's behavior, smiling when the child smiles, answering the child's questions, and in myriad ways respond to the child's cues (Barnard, Hammond, Booth et al., 1989; M. D. Lewis, 1993).

- They *talk to their child* often, using language that is descriptively rich and accurate (Hart & Risley, 1995; Sigman, Neumann, Carter et al., 1988).

- When they play with or interact with the child, they operate in what Vygotsky referred to as the *zone of proximal development* (described in Chapter 2), aiming their conversation, their questions, and their assistance at a level that is just above the level the child could manage on her own, thus helping the child to master new skills (e.g., Landry, Garner, Swank, & Baldwin, 1996).

- They *avoid excessive restrictiveness*, punitiveness, or control, instead giving the child room to explore, even opportunities to make mistakes (Bradley et al., 1989; S. Olson, Bates, & Kaskie, 1992). In a similar vein, they ask questions rather than giving commands (Hart & Risley, 1995).

- They *expect* their child to do well and to develop rapidly. They emphasize and press for school achievement (Entwisle & Alexander, 1990).

You'll remember from Chapter 1 that there is a problem in research of this type. Because parents provide *both* the genes and the environment, we can't be sure that these environmental characteristics are really causally important. Perhaps these are simply the environmental features provided by brighter parents and it is the parents' genes and not the environment they create that cause the higher IQs in their children. The way around this problem is to look at the link between environmental features and IQ scores in adopted children. Fortunately, we have a few studies of this type, and they point to the same critical environmental features, although the relationships are somewhat weaker. That is, among adoptive families, those that behave in the ways listed above have adopted children who score somewhat higher on IQ tests (Plomin, Loehlin, & DeFries, 1985).

School Experience and Special Interventions.
Home environments and family interactions are not the only source of environmental influence. Many children also spend a very large amount of time in group-care settings, including day care, special programs like Head Start, or regular preschools. How much effect do these environments have on the child's intellectual growth? I

Research Report

Three Other Models of Intelligence

Both the Stanford-Binet and the Wechsler tests, along with most standardized IQ tests, are based on the assumption that there is one central component of intellectual ability, sometimes called *g* (for general ability). A number of prominent psychologists dispute this assumption. Here are three popular alternative views.

Robert Sternberg's Triarchic Theory of Intelligence

Robert Sternberg (Sternberg, 1985; Sternberg & Wagner, 1993) proposes three aspects or types of intelligence:

- *componential intelligence* includes what we normally measure on IQ and achievement tests. Planning, organizing, remembering facts, and applying them to new situations are all part of componential intelligence.

- *experiential intelligence* includes what you might call creativity. A person with well-developed experiential intelligence can see new connections between things, can relate to experiences in insightful ways. A college student who can come up with good ideas for theories or experiments to test them or who can synthesize a great many facts into a new organization would be high in experiential intelligence.

- *contextual intelligence* is sometimes also called "street smarts." People who are skilled in this way are able to manipulate their environments, to see how they can fit in best, to know which people to cultivate and how to cultivate them, to adapt themselves to their setting or the setting to themselves. In college

we would see this form of intelligence in a student who went regularly to office hours to talk to the professor or who chose paper topics he knew the professor preferred. This is not just manipulation. It requires being attuned to a variety of fairly subtle signals and then acting on the information. Good salespeople, for example, would have to have a high level of contextual intelligence in order to tailor their sales pitch on the basis of subtle cues from each customer.

Daniel Goleman's Emotional Intelligence

Daniel Goleman proposes only one alternative form of intelligence, which he calls **emotional intelligence.** It includes

abilities such as being able to motivate oneself and persist in the face of frustrations; to control impulses and delay gratification; to regulate one's moods and keep distress from swamping the ability to think; to empathize and to hope. (1995a, p. 34)

As defined, emotional intelligence obviously has some overlap with Sternberg's contextual intelligence, but it includes other elements as well, such as the very kind of emotional control or modulation that is an important learning task in the preschool years.

Howard Gardner's Multiple Intelligences

Drawing in part from studies of genius and remarkable talent, Howard Gardner (1983) argues that instead of a single *g* factor, at least six intelligences exist, which he sometimes calls "frames of mind."

talked about some of the day-care effects in the last chapter, but I need to expand a bit.

On a theoretical level, this question is of interest because it may tell us something both about early experience in general and about the resilience of children. Are the effects of an initially impoverished environment permanent, or can they be offset by an enriched experience, such as a special preschool? At a practical level, programs like Head Start are based squarely on the assumption that it *is* possible to modify the trajectory of a child's intellectual development, especially if you intervene early.

Attempts to test this assumption have led to a messy body of research. In particular, children are rarely assigned randomly to Head Start or non–Head Start groups, making interpretation difficult. Still, researchers have reached some agreement on the effects. Children enrolled in Head Start or other enriched preschool programs, compared with similar children without such preschool experience, normally show a gain of about ten IQ points during the year of the Head Start experience. This gain typically fades and then disappears within the first few years of school (Zigler & Styfco, 1993). On other measures, however, a clear residual

Research Report

Three Other Models of Intelligence (*Continued*)

- **linguistic intelligence** *is seen in poets as well as in others who are highly sensitive to language and its uses; includes the ability to use language to convince others or to explain.*

- **musical intelligence,** *a talent that nearly always appears very early in life, includes unusual sensitivity to pitch and rhythm, often expressed in precocious ability to play an instrument or compose music.*

- **logical-mathematical intelligence** *is highly similar to what Piaget refers to as intelligence and overlaps with Sternberg's componential intelligence. At the upper end of this ability are mathematicians and many kinds of scientists.*

- **spatial intelligence** *includes the capacity to perceive the visual world accurately and to transform that original perception in one's mind, such as by mentally rotating a picture so that you can imagine what the back would look like. Architects must have this skill in some abundance, as must top-level chess players and some types of mathematicians.*

- **bodily kinesthetic intelligence** *includes control of one's bodily motions and the capacity to handle objects skillfully. A gifted mime like Marcel Marceau has a great deal of this type of intelligence, as do dancers, many actors, and many athletes.*

- **personal intelligence** *includes two facets: an internal facet that involves access to one's own feelings and the ability to discriminate among them; and an external facet that involves the ability to notice and make distinctions among other individuals, to notice their moods, temperaments, motivations, and intentions. This is very similar to what Goleman means by emotional intelligence and overlaps with Sternberg's contextual intelligence.*

All three of these authors are arguing not only that standard IQ tests have failed to measure many of these qualities, but that in the world beyond the school walls, emotional, experiential, contextual, bodily, or other forms of intelligence may be required as much or more than the type of academic intelligence measured on an IQ test. Gardner goes further:

> The single most important contribution education can make to a child's development is to help him toward a field where his talents best suit him, where he will be satisfied and competent. We've completely lost sight of that. Instead we subject everyone to an education where, if you succeed, you will be best suited to be a college professor. (quoted in Goleman, 1995a, p. 37)

I think Gardner underestimates the extent to which the kind of intelligence measured on an IQ test makes a difference in jobs of many types, but he—and Goleman and Sternberg—certainly have a point.

---

effect can still be seen some years later. Children with Head Start or other quality preschool experience are less likely to be placed in special education classes, less likely to repeat a grade, and more likely to graduate from high school (W. Barnett, 1995; Darlington, 1991). They also have better health, better immunization rates, and better school adjustment than their peers (Zigler & Styfco, 1993). One very long-term longitudinal study even suggests that the impact may last well into adulthood. Young adults who had attended a particularly good experimental preschool program, the Perry Preschool Project in Milwaukee, had higher rates of high school graduation, lower rates of criminal behavior, lower rates of unemployment, and a lower probability of being on welfare than

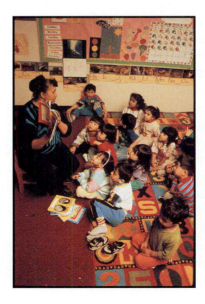

Children in Head Start programs or other enriched preschools don't have higher IQs later, but they are less likely to repeat a school grade or to be assigned to special education classes.

did their peers who had not attended such enriched preschools (W. Barnett, 1993). I should emphasize that the Perry Preschool Project was *not* a Head Start program; we have *no* equivalent information about children who have attended run-of-the-mill Head Start, so we can't be sure that the long-term effects would be as great as in the Perry Project, although it is reasonable to expect that well-run, comprehensive Head Start programs would have similar effects (Zigler & Styfco, 1996).

Despite these encouraging results, we should be careful about making assertions that are too sweeping about the benefits of Head Start. Edward Zigler—the nation's leading expert on Head Start—says, "early childhood intervention alone cannot transform lives. Its positive effects can be overpowered by the longer and larger experience of growing up in poverty" (Zigler & Styfco, 1996, p. 152). Programs like Head Start are well worth our support, but we should not expect them to solve all problems.

More promising still—although far more expensive and complex—are enrichment programs that begin in infancy rather than at age 3 or 4. Poverty-level children who have attended such programs continue to have higher IQs than comparison-group children, even well into school age. The best-designed and most meticulously reported of the infancy interventions is Craig Ramey's North Carolina study, called the Abecedarian Project (Campbell & Ramey, 1994; Ramey, 1993; Ramey & Campbell, 1987). Infants from poverty-level families, whose mothers had low IQ scores, were randomly assigned either to a special day-care program or to a control group that received nutritional supplements and medical care but no special enriched day care. The special day care, which began when the infants were 6 to 12 weeks of age and lasted until they began kindergarten, involved very much the kinds of "optimum" stimulation I just described.

Figure 8.5 shows the average IQ scores of the children in each of these two groups from age 2 to age 12. You can see that the IQs of the children who had been enrolled in the special program were higher at every age. Fully 44 percent of the control-group children had IQ scores below 85 (classified as borderline or retarded) compared with only 12.8 percent of the children who had been in the special

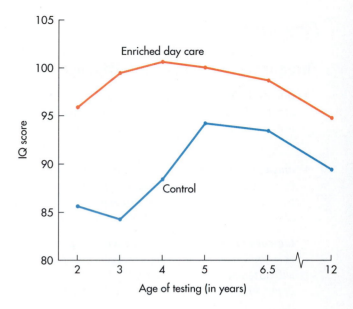

Figure 8.5

In the Ramey study children were randomly assigned to an experimental group with special day care or to a control group. At kindergarten, both groups entered public school. The difference in IQ between the experimental and control groups remained statistically significant even at age 12, seven years after the intervention ended. (Source: Ramey & Campbell, 1987, Figure 3, p. 135, with additional data from Ramey, 1993, Figure 2, p. 29.)

program. In addition, the enriched day-care group had significantly higher scores on both reading and mathematics tests at age 12 and were only half as likely to have repeated a grade (Ramey, 1992; 1993).

[?] *Critical Thinking*

Considering the results of Ramey's study, would you be in favor of providing such enriched day care to all infants from high-risk or poverty-level families? What are the arguments pro and con?

These results do *not* mean that all mental retardation could be "cured" by providing children with heavy doses of special education in infancy. What they do show is that the intellectual power of those children who begin life with few advantages can be significantly increased with early and extensive intervention (Bryant & Maxwell, 1997).

Racial Differences in IQ

So far I have sidestepped an extremely difficult set of questions, namely, racial differences in IQ scores or cognitive power. Debates about such differences were reenergized by the publication, in 1994, of a highly controversial book, *The Bell Curve*, in which Richard Herrnstein and Charles Murray (1994) reviewed and analyzed the evidence. Because these issues have powerful personal and political ramifications and can easily be blown out of proportion, I do not want to place too much emphasis on this topic. Even so, you should have some idea of what we know, what we don't know, and how we are trying to explain such differences.

The evidence shows a number of racial differences in intellectual performance, including consistently higher performance on achievement tests—particularly math and science tests—by Chinese and Japanese children (Geary, 1996; Geary, Bow-Thomas, Liu, & Siegler, 1996; Stevenson, Lee, Chen et al., 1990; Sue & Okazaki, 1990). But the basic finding that has been most troublesome for researchers and theorists (and that Herrnstein and Murray discuss at length) is that in the United States, African-American children consistently score lower than Euro-American children on standard measures of intelligence. This difference, which is on the order of 12 IQ points, is *not* found on infant tests of intelligence or on measures of infant habituation rate (Fagan & Singer, 1983), but it becomes apparent by the time children are 2 or 3 years old (Brody, 1992; Peoples, Fagan, & Drotar, 1995). There is some indication that the size of the difference between black and white children has been declining in the past several decades and may now be less than 10 points (Neisser et al., 1996). Yet a noticeable difference persists.

[?] *Critical Thinking*

Some psychologists have argued that the reason blacks achieve lower IQ scores than whites is that the tests are systematically biased against blacks or other minority group members. What kind of research results would demonstrate such a bias? What kind would argue against it?

Some scientists, including the authors of *The Bell Curve*, acknowledge that the environments of the two groups are, on average, substantially different. Yet they nonetheless conclude that the IQ-test difference must reflect—at least in part—basic genetic differences between the races (Jensen, 1980). Other scientists, while granting that intelligence is highly heritable, point out that the 10- or 12-point difference falls well within the presumed reaction range of IQ. They emphasize that the environments in which black and white children are typically reared differ sufficiently to account for the average difference in score (Brody, 1992). Black children in the United States are more likely to be born with low birth weight, more likely to suffer from subnutrition, more likely to have high blood levels of lead, less likely to be read to or provided with a wide range of intellectual stimulation. And each of these environmental characteristics is known to be linked to lower IQ scores.

Some of the most convincing research supporting such an environmental explanation comes from Sandra Scarr and her colleagues (Scarr & Weinberg, 1983; Weinberg, Scarr, & Waldman, 1992). For example, she has found that black children adopted at an early age into white middle-class families scored only slightly less well on IQ tests than did white children adopted into the same families. Findings like these persuade me that the IQ score difference we see is primarily a reflection of the fact that the tests, and schools, are designed by the majority culture to promote a particular form of intellectual activity and that many black or other minority families rear their children in ways that do not promote or emphasize this particular set of skills.

In a similar vein, Harold Stevenson and others have argued that the differences between Asian and Euro-American children in performance on mathematics achievement tests occur not because of genetic differences in capacity but because of differences in cultural emphasis on the importance of academic achievement, the number of hours spent on mathematics instruction in school and doing math homework, and differences in the quality of the math instruction in the schools (Chang & Murray, 1995; Geary et al., 1996; B. Schneider, Hieshima, Lee, & Plank, 1994; Stevenson & Lee, 1990; Stigler, Lee, & Stevenson, 1987)—a point I'll come back to in Chapter 11.

The fact that we may be able to account for such racial differences in IQ scores or achievement test performance by appealing to the concept of reaction range and to cultural or subcultural variations does not make the differences disappear, nor does it make them trivial. Perhaps, though, it puts such findings into a less explosive framework.

The Measurement of Intelligence: One More Look

One of the questions that students often ask at about this point is whether, given all the factors that can affect a test score, it is worth bothering with IQ tests at all. I think it is definitely worth it. Let me tell you why.

First, IQ tests are important tools for identifying children who have special school needs, including both gifted and retarded children. There are other methods for selecting children for special programs, such as teacher recommendations, but none of the alternatives is as reliable or valid as an IQ test for measuring that set of cognitive abilities that are demanded by school.

Second, IQ tests have been an invaluable research tool, providing us with a widely accepted measure of the effect of environmental variations. For example, Ramey used IQ scores as one critical measure of the success of his special day-care program. Similarly, physicians have used IQ scores as a way to demonstrate the detrimental effect of lead exposure on children's mental development. In this sense, the IQ test is a tool for detecting the effects of environmental variations, just as a thermometer is a tool for detecting variations in body temperature. If you use the tool correctly, not expecting it to tell you more than it is designed to say, it can be extremely valuable.

Summary

1. Language development moves at a rapid pace between ages 2 and 4, beginning with simple two-word sentences, followed by a grammar explosion when grammatical inflections are added, followed by complex sentences. A variety of meanings is conveyed in even the simplest sentences.

2. From the earliest sentences, children's language is creative, including forms and combinations the child has not heard but that follow apparent rules.

3. The development of word meanings (semantic development) follows a less-predictable course. Children appear to have many concepts or categories before they have words for them, but learning new words also creates new categories. The earliest words are normally highly specific and context-bound in meaning; later, children typically "overextend" their usage.

4. Some linguists have concluded that in figuring out word meanings, a child has built-in constraints or biases, such as the assumption that words refer to objects or actions but not both or to the principle of contrast.

5. Simple imitation or reinforcement theories of language development are not adequate to explain the phenomenon. More complex environmental theories, emphasizing the role of environmental richness or motherese, are more helpful but also not sufficient.

6. Innateness theorists assume the child is born with a set of "operating principles" that focus the child on relevant aspects of language input. Other theorists emphasize the child as a "little linguist" who constructs a language as he constructs all cognitive understandings. No one of these theories fully accounts for the process of language learning.

7. Piaget marked the beginning of the preoperational period at about 18 to 24 months, at the point when the child begins to use mental symbols. Despite this advance, the preschool child still lacks many sophisticated cognitive characteristics. In Piaget's view such children are still egocentric, rigid in their thinking, and generally captured by appearances.

8. Recent research on the cognitive functioning of preschoolers makes it clear that they are much less egocentric than Piaget thought. By age 4 they can distinguish between appearance and reality in a variety of tasks, and they develop a surprisingly sophisticated theory of how minds work. They understand that other people's actions are based on thoughts and beliefs, not on "reality."

9. By age 4 or 5, children also understand some of the links between specific situations and other people's likely emotions.

10. Language development proceeds at varying speeds in different children, with faster development associated with linguistically richer environments.

11. Children also differ in cognitive power, as measured by standard intelligence tests. Scores on such tests

are predictive of school performance and are at least moderately consistent over time.

12. Children with IQs below 70 or 75, and who also have difficulty with everyday adaptive tasks, are usually labeled retarded. In a minority of such children, the retardation is due to some physical damage or abnormality; in the remainder it appears to be due to some combination of genetic and environmental factors.

13. Children with IQs above 130 or 140, or those with striking abilities in specific areas such as music or mathematics, may be labeled as gifted.

14. Differences in IQ scores have been attributed to both heredity and environment. Twin and adoption studies make it clear that at least half the variation in IQ scores is due to genetic differences, the remainder to environment and the interaction of heredity and environment.

15. Qualities of the environment that appear to make a difference include the complexity of stimulation, the responsiveness and involvement of parents, the relative lack of restrictiveness, and high expectations for the child's performance.

16. The IQs of children reared in poverty environments can be raised by providing specially stimulating environments, such as enriched day care or preschools, but such interventions must be early, lengthy, and carefully planned for the effect to persist.

17. Several kinds of racial differences in IQ scores or test performance have been found consistently. Such differences seem more appropriately attributed to environmental variation rather than to genetics.

Key Terms

bodily kinesthetic intelligence   One of the six types of intelligence proposed by Howard Gardner. **(p. 281)**

componental intelligence   One of three types of intelligence in Sternberg's triarchic theory of intelligence; that type of intelligence typically measured on IQ tests, including analytic thinking, remembering facts, organizing information. **(p. 279)**

conservation   The concept that objects remain the same in fundamental ways, such as weight or number, even when there are external changes in shape or arrangement. Children begin to understand this concept at about age 5. **(p. 265)**

contextual intelligence   One of three types of intelligence in Sternberg's triarchic theory of intelligence; often also called "street smarts," this type of intelligence includes skills in adapting to an environment and in adapting an environment to one's own needs. **(p. 280)**

egocentrism   A cognitive state in which the individual (typically a child) sees the world only from his own perspective, without awareness that there are other perspectives. **(p. 263)**

emotional intelligence   A type of intelligence proposed by Daniel Goleman, including "abilities such as being able to motivate oneself and persist in the face of frustrations; to control impulses and delay gratification; to regulate one's moods and keep distress from swamping the ability to think; to empathize and to hope" (1995, p. 34). **(p. 280)**

experiential intelligence   One of three types of intelligence described by Sternberg in his triarchic theory of intelligence; includes creativity, insight, seeing new relationships among experiences. **(p. 280)**

false belief   Incorrectly believing something to be true and acting on that belief; the child's understanding of the principle of false belief is one key sign of the emergence of a representational theory of mind. **(p. 266)**

gifted   Normally defined in terms of very high IQ score (above 130 or 140), but may also be defined in terms of remarkable skill in one or more specific areas, such as mathematics or memory. **(p. 274)**

infant-directed speech   The formal scientific term for "motherese," that special form of simplified, higher-pitched speech adults use with infants and young children. **(p. 259)**

inflections   The various grammatical "markers" contained in every language, such as (in English) the *s* for plurals or the *-ed* for past tenses, auxiliary verbs such as *is*, and the equivalent. **(p. 252)**

intelligence quotient (IQ)   Originally defined in terms of a child's mental age and chronological age, IQs are now computed by comparing a child's performance with that of other children of the same chronological age. **(p. 273)**

Kaufman Assessment Battery for Children (K-ABC) A relatively new type of IQ test now quite widely used; includes measures of sequential processing, simultaneous processing, and achievement. **(p. 276)**

linguistic intelligence   One of the six types of intelligence proposed by Howard Gardner. **(p. 281)**

logical-mathematical intelligence   One of the six types of intelligence proposed by Howard Gardner. **(p. 281)**

mean length of utterance (MLU)   The average number of "meaningful units" in a sentence. Each basic word is one meaningful unit, as is each inflection, such as the *s* for plural or the *-ed* for a past tense. **(p. 272)**

mental age   Term used by Binet and Simon and Terman in the early calculation of IQ; the age level of IQ test items the child can successfully pass. When compared with the child's chronological age, allows calculation of an IQ score. **(p. 273)**

mentally retarded   Term used to describe children or adults with IQ scores of 75 or below in addition to poor adaptive behavior. **(p. 273)**

metacognition   General and rather loosely used term describing an individual's knowledge of his own thinking processes. Knowing what you know, and how you go about learning or remembering. **(p. 268)**

metamemory   A subcategory of metacognition; knowledge about your own memory processes. **(p. 268)**

motherese   See *infant-directed speech.* **(p. 259)**

musical intelligence   One of the six types of intelligence proposed by Howard Gardner. **(p. 280)**

overregularization   The tendency on the part of children to make the language regular by creating regularized versions of irregular speech forms as in past tenses or plurals; for example (in English), *beated* or *footses.* **(p. 253)**

Peabody Picture Vocabulary Test (PPVT)   A widely used measure of children's vocabulary. On each of 150 items, the examiner provides a word and the child must select the most appropriate picture from an array of four pictures. **(p. 259)**

personal intelligence   One of the six types of intelligence proposed by Howard Gardner. **(p. 281)**

pragmatics   The rules for the use of language in communicative interaction, such as the rules for taking turns, for selecting the style of speech appropriate to varying listeners, and the equivalent. **(p. 257)**

Raven's Progressive Matrices   A commonly used nonverbal measure of intelligence. The subject must select the pattern that correctly fills in a blank space left in a patterned display. **(p. 276)**

reaction range   Term used by some psychologists for the range of possible outcomes (phenotypes) on some variable, given basic genetic patterning (genotype). In the case of IQ, the reaction range is estimated at 20 to 25 points. **(p. 279)**

spatial intelligence   One of the six types of intelligence proposed by Howard Gardner. **(p. 281)**

Stanford-Binet   The best-known American intelligence test. It was written by Louis Terman and his associates, based upon the first tests by Binet and Simon. **(p. 273)**

telegraphic speech   Term used by Roger Brown to describe the earliest sentences created by most children because these sentences sound a bit like a telegram, in-cluding key nouns and verbs but generally omitting all other words and grammatical inflections. **(p. 252)**

theory of mind   Phrase used to describe one aspect of the thinking of 4- and 5-year-olds when they show signs of understanding not only that other people think differently, but that other people will base their behavior on what they believe or know or feel, rather than on the visible situation. **(p. 266)**

Wechsler Intelligence Scale for Children-III (WISC-III)   The most recent revision of this well-known American IQ test, which includes both verbal and performance (nonverbal) subtests. **(p. 275)**

Suggested Readings

Flavell, J. H. (1992). Cognitive development: Past, present, and future. *Developmental Psychology, 28,* 998–1005. This brief paper by one of the leading thinkers and researchers in the field of cognitive development gives you a quick tour of what Flavell thinks we now know, don't know, and are still arguing about. Flavell's 1993 text, *Cognitive Development,* mentioned in the suggested readings for Chapter 5, is also a wonderful source.

Goldstein, J. H. (Ed.). (1994). *Toys, play, and child development.* Cambridge, England: Cambridge University Press. A collection of current papers on the role of play in children's development. Included is an interesting chapter on war toys and their effect.

Hakuta, K. (1986). *Mirror on language: The debate on bilingualism.* New York: Basic Books. An elegant and comprehensible discussion of many of the issues about bilingualism and bilingual education I have discussed in the *Parenting* box on page 255.

Neisser, U., Boodoo, G., Bouchard, T. J., Jr., Boykin, A. W., Brody, N., Ceci, S. J., Halpern, D. F., Loehlin, J. C., Perloff, R., Sternberg, R. J., & Urbina, S. (1996). Intelligence: Knowns and unknowns. *American Psychologist, 51,* 77–101. A remarkable paper prepared as a collaborative effort by nearly all the leading experts on intelligence, designed in part as a response to *The Bell Curve.* These scientists were asked by the American Psychological Association to prepare a summary of the basic, agreed-upon facts about intelligence and its measurement. The paper is dense, but it includes good explanations of most of the key concepts. It is a wonderful source for further study.

Pinker, S. (1994). *The language instinct. How the mind creates language.* New York: William Morrow. This splendid book, written by one of the most articulate and easy-to-understand linguists, lays out the argument for a built-in language instinct.

Shatz, M. (1994). A *toddler s life. Becoming a person*. New York: Oxford University Press. Marilyn Shatz uses her grandson Ricky as an example throughout this engaging book, bringing in research as she goes along.

Shore, C. M. (1995). *Individual differences in language development*. Thousand Oaks, CA: Sage. A small book summarizing what we know about individual differences in rate and style of language development and about the alternative explanations of those differences.

CHAPTER 9

Social and Personality Development in the Preschool Years

Preview Questions

1 Are the "terrible twos" really so terrible?

2 Is rivalry really the most common type of sibling relationship?

3 Do preschool children have genuine friendships, or do they just play together?

4 How can a parent foster the development of altruistic behavior in a child?

5 Why are two-parent families better for children than single-parent families?

Chapter Outline

If you asked a random sample of adults to tell you the most important characteristics of children between the ages of 2 and 6, my hunch is that the first thing on the list would be the immense changes children make in their social abilities during these years. They go from being nay-saying, oppositional toddlers during the famed "terrible twos" to being skilled playmates and interesting conversationalists by age 5 or 6. Certainly, the huge improvements in the child's language skills are a crucial ingredient in this transition. But to many observers the most obvious thing about 5-year-olds is how socially "grown up" they seem compared with toddlers.

Children learn these new social skills in two rather different kinds of relationships, what Willard Hartup calls *vertical* and *horizontal* relationships (1989). A vertical relationship involves an attachment to someone who has greater social power or knowledge, such as a parent, a teacher,

or even an older sibling. Such relationships are complementary rather than reciprocal. The bond may be extremely powerful in both directions, but the actual behaviors the two partners show toward one another are not the same. Horizontal relationships, in contrast, are reciprocal and egalitarian. The individuals involved, such as same-age peers, have equal social power and their behavior toward one another comes from the same repertoire.

Hartup's point is that these two kinds of relationships serve different functions for the child, and both are needed for the child to develop effective social skills. Vertical relationships are necessary to provide the child with protection and security. In these relationships the child creates his basic internal working models and learns fundamental social skills. But it is in horizontal relationships—in friendships and in peer groups—that the child practices his social behavior and acquires those social skills that can only be learned in a relationship between equals: cooperation, competition, and intimacy. Let me begin by talking about the vertical relationships, in particular about the core relationship between child and parent.

I want to do it myself! The issues of independence and control are central to children in the preschool period.

Relationships with Parents

A parent's task changes rather dramatically after the baby leaves infancy. In the early months of life the key task for the parents is to provide enough warmth, predictability, and responsiveness to foster a secure attachment and to support basic physiological development. Once the child becomes physically, linguistically, and cognitively more independent, the need to instruct and control become more central aspects of the parents' task. As Eric Erikson pointed out in his description of this period (the stage of *autonomy versus shame and doubt* in his system), too much control and the child will not have sufficient opportunity to explore; too little control and the child will become unmanageable and fail to learn the social skills he will need to get along with peers as well as adults.

Yet, although the parents' task changes, it is a mistake to think of this new "stage" as unconnected to what went before. For one thing, the quality of the attachments to the parents continues to have an impact, not only in parent-child interactions but in the child's relationship with her peers.

Attachment

You'll remember from Chapter 6 that by 12 months of age, the baby has normally established a clear attachment to at least one caregiver. The infant displays this attachment in a wide variety of attachment behaviors, including smiling, crying, clinging, social referencing, and "safe base behavior." By age 2 or 3 the attachment appears no less strong, but many of these same attachment behaviors have become less continuously visible. Children this age are cognitively advanced enough to understand Mom if she explains why she is going away and that she will be back, so their anxiety at separation wanes. They can even use a photograph of the mother as a "safe base" for exploration in a strange situation (Passman & Longeway, 1982), which reflects the major cognitive advance of symbolic representation. Of course, attachment behaviors have not completely disappeared. Three-year-olds still want to sit on Mom's or Dad's lap; they are still likely to seek some closeness when Mom returns from an absence. But in nonfearful or nonstressful situations the preschool child is able to wander farther and farther from her safe base without apparent distress. She can also deal with her potential anxiety at separation by creating shared plans with the parents ("I'll be home after your nap time") (Crittenden, 1992).

Bowlby referred to this new form of attachment as a **goal-corrected partnership.** The infant's goal, to put it most simply, is always to have the attachment figure within sight or touch. The preschooler's goal is also to be "in contact" with the parent, but "contact" no longer requires constant physical presence. Further, the 3- or 4-year-old—especially the securely attached 3- or 4-year-old—can modify (or "correct") this goal in collaboration with the parent, agreeing on when and how the two will be together, or what the child will do if he gets scared or anxious, or who the replacement security person will be, whether a baby-sitter, Grandpa, or whomever.

For insecurely attached preschoolers, the task is more complex. Patricia Crittenden (1992) suggests that many avoidant children shift to a pattern she calls a **defended attachment.** These children,

Off she goes, into greater independence. Securely attached toddlers, because they are confident of the parents' support, are much more comfortable exploring away from home. An insecurely attached child, whose base feels less safe, is less adventuresome.

like all children, try to maintain some kind of contact with the parent. But because they anticipate the parent's anger or disinterest, they do not engage in negotiation with the parent, nor do they express their own feelings; instead, these children develop exceptionally acute awareness of what the parent may be thinking or feeling and adapt their own behavior to match—almost as if these youngsters were pushed to develop a more mature theory of mind at an early age, simply to achieve their attachment goals.

Crittenden similarly argues that many ambivalently attached children, and some formerly avoidant children, shift to a pattern she calls a **coercive attachment.** These children also do not engage in much negotiation or mutual goal-correction with the parent. Instead, they develop strategies for keeping the parent always available, either by being enticing and coy or threatening and angry. Thus the defended child adapts to the parent's inferred moods and needs; the coercive child tries to make the parent adapt to him.

Both these new styles or patterns of insecure attachment rest on the child's new cognitive abilities. The coercive child now understands something about the effects of her own smiles or cries and can use these behaviors deliberately; the defended child now understands something about how to read the parent's feelings, and adapts.

Table 9.1

Changes in Attachment Patterns Among Preschoolers, According to Crittenden

Infancy Attachment Category	Equivalent Preschool Attachment Category	Preschool Behavior
Secure	Secure	Feels confident that their attachment figure shares their basic goal of maintaining contact; develops a genuinely goal-corrected partnership, sharing with the parent(s) the task of arranging how to remain in contact and to reduce fear or anxiety.
Avoidant	Defended	Does not negotiate with parent because of fear or anxiety; instead becomes hyperaware of the parent's moods or needs and adapts her own behavior to the parent's, thus maintaining some kind of contact.
Ambivalent	Coercive	Maintains contact with the somewhat reluctant parent by coercing him or her, either through coy enticement or anger and crying. Child learns to manipulate the parent.

Sources: Crittenden, 1992; Fagot & Pears, 1996.

[?] *Critical Thinking*

Compare Crittenden's several types of attachment with the types of adult attachment models described in the *Research Report* in Chapter 6 (p. 196). Do you recognize yourself?

Attachment and Peer Relationships. These attachment patterns affect more than just the child's relationship with the parent; increasingly, preschool-age children generalize their internal models of attachment beyond the core family relationships to other people, including peers. The internal model, whether secure, defended, or coercive, becomes a kind of template the child applies to all relationships. The child who is coercive with parents is likely to be coercive with playmates; the securely attached preschooler is more likely to be altruistic or nurturant and to create more reciprocal friendships (Fagot & Pears, 1996).

The internal models also affect the way children interpret other people's behavior. For example, suppose a 4- or 5-year-old is happily drawing when along comes another child and spills paint on the drawing. Does the painter immediately assume that the paint-spiller meant harm? Or does she interpret the paint-spiller's behavior in some more neutral way—such as, "She was trying to help me" or "It was an accident"? Jude Cassidy and her colleagues (Cassidy, Kirsh, Scolton, & Parke, 1996) find that securely attached preschoolers are likely to apply benign or neutral explanations of the playmate's behavior, while insecurely attached preschoolers are more likely to assume the playmate meant some harm.

Compliance and Defiance

The preschooler's greater physical independence, which alters the child's attachment behaviors, shapes the relationship between parent and child in other ways as well. In particular, the toddler's growing insistence on autonomy brings him into more and more situations in which the parents want one thing and he wants another—precisely the sort of conflict that most of us think of as defining the "terrible twos." Yet, contrary to the popular image, 2-year-olds actually comply with parents' requests more often than not. They are more likely to comply with safety requests ("Don't touch that, it's hot!") or with prohibitions about care of objects ("Don't tear up the book"), than they are with requests to delay ("I can't talk to you now, I'm on the phone") or self-care, such as washing of hands or going to bed when requested. Still, on the whole, children this age comply fairly readily (Gralinski & Kopp, 1993). When they resist, it is most likely to be passively, by simply not doing what is asked.

Only a small percentage of the time does the child say no or actively defy the parent (Kuczynski, Kochanska, Radke-Yarrow, & Girnius-Brown, 1987). Overt refusals become more common by age 3 or 4.

Many psychologists think it is important to make a distinction between simple refusals or nay-saying ("I don't want to," or "No"), and defiance, in which the child's refusal is accompanied by anger, temper tantrums, or whining (e.g., Crockenberg & Litman, 1990). The former seems to be an important and healthy aspect of self-assertion and has been linked both to secure attachments and to greater maturity (Matas, Arend, & Sroufe, 1978). Defiance, on the other hand, has been linked to insecure attachment or to a history of abuse.

Direct defiance declines over the preschool years. We are less likely to see persistent whining, temper tantrums, or equivalent outbursts in a 6-year-old than in a 2-year-old, in part because the older child's cognitive and language skills have developed to the point where negotiation has become more possible.

Where does this then leave us in evaluating the stereotype of the "terrible twos"? It seems to be based partially on fact: Direct defiance is indeed at its peak at about age 2. On the other side of the coin are several facts: Plain refusals are more common at later ages than at age 2, and most 2-year-olds comply with adult requests most of the time. My hunch is that the impression so many parents have that their toddler is now suddenly difficult, oppositional, and negative comes in part from the simple contrast between the skills an infant brings to such interactions and the new skills of the toddler. Toddlers can *say* "NO!" They can turn their back on you and walk away. They are strong enough now to pull away from you if you try to hold on to them. Add to this the toddler's newfound awareness of his own identity (which I'll come to in a moment), and you get a mix that reinforces the common impression of toddler negativity, despite the fact that most toddlers are pretty compliant most of the time.

"No, I will not eat those peas" says this 2-year-old's body language. Toddlers and early preschoolers, like this young fellow, do indeed resist Mom and Dad more often than infants do, but the stereotype of the "terrible twos" is exaggerated for most children.

Relationships with Siblings

The family contains not just the vertical relationship with parents, but also—for many preschoolers—a highly formative type of "horizontal" relationship with brothers and sisters. In these early years, in fact, interactions with siblings may be a more important part of a child's social world than at any other age. Recent studies of sibling relationships have focused on several issues: (1) What is the nature of sibling relationships during the preschool years? (2) Why are siblings often so very different from one another? (3) What is the impact on a child of being first born or later born? Are oldest children consistently different from middle or youngest children?

The Quality of Sibling Relationships

Stories such as the tale of Cain and Abel might lead us to believe that rivalry or jealousy is the key ingredient of sibling relationships. Certainly the birth of a new brother or sister radically changes the life of the older sibling. The parents have less time for the older child, who may feel neglected and angry, leading both to more confrontations between the older child and the parents and to feelings of rivalry toward the new baby (Furman, 1995). Yet rivalry is not the only quality of these early sibling relationships; observations of preschoolers with their siblings point toward other ingredients as well. Toddlers and preschoolers help their brothers and sisters, imitate them, and share their toys. Judy Dunn (Dunn & Kendrick, 1982), in a detailed longitudinal study of a group of 40 families in England, observed that the older child often imitated a baby brother or sister; by the time the younger child was a year old, he or she began imitating the older sibling, and from then on most of the imitation flowed in that direction, with the younger child copying the older one.

At the same time, brothers and sisters also hit one another, snatch toys, threaten and insult each other. The older child in a pair of preschoolers is likely to be the leader and is therefore likely to show more of both aggressive and helpful behaviors (Abramovitch, Pepler, & Corter, 1982). For both members of the pair, however, the dominant feature seems to be ambivalence. Both supportive and negative behaviors are evident in about equal proportions. In Abramovitch's research, such ambivalence occurred whether the pair were close in age or further apart, and whether the older child

was a boy or a girl. Naturally, there are variations on this theme; some pairs show mostly antagonistic or rivalrous behaviors, while some show mostly helpful and supportive behaviors. Most sibling pairs show both types of behavior.

Why Are Siblings So Often Unlike One Another?

One apparent cause of such variations in sibling relationships seems to be the extent to which parents treat their children differently. Some of the best evidence comes from several studies by Dunn (Dunn & McGuire, 1994) in both England and the United States. She has found that parents may express warmth and pride toward one child and scorn toward another, may be lenient toward one and strict with another. Here's an example from one of Dunn's observations, of 30-month-old Andy and his 14-month-old sister, Susie.

> Andy was a rather timid and sensitive child, cautious, unconfident, and compliant. . . . Susie was a striking contrast—assertive, determined, and a handful for her mother, who was nevertheless delighted by her boisterous daughter. In [one] observation of Andy and his sister, Susie persistently attempted to grab a forbidden object on a high kitchen counter, despite her mother's repeated prohibitions. Finally, she succeeded, and Andy overheard his mother make a warm, affectionate comment on Susie's action: "Susie, you *are* a determined little devil!" Andy, sadly, commented to his mother, "I *m* not a determined little devil!" His mother replied, laughing, "No! What are you? A poor old boy!" (Dunn, 1992, p. 6)

Not only are such episodes common in family interactions, children are highly sensitive to such variations in treatment. Notice how Andy had monitored his mother's interaction with Susie, and then compared himself with his sister. Children this age are already aware of the emotional quality of exchanges between themselves and their parents as well as of the exchanges between their siblings and parents. Dunn finds that those who receive less affection and warmth from their mothers are likely to be more depressed, worried, or anxious than are their siblings. And the more differently the parents

Not exactly a joyous reaction to the birth of a baby brother! Three-year-old Mira, soothing herself by sucking her thumb, is probably feeling anxious, maybe a bit neglected. Her world has been turned upside down. These are normal feelings. In most families they don't lead to long-term rivalries. Instead, each child carves out her own niche within the family.

treat siblings, the greater the rivalry and hostility between the brothers and sisters (Brody, Stoneman, McCoy, & Forehand, 1992). When both parents favor one child over the other, the less favored child is also more likely to show significant behavior problems in other settings, such as school (McGuire, Dunn, & Plomin, 1995; Stocker, 1995).

Of course, parents treat children differently for many reasons, including the child's age. Susie's mother may be accepting of Susie's naughty behavior simply because the toddler is so young. Parents also respond to temperamental differences in the children. Whatever the causes, it now seems clear that such differences in treatment are an important ingredient in the child's emerging internal model of self, and contribute greatly to variations in behavior between children growing up in the same families.

Firstborns and Later-Borns

Children's relationships with their brothers and sisters, as well as their relationships with their parents, are also affected by where they stand in the family sequence (referred to as **birth order** or **ordinal position**). Early research suggested that birth order had, at most, very small effects. The most consistent finding was that oldest children (firstborns or onlies) are somewhat more likely to be achievement oriented. They have slightly higher IQ scores, are more likely to go on to college, and are more likely to achieve some degree of eminence as adults (Sutton-Smith, 1982). Various explanations of this slight difference have been offered, but most psychologists concluded that birth order was not the most helpful way of looking at the impact of family interaction patterns. Specific differences in the way parents treat their several children seem far more critical.

An intriguing new book by historian Frank Sulloway, *Born to Rebel* (1996), however, reopens the debate. Sulloway concludes that sibling rivalry, far from being a scientific *cul-de-sac*, is in fact the engine of history. After a detailed analysis of the lives of over 7000 historical figures as well as of many specific historical events, he finds that firstborns nearly always support the status quo while later-borns are the rebels, likely to support

new ideas or new political movements. His most central proposal is that each child must find some niche within the family configuration, some effective way to "curry parental favor." In this battle for successful niches, firstborns have a decided advantage. They are bigger and stronger and can defend the position of "biggest" or "most responsible." (My older sister used to chant at me, in that wonderful singsong voice children use to taunt one another, "I'm bigger 'n better than you, I'm bigger 'n better than you.") Firstborns, as a group, have more self-confidence and identify with authority and power. This combination allows them to achieve within the existing social system, committing them to the status quo from very early on.

Later-borns, in contrast, are automatically underdogs within the family. Sulloway argues that they are more open to experience because such an openness helps them find an unoccupied niche. Such openness also makes them more empathetic, imaginative, and independent-minded. Most explorers, heretics, and revolutionaries, according to Sulloway's research, were later-borns.

Sulloway's position is flexible enough to explain exceptions to these patterns. The key argument is that all children try to find some niche within the family. If the firstborn, perhaps because of a genetically patterned difficult temperament, becomes the family rebel, then the second child could capture the niche of the family achiever, the traditionalist. Birth order, then, is not destiny. But if Sulloway is right—and it remains for psychologists to test his theory in various ways—then birth order may turn out to give us further important clues about why children in the same family so often turn out so differently.

Relationships with Peers

The child's family experience is undeniably a central influence shaping her emerging personality and social relationships, particularly in these early years when children still spend a good portion of their time with their parents and siblings. At the same time, relationships with nonsibling peers become increasingly important over the years from 2 to 6.

Cultures and Contexts

China's One-Child Policy

A particularly fascinating cultural experiment regarding sibling effects and family size has been under way in China since 1979, when the government instituted an intense family-planning effort to reduce the normal family size to one child. This was done for economic and political reasons, since China has about twenty-one percent of the population of the world but only seven percent of the arable land. The Chinese were facing the prospect of enormous food shortages with attendant social unrest if something was not done about their population explosion. What they did was adopt a one-child policy. This policy, nowadays somewhat loosely followed in rural areas but still rigorously followed in urban areas, has had a variety of consequences, not the least of which is a sizeable number of girl babies abandoned because the culture places such a strong preference on sons. There is also some indication that girl fetuses are being deliberately aborted for the same reason. These consequences have been, and continue to be, serious problems.

At the inception of the one-child policy, the Chinese were also concerned about possible negative psychological effects of a culture full of only children (onlies). They feared that onlies would become family tyrants, spoiled by parents and grandparents. Recent studies do not confirm that fear. Toni Falbo (Falbo 1992; Falbo & Poston, 1993), an American researcher who has been involved in a series of large survey studies of Chinese children, reports that she can find few differences between only and nononly children, either in school performance or in personality. Another recent study (Yang, Ollendick, Dong, Xia, & Lin, 1995) reports, in fact, that children born after the only-child policy went into effect reported *less* fear, anxiety, and depression than did youngsters with siblings, born a few years before the one-child policy began. Thus, by the Chinese standards, the one-child policy has been a success. It has not led to a generation of "little emperors" as some had feared, although it is still early to know what effects this policy will have on the society as a whole in the decades ahead, when the only children have become adults. A culture made up of only children (with a preponderance of males) is likely to differ in a whole variety of ways, many of them unanticipated, from one in which larger families prevail. In particular, if Sulloway is right about firstborns (including onlies) being generally supportive of the status quo, then a whole culture of only children should create few pressures for societal change. An interesting thought.

Children first begin to show some positive interest in other infants as early as 6 months of age. If you place two babies that age on the floor facing each other, they will look at each other, touch, pull each other's hair, imitate each other's actions, and smile at one another. By 14 to 18 months we begin to see two or more children playing together with toys, sometimes cooperating together, sometimes simply playing side by side with different toys—a pattern Mildred Parten (1932) first described as **parallel play.** Toddlers this age express interest in one another, gazing at or making noises at each other. Only at around 18 months, however, do we begin to see much coordinated play, such as when one toddler chases another or when one imitates the other's action with some toy.

By age 3 or 4, children appear to prefer to play with peers rather than alone, and their play with one another is much more cooperative and coordinated. They build things together, play in the sand-box together, create pretend fantasies with each other. In all these interactions we see both positive and negative behaviors, both aggression and altruism (Hartup, 1992).

Aggression

The most common definition of **aggression** is behavior with the apparent intent to injure another person or object (Feshbach, 1970). Every child shows at least some behavior of this type, but the form and frequency of aggression changes over the preschool years, as you can see in the summary in Table 9.2.

When 2- or 3-year-old children are upset or frustrated, they are most likely to throw things or hit each other. As their verbal skills improve, however, they shift away from such overt physical aggression toward greater use of verbal aggression,

By age 3 most children play with one another in coordinated ways, rather than merely side by side.

Critical Thinking

Think about the groups you belong to. Do they have clear dominance hierarchies? Now imagine a group of adults coming together for the first time. Within a few weeks, a pecking order will have emerged. What determined that order? How does a dominant person establish such dominance?

such as taunting or name-calling, just as their defiance of their parents shifts from physical to verbal strategies.

The decline in physical aggression over these years also undoubtedly reflects the preschooler's declining egocentrism and increasing understanding of other children's thoughts and feelings. Yet another factor in the decline of physical aggression is the emergence of **dominance hierarchies.** As early as age 3 or 4, groups of children arrange themselves in well-understood pecking orders of leaders and followers (Strayer, 1980). They know who will win a fight and who will lose one, which children they dare attack and which ones they must submit to—knowledge that serves to reduce the actual amount of physical aggression.

A second change in the quality of aggression during the preschool years is a shift from primarily **instrumental aggression** to more **hostile aggression.** The latter is aimed at hurting another person or at gaining advantage; the former is aimed at gaining or damaging some object. So when 3-year-old Sarah pushes her playmate Doria in the sandbox in order to grab Doria's bucket, she is showing instrumental aggression. When Sarah gets angry at Doria and calls her a dummy, she is displaying hostile aggression.

Where does aggression come from? Why is it so common among children? What triggers it or controls it? Psychologists have identified several key factors.

Frustration. One early group of American psychologists (Dollard, Doob, Miller, Mowrer, & Sears, 1939) argued that aggression is always preceded by frustration and that frustration is always followed by aggression. This **frustration-aggression hypothesis** turns out to be too broadly stated; all frustration does not lead to aggression, but frustration does make aggression more likely. Toddlers

Table 9.2

Changes in the Form and Frequency of Aggression Between Ages 2 and 8

	2- to 4-year-olds	4- to 8-year-olds
Physical aggression	At its peak from 2 to 4	Declines in the period from 4 to 8
Verbal aggression	Relatively rare at 2; increases as the child's verbal skill improves	Dominant form of aggression from 4 to 8
Goal of aggression	Primarily "instrumental aggression," aimed at obtaining or damaging an object rather than directly hurting someone else	More "hostile aggression," aimed at hurting another person or another's feelings
Occasion for aggression	Most often after conflicts with parents	Most often after conflicts with peers

Sources: Goodenough, 1931; Hartup, 1974; Cummings et al., 1986.

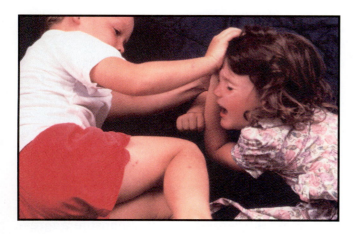

Six-year-old Christopher and his 4-year-old sister, Helen, may be less likely to get into this kind of physical fight than they were a few years ago, but clearly this kind of physical aggression does not disappear in the preschool years.

and preschoolers are often frustrated—because they cannot always do what they want and because they cannot express their needs clearly—so they often express that frustration through aggression. As the child acquires greater ability to communicate, plan, and organize her activities, her frustration level declines and overt aggression drops.

Reinforcement and Modeling. When Sarah pushes Doria away and grabs her toy, Sarah is reinforced for her aggression because she gets the toy. This straightforward effect of reinforcement clearly plays a vital role in children's development of aggressive patterns of behavior. One good example is Gerald Patterson's work, which I described in Chapter 1 (e.g., Patterson, Capaldi, & Bank, 1991). When parents give in to their young child's tantrums or aggression, they are reinforcing the very behavior they deplore, and they thereby help to establish a long-lasting pattern of aggression and defiance.

Modeling, too, plays a key role in children's learning of aggressive behaviors. Kids learn specific forms of aggression by watching other people perform them (e.g., Bandura, Ross, & Ross, 1961; 1963). As just one example, preschoolers today have learned special attack kicks from watching *Power Rangers* on television. Children also learn that aggression is an effective or approved way of solving problems by watching their parents and others behave aggressively. Indeed, parents who consistently use physical punishment with their

children have kids who are *more* aggressive than are children whose parents do not model aggression in this way (Eron, Huesmann, & Zelli, 1991)—a point I will expand on later in the chapter. When children have many different aggressive models, especially if those aggressive models appear to be rewarded for their aggression, then we should not be surprised that the child learns similar patterns of aggressive behavior. Certainly many inner-city neighborhoods in the United States appear to fit such a pattern.

Prosocial Behavior

At the other end of the spectrum of peer relationships is a set of behaviors psychologists call **prosocial behavior:** "Intentional, voluntary behavior intended to benefit another" (Eisenberg, 1992, p. 3). In everyday language, this is essentially what we mean by **altruism,** and it changes with age, just as other aspects of peer behavior change.

We first see altruistic behaviors in children of age 2 or 3—that is, at about the same time that they begin to show real interest in play with other children. They will offer to help another child who is hurt, offer a toy, or try to comfort another person (Marcus, 1986; Zahn-Waxler & Radke-Yarrow, 1982; Zahn-Waxler, Radke-Yarrow, Wagner, & Chapman, 1992). As I pointed out in the last chapter, children this young have only a beginning understanding of the fact that others feel differently from themselves, but they obviously understand enough about the emotions of others to respond in supportive and sympathetic ways when they see other children or adults hurt or sad.

After these early years, changes in prosocial behavior show a mixed pattern. Some kinds of prosocial behaviors seem to increase with age. For example, if you give children an opportunity to donate some treat to another child who is described as needy, school-age children donate more than younger children do. Helpfulness, too, seems to increase with age up through adolescence, although not all prosocial behaviors show this pattern. Comforting another child, for example, seems to be more common among preschool and early elementary school children than at older ages (Eisenberg, 1992).

Psychology in Action

Observation of Altruistic Behavior

Warning: This project, like many of the *Psychology in Action* suggestions given in this text, should not be undertaken without explicit permission and guidance from your instructor, who will have to obtain permission from your college or university's Human Subjects Review Committee for any project in which you interview or observe a child or parent directly. **Do not do this project on your own, without such permission.**

In this project, I want you to take an "anthropological" approach to an observation of preschool-age children. Your instructor will have arranged for you to observe in a preschool or other group-care setting containing children between 18 months and 4 years of age. Permission will ordinarily have been obtained through the center itself, but you will need to follow whatever process is required to obtain the appropriate informed consent.

Procedure

For this observation, assume you are a researcher who has become interested in the earliest forms of altruistic behavior in children, and further assume that there has not yet been any research on this subject. You want to begin simply by observing without any preconceived ideas about how frequently this might occur or under what circumstances.

Observe for at least two hours in a group-care setting, noting on paper in narrative form any episode that appears to you to fit some general criteria of "altruistic" or "compassionate" behavior. For each episode you will want to record the circumstances involved, the gender of the child, the approximate age of the child, the other children present, the words used (if any).

Analysis and Report

After the observation, look over your notes and try to answer the following questions:

1. What definition of altruism guided your observations? Did your definition change as a result of observing the children? Were there several types of "altruistic" actions that you observed that seem to be conceptually distinct?
2. What tentative hypotheses about the early development of altruism might you propose for further study, based on the episodes you have observed? For example: Are there hints of sex differences or age differences? Did the specific setting seem to have an effect? Was such behavior more common in pairs of children than in larger groups? Did this behavior occur primarily when one child was hurt or upset, or did it occur in other situations as well?
3. How might you test these tentative hypotheses with further research?

We also know that children vary a lot in the amount of such altruistic behavior they show, and that young children who show relatively more empathy and altruism are also those who regulate their own emotions well. They show positive emotions readily, and negative emotions less often (Eisenberg, Fabes, Murphy et al., 1996). These variations among children's level of empathy or altruism seem to be related to specific kinds of child rearing. I've translated some of the research into concrete advice in the *Parenting* box on page 300.

Friendships

Anna and Suzanne are not yet 2 years old. Their mothers became acquainted during their pregnancies and from their earliest weeks of life the little girls have visited each other's houses. When the girls were 6 months old they were enrolled in the same child care center. They now are frequent play partners, and sometimes insist that their naptime cots be placed side by side. Their greetings and play are often marked by shared smiles. Anna and Suzanne's parents and teachers identify them as friends. (Howes, 1996, p. 66)

The majority of toddlers do not yet have such individual friendships, but a few pairs show signs of specific playmate preferences as early as age 18 months. However, several studies show that, by age 3 or 4, more than half of children have at least one mutual friendship. Furthermore, the majority of these friendships last for at least six months,

Parenting

Rearing Helpful and Altruistic Children

If you want to encourage your own children to be more generous or altruistic, here are some specific things you can do, based on the work of Eisenberg and others (Eisenberg, 1992; Eisenberg & Murphy, 1995; Grusec, Goodnow, & Cohen, 1996):

1. *Capitalize on the child's capacity for empathy.* If your child injures someone else, point out the consequences of that injury for the other person: "When you hit Susan it hurts her," or "See, you made Jimmy cry." This strategy seems to be especially effective when parents use it regularly and when they don't combine it with physical punishment.

2. *Create a loving and warm family climate.* When parents express affection and warmth regularly toward their children, those children are more likely to be generous and altruistic. As a corollary, children who are securely attached are also more likely to show prosocial behavior.

3. *Provide rules or guidelines about helpful behavior.* Clear rules about what *to* do as well as what *not* to do are important—for example, "It's always good to be helpful to other people," or "We should share what we have with people who don't have so much." More direct instructions also foster prosocial behavior: "I'd like you to help Keisha with her puzzle," or "Please share your candy with John."

4. *Provide prosocial attributions.* Attribute your child's helpful or altruistic action to the child's own internal character: "You're such a helpful child!" or "You certainly do a lot of nice things for other people." This strategy begins to be effective with children

around age 7 or 8, at about the same time that they are beginning to develop global notions of self-esteem. In this way you may be able to affect the child's self scheme, which in turn may result in a generalized, internalized pattern of altruistic behavior.

5. *Have children do helpful things.* Assign your children regular household tasks. It doesn't seem to matter just what the tasks are, whether helping to cook or clean, take care of pets, or watch out for younger siblings. What matters is that the child have a regular role in everyday household routines, a pattern that seems to encourage the development of concern for others as well as a sense of responsibility. In school, too, children who have a chance to do helpful things such as tutoring younger students seem to develop more empathy and concern. This can backfire if the coercion required to get the child to do the helpful thing is too strong: The child may now attribute his "good" behavior to the coercion ("Mother made me do it") rather than to some inner trait of his own ("I am a helpful/kind person"), and no future altruism is fostered. But as a general rule, it is good for kids to practice performing helpful or generous actions.

6. *Model thoughtful and generous behavior.* Stating the rules clearly will do little good if your own behavior does not match what you say! Children (and adults) are simply much more likely to do generous or thoughtful things if they see other people performing those same actions, especially other people in authority such as parents.

---

many of them for far longer (Dunn, 1993; Howes, 1996).

To be sure, these early "friendships" are not nearly as deep or intimate as what we see among school-age or adolescent friend pairs. Toddler friends ignore one another's bids for interaction as often as not, and when they play together it is mostly around common toys. Still, these preschool friend pairs show unmistakable signs that their relationship is more than merely a passing fancy. They display more mutual liking, more reciprocity, more extended interactions, more positive and less negative behavior, more forgiveness, and more

supportiveness in a novel situation than is true between nonfriend pairs at this same age. Friends may actually quarrel more than nonfriends, but when they quarrel, preschool friends are more likely than are nonfriends to try to patch it up (Dunn, 1993; Hartup, Laursen, Stewart, & Eastenson, 1988).

There is every reason to believe that play with such a friend is a highly important arena for children to practice a whole host of social skills. As John Gottman says, in order to play collaboratively, friends "must coordinate their efforts with all the virtuosity of an accomplished jazz quartet"

Psychologists used to think that preschoolers were simply not capable of real friendships. Now we know that, by age 3 or 4, about half of preschoolers have at least one individual friend—like this pair.

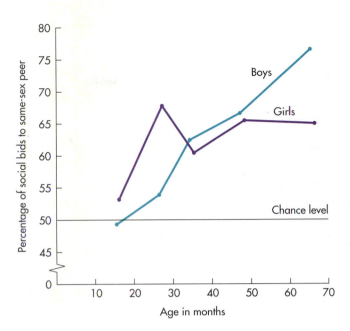

Figure 9.1

Same-sex playmate preference among preschoolers. (Source: La Freniere, Strayer, & Gauthier, 1984. Figure 1, p. 1961. Copyright by The Society for Research in Child Development, Inc.)

(1986, p. 3). Often, they must subdue their own desires in the interests of joint play, which requires not only some awareness of the other's feelings and wishes, but an ability to modulate one's own emotions. You already know that these cognitive and control skills emerge during the preschool years; what the research on friendships tells us is that play with peers, especially play with friends, may be a crucial ingredient in that development.

One of the really intriguing facts about such early friendships is that they are more likely between same-sex pairs, even among children as young as age 2 or 3. John Gottman (1986) reports that perhaps 65 percent of friendships in preschool children in the United States are with a same-sex peer. Social interactions with children other than the chosen friend(s) are also more likely to be with children of the same sex, beginning as early as age 2½ or 3 (Maccoby, 1988; 1990; Maccoby & Jacklin, 1987). By school age, peer relationships are almost exclusively same-sex.

You can see the early development of this preference in Figure 9.1, which shows the results of a study of preschool play groups by La Freniere, Strayer, and Gauthier (1984). By age 3, 60 percent of play groups were same-sex groupings and the rate rose from there.

[?] *Critical Thinking*

How many explanations can you think of for the fact that children begin to prefer to play with same-sex peers as early as age 3 or 4?

Sex Differences in Social Interactions. Not only are preschoolers' friendships and peer interactions increasingly sex-segregated, it is also becoming clear that boy-boy interactions and girl-girl interactions differ in quality, even in these early years. Eleanor Maccoby, one of the leading theorists in this area (1990), describes the girls' pattern as an *enabling style.* Enabling includes such behaviors as supporting the partner, expressing agreement, and making suggestions. All these behaviors tend to foster a greater equality and intimacy in the relationship and keep the interaction going. In contrast, boys are more likely to show what Maccoby calls a *constricting* or *restrictive* style. "A restrictive style is one that tends to derail the interaction—to inhibit the partner or cause the partner to withdraw, thus shortening the interaction or bringing it to an end" (1990, p. 517). Contradicting, interrupting, boasting, or other forms of self-display are all aspects of this style. You can get some sense of the difference from two examples drawn from Campbell Leaper's observations of pairs of previously unacquainted 7-year-olds, given in Table 9.3 (Leaper, 1991). Leaper's labels for these two exchanges are *cooperative* and *domineering*, but they seem clearly to match Maccoby's distinction between enabling and restrictive styles.

These two patterns begin to be visible in the preschool years. For example, Maccoby (1990) points out that beginning as early as age 3 or 4, boys and girls use quite different strategies in their attempts to influence each other's behavior. Girls generally ask questions or make requests; boys are much more likely to make demands or phrase things using imperatives ("Give me that!"). The really intriguing finding is that even at this early age, boys simply don't comply very much to the girls' style of influence attempt. So playing with boys yields little positive reinforcement for girls, and they begin to avoid such interactions and band together.

Similar differences in relationship style are evident in older children and adults. Girls and women have more intimate relationships with their friends. And in pairs or groups, girls and women seem to focus their attention on actions that will keep the interaction going. Adult men are more likely to be task oriented, women to be relationship oriented. I'll have more to say about these differences in later chapters. For now I only want to point out that these subtle and profound differences seem to begin very early in childhood (Buhrmester, 1996).

[?] *Critical Thinking*

Do your observations of adult relationships match the distinction Maccoby is making here? What do you think happens when one man and one woman interact in some nonromantic encounter? Is the resulting style some combination of enabling and constricting, or does one style dominate?

How might such differences arise so early? We are a long way from being able to answer that question. Still, we do know more and more about how a child figures out whether he is a boy or she is a girl,

---

Table 9.3

Examples of Enabling and Constricting Styles of Interaction

Girls' Interaction		Boys' Interaction	
Jennifer	Let's go play on the slide [sliding noises].	Andy	Mm, I don't like this.
Sally	Okay [sliding noises].	Patrick	[4 sec. silence; coughs, laughs]
	I'll do a choo-choo train with you.	Andy	Do this.
Jennifer	Okay.	Patrick	[4 sec. silence]
Sally	You can go first.	Andy	Do this.
Jennifer	Ch (gasp).	Patrick	I wish I could go.
Sally	Ch (gasp).	Andy	Do this. Kick your chair [kicking sounds]. Kick your chair!
		Patrick	I can't.
		Andy	Mm huh (sigh).
		Patrick	[7 sec. silence]

Source: Leaper, 1991, from Tables 2 and 3, p. 800.

an understanding that is, in turn, part of the more general emergence of the preschool child's sense of self.

The Emergence of the Sense of Self

When we left the 18- to 24-month-old in Chapter 6, he was beginning to understand that he is an object in the world with properties and qualities. By age 6 a child can give you quite a full description of himself on a whole range of dimensions. Still, these early self-definitions remain highly concrete. For example, Susan Harter (Harter, 1987; 1990; Harter & Pike, 1984) has found that children between 4 and 7 have clear notions of their own competence on a whole range of specific tasks, such as solving puzzles, counting, knowing a lot in school, climbing or skipping or jumping rope, or being able to make friends. However, these separate aspects of the **self scheme**—or internal working model of the self—have not yet coalesced into a global assessment of self-worth. For this reason, Harter argues that it is not appropriate to say of a preschooler that she has high or low self-esteem. She may have a high or low opinion of her ability to do some specific task or her ability to relate to others in specific situations, but high or low self-esteem in a more global sense does not seem to emerge until about age 7.

The self-concept of a preschool child is concrete in another way as well; he tends to focus on his own visible characteristics—whether he's a boy or girl, what he looks like, what or who he plays with, where he lives, what he is good or bad at doing—rather than on more enduring, inner qualities. This pattern obviously parallels what we see in cognitive development at the same ages; it is in these same years that children's attention tends to be focused on the external appearance of objects rather than on their enduring properties.

The Social Self. Another facet of the child's emerging sense of self is an increasing awareness of himself as a player in the social game. By age 2 the toddler has already learned a variety of social "scripts," that is, routines of play or interaction with others in her world. Case (1991) points out that the

toddler now begins to develop some implicit understanding of her own roles in these scripts. So she begins to think of herself as a "helper" in some situations or as "the boss" when she is telling some other child what to do. You can see this clearly in children's sociodramatic play, as they begin to take explicit roles: "I'll be the daddy and you be the mommy," or "I'm the teacher." As part of the same process, the preschool child also gradually understands her place in the network of family roles. She has sisters, brothers, father, mother, and so on.

The Gender Concept and Sex Roles

One of the most fascinating aspects of the preschool child's emerging sense of self is the development of a sense of gender. The child has several related tasks. On the cognitive side, she must learn the nature of the gender category itself—that boyness or girlness is permanent and unchanged by such things as modifications in clothing or hair length. This understanding is usually called the **gender concept.** On the social side, she has to learn what behaviors go with being a boy or a girl. That is, she must learn the **sex role** appropriate for her gender.

The Development of the Gender Concept. How soon does a child figure out that she is a girl or he is a boy? It depends on what we mean by "figure

Through their pretend play, Lucy and Rachel, at age 3, are not only learning about how to interact with a peer, they are also rehearsing various social scripts.

out." The earliest understanding is **gender identity,** which is simply a child's ability to label his own sex correctly and to identify other people as men or women, boys or girls. By 9 to 12 months, babies already treat male and female faces as if they were different categories (Fagot & Leinbach, 1993). Within the next year, they begin to learn the verbal labels that go with these categories. By age 2, if you show them a set of pictures of a same-sex child and several opposite-sex children and say "Which one is you?," most children can correctly pick out the same-sex picture (Thompson, 1975). By 2½ or 3, the majority of children can correctly label and identify the sex of others as well by pointing out "which one is a girl" or "which one is a boy" in a set of pictures (Fagot & Leinbach, 1989).

Accurate labeling, though, does not signify complete understanding. The child must also figure out that each person stays the same gender throughout life, called **gender stability.** Researchers have measured this by asking children such questions as "When you were a little baby, were you a little girl or a little boy?" or "When you grow up, will you be a mommy or a daddy?" Slaby and Frey, in their classic study (1975) found that most children understand this aspect of gender by age 4 or so.

The final component is the understanding that someone stays the same biological gender even though he may appear to change by wearing different clothes or changing his hair length, usually referred to as **gender constancy.** For example, boys

Even at age 2 these children have the beginning of a gender concept: They can correctly identify their own gender and that of other children.

don't change into girls by wearing dresses. This is an appearance/reality problem very much like Flavell's sponge/rock test I described in the last chapter. The child must figure out that although a boy wearing a dress may *look like* a girl, he is *really* still a boy, just as the sponge painted to look like a rock may *look like* a rock but is *really* still a sponge. When children are asked the question in this way, many 4-year-olds and most 5-year-olds can answer correctly, just as 4- and 5-year-olds understand other appearance/reality distinctions (Martin & Halverson, 1983). Sandra Bem has found that to reach this level of understanding a child must have at least some grasp of the basic genital differences between boys and girls and some understanding that genital characteristics are what makes you "really" a boy or a girl. In her study (Bem, 1989), 4-year-olds who did not yet understand genital differences also did not show gender constancy.

In sum, children as young as 2 or 2½ know their own sex and that of people around them, but they do not have a fully developed concept of gender until they are 4 or 5.

The Development of Sex-Role Concepts and Stereotypes.

Figuring out your gender and understanding that it stays constant is only part of the story. Learning what goes with, or ought to go with, being a boy or a girl is also a vital part of the child's task.

In every culture adults have clear sex-role stereotypes. Indeed, the content of those stereotypes is remarkably similar in cultures around the world. John Williams and Deborah Best (1990), who have studied gender stereotypes in 28 different countries, including non-Western countries such as Thailand, Pakistan, and Nigeria, find that the most clearly stereotyped traits are weakness, gentleness, appreciativeness, and softheartedness for women, and aggression, strength, cruelty, and coarseness for men. In most cultures, men are also seen as competent, skillful, assertive, and able to get things done, while women are seen as warm and expressive, tactful, quiet, gentle, aware of others' feelings, and lacking in competence, independence, and logic.

Studies of children show that these stereotyped ideas develop early, even in families that espouse gender equality. The 3-year-old daughter of an egalitarian-minded friend announced one day that mommies use the stove and daddies use the grill. Even 2-year-olds already associate certain tasks and possessions with men and women, such as vacuum cleaners and food with women and cars and tools with men. By age 3 or 4, children can assign occupations, toys, and activities to the stereotypic gender. (Another friend told me the story of a 4-year-old who came home from nursery school one day insisting that doctors were always men and nurses were always women—even though his own father was a nurse!) By age 5, children begin to associate certain personality traits with males or females, and such knowledge is well developed by age 8 or 9 (Martin, 1993; Serbin, Powlishta, & Gulko, 1993).

Studies of children's ideas about how men and women (or boys and girls) *ought* to behave add an interesting further element. An early study by William Damon (1977) illustrates the point particularly nicely. He told a story to children ages 4 through 9 about a little boy named George who likes to play with dolls. George's parents tell him that only little girls play with dolls; little boys shouldn't. The children were then asked a batch of questions about this, such as "Why do people tell George not to play with dolls?" or "Is there a rule that boys shouldn't play with dolls?"

Four-year-olds in this study thought it was okay for George to play with dolls. There was no rule against it, and he should do it if he wanted to. Six-year-olds, in contrast, thought it was *wrong* for

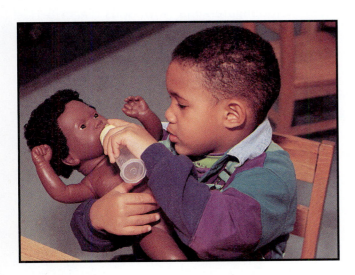

Four-year-olds and 9-year-olds are likely to think it's okay if a boy plays with dolls, but many 6-year-olds think it is simply wrong for boys to do girl things or for girls to do boy things.

George to play with dolls. By about age 9, children had differentiated between what boys and girls usually do and what is "wrong." One boy said, for example, that breaking windows was wrong and bad, but that playing with dolls was not bad in the same way: "Breaking windows you're not supposed to do. And if you play with dolls, well you can, but boys usually don't."

What seems to be happening is that the 5- and 6-year-old, having figured out that gender is permanent, is searching for a *rule* about how boys and girls behave (Martin & Halverson, 1981). The child picks up information from watching adults, from television, from listening to the labels that are attached to different activities (e.g., "Boys don't cry"). Initially, children treat these as absolute, moral rules. Later, they understand that these are social conventions, at which point sex-role concepts become more flexible and stereotyping declines somewhat (Katz & Ksansnak, 1994). In a similar way, many kinds of fixed, biased ideas about other people—such as bias against obese children, against those who speak another language, or against those of other races—are at their peak in the early school years and then decline throughout the remaining years of childhood and into adolescence (Doyle & Aboud, 1995; Powlishta, Serbin, Doyle, & White, 1994). Another way to put it is that children this age have a strong sense of "us" versus "them," of ingroup versus outgroup. They see other children as "like me" or "not like me" on whatever dimension, they develop strong preferences for those who are like themselves and highly stereotyped ideas about those who are "not like them." In the same way, and for the same reason, minority children begin to show strong preferences for those of their own ethnic group only at about age 7 or 8 (Aboud & Doyle, 1995). This entire process is totally normal, part of the child's attempt to create rules and order, to find patterns that can guide his understanding and his behavior. Just as a 2- or 3-year-old discovers the rule of adding -ed to a verb (in English) to make the past tense and overgeneralizes that rule, so the 6- or 7-year-old discovers the "rules" about boys and girls, men and women, "us" and "them," and overgeneralizes. In fact, most 6- and 7-year-olds believe that gender-role differences are determined by nature rather than nurture. By age 9 they understand that at least some differences in behavior between boys and girls are the result of training or experience rather than being built in (M. Taylor, 1996).

[?] *Critical Thinking*

In Western cultures it is far more common for young girls to be "tomboys" than it is for boys to show "girlish" behavior. Does this mean girls have a less clear gender concept? What do you think might be causing such a difference?

By age 2 or 3 we already see clear sex differences in children's toy choices. Left to their own devices, boys like this will select blocks or trucks to play with. Girls the same age are more likely to choose dolls or tea sets or dress-up clothes.

The Development of Sex-Role Behavior. The final element in the equation is the actual behavior children show with their own and with the opposite sex. The unexpected finding here is that children's behavior is sex-typed *before* they have developed clear ideas about gender differences or sex roles.

By 18 to 24 months children begin to show some preference for sex-stereotyped toys, such as dolls for girls or trucks or building blocks for boys, which is some months *before* they can consistently identify their own gender (O'Brien, 1992). By age 3, children begin to show a preference for same-sex playmates and are much more sociable with playmates of the same sex—at a time when many do not yet have a concept of gender stability (Maccoby, 1988; 1990; Maccoby & Jacklin, 1987).

The other intriguing pattern is that children in early elementary school seem to begin to pay more attention to the behavior of same-sex than opposite-sex adults or playmates, and to play more with new toys that are labeled as being appropriate for their own sex (e.g., Bradbard, Martin, Endsley, & Halverson, 1986). Overall then, we see many signs that children are both aware of and affected by gender from very early on, perhaps by age 1, certainly by age 2. Gender becomes a still more potent force in guiding behavior and attitudes at around age 5 or 6.

Explaining Sex-Role Development. Theorists from most of the major traditions have tried their hand at explaining these patterns of development. Freud relied on the concept of identification to explain the child's adoption of appropriate sex-role

behavior, but his theory founders on the fact that children begin to show clearly sex-typed behavior long before age 4 or 5, when Freud thought identification occurred.

Social learning theorists such as Bandura (1977a) and Mischel (1966; 1970) have naturally emphasized the role of parents in shaping children's sex-role behavior and attitudes. This model has been far better supported by research than have Freud's ideas. Parents do seem to reinforce sex-typed activities in children as young as 18 months old, not only by buying different kinds of toys for boys and girls but also by responding more positively when their sons play with blocks or trucks or when their daughters play with dolls (Fagot & Hagan, 1991; Lytton & Romney, 1991). Such differential reinforcement is particularly clear with boys, especially from fathers (Siegal, 1987). Some evidence also suggests that toddlers whose parents are more consistent in rewarding sex-typed toy choice or play behavior, and whose mothers favor traditional family sex roles, learn accurate gender labels earlier than do toddlers whose parents are less focused on the gender appropriateness of the child's play (Fagot & Leinbach, 1989; Fagot, Leinbach, & O'Boyle, 1992)—findings clearly consistent with the predictions of social-learning theory.

Cross-cultural evidence also supports a social-learning view. Anthropologist Beatrice Whiting (Whiting & Edwards, 1988), after examining patterns of gender socialization in 11 different cultures, concludes that "we are the company we keep." In most cultures, girls and boys keep different company, beginning quite early, with girls spending more time with women as well as in child-care responsibilities. To the extent that this is true, it would provide each sex with more same-sex than opposite-sex models and more opportunity for reinforcement of sex-appropriate behavior, such as nurturance directed at younger siblings.

Still, helpful as it is, a social-learning explanation is probably not sufficient. In particular, parents differentially reinforce boy behavior versus girl behavior less than you'd expect, and probably not enough in any case to account for the very early and robust discrimination children seem to make on the basis of gender (Fagot, 1995). Even children whose parents seem to treat their young sons and daughters in highly similar ways nonetheless learn gender labels and show same-sex playmate choices.

A third alternative, based strongly on Piagetian theory, is Lawrence Kohlberg's suggestion that the crucial aspect of the process is the child's understanding of the gender concept (Kohlberg, 1966; Kohlberg & Ullian, 1974). Once the child realizes that he is a boy or she is a girl forever, she or he becomes highly motivated to learn how to behave in the way that is expected or appropriate for that gender. Specifically, Kohlberg predicted that we should see systematic same-sex imitation only *after* the child has developed full gender constancy. Most studies designed to test this hypothesis have supported Kohlberg. Children do seem to become much more sensitive to same-sex models after they have understood gender constancy (Frey & Ruble, 1992). Yet Kohlberg's theory cannot handle the obvious fact that children show clear differential sex-role behavior, such as toy preferences, long before they have achieved full understanding of the gender concept.

The most fruitful current explanation is usually called **gender schema** theory (Bem, 1981; Martin, 1991; Martin & Halverson, 1981). Just as the self-concept can be thought of as a "scheme" or a "self theory," so the child's understanding of gender can be seen in the same way. The gender schema begins to develop as soon as the child notices the differences between male and female, knows his own gender, and can label the two groups with some consistency—all of which happens by age 2 or 3.

But why would children notice gender so early? Why is it such a salient category? One possibility, suggested by Maccoby, is that because gender is clearly an either/or category, children seem to understand very early that this is a key distinction, so the category serves as a kind of magnet for new information (Maccoby, 1988). Another alternative is that young children pay a lot of attention to gender differences because our culture is chockablock with gender references. Adults and other children emphasize gender distinctions in innumerable small ways. The first question we ask about a new baby is, "Is it a boy or a girl?" We buy blue baby clothes for boys and pink for girls; we ask toddlers about whether their playmates are boys or girls. A teacher emphasizes gender if she says "Good morning, boys and girls," or divides a group of preschoolers into a boys' team and a girls' team (Bigler, 1995). In all these ways, we signal to the child that this is an important category and thus further the very early development of a gender scheme that matches our cultural norms and beliefs. Whatever the origin of this early scheme, once it is established, a great many experiences are assimilated to it and children may begin to show preference for same-sex playmates or for gender-stereotyped activities (Martin & Little, 1990).

Preschoolers first learn some broad distinctions about what kinds of activities or behavior go with each gender, both by observing other children and through the reinforcements they receive from parents. They also learn a few gender "scripts"—whole sequences of events that normally go with a given gender, such as "fixing dinner" or "building with tools" (Levy & Fivush, 1993)—just as they learn other social scripts at about this age. Then, between ages 4 and 6, the child learns a more subtle and complex set of associations for his or her *own* gender—what children of his own gender like and don't like, how they play, how they talk, what kinds of people they associate with. Not until ages 8 to 10 does the child develop an equivalently complex view of the opposite gender (Martin, Wood, & Little, 1990).

The key difference between this theory and Kohlberg's is that for the initial gender schema to be formed, the child need not understand that gender is permanent. When gender constancy is understood at about 5 or 6, children develop a more elaborated rule or schema of "what people who are like me do" and treat this "rule" the same way they treat other rules—as absolutes. Later, the child's application of the "gender rule" becomes more flexible. She knows, for example, that most boys don't play with dolls, but that they *can* do so if they like.

The Development of Self-Control

Along with a self-concept, the preschooler must also develop another aspect of the self—self-control. Toddlers live in the here and now. When they want something, they want it immediately. When they are tired, they cry; when they are hungry, they insist on food. They are bad at waiting or at working toward distant goals and find it hard to resist temptation. There is a joyous side to this same quality: Because they live in the moment, they see things with new eyes—the bug on a leaf, the color of a particular flower, the delight in a favored food. But to function as acceptable social beings, they must learn self-control.

One aspect of this is the ability to modulate or regulate emotional expressions and emotion-based behavior (Dunn, 1994). When an infant is upset, it is the parents who help to regulate that emotion by cuddling or soothing or by removing the baby from the problem situation. With toddlers, parents help the child's control by giving instructions or prohibitions. Through the preschool years, this regulation process is taken over more and more by the child as the various prohibitions and instructions are internalized. Two-year-olds are only minimally able to modulate their feelings or behavior in this way, but by age 5 or 6 most children have made great strides in controlling the intensity of their expression of strong feelings—they don't, for example, automatically hit someone or something when they are angry, or cry inconsolably when they are frustrated, or sulk when they are denied (Sroufe, 1996). These are important skills, not just for the people who live with the child, but also for the children themselves. Indeed, we can think of them as aspects of what Daniel Goleman calls *emotional intelligence*—described in a *Research Report* in the last chapter (p. 280). Children who do *not* learn to control their emotional expression have more difficulty getting along in school at later ages (e.g., Eisenberg, Fabes, Guthrie et al., 1996).

One thing that makes it easier for parents to help their children learn self-control is that the preschooler's language is so vastly improved. Parents of 2- and 3-year-olds can begin to explain and give rules for behavior rather than simply saying no or removing the child from the situation. Not all parents provide such explanations, but it clearly helps to do so. Parents who explain why a child should or should not behave in some way (e.g., "sit down before you fall and hurt yourself") have children with better self-control; when parents instead express mostly irritation and anger, or give prohibitions without any explanation, their children are more defiant, more aggressive, and less compliant (Belsky, Woodworth, & Crnic, 1996). Good self-control and internalization of rules and standards are also fostered by the same kinds of family interactions that foster secure attachments in the first year of life: parental warmth, sensitivity, responsiveness, and child-centered methods of control (e.g., Kochanska, 1997).

Learning the Rules of Emotional Expression. Another aspect of the modulation of emotion is the learning of the social rules of specific emotional expressions. When and where is it permissible to express various feelings? What form may that expression take? When should you smile? When should you *not* frown or smile, regardless of the feeling you may be experiencing? For example, as early as age 3, children begin to learn that there are times when they ought to smile—even when they do not feel completely happy. Thus begins the "social smile," a facial expression that is quite distinct from the natural, delighted smile. Similarly, over the years of childhood, children learn to use abbreviated or constricted forms of other emotions, such as anger or disgust (Izard & Malatesta, 1987), and they learn to conceal their feelings in a variety of situations—a skill that may be particularly evident among children with a pattern of defended attachment. In all children such concealment appears to rest on the child's emerging theory of mind. For example, for a child to conceal some emotion in order not to hurt someone else's feelings requires that she have some sense of what will cause the other person's feelings to be hurt. Equally, the preschool child (perhaps especially the child with a coercive attachment pattern) learns to use her own emotional expression to get things she wants, by

This young fellow is still at an age when he needs Mom's help to handle his strong feelings. By school age he may still need help when his feelings are very strong, but most of the time he'll be able to control fairly well how he expresses his feelings.

crying or smiling as needed—a skill obviously based at least in part on her growing awareness that other people will judge her feelings by what they see her expressing.

[?] *Critical Thinking*

See if you can articulate five or ten rules about emotional expression that govern your own behavior. When do you smile? When should you not smile?

Individual Differences

So far I've been talking primarily about shared developmental patterns. But I am sure it is obvious to you that in the preschool years, children's relation-

ships, social behavior, and personalities become even more divergent than was true among infants. Some toddlers and preschoolers are tractable, compliant, and easy to handle; others are highly aggressive, defiant, and difficult to manage (Campbell & Ewing, 1990; Patterson et al., 1991). Some are shy and retiring while others are sociable and outgoing. These differences obviously have a variety of sources. Inborn temperament clearly plays some role, as does the security or insecurity of the child's first attachment, as you have already seen in Chapter 6. Yet another causal element seems to be the parents' style of child rearing—the way they deal with the need to discipline and control the child, the extent to which they show affection and warmth, the contingency of their responses. I've touched on these variations several times in this chapter and in earlier chapters, but it is time to make the differences more explicit.

Temperament Differences

As I mentioned in Chapter 6, variations in the child's temperament, such as "easiness" or "difficultness" or "inhibition," are reasonably stable over infancy, toddlerhood, and later ages. By preschool we also begin to see a link between difficultness of temperament and both concurrent and future behavior problems: Three- or 4-year-olds with difficult temperaments have more problems learning self-control and are more likely to show heightened aggressiveness, delinquency, or other forms of behavior problems in school, as teenagers, and as adults (Bates, 1989; Caspi, Henry, McGee, Moffitt, & Silva, 1995; Chess & Thomas, 1984; Newman, Caspi, Moffitt, & Silva, 1997). It is important to understand, though, that this is a statement about *probability*. The majority of preschoolers who are classed as having difficult temperaments do *not* develop later behavior problems, although the likelihood of such an outcome is greater. Perhaps the easiest way to think of it is that a difficult temperament creates a *vulnerability* in the child. If this vulnerable child has supportive and loving parents who are able to deal effectively with the child's difficultness, the trajectory is altered and the child does not develop broader behavior problems. But if the parents do not like the child, if they lack suitable child rearing skills, or if the family is facing other stresses, the

Temperament, whether we think of it as difficultness versus easiness or as gregariousness versus shyness, makes a difference for preschool children and for their future. Kids with a more difficult temperament are more likely to have trouble getting along with peers and to show behavior problems in elementary school or adolescence.

vulnerable, difficult child is highly likely to emerge from the preschool years with serious problems relating to others (Bates, 1989; Fish, Stifter, & Belsky, 1991).

The Impact of the Family: Styles of Parenting

The research on temperament gives us but one of many illustrations of the importance of understanding the family's role in the child's emerging personality or social behavior. Psychologists have struggled over the years to identify the best ways of describing the many dimensions along which families may vary. At the moment, the most fruitful conceptualization is one offered by Diana Baumrind (1972), who focuses on four aspects of family functioning: (1) warmth or nurturance; (2) level of expectations, which she describes in terms of "maturity demands"; (3) the clarity and consistency of rules; and (4) communication between parent and child.

Each of these four dimensions has been independently shown to be related to various child behaviors. Children with nurturant and warm parents, as opposed to those with more rejecting parents, are more securely attached in the first two years of life, have higher self-esteem, are more empathetic, more altruistic, more responsive to others' hurts or distress, have higher IQ scores in preschool and elementary school, do better in school, and are less likely to show delinquent behavior in adolescence or criminal behavior in adulthood (e.g., Maccoby, 1980; Maughan, Pickles, & Quinton, 1995; Simons,

Robertson, & Downs, 1989). High levels of affection can even buffer the child against the negative effects of otherwise disadvantageous environments. Several studies of children and teens growing up in poor, tough neighborhoods show that the single ingredient that most clearly distinguishes the lives of those who do *not* become delinquent from those who do is a high level of maternal love (Glueck & Glueck, 1972; McCord, 1982). In contrast, parental hostility is linked to declining school performance and higher risk of delinquency (Melby & Conger, 1996).

The degree and clarity of the parents' control over the child is also significant. Parents with clear rules, consistently applied, have children who are much less likely to be defiant or noncompliant—a pattern you'll remember from Gerald Patterson's research (Figure 1.2, p. 17). Such children are also more competent and sure of themselves (Kurdek & Fine, 1994) and less aggressive (Patterson, 1980). This same link between good parental control and positive outcomes for the child has been found among African-American as well as Euro-American youth. As one example, Craig Mason and his colleagues (Mason, Cauce, Gonzales, & Hiraga, 1996) found that among working-class black families, those in which the parents maintained the most consistent monitoring and control over their adolescents had teenagers who were least likely to show problem behavior. Interestingly and importantly, the link between parental control and lower rates of problem behavior in Mason's study was especially clear in cases in which the child had many peers who were engaging in problem behavior.

Thus the parents, by applying consistent rules and monitoring the child's activities, could at least partially counteract the negative effects of hanging out with problem peers.

Equally important is the *form* of control the parent uses. The most optimal outcomes for the child occur when the parent is not overly restrictive, explains things to the child, and avoids the use of physical punishments such as spanking—a control strategy I've discussed in the *Parenting* box on page 312.

We also find more optimal outcomes for children whose parents have high expectations, high "maturity demands" in Baumrind's language. Such children have higher self-esteem, show more generosity and altruism toward others, and show lower levels of aggression.

Finally, open and regular communication between parent and child has been linked to more positive outcomes. Listening to the child is as important as talking. Ideally, the parent needs to convey to the child that what the child has to say is *worth* listening to, that his ideas are important and should be considered in family decisions. Children from such families have been found to be more emotionally and socially mature (Baumrind, 1971; Bell & Bell, 1982).

While each of these characteristics of families may be significant individually, in fact they do not occur in isolation. They occur in combinations and patterns. Baumrind initially identified three such patterns or styles:

- The **authoritarian parental style** is high in control and maturity demands but low in nurturance and communication;
- The **permissive parental style** is high in nurturance but low in maturity demands, control, and communication; and
- The **authoritative parental style** is high in all four.

Eleanor Maccoby and John Martin (1983) proposed a variation of Baumrind's category system, shown in Figure 9.2, that I find even more helpful. They categorize families on two dimensions: the degree of demand or control and the amount of acceptance versus rejection. The intersection of these two dimensions creates four types, three of which

Figure 9.2

Maccoby and Martin expanded on Baumrind's categories in this two-dimensional typology. (Source: Adapted from Maccoby & Martin, 1983, Figure 2, p. 39.)

correspond quite closely to Baumrind's authoritarian, permissive, and authoritative types. Maccoby and Martin's conceptualization adds a fourth type, the uninvolved or **neglecting parental style,** which current research tells us may be the most detrimental of the four. Let me talk briefly about the effects of each style.

The Authoritarian Type. Children growing up in authoritarian families—with high levels of demand and control but relatively low levels of warmth or responsiveness—do less well in school, have lower self-esteem, and are typically less skilled with peers than are children from other types of families. Some of these children appear subdued; others may show high aggressiveness or other indications of being out of control.

Which of these two outcomes occurs may depend in part on how skillfully the parents use the various disciplinary techniques. Patterson finds that the "out of control" child is most likely to come from a family in which the parents are authoritarian by inclination but lack the skills to enforce the limits or rules they set.

These effects are not restricted to preschool-age children. In a series of large studies of high school students, including longitudinal studies of more than 6000 teens, Laurence Steinberg and Sanford Dornbusch and their coworkers (Dornbusch, Ritter, Liederman, Roberts, & Fraleigh, 1987; Lamborn, Mounts, Steinberg, & Dornbusch, 1991; Steinberg, Darling, Fletcher, Brown, & Dornbusch, 1995; Steinberg, Lamborn, Dornbusch, & Darling, 1992; Steinberg, Lamborn, Darling, Mounts, &

Parenting

To Spank or Not to Spank

There is a law in Sweden against physical punishment of children (Palmérus & Scarr, 1995). No such law exists in the United States, and nine out of ten parents of preschoolers say that they spank their children at least occasionally, most often in response to some aggressive act by the child (Holden, Coleman, & Schmidt, 1995). About half of parents of teenagers also report spanking their children (Straus, 1991a; Straus & Donnelly, 1993). Most of these parents think of spanking as an effective way of discipline. I think they are wrong. Let me tell you why.

Note please: I am not talking here about physical abuse, although certainly some parents do abuse their children by spanking excessively with a switch or a belt or fists. I'm talking about the ordinary kind of spanking that most people think of as normal and helpful: Two or three hard swats on the rear or (more likely with older children) a quick slap.

In the short term, spanking a child usually *does* get the child to stop the particular behavior you didn't like, and it seems to have a *temporary* effect of reducing the chance that the child will repeat the bad behavior. Since that's what you wanted, it may seem like a good strategy, but even in the short term there are some negative side effects. The child may have stopped misbehaving, but after a spanking he is likely to be crying, which may be almost as distressing as the original misbehavior. And crying is a behavior that spanking does not decrease: It is virtually impossible to get children to stop crying by spanking them! So you have exchanged one unpleasantness for another, and the second unpleasantness (crying) can't be dealt with by using the same form of punishment.

Another short-term side effect is that *you* are being negatively reinforced for spanking whenever the child stops misbehaving after you spank her. Thus you are being "trained" to use spanking the next time, and a cycle is being created.

In the longer term, the effects are clearly negative. First, when you spank, the child observes you using physical force or violence as a method of solving problems or getting people to do what you want. You thus serve as a model for a behavior you do *not* want your child to use with others. Second, by repeatedly pairing your presence with the unpleasant or painful event of spanking, you are undermining your own positive value for your child. Over time, this means that you are less able to use *any* kind of reinforcement effectively. Eventually, even your praise or affection will be less powerful in influencing your child's behavior. That is a very high price to pay.

Third, spanking frequently carries a strong underlying emotional message—namely, anger, rejection, irritation, and dislike of the child. Even very young children read this emotional message quite clearly (Rohner, Kean, & Cournoyer, 1991). Spanking therefore helps to create a family climate of rejection instead of warmth, with all the attendant negative consequences.

Dornbusch, 1994) have found that teenagers from authoritarian families have poorer grades in school and more negative self-concepts than do teenagers from authoritative families.

The Permissive (or Indulgent) Type. Children growing up with indulgent or permissive parents also show some negative outcomes. Steinberg and Dornbusch find that they do slightly worse in school during adolescence, are likely to be more aggressive—particularly if the parents are specifically permissive toward aggressiveness—and to be somewhat immature in their behavior with peers and in school. They are less likely to take responsibility and are less independent.

[?] Critical Thinking

It is somewhat surprising that children reared in permissive families are *less* independent and take *less* responsibility. You might think that such children have been specifically encouraged and reinforced for independence and decision making. Can you think of any reason why this pattern of results might occur?

The Authoritative Type. The most consistently positive outcomes have been associated with an authoritative pattern in which the parents are high in both control and warmth, setting clear limits but also responding to the child's individual needs.

Parenting

To Spank or Not to Spank (*Continued*)

Finally, we have research evidence that children who are spanked—just like children who are abused—at later ages show higher levels of aggression and less popularity with their peers, lower self-esteem, more emotional instability, higher rates of depression and distress, and higher levels of delinquency and later criminality (Laub & Sampson, 1995; Rohner et al., 1991; Strassberg, Dodge, Pettit, & Bates, 1994; Turner & Finkelhor, 1996). Further, as adults, children who have been spanked are more likely to be depressed than are those who were never or rarely spanked (Straus, 1995); they also have higher risks of various other types of adult problems, including problems holding a job, divorce or violence within a relationship, and criminality (Maughan et al., 1995). All these negative effects are especially clear if the physical punishment is harsh and erratic, but the risks for these poor outcomes are increased even with fairly mild levels of physical punishment.

I am *not* saying that you should never punish a child. I *am* saying that *physical punishment,* such as spanking, is not a good way to go about it. Yelling at the child is not a good alternative strategy either. Strong *verbal* aggression by a parent toward a child is also linked to many poor outcomes in the child, including increased risk of delinquency and adult violence (Straus, 1991b).

All in all, the bulk of the evidence is persuasive: Spanking and other forms of harsh discipline have neg-ative consequences for children. At the same time, an important caveat is in order. Virtually all the research showing such a link between physical punishment and poor outcomes has been done on European-American children. We now have a handful of studies suggesting that the same links may not occur in African-American families. For example, Deater-Deckard and his colleagues (Deater-Deckard, Dodge, Bates, & Pettit, 1996) found that white children whose parents used higher levels of physical punishment were more likely to be aggressive in school; the same link did not occur for black children in the same study—unless the physical discipline was severe. Just why such a difference may exist is not yet clear. It is possible that spanking or other forms of physical discipline are more likely to be combined with emotional coldness in European-American families than is true for African Americans; it is possible that the urban, black poor, in particular, use physical punishments as a means of maintaining tighter monitoring and control in a highly dangerous environment. Whatever the reason, results like this remind us once again that we must be very careful about generalizing from one group to another. For now, what I can tell you is that among European Americans, spanking seems to have consistently negative consequences and that *harsh* or erratic physical punishment has negative effects in every group studied.

Note, please, that this style of parenting is *not* one in which the parents let the child rule the roost. Authoritative parents have clear limits and are quite willing to discipline the child appropriately if the child misbehaves. They are less likely to use *physical* punishment than are authoritarian parents, preferring instead to use "time out" or other mild punishments, but it is important to understand that these parents are not a bit wishy-washy. Children reared in such families typically show higher self-esteem. They are more independent, but at the same time, they are more likely to comply with parental requests and may show more altruistic behavior as well. They are self-confident and achievement oriented in school and get better grades in elementary school, high school, or college (e.g., Crockenberg & Litman, 1990; Dornbusch et al.,

1987; Steinberg, Elmen, & Mounts, 1989; Weiss & Schwarz, 1996).

The Neglecting Type.   The most consistently negative outcomes are associated with the fourth pattern, the neglecting or uninvolved type. You may remember from the discussion of secure and insecure attachments in Chapter 6 that one of the family characteristics often found in children rated as insecure/avoidant is the "psychological unavailability" of the mother. The mother may be depressed or may be otherwise overwhelmed by other problems in her life and simply not have made any deep emotional connection with the child. Whatever the reason, such children continue to show disturbances in their relationships with peers and with adults for many years. At adolescence, for example, youngsters from neglecting families are more impulsive and antisocial, less competent with their peers, and much less achievement oriented in school (Block, 1971; Lamborn et al., 1991; Pulkkinen, 1982).

Figure 9.3 illustrates these contrasting outcomes with data from the Steinberg and Dornbusch study of adolescents (Steinberg, Lamborn, Darling et al., 1994), showing variations in grade point average as a function of family style. In a longitudinal analysis these same researchers have found that students who described their parents as most authoritative at the beginning of the study showed more *improvement* in academic competence and self-reliance and the smallest increases in psychological symptoms and delinquent behavior over the succeeding two years. So these effects persist.

The system is more complex than this makes it sound. For example, authoritative parents are much more likely to be involved with their child's school, attending school functions and talking to teachers, and this involvement seems to play a crucial role in their children's better school performance. When an otherwise authoritative parent is *not* also more involved with the school, the academic outcomes for the student are not so clearly positive. Similarly, a teenager whose parent is highly involved with the school but is not authoritative shows less optimal outcomes. It is the combination of authoritativeness and school involvement that is associated with the best academic results (Steinberg et al., 1992).

Despite these additional complexities—and the complexities discussed in the *Cultures and Contexts* box on facing page—we can draw several important conclusions from the research on family style. First, it seems clear that children are strongly affected by the family climate or style. Most likely, these effects persist well into adulthood. Second, many of us are accustomed to thinking about family styles as if permissive and authoritarian patterns were the only options. What the research on the authoritative pattern clearly shows is that one can be *both* affectionate and firm and that children respond to this combination in very positive ways.

Family Structure: Divorce and Other Variations

I cannot leave this discussion of family style and family functioning without at least some mention of the impact of variations in family structure. For those of us who live in cultures with high rates of divorce and single-parent families, this is an issue of profound practical importance.

Only about half of all children in the United States in 1995 live with both their biological parents (Hernandez, 1997). If we ask what percentage spend their *entire* childhood living with both natural parents, the numbers are even lower. Donald Hernandez, in his remarkable book, *America's Children* (1993), estimates that only about 40 percent of the children born in 1980—today's late teens—will spend all their years up to age 18 living with both natural parents. Among African Americans, Hernandez estimates, this figure is only 20 percent, while among European-Americans it is closer to 55 percent.

You can get some feeling for the variety of family structures in which children live today from Figure 9.4 (p. 316), which shows the percentages of five different family types among white, African-American, and Hispanic 13-year-olds in the United States, based on a nationally representative sam-

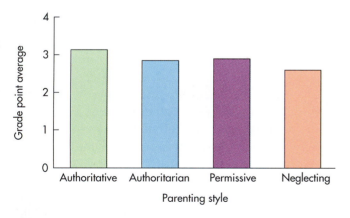

Figure 9.3

School grades vary as a function of parental style in Steinberg and Dornbusch's large sample of teenagers. (Source: Steinberg, Lamborn, Darling et al., 1994, from Table 5, p. 763.)

Cultures and Contexts

Ethnic Differences in Styles of Parenting

It is important for us to know something about the incidence of the various styles of parenting among the major ethnic groups in our culture. If we were to find, for example, that the authoritative pattern is found only among white families, then we could not be sure whether the more positive outcomes associated with this style were simply the result of belonging to the majority culture or whether they were really a consequence of the way the parents behaved. The best evidence on this point comes once again from the Dornbusch and Steinberg study of adolescents (Steinberg, Mounts, Lamborn, & Dornbusch, 1991).

They have studied a sample of roughly 10,000 ninth- through twelfth-grade students, chosen so as to be representative of four different ethnic groups: white, black, Hispanic, and Asian. Each subject answered questions about the acceptance, control, and autonomy they received from their parents. When the adolescent described his family as being above the average on all three dimensions, the family was classed as authoritative. The table below shows the percentages classed in this way in the four ethnic groups, broken down further by the social class and intactness of the family.

You can see that the authoritative pattern was most common among white families and least common among Asian Americans, but in each ethnic group, authoritative parenting was more common among the middle class and (with one exception) more common among intact families than in single-parent or stepparent families. Furthermore, these researchers found that some relationship between authoritative parenting and positive outcomes occurred in all ethnic groups. In all four groups, for example, teenagers from authoritative families showed more self-reliance and less delinquency than did those from nonauthoritative families. However, school grades were strongly linked to authoritative parental style for whites and Hispanics but only weakly for African Americans or Asian Americans. This last result raises a cautionary flag and points to a paradox that researchers are still exploring: Asian Americans as a group do extremely well in school, even though their parents are among the least authoritative. Perhaps the four categories of family style Maccoby and Martin (and Baumrind) suggest are at least partially ethnocentric and do not capture all the significant aspects of family style in every culture. Nonetheless, this four-category system seems to be a highly heuristic first approximation.

Percentage of Authoritative Families

Ethnic Group	Working Class		Middle Class	
	Intact[*]	Not Intact	Intact	Not Intact
White	17.2	11.5	25.0	17.6
Black	13.4	12.2	14.0	16.0
Hispanic	10.7	9.8	15.8	12.9
Asian	7.5	6.1	15.6	10.8

[*]"Intact" means the child is still living with both biological parents; "not intact" may mean single parent, stepfamily, or any family configuration other than both natural parents.

Source: Steinberg, Mounts, Lamborn, & Dornbusch, 1991, from Table 1, p. 25.

ple of over 21,000 children studied by Valerie Lee and her colleagues (Lee, Burkham, Zimiles, & Ladewski, 1994). Yet even this chart doesn't begin to convey the diversity of family structures or the number of changes in family structure a child may experience over time. Divorced mothers, for example, may have live-in relationships with one or more men before a remarriage, or they may have lived for a while with their own parents. And many children, especially children with never-married

Cultures and Contexts

Explaining the High Rate of Single Parenthood Among African Americans

Why is the rate of single parenthood so much higher among African Americans than other subgroups in the U.S. culture? Andrew Cherlin (1992a) suggests that it reflects historical trends in childbearing and marriage within the African-American community, rather than any increase in sexual activity among young black women. Unmarried black teens or young adults are no more likely to give birth today than they were in the 1960s. The *proportion* of all black births to unmarried young women has risen because the birth rate among older black women declined over those years, particularly among *married* women. At the same time, the rate of marriage declined steadily among blacks, a pattern that Cherlin attributes to two factors.

To begin with, economic conditions for many black males worsened as unemployment rose in the 1980s and early 1990s; even today, with unemployment at much lower levels nationally, job opportunities for unskilled men are severely limited. Furthermore, although black working women earn less than black working men, this gender difference is smaller among African Americans than among European Americans. Taken together, this means that black men, particularly inner-city black men, have been less and less able to take on the role of "provider" for a family, while black women are more and more able to support themselves. These conditions, according to Cherlin, made African-American women less likely to marry at all and less tolerant of unsatisfactory relationships.

Cultural traditions stemming from African styles of extended families have also contributed to this lesser emphasis on marriage as the foundation of family life. Instead, networks of relationships across several households or multiple generations within a single household are both common and approved.

These various factors help to put the large ethnic differences in the rate single-parent families into a wider context. Even so, explaining such a difference does not eliminate the effects on children. To be sure, extended kin networks can help to buffer children from the generally negative outcomes associated with single parenthood, but the risks are still higher.

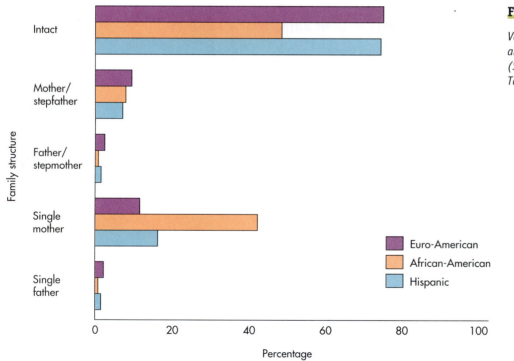

Figure 9.4

Variations in family structure among current 13-year-olds. (Source: Lee et al., 1994, from Table 2, p. 419.)

Cultures and Contexts

The Benefits of Extended Families

Because single-parent families have become so common in the United States, researchers here tend to develop a kind of tunnel vision when it comes to studies of "family structure." For us, the question nearly always translates to a comparison of single-parent families with two-parent families. However, in many parts of the world the normative form of family life is not the nuclear or two-parent family but rather an *extended* family—a family in which several generations live together in the same household. One study from the Sudan provides a kind of antidote to our typical cultural myopia.

Al Hassan al Awad and Edmund Sonuga-Barke (1992) compared the incidence of childhood problems for children who lived in Western-style nuclear families (mother and father only) versus those who lived in traditional extended families, in which three generations (at least) lived in the same household. All these families lived in towns near Khartoum (the capital of Sudan), and the two groups were matched for social status and approximate income. The mothers were interviewed about their child's behavior and problems.

The findings are very clear: Children reared in extended households were described as better off than were those living in nuclear households. They had fewer conduct problems, fewer sleep problems, better self-care, and were less likely to be overly dependent. The best single predictor of these good outcomes was the involvement of the child's grandmother in the child's care, and this was true within the group of nuclear families as well as in the comparison of nuclear and extended families.

How many different explanations for this result can you think of? Should we generalize this finding to Western cultures and conclude that extended families would typically be better for children? How could you check out such a hypothesis?

mothers, live in extended families with grandparents or other family members as well as a parent. All in all, the evidence makes it inescapably clear that the *majority* of children in the United States today experience at least two different family structures in the course of their growing up—and often, many more than that. This is especially true of African-Americans, but it is increasingly true of other ethnic groups in our culture as well.

In other industrialized countries, single-parent families are less common, but they are on the rise everywhere. By the mid-1980s, the proportions ranged from less than 5 percent in Japan to approximately 15 percent in Australia, the United Kingdom, and Sweden, to nearly 25 percent in the United States (Burns, 1992). Because cultures are complex, knowledge gleaned about the impact of family structure on children's development in one country may not be valid elsewhere, although the issue is growing in importance in many parts of the world.

What do we know about the impact on children of being reared in such varied or varying family structures?

The broadest statement I can make is that—at least in U.S. studies—the optimum family structure for children is to have two natural parents. All other structures, including never-married mothers, divorced mothers or fathers who have not remarried, and stepfamilies, are—on average—associated with poorer outcomes. Some examples:

- Children in intact families are substantially less likely to show behavior problems—such as excessive aggressiveness, delinquency, or drug abuse (McLanahan & Sandefur, 1994; Wills, Blechman, & McNamara, 1996). Figure 9.5 (p. 318) gives you one illustration, with findings drawn from the same large study reflected in Figure 9.4.

- Children growing up in single-parent families (whether the mother is divorced or never-married) are about twice as likely to drop out of high school, twice as likely to have a child before age 20, and less likely to have a steady job in their late teens or early twenties (McLanahan & Sandefur, 1994).

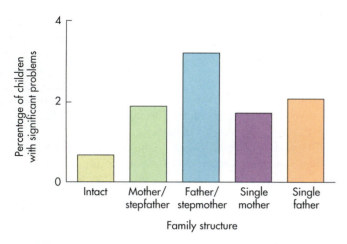

Figure 9.5

Children in intact families have lower rates of problem behavior than do children growing up in any other family structure. (Source: Lee et al., 1994, from Table 1, p. 417.)

- In the first few years after a divorce children typically show declines in school performance, and show more aggressive, defiant, negative, or depressed behavior (Furstenberg & Cherlin, 1991; Hetherington & Stanley-Hagan, 1995; Morrison & Cherlin, 1995). If they are adolescents, they are likely to show some increase in delinquent behavior (Kurtz & Tremblay, 1995).

- Negative effects of divorce may persist. Adults whose parents divorced are themselves more likely to divorce and are two to three times as likely to show long-term psychological problems, although it is important to point out that 70 to 80 percent of children whose parents divorce do not show such enduring problems but instead become "reasonably competent and well-adjusted individuals" (Hetherington & Stanley-Hagan, 1995b, p. 234).

- Children living in stepparent families also have higher rates of delinquency and lower school grades than do those in intact families (Lee et al., 1994).

As a general rule, these negative effects are more pronounced for boys than for girls, although some research suggests that among adolescents, girls show equally or even greater negative effects (Amato, 1993; Hetherington & Stanley-Hagan, 1995b). Age differences in the severity of the reaction, however, are typically not found. Specifically, al-

though Freud's theory might lead us to expect larger effects for children in the Oedipal period whose identification process would be disrupted by divorce, there is little indication that preschoolers are more severely affected than those of other ages.

[?] *Critical Thinking*

If children in the Oedipal period do not show more negative reactions to their parents' divorce, what might this say regarding Freud's theory about this stage?

Ethnicity, incidentally, does *not* appear to be a causal factor here. Yes, a larger percentage of African-American children grow up in single-parent families. But the same negative outcomes occur in white single-parent families, and the same positive outcomes are found in intact minority families. For example, the school dropout rate for a white child from a single-parent family is higher than the dropout rate for a Hispanic or African-American child reared in a two-parent family (McLanahan & Sandefur, 1994).

How are we to understand all these various findings? My own reading of this growing body of evidence is that nonintact family structures have less optimal effects for three key reasons.

First, single parenthood or divorce reduces the financial and emotional resources available to support the child. With only one parent, the household typically has only one income and only one adult to respond to the child's emotional needs. One ex-

Five-year-old Keith is a whole lot less sure than his mother is that her second marriage is a joyous occasion!

Parenting

Softening the Effects of Divorce

Given the rate of divorce in our culture, a significant percentage of you who are reading these words will go through a divorce when you have children still living at home. You cannot eliminate all the short-term disruptive effects of such an event on your children, but here are some specific things you can do that are likely to soften or shorten the effects:

1. Try to keep the number of separate changes the children have to cope with to a minimum. If at all possible, keep the children in the same school, in the same house or apartment, or in the same day-care setting. This advice holds not just for the period immediately following the divorce, but for several subsequent years as well (Buchanan, Maccoby, & Dornbusch, 1996).

2. If the children live with you full-time, help your children stay in touch with the noncustodial parent. Buchanan's large study of adolescents in divorced families (Buchanan et al., 1996) suggests that this is especially true for children with a custodial father. If they did not maintain regular contact with their noncustodial mother, then even a warm relationship with the father did not prevent a higher rate of emotional problems. If you are the noncustodial parent, maintain as much contact as possible with your children, calling regularly, seeing them regularly, attending school functions, and so on. If you live at some distance from your children, then phone calls and predictable visits in the summer or over school holidays may be sufficient, especially with older children. Whatever you do, don't forget the child's birthday or other special occasions!

3. Keep the conflict between you and your ex-spouse to a minimum. Most of all, try not to fight in front of the children; it is the conflict the children experience, rather than the conflict the parents feel, that seems to be critical (Buchanan et al., 1996). Open conflict has negative effects on children whether the parents are divorced or not (Amato, 1993; Coiro, 1995; Harold, Fincham, Osborne, & Conger, 1997; Insabella, 1995). So divorce is not the only culprit. But divorce *combined* with open conflict between the adults has worse effects.

4. Whatever else you do, do not use the child as a go-between or talk disparagingly about your ex-spouse to your child. Children who feel caught in the middle between the two parents are more likely to show various kinds of negative symptoms, such as depression or behavior problems (Buchanan et al., 1991).

5. Maintain your own network of support and use that network liberally. Stay in touch with friends, seek out others in the same situation, join a support group. In whatever way you can, nurture yourself and your own needs (Hetherington & Stanley-Hagan, 1995).

6. *Consider* the possibility of a dual residence arrangement in which the child moves back and forth regularly between the two households, such as weekly or monthly. Buchanan's large study of adolescents in divorced families suggested that children in this arrangement had slightly better adjustment than did those in mother- or father-custody situations. Such an arrangement will not work in every case. Certainly, if the level of acrimony between the divorcing couple is very high or they do not live close to one another, dual residence would be impossible. Still, when it is feasible, such an arrangement seems to be beneficial because it allows the child to maintain a close relationship with both parents.

In the midst of your own emotional upheaval from a divorce, these are not easy prescriptions to follow. But if you are able to do so, your children will suffer less.

ample: Data from the United States indicate that a woman's income drops an average of 40 to 50 percent after a divorce (Smock, 1993). Remarriage does indeed add a second adult to the family system, which alleviates these problems to some degree, but adds others.

Second, *any* family transition involves upheaval. This is true of the birth of a new sibling in an intact family. It is even more true of divorce or of remarriage. Both adults and children adapt slowly and with difficulty to the subtraction or addition of new adults to the family system (Hetherington & Stanley-Hagan, 1995). The period of maximum disruption appears to last several years, during which the parents often find it difficult to maintain good monitoring and control over their children. Parents can take specific actions to reduce this disruption (discussed in the *Parenting* box on p. 319), but some disruption is unavoidable.

Finally, and perhaps most importantly, single parenthood, divorce, and stepparenthood all increase the likelihood that the family climate or style will shift away from authoritative parenting toward less optimal forms. We see this in the first few years after a divorce when the custodial parent (usually the mother) is distracted or depressed and less able to manage warm control; we see it in stepfamilies as well, in which rates of authoritative parenting are lower than in intact families.

The key thing to understand is that authoritative child rearing is linked to low levels of disturbed behaviors and higher levels of psychological adjustment in the child, *no matter what family structure the child grows up in*; and authoritarian or neglecting parenting is linked to poor outcomes whether it is the normal family pattern or was triggered by a divorce, by a stressful remarriage, by the father's loss of a job, or by any other stress (Goldberg, 1990). Ultimately, it is this *process* within the family that is significant for the child. The likelihood of a nonoptimal family process is greater in single-parent families, but this does not mean that the probability is a hundred percent. Many single parents are able to find the strength within themselves to maintain a supportive process with their children. After all, we know that three-quarters of the children reared in single-parent or stepfamilies manage to finish high school, and roughly half those high school graduates go on to at least some college (McLanahan & Sandefur, 1994). Similarly, the great majority of children reared by a single parent or in a stepfamily do not become delinquent or show significant behavior problems. Indeed, one recent study of inner-city, African-American teenage boys suggests that those in single-parent households are no more likely to be delinquent than are those in two-parent households because, in this sample, the single mothers actually had more supportive relationships with their sons than did many of the married or remarried mothers (Zimmerman, Salem, & Maton, 1995). It is thus clearly possible for single or divorced parents to surmount the extra problems. Still, we need to face up to the fact that such family systems are less stable and, on average, less supportive for children.

Summary

1. Both vertical relationships, such as with parents and teachers, and horizontal relationships with peers are highly important in these years. Only in play with peers can the child learn about reciprocal relationships, both cooperative and competitive.

2. The child's attachment to the parent(s) remains strong, but except in stressful situations, attachment behaviors become less visible as the child gets older.

3. Preschoolers show more refusals and defiance of parental influence attempts than do infants. Outright defiance, however, declines from ages 2 to 6.

4. Both these changes are clearly linked to the child's language and cognitive gains.

5. Play with peers is visible before age 2 and becomes increasingly central through the preschool years.

6. Physical aggression toward peers increases and then declines during these years, while verbal aggression increases among older preschoolers. Aggression is often linked to frustration and is clearly affected by patterns of reinforcement and modeling.

7. Children as young as 2 also show altruistic behavior toward others, and this behavior seems to grow as the child's ability to take another's perspective increases.

8. Short-term friendships, mostly based on proximity, are evident in children in this age range. The majority of such pairs are same-sex.

9. As early as age 3 or 4, boys and girls show different patterns or styles of interaction with peers, a difference that continues well into adulthood.

10. The preschooler continues to define himself along a series of objective dimensions but does not yet have a global sense of self-esteem.

11. Children make major strides in self-control in the preschool years, as the parents gradually turn over the job of control to the child.

12. Between 2 and 6, most children move through a series of steps in their understanding of gender constancy, first labeling their own and others' gender, then understanding the stability of gender, and finally the constancy of gender at about age 5 or 6.

13. In these same years, children begin to learn what is "appropriate" behavior for their gender. By age 5 or 6 most children have developed fairly rigid rules about what boys or girls are supposed to do or be.

14. Neither Freud's nor Kohlberg's explanations of gender development have fared well. Social-learning ex-

planations are more persuasive because parents do appear to give some differential reinforcement of sex-appropriate behavior. The most useful current theory is gender schema theory, which combines some elements of Piagetian and social-learning models.

15. Children also differ widely in social behavior and personality. Temperament plays some role. Children with more difficult temperaments are more likely to show later behavior problems or delinquency.

16. Parental styles are also significant. Authoritative parenting, combining high warmth, clear rules and communication, and high maturity demands, is associated with the most positive outcomes. Neglecting parenting is associated with the least positive. Two other patterns, each with specific effects, are the authoritarian and the permissive.

17. Family structure also affects children. In U.S. data, any family structure other than two biological parents is linked to more negative outcomes. Following a divorce, children typically show disrupted behavior for several years. Parental styles also change, becoming less authoritative.

Key Terms

aggression   Behavior with the apparent intent to injure some other person or object. **(p. 296)**

altruism   Giving or sharing objects, time, or goods with others, with no obvious self-gain. **(p. 298)**

authoritarian parental style   One of the three styles described by Baumrind, characterized by high levels of control and maturity demands and low levels of nurturance and communication. **(p. 311)**

authoritative parental style   One of the three styles described by Baumrind, characterized by high levels of control, nurturance, maturity demands, and communication. **(p. 311)**

birth order   A child's position in the sequence of children within a family, such as firstborn, later-born, or only. **(p. 295)**

coercive attachment   Term used by Crittenden to describe the common preschool-age modification of an ambivalent attachment, in which the child coerces the parent's involvement through either coy enticement or anger. **(p. 291)**

defended attachment   Term used by Crittenden to describe a common preschool-age modification of an avoidant attachment, in which the child attempts to maintain contact with the parent by becoming hyper-

aware of the parent's moods or needs, adapting to the parent(s). **(p. 291)**

dominance hierarchy   A set of dominance relationships in a group that describes the rank order of "winners" and "losers" in competitive encounters; also called a "pecking order." **(p. 297)**

frustration-aggression hypothesis   Early psychological hypothesis that all aggression results from frustration and all frustration leads to aggression. Only partially supported by research. **(p. 297)**

gender concept   The understanding of one's own gender, including the permanence and constancy of gender. **(p. 303)**

gender constancy   The final step in developing a gender concept, in which the child understands that gender doesn't change even though there are external changes like clothing or hair length. **(p. 304)**

gender identity   The earliest aspect of gender concept development, in which the child labels herself correctly and categorizes others correctly as female or male. **(p. 304)**

gender schema   A fundamental schema created by children beginning at age 18 months or younger by which the child categorizes people, objects, activities, and qualities by gender. **(p. 307)**

gender stability   An aspect of the total gender concept in which the child understands that a person's gender continues to be stable throughout the lifetime. **(p. 304)**

goal-corrected partnership   Term used by Bowlby to describe the form of an appropriate child-to-parent attachment in the preschool years in which the two partners, through improved communication, negotiate the form and frequency of contact between them. **(p. 291)**

hostile aggression   Aggression aimed at hurting another person or gaining an advantage over another. **(p. 297)**

instrumental aggression   Aggression aimed at gaining or damaging some object. **(p. 297)**

neglecting parental style   A fourth style of parenting characterized by low levels of control, low acceptance or even outright rejection, and low levels of warmth. **(p. 311)**

ordinal position   See *birth order*.

parallel play   Form of play seen in toddlers in which two children play next to, but not with, one another. **(p. 296)**

permissive parental style   One of the three styles described by Baumrind, characterized by high levels of nurturance and low levels of control, maturity demands, and communication. **(p. 311)**

prosocial behavior   See *altruism*.

self-scheme   An internal model of self, not unlike the concept of an internal model of attachment. **(p. 303)**

sex role   The set of behaviors, attitudes, rights, duties, and obligations that are part of the "role" of being a boy or a girl, a male or a female in any given culture. **(p. 303)**

Suggested Readings

Boynton, R. S. (1996, October 7). The birth of an idea. *The New Yorker*, pp. 72–81. A fascinating review and analysis of Frank Sulloway's somewhat revolutionary ideas on the importance of birth order in shaping individual personality and behavior.

Dunn, J. (1993). *Young children s close relationships*. Newbury Park, CA: Sage. A wonderful small book, written in a clear and engaging style by one of the experts on children's social relationships.

Eisenberg, N. (1992). *The caring child*. Cambridge, MA: Harvard University Press. An excellent and thoughtful book on the origins of prosocial or altruistic behavior.

Furstenberg, F. F., Jr., & Cherlin, A. J. (1991). *Divided families: What happens to children when parents part*. Cambridge, MA: Harvard University Press. A relatively brief, current review of this important subject, aimed at lay readers and decision makers rather than at other psychologists.

Golombok, S., & Fivush, R. (1994). *Gender development*. Cambridge, England: Cambridge University Press. A basic, up-to-date description of all facets of gender development.

Lickona, T. (1983). *Raising good children*. Toronto: Bantam Books. One of the very best "how to" books for parents I have ever seen, with excellent concrete advice as well as theory. His emphasis is on many of the issues I raised in the *Parenting* box on rearing altruistic children.

Maccoby, E. E. (1990). Gender and relationships: A developmental account. *American Psychologist, 45,* 513–520. In this brief paper, Maccoby reviews the accumulating evidence suggesting that boys and girls show quite different styles of interaction, beginning in the preschool years.

McLanahan, S., & Sandefur, G. (1994). *Growing up with a single parent: What hurts, what helps*. Cambridge, MA: Harvard University Press. A sobering book, based on a careful reading of five major national studies, several of them longitudinal in design. It is well worth a look, if only because it raises some crucial issues. It is also written in a not-too-technical style that I think you will find comprehensible.

Summing Up Preschool Development

BASIC CHARACTERISTICS OF THE PRESCHOOL PERIOD

The table summarizes the changes in children's abilities and behavior between 2 and 6. The sense one gets of this period is that the child is making a slow but immensely important shift from dependent baby to independent child. The toddler and preschooler can now move around easily, can communicate more and more clearly, has a sense of himself as a separate person with

A Summary of the Threads of Development During the Preschool Years

Aspect of Development	Age in Years				
	2	3	4	5	6
Physical development	Runs easily; climbs stairs one step at a time; iron deficiency anemia common	Rides tricycle; uses scissors; draws; bed-wetting and bedtime struggles common	Climbs stairs one foot per step; kicks and throws large ball	Hops and skips; kicks, throws, and catches with more skill; grasps pencil maturely	Jumps rope, skips, rides bike
Cognitive development	Symbol use; 2- and 3-step play sequences	Flavell's Level 1 perspective taking	Level 2 perspective taking; understands false belief	Representational theory of mind clearly present; conservation of number and quantity	Some metacognition and metamemory
Language development	2-word sentences	3- and 4-word sentences and grammatical markers	Continued improvement of inflections, past tense, plurals, passive sentences, and other language complexities		
Self/personality development	Self-definition based on comparisons of size, age, gender		Self-definition based on physical properties or skills		
	Gender identity		Gender stability	Gender constancy	
	Erikson's stage of autonomy vs. shame and doubt		Erikson's stage of initiative vs. guilt		
	Freud's anal stage		Freud's phallic stage		
Social development	Attachment behavior becomes less and less overt, primarily shown under stress; child comfortable being at a greater and greater distance from parent				
		Attachment becomes "goal-corrected partnership"			
	Multistep turn-taking sequences in play with peers; aggression primarily physical	Some altruism; beginning same-sex peer choices	Beginning signs of individual friendships; aggression becomes more and more verbal	Negotiation rather than defiance becomes more common with parents; sociodramatic play	Roles in play with peers

specific qualities, and has the beginning cognitive and social skills that allow him to interact more fully and successfully with playmates. At the same time, the child's thinking is *decentering*, becoming less egocentric and less tied to the outside appearances of things.

In the beginning these newfound skills and newfound independence are not accompanied by much impulse control. Two-year-olds are pretty good at doing; they are lousy at *not* doing. If frustrated, they hit things, or wail, or scream, or shout (isn't language wonderful?). A large part of the conflict parents experience with children at this age comes about because the parent *must* limit the child, not only for the child's own survival but to help teach the child impulse control.

The preschool years also stand out as the period in which the seeds are sown for the child's—and perhaps the adult's—social skills and personality. The attachment process in infancy continues to be formative because it helps to shape the internal working model of social relationships the child creates. However, in the years from 2 to 6, this early model is revised, consolidated, and established more firmly. The resultant interactive patterns tend to persist into elementary school and beyond. The 3-, 4-, or 5-year-old who develops the ability to share, to read others' cues well, to respond positively to others, and to control aggression and impulsiveness, is likely to be a socially successful, popular 8-year-old. In contrast, the noncompliant, hostile preschooler is far more likely to become an unpopular, aggressive school child (Campbell, Pierce, March, & Ewing, 1991; Eisenberg, Fabes, Murphy et al., 1995; Patterson et al., 1991).

CENTRAL PROCESSES

Many forces are at play in creating these changes, beginning with two immense cognitive advances in this period: the 18- or 24-month-old child's new ability to use symbols and the rapid development of a more sophisticated theory of mind between ages 3 and 5.

Symbol Use. The development of symbol use is reflected in many different aspects of the child's life. We see it in the rapid surge of language development, in the child's approach to cognitive tasks, and in play, where the child now pretends, having an object *stand for* some-

thing else. The ability to use language more skillfully, in turn, affects social behavior in highly significant ways, such as in the increasing use of verbal rather than physical aggression and in the use of negotiation with parents in place of tantrums or defiant behavior.

Theory of Mind. The emergence of the child's more sophisticated theory of mind has equally broad effects, especially in the social arena, where the child's newfound abilities to read and understand others' behaviors form the foundation for new levels of interactions with peers and parents. It is probably not accidental that individual friendships between children are first visible at about the time that they also show the sharp drop in egocentrism that occurs with the emergence of a representational theory of mind.

We also see the seminal role of cognitive changes in the growing importance of several basic schemes. Not only does the 2- or 3-year-old have a more and more generalized internal model of attachment, she also develops a self scheme and a gender scheme, each of which forms part of the foundation of both social behavior and personality.

Social Contacts. Important as these cognitive changes are, they are clearly not the only causal forces. Equally central is the child's play with peers, which is itself made possible by the new physical and cognitive skills we see in the 2-year-old. When children play together, they expand each other's experience with objects and suggest new ways of pretending to one another, thus fostering still further cognitive growth. When two children disagree about how to explain something, or insist on their own different views, it enhances each child's awareness that there *are* other ways of thinking or playing, hence creating opportunities to learn about others' mental processes. Thus social interactions are the arena in which much cognitive growth occurs, just as Vygotsky proposed. For example, in one recent study, Charles Lewis finds that children who have many siblings or who interact regularly with a variety of adult relatives show more rapid understanding of other people's thinking and acting than do children with fewer social partners (C. N. Lewis, Freeman, & Maridaki-Kassotaki, 1995). Similarly, Jenkins and Astington (1996) find that children from larger families show more rapid development of a representational theory of mind. Some new research also indicates that children with secure attachments show a more rapid shift to understanding false belief and other aspects of a representational theory of mind than do children with insecure attachments (Charman, Redfern, & Fonagy, 1995; Steele, Holder, & Fonagy, 1995)—a result that points to the importance of the *quality* as well as the quantity of social interactions for the child's cognitive development.

Play with other children also forms the foundation of the child's emerging gender schema. Noticing whether other people are boys or girls and what toys boys and girls play with is itself the first step in the long chain of sex-role learning.

Naturally enough, it is also in social interactions, especially those with parents, that the child's pattern of social behaviors are modified or reinforced. The parents' style of discipline becomes critical here. Gerald Patterson's work shows clearly that parents who lack the skills to control the toddler's impulsivity and demands for independence are likely to end up strengthening noncompliant and disruptive behavior, even if the parent's intention is the reverse (Patterson et al., 1991).

INFLUENCES ON THE BASIC PROCESSES

The family's ability to support the child's development in these years is affected not only by the skills and

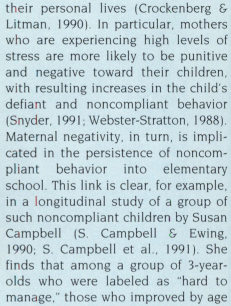

knowledge the parents bring to the process but also by the amount of stress they are experiencing from outside forces and by the quality of support they have in their personal lives (Crockenberg & Litman, 1990). In particular, mothers who are experiencing high levels of stress are more likely to be punitive and negative toward their children, with resulting increases in the child's defiant and noncompliant behavior (Snyder, 1991; Webster-Stratton, 1988). Maternal negativity, in turn, is implicated in the persistence of noncompliant behavior into elementary school. This link is clear, for example, in a longitudinal study of a group of such noncompliant children by Susan Campbell (S. Campbell & Ewing, 1990; S. Campbell et al., 1991). She finds that among a group of 3-year-olds who were labeled as "hard to manage," those who improved by age 6 had mothers who had been less negative.

The mother's stress is obviously not the only factor in her level of negativity toward the child. Depressed mothers are also more likely to show such behavior (Conrad & Hammen, 1989), as are mothers from working-class or poverty-level families, who may well have experienced such negativity and harsh discipline in their own childhoods. Still, stress and lack of personal social support are both part of the equation. Thus the preschooler, like children of every age, is affected by broader social forces outside the family as well as by the family interaction itself.

Physical Development and Health at School Age

Preview Questions

1 Why is it important for school children to have breakfast every day?

2 Why is the incidence of obesity rising so rapidly among school-age children in the United States and elsewhere in the world?

3 What are the arguments in favor of physical fitness for children?

4 What factors contribute to the higher rate of illness among children living in poverty?

5 Is it a good idea for parents to encourage their 6- and 7-year-olds to join organized sports teams?

Chapter Outline

School-age children have a wonderful kind of unthinking confidence about their bodies. They can do so many things well—riding a bike, climbing, jumping, skipping, throwing and catching a ball. The wobbliness and stiffness of early childhood is gone and the uncertainties of puberty have not yet begun. The child of this age can navigate the world with skill and begin to play sports with real enthusiasm. It is a pleasure to watch children this age, on the playground or in their neighborhoods; they so often have a kind of intense joyfulness about their physical play. Naturally enough, there are physical risks as well, including accidents resulting from all that joyful boisterousness. Let's start with some simple description.

Basic Changes in Size and Shape

The basic growth patterns established in the late preschool years continue at much the same rate for the next few years. Between ages 6 and 9, children

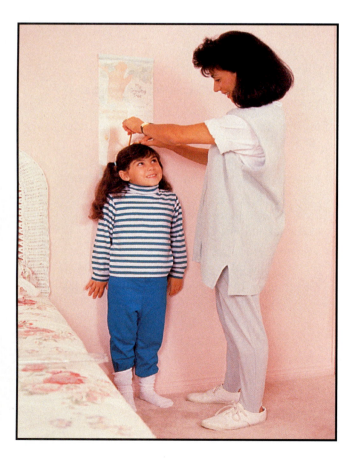

This girl is still in the stage of slow and steady growth; in a few years, when she's 9 or 10, her rate of growth will speed up, and for a few years she'll grow faster than the boys.

add 2 to 3 inches and 4 to 6 pounds each year. From age 9 to age 12, though, the pattern changes, as you can see clearly in Figure 10.1. First of all, the girls pass up the boys in both height and weight somewhere around age 9, a clear sign that girls are already beginning the first steps of pubertal changes in this period, while boys generally are not. Results from a recent large set of data collected by pediatricians all over the United States, involving over 17,000 girls seen in regular pediatric practices (Herman-Giddens, Slora, Wasserman et al., 1997), suggests that by age 8, more than a third of African-American and roughly ten percent of white girls already show the earliest stages of either breast or pubic hair development. By age 12, when virtually all girls are well into at least the early stages of puberty, girls are up to an inch taller than the boys at the equivalent percentile ranking. Tall girls at this age are taller than virtually *all* the boys—a fact I remember with crystal clarity because I was already 5 feet 6 inches at age 12, well above the 90th percentile line shown in Figure 10.1. There was not a single boy my age who was anywhere close to that size.

The figure also makes it clear that after about age 9, children's weight increases more rapidly than their height. Between ages 9 and 12, both boys and girls are adding 8 to 10 pounds a year; the heaviest girls are adding 10 to 14 pounds. Some of this disparity between height gains and weight gains reflects increases in obesity—a point I'll come back to in a moment. Some of it appears to reflect physical preparation for puberty, particularly among African-American girls.

Ethnic Differences in Growth Patterns. The basic shape of these curves is essentially the same for children all over the world, with slight variations from one ethnic group to another (Tanner, 1990). Asian children, for example, tend to be shorter at each age, although their growth trajectory does not differ. In contrast, African and African-American children are slightly taller at each age and follow a somewhat different trajectory. In particular, African-American girls show larger height gains (and early onset of pubertal changes) in the early school years than their European-American (or European) counterparts, so at age 10 or 11 they are, on average, about an inch taller (Webber, Wattigney, Srinivasan, & Berenson, 1995), and are typi-

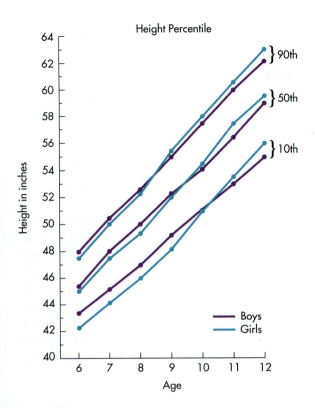 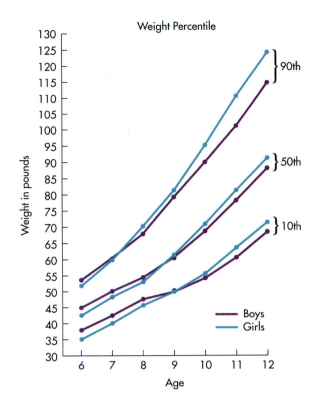

Figure 10.1

Basic changes in height and weight among U.S. children in the school years. The three lines for each sex show the 10th, 50th, and 90th percentile trajectories. (Source: Needlman, 1996, data from Table 13-1, pp. 50–51.)

cally the tallest children in a class. This difference disappears during puberty, when Euro-American girls catch up to their black peers.

The various ethnic groups also differ in body proportions, variations that begin to be apparent in this age range. Black school-age children begin to show longer legs for their heights and narrower hips in relation to their shoulder width in comparison to either whites or Asians. Thus whites and Asians have taller sitting heights than blacks, because their trunks are comparatively longer, while blacks have taller standing heights.

Abnormal Growth

Children are hardly ever taken to a pediatrician because they are too tall; when parents get concerned about a child's size it is nearly always because the child seems too short. Any child whose height falls at the 3rd percentile or below should probably be seen by a physician for a basic assess-

ment, in order to identify (or rule out) the several possible explanations.

The first step in such an assessment is to calculate the child's height in relation to the parents'. Many short children are short simply because they come from a line of short people. Their growth is perfectly normal. A physician can check to see how far a child's growth deviates from the expected pattern, given the parents' height, using something called a Parents-Allowed-For growth chart. For example, such a chart would make it clear that a child at the 3rd percentile of overall height whose parents are at the 60th percentile is abnormally short for his presumed heredity. A child of the same size whose parents are, on average, at the 10th percentile, is about at the size you'd expect. Only the first child needs further evaluation.

Such a further evaluation should cover at least the following:

- *Chromosomal anomalies.* Down syndrome will be obvious, but some others are not. For example,

Turner's syndrome (girls with an XO pattern), which is associated with shorter height in girls, is not so easy to spot.

- *Small-for-date birth weight*. Children born small for date very often end up shorter than you'd predict, given the height of their parents, with an average height at about the 30th percentile (Tanner, 1990). A subset of these children don't reach even the 30th percentile, but remain abnormally small, with characteristic facial appearance—a triangular face with large forehead and eyes and small lower jaw, and prominent and low-set ears. This syndrome, called Silver-Russell syndrome, is not linked to mental retardation or ill health, only to growth retardation and small stature.

- *Endocrine gland disorder*. Unusually small stature can also occur because of an insufficiency of growth hormone. This problem, which occurs in about one out of every 5000 children, most often has no known origin. It is usually detectable as early as age 2 or 3 when the child's size is already at the lowest end of the normal range. Curiously, this disorder is more common in cases of breech birth, although no one has yet explained why this might be so (Tanner, 1990). Growth-hormone insufficiency can be treated successfully with daily injections of genetically cloned growth hormone, beginning in childhood and continuing until growth would ordinarily stop at the end of adolescence. Such injections produce an immediate spurt or "catch up" in height that moves the child up into a more normal range and then help maintain a normal rate of growth thereafter.

A word of warning: The American Academy of Pediatrics has recommended that growth hormone should be used *only* in those cases where the child himself secretes too little; it is *not* recommended for children whose parents might wish they were a little taller. We have not yet reached (and likely never will reach) the point where parents can specify some desired height and a physician can tinker with the child's growth hormone. We simply know too little about the long-term risks of such hormones to make such tinkering safe.

[?] Critical Thinking

Why would parents *want* an otherwise normal child to be taller? Why do you think most of us have such a clear bias in favor of tallness, especially in men?

Malnutrition. An obvious alternative explanation for slow growth is malnutrition, or—more likely—subnutrition. You already know from Chapter 7 that children who are undernourished show slower physical development and end up shorter than their better nourished peers. But the effects are far broader than that. Malnourished or undernourished children also have less energy, which alters the quality of the child's interactions with both the objects and the people around him. For example, in a recent study of toddlers in Kenya, Egypt, Mexico, and the United States, Marian Sigman and her colleagues (Sigman, 1995; Wachs & Sigman, 1995) found that children who were chronically undernourished (but not clinically *mal*nourished) were less alert, less advanced in their forms of play, and less skilled in social interactions with other children than were their better nourished peers.

Similarly, Michael Espinosa and his colleagues (Espinosa, Sigman, Neumann, Bwibo, & McDonald, 1992), studying school-age children in Kenya, observed that undernourished kids were more soli-

Malnutrition as severe as what we see in these Philippine children is still common in many parts of the world; in the United States, we see more chronic undernutrition or periodic hunger, rather than severe malnutrition.

tary and less active on the playground than their well-nourished peers. Like the youngsters in Sigman's studies, the children in Espinosa's study were not severely malnourished. They were taking in about 1500 calories per day (including adequate protein), which is enough to sustain the child but not enough to provide the energy needed for play or perhaps for concentration in school over long periods.

Most of us are used to thinking that chronic malnutrition or subnutrition happens only in less technologically developed countries. In fact, however, hunger and malnutrition are surprisingly common in the United States. Among poor children, perhaps ten percent are so significantly underweight for their age that they are classed as chronically malnourished (Meyers, Frank, Roos et al., 1995). Many more are hungry at least part of the time. One striking statistic comes from the Community Childhood Hunger Identification Project (1991), who estimate that one out of every eight children under the age of 12 in the United States is hungry. These researchers arrived at this somewhat stunning number by interviewing samples of poverty-level families in seven different cities around the country, asking each family the eight questions listed in Table 10.1. Thirty-two percent of this sample of 2335 poor families answered yes to at least five of these questions, indicating a food shortage that affected the children.

Critical Thinking

Are you surprised by these estimates of the incidence of hunger in America? What practical steps can you think of to reduce the number of hungry children?

If 32 percent of poor children are hungry, then, given the number of poor children in the United States, at least one out of eight of all children is hungry. To be sure, not all these children are hungry all the time. In most poor households, hunger is more common right before payday or right before the welfare check and food stamps arrive (and half the poor families in this study lived on wages, not welfare). In four-fifths of these hungry households, parents reported that they had to limit their children's food for as much as a week every month.

The consequences of such chronic subnutrition are not only smaller body size. Hungry children are more tired, more irritable, and more likely to report dizziness or headaches, to have frequent ear infections or colds, and to have trouble concentrating. Because they are ill more often, they miss more school days. In the Community Childhood Hunger Identification Project, children from hungry families had missed an average of 6.5 days of school in the previous six months, compared with 4.3 days for children from nonhungry poor families. One societal answer to such hunger problems has been

Table 10.1

Measuring Family Hunger

- Does your household ever run out of money to buy food to make a meal?
- Do you or adult members of your household ever eat less than you feel you should because there is not enough money for food?
- Do you or adult members of your household ever cut the size of meals or skip meals because there is not enough money for food?
- Do your children ever eat less than you feel they should because there is not enough money for food?
- Do you ever cut the size of your children's meals or do they ever skip meals because there is not enough money for food?
- Do your children ever say they are hungry because there is not enough food in the house?
- Do you ever rely on a limited number of foods to feed your children because you are running out of money to buy food for a meal?
- Do any of your children ever go to bed hungry because there is not enough money to buy food?

Source: Community Childhood Hunger Identification Project, 1991, p. 2.

Social Policy Debate

School Feeding Programs

More than one-half of all youth in the United States eat one of their three main meals at school each school day (Gleason, 1995). Among elementary school students, two-thirds eat lunch at school. In schools that offer breakfast—a minority of schools, mostly located in poor neighborhoods—19 percent of elementary school children eat breakfast at school. Both meals are available free for those whose family income falls at 130 percent or below of the official poverty rate; those whose family income is between 130 percent and 185 percent of the poverty rate are eligible for reduced-price meals. The great majority of both eligible income groups participate in lunch programs. Participation is lower in breakfast programs; only about two-fifths of those who could receive free or reduced-price breakfasts actually do so. Some poor children do not participate because they get a good breakfast at home; sometimes, they (or their parents) simply don't know they are eligible and don't apply.

The breakfast program seems particularly important. Experimental studies in which children have been deliberately asked to fast by skipping breakfast show that such short-term reductions in nutrient supplies affect a child's memory and mental speed (Pollitt, 1995). When a child often misses breakfast, we shouldn't be surprised that he concentrates less well in school. School breakfast programs for children from poor or hungry families are an excellent response to this problem.

A particularly nice research demonstration of the effect comes from Alan Meyers and his colleagues (Meyers, Sampson, Weitzman, Rogers, & Kayne, 1989) who were able to study children in a school district in Massachusetts where breakfast programs were added in 1987. Not only was Meyers able to compare children who did or did not choose to participate in the program, he was also able to compare the children's achievement test scores and absence rates for the year before the breakfast program and the year after it was begun. He found that the children who ate breakfast at school showed significantly larger gains in achievement test scores over this one-year period than did the children who qualified for the program but chose not to participate. Breakfast-eating children also had comparatively fewer absences and lower rates of tardiness. Such beneficial effects have been found in studies in other countries as well, including developing countries (Pollitt, 1995). In general, the more severely undernourished a child, the more benefit he receives from school breakfast or other food programs.

In 1994, free breakfasts cost a total of $821 million nationwide in the United States. If all children who were economically eligible participated, the cost would rise, but so would the very real benefits.

school breakfast and lunch programs, described in the *Social Policy* box above.

Obesity

The other side of the coin from malnutrition is obesity, a problem that is growing in the United States, Canada, and many European countries. Although there is no standard definition of **obesity** or overweight for children, two definitions are common: (1) a body weight 20 percent or more above the normal weight for height, or (2) a **body mass index (BMI)** at the 85th percentile or above. (The BMI is described in detail in the *Research Report* on the facing page.) Those whose BMI falls at the 95th percentile or higher are sometimes called **superobese**. By the body mass index definition, more than 20 percent of elementary school–age children in the United States are significantly overweight, as you can see in Figure 10.2. More than 10 percent are superobese (Troiano, Flegal, Kuczmarski, Campbell, & Johnson, 1995). Equivalently high rates of obesity are common in other Western countries as well. For example, researchers in Italy found that 23.4 percent of a sample of 10-year-old boys and 12.7 percent of girls were obese (Maffeis, Schutz, Piccoli, Gonfiantini, & Pinelli, 1993), while Canadian researchers report rates of roughly twenty percent (Lechky, 1994).

U.S. surveys also tell us that obesity (at least in the United States) is more common among Hispanic and African-American children than among whites, with the highest rates among Mexican Americans (Troiano et al., 1995). In the latter group, 26.7 percent of the boys and 29 percent of the girls are classed as obese in the most recent

Research Report

Calculating a Body Mass Index (BMI)

The body mass index allows you to compare weights after adjusting for height. The formula is: weight in kilograms divided by the square of height in meters. Here's how to calculate your own:

1. Determine your weight in kilograms. One kilogram is 2.2 pounds, so divide your weight in pounds by 2.2.
2. Determine your height in meters. One meter is 39.37 inches, so divide your height in inches by 39.37.
3. Square the result of step 2.
4. Divide the result of step 3 into your weight in kilograms.

For example, suppose you are 5 feet 8 inches and weigh 140 pounds.

you weigh 63.64 kilograms (140 divided by 2.2)

your height in meters is 1.73 (68 divided by 39.37)

your height squared is 2.99

your BMI is 63.64 divided by 2.99 = 21.28

For adults, a BMI of 25 or less is classed as a healthy weight, although a number between 19 and 23.5 is better. A BMI between 26 and 30 is classed as overweight but not obese, and any BMI over 30.0 is classed as obese (Brownell & Fairburn, 1995). Given this guide, you can determine your own classification. Note, though, that the classification is only approximate. For example, a given volume of muscle weighs more than fat, so especially muscular folks, such as those who do heavy physical labor or weight lifters, are likely to have much higher BMIs even if they have low body fat.

Among children, normal BMIs are lower than this. The 50th percentile BMI for children ages 6 to 8 is approximately 16, with this number rising gradually over the succeeding years. By age 16 the average BMI is about 22. Among early elementary school children, a BMI of 19 or 20 or above would normally be classed as obese (Webber et al., 1995), but it is important to remember that judging obesity by BMI must be age-specific. Still, you may find it interesting to do this calculation not only for yourself, but for your own children or other children in this age group.

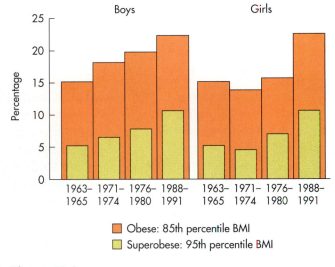

Figure 10.2

These figures show the steady rise in obesity in the United States among children ages 6 through 11, based on four national surveys conducted by the National Center for Health Statistics. (Source: Troiano et al., 1995, from Table 3, p. 1089.)

survey. In part, these ethnic differences are really poverty differences in disguise. Among poor children, obesity (as well as hunger) is more common for the simple reason that high-fat or high-calorie foods are likely to be cheaper than are fruits and vegetables.

Obesity in childhood is a problem for two reasons. First, fat children are more likely to be fat as adults, and we know that obesity in adulthood is linked to higher health risks of various kinds. The reassuring fact is that the connection between childhood fatness and adult overweight is not automatic. The more extreme the child's overweight, the more likely he is to remain fat throughout childhood and into adulthood, but almost 80 percent of fat infants and toddlers, and roughly half of overweight school-age children, are not obese as adults (Serdula, Ivery, Coates et al., 1993). (Conversely, more than half of obese adults were *not* fat as children.) Nonetheless, significantly overweight children are clearly at higher risk for adult obesity, a state linked to shorter life expectancies and higher risk of heart disease, high blood pressure, diabetes, gallbladder disease, and respiratory problems (Pi-Sunyer, 1995).

Obesity in childhood is also a problem because fat children are more likely than their thinner peers to be rejected or ridiculed. Albert Stunkard, one of the key figures in research on obesity, says:

> Obesity remains the last socially acceptable form of prejudice, and obese persons remain perhaps the only group toward whom social derogation can be directed with impunity. (Stunkard & Sobol, 1995, p. 417)

Elementary school children describe silhouettes of a fat child as "lazy, dirty, stupid, ugly, cheats, and liars" and are less likely to choose them as friends (Stunkard & Sobol, 1995). In general, kids this age express the same kind of prejudicial attitudes toward their fat peers as they do toward other "out groups," including children of the opposite gender, those with physical disabilities, or—sometimes—those of other ethnic groups.

Fear of fatness may also become a significant problem for some children. Serious eating disorders such as bulimia and anorexia—which I'll talk about in Chapter 13—don't become common until adolescence, but many school-age children, well aware of current cultural norms of thinness, are already dieting (Mellin, Irwin, & Scully, 1992). The balancing act required for the parents of an overweight child, then, is to try to help the child develop better eating and exercise habits without so emphasizing the importance of thinness that the child develops pathological patterns of dieting. Indeed, most experts argue that dieting (that is, restriction of caloric intake) is not appropriate at all for an overweight child because of the risk that a restricted diet would limit intake of key nutrients. Instead, a planned increase in physical activity, and a change in *what* the child eats, are better strategies.

Causes of Obesity.

Why are some children fat in the first place? Obesity in either childhood or adulthood appears to result from an interaction between a genetic predisposition and environmental factors that promote overeating or low levels of activity. Both twin and adoption studies show a

This overweight boy not only has different kinds of encounters with his peers, he is also more likely to be fat as an adult, with accompanying increased health risks.

clear genetic component. Adult identical twins have extremely similar adult weights, even if they are reared apart, while fraternal twins differ much more in weight (Stunkard, Harris, Pedersen, & McClearn, 1990). Even more persuasive are studies of adopted children, which show that those reared by obese parents are less likely to be obese than are the natural children of obese parents (Stunkard, Sorensen, Hanis et al., 1986).

Whether a child with a genetic propensity to fatness will actually become obese, however, depends on "energy balance"—the balance between the calories taken in and the number expended by exercise. In particular, obese children typically choose more sedentary activities or exercise some-what less.

Energy balance also quite obviously plays a role for the rising numbers of children who become obese even though they have no genetic propensity for fatness. Take another look at Figure 10.2 (p. 333). The *increase* in obesity over the past several decades shown in the figure—an increase documented by many researchers (e.g., Freedman, Srinivasan, Valdez, Williamson, & Berenson, 1997)—can't be explained by any hereditary factor; it *must* be due to environmental factors, specifically to some combination of poor diet and sedentary lifestyle.

The average school child in the United States today eats a diet too high in fat and too low in fruits, vegetables, and grains, a point I mentioned in Chapter 7. Table 10.2 gives you another look at the findings, comparing the average daily intake of various kinds of foods with the ideal amounts identified by the U.S. Department of Agriculture.

Clearly, children are not following the ideal diet. In fact, the picture is worse than the table suggests, because many school-age children eat no fruits or vegetables on a typical day; when they eat vegetables, it is more likely to be french fries than anything else. If you exclude the fried vegetables, as many as three in ten school-age children are eating less than one serving of fruits or vegetables each day (Krebs-Smith, Cook, Subar et al., 1996).

Table 10.2

Average Diet of 5– to 14-Year-Olds Compared with the Ideal

Food Group	Recommended Servings per Day	Actual Average Servings per Day
Grains	8	5.91
Vegetables	3.67	2.04
Fruit	3.67	1.41
Milk	2	2.50
Meat	2.25	1.65
Fat	<30% of calories	34%

Sources: Devaney, Gordon, & Burghardt, 1995; Kennedy, Ohls, Carlson, & Fleming, 1995; Nicklas, 1995a; 1995b; Krebs-Smith et al., 1996.

[?] Critical Thinking

College students, like school kids, are notorious for having bad diets. Write down everything you ate yesterday and compare it with the amounts listed in Table 10.2. Are you meeting these minimums?

Ironically, some of these flaws in children's daily diets are worse among children who eat school lunches and breakfasts than among those who don't. In particular, school lunches are notoriously high in fat, averaging about 37 percent of calories from fat (15 percent from saturated fat), compared with 33 percent in the average lunch of a child who brings lunch to school (Gordon, Devaney, & Burghardt, 1995). Part of the problem lies in the U.S. Department of Agriculture (USDA) regulations for school lunches (Pannell, 1995). They specify that whole milk must be offered, for example, and require a larger meat or meat alternative portion than is needed to meet children's protein needs, both of which add to the fat content of the meal. USDA-donated commodities, especially lard and cheese, have also increased the likelihood that the schools, trying to stay within their food budgets, will serve higher-fat foods. Furthermore, because children have learned to prefer high-fat foods, they begin to resist buying school lunches when the fat content drops below about 33 percent. Still, 33 percent is a good deal less than the 37 percent of fat in the typical current school lunch, so there is room for improvement, even without any food-choice education of students.

Obesity is also rising because children are getting less physical exercise, for a whole host of reasons. Many schools have cut back on aerobic exercise programs during physical education classes; some offer no physical education at all other than organized team sports. A second factor is the increasing number of families in which both parents work full-time. When children in these families get home from school, they are likely to stay at home, watching television or playing video games, rather than being physically active outdoors. One set of influential researchers, William Dietz and Steven Gortmaker (Dietz & Gortmaker, 1985; Gortmaker, Dietz, Sobol, & Wehler, 1987) have pushed this a step further, arguing that there is a causal connection between the amount of time a child spends watching television and the risk of obesity, not only because those who watch television are more sedentary, but because they are bombarded with ads for high-fat and high-sugar foods, resulting in less healthy eating habits and less healthy ideas about foods (Centers for Disease Control, 1996b). The prescription for children, and for our society as a whole, seems pretty clear: more exercise, healthier food, and less TV and other sedentary activities.

Other Normal Physical Changes

Children's bodies change in a whole variety of important ways beyond the highly visible changes in height and weight. Let me talk briefly about two such changes.

Bone Growth

Bones mature in such a regular and predictable way that physicians use **bone age** as the best single measure of a child's physical maturation, using X rays of the hand and wrist to judge the stage of development of wrist and finger bones. In general, bones continue to ossify during these years, with particular activity at sites at the ends of long bones (leg and arm bones as well as finger bones) called *epiphyses*. When the epiphyses have completely ossified, the bone stops growing and the child's height, arm length, and leg length are set (Tanner, 1990). These processes occur in all bones to at least some extent during the elementary school years, although the greatest bone growth is in the legs and feet (Bailey, Faulkner, & McKay, 1996). Parents will notice this effect indirectly: Children's shoe sizes are likely to increase faster than almost any other clothing size during these years, increasing as often as every three months. Parents must prepare themselves for the need to buy as many as four new pairs of shoes each year for their elementary school children—no small matter, given the price of today's shoes.

The process of bone development also gives us another powerful argument for increased exercise or physical activity for children. Children who exercise more also add more calcium to their bones (Ruiz, Mandel, & Garabedian, 1995), a fact that becomes especially important in adulthood because the level of bone calcium in early adulthood is as much as you will ever have. After about age 35, bone calcium begins to drop, faster in women than in men. This decline can be slowed down by maintaining exercise and by continuing a diet high in calcium, but the slow loss of calcium cannot be totally prevented. When the calcium drops below a critical level, physicians describe the condition as **osteoporosis,** and the risk of fractures increases substantially. Thus the level of bone calcium in early adulthood is highly important because the higher it is then, the later in life you are likely to fall below the critical level. By this argument, exercise in childhood is critical because it helps to increase bone density (Bailey et al., 1996).

Hormone Changes

Another important set of physical changes beginning in these years are the hormone changes that eventually lead to puberty. Such hormone changes may begin as early as age 6 or 7 in some girls, and at 9 or 10 for boys—an effect you've already seen in Figure 10.1 (p. 329). Since it is not until adolescence that we see these hormone changes in full flower, I will save the discussion of puberty until Chapter 13, where I can describe the whole process in one connected discussion, although those of you who will be elementary school teachers should bear clearly in mind that the average age for the earliest breast development in girls in the United States is between 9 and 10. Two to 3 percent of girls will begin menstruating at age 10 or younger, and another 15 percent will menstruate before age 12 (Herman-Giddens et al., 1997; Tanner, 1990), an age when most are still in elementary school.

Motor Development

Large muscle coordination continues to improve in these early school years, so that children become more and more skillful at things like bike riding. They also get both faster and stronger. As just one example, 5-year-olds can jump about 34 inches in a standing broad jump, while 11-year-olds can jump an average of about 64 inches (Cratty, 1979).

Girls in this age range are still ahead of boys in their overall rate of maturation. However, because girls also have slightly more body fat and slightly less muscle tissue than do boys, boys this age are slightly faster and stronger, which gives them an advantage in sports like baseball. Girls are slightly more flexible, which gives them an advantage in a sport like gymnastics. Still, the sex differences in both strength and speed are small at this age and the distributions overlap a great deal. For example, a 9-year-old boy can run 16.5 feet per second; a 10-year-old girl can run 17 feet per second (Cratty, 1979).

[?] *Critical Thinking*

Given these quite small sex differences in speed and strength, do you think it makes sense to have mixed-sex sports teams (such as soccer or swimming teams) in this age group? Why or why not?

Perhaps even more significant is the school-age child's increasingly good *ne* motor coordination. For example, a 5-year-old, with her greatly improved gross motor skills, can manage to hold her balance while standing on one leg by using her big muscles, using her arms and whole body to balance. The 8-year-old, with her growing fine motor skills, is able to balance by making many small adjustments. These same improvements in small muscle coordination allow the child to develop skill in writing, playing of most musical instruments, drawing, cutting, and many other skills. Improved fine motor skills also contribute greatly to the huge gains we see in children's abilities to play various sports and games.

Nevertheless, it is good for both parents and teachers to remember that 8- and 9-year-olds still do not have the level of speed, strength, or coordination that an adolescent or an adult has. Their reaction time—the time it takes to respond to some stimulus, such as pressing a button when you hear a buzzer or swinging the bat at the sight of a pitcher throwing the ball—is still significantly slower than an adult's, and their eye-hand coordination is far from perfect. So elementary school children may swing at a ball too late or judge the timing of kicking a ball inaccurately. Because children this age seem so confident and coordinated in their body movements, it is easy to forget that they still have a good deal of their physical maturation to go and cannot yet control their body movements completely.

Health

School-age children are generally healthier than are infants and toddlers; they are less likely to die than at any other period of childhood, and they have fewer colds and other acute illnesses. Still, children this age do get sick, and some do die.

Mortality

Table 10.3, which parallels Table 7.5 for the preschool period, shows you the most likely causes

Table 10.3

Primary Causes of Death Among Children Ages 5 to 14 in the United States

Cause	Number of Deaths per 100,000 Children	Rank Order of Causes for Each Ethnic/Racial Group		
		White	Black	Hispanic
Accidents	9.3	1	1	1
Cancer	4.1	2	3	2
Homicide	1.6	4	2	3
Congenital anomalies	1.2	3	4	4
Suicide	0.9	5	8	5

Source: National Center for Health Statistics, June 1996, data from Table 1, pp. 18, 21, 25, 28.

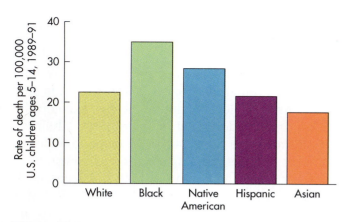

Figure 10.3

Although the likelihood of death among elementary school–age children is lower than at any other age in childhood, and has declined steadily over the past decades, it remains higher among African-American and Native American children than among other groups. (Source: Singh & Yu, 1996, from Table 1, p. 507.)

of death of school-age children in the United States. You can see in the table that accidents are the leading cause of death in every ethnic group, as was also true among preschoolers. Motor vehicle accidents account for 5.2 deaths per 100,000 children each year, and another 4.1 die of other kinds of accidents, including falls, fire, and drownings.

Counting all causes of death, 22.5 out of every 100,000 children this age will die in any given year, half the rate we see among preschoolers. Happily, this death rate has declined an average of approximately two percent every year for the past five decades in the United States (Singh & Yu, 1996), suggesting that, as a society, we have begun to control at least some of the causes of child deaths, such as through the use of seat belts and helmets. You will not be surprised, though, that death rates vary from one ethnic group to another, a pattern shown in Figure 10.3. African-American children—especially African-American boys—have the highest death rates, primarily because of much higher rates of accidents and homicide.

Illnesses and Accidents

School-age children suffer from essentially the same list of chronic illnesses as do preschoolers (go back and look at Table 7.6, p. 232), although ear infections become significantly less likely by school age because of the maturation of the structures of the inner ear. Acute illnesses like colds and flu are also a bit less common in these years. In the United States the average elementary school youngster has 4 to 6 such short-term illnesses each year.

While illnesses fall in frequency in the school years, the risk of nonfatal injuries from accidents rises in this age range. The annual rate of such injuries is about .4 for preschool children and .7 for elementary school children (Bussing, Menvielle, & Zima, 1996; Schor, 1987). The most common form of accident among school-age children is a fall, resulting in bruises, cuts, or broken bones, but children are also injured in bike accidents, by running into the street and being hit by a car, in fires, in fights, and by accidental poisonings (Shanon et al., 1992).

Such accidents are not equally distributed across all children, as you can see from Table 10.4, which lists some of the characteristics linked to increased risk of accident. Three factors seem to account for most of the items listed. First, children who are less well supervised have more accidents, whether the relative lack of supervision occurs because there is only one adult in the home, or because the parents are highly stressed, or for some other reason. Second, children who are physically more active have more accidents, a group that includes boys and any child who is physically more mature. This sex difference is actually quite large. Elementary school boys average approximately .8 accidents per year, while girls average only about .6, and boys' injuries tend to be more severe. As one example, Canadian researchers found that in a group of children treated for accidental injury in an emergency room in a large hospital, the boys were six times more likely than the girls to be so seriously injured that they were admitted to the hospital rather than being treated and sent home (Shanon et al., 1992). And third, Table 10.4 tells us that children whose behavior is wilder or more aggressive are more likely to have accidents (Bussing et al., 1996; Christoffel, Donovan, Schofer, Wills, & Lavigne, 1996).

Sports Injuries.   One item not listed in the table but that may be of particular interest to parents is the risk of injury among children who are involved in organized sports. The figures tell us that children's sports are not without risks. In the Canadian

Table 10.4

Groups with Higher Risk of Accidental Injuries Among School-Age Children

- Boys
- Children from single-parent families
- Children from highly stressed families
- Children from highly crowded households
- Children from crowded neighborhoods
- Highly aggressive, hyperactive, or antisocial children
- Bigger, more physically developed children

Sources: Bussing et al., 1996; Christoffel et al., 1996.

study I just mentioned, 17 percent of the injuries to children ages 5 to 10 were from sports activities; in the United States, 775,000 children under 15 are treated in hospital emergency rooms for sports injuries each year. Striking as this number is, it is probably not the crucial statistic. What a parent wants to know is the likelihood that a child participating in some sport will receive some significant injury and whether some sports are riskier than others. Unfortunately, there is no standard system for reporting sports injuries so we have no firm answer to these questions (Landry, 1992). In general, the *rate* of injuries seems to be fairly low. One study of soccer players ages 6 to 17 found an overall injury rate of 19 percent, but only 3 percent of those injuries required a player to miss more than one day of playing (Backous, Friedl, Smith, Par, & Carpine, 1988). The other broad conclusion we can draw from the research is that the older and bigger the athlete, and the more contact and collision involved in the sport, the higher the risk of injury. Among high school athletes, for example, the injury rate is highest in football, followed by wrestling and gymnastics (Garrick & Requa, 1978; McLain & Reynolds, 1989). Parents may try to steer their children away from such sports and into less injury-prone sports such as soccer, running, or swimming. Yet, as Gregory Landry, a pediatrician who specializes in sports injuries, points out:

> Despite a parent's best efforts, children tend to self-select sports based on their own desire, peer pressure, and their own talent regardless of injury rates. (1992, p. 166)

Poverty and Children's Health

A recurrent theme in what I've been saying about children's health here, and in Chapter 7, is that children living in poverty have considerably higher risks for almost every type of health problem. Barbara Starfield, a pediatrician and one of the leading experts on the epidemiology of children's health, has provided a striking summary (Table 10.5).

A sobering list, isn't it? This pattern is not unique to the United States. Equivalent risk differentials exist in virtually all countries. Nor are explanations hard to come by. I'm sure you could easily come up with a fairly complete list of potential causes and contributing factors. Your list would certainly include some of the following.

Access to Health Care. In any country lacking some kind of universal health coverage (such as the United States), poor parents are likely to have more limited access to health services for themselves or their children (Newacheck, 1994). In the United States, Medicaid, a federal program that provides medical coverage for those on welfare, helps to alleviate this problem for the poorest families. Still,

Table 10.5

Comparison of Health Problems of Poor Versus Nonpoor Children

Problem	Rate for Poor Compared with Rate for Nonpoor
Low birth weight	Double
Delayed immunization	Triple
Asthma	Higher
Lead poisoning	Triple
Neonatal mortality	1.5 times
Child deaths from accidents	Double–triple
Child deaths from disease	Triple–quadruple
Percent with conditions limiting school activity	Double–triple
Lost school days	40% more
Severely impaired vision	Double–triple
Severe iron-deficiency anemia	Double

Source: Starfield, 1991, adapted from Table 4, p. 522.

Parenting

What Parents and Teachers Can Do to Promote Better Health in School-Age Children

Once again, as in Chapters 4 and 7, let me list some highly specific things you can do to improve the chances that your school-age child will have good health and avoid accidents:

1. **Make sure your child has breakfast every morning.** Parents need either to provide breakfast at home or to have the child take breakfast at school if it is offered there. Teachers in schools that offer breakfast should encourage parents who are eligible for free or reduced-price breakfasts to take advantage of the opportunity. I cannot stress strongly enough how important it is for children's learning that they have breakfast before school.

2. **Make sure your child uses a seat belt every time she rides in a car and always uses a helmet when biking or skateboarding.** The latter point is especially critical for elementary school–age children who are much more likely to be riding bikes or boards over longer distances.

3. **Make sure your child is involved in some kind of vigorous physical activity every day.** Teachers and parents should lobby for the use of physical education periods in schools for aerobic activities and not just sports training; parents should encourage outdoor physical play where it is safe to do so or involve their children in some kind of organized sport activity.

4. **Encourage your child's school to shift toward lower-fat school lunches and low-fat snacks available in vending machines, and make sure you provide the same at home.** More fruits and vegetables would be good, too, though I know it is not always easy to get kids to eat them.

5. **Cut down on your child's TV-time.** It is simply not good for kids to spend hours every day watching the TV. Television viewing is linked to higher rates of aggressive behavior (a set of findings I'll be talking about in Chapter 12) and to higher risk of overweight. It encourages poor eating habits and reduces the amount of time a child has for either reading or physical play—both activities that are far more important for a child's physical health and intellectual development than almost anything she might see on television.

even for those poor who are covered by Medicaid, the barriers to regular health care for children can be substantial. Physicians who will take Medicaid patients (and a great many will not) may not be nearby; parents may face multiple bus trips and long waits at clinics or doctors' offices; and emergency room care, while often excellent, does not provide the kind of consistent monitoring of the child's health that is enjoyed by most middle-class families.

The situation for the working poor who are not eligible for Medicaid is considerably worse. Nicholas Zill (Zill, Moore, Smith, Stief, & Coiro, 1995) reports on one national survey showing that 43 percent of children in poor-but-not-on-welfare families were not covered by any form of health insurance, compared with only 12 percent of children in nonpoor families. Pregnant women who lack medical insurance are less likely to receive adequate prenatal care, thus increasing the likelihood of low birth weight and other neonatal problems; families who lack medical insurance are less likely to have their child fully immunized; when the child is ill, the child is seen later in the illness by a physician (usually in an emergency room); if the child suffers from a chronic condition (such as asthma), medication may be simply too expensive.

Dangerous Home and Neighborhood Environments. Children living in poverty also quite simply face more dangers.

- Their housing is more dilapidated, with attendant increased risks of cuts or falls.
- They are exposed to higher fire risks. Their buildings are less likely to have adequate smoke alarms; the wiring is more likely to be dangerously faulty.
- They are exposed to higher levels of lead, both in paint in their houses or apartments, and in inner-city air. Among other negative effects of elevated blood lead levels is a lower IQ score, as you can see from the results shown in Table 10.6, drawn from a famous Australian study of lead exposure.

Social Policy Debate

Changes in Immigration Law and Child Health

Legislation designed to address one set of problems often has unintended consequences. Here's one example.

In the fall of 1996, the state of California, interpreting one provision of the new federal welfare law, announced that they would begin cutting off funds to provide Medicaid-supported prenatal care to illegal immigrants (Golden, 1996). Epidemiological data clearly show that inadequate (or nonexistent) prenatal care in any group will lead to an increase in various kinds of prenatal and birth problems for that group. Lacking prenatal care, an increased percentage of illegal immigrant women, and their infants, will end up in emergency rooms and neonatal intensive care units—care that is enormously more expensive than is prenatal care.

One physician, the president of the California Association of Public-health Executives, says:

From a public-health perspective this is a no-brainer. In addition to the humanitarian and clinical considerations, it is an extremely prudent financial decision not to let any woman go without adequate prenatal care. (quoted in Golden, 1996, p. A1)

The counterargument, proposed by the governor of California and others, is that various federal requirements to provide services for illegal immigrants have resulted in a huge increase in health care costs, creating an unfair economic burden on state taxpayers. A spokesperson for the governor said:

Nobody is arguing about whether prenatal care benefits are good or bad. Obviously, it's a good thing. But we don't have enough resources. The Governor feels that it is unfair to deny people who are here obeying the laws when you're giving benefits to people who broke the law to come in. (quoted in Golden, 1996, p. C24)

Try thinking about this issue from two perspectives: in your role as a citizen/taxpayer and in your new role as a student of child development. In the end, what kind of policy do you think would be best?

Table 10.6

IQ Scores at Age 7 for Children with Varying Blood Lead Levels from the Port Pirie Study in Australia

Lead Level	Average IQ Score at Age 7
Category I (lowest)	109.6
Category II	107.7
Category III	102.7
Category IV (highest)	98.7

Note: Only Category I had blood lead levels below the level of 10 micrograms per deciliter now defined by the Centers for Disease Control as safe. Category IV had levels averaging 20 micrograms.

Source: Baghurst et al., 1992, Table 2, p. 1281.

- They are more likely to have to cross busy roads, leading to higher rates of pedestrian/car accidents.
- They encounter more violence both in their neighborhoods and in their homes.
- They live in more crowded conditions, with more changes—people moving in and out of their home, moves from one home to another,

and the like. They must thus deal with far higher levels of chronic stress than do children living in more sheltered environments. Stress-related diseases, such as asthma, are thus particularly frequent among poor children.

- They are more likely to live with someone who smokes. One survey shows that 58% of children living on welfare live with at least one adult who smokes, compared with 41% of children who are living in nonpoor families (Zill et al., 1995).
- When they travel by car, they are less likely to sit in special seats or wear seat belts; they are less likely to use bicycle helmets (Rivara, 1995).

The great majority of these differences flow fairly directly from financial poverty itself. A poor parent may be able to afford only dilapidated and dangerous housing. Similarly, a parent who has a hard time providing enough food for a child is unlikely to buy a bike helmet or a special car seat. Others of these increased risks flow from the greater stresses under which poor families live, making it just that much harder for the parent(s) to supervise their children closely.

Children living in poverty, whether in rural poverty like these Appalachian mountain children on the left or in urban poverty like the homeless family on the right, are simply exposed to higher risks for both disease and accident, one of several reasons that they get sick and injured two to three times as much as do more affluent children.

Single Parenthood. Living with a single parent also adds risks for a child—a point you've already seen illustrated in Figure 7.4 (p. 235) Even when they are not living in poverty, single parents simply have more difficulty managing all the myriad tasks of parenthood. As just one example, they have more trouble monitoring their children, so their children have more accidents (I. Roberts & Pless, 1995). Single parents' lives are also more likely to be chaotic, which adds stress for the child—stress that may be expressed in disease.

[?] *Critical Thinking*

Imagine that you were appointed by the President to a special commission to try to reduce the rate of illness and accidents among poor children. Given what you've read here, what three or four specific policy suggestions might you recommend?

Health Habits: Physical Exercise and Fitness

Another factor that may influence the child's health is exercise and overall physical fitness, measured either in terms of strength or speed or by assessing aerobic power (the body's ability to take in and transport oxygen.) Among adults, the linkages are clear: Physical exercise increases fitness, and greater fitness is linked to better health. Adults who exercise even moderately live longer and are less likely to suffer from such chronic illnesses as cardiovascular disease (Blair, Kohl, Barlow et al., 1995; Blair & Meredith, 1994; Lee, Hsieh, & Paffenbarger, 1995; Lissner, Bengtsson, Björkelund, &

Wedel, 1996). Among children, the immediate health benefits of greater fitness are less well established, although regular moderate or vigorous exercise does help to reduce or control some significant childhood medical problems, such as obesity and diabetes. Robert Malina (1989) also argues that exercise is essential for maintaining proper physical growth, including adding calcium to bone, as I mentioned earlier. Finally, the *habit* of exercise, established in childhood, may increase the likelihood that an individual will continue to exercise in adulthood—a highly desirable outcome (Blair & Meredith, 1994).

Physical Education in Schools. Physical education programs in schools have been one important mechanism for promoting fitness as well as providing training in individual sport skills. In recent years, in light of the accumulating evidence on the importance of exercise in adulthood, many physical education experts have emphasized the importance of training in so-called *lifetime physical activities*—activities or sports that are relatively easy to pursue into adulthood because they can be done alone or with only one or two others, such as swimming, walking, running, bicycling, racquet sports, aerobic dance, weight training, rowing, or skiing (e.g., Ross, 1994). Competitive team sports (football, basketball, volleyball, ice hockey, etc.), in contrast, are far more difficult to pursue in adulthood. When we look at what actually goes on during physical education (PE) classes in schools, several national surveys show that programs for elementary school students are doing a fairly decent job of promoting both general fitness and lifetime physical activities, with the greatest emphasis

Virtually all school-age children participate in some kind of organized physical activity, whether in physical education classes at school, like the one on the left, or in nonschool sports programs, like the coed soccer program on the right.

on aerobic activities. For high school students, the emphasis shifts much more toward team sport training.

Among fifth and sixth graders in the United States, the most common PE activities for boys are (in descending order) tag, tumbling, jumping or skipping rope, climbing ropes, and touch football. The most common activities for girls are aerobic dance, climbing ropes, touch football, some kinds of gymnastics, jumping or skipping rope, and running sprints (Ross, 1994).

A great many elementary school children also participate in organized sports outside of school, both in the United States and in other countries (e.g., Brettschneider & Sack, 1996). The most comprehensive U.S. survey available shows that among 10-year-olds, 43 percent played on a baseball team, 42 percent on a swimming team, and 40 percent on a basketball team (Weiss & Hayashi, 1996). These numbers begin to drop off at ages 11 and 12 and older—for reasons I've explored in the *Parenting* box on page 344—so that by age 14, only about half as many children are still involved in organized, nonschool sports.

Levels of Fitness.   Does some reasonable level of physical fitness result from all that exercise? Yes and no. One way to answer that question is to test children on some standard set of physical tests, such as the items in the *FitnessGram* test devised by the Institute for Aerobics Research (1987). For example, the FitnessGram standard for a mile run/walk is 13 minutes for 8-year-old boys and 14 minutes for 8-year-old girls. Both boys and girls that age are expected to be able to do 25 sit-ups and 1 pull-up. When Marilyn Looney and Sharon Plowman (1990) compared the results of

the National Children and Youth Fitness Surveys with the FitnessGram standards, they found that the majority of children did in fact reach these rather modest criteria of fitness (Table 10.7, p. 345 gives some examples)—except that most girls lacked the upper body strength to do even one pull-up.

The picture is not quite so rosy if you ask how many children could pass all five of the Fitness-Gram tests, a level that earns a child an "I'm Fit" award. Among the 12-year-olds (for whom Looney and Plowman had complete data on all five standards), only about 40 percent of the boys and 20 percent of the girls were eligible for this award. Looney and Plowman conclude that American children are "acceptably fit," although that seems to be true only if we set our standards at a fairly low level. Furthermore, levels of fitness appear to decline after elementary school, especially among girls. Less than half of high school girls can meet the standard for the mile run/walk, which is set at $10\frac{1}{2}$ minutes for those between ages 14 and 18; less than a third can manage even one pull-up. If one of the goals of physical education in school is to help students maintain a level of fitness that will allow them to pursue a variety of lifetime sports throughout adulthood, I'd say we are not fully reaching that goal. The result is that, for many young (and middle-aged and older) adults, it is much harder to get started again with some beneficial aerobic activity—a fact I can attest to personally. At age 38, when I decided to try to regain fitness, it took me a month of diligent daily effort before I was able to jog a full mile without stopping. Eventually, I was able to run a half marathon (13.5 miles) in under 2 hours, so I know it's possible. But my initial level of unfitness was a substantial hurdle to overcome.

Parenting

Sports for Children

In the United States, and increasingly in other industrialized countries, children no longer play much in the street or in backyards; they play on organized teams and groups: soccer teams, Little League baseball, swimming clubs, and the like. Many children begin such programs when they are 6 or 7, often with great enthusiasm. But participation peaks by age 10 or 11 and then declines rapidly. Why?

Kids drop out of such programs because the emphasis on competition and winning is so great (Anshel, 1990; Harvard Education Letter, 1992). Children of 6 or 7 get involved in sports mostly because they simply enjoy moving their bodies rather than out of any desire to defeat some opponent. They want to do their best, but they care more about having a chance to play than they do about winning. Yet coaches in many organized sports, even those for young children, emphasize winning rather than fun or fair play or even basic exercise—a process sometimes called the "professionalisation of play" (Hodge & Tod, 1993). Mark Anshel tells this story:

> The volunteer coach for the city league was meeting just before the game with his young athletes, boys aged nine and ten years. He was talking about how important it was for everyone to play well and win; this was a "big game." Then he asked whether anyone had any questions. A youngster raised his hand and asked, "Coach, will everyone get a chance to play?" "What's more important," the coach snapped back, "everyone playing, or winning?" In a nutshell, this actual story illustrates two things; first, the problem with youth sport today, and second, the different needs and priorities of child athletes as compared with those of the "mature," grown sport competitor. (1990, p. 327)

Further, amateur coaches often have poor understanding of normal motor skills among 6- or 7-year-olds. When they see a child who does not yet throw a ball skillfully or kicks a ball awkwardly they label this child as clumsy or uncoordinated. From then on, these perfectly normal kids get little playing time or encouragement. Only the stars—children with unusually good or early motor skill development—get maximum attention and exercise. Coaches may also overtly compare children's abilities, criticizing those who don't play as well rather than emphasizing effort and improvement. Kids drop out of sports by age 10 or 11 because they have a clear impression that they are "not good enough" (Anshel, 1990).

In fact, 6 or 7 is really too early for most children to be playing on full-size playing fields or in competitive games (Kolata, 1992). It would be far better to wait until age 9 or 10—if then—for competitive games, and to have kids spend the earlier years learning and perfecting basic skills in activities that are fun, regardless of their skill level, and that involve as much movement as possible. Among sports activities, soccer and swimming are particularly likely to meet these conditions, not only because everyone is likely to get at least some aerobic exercise but also because the basic skills are within the abilities of 6- or 7-year-olds. Baseball, in contrast, is *not* a good sport for most kids this age because it requires real eye-hand coordination to hit or catch the ball, coordination that most 7-year-olds do not yet have. Many children will be ready to play sports such as basketball by age 10 or so, but many organized sports such as tennis are still difficult for the average child of this age.

If you want to encourage your children to be involved in some organized sport (as opposed to simply encouraging active games or outdoor play), choose carefully. Let the child try several sports—individual sports as well as team sports—to see which one or ones he or she may enjoy. The child's body type or size may suggest which sports are likely to be best. A lean child of average or below-average height may find soccer or gymnastics a good choice; a larger child with broader shoulders may make a good swimmer; taller children may be inclined toward basketball—although small size certainly does not disqualify a child from this sport (Malina, 1994a). Whatever program you choose, make sure to select specific instructors or programs that deemphasize competition and offer skill training and encouragement to *all* children. Finally, don't push too fast or too hard. If you do, your child is likely to drop out of any type of organized sport by age 10 or 11, saying—as many do—that they feel inadequate or that it isn't fun anymore.

Table 10.7

Levels of Fitness in U.S. Children Compared with the FitnessGram Criteria

		8-year-olds			12-year-olds		
		Mile run/walk	Pull-ups	Sit-ups	Mile run/walk	Pull-ups	Sit-ups
Standard	Boys	13 min.	1	25	10 min.	1	35
	Girls	14 min.	1	25	12 min.	1	30
Percent meeting standard	Boys	84%	*	55%	71%	73%	65%
	Girls	85%	*	51%	69%	32%	70%

*Information not available because the younger children in the national survey were tested with chin-ups (palms facing body), whereas the standard refers to pull-ups (palms facing away from body).

Source: Looney & Plowman, 1990, from Table 1, p. 217.

[?] *Critical Thinking*

Why do you think more girls than boys lose fitness after elementary school? How could you check out your hypotheses?

Children with Special Problems

Any child who is not developing normally, such as children with physical disabilities, face special challenges when they begin formal education. Two other groups I haven't yet talked about—those with attention deficit disorder and those with learning disabilities—also face increased difficulty at school age. These are important subgroups of children for teachers to know something about, so let me describe them at least briefly.

Attention Deficit Hyperactivity Disorder

A mother in my home state of Wisconsin, Sue Munro, began to get calls from her son's teachers when he was in kindergarten.

> Chris was lying out in the hall, doing somersaults, standing on his head making weird noises. They couldn't get him in line with the rest of the class. He was bouncing off walls in Never-Never Land. (Martell, 1996, p. 1g)

Chris was later diagnosed with **attention deficit hyperactivity disorder (ADHD),** as were Sue Munro's two younger sons, Sam and Zach. A glance at the diagnostic criteria, listed in Table 10.8 (p. 346), will tell you quickly that the visible hallmarks of this disorder are physical restlessness and problems with attention, precisely as the label implies. Russell Barkley, one of the major researchers and theorists in this area, suggests that the underlying problem is a deficit in the child's ability to inhibit behavior—an inability to keep himself from starting some prohibited or unhelpful behavior or reacting to some compelling stimulus or to stop behaving in some fashion once he has started (1997). In busy, complex environments, with many stimuli (such as a classroom), ADHD children are unable to inhibit their reactions to all the sounds and sights around them, so they appear restless and cannot sustain attention on a single activity.

I should tell you that there is still a good deal of dispute among psychologists and psychiatrists, in the United States and Europe, about whether this is a single syndrome or whether it would be more fruitful to divide it into subtypes. European psychologists recognize only the hyperactivity subtype, which they label **hyperkinetic syndrome** (Taylor, 1995). American psychologists argue for a general syndrome with two subtypes (as shown in the table). Indeed, when the child shows an attention problem but not hyperactivity, U.S. practitioners normally use a different name, calling it **attention deficit disorder (ADD).** Because of these wide variations in definition, it is hard to arrive at

Table 10.8

Diagnostic Criteria for Attention Deficit Hyperactivity Disorder

- The child must show either significant *inattention* **or** significant *hyperactivity-impulsivity* or both.
- Inattention would be indicated by any six or more of the following:
  (1) often fails to give close attention to details or makes careless mistakes in schoolwork or other activities
  (2) often has difficulty sustaining attention in tasks or play
  (3) often does not seem to listen when spoken to directly
  (4) often does not follow through on instructions and fails to finish chores, homework, or duties
  (5) often has difficulty organizing tasks and activities
  (6) often avoids, dislikes, or is reluctant to engage in tasks that require sustained mental effort
  (7) often loses things necessary for tasks or activities (e.g., toys, pencils, books, tools)
  (8) often is easily distracted by extraneous stimuli
  (9) often is forgetful in daily activities
- Hyperactivity-impulsivity is indicated by the presence of six of the following, persisting over a period of at least six months:
  (1) often fidgets with hands or feet or squirms in seat
  (2) often leaves seat in classroom or in other situations in which remaining seated is expected
  (3) often runs about or climbs excessively or reports feelings of restlessness
  (4) often has difficulty playing quietly
  (5) is often "on the go" or often acts as if "driven by a motor"
  (6) often talks excessively
  (7) often blurts out answers before questions are completed
  (8) often has difficulty waiting for a turn
  (9) often interrupts or intrudes on others
- The onset of the problem must be before age 7.
- At least some of the symptoms must be present in at least two settings, such as home and school, or school and play with peers.
- The behavior must interfere with developmentally appropriate social, academic, or occupational functioning.

Source: Paraphrased from *Diagnostic and Statistical Manual of Mental Disorders* (4th ed.), 1994. Washington, DC: American Psychiatric Association, pp. 83–85. Copyright 1994 by the American Psychiatric Association.

a good estimate of just how common a problem this may be. The best current guess, based on studies from around the world, is that between 3 and 7 percent of children can be diagnosed with some form of ADHD. Perhaps 1.5 percent show hyperactivity alone, while ADD alone occurs in perhaps 1 percent of children (Barkley, 1997; Buitelaar & van Engeland, 1996). The remainder show both hyperactivity and attention difficulties. All these patterns are three to five times more common in boys than in girls (Heptinstall & Taylor, 1996)—yet another example of the greater vulnerability of boys.

A further diagnostic problem arises from the fact that a great many children are inattentive or overactive at least some of the time. It is tempting—for both teachers and parents—to label a boisterous or obstreperous child as ADD or ADHD. There is no doubt that a good deal of mislabeling of this kind does occur, especially in the United States, where ADD or ADHD are far more common diagnoses than is the case in Europe. In fact, however, the full syndrome is quite distinctive. ADHD-children's interactions with their peers are so strikingly different that novice observers need to watch videotapes for only a few minutes before they can reliably distinguish between a child diagnosed as ADHD and a normally behaving child, even when the hyperactive child displays no aggression and the sound is turned off (Henker & Whalen, 1989).

The body language is distinctive, the level of activity is different, and the child's social behavior is often inappropriate. About half such children *also* show problems with excessive aggressiveness, and most do poorly in school.

By definition, this is an early-developing disorder. The majority of hyperactive children already show some problems with attention and inhibition of activity by preschool age; many have problems making friends and playing effectively with peers because they are not well tuned to their playmates' cues, even at this early age (Sandberg, Day, & Gotz, 1996). ADHD persists into adolescence in half to three-quarters of cases and into adulthood in a third to a half of all instances (Barkley, 1997). The severity of the long-term problem seems to be strongly influenced by whether or not the child also develops what psychologists call a **conduct disorder,** a term that refers generally to excessive aggressiveness, bullying, cruelty, and delinquency (Martin & Hoffman, 1990). It is the combination of hyperactivity and aggressiveness that is especially likely to lead to later problems (Barkley, Fischer, Edelbrock, & Smallish, 1990). You can see one facet of this effect in the results of a longitudinal study by Terrie Moffitt (1990) of a group of 434 boys in New Zealand, including all boys born over a one-year period in a particular town. When the boys were 13 they were classed in one of four groups, based on the presence or absence of two factors: attention deficit disorder and delinquency. Moffitt then traced backward for each of these groups, looking at scores at earlier ages on measures of antisocial behavior, intelligence, and family adversity. You can see the results for antisocial behavior in Figure 10.4.

It is clear that the boys who showed *both* ADD (or ADHD) and delinquency as adolescents had been the most antisocial at every earlier age. ADD that was not accompanied by antisocial behavior at early ages was also not linked to delinquency at 13. Other research tells us that this same group of hyperactive *and* delinquent boys is also the most likely to have continued serious problems in adulthood, including criminal behavior.

Where might ADD or ADHD come from? Because the pattern begins so early and has such a strong physical component, most clinicians have assumed that these problems have some kind of biological origin. Surprisingly, early research failed

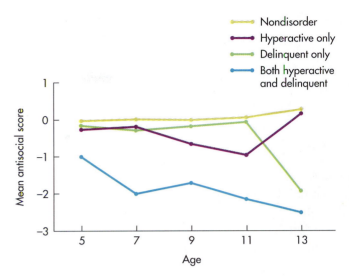

Figure 10.4

The boys in Moffitt's study had been studied every two years from the time they were 5. When they were 13, they were assigned to one of four hyperactivity/delinquency categories, then Moffitt backtracked from that age. You can see that those who were both delinquent and hyperactive at age 13 had shown markedly higher rates of antisocial behavior from the time they were 5, while those who were only hyperactive at 13 had been much less socially deviant at earlier ages. (Source: Moffitt, 1990, Figure 1, p. 899.)

to confirm such a biological hypothesis. Investigators could find no sign of overt brain damage, and typical neurological tests revealed no underlying physical problem. But three converging lines of evidence have revived the biological hypothesis.

To begin with, physicians and psychologists have known for some time that a biological *treatment* is very often effective in reducing or eliminating the deviant behavior. Roughly three-quarters of children diagnosed with ADHD in the United States (but many fewer in Europe) are treated with a stimulant medication called methylphenidate (most commonly, the drug Ritalin). The drug works by stimulating the part of the brain where attention is maintained. Most (but not all) children treated with this drug show decreases in demanding, disruptive, and noncompliant behaviors, lessened aggressiveness and noncompliance, more attentiveness in the classroom, and improved performance on many academic tasks (Schachar, Tannock, & Cunningham, 1996). This type of evidence is consistent with a biological explanation of ADHD, although of course it does not prove that the root cause of ADHD is biological.

More persuasive evidence for an underlying biological cause comes from behavior genetic research, which suggests that a pattern of hyperactivity is inherited, at least in certain families. About a quarter of the parents of hyperactive children themselves have a history of hyperactivity. Studies of twins also show a genetic contribution. Among identical twins, if one is diagnosed as hyperactive, the other is highly likely to have the same diagnosis; among fraternal twins this "concordance rate" is much lower (Kado & Takagi, 1996).

Finally, newer methods of assessing brain function have begun to reveal subtle differences in brain structure and brain function between hyperactive and nonhyperactive individuals. For example, studies using magnetic resonance imaging (MRI) suggest that the majority of ADHD children

have larger right than left brain hemispheres, while the majority of non-ADHD children show the reverse (Hynd, Hern, Novey et al., 1993). In another widely publicized study, Alan Zametkin and his colleagues (Zametkin, Nordahl, Gross et al., 1990) used positron-emission tomography (PET) scans to examine the glucose (sugar) metabolism in the brains of hyperactive and normal adults. All the hyperactive adults reported that they had also been hyperactive as children, and all had at least one offspring with the same diagnosis. Each subject was injected with a concentrated dose of glucose; then repeated PET scans were done to look at how the brain metabolized the sugar. Zametkin found that the hyperactive adults had significantly slower brain metabolism of the glucose, and this was especially so in the portions of the brain that are known to be involved in attentiveness and the ability to inhibit inappropriate responses.

Researchers have not yet zeroed in on the precise biological mechanism involved, but new research of this type strongly supports the basic hypothesis that ADHD has *some* biological basis. Still, being more confident about the origins of ADHD does not settle all the important questions. From the point of view of developmental psychopathology, we also need to understand how such an initially deviant biological pattern affects the child's interactions with parents and peers to produce the common combination of hyperactivity and antisocial behavior. For many hyperactive children, the pathway is very like the one Patterson has described for defiant or aggressive children. These kids are just plain hard to raise. Those parents whose child management skills are not up to the task of dealing with the hyperactive toddler's typically higher rates of noncompliance, or who face major family stresses that prevent them from maintaining good child-care routines, may find that their child's behavior becomes more and more disruptive, which in turn adversely affects the child's emerging social skills. By school age, parent-child conflict is high, as is child-peer conflict. Poor school performance makes it worse by lowering the child's self-esteem. Such children are then on a pathway that is highly likely to lead to continued problems in adolescence and adulthood (Campbell, 1990). In Moffitt's New Zealand study, for example, those boys who eventually showed the combination of hyperactivity and delinquency

This boy, diagnosed with attention deficit hyperactivity disorder, is likely to be given medication to help control his behavior.

Parenting

The Pros and Cons of Drug Treatment for Attention Deficit Hyperactivity Disorder

In the United States at least two million children (roughly five percent of all children in school) are taking Ritalin or an equivalent drug for some variant of hyperactivity or attention deficit. How should we interpret this fact? Does it mean that children with problems are being helped, or does it mean that far too many children are being identified as ADHD so that their normally boisterous behavior can be controlled in school? Both arguments have been made, as you can imagine. If you have a child diagnosed as ADHD or ADD, how do you decide whether your child should be medicated? If you're a teacher with such a child in your classroom, what advice do you give the parents? I am not going to try to settle this argument for you; I honestly don't know what choice I would have made if one of my children had been diagnosed with ADHD. If you find yourself in this situation you should do some serious research and ask a great many questions. What I can do here is to sketch some of the pros and cons so that you will know the kinds of questions to ask.

The arguments against Ritalin are several. First, many kids with mild forms of hyperactivity or attention deficits can be handled effectively without drugs, primarily by creating extra structure and reducing distractions in the child's immediate environment—good strategies for hyperactive children whether they are on medication or not. Second, the drugs have some possible side effects, including insomnia, stomachaches, and decreased appetite. Medicated children also may show increased talkativeness, anxiety, or motor and vocal tics (Schachar et al., 1996). The majority of children taking such drugs have minimal physical side effects, but as many as 40 percent of children can tolerate only low dosages. Third, we simply don't have enough infor-

mation about possible long-term effects of extended use of these drugs—an important question because the average child taking such drugs is taking them for three years or more. Some research hints at the possibility of some growth retardation; possible long-term effects on heart, liver, or kidneys are simply unknown.

The primary argument on the other side is that stimulant therapy *does* reduce symptoms for most children, allowing them to improve their school performance and their relationships with peers. The more severe the child's symptoms, the more necessary or helpful drug therapy may be. The use of drugs like Ritalin is also linked to lowered levels of defiance and aggressiveness. If it helps ADD children avoid the pathway toward pervasive and long-lasting conduct disorders, it may be worth the other risks or side effects.

If, after reviewing all the evidence and consulting with your physician, you decide that medication may be in order for your child, the next step is to find out whether your particular child will actually benefit. The best way to do that is with a "double-blind, placebo-controlled crossover trial" (Kemper, 1996). Your doctor arranges for a pharmacist to make up three sets of pills: a placebo, low-dose Ritalin, and higher-dose Ritalin. Neither you nor the physician knows which is which. The child takes one set of pills each week for three weeks, during which you (and perhaps the child's teacher) keep careful records of behavior, using some standardized symptom diary. At the end of three weeks, you try to guess which medication was which. If your child's behavior was notably better in a week that the pharmacist later says was a week with Ritalin, then you know that the medication has some beneficial effect.

All in all, not an easy decision.

came from families with much higher than average levels of stress and fewer resources. The hyperactive boys who did not develop the accompanying antisocial behavior came from families with lower than average levels of stress and more resources. Thus once again we find that the key for long-term problems or for recovery from difficulties lies in the interaction between the child's inborn or early-developed qualities and the capacity of the family and the environment more generally to support the child's optimum behavior.

Learning Disabilities

A second group of children who present special problems for teachers are who those who have difficulty learning to read, write, or do arithmetic, despite normal IQs and essentially good adaptive functioning. The typical label for this problem is **learning disability (LD),** although you will also hear terms like *dyslexia* (literally "nonreading") or *minimal brain damage.* The official definition of this problem includes the presumption that the difficulty arises from some type of central nervous system dysfunction or damage, in much the same way that definitions of ADHD assume some kind of biological underpinning. In fact, some children with attention deficit disorder are *also* diagnosed as learning disabled, so these two sets of problem children overlap. The overlap, however, is far from complete; most children diagnosed as learning disabled do not suffer from ADHD.

Diagnosing a learning disability is extremely tricky because it is basically a *residual* diagnosis. It is the label normally applied to a child who does not learn some school task, who is *not* generally retarded, and who does *not* show persistent or obvious emotional disturbance or a hearing or vision problem. In other words, we can say what learning disability is *not*; what we cannot say is what it *is*. Furthermore, the specific form of a child's learning disability may vary widely, with some displaying difficulties in reading only, some having trouble with reading and spelling (such as the boy whose writing sample is shown in Figure 10.5), and others having more difficulty with arithmetic.

Because of such fuzziness in the definition of the disability, there is a good deal of dispute about just how many LD children there really are. Sylvia Farnham-Diggory (1992), one of the leading experts in the field, argues that up to 80 percent of all children classified by school systems as learning disabled are misclassified. She claims that only about 5 out of every 1000 children are genuinely learning disabled. The remainder are more appropriately called slow learners, or they may suffer from another difficulty, perhaps temporary emotional distress, poor teaching, or whatever.

Practically speaking, however, the LD label is used very broadly within school systems (at least within the United States) to describe a grab bag of children who have unexpected or otherwise unexplainable difficulty with schoolwork, particularly reading. Nearly 5 percent of all children in the United States are currently labeled in this way (Farnham-Diggory, 1992).

The Nature of the Problem. Given such problems with definition, we shouldn't be surprised that the search for causes has been fraught with difficulties. As Farnham-Diggory says, "We are trying to find out what's wrong with children whom we won't be able to accurately identify until after we know what's wrong with them" (1986, p. 153).

The most central problem has been with the basic assumption that learning disability has a neurological basis. The difficulty is that children so labeled (like hyperactive children) rarely show signs of major brain damage on any standard tests—perhaps because many children are mislabeled or perhaps because the brain dysfunction is more subtle than what can be measured with standard tests.

The most promising current view is that a large number of small abnormalities develop in the brain during prenatal life, such as some irregularity of neuron arrangement, clumps of immature brain cells, scars, or congenital tumors. The growing brain compensates for these problems by "rewiring" around the problem areas. These rewirings, in turn, may scramble normal information processing procedures just enough to make reading, calculation, or some other specific task very difficult (Farnham-Diggory, 1992).

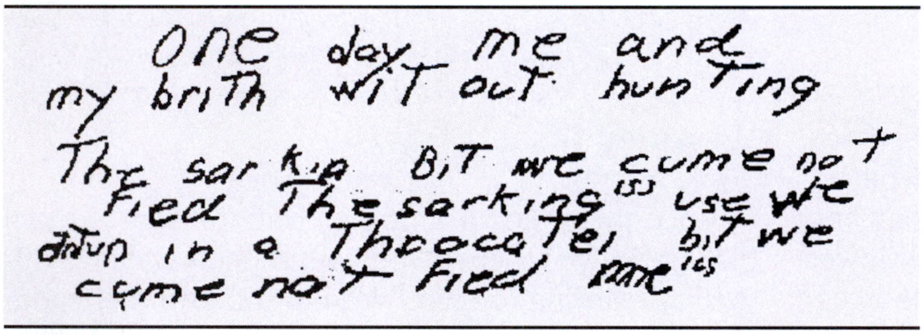

Figure 10.5

This story, written by 13-year-old Luke, diagnosed as learning disabled, translates as follows: "One day me and my brother went out hunting the Sark. But we could not find the Sark. So we went up in a helicopter but we could not find him." The little numbers next to some of the words are Luke's word counts. They show that despite his severe writing handicap, his counting abilities were intact (Source: Farnham-Diggory, 1978, p. 61).

School can surely be a discouraging and frustrating place for a child with a learning disability.

explanation of learning disability occur despite thousands of research studies and a great deal of theorizing by thoughtful and capable people. Not surprisingly, the uncertainty at the theoretical level is reflected in confusion at the practical level. Children are labeled "learning disabled" and assigned to special classes or given special help in a regular classroom, but whether the child will be helped by a particular type of intervention program will depend on whether that specific program is (a) any good, and (b) happens to match his or her type of disability or problem. Remediation does seem to be possible, but it is *not* simple, and a program that works well for one child may not work at all for another. Of course, this is not good news for parents whose child may be having difficulty with some aspect of schooling, whose only recourse is trial and error and eternal vigilance. But it reflects the disordered state of our knowledge.

Inclusive Education

Parents of children with any kind of disability should know that Public Law (P.L.) 94-142, called the Education for All Handicapped Children Act, passed in 1975, specifies that every child in the United States must be given access to an *appropriate* education in the *least restrictive environment* possible. P.L. 94-142 does not say that every child, no matter what the nature or degree of his or her disability may be, must be educated full-time in a regular classroom. The law allows schools to offer a continuum of services, including separate schools or special classrooms, although the law also indicates that a child should be placed in a regular classroom as a first choice, and be removed from that setting only if the child's disability is such that he cannot be satisfactorily educated there.

P.L. 94-142 and the supplementary laws that followed it (including P.L. 99-457, the Education of the Handicapped Act Amendments of 1986, and P.L. 102-119, the Individuals with Disabilities Education Act [IDEA] of 1990) rest most centrally on the philosophical position that children with disabilities have a right to participate in normal school environments (e.g., Stainback & Stainback, 1985). Proponents have further argued that such *inclusive education* aids the disabled child by integrating him into the nondisabled world, thus facilitating the development of important social

Another explanation of the problem, one I'll be exploring more fully in the next chapter, is that reading disability may reflect a more general problem with understanding the sound and structure of language. The research findings supporting this conclusion have been very helpful in pointing educators toward possible remedial programs for some children with reading difficulties, but they do not tell us why a child might have such language deficits in the first place. The problem may indeed lie in some type of brain dysfunction, or it may be that children whose reading problem has a linguistic origin are among the 80 percent Farnham-Diggory says are misclassified. They do indeed have a reading problem, but they may not have a neurological problem underlying it.

I want to emphasize that the continuing confusions and disagreements about identification and skills as well as providing more appropriate academic challenges than are often found in separate classrooms or programs designated for the disabled (Siegel, 1996). Advocates of **inclusion** are convinced that mildly retarded and learning disabled children will show greater academic achievement if they are in regular classrooms full-time.

Schools and school districts differ widely in the specific model of inclusion they use, although virtually all systems involve a team of educators, including combinations of the classroom teacher, one or more special education teachers, classroom aides, and volunteers. Some schools follow a plan in which the disabled student is placed in a regular classroom part of each day, with the remainder of the time spent working with a special education teacher in a special class or resource room, a system often called a *pull-out program*. More common today are *full inclusion systems*, in which the child spends his entire school day in a regular class, receiving help from volunteers, aides, or special education teachers who come to the classroom to work with the child there. In some districts, a group of disabled children are clustered in a single classroom; in others, no more than one such child is normally assigned to any one class (Baker & Zigmond, 1995).

I don't think we need to argue about the desirability of the overall goal: to provide every child with the best education possible, one that challenges optimally and gives the child the best possible chance to learn the basic intellectual and social skills needed to function in our increasingly complex society. (No small task!) What the experts (and parents) do argue about is whether current inclusion programs are meeting this goal. The arguments are not calm! (See e.g., Gerber, 1995; Roberts & Mather, 1995.) Some academicians ac-

cuse each other of "selling out" by questioning the value of full inclusion (McLeskey & Pugach, 1995). Others say their "worst fears" have been realized by the existing evidence on inclusion programs (Martin, 1995). All in all, there is definitely more heat than light on this whole issue.

From my point of view, as both a psychologist and a scientist, I would like answers to the most basic questions, such as whether learning disabled, retarded, or physically disabled children are *better off* intellectually and socially in inclusion programs than in special classes. Do they make more progress in reading or math? Do they learn better social skills—skills that will enable them to function later in a job situation, or with peers? Do they make friends?

For those of you who plan to be teachers, these theoretical questions are entirely moot. Inclusion programs are legally mandated and here to stay (Putnam, Spiegel, & Bruininks, 1995). For teachers, the crucial question is more practical: What works best? Among the many varieties of inclusion programs, can we identify features that are consistently associated with better results or poorer results?

All these questions—mine and yours—are extremely hard to answer. For all kinds of perfectly understandable reasons, we have little of the kind of research we need to answer them. Inclusion programs vary widely in design and serve children with diverse problems. The teachers who implement them range from highly skilled and inventive to overwhelmed and unskilled. If a particular program pattern appears to work in one school, it is often difficult to tell whether it is successful because of the specific teachers involved, because of the specific characteristics of the children being served, or because the program itself is especially well designed.

Both David, the Down syndrome boy on the right, and Gina, a child with spina bifida on the left, are in inclusive elementary school classrooms, participating as fully as possible in all activities and assignments.

Given all this, it is not surprising that we lack clear answers to either the practical or theoretical questions. Still, educators and psychologists have struggled to summarize the information we do have. Most would agree with the following conclusions:

- Taken as a group, children with disabilities appear to show equivalent academic gains in inclusive programs as they do in special classes (Buysse & Bailey, 1993; MacMillan, Keogh, & Jones, 1986; Odom & Kaiser, 1997). For children with a physical disability but without any learning problem, full inclusion is clearly optimal.

- However, for the subset of children with learning disabilities, full inclusion programs may be less academically supportive than are pull-out programs or "resource rooms." As Vaughn and Schumm say: "The evidence that does exist for students with learning disabilities suggests that they do not fare well academically in the general education classroom, where undifferentiated, large-group instruction is the norm" (1995, p. 264). Success for LD children in a regular classroom depends heavily on the ability of the teacher to implement an individualized program.

- Although there may be some social benefits from inclusion, there are also social risks. Some research shows gains in self-esteem and social skills for disabled children in inclusion programs (e.g., Banerji & Dailey, 1995; Cole, 1991b). Yet virtually all groups of disabled children, including the learning disabled, mildly retarded, and physically disabled, are more likely to experience rejection from their peers in regular classes than are nondisabled children (e.g., Sale & Carey, 1995). Learning disabled students, in particular, are often notably unpopular with their peers (Roberts & Mather, 1995).

- Effective inclusion programs require, at a minimum, that teachers be given extensive additional training and substantial support from specialists, aides, or volunteers (Roberts & Mather, 1995)—conditions that are very often not met because of budgetary or other reasons. The majority of teachers feel they are not prepared to teach students with disabilities; many who have such children in their classrooms feel that they do not receive adequate support (Schumm & Vaughn, 1995).

Reading through this set of statements will convince you that there is no magic bullet here, no single solution for educators, for parents, or for disabled children. If you are planning to become a teacher, you will need to learn as much as possible about the needs of children with various kinds of disabilities as well as about successful strategies for teaching them; if you are a parent of a disabled child, you will need to inform yourself about all the educational alternatives and to be ready to act as the child's consistent advocate within the school system.

Summary

1. Children gain 2 to 3 inches and 4 to 6 pounds per year between ages 6 and 9. Past age 9, girls gain in height more rapidly than boys, and both boys and girls gain weight faster than height.

2. There are some slight ethnic differences in growth patterns, but the overall pattern is highly similar for all children.

3. Children who are extremely small for their age and family height pattern should be evaluated by a physician. Possible explanations include chromosomal anomalies, prenatal growth retardation, endocrine gland disorders, or malnutrition or chronic subnutrition.

4. Undernourished children grow more slowly, and they have less energy and are less able to maintain focused attention in school. They also get sick more often. A surprising number of children (perhaps one in eight) in the United States are hungry at least occasionally.

5. Obesity is also very common and increasing in frequency in the United States and many other countries. At present, more than one-fifth of elementary school children are obese; one-tenth are superobese.

6. Obesity is a problem not only because fatness tends to persist, bringing higher rates of health problems in adulthood, but because obese children are more likely to be rejected by their peers.

7. Obesity is at least partially genetically influenced, but diet and lack of exercise also play a role, especially in accounting for the rise in obesity. The majority of U.S. schoolchildren eat too few fruits and vegetables and too much fat.

8. Children gain in both large muscle and small muscle coordination in the elementary school years, making

possible more skillful writing and drawing as well as more coordinated and skillful sports performance.

9. School-age children have the lowest death rates of any age group in childhood or adolescence. Accidents are the most common cause of death in this age range. Nonfatal accident rates, however, are higher at this age than among preschoolers, in part because children are less closely supervised and engage in more physically active play.

10. Virtually all forms of physical disability, chronic illness, acute illness, and accidents are more frequent among children living in poverty. Explanations focus on lowered access to health care, on more dangerous home and neighborhood situations among the poor, as well as on higher levels of general stress.

11. Adequate physical exercise to achieve real fitness is important for children's health. Physical education programs in schools are designed to meet this need, yet a significant fraction of children cannot pass minimal tests of fitness.

12. Children with special problems include those diagnosed with attention deficit hyperactivity disorder, a pattern that normally begins in early childhood and persists. It includes problems with both attention and excessive restlessness and activity.

13. Hyperactivity appears to have an initial biological cause, but deviant patterns are aggravated or ameliorated by subsequent experience.

14. Nearly 5 percent of the school population in the United States is labeled as learning disabled. There is still considerable dispute about how to identify genuine learning disability, and many children may be misclassified.

15. Learning disability may be caused by small anomalies in brain function; alternatively, it may reflect broader language or cognitive deficits, or both.

16. Inclusive education—in which children with disabilities are primarily educated in regular classrooms alongside nondisabled children—is mandated by law in the United States, although many questions and problems remain. Programs vary widely; some are effective, others are not.

Key Terms

attention deficit hyperactivity disorder (ADHD) The current technical term for what is often called hyperactivity, characterized by short attention span, distractibility, and heightened levels of physical activity. **(p. 345)**

attention deficit disorder (ADD) Term sometimes used interchangeably with ADHD, but also used more narrowly to describe the subset of children who show attention problems without hyperactivity. **(p. 345)**

body mass index (BMI) A measure of fatness in which weight is adjusted for height. The specific formula is: weight in kilograms/(height in centimeters)^2. **(p. 332)**

bone age A measure of physical maturation based on X-ray examination of bones, typically the wrist and hand bones. Two children of the same chronological age may have different bone age because they differ in rate of physical maturation. **(p. 336)**

conduct disorder Diagnostic term for a pattern of deviant behavior including any or all of excessive aggressiveness, bullying, cruelty, or delinquency. **(p. 347)**

hyperkinetic syndrome Label used in Europe in place of attention deficit disorder; diagnosed much more rarely than ADD in the United States. **(p. 345)**

inclusion Term used to describe the full-time placement of physically, mentally, or emotionally disabled children in regular classrooms, with any special services required by the child provided in that classroom. **(p. 352)**

learning disability (LD) Term broadly used to describe any child with an unexpected or unexplained problem in learning to read, spell, or calculate. More precisely used to refer to conditions in a subgroup of such children who have some neurological dysfunction. **(p. 349)**

obesity Most often defined as a body weight 20 percent or more above the normal weight for height, or a body mass index at the 85th percentile or above. **(p. 332)**

osteoporosis Loss of bone mass after middle age, resulting in more brittle and porous bones and a substantially increased risk of fracture. **(p. 336)**

superobese An individual with a body mass index at the 95th percentile or higher. **(p. 332)**

Suggested Readings

Alper, S., Schloss, P. J., Etscheidt, S. K., & Macfarlane, C. A. (1995). *Inclusion. Are we abandoning or helping students?* Thousand Oaks, CA: Corwin Press. A small book aimed at teachers, full of highly practical suggestions about strategies for including disabled children in a classroom.

Brownell, K. D., & Fairburn, C. G. (Eds.). (1995). *Eating disorders and obesity*: A *comprehensive handbook*. New York: Guilford Press. Short, comprehensible chapters on every aspect of eating disorders and obesity. Much of the focus is on adolescents and adults, but the basic principles are much the same.

Farnham-Diggory, S. (1992). *The learning-disabled child*. Cambridge, MA: Harvard University Press. This revision of an excellent book will give you an up-to-date source, pitched at the level of the lay reader.

Sandberg, S. (Ed.). (1996). *Hyperactivity disorders of childhood*. Cambridge, England: Cambridge University Press. Dense, detailed chapters on every aspect of this problem, written by European experts.

Cognitive Development at School Age

Preview Questions

1 How would a teacher committed to a Piagetian-style constructivist theory of cognitive development organize her classroom?

2 Do young children make good court witnesses?

3 What is the best single predictor of a child's ease in learning to read?

4 What are some of the key characteristics of highly effective schools?

5 Why do boys score higher on tests of upper-level mathematics?

Chapter Outline

The years of middle childhood are often passed over rather briefly, as if they were somehow insignificant for our understanding of cognitive development. Far less research has been done on the thinking of children in this age group than on either preschoolers or adolescents. Yet surely the beginning of formal schooling is a seminal event—both a response to the cognitive gains the child has already made and an important stimulus for further intellectual gains. It is not accidental that children in virtually every country in the world begin school at age 5, 6, or 7. Children this age are ready for the demands of formal schooling in a way that younger children are not. In the years that follow, they must acquire a wide range of quite specific competencies, including the three Rs. Broader cognitive changes also occur during these years, much as Piaget described. For those of you who will be elementary school teachers, it is vital to understand all these intellectual changes as well as the factors that affect them. Let's start with perhaps the most basic skill, language.

Language Development

By age 5 or 6 virtually all children have mastered the basic grammar and pronunciation of their native tongue. They can create remarkably complex sentences and have a vocabulary of perhaps 15,000 words. Yet anyone who has talked recently with a 6-year-old is well aware that the child still has a fair distance to go before reaching adultlike facility with language. During middle childhood, children learn such things as how to maintain the topic of conversation, how to create unambiguous sentences, and how to speak politely or persuasively (Anglin, 1993).

They also continue to add new vocabulary at a fairly astonishing rate of 5000 to 10,000 words per year. This estimate comes from several recent, careful studies by Jeremy Anglin (1993; 1995), who estimates children's total vocabularies by testing them on a sample of words drawn at random from a large dictionary. Figure 11.1 shows Anglin's estimates for grades 1, 3 and 5. Anglin finds that, between the third and fifth grades, the largest gain occurs in knowledge of the type of words he calls *derived words*: words that have a basic root to which some prefix or suffix is added, such as happ*ily* or *un*wanted.

Anglin argues that at about age 8 or 9 the child shifts to a new level of understanding of the structure of language, figuring out relationships between whole categories of words, such as between adjectives and adverbs (happy and happily, sad and sadly), or between adjectives and nouns

The children in these photos, from Guatemala and the Czech Republic, start school at about age 5 or 6—as do children in nearly every other part of the world.

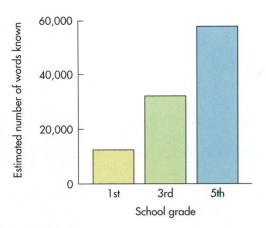

Figure 11.1

Anglin's estimates of the total vocabulary of first, third, and fifth graders. (Source: Anglin, 1995, from Figure 6, p. 7.)

(happy and happiness), and the like. Having understood these relationships, the child can now understand and create a whole class of new words and his vocabulary thereby increases rapidly.

Cognitive Changes

Such an understanding of underlying patterns is just what Piaget also thought was new about these years of middle childhood. Piaget argued that this new quality of children's learning and understanding, which becomes apparent at about age 6 or 7, was as striking, and as significant, as the acquisition of symbol usage at age 2.

Piaget's View of Concrete Operations

The new skills we see at age 6 or 7 build on all the small changes we have already seen in the preschooler, but from Piaget's perspective a great leap forward occurs when the child discovers or develops a set of immensely powerful, abstract, general "rules" or "strategies" for examining and interacting with the world. You'll remember from Chapter 2 that Piaget calls these new skills *concrete operations*. By an "operation," Piaget means any of a set of powerful, abstract, internal schemes such as reversibility, addition, subtraction, multiplication, division, and serial ordering. All these opera-

tions are critical building blocks of logical thinking, providing internal rules about objects and their relationships. The child now understands the *rule* that adding something makes it more and subtracting makes it less; she understands that objects can belong to more than one category at once and that categories have logical relationships.

Of all the operations, Piaget thought the most critical was **reversibility**—the understanding that both physical actions and mental operations can be reversed. The clay sausage in a conservation experiment (described in a *Research Report* in Chapter 2, p. 53) can be made back into a ball; the water can be poured back into the shorter, fatter glass. This understanding of the basic reversibility of actions underlies many of the gains made during this period. For example, if you understand reversibility, then knowing that A is larger than B also tells you that B is smaller than A. The ability to understand hierarchies of classes, such as Fido, spaniel, dog, and animal also rests on this ability to go backward as well as forward in thinking about relationships.

Piaget also proposed that during this third stage the child develops the ability to use **inductive logic.** He can go from his own experience to a general principle. For example, he can move from the observation that when you add another toy to a set and then count the set, it has one more than it did before, to a general principle that adding always makes it more.

Elementary school children are pretty good observational scientists and will enjoy cataloging, counting species of trees or birds, or figuring out the nesting habits of guinea pigs. What they are not yet good at is *deductive logic*, which requires starting with a general principle and then predicting some outcome or observation, such as going from a theory to a hypothesis. For example, suppose I asked you to think of all the ways human

[?] *Critical Thinking*

Try thinking about this question and watch yourself as you are thinking about it. Can you see how your deductive logic works? Can you think of everyday situations in which you use inductive or deductive logic?

Psychology in Action

Conservation of Number and Weight

Warning: This project, like many of the *Psychology in Action* suggestions given in this text, should not be undertaken without explicit permission and guidance from your instructor, who will have to obtain permission from your college or university's Human Subjects Review Committee for any project in which you interview or observe a child or parent directly. **Do not do this project on your own, without such permission.**

For this project you need to locate a child between ages 5 and 10 and obtain permission from the parents, or from both the parents and the child, following the procedures specified by your instructor. You will be testing this child for two kinds of conservation: number and weight. Recall that the concept of conservation involves the understanding that some features of objects remain invariant despite changes in other features. The weight of an object remains the same regardless of how its shape is changed; the number of objects in a row remains the same regardless of how widely spaced the objects are. Typically, number conservation is learned (or discovered) at about age 5 or 6, while conservation of weight is learned later, at perhaps age 8 or 9.

Procedure

The testing can ordinarily be done most easily in the child's home although other settings are quite OK if they can be arranged. Present the child with the two tasks in the order given here, following instructions precisely.

Conservation of Number. For this part of the process you will need 14 pennies or identical buttons. Start with ten items and place them between yourself and the child (preferably on a table, but the floor will do), spaced equally in two rows of five, as follows:

```
X  X  X  X  X
X  X  X  X  X
```

Ask the child:

Are there the same number of pennies (buttons) in this row as there are in this row, or are there more here (pointing to the child's row), or more here (pointing to your row)?

The child may want to move the objects around a bit before he agrees the two rows are the same, which is fine. Once the child has agreed they are the same, spread the objects in your row so that it is now noticeably longer than the child's row but still contains only five objects; for example:

```
X    X    X    X    X
  X  X  X  X  X
```

Now ask the following questions, and record the child's exact answers:

Are there the same number of pennies in this row as there are in this row, or are there more here, or more here?

Depending on the child's answer to this question, ask either of the following probe questions:

Why are they the same? or *Why are there more here?*

Now spread out the child's row and add two objects to each row, so that your row and the child's row are again exactly matched, with seven items equally spaced in each. Ask question 2 and the probe question as above, and record the child's answers precisely.

Now move the objects in your row closer together so that the child's row is now longer. Ask question 2 and the probe question again and record the answers.

Conservation of Weight. Put away the pennies (or give them to the child), and bring out two equal balls of clay or Play-Doh, each a size that can be readily handled in a child's palm. Handle them yourself, rounding

relationships would be different if women were physically as strong as men. Coming up with answers to this question requires deductive, not inductive, logic; the problem is hard because you must imagine things that you have not experienced. The child using concrete operations logic is good at dealing with things he knows or can see and manipulate—that is, he is good with *concrete* things; he

does not do well with mentally manipulating ideas or possibilities. Piaget thought that deductive reasoning did not develop until the period of formal operations in junior high or high school.

Piaget did not say, by the way, that all these concrete operations skills popped out all at the same moment, as if a lightbulb had gone on in the child's head. He understood that it took the child

Psychology in Action

Conservation of Number and Weight (*Continued*)

each into a ball, and then hand them to the child and ask:

> Do these two balls weigh *the same? Do they have the same amount of weight?*

If the child agrees that they weigh the same, proceed. If not, say, *Make them the same,* and let him manipulate the balls until he agrees they are equal. Once he has agreed, say,

> *Now I am going to make this ball into a hot dog.*

Roll one of the two balls into a hot dog shape. When you have completed the transformation, put the two pieces of clay in front of the child and ask:

> *Does this one* (pointing to the hot dog) *weigh the same as this one* (pointing to the ball), *or does this one* (the hot dog) *weigh more, or does this one* (the ball) *weigh more?*

Depending on the child's answer to question 3, ask one of the following probe questions and record the answers carefully:

> *Why do they weigh the same?* or *Why does this one weigh more?*

This ends the procedure, so you should praise and thank the child. You might also want to play a bit with the child with some other toy of the child's choosing, to make sure that the whole process is pleasant to the child.

Analysis and Report

For each of the crucial questions, decide whether or not the child "conserved." To be judged as having con-

served, the child must not only have said the two objects or sets were the same after transformation, he must also give a valid reason, such as:

> You haven't added any or taken any away so they have to be the same.
>
> One is longer but it is also skinnier so it is still the same.
>
> If I made it back into a ball, it would be the same.

Compare the child's performance on the two types of conservation. Did the child conserve on both, neither, or only one? Was the child's performance consistent with the typically observed sequence and age of acquisition of these two conservations? (If the child conserved weight but not number, that would be contrary to research data.) What else, other than the child's basic comprehension of conservation, might affect the child's answers in a test of this kind? Was the child interested or bored? Were there distractions in the environment? Might the sequence in which the items were given have any effect? Do you think it would have mattered, for example, if conservation of weight had been tested before conservation of number? If you were designing a study to examine the acquisition of these conservations, would you want to have all children given the items in the same order, or should the order be randomized?

If several students have completed this project, you may want to combine your data and analyze children's success on these three conservations as a function of age. Do your collective findings match the results of existing research?

some years to apply these new cognitive skills to all kinds of problems. At the same time, he argued that the shift to concrete operations involved a profound change in the *way* the child thinks, the strategies she uses, and the depth of understanding she can achieve.

Direct Tests of Piaget's Ideas

Researchers who have followed up on Piaget's descriptions of the concrete operational period have generally found that Piaget was right about the ages at which children first show various skills or under-

standings. Studies of conservation, for example, consistently show that children grasp conservation of mass or substance by about age 7. That is, they understand that the amount of clay is the same whether it is in a pancake or a ball or some other shape. They generally understand conservation of weight (that the two balls of clay weigh the same amount no matter their shape) at about age 8, but they understand conservation of volume (that an amount of water or clay takes up the same amount of *space* no matter its shape) only at about age 11.

Studies of classification skills show that at about age 7 or 8 the child first grasps the principle

Because elementary school–age children are good at observational science, field trips like this one to hunt fossils are a particularly effective way of teaching.

A good illustration of these several cognitive changes comes from an early longitudinal study of concrete operations tasks by Carol Tomlinson-Keasey and her colleagues (Tomlinson-Keasey, Eisert, Kahle, Hardy-Brown, & Keasey, 1979). They followed a group of 38 children from kindergarten through third grade, testing them with five traditional concrete operations tasks each year: conservation of mass, weight, and volume, class inclusion, and hierarchical classification. You can see from Figure 11.2 that the children got better at all five tasks over the 3-year period, with a spurt between the end of kindergarten and the beginning of first grade (about the age Piaget thought that concrete operations really began), and another spurt during second grade.

of **class inclusion,** that subordinate classes are *included in* larger, superordinate classes. Bananas are included in the class of fruit, and fruit are included in the class of food, and so forth. Preschool children understand that bananas are *also* fruit, but they do not yet fully understand the relationship between the classes—that the class of fruit is superordinate, including all bananas as well as all other subtypes, such as oranges or apples.

New Themes: Memory and Strategy Development

Some researchers, rather than simply repeating Piaget's tasks, have tried to devise other ways to test the proposition that school-age children, compared with younger children, approach tasks in ways that are more general, based on broader principles. In particular, the notion that older children consciously

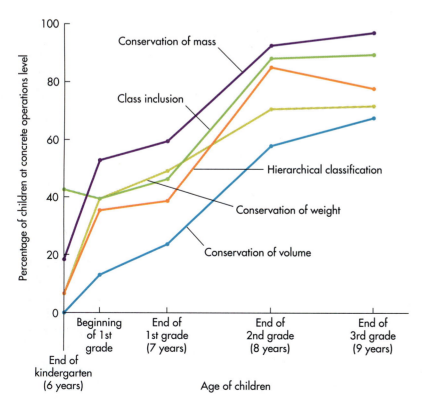

Figure 11.2

These results are from a longitudinal study in which the same children were given a set of concrete operations tasks five different times, beginning in kindergarten and ending in the third grade. (Source: Tomlinson-Keasey et al., 1979, adapted from Table 2, p. 1158.)

Teaching

Piaget's and Vygotsky's Theories in the Classroom

Many psychologists and educators have attempted to translate Piaget's and Vygotsky's ideas into specific educational practices. Two critical ideas are at the heart of all these educational applications: Piaget's basic concept of *constructivism,* which is that children *construct* their understanding of any given object, concept, or idea based on their own explorations; and Vygotsky's idea that *social interaction* is a critical ingredient in furthering the child's understanding (Brown, Metz, & Campione, 1996). In a classroom, these two ideas together argue for providing children with opportunities to explore together—to experiment and discover jointly, with children correcting and questioning each other. Here's a wonderful example of how this can work in a first grade classroom.

The teacher in this class, Anne Hendry, describes her efforts to teach her class about measurement (Hendry, 1996). On her classroom floor she taped the shape of a boat 16 by 6 feet, to represent the *Mayflower.* She told them that the King had proclaimed an edict that the ship could not sail until the children told him how big it was.

> "Well, what should we do? Who has an idea?" I asked. Thus our discussion of measurement began . . . or I thought it would begin. But there was a . . . long period of silence. . . . I watched as they looked from one to another, and I could see that they had no idea where to begin. Surely, I thought, there must be something they could use as a point of reference to expand on. Someone always has an idea. But the silence was long as the children looked again from one to another.

One of the children proposed that the boat was 3 feet long, which prompted a brief discussion but no progress. Finally,

> Tom raised his hand and said, "Mrs. Hendry, I know it can't be three feet because the nurse just measured me last week and said that I was four feet, and this boat is much bigger than me!" . . . "Let's see how many times Tom can fit in the boat," someone suggested. Tom got down and up several times along the length of the boat: the children decided that the boat was four "Toms" long.
>
> "How can we tell that to the King, since he does not know Tom?" I asked. "Send Tom to the King," was their easy solution. . . . I was really hoping that they would relate to the information Tom had already given us about his size. I thought someone might add four feet, four times, presenting us with a quick solution. . . . But this was not the route they decided to take.

Another child suggested they measure with hands instead of with Toms. So the children measured how many of Mark's hands were the length of the boat, ar-

riving at a length of 36 Mark hands. Mrs. Hendry then suggested that, just to make sure, they also have Sue (the smallest child in the class) use her hands—and it turned out to be 44 hands long.

> "Why are they different?" I asked. "Can we use hands to measure?" "No" the children decided, this would not work either, since everyone's hands were not the same size. Al suggested using feet. We tried this, but once again, when someone else double-checked with their feet, we found two different measurements.

The discussion began again during the next day's math period. One child suggested that they might use Zeb's foot to measure. Zeb had been the child assigned to read the original "Edict" from the King. The children reasoned that since Zeb knew the King, and the King knew Zeb, the King would understand Zeb's foot size.

> "Measure it on a piece of paper and measure everything in Zeb's foot." Using this form of measurement, the children related to the King that the boat was 24 "Zeb's foot" long and 9 "Zeb's foot" wide.

The children then proceeded to measure everything in the classroom, using their new "ruler." Over the next several days, Hendry asked the children why it was important for everyone to use the same measuring strategy; later, she had them explore the use of rulers and other conventional units of measurement.

Notice that Hendry *did not tell the children how to get the answer.* She used the group process (a Vygotskian aspect), but she allowed the children to struggle and to try a variety of "wrong" solutions, discovering for themselves why they wouldn't work. At the end of this lesson, these children *understood* measurement in a completely new way. Many teachers would not have had the patience to wait so long for the children to arrive at an answer; many would have been unable to resist bringing out a ruler and showing them how to use it. But Hendry's approach is a clearer application of Piaget's and Vygotsky's principles. It is not just that children need to measure for themselves, but that they need to discover the *principle* of measuring. Hands-on experience, then, is not enough to make some classroom technique "Piagetian" or "Vygotskian." What is crucial is that the child or a group of children have a more unfettered opportunity to try to solve puzzles or discover a basic process or principle (Schifter, 1996). The teacher's role, however, remains crucial. She must pose interesting problems, have information available for the students to turn to if they want to find answers, group children in sets that can work effectively together. In Vygotsky's terms, she must create an appropriate *zone of proximal development.*

use *strategies* for solving problems or for remembering things has been the basis for a whole new look at cognitive development. Work on memory and memory strategies is a particularly good example.

Rehearsal Strategies. Suppose you need to run a set of errands: stop at the cleaners, buy some stamps, copy your IRS forms, and buy milk, bread, orange juice, carrots, lettuce, spaghetti, and spaghetti sauce at the grocery store. To remember such a list, you might use any one of several possible strategies, some of which I have listed (with examples) in Table 11.1. You could rehearse the list, you could organize the route in your mind, you could remember your menu for dinner when you get to the grocery store.

[?] *Critical Thinking*

How would you go about remembering this list of things to do? Would you write down the list? What other strategies might you use?

Do children do these things when they try to remember? One classic early study (Keeney, Cannizzo, & Flavell, 1967) indicated that school-age children did but younger children did not. Keeney showed children a row of seven cards with pictures on them and told them to try to remember all the

pictures in the same order as they were laid out. A space helmet, then placed over the child's head, kept the child from seeing the cards but allowed the experimenter to see if the child seemed to be rehearsing the list by muttering under his breath. Children under 5 almost never showed any rehearsal, while 8- to 10-year-old children usually did. Interestingly, when 5-year-olds were *taught* to rehearse, they were able to do so, and their memory scores improved. But when these same 5-year-olds were then given a new problem without being reminded to rehearse, they stopped rehearsing. That is, they could use the strategy if they were reminded, but they did not produce it spontaneously, a pattern described as a **production deficiency.**

More recent work suggests that preschool-age children can show some kinds of strategies in their remembering if the task is quite simple, such as the game of hide-and-seek (DeLoache, 1989). In one of Judy DeLoache's research techniques, the child watches the experimenter hide an attractive toy in some obvious place (e.g., behind a couch), and is then told that when a buzzer goes off she can go and find the toy. While playing with other toys during the 4-minute delay interval, 2-year-olds often talked about, pointed to, or looked at the toy's hiding place—all of which seem clearly to be early forms of mnemonic strategies.

These results and others like them tell us that no magic shift from nonstrategic to strategic behav-

---

Table 11.1

Some Common Information Processing Strategies Involved in Remembering

Rehearsal	Either mental or vocal repetition, or repetition of movement (as in learning to dance). May occur in children as young as 2 years under some conditions; is common in older children and adults.
Clustering	Grouping ideas or objects or words into clusters to help you remember them, such as "all animals," or "all the ingredients in the lasagna recipe," or "the chess pieces involved in the move called castling." This strategy is more easily applied in an area where you have experience or particular knowledge. Primitive clustering occurs in 2-year-olds.
Elaboration	Finding shared meaning or a common referent for two or more things that need to be remembered. The helpful mnemonic for recalling the notes for the lines on the musical staff ("Every Good Boy Does Fine") is a kind of elaboration, as is associating the name of a person you have just met with some object or other word. This form of memory aid is not used spontaneously by all individuals, and is not used skillfully until fairly late in development, if then.
Systematic searching	When you try to remember something, you can "scan" your memory for the whole domain in which it might be found. Three- and 4-year-old children can begin to do this when they search for actual objects in the real world, but are not good at doing this in memory. So search strategies may be first learned in the external world and then applied to inner searches.

Source: Flavell, 1985.

ior occurs at age 5 or 6 or 7. Children as young as 2 use primitive strategies, but school-age children seem to use strategies far more flexibly and efficiently, a quality of thinking that becomes increasingly evident in older school children (Bjorklund & Coyle, 1995). For example, when learning a list of words, 8-year-olds are more likely to practice the words one at a time ("cat, cat, cat") while still older children practice them in groups ("desk, lawn, sky, shirt, cat"). The 8-year-olds, tested again a year later, show signs of a shift toward the more efficient strategy (Guttentag, Ornstein, & Siemens, 1987).

Other Memory Strategies.   Other strategies that help improve memory involve putting the items to be learned or remembered into some meaningful organization. When you mentally organize your grocery list with all the fruits and vegetables in one group and all the canned food in another, you are using this principle, which is called *clustering* or *chunking*.

Studies of clustering often involve having children or adults learn lists of words that have potential categories built into them. For example, I might ask you to remember this list of words: *chair, spaghetti, lettuce, cat, desk, chocolate, duck, lion, table*. I give you two minutes to try to memorize the list, using whatever method(s) you want, making sure you understand that you don't have to remember them in the order I listed them, but in any order you like. I'm only interested in how many you can recall. Then I ask you to list the words for me. If you have used some kind of clustering technique, you are likely to list the same-category words together (*cat, duck, lion; chair, desk, table;* and *spaghetti, chocolate, lettuce*).

School-age children do show this kind of internal organization when they recall things, while preschoolers do not. And among school-age children, older children use this strategy more efficiently, using a few large categories rather than many smaller ones (Bjorklund & Muir, 1988).

In sum, we can see some primitive signs of memory strategies under optimum conditions as early as age 2 or 3; but with increasing age children use more and more powerful ways of helping themselves remember things. In the use of each strategy children also appear to shift from a period in which they don't use it at all, to a period in which they will use it if reminded or taught, to one in which

they use it spontaneously. Finally, they use these strategies more and more skillfully and generalize them to more and more situations. These are obviously changes in the *quality* of the child's strategies as well as the quantity.

Expertise

However—and this is a big however—all these apparent developmental changes may well turn out to be as much a function of expertise as they are of age. That may sound like one of those statements that only theorists care about, but this particular issue has major implications for education. Piaget's theory suggests that elementary-age children are "in" the concrete operations stage; they are making cognitive progress, to be sure, but their thinking is still limited in certain general ways, regardless of the amount of experience they may have had with some particular kind of problem. If that's true, then your teaching strategies have to take those cognitive limitations into account. The alternative possibility is that children this age are quite able to perform complex cognitive feats when they are dealing with something they know a lot about—when they have **expertise,** to use the psychologist's term. If this possibility turns out to be supported, then a teacher need not think of being limited in what she might try to teach her class on some specific topic. The children might still need to learn the material in some sequence, perhaps beginning with more concrete approaches, but they could move toward very complex ways of thinking and analyzing as their expertise develops.

The research supports this second possibility. Specific knowledge makes a huge difference. Children and adults who know a lot about some subject or some set of materials (dinosaurs, baseball cards, mathematics, or whatever) not only categorize information in that topic area in more complex and hierarchical ways, they are also better at remembering new information on that topic and better at applying more advanced forms of logic to material in that area. Furthermore, such expertise seems to generalize very little to other tasks (Ericsson & Crutcher, 1990). A child who is a devout soccer fan will be better than a nonfan at recalling lists of soccer words or the content of a story about soccer, but the two children are likely to be equally

Research Report

Memory and the Child as Witness

In a case in England, a 7-year-old was able to provide the police with details of her experience after a sexual assault and was later able to identify her attacker in a lineup (Davies, 1993). In several famous cases in the United States, children as young as 3 have testified in court about physical or sexual abuse by nursery school teachers, testimony that has sometimes (but not always) led to convictions. Such testimony by children has raised a storm of controversy, centering on two main issues: (1) Can young children accurately remember faces or events and report on their experiences, even after a period of time has passed? (2) Are children more suggestible than adults about what they might have seen or experienced? (Will they report what they have been told to say, what may have been suggested to them, or what they actually saw or felt?) The answer to both questions seems to be yes, which leaves us in a real dilemma regarding the overall accuracy of children's testimony (Ceci & Bruck, 1995). What is the evidence that supports this mixed conclusion?

To begin, recall of specific events or of the faces of people seen at a previous time does improve with age, but even preschoolers can recall action-related events with considerable accuracy. When experimenters have staged various crises or happenings, preschoolers and school-age children can describe what happened and can pick out a photo of the "culprit" almost as well as adults can. They report less detail than adults do, but they rarely report something that didn't actually occur (Baker-Ward, 1995; Baker-Ward, Gordon, Ornstein, Larus, & Clubb, 1993; Ceci & Bruck, 1993; Davies, 1993). In several real-life studies, Margaret Steward (Steward, 1993; Steward & Steward, 1996) has asked preschool children to describe their experiences on a recent visit to a medical clinic—visits that had been videotaped. The children reported only a quarter of the actual occasions when they had been touched on some part of their body by a medical person, but 94 percent of the reports they did give were accurate. When the same children were interviewed again after six months, their reports were not always consistent, but the items they did report consistently were nearly always accurate. Even when children were under stress at the time of some event, such as those who were injured in an accident and treated at a hospital, young children remembered the event quite accurately (Peterson & Bell, 1996).

At the same time, younger children, particularly preschoolers, *are* more suggestible than older children

or adults (Ceci & Bruck, 1995). One common way to study this is to show a film or tell a story to children and adults. Then, while asking questions about what the subject saw, the investigator injects some misleading question into the set—a question that assumes something that didn't really happen (e.g., "He was carrying a pipe wrench when he came into the room, wasn't he?"). Some days or weeks later the subjects are again asked to describe what happened in the film or story. In this way you can check to see whether the inaccurate or misleading suggestion has been absorbed into the story. Young children are more affected than are older children or adults by such misleading suggestions (Leichtman & Ceci, 1995). Indeed, it is possible to mislead young children enough so that they will report inaccurately about specific physical events, such as having been kissed while being bathed or having been spanked (Bruck, Ceci, Francoeur, & Barr, 1995; Ceci & Bruck, 1993).

Thus it *is* possible for an interviewer—a psychologist, social worker, attorney, or whomever—to nudge a child's testimony in one direction or another, unintentionally or intentionally. This seems to be particularly true when the child is questioned repeatedly about some event that may or may not have occurred. Even when the event did *not* happen, many preschoolers and some school-age children will say that it did after they have been asked about it many times (Muir-Broaddus, 1997). Thus, when the interviewer believes that some misbehavior has occurred—sexual abuse, for example—such a belief may affect the way she conducts the interview and can influence the content of the child's recall, especially with preschool children (Ceci & Bruck, 1995). When misinformation comes from parents, children are even more likely to incorporate the parents' version into their own free recall (Ricci, Beal, & Dekle, 1995). Furthermore, these incorporated false reports persist over time; when children are reinterviewed later, many of the false reports are repeated. Adult witnesses are *also* susceptible to suggestions of various kinds, a point made in repeated clever studies by Elizabeth Loftus (e.g., Loftus, 1992). So the difference here is one of degree and not of kind. From the legal point of view, this does not mean that children should not testify; it speaks only to the weight one might give their recollections and the care that should be used in framing questions, beginning with the very first interview with the child.

good at remembering random lists of words (Schneider & Bjorklund, 1992; Schneider, Reimers, Roth, & Visé, 1995).

The research on expertise also tells us that even the typical age differences in strategy use or memory ability disappear when the younger group has more expertise than the older. For example, Michelene Chi, in her now classic early study (1978), showed that expert chess players can remember the placement of chess pieces on a board much more quickly and accurately than can novice chess players, *even when the expert chess players are children and the novices are adults.* To paraphrase Flavell (1985), expertise makes any of us look very smart, very cognitively advanced; lack of expertise makes us look very dumb.

[?] *Critical Thinking*

Think about your own areas of expertise and the areas about which you have little knowledge. Can you see any differences in the *way* you think about these different areas, either in the form of logic you use or in the way you go about remembering?

Since young children are novices at almost everything, while older children are more expert at many things, perhaps the apparent age difference in the use of cognitive strategies is just the effect of the accumulation of more specific knowledge, and *not* the result of stagelike changes in fundamental cognitive structures.

These school-age chess players, unless they are rank novices, would remember a series of chess moves or the arrangement of chess boards far better than I could, since they have expertise and I do not.

Variability in Children's Thinking

Yet another strong argument against strict stage-like change comes from recent work of Robert Siegler (1996), who has shown that individual children may use a wide variety of types of reasoning or strategies—from very simple to quite sophisticated—on the same type of problem on different attempts. For example, if you give first or second graders simple addition problems (3 + 6; 9 + 4; etc.), they may solve each problem in any of a variety of ways. If they have committed a particular sum to memory, they may retrieve the answer directly from memory without calculation—the strategy most adults use with simple addition problems. On other problems, children may simply count, starting at one, until they reach the sum. So 3 + 6 becomes "one, two, three, four, five, six, seven, eight, nine." Alternatively, they may use what the researchers call a *min strategy*, a somewhat more sophisticated technique in which the child starts with the larger number and then adds the smaller one by counting. In this method, the 3 + 6 sum is arrived at by saying to yourself, "Six, seven, eight, nine." Finally, a child might use a still more sophisticated *decomposition* strategy, which involves dividing a problem into several simpler ones. So a child might add 9 + 4 by thinking "10 + 4 = 14, 9 is one less than 10, 14 − 1 = 13, so 9 + 4 = 13" (Siegler, 1996, p. 94). (You may use this method for more complicated problems, such as multiplying 16 × 9. You might think 9 × 10 = 90; 9 × 6 = 54; 54 + 90 = 144.) With increasing age, elementary school children use counting less and less, while increasing their use of retrieval, the min strategy, and decomposition—a finding that is entirely consistent with the notion of a gradual increase in use of more complex strategies. What Siegler has added to this information is the finding that the same child may use all these different strategies on different addition problems on the same day. So it isn't that each child systematically shifts from one level of strategy to another, but rather that at any given time the child may have a whole variety of strategies and use all of them on different problems. Over time, the child's repertoire of likely strategies does indeed shift toward more and more complex or sophisticated ones, just as Piaget and others have described. However, the process is not steplike but rather like a series of waves, as in Figure 11.3.

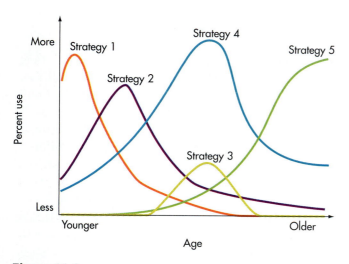

Figure 11.3

Siegler's "overlapping wave" model of cognitive development is probably a better description of the way children move toward more complex forms of thinking than is the steplike stage model Piaget originally proposed.

When children add a new strategy, they do not immediately give up old ones; instead, they continue to use the old and new for some while. Gradually, as the new strategies become more firmly established and better rehearsed, the simpler strategy drops out.

Siegler's model fits nicely with what we now know about expertise. A child who has a lot of experience with some particular problem or subject is far more likely to use the most sophisticated strategies in his repertoire when working on that particular kind of problem; when he is dealing with a subject he knows little about, or a type of problem with which he has little experience, he is much more likely to use the most primitive or simplistic strategies in his repertoire.

If we pull together all we know about cognitive development in this period, we thus find both support and nonconfirmations of Piaget's broad ideas. On the one hand, Piaget's core concept of **constructivism**—that children are active thinkers, constantly trying to construct new strategies and advanced understandings—is strongly supported. Siegler points out that children will continue to construct new strategies for solving some given kind of problem, such as addition problems, "even when they already know perfectly adequate ones for solving them" (Siegler & Ellis, 1996, p. 211). Piaget also seems to have been on the mark in argu-

ing for genuine qualitative change in the form of the child's thinking. The 8-year-old, in contrast to a 4-year-old, approaches new tasks differently. He is more likely to attempt a complex strategy; if that strategy fails, he is more likely to try another one.

However, it looks very much as if these new cognitive skills do not arise from any broad reorganization of schemes at about age 6 or 7, as Piaget proposed. Instead, the developmental process appears to be both gradual and heavily affected by the amount of experience the child has in a particular domain. The third major approach to cognitive development, the *information processing* approach, seems especially helpful in understanding just such a pattern of gradual qualitative change.

Information Processing: Another View of Cognitive Development

The information processing approach is not really a theory of cognitive development; it is an approach to studying thinking and remembering—a set of questions and some methods of analysis. The basic metaphor underlying this approach has been that of the human mind as computer. Like a computer, we can think of the "hardware" of cognition, such as the physiology of the brain, and the "software" of cognition, which would be the set of strategies or "programs" using the basic hardware. To understand thinking in general, we need to understand the processing capacity of the hardware and just what programs have to be "run" to perform any given task. What inputs (facts or data) are needed, what coding, decoding, remembering, or analyzing is required? To understand cognitive *development*, we need to discover whether either the basic processing capacity of the system or the programs change in any systematic way with age. Do children develop new types of processing (new programs)? Or do they simply learn to use basic programs on new material?

Changes in Processing Capacity. One obvious place to look for an explanation of developmental changes in cognitive skills is in the hardware itself. Any computer has physical limits on the number of different operations it can perform at one time or in a given space of time. As the brain and nervous system develop in the early years of life, with synapses formed and then pruned to remove redundancies, perhaps the capacity of the system increases.

One type of evidence consistent with this possibility is the finding that over the years of childhood, children are able to remember longer and longer lists of numbers, letters, or words, a pattern clear in the data shown in Figure 11.4. Alternatively, these results might simply be yet another reflection of age differences in expertise because older children naturally will have more experience with numbers, letters, or words. Hence, the memory-span data don't give us a clear-cut answer to the question of whether basic processing capacity increases with age.

Even if no change in basic capacity occurs, psychologists agree that processing *ef ciency* increases steadily with age, a change that most developmentalists now see as the basis on which cognitive development occurs (Case, 1985; Halford, Maybery, O'Hare, & Grant, 1994; Kuhn, 1992).

Processing Efficiency. The best evidence that cognitive processing becomes more efficient is that it gets steadily faster with age. Robert Kail (Kail, 1991; Kail & Hall, 1994) has found virtually the same exponential increase with age in processing speed for a wide variety of tasks, including such perceptual-motor tasks as tapping, simple response time to a stimulus (such as pressing a button when you hear a buzzer), and cognitive tasks (such as mental addition). He has found virtually identical patterns of speed increases in studies in Korea as well as in the United States, which adds a useful bit of cross-cultural validity to the argument.

The most plausible explanation for this common pattern is that over time the physical system changes in some fundamental way that allows greater and greater speed of both response and mental processing. The most likely candidate for such a basic change is the "pruning" of synapses, a process I talked about in Chapter 4 (Hale, Fry, & Jessie, 1993). If pruning begins at about 18 months and then continues steadily throughout childhood, one effect could be to make the "wiring diagram" steadily more efficient and thus faster.

Changes in the Software: The Development of Metacognition and Executive Processes. Greater efficiency in processing is also gained because the child acquires new strategies for solving problems or recalling information. Of course, the new strategies themselves may appear because of increased underlying capacity or efficiency. Or new strategies may arise because of the child's experimentation and experience with a particular kind of problem or material. Once present, however, these more powerful strategies make the whole system more efficient, much as we see in the behavior of experts at some task, who can perform that type of task with remarkable speed and directness.

One form of new strategy—or new "software"—is the child's increasing awareness of her own mental processes. If I asked you how you had tried to recall the list of nine items (chair, spaghetti, lettuce . . .) I listed earlier, I am sure you could describe your mental processes. You may even have consciously considered the various alternative strategies and then selected the best one. You could also tell me other things about the way your mind works, such as good ways to study particular subjects, or which kinds of tasks will be hardest, and why. These are all examples of metamemory or metacognition—knowing about remembering or knowing about knowing. Such skills are a part of a larger category that information processing theo-

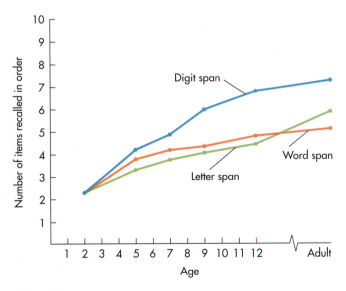

Figure 11.4

Psychologists have tried to measure basic memory capacity by asking subjects to listen to a list of numbers, letters, or words, and then to repeat back the list in order. This figure shows the number of such items that children of various ages are able to remember and report accurately. (Source: Dempster, 1981, from Figures 1, 2, and 3, pp. 66, 67, 68.)

rists refer to as **executive processes:** planning what to do and considering alternative strategies.

[?] *Critical Thinking*

Write down four good ways to study. In choosing one of these methods, does it matter what subject you are studying? How do you know all this? Do you think about it consciously when you are starting to study?

These skills are of particular interest because there is some suggestion that it may be precisely such metacognitive or executive skills that emerge (gradually) with age. Performance on a whole range of tasks will be better if the child can monitor her own performance or can recognize when a particular strategy is called for and when it is not. I pointed out in Chapter 8 that 4- and 5-year-old children do show some such monitoring, but it is rarely found earlier than that and it clearly improves fairly rapidly after school age. School children begin to understand what they will need to do in order to learn something; they are aware of what they know and do not know. Among other things, some metacognitive ability is critical for learning skillful reading. A child learning to read needs to recognize which words he knows and which he does not, or which sentences he understands and which he does not, and have some idea of how to get the information he needs. He needs to be able to recognize the difference between easy sentences and hard ones so that he can concentrate more and put more effort into the harder ones. A variety of research tells us that younger and poorer readers are less skilled at all these metacognitive tasks, while better or older readers can do them more readily and skillfully (Flavell et al., 1993).

Such metacognitive and executive skills may well form the foundation of some of the age changes Piaget described.

A Summary of Developmental Changes in Information Processing

If I add up all the bits and pieces of evidence about information processing capacity and skills, I arrive at a set of tentative generalizations:

1. There may or may not be any increase in the basic processing capacity of the system (the hardware), but there clearly is an increase in the efficiency with which the hardware is used, resulting in steadily greater processing speed.

2. The sheer amount of specific knowledge the child has about any given task increases as the child experiments, explores, and studies things. This leads to more and more "expert" approaches to remembering and solving problems, which in turn improves the efficiency of the processing system.

3. Genuinely new strategies are acquired, probably in some kind of order. In particular, a school-age child seems to develop some "executive" or metacognitive abilities—she knows that she knows, and she can *plan* a strategy for the first time.

4. Existing strategies are applied to more and more different domains and more and more flexibly. If a child learned to rehearse on one kind of memory problem, the older child is more likely to try to rehearse on a new memory task; the younger child (particularly younger than 5 or 6) is not likely to generalize the strategy to the new task.

5. With increasing age, a wider range of different strategies can be applied to the same problem, so that if the first doesn't work, a back-up or alternative strategy can be used. If you can't find your misplaced keys by retracing your steps, you try another tack, such as looking in your other purse or the pocket of your jacket or searching each room of the house in turn. Young children do not do this; school-age children and adolescents do.

Collectively, these various points suggest that some of the changes that Piaget observed and chronicled with such detail and richness are the result simply of increased experience with tasks and problems and increased speed and efficiency of processing (all quantitative changes, if you will). But there also seems to be a real qualitative change in the complexity, generalizability, and flexibility of strategies used by the child.

Having lost one of his shoes, this school-age boy first searches in the most obvious places. If that strategy doesn't work, he is likely to have a number of fall-back options, unlike a preschooler, who tends to get stuck in his first strategy.

Schooling and Its Impact

Although I started this chapter by pointing out that children all over the world begin school at age 5, 6, or 7, thus far I have been talking about cognitive development as if it were entirely separate from the experience of schooling. Surely, though, schooling itself must have some impact—on the child's thinking, on the child's skills, on the child's beliefs about his own skills.

Schooling and Cognitive Development

One question is whether some kind of school experience is itself necessary for the child to develop the full range of strategic abilities that we commonly see in children this age. Researchers have attempted to answer this question in several ways. One strategy has been to study children in societies or cultures in which schooling is not compulsory or is not universally available. By comparing similar groups of children, some of them in school and some of them not, it may be possible to discover the role that schooling plays in cognitive development.

A second strategy, developed recently, is to compare children whose birthdays are just before versus just after the arbitrary school district cutoffs for entrance into kindergarten or first grade. If a particular school district sets September 15 as the

cutoff, for example, then a child born on September 10 would be eligible for first grade five days after he turned 6, while a child born on September 20 would not be eligible for another year, even though he is only 10 days younger. A year later these two children are still essentially the same age but one has had a year of school and the other has not, which permits us to look at the effect of schooling with age held constant (e.g., Morrison, Smith, & Dow-Ehrensberger, 1995; Stelzl, Merz, Ehlers, & Remer, 1995).

The cross-cultural studies—in Mexico, Peru, Colombia, Liberia, Zambia, Nigeria, Uganda, Hong Kong, and many other countries—support the conclusion that school experiences are indeed *causally* linked to the emergence of some advanced cognitive skills. Children who do not attend schools not only do not learn some complex concepts and strategies, they are also not as good at generalizing a learned concept or principle to some new setting. So attending school helps children learn to think—precisely what it is intended to do.

A good example comes from Harold Stevenson's study of the Quechua Indian children of Peru (Stevenson & Chen, 1989; Stevenson, Chen, Lee, & Fuligni, 1991). He and his associates tested 6- to 8-year-old children, some of whom had been in school for about six months and some who had not yet started school or who were living in an area where a school was not available. Stevenson found that in both rural and urban areas, schooled children performed better on virtually all tasks, including a measure of seriation (putting things in serial order, such as by size or length) and a measure of concept formation. These differences remained even if the parents' level of education, the nutritional status of the child, and the amount of educational enrichment offered at home were taken into account.

Similarly, studies comparing early versus late school starters in the United States show that schooling itself, rather than merely age, has a direct effect on some kinds of cognitive skills, such as the ability to use good memory strategies. In one such study, Fred Morrison and his colleagues (F. Morrison et al., 1995) found that a big improvement in memory strategy use occurred in first grade; same-age children who spent the year in kindergarten because they just missed the cutoff did not show the same gain in memory skill—although these children would, of course, acquire such skill in the following year, when they were in first grade.

[?] *Critical Thinking*

Suppose your child's birthday were right after your local school district's cutoff for starting kindergarten or first grade. In light of the evidence about the effects of schooling, would you try to get your child in early? Or wouldn't it make any difference in the long run?

This does not mean that schooling is the only way for children to acquire complex forms of thinking. Specific experience in some area can also promote expertise, even without any school experience. As just one example, Brazilian street children who sell in the markets are able to make change unerringly, despite their lack of formal schooling (Carraher, Carraher, & Schliemann, 1985). Nonetheless, schooling exposes children to many specific skills and types of knowledge and appears to stimulate the development of more flexible, generalized strategies for remembering and solving problems.

Adjusting to School

In the early years of schooling, the child faces a whole host of tasks. He must adapt to the rules of the classroom, he must get along with several dozen other children, and he must learn to read.

Learning to Read. A wide range of research tells us that what most strongly affects a child's speed or ease of learning to read is the child's specific understanding of the structure and sound of language. Especially significant are the child's ability to recognize individual letters and her awareness that spoken and written words are made up of individual sounds (Adams, 1990).

I already mentioned in Chapter 5 that very young babies pay attention to individual sounds, which linguists call *phonemes*. The understanding that words are made up of strings of such sounds—an understanding referred to as *phonemic awareness*—seems to be a more advanced understanding, one that is essential to reading.

Suppose you say to a child, "Tell me a word that starts the same as tap." To respond to such a request correctly, the child has to be able to identify which sound in the string of sounds comes first in the word *tap*. He must also be able to recognize this same sound in other words. You can get at this same skill in other ways, such as by asking children to recognize or produce rhyming words or by reading them two words that differ in only one sound, such as *sing* and *sink*, and then asking the child if the two words are the same or different. We now have abundant evidence that children who are more skilled at such tasks at age 3, 4, or 5, later learn to read much more easily (Bryant, MacLean, Bradley, & Crossland, 1990; Hansen & Bowey, 1994; Whitehurst, 1995). Furthermore, if you train preschoolers or kindergartners in phonemic awareness, their reading skills in first grade improve, a result that has been found in studies in Scandinavia and Germany as well as the United States (Schneider et al., 1995).

Where does such early language awareness come from? How does it happen that some 5- and 6-year-olds have extensive understanding of the way words are put together, while others have little? The answer seems to be quite simple: exposure and expertise. For a child to learn about letters and sounds, he has to have had a great deal of exposure to language, both written and spoken. Such children are talked to a lot as infants, read to regularly, taught nursery rhymes, given toy letters to play with, and told the sounds that go with each letter or quite specifically taught the alphabet at an early age.

Of all the types of early experience that may contribute to such expertise, the most crucial seems to be the experience of being read to, regularly and in a fashion that invites the child's attention and response—a point I made in a *Research Report* in Chapter 8 (p. 260). Families who do not engage in such reading, or who do not encourage other prereading experiences, have children who have far more difficulty learning to read once they begin school.

Cultures and Contexts

How Asian Teachers Teach Math and Science So Effectively

The way school subjects are taught may also make a major difference in children's intellectual development, a possibility that emerges especially clearly from comparisons of mathematics and science teaching in Asia and America. James Stigler and Harold Stevenson (Stevenson, 1994; Stigler & Stevenson, 1991) have observed such teaching in 120 classrooms in Japan, Taiwan, and the United States, and are convinced that Asian teachers have devised a particularly effective mode of presenting these subjects.

Japanese and Chinese teachers approach mathematics and science by crafting a series of "master lessons," each organized around a single theme or idea and each involving specific forms of student participation. These lessons are like good stories, with a beginning, a middle, and an end. They frequently begin with a problem posed for the students (not unlike the measurement problem posed by Anne Hendry to her first graders described in the *Teaching* box earlier). Here is one example from a fifth grade class in Japan:

> The teacher walks in carrying a large paper bag full of clinking glass. . . . She begins to pull items out of the bag, placing them, one-by-one, on her desk. She removes a pitcher and a vase. A beer bottle evokes laughter and surprise. She soon has six containers lined up on her desk. . . . The teacher, looking thoughtfully at the containers, poses a question: "I wonder which one would hold the most water?" Hands go up, and the teacher calls on different students to give their guesses: "the pitcher," "the beer bottle," "the teapot." The teacher stands aside and ponders: "Some of you said one thing, others said something different. . . . There must be some way we can find out who is correct. How can we know who is correct?" (Stigler & Stevenson, 1991, p. 14)

The lesson continues as the students agree on a plan for determining which will hold the most. For such lessons, students are frequently divided into small groups, each assigned to work on part of the problem. These small groups then report back to the class as a whole. At the end of the lesson, the teacher reviews the original problem and what they have learned. In this particular case, the children have learned something not only about measurement but about the process of hypothesis testing.

In United States classrooms, in contrast, it is extremely uncommon for a teacher to spend 30 or 60 minutes on a single coherent math or science lesson involving the whole class of children and a single topic. Instead, teachers shift often from one topic to another during a single math or science "lesson." They might do a brief bit on addition, then talk about measurement, then about telling time, and back to addition. Asian teachers shift *activities* in order to provide variety, such as shifting from lecture format to small-group discussions; American teachers shift *topics* for the same apparent purpose.

Stigler and Stevenson also found striking differences in the amount of time teachers actually spend leading instruction for the whole class. In the United States classrooms they observed, this occurred only 49 percent of the time; group instruction occurred 74 percent of the time in Japan and 91 percent in Taiwan.

Stigler and Stevenson point out that the Asian style of teaching is not new to Western teachers. American educators frequently recommend precisely such techniques. "What the Japanese and Chinese examples demonstrate so compellingly is that when widely implemented, such practices can produce extraordinary outcomes" (Stigler & Stevenson, 1991, p. 45).

The form of teaching is clearly not the only factor contributing to higher math and science scores among Asian children. Asian parents also prepare their children for school more intensely, have higher standards for their child and for the school, and are highly involved in the school and in supervising their child's homework—all factors that we know make a difference (Stevenson & Lee, 1990). Still, the form of teaching is also a significant element.

For those lacking such expertise at the start of school, the only solution is to try to build a parallel base of knowledge through many of the same kinds of experiences that more expert readers have had at home. This means that poor readers need a great deal of exposure to sound/letter combinations. They also need to learn how to recognize patterns of letters in words. One need not—indeed must not—choose between those two hotly debated educational systems, phonics and "whole

Reading requires concentration when you're a first grader like young Thomas, but it can also bring delight, as it opens the doors to a huge new world.

naturally occurring home experiences of good readers: a great deal of reading, "play" with words, active questioning, and experimentation.

Fitting In and Adapting.

Whether a child comes to school ready to learn to read is clearly one of the key factors influencing his overall adjustment to school. But it is not the only factor. Parent involvement in the school also matters, as do some aspects of the child's temperament.

When parents come to parent-teacher conferences, attend school events, and get involved in supervising the child's homework, children are more strongly motivated, feel more competent, and adapt better to school. They learn to read more readily, get better grades through elementary school, and stay in school for more years (Brody, Stoneman, & Flor, 1995; Grolnick & Slowiaczek, 1994; Reynolds & Bezruczko, 1993). As Laurence Steinberg puts it, "All other things being equal, chil-

Being involved with your child's school and schooling, as third grader Brian's dad is doing here, is one of the most important things a parent can do to promote learning and achievement.

word" training. Both are needed, along with instruction in syntax, so that the child will understand better what words *could* appear in certain places in sentences.

Marilyn Adams, who has analyzed all the evidence on early reading, also makes a persuasive case that the poor reader must have maximum possible success in oral reading, preferably with texts that are full of the sort of rhyme and repetition that will help to foster phonemic awareness and learning of language regularities (1990). Programs with this emphasis, such as the Reading Recovery Program devised by Marie Clay (1979), have been highly successful with poor readers while more drill-like phonics programs have not (Hatcher, Hulme, & Ellis, 1994). In other words, poor readers seem to learn to read most easily through programs that to some degree mimic the

Research Report

Bilingual Education

In the United States today, there are 2.5 million school-age children for whom English is not the primary language of the home (Hakuta & Garcia, 1989). In California, 19 percent of all the children enrolled in public schools are Spanish-speaking with limited proficiency in English. What is the best way to teach children a second language at the same time that the child is being taught basic subject matter such as reading and mathematics? Let me describe the alternatives as they exist in U.S. classrooms (Rossell & Baker, 1996).

The most common system in the United States is **bilingual education,** in which the instruction in reading, writing, and other basic subject matter (social studies, science, etc.) is in the children's native tongue during the first two or three years of schooling. The children then make a gradual transition to full English instruction over several years. A much smaller number of children are in **English as a Second Language (ESL)** programs, in which the child spends most of her day in a regular English-speaking classroom, but also has an hour or two of special instruction in English in a separate classroom with other children of limited English proficiency.

A third choice is called **structured immersion,** in which all the children in the classroom speak the same non-English native tongue and the teacher speaks both English and the children's native language. The basic instruction in such classrooms is in English, paced so that the children can comprehend, with the teacher translating only when absolutely necessary.

Finally, there is **submersion,** sometimes called "sink or swim" programs, in which the non-English-speaking child is simply assigned to a regular English-speaking classroom, without any added support or supplemental instruction.

The only way to find out which of these alternatives is best is with studies in which children are assigned randomly to each of several of these types of programs and then followed over time. Christine Rossell and Keith Baker, in their recent comprehensive review of all such controlled, comparative studies (1996), report that bilingual education is not consistently better than submersion, ESL, or structured immersion. Indeed, on measures of English reading proficiency, students in structured immersion programs were consistently better than those in traditional bilingual education programs or those in ESL programs. Rossell and Baker conclude that some version of structured immersion—similar to programs used in Canada—is best. Note, though, that such a system would not be feasible for a school system in which the student body includes a few children speaking each of many different native languages. For such children, either submersion or some version of an ESL program is presently the only alternative.

As a further caveat, let me hasten to add that the research findings are extremely messy and the whole issue remains fraught with controversy (e.g., Crawford, 1991; Goldenberg, 1996; Rossell & Baker, 1996). Different observers draw varying conclusions from the existing research evidence, and the great majority of bilingual educators remain committed to some version of traditional bilingual education.

Finally, note that even the very best program will not be effective for children who come to school without good spoken language in their native tongue. Learning to read, in any language, requires that the child have a fairly extensive awareness of the structure of language. Any child who lacks such awareness—because she has been exposed to relatively little language, or was not read to or talked to sufficiently in infancy and preschool years—will have difficulty learning to read, whether the instruction is given in the native language or in English.

dren whose parents are involved in school do better than their peers" (1996, pp. 124–125). This effect of parent involvement has been found within groups of poor children as well as among the middle class, which tells us that the effect is not just a social-class difference in disguise (e.g., Luster & McAdoo, 1996; Reynolds & Bezruczko, 1993). That is, among poverty-level children, those whose parents are most involved with their school and schooling have a better chance of doing well in school. At the same time, of course, such involvement is less common among poverty-level families, sometimes because they are so overstressed with other aspects of their lives that they simply do not find time, and sometimes because they are simply unaware that such involvement will help their child.

Parent involvement is important not just for the child, but for the parent and for the school.

Parenting

Getting Involved in Your Child's Schooling

Being an "involved" parent takes more than just attending the occasional parent-teacher conference, although that is important. Insofar as possible, you should also:

Attend as many school functions as you can. Go to school plays and take your child along, even if the child isn't in the play; attend the school open house.

Volunteer in your child's classroom. If you work full-time, you might still spend some time at school early in the morning, or help make decorations for special events, or take a vacation day to go on a field trip with your child's class.

Encourage your child's participation in extracurricular activities at school, be it sports, music, chess club, or whatever. Children who are more involved in the school life are more likely to be enthusiastic about going to school.

Maintain communication with your child's teacher. Ask your child daily whether the teacher sent home any notes or announcements. Ask your child's teacher for the best time to call her or him, and check in with the teacher regularly.

Make homework a priority. At the beginning of the year, ask your child's teacher what kind and amount of homework she is likely to assign and how long she expects the child to spend on homework each day. For elementary school children, this is likely to be between 30 and 60 minutes a day. Help your child set up a specific time and place to do the homework, and supervise to make sure the work is completed. Check it over, find things to praise; correct (but don't criticize) any mistakes.

Ask about the child's day. Asking "How was your day?" isn't likely to generate much of an answer other than "fine" or "lousy." Instead, try asking "What did you learn today that surprised you?" or "What was the most fun thing you did today?"

At the first sign of trouble, get help. If your child seems to be falling behind, is unable to do the assigned homework, or says she hates school, talk to the teacher immediately and try to figure out what the problem may be. Arrange for whatever further assessment or help your child needs.

Schools that invite and encourage parent participation help to create a stronger sense of community, linking parents with one another and with the teachers. Stronger communities, in turn—be they in poverty-stricken inner cities or middle-class suburbs—provide better supervision and monitoring of the children in their midst, which benefits the children. Parents who get involved with their child's school also learn ways to help their children; they may even be motivated to continue their own education (Haynes, Ben-Avie, Squires et al., 1996).

[?] Critical Thinking

Imagine that you're the newly appointed principal of a school in an inner-city neighborhood. You discover that parent participation or involvement with the school is very low. What concrete steps might you take in order to increase parent involvement with the school?

A child's early success in school is also affected by whether her own personality or temperament matches the qualities valued and rewarded within the school setting. For example, Karl Alexander and his colleagues (Alexander, Entwisle, & Dauber, 1993) have found that children who are enthusiastic, interested in new things, easygoing, and cheerful do better in the early years of school than those who are more withdrawn, moody, or high-strung.

What all this research indicates is that how a child starts out in the first few years of school has a highly significant effect on the rest of her school experience and success. Children who come to school with good skills quickly acquire new academic skills and knowledge and thereby adapt to later school demands more easily. Children who enter school with poor skills, or with less optimal temperamental qualities, learn less in the early years and are likely to move along a slower achievement trajectory throughout their school years. Such a slow trajectory is not immutable. Parent involvement can improve the chances of a less-advantaged child, as can a particularly skillful kindergarten or first grade teacher (Pianta, Steinberg, & Rollins, 1995). The key point is that the child does not enter school with a blank slate; she brings her history and her qualities with her.

Self-Judgments in School.   The child's success at the various school tasks, in turn, affects his view of himself and his own abilities. Kindergarten and first grade children seem to judge themselves and their abilities mostly on direct information of their own success or failure. They pay relatively little attention to how well others do at a particular task. In fact, the great majority will confidently tell you that they are the smartest kid in their class. By about third grade, though, children begin to compare themselves with others and judge themselves accordingly. They notice whether their classmates finish a test sooner than they did or whether someone else got a better grade or more corrections on his spelling paper (Stipek, 1992).

Teachers' behavior shows a similar change: In the first few grades teachers emphasize effort and work habits. Then, over the succeeding years, they gradually begin to use more comparative judgments. By junior high, teachers compare children not only with each other but to fixed standards, other schools, or national norms (Stipek, 1992). These comparative processes are sometimes subtle, but they can be powerful. Robert Rosenthal, in his famous "Pygmalion in the classroom" studies, has shown that a teacher's belief about a given student's ability and potential has a small but significant effect on her behavior toward that student and on the student's eventual achievement (1994). When the teacher believes a student can achieve, that student does better.

The beliefs about their own abilities that students develop through these processes are usually quite accurate. Students who consistently do well in comparison to others come to believe that they are academically competent and that they are in control of academic outcomes. Interestingly, this seems to be less true of girls than of boys, at least in American culture. On average, girls get better school grades than boys do, but they have lower perceptions of their own ability. When they do well, they are more likely to attribute it to hard work

These fourth graders are already developing fairly clear ideas about their own academic abilities, comparing their own successes and failures to those of other children in their class.

than ability; when they do poorly, they see it as their own fault (Stipek & Gralinski, 1991).

Collectively, these experiences of success and failure mean that by seventh or eighth grade, most students have well-established ideas about their own academic skills and their ability to control the events around themselves.

Assessing Students' Progress: IQ and Achievement Tests in the Schools

One source of information children have about how well they are doing academically is their performance on various kinds of standardized tests. There are two basic types, IQ tests—which you read about in Chapter 8—and achievement tests.

IQ Tests in the Schools.   You already know that IQ test scores are good predictors of school performance. It is for this reason that such tests are most often used within school systems as a method of selecting or identifying children who might benefit from special programs, whether in the form of separate special classes or supplementary services provided in an inclusive classroom. Children whose speed of learning seems to be much faster or slower than normal may be given an IQ test to see if they might be retarded or gifted. Similarly, a child who is having difficulty learning to read but is otherwise doing okay might be given a test like the

WISC-III or other special tests designed to help diagnose specific learning disabilities. In each case, the pattern of scores on the test as a whole, or on individual subtests, is then used along with other data to decide if the child needs special help.

Such uses of IQ tests are very close to what Binet envisioned nearly a hundred years ago. Nonetheless, such diagnostic functions for IQ tests have been the subject of extensive debate, much of it heated.

Everyone agrees that schools must often diagnose or sort children into groups. Clearly, some children do require additional assistance. The arguments center on whether IQ tests ought to be used as the central basis for such sorting. There are several strong reasons usually given against such a use.

First, as I pointed out in Chapter 8, IQ tests do not measure all the facets of a child's functioning that may be relevant. For example, clinicians have found that some children with IQ scores below 70, who would be considered retarded if the score alone were used for classification, nonetheless have sufficient social skills to enable them to function well in a regular classroom. If we used only the IQ score, these children might be incorrectly placed in special classes. Second, there is the problem of the self-fulfilling prophecy of an IQ test score. Because many parents and teachers still believe that IQ scores are a permanent feature of a child, once a child is labeled as "having" a particular IQ, that label tends to be difficult to remove later.

The third and most important negative argument is that tests may simply be biased in such a way that some subgroups of children are more likely to score high or low, even though their underlying ability is the same. For example, the tests may contain items that are not equally accessible to minorities and whites; taking such tests and doing well may also require certain test-taking skills, motivations, or attitudes less common among some minority children, especially African-American children (Kaplan, 1985; Reynolds & Brown, 1984).

In response to these arguments, most major tests have been revised to eliminate all obvious types of bias. Yet a troubling fact remains: When IQ tests are used for diagnosis in schools, proportionately more minority than white children continue to be diagnosed as retarded or slow. This

fact has led to a number of lawsuits, including *Larry* P. v. *Riles*, a case in which a group of parents of black children sued the California school system for bias. The parents argued that there was no underlying difference in basic ability between black and white children, so if differences in test scores led to larger numbers of black children being assigned to special classes, the tests must clearly be biased.

The school system argued that IQ tests don't measure underlying capacity or ability, but only a child's existing repertoire of basic intellectual skills. In the terms I used in Chapter 8, this is like saying that an IQ test cannot tell you what the upper limit of some child's intellectual "reaction range" may be; all it can tell you is where the child is now functioning within that range. By school age the child's level of functioning has already been affected by such environmental factors as prenatal care, diet, health, and family stability—all of which tend to be less optimal among African Americans. Thus the test may accurately reflect a child's current abilities and be a proper basis for assigning the child to a special program, even though that child might have a greater underlying capacity or competence that could have been expressed under more ideal life circumstances.

In this particular case the judge ruled in favor of the parents and prohibited the use of standardized IQ test scores for placement in special classes in California. Other legal decisions, including subsequent rulings in the California case, have gone the other way (Elliott, 1988). So the legal question is not settled, although there are places in the United States in which the use of IQ tests for diagnosis and placement of African-American or other minority children is forbidden. One unintended consequence of this is that since placement decisions must still be made, they are now being made based on evidence that may be even more culturally biased, such as less-standardized tests or teacher evaluations.

I have no quick or easy solution to this dilemma. It is certainly true that schools in the United States reflect the dominant middle-class Euro-American culture, with all its values and assumptions. It is also true that succeeding in these schools is essential if the child is to acquire the basic skills needed to cope with the complexities of life in an industrialized country. For a host of reasons, including poorer prenatal care, greater poverty, and different familial patterns, more African-American children appear to *need* added assistance in order to acquire the skills they lack. However, I am well aware that placing a child in a special class, or leaving the child in an inclusive class but labeling him in some way that implies "slow," may create a self-fulfilling prophecy. Teachers may have lower expectations for children labeled in this way, so the children—who were already learning more slowly—are challenged still less and so proceed even more slowly. Yet to offer no special help to children who come to school lacking the skills needed to succeed there seems equally unacceptable to me. In the end, I conclude that IQ tests are more reliable and valid than the alternatives. I would not want a single IQ test used as the sole basis for a placement decision, especially early in elementary school when IQ test scores are still relatively variable. At the very least, I would want to take into account the level of stress in the child's life at the time the test was

given. But it seems foolish to me to throw out the tests altogether.

[?] *Critical Thinking*

Do you agree with me? Why or why not?

Achievement Tests.   The second major type of test used in schools is an **achievement test,** a type of exam with which nearly all of you have doubtless had personal experience. Achievement tests are designed to assess *specific* information learned in school, using items like those in Table 11.2. The child taking an achievement test doesn't end up with an IQ score, but his performance is still compared with that of other children in the same grade across the country.

How is this type of test different from an IQ test? The designers of IQ tests thought they were measuring the child's basic capacity, her underlying **competence.** An achievement test, in contrast,

Table 11.2
Some Sample Items from a Fourth Grade Achievement Test

VOCABULARY

jolly old man
1. angry
2. fat
3. merry
4. sorry

LANGUAGE EXPRESSION

Who wants _____ books?
1. that
2. these
3. them
4. this

MATHEMATICS

What does the "3" in 13 stand for?
1. 3 ones
2. 13 ones
3. 3 tens
4. 13 tens

REFERENCE SKILLS

Which of these words would be first in ABC order?
1. pair
2. point
3. paint
4. polish

SPELLING

Jason took the *cleanest* glass.
    right ___ wrong ___

MATHEMATICS COMPUTATION

79	149	62
+ 14	− 87	× 3

Source: From Comprehensive Tests of Basic Skills, Form S. Reprinted by permission of the publisher, CTB/McGraw-Hill, Del Monte Research Park, Monterey, CA 93940. Copyright © 1973 by McGraw-Hill, Inc. All rights reserved. Printed in the USA.

is intended to measure what the child has actually learned (her **performance**). This is an important distinction. Each of us presumably has some upper limit of ability—what we could do under ideal conditions, when we are maximally motivated, well, and rested. Yet, because everyday conditions are rarely ideal, we typically perform below our hypothetical ability.

The authors of the famous IQ tests believed that by standardizing the procedures for administering and scoring the tests they could come close to measuring competence. But because we can never be sure that we are assessing any ability under the best of all possible circumstances, we are *always* measuring performance at the time the test is taken. What this means in practical terms is that the distinction between IQ tests and achievement tests is one of degree rather than of kind. IQ tests include items that are designed to tap fairly fundamental intellectual processes like comparison or analysis; the achievement tests call for specific information the child has learned in school or elsewhere. College entrance tests like the Scholastic Aptitude Tests (SATs) fall somewhere in between. They are designed to measure basic "developed abilities"—for example, the ability to reason with words—rather than just specific knowledge. But all three types of tests measure aspects of a child or young person's performance and not competence.

The use of achievement tests in schools has been almost as controversial as the use of IQ tests. I've explored some of the arguments and counter-arguments in the *Social Policy* discussion on page 382.

School Quality

A very different set of questions about school experience has to do with variations in the quality of the schools themselves. Real estate agents have always touted a "good school district" as a reason for settling in one town or neighborhood rather than another. Now we have research to show that the real estate agents are right: Specific characteristics of schools and teachers do affect children's development.

Researchers interested in possible effects of good and poor schools have most often approached the problem by identifying unusually "effective" or "successful" schools (Good & Weinstein, 1986; Rutter, 1983). In this research an effective school is defined as one in which pupils show one or more of the following characteristics at higher rates than you would predict, given the kind of families or neighborhoods the pupils come from: high scores on standardized tests, good school attendance, low rates of disruptive classroom behavior or delinquency, a high rate of later college attendance, or high self-esteem. Some schools seem to achieve such good outcomes year after year, so the effect is not just chance variation. When these successful schools are compared with others in similar neighborhoods that have less impressive track records, certain common themes emerge, summarized in Table 11.3.

What strikes me when I read this list is how much effective schools sound like authoritative parenting. Such schools have clear goals and rules, good control, good communication, and high nurturance. The same seems to be true of effective teachers: It is the "authoritative" teachers whose pupils do best academically. Such teachers have clear goals, clear rules, effective management strategies, and personal and warm relationships with their pupils (Linney & Seidman, 1989). They also have high expectations for their students and make sure that virtually all the students in their classes complete the year's normal work (Mac Iver, Reuman, & Main, 1995).

Each school also has an overall climate or ethos that affects its students. The most positive

In the United States virtually all fourth graders—like these in Austin, Texas—are given achievement tests in order to allow schools to compare their students' performance against national norms.

Table 11.3
Characteristics of Unusually Effective Schools

- **Qualities of pupils.** Pupils represent a *mixture* of backgrounds or abilities but with a reasonably large concentration of pupils who come to school with good academic skills.
- **Goals of the school.** School leaders place strong emphasis on academic excellence, with high standards and high expectations.
- **Organization of classrooms.** Classes are focused on specific academic learning. Daily activities are structured, with a high percentage of time in actual group instruction.
- **Homework.** Homework is assigned regularly, and graded quickly.
- **Discipline.** Most discipline is handled within the classroom, with relatively little fallback to "sending the child to the principal." In really effective schools, not much class time is actually spent in discipline because these teachers have very good control of the class.
- **Praise.** Pupils receive high doses of praise for good performance, or for meeting stated expectations.
- **Teacher experience.** The school staff includes many teachers with extensive teaching experience, presumably because it takes time to learn effective class management and instruction strategies.
- **Building surroundings.** The school building, even if it is old, is clean, attractive, and orderly.
- **School leadership.** The school principal states his or her goals clearly and often and backs up these intentions with actions.
- **Responsibilities for children.** Children are given real responsibilities—in individual classrooms and in the school as a whole.
- **Size.** As a general rule, smaller schools are more effective, in part because in such schools children feel more involved and are given more responsibility. This effect is particularly clear in studies of high schools.
- **Money.** Increasing the amount of money spent on schools (above the basic amount needed to provide a physically safe, clean environment, staffed with highly competent teachers) does not *automatically* improve quality, but if the added money is carefully spent, it can have positive effects. For example, reducing class size doesn't automatically result in better school performance, but if smaller classes are combined with new methods of instruction, it can be beneficial.

Source: Rutter, 1983; Linney & Seidman, 1989; Stringfield & Teddlie, 1991; Mosteller, 1995; Sadowski, 1995.

school climate occurs when the principal provides clear and strong leadership, is dedicated to effective teaching, and provides concrete assistance for such teaching, and when goals are widely shared. In such schools parents also typically participate in school activities at a high rate. If you are making a decision about a city or a neighborhood in which to rear your children, these are the qualities to look for.

Individual Differences

I have already raised a number of issues of individual differences—differences in children's early reading ability, the use of IQ tests to identify students for special services, and the like. Let me explore here three other individual difference questions, all of which have considerable practical relevance.

Individual Differences in Information Processing

In my earlier discussion of information processing, I focused on the *developmental* aspects—those changes in processing capacity or efficiency of strategies that appear to be common across children. Information processing researchers have also turned their attention to questions of individual differences, asking what fundamental processes lie behind an individual's performance on an IQ test or other measure of cognitive skill. A few preliminary answers have emerged.

Social Policy Debate

Achievement Tests in Schools

The major arguments for using achievement tests in schools are that they provide parents and taxpayers with a way of assessing the quality of their schools and that they provide teachers with important information about the strengths and weaknesses of their class or individual students.

Do such tests actually serve these purposes well? Maybe not. One important point is that when schools know that they are being evaluated based on test scores, they have a strong incentive to "teach to the test" (Corbett & Wilson, 1989). Further, teachers report that even when they do not spend time teaching specific material that is likely to be tested, they do spend more time on the general subject matter covered by the tests, and therefore have less time for skills that are not included in most achievement tests, such as discussing ideas, solving problems inductively, writing, or engaging in creative activities (Darling-Hammond & Wise, 1985).

The failure of most standardized tests to tap the child's ability to draw inferences, apply information, or ask good questions seems especially troublesome, because these are all problem-solving skills that appear to have long-range significance for adult success.

Overall, it seems clear that achievement tests will be useful as measures of the quality of schools only if

there is a good match between what the tests measure and our basic educational goals. If one of our goals is to teach children how to write, then the usual achievement tests are not helpful because they do not measure such a skill. In contrast, if one of our goals is to teach basic computational skills, an achievement test can be a good measure of how well we have succeeded.

A second argument against achievement tests is that they are not terribly helpful for teachers trying to design programs for individual children. Teachers report that they rarely use test scores as a basis for diagnosing a specific child's strengths and weaknesses. Most feel that a child's day-to-day classroom performance yields better diagnostic information than a one-shot test under high-stress conditions.

The answers are not obvious, are they? (See Harvard Education Letter, 1988.) We need better tests that tap more basic problem-solving skills rather than merely rote learning; we need other ways of judging whether our schools are meeting our social mandate. At the very least, you need to be a very skeptical reader of those annual "school report cards" that purport to tell us how well a given school or school district is performing its job. Better yet, take a course on tests and measurements so that you can be a really sophisticated consumer.

Speed of Information Processing. Given that increases in speed or efficiency of processing appear to be one of the underpinnings of age changes in cognitive skills, it makes sense to hypothesize that differences in speed may also underlie individual differences in IQ. A number of different investigators have found just such a link: Subjects with faster reaction times or speed of performance on a variety of simple tasks also have higher IQ scores on standard tests (Fry & Hale, 1996; Vernon, 1987). We even have a few studies in which speed of processing has been directly linked to central nervous system functioning and to IQ. For example, it is now possible to measure the speed of conduction of impulses along individual nerves, such as nerves in the arm. Philip Vernon (Vernon, 1993; Vernon & Mori, 1992) has found that such a measure of neural speed correlates about .45 with IQ scores.

Most of this research has been done with adults, but a link between speed of reaction time and IQ score has also been found in a few studies

with children (Keating, List, & Merriman, 1985; Saccuzzo, Johnson, & Guertin, 1994). Furthermore, we have some pretty clear indications that such speed-of-processing differences may be built in at birth. In particular, recall the research I talked about in Chapter 5, linking speed of infant habituation and recognition memory with later IQ.

Critical Thinking

One of the synonyms of "intelligent" is "quick." Do you think this reflects some basic assumption that speed of processing is a central ingredient of what we think of as intelligent behavior? Can one be very intelligent and slow?

Other IQ–Processing Links. Another research approach has been to compare the information processing strategies used by normal-IQ and retarded children. For example, Judy DeLoache (DeLoache & Brown, 1987) has compared the searching strategies of groups of 2-year-olds who were either developing normally or showed delayed development. When the search task was very simple, such as searching for a toy hidden in some distinctive location in a room, the two groups did not differ in search strategies or skill. But when the experimenter surreptitiously moved the toy before the child was allowed to search, normally developing children were able to search in alternative, plausible places, such as in nearby locations; developmentally delayed children simply persisted in looking in the place where they had seen the toy hidden. They either could not change strategies or did not have alternative, more complex strategies in their repertoires.

Research with older children confirms this difference in the flexibility of strategy use. Retarded children can learn fairly complex tasks, but they have much more trouble generalizing or transferring their learning to slightly different problems or tasks (Bray, Fletcher, & Turner, 1997; Campione, Brown, Ferrara, Jones, & Steinberg, 1985). Thus one aspect of "intelligence" is just this ability to transfer, to generalize from one task to another. Older children generalize more readily, as do those with higher IQ scores.

Sex Differences in Cognitive Skills

The cover story of a recent issue of the British magazine *The Economist* described males as "tomorrow's second sex." Much of the article detailed the difficulties of adult males in a rapidly changing economy, but *The Economist* also pointed out that girls do better in school and on achievement tests beginning as early as age 4—differences you can see illustrated in Figure 11.5. Further, British studies suggest that while boys used to catch up when they reached high school and college age, this is no longer true, a point illustrated in the right-hand side and bottom portion of Figure 11.5.

Some of these conclusions are echoed by U.S. research. On average, elementary school girls are slightly better on verbal tasks and at arithmetic computation. Because computation skills make up a large portion of math achievement tests in these early years, girls typically get higher scores on such tests and get better school grades through elementary school. Boys, on the other hand, are slightly better at numerical reasoning, a difference that becomes clearer on tests in high school, when rea-

soning problems make up a larger portion of math exams. For example, on the math portion of the Scholastic Aptitude Tests (SATs), the average score for boys is consistently higher than the average score for girls. Unlike the British findings, however, U.S. data suggest that these SAT mathematics score differences have not gotten smaller over the past several decades (Brody, 1992; Byrnes & Takahira, 1993; Jacklin, 1989).

Two related differences also favor boys. More boys than girls are found among children who test as gifted in mathematics (Benbow, 1988; Lubinski & Benbow, 1992). And on tests of spatial visualiza-

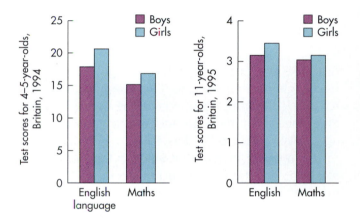

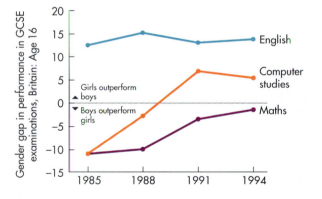

Figure 11.5

In Britain—as in the United States—girls score higher on achievement tests and get better grades in school. The lower panel of the figure also shows that over the past decade, girls' advantage has widened among high school students—an age when boys used to catch up. The GCSE examinations represented in the 16-year-old data are standardized achievement tests given to all English and Welsh students. (Source: The Economist, September 28, 1996, p. 24, Surrey Educational Psychology Service, and Equal Opportunities Commission.)

In elementary school, girls get better grades and higher scores on achievement tests than boys. What explanations can you think of for such a difference?

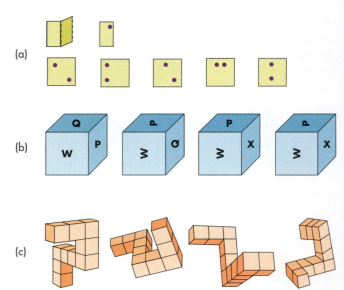

Figure 11.6

Three illustrations of spatial ability tests: (a) Spatial visualization: The figure at the top represents a square piece of paper being folded. A hole is punched through all the thicknesses of the folded paper. Which figure shows what the paper looks like when it is unfolded? (b) Spatial orientation: Compare the three cubes on the right with the one on the left. No letter appears on more than one face of a given cube. Which of the three cubes on the right could be a different view of the cube on the left? (c) Mental rotation: In each pair, can the three-dimensional objects be made congruent by rotation? (Source: Halpern, 1986, Figure 3.1, p. 50, and Figure 3.2, p. 52.)

tion, like the ones illustrated in Figure 11.6, boys have higher average scores. On measures of mental rotation (illustrated by item *c* in the figure), the sex difference is quite large and becomes larger with age (Voyer, Voyer, & Bryden, 1995).

I want to point out that even on tests of mental rotation, the two distributions overlap. That is, many girls and women are good at this type of task, and many boys and men are not, although the average difference is quite large.

Where might such differences come from? The explanatory options should be familiar by now. Biological influences have been most often argued in the case of sex differences in spatial abilities, where there may be both genetic differences and—more speculatively—differences in brain functioning resulting from prenatal variations in hormones (Newcombe & Baenninger, 1989). These initial differences in potential ability may then be shaped further by sex-related differences in play activities in childhood and school experiences in high school. Young boys play more with construction toys, for example, and in high school they are more likely to take the kind of math and science classes that will strengthen spatial abilities. Girls who are very good at spatial skills seem to share both these characteristics: They are likely to have inherited some potential for spatial skill, and they have been given (or have chosen) many opportunities to develop that skill (Casey, 1996).

In contrast, more purely environmental explanations have been prominent in discussions of the sex differences in mathematical or verbal reason-

ing. Especially in the case of mathematics, we have considerable evidence that girls' and boys' skills are systematically shaped by a series of environmental factors characteristic of U.S. culture:

- Boys take more math courses than girls do, primarily because they have more positive attitudes about mathematics, not because boys have higher math aptitude (Eccles & Jacobs, 1986). When the number of math courses girls and boys have taken is held constant, the sex difference in math test scores becomes much smaller.

- Parental attitudes about mathematics are markedly different for boys and girls. Parents are more likely to attribute a daughter's success in mathematics to effort or good teaching; poor performance by a girl is attributed to lack of ability. In contrast, parents attribute a boy's success to ability and his failure to lack of application (Holloway & Hess, 1985; Parsons, Adler, & Kaczala, 1982).

- Girls and boys have different experiences in math classes. In elementary school, teachers pay more attention to boys during math instruction (and more attention to girls during reading instruction). In high school, math teachers direct more of their questions and comments to boys, even when girls are outspoken in class.

The cumulative effect of these differences in expectation and treatment show up in high school, when sex differences on standardized math tests usually become evident. In part, then, the sex differences in math achievement test scores appear to be perpetuated by subtle family and school influences on children's attitudes. Whether these differences can explain the greater percentage of boys than girls who show real giftedness in mathematics is not so clear. One possibility is that because tests of mathematical ability involve at least some items that require mental rotation ability, very high scores on such tests are less likely for girls. Indeed, one recent study (Casey, Nuttall, Pezaris, & Benbow, 1995) shows that when mental rotation ability is subtracted out, the sex difference in SAT math scores among high ability groups disappears. Still, this issue, like many of the issues I have touched on in this chapter, remains hotly debated.

Summary

1. During the school years, children learn a great deal about the conversational customs of language; they also add many thousands of new words to their vocabularies.

2. Piaget proposed a major change in the child's thinking at about age 6, when powerful "operations," such as reversibility, addition, or multiple classification, are understood. The child also learns to use inductive logic, but does not yet use deductive logic.

3. Recent research on this period confirms many of Piaget's descriptions of sequences of development but calls into question Piaget's basic concept of stages.

4. Studies of expertise also point to a more important role of specific task experience in the sophistication of the child's thinking than Piaget believed.

5. Siegler's work shows that cognitive development is less stepwise than Piaget proposed; children may use a variety of different strategies, varying in com-

plexity, on the same kind of problem. Still, the strategy repertoire does become more complex with age.

6. Information processing theorists have searched for the basic building blocks of cognition, both the "hardware" and the "software."

7. Most theorists conclude that there are no age-related changes in the capacity of the mental hardware, but there are clearly improvements in speed and efficiency.

8. One form of increased efficiency is the greater and greater use of various types of processing strategies with age, including strategies for remembering. Preschoolers use some strategies, but school-age children use them more often and more flexibly. Indeed, the inability to use strategies flexibly is one of the hallmarks of mental retardation.

9. At school age, most children also develop some "executive skills," the ability to monitor their own cognitive processes, and thus to plan their mental activity.

10. School has a significant effect in fostering this shift to a more abstract or strategic form of thinking. Children who lack school experience show fewer such skills.

11. The best single predictor of the child's ease of learning to read in first and second grade is the child's "phonemic awareness," an awareness fostered by being read to, by rhyming experience, and by extensive exposure to rich language.

12. The child's adaptation to the school setting is affected by cognitive readiness, by parental involvement with the child's school and schooling, and by the child's temperament.

13. One of the main effects of school experience is to shape a child's sense of her own academic abilities. By adolescence children have clearly developed ideas of their comparative skills and abilities.

14. Children's intellectual or school performance is assessed with both IQ tests and achievement tests. Both must be understood as measures of performance, not competence. Both are controversial.

15. Children's intellectual and social development is affected by the quality of the schools they attend. Successful or effective schools have many of the same qualities we see in "authoritative" families: clear rules, good control, good communication, and high warmth.

16. Studies of individual differences in information processing suggest that variations in IQ scores are linked both to speed of basic neural processing and to flexibility and generality of strategy use.

17. On average, girls have better grades in school and higher scores on achievement tests in elementary school. On specific tests, girls are better on most verbal tasks; boys are typically better at tasks involving spatial visualization and on tests of advanced mathematical ability. There is as yet no clear agreement on how to explain such differences.

Key Terms

achievement test   Test designed to assess a child's learning of specific material taught in school, such as spelling or arithmetic computation, and typically given to all children in designated grades. **(p. 379)**

bilingual education   As practiced in the United States, a system of education for non-English-proficient students in which the instruction in reading, writing, and basic subject matter is in the children's native tongue during the first two or three years of schooling, with a gradual transition to full English instruction over several years. **(p. 375)**

class inclusion   The relationship between classes of objects such that a subordinate class is included in a superordinate class; for example, bananas are part of the class "fruit," and the class fruit is included in the class "food." **(p. 362)**

competence   The level of skill displayed by a person under ideal or perfect circumstances. It is not possible to measure competence directly. **(p. 379)**

constructivism   A key concept in Piaget's theory, that from birth a child is actively engaged in a process of constructing an understanding both of his own actions and of the external world. **(p. 368)**

English as a Second Language (ESL)   An alternative to bilingual education; non-English-proficient students spend most of their school day in a full-English classroom but then spend several hours in a separate class with special instruction in English. **(p. 375)**

executive processes   Proposed subset of information processes involving organizing and planning strategies. Similar in meaning to metacognition. **(p. 370)**

expertise   Knowledge of a particular subject or skill at some particular task or physical activity that is based on extensive practice or study. **(p. 365)**

inductive logic   Reasoning from the particular to the general, from experience to broad rules. Characteristic of concrete operational thinking. **(p. 359)**

performance   The behavior shown by a person under real-life rather than perfect or ideal circumstances. Even

when we are interested in competence, all we can ever measure is performance. **(p. 380)**

production deficiency   Phrase used to describe a situation in which an individual can use some physical or mental strategy if reminded to do so, but fails to "produce" the strategy spontaneously. **(p. 364)**

reversibility   One of the most critical of the "operations" Piaget identified as part of the concrete operations period. The child understands that actions can be reversed, thus returning to a previous state. **(p. 359)**

structured immersion   An alternative to traditional bilingual education in which all children in a given classroom speak the same non-English native tongue. All basic instruction is in English, paced so that the children can comprehend, with the teacher translating only when absolutely necessary. **(p. 375)**

submersion   Label used to describe programs for non-English-proficient students in which they are simply assigned to a regular English-speaking classroom without any supplemental language assistance. Also known as "sink or swim" programs. **(p. 375)**

Suggested Readings

Adams, M. J. (1990). *Beginning to read: Thinking and learning about print*. Cambridge: Massachusetts Institute of Technology Press. This is a wonderful book about reading. It is easy to read, complete, thoughtful, and up to date. If you are planning a career as a teacher, especially if you expect to teach early elementary school grades, you should go right out and buy a copy.

Ceci, S. J., & Bruck, M. (1995). *Jeopardy in the courtroom. A scientic analysis of children s testimony*. Washington, DC: American Psychological Association. A highly readable, sobering discussion of children's testimony in child abuse cases and the factors that can influence that testimony.

Collins, W. A. (Ed.). (1984). *Development during middle childhood. The years from six to twelve*. Washington, DC: National Academy Press. This book covers the exact age range I'm discussing in this chapter and the next. It includes chapters on most aspects of the child's functioning, including physical development, health, and cognitive change.

Comer, J. P., Haynes, N. M., Joyner, E. T., & Ben-Avie, M. (Eds.). (1996). *Rallying the whole village. The Comer process for reforming education*. New York: Teachers College Press. If you plan to be a teacher, you will want to read this book—the product of many years of educational experimentation led by James Comer. The demonstrated success of his School Development Program has influenced many current-day thinkers about education reform. Among other features, Comer schools place a strong emphasis on creating a school community, including parents and teachers working together.

Flavell, J. H., Miller, P. H., & Miller, S. A. (1993). *Cognitive development* (3rd ed.). Englewood Cliffs, NJ: Prentice Hall. Once again I recommend this excellent book. See especially Chapter 4, which covers many of the same topics I have discussed in this chapter.

CHAPTER 12

Social and Personality Development at School Age

Preview Questions

1 *School-age children don't hug or touch their parents as often as they did earlier. Does this mean their attachment has weakened?*

2 *Why do school-age children, almost universally, choose to play with same-gender peers?*

3 *Are boys more aggressive than girls, or do girls just show their aggression differently?*

4 *What are the ingredients in high self-esteem among children?*

5 *Would it be better for children if we turned off all the television sets?*

Chapter Outline

At age 8 Roger was prone to emotional outbursts, insisted on his own way when he played with other children, and bullied weaker children on the playground. At 13 he was arrested for shoplifting; at 17 he dropped out of school. As an adult he had a hard time finding and keeping a job, and his marriage lasted only a few years. His wife claimed that she couldn't deal with his temper.

David, in contrast, was very shy at age 8. He rarely joined groups of other children when they were playing, although he would join in if asked or urged. He had a few friends in school, but was mostly a loner. He went to college, but had a very hard time settling on a career and changed jobs frequently until his late twenties. His marriage has been stable, but he has been disappointed at his rate of progress in his job. His job supervisors say that David has a habit of withdrawing whenever they press him for something or when the stress level at work gets high, so they are reluctant to promote him.

Both cases are fictitious, but the links between these types of childhood social behaviors and adult outcomes are not. Certainly the cognitive changes I described in the last chapter play a central role in preparing the child for the demands of adolescence and adulthood. But relationships in middle childhood also play a significant part in shaping the life course.

Let me build a bridge between cognition and social relationships by beginning with a look at how children in this age range *understand* themselves and their relationships. Such understandings form part of the basis of the relationships themselves.

Children's Understanding of Self and Relationships

The Self-Concept at School Age

In Chapter 9 I pointed out that by age 5 or 6, most children define themselves along a number of different dimensions, such as size or gender. But these early self-descriptions are highly concrete, often quite situation-specific. Over the elementary school years we see a shift toward a more abstract, more comparative, more generalized self-definition. A 6-year-old might describe herself as "smart" or "dumb"; a 10-year-old is more likely to say that he is "smarter than most other kids," or "not as good at baseball as my friends" (Rosenberg, 1986; Ruble, 1987). In these same years the child's self-concept also becomes gradually less focused on external characteristics and more on enduring internal qualities.

A number of these themes are illustrated in the results of a particularly nice older study by Montemayor and Eisen of self-concepts in 9- to 18-year-olds (1977), each of whom was asked to give 20 answers to the question, "Who am I?" The researchers found that the younger children were still using mostly surface qualities to describe themselves, such as in this description by a 9-year-old:

[?] *Critical Thinking*

Before you go on and read any of the examples, take a moment and write down 20 answers to the "Who am I?" question yourself. Then, after you have read the examples, go back and look at your own answers to the question again. What types of descriptions did you include?

My name is Bruce C. I have brown eyes. I have brown hair. I have brown eyebrows. I am nine years old. I LOVE! Sports. I have seven people in my family. I have great! eye site. I have lots! of friends. I live on 1923 Pinecrest Dr. I am going on 10 in September. I'm a boy. I have a uncle that is almost 7 feet tall. My school is Pinecrest. My teacher is Mrs. V. I play Hockey! I'm almost the smartest boy in the class. I LOVE! food. I love fresh air. I LOVE school. (Montemayor & Eisen, 1977, pp. 317–318)

In contrast, look at the self-description of this 11-year-old girl in the sixth grade:

My name is A. I'm a human being. I'm a girl. I'm a truthful person. I'm not very pretty. I do so-so in my studies. I'm a very good cellist. I'm a very good pianist. I'm a little bit tall for my age. I like several boys. I like several girls. I'm old-fashioned. I play tennis. I am a *very* good swimmer. I try to be helpful. I'm always ready to be friends with anybody. Mostly I'm good, but I lose my temper. I'm not well-liked by some girls and boys. I don't know if I'm liked by boys or not." (Montemayor & Eisen, 1977, pp. 317–318)

This girl, like the other youngsters of this age in the Montemayor and Eisen study, describes her external qualities, but she also emphasizes her beliefs, the quality of her relationships, and her general personality traits. Thus, as the child moves through the elementary school years, her self-definition becomes more complex, more comparative, less tied to external features, more centered on feelings and ideas.

Describing Other People

In these same school years children's descriptions of others move through highly similar changes, from the concrete to the abstract, from the ephemeral to the stable. If you ask a 6- or 7-year-old to describe others, he will focus almost exclusively on external features—what the person looks like, where he lives, what he does. This description by a 7-year-old boy in England, taken from another informative early study (Livesley & Bromley, 1973), is typical:

> He is very tall. He has dark brown hair, he goes to our school. I don't think he has any brothers or sisters. He is in our class. Today he has a dark orange [sweater] and gray trousers and brown shoes. (p. 213)

When young children do use internal or evaluative terms to describe people, they are likely to use quite global terms, such as "nice" or "mean," "good" or "bad." Further, young children do not seem to see these qualities as lasting or general traits of the individual, applicable in all situations or over time (Rholes & Ruble, 1984). In other words, the 6- or 7-year-old has not yet developed a concept we might think of as "conservation of personality."

Then, beginning at about age 7 or 8, a rather dramatic shift occurs in children's descriptions of others. The child begins to focus more on the inner traits or qualities of another person and to assume

If you asked 4-year-olds to describe this boy, they would probably describe his physical characteristics. Eight-year-olds given the same task would be much more likely to describe the boy's feelings or general qualities.

that those traits will be visible in many situations (Eder, 1989; Gnepp & Chilamkurti, 1988). Children this age still describe others' physical features, but now those descriptions are used as examples of more general points about internal qualities. You can see the change when you compare the 7-year-old's description with this (widely quoted) description by a nearly 10-year-old:

> He smells very much and is very nasty. He has no sense of humour and is very dull. He is always fighting and he is cruel. He does silly things and is very stupid. He has brown hair and cruel eyes. He is sulky and 11 years old and has lots of sisters. I think he is the most horrible boy in the class. He has a croaky voice and always chews his pencil and picks

his teeth and I think he is disgusting. (Livesley & Bromley, 1973, p. 217)

This description still includes many external, physical features but goes beyond such concrete, surface qualities to the level of personality traits, such as lack of humor or cruelty.

I can illustrate these changes less anecdotally with some findings from a study by Carl Barenboim (1981). He asked 6-, 8-, and 10-year-olds to describe three people; a year later, he asked them to do the same thing again. This variation of a *cohort-sequential* research design gives Barenboim both longitudinal and cross-sectional information. Figure 12.1 shows the results for two of the categories Barenboim used in his analysis. A *behavioral comparison* was any description that involved comparing a child's behaviors or physical features with another child or with a norm. Examples would be "Billy runs a lot faster than Jason," or "She draws the best in our whole class." Statements that involved some internal personality trait he called *psychological constructs*, such as "Sarah is so kind," or "He's a real stubborn idiot!" You can see that behavioral comparisons peaked at around age 8 or 9 but that psychological constructs rose steadily throughout middle childhood.

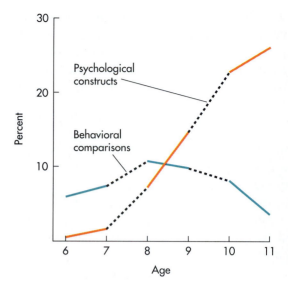

Figure 12.1

These data from Barenboim's study show the change in children's descriptions of their peers during the years of middle childhood. The colored lines represent longitudinal data, the dashed lines cross-sectional comparisons. (Source: Barenboim, 1981, Figure 1, p. 134.)

[?] *Critical Thinking*

Write down a description of your best friend. How does your description compare with the ones given by children? Can you define the difference in precise terms?

Understanding Friendships

A very similar developmental progression emerges when we ask children to describe or define various kinds of relationships. Let me use descriptions of friendships as an illustration.

Preschool children seem to understand friendships mostly in terms of common activities. If you ask a young child how people make friends, the answer is usually that they "play together," or spend time physically near each other (Damon, 1977; 1983; Hartup & Stevens, 1997; Selman, 1980). Children this age think of friendship as something that involves sharing toys or giving things to one another.

Robert Selman's research and extensive studies by Thomas Berndt (1983; 1986) show that in elementary school this early view of friendship gives way to one in which the key concept seems to be *reciprocal trust*. Friends are now seen as special people with desired qualities other than mere proximity, as people who are generous with one another, who help and trust one another. They expect to spend time with their friends and to disclose their own inner feelings and needs to a friend.

Linking Cognition and Social Behavior

When we put all these various jigsaw pieces together, we find a picture of a child whose attention has shifted from externals to internals. Just as the school child can understand conservation in part because he can set aside the *appearance* of change and focus on the underlying continuity, so the child of this same age looks beyond (or behind) physical appearance and searches for deeper consistencies that will help her to interpret both her own and other people's behavior.

Selman suggests another link between thinking and relationships in these years. The preschool child may have a theory of others' minds, but he does not yet understand that other people also read *his* mind. As I noted in Chapter 8, the 4-year-old may understand the statement "I know that you know." But he does not yet understand the next step in this potentially infinite regress: "I know that you know that I know." This reciprocal aspect of perspective taking seems to be grasped some time in the early elementary school years. Selman's point is that only when the child understands reciprocality of perspective do we see really reciprocal relationships between friends. Only then do qualities like fairness and trust become central to children's ideas of friendship.

Just what is cause and what is effect is not so obvious. We should not necessarily assume that the cognitive horse is pulling the relationship cart, although that is one possibility. It is also plausible (as Vygotsky would argue) that the child learns important lessons about the distinction between appearance and reality, and between external and internal qualities, in play with peers and interactions with parents and teachers. Whichever way the causality runs, the central point is that children's relationships with others both reflect, and shape, their *understanding* of themselves and of relationships (Hartup, 1996b). With that in mind, let's look at the relationships themselves.

Relationships with Parents

Because overt attachment behaviors like clinging or crying are far less visible in these school-age years, it is easy to lose sight of the fact that children are still strongly attached to their parents. Parents can and do fill the child's need for a secure base by being accessible, available, responsive, and willing to communicate openly with their children. However, at this age, the child takes more responsibility for maintaining contact with the parent (Kerns, 1996). The child of 8 or 9 is off encountering the world, yet he wants to know that Mom or Dad is there when he needs them. Such a need is most likely to arise when the child faces some stressful situation—such as the first day of school, illness or upheaval in the family, or the death of a pet. Because fewer experiences are new and potentially stressful to the 7- or 8-year-old

Because school-age children, like these skaters, roam farther from home, spending more and more time with peers, we might be tempted to assume that they are less strongly attached to their parents. But this assumption is wrong. Children this age still depend on their parents to be a safe base.

than to the preschooler, we see much less obvious safe-base behavior, and less open affection from child to parent (Maccoby, 1984).

Critical Thinking

Seven- and 8-year-olds often seem to actively reject public displays of affection from their parents, squirming away from hugs or refusing kisses—especially in front of peers. Do you have any guesses about how to explain such behavior?

Despite these changes, it would be a great mistake to assume that the attachment has weakened. School children continue to rely on their parents' presence, support, and affection, and they continue to be strongly influenced by their parents' judgments. What does change is the agenda of issues between parent and child. Parents of preschoolers are most concerned with teaching the child some level of physical independence and controlling the child's behavior. They worry about toilet training, temper tantrums, defiance, and

Research Report

Sibling Relationships in Middle Childhood

When psychologists talk about families, we most often talk about "parents" and "children" and the relationships between the two. But what about brothers' and sisters' relationships to each other? I introduced some of the themes in studies of sibling relationships in Chapter 9; how do those themes play out in middle childhood?

First of all, as a general rule, sibling relationships seem to be less central in the lives of school-age children than are relationships with either friends or parents (Buhrmester, 1992). Elementary school–age children are less likely to turn to a sibling for affection than they are to parents, and less likely to turn to a brother or sister for companionship or intimacy than they are to a friend.

While this is true in general, sibling relationships also vary enormously. Based on direct studies of young children as well as retrospective reports by young adults about their sibling relationships when they were at school age, researchers have identified several patterns or styles of sibling relationships: (1) a *caregiver* relationship, in which one sibling serves as a kind of quasi parent for the other, a pattern that seems to be more common between an older sister and younger brother

than in any other combination; (2) a *buddy* relationship, in which both members of the pair try to be like one another and take pleasure in being together; (3) a *critical* or *conflictual* relationship, which includes attempts by one sibling to dominate the other, teasing, and quarreling; (4) a *rival* relationship, which contains many of the same elements as a critical relationship but is also low in any form of friendliness or support; and (5) a *casual* or *uninvolved* relationship, in which the siblings have relatively little to do with one another (Murphy, 1993; Stewart, Beilfuss, & Verbrugge, 1995).

Rivalrous or critical relationships seem to be more common when siblings are close together in age (four or fewer years apart) and in families in which the parents are less satisfied with their marriage (Buhrmester & Furman, 1990; McGuire, McHale, & Updegraff, 1996); friendly and intimate relationships appear to be somewhat more common in pairs of sisters (Buhrmester & Furman, 1990), while rivalry seems to be highest in boy-boy pairs (Stewart et al., 1995).

Do you recognize your own middle-childhood sibling relationships in these categories? Has your relationship with your brothers and sisters changed in the years since you were in elementary school?

fights with siblings. Occasions requiring discipline are common. When the child reaches elementary school, disciplinary encounters decline. The agenda now includes such issues as whether the child will do regular chores, the standards for the child's school performance, and the level of independence that will be allowed (Maccoby, 1984). Is it okay for Joe to stop off at his friend's house after school without asking ahead of time? How far from home may Diana ride her bike? In many non-Western cultures, parents must also now begin to teach children quite specific tasks, such as agricultural work and care of younger children or animals, all tasks that may be necessary for the survival of the family.

When we look at the various ways parents try to accomplish all these tasks, we see the same parental styles I talked about in Chapter 9: authoritarian, authoritative, permissive, and neglecting.

For children in this age range, as for younger children, the authoritative style seems far the best for fostering and supporting the child's emerging competence.

Baumrind (1991) has provided illustrative data in a recent analysis of her small longitudinal sample. She classified each parent's style of interaction on the basis of extensive interviews and direct observation when the children were preschoolers. When the children were age 9, she measured their level of social competence. Those rated "optimally competent" were seen as both assertive and responsible in their relationships; those rated "partially competent" typically lacked one of these skills; those rated as incompetent showed neither. You can see in Table 12.1 that the children from authoritative families were nearly all rated as fully competent, while those from neglecting families were most often rated as incompetent.

Table 12.1

Social Competence in 9-Year-Olds as a Function of Parental Style

	Percentage of Children Rated		
Parental Style	Competent	Partially Competent	Incompetent
Authoritative	85	15	0
Authoritarian	30	57	13
Permissive	8	67	25
Neglecting	0	47	53

Source: Baumrind, 1991, adapted from Table 5.1, p. 129.

Relationships with Peers

The biggest shift in relationships in the years of middle childhood is the increasing centrality of the peer group. The vertical relationships with parents or teachers obviously don't disappear, but playing with other kids is what children who are 7, 8, 9, or 10 years old prefer. Such activities—along with watching television—take up virtually all children's time when they are not in school, eating, or sleeping (Timmer, Eccles, & O'Brien, 1985).

Shared play interests continue to form the major basis of these school-age peer relationships. Furthermore, kids this age *de ne* play groups in terms of common activities, rather than in terms of common attitudes or values. You can see this pattern in Figure 12.2, which shows the results of a study by Susan O'Brien and Karen Bierman (1988). They asked fifth, eighth, and eleventh grade subjects to tell them about the different groups of kids that hang around together at their school, and then to say how they could tell that a particular bunch of kids was "a group." For the fifth graders, the single best criterion for defining a group was that the kids did things together. For eighth graders, shared attitudes and common appearance became much more important—yet another example of the broad shift from concrete to abstract views of relationships.

Gender Segregation

Beyond the centrality of shared activities, the most striking thing about peer group interactions in the elementary school years is how gender-segregated

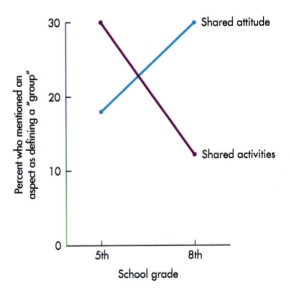

Figure 12.2

O'Brien and Bierman's results illustrate the change between elementary and high school in children's ideas about what defines a "group" of peers. (Source: O'Brien & Bierman, 1988, Table 1, p. 1363.)

they are, a pattern that seems to occur in every culture in the world (Cairns & Cairns, 1994; Harkness & Super, 1985) and that is frequently visible in children as young as 3 or 4. Boys play with boys, girls play with girls, each in their own areas and at their own kinds of games. There are some ritualized "boundary violations" between these separate territories, such as chasing games (e.g., "You can't catch me, nyah nyah," followed by chasing accompanied by screaming by the girls) (Thorne, 1986). On the whole, though, girls and boys between the ages of 6 and 12 actively avoid interacting with one another and show strong favoritism toward their

In this age range gender segregation in play groups is almost total: Boys play with boys, girls with girls.

own gender and negative stereotyping of the opposite gender (Powlishta, 1995). Given a forced choice between playing with a child of the opposite gender or a child of a different race, researchers have found that elementary school–age children will make the cross-race choice rather than the cross-gender choice (Maccoby & Jacklin, 1987).

Why is this preference for same-gender playmates so very strong at this age? Eleanor Maccoby, whose ideas about sex differences in styles of interaction I talked about in Chapter 9, suggests two reasons (Maccoby, 1990). First, girls appear to be put off by boys' rough-and-tumble play style and by the strong emphasis on competition and dominance that is so much a part of boy-boy interactions. Second, Maccoby argues that girls find it hard to influence boys. Girls make polite suggestions to each other, a style of influence attempt that school-age boys simply don't comply with very often. In response, argues Maccoby, girls withdraw into their own pairs or groups among whom their own "rules" of behavior are familiar and effective. Why boys avoid girls is more of a mystery, although it is clear that they do. Indeed, boys' preference for same-gender playmates is, if anything, even stronger than is girls' preference for playing with girls.

Friendships

This pattern is even more pronounced when we look at friendships. By age 7 gender segregation in friendships is the rule. Parents in one U.S. study reported that about a quarter of the friendships of their 5- or 6-year-olds but *none* of the friendships of their 7- and 8-year-olds were cross-sex (Gottman, 1986). In a more recent large study of third and fourth graders, researchers found that only 14 per-

cent had a cross-sex friendship; for only 3 percent of these children was the cross-sex relationship the child's primary or most central friendship (Kovacs, Parker, & Hoffman, 1996).

School-age children spend more time with their friends than do preschoolers, and they gradually develop a larger collection of **reciprocal friendships,** as you can see in Figure 12.3, which is based on two studies by Thomas Berndt (Berndt & Hoyle, 1985). Berndt used a fairly typical procedure in which he asked children to name their "best friends." He counted a reciprocal friendship each time two children each named the other.

In these same years, friendships also become more stable—more likely to endure for a year or longer (Cairns & Cairns, 1994). Children in this age range also behave differently with friends than they do with strangers. School-age children are more open and more supportive with chums, smiling,

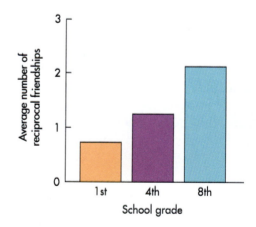

Figure 12.3

Among both boys and girls, the number of mutual (reciprocal) friendships increases over the elementary school years. (Source: Berndt & Hoyle, 1985.)

Cultures and Contexts

Gender Segregation in Other Cultures

Many of the statements I make about "children's development" are based exclusively on research done in the United States or other Western industrialized countries. It is always appropriate to ask whether the same developmental changes, the same behavioral patterns, would appear in children reared in very different environments. In the case of gender segregation, the answer seems quite clear: What we observe on United States school playgrounds is true all over the world.

A good example is an observational study of children in a Kipsigis settlement in rural Kenya (Harkness & Super, 1985). This particular settlement consists of 54 households engaged in traditional hoe agriculture and cattle raising. Women care for the children, cook, and carry firewood and water. Men are in charge of the cows, plow the fields when needed, maintain the dwellings, and participate in the political business of the community.

For this study, observers went to the settlement at different times of day to record the gender of each child's companions. They found little sex segregation among children younger than 6, but clear separation for children between 6 and 9. In this age group, two-thirds of boys' and three-fourths of girls' companions were of

the same gender. The differences were even larger when they looked at the sex of the child to which each youngster addressed his or her specific bids for attention: Fully 72 percent of boys' and 84 percent of girls' bids were made to another child of the same gender.

These numbers reflect somewhat less sex segregation than we commonly observe in the United States. But what impresses me is that even this much sex segregation exists in a culture in which children spend much of their time in their own compound, with only siblings and half-siblings available as playmates.

This is not to say that context and culture have no effect. They clearly do. The Kipsigis encourage certain kinds of sex segregation by assigning somewhat different tasks to boys and girls. Additionally, in Western countries, children attending "progressive" schools in which equality of sex roles is a specific philosophy show less sex segregation in their play than is true in more traditional schools (Maccoby & Jacklin, 1987). Yet even in progressive schools, the majority of contacts are still with children of the same gender. All in all, it seems to be the case universally that when children this age are free to choose their playmates, they strongly prefer playmates of the same sex.

looking, laughing, and touching one another more than with nonfriends; they talk more with friends and cooperate and help one another more. Pairs of friends are also more successful than are nonfriends in solving problems or performing some task together (Newcomb & Bagwell, 1996). Yet school-age children are also more critical of friends and have more conflicts with them (Hartup, 1996a); they are more polite with strangers. At the same time, when such conflicts with friends occur, children are more concerned about resolving them than is true of disagreements among nonfriends. Thus friendships are an arena in which children can learn how to manage conflicts (Newcomb & Bagwell, 1995).

[?] Critical Thinking

Do you still have any friends from your elementary school years? If not, why do you think those early friendships did not survive? If yes, what do you think differentiates an early friendship that survives from one that does not?

The quality of girls' and boys' friendships also differ in intriguing ways. Waldrop and Halverson (1975) refer to boys' relationships as *extensive* and to girls' relationships as *intensive*. Boys' friendship groups are larger and more accepting of newcomers than are girls'. They play more outdoors and roam over a larger area in their play. Girl friends are more likely to play in pairs or in smaller, more exclusive groups, and they spend more playtime indoors or near home or school (Benenson, 1994; Gottman, 1986).

We also see sex differences at the level of actual interaction—a fact that won't surprise you, given what I've already said about the reasons for gender segregation in this age group. Boys' groups and boys' friendships appear to be focused more on competition and dominance than are girls' friendships (Maccoby, 1995). In fact, among school-age boys, we see *higher* levels of competition between pairs of friends than between strangers, the opposite of what we see among girls. Friendships between girls also include more agreement, more compliance, and more self-disclosure than is true for boys. For example, Campbell Leaper (1991), whose work you may remember from Table 9.3 (p. 302), finds that "controlling" speech—a category that includes rejecting comments, ordering, manipulating, challenging, defiance, refutation, or resistance of other's attempt to control—is twice as common among pairs of 7- and 8-year-old male friends as among pairs of female friends. Among the 4- and 5-year-olds in this study, there were no sex differences in controlling speech.

None of this should obscure the fact that the interactions of male and female friendship pairs have a great many characteristics in common. For example, collaborative and cooperative exchanges are the most common forms of communication in both boys' and girls' friendships in these years. Nor should we necessarily conclude that boys' friendships are less important to them than are girls' friendships. Nevertheless, it seems clear that there are differences in form and style that may well have enduring implications for the patterns of friendship over the full life span.

Patterns of Aggression

I pointed out in Chapter 9 that physical aggression declines over the preschool years, while verbal ag-

gression increases. In the years of middle childhood and adolescence, physical aggression becomes still less common as children learn the cultural rules about when and how much it is acceptable to display anger or aggression. In most cultures this means that anger is more and more disguised and aggression more and more controlled with increasing age (Underwood, Coie, & Herbsman, 1992).

One interesting exception to this general pattern—consistent with what I've just said about boys' friendship patterns—is that in all-boy pairs or groups, at least in United States studies, physical aggression seems to remain both relatively high and constant over the years of childhood. Indeed, at every age, boys show more physical aggression and more assertiveness than do girls, both within friendship pairs and in general (Fabes, Knight, & Higgins, 1995). Table 12.2 gives some highly representative data from a very large, careful survey in Canada (Offord, Boyle, & Racine, 1991) in which teachers completed checklists describing each child's behavior—the same study, by the way, from which the data in Figure 1.4 (p. 24) were drawn. It is clear that boys are described as far more aggressive on nearly any measure of physical aggressiveness.

Relational Aggression. Results like these have been so clear and so consistent that most psychologists concluded that boys are simply "more aggressive" in every possible way. But that may turn out to be wrong or at least misleading.

Why do you think it is that among boys, competition is such a strong feature of friendship interactions? Do you think this is true in every culture?

Table 12.2

Percentage of Boys and Girls Ages 4 to 11 Rated by Their Teachers as Displaying Each Type of Aggressive Behavior

Behavior	Boys	Girls
Mean to others	21.8	9.6
Physically attacks people	18.1	4.4
Gets in many fights	30.9	9.8
Destroys own things	10.7	2.1
Destroys others' things	10.6	4.4
Threatens to hurt people	13.1	4.0

Source: Offord, Boyle, & Racine, 1991, from Table 2.3, p. 39.

Research Report

Bullies and Victims

Some physically or relationally aggressive children may also fall into the category of **bully.** Psychologists such as Dan Olweus, who has done the most significant work on bullies and victims, define a bully as one who repeatedly torments some other child with words, gestures, intentional exclusion from a group, or physical aggression (1995). The target of such repeated torment is referred to as the **victim.** Olweus's studies in Sweden indicate that as many as 9 percent of elementary school children are regularly victims, while 7 percent could be called bullies, percentages confirmed in studies in other countries (e.g., Perry, Kusel, & Perry, 1988).

Victims have certain characteristics in common, including passivity, sensitivity, low self-esteem, and quietness (Egan & Perry, 1997; Olweus, 1995). Among boys, victims are also often physically smaller or weaker than their peers. Whether boys or girls, victims seldom assert themselves with their peers, making neither suggestions for play activities nor prosocial actions. Instead, they submit to whatever suggestions others may make. Other children do not like this behavior, and thus do not like the victim (Crick & Grotpeter, 1996; Schwartz, Dodge, & Coie, 1993). The consequences of such victimization can include loneliness, school-avoidance, lower self-esteem, and significant depression at later ages (Kochenderfer & Ladd, 1996; Olweus, 1995).

Not every child, faced with a passive and unresponsive playmate, turns into a bully. Bullies are distinctive because they are typically aggressive in a variety of situations, not just in relation to selected victims. Bullies also tend to be more aggressive toward adults than do nonbullies, have little empathy for their victim's pain or unhappiness, and are often impulsive. Olweus's studies do *not* support the common assumption that bullies are basically insecure children who have developed a tough exterior to cover up their insecurity. In fact, the opposite appears to be true. Bullies most often have *low* levels of anxiety and insecurity. Olweus proposes four child-rearing factors instrumental in the development of bullying behavior:

- *indifference and lack of warmth from the parent toward the child in the early years;*
- *lack of clear or adequate limits on aggressive behavior set by the parents;*
- *the parents' use of physical punishment;*
- *a difficult, impulsive temperament in the child.*

If you compare this list with the qualities of authoritative and neglecting parenting I described in Chapter 9, you'll see that the parents Olweus is describing are those who are authoritarian by inclination but lacking good limit-setting skills—the same pattern Gerald Patterson has described in families of "out of control" children. These children tyrannize their families and terrorize their peers. In adolescence and adulthood they are highly likely to be involved in law-breaking, a point I'll expand on more fully in a *Research Report* later in the chapter (p. 402).

Rather, it begins to look as if girls express aggressiveness in a different way, using what has recently been labeled **relational aggression,** instead of either physical aggression or nasty words. Physical aggression hurts others through physical damage or threat of such damage; relational aggression is aimed at damaging the other person's self-esteem or peer relationships, such as by cruel gossiping, facial expressions of disdain, or ostracism or threats of ostracism ("I won't invite you to my birthday party if you do that"). Children experience such indirect aggression as genuinely hurtful, and they are likely to shun other kids who use this form of aggression a lot, just as they tend to reject peers who are physically aggressive (Crick & Grotpeter, 1995; Rys & Bear, 1997).

Girls are much more likely to use relational aggression than are boys, especially toward other girls, a difference that begins as early as the preschool years and becomes very marked by the fourth or fifth grade. For example, in one recent study of nearly 500 children in the third through sixth grades, Nicki Crick found that 17.4 percent of the girls but only 2 percent of the boys were high in relational aggression—almost precisely the reverse of what we see for physical aggression (Crick & Grotpeter, 1995). Whether this difference in the form of aggression has some hormonal/biological basis or is trained at an early age, or both, we do not know. We do know that higher rates of physical aggression in males have been observed in every human society and in all varieties of primates. We also know that girls who have a disorder called *congenital adrenal hyperplasia* and who received heightened levels of androgen (male hormone) prenatally, show more aggression with playmates than do their normal siblings or cousins (Berenbaum, 1997). Among boys, we also have some evidence of a link between rates of physical aggression and testosterone levels (e.g., Susman, Inoff-Germain, Nottelmann et al., 1987), particularly at adolescence and later ages. Just where the apparent propensity toward relational aggression comes from among girls, however, is still an open question.

Individual Differences

I've spent a good part of this chapter talking about common developmental patterns. Yet, if we are to understand development, we must understand the individual pathways as well as the common ones. Sex differences represent one form of differential pathway. We also need to look at more individual variations, of which three seem particularly important and pervasive in this age range: excessive aggressiveness or conduct disorder, popularity versus rejection or neglect by peers, and variations in self-esteem.

Conduct Disorders

While all children can be mean, cruel, or aggressive toward one another at least occasionally, school-age children do differ widely in their propensities for such behaviors. A child who displays them regularly is usually said to have a *conduct disorder*, which I defined in Chapter 10 as a combination of excessive aggressiveness, bullying, cruelty, and delinquency.

It has been clear for a long while that there are a number of subvarieties of conduct disorders (e.g.,

Achenbach, 1993). In particular, Stephen Hinshaw and his colleagues (Hinshaw, Lahey, & Hart, 1993) argue that the crucial issue is when the deviant behavior begins. **Childhood-onset conduct disorders** are more serious, with high levels of aggression that tend to persist not only throughout childhood but into adulthood. **Adolescent-onset conduct disorders** appear to be milder, more transitory, more a function of hanging about with bad companions than a deeply ingrained behavior problem.

? Critical Thinking

What kind of social policy implications (if any) do you see in the fact that early-onset conduct disorders are most likely to persist and be followed by adult criminality or violence?

The developmental pathway for early-onset conduct disorders is one you are familiar with by now from all I have said about Patterson's research on aggressive children. In early life, these are children who throw tantrums and defy parents; many have disorganized attachments early in life; many also suffer from some form of attention deficit disorder as well (Lynam, 1996; Shaw, Owens, Vondra, Keenan, & Winslow, 1996). If the parents are not up to the task of controlling the child, the child's behavior worsens to overt aggression toward others, who then reject the child. Such peer rejection aggravates the problem, pushing the seriously aggressive child in the direction of other children with similar problems, who become the child's only supportive peer group (Shaw, Kennan, & Vondra, 1994). By adolescence these youngsters are firmly established in delinquent or antisocial behavior with friends drawn almost exclusively from among other delinquent teens (Tremblay, Masse, Vitaro, & Dobkin, 1995). They are also highly likely to display a whole cluster of other problem behavior, including drug and alcohol use, truancy or dropping out of school, and early and risky sexual behavior, including multiple sexual partners (Dishion, French, & Patterson, 1995).

The degree of continuity of this form of deviant behavior is quite striking. The correlation

Children who are consistently aggressive, cruel, or bullying toward their peers are said to have a conduct disorder. When such behavior is visible at an early age it tends to persist, not just into adolescence but into adulthood.

between aggression in childhood and aggression in adulthood averages .60 to .70—very high correlations for data of this kind, and replicated in studies in both England and the United States (Farrington, 1991)—described in the *Research Report* box.

There is also some indication that the early-onset/aggressive syndrome has a much stronger genetic component than is true for the later-onset/delinquent pattern (Achenbach, 1993). Thus the preschooler who already shows defiant and oppositional behavior as well as aggressiveness may have strong inborn propensities for such behavior. But if Patterson is correct—and I think he is—then whether that propensity will develop into a full-fledged, persisting, conduct disorder will depend on the unfolding sequence of events, including the parents' ability to handle the child's early defiance as well as the general environment in which the child lives, such as inner city versus small town (Gottesman & Goldsmith, 1994; Loeber, Tremblay, Gagnon, & Charlebois, 1989).

One confirmation of Patterson's basic model comes from a remarkable new intervention project, called the Fast Track Project, aimed at altering the behavior of children who are already showing strong signs of excessive aggression or conduct disorders in early elementary school

(McMahon, 1997). The researchers are working with nearly 900 such children, in 395 different classrooms in four different cities. For half the children, a special intervention was designed to change the child and his environment at all possible levels, including teaching entire classrooms of children about how to express and label emotions, how to interact with peers, and how to solve social problems. Parents of children in the intervention group are also given special help in learning better child management skills and are encouraged as well to create better connections with their child's school. Early results indicate that after two years, the intervention seems to be working. The parents are using less physical punishment and are more appropriate and effective in their discipline; the children are better at recognizing their own emotions, are more competent in their social relationships, are rated as less aggressive by their peers, and are less likely to be placed in special education programs than are the equivalent children who have had no intervention (Coie, 1997; Dodge, 1997). This is not an inexpensive program, but if the early results hold up, it not only confirms Patterson's overall model, it also points toward methods of altering the developmental trajectory for children with early-onset conduct disorders.

Popularity and Rejection

Our understanding of the longitudinal dynamics of conduct disorders has been enriched by research on popularity and rejection among children, because rejection by peers is one clear consequence of the set of aggressive behaviors characteristic of conduct-disordered children.

Psychologists who study popularity in children have concluded that it is important to distinguish between several subgroups of unpopular children. The most frequently studied are **rejected children.** If you ask children to list peers they would *not* like to play with, or if you observe which children are avoided on the playground, you can get a measure of rejection of this type. **Neglected children** form a second group among the less popular.

Research Report

Long-Term Consequences of Childhood Aggression and Peer Rejection

A growing body of research points to significant links between early aggressiveness and rejection by peers and behavior problems or emotional disturbances in adolescence and adulthood. Let me give you a sampling of the findings.

- *Leonard Eron, in a 22-year longitudinal study, has found that a high level of aggressiveness toward peers at age 8 is related to various forms of aggressiveness at age 30, including "criminal behavior, number of moving traffic violations, convictions for driving while intoxicated, aggressiveness toward spouses, how severely the subjects punished their own children" (1987, p. 439).*

- *In the Concordia Project in French Canada, Lisa Serbin (Serbin, Moskowitz, Schwartzman, & Ledingham, 1991) has studied several thousand children who were initially identified by their peers in grade 1, 4, or 7 as either highly aggressive, withdrawn, or both. A large comparison group of nonaggressive and nonwithdrawn children was also studied. Both aggressive girls and aggressive boys later showed poorer school achievement in high school. In adulthood, 45.5 percent of the aggressive but only 10.8 percent of the nonaggressive men had appeared in court. For women, the ratio was about two to one (3.8 percent vs. 1.8 percent).*

- *Farrington (1991) has studied a group of 400 working-class boys in England, beginning when they were 8 and continuing into their 30s. Those who were rated by their teachers as most aggressive at ages 8, 10, and 12 were more likely to describe themselves at 32 as getting into fights, carrying a weapon, or fighting police officers. They were also twice as likely as were less aggressive children to commit a violent offense (20.4 percent vs. 9.8 percent), twice as likely to be unemployed, more likely to hit their wives, and half again as likely to have a drunk driving conviction.*

- *John Coie and his colleagues (Coie, Terry, Lenox, Lochman, & Hyman, 1995) have followed a group of over a thousand children from the third to the tenth grade. Among the boys, those who were both aggres-sive and rejected in third grade were far more likely to show delinquency or other behavior problems in high school than were any other group of boys. Among girls, aggressiveness but not peer rejection was linked to later behavior problems.*

- *Studies in Sweden show that high levels of aggression as early as age 4 or 5 are predictive of delinquency or criminality in early adulthood (Stattin & Magnusson, 1996).*

We could explain such a link between early aggression or unpopularity and later behavior problems in any of several ways. The simplest explanation is that problems with peers arise out of high levels of aggression and that such aggression simply persists as the individual's primary mode of interaction. It is also possible that a failure to develop friendships itself causes problems that later become more general. Or it could signify a seriously warped internal working model of relationships, or all the above.

Whatever the explanation, the point to remember is that such deviant behavior does tend to persist and may have profound effects on an individual's entire life pattern. If you are a preschool or elementary school teacher and observe aggressive, cruel, or bullying behavior in any child in your care, you should not shrug it off with some internal comment such as, "Boys will be boys." Boys *are* more aggressive than girls, but persistent aggression or cruelty is not a normal aspect of child behavior and should not be tolerated. Intervention is required, with the family as well as with the child. If you see aggression or cruelty on the playground, step in immediately; explain to the aggressing child that this behavior is not acceptable, that it hurts others; agree with the other teachers in your school on some consistent set of consequences for children who are aggressive or cruel, such as time-out; if a child is consistently aggressive or bullying, speak to the parents, perhaps suggesting a parenting class or directly helping them to control the child's behavior better at home. Once firmly established, aggression is a very difficult behavior pattern to alter. However, that fact does not mean you should not try.

Children in this category are reasonably well liked but lack individual friends and are rarely chosen as most preferred by their peers. Neglect seems to be much less stable over time than is rejection, but children who are neglected nonetheless seem to share certain qualities. Interestingly, such children often do quite well in school (Wentzel & Asher, 1995), but they are more prone to depression and loneliness than are accepted children, especially if the neglect has persisted over several years (Burks, Dodge, & Price, 1995; Cillessen, van IJzendoorn, van Lieshout, & Hartup, 1992; Rubin, Hymel, Mills, & Rose-Krasnor, 1991). Where might such differences in popularity or peer acceptance come from?

We can't tell from this photograph whether this child is rejected or neglected by her peers or if this is just a sad moment. We do know that neglected children have better long-term prognosis than is true for rejected children, but the neglected are more likely to be depressed in childhood and adolescence—as this girl seems to be.

Critical Thinking

One reasonable hypothesis might be that neglected children would be more likely to have had insecure attachments as infants. Can you think of refinements of this hypothesis? And how could you test it?

Qualities of Rejected and Popular Children. Some of the characteristics that differentiate popular and unpopular children are factors outside a child's control. In particular, attractive children and physically larger children are more likely to be popular—perhaps merely a continuation of the preference for attractive faces that Langlois detected in young infants and that I described in Chapter 5. The most crucial ingredient, though, is not how the child looks but how the child behaves.

Popular children behave in positive, supporting, nonpunitive, and nonaggressive ways toward most other children. They explain things, take their playmates' wishes into consideration, take turns in conversation, and are able to regulate the expression of their strong emotions. Not surprisingly, these more popular children are also more likely than are rejected children to have close reciprocal friendships (Franco & Levitt, 1997), giving them still more opportunity to practice important social skills. Rejected children, in contrast, are aggressive, disruptive, uncooperative, and often unable to control the expression of their strong feelings (Eisenberg et al., 1995; Pettit, Clawson, Dodge, & Bates, 1996). They interrupt their play partners more often, fail to take turns in a systematic way, and are less empathetic toward peers (Cohen & Strayer, 1996).

These conclusions emerge from a variety of types of research, including at least a few cross-cultural studies. For example, aggression and disruptive behavior are linked to rejection and unpopularity among Chinese children, just as they are among American children (Chen, Rubin, & Li, 1995; Chen, Rubin, & Sun, 1992). Among the best sources of evidence are studies involving direct observation of groups of previously unacquainted children who spend several sessions playing with one another and then pick their favorite playmates from among the group (e.g., Coie & Kupersmidt, 1983; Dodge, 1983; Shantz, 1986). In these studies, children who are most consistently positive and supportive during the play sessions are those who end up being chosen as leaders or as friends; those who consistently participate in conflicts are most often rejected.

Rejected children also seem to have quite different internal working models of relationships and of aggression from those of popular children. In a series of studies, Kenneth Dodge (Dodge, Coie, Pettit, & Price, 1990; Dodge & Feldman, 1990; Dodge & Frame, 1982; Quiggle, Garber, Panak, & Dodge, 1992) has shown that aggressive/rejected children are much more likely to see aggression as a useful way to solve problems. They are also much more likely to interpret someone else's behavior as hostile or attacking than is true for less aggressive or more popular children. Given an ambiguous event, such as being hit in the back with a kickball, aggressive or rejected children—especially boys—are much more likely to assume that the ball was thrown on purpose, and they retaliate. Of course, such retaliation, in turn, is likely to elicit hostility from others, so their expectation that other people are hostile to them is further confirmed.

Happily, not all rejected children remain rejected; not all develop serious behavior problems or delinquency. Further, not all aggressive children are rejected. Recent research gives us a few hints about what may differentiate between these several subgroups. For example, some aggressive children also show fairly high levels of altruistic or prosocial behavior, and this mixture of qualities carries a much more positive prognosis than does aggression unleavened by helpfulness (Coie & Cillessen, 1993; Newcomb, Bukowski, & Pattee, 1993). Distinctions like these may help us not only to refine our predictions but to design better intervention programs for rejected/aggressive children.

Self-Esteem

Finally, we come to an aspect of individual differences that has been the subject of a great many popular books and talk-show conversations, namely, self-esteem. Thus far I have talked about the self-concept as if there were few values attached to the categories by which we define ourselves. Yet the self-concept obviously contains an evaluative aspect as well. Note, for example, the differences in

tone in the answers to the "Who am I?" question that I have already quoted. The 9-year-old makes a lot of positive statements about himself, while the 11-year-old gives a more mixed self-evaluation.

These evaluative judgments have several interesting features. Over the years of elementary school and high school, children's evaluations of their own abilities become increasingly differentiated, with quite separate judgments about skills in academics or athletics, physical appearance, peer social acceptance, friendships, romantic appeal, and relationships with parents (Harter, 1990).

Paradoxically, however, it is at school-age—around age 7—that children first develop a *global* self-evaluation. Seven- and 8-year-olds (but not younger children) readily answer questions about how well they like themselves as people, how happy they are, or how well they like the way they are leading their lives. It is this global evaluation of one's own worth that is usually referred to as **self-esteem,** and this global evaluation is *not* merely the sum of all the separate assessments the child makes about his skills in different areas.

Instead, as Susan Harter's extremely interesting research on self-esteem tells us, each child's level of self-esteem is a product of two internal assessments or judgments (1987; 1990). First, each child experiences some degree of discrepancy between what he would like to be (or thinks he *ought* to be) and what he thinks he is. When that discrepancy is low, the child's self-esteem is generally high. When the discrepancy is high—when the child sees himself as failing to live up to his *own* goals or values—self-esteem will be much lower.

The standards are not the same for every child. Some children value academic skills highly, others value sports skills or having good friends. Whatever the child's goals, the key to self-esteem, according to Harter, is the amount of discrepancy between what the child desires and what the child thinks he has achieved. In other words, a child who values sports prowess but who isn't big enough or coordinated enough to be good at sports will have lower self-esteem than will an equally small or uncoordinated child who does not value sports skill so highly. Similarly, being good at something, like singing or playing chess, won't raise a child's self-esteem unless the child values that particular skill.

Culture obviously plays some role here. Each culture or subculture assigns value to particular

In some parts of the United States (such as Texas, where this photo was taken), school football is often the center of community life, and in such circumstances it would be hard for a boy to avoid placing a high value on being able to play well. His self-esteem will then be affected by how well he is able to perform.

qualities or skills, whether intellectual skills, sports prowess, kindness, or whatever. Children's own choices of goals or desired qualities are clearly shaped by such cultural values. At the very broadest level, children growing up in individualist cultures are likely to compare themselves with individual achievement standards—getting good grades, winning a blue ribbon at the county fair, or scoring the winning goal in a soccer game. Children growing up in collectivist cultures would be more likely to judge themselves against community qualities, such as the ability to get along with others.

Culture also operates at a highly local level. A friend described to me the pangs of inadequacy suffered by her 12-year-old daughter who feels like a failure at soccer, a highly valued team sport in her school. Yet this same 12-year-old is a gifted ballet dancer, highly trained, coordinated, and skilled. Harter's model tells us that this child's self-esteem would not suffer from her lack of ability at soccer *unless* she valued it—which she does. This 12-year-old has internalized some of the specific values of her school's "culture," which includes skill at soccer or other team sports, and thus compares herself with this standard. Her ballet prowess helps somewhat to balance the scale in her own mind, but not completely, because she feels she is failing at something "important."

The second major influence on a child's self-esteem, according to Harter, is the overall sense of support the child feels from the important people around her, particularly parents and peers. Children who feel that other people generally like them the way they are have higher self-esteem scores than do children who report less overall support.

Both these factors are clear in the results of Harter's own research. She asked third, fourth, fifth, and sixth graders how important it was to them to do well in each of five domains (physical appearance, social acceptance, scholastic competence, athletic competence, and behavioral conduct), and then how well they thought they actually did in each. The total discrepancy between these sets of judgments comprised the discrepancy score. Remember that a high discrepancy score indicates that the child didn't feel he was doing well in areas that mattered to him. The social support score was based on children's replies to a set of questions about whether they thought others (parents and peers) liked them as they were, treated them as a person, or felt that they were important. Figure 12.4 shows the results for the third and fourth graders; the findings for the fifth and sixth graders are virtually identical, and both sets of data sup-

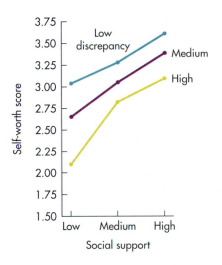

Figure 12.4

For these children in Harter's studies, self-esteem was about equally influenced by the amount of support the child saw herself as receiving from parents and peers and by the degree of discrepancy between the value the child places on various domains and the skill she sees herself having in each of those domains. (Source: Harter, 1987, Figure 9.2, p. 227.)

port Harter's hypothesis, as does other research, including studies of African-American youth (DuBois, Felner, Brand, Phillips, & Lease, 1996; Luster & McAdoo, 1995). Note that a low discrepancy score alone does not protect a child completely from low self-esteem if she lacks sufficient social support. Similarly, a loving and accepting family and peer group does not guarantee high self-esteem if the youngster does not feel she is living up to her own standards.

[?] *Critical Thinking*

Think about the following somewhat paradoxical proposition: If Harter's model of self-esteem is correct, then our self-esteem is most vulnerable in the area in which we may appear (and feel) the most competent. Does this fit with your experience?

A particularly deadly combination occurs when the child perceives that the parents' support is *contingent* on good performance in some area—getting good grades, making the first-string football team, winning the audition to play with the school orchestra, being popular with other kids. Then, if the child does not measure up to the standard, he experiences both an increased discrepancy between ideal and achievement and a loss of support from the parents.

Consistency of Self-Esteem Over Time.

How stable are these self-judgments? Is a third grader with low self-esteem doomed to feel less than worthy for the rest of his life? A number of longitudinal studies of elementary school–age children and teenagers show that global self-esteem is quite stable in the short term but somewhat less so over periods of several years. The correlation between two self-esteem scores obtained a few months apart is generally about .60. Over several years, this correlation drops to something more like .40 (Alsaker & Olweus, 1992; Block & Robins, 1993). So it is true that a child with high self-esteem at age 8 or 9 is more likely to have high self-esteem at age 10 or 11. It is also true that considerable variation occurs around that stability.

Consequences of Variations in Self-Esteem.

Harter and others have found that the child's level of self-esteem is *strongly* negatively correlated with depression in both middle childhood and adolescence. That is, the lower the self-esteem score, the more depressed the child describes himself to be. The correlations in several of Harter's studies range from −0.67 to −0.80—remarkably high for research of this type (Harter, 1987; Renouf & Harter, 1990). Bear in mind, though, that this is still correlational evidence. These findings don't prove a causal connection between low self-esteem and depression. More persuasive is Harter's finding from her longitudinal studies that when a child's self-esteem score rises or falls, her depression score drops or rises accordingly.

Origins of Differences in Self-Esteem.

If we accept Harter's model and assume that self-esteem is a product of each person's comparison of her own qualities with her desired or valued qualities, we still have to ask where each child's values and self-judgments come from. How does a child come to think of herself as good at something or bad at something else? Why does she value one quality and not another? There are at least three sources of information. First, of course, a child's own direct experience with success or failure in various arenas plays an obvious role. I pointed out in the last chapter that children in elementary school become aware of their relative academic successes; they gain equally direct comparative information when they play sports, take clarinet lessons, or try out for the school play.

Second, the value a child attaches to some skill or quality is obviously affected fairly directly by peers' and parents' attitudes and values, as I've already mentioned. Peer (and general cultural) standards for appearance establish benchmarks for all children and teens. A child who is "too tall" or "too fat" or deviates in some other way from the accepted norms is likely to feel a sense of inadequacy. Similarly, the degree of emphasis parents place on the child's performing well in some domain, whether it is school, athletics, or playing chess, is an important element in forming the child's aspirations in each area.

And third, labels and judgments from others play a highly significant role. To a very considerable

Playing catch with Dad is a classic father-son activity in American culture. One of the side effects is likely to be that the son comes to believe that skill in sports is something his dad values highly.

extent we come to think of ourselves as others think of us (Cole, 1991a). Children who are repeatedly told that they are "smart," "a good athlete," or "pretty" are likely to have higher self-esteem than are children who are told that they are "dumb," "clumsy," or a "late bloomer." A child who brings home a report card with Cs and Bs on it and hears the parent say, "That's fine, honey. We don't expect you to get all As," draws conclusions both about the parents' expectations and about their judgments of his abilities.

From all these sources, the child fashions his ideas (his internal model) about what he should be and what he is. Like the child's internal model of attachment, a child's self scheme is not fixed in

stone. It is responsive to changes in others' judgments as well as to changes in the child's own experience of success or failure. Once created, however, the model does tend to persist, both because the child will tend to choose experiences that will confirm and support his self scheme, and because the social environment—including the parents' evaluations of the child—tends to be at least moderately consistent.

[?] *Critical Thinking*

Think back to your own early school years. Can you remember what labels or descriptors your parents and others applied to you? Were you "the smart one" or "the pretty one" or "the one who's good at music"? Think about how those labels—whatever they were— affected your self-image and self-esteem.

The Role of the Larger Society

As at earlier ages, the daily life of the school-age child is shaped not just by the hours she spends in school or playing with pals. She is also affected by her family's economic circumstances, by the neighborhood she lives in, by the television programs she watches. Within the family, the pattern of interaction between parent and child is shaped by many of these same forces, as it is also affected by the quality of the parent's job, the amount of emotional support the parent(s) have from family or friends, and many other factors I've talked about in earlier chapters. Let me talk about two of these components of the larger culture that seem especially important in these elementary school years: the effects of poverty and the effects of television.

The General Effects of Poverty

In Chapter 10 I talked about the impact of poverty on a child's physical health, but of course the effects are far broader than that. Figure 12.5 (p. 408) shows the most recent U.S. national data on the percentage of children who live below the poverty line, defined in 1995 as an income for a family of four of $15,771 per year or less. Happily, these percentages have dropped somewhat in the past few years. In 1993, for example, 45.9% of African-American children lived in poverty, compared with the 41.9% shown in Figure 12.5 for 1995. Still, *proportionately more children in the United States live in poverty than in any other industrialized country in the world.* By way of specific contrast, the poverty rate for children in Canada is roughly nine percent; in Sweden it is about two percent.

Poverty is unequally distributed across ethnic groups in the United States, a fact that is plain in Figure 12.5. It is also unequally distributed across family structures: Children reared by single mothers are far more likely to be living in poverty. Approximately sixty percent of black and Hispanic children and forty percent of white children reared by single mothers in the United States live in poverty (Zill & Nord, 1994). Many of these mothers have jobs, but the jobs pay too little to lift the family out of poverty.

The Effects of Poverty on Families and Children.
Among many other things, poverty reduces options for parents. They may not be able to afford prenatal care, so their children are more likely to be born with some sort of disability. When the mother works, she is likely to have fewer choices of affordable child care. Such children spend more time in poor-quality care and shift more often from one

care arrangement to another. Poor families also live in smaller and less-adequate housing, often in decaying neighborhoods with high rates of violence; consequently, many of them move frequently, which means their children change schools often. The parents are less likely to feel they have adequate social support, and the children often lack a stable group of playmates (Dodge, Pettit, & Bates, 1994). Overall, poverty environments are more chaotic, more highly stressed, with fewer psychological and social resources (Brooks-Gunn, 1995b; McLoyd & Wilson, 1991).

Mothers and fathers living in poverty also treat their children quite differently than do parents in working-class or middle-class families in the United States. They talk and read to them less, provide fewer age-appropriate toys, spend less time with them in intellectually stimulating activities, explain things less often and less fully, are less warm, and are stricter and more physical in their discipline (Dodge et al., 1994; Sampson & Laub, 1994). In the terms I introduced in Chapter 9, poor parents are more likely to be either neglecting or authoritarian and less likely to be authoritative.

Some of this pattern of parental behavior is undoubtedly a response to the extraordinary stresses and special demands of the poverty environment, a point buttressed by the repeated observation that those parents living in poverty who nonetheless feel they have enough social support are much less likely to be harshly punitive or unsupportive toward their children (Hashima & Amato, 1994; Taylor & Roberts, 1995). To some extent the stricter discipline and emphasis on obedience we see in poor parents may be thought of as a logical response to the realities of life in a very poor neighborhood.

Some of the differences in child-rearing patterns between poor and nonpoor parents may also result from straightforward modeling of the way these same parents were reared; some may be a product of ignorance of children's needs. Poor parents with relatively more education, for example, typically talk to their children more, are more responsive, and provide more intellectual stimulation than do equally poor parents with lower levels of education (Kelley, Sanches-Hucles, & Walker, 1993). Whatever the cause, children reared in poverty experience both different physical condi-

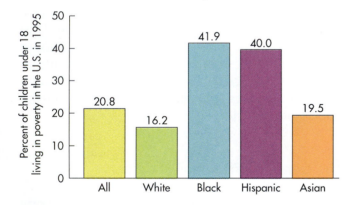

Figure 12.5

The percentage of children under age 18 living in poverty in the United States in 1995. (Source: Kilborn, 1996, p. 8, from Census Bureau data.)

Parenting

Latchkey Children

Many parents find themselves unable to afford, or unable to arrange, after-school care for their elementary school children. This leaves the child to care for herself in the hours between the end of school and the parent(s)' return from work. Such children are referred to as **latchkey children.**

It has been very difficult to discover just how many latchkey children there are, in part because such a practice has had a lot of bad press, so parents are not always willing to acknowledge that their children care for themselves part of the time. Most current estimates are that between 5 and 10 percent of children between ages 6 and 13 in the United States spend at least some part of their days in "self-care" (Zigler & Gilman, 1996). In families in which all the adults are working, the rate is about twice that high (Cain & Hofferth, 1989).

Self-care is most likely for children 10 and over, and for only a short time each day, most often after school. Contrary to what you may assume, such care arrangements are *not* found primarily among families in poverty environments. On the contrary, they are more common among middle- and upper-class white families in suburban or rural areas.

There is very little decent research to tell us what effect such self-care may have on children. Some studies suggest that latchkey children are more vulnerable to peer pressure and substance abuse (Zigler & Gilman, 1996). Other evidence suggests that latchkey children do not differ from other kids in their school performance, self-concept, or susceptibility to peer pressure *if* the child has a clear routine, is in daily contact with the parent(s) by phone during the self-care hours, and has neighbors or others to turn to in case of need (Cole & Rodman, 1987). When these conditions cannot be met—as may be the case for children living in public housing developments or in other environments without good support—self-care may simply exacerbate existing problems.

Among adolescents who lack supervision for parts of each day, those who stay in their own homes for the unsupervised hours seem to do better than those who spend the time "hanging out" or at a friend's house. The latter groups seem to be especially susceptible to peer pressure during the peer-sensitive years of early adolescence (Steinberg, 1986).

Overall, the relatively scant research literature suggests that self-care by children is not the unmitigated disaster many popular press reports would have us believe. Still, there are enough red flags to suggest that we need to know much more about the specific conditions needed to support children who must care for themselves for part of each day.

tions and quite different interactions with their parents.

Not surprisingly, such children turn out differently. Children from poverty environments have higher rates of illness and disabilities, as you've already seen in Chapter 10. On average, they also have lower IQs and move through the sequences of cognitive development more slowly. They come to school less ready to learn to read, and thereafter they do consistently less well in school. They are twice as likely as nonpoor children to repeat a grade and are less likely to go on to college (Brooks-Gunn, 1995b; Huston, 1994; Zill et al., 1995). As adults they are more likely to be poor, thus continuing the cycle through another generation. All these effects are greater for those children who live in poverty in infancy and early childhood as well as for those who have lived continuously in poverty compared to children who have experienced some mixture of poverty and greater affluence (Bolger, 1997; Duncan, Brooks-Gunn, & Klebanov, 1994; Shanahan, Sayer, Davey, & Brooks, 1997).

The Special Case of Inner-City Poverty. These negative effects are also exacerbated for children growing up in poverty-ravaged urban neighborhoods. They are exposed to street gangs and street violence, drug pushers, overcrowded homes, and abuse. Whole communities have become like war zones.

In the United States almost 13 million children live in such urban poverty (Garbarino, Kostelny, & Dubrow, 1991). More than 1.5 million live in public housing developments, including some in settings with the highest crime rates in the country. Surveys in a number of large cities indicate that nearly half of inner-city elementary and high school students have witnessed at least one violent crime in the past year (Osofsky, 1995); nearly all have heard guns being fired, seen someone being beat up, or observed a drug deal (White, Bruce, Farrell, & Kliewer, 1997). Guns are common in schools as well as on the streets. In a 1993 national survey by the Centers for Disease Control, 22.1 percent of high school students reported that they had carried a weapon (gun, knife, or club) some time in the previous 30 days; 7.9 percent had carried a gun (Kann, Warren, Harris et al., 1995).

[?] Critical Thinking

Are you shocked by such statistics? What do you think we ought to do about it?

A growing body of evidence shows that the effect of living in such a concentrated pocket of poverty is to intensify all the ill effects of family poverty (Klebanov, Brooks-Gunn, Hofferth, & Duncan, 1995; Kupersmidt, Griesler, DeRosier, Patterson, & Davis, 1995). When the whole neighborhood is poor, especially when residence in the neighborhood is in constant flux, parents have fewer other resources to rely on and children have more violent and fewer supportive adult models; rates of child abuse rise, as do rates of aggression and delinquency in the children (Coulton, Korbin, Su, & Chow, 1995; McLoyd, 1997). When the whole neigh-

When you look at scenes of urban poverty like this, you can see why some refer to them as "war zones."

borhood also lacks what sociologist William Wilson calls *connectedness* and *stability*—when the adults do not collaborate to monitor the children and do not provide practical or emotional support to one another—the effects are still worse (Sampson, 1997; Wilson, 1995).

Many children living in such neighborhoods show all the symptoms of posttraumatic stress disorder (Garbarino, Dubrow, Kostelny, & Pardo, 1992), including sleep disturbances, irritability, inability to concentrate, angry outbursts, and hypervigilance. Many experience flashbacks or intrusive memories of traumatic events. And because they are likely to have missed out on many of the forms of intellectual stimulation and consistent family support that would allow them to succeed in school, they have high rates of behavior problems and academic failures. Less than half of urban poor children graduate from high school (Garbarino et al., 1991). The reasons for such school failures are complex but there is little doubt that the chronic stress experienced by poor children is one highly significant component.

James Garbarino expresses my own feelings about such poverty with particular eloquence:

> What is truly needed in America's urban war zones is restoration of a safe environment where children can have a childhood, and where parents can exert less energy on protecting children from random gunfire and more on helping children to grow. No one can eliminate all risk from the lives of families. But America does have the resources to make a real childhood a real possibility even for the children of the urban poor. But sometimes the war close to home is the most difficult to see. (Garbarino et al., 1991, p. 148)

The Role of Stress and Protective Factors. Arnold Sameroff and his colleagues have argued that the effects of various different kinds and numbers of stresses accumulate. A child may be able to handle one or two, but as the stresses and risks pile up, the probability that a child will thrive intellectually, emotionally, or socially declines steadily (Sameroff, Seifer, Barocas, Zax, & Greenspan, 1987). For a child growing up in poverty, perhaps especially urban poverty, the chances of experiencing multiple separate types of stress are very high indeed.

At the same time, studies of resilient and vulnerable children (Easterbrooks, Davidson, & Chazan, 1993; Furstenberg & Hughes, 1995; Garmezy & Masten, 1991; Masten et al., 1990; Winfield, 1995) suggest that certain characteristics or circumstances may help to protect some children from the detrimental effects of repeated stresses and upheavals. Some of the key protective factors are:

- High intelligence in the child;
- Competent adult parenting, such as an authoritative style, with good supervision and monitoring of the child;
- Effective schools;
- A secure initial attachment of the child to the parent;
- A strong community help network, including friends or family or neighbors.

For example, in a major longitudinal study in Kauai, Hawaii, Emmy Werner (Werner & Smith, 1992) has found that a subset of those children reared in poverty nonetheless became competent, able, autonomous adults. The families of these resilient children were clearly more authoritative, more cohesive, and more loving than were the equivalently poor families whose children had worse outcomes. Similarly, studies of boys reared in high-crime, inner-city neighborhoods show that high intelligence and at least a minimum level of family cohesion increase a boy's chance of creating a successful adult life pattern (Long & Vaillant, 1984; McCord, 1982; Sampson & Laub, 1994). Boys reared in poverty-level families in which the parents have strong antisocial tendencies, high use of alcohol, or low IQ are much less likely to develop the competence needed to bootstrap themselves out of their difficult circumstances.

Thus the outcome depends on some joint effect of the number of stresses the child must cope with and the range of competencies or advantages the child (and her family) brings to the situation. Poverty does not guarantee bad outcomes, but it stacks the deck against most children. As Judith Musick puts it, these environments are "densely layered with risk" (1994, p. 1).

Television and Its Effects

Another major influence on children, particularly in industrialized countries, is television. Ninety-eight percent of American homes have a TV set. Children between the ages of 2 and 11 spend an average of about 22 hours a week watching television, adolescents a bit less (American Psychological Association, 1993; Fabrikant, 1996). This number has declined in the past decade, dropping from more than 26 hours a week in 1984, but it is still the case that "By the time American children are 18 years old, they have spent more time watching television than in any other activity except sleep" (Huston, Wright, Rice, Kerkman, & St. Peters, 1990). In the United States, high levels of viewing are more common among African-American children than among whites or Hispanics and more common in families in which the parents are less well educated (Anderson, Lorch, Field, Collins, & Nathan, 1986).

Viewing rates are not as high in most other countries, but TV set ownership is above 50 percent of households in Latin America and in most of Eastern and Western Europe, so this is not an exclusively American phenomenon (Comstock, 1991).

I can give you only a few tidbits from the vast amount of research designed to detect any effects such viewing may have on children and on adults. Still, a taste is better than no meal at all.

Positive Educational Effects. Programs specifically designed to be educational or to teach children positive values do indeed have demonstrable positive effects. This is particularly clear among preschoolers, for whom most such programming is largely designed. For example, children who watch *Sesame Street* more regularly develop larger vocabularies than do children who do not watch or watch less often (Rice, Huston, Truglio, & Wright, 1990). Moreover, those who watch programs that emphasize sharing, kindness, and helpfulness, such as *Mister Rogers Neighborhood*, *Sesame Street*, or even *Lassie*, show more kind and helpful behavior (Murray, 1980). Results like these show that, as Huston and Wright say, "television can be an ally, not an enemy, for parents. Parents can use television programs for their children's benefit just as they use books and toys" (Huston & Wright, 1994, p. 80).

Research Report

Family Viewing Patterns

The mythical "average child" in the United States watches three to four hours of television a day. Such averages obviously disguise very large variations among families in both viewing patterns and attitudes about television. To a considerable extent, parents control their children's TV viewing through explicit rules and through attitudes—an example of the way in which broad cultural forces interact with individual family styles. Nearly half of families have consistent rules about what type or which programs a child may view. Forty percent restrict the number of hours a child can watch, while another 40 percent encourage the child's viewing at least some of the time (Comstock, 1991).

Michelle St. Peters (St. Peters, Fitch, Huston, Wright, & Eakins, 1991) found that she could classify families into one of four types, on the basis of the degree of regulation and degree of encouragement of TV viewing parents imposed: *laissez-faire* parents had few regulations but did not specifically encourage viewing; *restrictive* parents had high regulations and little encouragement; *promotive* parents had few regulations and high levels of encouragement for TV viewing; and *selective* parents had high regulations but encouraged some types of viewing.

In a 2-year longitudinal study of 5-year-olds and their parents, St. Peters found that children in restrictive families watched the least amount of television (11.9 hours per week). When they watched, it was most likely to be entertainment or educational programs aimed specifically at children (such as *Sesame Street, Mister Rogers' Neighborhood,* or a Walt Disney program). The heaviest viewers were children with parents classed as promotive, who watched an average of 21.1 hours per week. They watched not only children's programs but also adult comedy, drama, game shows, and action adventure. Both laissez-faire families (16.7 hours) and selective families (19.2 hours) watched an intermediate number of hours each week.

The key point here is that families create the conditions for children's viewing and thus for what children learn from television. Parents not only establish a degree of regulation, they may also watch with the child and interpret what the child sees. A family that wants to do so can take advantage of the beneficial things television has to offer and minimize exposure to programs with aggressive, violent, or sexist content. The difficulty for many families, however, is that such a planned approach to TV may mean that the parents will have to give up their own favorite programs....

Negative Effects of Television on Cognitive Skills. However, among elementary and high school students, heavy television viewing is associated with *lower* scores on achievement tests, including measures of such basic skills as reading, arithmetic, and writing. This is particularly clear in the results of an enormous study in California that included more than 500,000 sixth and twelfth graders (California Assessment Program, 1980). The researchers found that the more hours the students watched television, the lower their scores on standardized tests. This relationship was actually *stronger* among children from well-educated families, so this result is not an artifact of the fact that working-class or low-education families watch more television. However, among children with limited English fluency, high levels of viewing were associated with somewhat higher school achievement. Thus television can help to teach children things they did not already know (including language), but among children with basic skills at the start of school, TV viewing time appears to have a negative effect on school performance.

Critical Thinking

How many different explanations can you think of for the relationship between amount of television viewing and school performance? What kind of data would you need in order to check the plausibility of each of your explanations?

Television and Aggression. By far the largest body of research has focused on the potential impact of television on children's aggressiveness. The level of violence on U.S. television is remarkably high and has remained high over the past two decades, despite many congressional investiga-

In the United States, elementary school–age children watch an average of 22 hours of television every week. Amazing.

tions and cries of alarm. On prime-time programs, a violent act occurs 5 or 6 times per hour; on Saturday morning cartoons, the rate is 20 to 25 times per hour. The highest rates of violence are generally found in programs broadcast between six and nine in the morning and two and five in the afternoon—times of day when young children are likely to be watching (Donnerstein, Slaby, & Eron, 1994). Cable television, now available in roughly sixty percent of homes in the United States, adds to this diet of violence, as do violent video games that are increasingly popular as replacements of TV viewing time. The violence portrayed on these various programs and media is typically shown as a successful way of solving problems and is frequently rewarded: People who are violent often get what they want. In many video games symbolic violence is the approved means to achieve the game's goal.

Does the viewing of such a barrage of violence *cause* higher rates of aggression or violence in children? Demonstrating such a causal link is a bit like

demonstrating a causal connection between smoking and lung cancer. Unequivocal findings would require an experimental design—a strategy ruled out for obvious ethical reasons. One cannot assign some people randomly to smoke for 30 years, nor assign some children to watch years of violent television programming, while others watch none. But we have three other types of research that all point strongly toward the existence of a causal link.

First, we have a few genuinely experimental studies in which one group of children has been exposed to a few episodes of moderately aggressive programs while others watched neutral programs. Collectively, these studies show a significant short-term increase in aggression among those who watched the aggressive TV programs (Paik & Comstock, 1994). In a recent example of this type of study, Chris Boyatzis (Boyatzis, Matillo, Nesbitt, & Cathey, 1995) found that early elementary school–age children who were randomly assigned to watch episodes of a popular (and highly violent) children's program, *The Mighty Morphin Power Rangers*, showed seven times as many aggressive acts during subsequent free play with peers as did comparable children who had not just viewed the violent program.

A second type of research involves comparing levels of aggression among children who vary in the amount of television they watch in their everyday lives. The almost universal finding is that those who watch more TV are more aggressive than their low-TV-watching peers. Of course, this leaves us with a problem of interpretation. In particular, children who already behave aggressively may *choose* to watch more television and more violent television programming; similarly, families who watch TV a great deal may also be more likely to use patterns of discipline that will foster aggressiveness in the child. One partial solution to this dilemma is to study children longitudinally, as Leonard Eron did in a 22-year-long study of aggressiveness from age 8 to age 30 (Eron, 1987).

Eron found that the best predictor of a young man's aggressiveness at age 19 was the violence of television programs he watched when he was 8. When Eron interviewed the men again when they were 30, he found that those who had had higher rates of TV viewing at age 8 were much more likely to have a record of serious criminal behavior in

Psychology in Action

Television Aggression

Using the definition of violence offered by George Gerbner ("the overt expression of physical force against others or self, or the compelling of action against one's will on pain of being hurt or killed"), select a minimum of four half-hour television programs normally watched by children and count the number of physically aggressive or violent episodes in each. At the same time, devise a definition of verbal aggression and count episodes of this type of aggression as well.

You may select any four (or more) programs, but I would strongly recommend that you distribute them in the following way:

1. At least one "educational" television program, such as *Sesame Street* or *Mister Rogers' Neighborhood*.
2. At least one Saturday morning cartoon. Select at random.
3. At least one early evening adult program that is watched by young children, such as a situation comedy or a crime film.

For each program you watch, record the number of violent episodes, separating the instances of verbal and physical violence.

Analysis and Report

In thinking or writing about the details of your observations, consider the following questions:

1. Did you have difficulty devising a useful definition of verbal aggression?
2. What kind of variation in the number of violent episodes is there among the programs that you watched?
3. Are some programs more verbally aggressive, some more physically aggressive?
4. Do the numbers of violent episodes per program correspond to the numbers reported in the text?
5. What about the consequences of aggression in the television films? Are those who act violently rewarded or punished? How often do reward and punishment occur?
6. What behaviors other than aggression might a child have learned from watching the programs you viewed? This question is particularly relevant for *Sesame Street* or *Mister Rogers,* but applies to more traditional entertainment programs as well.
7. In view of the material in this chapter, and your own observations for this project, what rules or limits (if any) would you place on TV viewing for your own child?

adulthood, a set of results shown in Figure 12.6. The pattern is the same for women, by the way, but the level of criminal offenses is far lower, just as the level of aggression is lower among girls in childhood.

The results shown in the figure, of course, are still a form of correlation. They don't prove that the TV viewing contributed in any causal way to the later criminality because those children who chose to watch a lot of violent TV at age 8 may already have been the most violent children. Indeed, Eron found just such a pattern: Eight-year-old boys who watched a lot of violent television were already more aggressive with their peers, indicating that aggressive boys select more violent TV programs. However, the longitudinal design allowed Eron to tease out some additional patterns. In particular,

he found that among the *already*-aggressive 8-year-olds, those who watched the most television were more delinquent or aggressive as teenagers and as adults than were those who watched television for fewer hours (Eron, 1987; Huesmann, Lagerspetz, & Eron, 1984).

Shorter-term longitudinal studies in Poland, Finland, Israel, and Australia show similar links between TV viewing and later increased aggression among children (Eron et al., 1991). Collectively, the evidence suggests that the causality runs both ways: "Aggressive children prefer violent television, and the violence on television causes them to be more aggressive" (Eron, 1987, p. 438).

The newest type of evidence comes from epidemiologist Brandon Centerwall (1989; 1992), who proposes that we think of societal violence as an

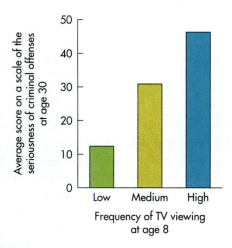

Figure 12.6

These data from Leonard Eron's 22-year longitudinal study show the relationships between the amount of television a group of boys watched when they were 8 and the average severity of criminal offenses they had committed by the age of 30. (Source: Eron, 1987, Figure 3, p. 440.)

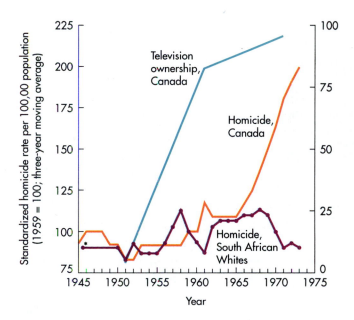

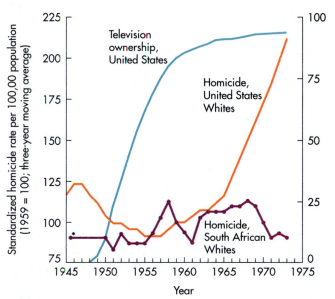

Figure 12.7

Centerwall looked at societal violence as if it were a disease and asked what relationship the introduction of television in each culture had to the rate of such violence. (Source: Centerwall, 1989, Figure 1, p. 6, and Figure 2, p. 7.)

epidemic disease and use exactly the same strategies to study it that an epidemiologist would use in trying to trace the causal factors in any other epidemic. One such strategy is to examine the conditions surrounding the emergence of a particular disease in a series of different countries, to see if it is possible to identify common antecedents. In his study of societal violence Centerwall looked at changes in the homicide rates in Canada as a whole and among whites in the United States and South Africa as a function of the time since television was introduced into each country.

Television was introduced in both the United States and Canada in about 1950; in South Africa widespread television was available only about 25 years later. In each of these three countries, the homicide rate began to rise rapidly 10 to 15 years after TV viewing became widespread, as you can see in Figure 12.7. That is, as soon as the first generation of children who had grown up watching television became adults, homicide rates soared.

Naturally, this is *also* correlational evidence. You might well argue that other changes in these three societies might have caused a rise in violence in those particular years. To try to rule out such alternative explanations, Centerwall checked out a number of the more obvious possibilities, such as changes in the age distribution of the populations (since young people are more violent), in urbanization, economic conditions, alcohol consumption, civil unrest, or in the availability of firearms. He found that the pattern of changes on each of these dimensions in the three countries did *not* match the shifts in the homicide rates. Only the introduction of television was temporally linked to the rise in violence.

Virtually all psychologists, after reviewing the combined evidence, would agree with Eron's testimony before a Senate committee:

> There can no longer be any doubt that heavy exposure to televised violence is one of the causes of aggressive behavior, crime, and violence in society. The evidence comes from both the laboratory and real-life studies. Television violence affects youngsters of all ages, of both genders, at all socioeconomic levels and all levels of intelligence. The effect is not limited to children who are already disposed to being aggressive and is not restricted to this country. (Eron, 1992, p. S8539)

Other evidence suggests that repeated viewing of TV violence leads to emotional desensitization toward violence, to a belief that aggression is a good way to solve problems, and to a reduction in prosocial behavior (Donnerstein et al., 1994). Violent television is clearly not the only, or even the major, cause of aggressiveness among children or adults. It is nonetheless a significant influence, both individually and at the broader cultural level.

[?] *Critical Thinking*

Given all that you have now read about television and children's development, how could you as a parent maximize the benefits and limit the negative effects? Would you be willing to give up having a television altogether if you thought that was necessary for your child's optimum development?

For parents, the clear message from all the research on television is that it is an educational medium. Children learn from what they watch—vocabulary words, helpful behaviors, dietary preferences, and aggressive behaviors and attitudes. The overall content of television—violence and all—may indeed reflect general cultural values. But an individual family can pick and choose among the various cultural messages by controlling what the child watches on TV.

Summary

1. Patterns of relationships established in elementary school may have greater impact on adolescent and adult life than do cognitive changes in these same years.

2. In middle childhood the self-concept becomes more abstract, more comparative, more generalized.

3. Similar changes occur in children's descriptions of others and in their understanding of relationships such as friendships. Friendships are increasingly seen as reciprocal relationships in which generosity and trust are important elements.

4. These changes parallel the cognitive changes we see in the same years, particularly the child's reduced reliance on appearances.

5. Relationships with parents become less overtly affectionate, with fewer attachment behaviors, in middle childhood. The strength of the attachment, however, appears to persist and the parents continue to function as a "safe base" for the child.

6. Peer relationships become increasingly central. Gender segregation of peer group activities, which appears in every culture, is at its peak in these years.

7. Individual friendships also become more common and more enduring; they are almost entirely sex-segregated. Boys' and girls' friendships appear to differ in quite specific ways. Boys' relationships are more extensive and more "restrictive," with higher levels of competition and aggression; girls' relationships are more intensive and enabling, with more compliance and agreement.

8. Physical aggression declines, while verbal insults and taunts increase. Boys show markedly higher levels of physical and direct verbal aggression, and higher rates of conduct disorders, but girls show higher rates of "relational aggression."

9. When a child shows persistent aggression, cruelty, or bullying, he may be diagnosed with a conduct disorder. When such problems are evident early in childhood, the deviant behavior tends to be more serious and persistent.

10. Early-onset conduct disorders appear to have a genetic component and to be exacerbated by poor family interactions and subsequent poor peer relations.

11. Socially rejected children are most strongly characterized by high levels of aggression or bullying and low levels of agreement and helpfulness. Aggres-

sive/rejected children are likely to show behavior problems in adolescence and a variety of disturbances in adulthood.

12. Rejected children are more likely to interpret others' behavior as threatening or hostile. Thus they have different internal models of relationship.

13. Self-esteem appears to be shaped by two factors: the degree of discrepancy a child experiences between goals and achievements and the degree of perceived social support from peers and parents.

14. Low self-esteem is strongly associated with depression in children this age.

15. A large fraction of children in the United States grow up in poverty. Such children, especially those experiencing persistent urban poverty, are markedly disadvantaged in many ways, including lower access to medical care and exposure to multiple stresses. They do worse in school and drop out of school at far higher rates.

16. Some protective factors, including a secure attachment, higher IQ, authoritative parenting, and effective schools, can counterbalance poverty effects for some children.

17. The average American child watches four hours of television per day. Preschoolers can learn vocabulary, politeness, or other skills. Among schoolchildren, the more TV watched, the lower the grades.

18. Experts agree that watching violence on television also increases the level of personal aggression or violence shown by a child.

Key Terms

adolescent-onset conduct disorder A conduct disorder that begins only in adolescence. Typically less severe and persistent than childhood-onset disorders. **(p. 400)**

bully A child who repeatedly torments some other child with words, gestures, intentional exclusion from a group, or physical aggression. **(p. 399)**

childhood-onset conduct disorder Conduct disorder beginning in childhood; linked to rejection by peers and to persistent conduct problems into adolescence and adulthood. **(p. 400)**

latchkey children Children in "self-care" before or after school because the parents are working or otherwise unavailable and no other supervision has been arranged. **(p. 409)**

neglected children Type of unpopular children who are not overtly rejected, are reasonably well liked, but are not often chosen as friends. **(p. 401)**

reciprocal friendship Any friendship in which the two partners each name the other as a friend; also a quality of friendship in school-age children, when friendship is perceived for the first time as being based on reciprocal trust. **(p. 396)**

rejected children Unpopular children who are not just ignored but are explicitly avoided, not chosen as playmates or friends. **(p. 401)**

relational aggression A form of aggression aimed at damaging the other person's self-esteem or peer relationships, such as by ostracism or threats of ostracism, cruel gossiping, or facial expressions of disdain. **(p. 399)**

self-esteem A global judgment of self-worth; how well you like the person you perceive yourself to be; how well you measure up when judged against your own valued qualities or skills. **(p. 404)**

victim The target of a bully. Child victims tend to be passive, sensitive, quiet, and physically somewhat smaller or less strong. **(p. 399)**

Suggested Readings

Asher, S. R., & Coie, J. D. (Eds.). (1990). *Peer rejection in childhood*. Cambridge, England: Cambridge University Press. This edited volume contains papers by all the leading researchers on this important subject. The papers are aimed at an audience of fellow psychologists, so the technical level is fairly high. Still, it is a wonderful next source if you are interested in this subject.

Chase-Lansdale, P. L., & Brooks-Gunn, J. (Eds.). (1995). *Escape from poverty. What makes a difference for children?* Cambridge, England: Cambridge University Press. A fine collection of papers on many aspects of poverty in the United States in the middle 1990s, including a discussion of early welfare-to-work programs.

Eron, L. D., Gentry, J. H., & Schlegel, P. (Eds.). (1994). *Reason to hope. A psychosocial perspective on violence and youth*. Washington, DC: American Psychological Association. The chapter on the effect of television on violence is a good current review of this material. The book also includes many other fascinating chapters.

Garbarino, J., Dubrow, N., Kostelny, K., & Pardo, C. (1992). *Children in danger. Coping with the consequences of community violence*. San Francisco: Jossey-Bass. A striking, frightening book about children growing up in "war zones," including those in urban poverty zones in the United States as well as those in literal war zones in other countries.

Huston, A. C. (Ed.). (1991). *Children in poverty. Child development and public policy*. Cambridge, England: Cambridge University Press. An excellent collection of papers on all aspects of poverty.

Kozol, J. (1995). *Amazing grace*. New York: Crown. A deeply affecting book about children growing up in one of the most concentrated pockets of poverty in the United States, the south Bronx. It will astonish you—and make you weep.

Summing Up Development at School Age

BASIC CHARACTERISTICS OF MIDDLE CHILDHOOD

You can see from the following table, which summarizes the changes and continuities of middle childhood, that many of the changes in this period are gradual ones: greater and greater physical skill, less and less reliance on appearance and more and more attention to underlying qualities and attributes, greater and greater role of peers. The one interval during these years in which there seems to be a more rapid change is right at the beginning of middle childhood, at the point of transition from the preschooler to the school child. And of course at the other end of this age range, puberty causes another set of rapid changes.

The Transition Between 5 and 7. Some kind of a transition into middle childhood has been noted in a great many cultures. There seems to be widespread recognition that a 6-year-old is somehow qualitatively different from a 5-year-old: more responsible, more able to understand complex ideas. Among the Kipsigis of Kenya, for example, the age of 6 is said to be the first point at which the child has *ng omnotet*, translated as "intelligence" (Harkness & Super, 1985). The fact that schooling begins at this age seems to reflect an implicit or explicit recognition of this fundamental shift.

Psychologists who have studied development across this transition have pointed to a whole series of changes.

- Cognitively, we see a shift to what Piaget calls concrete operational thinking. The child now understands conservation problems, seriation, and class inclusion. More generally, the child seems to pay less attention to surface properties of objects and more to underlying continuities and patterns. We see this not only in children's understanding of physical objects but in their understanding of others, of relationships, and of themselves. In studies of information processing, we see a parallel rapid increase in the child's use of executive strategies.

- In the self-concept, we first see a global judgment of self-worth at about age 7 or 8.

- In peer relationships, gender segregation becomes virtually complete by age 6 or 7, especially in individual friendships.

A Summary of the Threads of Development During Middle Childhood

Aspect of Development	Age in Years						
	6	7	8	9	10	11	12
Physical development	Jumps rope; skips; may ride bike	Rides two-wheeled bike	Rides bike well Uses pencil well	Puberty begins for some girls		Puberty begins for some boys	
Cognitive development	Gender constancy; various concrete operations skills, including some conservation, class inclusion, various memory strategies, executive processes (metacognition)		Inductive logic; better and better use of concrete operations skills; conservation of weight			Conservation of volume	
Self/ personality development	Concept of self increasingly more abstract, less tied to appearance; descriptions of others increasingly focused on internal, enduring qualities						
			Global sense of self-worth				
			Friendship based on reciprocal trust				
	Gender segregation in play and friendship almost total						
	Enduring friendships appear, continue throughout these years						

The apparent confluence of these changes is impressive and seems to provide some support for the existence of a Piaget-like stage. On the surface, at least, it looks as if some kind of change in the basic structure of the child's thinking has occurred that is reflected in all aspects of the child's functioning. Impressive as these changes are, however, it is not so clear that what is going on here is a rapid, pervasive, structural change to a whole new way of thinking and relating. Children don't make this shift all at once in every area of their thinking or relationships. For example, while the shift from a concrete to a more abstract self-concept may become noticeable at 6 or 7, it occurs quite gradually and is still going on at ages 11 and 12. Similarly, a child may grasp conservation of quantity at age 5 or 6, but typically does not understand conservation of weight until several years later.

Furthermore, expertise, or the lack of it, strongly affects the pattern of the child's cognitive progress. Thus, while I think most psychologists would agree that a set of important changes normally emerge together at about this age, most would also agree that there is no rapid or abrupt reorganization of the child's whole mode of operating.

CENTRAL PROCESSES

In trying to account for the developmental shifts we see during middle childhood, my bias has been to see the cognitive changes as most central, the necessary but not sufficient condition for the alterations in relationships and in the self scheme during this period. A good illustration is the emergence of a global sense of self-worth, which seems to require not only a tendency to look beyond or behind surface characteristics, but also the use of inductive logic. The child appears to arrive at a global sense

of self-worth by some summative, inductive process.

Similarly, the quality of the child's relationships with peers and parents seems to rest, in part, on a basic cognitive understanding of reciprocity and perspective taking. The child now understands that others read him as much as he reads them.

Children of 7 or 8 will now say of their friends that they "trust each other," something you would be very unlikely to hear from a 5-year-old.

Such a cognitive bias dominated theories and research on middle childhood for many decades, largely as a result of the powerful influence of Piaget's theory. This imbalance has begun to be redressed in recent years, as the central importance of the peer group and the child's social experience have been better understood. There are two aspects to this revision of thinking. First, we have reawakened to the (obvious) fact that a great deal of the experience on which the child's cognitive progress is based occurs in social interactions, particularly in play with other children. Second, we have realized that social relationships make a unique set of demands, both cognitive and interactive, and have unique consequences for the child's social and emotional functioning. It is in these elementary school years, for example, that patterns of peer rejection or acceptance are consolidated, with reverberations through adolescence and into adult life.

As objects of thought, people are simply not the same as rocks, beakers of water, or balls of clay. Among many other things, people behave *intentionally*, and they can reveal or conceal information about themselves. Further, unlike relationships with objects, relationships with people are mutual and reciprocal. Other people talk back, respond to your distress, offer things, get angry.

Children also have to learn social scripts, those special rules that apply to social interactions, such as politeness rules, or rules about when you can and cannot speak, about when you should or should not display emotions, or about power or dominance hierarchies. Such scripts change with age, so at each new age the child must learn a new set of roles, a new set of rules about what she may and may not do. To be sure, these changes in the scripts are partly in *response* to the child's growing cognitive sophistication. But they also reflect changes in the child's role in the social system. One obvious example is the set of changes when children start school. The script associated with the role of "student" is simply quite different from the one connected with the role of "little kid." School classrooms are more tightly organized than are preschools or day care centers, expectations for obedience are higher, many new drills and routines must be learned. These changes are bound to affect the child's pattern of thinking.

Just what role physical change plays in this collection of developments I do not know. Clearly, physical changes *are* going on. Girls, in particular, begin the early steps of puberty during elementary school. What we don't know is whether the rate of physical development in these years is connected in any way to the rate of the child's progress through the sequence of cognitive or social understandings. There has been virtually no research linking the first row in the summary table with any of the other rows. We do have data showing that bigger, more coordinated, early-developing children are likely to have slightly faster cognitive development and be somewhat more popular with peers, but this is only one piece of the puzzle. Obviously, this is an area in which we need far more knowledge.

INFLUENCES ON THE BASIC PROCESSES

Most of what I have said about middle childhood—and about other ages as well—is based almost entirely on research on children growing up in Western cultures. I've tried to balance the scales a bit as I've gone along, but we must still ask, again and again, whether the patterns we see are specific to particular cultures or whether they reflect underlying developmental processes common to all children everywhere.

In the case of middle childhood, there are some obvious differences in the experiences of children in Western cultures versus those growing up in parts of the world where families live by subsistence agriculture and schooling is not a dominant force in children's lives (Weisner, 1984). In many such cultures children of 6 or 7 are thought of as "intelligent" and responsible and are given almost adultlike roles. They are highly likely to be given the task of caring for younger siblings or to begin an apprenticeship in the skills they will need as adults, such as agricultural skills or animal husbandry, learning alongside the adult. In some West African and Polynesian cultures, it is also common for children this age to be sent out to foster care, either with relatives or to apprentice with a skilled tradesperson.

Children growing up in such cultures obviously have a very different set of social tasks to learn in the middle childhood years. They do not need to learn how to relate to or make friends with strangers. Instead, from an early age they need to learn their place in an existing network of roles and relationships. For the Western child, the roles are less prescribed, the choices for adult life are far more varied.

Yet the differences in the lives of Western and non-Western children should not obscure the very real similarities. In all cultures children this age develop individual friendships, segregate their play groups by gender, develop the cognitive underpinnings of reciprocity, learn the beginnings of what Piaget calls concrete operations, and acquire some of the basic skills that will be required for adult life. These are not trivial similarities. They speak to the power of the common process of development, even in the midst of obvious variation in experience.

Physical Development and Health in Adolescence

Preview Questions

1 Are teenagers really more awkward or uncoordinated than children of other ages?

2 Why do girls who begin puberty early have more psychological problems?

3 Which teenage girls are most likely to become pregnant?

4 Why do adolescents engage in so many risky behaviors?

5 How are eating disorders and illegal steroid use related to each other?

Chapter Outline

When you think back to your own adolescence, can you pick out a particular time, a particular age, when you began to think of yourself as an "adolescent"? Was it when you noticed the first physical changes of puberty? Was it when you changed from elementary school to junior high? Or was the whole set of changes so gradual that there was no clear starting point—no time when you suddenly thought of yourself as an adolescent? And when did you stop being an adolescent? When you left high school? When you stopped growing? When you had a full-time job?

Many of us use the word *adolescent* as if it were a precise label, more or less equivalent to "teenager," but in fact the definition is quite fuzzy. If we want to include all the physical processes of puberty within the years of adolescence, then we need to think of adolescence as beginning before the teenage years, especially for girls, some of whom begin puberty at 8 or 9. On the other end of the teenage years, it is not clear that it is still appropriate to refer to a young man of 18 with a job and a wife and child as an adolescent.

It makes more sense to think of adolescence as the period that lies psychologically and culturally between childhood and adulthood rather than as a specific age range. It is the period of transition in which the child changes physically, mentally, and emotionally into an adult—however adulthood may be defined in the particular culture in which the young person is growing up. The timing of this transition differs from one society to another and from one individual to another within a culture. But every child must cross through such a transitional period, including the transition to sexual maturity, in order to achieve adult status. In most industrialized cultures today, this transitional stage is quite lengthy, lasting from perhaps age 12 to 18 or 20. Indeed, as the level of technical skill needed for adult work has risen in recent decades, the period of "preparation for adulthood" has tended to expand still further, with marriage and childbearing more and more often delayed into the middle 20s. In contrast, in less technologically advanced eras, when young people were expected to take up adult work in their teens—on the farm, in factories, or at home—the period of transition from childhood to adulthood was far shorter.

In the initiation rite of the Kota tribe of the Congo, boys' faces are painted blue to make them appear ghostlike, to symbolize the phantom of their now-departed childhood.

Because the physical and emotional changes that are part of this transition are so striking, the period of adolescence has acquired a reputation as being full of storm and stress. Such a description considerably exaggerates the degree of emotional upheaval most adolescents experience. Nonetheless, the *importance* of the process is difficult to exaggerate. In this chapter I'll be looking at the physical changes linked to this period, including the pervasive process of **puberty** (with its attendant changes in sexual behavior) and health habits and behaviors. In later chapters I'll explore some of the equally striking shifts in cognitive skills and social behavior.

Cultures and Contexts

Adolescent Initiation Rituals

So important is the change in status from child to adult that many societies have marked this passage with some kind of rite or ritual. Such rituals vary enormously in content, but certain practices are especially common (Cohen, 1964).

One such practice, more common for boys than for girls, is the separation of the child from the family, referred to by anthropologists as *extrusion*. The child may spend the day with his family, but sleep elsewhere, or may live in a separate dwelling with other boys or with relatives. For example, among the Kurtatchi of Melanesia, boys go through an extrusion ceremony at about age 9 or 10, after which they sleep in a special hut used by boys and unmarried men (Cohen, 1964). This practice obviously symbolizes the separation of the child from the birth family, marking a coming-of-age. It also emphasizes that the child "belongs" not just to the family but to the larger group of kin or societal/tribal members.

A related theme is the accentuation of differences between females and males. In many cultures, for example, nudity taboos begin only at adolescence. In other societies adolescents are forbidden to speak to any opposite-sex siblings, a taboo that may extend until one of the siblings marries (Cohen, 1964). This practice seems to have at least two purposes. First and most obviously, it strengthens the incest taboo, which is essential to the avoidance of inbreeding. Second, it signifies the beginning of the time in life when males and females have quite different life patterns. Girls and boys have begun to learn gender-appropriate tasks long before adolescence, but at adolescence they take up their distinct roles far more completely.

These two patterns may form the backdrop for the initiation ritual itself, which is usually brief and fairly intense, often including considerable drama and pageantry. During this time—usually in groups and separately for each sex—youth are indoctrinated by the elders into the customary practices of their tribe or society. They may learn the history and songs of their people as well as special religious rituals or practices, such as the learning of Hebrew as preparation for the *bar mitzvah* or *bas mitzvah* in the Jewish tradition.

Physical mutilation or trials of endurance also play a part in the initiation in some cases. Boys may be circumcised or cut so as to create certain patterns of scars; or they may be sent out into the wilderness to undergo spiritual purification or to prove their manhood by achieving some feat. This is less common in girls' initiation rituals, but physical trials or mutilation do occur, such as the removal of the clitoris, whipping, or scarification.

Among the Hopi, for example, both boys and girls go through specific rituals in which they are taught the religious ceremonies of the Kachina cult and are also whipped. After these ceremonies, they may participate fully in the adult religious practices.

In modern United States culture, as in most other Western cultures, we have no universally shared initiation rites, but there are still many changes of status and a few experiences that have some properties in common with traditional adolescent rites of passage. For example, we do not deliberately separate adolescents from family or from adults, but we do send adolescents to a new level of school, thus effectively segregating them from all but their peers. Boot camp, for those who enter the military, is a more obvious parallel because the recruits are sent to a separate location and undergo various physical trials before they are accepted. Until relatively recent times, it was also common for adolescent boys and girls in our culture to attend separate schools. Even within coeducational schools, physical education classes were sex-segregated until very recently, as were such traditional gender-stereotyped classes as home economics and shop.

Various other changes in legal standing also mark the passage to adult status in modern Western cultures. In the United States, for example, young people can have a driver's license at 16 and can see R-rated movies at 17. At 18, they can vote, marry, or enter the military without parental consent, and be tried in adult rather than juvenile court for any legal offense.

These various remnants of older initiation patterns are considerably less condensed in modern society than are traditional initiation rites. One result of this is that the passage into adult status is much fuzzier for young people in most industrialized countries. Perhaps this is one reason why adolescents in our society often create their own separation and distinctness, such as by wearing unusual or even outlandish clothing or hair styles.

[?] **Critical Thinking**

What do you think are some of the consequences of the lack of clear initiation rituals and of the relatively long period of adolescence in modern Western societies? How might our culture be different if we did have shared initiation rites?

Basic Physical Changes

The many body changes associated with puberty are largely controlled by hormones, which play a central role in the physical drama of adolescence.

Hormones

Hormones, which are secretions of the various **endocrine glands** in the body, govern pubertal growth and physical changes in several ways, summarized in Table 13.1. Of all the endocrine glands, the most critical is the **pituitary** because it provides the trigger for release of hormones from other glands. For example, the thyroid gland secretes thyroxine only when it has received a signal to do so through the action of a special thyroid-stimulating hormone secreted by the pituitary. The pituitary hormones are, in turn, controlled by the hypothalamus, a brain structure near the pituitary and linked to it by special blood vessels. Nerve cells in the hypothalamus release chemical messengers to the pituitary, with each pituitary hormone having its own unique chemical trigger (Tanner, 1990).

Many of these same hormones play a central role in growth and development at earlier ages as well. Thyroid hormone (thyroxine) is present from about the fourth month of gestation, and appears to be involved in stimulating normal brain development prenatally. The pituitary secretes growth hormone as early as ten weeks after conception, thus helping to stimulate the very rapid growth of cells and organs of the body. And as I mentioned in Chapter 3, testosterone is produced prenatally in the testes of the developing male, influencing both the development of male genitals and some aspects of brain development.

After birth, the rate of growth is governed largely by thyroid hormone and pituitary growth hormone. Thyroid hormone is secreted in greater quantities for the first two years of life and then falls to a lower level and remains steady until adolescence, when it again rises, peaking at the time of the maximum growth spurt and then falling off again. Secretions from the testes and ovaries, as well as adrenal androgen, are also at very low levels in the early years of childhood. This changes at age 7 or 8, when adrenal androgen begins to be secreted—the first signal of the changes of puberty.

Following this first step, there is a complex sequence of hormone changes, beginning with a signal from the hypothalamus to the pituitary to begin secreting increased levels of **gonadotrophic hormones** (two in males, three in females). These, in turn, stimulate the development of the glands in the testes and ovaries that then begin to secrete more hormones, *testosterone* in boys and a form of **estrogen** called *estradiol* in girls. Over the course of puberty, the levels of testosterone increase 18-fold in boys, while levels of estradiol increase 8-fold in girls (Biro, Lucky, Huster, & Morrison, 1995; Nottelmann, Susman, Blue et al., 1987).

At the same time, the pituitary also secretes three other hormones that interact with the specific sex hormones and affect growth: adrenal androgen, thyroid-stimulating hormone, and general growth hormone. The role of adrenal androgen, which is chemically very similar to testosterone, remains a bit of a mystery. It used to be thought that it was critical in the development of secondary sex characteristics in girls, particularly the development of pubic and underarm hair. Recent research calls that into question (Tanner, 1990). At the moment, the only established role of this hormone is in prompting and controlling skeletal development, which suggests that it plays some part in the adolescent growth spurt, perhaps particularly for girls (Tanner, 1990).

It is somewhat misleading, by the way, to talk about "male" and "female" hormones. Both males and females have at least some of each (estrogen or estradiol and testosterone or androgen); the difference is essentially in the relative proportion of the two.

All these hormonal changes are reflected in two sets of body changes: the well-known changes

Table 13.1

Major Hormones Involved in Physical Growth and Development

Gland	Some of the Key Hormone(s) Secreted	Aspects of Growth Influenced
Thyroid	Thyroxine	Normal brain development and overall rate of growth.
Adrenal	Adrenal androgen (chemically highly similar to testosterone)	Some changes at puberty, particularly the development of skeletal maturity and mature muscles, especially in boys.
Leydig cells in the testes (in boys)	Testosterone	Crucial in the formation of male genitals prenatally; triggers the sequence of primary and secondary sex characteristic changes at puberty in the male; also stimulates increased output of growth hormone and affects bones and muscles.
Ovaries (in girls)	Several estrogens, the most critical of which is estradiol	Development of the menstrual cycle, breasts, and pubic hair in girls.
Pituitary	Growth hormone (GH); thyroid-stimulating hormone (TSH); and the gonadotrophic hormones: follicle-stimulating hormone (FSH) and luteinizing hormone (LH)	Growth hormone governs the rate of physical maturation; other pituitary hormones signal the respective sex glands to secrete; follicle-stimulating hormone and luteinizing hormone help control the menstrual cycle.

Source: Tanner, 1990.

in sex organs and a much broader set of changes in muscles, fat, bones, and body organs.

Height and Weight

One of the most striking physical changes of adolescence is in height. You'll remember from earlier chapters that in infancy, the baby gains in height very rapidly, adding 10 to 12 inches in length in the first year. The toddler and school child grows much more slowly. The third phase begins with the dramatic adolescent growth spurt, triggered by the big increases in growth hormones. During this phase, the child may add 3 to 6 inches a year for several years. After the growth spurt, in the fourth phase, the teenager again adds height and weight slowly until his or her final adult size is reached. I've graphed these changes in two different ways to give you the full effect. Figure 13.1 (p. 428) parallels the equivalent figures in earlier chapters, showing the changes in height and weight for the 10th, 50th, and 90th percentiles of boys and girls ages 12 to 18, based on U.S. data. Figure 13.2 (p. 429) shows

the *gain* in height each year over the full sweep of years from infancy through adolescence, making the growth spurt particularly clear.

The sex difference in the timing of the growth spurt is evident in both figures. Boys start their growth spurt later and continue longer. They catch up to the girls by age 13 or 14, and then continue growing for several more years. By age 16, as you can see vividly in Figure 13.1, boys at the 10th percentile of height are taller than girls at the 50th percentile.

Exercise, by the way, does not affect the pattern of growth in height. Robert Malina, a prominent researcher on children's physical development, analyzed data from a number of studies, from four different countries (Canada, Belgium, Poland, and the Czech Republic), in which highly active and inactive teenage boys were studied over a period of several years in adolescence (Malina, 1994b). In each case, the active boys showed essentially identical patterns of increases in height through adolescence as did the inactive boys. The two groups did differ in weight, however, with the inactive boys typically weighing more at each age. Malina concludes that regular physical activity has no impact

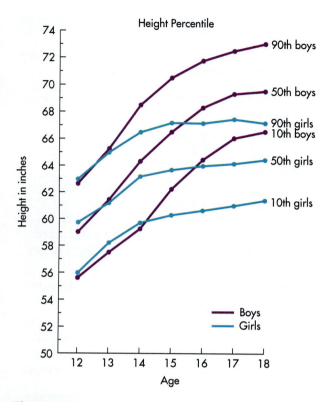

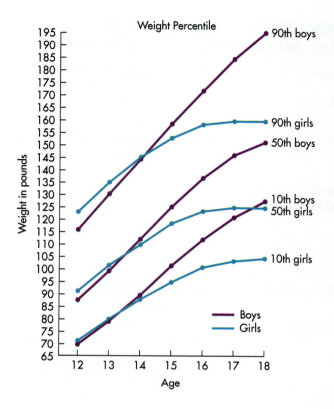

Figure 13.1

Basic changes in height and weight for U.S. children in the teenage years. The three lines for each sex show the 10th, 50th, and 90th percentile trajectories. (Source: Needlman, 1996, data from Table 13-1, pp. 50–52.)

on a child's attained stature (final height) or the timing of the growth spurt.

Body Shape

Figures 13.1 and 13.2 may give the impression that the teenager's growth is a smooth process. In fact, the different parts of the child's body do not all grow to full adult size at the same pace. This means that the shape and proportions of the adolescent's body go through a series of changes. As you may remember from Chapter 10, the child's hands and feet grow to full adult size earliest, followed by the arms and legs, with the trunk usually the slowest part to grow. Because of this asymmetry in the relative size of body parts, we often think of an adolescent as "awkward" or uncoordinated. Interestingly, research does not bear out such an impression. Robert Malina has found no point in the adolescent growth process at which teenagers become

consistently less coordinated or less skillful at physical tasks (Malina, 1990).

Children's heads and faces also change in childhood and adolescence. During the elementary school years, the size and shape of a child's jaw changes when the permanent teeth come in. In adolescence both jaws grow forward and the forehead becomes more prominent. This set of changes often gives teenagers' faces (especially boys') an angular, bony appearance, quite unlike their earlier look—as you can see in the set of pictures in Figure 13.3, drawn from a classic early study by J. M. Tanner (1962), one of the most renowned researchers on physical development.

Muscles and Fat

Muscles. Muscle fibers, like bone tissues, go through a growth spurt at adolescence, becoming thicker and denser, so that adolescents become

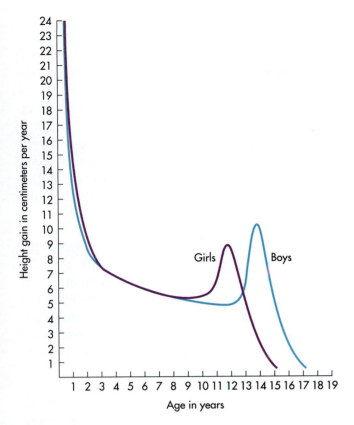

Figure 13.2

These curves show the gain in height for each year from birth through adolescence. You can see the clear phases: very rapid growth in infancy, slower growth in the preschool and elementary school years, a growth spurt at adolescence, and the cessation of growth at adulthood. (Sources: Malina, 1990; Tanner, 1990, p. 14.)

quite a lot stronger in just a few years. Both boys and girls show this increase in strength but the in-crease is much greater in boys. For example, in a cross-sectional study in Canada involving 2673 children and teenagers, Smoll and Schutz (1990) measured strength by having each child hang from a bar, with eyes level with the bar, for as long as possible. Table 13.2 (p. 430) shows the number of seconds boys and girls of several ages can hold this arm hang. In this sample of children, boys in-creased the average length of their bar hang by 160 percent between ages 9 and 17. Girls increased in strength between ages 8 and 12, and then actually declined, so that by age 17, the boys in this study were three times as strong as the girls. This sub-stantial difference in strength reflects the underly-ing sex difference in muscle tissue that is accentu-ated at adolescence: Among adult men, about forty percent of total body mass is muscle compared with only about twenty-four percent in adult women.

Such a sex difference in muscle mass (and ac-companying strength) seems to be largely a result of hormone differences, although sex differences in exercise patterns or fitness may also play some role. For example, the sex difference in *leg* strength is much less than the difference in arm strength, a pattern that makes sense if we assume that all teenagers walk and use their legs a similar amount but that boys use their arm muscles in various sports activities more than girls do, especially in the teenage years when girls increasingly drop out of sports programs (Tanner, Hughes, & White-house, 1981). Still, there does seem to be a basic hormonal difference as well, because we know that very fit girls and women are still not as strong as very fit boys and men.

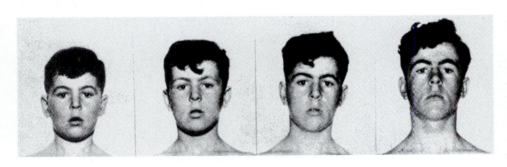

Figure 13.3

These photos of the same boy be-fore, during, and after puberty show the striking changes in the jaws and forehead that dramati-cally alter appearance in many teenage boys. The same changes occur in girls' faces, but the changes are not as dramatic. (These photos, by the way, may look old and out of date, but they are the only longitudinal photos of this kind available. The basic processes they describe have surely not changed in the years since they were taken.) (Source: Tanner, 1962, Plate 1, p. 17.)

Table 13.2

Length of Arm Hang in Seconds for Boys and Girls in Several Grades

	School Grade (Age)		
	3rd (age 8–9)	7th (age 12–13)	11th (age 16–17)
Boys	19.0	32.4	50.2
Girls	13.2	20.0	18.1

Source: Smoll & Schutz, 1990, from Table 1, p. 363.

Fat.   Another major component of the body is fat, most of which is stored immediately under the skin. This *subcutaneous fat* is first laid down beginning at about 34 weeks prenatally and has an early peak at about 9 months after birth. The thickness of this layer of fat then declines until about age 6 or 7, then rises until adolescence.

Here, too, there is a sex difference. From birth, girls have slightly more fat tissue than boys do, and this discrepancy becomes gradually more marked during childhood and adolescence. The size of the difference is illustrated nicely in the results of the same Canadian study reflected in Table 13.2 (Smoll & Schutz, 1990). Between age 13 and age 17, the percentage of body weight made up of fat rose from 21.8 to 24.0 percent among girls in this study but dropped from 16.1 to 14.0 percent among boys. So, during and after puberty, proportions of fat rise among girls and decline among boys, while the proportion of weight that is muscle rises in boys and declines in girls.

Other Body Changes

Puberty also brings important changes in other body organs, including the brain and the heart and lungs.

Brain Growth in Adolescence.   I mentioned in earlier chapters that virtually all the neurons a child will ever have are already present at birth; the great bulk of myelination has also been completed by age 5 or 6. These facts led a great many psychologists and physiologists to conclude that the brain didn't change much in puberty. Newer evidence, however, is beginning to point to a variety of subtle but probably critical changes. For one thing, a significant amount of "pruning" of neural connections occurs in adolescence, thus further improving the efficiency of the "wiring diagram." Some myelination also continues into adolescence, as does some increase in the number of glial cells (Crockett & Petersen, 1993). A number of authors, including Tanner, argue that there is very likely a causal connection between these changes in the nervous system and parallel changes in the child's cognitive skills we see in adolescence. Tanner says:

> There is clearly no reason to suppose that the link between maturation of structure and appearance of function suddenly ceases at age 6 or 10 or 13. On the contrary, there is every reason to think that the higher intellectual abilities also appear only when maturation of certain structures or cell assemblies, widespread in location throughout the cortex, is complete. (1990, p. 113)

Such a link is still speculative. We lack the research that would connect specific brain changes with specific shifts in adolescents' intellectual competencies, but it is an attractive and logical hypothesis.

Heart and Lungs.   Less subtle changes occur in the heart and lungs during adolescence, both of which increase considerably in size in adolescence, while the heart rate drops. These changes are more marked for boys than for girls—another of the factors that increases the capacity for sustained effort by boys relative to girls. Before about age 12, boys and girls have similar physical strength, speed, and endurance, although even at these earlier ages, when there is a difference it favors the boys because of their lower levels of body fat. After puberty, boys have a clear advantage in all three (Smoll & Schutz, 1990).

[?] *Critical Thinking*

Assume that you are a member of a local school board, faced with a decision about whether to have teenage boys and girls play on the same competitive teams, such as volleyball, soccer, or baseball. Given all that I have said about sex differences in physical characteristics at puberty, how would you decide? Why?

The fact that, in adolescence, boys develop more strength and speed than do girls, is no argument for girls to give up athletic competition or fitness training. On the contrary, participating in sports like track, cross country, basketball, or soccer brings all the same benefits for girls that equivalent sports participation does for boys—with the added bonus of building up higher reserves of bone calcium, needed more by adult women.

Development of Sexual Maturity

The hormone changes of puberty also trigger the development of full sexual maturity, including changes in *primary sex characteristics*, such as the testes and penis in the male, and the ovaries, uterus, and vagina in the female, and changes in *secondary sex characteristics*, such as breast development in girls, changing voice pitch and beard growth in boys, and the growth of body hair in both sexes.

Each of these physical developments occurs in a defined sequence, customarily divided into five stages, following a system originally suggested by J. M. Tanner (1978). Stage 1 always describes the preadolescent stage, stage 2 the first signs of pubertal change, stages 3 and 4 the intermediate

steps, and stage 5 the final adult characteristic. Table 13.3 (p. 432) gives one example of these sequences for each sex. These stages have proven to be extremely helpful not only for describing the normal progress through puberty, but for assessing the rate of development of individual youngsters.

Sexual Development in Girls. Studies of preteens and teens in both Europe and North America (Malina, 1990) show that in girls, the various sequential changes are interlocked in a particular pattern, shown schematically in the upper part of Figure 13.4 (p. 433). The first steps are typically the early changes in breasts and pubic hair, followed by the peak of the growth spurt and by stage 4 of both breast and pubic hair development. Only then does first menstruation occur, an event called **menarche** (pronounced men-ARE-kee). Menarche typically occurs two years after the beginning of other visible changes and is succeeded only by the final stages of breast and pubic hair development. Among girls in industrialized countries today, menarche occurs, on average, between ages 12 and 13½. The most recent U.S. data (Herman-Giddens et al., 1997) show that African-American girls pass through this transition somewhat earlier, at a bit older than 12, while the average age for Euro-American girls is closer to 13. Ninety-five percent of all girls experience this event between the ages of 11 and 15 (Malina, 1990).

Interestingly, the timing of menarche has changed rather dramatically over the past centuries. In 1840, the average age of menarche in Western industrialized countries was about age 17; that average then dropped about four months a decade to a level of approximately age 13 in 1970, after which it leveled off (Roche, 1979), an example of what psychologists call a **secular trend.** In this case, the change has most likely been caused by significant changes in lifestyle and diet, particularly increases in protein intake.

Menarche does not signal full adult fertility. Most girls menstruate irregularly for some months or years, and in as many as three-quarters of the cycles in the first year, and half the cycles in the second and third years after menarche, no ovum is produced (Vihko & Apter, 1980). Full adult fertility thus develops over a period of years.

This initial menstrual irregularity has some significant practical consequences for sexually active teenagers. For one thing, such irregularity no doubt

Table 13.3

Examples of Tanner's Stages of Pubertal Development

Stage	Breast Development	Male Genital Development
1	No change except for some elevation of the nipple.	Testes, scrotum, and penis are all about the same size and shape as in early childhood.
2	Breast bud stage: Elevation of breast and the nipple as a small mound; areolar diameter is enlarged over stage 1.	Scrotum and testes are slightly enlarged. Skin of the scrotum is reddened and changed in texture but little or no enlargement of the penis.
3	Breast and areola both enlarged and elevated more than in stage 2, but no separation of their contours.	Penis slightly enlarged, at first mainly in length. Testes and scrotum are further enlarged.
4	Areola and nipple form a secondary mound projecting above the contour of the breast.	Penis further enlarged, with growth in breadth and development of glans. Testes and scrotum further enlarged and scrotum skin still darker.
5	Mature stage. Only the nipple projects, with the areola recessed to the general contour of the breast.	Genitalia are adult in size and shape.

Source: Petersen & Taylor, 1980, p. 127.

contributes to the widespread assumption among early-teenage girls that they cannot get pregnant because they are "too young." In fact, pregnancy *can* occur any time after the first menstruation. Menstrual irregularity also makes any form of rhythm contraception unreliable, even among teenagers who have enough basic reproductive knowledge to realize that the time of ovulation is normally the time of greatest fertility—knowledge that is not widespread.

Sexual Development in Boys. In boys, as in girls, the peak of the growth spurt typically comes fairly late in the sequence, as you can see in the bottom part of Figure 13.4. Malina's data suggest that, on average, a boy completes stages 2, 3, and 4 of genital development and stages 2 and 3 of pubic hair development before the growth peak is reached (Malina, 1990). The development of a beard and the lowering of the voice typically occur near the end of the sequence. Precisely when in this sequence the boy begins to produce viable sperm is very difficult to determine, although current evidence places this event sometime between ages 12 and 14, usually *before* the boy has reached the peak of the growth spurt (Brooks-Gunn & Reiter, 1990).

Two things are particularly interesting about these sequences. First, while boys begin the early stages of pubertal change only a short time later than do girls, the growth spurt comes about two years later in boys—a point already apparent in Figures 13.1 and 13.2.

A second intriguing thing is that while the order of development seems to be highly consistent *within* each sequence (such as breast development or pubic hair development), there is quite a lot of variability *across* sequences. I've shown the normative or average pattern in Figure 13.4, but individual teenagers often deviate from the norm. For instance, a girl might move through several stages of pubic hair development before the first clear breast changes or experience menarche much earlier in the sequence than normal. It is important to keep this variation in mind if you are trying to make a prediction about an individual teenager.

Early Versus Late Pubertal Development

Yet another form of variation in the pattern of puberty is the *timing* of the entire process. In any random sample of 12- or 13-year-olds, you will find some who are already at stage 5 and others still at stage 1 in the steps of sexual maturation. What is the psychological effect of such variation on the child who is very early or very late?

The cumulative body of research on this question points to an interesting and complex hypothesis that once again underlines the importance of

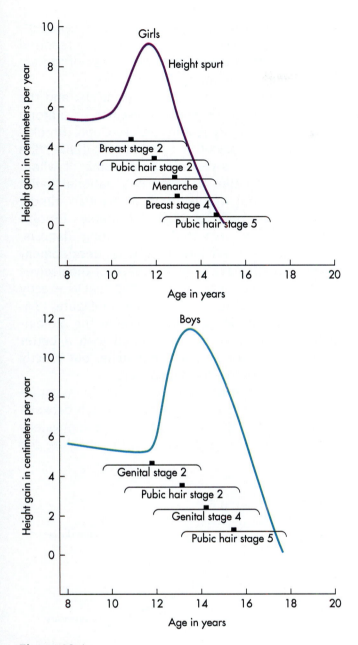

Figure 13.4

The typical sequence of pubertal development for girls (upper figure) and boys (lower figure). The colored curved line shows the gains in height at various ages; the box on each black line represents the average attainment of that change, while the line shows the range of normal times. Note the wide range of normality for all of these changes. Also note how late in the sequence menarche occurs for girls, and that girls are about two years ahead of boys. (Sources: Garn, 1980; Chumlea, 1982; Malina, 1990; Tanner, 1990; Biro et al., 1995.)

internal models. The general idea is that each young child or teenager has an internal model about the "normal" or "right" timing for puberty (Faust, 1983; Lerner, 1987; Petersen, 1987). Each

girl has an internal model about the "right age" to develop breasts or begin menstruation; each boy has an internal model or image about when it is right to begin to grow a beard or to grow to adult size. According to this hypothesis, it is the discrepancy between an adolescent's expectation and what actually happens that determines the psychological effect, just as it is the discrepancy between goals and achievements that determines self-esteem. Those whose development occurs outside their own desired or expected range are likely to think less well of themselves, to be less happy with their bodies and with the process of puberty, perhaps have fewer friends or experience other signs of distress.

In American culture today, most young people seem to share the expectation that pubertal changes will happen sometime between age 12 and 14; anything earlier is seen as "too soon," anything later is thought of as "late." If you compare these expectations with the actual average timing of pubertal changes, you'll see that such a norm includes girls who are average in development and boys who are *early*. So we should expect that these two groups—normal-developing girls and early-developing boys—should have the best psychological functioning. Early-maturing boys may have an added advantage because they are more likely to be of the *mesomorphic* body type, with wide shoulders and a large amount of muscle. This body type is consistently preferred for boys at all ages, and because boys with this body type tend to be good at sports, the early-developing boy should be particularly advantaged. Late-developing boys, and to a lesser extent late-developing girls, in contrast, should be at some psychological disadvantage.

Research in the United States generally confirms these predictions. Girls who are early developers (before 11 or 12 for major body changes) show consistently more negative body images, such as thinking themselves too fat. Such girls are also more likely to engage in risky behavior like smoking or drinking, more often become involved with misbehaving peer groups, become sexually active at an earlier age, and are more likely to be depressed later in adolescence (Alsaker, 1995; Brooks-Gunn & Paikoff, 1993; Ge, Conger, & Elder, 1996; Silbereisen & Kracke, 1993). Very late development in girls also appears to be somewhat negative, but the effect of lateness is not so striking for girls as it is for boys. Among boys, the relationship is essentially linear. The earlier the boy's development, the more positive his body image, the better he does in school, the less trouble he gets into, and the more friends he has (Duke, Carlsmith, Jennings et al., 1982).

[?] *Critical Thinking*

Do you remember your own puberty as very early, early, on time, or late? Do you think that perception had any effect on your overall experience of adolescence?

In nearly all these studies, earliness or lateness has been defined in terms of the actual physical changes. The results are even clearer when researchers have instead asked teenagers about their internal model of earliness or lateness. For example, Rierdan, Koff, and Stubbs (1989) found that the negativeness of a girl's menarcheal experience

Early-developing girls, like the one on the right, report much less positive adolescent experiences and more depression than on-time or later-developing girls.

was predicted by her *subjective* sense of earliness; those who perceived themselves as early reported a more negative experience, regardless of the actual chronological timing of menarche.

This link between the internal model and the outcome is especially vivid in research on a group of ballet dancers by Jeanne Brooks-Gunn (Brooks-Gunn, 1987; Brooks-Gunn & Warren, 1985). She studied 14- to 18-year-old girls, some of whom were serious ballet dancers at a national ballet company school. In this group, a very lean, almost prepubescent body is highly desirable. Brooks-Gunn therefore expected that among dancers, those who were very late in pubertal development would actually have a better image of themselves than those who were on time. And that is exactly what she found, as you can see in Figure 13.5. Among the nondancers, menarche at the biologically average time was associated with a better body image than was late menarche, but exactly the reverse was true for the dancers.

These studies are consistent with the hypothesis that it is the discrepancy or mismatch between the desired or expected pattern and a youngster's actual pattern that is critical, not the absolute age

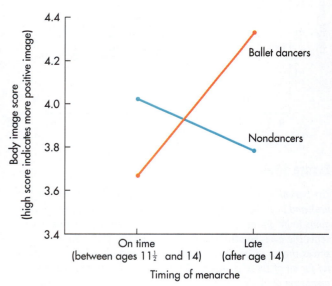

Figure 13.5

Serious ballet dancers clearly prefer to have a very late puberty. In this study those dancers whose menarche was "on time" by ordinary standards actually had poorer body images than did those who were objectively quite late, while the reverse was true for nondancers. Thus it is perception of timing and not actual timing that is critical. (Source: Brooks-Gunn & Warren, 1985, from Table 1, p. 291.)

of pubertal development. Because the majority of young people in any given culture share similar expectations, we can see common effects of early or late development. To predict the effect of early or late development in any individual teenager, however, we would need to know more about her or his internal model or the shared internal models of his cultural subgroup.

Adolescent Sexuality and Pregnancy

The many physical changes of puberty mean that the young person is stronger and faster and better coordinated than before. They also obviously make mature sexual attraction and behavior possible. Recent studies suggest that, on average, children experience their first feeling of sexual attraction—heterosexual or homosexual—very early in the pubertal process, at about age 10 or 11 (McClintock & Herdt, 1996). Most, however, do not become sexually active as early as that. What do we know about the choices teenagers make about their sexual activity?

As is usually the case, what I can tell you about this is almost entirely specific to the United States or to other industrialized countries. It is good to keep in mind that the whole question of adolescent sexuality is a central issue for those of us in such cultures in large part because we have created a long delay between physical sexual maturity and social maturity: Young people are physically mature at 13 or 14 but they are not financially independent or fully trained until age 20 or later. In cultures in which 12- or 14-year-olds are considered ready to take on adult tasks and responsibilities, to marry, and to bear children, adolescent sexuality is handled very differently. In the United States, where teen pregnancy has become extremely common, it is perceived as a significant problem.

Adolescent sexual activity has increased fairly dramatically in the United States since the late 1950s (Miller, Christopherson, & King, 1993). By 1993, roughly half of teens reported they had had intercourse at least once (Kann et al., 1995). Figure 13.6 shows the most current findings from a 1993 national survey by the Centers for Disease Control. You can see that the percentage of those reporting sexual activity increases steadily with age and that, at every age, more boys than girls report such activity—although this difference is far smaller now

than it was a decade ago. Comparable surveys in Canada show that half of 16-year-olds and two-thirds of 18-year-olds have experience of intercourse (Herold & Marshall, 1996).

At every age, we find consistent ethnic differences in sexual activity. In the same 1993 Centers for Disease Control survey, 79.7 percent of black high school students reported at least one experience of intercourse compared with 56.0 percent of Hispanics and 48.4 percent of whites.

Although sexual activity is somewhat correlated with the amount of testosterone in the blood among boys (Halpern, Udry, Campbell, & Suchindran, 1993; Udry & Campbell, 1994), social factors are much better predictors of teen sexual activity than are hormones. Those who begin sexual activity early are more likely to live in poor neighborhoods in which young people have little monitoring by adults; they come from poorer families or from families in which sexual activity is condoned and dating rules are lax; they are more likely to use alcohol. Among girls, those who are sexually active are also more likely to have had early menarche, to have low interest in school, and to have a history of sexual abuse (Billy, Brewster, & Grady, 1994; Hovell, Sipan, Blumberg et al., 1994; Small & Luster, 1994). In general, these same factors predict sexual activity among whites, blacks, and Hispanics; and in every group, the greater the number of these risk factors present in the life of an individual teenager, the greater the likelihood that he or she will be sexually active.

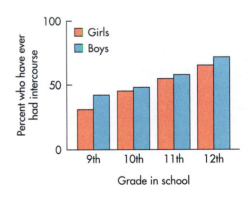

Figure 13.6

These data are from a nationally representative sample of 16,296 U.S. high school students interviewed in 1993 by the Centers for Disease Control. (Source: Kann et al., 1995, from Table 20, p. 47.)

Research Report

Homosexuality Among Adolescents

For the great majority of teenagers, "sexual activity" is heterosexual activity. A minority, however, are sexually drawn to their own gender. In a recent study of nearly 35,000 youth in Minnesota public schools, Gary Remafedi (Remafedi, Resnick, Blum, & Harris, 1992) found that slightly fewer than 1 percent of the adolescent boys and only 0.4 percent of the girls *defined* themselves as homosexual, but roughly one in ten said they were "unsure" of their sexual orientation and 2 to 6 percent reported that they were attracted to others of the same sex. Similarly, in a smaller study of nearly 500 tenth through twelfth graders in Australia, Simone Buzwell and Doreen Rosenthal (1996) found that only two subjects described themselves as homosexual, while 4.2 percent had had at least one homosexual experience but still labeled themselves as heterosexual.

These figures are a bit lower than but still generally consistent with the newest and most comprehensive data on sexual orientations among U.S. adults (Laumann, Gagnon, Michael, & Michaels, 1994): Two to 3 percent of adults say they think of themselves as homosexual or bisexual; roughly twice that many say they are attracted to those of the same sex.

Recent evidence has greatly strengthened the hypothesis that homosexuality has a biological basis (Gladue, 1994; Pillard & Bailey, 1995). For example, several new twin studies show that when one twin is homosexual, the probability that the other will also be homosexual is 50 to 60 percent. For fraternal twins, this "concordance rate" is only about twenty percent and only about eleven percent among pairs of biologically unrelated boys adopted into the same families (Bailey & Pillard, 1991; Bailey, Pillard, Neale, & Agyei, 1993; Whitam, Diamond, & Martin, 1993). More direct comparisons of gene patterning and brain architecture of homosexual and heterosexual men also point to the possibility (not yet firmly established) that homosexual behavior may be hardwired (e.g., Hamer, Hu, Magnuson, Hu, & Pattatucci, 1993; LeVay, 1991).

Additional studies suggest that prenatal hormone patterns may also be causally involved in homosexuality. For example, women whose mothers took the drug diethylstilbestrol (DES, a synthetic estrogen) during pregnancy are more likely to be homosexual as adults than are women who did not have such DES exposure (Meyer-Bahlburg, Ehrhardt, Rosen et al., 1995).

Finally, there is accumulating information showing that boys who show strong cross-sex-typed behavior in infancy and early childhood are highly likely to show homosexual preferences when they reach adolescence (Bailey & Zucker, 1995), findings that are consistent with the hypothesis that homosexuality is built in by the time of birth.

Such biological evidence does not mean that environment plays no role in homosexuality. No behavior is entirely controlled by either nature or nurture, as I have said many times. At the very least, we know that 40 or 50 percent of identical twins do *not* share the same sexual orientation. Something beyond biology must be at work, although we do not yet know what environmental factors may be involved.

Whatever the cause, homosexual teenagers are a minority who face high levels of prejudice and stereotyping. Many are verbally attacked or ridiculed; as many as a third are physically assaulted by their peers (Remafedi, Farrow, & Deisher, 1991; Savin-Williams, 1994). For these and other reasons, these young people are at high risk for a variety of problems. In Remafedi's Minneapolis study, for example, four-fifths of homosexual teens showed deteriorating school performance and more than one-fourth dropped out of high school (Remafedi, 1987a). They must also cope with the decision about whether to "come out" about their homosexuality. Those who do come out are far more likely to tell peers than parents, although telling peers carries some risk: In his Minneapolis study, Remafedi found that 41 percent of homosexual male youths had lost a friend over the issue (Remafedi, 1987b). Some research suggests that as many as two-thirds of homosexual youth have not told their parents (Rotheram-Borus, Rosario, & Koopman, 1991).

There is obviously much that we do not know about homosexual adolescents. What is clear is that the years of adolescence are likely to be particularly stressful for this subgroup.

Critical Thinking

Imagine yourself as the parent of a teenager. How do you think you would react if your son or daughter revealed to you that he or she is a homosexual? Why is this such a difficult issue for so many parents?

Reproductive Knowledge and Contraceptive Use. Despite their high levels of sexual activity, teenagers know relatively little about physiology and reproduction, a fact that highlights widespread weaknesses in sex education programs in schools (or at home.) For example, only about half of white and a quarter of black teenagers can describe the time of greatest fertility in the menstrual cycle (Freeman & Rickels, 1993; Morrison, 1985). Despite such ignorance, contraceptive use has risen significantly in recent years. Two-thirds of young people now report using some form of contraception (including withdrawal and some form of rhythm method) at their first sexual intercourse (Sells & Blum, 1996). Roughly half report having used a condom during their last experience of intercourse; another 18 percent report that they or their partner used birth control pills (Kann et al., 1995). Contraceptive use is lower among Hispanics than among Anglos, and in all groups is least likely among younger girls. Contraceptive use is even more widespread in several European countries (e.g., Sweden and the Netherlands) in which such use is culturally acceptable and contraceptive information is readily available (Jones, Forrest, Goldman et al., 1986).

Critical Thinking

How many different reasons can you think of why teenagers would *not* use contraceptives? Which of those explanations might account for the lower use of contraception among Hispanic Americans?

Teenage Pregnancy. Despite these recent increases in contraceptive use, the rate of teenage pregnancy remains higher in the United States than in any other developed Western country (Ambuel, 1995). In the Netherlands, for example, only 14 girls out of every 1000 between the ages of 15 and 19 become pregnant each year. In the United

States the equivalent rate is about 120 pregnancies per 1000 girls per year, of which four-fifths are unintended (Henshaw, 1994). The pregnancy rate is about four times higher among African-American teen girls than among whites; Hispanic Americans fall in between (Centers for Disease Control, 1993b). Sandra Hofferth estimates that fully 44 percent of all teenage girls in the United States will be pregnant at least once before the age of 20 (1987a). About half these pregnancies are carried to term.

Let me try to put these fairly astonishing numbers into some kind of context. Birthrates have actually dropped among the entire U.S. population since the 1960s and early 1970s, *including among*

Teenage sexual activity is not more common in the United States than in most Western industrialized countries, but teen pregnancy is. Girls such as this one who give birth during their teens are more likely to have problems in adulthood, including lower income, less education, and higher risk of divorce, although many teenage moms manage to surmount these problems.

Research Report

Which Teenage Girls Become Pregnant?

Whether a girl becomes pregnant during her teenage years depends on many of the same factors that predict sexual activity in general, including family background, educational aspirations, timing of sexual activity, and subcultural attitudes. The likelihood of pregnancy is higher:

• *The younger a girl is when she becomes sexually active;*

• *Among girls from poor families, from single-parent families, or from families with relatively uneducated parents;*

• *Among girls whose mothers became sexually active early and who bore their first child early;*

• *Among girls who were rejected by their peers in elementary school, especially if they were high in aggressiveness (Underwood, Kupersmidt, & Coie, 1996).*

The likelihood of pregnancy is *reduced:*

• *Among girls who do well in school and have strong educational aspirations, and these girls are more*

likely to use contraception if they are sexually active;

• *Among girls with more stable and committed relationships with their sexual partners;*

• *Among girls who have good communication about contraception with their mothers and whose mothers support the use of contraception;*

• *Among girls who were popular with their peers in elementary school.*

Black and Hispanic teenagers are more likely than are Anglo teens to become pregnant, but for different reasons. Blacks are more likely to be sexually active, while Hispanics, who have lower rates of sexual activity, are less likely to use contraception than are Anglos.

The riskiest time for teen pregnancy is in the first year or so after a girl has become sexually active. It is during these early months that girls are least likely to seek out contraceptive information or to use contraception consistently.

---

teenagers. Indeed, the proportion of all births in the United States that are teenage births has declined steadily since 1975. What has increased steadily since the 1960s is the rate of births to *nonmarried* teens. In 1993, 73 percent of all girls under 18 who gave birth in the United States were unmarried, compared with only 53 percent in 1970; among black girls, the current rate is 95 percent (U.S. Bureau of the Census, 1996). Thus it is not that more and more teenagers are bearing children but that more and more teenage girls are choosing to rear their children without marrying.

Whether one sees this as a worrisome trend or not depends not only on one's religious or moral beliefs but also on evidence about the long-term consequences of adolescent childbearing for the adult lives of the girls involved and for the lives of the children they bear. The bulk of that evidence points to negative consequences for the teenage mothers, although it has been difficult to sort out which effects are due to early childbearing itself

and which might be due to self-selection or the impact of poverty. Most studies indicate that teenage childbearing—whether the woman was married or unmarried—is associated with a larger total number of children, more closely spaced, fewer years of total education throughout adult life, lower levels of occupational success, lower income in adulthood, and higher likelihood of divorce in adult life. These relationships are found among African-American, Hispanic, and Anglo teens, so these negative outcomes are not just ethnic differences in disguise (Astone, 1993; Hofferth, 1987b; Moore, Myers, Morrison et al., 1993).

The picture is certainly not entirely bleak. Pregnant teens who manage to complete their high school education, often through the support of special school programs, have better prospects. Happily, more than half of girls who become pregnant before age 18 do manage to complete high school by the time they are in their early twenties (Upchurch, 1993). Further, many teenage moms who struggle economically in their early adult years manage to recover in their thirties and forties. As one example, Emmy Werner, in her longitudinal study in Kauai, Hawaii, describes a young woman who, at age 18, had a 1-year-old and another baby on the way. When interviewed, she said, "I always wanted things to be perfect; get married, get my own place, be happy; but nothing seems to be going smoothly. I feel life is so hard, and now we are going to have two children, and I don't want them to go through what I went through" (Werner & Smith, 1992, p. 83). Yet, 14 years later, when this same woman was 32, she had gone a long way toward overcoming the early obstacles. At that age, she said, "I am happy.... I think I have accomplished everything that I want. I have a good position at work; my children are older and soon will be on their own; I am in the process of buying my own home, and I look forward to the future" (Werner & Smith, 1992, p. 83).

Examples like this are not as rare as you might think. Nonetheless, it is still true that teenage mothers as a group are disadvantaged. For black inner-city girls in particular, the chances of moving out of poverty in adulthood seem to be far better for those who delay childbearing into their twenties than for those who bear children in adolescence (Freeman & Rickels, 1993).

For the children of these teenage mothers, the news is not good. These children are simply far more likely to grow up in poverty, with all the accompanying negative consequences for the child's optimum development (Osofsky, Hann, & Peebles, 1993).

Health

In adolescence the risk of most kinds of acute illnesses decline, but death rates rise over what we see among school-age children, as does the incidence of various kinds of accidents.

Mortality

The U.S. Bureau of the Census divides up the age range in a somewhat awkward way for our purposes, using a single grouping from age 15 to age 24, thus combining young adults with adolescents. Keep this in mind when you look at the numbers in Table 13.4, which gives the mortality rates from various causes for those in this age range. Even with this caveat in mind, though, the contrast with the equivalent numbers in Table 10.3 (p. 337) are striking. Just look at the Number of Deaths column for the two tables and you can see a huge change. The leading cause of death in both cases is accidents, but the rate is four times as high among youth ages 15 to 24 than among those ages 5 to 14. The increase in death from homicide is even more enormous, from 1.6 per 100,000 in the younger group to 22.2 per 100,000 in the older age bracket.

The largest single cause of death among youth in the 15–24 bracket in the United States is motor vehicle accidents, which cause more than 20 deaths per 100,000 young people per year—the highest rate for any age group. Why might this be so? One key reason is alcohol. As Ralph Hingson

Table 13.4
Primary Causes of Death Among Youth Ages 15 to 24 in the United States

Cause	Number of Deaths per 100,000 Teens and Young Adults	Rank Order of Causes for Each Ethnic/Racial Group		
		White	Black	Hispanic
Accidents	37.8	1	2	2
Homicide	22.2	3	1	1
Suicide	13.0	2	3	3
Cancer	5.0	4	6	4
Heart disease	2.7	5	4	6
AIDS	1.6	7	5	5

Source: National Center for Health Statistics, June 1996, data from Table 1, pp. 18, 22, 25, 29.

Research Report

Adolescent Suicide and Its Prevention

You can see in Table 13.4 (p. 439) that suicide is the third leading cause of death among U.S. adolescents and young adults; among whites in this age group, it is the second leading cause. The rate has also been rising in the past several decades (Sells & Blum, 1996). Furthermore, recent national survey data tell us that as many as one-fourth of all teens in the United States have had thoughts about suicide, 19% say they have made a suicide plan, and 8.6% say they have made an attempt (Kann et al., 1995)—numbers I find highly disturbing.

Boys are far more likely than girls to die by suicide. The highest rate is among Native American males, with a rate of 26.3 deaths per 100,000 per year, followed by young white males at 22.7, black males at 18.0, and Hispanic males at 16.3. The rates for girls are far lower, averaging 3.7 deaths per 100,000 per year (Centers for Disease Control, 1994a; National Center for Health Statistics, 1996). In contrast, suicide *attempts* are estimated to be as much as four times more common in girls than in boys (Group for the Advancement of Psychiatry, 1996). The major reason for the difference appears to be that girls, more often than boys, use less "successful" methods, such as self-poisoning, whereas boys are more likely to use firearms.

It is obviously very difficult to uncover the contributing factors in successful or completed suicides because the crucial individual is no longer available to be interviewed. Researchers and clinicians are forced to rely on secondhand reports by parents or others about the mental state of the suicide before the act—reports that are bound to be at least partially invalid because, in many cases, the parents or friends had no suspicion that a suicide attempt was imminent. Nonetheless, we do have some information about risk factors. First and foremost, some kind of significant emotional disturbance in the suicide or potential suicide is virtually a universal ingredient, including but not restricted to depression. Behavior problems such as aggression are also common in the histories of completed suicides, as is a history of physical or sexual abuse, the loss of a caregiver from separation or death, and a family history of psychiatric disorder or suicide (Garland & Zigler, 1993; Wagner, 1997).

These factors alone, however, are not enough to explain suicidal behavior. After all, many teenagers (or adults) have one or more of these risk factors, and very few actually commit suicide. David Shaffer (Shaffer,

Garland, Gould, Fisher, & Trautman, 1988) suggests at least three other important elements:

1. Some triggering stressful event. Studies of suicides suggest that among adolescents, this triggering event is often a disciplinary crisis with the parents or some rejection or humiliation, such as breaking up with a girlfriend or boyfriend or failure in a valued activity.
2. An altered mental state, which might be an attitude of hopelessness, reduced inhibitions from alcohol consumption, or rage (Swedo, Rettew, Kuppenheimer et al., 1991). Among girls, in particular, the sense of hopelessness seems to be common: a feeling that the world is against them *and that they can't do anything about it.*
3. There must be an opportunity—a loaded gun available in the house, a bottle of sleeping pills in the parents' medicine cabinet, or the like. Indeed, one likely contributor to the rising teenage suicide rates, especially among boys, is the increased availability of firearms among adolescents.

Attempts to prevent teen suicide have not been notably successful. Despite the fact that most suicides and suicide attempters have displayed significantly deviant behavior for some time before the event, most do not find their way to mental health clinics or other professionals; and increasing the availability of such clinics or of hot lines or crisis phones has not proven effective in reducing suicide rates.

Other prevention efforts have focused on education, such as providing training to teachers or to teenagers on how to identify students who are at risk for suicide, in the hope that vulnerable individuals might be reached before they attempt suicide. Risk factors include withdrawal from friends, recent social stresses such as an emotional loss of some kind, self-destructive behavior such as extreme risk taking, and any talk of suicide (Group for the Advancement of Psychiatry, 1996). The problem is that a great many adolescents show several of these risk factors at one time or another, and most do not attempt suicide. So it is hard for peers or teachers to single out those at specially high risk.

Another prevention strategy has been to offer special training in coping skills to students, so that teenagers might be able to find a nonlethal solution to their problems. Unfortunately, most such programs appear to be ineffective in changing student attitudes or

Research Report

Adolescent Suicide and Its Prevention (*Continued*)

knowledge (Shaffer, Garland, Vieland, Underwood, & Busner, 1991).

These discouraging results are not likely to change until we know a great deal more about the developmental pathways that lead to this particular form of psychopathology. What makes one teenager particularly vulnerable and another able to resist the temptation?

What combination of stressful circumstances is most likely to trigger a suicide attempt, and how do those stressful circumstances interact with the teenager's personal resources? Only when we can answer questions of this kind will we be on the road to understanding teenage suicide.

and Jonathan Howland point out, "Teenagers are not only the least experienced drivers, they are the least experienced drinkers" (1993, p. 307). When they drink, adolescents are more likely to drink to excess. Roughly half of all traffic fatalities in this age group are linked with alcohol. Another factor is the teenager's sense of immortality and his willingness to take risks while driving. Teens are more likely than are other age groups to speed, run red lights, make illegal turns, fail to wear seat belts, and drive while intoxicated.

Happily, the rate of motor vehicle fatalities among teens and young adults has dropped 38 percent since 1979 (Sells & Blum, 1996). What is increasing is the rate of homicide in this age group. In 1993, 3661 youth between the ages of 10 and 19 died from homicide, and another 526 from accidents involving firearms. Among black males ages 15 to 19, guns are the leading cause of death. In this group the rate of death from guns is 153.1 per 100,000 per year—an astonishing number—compared with 28.8 among white males in the same age group (Guns, 1996). A sizeable fraction of these black-youth deaths by firearms occur in dense pockets of inner-city poverty, which I talked about in the last chapter and earlier.

Finally, before leaving the depressing subject of adolescent mortalities, I need to say a word about deaths from AIDS, which appears on the list of significant causes of death for the first time in this age range. There are roughly 8000 reported cases of AIDS among U.S. teens and young adults (ages 13 to 29); an additional 36,000 are likely infected with HIV, based on estimates from the Centers for Disease Control. The teens at greatest risk for infection are runaways, those with homosexual experiences, those engaged in prostitution, and intravenous drug users. However, *all* sexually active teens are at some risk because the disease has begun to spread beyond these risk groups within the adolescent population in the United States (Sells & Blum, 1996; Panel on High Risk Youth, 1993). African-American and Hispanic youth are disproportionately represented in all these groups, accounting for more than a third of the cases among males and more than half the cases among females. The good news is that information about AIDS provided to young people has apparently led to an increase in the use of condoms, although the numbers are still too low. In the 1993 national high school survey by the Centers for Disease Control, 46% of white, 48% of black, and 39% of Hispanic teenage girls reported that they had used a condom the last time they had intercourse (Kann et al., 1995). Boys in this survey reported nearly sixty percent condom use, but these numbers are still too low to provide consistent protection against AIDS or less lethal sexually transmitted diseases.

Illnesses

While the rate of death rises in adolescence, the rate of acute illnesses—flu, colds, and the like—goes down, as does the risk of some kinds of chronic illnesses, such as ear infections. The incidence of acute asthma attacks, however, rises in the teenage years, especially among blacks (Centers for Disease Control, 1996a). Also increasing in these years is the likelihood of sexually transmitted diseases.

Sexually Transmitted Diseases.   The leading cause of infertility in adult women is pelvic inflammatory disease, most often caused by some type of **sexually transmitted disease (STD),** also called **venereal disease**, the label for any one of a cluster of diseases (described in Table 13.5) spread by sexual contact. STDs are more common among teenagers and young adults than in any other age group: Those under age 25 account for two-thirds of all the cases. **Chlamydia** and **genital warts** (technically called *human papillomavirus*) are apparently the most common among adolescents, although exact figures are hard to come by. Various reports place the incidence of both of these diseases at between 10 and 40 percent among sexually active girls (Sells & Blum, 1996).

If you read the various entries in the table, you can readily see that these are generally not trivial diseases. All carry significant risks, including sterility, cancer, or death. Adolescents and young adults appear to be at special risk for such diseases for a whole set of interlinked reasons (Biro & Rosenthal, 1995).

- They are more likely to have multiple sexual partners. Among all high school students (grades 9–12), 18.8% have had four or more partners; among black males, the rate is 58.8%; among high school seniors, 27% have had four or more partners (Kann et al., 1995).

- They do not use condoms consistently. Teenagers may use other forms of pregnancy prevention, but only condoms protect against transmission of STDs.

- They may have mistaken beliefs that STDs are easily cured.

- They may know in some abstract way that unprotected sex is risky, but still not think that something bad could happen to *them*.

- They are less likely to go for treatment if they have symptoms, out of fear that their parents will find out, because it is embarrassing, or because they do not know where to go for help.

Table 13.5

Common Forms of Sexually Transmitted Diseases

Disease	Symptoms	Treatment	If Untreated:
Chlamydia	1/3 have no symptoms. May involve pain during urination and discharge; in females, may also be some abdominal discomfort	Antibiotics	Can cause pelvic inflammatory disease, which may in turn cause sterility
Genital warts (human papillomavirus)	Painless growths on genitalia and anus	Removal of warts	May increase risk of cervical cancer
Herpes simplex	Painful blisters on the genitalia; in women, sometimes accompanied by fever	No known cure; can be controlled with the drug acyclovir	Increased risk of cervical cancer; risk of transmitting virus to infant at birth
Gonorrhea	Similar to chlamydia: discharge from penis or vagina; discomfort during urination	Antibiotics, especially penicillin	Can cause pelvic inflammatory disease; also linked to arthritis and meningitis
Syphilis	In first stage, reddish brown sores on mouth and genitalia, which may then disappear; second stage may have a widespread skin rash	Antibiotics	In later stages of untreated disease: paralysis, brain damage, convulsions, sometimes death
HIV	Extreme fatigue, fever, weight loss, diarrhea, night sweats, susceptibility to infections	Combination of three experimental drugs appears to suppress virus in many patients	Death, after extended illness, usually from some infection

Sources: Biro & Rosenthal, 1995; Centers for Disease Control, 1994e.

The good news is that the use of condoms among sexually active teens has risen in recent years, as has their knowledge about sexually transmitted diseases, especially through AIDS instruction in schools. Despite these gains in prevention, STDs remain a significant problem among U.S. adolescents.

Other Risky Behavior

Risky sexual behavior is only one part of a far more general pattern among adolescents. Teenagers in every culture appear to have what Jeffrey Arnett (1995) describes as a heightened level of sensation seeking and recklessness, leading to markedly increased rates of accidents and injuries in this age range. The form this recklessness takes, and the extent to which it is allowed expression, vary from one culture and one historical time to the next. In the United States at this time, the cultural mores allow—perhaps even encourage—a wide variety of risky behaviors, including all the elements that cause heightened mortality from automobile accidents I already mentioned: driving too fast, tailgating, not using seat belts, driving while intoxicated. Similarly, teens who ride bicycles or motorcycles are less likely than are adults to wear helmets regularly. The Centers for Disease Control's recent national survey of risky behavior among adolescents shows that 92% of teens rarely or never use bicycle helmets (Kann et al., 1995).

Alcohol and Drug Use.   Another major type of risk-taking behavior among teenagers is alcohol and drug use. National data suggest that many types of teenage drug use declined in the United States over the past several decades, reaching a low point in 1992. For example, 23 percent of teenagers in 1974 reported that they had used marijuana, compared with only 11.7 percent in 1992 (U.S. Bureau of the Census, 1995). Since 1992, however, illegal drug use among teenagers has risen rather rapidly. In 1996, 40 percent of high school seniors said they had used some kind of illegal drug (most often marijuana) at least once in the past year, up from 30 percent in 1991. Among tenth graders, the rise has been even more substantial, from 21 percent in 1991 to 37.5 percent in 1996, while among eighth graders the rate of those who say they have used any illegal drug in the past year doubled between 1991 and 1996, from 11 to 23.6 percent (Wren, 1996).

Alcohol use by teens is also high and rising, after a drop during the 1980s. Recent U.S. national figures, from 1993, shown in Table 13.6, illustrate the point. The overall rates of alcohol use are about the same for girls and boys, although teenage boys are more likely to engage in binge drinking than are girls (33.7% versus 26.0%, respectively). Similarly, there are few ethnic group differences in overall alcohol use, but African Americans—especially African-American girls—are less likely than other groups to drink in binges.

Risky Behavior in Context

These various risky behaviors appear to be unusually common in adolescence because they help many teenagers meet important psychological and social goals, including gaining peer acceptance or respect, establishing autonomy from parents and from other authority figures, coping with anxiety or fear of failure, and affirming maturity. Richard Jessor

---

Table 13.6

Alcohol Use by United States Teens in 1993 (in percents)

School Grade	Ever Used Alcohol	Used Alcohol in Last Month	Binge Drinking* in Last Month
9th	72.9	40.5	22.0
10th	76.8	44.0	26.2
11th	84.9	49.7	31.3
12th	87.6	56.4	39.1
Total	80.9	48.0	33.7

*Binge drinking is defined as five or more drinks on one occasion.

Source: Kann et al., 1995, from Table 14, p. 38.

Parenting

How to Get Your Teenager to Stop Smoking, or Not to Start

Nearly half of eighth graders think that smoking a pack or two of cigarettes a day carries no great risk. By senior year, only about thirty percent still believe this, but by then many have a well-established smoking habit. In fact, nearly all first tobacco use occurs before high school graduation; most of those who do not smoke in high school never develop the habit, while most of the 3 million adolescents who smoke regularly become addicted and are unable to quit, even when they try (Centers for Disease Control, 1994c).

Ethnic groups differ widely in tobacco use, with African-American youth smoking the least and white youth smoking the most (Kandel, Chen, Warner, Kessler, & Grant, 1997; Wills & Cleary, 1997). In one study researchers found that less than five percent of African-American high school seniors smoke daily, compared with about twelve percent of Hispanics and more than twenty percent of whites (Hilts, 1995).

The health risks linked to smoking are well established. What is not well established is how to prevent young people from taking up this habit. Among young blacks, family and peer pressure seems to be strongly *against* smoking, which clearly contributes to their lower smoking rates. Among white teens, there appears to be pressure in the other direction. So how can a parent change this? Reminding young people of the long-term health risks turns out not to be an especially effective strategy, at least not in isolation. Several other strategies are much more successful.

Stop Smoking Yourself. If you are a smoker but want your children *not* to smoke, the first step is for you to quit. The data are clear: Children of parents who smoke are more likely to smoke themselves—a pattern that is especially clear for mothers and daughters (Kandel & Wu, 1995).

Emphasize the Bad Breath. Tell them about all the negative *social* consequences of smoking. Their breath will smell bad, their teeth will turn yellow, their hair

and clothes will smell like smoke all the time, and their stamina—and thus their ability to do well in athletics—may be impaired. Tell them that teenagers themselves say that they find smokers less attractive (Centers for Disease Control, 1994d).

Encourage Your Schools to Adopt Antismoking Programs. All these messages are more effective if they come from other teenagers rather than from Mom and Dad, so lobby the local high school to organize systematic school-based prevention programs, with teens as models. The Minnesota Heart Health Program, for example, which used teen-led antismoking sessions in high schools in two communities, found that the rates of smoking in those communities was only half as high as in nearby communities that had not had any school intervention (Perry, Klep, & Sillers, 1989). You could also lobby your school board to adopt a complete ban on smoking on the school premises, including among teachers. In schools that allow smoking, 25 percent more of the students become smokers than in schools that forbid it on the school grounds. The Centers for Disease Control, in their "Guidelines for School Health Programs to Prevent Tobacco Use and Addiction" (1994d), list a complete school ban on tobacco use as its very first recommendation.

Focus on the Manipulation. Remind your children that the cigarette companies are trying to manipulate them through their advertising. You may want to get them to look at specific ads and talk about the particular forms of manipulation involved.

Pay Attention to Your Child's Friends. Teenagers whose friends smoke are more likely to take up the habit. You need to start paying attention to this *very* early—certainly by junior high school, when you may still have enough influence over the child's choice of friends to help steer the child toward a different crowd of kids.

(1992) argues that these are absolutely normal, central goals of adolescence. So when some risky behavior, such as smoking, drinking, or early sexual activity, helps individual teenagers meet those goals, such behaviors will be hard to change *unless* alternative ways of meeting these same goals are available or encouraged.

Jessor's argument also implies that those teenagers who will be most likely to show high risk behaviors are those who enter adolescence with few social skills and hence few alternative avenues for meeting their social and personal goals. And that is indeed what researchers have found. We know, for example, that reckless behaviors tend to

During adolescence we see a rise in a whole range of high-risk behaviors, particularly those that involve sensation seeking, such as drinking and driving fast and smoking (cigarettes and marijuana).

cluster together; the same teenager who smokes is also more likely to drink in binges, use marijuana, have multiple sexual partners, not use a bike helmet, and get into fights or carry a weapon (Escobedo, Reddy, & DuRant, 1997). Furthermore, those teens who show high rates of such reckless behaviors are likely to have had poor school records, early rejection by peers, neglect at home, or some combination of these early problems (Robins & McEvoy, 1990). By default, such children or teens are drawn to peers who share their patterns and their internal models of the world.

Bulimia and Anorexia

Another major health problem among adolescents, particularly among adolescent girls, are two forms of eating disorder, bulimia and anorexia nervosa. Many psychologists argue that these disorders are in fact only the extreme end of a continuum of problems related to dieting and obsession about body shape and size that appear to be epidemic among white teenage (and increasingly preteen) girls in the United States, Britain, and some other European countries (e.g., Smolak, Levine, & Streigel-Moore, 1996).

Bulimia (sometimes called *bulimia nervosa*) involves three elements: (1) a preoccupation with eating and an irresistible craving for food, leading to episodes of binge eating; (2) an intense fear of fatness; and (3) some method of "purging" to counteract the effects of the binge eating so as to avoid weight gain. Typical purging methods are self-induced vomiting, excessive use of laxatives, or excessive exercise (Garfinkel, 1995). Alternating periods of restrained and binge eating are common among individuals in all weight groups. Only when binge eating occurs as often as twice a week and is

combined with repeated episodes of some kind of purging is the syndrome properly called bulimia. Bulimics are ordinarily not exceptionally thin, but they are obsessed with their weight, feel intense shame about their abnormal behavior, and often experience significant depression. The physical consequences can include marked tooth decay (from repeated vomiting), stomach irritation, dehydration, lowered body temperature, disturbances of body chemistry, loss of hair, and, in extreme cases, cardiovascular problems (Mitchell, 1995; Muscari, 1996).

The incidence of bulimia appears to have been increasing in recent decades in many Western countries, but firm figures have been hard to establish. Current estimates are that from 1 to 3 percent of adolescent girls and young adult women show the full syndrome of bulimia; as many as 20 percent of girls in Western industrialized countries show at least some bulimic behaviors, such as occasional purging (Attie & Brooks-Gunn, 1995; Brooks-Gunn & Attie, 1996; Graber, Brooks-Gunn, Paikoff, & Warren, 1994). Many more are sufficiently concerned about their weight to diet regularly or constantly. None of these behaviors is found in countries where food is scarce.

Those adolescents most at risk for bulimia are those in cultural settings where slenderness is strongly emphasized, particularly if the girl herself wishes to pursue a career in which thinness is required (for example, dancers, gymnasts, models, or actors) (Brownell & Fairburn, 1995).

Anorexia nervosa is less common but potentially more deadly. It is characterized by a refusal to maintain body weight at or above a minimally normal level, with extreme dieting to maintain an abnormally low weight, an intense fear of gaining weight, and obsessive exercise. The weight loss can eventually produce a variety of physical symptoms associated with starvation: sleep disturbance, cessation of menstruation, insensitivity to pain, endocrine disorders, loss of hair on the head, low blood pressure, a variety of cardiovascular problems, and reduced body temperature. An anorexic's body image is so distorted that she can look in the mirror at a skeletally thin body and remain convinced that she is "too fat." As many as 10 percent of anorexics die as a result of their eating disorder. Some literally starve themselves to death; others die because of some type of cardiovascular dysfunction (Litt, 1996).

As is true for bulimia, anorexia is far more common among girls and women than among boys or men. Perhaps 1 girl out of every 500 in Western countries (0.2%) is anorexic. Among European and white American girls, especially those from professional families, the rate may be as high as 1 out of

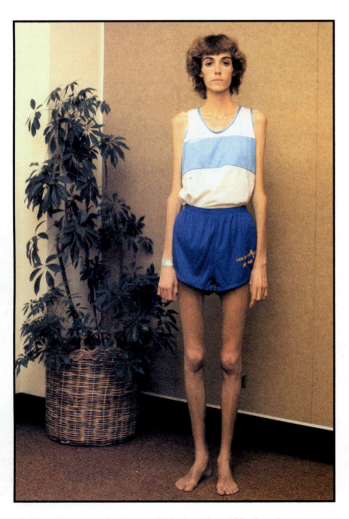

When this anorexic 15-year-old looks at herself in the mirror, chances are she sees herself as "too fat," despite her obvious emaciation.

100 (Brooks-Gunn & Attie, 1996; Litt, 1996). As is true for bulimia, the rate is considerably higher among subgroups who are under pressure to maintain extreme thinness, such as ballet dancers and high-performance athletes in sports in which thinness is greatly valued, such as gymnastics (Stoutjesdyk & Jevne, 1993).

Both bulimia and anorexia typically begin with persistent dieting, reinforcing the idea that eating disorders represent the extreme end of a continuum that includes other forms of concern about weight (Cooper, 1995; Polivy & Herman, 1995). Such a link between dieting and eating disorders is further strengthened by recent evidence that in countries such as Taiwan, Singapore, and China, where dieting has become a recent fad, eating disorders—almost never seen earlier—are becoming more common (Goleman, 1995b).

Yet a great many young women (and some young men) diet regularly, even obsessively, but never shift into an outright eating disorder. What tips a dieter into bulimia or anorexia?

Linda Smolak and Michael Levine propose the following scenario (1996). A key factor is a strong "thinness schema"—a firm belief that thinness is an essential ingredient of beauty—a common belief in many Western cultures. Denise Wilfley and Judith Rodin point out that "a healthy woman of normal weight has 22% to 25% body fat, yet our current aesthetic ideal is based on actresses and models who have only 10% to 15% body fat" (1995, p. 80). Many teenagers, especially white teens in the United States and Europe, accept this ideal and make valiant efforts to achieve it. Current research, for example, shows that roughly three-quarters of teenage girls have dieted or are dieting. If you look only at chronic dieters (those who have dieted at least ten times in the past year), the percentages are lower but still striking, as you can see in Figure 13.7. These numbers come from a questionnaire study of all junior and senior high school students in Minnesota in 1987 and 1988—a total of more than 36,000 teenagers (Story, Rosenwinkel, Himes et al., 1991). You can see that chronic dieting is far less common among boys than among girls; such dieting was also less common among black than among Hispanic and white girls.

When an adolescent combines such a thinness schema with perfectionism, body dissatisfaction (such as might be caused by teasing an overweight

Research Report

An Australian Study Illustrating Sex Differences in Body Image Among Adolescents

Susan Paxton's study of Australian high school students illustrates that the preoccupation with thinness among teenage girls is not restricted to the United States and shows what such a preoccupation can do to girls' body images (Paxton, Wertheim, Gibbons et al., 1991).

A total of 562 teenagers in grades 7 through 11 reported on their current weight and height and their judgment of that weight as underweight, a good weight, or overweight. They also responded to questions about the effect being thinner might have on their lives, and they described their weight control behaviors, including dieting and exercise.

Paxton reports that among teenagers who were actually *normal* in weight for their height, 30.1 percent of the girls but only 6.8 percent of the boys described themselves as overweight. Thus many girls *perceive* themselves as too fat when they are actually normal. Furthermore, the majority of girls thought that being thinner would make them happier; a few even thought that being thinner would make them more intelligent. Boys, in contrast, thought that being thinner would actually have some negative effects.

Not surprisingly, these differences in the perception of thinness were reflected in dieting behavior in this sample. Twenty-three percent of the girls reported that they went on a crash diet at least occasionally; 4 percent said they did so once or twice a week. The comparable percentages for boys were 9 and 1 percent, respectively. More girls than boys also reported using diet pills, laxatives, and vomiting, although the rates were low for both sexes.

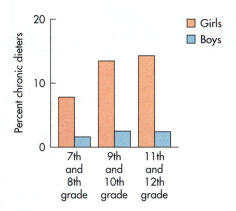

Figure 13.7

Percentage of junior high and high school students in Minnesota in 1987–88 who reported having dieted at least ten times in the previous year. (Source: Story et al., 1991, from Table 3, p. 995.)

child), a strong emphasis on weight and shape within the family, and low self-esteem, she (or, less often, he) is more likely to shift from chronic dieting to an eating disorder.

The final ingredient in Smolak and Levine's scenario is some kind of precipitator or trigger. For some, this can be early puberty. One of the effects of puberty in girls is to increase the amount of body fat. This is particularly true of early-developing girls, who characteristically acquire and retain higher fat levels than do later-maturing girls. Indeed, early-developing girls are nearly twice as likely to have an eating disorder as are normal- or late-developing girls (Graber et al., 1994; Killen, Hayward, Litt et al., 1992).

For others, the trigger may be some significant stressful life event, such as breaking up with a boyfriend. When several significant changes occur together (for example, a girl who hits puberty just as she switches to junior high school and just as her parents divorce), the risk of an eating disorder seems especially high. Smolak and Levine propose that when a teenager with a strong thinness schema is able to deal with the stresses and tasks of adolescence one at a time, most often she develops only some kind of disturbed eating pattern or chronic dieting, but does not develop bulimia or anorexia. When stresses pile up, though, for a teenager with a strong thinness schema, perfectionism, low self-esteem, and poor familial relationships, the likelihood of an eating disorder is very high.

[?] Critical Thinking

If you had the power to change our culture in such a way that the rate of bulimia and anorexia would decline substantially, what changes would you want to make? Why and how?

Of the two problems, bulimia is considerably easier to treat; anorexics frequently have relapses, even after extensive treatment. Newer treatment programs, however, offer some promise. In particular, treatment of both types of eating disorders increasingly involves antidepressant drugs, because depression very frequently accompanies the eating problem. Among bulimics, antidepressant medication appears to be effective in about a third of the cases. Another successful treatment for bulimia is cognitive-behavioral therapy, in which the patient is taught how to eat sensibly at the same time that she works to identify the emotional signals that trigger a binge-eating episode, such as a bad mood, some disappointment, or a sense of failure. The therapist then helps the patient develop alternative strategies for dealing with these triggering experiences and feelings.

Steroid Use

A parallel health problem, found far more often among boys, is the use of steroids to help create the mesomorphic, muscular physique associated with male attractiveness in most Western societies. In the Centers for Disease Control 1993 survey of high school students, 3.1% of the boys and 1.2% of the girls reported the use of illegal steroids (Kann et al., 1995). Other investigators have reported rates as high as 8% among high school boys (Rogol & Yesalis, 1992). Use of these drugs is especially likely among athletes in sports in which muscular bulk is valued, such as swimming, football, or power weight lifting. Yet as many as a third of boys who use steroids are not involved in any sports. They use the drugs in order to try to achieve the culturally ideal body type.

Gonadal steroid hormones are a *normal* part of adolescent growth patterns in boys, involved in the growth spurt and the increase in muscle tissue. Anabolic steroid drugs, all derivatives of testosterone, are also sometimes prescribed by physicians to accelerate markedly delayed puberty—so these are not totally foreign substances. When taken by otherwise normally developing boys (or girls), however, they can have unpleasant physical side effects, including increased acne and possibly smaller final stature. The latter effect occurs because steroids stimulate the closure of the epiphy-

Well-muscled bodies are clearly part of the U.S. cultural ideal for boys and men, contributing not only to the use of body-building equipment but—for some boys—to the use of steroids.

ses at the end of the long bones. Once the epiphyses are closed, no further growth in length of that bone can occur. Added steroids stimulate earlier closure, thus reducing final height. There are also hints from a variety of studies and anecdotal reports that steroid use can increase aggressive or violent behavior and foster more severe mood swings, although the data are simply not clear enough to allow a firm conclusion about such behavioral changes (Rogol & Yesalis, 1992).

When steroids are taken in larger doses and over longer periods of time, the physical side effects can be far more severe, including sustained penile erection, body swelling, and liver dysfunction. Among girls, even relatively low levels of steroid use can have profound and irreversible effects, including a deepened voice, greater body hair, changes in the clitoris, and cessation of menstruation.

Steroid use by teenagers, especially by young athletes, is undoubtedly both fostered and exacerbated by the great emphasis in U.S. culture on sports success. Many coaches express a "win at any cost" philosophy. Add to this the strong cultural emphasis, in the media and elsewhere, on "ideal" physical appearance, which for boys involves low body fat and high muscle definition, and you can begin to understand why so many boys (and some girls) are tempted. In the same way, you can understand why so many girls (and adult women!), steeped in the societal preference for slenderness and low body fat, choose to diet again and again, sometimes slipping over into frank eating disorders. The ultimate answer has to be a change in the culture—no small task.

Poverty and Health

Given what I have already said about the link between poverty and health in Chapter 10, you will not be surprised that poor teenagers, like poor elementary school children or preschoolers, are less healthy than their more economically advantaged peers. Still, I want to give you a few statistics. Several national surveys show that only 38 percent of poor teens, compared with 56 percent of those in nonpoor households, are in excellent health. Poor teens, like their younger peers, miss more days of school because of illness and have more chronic illnesses (Klerman, 1993; Newacheck, 1989).

Poor teens are also less likely to get good medical or dental care, to eat a good diet, or to get adequate exercise. They are also somewhat more likely to engage in various kinds of risky behavior, including riding a bike or motorcycle without a helmet or in a car without a seat belt and having sex without a contraceptive. In contrast, neither smoking nor drug use is consistently associated with poverty. Kids who drop out of school are more likely to be involved in smoking or drug taking, and more poor than affluent teens drop out of school, but poverty itself doesn't seem to be implicated with either of these behaviors.

Good and Poor Health Habits

Teenagers, at least those in the United States, are famous for their *lack* of a healthy lifestyle. They not only engage in the various risky behaviors I've al-

ready described, they eat poorly, get too little sleep, and don't exercise as much as they did in elementary school. Only 15 percent of high school students, for example, say they eat at least five servings of fruits and vegetables a day; a third eat three or more servings of high-fat food snacks every day, such as hamburgers, hot dogs, french fries, potato chips, cookies, doughnuts, pie, or cake. These poor eating habits are about as common in ninth graders as they are among twelfth graders; they're *all* eating poorly.

Levels of exercise also decline steadily over the high school years, especially among girls. You can see the trend clearly in Figure 13.8, which is based on the same 1993 national survey I've quoted several times (Kann et al., 1995). The figure shows the percentage of teens in each grade who reported that they participated in activities that made them sweat and breathe hard for at least 20 minutes on at least three days of the previous week. By grade 12, less than half the girls were that active. The reasons are multiple, but a significant factor is that many high schools no longer require physical education for all students, relying instead on sports participation for physical fitness. By twelfth grade, only 29% of girls in this survey said they were enrolled in PE; only 17% attended PE daily. Boys are more likely to choose PE when it is optional and are more likely to be involved in organized sports.

These poor health habits are not immediately fatal. Teenagers can and do survive their years of

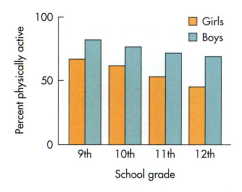

Figure 13.8

The percentage of high school students in a large national survey who reported that they exercised hard enough, at least three times in the past week, to make them sweat and breathe hard. (Source: Kann et al., 1995, from Table 24, p. 53.)

potato chips and increasingly sedentary living. The problem is that these habits are carried forward into adulthood, when the poor-health-habit chickens eventually come home to roost in the form of increased risks of heart disease and cancer. For most teens—and arguably for most young adults—these connections between daily health habits and long-term health risks are either unknown or seen as unimportant. Again, as with eating disorders and steroid use, we may need to change the whole culture in order to improve teenagers' health behaviors. What about banning ads for high-fat foods?

A Final Word

The facts and figures I have been talking about in this chapter are a nice illustration of the way in which physical development interacts with culture and internal models. The physical changes of puberty are one of the most obviously maturationally controlled aspects of development. Yet the way in which each youngster experiences the adolescent period, including puberty, is just as obviously shaped by cultural expectations and definitions and by each young person's own internal model of self. Similarly, the striving for autonomy and acceptance that partially motivates risky behaviors may be a normal part of the adolescent tradition in every culture. Of course, the specific risky behaviors we see are obviously affected by culture, just as each adolescent's own internal models affect the likelihood that he or she will choose risky behaviors as a way to express independence. Thus we cannot understand development, in general or in particular, without looking simultaneously at all three of these elements.

Summary

1. Adolescence is defined not only as a time of pubertal change, but as the transitional period between childhood and full adult role adoption.

2. Because of the importance of this transition, it is marked by rites and rituals in many cultures—although not in most modern Western countries.

3. The physical changes of adolescence are triggered by a complex set of hormonal changes, beginning at about age 8 or 9. Very large increases in go-nadotrophic hormones, including estrogen and testosterone, are central to the process.

4. Effects are seen in a rapid growth spurt in height and an increase in muscle mass and in fat. Boys add comparatively more muscle and girls more fat. A further pruning of dendrites also occurs, as does an increase in size of both heart and lungs.

5. In girls, mature sexuality is achieved in a set of changes beginning as early as age 8 or 9. Menarche occurs relatively late in the sequence.

6. Sexual maturity is later in boys, with the growth spurt occurring a year or more after the start of genital changes.

7. Variations in the rate of pubertal development have some psychological effects. In general, children whose physical development is markedly earlier or later than they expect or desire show more negative effects than do those whose development is "on time."

8. Sexual activity among teens has increased in recent decades in the United States, where roughly half of all high school students are sexually active and one in ten teenage girls becomes pregnant each year.

9. Long-term consequences for girls who bear children during adolescence are negative on average, although a significant minority of such girls are able to overcome their early disadvantages.

10. Adolescents have fewer acute illnesses than younger children but higher death rates. The three leading causes of death are accidents (primarily auto accidents), homicide, and suicide.

11. Girls are more likely to attempt suicide; boys are more likely to succeed. A very large fraction of adolescents report they have had thoughts of suicide.

12. Adolescents show higher rates of almost all kinds of risky behavior, including unprotected sex, drug use, fast driving, bike riding without helmets, and so on.

13. After several decades of decline, alcohol and drug use among teenagers in the United States began to rise again after 1992. Eighty percent of high school students report using alcohol at least once; a third report recent binge drinking.

14. Eating disorders such as bulimia and anorexia, more common in teenage girls than boys, are rising in frequency in most Western countries. A primary cause appears to be societal emphasis on an ideal thin body, leading to dieting, a pattern that shifts to a more serious eating disorder in many girls who face unusual stresses.

15. Some teen boys respond to the cultural ideal of a muscular body by taking steroids; such use may

also be fostered by an emphasis on sports prowess for both boys and girls.

16. As at earlier ages, teenagers living in poverty have poorer health than do those in more affluent circumstances.

17. Teenagers as a group have generally poor health habits, including poor diet and decreasing levels of exercise, in addition to various risky behaviors.

18. While maturational changes are clearly at the heart of the physical transition of puberty, the teenager's experience of puberty and adolescence is also strongly shaped by culture and by internal models and expectations.

Key Terms

anorexia nervosa   A serious eating disorder characterized by extreme dieting, intense fear of gaining weight, and distorted body image. **(p. 445)**

bulimia   An eating disorder characterized by an intense concern about weight combined with binge eating followed by purging, either through self-induced vomiting, excessive use of laxatives, or excessive exercise. **(p. 445)**

chlamydia   A sexually transmitted disease found fairly frequently among teenagers; symptoms include pain at urination and discharge, although one-third of infected persons have no symptoms. Can lead to pelvic inflammatory disease in women, which in turn can lead to sterility. **(p. 442)**

endocrine glands   These glands—including the adrenals, the thyroid, the pituitary, the testes, and the ovaries—secrete hormones governing overall physical growth and sexual maturing. **(p. 426)**

estrogen   The female sex hormone secreted by the ovaries. **(p. 426)**

genital warts   A sexually transmitted disease (technically called human papillomavirus) found fairly frequently among adolescents. Symptoms involve warts on the genitalia. **(p. 442)**

gonadotrophic hormones   Hormones produced in the pituitary gland that stimulate the sex organs to develop. **(p. 426)**

menarche   Onset of menstruation in girls. **(p. 431)**

pituitary   One of the endocrine glands. The pituitary plays a central role in controlling the rate of physical maturation and sexual maturing. **(p. 426)**

puberty   The collection of hormonal and physical changes at adolescence that brings about sexual maturity. **(p. 424)**

secular trend   A pattern of change in some characteristic over several cohorts, such as systematic changes in the average timing of menarche or average height or weight. **(p. 431)**

sexually transmitted diseases (STDs)   Also called venereal diseases. Category of disease spread by sexual contact, including chlamydia, genital warts, syphilis, gonorrhea, and HIV. The two most common of these infections among adolescents are chlamydia and genital warts. **(p. 442)**

venereal diseases   See *sexually transmitted diseases.*

Suggested Readings

Brownell, K. D., & Fairburn, C. G. (Eds.). (1995). *Eating disorders and obesity: A comprehensive handbook.* New York: Guilford Press. A first-class compendium of short summaries of what we know about every aspect of this subject.

Gullotta, T. P., Adams, G. R., & Montemayor, R. (Eds.). (1993). *Adolescent sexuality.* Newbury Park, CA: Sage. A first-rate volume of papers on all aspects of this important subject. Of particular interest are a paper by Dyk reviewing information on physical changes at adolescence and one by Miller et al. on sexual behavior in adolescents.

Malina, R. M. (1990). Physical growth and performance during the transitional years. In R. Montemayor, G. R. Adams, & T. P. Gullotta (Eds.), *From childhood to adolescence: A transitional period?* (pp. 41–62). Newbury Park, CA: Sage. Malina and Tanner together give us excellent normative information on normal physical growth. This particular paper focuses on puberty.

Millstein, S. G., Petersen, A. C., & Nightingale, E. O. (Eds.). (1993). *Promoting the health of adolescents. New directions for the twenty-first century.* New York: Oxford University Press. An excellent volume covering all aspects of the important question of how we can promote better health and health habits in adolescence.

Tanner, J. M. (1990). *Foetus into man. Physical growth from conception to maturity* (revised and enlarged ed.). Cambridge, MA: Harvard University Press. A detailed but very thorough and remarkably understandable book that covers all aspects of physical growth from conception through puberty.

Cognitive Development in Adolescence

Preview Questions

1 *Are teenagers really capable of more advanced forms of thinking than younger children?*

2 *What stage of moral reasoning is reflected in the statement "If it's the law, you have to obey it, no matter what"?*

3 *Do boys and girls, men and women, use different kinds of reasoning about moral questions?*

4 *Why do so few U.S. high school students think it is important to get good grades in school?*

5 *Is it a good idea, or a bad idea, for teenagers to have part-time jobs?*

Chapter Outline

Ask an 8-year-old what she wants to be when she grows up and she is likely to give you a very specific answer—"a fireman," "a veterinarian," or "an artist." Ask a 15-year-old the same question and you are likely to get a quite different answer: "Well, I'm thinking about several things. I know I want to go to college, but I don't know where, and I'm not sure what I want to study. Maybe science." The teenager's response is typically more future-oriented, more thoughtful, more questioning. Such a change might merely reflect the fact that the adolescent is much closer to significant life decisions and so is more aware of their complexity. It could also reflect an underlying change in the kind of thinking the teenager is now capable of performing. Piaget proposed just such a major shift at adolescence, to what he called the *formal operational stage*.

Piaget's View of Formal Operational Thought

Piaget's observations led him to conclude that this new level of thinking emerged fairly rapidly in early adolescence, roughly between ages 12 and 16. It has a number of key elements (summarized in Table 14.1.):

From the Actual to the Possible.   One of the first steps in the process is for the child to extend her concrete operational reasoning abilities to objects and situations that she has not seen or experienced firsthand, or that she cannot see or manipulate directly. Instead of thinking only about real things and actual occurrences, as the younger child can do, she must start to think about possible occurrences. The preschool child plays "dress up" by putting on real clothes. The teenager *thinks* about options and pos-

sibilities, imagining herself in different roles, going to college or not going to college, marrying or not marrying, having children or not having them. She can imagine future consequences of actions she might take now, so that some kind of long-term planning becomes possible.

Systematic Problem Solving.   Another important feature of formal operations is the ability to search systematically and methodically for the answer to a problem. To study this, Piaget and his colleague Barbel Inhelder (Inhelder & Piaget, 1958) presented adolescents with complex tasks, mostly drawn from the physical sciences. In one of these tasks, subjects were given varying lengths of string and a set of objects of various weights that could be tied to the strings to make a swinging pendulum. They were shown how to start the pendulum by pushing the weight with differing amounts of force and by holding the weight at different heights. The subject's task was to figure out which one or which combination of length of string, weight of object, force of push, or height of push determines the "period" of the pendulum—that is, the amount of time for one swing. (In case you have forgotten your high school physics, the answer is that only the length of the string affects the period of the pendulum.)

[?] *Critical Thinking*

Suppose you find yourself with what seems like one cold after another or one sinus infection after another. Could it be an allergy? Could it be some more basic health problem? How might you go about finding out? Would you need to use some kind of systematic problem solving to find the answer?

Table 14.1

Key Features of Adolescent Thought in Piaget's Theory

- **From Actual to Possible:** The adolescent can now think about things she imagines, or about possibilities, as well as about things that she has seen or known.
- **Systematic Problem Solving:** Faced with a problem or a task that has several variables or hypotheses—such as figuring out why a bicycle's brakes don't work or choosing a college from among many choices—the teenager can examine the several factors systematically and fully.
- **Hypothetico-Deductive Reasoning:** The teenager can use deductive as well as inductive logic, can consider hypothetical premises as well as known possibilities. The combination of systematic problem solving and some form of deductive logic is required for almost all scientific reasoning.

If you give this task to a concrete-operational child, she will usually try out many different combinations of length, weight, force, and height in an inefficient way. She might try a heavy weight on a long string, and then a light weight on a short string. Because both string length and weight have changed, there is no way to draw a clear conclusion about either factor.

In contrast, an adolescent using formal operations is likely to be more organized, attempting to vary just one of the four factors at a time. She may try a heavy object with a short string, then with a medium string, then with a long one. After that, she might try a light object with the three lengths of string. Of course, not all adolescents (or all adults, for that matter) are quite this methodical in their approach. Still, there is a very dramatic difference in the overall strategy used by 10-year-olds versus 15-year-olds that marks the shift from concrete to formal operations.

Logic.   Another facet of this shift is the appearance of what Piaget called **hypothetico-deductive reasoning** in the child's repertoire of skills. I mentioned in Chapter 11 that the concrete-operational child is able to use inductive reasoning, which involves arriving at a conclusion or a rule based on a lot of individual experiences. The more difficult kind of reasoning, using **deductive logic,** involves considering hypotheses or hypothetical premises, and then deriving logical outcomes from those hypotheses. For example, the statement "If all people are equal, then you and I must be equal" involves logic of this type. Although children as young as 4 or 5 can understand some deductive relationships if the premises given are factually true, only at adolescence are young people able to understand and use the basic *logical* relationships (e.g., Ward & Overton, 1990).

A great deal of the logic of science is of this hypothetico-deductive type. We begin with a theory and propose, "If this theory is correct, then I should observe such and such." In doing this, we are going well beyond our observations. We are conceiving things that we have never seen that *ought* to be true or observable. We can think of this change as part of a general decentering process that began much earlier in cognitive development. The preoperational child gradually moves away from his egocentrism and comes to be able to take the physical or emotional perspective of others.

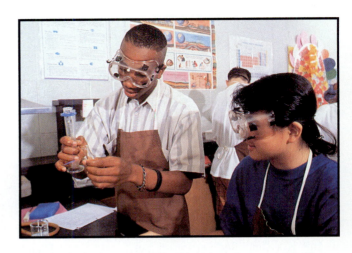

High school science classes like this biology class may be the first places where adolescents are required to use deductive logic—a skill Piaget did not think was present until the period of formal operations.

During formal operations, the child takes another step by freeing himself even from his reliance upon specific experiences.

Post-Piagetian Work on Adolescent Thought

Edith Neimark summarizes the accumulated information succinctly:

> An enormous amount of evidence from an assortment of tasks shows that adolescents and adults are capable of feats of reasoning not attained under normal circumstances by [younger] children, and that these abilities develop fairly rapidly during the ages of about 11 to 15. (1982, p. 493)

Furthermore, many of the qualities of adolescent thought Piaget identified do seem to emerge during this period. Adolescents, much more than school-age children, operate with possibilities in addition to reality, and they are more likely to use deductive logic. As Flavell puts it (1985, p. 98), the thinking of the school-age child "hugs the ground of . . . empirical reality," while the teenager is more likely to soar into the realm of speculation and possibility. An 8-year-old thinks that "knowing" something is a simple matter of finding out the facts; a teenager is more likely to see knowledge as relative, as less certain (Bartsch, 1993). Deanna

Psychology in Action

Understanding a Pendulum

Warning: This project, like many of the *Psychology in Action* suggestions given in this text, should not be undertaken without explicit permission and guidance from your instructor, who will have to obtain permission from your college or university's Human Subjects Review Committee for any project in which you interview or observe a child or parent directly. **Do not do this project on your own, without such permission.**

This is a simplified version of the Inhelder and Piaget pendulum problem described in the text. To complete this project, you should locate a child between ages 8 and 16, obtaining the parents' permission for the testing in whatever way prescribed by your instructor.

Equipment

Because the physical objects are so important for this problem, you need to collect your equipment carefully and test it before you start. You will need three pieces of strong, flexible string of three lengths (say, 25 cm, 37 cm, and 50 cm long). You will also need three similar objects of varying weights. Fishing sinkers work well, as do keys, but the lightest one should be heavy enough so that it will weight down the string and allow it to swing.

If you can complete the testing in some location in which you have a chance to tie all three strings to an overhead rod or other object, that would be best, since it leaves you free to write down what your subject does. Otherwise, you will have to hold the top of each string when your subject wishes to use that string in a test.

Procedure

Tell your subject:

> *I am doing a class project about how different people go about solving a problem. The problem I would like you to solve is to find out what makes a pendulum swing faster or slower.*

Pause at this point and demonstrate how you can attach a weight to the string and push the weight to start the pendulum swinging. Demonstrate this with more than one weight/string combination so that it is clear that there is variability in the speed of the pendulum swing. Then say:

> *You need to figure out what makes the pendulum swing faster or slower. You can use any of these three strings and these three weights to help you figure this out. I'll be taking notes about what you do and say while you are working on the problem.*

Record each combination the subject tries, in the order of the attempts. If you can, you should also record any comments the subject makes in the process. Allow the subject to continue until he/she gives you an answer; if no answer is forthcoming, you may ask after a period of time a question such as, *Can you figure out what makes the pendulum move fast or slow?* If that does not promote an answer, or the subject seems very frustrated or bored, you may terminate the procedure and thank the subject for his/her help. If the subject has not solved the problem, you'll want to reassure him/her by pointing out that this is a really hard problem and that lots of kids his/her age have a hard time figuring it out.

Analysis and Report

In reporting on your project, make sure to discuss the following points:

- *Did your subject solve the problem? (That is, did he/she figure out that it is the length of string and not the weight that determines the speed of the pendulum?)*

- *How many separate string/weight combination tests did it take to reach some conclusion, whether the conclusion was correct or not?*

- *Did the subject try various string/weight combinations in any systematic order? Or were the various attempts more random?*

- *Did the subject talk to himself/herself while working on the problem? Was this self-talk directed at keeping track of things he/she had tried, or at thinking through the problem?*

- *Did your subject's performance fit the findings from Piaget's and others' studies on the age at which formal operations develops?*

Kuhn and her colleagues have also found that teenagers and young adults, faced with disconfirming evidence, are more likely than are younger children to change their theory or their initial guesses; they are also more systematic in seeking out new information that will help hone their hypotheses—both hallmarks of formal operations reasoning (Kuhn, Garcia-Mila, Zohar, & Andersen, 1995).

Some research illustrations would probably make the change clearer. In an early cross-sectional study, Susan Martorano (1977) tested 20 girls at each of four grades (grades 6, 8, 10, and 12) on ten different tasks that require one or more of what Piaget called formal operations skills. Indeed, many of the tasks she used were those Piaget himself had devised. Results from two of these tasks are in Figure 14.1. The pendulum problem is the same one I described earlier; the "balance" problem requires a youngster to predict whether or not two varying weights, hung at varying distances on either side of a scale, will balance. To solve this problem using formal operations, the teenager must consider both weight and distance simultaneously. You can see in the figure that older students generally did better, with the biggest improvement in scores between ages 13 and 15.

In a more practical vein, Catherine Lewis (1981) has shown that these new cognitive abilities alter the ways teenagers go about making decisions. Older teenagers are more focused on the future, on possibilities, and on options, when they consider decisions. Lewis asked eighth-, tenth-, and twelfth-grade students to respond to a set of dilemmas, each of which involved a person facing a difficult decision, such as whether or not to have an operation to remove a facial disfigurement or how to decide which doctor to trust when the doctors give differing advice. Forty-two percent of the twelfth graders, but only 11 percent of the eighth graders, mentioned future possibilities in their answers to these dilemmas.

In answer to the cosmetic surgery dilemma, for example, a twelfth grader said:

> Well, you have to look into the different things . . . that might be more important later on in your life. You should think about, will it have any effect on your future and with, maybe, the people you meet. . . . (p. 541)

An eighth grader, in response to the same dilemma, said:

> The different things I would think about in getting the operation is like if the girls turn you down on a date, or the money, or the kids teasing you at school. . . . (p. 542)

The eighth grader, as is characteristic of the preadolescent or early adolescent, is focused on the here and now, on concrete things. The teenager is considering things that *might* happen in the future.

Critical Thinking

Think for a minute about how you went about making the last major decision you faced. What factors did you consider? Did you think about future consequences, or only about the here and now?

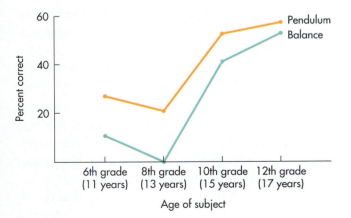

Figure 14.1

Results from two of the ten different formal operational tasks used in Martorano's cross-sectional study. (Source: Martorano, 1977, p. 670. Copyright by the American Psychological Association.)

Note, though, that even among the twelfth grade students in Lewis's study, nearly three-fifths did not show this type of future orientation. And take another look at Figure 14.1; only 50 to 60 percent of twelfth graders solved the two formal operations problems. In Martorano's study, in fact, only 2 of the 20 twelfth-grade subjects used formal operations logic on all ten problems.

These findings reflect a common pattern in research on adolescent thinking: By no means do all teenagers (or adults) use these more abstract forms of logic and thought. Keating (1980) estimates that only 50 to 60 percent of 18- to 20-year-olds in Western countries use formal operations at all, let alone consistently. The rates are even lower in non-Western countries.

Why Doesn't Every Teenager Use Formal Logic?

There are several possible explanations for such low levels of formal operations thought. One interpretation is that expertise is once again the crucial element. That is, most of us have some formal operational ability, but we can only apply it to topics or tasks with which we are highly familiar. For example, I use formal operations reasoning about psychology because it is an area I know well, but I am a lot less skillful at applying the same kind of reasoning to fixing my car—about which I know next to nothing. Willis Overton and his colleagues (Overton, Ward, Noveck, Black, & O'Brien, 1987) have found considerable support for this possibility in their research. They have found that as many as 90 percent of adolescents can solve a quite complex logic problem if the problem is stated using familiar content, while only half can solve the identical logic problem when it is stated in abstract language.

Another possibility is that most of our everyday experiences and tasks do not require formal operations. Inductive reasoning or other simpler forms of logic are quite sufficient most of the time. So we get into a cognitive rut, applying our most habitual mode of thinking to new problems as well. We can kick our thinking up a notch under some circumstances, especially if someone reminds us that it would be useful to do so, but we simply don't rehearse formal operations very much.

The fact that formal operations thinking is found more often among young people or adults in Western cultures may be interpreted in the same way. Industrialized cultures include high levels of technology and complex lifestyles. They may therefore demand more formal operational thought. By this argument, all nonretarded teenagers and adults are thought to have the *capacity* for formal logic, but only those of us whose lives demand its development will actually acquire it.

[?] *Critical Thinking*

Which of these explanations of the relative lack of formal operations among adolescents and adults do you find most persuasive? Think about your own experience. Do you use this type of thinking consistently, or only in certain situations? What sort of circumstances are most likely to trigger its use?

Notice that all of these explanations undermine the very notion of a universal "stage" of thinking in adolescence. Yes, more abstract forms of thinking may develop in adolescence, but they are neither universal nor broadly used by individual teenagers or adults. Whether one develops or uses these forms of logic depends heavily on experience, expertise, and environmental demand.

An Evaluation of Piaget's Theory and Some Remaining Questions

Each time I have talked about cognitive development I have raised some issues about Piaget's theory, or about the general notion of underlying stages, so the issues are not new to you. Still, it is useful to pull the threads together for one last look.

The child clearly comes a long way in the brief span of 15 years. As Robert Siegler puts it,

> Among the most remarkable characteristics of human beings is how much our thinking changes with age. When we compare the thinking of an infant, a toddler, an elementary school student, and an adolescent, the magnitude of the change is immediately apparent. (1994, p. 1)

In broad outline, Piaget's observations about this sequence have been frequently confirmed. Children do clearly change not only in what they know but in the way they approach problems.

Yet it now seems quite unlikely that this developmental progression involves coherent, general stages of the kind Piaget envisioned. Children's performance is much more variable than that. The same child may use quite sophisticated strategies for one kind of problem and very primitive strategies on another, or use widely varying strategies

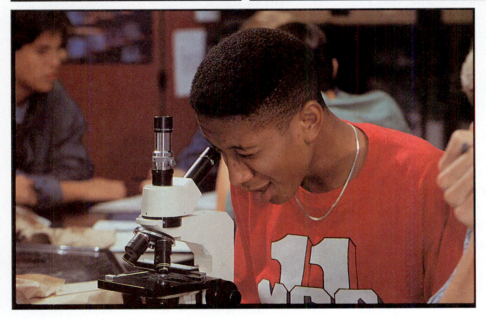

Everything we know about children's cognitive development tells us that this toddler, this school-age girl, and this teenager are using different types of thinking, different forms of logic or strategies. But we are still a long way from having a good explanation of how or why the change occurs.

on the identical problem on separate occasions (Siegler, 1994; 1996). The expert child chess player, who can demonstrate quite extraordinary feats of memory and conceptual sophistication playing chess probably has no better memory for strings of numbers than does another child of the same age. In the current language used by cognitive theorists, children's thinking is quite *domain speci c* (Hirschfeld & Gelman, 1994).

Nor do new cognitive skills emerge full-blown. Rather, they are preceded by more rudimentary or partial versions of the same skills at earlier ages. For example, virtually all the achievements of the concrete operational period are present in at least rudimentary or fragmentary form in the preschool years. This observation undermines the basic notion of a stage in the sense that Piaget proposed it.

Still, even if we are now able to reject Piaget's highly "domain-general" theory, we are nevertheless left with a wide range of possibilities. Development might be *totally* situation (domain) specific, or it might have at least some generality, with some basic skills or understandings changing with age and being applied across several different domains or tasks. We see some sign of just such a semigeneral, almost stagelike shift in children's theory of mind at about age 4. Indeed, the very use of the word *theory* in this label implies that the child has some kind of coherent model that gets applied to a variety of situations (Gopnik & Wellman, 1994). On the other side of the coin, the research on expertise makes thinking look highly domain specific.

A second key issue with roots in Piagetian theory is the question of why particular new intellectual skills emerge at the time that they do. Why does vocabulary explode at about age 18 months? Why does the ability to understand conservation appear only at about age 5 or 6? Piaget's theory obviously offered one answer to this question. If we conclude that he is wrong about broad stages, we still are left with the task of explaining the overall timing of cognitive development (Siegler, 1992). One possible model, common among information processing theorists, is to propose some kind of built-in constraints, such as systematic improvements in the efficiency of the neural wiring at particular age points. Such models may help us understand *change* in children's thinking, but whether they will help us understand *qualitative* changes in children's thinking, such as from nonsystematic to systematic, or from attention to appearances to attention to underlying principles, is not yet clear.

The theoretical issues are obviously highly complex, and well beyond the scope of this book. I raise them here so that you can see the direction of our current struggles, and also so that you can understand why Piaget's theory remains so central in our discussions. Piaget was clearly wrong in several important respects, but at this time, we have no alternative that handles all the facts any better.

The Development of Moral Reasoning

Another aspect of cognitive development that interested Piaget and has continued to fascinate researchers, is the child's reasoning about moral questions. How does a child decide what is good or bad, right or wrong, in his own and other people's behavior? When you serve on a jury, you must make such a judgment, as you do in everyday life: Should you give the store clerk back the excess change she handed you? Should you turn in a classmate you see cheating on an exam? What

about someone who lies in a job interview? Does your judgment change if you know that the person desperately needs the job to support his handicapped child?

These questions do not become relevant only at adolescence. Children younger than adolescents clearly make such judgments as well. Nevertheless, because several key changes in moral reasoning appear to coincide with adolescence or with the emergence of formal operations reasoning, this is a good place to introduce you to this very intriguing body of theory and research.

Kohlberg's Theory

Piaget was the first to offer a description of the development of moral reasoning (Piaget, 1932), but Lawrence Kohlberg's work has had the most powerful impact (Colby, Kohlberg, Gibbs, & Lieberman, 1983; Kohlberg, 1964; 1976; 1980; 1981). Building on and revising Piaget's ideas, Kohlberg pioneered the practice of assessing moral reasoning by presenting a subject with a series of hypothetical dilemmas in story form, each of which highlighted a specific moral issue, such as the value of human life. One of the most famous is the dilemma of Heinz:

> In Europe, a woman was near death from a special kind of cancer. There was one drug that the doctors thought might save her. It was a form of radium that a druggist in the same town had recently discovered. The drug was expensive to make, but the druggist was charging ten times what the drug cost him to make. He paid $200 for the radium and charged $2000 for a small dose of the drug. The sick woman's husband, Heinz, went to everyone he knew to borrow the money, but he could only get together about $1000, which is half what it cost. He told the druggist that his wife was dying, and asked him to sell it cheaper or let him pay later. But the druggist said, "No, I discovered the drug and I'm going to make money from it." So Heinz got desperate and broke into the man's store to steal the drug for his wife. (Kohlberg & Elfenbein, 1975, p. 621)

After hearing this story, the child or young person is asked a series of questions, such as whether Heinz should have stolen the drug. What if Heinz didn't love his wife? Would that change anything?

What if the person dying was a stranger? Should Heinz steal the drug anyway?

On the basis of answers to dilemmas like this one, Kohlberg concluded that there were three main levels of moral reasoning, with two stages within each level. These are summarized briefly in Table 14.2.

At Kohlberg's Level I, **preconventional morality,** the child's judgments are based on sources of authority who are close by and physically superior to himself—usually the parents. Just as his descriptions of others at this same stage are largely external, so the standards the child uses to judge rightness or wrongness are external rather than internal. In particular, it is the outcome or consequences of his actions that determine the rightness or wrongness of those actions.

In stage 1 of this level—the *punishment and obedience orientation*—the child relies on the physical consequences of some action to decide if it is right or wrong. If he is punished, the behavior was wrong; if he is not punished, it was right. He is obedient to adults because they are bigger and stronger.

In stage 2—*individualism, instrumental purpose, and exchange*—the child begins to do things that are rewarded and avoid things that are punished. (For this reason, the stage is sometimes called a position of "naive hedonism.") If it feels good, or brings pleasant results, it is good. This phase is marked by some beginning concern for other people, but only if that concern can be expressed as something that benefits the child himself as well. So he can enter into agreements such as, "If you help me, I'll help you."

To illustrate, here are some responses to variations of the Heinz dilemma, drawn from studies of children and teenagers in a number of different cultures, all of which would be rated as stage 2:

He should steal the food for his wife because if she dies he'll have to pay for the funeral, and that costs a lot. (Taiwan)

[He should steal the drug because] he should protect the life of his wife so he doesn't have to stay alone in life. (Puerto Rico)

[*Suppose it wasn't his wife who was starving but his best friend. Should he steal the food for his friend?*] Yes, because

---

Table 14.2

Kohlberg's Stages of Moral Development

Level I: Preconventional Morality
- *Stage 1: Punishment and obedience orientation.* The child decides what is wrong on the basis of what is punished. Obedience is valued for its own sake, but the child obeys because the adults have superior power.
- *Stage 2: Individualism, instrumental purpose, and exchange.* The child follows rules when it is in his immediate interest. What is good is what brings pleasant results.

Level II: Conventional Morality
- *Stage 3: Mutual interpersonal expectations, relationships, and interpersonal conformity.* Moral actions are those that live up to the expectations of the family or other significant group. "Being good" becomes important for its own sake.
- *Stage 4: Social system and conscience (law and order).* Moral actions are those so defined by larger social groups or the society as a whole. One should fulfill duties one has agreed to and uphold laws, except in extreme cases.

Level III: Principled or Postconventional Morality
- *Stage 5: Social contract or utility and individual rights.* Acting so as to achieve the "greatest good for the greatest number." The teenager or adult is aware that most values are relative and laws are changeable, although rules should be upheld in order to preserve the social order. Still, some basic nonrelative values exist, such as the importance of each person's life and liberty.
- *Stage 6: Universal ethical principles orientation.* The adult develops and follows self-chosen ethical principles in determining what is right. These ethical principles are part of an articulated, integrated, carefully thought-out and consistently followed system of values and principles.

Sources: After Kohlberg, 1976; and Lickona, 1978.

one day when he is hungry his friend would help. (Turkey) (all quotes from Snarey, 1985, p. 221)

At the next major level, **conventional morality,** there is a shift from judgments based on external consequences and personal gain to judgments based on rules or norms of a group to which the child belongs, whether that group is the family, the peer group, a church, or the nation. What the chosen reference group defines as right or good *is* right or good in the child's view, and the child internalizes these norms to a considerable extent.

Stage 3 (the first stage of Kohlberg's Level II) is the stage of *mutual interpersonal expectations, relationships, and interpersonal conformity* (sometimes also called the *good boy/nice girl* stage). Children at this stage believe that good behavior is what pleases other people. They value trust, loyalty, respect, gratitude, and maintenance of mutual relationships. Andy, a boy Kohlberg interviewed who was at stage 3, said:

> I try to do things for my parents, they've always done things for you. I try to do everything my mother says, I try to please her. Like she wants me to be a doctor and I want to, too, and she's helping me get up there. (Kohlberg, 1964, p. 401)

Another mark of this third stage is that the child begins to make judgments based on intentions as well as on outward behavior. If someone "means well" or "didn't mean to do it," their wrongdoing is seen as less serious than if they did it "on purpose."

Given their age, it is most likely that these students, participating in the Hispanic Youth Legislature, are reasoning at stage 3 of Kohlberg's stages of moral reasoning: What is good is what family or peers define as good and right.

Stage 4, the second stage of the conventional level, shows the child turning to larger social groups for her norms. Kohlberg labeled this the stage of *social system and conscience;* it is also sometimes called the *law and order orientation.* People reasoning at this stage focus on doing their duty, respecting authority, following rules and laws. The emphasis is less on what is pleasing to particular people (as in stage 3) and more on adhering to a complex set of regulations. The regulations themselves are not questioned.

The transition to Level III, **principled morality** (also called **postconventional morality**), is marked by several changes, the most important of which is a shift in the source of authority. According to Kohlberg, at Level I children see authority as totally outside themselves; at Level II, the judgments or rules of external authority are internalized, but they are not questioned or analyzed; at Level III, a new kind of personal authority emerges in which individual choices are made, with individual judgments based on self-chosen principles.

In stage 5 at this level—called the *social contract* orientation by Kohlberg—we see the beginning of such self-chosen principles. People operating at this level see rules, laws, and regulations as important because they insure fairness, while at the same time arguing that there are times when the rules, laws, and regulations need to be ignored or changed. The U.S. system of government is based on moral reasoning of this kind, since we have provisions for changing laws and for allowing personal protests against a given law, such as during the civil rights protests of the 1960s, the Vietnam War protests of the 1960s and 1970s, or the protests against apartheid in the 1980s.

[?] *Critical Thinking*

Imagine a society in which everyone handled moral issues at Kohlberg's stage 3. Now think about one in which everyone operated at stage 5. How would those two societies be likely to differ?

In his original writing about moral development, Kohlberg also included a sixth stage, the *universal ethical principles orientation.* People who reason in this way assume personal responsibility for their own actions, based upon fundamental and universal principles, such as justice and basic respect for persons. Kohlberg later waffled a good bit on whether such a stage was the logical and necessary end point of the sequence, and on whether people reasoning at such a level actually existed (Kohlberg, 1978; 1984; Kohlberg, Levine, & Hewer, 1983). If they exist at all, it seems likely that such universal ethical principles guide the moral reasoning of only a few very unusual individuals—perhaps those who devote their lives to humanitarian causes, such as Mother Teresa or Gandhi.

In all this, it is *very* important to understand that what defines the stage or level of a person's moral judgment is not the specific moral choice but the *form of reasoning* used to justify that choice. For example, the choice either that Heinz should steal the drug or that he should not could be justified with logic at any given stage. I've already given you some examples of a stage 2 justification for Heinz's stealing the drug; here's a stage 5 justification of the same choice, drawn from a study in India:

> [What if Heinz was stealing to save the life of his pet animal instead of his wife?] If Heinz saves an animal's life his action will be commendable. The right use of the drug is to administer it to the needy. There is some difference, of course—human life is more evolved and hence of greater importance in the scheme of nature—but an animal's life is not altogether bereft of importance. . . . (Snarey, 1985, p. 223, drawn originally from unpublished work by Vasudev, 1983)

If you compare this answer with the ones I quoted before, you can clearly see the difference in the form of reasoning used, even though the action being justified is precisely the same.

Kohlberg argued that this sequence of reasoning is both universal and hierarchically organized, just as Piaget thought his proposed stages of cognitive development were universal and hierarchical. That is, each stage follows and grows from the preceding one and has some internal consistency. Individuals should not move "down" the sequence, but only "upward" along the stages, if they move at all. Kohlberg did *not* suggest that all individuals eventually progress through all six stages, nor even that each stage is tied to specific ages. He did argue that the order is invariant and universal. Let me take a critical look at these claims.

Kohlberg thought that there were at least a few people, perhaps like Mother Teresa, whose moral reasoning is based on universal ethical principles.

Age and Moral Reasoning

Kohlberg's own findings, confirmed by many other researchers (e.g., L. Walker, de Vries, & Trevethan, 1987), show that preconventional reasoning (stages 1 and 2) is dominant in elementary school, and stage 2 reasoning is still evident among many early adolescents. Conventional reasoning (stages 3 and 4) emerges as important in middle adolescence and remains the most common form of moral reasoning in adulthood. Postconventional reasoning (stages 5 and 6) is relatively rare, even in adulthood. For example, in one study of men in their 40s and 50s, only 13 percent were rated as using stage 5 moral reasoning (Gibson, 1990).

Research Report

Eisenberg's Model of Prosocial Reasoning

Most of the moral dilemmas Kohlberg posed for his subjects deal with wrongdoing—with stealing, punishment, disobeying laws. Few tell us anything about the kind of reasoning children use in justifying *prosocial behavior*. I mentioned in Chapter 9 that altruistic behavior is visible in children as young as 2 and 3; but how do children explain and justify such behavior?

Nancy Eisenberg and her colleagues (Eisenberg, 1986; Eisenberg, Carlo, Murphy, & Van Court, 1995; Eisenberg, Shell, Pasternack et al., 1987) have explored such questions by proposing dilemmas to children in which self-interest is set against the possibility of helping another person. One story for younger children, for example, involves a child walking to a friend's birthday party. On the way, he comes upon another child who has fallen and hurt himself. If the party-bound child stops to help, he will probably miss the cake and ice cream. What should he do?

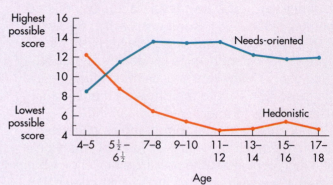

In response to dilemmas like this, preschool children most often use what Eisenberg calls **hedonistic reasoning,** in which the child is concerned with self-oriented consequences rather than moral considerations. Children this age say things like "I'd help because she'd help me the next time," or "I wouldn't help because I'd miss the party." This approach gradually shifts to one Eisenberg calls **needs-oriented reasoning,** in which the child expresses concern directly for the other person's need, even if the other's need conflicts with the child's own wishes or desires. Children operating on this basis say things like, "She'd feel better if I helped." At this stage, children do not express their choices in terms of general principles or indicate any reflectiveness about generalized values; they simply respond to the other's needs.

Still later, typically in adolescence, children say they will do good things because it is expected of them, a pattern highly similar to Kohlberg's stage 3 reasoning, and in late adolescence, some young people give evidence that they have become more self-reflective in

their judgments, trying to put themselves in the other person's place, or developing clear, internalized values that guide their prosocial behavior: "I'd feel a responsibility to help because of my values," or "If everyone helped, society would be a lot better."

The figure (drawn from Eisenberg, Carlo, Murphy, & Van Court, 1995, Table 1, p. 1187) gives some sample data from Eisenberg's longitudinal study of a small group of American children that illustrate the shift from hedonistic to needs-oriented reasoning. Clearly, by adolescence, hedonistic reasoning has virtually disappeared (the lowest possible score on this scale is 4), while needs-oriented reasoning dominates in early adolescence. Eisenberg reports that similar patterns have been found among children in West Germany, Poland, and Italy, but that kibbutz-reared Israeli elementary school children show little needs-oriented reasoning (Eisenberg, 1986). Instead, this particular group of Israeli children is more likely to reason on the basis of the humanness of recipients and on internalized values and norms, a pattern consistent with the strong emphasis on egalitarianism and communal values in the kibbutzim. These findings point to perhaps a larger role of culture in children's prosocial reasoning than in reasoning about justice, although that is still a highly tentative conclusion.

Let me give you two examples illustrating these overall age trends. The first, shown in Figure 14.2, comes from Kohlberg's own longitudinal study of 58 boys, first interviewed when they were 10, and subsequently followed for more than 20 years (Colby et al., 1983). Table 14.3 shows cross-sectional data from a study by Lawrence Walker and his colleagues

(L. Walker et al., 1987). They studied ten boys and ten girls at each of four ages, and interviewed the parents of each child as well. Note that Walker scored each response on a 9-point scale rather than just scoring the five main stages. This system, which has become quite common, allows for the fact that many people's reasoning falls between two specific stages.

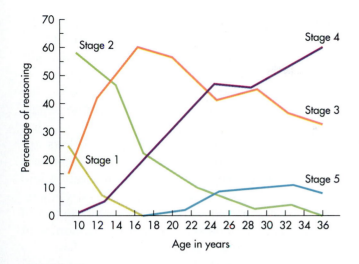

Figure 14.2

These findings are from Colby & Kohlberg's long-term longitudinal study of a group of boys who were asked about Kohlberg's moral dilemmas every few years from age 10 through early adulthood. Note that postconventional or principled reasoning was quite uncommon, even in adulthood. (Source: Colby et al., 1983, Figure 1, p. 46. © The Society for Research in Child Development.)

The results of these two studies are not identical, but there is nonetheless remarkable agreement on the order of emergence of the various stages and on the approximate ages at which they predominate. In both studies stage 2 reasoning dominates at age 10, and stage 3 reasoning is most common at about age 16.

Sequence of Stages

The evidence also seems fairly strong that the stages follow one another in the sequence Kohlberg proposed. There have been a number of long-term longitudinal studies of teenagers and young adults, in the United States (Colby et al., 1983), in Israel (Snarey, Reimer, & Kohlberg, 1985), and in Turkey. In each study the changes in subjects' reasoning nearly always occurred in the hypothesized order. Subjects did not skip stages, and only about 5 to 7 percent of the time was there any indication of regression (movement down the sequence rather than up). Similarly, when Walker retested the subjects in his study two years later, he found only 6 percent had moved down, mostly only half a stage, while 22 percent had moved up, and none had skipped a stage (Walker, 1989). Such a rate of regression is about what you would expect to find, given the fact that the measurements of stage reasoning are not perfect. On the whole, I agree with James Rest (1983) that the evidence is "fairly compelling" that moral judgment changes over time, in the sequence Kohlberg describes.

Universality of Stages of Moral Reasoning

Might this sequence of stages be only a phenomenon of Western culture? Or has Kohlberg uncovered a genuinely universal process? Thus far, variations of Kohlberg's dilemmas have been presented to children or adults in 27 different cultural areas, including both Western and non-Western, industrialized and nonindustrialized (Snarey, 1985).

John Snarey, who has reviewed and analyzed these many studies, notes several things in support of Kohlberg's position: (1) In studies of children, an increase with age in the stage of reasoning used is found consistently in every culture; (2) The

Table 14.3

Percentage of Children and Parents Who Show Moral Reasoning at Each of Kohlberg's Stages

Age	Stage 1	1–2	2	2–3	3	3–4	4	4–5	5
6 (1st grade)	10	70	15	5	—	—	—	—	—
9 (4th grade)	—	25	40	35	—	—	—	—	—
12 (7th grade)	—	—	15	60	25	—	—	—	—
15 (10th grade)	—	—	—	40	55	5	—	—	—
Parents	—	—	—	1	15	70	11	3	—

Source: L. Walker et al., 1987, Table 1, p. 849.

few longitudinal studies report "strikingly similar findings" (1985, p. 215), with subjects moving upward in the stage sequence with few reversals; (3) Cultures differ in the highest level of reasoning observed. In complex urban societies (both Western and non-Western), stage 5 is typically the highest stage observed, while in those cultures Snarey calls "folk" societies, stage 4 is typically the highest. Collectively, this evidence seems to provide quite strong support for the universality of Kohlberg's stage sequence.

Moral Judgment and Moral Behavior

A final issue often raised about Kohlberg's theory has to do with the link between children's or adults' moral reasoning and their moral behavior. Kohlberg never said that there should be a one-to-one correspondence between the two. Reasoning at stage 4 (conventional reasoning) does not mean that you will never cheat or that you will always be kind to your mother. Still, the form of reasoning a young person typically applies to moral problems should have at least *some* connection with real-life choices or behavior.

One such connection proposed by Kohlberg is that the higher the level of reasoning a young person shows, the stronger the link to behavior ought to become. Thus young people reasoning at stage 4 or stage 5 should be more likely to follow their own rules or reasoning than should children reasoning at lower levels.

[?] *Critical Thinking*

Do you think that a person's stage or level of moral reasoning has any impact on political behavior, such as on whether or not a person votes, or on liberal/conservative party or independent preferences? Can you generate a hypothesis about such a link and figure out how you might test it?

For example, Kohlberg and Candee (1984) studied students involved in the early "Free Speech" movement at Berkeley in the late 1960s (a precursor to the Vietnam War protests). They interviewed and tested the moral judgment levels of a group that had participated at a sit-in in the university administration building plus a group randomly chosen from the campus population. Of those who thought it was morally right to sit in, nearly three-quarters of those reasoning at stages 4 or 5 actually did so, compared with only about a quarter of those reasoning at stage 3. Thus the higher the stage of reasoning, the more consistent the behavior was with the reasoning.

In different research Kohlberg and others approached the question simply by asking whether a link exists between stage of moral reasoning and the probability of making some "moral choice," such as not cheating. In one study Kohlberg (1975) found that only 15 percent of students reasoning at the principled level (stage 5) cheated when they were given an opportunity, while 55 percent of conventional-level and 70 percent of preconventional students cheated.

A similar argument lies behind studies in which the moral reasoning of delinquents, or highly aggressive younger children, is compared with that of nondelinquent peers. The repeated finding is that delinquents (male or female) have lower levels of moral reasoning than do nondelinquents, even when the two groups are carefully matched for levels of education, social class, and IQ scores (Smetana, 1990). In one recent study, for example, Virginia Gregg and her colleagues (Gregg, Gibbs, & Basinger, 1994) found that only 20 percent of a group of incarcerated male and female delinquents were reasoning at stage 3 or higher, while 59 percent of a carefully matched comparison group of nondelinquents were reasoning at this stage. Like younger children who act out more in school, delinquents are most likely to use highly hedonistic reasoning, scored at Kohlberg's stage 2 (Richards, Bear, Stewart, & Norman, 1992).

However, despite this abundant evidence for a link between moral reasoning and behavior, no one has found the correspondence to be perfect. After all, in Kohlberg's studies, 15 percent of the principled moral reasoners did cheat, and a quarter of stage 4 and stage 5 reasoners who thought it morally right to participate in a sit-in did not do so. As Kohlberg says, "One can reason in terms of principles and not live up to those principles" (1975, p. 672).

Besides level of reasoning, what else might matter? We don't have all the answers to that question yet, but some influences are clear (summarized in Table 14.4). First, simple habits are involved. Every day each of us faces small moral situations that we have learned to handle in a completely automatic way. Sometimes these automatic choices may be at a lower level of reasoning than we would use if we sat down and thought about it. For example, I may make the same donation to a particular charity every year without stopping to consider whether I could now afford more or whether that particular charity is really the place where my money could best be used.

Second, in any given situation, even though you might think it morally right to take some action, you may not see that action as morally *necessary* or obligatory. I might be able to make a good argument for the moral acceptability of a sit-in protest but still not see it as my *own* duty or responsibility to participate.

Third, the cost to the person of doing something helpful (or refraining from doing something morally "wrong," like cheating) may be an important factor. If helping someone else has little cost in time, money, or effort, then most children, teenagers, and adults will help, regardless of their overall level of social-cognitive reasoning. It is when there is some cost—in time, money, energy, or whatever—that we find a more consistent correlation between level of reasoning and behavior. This suggests the more general principle that moral reasoning becomes a factor in moral behavior only when something about the situation heightens the sense of moral conflict, such as when a cost is involved or when the individual feels personally responsible.

Table 14.4

Some Factors That Affect a Person's Moral Behavior

- Level of moral reasoning.
- Habits; we all tend to repeat old patterns without further reflection, even if our level of moral reasoning has changed.
- The degree to which the person feels personally responsible in a given situation.
- The personal cost involved; the higher the cost, the more closely the moral behavior matches the individual's level of moral reasoning.
- Presence of competing influences, such as peer pressure or motives for self-protection.

Most teenagers or adults will readily show helpful behavior like this if little personal cost is attached. But if the cost of helping goes up—as when you're in a hurry to get somewhere else—then those with higher levels of moral reasoning are more likely to help.

Fourth and finally, competing motives or ethics are often at work as well, such as pressure from a peer group or motives for self-protection or self-reward. Gerson and Damon found this very clearly in an early study in which they asked groups of four children to divide up ten candy bars (1978). The candy was a reward for work the children had done on a project on which some of the group members had worked harder than others. When asked separately about how the candy bars ought to be divided, children usually argued for various kinds of fair arrangements, such as a model in which the child who worked the hardest should get the most. Yet, faced with the actual distribution of the candy bars, some children gave themselves the most; others went along with a group consensus and divided the candy equally. We might expect that in early adolescence, when the impact of the peer group is particularly strong, this group effect on moral actions might be especially strong as well.

Thus moral *behavior* results from a complex of influences, of which the level of moral reasoning is only one element. Our knowledge about these links is improving, but we very much need to know more, both about group pressure and about all the other factors that lead each of us to behave in ways that are less thoughtful, considerate, or fair than we "know how" to do. Kohlberg's own fascination with this set of questions, and with the question of how one raises a person's level of moral reasoning, led him and his colleagues to a series of bold attempts to apply the theory to schooling. I've explored some of this research in the *Research Report* box on the facing page.

Moral Development: A Critique

Kohlberg's theory about the development of moral reasoning has been one of the most provocative theories in developmental psychology. There have been over 1000 studies exploring or testing aspects of the theory, and several competing theories have been proposed. What is remarkable is how well the theory has stood the test of this barrage of research and commentary. There does appear to be a clear set of stages in the development of moral reasoning, and these stages seem to be universal.

Still, the theory has not emerged unscathed. Some psychologists are less impressed than

Snarey with the data on universality (Shweder, Mahapatra, & Miller, 1987). Also troubling is the fact that so few teenagers or adults seem to reason at the postconventional level (stage 5 or 6). Shweder points out that the effective range of variation is really only from stage 2 to stage 4, which is not nearly so interesting or impressive as is the full range of stages.

Even more vocal critics have been those who argue that Kohlberg is really not talking about all aspects of "moral reasoning." Instead, as Kohlberg himself acknowledged in his later writings (Kohlberg et al., 1983), he is talking about the development of reasoning about *justice and fairness*. We might also want to know about other ethical bases than justice, such as an ethic based on concern for others or for relationships. In this category, the best-known critic has been Carol Gilligan.

Gilligan's Ethic of Caring. Carol Gilligan (Gilligan, 1982; Gilligan & Wiggins, 1987) is fundamentally dissatisfied with Kohlberg's focus on justice and fairness as the defining features of moral reasoning. Gilligan argues that there are at least two distinct "moral orientations": namely, justice and care. Each has its own central injunction: not to treat others unfairly (justice) and not to turn away from someone in need (caring). Boys and girls learn both of these injunctions, but Gilligan has hypothesized that girls are more likely to operate from an orientation of caring or connection, while boys are more likely to operate from an orientation of justice or fairness. Because of these differences, she argues, they tend to perceive moral dilemmas quite differently.

Given the emerging evidence on sex differences in styles of interaction and in friendship patterns, which I have talked about in earlier chapters, Gilligan's hypothesis makes some sense. Perhaps girls, focused more on intimacy in their relationships, judge moral dilemmas by different criteria. In fact, though, research on moral dilemmas has not shown that boys are more likely to use justice reasoning or that girls more often use care reasoning. Several studies of adults do show such a pattern (e.g., Lollis, Ross, & Leroux, 1996; Lyons, 1983), but studies of children, adolescents, or college students generally have not (Jadack, Hyde, Moore, & Keller, 1995; Smetana, Killen, & Turiel, 1991; L. Walker et al., 1987).

Research Report

Application of Kohlberg's Theory to Education

A lot of what I have said about Kohlberg's theory may seem fairly abstract to you. In Kohlberg's own view, though, there were many potential practical implications for education. The question that interested him was whether children or young people can be taught higher stages of moral reasoning, and if so, whether such a change in moral reasoning would change their behavior in school.

We know from early research by Elliot Turiel (1966) that, at least under some conditions, exposing young people to moral arguments one step above their own level of reasoning can lead to an increase in their level of moral judgment. Young people who attend college also continue to show increases in moral stage scores, while those who quit school after high school typically show no further increase (Rest & Thoma, 1985). Because arguments about moral and philosophical issues in class and over coffee (or a few beers) in the wee small hours of the night are one of the hallmarks of the college experience for many young people, perhaps it is the discussion—the exposure to other people's ideas, other people's logic—that makes a difference.

If that's true, what would happen if high school students were given systematic opportunities to explore moral dilemmas; would that change them too? Apparently it can.

One educational application has involved the creation of special discussion classes in which moral dilemmas similar to those Kohlberg devised are presented and argued. In the process, the teacher attempts to model higher levels of reasoning. Other programs are broader based, involving not just discussion, but also cross-age teaching (to encourage nurturance and caring), empathy training, cooperation games, volunteer service work, and the like. The dozens of studies on the effectiveness of programs of this kind show that, on average, the programs succeed in shifting young people's moral reasoning upward about a half a stage (Schaefli, Rest, & Thoma, 1985). The largest effects are generally found in programs focusing exclusively on discussions of moral dilemmas, but broader-based programs also work. Courses lasting longer than three or four weeks seem to work better than very short programs, and the effects are generally larger with older students—college students and even post–college age adults. Among high school students, there is some impact, but it is not as large.

An even broader-based educational application, designed to change students' moral behavior as much as their moral reasoning, has been the development of the so-called just community. These experimental schools, typically set up as a "school within a school," operate as a kind of laboratory for moral education (Higgins, 1991; Higgins, Power, & Kohlberg, 1984; Kohlberg & Higgins, 1987; Power & Reimer, 1978).

Kohlberg insisted that the crucial feature of these just communities must be complete democracy: Each teacher and student has one vote, and community issues and problems have to be discussed in open forum. Rules are typically created and discussed at weekly community-wide meetings. In this way, students become *responsible* for the rules and for one another.

In the experimental schools following this model, Kohlberg and his coworkers found that as the students' level of Kohlbergian moral reasoning shifted upward, so did their reasoning about responsibility and caring. The link between moral reasoning and moral behavior was strengthened as well. For example, stealing and other petty crime virtually disappeared in one school after the students had repeatedly discussed the problem and arrived—painfully—at a solution that emphasized the fact that stealing damaged the whole community, and thus the whole community had to be responsible. For example, after one stealing episode the group agreed that if the stolen money had not been returned (anonymously) by a specified date, each community member would be assessed 15 cents to make up the victim's loss (Higgins, 1991).

This effect of just communities makes sense when you think about the factors that seem to affect moral behavior. In these schools two elements were added that would tend to support more moral behavior: a sense of personal responsibility and a group norm of higher moral reasoning and caring.

Among teenagers, the emotional impact of group pressure may be especially significant, in addition to whatever effect there may be from exposure to more mature arguments. If you are arguing your position about some moral dilemma, but find yourself in the minority, the "social disequilibrium" you feel may help to make you more open to other arguments, and thus to change your view. Certainly in experimental schools like those studied by Kohlberg, this added emotional impact is no doubt part of the process (Haan, 1985).

Classes in moral education have not proven to be the "quick fix" that many educators hoped for. The gains in moral reasoning are not huge, and they may not be reflected in increases in moral behavior in the school unless there is an effort to alter the overall moral atmosphere of the entire school. Yet these programs do show that there are provocative and helpful applications of at least some of the abstract developmental theories.

Gilligan argues that these girls are much more likely to be using an "ethic of caring" than an "ethic of justice" as a basis for their moral judgments. This *may* be true among adult women; it appears not to be true among children or adolescents.

For example, Lawrence Walker (L. Walker et al., 1987) scored children's answers to moral dilemmas, using both Kohlberg's fairness scheme and Gilligan's criteria for a care orientation. He found no sex difference for either hypothetical dilemmas like the Heinz dilemma or the real-life dilemmas suggested by the children themselves. Only among adults did Walker find a difference, in the direction that Gilligan would expect.

[?] Critical Thinking

Suppose Gilligan were right that adult women typically reason with an ethic of care, while adult men reason with an ethic of justice. What do you think would be the implications of such a difference—for male/female relationships, for men and women as political leaders, or in other ways?

Gilligan's arguments have often been quoted in the popular press as if they were already proven, when in fact the empirical base is really quite weak. Gilligan herself has done no systematic studies of children's (or adults') care reasoning. Yet despite these weaknesses, I am not ready to discard all her underlying points, primarily because the questions she is asking seem to me to fit so well with the newer research on sex differences in styles of relationships. The fact that we typically find no differences between boys and girls in their tendencies to use care versus justice orientations does not mean that there are no differences in the assumptions males and females bring to relationships or to moral judgments. This seems to me to be clearly an area in which we need to learn a great deal more.

Moral Reasoning and Cognitive Development

Before I leave this subject, I need to explore one other set of linkages, namely, the potential connection between the sequences of development of moral reasoning and the broader sequences of cognitive development I have been talking about throughout the book.

Kohlberg's own hypothesis was that the child first moves to a new level of logical thought, then applies this new kind of logic to relationships as well as objects, and only then applies this thinking to moral problems. More specifically, Kohlberg argued that at least some formal operations, and at least some mutual perspective taking in relationships, are necessary (but not sufficient) for the emergence of conventional moral reasoning. Full formal operations and still more abstract social understanding may be required for postconventional reasoning.

The research examining such a sequential development is scant, but supports Kohlberg's hypothesis. Lawrence Walker (1980) found that among a group of fourth to seventh graders he tested on all three dimensions (concrete and formal operations, social understanding, and moral reasoning), one-half to two-thirds were reasoning at the same level across the different domains, which makes the whole thing look unexpectedly "stagelike." When a child was ahead in one progression, the sequence was always that the child developed logical thinking first, then more advanced social understanding, and then the parallel moral judgments.

This research seems to tell us that there is *some* coherence in a child's or young person's thinking or reasoning about quite different problems. Children who have not yet understood principles of conservation are not likely to understand that another person's behavior may not match his feelings. Once conservation is understood, however, the child begins to extend this principle to people and to relationships. Similarly, a young person still using concrete operations is unlikely to use postconventional moral reasoning. Still, the coherence is not automatic. The basic cognitive understanding makes advances in social and moral reasoning *possible*, but does not guarantee them. Experience in relationships, and with moral dilemmas, is necessary too.

The moral of this (if you will excuse the pun) is that just because a young person or adult shows signs of formal operations, it does *not* necessarily follow that the teenager or young adult will show sensitive, empathetic, and forgiving attitudes toward friends or family. You may find it helpful to bear this in mind in your own relationships.

Schooling During the Adolescent Years

I cannot end this chapter on cognitive development in adolescence without saying a further word about the impact of school experiences. Such experiences are clearly formative in middle childhood, as you'll recall from Chapter 11. School is no less a central force in the lives of adolescents, but the effect is different for the two age groups. In middle childhood school experience is focused on learning a whole set of basic skills and specific knowledge—how to read, to do mathematics, to write. In adolescence, while additional specific knowledge is obviously conveyed in school, and while schooling may contribute to the development of formal operational thought, the school setting serves a host of other functions as well. Not only is it an arena in which teenagers can practice new social skills, it is also the setting in which society attempts to shape young people's attitudes and behaviors in order to prepare them for adult life. High schools teach driver's education, "family life" education, including sexuality, home economics, civics, and current affairs; guidance counselors help the teenager decide about college or about future job options; organized sports programs and other extracurricular activities offer opportunities for nonacademic success (or failure).

Some students are highly "engaged" in this entire process—to use Laurence Steinberg's term.

They not only enjoy school, they are involved in all aspects of it, participating in activities, doing their homework, learning the skills they need. Others, including many middle-class teenagers in suburban schools, are "disengaged" from schooling, particularly the academic part of the process. Steinberg argues—persuasively I think—that this quality of engagement or disengagement is a critical one for the teenager and her future. So let me say something about the two ends of the continuum: the engaged and the disengaged.

Disengaged Students

Steinberg paints quite a gloomy picture of the typical level of engagement of U.S. high school students today, based on interviews with and observations of over 20,000 teenagers and their families (Steinberg, 1996). A high proportion don't take school or their studies seriously; outside of class, they don't often participate in activities that reinforce what they are learning in school (such as doing their homework); the peer culture denigrates academic success and scorns students who try to do well in school. Some of the specifics that support these conclusions are summarized in Table 14.5 (p. 472).

Furthermore, the majority of U.S. parents today are just as disengaged from their children's schooling as their teenagers are. In Steinberg's study, more than half the high school students said they could bring home grades of C or worse without their parents getting upset; a third said their parents don't know what they are studying at school; only about a fifth of parents consistently attend school programs. Given what I said in Chapter 11 about the importance of parent involvement as a factor in children's school achievement, this pervasive disinterest by parents of teenagers is a particularly disturbing finding.

Steinberg takes the position that such widespread disengagement by U.S. teenagers is not primarily a reflection of a failure of the schools to be interesting or well run, but is instead a reflection of more general patterns in our culture and in family interactions. One key factor, for example, is the beliefs students have about the importance of school success or failure for their own future lives. Most of the teenagers in Steinberg's study agreed that doing well in school—by which they mostly meant

Source: Steinberg, 1996, from pp. 18–19.

Table 14.5

Evidence for Widespread Disengagement from Schooling Among Teenagers in Steinberg's Study

- Over one-third of students said they get through the school day mostly by "goofing off with their friends."
- Two-thirds of the students said they cheated on a school test in the past year; nine of ten said they had copied homework from someone else.
- The average U.S. high school student spends only about four hours per week on homework, compared with four hours per *day* among students in other industrialized countries.
- One-half the students in Steinberg's sample said they did not do the homework they were assigned.
- Two-thirds of U.S. high school students hold down paying jobs; one-half work 15 or more hours per week.
- Only about twenty percent of students in Steinberg's study say their friends think it is important to get good grades in school.
- Nearly twenty percent of students in the sample say they do not try as hard as they can in school because they are afraid about what their friends might think.

completing high school—would bring long-term benefits. At the same time, a great many did not draw the parallel conclusion that doing *poorly* (getting bad grades) would hurt their chances later.

An interesting ethnic group difference exists on this point. Asian-American students, who as a group are more strongly engaged in school than any other ethnic group among U.S. teenagers, also have the strongest belief in the negative consequences of school failure. Black and Latino students, in contrast, see little in the way of bad consequences for getting bad grades—so why try very hard? These differences in belief contribute to the differences in school engagement (and thus in school achievement) we see among these various ethnic groups.

Disengaged students also come from different kinds of families. Using the category system I described in Chapter 9, Steinberg finds that youth from authoritative families are most likely to be engaged in school, while those from either permissive or authoritarian families are less engaged. One result is that teenagers from authoritative families get better school grades, as you've already seen from Figure 9.3 (p. 314). Authoritative parents are also more involved in their child's schooling than are other parents. These are the moms and dads who come to school events, confer with the child's teachers, keep track of how well the child is doing, and try to nip problems in the bud. At the other end of the continuum is a large group of parents—perhaps as many as a quarter by Steinberg's estimate—who are disengaged from the role of parent as well as from the child's school. These parents

(middle class as well as poor) don't keep track of their child's activities, don't pay much attention to the child's grades, don't supervise or insist on homework, don't attend school functions. Not surprisingly, the teenage children of these parents are highly likely to be—or to become—disengaged from school.

Parents are not the whole story. Peer group norms and values play an equally important role. Asian students, for example, are far more likely than are African-American or Latino students to have friends who value good grades and effort in school; African-American and Latino peer groups are much more likely to devalue academic effort or achievement. In these groups, parental involvement in school or emphasis on the importance of school is undermined by peer norms. To work hard, to try to achieve, is thought of as "acting white" and is thus denigrated. As Steinberg puts it, "the sad truth is that many students, and many Black students in particular, are forced to choose between doing well in school and having friends" (1996, p. 161).

This problem is not unique to African-American or Hispanic students. The dominant white teen culture in the United States today also takes as one of its central values that you should not seem to be working hard—that you should get by, but not show off in the process. To put it another way, the widespread peer norm or goal is the *appearance* of uninvolvement. Not surprisingly, many teenagers take this a step too far and become genuinely uninvolved with their schooling, with long-term negative consequences for adult life.

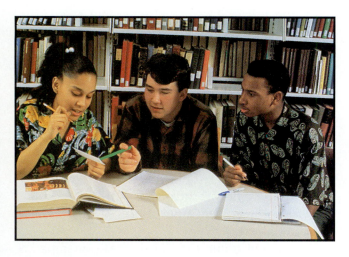

Teenagers openly studying together, as these three are doing, is a fairly rare sight in most U.S. high schools, where the dominant peer value system denigrates visible academic effort.

[?] *Critical Thinking*

Think about your own high school years. Does any of this ring true? Did you risk disapproval from some of your peers if you were diligent in your studies? How did you deal with this?

Those Who Drop Out. At the extreme end of the continuum of uninvolvement are the teenagers who actually drop out of school before completing high school. The good news is that dropping out is a rarer occurrence than you might guess. Roughly three-fourths of young adults in the United States have received a high school diploma and another 12 percent receive a General Equivalency Diploma (GED) at some later age. Thus only about 15 percent of current young adults failed to graduate from high school (McLanahan & Sandefur, 1994). Among students in the most recent high school classes, the rate is even lower. For example, among those students who entered high school in 1988, only 11 percent had failed to graduate by 1993. Hispanics have the highest dropout rates (roughly thirty percent). Until quite recently, African Americans had higher dropout rates than European Americans, but this difference has disappeared in the most recent comparisons. Today, in both groups, 86 to 87 percent of young adults have a high school diploma (Holmes, 1996). Overall, social class is a better predictor of school completion than is ethnicity. Kids growing up in poor families—especially poor families with a single par-

ent—are considerably more likely to drop out of high school than are those from more economically advantaged or intact families.

Teenagers who drop out of school list many reasons for such a decision, including not liking school, getting poor grades, being suspended, or needing to find work to support a family. For girls, additional factors are involved. They most often say that they dropped out because they planned to marry, were pregnant, or felt that school was simply not for them (National Center for Health Statistics, 1987).

Some of these same factors appear when we try to *predict* which kids will drop out. For example, in their longitudinal study of more than 500 children, Robert Cairns and Beverly Cairns (1994) found two strong predictors of subsequent dropout: whether the teenager had a history of low academic success, often including repeating a grade, and whether the child/teenager had shown a pattern of aggressive behavior. More than eighty percent of boys and about fifty percent of girls who had shown *both* characteristics in seventh grade later dropped out of school before completing high school. For girls in this study, giving birth or getting married were also strongly linked to dropping out—although it was also true that early pregnancy was more likely among girls who had a history of poor school performance or high levels of aggression. So it is unclear what is cause and what is effect here.

Robert Cairns and his colleagues (e.g., Mahoney & Cairns, 1997) have also found that among those students who were less academically skilled,

On average, we'd expect at least one of these ninth graders to drop out of school before completing high school.

those who had participated in one or more extracurricular activities in their early years of high school were less than half as likely to drop out as were those who were not involved in school activities. This finding provides further support for Steinberg's basic point about engagement and disengagement: Some kind of connection with the school, even among those who are academically less successful, can act as a counterweight to poor academic performance and help keep many young people in school long enough to graduate.

On the other side of the ledger for some adolescents is their perception that a high school diploma won't give them much extra in the job world. Some of the young men in the Cairns study, for example, were already working part-time at jobs that paid above the minimum wage and saw no rationale for staying in school when they could earn more by working full-time. Here are two voices:

> [School] was boring, I felt like I knew all I had to know. . . . I was going to go back . . . , but I figure I was making $6 an hour and nothing in school, so . . . (Chuck)

> I just hate it. I said well if I could go to school 8 hours a day, I could get me a job 8 hours a day, 5 days a week. I said I'm going to school 40 hours a week and I said I'm not getting paid for it and I said well I'm gonna go get me a job and get paid. (Amy) (Cairns & Cairns, 1994, pp. 180, 181)

Yet in the long term, teens who use such a rationale for dropping out of high school (or for cruising through high school with poor grades) are wrong. Unemployment is higher among high school dropouts than in any other education group, and dropouts who do manage to find jobs earn lower wages than do those with a high school diploma. In 1993, for example, the average income for young adults ages 25 to 34 who had not completed high school was $11,232, compared with $15,720 for those with a high school education but no more, and $28,092 for those with a college degree (U.S. Bureau of the Census, 1996). A high school diploma by itself does not provide as much benefit as it once did; a man or woman with a high school education can no longer count on finding good-paying, skilled industrial jobs, as was the case even a decade ago. A high school education, nonetheless, still offers distinct advantages. Those who drop out enter a very different—and far less optimal—life trajectory.

Engaged Students: Those Who Achieve

The other side of the coin are those engaged students who do well in school. Engaged students spend more time on homework, cut class less often, pay more attention in class, and don't cheat. They also tend to hang out with other kids who are engaged, or at least do not ridicule those who make some effort in school, and they tend to have parents who expect them to get good grades (As and Bs) and who are involved with the child and the school (Brooks-Gunn, Guo, & Furstenberg, 1993; Steinberg, 1996).

You might argue that all the relationships I've just described exist simply because brighter kids have an easier time with school work. There is some truth to that. In fact, the best single predictor of a student's academic performance in high school is his IQ score. Bright kids also have the advantage

As Steinberg uses the term, an "engaged" student, like this girl, is not just one who has the advantage of high IQ and thus finds school easy; engagement also includes an attitude of interest in school and a willingness to expend effort to do well.

Social Policy Debate

Steinberg's Suggested Solutions for Student Disengagement and Poor Achievement

If one of the major causes of the poor (and declining) achievement of U.S. high school students is a pervasive disengagement from school and schooling—as Steinberg argues—then what ought to be done about it? Here are his answers for you to think about (1996, pp. 188–193). You may not agree with all of them, but they are well worth your consideration.

1. **Refocus the discussion.** Recognize that the problem is larger than the schools; simply changing the curriculum or teaching methods will not be enough.
2. **Establish academic excellence as a national priority.** Make clear, by all possible means, that schooling is the primary activity of childhood and adolescence. It is more important than playing varsity sports; it is more important than working at a job after school; it is more important than television; it is more important than talking to friends on the phone; it is more important than surfing the Internet.
3. **Increase parental effectiveness.** Be willing to discuss openly the "high rate of parental irresponsibility in this country" (p. 189). Mount a systematic effort to educate parents about the fundamentals of good parenting. Parenting skills can be taught, through such means as school-sponsored "clinics" for parents and public service programs.
4. **Increase parental involvement in school.** "Merely asking parents to help monitor their children's homework assignments . . . is not sufficient" (p. 189). Schools need to make major efforts to draw parents

into school programs—even if this means rearranging programs to fit the schedules of working parents.
5. **Make school performance really count.** Many students get by with poor grades in school because they know they can still get into *some* college or think they can get some job. We need to find ways to make school performance matter more.
6. **Adopt a system of national standards and examinations.** Graduation from high school, or promotion from one grade to the next, should be based on meeting at least minimum national standards.
7. **Develop uniform national standards for school transcripts.** Transcripts should provide information about what a student has actually learned and what competencies she has.
8. **Eliminate remedial education at four-year colleges and universities.** A great many colleges and universities provide remedial writing and mathematics classes because their entering students do not have basic competencies. This trivializes the meaning of college admission and a college degree.
9. **Support appropriate school-sponsored extracurricular activities.** Nonacademic school activities like sports, choir, band, or the like, are still important and should be supported. Even so, students should not be devoting more time to these activities than to academic work.
10. **Limit youngsters' time in after-school jobs.** The upper limit ought to be 20 hours a week; less would be better.

of many years of successful schooling, which fosters a greater sense of self-efficacy in these intellectually more able students, in turn increasing their sense of involvement with schooling. Yet Steinberg is also right that the sense of involvement has many other ingredients, which jointly have a strong impact on a teenager's effort and success in school.

That effort and success, in turn, predicts more years of subsequent education, a link that exists among children reared in poverty as well as among the middle class (Barrett & Depinet, 1991). Those extra years of education then have a powerful effect on the career path a young person enters in early adulthood, influencing lifetime income and job

success (Featherman, 1980; Rosenbaum, 1984). These are not trivial effects, which is why Steinberg's conclusions about the typical level of school engagement among U.S. high school students today are so disturbing.

Joining the Work World

One possible contributor to the pervasive school disengagement among U.S. high school students is an increasing pattern of part-time jobs for teenagers. Certainly, teenage employment is not a new phenomenon. In earlier historical eras (and in many cultures around the world today), teenagers already fulfilled normal adult work responsibilities. They worked in the mines and in the fields, herded animals, and fished. Child labor laws changed this picture drastically in the nineteenth century in most industrialized countries. Today, adolescents are in school for many hours each day and are not generally available for full-time adult work. Yet increasingly, adolescents have jobs. In the United States, teenage employment rates have risen steadily since the 1950s. Today, roughly three-fifths of all high school juniors have some kind of formal part-time job during at least part of the school year, and the great majority of students have had at least some work experience before they graduate (Bachman & Schulenberg, 1993).

For some, such work is an economic necessity. Others work to earn money for college or to support their favorite hobbies or habits—a car, pizza with friends, or whatever. Parents are frequently very supportive of such work on the grounds that it "builds character" and teaches young people about "real life." Here's one parental voice:

> Let's face it . . . some time in life, someone is going to tell you what to do. . . . I think work is the only place to learn to deal with it. . . . Parents can give you a little discipline, but it isn't accepted. . . . You can't learn that in school, because there is another so-called tyrant, the teacher. But then they get . . . a boss, and you get out there and learn it. (Greenberger & Steinberg, 1986, p. 39)

Are parents right about such beneficial effects of work? Does it really teach responsibility and reliability? Maybe, but maybe not. If you look again at Table 14.5 (p. 472), you'll see that Steinberg lists teenage employment as one of the symptoms (or causes) of widespread school disengagement. From his view, the high rate of teenage employment is one aspect of our current culture that needs changing. Other investigators have come to somewhat more optimistic conclusions about the possible beneficial effects of teenage work experience. What does the evidence tell us?

The Pessimistic View. On the pessimistic side we find several major studies that suggest that the more hours adolescents work, the more *negative* the consequences. In the largest single study, Jerald Bachman and John Schulenberg (1993) accumulated information from more than 70,000 students,

seniors in the graduating classes of 1985 through 1989. Subjects were drawn each year from both private and public schools in every state in the country. Roughly four-fifths of the students worked at least a few hours per week, most of them for pay. Nearly half the boys (46.5%) and more than a third of the girls (38.4%) worked more than 20 hours per week.

Bachman and Schulenberg found that the more hours students worked, the more they used drugs (alcohol, cigarettes, marijuana, cocaine), the more aggression they showed toward peers, the more arguments they had with parents, the less sleep they got, the less often they ate breakfast, the less exercise they had, and the less satisfied they were with life. An impressive list of negatives, isn't it?

Most part-time teen jobs are low-skill and low-paying, like this one. Such jobs do not appear to build character, but rather have negative effects on school involvement and achievement.

The second major piece of pessimistic evidence comes from Steinberg's own study (Steinberg & Dornbusch, 1991; Steinberg, Fegley, & Dornbusch, 1993). Steinberg and his colleagues have employment information from 5300 of their sample of ninth to twelfth graders, data collected in 1987 and 1988. Like Bachman and Schulenberg, they find that work has a variety of negative effects on teenagers, including lower school grades and weaker commitment to school.

Figure 14.3 gives one finding from each of these studies, so you can see the size of the effects. I should note, by the way, that Steinberg and Dornbusch found essentially the same pattern of results for all the ethnic groups in their study, as well as for students from every economic level. So this is a widespread and significant effect.

At this point some of you are undoubtedly thinking that results like those in Figure 14.3 may not mean that working during the high school years *causes* bad effects. Instead, the findings might reflect self-selection: Those students who are least engaged in school, who already hang out with others who smoke or drink more, may be the same ones who choose to work more. Bachman and Schulenberg's data are consistent with such an interpretation. They find that those high school seniors who are getting the best grades, who are planning to go on to college, are least likely to work. Note, though, that this is still correlational evidence and doesn't solve the problem. Steinberg and his colleagues are able to help unravel these two factors because they have longitudinal data. They found that those who later worked 20 hours a week had indeed been less involved with or committed to school in earlier years, which illustrates the effect of self-selection. But these same students became even *more* withdrawn from school and showed not only increases in drug use and delinquency but a *decline* in self-reliance after they began working.

The Optimistic View.   A quite different answer to the question of the impact of teenage employment comes from a recent study by Jeylan Mortimer and her colleagues (Mortimer & Finch, 1996 ; Mortimer, Finch, Dennehy, Lee, & Beebe, 1995), who have followed a group of more than 1000 Minnesota students from grades 9 through 12. She found that

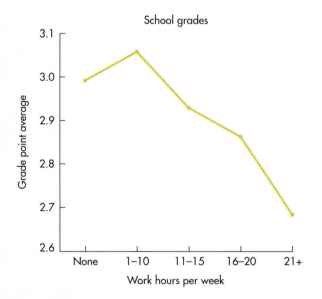

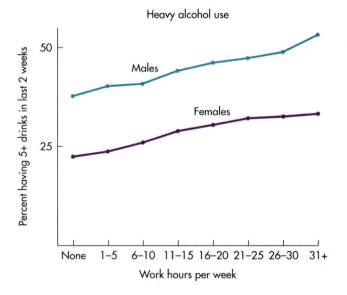

<u>Figure 14.3</u>

Evidence for the negative effect of teenage employment: The data on the left come from Steinberg and Dornbusch's study; the data on the right come from Bachman and Schulenberg. (Sources: Steinberg & Dornbusch, 1991, upper section of Figure 1, p. 308; Bachman & Schulenberg, 1993, upper right section of Figure 1, p. 226.)

over these years, teenagers worked more and more hours and their work became somewhat more complex. She also found no correlation between the number of hours students work and their school grades or risk for problem behavior—with the exception of alcohol use, which was higher among those students who work more. What mattered more than work *per se*, in this group of young people, was the quality of work they were doing. Students who had positive work experiences developed increased feelings of competence and efficacy; those students who saw themselves gaining useful skills through their work also seemed to develop that constellation of work-related values and attitudes that most adults mean when they say that work "builds character."

It is not clear how we should add up the results of these several studies. One possible resolution is suggested by Kristelle Miller (Miller & Pedersen-Randall, 1995), who finds that only work on weekdays, and *not* weekend work, has a detrimental effect on high school students' grades. This suggests the hypothesis that work is academically detrimental to the extent that it distracts young people from academic tasks. Even Mortimer's findings are consistent with this. In her study the employed eleventh and twelfth graders often said that the time on the job made it hard to get homework done and meant they often came to school tired. On the other hand, Mortimer is probably right that the quality of work is a critical ingredient in the equation. Low-skilled work that affords little opportunity for independence and little chance to learn long-term job skills is much more likely to be associated with poor outcomes than is complex, skilled work.

[?] Critical Thinking

What was your own work experience as a teenager? What lessons do you think you learned from that work, if any? In light of your own experience and the data from this study, would you want your own children to work when they are teenagers?

Collectively, these findings are a good illustration of why it is so very difficult to arrive at clear social policy recommendations. At the very least, however, this mixture of results should make parents think twice before they (we) encourage teenagers to work 15 or 20 hours a week.

Summary

1. Piaget proposed a fourth major level of cognitive development in adolescence, called formal operational thought. It is characterized by the ability to apply basic operations to ideas and possibilities as well as to actual objects.

2. Hypothetico-deductive logic and systematic problem solving are also part of formal operational thought.

3. Researchers have found clear evidence of such advanced forms of thinking in at least some adolescents. However, formal operational thinking is not universal, nor is it consistently used, even by those who possess the ability.

4. Such evidence once more calls Piaget's general model into question; it is not clear that general stages of cognitive development exist. Yet no alternative theory can explain why certain cognitive skills emerge for the first time at particular ages.

5. Theorists are also still arguing about how general, or how specific, a child's knowledge or cognitive skills are.

6. Another facet of adolescent thinking is the development of new levels of moral reasoning. Kohlberg proposes three levels of such reasoning, organized into six stages.

7. Preconventional moral reasoning includes reliance on external authority: What is punished is bad, what feels good is good.

8. Conventional morality is based on rules and norms provided by outside groups, the family, church, or society. This is the dominant form of moral reasoning among teenagers and adults.

9. Principled or postconventional morality is based on self-chosen principles. Only about fifteen percent of adults reason at this level.

10. Research evidence suggests that these levels and stages do develop in a specified order, and that they are found in this same sequence in all cultures studied so far.

11. Moral reasoning is not perfectly correlated with moral behavior. Moral behavior is also affected by habits, by the degree of responsibility the individual feels, and by the cost associated with behaving morally.

12. Kohlberg's model has been criticized on the grounds that it deals only with reasoning about justice and fairness. Gilligan suggests that people may also reason based on caring and connection, and that girls are more likely to use the latter model. Research does not support Gilligan on the latter point.

13. There appears to be some link between the emergence of formal operations logic and the development of conventional moral reasoning. The former may be necessary but not sufficient for the latter.

14. A critical feature of adolescents' school experience is their degree of engagement or disengagement with the entire schooling and learning process. In the United States today, a significant fraction of students appear to be disengaged.

15. Engaged students are more likely to come from families using authoritative child-rearing practices; in addition, their parents are more likely to be involved with the school. Engaged students are also more likely to believe that doing poorly in school will have long-term negative consequences.

16. Asian-American students are most likely to be highly engaged in school; African-American and Hispanic students are least likely to be highly engaged, with Euro-American students falling in between. The peer culture of the latter three groups includes some disparagement of visible academic effort, with an antiacademic norm clearest among African-American students.

17. Roughly fifteen percent of U.S. students fail to complete high school. Hispanics are more likely than either African Americans or European Americans to drop out. Those who have repeated a grade in school are also more likely to drop out.

18. Part-time employment by teenagers has become very common. Most—but not all—researchers find that such work is associated with lower school performance and higher rates of delinquent behavior. An exception may exist when the specific work is interesting and provides real skill training.

Key Terms

conventional morality   The second level of moral judgment proposed by Kohlberg, in which the person's judgments are dominated by considerations of group values and laws. **(p. 462)**

deductive logic   Reasoning from the general to the particular, from a rule to an expected instance, or from a

theory to a hypothesis. Characteristic of formal operational thought. **(p. 456)**

hedonistic reasoning   A form of prosocial moral reasoning described by Eisenberg in which the child is concerned with self-oriented consequences rather than moral considerations. Roughly equivalent to Kohlberg's stage 2. **(p. 464)**

hypothetico-deductive reasoning   Piaget's term for the form of reasoning that is part of formal operational thought, involving not just deductive logic but, more broadly, the ability to consider hypotheses and hypothetical possibilities. **(p. 456)**

needs-oriented reasoning   A form of prosocial moral reasoning proposed by Eisenberg in which the child expresses concern directly for the other person's need, even if the other's need conflicts with the child's own wishes or desires. **(p. 464)**

preconventional morality   The first level of morality proposed by Kohlberg, in which moral judgments are dominated by consideration of what will be punished and what feels good. **(p. 461)**

postconventional morality   See *principled morality*.

principled morality   The third level of morality proposed by Kohlberg, in which considerations of justice, individual rights, and contracts dominate moral judgment. **(p. 462)**

Suggested Readings

Kurtines, W. M., & Gewirtz, J. L. (Eds.). (1991). *Handbook of moral behavior and development*. (Vols. 1–3). Hillsdale, NJ: Erlbaum. This massive three-volume work was prepared as a commemoration of the work of Lawrence Kohlberg. Volume 1 deals with theory, volume 2 with research, and volume 3 with application. If this area intrigues you, there is no more complete source.

Steinberg, L. (1996). *Beyond the classroom. Why school reform has failed and what parents need to do*. New York: Simon & Schuster. Steinberg is one of my favorite researchers and authors—as I'm sure you have gathered after reading this chapter! This excellent book is basically an account of the major study by Steinberg and Dornbusch, written for a lay audience. It is highly readable, and Steinberg does not hesitate to talk about the practical educational and societal applications of his findings. "Must" reading for any of you who plan to be teachers; highly recommended for parents or would-be parents.

CHAPTER 15

Social and Personality Development in Adolescence

Preview Questions

1 *Do all adolescents go through some kind of identity crisis?*

2 *How do friendships change in adolescence?*

3 *Do teenagers become emotionally detached from their parents as the importance of the peer group grows?*

4 *Does the peer group really lure teenagers into bad behavior?*

5 *Why are more teenage girls than boys depressed?*

Chapter Outline

In my own memories of adolescence, the physical changes loom large. Certainly the fact that I grew 6 inches the year I was 12, towering over absolutely everyone, was a highly important event. I recall very vividly that I had little notion how long my arms and legs were during this period, and regularly hit people as I was making grand gestures; I recall my mother's despair at keeping me in clothes that fit; I know that this experience colored all my relationships and deeply affected my self-concept.

Significant as these physical changes were, my memories of those years are equally colored by another set of adolescent tasks: gaining some independence from my family, figuring out who I was and what I could or should do with my life, discovering some of the mysteries of relationships with that other species, *boys*. It is these tasks of independence, identity, and relationship that are the central story of this chapter.

Understanding the Self and Relationships

Let me begin, as I did in Chapter 12, by looking at the cognitive aspect of these tasks. How does the child's understanding of himself and his relationships change at adolescence?

Teenagers like these face a whole new set of social and emotional tasks: to become independent, to figure out who they are, and to take steps toward developing an enduring relationship with a sexual partner/spouse.

The Self-Concept

Through the elementary school years, the child's self-concept becomes less and less tied to outer qualities, more and more focused on enduring internal characteristics. This trend continues in adolescence, with self-definitions becoming more and more abstract. You may remember the replies of a 9-year-old and an 11-year-old to the question, "Who am I?" in Montemayor and Eisen's study, quoted in Chapter 12 (pp. 390–391). Here's a 17-year-old's answer to the same question:

> I am a human being. I am a girl, I am an individual. I don't know who I am. I am a Pisces. I am a moody person. I am an indecisive person. I am an ambitious person. I am a very curious person. I am not an individual. I am a loner. I am an American (God help me). I am a Democrat. I am a liberal person. I am a radical. I am a conservative. I am a pseudoliberal. I am an atheist. I am not a classifiable person (i.e., I don't want to be). (Montemayor & Eisen, 1977, p. 318)

Clearly, this girl's self-concept is even less tied to her physical characteristics or to her abilities than are those of the younger children. She is describing abstract traits or ideology.

You can see the change very graphically in Figure 15.1 based on the answers of all 262 subjects in the Montemayor and Eisen study. Each of the subjects' answers to the "Who am I?" question was placed in one or more specific categories, such as references to physical properties ("I am tall," "I have blue eyes") or references to ideology ("I am a Democrat," "I believe in God," etc.). As you can see, appearance is a salient dimension in the preteen and early teen years but becomes less dominant in late adolescence, at a time when ideology and belief become more salient. By late adolescence, most teenagers think of themselves in terms of enduring traits, beliefs, personal philosophy, and moral standards (Damon & Hart, 1988).

At the same time, the adolescent's self-concept becomes more differentiated, as the teenager comes to see herself somewhat differently in each of several roles: as a student, with friends, with parents, and in romantic relationships (Harter & Monsour, 1992). Self-concepts also become more flexible in the sense that categories are held less

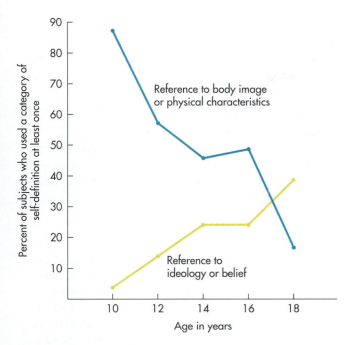

Figure 15.1

As they get older, children and adolescents define themselves less and less by what they look like and more and more by what they believe or feel. (Source: Montemayor & Eisen, 1977, from Table 1, p. 316.)

rigidly. One example of this is the greater flexibility adolescents show in their views about what is acceptable behavior for people of their gender.

Sex Role Concepts in Adolescence. Seven- and 8-year-olds appear to treat gender categories as if they were fixed rules. By adolescence they understand that these are social conventions, and sex-role concepts become more flexible (Katz & Ksansnak, 1994). Teenagers have largely abandoned the automatic assumption that whatever their own gender does is better or preferable (Powlishta, Serbin, Doyle, & White, 1994). Indeed, a significant minority of teenagers and youths begin to define themselves as having both masculine and feminine traits.

In the early days of research on masculinity and femininity, psychologists conceived of these two qualities as opposite ends of a single continuum. A person could be masculine *or* feminine, but could not be both. Research by Sandra Bem (1974) and Janet Spence and Robert Helmreich (1978), however, makes it clear that masculinity and femininity

should be thought of as independent dimensions or aspects. A person can be high or low on either or both. Indeed, if we categorize people as high or low on each of these two dimensions, based on each individual's self-description, we end up with four basic sex-role types, called **masculine, feminine, androgynous,** and **undifferentiated.** The masculine and feminine types are the traditional combinations, in which a person sees himself or herself as high in one quality and low in the other. A masculine teenager or adult, by this conceptualization, is therefore one who perceives himself (or herself) as having many traditional masculine qualities and few traditional feminine qualities. A feminine teenager or adult shows the reverse pattern. In contrast, androgynous individuals see themselves as having *both* masculine and feminine traits; undifferentiated individuals describe themselves as lacking both.

[?] Critical Thinking

Make yourself a 2 by 2 grid to show these four types: masculine, feminine, androgynous, and undifferentiated. Why does this conceptualization of masculinity and femininity radically alter the way we think about these qualities, compared with a conceptualization of the two qualities as opposite ends of the same continuum?

Between 25 and 35 percent of U.S. high school students define themselves as androgynous (e.g., Lamke, 1982; Rose & Montemayor, 1994). More girls than boys seem to show this pattern, and more girls place themselves in the masculine category than boys do in the feminine group.

More striking is the finding that either an androgynous or a masculine sex role self-concept is associated with higher self-esteem among *both* boys and girls (Burnett, Anderson, & Heppner, 1995; Rose & Montemayor, 1994). This finding makes sense if we assume the existence of a kind of "masculine bias" in American and other Western societies, such that traditionally masculine qualities like independence and competitiveness are more valued by both men and women than are many traditionally female qualities. If such a bias exists—and there is good reason to think it does— then the teenage boy's task is simpler than the

Psychology in Action

Who Am I?

Warning: This project, like many of the *Psychology in Action* suggestions given in this text, should not be undertaken without explicit permission and guidance from your instructor, who will have to obtain permission from your college or university's Human Subjects Review Committee for any project in which you interview or observe a child or parent directly. **Do not do this project on your own, without such permission.**

The purpose of this project is to replicate, on a small scale, the research by Montemayor and Eisen (1977), some of whose results appear in Figure 15.1 (p. 483). For the project you will need to find three or four teenagers, preferably one or two who are in early adolescence (12 to 14 years) and several who are near the end of high school (16 to 18 years). Obtain the appropriate informed consent from each of these youngsters, following whatever procedure your instructor specifies.

Procedure

For each subject, prepare a sheet of paper with 20 numbered spaces on it. At the top, write the instructions:

In the spaces below, write 20 different answers to the question, "Who am I?"

Each subject should be interviewed/tested alone. Hand the teenager the sheet, and ask him to fill out all 20 blanks, in each space giving one answer to the "Who am I?" question.

Analysis and Report

Analyze the answers your several subjects give, using the categories shown in Figure 15.1 (physical appearance and ideology) or any other categories you may identify. Do your subjects' answers match the pattern Montemayor and Eisen report? Are there any differences in the responses given by your younger and older subjects?

Reference

Montemayor, R., & Eisen, M. (1977). The development of self-conceptions from childhood to adolescence. *Developmental Psychology, 13,* 314–319.

---

teenage girl's. He can achieve high self-esteem and success with his peers by adopting a traditional masculine sex role, while a girl who adopts a traditional gender role is adopting a less-valued role, with attendant risks of lower self-esteem and a reduced sense of competence (Massad, 1981; Rose & Montemayor, 1994).

Findings like these suggest the possibility that while the creation of rigid rules or schemas for sex roles is a normal—even essential—process in young children, a blurring of those rules may be an important process in adolescence, particularly for girls, for whom a more masculine or androgynous self-concept is associated with more positive outcomes.

Identity in Adolescence

A somewhat different way to look at adolescent self-concept is through the lens of Erikson's theory. In this model the central task or dilemma of adolescence is that of *identity versus role confusion.*

Erikson argued that the child's early sense of identity comes partly unglued in early adolescence because of the combination of rapid body growth and the sexual changes of puberty. He referred to this period as one in which the adoles-

Teenage boys like these may have an easier time than do girls in achieving high self-esteem because both boys and girls seem to place a higher value on certain traditionally "masculine" qualities than on traditionally "feminine" qualities.

cent mind is in a kind of *moratorium* between childhood and adulthood. The old identity will no longer suffice; a new identity must be forged, one that must serve to place the young person among the myriad roles of adult life—occupational roles, sexual roles, religious roles. Confusion about all these role choices is inevitable. Erikson put it this way:

> In general it is primarily the inability to settle on an occupational identity which disturbs young people. To keep themselves together they temporarily overidentify, to the point of apparent complete loss of identity, with the heroes of cliques and crowds. . . . They become remarkably clannish, intolerant, and cruel in their exclusion of others who are "different," in skin color or cultural background . . . and often in entirely petty aspects of dress and gesture arbitrarily selected as *the* signs of an in-grouper or out-grouper. It is important to understand . . . such intolerance as the necessary *defense against a sense of identity confusion*, which is unavoidable at [this] time of life. (1980a, pp. 97–98)

The teenage clique or group thus forms a base of security from which the young person can move toward a unique solution of the identity process. Ultimately, each teenager must achieve an integrated view of himself, including his own pattern of beliefs, occupational goals, and relationships.

Nearly all the current work on the formation of adolescent identity has been based on James Marcia's descriptions of **identity statuses** (Marcia, 1966; 1980), which are rooted in, but go beyond, Erikson's general conceptions of the adolescent identity process. Following one of Erikson's ideas, Marcia argues that adolescent identity formation has two key parts: a *crisis* and a *commitment*. By a "crisis" Marcia means a period of decision making when old values and old choices are reexamined. This may occur as a sort of upheaval—the classic notion of a crisis—or it may occur gradually. The outcome of the reevaluation is a commitment to some specific role, some particular ideology.

If you put these two elements together, as in Figure 15.2, you can see that four different "identity statuses" are possible.

- **Identity achievement:** The person has been through a crisis and reached a commitment to ideological or occupational goals.

Figure 15.2

The four identity statuses proposed by Marcia, based on Erikson's theory. For a fully achieved identity, the young person must both have reexamined his or her values or goals and have reached a firm commitment. (Source: Marcia, 1980.)

- **Moratorium:** A crisis is in progress, but no commitment has yet been made.
- **Foreclosure:** A commitment has been made without having gone through a crisis. No reassessment of old positions has been made. Instead, the young person has simply accepted a parentally or culturally defined commitment.
- **Identity diffusion:** The young person is not in the midst of a crisis (although there may have been one in the past), and no commitment has been made. Diffusion may thus represent either an early stage in the process (before a crisis) or a failure to reach a commitment after a crisis.

Erikson's theory and Marcia's model assume that some kind of identity crisis is both normal and healthy. These assumptions have not always been supported by the evidence. For one thing, the whole process of identity formation may occur later than Erikson thought, when it occurs at all. In one combined analysis of eight separate cross-sectional studies, Alan Waterman (1985) found that the identity achievement status occurred most often in college, not during the high school years. Among these subjects, the moratorium status was relatively uncommon, except in the early years of college. So, if most young people are going through an identity crisis, the crisis is occurring fairly late in adolescence and not lasting terribly long. What's more, about a third of the young people at every age were in the foreclosure status, which may indicate that many young people simply do not go through a crisis at all, but follow well-defined grooves.

As a further caveat, I should point out that all the subjects in the studies Waterman analyzed were either in college or in college-preparatory high school programs. This may give a false impression of the process of identity formation for young people who do not go to college, who do not have the luxury of a long period of questioning but must work out some kind of personal identity while still in their teens.

The whole conception of an adolescent identity crisis has also been strongly influenced by current cultural assumptions in Western societies, in which full adult status is postponed for almost a decade after puberty. In these cultures young people do not normally or necessarily adopt the same roles or occupations as their parents. Indeed, they are encouraged to choose for themselves. In such a cultural system adolescents are faced with what may be a bewildering array of options, a pattern that might well foster the sort of identity crisis Erikson described. In less-industrialized cultures, especially those with clear initiation rites of the type I described in Chapter 13, there may well be a shift in identity from that of child to that of adult, but without a crisis of any kind. Some anthropologists, in fact, refer to such cultures as *foreclosed*, in the sense that adolescent identity alternatives are distinctly limited (Coté, 1996).

For all these reasons, both Marcia and Waterman would now agree that the various identity statuses do not form a clear developmental pathway followed by all or most teenagers and young adults, even in Western cultures. Teens do not routinely move from foreclosure through moratorium to a clear identity status. Instead, the four types may more reasonably be thought of as different approaches young people may take to the task of identity formation, depending on culture as well as on the young person's individual situation (Marcia, 1993; Waterman, 1988). In this view, it is not correct to say that a young person in the foreclosure status has not achieved any identity. She *has* an identity, but one that is adopted from parental or other societal rules, without serious questioning.

Therefore, the *developmental* aspect of the Erikson/Marcia model may not be correct. Interestingly, however, the second half of the model—the notion that an identity crisis and its resolution is a psychologically healthy process—is confirmed by a whole variety of research. In Western cultures, at least, young people who have made a commitment to some identity (that is, those who are classed in either identity achievement or foreclosure statuses) have higher self-esteem, lower levels of depression, and are more goal directed. Identity achievers, more than those in any of the other statuses, are also more likely to be using formal operations reasoning, to be using moral reasoning at higher stages in Kohlberg's system, and to have greater capacity for intimacy in their personal relationships. In this last area, those in a foreclosure status tend to be more stereotyped in their approach to relationships, while those in identity diffusion have the most difficulties with intimacy (Waterman, 1992). All this evidence suggests that while a variety of roads may lead to some kind of personal identity, not all roads are psychologically equivalent. What Marcia calls the identity achievement status is linked with more mature and emotionally healthy behavior in a variety of other domains.

Ethnic Identity

Minority teenagers, especially those of color in a predominantly white culture, face another task in creating an identity in adolescence: They must develop an ethnic or racial identity, including self-identification as a member of some specific group, commitment to that group and its values and attitudes, and some positive (or negative) attitudes about the group to which they belong. Some of this self-identification occurs in middle childhood, as I pointed out in Chapter 9. Seven- and 8-year-old minority children not only understand the differences between themselves and majority children, they typically prefer their own subgroup.

Further steps in the ethnic identity process occur in adolescence. Jean Phinney (Phinney, 1990; Phinney & Rosenthal, 1992) has proposed three rough stages in these later years. The first stage is an "unexamined ethnic identity," equivalent to what Marcia calls a foreclosed status. For some subgroups in U.S. society, such as African Americans and Native Americans, this unexamined identity typically includes the negative images and stereotypes common in the wider culture. Indeed, it may be especially at adolescence, with the advent of the cognitive ability to reflect and interpret, that the young person becomes keenly aware of the way in which his own group is perceived by the majority. As Spencer and Dornbusch (1990) put it, "The young African-American may learn as a child that black is beautiful but conclude as an adolescent that white is powerful" (p. 131).

Many minority teenagers initially prefer the dominant white culture or wish they had been born into the majority. An African-American journalist, Sylvester Monroe, who grew up in an urban housing project, clearly describes this initial negative feeling:

> If you were black, you didn't quite measure up. . . . For a black kid there was a certain amount of self-doubt. It came at you indirectly. You didn't see any black people on television, you didn't see any black people doing certain things. . . . You don't think it out but you say, "Well, it must mean that white people are better than we are. Smarter, brighter—whatever. (Spencer & Dornbusch, 1990, pp. 131–132)

Not all minority teens arrive at such negative views of their own group. Individual youngsters may have very positive ethnic images, conveyed by parents or others around the child. Phinney's point is that this initial ethnic identity is not arrived at independently but comes from outside sources.

The second stage is the "ethnic identity search," parallel to the crisis in Marcia's analysis of ego identity. This search is typically triggered by some experience that makes ethnicity salient— perhaps an example of blatant prejudice or merely the widening experience of high school. At this point the young person begins to compare her own ethnic group with others, to try to arrive at her *own* judgments.

This exploration stage is eventually followed by a resolution of the conflicts and contradictions—analogous to Marcia's status of identity achievement. It is often a difficult process. For example, I pointed out in the last chapter that some African-American adolescents who want to try to compete in and succeed in the dominant culture can experience ostracism from their black friends,

who accuse them of "acting white" and betraying their blackness. Latinos often report similar experiences. Some resolve this by keeping their own ethnic group at arm's length; some search for a middle ground, adopting aspects of both the majority and minority cultures, a pattern Phinney calls a "blended bicultural" identity (Phinney & Devich-Navarro, 1997); others deal with it by creating essentially two identities (a pattern Phinney calls an "alternating bicultural" identity), as expressed by one young Chicano who was interviewed by Phinney:

> Being invited to someone's house, I have to change my ways of how I act at home, because of culture differences. I would have to follow what they do . . . I am used to it now, switching off between the two. It is not difficult. (Phinney & Rosenthal, 1992, p. 160)

Still others resolve the dilemma by wholeheartedly choosing their own ethnic group's patterns and values, even when that choice may limit their access to the larger culture.

In both cross-sectional and longitudinal studies, Phinney has found that African-American teens and young adults do indeed move through these steps or stages toward a clear ethnic identity. Furthermore, research shows that African-American, Asian-American, and Mexican-American teens and college students who have reached the second or third stage in this process—those who are searching for or who have reached a clear identity—have higher self-esteem and better psychological adjustment than do those who are still in the "unexamined" stage (Phinney, 1990). In contrast, among Caucasian students, ethnic identity has essentially no relationship to self-esteem or adjustment.

This stagelike model may be a decent beginning description of the process of ethnic identity formation. However, let us not lose sight of the fact that the details and the content of ethnic identity will differ markedly from one subgroup to another. Those groups who encounter more overt prejudice will have a different road to follow than will those who may be more easily assimilated; those whose own ethnic culture espouses values that are close to those of the dominant culture will have less difficulty resolving the contradictions than will those whose subculture is at greater variance with the

All adolescents must struggle with the task of forming a clear individual identity, but for minority youth, this task has added complexities because of the need to achieve some kind of ethnic identity as well.

majority. Whatever the specifics, young people of color and those from clearly defined ethnic groups have an important additional identity task in their adolescent years.

Self-Esteem

Self-esteem also shows interesting shifts during the teenage years. The overall trend is a steady rise in esteem through the years of adolescence; the average 19- or 20-year-old has a considerably more positive sense of her global self-worth than she did at age 8 or 11 (Harter, 1990; Wigfield, Eccles, MacIver, Reuman, & Midgley, 1991). At the same time, there is an interesting glitch in this pattern: At the very beginning of adolescence, self-esteem very often drops rather abruptly. In one study Edward Seidman and his colleagues followed a group of nearly 600 Latino, black, and white youngsters over the two years from sixth grade to junior high (ages 12 to 14) (Seidman, Allen, Aber, Mitchell, & Feinman, 1994). Seidman found a significant average drop in self-esteem over that period, a decline that occurred in each of the three ethnic groups. Similarly, David DuBois and his colleagues (DuBois et al., 1996), in a cross-sectional study of 1800 children in grades 5 through 8, found that eighth graders had significantly lower global self-esteem than did fifth graders.

This decline seems to be linked not so much to age as to stress and major life changes, such as changing schools at the same time as puberty (DuBois et al., 1996; Harter, 1990). Researchers have noted it especially among students—both white and black—who shift to junior high school at seventh grade (Seidman et al., 1994; Wigfield et al., 1991). When the transition process is more gradual, such as for children in a middle school that includes grades 5 through 8, we see no parallel drop in self-esteem in early adolescence.

Underlying this average pattern are, not surprisingly, wide individual variations. Some teenagers manage to maintain high self-esteem throughout adolescence; some enter adolescence with low self-esteem and remain low. Only a subset appear to show a sharp drop in self-esteem. In one recent study, for example (Zimmerman, Copeland, Shope, & Dielman, in press), about 20 percent of the 1103 students showed major declines in self-esteem over the period from grade 6 to grade 10. Such declines were equally likely among African-American and white youth, but girls were significantly more likely than boys to show such a pattern of steady decline in self-esteem. Those who showed such a decline also typically showed a drop in school grades over the same years and a greater susceptibility to peer pressure for deviant behavior. Thus the subset of teens whose self-esteem shows the largest drop in the adolescent years are also those who are vulnerable in a whole host of other ways. Just what is cause and what is effect in this cluster of problems is not yet clear; what is clear is that for these young people, adolescence is accurately described as a time of "storm and stress."

Summary of Developmental Changes in the Self-Concept

Let me combine the bits of information I have given in several chapters, and sum up this developmental progression. The infant and toddler develops first a primitive sense of her own separateness, followed quickly by an understanding of her own constancy and of herself as an actor or agent in the world. By 18 to 24 months, most children achieve self-awareness; they grasp the fact that they are also *objects* in the world. At that point children begin to define themselves in terms of their physical properties (age, size, gender) and in terms of their activities and skills. Over the period of concrete and formal operations (from age 6 through adolescence), the content of the child's self-concept becomes gradually more abstract, less and less tied to outward physical qualities, more based on the assumption of enduring inner qualities. During late adolescence, the whole self-concept also appears to undergo a kind of reorganization, with a new, future-oriented sexual, occupational, ideological, and ethnic identity created.

As a final point, I want to emphasize once again that a child's self-concept, including her level of self-esteem, appears to be a highly significant mediating concept. Once such a "theory" of the self is well established, once a global judgment of one's own self-worth is created, it reverberates throughout a child's behavior. Among other things, each child systematically chooses experiences and environments that are consistent with her beliefs about herself. A child who believes that she can't do long division will behave quite differently in the classroom from the child whose self-concept includes the idea "I am good at math." A child who believes she can't make friends makes different choices than one who sees herself as having many friends. These beliefs are pervasive, many develop early, and although they are somewhat responsive to changing circumstances (including personal stresses), they also act as self-fulfilling prophecies and thus help to shape the trajectory of the person's life throughout adulthood.

Critical Thinking

Can you think of examples of how your own self-concept affects your choices and your behavior?

Concepts of Relationships

In a parallel fashion the teenager's understanding of others and of relationships becomes more and more abstract, less and less tied to externals. For example, teenagers' descriptions of other people contain more comparisons of one trait with another or one person with another, more recognition of inconsistencies and exceptions, more shadings of gray than we hear in descriptions given by younger children (Shantz, 1983). To illustrate, here's a description by a 15-year-old:

> Andy is very modest. He is even shyer than I am when near strangers and yet is very talkative with people he knows and likes. He always seems good tempered and I have never seen him in a bad temper. He tends to degrade other people's achievements, and yet never praises his own. He does not seem to voice his opinions to anyone. He easily gets nervous. (Livesley & Bromley, 1973, p. 221)

We see similar changes in children's descriptions of friendships. By age 11 or 12, children begin to talk about *intimacy* as an important ingredient in friendship; by middle adolescence they expect a friend to be a confidant and to be supportive and trustworthy (Hartup & Stevens, 1997).

Table 15.1
Summary of Changes in the Self-Concept from Infancy Through Adolescence

Age	Self-Concept
Infant	Primitive sense of separate self; beginning sense of self-constancy and awareness of self as an actor in the world
Toddler	Awareness of self as an object with properties; defines self in terms of major categories, such as gender and size
Preschooler	Definition of self almost entirely in terms of observable properties
School age	Global sense of self-esteem develops; self-definition becomes gradually more abstract, less and less tied to externals
Adolescent	Greater focus on such internal qualities as beliefs and values; new, future-oriented sexual, occupational, ideological, and ethnic identity created

Understanding of friendship also becomes more qualified, more shaded. Damon's research (1983) suggests that in late adolescence, young people understand that even very close friendships cannot fill every need and that friendships are not static: They change, grow, or dissolve, as each member of the pair changes. A really good friendship, then, is one that *adapts* to these changes. At this age, young people say things about friendship like "trust is the ability to let go as well as to hang on" (Selman, 1980, p. 141).

In an intriguing series of interviews, Robert Selman (1980) has also studied friendships by asking children and adolescents how they settle disagreements or arguments with friends. Table 15.2 lists some of the answers given by children of various ages, illustrating the kind of progression I have been describing.

[?] *Critical Thinking*

Can you recognize your own thinking in the comments in Table 15.2? How would you describe your ways of settling arguments with your friends?

Relationships

All these cognitive changes in the teenager's understanding of herself and her relationships form an important part of the foundation of the actual relationships she creates, although the causality clearly runs both ways: Relationships affect the child's or adolescent's thinking just as much as the changes in her understanding affect her relationships. The key relationships in adolescence continue to be with parents and with peers.

Relationships with Parents

Teenagers have two apparently contradictory tasks in their relationships with their parents: to establish autonomy from the parents and to maintain their sense of relatedness with their parents. The push for autonomy shows itself in increases in conflict between parent and adolescent; the maintenance of connection is seen in the continued strong attachment of child to parent.

Increases in Conflict. The rise in conflict between parents and their teenagers has now been repeatedly documented by researchers (e.g., Flannery, Montemayor, & Eberly, 1994; Laursen, 1995; Steinberg, 1988). In the great majority of families it seems to consist of an increase in mild bickering or conflicts over everyday issues like chores or personal rights—for example, whether and when the teen should be required to do family chores, or whether the adolescent should be allowed to wear a bizarre hairstyle or black clothes held together with safety pins. Teenagers and their parents also

---

Table 15.2

Comments by Children of Various Ages About How to Solve Disagreements or Arguments Between Friends

- "Go away from her and come back later when you're not fighting." (age 5)
- "Punch her out." (age 5)
- "Around our way the guy who started it just says he's sorry." (age 8)
- "Well if you say something and don't really mean it, then you have to mean it when you take it back." (age $8\frac{1}{2}$)
- "Sometimes you got to get away for a while. Calm down a bit so you won't be so angry. Then get back and try to talk it out." (age 14)
- "If you just settle up after a fight, that is no good. You gotta really feel that you'd be happy the way things went if you were in your friend's shoes. You can just settle up with someone who is not a friend, but that's not what friendship is really about." (age $15\frac{1}{2}$)
- "Well, you could talk it out, but it usually fades itself out. It usually takes care of itself. You don't have to explain everything. You do certain things and each of you knows what it means. But if not, then talk it out." (age 16)

Source: Selman, 1980, pp. 107–113.

interrupt each other more often and become more impatient with one another.

This increase in discord is widely found, but we need to be careful not to assume that it signifies a major disruption of the quality of the parent-child relationships. Laurence Steinberg, one of the key researchers in this area, estimates that only 5 to 10 percent of families in the United States experience a substantial or pervasive deterioration in the quality of the parent-child relationship in these years of early adolescence (Steinberg, 1990). Those families at highest risk for persistently heightened conflict between parents and adolescents are those in which the parents have a history of low levels of warmth and supportiveness toward their child in earlier years as well as during adolescence (Rueter & Conger, 1995; Silverberg & Gondoli, 1996). When parents continue to express warmth and supportiveness and are open to hearing the teenager's opinions and disagreements, the period of heightened conflict seems to be relatively brief.

If the rise in conflict doesn't signify that the relationship is falling apart, what does it mean? A variety of theorists have suggested that the temporary discord, far from being a negative event, may instead be a developmentally healthy and necessary part of the adolescent's identity-formation process. In order to become his own person, the teenager needs to push away from the parents, disagree with them, try out his own limits—an **individuation** process not unlike what we see in the

Conflict between parents and children rises in the early adolescent years, apparently as part of a normal individuation process. Most families adjust to the teenager's new autonomy, and conflict then declines.

toddler who begins to say no to the parents during the famous period called the terrible twos (Grotevant & Cooper, 1985). We see the same kind of increase in conflict among primates, especially between adult males and newly adolescent males. The young males begin to make competitive gestures and may be driven off into a brief period of independent life before returning to the troop. Among humans, we have accumulating evidence that the increase in family conflict is linked with the hormonal changes of puberty rather than age, which would lend further support to the argument that this is a normal and even necessary process.

For example, Steinberg (1988) followed a group of teenagers over a 1-year period, assessing their stage of puberty and the quality of their relationship with their parents at the beginning and end of the year. He found that as the early pubertal stages began, family closeness declined, parent-child conflict rose, and the child's autonomy increased. Other researchers (e.g., Inoff-Germain, Arnold, Nottelmann et al., 1988) have taken this a step further by measuring actual hormone levels and showing links between the rise of the various hormones of puberty and the rise in aloofness toward or conflict with parents. Among girls conflict seems to rise after menarche (Holmbeck & Hill, 1991).

The pattern of causes is obviously complex. Hormonal changes may be causally linked to increases in assertiveness, perhaps especially among boys. Parents' reactions to pubertal changes may also be highly important parts of the mix. Visible pubertal changes, including menarche, change parents' expectations for the child and increase their concern about guiding and controlling the adolescent to help her avoid the shoals of too much independence.

In fact, adolescence may actually be more stressful to *parents* than to the young people themselves (Gecas & Seff, 1990). Almost two-thirds of parents perceive their children's adolescence as the most difficult stage of parenting, because of both loss of control over the adolescent and fear for the adolescent's safety.

In the midst of the increased conflict, and perhaps partially as a result of it, the overall level of the teenager's autonomy within the family increases steadily throughout the adolescent years. Parents give the youngster more and more room to make independent choices and to participate in family decision making. Steinberg argues that this "distancing" is an essential part of the adolescent development process.

Attachment to Parents. Paradoxically, despite this distancing and temporarily heightened family conflict, teenagers' underlying emotional attachment to their parents remains strong. Results from a study by Mary Levitt and her colleagues (Levitt, Guacci-Franco, & Levitt, 1993) illustrate the point.

Levitt interviewed African-American, Hispanic-American, and Anglo-American children ages 7, 10, and 14. Each child was shown a drawing with a set of concentric circles and was asked to place in the middle circle those "people who are the most close and important to you—people you love the most and who love you the most." In the next circle outward from the middle, children were asked to place the names of "people who are not quite as close but who are still important—people you really love or like, but not quite as much as the people in the first circle." A third circle contained names of somewhat more distant members of this personal "convoy." The interviewer then asked about the kind of support each listed person provided to the subject.

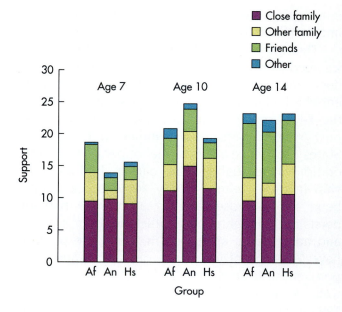

Figure 15.3

African-American (Af), Anglo-American (An), and Hispanic-American (Hs) children and teens were asked about the amount and type of support they received from various members of their "personal convoy." Note that for teens, friends become more significant sources of support, but parents do not become less important. (Source: Levitt et al., 1993, Figure 2, p. 815.)

[?] *Critical Thinking*

You might find it interesting to complete such a "personal convoy" map for your own relationships. Are your parents in the center circle? Friends? Partner?

Levitt found that for all three ethnic groups, at all three ages, parents and other close family members were by far the most likely to be placed in the inner circle. Even 14-year-olds rarely placed friends in this position. So the parents remain central. At the same time, it is clear from Levitt's results that peers become increasingly important as providers of support, as you can see in Figure 15.3, which shows the total amount of support the children and adolescents described from each source. Friends clearly provided more support among the 14-year-olds than among the younger children, a pattern that occurred in all three ethnic groups.

A recent large study in the Netherlands (van Wel, 1994) suggests that the teenager's bond with his parents may weaken somewhat in the middle of adolescence (ages 15 and 16) and then recover.

This one finding, however, does not significantly alter the conclusion drawn by virtually all the current researchers who have explored this question, who find that a teenager's sense of well-being or happiness is more strongly correlated with the quality of his attachment to the parents than with the quality of his attachments to his peers (e.g., Greenberg, Siegel, & Leitch, 1983; Raja, McGee, & Stanton, 1992). Thus, even while the teenager is becoming more autonomous, he needs his parents to provide a highly important psychological safe base.

Variations in Family Relationships

During these adolescent years, as at all earlier times, some parents are better than others at creating such a safe base. I already talked at length in Chapter 9 about differences in family interactive style and their effects on children and teenagers. Among adolescents, as among younger children, authoritative parenting is consistently associated with more positive outcomes. I mentioned in both Chapter 9 and Chapter 14 that teenagers whose

Table 15.3

Average Scores on Various Measures of Adolescent Behavior for Teenagers from Families with Different Styles of Discipline and Control

Outcome Measure	Style of Parenting			
	Authoritative	Authoritarian	Permissive	Neglectful
Self-reliance	3.09*$_a$	2.96$_b$	3.03$_a$	2.98$_b$
Psychological symptoms	2.36$_a$	2.46$_a$	2.43$_a$	2.65$_b$
School misconduct	2.16$_a$	2.26$_b$	2.38$_c$	2.43$_c$
Drug use	1.41$_a$	1.38$_a$	1.69$_b$	1.68$_b$

*Each number represents the average score on a 4-point scale, in which a 1 always indicates a low amount of the particular behavior and a 4 means the maximum amount.

Note also that in each row, numbers with different subscripts are significantly different from one another.

Source: Lamborn et al., 1991, Table 9 and Table 10, pp. 1060 and 1061.

parents use an authoritative style do better in school than do those whose parents use authoritarian or other styles. The same benefit of authoritative parenting is also found when we look at aspects of emotional and mental health.

Table 15.3 shows one set of results from the very large, multiethnic study by Steinberg, Dornbusch, and their colleagues that I've described a number of times (Lamborn et al., 1991). In this particular analysis they report on responses of approximately ten thousand high school students, in Wisconsin and California, who reported on their family patterns and answered a set of questions about each of several aspects of their own behavior and feelings. Each question offered a 4-point scale, in which 1 always meant a low amount and 4 always meant the highest amount. The numbers entered in the table are the average scores on these 4-point scales. When you look at the numbers, it is clear that the social and emotional outcomes were best for the students who described their families as authoritative and least good for those from neglectful families.

Family Structure. Family structure, too, continues to be an important factor in the teenager's life. The general rule still holds: Teenagers in intact families (living with both natural parents) are the best off on almost every measure (e.g., Demo & Acock, 1996). In adolescence, however, we see an interesting exception to the typical pattern of effects. You'll remember from Chapter 9 that boys are usually more negatively affected than girls by

parental divorce or remarriage. Among adolescents, it is girls who show more distress, both in families in which the girl lives with her still-single mother and in stepparent families (Amato, 1993; Hetherington & Clingempeel, 1992). Adolescent girls, but apparently not preschool or elementary school–age girls, have more trouble interacting with the new stepfather than do their brothers, and they tend to treat him more as an intruder. They are resistant, critical, sulky, and try to avoid contact with him, despite the obvious effort of many stepfathers to be thoughtful and nonauthoritarian. Girls in this situation are more likely to become de-

In blended families like this one, teenage girls seem to have a harder time than do their brothers adapting to having a stepfather. They are more likely to become depressed or defiant.

Parenting

The Key Ingredients in Successful Families of Adolescents

In a recent summary of what we know about how best to parent adolescents, Grayson Holmbeck, Roberta Paikoff, and Jeanne Brooks-Gunn (1995) offer the following list of ideal parent behaviors (paraphrased and adapted from p. 104):

1. Set clear standards for your child's behavior; this seems to be especially effective if you allow some give-and-take with your teenager about what the rules are.
2. Enforce rules and regulations with sanctions (penalties) without physical punishment; try to keep the sanctions to the lowest level possible, while still enforcing the rules.
3. Provide consistent discipline and explain why each time.
4. Permit give-and-take in family discussions the teenager participates in, whatever the subject matter. Teenagers need to try out their arguments and ideas, sometimes to disagree vehemently.
5. Remain involved in the adolescent's daily life and monitor the teen's whereabouts—but without being overly protective. Monitoring is important at every age, but is vitally important with adolescents.

Everything we know about outcomes for teenagers tells us that parents who fail to monitor their teen, even when they do all the other good things on this list, have a child who is more likely to get into difficulty in school and engage in various kinds of risky behavior, including drugs, alcohol, sex, and delinquency. Parents need to know where their child is, with whom, doing what—even when they allow a fair amount of freedom in the child's movements. Involvement also implies involvement with the child's school, as well as knowing the child's friends and the families of those friends.

6. Provide a warm, cohesive, and responsive family environment. Easier said than done, at times, but there is no doubt that the warmth and support offered to the teenager is important, as it is for children of every age.
7. Provide information to the teenager and help her to develop useful skills, particularly where risks are likely, such as knowing how to say no to drugs, or smoking, or sex.

Doing all these things is hard, but it makes a difference.

pressed; they are also more likely than are boys in stepfamilies to become involved with drugs.

Why this pattern occurs is not so obvious. The daughter may feel displaced from a special or more responsible position in the family system that she held after her parents' divorce and before the mother's remarriage; she may feel disturbed by the mother's romantic and clearly sexual involvement with the stepfather. In contrast, the teenage boy may have more to gain by the addition of the stepfather because he acquires a male role model. Whatever the explanation, findings like these remind us once again that family systems are astonishingly complex. Simple categories like "intact" and "stepparent" families will need to give way, ultimately, to more fine-grained analyses that take into account not only the child's age and gender, but family style, the history and sequence of family structures, the presence of other relatives in the system, and so forth.

Relationships with Peers

I've been making the case that the teenager's relationship with his parents continues to be highly significant and formative. At the same time, there is no gainsaying the fact that peer relationships become far more significant at adolescence than they have been at any earlier stage—and perhaps than they will be at any later time in life. Teenagers spend more than half their waking hours with other teenagers, and less than 5 percent of their time with either parent. Their friendships are also increasingly intimate, in the sense that adolescent friends share more and more of their inner feelings and secrets and are more knowledgeable about each other's feelings. These friendships are also more likely to endure for a year or longer. In one longitudinal study, Robert Cairns and Beverly Cairns found that only about twenty percent of friendships among fourth graders lasted as long as

Research Report

Sex Differences in Friendships in Adolescence

In earlier chapters I talked about some of the sex differences in the pattern of children's interactions with one another, beginning as early as preschool age or even toddlerhood. These same differences persist into adolescence, when girls' friendships (in U.S. culture as well as many other societies) are much more focused on intimacy, self-disclosure, and mutual support. Teenage boys' friendships are much more focused on "the enhancement of individual status," with higher rates of competition and much less personal disclosure.

An excellent illustration of this difference comes from a study by Duane Buhrmester (1996), who interviewed 200 adolescents, all 12 to 15 years old, each evening for five consecutive days, asking each teen to describe the social events of the preceding 24-hour period. Each time the teenage respondent described a social encounter that had lasted 10 minutes or longer, the interviewer asked the subject to rate the level or extent of self-disclosure and emotional support in that relationship, using a 7-point scale. The differences in the responses of the boys and girls in this study are shown in the accompanying table.

The findings in the table show strikingly different friendship patterns for teenage boys and girls. Girls

Gender Differences in Adolescents' Daily Interactions with Same-Sex Friends

Interaction Measure	Males	Females
Number of interactions with all same-sex friends	5.51	7.76
Number of interactions with best friends	1.30	1.92
Rated self-disclosure when interacting with best friend	2.74	3.91
Rated emotional support when interacting with best friend	3.04	4.26

Note: All the sex differences shown here are statistically significant.

Source: Buhrmester, 1996, Table 8.2, p. 170.

spend more time with other girls, especially with their best friend, and they receive more emotional support and disclose more with that best friend. All these patterns appear to persist into adulthood, creating quite different social and emotional experiences for men and women.

a year; about twice as many of the friendships formed by these same youngsters when they were tenth graders were long-lasting (1994).

Beyond these changes in individual relationships, the *function* of the peer group changes in adolescence. In elementary school peer groups are mostly the setting for mutual play and for all the learning about relationships and the natural world that is part of such play. But the teenager uses the peer group in another way. He is struggling to make a slow transition from the protected life of the family to the independent life of adulthood; the peer group becomes the *vehicle* for that transition. One sign of this shift is that teenagers begin to use their peers, rather than their parents, as their primary confidants. You've seen one illustration of this change in Figure 15.3 (p. 493). An equally striking set of findings comes from research by Duane Buhrmester (1996), whose research on gender differences are described in the *Research Report* box above. Figure 15.4 shows the combined findings

from several studies in which children, teenagers, or adults were asked to rate the level of intimate disclosure they experienced with parents, friends, and a romantic partner. You can see three clear stages. Before adolescence, children report higher levels of self-disclosure with their parents. At adolescence this changes in a major way: Self-disclosure with parents drops abruptly, while self-disclosure with friends becomes dominant. Then, in adulthood, a second shift occurs, as a romantic partner takes the dominant role. Clearly, in the adolescent years, peers are in the ascendant.

Another facet of this change in the centrality of peer relationships is a strong clannishness and an intense conformity to the group. Such conformity, which Erikson saw as an entirely normal aspect of adolescence, seems to peak at about age 13 or 14 (at about the same time that we see a drop in self-esteem) and then wanes as the teenager begins to arrive at a sense of identity that is more independent of the peer group.

Friendships in adolescence are more intimate, more based on mutual disclosure, than was true at earlier ages—a pattern that is especially clear among girls.

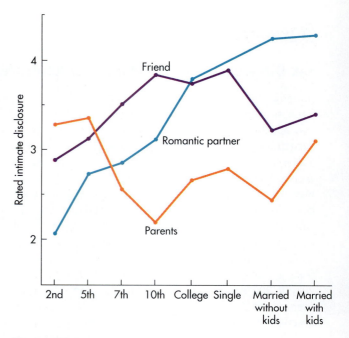

Figure 15.4

Before adolescence, parents are most often a child's closest confidant; in adolescence, it is peers in whom the young person confides. (Source: Buhrmester, 1996, p. 168.)

However, while it is very clear that peers do indeed put pressure on each other to conform to peer group behavior standards, it is also true that peer group pressures are less potent and less negative than popular cultural stereotypes might lead you to believe (Berndt, 1992). To begin with, let us remember that adolescents *choose* their friends, their crowd. They are likely to choose to associate with a group that shares their values, attitudes, and behaviors. If the discrepancy between their own ideas and those of their friends becomes too great, teens are more likely to move toward a more compatible group of friends than to be persuaded to shift toward the first group's values or behaviors. Furthermore, teenagers report that when explicit peer pressure is exerted, it is likely to be pressure toward positive activities, such as school involvement, and *away* from misconduct. Only in "druggie-tough" crowds does there seem to be explicit pressure toward misconduct or law-breaking, and here

the motive may be as much a desire to prove "I'm as tough as you are" as it is explicit pressure from peers (Berndt & Keefe, 1995b; Brown, Dolcini, & Leventhal, 1995). Thus, while Erikson appears to be quite correct in saying that peers are a major force in shaping a child's identity development in adolescence, peer influence is neither monolithic nor uniformly negative.

Changes in Peer Group Structure in Adolescence.

The structure of the peer group also changes over the years of adolescence. The classic, widely quoted early study is Dunphy's observation of the formation, dissolution, and interaction of teenage groups in a high school in Sydney, Australia, between 1958 and 1960 (Dunphy, 1963). Dunphy identified two important subvarieties of groups. The first type, which he called a **clique,** is made up of four to six young people who appear to be strongly attached to one another. Cliques have strong cohesiveness and high levels of intimate sharing. In the early years of adolescence, these cliques are almost entirely same-sex groups—a residual of the preadolescent pattern. Gradually, however, the cliques combine into larger sets Dunphy called **crowds,** which include both males and females. Fi-

Research Report

Are African-American Adolescents More Susceptible to Peer Influence?

One assumption made by a great many adults, including many social scientists, is that African-American youth, more than any other group, are likely to be strongly peer-oriented and to be more vulnerable to peer pressure. One typical argument is that because black teenagers more often live in single-parent families, they are more likely to depend more on peers for affiliation and support. Several recent studies call this assumption into question.

Peggy Giordano and her colleagues (Giordano, Cernkovich, & DeMaris, 1993) studied a group of 942 teenagers, chosen as a representative sample of all adolescents living in Toledo, Ohio. Half the group was black; the remainder was mostly non-Hispanic whites. These teens were asked a wide variety of questions about their friendships and their relationships with peers, such as:

"How important is it to you to do things your friends approve of?"

"How important is it to you to have a group of friends to hang around with?"

They were also asked about family intimacy (e.g., "I'm closer to my parents than a lot of kids my age are") and about parental supervision and control.

In this sample African-American adolescents reported significantly *more* family intimacy, *more* parental supervision and control, *less* need for peer approval, and *less* peer pressure than did white teens.

Similarly, Vicki Mack (Mack, Urberg, Lou, & Tolson, 1995), in a study of nearly 1000 teens in Detroit, found that the African-American youth described *lower* levels of compliance to friends and *higher* scores on measures of the importance of their relationship with their parents. These two studies certainly raise questions about widespread cultural assumptions.

nally, the crowd breaks down again into heterosexual cliques and then into loose associations of couples. In Dunphy's study, the period of the fully developed crowd was typically between ages 13 and 15—the very years when we see the greatest conformity to peer pressure.

Bradford Brown and others of the current generation of adolescence researchers have changed Dunphy's labels somewhat (Brown, 1990; Brown, Mory, & Kinney, 1994). Brown uses the word *crowd* to refer to the "reputation-based" group with which a young person is identified, either by choice or by peer designation. In U.S. schools these groups have labels like *jocks, brains, nerds, dweebs, punks, druggies, toughs, normals, populars, preppies,* or *loners.* Studies in U.S. junior and senior high schools make it clear that teenagers can readily identify and have quite stereotypic—even caricatured—descriptions of each of the major crowds in their school (e.g., "The partyers goof off a lot more than the jocks do, but they don't come to school stoned like the burnouts do"). Each of these descriptions serves, according to Brown, as an "identity prototype" (Brown et al., 1994, p. 133): Labeling others and labeling oneself as belonging to one or more of these

groups helps to create or reinforce the adolescent's own identity. Such labeling also helps the adolescent identify potential friends or foes. Thus membership in one crowd or another channels each adolescent toward particular activities and particular relationships.

Within any given school, these various crowds are organized into a fairly clear, widely understood pecking order. In U.S. schools, the groups labeled as some variant of "jocks," "populars," or "normals" are typically at the top of the heap, with "brains" somewhere in the middle and "druggies," "loners," and "nerds" at the bottom (Brown et al., 1994).

Through the years of junior high and high school, the social system of crowds becomes increasingly differentiated, with more and more distinct groups. For example, in one Midwest school system, Kinney (1993) found that junior high students labeled only two major crowds: one small, high-status group (called *trendies* in this school) and the great mass of lower-status students (called *dweebs*). A few years later the same students named five distinct crowds, three with comparatively high social status and two low-status groups (*grits* and *punkers*). By late high school these same students

| From one kind of clique to another.

identified seven or eight crowds, but by this age the crowds seemed to be less significant in the social organization of the peer group; mutual friendships and dating pairs had become more central (Urberg, Degirmencioglu, Tolson, & Halliday-Scher, 1995).

[?] *Critical Thinking*

Think back to your own high school. Can you draw some kind of diagram or map to describe the organization of crowds and cliques? Were those crowds or cliques more or less important in the last few years of high school than they had been earlier?

Within (and sometimes across) these crowds, adolescents create smaller friendship groups Brown calls *cliques*—a usage that is very similar to Dunphy's meaning for the same term. These groups, as Dunphy observed, are almost entirely same-sex in early adolescence; by late adolescence they have become mixed in gender, often composed of groups of dating couples.

Whatever specific clique or crowd a teenager may identify with, theorists agree that the peer group performs the highly important function of helping the teenager shift from friendships to "partner" social relationships. The 13- or 14-year-old can begin to try out her new relationship skills in the wider group of the crowd or clique; only after some confidence is developed do we see the beginnings of dating and of more committed pair relationships.

Heterosexual Relationships in Adolescence

Of all the changes in social relationships in adolescence, perhaps the most profound is this shift from the total dominance of same-sex friendships to heterosexual relationships. These new relationships are clearly part of the preparation for assuming a full adult sexual identity. Physical sexuality is part of that role, but so are the skills of personal intimacy with the opposite sex, including flirting, communicating, and reading the form of social cues used by the other gender.

In Western societies these skills are learned first in larger crowds or cliques and then in dating pairs (Zani, 1993). Studies of adolescents in the United States suggest that dating begins most typically at 15 or 16, as you can see from Table 15.4,

Table 15.4

Age at First Date Among U.S. Adolescents (in Percentages)

Age	Males	Females
13 or younger	21.2	8.6
14	17.9	16.2
15	21.2	33.6
16	29.5	29.3
17–18	7.2	10.0

Source: Thornton, 1990, Table 1, pp. 246–247.

which shows results from a representative sample of Detroit teenagers (Thornton, 1990). More than half of both boys and girls in this same study had become sexually active by the time they were 18, following the same kind of steady increase with age you saw in Figure 13.6 (p. 435).

You'll also recall from Chapter 13 that heterosexual behavior varies across ethnic groups within American society. African-American teens begin dating and sexual experimentation earlier than do Euro-American and Hispanic teens. Early dating and early sexual activity are also more common among the poor of every ethnic group and among those who experience relatively early puberty. Religious teachings and individual attitudes about the appropriate age for dating and sexual behavior also make a difference, as does family structure. Girls from divorced or remarried families, for example, report earlier dating and higher levels of sexual experience than do girls from intact families, and those with strong religious identity report later dating and lower levels of sexuality (Bingham, Miller, & Adams, 1990; Miller & Moore, 1990). In every one of these subgroups, however, these are years of experimentation with presexual and sexual relationships.

Individual Differences

These shared developmental patterns are obviously a central part of the story of adolescence. At the same time, young people's experience of these years clearly varies widely. Most generally, young people vary in personality, just as infants and young children differ in temperament, and these

variations affect the adolescent's experience and her behavior.

Personality in Adolescence

You'll recall from Chapter 6 that most psychologists today think of personality as being built on the matrix or substrate of the child's inborn temperament. But just how should we describe personality? What are the key dimensions on which personalities differ? Over the years, researchers and theorists have disagreed vehemently on how many such dimensions there might be, how they should be measured, or even whether there were any stable personality traits at all. In the past decade, however, somewhat to the surprise of many psychologists, researchers in this disputatious field have reached consensus that adult personality can be adequately described as a set of variations along five major dimensions, often referred to as the **Big Five,** described in Table 15.5 (p. 500): **extraversion, agreeableness, conscientiousness, neuroticism,** and **openness/intellect** (Digman, 1990; McCrae & John, 1992). To link up this list with the key temperament dimensions I described in Chapter 6, I've suggested some of the possible connections in the table—although these links are still quite speculative (e.g., Ahadi & Rothbart, 1994; Digman, 1994).

These Big Five dimensions have now been found in studies of adults in a variety of countries, including some non-Western cultures (Bond, Nakazato, & Shiraishi, 1975; Borkenau & Ostendorf, 1990). We also have good evidence that these five are stable traits; among adults, scores on these five dimensions have been shown to be stable over periods as long as a decade or two (e.g., Costa & McCrae, 1988).

[?] Critical Thinking

How would you rate your own personality on each of the Big Five?

New research suggests that these same five dimensions also describe adolescent personality. For example, Cornelis van Lieshout and Gerbert Haselager, in a large study of children and adolescents

Table 15.5

The Big Five Personality Traits

Trait	Qualities of Individual High in That Trait	Possible Temperament Components
Extraversion	Active, assertive, energetic, enthusiastic, outgoing, talkative	High activity level; sociability; positive emotionality
Agreeableness	Affectionate, forgiving, generous, kind, sympathetic, trusting	Perhaps high approach/positive emotionality; perhaps effortful control
Conscientiousness	Efficient, organized, planful, reliable, responsible, thorough	Effortful control/task persistence
Neuroticism (also called emotional [in]stability)	Anxious, self-pitying, tense, touchy, unstable, worrying	Negative emotionality; irritability
Openness/Intellect	Artistic, curious, intuitive, insightful, original, flexible, intellectually engaged, absorbed	Approach; low inhibition

Sources: McCrae & Costa, 1990; Ahadi & Rothbart, 1994; John et al., 1994, Table 1, p. 161; McCrae, 1996.

in the Netherlands (1994), found that the five clearest dimensions characterizing their young subjects matched the Big Five very well. In this sample, agreeableness and emotional (in)stability were the clearest dimensions, followed by conscientiousness, extraversion, and openness.

Similar results have come from a study in the United States by Oliver John and his colleagues (John, Caspi, Robins, Moffitt, & Stouthamer-Loeber, 1994), who studied a group of 350 ethnically diverse 12- and 13-year-old boys, drawn at random from the Pittsburgh public school system. Like the Dutch researchers, John found strong evidence that the five-factor model captures the personality variations among these early teen boys. John's study is also helpful as a test of the five-factor model because he has information on other aspects of the boys' behavior, such as their school success or delinquent behavior. By comparing the personality profiles of boys who differ in some specified behavior, he can check to see if the personality patterns differ in ways that make theoretical and conceptual sense. For example, Figure 15.5 contrasts the personality profiles of boys who reported delinquent activity versus boys who reported none. As John predicted, delinquent boys were markedly lower than nondelinquent boys in both conscientiousness and agreeableness. John also found that boys higher in conscientiousness did slightly better in school, just as you would expect.

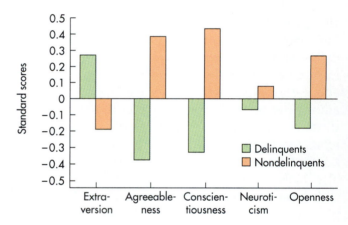

Figure 15.5

Delinquent 12-year-olds have quite different personality profiles from nondelinquents of the same age—a set of results that helps to validate the usefulness of the Big Five personality traits as a description of adolescent personality. (Source: John et al., 1994, Figure 1, p. 167.)

These early results are impressive and point to the usefulness of the five-factor model in describing child and adolescent personality.

Two Common Problems: Depression and Delinquency

Adolescents also differ in the extent to which they experience two of the most common psychological/social problems of this age period: depression and delinquency. Delinquency gets more press, but depression is an equally significant problem among teens.

Depression. For many years, psychiatrists took the position that significant depression could not occur in children or adolescents. This turns out to be quite wrong. We now have abundant evidence that depression is actually quite common in adolescence and occurs at least occasionally among younger children. Perhaps ten percent of preadolescent children and 30 to 40 percent of adolescents experience significant short-term depressed mood or misery (Compas, Hinden, & Gerhardt, 1995; Harrington, Rutter, & Fombonne, 1996; Petersen, Compas, Brooks-Gunn et al., 1993). When such a depressed mood lasts six months or longer and is accompanied by other symptoms, such as disturbances of sleeping and eating and difficulty concentrating, it is usually referred to as **clinical depression** or a *depressive disorder.* Recent epidemiological studies tell us that at any given time, 1 to 2 percent of preadolescents and 5 to 7 percent of adolescents are in the midst of such an enduring depression. Perhaps twice that many will experience a serious depression at some time in their adolescent years (Compas et al., 1993; Merikangas & Angst, 1995). These are not trivial states of unhappiness. A significant portion of depressed teens say they think about suicide. In one longitudinal study of youth growing up in a working-class neighborhood in the United States, a fifth of those who had had a serious depression by age 18 had also attempted suicide (Reinherz, Giaconia, Pakiz et al., 1993).

Interestingly, among preadolescents, boys appear to be slightly more likely than girls to be unhappy or depressed; but beginning at about age 13, girls are twice as likely to report high or chronic levels of depression, a sex difference that exists throughout adulthood and has been found in a number of industrialized countries and among African Americans, Hispanic Americans, and European Americans (Culbertson, 1997; Nolen-Hoeksema & Girgus, 1994; Roberts & Sobhan, 1992).

Where do such depressions come from, and why do girls have more of them? The search for the developmental pathways leading to later depression begins with the clear finding that children growing up with depressed parents are much more

From just this photo we can't tell what has caused this teenager's dejected look, but we do know that depressed mood and significant clinical depressions are considerably more common in the adolescent years than most psychiatrists or psychologists once thought. Such depression is also much more likely among teen girls than boys.

likely than are those growing up with nondepressed parents to develop depression themselves (Merikangas & Angst, 1995). Of course, this could indicate a genetic factor at work here, a possibility supported by at least a few studies of twins and adopted children (Petersen et al., 1993). Or we could understand this link between parental and child depression in terms of the changes in the parent-child interaction that are caused by the parent's depression.

I mentioned in Chapter 6 that depressed mothers are much more likely than are nondepressed mothers to have children who are insecurely attached. In particular, their behavior with their child is often so nonresponsive that it seems to foster in the child a kind of helpless resignation. Such a sense of helplessness has been found to be strongly related to depression in both adults and adolescents (Dodge, 1990).

Certainly, not all children of depressed parents are themselves depressed; about 60 percent show no abnormality at all. Whether a child moves along a pathway toward depression or not seems to be largely a function of the number of other stresses that are present in the family life, such as an illness, family arguments, work stress, loss of income, job loss, or marital separation.

The detrimental role of stress in the emergence of depression is just as clear among children whose parent or parents are not depressed. Any combination of stresses, such as the parents' divorce, the death of a parent or another loved person, the father's loss of job, a move, or a change of schools, increases the likelihood of depression in the child (Compas et al., 1993). Indeed, the role of such individual life stresses may help to explain the sex differences in depression among adolescents. Anne Petersen (Petersen, Sarigiani, & Kennedy, 1991) has proposed that girls are more likely to experience simultaneous stressful experiences in adolescence, such as pubertal changes combined with a shift in schools. In her own longitudinal study, Petersen found that depression was *not* more common among girls than among boys when both groups had encountered equal levels of life stress or simultaneous stressful experiences.

Susan Nolen-Hoeksema agrees with Petersen that one of the keys is that teenage girls face more stresses than do teenage boys (Nolen-Hoeksema, 1994; Nolen-Hoeksema & Girgus, 1994). She also argues that girls respond to their "down" moods quite differently than do boys. Girls (and women) are more likely to *ruminate* about their sadness or distress, a coping strategy that actually accentuates the depression ("What does it mean that I feel this way?" "I just don't feel like doing anything"), producing longer-lasting depressive episodes. Boys (and men), on the other hand, are more likely to use distraction to deal with their blue moods—exercising, playing a game, or working—a coping strategy that tends to reduce depression.

You'll remember from Chapter 12 that low self-esteem is also part of the equation. Susan Harter's studies tell us that a young person who feels she (or he) does not measure up to her own standards is much more likely to show symptoms of a clinical depression (e.g., Harter & Whitesell, 1996). The fact that depression increases markedly in adolescence makes good sense from this point of view. We know

that in adolescence children are much more likely to define themselves and others in *comparative* terms—to judge against some standard or to see themselves as "less than" or "more than" some other person. We also know that at adolescence appearance becomes highly salient and that a great many teenagers are convinced that they do not live up to the culturally defined appearance standards. Self-esteem therefore drops in early adolescence, and depression rises. Girls in current Western cultures seem especially vulnerable to this process because the increase in body fat that is typical for girls in adolescence runs counter to the desired slim body type.

Critical Thinking

Can you think of any other possible explanations of the higher rates of depression among teenage girls than teenage boys? What sort of study would you have to do to test your hypotheses?

All this research has taken us a fair distance in our efforts to understand both the rise in depression in adolescence and the marked gender difference in rates of depression. Still, teenagers vary widely in their responses to what appear to be the same levels of stress. Not every teenager who faces multiple stresses or fails to live up to some standard is inclined to ruminate rather than use distraction, or who is temperamentally shy ends up being clinically depressed. These are all risk factors, but even with these risk factors, some are more vulnerable than others.

Juvenile Delinquency. **Delinquency** is a subvariety of what psychologists call *conduct disorders*—a pattern I described in some detail in Chapter 12 that includes high levels of aggression, argumentativeness, bullying, disobedience, high irritability, and threatening and loud behavior. Delinquency is defined more narrowly to include only intentional law-breaking, although a great many teenagers who break laws also show other aspects of a conduct disorder, thus the two categories overlap considerably (American Psychiatric Association, 1994).

It is extremely difficult to estimate how many teenagers engage in delinquent behavior. One window on the problem is to look at the number of arrests—although arrest rates are arguably only the tip of the iceberg. More than two million juveniles were arrested in the United States in 1994, which is almost seven percent of all youngsters between ages 10 and 17. Among those aged 15 to 17, the arrest rate is roughly ten percent (U.S. Bureau of the Census, 1996), a higher rate than we see for any other age group across the entire life span. Many of these arrests are for relatively minor infractions, but about a third are for serious crimes, including murder, burglary, rape, and arson.

When adolescents themselves describe their own law-breaking, they report even higher rates. Four-fifths of U.S. youngsters between ages 11 and 17 say that they have been delinquent at some time or another. One-third admit truancy and disorderly conduct and one-fifth say they have committed criminal acts, most often physical assaults or thefts (Dryfoos, 1990). Terrie Moffitt (1993) reports similar figures from a large New Zealand sample, among whom 93 percent of males acknowledged some form of delinquent activity by age 18.

Just as conduct disorders are much more common among preschool and elementary school–age boys than girls, delinquent acts and arrests are far more common among teenage males than females. Among those actually arrested, the ratio is more than four to one; in self-reports the ratios vary, but the more physically violent the act, the more common it is among boys.

Persistent delinquency is also more common among lower-IQ-score teens (Lynam, Moffitt, & Stouthamer-Loeber, 1993). This link between IQ

These boys at the Cook County (Illinois) Juvenile Temporary Detention Center are among the two million juveniles arrested each year in the United States.

score and delinquency cannot be explained away by arguing that the less-bright delinquents are more likely to be caught; nor is it simply an artifact of social class or ethnic differences in both delinquency and IQ because among white middle-class teens, it is also the case that delinquents have lower IQs than their nondelinquent peers. Instead, low IQ scores appear to be a genuine risk factor for delinquency, particularly for those children who experience some school failure (Hämäläinen & Pulkkinen, 1996). The argument offered by Donald Lynam and others is that school failure reduces a young person's engagement with school and the values it represents. School failure also increases the child's or adolescent's frustration, which increases the likelihood of aggression of some kind. Thus, for many less intelligent young people, traditional social constraints on delinquent behavior are simply weaker.

Such a link between IQ score and delinquency seems to be particularly valid for *childhood-onset* as opposed to *adolescent-onset* delinquency, a distinction I mentioned in Chapter 12. Childhood-onset disorders are more serious, with high levels of persisting aggression and high likelihood of adult criminality. Adolescent-onset problems are typically milder and more transitory, apparently more a reflection of peer group processes or testing the limits of authority than of a deeply ingrained behavior problem. This second group is less likely to be convicted in court, and in particular is much less likely to be convicted of any violent offense (Moffitt, Caspi, Dickson, Silva, & Stanton, 1996).

I described the developmental pathway for early-onset disorders in Chapter 12, beginning perhaps with some basic personality or temperamental tendencies toward aggression or anger, perhaps lower IQ, combined with ineffective parenting, with poor school success and poor peer relations as possible results. For young people whose delinquency appears first in adolescence, the pathway is different. These seem to be primarily young people whose parents provide insufficient monitoring, whose individual friendships are not very supportive or intimate, and who are drawn to a clique or crowd that includes some teens who are experimenting with drugs or mild law-breaking. After a period of months of hanging out with such a group of peers, this particular subgroup of previously nondelinquent kids show some increase in risky or

Research Report

Delinquency Among Girls

When we use the term *delinquent,* most of us think immediately of teenage boys. Yet, although the incidence of delinquency or criminality in girls is much lower, it is not zero. Girls are much less likely to be involved in forms of delinquency that involve violence, just as girls are consistently less physically aggressive at every age. However, girls do get involved in delinquent behaviors such as shoplifting or the use of illegal drugs (Zoccolillo, 1993).

A study in New Zealand by Avshalom Caspi and his colleagues (Caspi et al., 1993) provides some interesting insights into the possible origins of such delinquent behavior. The sample of students involved in this study included all the children born in one town in one year (1972–1973), a group of more than 1000. The children were tested and assessed repeatedly, at ages 3, 5, 7, 9, 11, 13, and 15. In one analysis, Caspi looked at rates of delinquency among the girls as a function of the earliness or lateness of their menarche and of

whether they went to an all-girls or a mixed-sex high school. Caspi's hypothesis was that girls who attended a mixed-sex secondary school would be more likely to be involved in delinquent activities because they would have more rule-breaking models (delinquent boys) among their peers. He also expected to find that girls with early puberty would be more likely to become delinquent, especially in mixed-sex schools.

These hypotheses were generally confirmed, although there were some interesting wrinkles. At age 13 the girls were asked to report on "norm violations," which included a variety of mild delinquent acts, such as breaking windows, stealing from schoolmates, getting drunk, swearing loudly in public, or making prank telephone calls. As you can see in the figure, such norm violations were most common among early-maturing girls attending coed schools. Further analysis shows that this difference is almost entirely contributed by a small group of girls who had had a history of high levels of aggression earlier in childhood *and* who had early puberty. Early-maturing girls in coed schools who had no such history of early problems showed no heightened rate of delinquency.

To make it still more complicated, Caspi found that at age 15, early-developing girls in coed schools continued to have high rates of delinquency, but at this age the highest rate of delinquency was found among *on-time-puberty* girls attending coed schools. Puberty, whether early or on time, thus seems to increase the likelihood that vulnerable girls will get involved with antisocial peers, but this is only true of girls in coed schools.

I find this study fascinating not only because it points to the complex relationships between physical maturation and social relationships, but also because it offers an interesting argument in favor of all-girls schools...

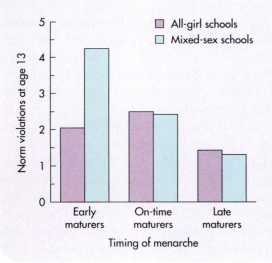

antisocial behaviors, such as increased drug taking (Berndt & Keefe, 1995a; Dishion, Capaldi, Spracklen, & Li, 1995; Steinberg, Fletcher, & Darling, 1994). At the same time, parents continue to have an important role in this process: When parents *do* provide good monitoring and emotional support for their teenager, the adolescent is unlikely to get involved in delinquent acts or drug use even if he hangs around with a tougher crowd or

has a close friend who engages in such behavior (Brown & Huang, 1995; Mounts & Steinberg, 1995).

Thus adolescent-onset delinquency reflects a type of peer pressure, a finding that confirms the assumption by many adults that kids would be okay if they just didn't fall in with "bad companions." Still, let us be very careful about making too broad a claim about the effect of adolescent peer groups in seducing young people into delinquency.

First, as I have already said, among *early*-onset delinquents there is no "seduction" into bad behavior; the teenager who is already deviant chooses to hang out with other deviant kids. Collectively, these kids then reinforce one another's delinquent behavior. Second, the majority of initially nondelinquent teens become involved with *non*delinquent peer groups, which continue to reinforce *non*delinquency. Only a subgroup is "lured" into significant delinquency or misbehavior by contact with "bad companions," and kids in this subgroup are already subtly different before they hit adolescence. Their early behavior is not overtly deviant, as is the case with the early-onset delinquents, but they seem to lack the kind of skills in friendship making that would help to buffer them from the effects of peer pressure (Berndt & Keefe, 1995a). And very often they have parents who do not provide adequate supervision or monitoring. So it is only the minority whose behavior is negatively influenced by a crowd that encourages and reinforces disruptive or risky behavior.

Pathways and Trajectories

One way to conceptualize these variations among teens is in terms of "pathways" through adolescence. Bruce Compas and his colleagues (Compas et al., 1995) have provided a very useful visual model to describe such pathways, shown in Figure 15.6. Path 1 in this model describes the young person who sails through adolescence with little depression or delinquency, with supportive friendships and decent academic success. These youths most often come from low-risk environments. On the other end of the continuum is path 2, which describes a consistently *poor* adaptation. This group includes the early-onset delinquents as well as some young people who enter adolescence with poor self-esteem and relatively high levels of depression, patterns that tend to persist in them.

The remaining three paths all involve change of some type during adolescence. Path 3 describes a turnaround or recovery from some previous negative pattern. This might happen because of a new relationship with a particularly attentive and helpful teacher; for some, military service in the late teens provides a kind of "recovery" experience (Elder, 1986). Path 4 is the reverse of 3—a decline in functioning

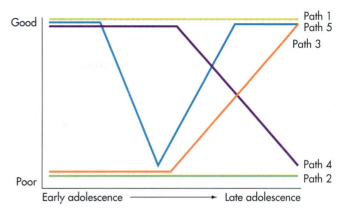

Figure 15.6

Five paths through adolescence. The majority of teens follow paths 1 and 2; a smaller number shows significant change during the adolescent years. (Source: Compas, Hinden, & Gerhardt, 1995, Figure 1, p. 272.)

during adolescence that is not presaged by obvious problems at earlier ages and that seems to persist. The 20 percent of young people in Zimmerman's study of self-esteem who showed steadily declining levels of confidence and self-esteem, for example, may be following such a deteriorating path (Zimmerman et al., in press), although some may well recover at later ages. At this point we know far too little about what might trigger such a loss of competency or adequacy of functioning. It might occur because of some major upheaval in the child's family; in some cases it can be triggered by genetic effects that do not "turn on" until adolescence, such as some forms of schizophrenia (Rutter & Rutter, 1993). Clearly, we need to know far more about this group.

Finally, path 5 describes a pattern of temporary deviance, often reflecting short-term experimentation with risk-taking behaviors or delinquent acts that is not embedded in a broader pattern of deviance (Moffitt, 1993)—precisely the group I was just talking about.

I cannot tell you how many teenagers follow each of these five paths. Answering such a question obviously requires large-scale, long-term longitudinal studies, of which we have very few. What we do know is that the stable pathways (paths 1 and 2) are more common than the unstable ones. Thus, although adolescence is a time of change for virtually all teens—changes in body, form of thinking, identity, and social relationships—the majority of young people respond to the special demands of this period of life in a way that is consistent with their earlier patterns. Competent and secure young people are not typically thrown off course by adolescence. When we see deviant behavior in adolescence, it nearly always has roots in earlier developmental periods.

Summary

1. Self-definitions become increasingly abstract at adolescence, with more emphasis on enduring, internal qualities and ideology.

2. Teenagers also increasingly define themselves in terms that include both masculine and feminine traits. When both are high, the individual is described as androgynous. High levels of androgyny are associated with higher self-esteem in both male and female adolescents.

3. Erikson emphasized that adolescents must go through a crisis and a redefinition of the self. Many adolescents clearly do so, but we do not know whether all do.

4. Young people of color or those in clearly identifiable minority groups have the additional task in adolescence of forming an ethnic identity, a process that appears to have several steps analogous to Marcia's model of identity formation.

5. Self-esteem drops somewhat at the beginning of adolescence and then rises steadily through the teen years.

6. Concepts of relationships also undergo change, becoming more flexible, more shaded. Friendships are increasingly seen as adaptive and changeable.

7. Adolescent-parent interactions typically become somewhat more conflicted in early adolescence, possibly linked to the physical changes of puberty. But the attachment to parents remains strong.

8. Authoritative family interactions continue to be the optimal pattern at adolescence. Teenagers in such families are more self-reliant, use fewer drugs, and have higher self-esteem than do those in neglecting or authoritarian families.

9. The parents' divorce and remarriage during the child's adolescence appears to have a more negative effect for girls than for boys.

10. Peer relationships become increasingly important, both quantitatively and qualitatively. Theorists emphasize that peers serve an important function as a bridge between the dependence of childhood and the independence of adulthood.

11. Reputation-based groups, called "crowds" by current researchers, are an important part of adolescent social relationships, particularly in the early high school years. Smaller groups of friends, called "cliques," are also present and gradually shift from same-sex to mixed-sex to dating pairs.

12. Susceptibility to peer group pressure appears to be at its peak at about age 13 or 14, but peer pressure is as often away from deviant behavior as toward it, and individual teens vary considerably in their susceptibility to such pressure.

13. On average in Western cultures, dating begins at about age 15, but there is wide variability.

14. Researchers studying adult personality have agreed on a set of five dimensions (the Big Five) that capture most of the variation among individuals: extraversion, agreeableness, conscientiousness, neuroticism, and openness/intellect.

15. Recent research suggests that the same five dimensions may give us an accurate picture of variations in adolescent personality as well.

16. Rates of depression increase sharply at adolescence, and are higher among girls than boys. Depressed teens are more likely to come from families with at least one depressed parent, but there are other pathways, including poor peer acceptance in elementary school, low self-esteem, and high levels of life change or stress at adolescence.

17. Delinquent acts also increase at adolescence, especially among boys. Early-onset delinquency and adolescent-onset delinquency have quite different causes and patterns.

Key Terms

agreeableness   One of the Big Five personality traits, characterized by trust, generosity, kindness, and sympathy. **(p. 499)**

androgynous   Label applied to a person whose self-concept includes and whose behavior expresses high levels of both masculine and feminine qualities. **(p. 483)**

Big Five   The five primary dimensions of personality variation identified by researchers, including extraversion, agreeableness, conscientiousness, neuroticism, and openness/intellect. **(p. 499)**

clinical depression   A combination of sad mood, sleep and eating disturbances, and difficulty concentrating, lasting six months or longer. **(p. 501)**

clique   Defined by Dunphy as a group of six to eight friends with strong affectional bonds and high levels of group solidarity and loyalty; currently used by researchers to describe a self-chosen group of friends, in contrast to reputation-based crowds. **(p. 496)**

conscientiousness One of the Big Five personality traits, characterized by efficiency, organization, planfulness, and reliability. **(p. 499)**

crowd Defined by Dunphy as a larger and looser group of friends than a clique, normally made up of several cliques joined together; defined by current researchers as a reputation-based group, common in adolescent subculture, with widely agreed-upon characteristics (e.g., "brains," "jocks," or "druggies"). **(p. 496)**

delinquency A subcategory of conduct disorders involving explicit law-breaking. **(p. 502)**

extraversion One of the Big Five personality traits, characterized by assertiveness, energy, enthusiasm, and outgoingness. **(p. 499)**

feminine One of four sex-role types suggested by the work of Bem and others; a pattern of high scores on femininity measures and low scores on masculinity. **(p. 483)**

foreclosure One of four identity statuses proposed by Marcia; it signifies an ideological or occupational commitment without having gone through a reevaluation. **(p. 485)**

identity achievement One of four identity statuses proposed by Marcia; it involves the successful resolution of an identity "crisis," which results in a new commitment. **(p. 485)**

identity diffusion One of four identity statuses proposed by Marcia; it involves neither a current reevaluation nor a firm personal commitment. **(p. 485)**

identity statuses Four categories suggested by James Marcia, created by combining high and low identity crises and high and low identity commitment. Includes foreclosure, moratorium, identity diffusion, and identity achievement. **(p. 485)**

individuation Label used by some theorists for the process of psychological, social, and physical separation from parents that begins in adolescence. **(p. 491)**

masculine One of four sex-role types suggested by the work of Bem and others; a pattern of high scores on masculinity measures and low scores on femininity measures. **(p. 483)**

moratorium One of four identity statuses proposed by Marcia; it involves an ongoing reexamination but without a new commitment as yet. **(p. 485)**

neuroticism One of the Big Five personality traits, characterized by anxiety, self-pity, tenseness, and emotional instability. **(p. 499)**

openness/intellect One of the Big Five personality traits, characterized by curiosity, imagination, insight, originality, and wide interest. **(p. 499)**

undifferentiated One of four sex-role types suggested by the work of Bem and others; a pattern of low scores on both masculinity and femininity measures. **(p. 483)**

Suggested Readings

Adams, G. R., Gullotta, T. P., & Montemayor, R. (Eds.). (1992). *Adolescent identity formation*. Newbury Park, CA: Sage. One of a series of excellent books on facets of adolescence edited by these same three psychologists. It includes a discussion of the Erikson/Marcia view of identity by Waterman as well as Phinney's paper on ethnic identity.

Crockett, L. J., & Crouter, A. C. (Eds.). (1995). *Pathways through adolescence*. Mahwah, NJ: Erlbaum. Another excellent collection of papers on adolescence, written by many of the current leading researchers.

Eron, L. D., Gentry, J. H., & Schlegel, P. (Eds.). (1994). *Reason to hope. A psychosocial perspective on violence and youth*. Washington, DC: American Psychological Association. A comprehensive discussion of what we know about the causes, consequences, and possible cures of youth violence.

Montemayor, R., Adams, R. G., & Gullotta, T. P. (Eds.). (1994). *Personal relationships during adolescence*. Thousand Oaks, CA: Sage. A first-rate collection of papers, including an especially fascinating discussion of teen crowds by Bradford Brown.

Rutter, M. (Ed.). (1995). *Psychosocial disturbances in young people. Challenges for prevention*. Cambridge, England: Cambridge University Press. An excellent recent collection of papers on many of the emotional and social problems of adolescence.

Steinberg, L., & Levine, A. (1990). *You and your adolescent. A parent s guide for ages 10 to 20*. New York: Harper & Row. The best book for parents of adolescents I have seen. I strongly recommend it.

Summing Up Development in Adolescence

BASIC CHARACTERISTICS OF ADOLESCENCE

A number of experts on adolescence argue that it makes sense to divide the period of years from 12 to about 20 into two subperiods, one beginning at 11 or 12, the other perhaps at 16 or 17, a categorization I have followed in the summary table. Some label these as *adolescence* and *youth* (Keniston, 1970), others as *early* and *late* adolescence (e.g., Brooks-Gunn, 1988). However we label them, there are distinct differences.

Early adolescence is, almost by definition, a time of transition, a time in which significant change occurs in virtually every aspect of the child's functioning. Late adolescence is more a time of consolidation, when the young person establishes a cohesive new identity, with clearer goals and role commitments. Norma Haan (1981), borrowing Piaget's concepts, suggests that early adolescence is a time dominated by assimilation, while late adolescence is primarily a time of accommodation.

The 12- or 13-year-old is assimilating an enormous amount of new physical, social, and intellectual experi-

A Summary of the Threads of Development During Early and Late Adolescence

Aspect of Development	Age in Years							
	12	13	14	15	16	17	18	19+
		Early Adolescence				Late Adolescence (Youth)		
Physical development	Major pubertal change begins for boys		Boys' height spurt				Puberty completed for boys	
	Girls' height spurt	Average age of menarche			Puberty completed for girls			
Cognitive development	Beginning formal operations: systematic analysis; some deductive logic				Consolidated formal operations (for some)			
	Kohlberg's stage 3 ("good boy, nice girl" orientation) continues to dominate							
					Kohlberg's stage 4 ("law and order") for a few			
		Descriptions of self and others begin to include exceptions, comparisons, special conditions; deeper personality traits						
Personality and social development	Self-esteem declines	Self-esteem begins to rise and continues to rise for remainder of adolescence						
	Rate of depression rises sharply and remains high						Clear identity achievement for perhaps half	
	Erikson's stage of identity vs. role diffusion							
	Parent-child conflict peaks at beginning of puberty		Maximum impact of peer group pressure	Normal time for first dating				

ences. While all this absorption is going on, but before it is digested, the young person is in a more or less perpetual state of disequilibrium. Old patterns, old schemes, no longer work very well, but new ones have not yet been established. It is during this early period that the peer group is so centrally important. Ultimately, the 16- or 17- or 18-year-old begins to make the needed accommodations, pulls the threads together, and establishes a new identity, new patterns of social relationships, new goals, and new roles.

EARLY ADOLESCENCE

As I mentioned in the last chapter, the early years of adolescence have certain characteristics in common with the early years of toddlerhood. Two-year-olds are famous for their negativism and for their constant push for more independence. At the same time they are struggling to learn a vast array of new skills. Teenagers show many of these same qualities, albeit at much more abstract levels. Many of them go through a period of negativism right at the beginning of the pubertal changes, particularly with parents. And many of the conflicts with parents center on issues of independence—they want to come and go when they please, listen to the music they prefer at maximum volume, and wear the clothing and hair styles that are currently "in."

Like the negativism of the 2-year-old, it is easy to overstate the depth or breadth of the conflict between young teenagers and their parents. It is important to keep in mind that for most teens, we are not talking here about major turmoil but only a temporary increase in disagreements or disputes. The depiction of adolescence as full of storm and stress is as much an exaggeration as is the phrase *terrible twos*. What is true is that both are characterized by a new push for independence that is inevitably accompanied by more confrontations with parents over limits.

While this push for independence is going on, the young adolescent is also facing a whole new set of demands and skills to be learned—new social skills, new and more complex school tasks, major changes in her body, a need to form an adult identity. The sharp increases in the rate of depression (especially among girls) and the drop in self-esteem we see at the beginning of adolescence seem to be linked to this surplus of new demands and changes. A number of investigators have found that those adolescents who have the great-

est number of simultaneous changes at the beginning of puberty—changing to junior high school, moving to a new town or new house, perhaps a parental separation or divorce—also show the greatest loss in self-esteem, the largest rise in problem behavior, and the biggest drop in grade point average (Simmons, Burgeson, & Reef, 1988). Young adolescents who can cope with these changes one at a time, as when the youngster remains in the same school through eighth or ninth grade before shifting to junior or senior high school, show fewer symptoms of stress.

Facing major stressful demands, the 2-year-old uses Mom (or some other central attachment figure) as a safe base for exploring the world, returning for reassurance when fearful. Young adolescents seem to do the same with the family, using it as a safe base from which to explore the rest of the world, including the world of peer relationships. Parents of young adolescents must try to find a difficult balance between providing the needed security, including clear rules and limits, and still allowing independence—just as the parent of a 2-year-old must walk the fine line between allowing exploration and keeping the child safe. Among teenagers, as among toddlers, the most confident and successful are those whose families manage this balancing act well.

Still a third way in which theorists have likened the young teenager to the 2-year-old is in egocentrism. David Elkind (1967) suggested some years ago that egocentrism rises in adolescence. This new egocentrism, according to Elkind, has two facets: (1) the belief that "others in our immediate vicinity are as concerned with our thoughts and behavior as we ourselves are" (Elkind & Bowen, 1979, p. 38), which Elkind describes as having an *imaginary audience*, and (2) the possession of a *personal fable*, a tendency by the teenager to consider her own ideas and feelings unique and singularly important. This is typically accompanied by a sense of invulnerability—a feeling that may lie behind the adolescent's apparent attraction to high-risk behavior, such as unprotected sex, drugs, drinking, high-speed driving, and the like (Arnett, 1995).

Elkind's own research (Elkind & Bowen, 1979) shows that preoccupation with others' views of the self (imaginary audience behavior) peaks at about age 13 to 14. Teenagers this age are most likely to say that if they went to a party where they did not know most of the kids, they would wonder *a lot* about what the other kids were thinking of them. They also report that they worry a lot when someone is watching them work, and they feel desperately embarrassed if they discover a grease spot on their clothes or newly erupted pimples. Of course, younger children and adults may also worry about these things, but they seem to be much less disturbed or immobilized by these worries than are 13- and 14-year-olds, an age when the dominance of the peer crowd or clique is at its peak.

Drawing a parallel between the early adolescent and the toddler makes sense in that both age groups face the task of establishing a separate identity. The toddler must separate herself from the symbiotic relationship with Mom or central caregiver. She must figure out not only that she is separate but that she has abilities and qualities. Physical maturation also allows her new levels of independent exploration. The young adolescent must separate himself from his family, and from his identity as a child, and begin to form a new identity as an adult. This, too, is accompanied by major maturational changes that make new levels and kinds of independence possible.

LATE ADOLESCENCE

To carry the basic analogy further, late adolescence is more like the preschool years. Major changes have been weathered and a new balance has been achieved. The physical upheavals of puberty are mostly complete, the family system has changed to allow the young person more independence and freedom, and the beginnings of a new identity have been created. This period is not without its strains. For most young people a clear identity is not achieved until college age, if then, so the identity process continues. Also, the late adolescent faces the often difficult task of forming an emotionally intimate sexual or presexual partnership. Nonetheless, I think Haan is correct about this later period being more one of accommodation than assimilation. At the very least we know that it is accompanied by rising levels of self-esteem and declining levels of family confrontation or conflict.

CENTRAL PROCESSES AND THEIR CONNECTIONS

In other interludes I have suggested that changes in one or another of the facets of development may be central to the constellation of transformations we see at a given age. In infancy underlying physiological changes along with the creation of a first central attachment appear to have such key causal roles; in the preschool years cognitive changes seem especially dominant, while among school-age children both cognitive and social changes appear to be formative. *Every* domain shows significant change in adolescence. At this point, we simply do not have the research data to clarify the basic causal connections among the transformations in these various areas. Still, we have *some* information about linkages.

THE ROLE OF PUBERTY

The most obvious place to begin is with puberty itself. Puberty not only defines the beginning of early adolescence, it clearly affects all other facets of the young person's development, either directly or indirectly.

Direct effects might be seen in several ways. Most clearly, the surges of pubertal hormones stimulate sexual interest, while they also trigger body changes that make adult sexuality and fertility possible. These changes seem inescapably causally linked to the gradual shift (for the great majority of teens) from same-sex peer groupings to heterosexual crowds and finally to heterosexual pair relationships.

Hormones and Family Relationships. Hormone changes may also be directly implicated in the increases in confrontation or conflict between parents and children and in the rise in various kinds of aggressive or delinquent behavior as well. Steinberg's research (1988) suggests such a direct link because he finds pubertal stage and not age to be the critical variable in predicting the level of adolescent-parent conflict. Other investigators have found that, in girls, the rise in estradiol at the beginning of puberty is associated with increases in verbal aggression and a loss of impulse control, while in boys, increases in testosterone are correlated with increases in irritability and impatience (Paikoff & Brooks-Gunn, 1990). However, many studies find no such connection (e.g., Coe, Hayashi, & Levine, 1988), which has led most theorists to conclude that the connections between pubertal hormones and changes in adolescent social behavior are considerably more complicated than we had first imagined.

One of the complications is that the physical changes of puberty have highly significant indirect effects as well. When the child's body grows and becomes more like that of an adult, the parents begin to treat the child differently and the child begins to see himself as a soon-to-be-adult. Both of these changes may be linked to the brief rise in parent-adolescent confrontation and may help to trigger some of the searching self-examinations that are part of this period of life.

The adolescent's pubertal changes also require other adaptations from the parents that change the family dynamics. It can be very confusing to parents to deal with a young teenager who seems, simultaneously, to demand both more independence, authority, and power and more nurturance and guidance. What is more, the presence of a sexually charged pubescent teen may reawaken the parents' own unresolved adolescent issues, just when they are themselves facing a sense of physical decline in their 40s or 50s. Then, too, teenagers may stay up late, severely restricting private time for parents. Perhaps, then, it is not surprising that many parents (particularly fathers) report that marital satisfaction is at its lowest ebb during their children's adolescence (Glenn, 1990). Taking all this together, you can see why it is so difficult to sort out the direct and the indirect effects of pubertal hormone changes on social behavior.

Puberty and Cognitive Change. Physiological changes may also play some role in the shift to formal operations. We have some indication, for example, that a second major synaptic and dendritic "pruning" occurs at adolescence. At the same time, any link between formal operational thinking and pubertal change cannot be inevitable because we know that all adolescents experience puberty but not all make the transition to formal operations. The best guess at the moment is that neurological or hormonal changes at adolescence may be *nec-*

essary for further cognitive gains, but they cannot be *sufficient* conditions for such developments.

THE ROLE OF COGNITIVE CHANGES

An equally attractive possibility to many theorists has been the proposition that it is the cognitive changes that are pivotal in adolescence. The cognitive shift from concrete to formal operations obviously does not cause pubertal changes, but cognitive development may be central to many of the other changes we see at adolescence, including changes in the self-concept, the process of identity formation, increases in level of moral reasoning, and changes in peer relationship.

There is ample evidence, for example, that the greater abstractness of the child's self-concept and of his descriptions of others are intimately connected to the broader changes in cognitive functioning (Harter, 1990). The emergence of concrete operations at 7 or 8 is reflected in the child's use of trait labels to describe himself and others; the emergence of formal operations is reflected in self-descriptions that focus more and more on interior states and in descriptions of others that are both flexible and based on subtle inferences from behavior.

A somewhat broader proposal about connections between cognitive and other changes at adolescence is Kohlberg's hypothesis about the linkages between formal operations, moral reasoning, and social cognitive reasoning—a hypothesis I talked about in Chapter 14 (Kohlberg, 1973; 1976). The limited data support the proposition that young people must develop at least some formal operations and at least some mutual perspective taking in relationships before they begin to use conventional moral reasoning. Full formal operations and still more abstract social understanding may be required for postconventional reasoning.

Some ability to use formal operations may also be necessary but not sufficient for the formation of a clear identity. One of the characteristics of formal operations thinking is the ability to imagine possibilities that you have never experienced and to manipulate ideas in your head. These new skills may help to foster the broad questioning of old ways, old values, and old patterns that are a central part of the identity-formation process. Several studies show that among high school and college students, those in Marcia's identity achievement or moratorium statuses are much more likely also to be using formal operations reasoning than are those in the diffusion or foreclosure statuses (e.g., Leadbeater & Dionne, 1981; Rowe & Marcia, 1980). In Rowe and Marcia's study, the *only* individuals who showed full identity achievement were those who were also using full formal operations. But the converse was not true. That is, there were a number of subjects who used formal operations who had not yet established a clear identity. Thus formal operations thinking may *enable* the young person to rethink many aspects of his life, but it does not guarantee that he will do so.

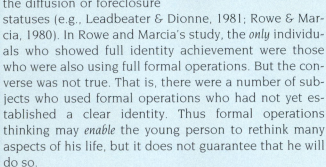

Overall, we are left with the impression that both the physical changes of puberty and the potential cognitive changes of formal operations are central to the phenomena of adolescence, but the connections between them, and their impact on social behavior, are still largely a mystery. I know it is frustrating to have me keep saying that we don't know, but that's an accurate statement of our current knowledge.

INFLUENCES ON THE BASIC PROCESSES

I do not have space enough to detail all the many factors that will influence the teenager's experience of adolescence. Many I have already mentioned, including such cultural variations as the presence or absence of initiation rites, the timing of the child's pubertal development, and the degree of personal or familial stress. But one more general point is worth repeating: Adolescence, like every other developmental period, does not begin with a clean slate. The individual youngster's own temperamental qualities, behavioral habits, and internal models of interaction, established in earlier years of childhood, obviously have a profound effect on the experience of adolescence. Examples are easy to find.

- Sroufe's longitudinal study, which I described in Chapter 6 (Sroufe, 1989), shows that those who had

been rated as having a secure attachment in infancy were more self-confident and more socially competent with peers at the beginning of adolescence.

- Delinquency and heightened aggressiveness in adolescence are most often presaged by earlier behavior problems, and by inadequate family control as early as the years of toddlerhood (Dishion, French, & Patterson, 1995). Even those delinquents who show such antisocial behavior for the first time as teenagers enter adolescence with different qualities, including poorer quality friendships (Berndt & Keefe, 1995a).

- Depression in the teenage years is more likely among those who enter adolescence with lower self-esteem (Harter, 1987).

Avshalom Caspi and Terrie Moffitt (1991) make the more general point that *any* major life crisis or transition, including adolescence, has the effect of *accentuating* earlier personality or behavioral patterns rather than creating new ones. This is not unlike the observation that the child's attachment to the parent is only revealed when the child is under stress. As one example of the more general process, Caspi and Moffitt point out that girls with very early puberty, on average, have higher rates of psychological problems than do those with normal-onset puberty. However, closer analysis reveals that it is only the early-puberty girls who already had social problems before puberty began whose pubertal experience and adolescence is more negative. Very early puberty does not increase psychological problems for girls who were psychologically healthier to begin with.

I think this is an important point for understanding all the various transitions of adult life as well as those of adolescence. Not only do we carry ourselves with us as we move through the roles and demands of adult life, but those existing patterns may be most highly visible when we are under stress. This does not mean that we never change or learn new and more effective ways of responding. Many do. Still, we must never lose sight of the fact that by adolescence, and certainly by adulthood, our internal working models and our repertoire of coping behaviors are already established, creating a bias in the system. Another way of putting it is that while change is possible, continuity is the default option.

Glossary

accommodation That part of the adaptation process by which a person modifies existing schemes in order to fit new experiences or creates new schemes when old ones no longer handle the data. **(p. 49)**

achievement test Test designed to assess a child's learning of specific material taught in school, such as spelling or arithmetic computation, and typically given to all children in designated grades. **(p. 379)**

acuity Sharpness of perceptual ability—how well or how clearly one can see or hear or use other senses. **(p. 154)**

acute illness Brief (rather than chronic) illnesses, such as colds, the flu, or diarrhea. **(p. 234)**

adolescent-onset conduct disorder A conduct disorder that begins only in adolescence. Typically less severe and persistent than childhood-onset disorders. **(p. 400)**

affectional bond A "relatively long-enduring tie in which the partner is important as a unique individual and is interchangeable with none other." **(p. 184)**

aggression Behavior with the apparent intent to injure some other person or object. **(p. 296)**

agreeableness One of the Big Five personality traits, characterized by trust, generosity, kindness, and sympathy. **(p. 499)**

alpha-fetoprotein test A prenatal diagnostic test frequently used to screen for the risk of neural tube defects. May also be used in combination with other tests to diagnose Down syndrome and other chromosomal anomalies. **(p. 88)**

altruism Giving or sharing objects, time, or goods with others, with no obvious self-gain. **(p. 298)**

amniocentesis A medical test for genetic abnormalities in the embryo/fetus that may be done at 15–18 weeks of gestation. **(p. 88)**

amnion The sac or bag, filled with liquid, in which the embryo and fetus floats during prenatal life. **(p. 80)**

androgynous Label applied to a person whose self-concept includes and whose behavior expresses high levels of both masculine and feminine qualities. **(p. 483)**

anorexia nervosa A serious eating disorder characterized by extreme dieting, intense fear of gaining weight, and distorted body image. **(p. 445)**

Apgar score A rating system for newborns with a maximum of 10 points, based on assessment of heart and respiratory rates, muscle tone, response to stimulation, and color. **(p. 114)**

assimilation That part of the adaptation process that involves the "taking in" of new experiences or information into existing schemes. Experience is not taken in "as is," however, but is modified (or interpreted) somewhat so as to fit the preexisting schemes. **(p. 49)**

asthma The most common chronic disease of childhood, increasing in frequency in recent decades. Symptoms include chronic cough, wheezing, tightness in the chest, and difficulty breathing. **(p. 233)**

attachment An especially intense and central type of affectional bond in which the presence of the partner adds a special sense of security, a "safe base," for the individual. Characteristic of the child's bond with the parent. **(p. 184)**

attachment behaviors The collection of (probably) instinctive behaviors of one person toward another that bring about or maintain proximity and caregiving, such as the smile of the young infant; behaviors that reflect an attachment. **(p. 185)**

attention deficit hyperactivity disorder (ADHD) The current technical term for what is often called hyperactivity, characterized by short attention span, distractibility, and heightened levels of physical activity. **(p. 345)**

attention deficit disorder (ADD) Term sometimes used interchangeably with ADHD, but also used more narrowly to describe the subset of children who show attention problems without hyperactivity. **(p. 345)**

authoritarian parental style   One of the three styles described by Baumrind, characterized by high levels of control and maturity demands and low levels of nurturance and communication. **(p. 311)**

authoritative parental style   One of the three styles described by Baumrind, characterized by high levels of control, nurturance, maturity demands, and communication. **(p. 311)**

axon   The long appendage-like part of a neuron; the terminal fibers of the axon serve as transmitters in the synaptic connection with the dendrites of other neurons. **(p. 82)**

babbling   The frequently repetitive vocalizing of consonant-vowel combinations by an infant, typically beginning at about age 6 months. **(p. 169)**

Babinski reflex   A reflex found in very young infants in which they splay out their toes in response to a stroke on the bottom of the foot. **(p. 115)**

Bayley Scales of Infant Development   The best-known and most widely used test of infant "intelligence," revised most recently in 1993. **(p. 173)**

behavior genetics   The study of the genetic basis of behavior, such as intelligence or personality. **(p. 11)**

Big Five   The five primary dimensions of personality variation identified by researchers, including extraversion, agreeableness, conscientiousness, neuroticism, and openness/intellect. **(p. 499)**

bilingual education   As practiced in the United States, a system of education for non-English-proficient students in which the instruction in reading, writing, and basic subject matter is in the children's native tongue during the first two or three years of schooling, with a gradual transition to full English instruction over several years. **(p. 375)**

birth order   A child's position in the sequence of children within a family, such as firstborn, later-born, or only. **(p. 295)**

blastocyst   Name for the mass of cells from roughly four to ten days after fertilization. **(p. 80)**

bodily kinesthetic intelligence   One of the six types of intelligence proposed by Howard Gardner. **(p. 281)**

body mass index (BMI)   A measure of fatness in which weight is adjusted for height. The specific formula is: weight in kilograms/(height in centimeters)^2. **(p. 332)**

bone age   A measure of physical maturation based on X-ray examination of bones, typically the wrist and hand bones. Two children of the same chronological age may

have different bone age because they differ in rate of physical maturation. **(p. 336)**

bulimia   An eating disorder characterized by an intense concern about weight combined with binge eating followed by purging, either through self-induced vomiting, excessive use of laxatives, or excessive exercise. **(p. 445)**

bully   A child who repeatedly torments some other child with words, gestures, intentional exclusion from a group, or physical aggression. **(p. 399)**

categorical self   Term used by Michael Lewis to describe the aspect of the self-concept that develops in the second year of life and later, when the child categorizes himself along important dimensions, such as gender, size, or ability. **(p. 195)**

cephalocaudal   One of two basic patterns of physical development in infancy (the other is proximodistal); the term describes development that proceeds from the head downward. **(p. 126)**

cesarean section   Delivery of the child through an incision in the mother's abdomen rather than vaginally. **(p. 105)**

childhood-onset conduct disorder   Conduct disorder beginning in childhood; linked to rejection by peers and to persistent conduct problems into adolescence and adulthood. **(p. 400)**

chlamydia   A sexually transmitted disease found fairly frequently among teenagers; symptoms include pain at urination and discharge, although one-third of infected persons have no symptoms. Can lead to pelvic inflammatory disease in women, which in turn can lead to sterility. **(p. 442)**

chorion   The outer layer of cells during the blastocyst stage of prenatal development, from which both the placenta and the umbilical cord are formed. **(p. 80)**

chorionic villus sampling   A technique for prenatal genetic diagnosis that involves taking a sample of cells from the placenta. Can be performed earlier in the pregnancy than amniocentesis but carries slightly higher risks. **(p. 88)**

chromosomes   The structures—arrayed in 23 pairs and contained in each cell in the body—that carry genetic information. Each chromosome is made up of many segments, called genes. **(p. 75)**

chronic illness   Any illness that persists six months or longer. In children this category includes asthma, cancer, diabetes, sickle-cell disease, and others. **(p. 232)**

classical conditioning   One of three major types of learning. An automatic unconditioned response, such as an emotion or a reflex, comes to be triggered by a new cue, called the conditioned stimulus (CS), after the CS has been paired several times with the original unconditional stimulus. **(p. 54)**

class inclusion The relationship between classes of objects such that a subordinate class is included in a superordinate class; for example, bananas are part of the class "fruit," and the class fruit is included in the class "food." **(p. 362)**

clinical depression A combination of sad mood, sleep and eating disturbances, and difficulty concentrating, lasting six months or longer. **(p. 501)**

clique Defined by Dunphy as a group of six to eight friends with strong affectional bonds and high levels of group solidarity and loyalty; currently used by researchers to describe a self-chosen group of friends, in contrast to reputation-based crowds. **(p. 496)**

coercive attachment Term used by Crittenden to describe the common preschool-age modification of an ambivalent attachment, in which the child coerces the parent's involvement through either coy enticement or anger. **(p. 291)**

cohort A group of persons of approximately the same age who have shared similar major life experiences, such as cultural training, historical events, or general economic conditions. **(p. 24)**

colic A pattern of persistent and often inconsolable crying, totaling more than three hours per day, found in some infants in the first three months of life. **(p. 122)**

collectivism A cultural perspective or belief system, contrasted with individualism, in which the emphasis is on collective rather than individual identity and on group solidarity, decision making, duties, and obligations. Characteristic of most Asian, Hispanic, and African cultures. **(p. 17)**

competence The level of skill displayed by a person under ideal or perfect circumstances. It is not possible to measure competence directly. **(p. 379)**

componential intelligence One of three types of intelligence in Sternberg's triarchic theory of intelligence; that type of intelligence typically measured on IQ tests, including analytic thinking, remembering facts, organizing information. **(p. 279)**

concrete operational stage The stage of development between ages 6 and 12, proposed by Piaget, in which mental operations such as subtraction, reversibility, and multiple classification are acquired. **(p. 51)**

conditional stimulus Term in classical conditioning for the stimulus that, after being paired a number of times with an unconditioned stimulus, comes to trigger the unconditioned response. For example, the sound of the mother's footsteps may become a conditional

stimulus for the baby's turning his head as if to suck. **(p. 54)**

conditioned response Term in classical conditioning for the response to the conditional stimulus. In appearance this behavior may look very much like the unconditioned response, but because it is triggered by a new, learned stimulus it is given a different name. **(p. 54)**

conduct disorder Diagnostic term for a pattern of deviant behavior including any or all of excessive aggressiveness, bullying, cruelty, or delinquency. **(p. 347)**

conscientiousness One of the Big Five personality traits, characterized by efficiency, organization, planfulness, and reliability. **(p. 499)**

conservation The concept that objects remain the same in fundamental ways, such as weight or number, even when there are external changes in shape or arrangement. Children begin to understand this concept at about age 5. **(p. 265)**

constructivism A key concept in Piaget's theory, that from birth a child is actively engaged in a process of constructing an understanding both of his own actions and of the external world. **(p. 368)**

contextual intelligence One of three types of intelligence in Sternberg's triarchic theory of intelligence; often also called "street smarts," this type of intelligence includes skills in adapting to an environment and in adapting an environment to one's own needs. **(p. 280)**

control group The group of subjects in an experiment that receives either no special treatment or some neutral treatment. **(p. 29)**

conventional morality The second level of moral judgment proposed by Kohlberg, in which the person's judgments are dominated by considerations of group values and laws. **(p. 462)**

cooing An early stage during the prelinguistic period, typically from 1 to 4 months of age, when vowel sounds are repeated, particularly the *uuu* sound. **(p. 169)**

correlation A statistic used to describe the degree or strength of a relationship between two variables. It can range from +1.00 to −1.00. The closer it is to ±1.00, the stronger the relationship being described. **(p. 32)**

cortex The convoluted gray portion of the brain that governs most complex thought, language, and memory. **(p. 126)**

critical period Any time period during development when the organism is especially responsive to and learns from a specific type of stimulation. The same stimulation at other points in development has little or no effect. **(p. 14)**

cross-cultural research Research involving in-depth study of another culture or comparisons of several cultures or subcultures. **(p. 24)**

cross-modal transfer The ability to transfer information gained through one sense to another sense at a later time; for example, identifying visually something you had previously explored only tactually. **(p. 161)**

cross-sectional design A form of research in which samples of subjects from several different age groups are studied at the same time. **(p. 24)**

cross-sequential design A complex combination of cross-sectional and longitudinal research designs in which groups of subjects of several different ages are initially selected and compared, and then all groups are followed longitudinally. **(p. 26)**

crowd Defined by Dunphy as a larger and looser group of friends than a clique, normally made up of several cliques joined together; defined by current researchers as a reputation-based group, common in adolescent subculture, with widely agreed-upon characteristics (e.g., "brains," "jocks," or "druggies"). **(p. 496)**

culture A system of meanings and customs, shared by some identifiable group or subgroup, and transmitted from one generation of that group to the next. **(p. 16)**

deductive logic Reasoning from the general to the particular, from a rule to an expected instance, or from a theory to a hypothesis. Characteristic of formal operational thought. **(p. 456)**

defended attachment Term used by Crittenden to describe common preschool-age modification of an avoidant attachment, in which the child attempts to maintain contact with the parent by becoming hyperaware of the parent's moods or needs, adapting to the parent(s). **(p. 291)**

delinquency A subcategory of conduct disorders involving explicit law-breaking. **(p. 502)**

dendrites The branchlike parts of a neuron that form one-half of the synaptic connection to other nerves. Dendrites develop rapidly in the final three prenatal months and the first year after birth. **(p. 82)**

deoxyribonucleic acid (DNA) The chemical of which genes are composed. **(p. 75)**

dependent variable The variable in an experiment that is expected to show the impact of manipulations of the independent variable; also called the outcome variable. **(p. 29)**

design stage Third stage in the development of children's drawings, as proposed by Kellogg; the mixing of several basic shapes into more complex designs. **(p. 231)**

developmental disabilities Permanent physical problems, such as blindness, deafness, cerebral palsy, limb deformations, and the like. Mental retardation is also typically classed in this category. Combined with chronic illnesses to create the larger category of "chronic conditions." **(p. 232)**

developmental psychopathology A relatively new approach to the study of deviance that emphasizes that normal and abnormal development are part of a continuum, with common roots, and that pathology can arise from many different pathways or systems. **(p. 64)**

difficult child One of three temperamental patterns described by Chess and Thomas; a child who is irregular in pattern, relatively inflexible, and generally negative in emotional tone. **(p. 199)**

dizygotic twins See *fraternal twins*. **(p. 79)**

dominance hierarchy A set of dominance relationships in a group that describes the rank order of "winners" and "losers" in competitive encounters; also called a "pecking order." **(p. 297)**

Down syndrome A genetic anomaly in which every cell contains three copies of chromosome 21 rather than two. Children born with this genetic pattern are usually mentally retarded and have characteristic physical features. **(p. 84)**

easy child One of three temperamental patterns described by Chess and Thomas; an adaptable child, with regular patterns and a generally positive emotional quality. **(p. 199)**

ego Term in Freudian theory for that portion of the personality that organizes, plans, and keeps the person in touch with reality. Language and thought are both ego functions. **(p. 42)**

egocentrism A cognitive state in which the individual (typically a child) sees the world only from his own perspective, without awareness that there are other perspectives. **(p. 263)**

embryo The name given to the organism during the period of prenatal development from about two to eight weeks after conception, beginning with implantation of the blastocyst into the uterine wall. **(p. 80)**

emotional intelligence A type of intelligence proposed by Daniel Goleman, including "abilities such as being able to motivate oneself and persist in the face of frustrations; to control impulses and delay gratification; to regulate one's moods and keep distress from swamping the ability to think; to empathize and to hope" (1995, p. 34). **(p. 280)**

emotional maltreatment A form of child abuse involving deliberate thwarting of a child's basic emotional needs. Includes belittling, ridicule, intimidation, and threats. **(p. 239)**

endocrine glands   These glands—including the adrenals, the thyroid, the pituitary, the testes, and the ovaries—secrete hormones governing overall physical growth and sexual maturing. **(p. 426)**

English as a Second Language (ESL)   An alternative to bilingual education; non-English-proficient students spend most of their school day in a full-English classroom but then spend several hours in a separate class with special instruction in English. **(p. 375)**

enuresis   The technical medical term for bed-wetting. **(p. 226)**

equilibration   The third part of the adaptation process as proposed by Piaget, involving a periodic restructuring of schemes into new structures. **(p. 49)**

estrogen   The female sex hormone secreted by the ovaries. **(p. 426)**

ethnic group   "A subgroup whose members are perceived by themselves and others to have a common origin and culture, and shared activities in which the common origin or culture is an essential ingredient" (Porter & Washington, 1993, p. 140). **(p. 18)**

ethnography   A detailed description of a single culture or context, based on extensive observation by a resident observer. **(p. 27)**

executive processes   Proposed subset of information processes involving organizing and planning strategies. Similar in meaning to metacognition. **(p. 370)**

exercise-induced asthma   A form of asthma triggered by heavy exercise, especially in cold, dry air. Common among top-level athletes, such as Jackie Joyner-Kersee. **(p. 233)**

exosystem   Concept in Bronfenbrenner's ecological model; it is that set of system elements that affects the child indirectly, through its influence on the family or on some other microsystem in which the child exists. For example, the parents' jobs and their network of friends are part of the exosystem for the child. **(p. 62)**

experiential intelligence   One of three types of intelligence described by Sternberg in his triarchic theory of intelligence; includes creativity, insight, seeing new relationships among experiences. **(p. 280)**

experiment   A research strategy in which subjects are assigned randomly to experimental and control groups. The experimental group is then provided with some designated experience that is expected to alter behavior in some fashion. **(p. 29)**

experimental group   The group (or groups) of subjects in an experiment given a special treatment intended to produce some specific consequence. **(p. 29)**

expertise   Knowledge of a particular subject or skill at some particular task or physical activity that is based on extensive practice or study. **(p. 365)**

expressive language   The term used to describe the child's skill in speaking and communicating orally. **(p. 169)**

expressive style   One of two styles of early language proposed by Nelson, characterized by low rates of nounlike terms, and high use of personal-social words and phrases. **(p. 172)**

extinction   A decrease in and eventually the elimination of the strength of some response after nonreinforcement. **(p. 56)**

extraversion   One of the Big Five personality traits, characterized by assertiveness, energy, enthusiasm, and outgoingness. **(p. 499)**

extremely low birth weight   Any birth weight below 1000 grams. **(p. 105)**

fallopian tube   The tube between the ovary and the uterus down which the ovum travels to the uterus and in which conception usually occurs. **(p. 74)**

false belief   Incorrectly believing something to be true and acting on that belief; the child's understanding of the principle of false belief is one key sign of the emergence of a representational theory of mind. **(p. 266)**

family day care   Nonparental care in which the child is cared for in someone else's home, usually with a small group of other children. **(p. 202)**

family preservation program   A type of treatment program for abusing families that focuses on providing intensive, short-term assistance to the family so that the abused child may remain with the family. **(p. 246)**

feminine   One of four sex-role types suggested by the work of Bem and others; a pattern of high scores on femininity measures and low scores on masculinity. **(p. 483)**

fetal alcohol syndrome (FAS)   A pattern of physical and mental abnormalities, including mental retardation and minor physical anomalies, found often in children born to alcoholic mothers. **(p. 91)**

fetus   The name given to the developing organism from about eight weeks after conception until birth. **(p. 80)**

fontanels   The "soft spots" in the skull present at birth. These disappear when the several bones of the skull grow together. **(p. 129)**

foreclosure   One of four identity statuses proposed by Marcia; it signifies an ideological or occupational commitment without having gone through a reevaluation. **(p. 485)**

formal operational stage   Piaget's name for the fourth and final major stage of cognitive development, occurring during adolescence, when the child becomes able to manipulate and organize ideas as well as objects. **(p. 51)**

foster care   A form of treatment for abused children involving removal of the child from the family and placement of him with another family for temporary care. **(p. 246)**

fraternal twins   Children carried in the same pregnancy but resulting from two separate fertilized ova; they are no more alike genetically than other pairs of brothers and sisters. Also called dizygotic twins. **(p. 79)**

frustration-aggression hypothesis   Early psychological hypothesis that all aggression results from frustration and all frustration leads to aggression. Only partially supported by research. **(p. 297)**

gametes   Sperm and ova. These cells, unlike all other cells of the body, contain only 23 chromosomes rather than 23 pairs. **(p. 75)**

gender concept   The understanding of one's own gender, including the permanence and constancy of gender. **(p. 303)**

gender constancy   The final step in developing a gender concept, in which the child understands that gender doesn't change even though there are external changes like clothing or hair length. **(p. 304)**

gender identity   The earliest aspect of gender concept development, in which the child labels herself correctly and categorizes others correctly as female or male. **(p. 304)**

gender schema   A fundamental schema created by children beginning at age 18 months or younger by which the child categorizes people, objects, activities, and qualities by gender. **(p. 307)**

gender stability   An aspect of the total gender concept in which the child understands that a person's gender continues to be stable throughout the lifetime. **(p. 304)**

gene   A uniquely coded segment of DNA in a chromosome that affects one or more specific body processes or developments. **(p. 75)**

genital warts   A sexually transmitted disease (technically called human papillomavirus) found fairly frequently among adolescents. Symptoms involve warts on the genitalia. **(p. 442)**

genotype   The pattern of characteristics and developmental sequences mapped in the genes of any specific individual. Will be modified by individual experience into the phenotype. **(p. 75)**

gifted   Normally defined in terms of very high IQ score (above 130 or 140), but may also be defined in terms of remarkable skill in one or more specific areas, such as mathematics or memory. **(p. 274)**

glial cells   One of two major classes of cells making up the nervous system, glial cells provide the firmness and structure, the "glue," to hold the system together. **(p. 82)**

goal-corrected partnership   Term used by Bowlby to describe the form of an appropriate child-to-parent attachment in the preschool years in which the two partners, through improved communication, negotiate the form and frequency of contact between them. **(p. 291)**

gonadotrophic hormones   Hormones produced in the pituitary gland that stimulate the sex organs to develop. **(p. 426)**

grand schemes   Phrase used in this book to describe the three most comprehensive theories of development: psychoanalytic, cognitive-developmental, and learning theories. **(p. 41)**

habituation   An automatic decrease in the intensity of a response to a repeated stimulus, which enables the child or adult to ignore the familiar and focus attention on the novel. **(p. 151)**

hedonistic reasoning   A form of prosocial moral reasoning described by Eisenberg in which the child is concerned with self-oriented consequences rather than moral considerations. Roughly equivalent to Kohlberg's stage 2. **(p. 464)**

hemispheric lateralization   The specialization of tasks in the two hemispheres of the brain. Verbal tasks are primarily handled in the left brain, spatial tasks and emotional responses in the right. Left-handed individuals are usually somewhat less firmly lateralized. **(p. 221)**

heterozygous   Term describing the genetic pattern when the pair of genes at any given genetic locus carry different instructions, such as a gene for blue eyes from one parent and for brown eyes from the other parent. **(p. 76)**

holophrases   A combination of a gesture with a single word that conveys a sentencelike meaning; often seen/heard in children between 12 and 18 months. **(p. 170)**

homozygous   Term describing the genetic pattern when the pair of genes at any given genetic locus carry the same instructions. **(p. 76)**

hostile aggression   Aggression aimed at hurting another person or gaining an advantage over another. **(p. 297)**

hyperkinetic syndrome   Label used in Europe in place of attention deficit disorder; diagnosed much more rarely than ADD in the United States. **(p. 345)**

hypothetico-deductive reasoning   Piaget's term for the form of reasoning that is part of formal operational thought, involving not just deductive logic but, more broadly, the ability to consider hypotheses and hypothetical possibilities. **(p. 456)**

id   Term in Freudian theory for the first, primitive portion of the personality; the storehouse of basic energy, continually pushing for immediate gratification. **(p. 42)**

identical twins   Children carried in the same pregnancy who come from the *same* originally fertilized ovum; they are genetically identical to one another. Also called monozygotic twins. **(p. 79)**

identification   The process of taking into oneself ("incorporating") the qualities and ideas of another person, which Freud thought was the result of the Oedipal crisis between ages 3 and 5. The child attempts to make himself or herself like the parent of the same sex. **(p. 42)**

identity   Term used in Erikson's theory to describe the gradually emerging sense of self, changing through a series of eight stages. **(p. 44)**

identity achievement   One of four identity statuses proposed by Marcia; it involves the successful resolution of an identity "crisis," which results in a new commitment. **(p. 485)**

identity diffusion   One of four identity statuses proposed by Marcia; it involves neither a current reevaluation nor a firm personal commitment. **(p. 485)**

identity statuses   Four categories suggested by James Marcia, created by combining high and low identity crises and high and low identity commitment. Includes foreclosure, moratorium, identity diffusion, and identity achievement. **(p. 485)**

implantation   Process by which the blastocyst attaches itself to the wall of the uterus, generally during the second week after fertilization. **(p. 80)**

inclusion   Term used to describe the full-time placement of physically, mentally, or emotionally disabled children in regular classrooms, with any special services required by the child provided in that classroom. **(p. 352)**

independent variable   A condition or event an experimenter varies in some systematic way in order to observe the impact of that variation on the subjects' behavior. **(p. 29)**

individualism   A cultural perspective or belief system, contrasted with collectivism, in which the emphasis is placed on the separateness and independence of individual development and behavior. Characteristic of most Western cultures. **(p. 17)**

individuation   Label used by some theorists for the process of psychological, social, and physical separation from parents that begins in adolescence. **(p. 491)**

inductive logic   Reasoning from the particular to the general, from experience to broad rules. Characteristic of concrete operational thinking. **(p. 359)**

infant-directed speech   The formal scientific term for "motherese," that special form of simplified, higher-pitched speech adults use with infants and young children. **(p. 259)**

infant mortality rate   Number of deaths in the first year, out of each 1000 live births. **(p. 138)**

inflections   The various grammatical "markers" contained in every language, such as (in English) the *s* for plurals or the *-ed* for past tenses, auxiliary verbs such as *is*, and the equivalent. **(p. 252)**

information processing   Phrase used to refer to a new, third approach to the study of intellectual development that focuses on changes with age and on individual differences in fundamental intellectual skills. **(p. 147)**

insecure attachment   Internal working model of relationships in which the child does not as readily use the parent as a safe base and is not readily consoled by the parent if upset. Includes three subtypes of attachment: ambivalent, avoidant, and disorganized/disoriented. **(p. 190)**

instrumental aggression   Aggression aimed at gaining or damaging some object. **(p. 297)**

intelligence quotient (IQ)   Originally defined in terms of a child's mental age and chronological age, IQs are now computed by comparing a child's performance with that of other children of the same chronological age. **(p. 273)**

internal working model (of social relationships)   Cognitive construction, for which the earliest relationships may form the template, of the workings of relationships, such as expectations of support or affection, trustworthiness, and so on. **(p. 190)**

intersensory integration   The combining of information from two or more senses to form a unified perceptual whole, such as the sight of mouth movements combined with the sound of particular words. **(p. 161)**

intrinsic reinforcements   Concept emphasized in Bandura's theory; those inner sources of pleasure, pride, or satisfaction that serve to increase the likelihood that an individual will repeat the behavior that led to the feeling. **(p. 56)**

jargon   A form of babbling in which the infant strings together a series of different vowel-consonant combinations rather than repeating the same combination over and over. **(p. 169)**

Kaufman Assessment Battery for Children (K-ABC)   A relatively new type of IQ test now quite widely used; includes measures of sequential processing, simultaneous processing, and achievement. **(p. 276)**

latchkey children   Children in "self-care" before or after school because the parents are working or otherwise unavailable and no other supervision has been arranged. **(p. 409)**

learning disability (LD)   Term broadly used to describe any child with an unexpected or unexplained problem in learning to read, spell, or calculate. More precisely used to refer to conditions in a subgroup of such children who have some neurological dysfunction. **(p. 349)**

libido   Term used by Freud to describe the pool of sexual energy in each individual. **(p. 42)**

linguistic intelligence   One of the six types of intelligence proposed by Howard Gardner. **(p. 281)**

logical-mathematical intelligence   One of the six types of intelligence proposed by Howard Gardner. **(p. 281)**

longitudinal design   A research design in which the same subjects are observed or assessed repeatedly over a period of months or years. **(p. 24)**

low birth weight (LBW)   Any baby born with a weight below 2500 grams is given this label, including both those born too early (preterm) and those who are "small for date." **(p. 105)**

macrosystem   Term used by Bronfenbrenner in his ecological model to describe the larger culture or subcultural setting in which both the microsystems and exosystems exist. **(p. 62)**

masculine   One of four sex-role types suggested by the work of Bem and others; a pattern of high scores on masculinity measures and low scores on femininity measures. **(p. 483)**

maturation   The sequential unfolding of physical characteristics, governed by instructions contained in the genetic code and shared by all members of a species. **(p. 9)**

mean length of utterance (MLU)   The average number of "meaningful units" in a sentence. Each basic word is one meaningful unit, as is each inflection, such as the *s* for plural or the *-ed* for a past tense. **(p. 272)**

menarche   Onset of menstruation in girls. **(p. 431)**

mental age   Term used by Binet and Simon and Terman in the early calculation of IQ; the age level of IQ test items the child can successfully pass. When compared with the child's chronological age, allows calculation of an IQ score. **(p. 273)**

mentally retarded   Term used to describe children or adults with IQ scores of 75 or below in addition to poor adaptive behavior. **(p. 273)**

metacognition   General and rather loosely used term describing an individual's knowledge of his own thinking processes. Knowing what you know, and how you go about learning or remembering. **(p. 268)**

metamemory   A subcategory of metacognition; knowledge about your own memory processes. **(p. 268)**

microsystem   Term used by Bronfenbrenner in his ecological model to describe any setting a child experiences directly, such as the family, the school, or a day care center. **(p. 62)**

minitheories   Term used in this text to describe the narrower, more limited types of theories designed to explain only a particular, somewhat specific phenomenon. **(p. 41)**

modeling   Term used by Bandura and others to describe observational learning. **(p. 56)**

models   Term used in this book to describe the middle level of theories, less comprehensive than a grand scheme but broader than a minitheory; examples are biological and ecological models. **(p. 41)**

monozygotic twins   See *identical twins*. **(p. 79)**

moral-legal-educational maltreatment   A form of child abuse in which the parent fails to provide the child with the needed opportunities to become integrated in society or exposes the child to illegal activities. Failure to ensure the child's attendance at school would be one example. **(p. 239)**

moratorium   One of four identity statuses proposed by Marcia; it involves an ongoing reexamination but without a new commitment as yet. **(p. 485)**

Moro reflex   When startled (e.g., by a loud sound or a sensation of being dropped), the infant extends his legs, arms, and fingers, arches his back, and draws back his head. **(p. 115)**

motherese   See *infant-directed speech*. **(p. 259)**

musical intelligence   One of the six types of intelligence proposed by Howard Gardner. **(p. 280)**

myelin   Material making up a sheath that develops around most axons. This sheath is not completely developed at birth. **(p. 128)**

myelination   The process by which myelin is added. **(p. 128)**

needs-oriented reasoning   A form of prosocial moral reasoning proposed by Eisenberg in which the child expresses concern directly for the other person's need, even if the other's need conflicts with the child's own wishes or desires. **(p. 464)**

negative reinforcement   The strengthening of a behavior because of the removal, cessation, or avoidance of an unpleasant stimulus. **(p. 55)**

neglected children   Type of unpopular children who are not overtly rejected, are reasonably well liked, but are not often chosen as friends. **(p. 401)**

neglecting parental style   A fourth style of parenting characterized by low levels of control, low acceptance or even outright rejection, and low levels of warmth. **(p. 311)**

neuron   The second major class of cells in the nervous system, neurons are responsible for transmission and reception of nerve impulses. **(p. 82)**

neuroticism   One of the Big Five personality traits, characterized by anxiety, self-pity, tenseness, and emotional instability. **(p. 499)**

neurotransmitters   Chemicals at synapses that accomplish the transmission of signals from one neuron to another. **(p. 82)**

nightmares   Scary, upsetting dreams, occurring normally in the early morning. **(p. 226)**

night terrors   A form of sleep disruption occurring early in a night's sleep for some children. The child may scream but is not fully awake and returns to sleep readily. **(p. 226)**

nursing bottle syndrome   Pattern of tooth decay in the primary teeth that can occur when an infant continues to drink from a bottle past about age 1, especially if the child is given a bottle at bedtime or nap time. **(p. 126)**

obesity   Most often defined as a body weight 20 percent or more above the normal weight for height, or a body mass index at the 85th percentile or above. **(p. 332)**

object permanence   The understanding that an object continues to exist even when it is temporarily out of sight. More generally, the basic understanding that objects exist separate from one's own action on them. **(p. 163)**

observational learning   Learning of motor skills, attitudes, or other behaviors through observing someone else perform them. **(p. 56)**

Oedipus conflict   The pattern of events Freud believed occurred between ages 3 and 5 when the child experiences a "sexual" desire for the parent of the opposite sex; the resulting fear of possible reprisal from the parent of the same sex is resolved when the child "identifies" with the parent of the same sex. **(p. 42)**

openness/intellect   One of the Big Five personality traits, characterized by curiosity, imagination, insight, originality, and wide interest. **(p. 499)**

operant conditioning   That type of learning in which the probability of a person's performing some behavior is strengthened by positive or negative reinforcements. **(p. 55)**

operations   Piaget's term for the new and powerful class of mental schemes he saw as developing between roughly ages 5 and 7, including reversibility, addition, and subtraction. **(p. 51)**

ordinal position   See *birth order*.

ossification   The process of hardening by which soft tissue becomes bone. **(p. 129)**

osteoporosis   Loss of bone mass after middle age, resulting in more brittle and porous bones and a substantially increased risk of fracture. **(p. 336)**

otitis media   The medical name for what most parents call an ear infection: the collection of fluid in the middle ear, often accompanied by other symptoms of acute illness. **(p. 136)**

overregularization   The tendency on the part of children to make the language regular by creating regularized versions of irregular speech forms as in past tenses or plurals; for example (in English), *beated* or *footses*. **(p. 253)**

ovum   The gamete produced by a woman, which, if fertilized by a sperm from a male, forms the basis for the developing organism. **(p. 74)**

parallel play   Form of play seen in toddlers in which two children play next to, but not with, one another. **(p. 296)**

parental enhancement programs   A form of treatment focused on providing abusing parents with improved parenting skills as well as support in solving other life crises. **(p. 246)**

partial reinforcement   Reinforcement of behavior on some schedule less frequent than every occasion. **(p. 56)**

Peabody Picture Vocabulary Test (PPVT)   A widely used measure of children's vocabulary. On each of 150 items, the examiner provides a word and the child must select the most appropriate picture from an array of four pictures. **(p. 259)**

performance   The behavior shown by a person under real-life rather than perfect or ideal circumstances. Even when we are interested in competence, all we can ever measure is performance. **(p. 380)**

permissive parental style   One of the three styles described by Baumrind, characterized by high levels of nurturance and low levels of control, maturity demands, and communication. **(p. 311)**

personal intelligence   One of the six types of intelligence proposed by Howard Gardner. **(p. 281)**

personality   The collection of individual, relatively enduring patterns of reacting to and interacting with others that distinguishes each child or adult; temperament is thought of as the emotional substrate of personality. **(p. 198)**

phenotype   The expression of a particular set of genetic information in a specific environment; the observable result of the joint operation of genetic and environmental influences. **(p. 79)**

physical abuse   A form of child abuse involving the nonaccidental inflicting of bodily injury on a child. **(p. 239)**

physical neglect   A form of child abuse that includes both the failure to provide adequately for the child's nurturance and basic care and the failure to provide adequate supervision. **(p. 239)**

pictorial stage   Fourth stage in the development of children's drawings, as proposed by Kellogg; the child draws pictures of real-life objects such as people or houses, using combinations of the basic shapes. **(p. 231)**

pituitary   One of the endocrine glands. The pituitary plays a central role in controlling the rate of physical maturation and sexual maturing. **(p. 426)**

placenta   An organ that develops during gestation between the fetus and the wall of the uterus. The placenta filters nutrients from the mother's blood, acting as liver, lungs, and kidneys for the fetus. **(p. 80)**

polygenic inheritance   Any pattern of genetic transmission in which multiple genes contribute to the outcome, like that presumed to occur for complex behaviors such as intelligence or temperament. **(p. 78)**

positive reinforcement   Strengthening of a behavior by the presentation of some pleasurable or positive stimulus. **(p. 55)**

postconventional morality   See *principled morality*.

postpartum depression   A severe form of the common experience of postpartum blues. Affecting perhaps 10 percent of women, this form of clinical depression typically lasts six to eight weeks. **(p. 182)**

pragmatics   The rules for the use of language in communicative interaction, such as the rules for taking turns, for selecting the style of speech appropriate to varying listeners, and the equivalent. **(p. 257)**

preconventional morality   The first level of morality proposed by Kohlberg, in which moral judgments are dominated by consideration of what will be punished and what feels good. **(p. 461)**

preterm infant   Descriptive phrase widely used to label infants born before a 38-week gestational age. **(p. 105)**

preoperational stage   Piaget's term for the second major stage of cognitive development, generally from ages 2 to 6, marked at the beginning by the ability to use symbols and later by the development of basic classification and logical abilities. **(p. 51)**

primary circular reactions   Piaget's phrase to describe the baby's simple repetitive actions in the second substage of the sensorimotor stage, organized around the baby's own body; the baby repeats some action in order to have some desired outcome occur again, such as putting his thumb in his mouth to repeat the good feeling of sucking. **(p. 148)**

primary teeth   The "baby teeth" that begin erupting at 5 or 6 months and then are lost, beginning at age 5 or 6, to be replaced by the permanent, or secondary, teeth. **(p. 129)**

primitive reflexes   Collection of reflexes seen in young infants, controlled by the more primitive parts of the brain, that gradually disappear during the first year of life, including the Moro, Babinski, stepping, and others. **(p. 115)**

principled morality   The third level of morality proposed by Kohlberg, in which considerations of justice, individual rights, and contracts dominate moral judgment. **(p. 462)**

production deficiency   Phrase used to describe a situation in which an individual can use some physical or mental strategy if reminded to do so, but fails to "produce" the strategy spontaneously. **(p. 364)**

prosocial behavior   See *altruism*.

proximodistal   One of two basic patterns of physical development in infancy (the other is cephalocaudal); the term describes development that proceeds from the center outward, such as from the trunk to the limbs. **(p. 126)**

psychosexual stages   The stages of personality development suggested by Freud, including the oral, anal, phallic, latency, and genital stages. **(p. 42)**

psychosocial stages   The stages of personality development suggested by Erikson, including trust, autonomy, initiative, industry, identity, intimacy, generativity, and ego integrity. **(p. 44)**

puberty   The collection of hormonal and physical changes at adolescence that brings about sexual maturity. **(p. 424)**

punishment   Unpleasant consequences, administered after some undesired behavior by a child or adult, with the intent of extinguishing the behavior. **(p. 56)**

Raven's Progressive Matrices   A commonly used nonverbal measure of intelligence. The subject must select the pattern that correctly fills in a blank space left in a patterned display. **(p. 276)**

reaction range   Term used by some psychologists for the range of possible outcomes (phenotypes) on some variable, given basic genetic patterning (genotype). In the case of IQ, the reaction range is estimated at 20 to 25 points. **(p. 279)**

receptive language   Term used to describe the child's ability to understand (receive) language, in contrast to his ability to express language. **(p. 169)**

reciprocal friendship   Any friendship in which the two partners each name the other as a friend; also a quality of friendship in school-age children, when friendship is perceived for the first time as being based on reciprocal trust. **(p. 396)**

referential style   Second style of early language proposed by Nelson, characterized by emphasis on objects and their naming and description. **(p. 172)**

reflexes   Automatic body reactions to specific stimulation, such as the knee jerk or the Moro reflex. Many reflexes remain among adults, but the newborn also has some "primitive" reflexes that disappear as the cortex is fully developed. **(p. 115)**

rejected children   Unpopular children who are not just ignored but are explicitly avoided, not chosen as playmates or friends. **(p. 401)**

relational aggression   A form of aggression aimed at damaging the other person's self-esteem or peer relationships, such as by ostracism or threats of ostracism, cruel gossiping, or facial expressions of disdain. **(p. 399)**

respiratory distress syndrome   A problem frequently found in infants born more than six weeks before term, in which the infant's lungs lack the chemical surfactant needed to keep the air sacs inflated. **(p. 106)**

reversibility   One of the most critical of the "operations" Piaget identified as part of the concrete operations period. The child understands that actions can be reversed, thus returning to a previous state. **(p. 359)**

rooting reflex   Stroke an infant on the cheek near the mouth and the baby will, reflexively, turn toward the touch, open his mouth, and make sucking movements. **(p. 115)**

rubella   A form of measles that, if contracted during the first few weeks of a pregnancy, may have severe effects on the developing baby. **(p. 87)**

scaffolding   Term used by Bruner to describe a Vygotskian idea: a teacher (parent, older child, or person in the official role of teacher) structures a learning encounter with a child, so as to lead the child from step to step. **(p. 52)**

scatter plot   A way to display the type of data on which a correlation is based. **(p. 32)**

schematic learning   The development of expectancies of what actions lead to what results or what events tend to go together. Classical conditioning may be thought of as a subset of schematic learning. **(p. 151)**

scheme   Piaget's word for the basic actions of knowing, including both physical actions (sensorimotor schemes, such as looking or reaching) and mental actions, such as classifying or comparing or reversing. An experience is assimilated to a scheme, and the scheme is modified or created through accommodation. **(p. 49)**

scribble   First stage in the development of children's drawings, as proposed by Kellogg; she identifies 20 basic scribbles which form the foundation of the basic shapes. **(p. 231)**

secondary circular reactions   Repetitive actions in the third substage of the sensorimotor period, oriented around external objects; the infant repeats some action in order to have some outside event recur, such as hitting a mobile repeatedly to watch it move. **(p. 148)**

secular trend   A pattern of change in some characteristic over several cohorts, such as systematic changes in the average timing of menarche or average height or weight. **(p. 431)**

secure attachment   Demonstrated by the child's ability to use the parent as a safe base and to be consoled after separation, when fearful, or when otherwise stressed. **(p. 190)**

self-esteem   A global judgment of self-worth; how well you like the person you perceive yourself to be; how well you measure up when judged against your own valued qualities or skills. **(p. 404)**

self-scheme   An internal model of self, not unlike the concept of an internal model of attachment. **(p. 303)**

sensitive period   Similar to a critical period, except broader and less specific. A time in development when a particular type of stimulation is particularly important or effective. **(p. 15)**

sensorimotor stage   Piaget's term for the first major stage of cognitive development, from birth to about age 2, when the child moves from reflexive to voluntary action. **(p. 51)**

sequential design   A family of research designs involving multiple cross-sectional or multiple longitudinal studies, or a combination of the two. **(p. 24)**

sex-linked transmission   Pattern of genetic transmission that occurs when the critical gene is carried on a portion of the X chromosome that is not matched by genetic material on the Y chromosome. Diseases such as hemophilia follow this genetic pattern. **(p. 78)**

sex role   The set of behaviors, attitudes, rights, duties, and obligations that are part of the "role" of being a boy or a girl, a male or a female in any given culture. **(p. 303)**

sexual abuse   A form of child abuse that includes any kind of sexual contact between a child and a responsible adult that is for the purpose of the *adult s* gratification or gain. **(p. 239)**

sexually transmitted diseases (STDs)   Also called venereal diseases. Category of disease spread by sexual contact, including chlamydia, genital warts, syphilis, gonorrhea, and HIV. The two most common of these infections among adolescents are chlamydia and genital warts. **(p. 442)**

shape stage   Second stage in the development of children's drawings, as proposed by Kellogg; the child begins to draw specific shapes (lines, circles, squares) deliberately. **(p. 231)**

slow-to-warm-up child   One of three temperament patterns described by Chess and Thomas; a child who has moderate emotional reactions but who is relatively inflexible in the face of novelty. **(p. 199)**

small for date   Term for an infant who weighs less than is normal for the number of weeks of gestation completed. **(p. 105)**

social referencing   Using another person's reaction to some situation as a basis for deciding one's own reaction. A baby does this when she checks her parent's facial expression or body language before responding positively or negatively to something new. **(p. 160)**

spatial intelligence   One of the six types of intelligence proposed by Howard Gardner. **(p. 281)**

Stanford-Binet   The best-known American intelligence test. It was written by Louis Terman and his associates, based upon the first tests by Binet and Simon. **(p. 273)**

states of consciousness   Five main sleep/awake states identified in infants, from deep sleep to active awake states. **(p. 119)**

Strange Situation   A series of eight episodes used by Mary Ainsworth and others in studies of attachment. The child is observed with the mother, with a stranger, when left alone, and when reunited with both stranger and mother. **(p. 190)**

structured immersion   An alternative to traditional bilingual education in which all children in a given classroom speak the same non-English native tongue. All basic instruction is in English, paced so that the children can comprehend, with the teacher translating only when absolutely necessary. **(p. 375)**

submersion   Label used to describe programs for non-English-proficient students in which they are simply assigned to a regular English-speaking classroom without any supplemental language assistance. Also known as "sink or swim" programs. **(p. 375)**

sudden infant death syndrome (SIDS)   The unexpected death of an infant who otherwise appears healthy; also called crib death. Cause is unknown, but certain risk factors are known. **(p. 138)**

superego   Term in Freudian theory for the "conscience" part of personality, which develops as a result of the identification process. The superego contains the parental and societal values and attitudes incorporated by the child. **(p. 42)**

superobese   An individual with a body mass index at the 95th percentile or higher. **(p. 332)**

synapse   The point of communication between two neurons, where nerve impulses are passed from one neuron to another by means of chemicals called neurotransmitters. **(p. 82)**

telegraphic speech   Term used by Roger Brown to describe the earliest sentences created by most children because these sentences sound a bit like a telegram, including key nouns and verbs but generally omitting all other words and grammatical inflections. **(p. 252)**

temperament   Term sometimes used interchangeably with "personality," but best thought of as the emotional substrate of personality; at least partially genetically determined. **(p. 60)**

temperament   Term sometimes used interchangeably with "personality," but best thought of as the emotional substrate of personality; at least partially genetically determined. **(p. 198)**

teratogen   Any outside agent, such as a disease or a chemical, the presence of which significantly increases the risk of deviations or abnormalities in prenatal development. **(p. 14)**

tertiary circular reactions   The deliberate experimentation with variations of previous actions, characteristic of the fifth substage of sensorimotor intelligence, according to Piaget. **(p. 149)**

theory of mind   Phrase used to describe one aspect of the thinking of 4- and 5-year-olds when they show signs of understanding not only that other people think differently, but that other people will base their behavior on what they believe or know or feel, rather than on the visible situation. **(p. 266)**

time-lag design   A comparison of groups of subjects of the *same* age in different cohorts, such as studying drug use in a separate sample of 15-year-olds each year for 20 years; allows a direct examination of cohort changes in some behavior. **(p. 26)**

tracking   Also called smooth pursuit. The smooth movements of the eye used to follow the track of some moving object. **(p. 154)**

transitional object   An object such as a "security blanket" or a favored toy used by a child to aid the transition from waking to sleeping or from being with people to being alone. **(p. 224)**

ultrasound   A form of prenatal diagnosis in which high frequency sound waves are used to provide a picture of the moving fetus. Can be used to detect many physical deformities, such as neural tube defects, as well as multiple pregnancies and gestational age. **(p. 88)**

umbilical cord   The cord connecting the embryo/fetus to the placenta, containing two arteries and one vein. **(p. 80)**

unconditioned response Term in classical conditioning for the basic unlearned response that is triggered by the unconditional stimulus. A baby's turning of his head when touched on the cheek is an unconditional response. **(p. 54)**

unconditional stimulus Term in classical conditioning for the cue or signal that automatically triggers the unconditioned response. A touch on a baby's cheek, triggering head turning, is an unconditional stimulus. **(p. 54)**

undifferentiated One of four sex-role types suggested by the work of Bem and others; a pattern of low scores on both masculinity and femininity measures. **(p. 483)**

uterus The female organ in which the blastocyst implants itself and within which the embryo/fetus develops. (Popularly referred to as the womb.) **(p. 74)**

venereal diseases See *sexually transmitted diseases.*

very low birth weight Any birth weight below 1500 grams (3.3 pounds). **(p. 105)**

victim The target of a bully. Child victims tend to be passive, sensitive, quiet, and physically somewhat smaller or less strong. **(p. 399)**

visual cliff Apparatus designed by Gibson and Walk for their studies of depth perception in infants. **(p. 156)**

Wechsler Intelligence Scale for Children-III (WISC-III) The most recent revision of this well-known American IQ test, which includes both verbal and performance (nonverbal) subtests. **(p. 275)**

zone of proximal development A concept in Vygotsky's theory describing that range of tasks or problems that are too hard for the child to do alone but that she can manage with guidance. **(p. 52)**

References

Aboud, F. E., & Doyle, A. B. (1995). The development of in-group pride in black Canadians. *Journal of Cross-Cultural Psychology, 26,* 243–254.

Abramovitch, R., Pepler, D., & Corter, C. (1982). Patterns of sibling interaction among preschool-age children. In M. E. Lamb & B. Sutton-Smith (Eds.), *Sibling relationships: Their nature and significance across the lifespan* (pp. 61–86). Hillsdale, NJ: Erlbaum.

Abrams, B. (1994). Weight gain and energy intake during pregnancy. *Clinical Obstetrics and Gynecology, 37,* 515–527.

Abrams, E. J., Matheson, P. B., Thomas, P. A., Thea, D. M., Krasinski, K., Lambert, G., Shaffer, N., Bamji, M., Hutson, D., Grimm, K., Kaul, A., Bateman, D., Rogers, M., & New York City Perinatal HIV Transmission Collaborative Study Group, (1995). Neonatal predictors of infection status and early death among 332 infants at risk of HIV-1 infection monitored prospectively from birth. *Pediatrics, 96,* 451–458.

Achenbach, T. M. (1982). *Developmental psychopathology* (2nd ed.). New York: Wiley.

Achenbach, T. M. (1993). Taxonomy and comorbidity of conduct problems: Evidence from empirically based approaches. *Development and Psychopathology, 5,* 51–64.

Achenbach, T. M., & Edelbrock, C. S. (1981). Behavioral problems and competencies reported by parents of normal and disturbed children aged 4 through 16. *Monographs of the Society for Research in Child Development , 46*(1, Serial No. 188).

Adair, R. H., & Bauchner, H. (1993, April). Sleep problems in childhood. *Current Problems in Pediatrics,* 147–170.

Adams, G. R., Gullotta, T. P., & Montemayor, R. (Eds.). (1992). *Adolescent identity formation.* Newbury Park, CA: Sage.

Adams, M. J. (1990). *Beginning to read: Thinking and learning about print.* Cambridge: Massachusetts Institute of Technology Press.

Adashek, J. A., Peaceman, A. M., Lopez-Zeno, J. A., Minogue, J. P., & Socol, M. L. (1993). Factors contributing to the increased cesarean birth rate in older parturient women. *American Journal of Obstetrics and Gynecology, 169,* 936–940.

Adesman, A. R. (1996). Fragile X syndrome. In A. J. Capute & P. J. Accardo (Eds.), *Developmental disabilities in infancy and childhood* (2nd ed.). Vol. 2, *The spectrum of developmental disabilities* (pp. 255–269). Baltimore: Paul H. Brookes.

Ahadi, S. A., & Rothbart, M. K. (1994). Temperament, development, and the big five. In C. F. Halverson Jr., G. A. Kohnstamm, & R. P. Martin (Eds.), *The developing structure of temperament and personality from infancy to adulthood* (pp. 189–207). Hillsdale, NJ: Erlbaum.

Ahlsten, G., Cnattingius, S., & Lindmark, G. (1993). Cessation of smoking during pregnancy improves foetal growth and reduces infant morbidity in the neonatal period. A population-based prospective study. *Acta Paediatrica, 82,* 177–182.

Ainsworth, M. D. S. (1967). *Infancy in Uganda: Infant care and the growth of love.* Baltimore: Johns Hopkins University Press.

Ainsworth, M. D. S. (1972). Attachment and dependency: A comparison. In J. L. Gewirtz (Ed.), *Attachment and dependency* (pp. 97–138). Washington, DC: V. H. Winston.

Ainsworth, M. D. S. (1982). Attachment: Retrospect and prospect. In C. M. Parkes & J. Stevenson-Hinde (Eds.), *The place of attachment in human behavior* (pp. 3–30). New York: Basic Books.

Ainsworth, M. D. S. (1989). Attachments beyond infancy. *American Psychologist, 44,* 709–716.

Ainsworth, M. D. S., Blehar, M., Waters, E., & Wall, S. (1978). *Patterns of attachment.* Hillsdale, NJ: Erlbaum.

Ainsworth, M. D. S., & Marvin, R. S. (1995). On the shaping of attachment theory and research: An interview with Mary D. S. Ainsworth (Fall 1994). *Monographs of the Society for Research in Child Development, 60*(2–3, Serial No. 244), pp. 3–21.

Aksu-Koc, A. A., & Slobin, D. I. (1985). The acquisition of Turkish. In D. I. Slobin (Ed.), *The crosslinguistic study of language acquisition.* Vol. 1, *The data* (pp. 839–878). Hillsdale, NJ: Erlbaum.

Alaimo, K., McDowell, M. A., Briefel, R. R., Bischof, A. M., Caughman, C. R., Loria, C. M., & Johnson, C. L. (1994). Dietary intake of vitamins, minerals, and fiber of persons ages

2 months and over in the United States: Third National Health and Nutrition Examination Survey, Phase 1, 1988–91. *Vital and Health Statistics, Centers for Disease Control and Prevention, Advance Data, 258*(November 14).

Al Awad, A. M. E. L., & Sonuga-Barke, E. J. S. (1992). Childhood problems in a Sudanese city: A comparison of extended and nuclear families. *Child Development, 63,* 906–914.

Alexander, K. L., Entwisle, D. R., & Dauber, S. L. (1993). First-grade classroom behavior: Its short and long-term consequences for school performance. *Child Development, 64,* 801–814.

Alho, O., Läärä, E., & Oja, H. (1996). How should relative risk estimates for acute otitis media in children aged less than 2 years be perceived? *Journal of Clinical Epidemiology, 49,* 9–14.

Allen, M. C. (1996). Preterm development. In A. J. Capute & P. J. Accardo (Eds.), *Developmental disabilities in infancy and childhood* (2nd ed.). Vol. 2, *The spectrum of developmental disabilities* (pp. 31–47). Baltimore: Paul H. Brookes.

Allen, M. C., Donohue, P. K., & Dusman, A. E. (1993). The limit of viability—Neonatal outcome of infants born at 22 to 25 weeks' gestation. *The New England Journal of Medicine, 329,* 1597–1601.

Alper, S., Schloss, P. J., Etscheidt, S. K., & Macfarlane, C. A. (1995). *Inclusion. Are we abandoning or helping students?* Thousand Oaks, CA: Corwin Press.

Alsaker, F. D. (1995). Timing of puberty and reactions to pubertal change. In M. Rutter (Ed.), *Psychosocial disturbances in young people. Challenges for prevention* (pp. 37–82). Cambridge, England: Cambridge University Press.

Alsaker, F. D., & Olweus, D. (1992). Stability of global self-evaluations in early adolescence: A cohort longitudinal study. *Journal of Research on Adolescence, 2,* 123–145.

Amador, M., Silva, L. C., & Valdes-Lazo, F. (1994). Breast-feeding trends in Cuba and the Americas. *Bulletin of the Pan American Health Organization, 28,* 220–227.

Amato, P. R. (1993). Children's adjustment to divorce: Theories, hypotheses, and empirical support. *Journal of Marriage and the Family, 55,* 23–38.

Ambert, A. (1994). An international perspective on parenting: Social change and social constructs. *Journal of Marriage and the Family, 56,* 529–543.

Ambuel, B. (1995). Adolescents, unintended pregnancy, and abortion: The struggle for a compassionate social policy. *Current Directions in Psychological Science, 4,* 1–5.

American Academy of Pediatrics Committee on Nutrition. (1986). Prudent life-style for children: Dietary fat and cholesterol. *Pediatrics, 78,* 521–525.

American Academy of Pediatrics Committee on Nutrition. (1992). Statement on cholesterol. *Pediatrics, 90,* 469–473.

American Psychiatric Association. (1994). *Diagnostic and statistical manual of mental disorders* (4th ed.). Washington: DC: American Psychiatric Association.

American Psychological Association. (1993). *Violence and youth: Psychology's response.* Vol. 1, *Summary report of the American Psychological Association Commission on Violence and Youth.* Washington, DC: American Psychological Association.

Anderson, D. R., Lorch, E. P., Field, D. E., Collins, P. A., & Nathan, J. G. (1986). Television viewing at home: Age trends in visual attention and time with TV. *Child Development, 57,* 1024–1033.

Andersson, B. (1989). Effects of public day-care: A longitudinal study. *Child Development, 60,* 857–886.

Andersson, B. (1992). Effects of day-care on cognitive and socioemotional competence of thirteen-year-old Swedish schoolchildren. *Child Development, 63,* 20–36.

Anglin, J. M. (1993). Vocabulary development: A morphological analysis. *Monographs of the Society for Research in Child Development, 58*(Serial No. 238).

Anglin, J. M. (1995, April). *Word learning and the growth of potentially knowable vocabulary.* Paper presented at the biennial meetings of the Society for Research in Child Development, Indianapolis.

Anisfeld, E., Casper, V., Nozyce, M., & Cunningham, N. (1990). Does infant carrying promote attachment? An experimental study of the effects of increased physical contact on the development of attachment. *Child Development, 61,* 1617–1627.

Anisfeld, M. (1991). Neonatal imitation. *Developmental Review, 11,* 60–97.

Anshel, M. H. (1990). *Sport psychology: From theory to practice.* Scottsdale, AZ: Gorsuch Scarisbrick.

Apgar, V. A. (1953). A proposal for a new method of evaluation of the newborn infant. *Current Research in Anesthesia and Analgesia, 32,* 260–267.

Arn, P., Chen, H., Tuck-Muller, C. M., Mankinen, C., Wachtel, G., Li, S., Shen, C.-C., & Wachtel, S. S. (1994). SRVX, a sex reversing locus in Xp21.2 → p22.11. *Human Genetics, 93,* 389–393.

Arnett, J. (1995). The young and the reckless: Adolescent reckless behavior. *Current Directions in Psychological Science, 4,* 67–71.

Arnold, L. D. W., & Larson, E. (1993). Immunologic benefits of breast milk in relation to human milk banking. *American Journal of Infection Control, 21,* 235–242.

Asendorpf, J. B., Warkentin, V., & Baudonnière, P. (1996). Self-awareness and other-awareness II: Mirror self-recognition, social contingency awareness, and synchronic imitation. *Developmental Psychology, 32,* 313–321.

Asher, S. R., & Coie, J. D. (Eds.). (1990). *Peer rejection in childhood.* Cambridge, England: Cambridge University Press.

Aslin, R. N. (1981). Experiential influences and sensitive periods in perceptual development: A unified model. In R. N. Aslin, J. R. Alberts, & M. R. Petersen (Eds.), *Development of perception. Psychobiological perspectives.* Vol. 2, *The visual system* (pp. 45–93). New York: Academic Press.

Aslin, R. N. (1987). Motor aspects of visual development in infancy. In P. Salapatek & L. Cohen (Eds.), *Handbook of infant perception*. Vol. 1, *From sensation to perception* (pp. 43–113). Orlando, FL: Academic Press.

Astington, J. W., & Gopnik, A. (1991). Theoretical explanations of children's understanding of the mind. In G. E. Butterworth, P. L. Harris, A. M. Leslie, & H. M. Wellman (Eds.), *Perspectives on the child's theory of mind* (pp. 7–31). New York: Oxford University Press.

Astington, J. W., & Jenkins, J. M. (1995, April). *Language and theory of mind: A theoretical review and a longitudinal study*. Paper presented at the biennial meetings of the Society for Research in Child Development, Indianapolis.

Astone, N. M. (1993). Are adolescent mothers just single mothers? *Journal of Research on Adolescence, 3*, 353–371.

Attie, I., & Brooks-Gunn, J. (1995). The development of eating regulation across the life span. In D. Cicchetti & D. J. Cohen (Eds.), *Developmental psychopathology*. Vol. 2, *Risk, disorder, and adaptation* (pp. 332–368). New York: Wiley.

Avis, J., & Harris, P. L. (1991). Belief-desire reasoning among Baka children: Evidence for a universal conception of mind. *Child Development, 62*, 460–467.

Bachman, J. G., & Schulenberg, J. (1993). How part-time work intensity relates to drug use, problem behavior, time use, and satisfaction among high school seniors: Are these consequences or merely correlates? *Developmental Psychology, 29*, 220–235.

Backous, D. D., Friedl, K. E., Smith, N. J., Par, T. J., & Carpine, W. D., Jr. (1988). Soccer injuries and their relation to physical maturity. *American Journal of Diseases of Children, 142*, 839–842.

Baghurst, P. A., McMichael, A. J., Tong, S., Wigg, N. R., Vimpani, G. V., & Robertson, E. F. (1995). Exposure to environmental lead and visual-motor integration at age 7 years: The Port Pirie cohort study. *Epidemiology, 6*(104–109).

Baghurst, P. A., McMichael, A. J., Wigg, N. R., Vimpani, G. V., Robertson, E. F., Roberts, R. J., & Tong, S. (1992). Environmental exposure to lead and children's intelligence at the age of seven years. *The New England Journal of Medicine, 327*, 1279–1284.

Bailey, D. A., Faulkner, R. A., & McKay, H. A. (1996). Growth, physical activity, and bone mineral acquisition. In J. O. Holloszy (Ed.), *Exercise and sport sciences reviews* (pp. 233–265). Baltimore: Williams & Wilkins.

Bailey, J. M., & Pillard, R. C. (1991). A genetic study of male sexual orientation. *Archives of General Psychiatry, 48*, 1089–1096.

Bailey, J. M., Pillard, R. C., Neale, M. C., & Agyei, Y. (1993). Heritable factors influence sexual orientation in women. *Archives of General Psychiatry, 50*, 217–223.

Bailey, J. M., & Zucker, K. J. (1995). Childhood sex-typed behavior and sexual orientation: A conceptual analysis and quantitative review. *Developmental Psychology, 31*, 43–55.

Baillargeon, R. (1987). Object permanence in very young infants. *Developmental Psychology, 23*, 655–664.

Baillargeon, R. (1994). How do infants learn about the physical world? *Current Directions in Psychological Science, 3*, 133–140.

Baillargeon, R., & DeVos, J. (1991). Object permanence in young infants: Further evidence. *Child Development, 62*, 1227–1246.

Baillargeon, R., Spelke, E. S., & Wasserman, S. (1985). Object permanence in five-month-old infants. *Cognition, 20*, 191–208.

Baker, J. M., & Zigmond, N. (1995). The meaning and practice of inclusion for students with learning disabilities: Themes and implications from the five cases. *The Journal of Special Education, 29*, 163–180.

Baker-Ward, L. (1995, April). *Children's reports of a minor medical emergency procedure*. Paper presented at the biennial meetings of the Society for Research in Child Development, Indianapolis.

Baker-Ward, L., Gordon, B. N., Ornstein, P. A., Larus, D. M., & Clubb, P. A. (1993). Young children's long-term retention of a pediatric examination. *Child Development, 64*, 1519–1533.

Balaban, M. T. (1995). Affective influences on startle in five-month-old infants: Reactions to facial expressions of emotion. *Child Development, 66*, 28–36.

Baldwin, D. A. (1995, April). *Understanding relations between constraints and a socio-pragmatic account of meaning acquisition*. Paper presented at the biennial meetings of the Society for Research in Child Development, Indianapolis.

Bamford, F. N., Bannister, R. P., Benjamin, C. M., Hillier, V. F., Ward, B. S., & Moore, W. M. O. (1990). Sleep in the first year of life. *Developmental Medicine and Child Neurology, 32*, 718–724.

Bandura, A. (1977). *Social learning theory*. Englewood Cliffs, NJ: Prentice Hall.

Bandura, A. (1986). *Social foundations of thought and action: A social cognitive theory*. Englewood Cliffs, NJ: Prentice Hall.

Bandura, A. (1989). Social cognitive theory. *Annals of Child Development, 6*, 1–60.

Bandura, A., Ross, D., & Ross, S. A. (1961). Transmission of aggression through imitation of aggressive models. *Journal of Abnormal and Social Psychology, 63*, 575–582.

Bandura, A., Ross, D., & Ross, S. A. (1963). Imitation of film-mediated aggressive models. *Journal of Abnormal and Social Psychology, 66*, 3–11.

Banerji, M., & Dailey, R. A. (1995). A study of the effects of an inclusion model on students with specific learning disabilities. *Journal of Learning Disabilities, 28*(511–522).

Bardoni, B., Zanaria, E., Guioli, S., Floridia, G., Worley, K. C., Tonini, G., Ferrante, E., Chiumello, G., McCabe, E. R. B., Fraccaro, M., Zuffardi, O., & Camerino, G. (1994). A dosage sensitive locus at chromosome Xp21 is involved in male to female sex reversal. *Nature Genetics, 7,* 497–501.

Barenboim, C. (1981). The development of person perception in childhood and adolescence: From behavioral comparisons to psychological constructs to psychological comparisons. *Child Development, 52,* 129–144.

Barkley, R. A. (1997). Behavioral inhibition, sustained attention, and executive functions: Constructing a unifying theory of ADHD. *Psychological Bulletin, 121,* 65–94.

Barkley, R. A., Fischer, M., Edelbrock, C. S., & Smallish, L. (1990). The adolescent outcome of hyperactive children diagnosed by research criteria: I. An 8-year prospective follow-up study. *Journal of the American Academy of Child and Adolescent Psychiatry, 29,* 546–557.

Barnard, K. E., Hammond, M. A., Booth, C. L., Bee, H. L., Mitchell, S. K., & Spieker, S. J. (1989). Measurement and meaning of parent-child interaction. In J. J. Morrison, C. Lord, & D. P. Keating (Eds.), *Applied developmental psychology* (Vol. 3) (pp. 40–81). San Diego: Academic Press.

Barness, L. A., & Curran, J. S. (1996). Nutrition. In R. E. Behrman, R. M. Kliegman, & A. M. Arvin (Eds.), *Nelson textbook of pediatrics* (15th ed.) (pp. 141–184). Philadelphia: W. B. Saunders.

Barnett, D. (1997). The effects of early intervention on maltreating parents and their children. In M. J. Guralnick (Ed.), *The effectiveness of early intervention* (pp. 147–170). Baltimore: Paul H. Brookes.

Barnett, D., Manly, J. T., & Cicchetti, D. (1993). Defining child maltreatment: The interface between policy and research. In D. Cicchetti & S. L. Toth (Eds.), *Child abuse, child development, and social policy* (pp. 7–73). Norwood, NJ: Ablex.

Barnett, W. S. (1993). Benefit-cost analysis of preschool education: Findings from a 25-year follow-up. *American Journal of Orthopsychiatry, 63,* 500–508.

Barnett, W. S. (1995). Long-term effects of early childhood programs on cognitive and school outcomes. *The Future of Children, 5*(3), 25–50.

Barrett, G. V., & Depinet, R. L. (1991). A reconsideration of testing for competence rather than for intelligence. *American Psychologist, 46,* 1012–1024.

Bartsch, K. (1993). Adolescents' theoretical thinking. In R. M. Lerner (Ed.), *Early adolescence. Perspectives on research, policy, and intervention* (pp. 143–157). Hillsdale, NJ: Erlbaum.

Bates, E. (1993). Commentary: Comprehension and production in early language development. *Monographs of the Society for Research in Child Development, 58*(3–4, Serial No. 233), 222–242.

Bates, E., Bretherton, I., Beeghly-Smith, M., & McNew, S. (1982). Social bases of language development: A reassessment. In H. W. Reese & L. P. Lipsitt (Eds.), *Advances in child development and behavior* (Vol. 16) (pp. 8–68). New York: Academic Press.

Bates, E., Bretherton, I., & Snyder, L. (1988). *From first words to grammar. Individual differences and dissociable mechanisms.* Cambridge, England: Cambridge University Press.

Bates, E., O'Connell, B., & Shore, C. (1987). Language and communication in infancy. In J. D. Osofsky (Ed.), *Handbook of infant development* (2nd ed.) (pp. 149–203). New York: Wiley.

Bates, J. E. (1989). Applications of temperament concepts. In G. A. Kohnstamm, J. E. Bates, & M. K. Rothbart (Eds.), *Temperament in childhood* (pp. 321–356). Chichester, England: Wiley.

Bates, J. E., Marvinney, D., Kelly, T., Dodge, K. A., Bennett, D. S., & Pettit, G. S. (1994). Child-care history and kindergarten adjustment. *Developmental Psychology, 30,* 690–700.

Baumrind, D. (1971). Current patterns of parental authority. *Developmental Psychology Monograph, 4*(1, Part 2).

Baumrind, D. (1972). Socialization and instrumental competence in young children. In W. W. Hartup (Ed.), *The young child: Reviews of research* (Vol. 2) (pp. 202–224). Washington, D.C.: National Association for the Education of Young Children.

Baumrind, D. (1991). Effective parenting during the early adolescent transition. In P. A. Cowan & M. Hetherington (Eds.), *Family transitions* (pp. 111–163). Hillsdale, NJ: Erlbaum.

Baydar, N., & Brooks-Gunn, J. (1991). Effects of maternal employment and child-care arrangements on preschoolers' cognitive and behavioral outcomes: Evidence from the children of the National Longitudinal Survey of Youth. *Developmental Psychology, 27,* 932–945.

Baydar, N., Brooks-Gunn, J., & Furstenberg, F. F. (1993). Early warning signs of functional illiteracy: Predictors in childhood and adolescence. *Child Development, 64,* 815–829.

Bayley, N. (1969). *Bayley scales of infant development* (rev. 1993). New York: Psychological Corporation.

Beaudry, M., Dufour, R., & Marcoux, S. (1995). Relation between infant feeding and infections during the first six months of life. *Journal of Pediatrics, 126,* 191–197.

Becker, J. A. (1982). Children's strategic use of requests to mark and manipulate social status. In S. A. Kuczaj, II (Ed.), *Language development.* Vol. 2, *Language, thought, and culture* (pp. 1–36). Hillsdale, NJ: Erlbaum.

Beckwith, L., & Rodning, C. (1991). Intellectual functioning in children born preterm: Recent research. In L. Okagaki & R. J. Sternberg (Eds.), *Directors of development* (pp. 25–58). Hillsdale, NJ: Erlbaum.

Bee, H. L., Barnard, K. E., Eyres, S. J., Gray, C. A., Hammond, M. A., Spietz, A. L., Snyder, C., & Clark, B. (1982). Prediction of IQ and language skill from perinatal status, child performance, family characteristics, and mother-infant interaction. *Child Development, 53,* 1135–1156.

Bell, L. G., & Bell, D. C. (1982). Family climate and the role of the female adolescent: Determinants of adolescent functioning. *Family Relations, 31,* 519–527.

Belsky, J. (1980). Child maltreatment: An ecological integration. *American Psychologist, 35*, 320–335.

Belsky, J. (1985). Prepared statement on the effects of day care. In *Select Committee on Children, Youth, and Families, House of Representatives, 98th Congress, Second Session, Improving child care services: What can be done?* Washington, DC: U.S. Government Printing Office.

Belsky, J. (1992). Consequences of child care for children's development: A deconstructionist view. In A. Booth (Ed.), *Child care in the 1990s. Trends and consequences* (pp. 83–94). Hillsdale, NJ: Erlbaum.

Belsky, J. (1996). Parent, infant, and social-contextual antecedents of father-son attachment security. *Developmental Psychology, 32*, 905–913.

Belsky, J., Hsieh, K., & Crnic, K. (1996). Infant positive and negative emotionality: One dimension or two? *Developmental Psychology, 32*, 289–298.

Belsky, J., Lang, M. E., & Rovine, M. (1985). Stability and change in marriage across the transition to parenthood: A second study. *Journal of Marriage and the Family, 47*, 855–865.

Belsky, J., Rosenberger, K., & Crnic, K. (1995). The origins of attachment security: "Classical" and contextual determinants. In R. Muir, S. Goldberg, & J. Kerr (Eds.), *John Bowlby's attachment theory: Historical, clinical and social significance* (pp. 115–124). Hillsdale, NJ: Erlbaum.

Belsky, J., & Rovine, M. (1988). Nonmaternal care in the first year of life and the security of infant-parent attachment. *Child Development, 59*, 157–167.

Belsky, J., Woodworth, S., & Crnic, K. (1996). Troubled family interaction during toddlerhood. *Development and Psychopathology, 8*, 477–495.

Bem, S. L. (1974). The measurement of psychological androgyny. *Journal of Consulting and Clinical Psychology, 42*, 155–162.

Bem, S. L. (1981). Gender schema theory: A cognitive account of sex-typing. *Psychological Review, 88*, 354–364.

Bem, S. L. (1989). Genital knowledge and gender constancy in preschool children. *Child Development, 60*, 649–662.

Benbow, C. P. (1986). Physiological correlates of extreme intellectual precocity. *Neuropsychologia, 24*, 719–725.

Benbow, C. P. (1988). Sex differences in mathematical reasoning ability in intellectually talented preadolescents: Their nature, effects, and possible causes. *Behavioral and Brain Sciences, 11*, 169–232.

Bender, B. G., Harmon, R. J., Linden, M. G., & Robinson, A. (1995). Psychosocial adaptation of 39 adolescents with sex chromosome abnormalities. *Pediatrics, 96*, 302–308.

Bender, S. L., Word, C. O., DiClemente, R. J., Crittenden, M. R., Persaud, N. A., & Ponton, L. E. (1995). The developmental implications of prenatal and/or postnatal crack cocaine exposure in preschool children: A preliminary report. *Developmental and Behavioral Pediatrics, 16*, 418–424.

Bendersky, M., & Lewis, M. (1994). Environmental risk, biological risk, and developmental outcome. *Developmental Psychology, 30*, 484–494.

Benenson, J. F. (1994). Ages four to six years: Changes in the structures of play networks of girls and boys. *Merrill-Palmer Quarterly, 40*, 478–487.

Benoit, D., & Parker, K. C. H. (1994). Stability and transmission of attachment across three generations. *Child Development, 65*, 1444–1456.

Berch, D. B., & Bender, B. G. (1987). Margins of sexuality. *Psychology Today, 21*(December), 54–57.

Berenbaum, S. A. (1997, April). *How and why do early hormones affect sex-typed behavior?* Paper presented at the biennial meetings of the Society for Research in Child Development, Washington, DC.

Bergmann, B. R. (1996). *Saving our children from poverty: What the United States can learn from France.* New York: Russell Sage Foundation.

Berkowitz, G. S., Skovron, M. L., Lapinski, R. H., & Berkowitz, R. L. (1990). Delayed childbearing and the outcome of pregnancy. *The New England Journal of Medicine, 322*, 659–664.

Berndt, T. J. (1983). Social cognition, social behavior, and children's friendships. In E. T. Higgins, D. N. Ruble, & W. W. Hartup (Eds.), *Social cognition and social development. A sociocultural perspective* (pp. 158–192). Cambridge, England: Cambridge University Press.

Berndt, T. J. (1986). Children's comments about their friendships. In M. Perlmutter (Ed.), *Minnesota symposia on child psychology* (Vol. 18) (pp. 189–212). Hillsdale, NJ: Erlbaum.

Berndt, T. J. (1992). Friendship and friends' influence in adolescence. *Current Directions in Psychological Science, 1*, 156–159.

Berndt, T. J., & Hoyle, S. G. (1985). Stability and change in childhood and adolescent friendships. *Developmental Psychology, 21*, 1007–1015.

Berndt, T. J., & Keefe, K. (1995a). Friends' influence on adolescents' adjustment to school. *Child Development, 66*, 1312–1329.

Berndt, T. J., & Keefe, K. (1995b, April). *Friends' influence on school adjustment: A motivational analysis.* Paper presented at the biennial meetings of the Society for Research in Child Development, Indianapolis.

Bertenthal, B. I., & Campos, J. J. (1987). New directions in the study of early experience. *Child Development, 58*, 560–567.

Bertenthal, B. I., Campos, J. J., & Kermoian, R. (1994). An epigenetic perspective on the development of self-produced locomotion and its consequences. *Current Directions in Psychological Science, 3*, 140–145.

Bérubé, M. (1996). *Life as we know it. A father, a family, and an exceptional child.* New York: Pantheon Books.

Betancourt, H., & Lopez, S. R. (1993). The study of culture, ethnicity, and race in American psychology. *American Psychologist, 48*, 629–637.

Bettes, B. A. (1988). Maternal depression and motherese: Temporal and intonational features. *Child Development, 59*, 1089–1096.

Bhatt, R. S., & Rovee-Collier, C. (1996). Infants' forgetting of correlated attributes and object recognition. *Child Development, 67*, 172–187.

Bigler, R. S. (1995). The role of classification skill in moderating environmental influences on children's gender stereotyping: A study of the functional use of gender in the classroom. *Child Development, 66*, 1072–1087.

Billy, J. O. G., Brewster, K. L., & Grady, W. R. (1994). Contextual effects on the sexual behavior of adolescent women. *Journal of Marriage and the Family, 56*, 387–404.

Binet, A., & Simon, T. (1905). Methodes nouvelles pour le diagnostic du niveau intellectual des anormaux. *L'Anee Psychologique, 11*, 191–244.

Bingham, C. R., Miller, B. C., & Adams, G. R. (1990). Correlates of age at first sexual intercourse in a national sample of young women. *Journal of Adolescent Research, 5*, 18–33.

Biro, F. M., Lucky, A. W., Huster, G. A., & Morrison, J. A. (1995). Pubertal staging in boys. *Journal of Pediatrics, 127*, 100–102.

Biro, F. M., & Rosenthal, S. L. (1995). Adolescents and sexually transmitted diseases: Diagnosis, developmental issues, and prevention. *Journal of Pediatric Health Care, 9*, 256–262.

Biswas, M. K., & Craigo, S. D. (1994). The course and conduct of normal labor and delivery. In A. H. DeCherney & M. L. Pernoll (Eds.), *Current obstetric and gynecologic diagnosis and treatment* (pp. 202–227). Norwalk, CT: Appleton & Lange.

Bivens, J. A., & Berk, L. E. (1990). A longitudinal study of the development of elementary school children's private speech. *Merrill-Palmer Quarterly, 36*, 443–463.

Bjorklund, D. F., & Coyle, T. R. (1995, April). *Utilization deficiencies, multiple strategy use, and memory development.* Paper presented at the biennial meetings of the Society for Research in Child Development, Indianapolis.

Bjorklund, D. F., & Muir, J. E. (1988). Remembering on their own: Children's development of free recall memory. In R. Vasta (Ed.), *Annals of child development* (Vol. 5) (pp. 79–124). Greenwich, CT: JAI Press.

Black, K. A., & McCartney, K. (1995, April). *Associations between adolescent attachment to parents and peer interactions.* Paper presented at the biennial meetings of the Society for Research in Child Development, Indianapolis.

Blair, S. N., Kohl, H. W., III, Barlow, C. E., Paffenbarger, R. S., Jr., Gibbons, L. W., & Macera, C. A. (1995). Changes in physical fitness and all-cause mortality. *Journal of the American Medical Association, 273*, 1093–1098.

Blair, S. N., & Meredith, M. D. (1994). The exercise-health relationship: Does it apply to children and youth? In R. R. Pate & R. C. Hohn (Eds.), *Health and fitness through physical education* (pp. 11–19). Champaign, IL: Human Kinetics.

Blake, I. K. (1994). Language development and socialization in young African-American children. In P. M. Greenfield & R. R. Cocking (Eds.), *Cross-cultural roots of minority child development* (pp. 167–195). Hillsdale, NJ: Erlbaum.

Blass, E. M., Ganchrow, J. R., & Steiner, J. E. (1984). Classical conditioning in newborn humans 2–48 hours of age. *Infant Behavior and Development, 7*, 223–235.

Block, J. (1971). *Lives through time.* Berkeley, CA: Bancroft.

Block, J. (1987, April). *Longitudinal antecedents of ego-control and ego-resiliency in late adolescence.* Paper presented at the biennial meetings of the Society for Research in Child Development, Baltimore.

Block, J., & Robins, R. W. (1993). A longitudinal study of consistency and change in self-esteem from early adolescence to early adulthood. *Child Development, 64*, 909–923.

Bloom, L. (1973). *One word at a time.* The Hague: Mouton.

Bloom, L. (1991). *Language development from two to three.* Cambridge, England: Cambridge University Press.

Bloom, L. (1993). *The transition from infancy to language. Acquiring the power of expression.* Cambridge, England: Cambridge University Press.

Bloom, L. (1997, April). *The child's action drives the interaction.* Paper presented at the biennial meetings of the Society for Research in Child Development, Washington, DC.

Bolger, K. (1997, April). *Children's adjustment as a function of timing of family economic hardship.* Paper presented at the biennial meetings of the Society for Research in Child Development, Washington, DC.

Bond, M. H., Nakazato, H., & Shiraishi, D. (1975). Universality and distinctiveness in dimensions of Japanese person perception. *Journal of Cross-Cultural Psychology, 6*, 346–357.

Borkenau, P., & Ostendorf, F. (1990). Comparing exploratory and confirmatory factor analysis: A study on the five-factor model of personality. *Personality and Individual Differences, 11*, 515–524.

Bornstein, M. H. (1987). Sensitive periods in development: Definition, existence, utility, and meaning. In M. H. Bornstein (Ed.), *Sensitive periods in development: Interdisciplinary perspectives* (pp. 3–18). Hillsdale, NJ: Erlbaum.

Bornstein, M. H. (1995). Parenting infants. In M. H. Bornstein (Ed.), *Handbook of parenting. Vol. 1, Children and parenting* (pp. 3–39). Mahwah, NJ: Erlbaum.

Bornstein, M. H., Tamis-LeMonda, C. S., Tal, J., Ludemann, P., Toda, S., Rahn, C. W., Pecheux, M., Azuma, H., & Vardi, D. (1992). Maternal responsiveness to infants in three societies: The United States, France, and Japan. *Child Development, 63,* 808–821.

The Boston Women's Health Collective. (1992). *The new our bodies, ourselves: A book by and for women.* New York: Simon & Schuster.

Bouchard, T. J. J., & McGue, M. (1981). Familial studies of intelligence: A review. *Science, 212,* 1055–1059.

Boukydis, C. F. Z., & Burgess, R. L. (1982). Adult physiological response to infant cries: Effects of temperament, parental status, and gender. *Child Development, 53,* 1291–1298.

Boulton, T. J. C., & Magarey, A. M. (1995). Effects of differences in dietary fat on growth, energy and nutrient intake from infancy to eight years of age. *Acta Paediatrica, 84,* 146–150.

Bowerman, M. (1985). Beyond communicative adequacy: From piecemeal knowledge to an integrated system in the child's acquisition of language. In K. E. Nelson (Ed.), *Children's language* (Vol. 5) (pp. 369–398). Hillsdale, NJ: Erlbaum.

Bowlby, J. (1969). *Attachment and loss.* Vol. 1, *Attachment.* New York: Basic Books.

Bowlby, J. (1973). *Attachment and loss.* Vol. 2, *Separation, anxiety, and anger.* New York: Basic Books.

Bowlby, J. (1980). *Attachment and loss.* Vol. 3, *Loss, sadness, and depression.* New York: Basic Books.

Bowlby, J. (1988a). Developmental psychiatry comes of age. *The American Journal of Psychiatry, 145,* 1–10.

Bowlby, J. (1988b). *A secure base.* New York: Basic Books.

Boyatzis, C. J., Matillo, G., Nesbitt, K., & Cathey, G. (1995, April). *Effects of "The Mighty Morphin Power Rangers" on children's aggression and prosocial behavior.* Paper presented at the biennial meetings of the Society for Research in Child Development, Indianapolis.

Boyce, W. T., Chesney, M., Alkon, A., Tschann, J. M., Adams, S., Chesterman, B., Cohen, F., Kaiser, P., Folkman, S., & Wara, D. (1995). Psychobiologic reactivity to stress and childhood respiratory illnesses: Results of two prospective studies. *Psychosomatic Medicine, 57,* 411–422.

Boynton, R. S. (1996, October 7). The birth of an idea. *The New Yorker,* pp. 72–81.

Bradbard, M. R., Martin, C. L., Endsley, R. C., & Halverson, C. F. (1986). Influence of sex stereotypes on children's exploration and memory: A competence versus performance distinction. *Developmental Psychology, 22,* 481–486.

Bradley, R. H., Caldwell, B. M., Rock, S. L., Barnard, K. E., Gray, C., Hammond, M. A., Mitchell, S., Siegel, L., Ramey, C. D., Gottfried, A. W., & Johnson, D. L. (1989). Home environment and cognitive development in the first 3 years of life: A collaborative study involving six sites and three ethnic groups in North America. *Developmental Psychology, 25,* 217–235.

Bradley, R. H., Whiteside, L., Mundfrom, D. J., Casey, P. H., Kelleher, K. J., & Pope, S. K. (1994). Early indications of resilience and their relation to experiences in the home environments of low birthweight, premature children living in poverty. *Child Development, 65,* 346–360.

Bray, N. W., Fletcher, K. L., & Turner, L. A. (1997). Cognitive competencies and strategy use in individuals with mental retardation. In W. E. MacLean Jr. (Ed.), *Ellis' handbook of mental deficiency, psychological theory and research (3rd ed.)* (pp. 197–217). Mahwah, NJ: Erlbaum.

Brazelton, T. B. (1984). *Neonatal Behavioral Assessment Scale.* Philadelphia: Lippincott.

Breitmayer, B. J., & Ramey, C. T. (1986). Biological nonoptimality and quality of postnatal environment as codeterminants of intellectual development. *Child Development, 57,* 1151–1165.

Breslau, N., DelDotto, J. E., Brown, G. G., Kumar, S., Ezhuthachan, S., Hufnagle, K. G., & Peterson, E. L. (1994). A gradient relationship between low birth weight and IQ at age 6 years. *Archives of Pediatric and Adolescent Medicine, 148,* 377–383.

Bretherton, I. (1991). Pouring new wine into old bottles: The social self as internal working model. In M. R. Gunnar & L. A. Sroufe (Eds.), *Minnesota symposia on child development* (Vol. 23) (pp. 1–42). Hillsdale, NJ: Erlbaum.

Bretherton, I. (1992a). The origins of attachment theory: John Bowlby and Mary Ainsworth. *Developmental Psychology, 28,* 759–775.

Bretherton, I. (1992b). Attachment and bonding. In V. B. Van Hasselt & M. Hersen (Eds.), *Handbook of social development. A lifespan perspective* (pp. 133–155). New York: Plenum Press.

Brettschneider, W., & Sack, H. (1996). Germany. In P. De Knop, L. Engström, B. Skistad, & M. R. Weiss (Eds.), *Worldwide trends in youth sport* (pp. 139–151). Champaign, IL: Human Kinetics.

Broberg, A. G., Wessels, H., Lamb, M. E., & Hwang, C. P. (1997). Effects of day care on the development of cognitive abilities in 8-year-olds: A longitudinal study. *Developmental Psychology, 33,* 62–69.

Brody, G. H., Stoneman, Z., & Flor, D. (1995). Linking family processes and academic competence among rural African American youths. *Journal of Marriage and the Family, 47,* 567–579.

Brody, G. H., Stoneman, Z., McCoy, J. K., & Forehand, R. (1992). Contemporaneous and longitudinal associations of sibling conflict with family relationship assessments and family discussions about sibling problems. *Child Development, 63,* 391–400.

Brody, N. (1992). *Intelligence* (2nd ed.). San Diego: Academic Press.

Broman, S., Nichols, P. L., Shaughnessy, P., & Kennedy, W. (1987). *Retardation in young children.* Hillsdale, NJ: Erlbaum.

Bronfenbrenner, U. (1979). *The ecology of human development.* Cambridge, MA: Harvard University Press.

Bronfenbrenner, U. (1989). Ecological systems theory. *Annals of Child Development, 6,* 187–249.

Bronfenbrenner, U. (1993). The ecology of cognitive development: Research models and fugitive findings. In R. H. Wozniak & K. W. Fischer (Eds.), *Development in context. Acting and thinking in specific environments* (pp. 3–44). Hillsdale, NJ: Erlbaum.

Bronson, G. W. (1994). Infants' transitions toward adult-like scanning. *Child Development, 65,* 1253–1261.

Brooks-Gunn, J. (1987). Pubertal processes and girls' psychological adaptation. In R. M. Lerner & T. T. Foch (Eds.), *Biological-psychosocial interactions in early adolescence* (pp. 123–154). Hillsdale, NJ: Erlbaum.

Brooks-Gunn, J. (1988). Commentary: Developmental issues in the transition to early adolescence. In M. R. Gunnar & W. A. Collins (Eds.), *Minnesota symposia on child psychology* (Vol. 21) (pp. 189–208). Hillsdale, NJ: Erlbaum.

Brooks-Gunn, J. (1995a). Strategies for altering the outcomes of poor children and their families. In P. L. Chase-Lansdale & J. Brooks-Gunn (Eds.), *Escape from poverty. What makes a difference for children?* (pp. 87–117). Cambridge, England: Cambridge University Press.

Brooks-Gunn, J. (1995b). Children in families in communities: Risk and intervention in the Bronfenbrenner tradition. In P. Moen, G. H. Elder Jr., & K. Lüscher (Eds.), *Examining lives in context: Perspectives on the ecology of human development* (pp. 467–519). Washington, DC: American Psychological Association.

Brooks-Gunn, J., & Attie, I. (1996). Developmental psychopathology in the context of adolescence. In M. F. Lenzenweger & J. J. Haugaard (Eds.), *Frontiers of developmental psychopathology* (pp. 148–189). New York: Oxford University Press.

Brooks-Gunn, J., Guo, G., & Furstenberg, F. F., Jr. (1993). Who drops out of and who continues beyond high school? A 20-year follow-up of black urban youth. *Journal of Research on Adolescence, 3,* 271–294.

Brooks-Gunn, J., & Matthews, W. S. (1979). *He and she: How children develop their sex-role identity.* Englewood Cliffs, NJ: Prentice Hall.

Brooks-Gunn, J., & Paikoff, R. L. (1993). "Sex is a gamble, kissing is a game": Adolescent sexuality and health promotion. In S. G. Millstein, A. C. Petersen, & E. O. Nightingale (Eds.), *Promoting the health of adolescents* (pp. 180–208). New York: Oxford University Press.

Brooks-Gunn, J., & Reiter, E. O. (1990). The role of pubertal processes. In S. S. Feldman & G. R. Elliott (Eds.), *At the threshold. The developing adolescent* (pp. 16–53). Cambridge, MA: Harvard University Press.

Brooks-Gunn, J., & Warren, M. P. (1985). The effects of delayed menarche in different contexts: Dance and nondance students. *Journal of Youth and Adolescence, 13,* 285–300.

Brown, A. L., Metz, K. E., & Campione, J. C. (1996). Social interaction and individual understanding in a community of learners: The influence of Piaget and Vygotsky. In A. Tryphon & J. Vonèche (Eds.), *Piaget–Vygotsky: The social genesis of thought* (pp. 145–170). Hove, England: Psychology Press.

Brown, B. B. (1990). Peer groups and peer cultures. In S. S. Feldman & G. R. Elliott (Eds.), *At the threshold. The developing adolescent* (pp. 171–196). Cambridge, MA: Harvard University Press.

Brown, B. B., Dolcini, M. M., & Leventhal, A. (1995, April). *The emergence of peer crowds: Friend or foe to adolescent health?* Paper presented at the biennial meetings of the Society for Research in Child Development, Indianapolis.

Brown, B. B., & Huang, B. (1995). Examining parenting practices in different peer contexts: Implications for adolescent trajectories. In L. J. Crockett & A. C. Crouter (Eds.), *Pathways through adolescence* (pp. 151–174). Mahwah, NJ: Erlbaum.

Brown, B. B., Mory, M. S., & Kinney, D. (1994). Casting adolescent crowds in a relational perspective: Caricature, channel, and context. In R. Montemayor, G. R. Adams, & T. P. Gullotta (Eds.), *Personal relationships during adolescence* (pp. 123–167). Thousand Oaks, CA: Sage.

Brown, L., Karrison, T., & Cibils, L. A. (1994). Mode of delivery and perinatal results in breech presentation. *American Journal of Obstetrics and Gynecology, 171,* 28–34.

Brown, R. (1973). *A first language: The early stages.* Cambridge, MA: Harvard University Press.

Brown, R., & Hanlon, C. (1970). Derivational complexity and order of acquisition. In J. R. Hayes (Ed.), *Cognition and the development of language* (pp. 155–207). New York: Wiley.

Brownell, C. A. (1990). Peer social skills in toddlers: Competencies and constraints illustrated by same-age and mixed-age interaction. *Child Development, 61,* 836–848.

Brownell, K. D., & Fairburn, C. G. (Eds.). (1995). *Eating disorders and obesity: A comprehensive handbook.* New York: Guilford Press.

Bruck, M., Ceci, S. J., Francoeur, E., & Barr, R. (1995). "I hardly cried when I got my shot!" Influencing children's reports about a visit to their pediatrician. *Child Development, 66,* 193–208.

Bryant, D., & Maxwell, K. (1997). The effectiveness of early intervention for disadvantaged children. In M. J. Guralnick (Ed.), *The effectiveness of early intervention* (pp. 23–46). Baltimore: Paul H. Brookes.

Bryant, P. E., MacLean, M., Bradley, L. L., & Crossland, J. (1990). Rhyme and alliteration, phoneme detection, and learning to read. *Developmental Psychology, 26,* 429–438.

Buchanan, C. M., Maccoby, E. E., & Dornbusch, S. M. (1991). Caught between parents: Adolescents' experience in divorced homes. *Child Development, 62,* 1008–1029.

Buchanan, C. M., Maccoby, E. E., & Dornbusch, S. M. (1996). *Adolescents after divorce.* Cambridge, MA: Harvard University Press.

Buhrmester, D. (1992). The developmental courses of sibling and peer relationships. In F. Boer & J. Dunn (Eds.), *Children's sibling relationships: Developmental and clinical issues.* Hillsdale, NJ: Erlbaum.

Buhrmester, D. (1996). Need fulfillment, interpersonal competence, and the developmental contexts of early adolescent friendship. In W. M. Bukowski, A. F. Newcomb, & W. W. Hartup (Eds.), *The company they keep. Friendship in childhood and adolescence* (pp. 158–185). Cambridge, England: Cambridge University Press.

Buhrmester, D., & Furman, W. (1990). Perceptions of sibling relationships during middle childhood and adolescence. *Child Development, 61,* 1387–1398.

Buitelaar, J. K., & van Engeland, H. (1996). Epidemiological approaches. In S. Sandberg (Ed.), *Hyperactivity disorders of childhood* (pp. 26–68). Cambridge, England: Cambridge University Press.

Burks, V. S., Dodge, K. A., & Price, J. M. (1995). Models of internalizing outcomes of early rejection. *Development and Psychopathology, 7,* 683–695.

Burnett, J. W., Anderson, W. P., & Heppner, P. P. (1995). Gender roles and self-esteem: A consideration of environmental factors. *Journal of Counseling and Development, 73,* 323–326.

Burns, A. (1992). Mother-headed families: An international perspective and the case of Australia. *Social Policy Report, Society for Research in Child Development, 6*(1), 1–22.

Buss, A. H. (1989). Temperaments as personality traits. In G. A. Kohnstamm, J. E. Bates, & M. K. Rothbart (Eds.), *Temperament in childhood* (pp. 49–58). Chichester, England: Wiley.

Buss, A. H., & Plomin, R. (1984). *Temperament: Early developing personality traits.* Hillsdale, NJ: Erlbaum.

Buss, A. H., & Plomin, R. (1986). The EAS approach to temperament. In R. Plomin & J. Dunn (Eds.), *The study of temperament: Changes, continuities and challenges* (pp. 67–80). Hillsdale, NJ: Erlbaum.

Bussing, R., Menvielle, E., & Zima, B. (1996). Relationship between behavioral problems and unintentional injuries in US children. *Archives of Pediatric and Adolescent Medicine, 150,* 50–56.

Butterworth, C. E., Jr., & Bendich, A. (1996). Folic acid and the prevention of birth defects. *Annual Review of Nutrition, 16,* 73–97.

Buysse, V., & Bailey, D. B., Jr. (1993). Behavioral and developmental outcomes in young children with disabilities in integrated and segregated settings: A review of comparative studies. *The Journal of Special Education, 26,* 434–461.

Buzwell, S., & Rosenthal, D. (1996). Constructing a sexual self: Adolescents' sexual self-perceptions and sexual risk-taking. *Journal of Research on Adolescence, 6,* 489–513.

Byrnes, J. P., & Takahira, S. (1993). Explaining gender differences on SAT-Math items. *Developmental Psychology, 29,* 805–810.

Cain, V. S., & Hofferth, S. L. (1989). Parental choice of self-care for school-age children. *Journal of Marriage and the Family, 51,* 65–77.

Cairns, R. B., & Cairns, B. D. (1994). *Lifelines and risks. Pathways of youth in our time.* Cambridge, England: Cambridge University Press.

California Assessment Program (1980). *Student achievement in California schools. 1979–1980 annual report: Television and student achievement.* Sacramento: California State Department of Education.

Campbell, D. W., & Eaton, W. O. (1995, April). *Sex differences in the activity level in the first year of life: A meta-analysis.* Paper presented at the biennial meetings of the Society for Research in Child Development, Indianapolis.

Campbell, F. A., & Ramey, C. T. (1994). Effects of early intervention on intellectual and academic achievement: A follow-up study of children from low-income families. *Child Development, 65,* 684–698.

Campbell, R. L., & Bickhard, M. H. (1992). Types of constraints on development: An interactivist approach. *Developmental Review, 12,* 311–338.

Campbell, S. B. (1990). The socialization and social development of hyperactive children. In M. Lewis & S. M. Miller (Eds.), *Handbook of developmental psychopathology* (pp. 77–92). New York: Plenum Press.

Campbell, S. B., Cohn, J. F., Flanagan, C., Popper, S., & Meyers, T. (1992). Course and correlates of postpartum depression during the transition to parenthood. *Development and Psychopathology, 4,* 29–47.

Campbell, S. B., & Ewing, L. J. (1990). Follow-up of hard-to-manage preschoolers: Adjustment at age 9 and predictors of continuing symptoms. *Journal of Child Psychology and Psychiatry, 31,* 871–889.

Campbell, S. B., Pierce, E. W., March, C. L., & Ewing, L. J. (1991). Noncompliant behavior, overactivity, and family stress as predictors of negative maternal control with preschool children. *Development and Psychopathology, 3,* 175–190.

Campione, J. C., Brown, A. L., Ferrara, R. A., Jones, R. S., & Steinberg, E. (1985). Breakdowns in flexible use of information: Intelligence-related differences in transfer following equivalent learning performance. *Intelligence, 9,* 297–315.

Capron, C., & Duyme, M. (1989). Assessment of effects of socio-economic status on IQ in a full cross-fostering study. *Nature, 340,* 552–554.

Capute, A. J., Palmer, F. B., Shapiro, B. K., Wachtel, R. C., Ross, A., & Accardo, P. J. (1984). Primitive reflex profile: A quantification of primitive reflexes in infancy. *Developmental Medicine and Child Neurology, 26,* 375–383.

Carey, S., & Bartlett, E. (1978). Acquiring a single new word. *Papers and Reports on Child Language Development, 15,* 17–29.

Carlson, E. A., & Sroufe, L. A. (1995). Contribution of attachment theory to developmental psychopathology. In D. Cicchetti & D. J. Cohen (Eds.), *Developmental psychopathology.* Vol. 1, *Theory and methods* (pp. 581–617). New York: Wiley.

Caron, A. J., & Caron, R. F. (1981). Processing of relational information as an index of infant risk. In S. Friedman & M. Sigman (Eds.), *Preterm birth and psychological development* (pp. 219–240). New York: Academic Press.

Carraher, T. N., Carraher, D. W., & Schliemann, A. D. (1985). Mathematics in the streets and in the schools. *British Journal of Developmental Psychology, 3,* 21–29.

Carver, R. P. (1990). Intelligence and reading ability in grades 2–12. *Intelligence, 14,* 449–455.

Case, R. (1985). *Intellectual development: Birth to adulthood.* New York: Academic Press.

Case, R. (1991). Stages in the development of the young child's first sense of self, *Developmental Review, 11,* 210–230.

Caselli, C., Casadio, P., & Bates, E. (1997). *A cross-linguistic study of the transition from first words to grammar* (Technical Report No. CND-9701). Center for Research in Language, University of California, San Diego.

Casey, M. B. (1996). Understanding individual differences in spatial ability within females: A nature/nurture interactionist framework. *Developmental Review, 16,* 241–260.

Casey, M. B., Nuttall, R., Pezaris, E., & Benbow, C. P. (1995). Influence of spatial ability on gender differences in mathematics college entrance test scores across diverse samples. *Developmental Psychology, 31,* 697–705.

Caspi, A., Henry, B., McGee, R. O., Moffitt, T. E., & Silva, P. A. (1995). Temperamental origins of child and adolescent behavior problems: From age three to age fifteen. *Child Development, 66,* 55–68.

Caspi, A., Lynam, D., Moffitt, T. E., & Silva, P. A. (1993). Unraveling girls' delinquency: Biological, dispositional, and contextual contributions to adolescent misbehavior. *Developmental Psychology, 29,* 19–30.

Caspi, A., & Moffitt, T. E. (1991). Individual differences are accentuated during periods of social change: The sample case of girls at puberty. *Journal of Personality and Social Psychology, 61,* 157–168.

Cassidy, J., & Berlin, L. J. (1994). The insecure/ambivalent pattern of attachment: Theory and research. *Child Development, 65,* 971–991.

Cassidy, J., Kirsh, S. J., Scolton, K. L., & Parke, R. D. (1996). Attachment and representations of peer relationships. *Developmental Psychology, 32,* 892–904.

Caughy, M. O., DiPietro, J. A., & Strobino, D. M. (1994). Daycare participation as a protective factor in the cognitive development of low-income children. *Child Development, 65,* 457–471.

Ceci, S. J., & Bruck, M. (1993). Suggestibility of the child witness: A historical review and synthesis. *Psychological Bulletin, 113,* 403–439.

Ceci, S. J., & Bruck, M. (1995). *Jeopardy in the courtroom. A scientific analysis of children's testimony.* Washington, DC: American Psychological Association.

Center for Educational Statistics. (1987). *Who drops out of high school? From high school and beyond.* Washington, DC: Office of Educational Research and Improvement, U.S. Department of Education.

Centers for Disease Control. (1992). Pregnancy risks determined from birth certificate data—United States, 1989. *Morbidity and Mortality Weekly Report, 41*(30), 556–563.

Centers for Disease Control. (1993a). Rates of cesarean delivery—United States, 1991. *Journal of the American Medical Association, 269*(18), 2360.

Centers for Disease Control. (1993b). Childbearing patterns among selected racial/ethnic minority groups—United States, 1990. *Morbidity and Mortality Weekly Report, 42,* 399–403.

Centers for Disease Control. (1994a). Programs for the prevention of suicide among adolescents and young adults. *Morbidity and Mortality Weekly Report, 43* (April 22), 3–7.

Centers for Disease Control. (1994b). Recommendations of the U.S. Public Health Service task force on the use of zidovudine to reduce perinatal transmission of human immunodeficiency virus. *Morbidity and Mortality Weekly Report, 43*(August 5), 1–20.

Centers for Disease Control. (1994c). Preventing tobacco use among young people. A report of the Surgeon General. Executive summary. *Morbidity and Mortality Weekly Report, 43.* 2–10.

Centers for Disease Control. (1994d). Guidelines for school health programs to prevent tobacco use and addiction. *Morbidity and Mortality Weekly Report, 43,* 1–17.

Centers for Disease Control. (1994e). Health-risk behaviors among persons aged 12–21 years—United States, 1992. *Morbidity and Mortality Weekly Report, 43,* 231–235.

Centers for Disease Control. (1995a). Chorionic villus sampling and amniocentesis: Recommendations for prenatal counseling. *Morbidity and Mortality Weekly Report, 44,* 1–12.

Centers for Disease Control. (1995b). U.S. Public Health Service recommendations for human immunodeficiency virus counseling and voluntary testing for pregnant women. *Mortality and Morbidity Weekly Report, 44,* 1–15.

Centers for Disease Control. (1996a). Asthma mortality and hospitalization among children and young adults—United States, 1980–1993. *Morbidity and Mortality Weekly Report, 45*(17), 350–353.

Centers for Disease Control. (1996b). Guidelines for school health programs to promote lifelong healthy eating. *Morbidity and Mortality Weekly Report, 45*, 1–41.

Centers for Disease Control. (1997a). Recommended childhood immunization schedule—United States, 1997. *Morbidity and Mortality Weekly Report, 46*(2), 35–40.

Centers for Disease Control. (1997b). Rates of homicide, suicide, and firearm-related death among children—26 industrialized countries. *Morbidity and Mortality Weekly Report, 46*(5), 101–105.

Centers for Disease Control. (1997c). State-specific variation in rates of twin births—United States, 1992–1994. *Morbidity and Mortality Weekly Report, 46*(2), 121–125.

Centers for Disease Control. (1997d). Update: Blood lead levels—United States, 1991–1994. *Morbidity and Mortality Weekly Report, 46*(7), 141–145.

Centerwall, B. S. (1989). Exposure to television as a cause of violence. In G. Comstock (Ed.), *Public communication and behavior* (pp. 1–58). San Diego: Academic Press.

Centerwall, B. S. (1992). Television and violence. The scale of the problem and where to go from here. *Journal of the American Medical Association, 267*(22), 3059–3063.

Cernoch, J. M., & Porter, R. H. (1985). Recognition of maternal axillary odors by infants. *Child Development, 56*, 1593–1598.

Chang, L., & Murray, A. (1995, April). *Math performance of 5- and 6-year-olds in Taiwan and the U.S.: Maternal beliefs, expectations, and tutorial assistance.* Paper presented at the biennial meetings of the Society for Research in Child Development, Indianapolis.

Charman, T., Redfern, S., & Fonagy, P. (1995, April). *Individual differences in theory of mind acquisition: The role of attachment security.* Paper presented at the biennial meetings of the Society for Research in Child Development, Indianapolis.

Chase-Lansdale, P. L., & Brooks-Gunn, J. (Eds.). (1995). *Escape from poverty. What makes a difference for children?* Cambridge, England: Cambridge University Press.

Chen, X., Rubin, K. H., & Li, Z. (1995). Social functioning and adjustment in Chinese children: A longitudinal study. *Developmental Psychology, 31*, 531–539.

Chen, X., Rubin, K. H., & Sun, Y. (1992). Social reputation and peer relationships in Chinese and Canadian children: A cross-cultural study. *Child Development, 63*, 1336–1343.

Cherlin, A. J. (1992a). *Marriage, divorce, remarriage.* Cambridge, MA: Harvard University Press.

Cherlin, A. J. (1992b). Infant care and full-time employment. In A. Booth (Ed.), *Child care in the 1990s. Trends and consequences* (pp. 209–214). Hillsdale, NJ: Erlbaum.

Chess, S., & Thomas, A. (1984). *Origins and evolution of behavior disorders: Infancy to early adult life.* New York: Brunner/Mazel.

Chi, M. T. (1978). Knowledge structure and memory development. In R. S. Siegler (Ed.), *Children's thinking: What develops?* (pp. 73–96). Hillsdale, NJ: Erlbaum.

Chisholm, J. S. (1989). Biology, culture, and the development of temperament: A Navaho example. In J. K. Nugent, B. M. Lester, & T. B. Brazelton (Eds.), *The cultural context of infancy.* Vol. 1, *Biology, culture, and infant development.* Norwood, NJ: Ablex.

Chomsky, N. (1965). *Aspects of a theory of syntax.* Cambridge: Massachusetts Institute of Technology Press.

Chomsky, N. (1975). *Reflections on language.* New York: Pantheon Books.

Chomsky, N. (1986). *Knowledge of language: Its nature, origin, and use.* New York: Praeger.

Chomsky, N. (1988). *Language and problems of knowledge.* Cambridge: Massachusetts Institute of Technology Press.

Christoffel, K. K., Donovan, M., Schofer, J., Wills, K., & Lavigne, J. V. (1996). Psychosocial factors in childhood pedestrian injury: A matched case-control study. *Pediatrics, 97*, 33–42.

Christophersen, E. R. (1989). Injury control. *American Psychologist, 44*, 237–241.

Chumlea, W. C. (1982). Physical growth in adolescence. In B. B. Wolman (Ed.), *Handbook of developmental psychology* (pp. 471–485). Englewood Cliffs, NJ: Prentice Hall.

Cicchetti, D., & Barnett, D. (1991). Attachment organization in maltreated preschoolers. *Development and Psychopathology, 3*, 397–411.

Cicchetti, D., & Cohen, D. J. (1995). Perspectives on developmental psychopathology. In D. Cicchetti & D. J. Cohen (Eds.), *Developmental psychopathology.* Vol. 1, *Theory and methods* (pp. 3–20). New York: Wiley.

Cicchetti, D., & Lynch, M. (1995). Failures in the expectable environment and their impact on individual development: The case of child maltreatment. In D. Cicchetti & D. J. Cohen (Eds.), *Developmental psychopathology.* Vol. 2, *Risk, disorder, and adaptation* (pp. 32–71). New York: Wiley.

Cillessen, A. H. N., van IJzendoorn, H. W., van Lieshout, C. F. M., & Hartup, W. W. (1992). Heterogeneity among peer-rejected boys: Subtypes and stabilities. *Child Development, 63*, 893–905.

Clark, E. V. (1975). Knowledge, context, and strategy in the acquisition of meaning. In D. P. Date (Eds.), *Georgetown University round table on language and linguistics.* Washington, DC: Georgetown University Press.

Clark, E. V. (1983). Meanings and concepts. In J. H. Flavell & E. M. Markman (Eds.), *Handbook of child psychology: Cognitive development* (Vol. 3) (pp. 787–840). New York: Wiley.

Clark, E. V. (1990). On the pragmatics of contrast. *Journal of Child Language, 41*, 417–431.

Clarke-Stewart, A. (1990). "The 'effects' of infant day care reconsidered" reconsidered: Risks for parents, children, and researchers. In N. Fox & G. G. Fein (Eds.), *Infant day care: The current debate* (pp. 61–86). Norwood, NJ: Ablex.

Clarke-Stewart, A. (1992). Consequences of child care for children's development. In A. Booth (Ed.), *Child care in the 1990s. Trends and consequences* (pp. 63–82). Hillsdale, NJ: Erlbaum.

Clarke-Stewart, K. A., Gruber, C. P., & Fitzgerald, L. M. (1994). *Children at home and in day care.* Hillsdale, NJ: Erlbaum.

Clay, M. M. (1979). *The early detection of reading difficulties.* Portsmouth, NH: Heinemann.

Cnattingius, S., Berendes, H. W., & Forman, M. R. (1993). Do delayed childbearers face increased risks of adverse pregnancy outcomes after the first birth? *Obstetrics and Gynecology, 81,* 512–516.

Coe, C., Hayashi, K. T., & Levine, S. (1988). Hormones and behavior at puberty: Activation or concatenation? In M. R. Gunnar & W. A. Collins (Eds.), *Development during the transition to adolescence. Minnesota symposia on child psychology* (Vol. 21) (pp. 17–42). Hillsdale, NJ: Erlbaum.

Cohen, D., & Strayer, J. (1996). Empathy in conduct-disordered and comparison youth. *Developmental Psychology, 32,* 988–998.

Cohen, S., & Williamson, G. M. (1991). Stress and infectious disease in humans. *Psychological Bulletin, 109,* 5–24.

Cohen, Y. A. (1964). *The transition from childhood to adolescence.* Chicago: Aldine.

Cohn, A. H., & Daro, D. (1987). Is treatment too late: What ten years of evaluative research tell us. *Child Abuse and Neglect, 11,* 433–442.

Coie, J. D. (1997, April). *Initial outcome evaluation of the prevention trial.* Paper presented at the biennial meetings of the Society for Research in Child Development, Washington, DC.

Coie, J. D., & Cillessen, A. H. N. (1993). Peer rejection: Origins and effects on children's development. *Current Directions in Psychological Science, 2,* 89–92.

Coie, J. D., & Kupersmidt, J. B. (1983). A behavioral analysis of emerging social status in boys' groups. *Child Development, 54,* 1400–1416.

Coie, J. D., Terry, R., Lenox, K., Lochman, J., & Hyman, C. (1995). Childhood peer rejection and aggression as predictors of stable patterns of adolescent disorder. *Development and Psychopathology, 7,* 697–713.

Coiro, M. J. (1995, April). *Child behavior problems as a function of marital conflict and parenting.* Paper presented at the biennial meetings of the Society for Research in Child Development, Indianapolis.

Colby, A., Kohlberg, L., Gibbs, J., & Lieberman, M. (1983). A longitudinal study of moral judgment. *Monographs of the Society for Research in Child Development, 48*(1–2, Serial No. 200).

Cole, D. A. (1991a). Change in self-perceived competence as a function of peer and teacher evaluation. *Developmental Psychology, 27,* 682–688.

Cole, D. A. (1991b). Social integration and severe disabilities: A longitudinal analysis of child outcomes. *The Journal of Special Education, 25,* 340–351.

Cole, D. A., & Rodman, H. (1987). When school-age children care for themselves: Issues for family life educators and parents. *Family Relations, 36,* 92–96.

Cole, M. (1992). Culture in development. In M. H. Bornstein & M. E. Lamb (Eds.), *Developmental psychology: An advanced textbook* (3rd ed.) (pp. 731–789). Hillsdale, NJ: Erlbaum.

Collaer, M. L., & Hines, M. (1995). Human behavioral sex differences: A role for gonadal hormones during early development? *Psychological Bulletin, 118,* 55–107.

Collet, J. P., Burtin, P., Gillet, J., Bossard, N., Ducruet, T., & Durr, F. (1994). Risk of infectious diseases in children attending different types of day-care setting. Epicreche Research Group. *Respiration, 61,* 16–19.

Collins, W. A. (Ed.). (1984). *Development during middle childhood. The years from six to twelve.* Washington, DC: National Academy Press.

Colombo, J. (1993). *Infant cognition. Predicting later intellectual functioning.* Newbury Park, CA: Sage.

Colton, M., Buss, K., Mangelsdorf, S., Brooks, C., Sorenson, D., Stansbury, K., Harris, M., & Gunnar, M. (1992). Relations between toddler coping strategies, temperament, attachment and adrenocortical stress responses. Poster presented at the 8th International Conference on Infant Studies, Miami, FL.

Comer, J. P., Haynes, N. M., Joyner, E. T., & Ben-Avie, M. (Eds.). (1996). *Rallying the whole village. The Comer process for reforming education.* New York: Teachers College Press.

Committee on Diet and Health. (1989). *Diet and health. Implications for reducing chronic disease risk.* Washington, DC: National Academy Press.

Committee on Infectious Diseases. (1996). Recommended childhood immunization schedule. *Pediatrics, 97,* 143–146.

Community Childhood Hunger Identification Project. (1991). *A survey of childhood hunger in the United States.* Washington, DC: Food Research and Action Center.

Compas, B. E., Ey, S., & Grant, K. E. (1993). Taxonomy, assessment, and diagnosis of depression during adolescence. *Psychological Bulletin, 114,* 323–344.

Compas, B. E., Hinden, B. R., & Gerhardt, C. A. (1995). Adolescent development: Pathways and processes of risk and resilience. *Annual Review of Psychology, 46,* 265–293.

Comstock, G. (1991). *Television and the American child.* San Diego: Academic Press.

Conger, R. D., Conger, K. J., Elder, G. H., Jr., Lorenz, F. O., Simons, R. L., & Whitbeck, L. B. (1992). A family process model of economic hardship and adjustment of early adolescent boys. *Child Development, 63,* 526–541.

Conger, R. D., Ge, X., Elder, G. H., Jr., Lorenz, F. O., & Simons, R. L. (1994). Economic stress, coercive family process, and developmental problems of adolescence. *Child Development, 65,* 541–561.

Conger, R. D., Patterson, G. R., & Ge, X. (1995). It takes two to replicate: A mediational model for the impact of parents' stress on adolescent adjustment. *Child Development, 66,* 80–97.

Connolly, K., & Dalgleish, M. (1989). The emergence of a tool-using skill in infancy. *Developmental Psychology, 25,* 894–912.

Conrad, M., & Hammen, C. (1989). Role of maternal depression in perceptions of child maladjustment. *Journal of Consulting and Clinical Psychology, 57,* 663–667.

Cooper, P. J. (1995). Eating disorders and their relationship to mood and anxiety disorders. In K. D. Brownell & C. G. Fairburn (Eds.), *Eating disorders and obesity: A comprehensive handbook* (pp. 159–164). New York: Guilford Press.

Cooper, R. P., & Aslin, R. N. (1994). Developmental differences in infant attention to the spectral properties of infant-directed speech. *Child Development, 65,* 1663–1677.

Corbet, A., Long, W., Schumacher, R., Gerdes, J., & Cotton, R. (1995). Double-blind developmental evaluation at 1-year corrected age of 597 premature infants with birth weights from 500 to 1350 grams enrolled in three placebo-controlled trials of prophylactic synthetic surfactant. *Journal of Pediatrics, 126,* S5–12.

Corbett, H. D., & Wilson, B. (1989). Two state minimum competency testing programs and their effects on curriculum and instruction. In R. Stake (Ed.), *Effects of changes in assessment policy.* Vol. 1, *Advances in program evaluation.* Greenwich, CT: JAI Press.

Corter, C. M., & Fleming, A. S. (1995). Psychobiology of maternal behavior in human beings. In M. H. Bornstein (Ed.), *Handbook of parenting.* Vol. 2, *Biology and ecology of parenting* (pp. 87–116). Mahwah, NJ: Erlbaum.

Cossette, L., Malcuit, G., & Pomerleau, A. (1991). Sex differences in motor activity during early infancy. *Infant Behavior and Development, 14,* 175–186.

Costa, P. T., Jr., & McCrae, R. R. (1988). Personality in adulthood: A six-year longitudinal study of self-reports and spouse ratings on the NEO personality inventory. *Journal of Personality and Social Psychology, 54,* 853–863.

Coté, J. E. (1996). Identity: A multidimensional analysis. In J. G. Adams, R. Montemayor, & T. P. Gullotta (Eds.), *Psychosocial development during adolescence: Progress in developmental contextualism* (pp. 131–180). Thousand Oaks, CA: Sage.

Coulton, C. J., Korbin, J. E., Su, M., & Chow, J. (1995). Community level factors and child maltreatment rates. *Child Development, 66,* 1262–1276.

Crain, E. F., Weiss, K. B., Bijur, P. E., Hersh, M., Westbrook, L., & Stein, R. E. K. (1994). An estimate of the prevalence of asthma and wheezing among inner city children. *Pediatrics, 94,* 356–362.

Crain-Thoreson, C., & Dale, P. S. (1995, April). *Parent vs. staff storybook reading as an intervention for language delay.* Paper presented at the biennial meetings of the Society for Research in Child Development, Indianapolis.

Cratty, B. (1979). *Perceptual and motor development in infants and children* (2nd ed.). Englewood Cliffs, NJ: Prentice Hall.

Crawford, J. (1991). *Bilingual education: History, politics, theory, and practice* (2nd ed.). Los Angeles: Bilingual Education Services.

Crick, N. R., & Grotpeter, J. K. (1995). Relational aggression, gender, and social-psychological adjustment. *Child Development, 66,* 710–722.

Crick, N. R., & Grotpeter, J. K. (1996). Children's treatment by peers: Victims of relational and overt aggression. *Development and Psychopathology, 8,* 367–380.

Crittenden, P. M. (1992). Quality of attachment in the preschool years. *Development and Psychopathology, 4,* 209–241.

Crnic, K. A., Greenberg, M. T., Ragozin, A. S., Robinson, N. M., & Basham, R. B. (1983). Effects of stress and social support on mothers and premature and full-term infants. *Child Development, 54,* 209–217.

Crockenberg, S. B. (1981). Infant irritability, mother responsiveness, and social support influences on the security of infant-mother attachment. *Child Development, 52,* 857–865.

Crockenberg, S. B., & Litman, C. (1990). Autonomy as competence in 2-year-olds: Maternal correlates of child defiance, compliance, and self-assertion. *Developmental Psychology, 26,* 961–971.

Crockett, L. J., & Crouter, A. C. (Eds.). (1995). *Pathways through adolescence.* Mahwah, NJ: Erlbaum.

Crockett, L. J., & Petersen, A. C. (1993). Adolescent development: Health risks and opportunities for health promotion. In S. G. Millstein, A. C. Petersen, & E. O. Nightingale (Eds.), *Promoting the health of adolescents* (pp. 13–37). New York: Oxford University Press.

Cromer, R. F. (1991). *Language and thought in normal and handicapped children.* Oxford, England: Basil Blackwell.

Crook, C. (1987). Taste and olfaction. In P. Salapatek & L. Cohen (Eds.), *Handbook of infant perception.* Vol. 1, *From sensation to perception* (pp. 237–264). Orlando, FL: Academic Press.

Crowell, J. A., & Feldman, S. S. (1988). Mothers' internal models of relationships and children's behavioral and developmental status: A study of mother-child interaction. *Child Development, 50,* 1273–1285.

Crowell, J. A., & Feldman, S. S. (1991). Mothers' working models of attachment relationships and mother and child behavior during separation and reunion. *Developmental Psychology, 27,* 597–605.

Culbertson, F. M. (1997). Depression and gender: An international review. *American Psychologist, 52*, 25–31.

Cummings, E. M., Hollenbeck, B., Iannotti, R., Radke-Yarrow, M., & Zahn-Waxler, C. (1986). Early organization of altruism and aggression: Developmental patterns and individual differences. In C. Zahn-Waxler, E. M. Cummings, & R. Iannotti (Eds.), *Altruism and Aggression* (pp. 165–188). Cambridge, England: Cambridge University Press.

Cunningham, A. S., Jelliffe, D. B., & Jelliffe, E. F. P. (1991). Breast-feeding and health in the 1980s: A global epidemiologic review. *Journal of Pediatrics, 118*, 659–666.

Cunningham, F. G., MacDonald, P. C., Leveno, K. J., Gant, N. F., & Gilstrap, L. C. (1993). *Williams Obstetrics* (19th ed.). Norwalk, CT: Appleton & Lange.

Daly, K. A. (1997). Definition and epidemiology of otitis media. In J. E. Roberts, I. F. Wallace, & F. W. Henderson (Eds.), *Otitis media in young children: Medical, developmental, and educational considerations* (pp. 3–42). Baltimore: Paul H. Brookes.

Damon, W. (1977). *The social world of the child*. San Francisco: Jossey-Bass.

Damon, W. (1983). The nature of social-cognitive change in the developing child. In W. F. Overton (Ed.), *The relationship between social and cognitive development* (pp. 103–142). Hillsdale, NJ: Erlbaum.

Damon, W., & Hart, D. (1988). *Self-understanding in childhood and adolescence*. New York: Cambridge University Press.

Darling-Hammond, L., & Wise, A. E. (1985). Beyond standardization: State standards and school improvement. *Elementary School Journal* (January), 315–336.

Darlington, R. B. (1991). The long-term effects of model preschool programs. In L. Okagaki & R. J. Sternberg (Eds.), *Directors of development* (pp. 203–215). Hillsdale, NJ: Erlbaum.

Das Eiden, R., & Leonard, K. E. (1996). Paternal alcohol use and the mother-infant relationships. *Development and Psychopathology, 8*, 307–323.

Davies, G. M. (1993). Children's memory for other people: An integrative review. In C. A. Nelson (Ed.), *Minnesota symposia on child psychology* (Vol. 26) (pp. 123–157). Hillsdale, NJ: Erlbaum.

Davis, S. F., Byers, R. H., Jr., Lindegren, M. L., Caldwell, M. B., Karon, J. M., & Gwinn, M. (1995). Prevalence and incidence of vertically acquired HIV infection in the United States. *Journal of the American Medical Association, 274*, 952–955.

Dawson, D. A. (1991). Family structure and children's health and well-being: Data from the 1988 National Health Interview Survey on child health. *Journal of Marriage and the Family, 53*, 573–584.

Deater-Deckard, K., Dodge, K. A., Bates, J. E., & Pettit, G. S. (1996). Physical discipline among African American and European American mothers: Links to children's externalizing behaviors. *Developmental Psychology, 32*, 1065–1072.

DeCasper, A. J., & Fifer, W. P. (1980). Of human bonding: Newborns prefer their mothers' voices. *Science, 208*, 1174–1176.

DeCasper, A. J., Lecaneut, J., Busnel, M., Granier-Deferre, C., & Maugeais, R. (1994). Fetal reactions to recurrent maternal speech. *Infant Behavior and Development, 17*, 159–164.

DeCasper, A. J., & Spence, M. J. (1986). Prenatal maternal speech influences newborns' perception of speech sounds. *Infant Behavior and Development, 9*, 133–150.

de Chateau, P. (1980). Effects of hospital practices on synchrony in the development of the infant-parent relationship. In P. M. Taylor (Ed.), *Parent-infant relationships* (pp. 137–168). New York: Grune & Stratton.

de Haan, M., Luciana, M., Maslone, S. M., Matheny, L. S., & Richards, M. L. M. (1994). Development, plasticity, and risk: Commentary on Huttenlocher, Pollit and Gorman, and Gottesman and Goldsmith. In C. A. Nelson (Ed.), *Minnesota symposia on child psychology* (Vol. 27) (pp. 161–178). Hillsdale, NJ: Erlbaum.

DeLoache, J. S. (1989). The development of representation in young children. In H. W. Reese (Ed.), *Advances in child development and behavior* (Vol. 22) (pp. 2–37). San Diego: Academic Press.

DeLoache, J. S. (1995). Early understanding and use of symbols: The model model. *Current Directions in Psychological Science, 4*, 109–113.

DeLoache, J. S., & Brown, A. L. (1987). Differences in the memory-based searching of delayed and normally developing young children. *Intelligence, 11*, 277–289.

DeMeis, D. K., Hock, E., & McBride, S. L. (1986). The balance of employment and motherhood: Longitudinal study of mothers' feelings about separation from their first-born infants. *Developmental Psychology, 22*, 627–632.

Demo, D. H., & Acock, A. C. (1996). Family structure, family process, and adolescent well-being. *Journal of Research on Adolescence, 6*, 457–488.

Dempster, F. N. (1981). Memory span: Sources of individual and developmental differences. *Psychological Bulletin, 89*, 63–100.

Dennis, W. (1960). Causes of retardation among institutional children: Iran. *Journal of Genetic Psychology, 96*, 47–59.

Den Ouden, L., Rijken, M., Brand, R., Verloove-Vanhorick, S. P., & Ruys, J. H. (1991). Is it correct to correct? Developmental milestones in 555 "normal" preterm infants compared with term infants. *Journal of Pediatrics, 118*, 399–404.

Desrochers, S., Ricard, M., Décarie, T. G., & Allard, L. (1994). Developmental synchrony between social referencing and Piagetian sensorimotor causality. *Infant Behavior and Development, 17*, 303–309.

Devaney, B. L., Gordon, A. R., & Burghardt, J. A. (1995). Dietary intakes of students. *American Journal of Clinical Nutrition, 61*, 205S–212S.

de Villiers, P. A., & de Villiers, J. G. (1992). Language development. In M. H. Bornstein & M. E. Lamb (Eds.), *Developmental psychology: An advanced textbook* (3rd ed.) (pp. 337–418). Hillsdale, NJ: Erlbaum.

The Diagram Group. (1977). *Child's body.* New York: Paddington.

Diamond, A. (1991). Neuropsychological insights into the meaning of object concept development. In S. Carey & R. Gelman (Eds.), *The epigenesis of mind: Essays on biology and cognition* (pp. 67–110). Hillsdale, NJ: Erlbaum.

Díaz, R. M., Neal, C. J., & Amaya-Williams, M. (1990). The social origins of self-regulation. In L. C. Moll (Ed.), *Vygotsky and education* (pp. 127–154). Cambridge, England: Cambridge University Press.

Dietrich, K. N., Berger, O. G., Succop, P. A., Hammond, P. B., & Bornschein, R. L. (1993). The developmental consequences of low to moderate prenatal and postnatal lead exposure: Intellectual attainment in the Cincinnati Lead Study cohort following school entry. *Neurotoxicology and Teratology, 15,* 37–44.

Dietz, W. H., & Gortmaker, S. L. (1985). Do we fatten our children at the television set? Obesity and television viewing in children and adolescents. *Pediatrics, 75,* 807–812.

DiFranza, J. R., & Lew, R. A. (1996). Morbidity and mortality in children associated with the use of tobacco products by other people. *Pediatrics, 97,* 560–568.

Digman, J. M. (1990). Personality structure: Emergence of the five-factor model. *Annual Review of Psychology, 41,* 417–440.

Digman, J. M. (1994). Child personality and temperament: Does the five-factor model embrace both domains? In C. F. Halverson Jr., G. A. Kohnstamm, & R. P. Martin (Eds.), *The developing structure of temperament and personality from infancy to adulthood* (pp. 323–338). Hillsdale, NJ: Erlbaum.

Dishion, T. J., Capaldi, D., Spracklen, K. M., & Li, F. (1995). Peer ecology of male adolescent drug use. *Development and Psychopathology, 7,* 803–824.

Dishion, T. J., French, D. C., & Patterson, G. R. (1995). The development and ecology of antisocial behavior. In D. Cicchetti & D. J. Cohen (Eds.), *Developmental psychopathology.* Vol. 2, *Risk, disorder, and adaptation* (pp. 421–471). New York: Wiley.

Dishion, T. J., Patterson, G. R., Stoolmiller, M., & Skinner, M. L. (1991). Family, school, and behavioral antecedents to early adolescent involvement with antisocial peers. *Developmental Psychology, 27,* 172–180.

Dockett, S., & Smith, I. (1995, April). *Children's theories of mind and their involvement in complex shared pretense.* Paper presented at the biennial meetings of the Society for Research in Child Development, Indianapolis.

Dodge, K. A. (1983). Behavioral antecedents of peer social status. *Child Development, 54,* 1386–1399.

Dodge, K. A. (1990). Developmental psychopathology in children of depressed mothers. *Developmental Psychology, 26,* 3–6.

Dodge, K. A. (1997, April). *Testing developmental theory through prevention trials.* Paper presented at the biennial meetings of the Society for Research in Child Development, Washington, DC.

Dodge, K. A., Coie, J. D., Pettit, G. S., & Price, J. M. (1990). Peer status and aggression in boys groups: Developmental and contextual analysis. *Child Development, 61,* 1289–1309.

Dodge, K. A., & Feldman, E. (1990). Issues in social cognition and sociometric status. In S. R. Asher & J. D. Coie (Eds.), *Peer rejection in childhood* (pp. 119–155). Cambridge, England: Cambridge University Press.

Dodge, K. A., & Frame, C. L. (1982). Social cognitive biases and deficits in aggressive boys. *Child Development, 53,* 620–635.

Dodge, K. A., Pettit, G. S., & Bates, J. E. (1994). Socialization mediators of the relation between socioeconomic status and child conduct problems. *Child Development, 65,* 649–665.

Dollard, J., Doob, L. W., Miller, N. E., Mowrer, O. H., & Sears, R. R. (1939). *Frustration and aggression.* New Haven, CT: Yale University Press.

Donnerstein, E., Slaby, R. G., & Eron, L. D. (1994). The mass media and youth aggression. In L. D. Eron, J. H. Gentry, & P. Schlegel (Eds.), *Reason to hope. A psychosocial perspective on violence and youth* (pp. 219–250). Washington, DC: American Psychological Association.

Dornbusch, S. M., Ritter, P. L., Liederman, P. H., Roberts, D. F., & Fraleigh, M. J. (1987). The relation of parenting style to adolescent school performance. *Child Development, 58,* 1244–1257.

Doyle, A. B., & Aboud, F. E. (1995). A longitudinal study of white children's racial prejudice as a social-cognitive development. *Merrill-Palmer Quarterly, 41,* 209–228.

Dryfoos, J. (1990). *Adolescents at risk. Prevalence and prevention.* New York: Oxford University Press.

DuBois, D. L., Felner, R. D., Brand, S., Phillips, R. S. C., & Lease, A. M. (1996). Early adolescent self-esteem: A developmental-ecological framework and assessment strategy. *Journal of Research on Adolescence, 6,* 543–579.

Duke, P. M., Carlsmith, J. M., Jennings, D., Martin, J. A., Dornbusch, S. M., Gross, R. T., & Siegel-Gorelick, B. (1982). Educational correlates of early and late sexual maturation in adolescence. *Journal of Pediatrics, 100,* 633–637.

Duncan, G. J., Brooks-Gunn, J., & Klebanov, P. K. (1994). Economic deprivation and early childhood development. *Child Development, 65,* 296–318.

Duncan, R. M. (1995). Piaget and Vygotsky revisited: Dialogue or assimilation? *Developmental Review, 15,* 458–472.

Dunham, P., & Dunham, F. (1995). Developmental antecedents of taxonomic and thematic strategies at 3 years of age. *Developmental Psychology, 31,* 483–493.

Dunn, J. (1992). Siblings and development. *Current Directions in Psychological Science, 1,* 6–9.

Dunn, J. (1993). *Young children's close relationships*. Newbury Park, CA: Sage.

Dunn, J. (1994). Experience and understanding of emotions, relationships, and membership in a particular culture. In P. Ekman & R. J. Davidson (Eds.), *The nature of emotion: Fundamental questions* (pp. 352–355). New York: Oxford University Press.

Dunn, J., & Kendrick, C. (1982). Siblings and their mothers: Developing relationships within the family. In M. E. Lamb & B. Sutton-Smith (Eds.), *Sibling relationships: Their nature and significance across the lifespan* (pp. 39–60). Hillsdale, NJ: Erlbaum.

Dunn, J., & McGuire, S. (1994). Young children's nonshared experiences: A summary of studies in Cambridge and Colorado. In E. M. Hetherington, D. Reiss, & R. Plomin (Eds.), *Separate social worlds of siblings. The impact of nonshared environment on development* (pp. 111–128). Hillsdale, NJ: Erlbaum.

Dunphy, D. C. (1963). The social structure of urban adolescent peer groups. *Sociometry, 26,* 230–246.

Dwyer, J. T. (1995). Dietary fiber for children: How much? *Pediatrics, 96,* 1019–1022.

Easterbrooks, M. A., Davidson, C. E., & Chazan, R. (1993). Psychosocial risk, attachment, and behavior problems among school-aged children. *Development and Psychopathology, 5,* 389–402.

Eccles, J. S., & Jacobs, J. E. (1986). Social forces shape math attitudes and performance. *Signs: Journal of Women in Culture and Society, 11,* 367–389.

Eder, R. A. (1989). The emergent personologist: The structure and content of $3\frac{1}{2}$-, $5\frac{1}{2}$-, and $7\frac{1}{2}$-year-olds' concepts of themselves and other persons. *Child Development, 60,* 1218–1228.

Egan, S. K., & Perry, D. G. (1997, April). *Self-concept and victimization by peers: Concurrent and predictive relations.* Paper presented at the biennial meetings of the Society for Research in Child Development, Washington, DC.

Eisenberg, N. (1986). *Altruistic emotion, cognition, and behavior.* Hillsdale, NJ: Erlbaum.

Eisenberg, N. (1992). *The caring child.* Cambridge, MA: Harvard University Press.

Eisenberg, N., Carlo, G., Murphy, B., & Van Court, P. (1995). Prosocial development in late adolescence. *Child Development, 66,* 1179–1197.

Eisenberg, N., Fabes, R. A., Guthrie, I. K., Murphy, B. C., Maszk, P., Holmgren, R., & Suh, K. (1996). The relations of regulation and emotionality to problem behavior in elementary school children. *Development and Psychopathology, 8,* 141–162.

Eisenberg, N., Fabes, R. A., Murphy, B., Karbon, M., Smith, M., & Maszk, P. (1996). The relations of children's dispositional empathy-related responding to their emotionality, regulation, and social functioning. *Developmental Psychology, 32,* 195–209.

Eisenberg, N., Fabes, R. A., Murphy, B., Maszk, P., Smith, M., & Karbon, M. (1995). The role of emotionality and regulation in children's social functioning: A longitudinal study. *Child Development, 66,* 1360–1384.

Eisenberg, N., & Murphy, B. (1995). Parenting and children's moral development. In M. H. Bornstein (Ed.), *Handbook of parenting.* Vol. 4, *Applied and practical parenting* (pp. 227–257). Mahwah, NJ: Erlbaum.

Eisenberg, N., Shell, R., Pasternack, J., Lennon, R., Beller, R., & Mathy, R. M. (1987). Prosocial development in middle childhood: A longitudinal study. *Developmental Psychology, 23,* 712–718.

Ekman, P. (1972). Universals and cultural differences in facial expressions of emotion. In J. Cole (Ed.), *Nebraska symposium on motivation, 1971* (pp. 207–282). Lincoln: University of Nebraska Press.

Ekman, P. (1973). Cross-cultural studies of facial expression. In P. Ekman (Ed.), *Darwin and facial expression* (pp. 169–222). New York: Academic Press.

Ekman, P. (1989). The argument and evidence about universals in facial expressions of emotion. In H. Wagner & A. Manstead (Eds.), *Handbook of social psychophysiology* (pp. 143–164). Chichester, England: Wiley.

Elder, G. H., Jr. (1986). Military times and turning points in men's lives. *Developmental Psychology, 22,* 233–245.

Elkind, D. (1967). Egocentrism in adolescence. *Child Development, 38,* 1025–1034.

Elkind, D., & Bowen, R. (1979). Imaginary audience behavior in children and adolescents. *Developmental Psychology, 15,* 38–44.

Elliott, R. (1988). Tests, abilities, race, and conflict. *Intelligence, 12,* 333–350.

Emde, R. N., Plomin, R., Robinson, J., Corley, R., DeFries, J., Fulker, D. W., Reznick, J. S., Campos, J., Kagan, J., & Zahn-Waxler, C. (1992). Temperament, emotion, and cognition at fourteen months: The MacArthur longitudinal twin study. *Child Development, 63,* 1437–1455.

Endresen, E., & Helsing, E. (1995). Changes in breastfeeding practices in Norwegian maternity wards: National surveys, 1973, 1982, and 1991. *Acta Paediatrica, 84,* 719–724.

Entwisle, D. R., & Alexander, K. L. (1990). Beginning school math competence: Minority and majority comparisons. *Child Development, 61,* 454–471.

Entwisle, D. R., & Doering, S. G. (1981). *The first birth.* Baltimore: Johns Hopkins University Press.

Epstein, S. (1991). Cognitive-experiential self theory: Implications for developmental psychology. In M. R. Gunnar & L. A. Sroufe (Eds.), *Minnesota symposia on child development* (Vol. 23) (pp. 79–123). Hillsdale, NJ: Erlbaum.

Ericsson, K. A., & Crutcher, R. J. (1990). The nature of exceptional performance. In P. B. Baltes, D. L. Featherman, &

R. M. Lerner (Eds.), *Life-span development and behavior* (Vol. 10) (pp. 188–218). Hillsdale, NJ: Erlbaum.

Erikson, E. H. (1950). *Childhood and society.* New York: Norton.

Erikson, E. H. (1980a). *Identity and the life cycle.* New York: Norton. (Originally published 1959)

Erikson, E. H. (1980b). Themes of adulthood in the Freud-Jung correspondence. In N. J. Smelser & E. H. Erikson (Eds.), *Themes of work and love in adulthood* (pp. 43–76). Cambridge, MA: Harvard University Press.

Erikson, E. H. (1982). *The life cycle completed.* New York: W. W. Norton.

Erikson, E. H., Erikson, J. M., & Kivnick, H. Q. (1986). *Vital involvement in old age.* New York: W. W. Norton.

Eron, L. D. (1987). The development of aggressive behavior from the perspective of a developing behaviorism. *American Psychologist, 42,* 435–442.

Eron, L. D. (1992). Testimony before the Senate Committee on Governmental Affairs. *Congressional Record, 88*(June 18), S8538–S8539.

Eron, L. D., Gentry, J. H., & Schlegel, P. (Eds.). (1994). *Reason to hope. A psychosocial perspective on violence and youth.* Washington, DC: American Psychological Association.

Eron, L. D., Huesmann, L. R., & Zelli, A. (1991). The role of parental variables in the learning of aggression. In D. J. Pepler & K. H. Rubin (Eds.), *The development and treatment of childhood aggression* (pp. 169–188). Hillsdale, NJ: Erlbaum.

Escobedo, L. G., Reddy, M., & DuRant, R. H. (1997). Relationship between cigarette smoking and health risk and problem behaviors among US adolescents. *Archives of Pediatric and Adolescent Medicine, 151,* 66–71.

Escorihuela, R. M., Tobena, A., & Fernández-Teruel, A. (1994). Environmental enrichment reverses the detrimental action of early inconsistent stimulation and increases the beneficial effects of postnatal handling on shuttlebox learning in adult rats. *Behavioural Brain Research, 61,* 169–173.

Eskes, T. K. A. B. (1992). Home deliveries in the Netherlands—Perinatal mortality and morbidity. *International Journal of Gynecology and Obstetrics, 38,* 161–169.

ESPGAN Committee on Nutrition. (1994). Committee report: Childhood diet and prevention of coronary heart disease. *Journal of Pediatric Gastroenterology and Nutrition, 19,* 261–269.

Espinosa, M. P., Sigman, M. D., Neumann, C. G., Bwibo, N. O., & McDonald, M. A. (1992). Playground behaviors of school-age children in relation to nutrition, schooling, and family characteristics. *Developmental Psychology, 28,* 1188–1195.

Evans, R. I. (1969). *Dialogue with Erik Erikson.* New York: Dutton.

Fabes, R. A., Knight, G. P., & Higgins, D. A. (1995, April). *Gender differences in aggression: A meta-analytic reexamination of time and age effects.* Paper presented at the biennial meetings of the Society for Research in Child Development, Indianapolis.

Fabrikant, G. (1996, April 8). The young and restless audience. Computers and videos cut into children's time for watching TV and ads. *New York Times,* p. C1.

Fagan, J. F., III (1992). Intelligence: A theoretical viewpoint. *Current Directions in Psychological Science, 1,* 82–86.

Fagan, J. F., & Singer, L. T. (1983). Infant recognition memory as a measure of intelligence. In L. P. Lipsett (Ed.), *Advances in infancy research* (Vol. 2) (pp. 31–78). Norwood, NJ: Ablex.

Fagard, J., & Jacquet, A. (1989). Onset of bimanual coordination and symmetry versus asymmetry of movement. *Infant Behavior and Development, 12,* 229–235.

Fagot, B. I. (1995). Parenting boys and girls. In M. H. Bornstein (Ed.), *Handbook of parenting.* Vol. 1, *Children and parenting* (pp. 163–183). Mahwah, NJ: Erlbaum.

Fagot, B. I., & Hagan, R. (1991). Observations of parent reactions to sex-stereotyped behaviors: Age and sex effects. *Child Development, 62,* 617–628.

Fagot, B. I., & Leinbach, M. D. (1989). The young child's gender schema: Environmental input, internal organization. *Child Development, 60,* 663–672.

Fagot, B. I., & Leinbach, M. D. (1993). Gender-role development in young children: From discrimination to labeling. *Developmental Review, 13,* 205–224.

Fagot, B. I., Leinbach, M. D., & O'Boyle, C. (1992). Gender labeling, gender stereotyping, and parenting behaviors. *Developmental Psychology, 28,* 225–230.

Fagot, B. I., & Pears, K. C. (1996). Changes in attachment during the third year: Consequences and predictions. *Development and Psychopathology, 8,* 325–344.

Falbo, T. (1992). Social norms and the one-child family: Clinical and policy implications. In F. Boer & J. Dunn (Eds.), *Children's sibling relationships. Developmental and clinical issues* (pp. 71–82). Hillsdale, NJ: Erlbaum.

Falbo, T., & Poston, D. L., Jr. (1993). The academic, personality, and physical outcomes of only children in China. *Child Development, 64,* 18–35.

Farber, S. L. (1981). *Identical twins reared apart. A reanalysis.* New York: Basic Books.

Farnham-Diggory, S. (1978). *Learning disabilities.* Cambridge, MA: Harvard University Press.

Farnham-Diggory, S. (1986). Time, now, for a little serious complexity. In S. J. Ceci (Ed.), *Handbook of cognitive, social, and neuropsychological aspects of learning disability* (Vol. 1). Hillsdale, NJ: Erlbaum.

Farnham-Diggory, S. (1992). *The learning-disabled child.* Cambridge, MA: Harvard University Press.

Farrar, M. J. (1992). Negative evidence and grammatical morpheme acquisition. *Developmental Psychology, 28,* 90–98.

Farrington, D. P. (1991). Childhood aggression and adult violence: Early precursors and later life outcomes. In D. J.

Pepler & K. H. Rubin (Eds.), *The development and treatment of childhood aggression* (pp. 5–30). Hillsdale, NJ: Erlbaum.

Farver, J. M., Kim, Y. K., & Lee, Y. (1995). Cultural differences in Korean- and Anglo-American preschoolers' social interaction and play behaviors. *Child Development, 66,* 1088–1099.

Faust, M. S. (1983). Alternative constructions of adolescent growth. In J. Brooks-Gunn & A. C. Petersen (Eds.), *Girls at puberty. Biological and psychosocial perspectives* (pp. 105–126). New York: Plenum Press.

Featherman, D. L. (1980). Schooling and occupational careers: Constancy and change in worldly success. In O. G. Brim Jr. & J. Kagan (Eds.), *Constancy and change in human development* (pp. 675–738). Cambridge, MA: Harvard University Press.

Feldman, S. S. (1987). Predicting strain in mothers and fathers of 6-month-old infants: A short-term longitudinal study. In P. W. Berman & F. A. Pedersen (Eds.), *Men's transitions to parenthood* (pp. 13–36). Hillsdale, NJ: Erlbaum.

Fenson, L., Dale, P. S., Reznick, J. S., Bates, E., Thal, D. J., & Pethick, S. J. (1994). Variability in early communicative development. *Monographs of the Society for Research in Child Development, 59*(5, Serial No. 242).

Ferber, R. A. (1985). *Solve your child's sleep problem.* New York: Simon & Schuster.

Ferber, R. A. (1987a). The sleepless child. In C. Guilleminault (Ed.), *Sleep and its disorders in children* (pp. 141–163). New York: Raven Press.

Ferber, R. A. (1987b). Sleeplessness, night awakening, and night crying in the infant and toddler. *Pediatric Review, 9,* 69–82.

Fergusson, D. M., & Horwood, L. J. (1994). Nocturnal enuresis and behavior problems in adolescence: A 15-year longitudinal study. *Pediatrics, 94,* 662–668.

Fernald, A., & Kuhl, P. (1987). Acoustic determinants of infant preference for motherese speech. *Infant Behavior and Development, 10,* 279–293.

Fernald, A., & Morikawa, H. (1993). Common themes and cultural variations in Japanese and American mothers' speech to infants. *Child Development, 64,* 637–656.

Fernald, A., Taeschner, T., Dunn, J., Papousek, M., Boysson-Bardies, B., & Fukui, I. (1989). A cross-language study of prosodic modifications in mothers' and fathers' speech to preverbal infants. *Journal of Child Language, 16,* 477–501.

Feshbach, S. (1970). Aggression. In P. H. Mussen (Ed.), *Carmichael's manual of child psychology* (Vol. 2, 3rd ed.) (pp. 159–260). New York: Wiley.

Field, T. M. (1977). Effects of early separation, interactive deficits, and experimental manipulations on infant-mother face-to-face interaction. *Child Development, 48,* 763–771.

Field, T. M. (1990). *Infancy.* Cambridge, MA: Harvard University Press.

Field, T. M. (1991). Quality infant day-care and grade school behavior and performance. *Child Development, 62,* 863–870.

Field, T. M. (1995). Psychologically depressed parents. In M. H. Bornstein (Ed.), *Handbook of parenting.* Vol. 4, *Applied and practical parenting* (pp. 85–99). Mahwah, NJ: Erlbaum.

Field, T. M., De Stefano, L., & Koewler, J. H. I. (1982). Fantasy play of toddlers and preschoolers. *Developmental Psychology, 18,* 503–508.

Field, T. M., Woodson, R., Greenberg, R., & Cohen, D. (1982). Discrimination and imitation of facial expressions by neonates. *Science, 218,* 179–181.

Fields, S. A., & Wall, E. M. (1993). Obstetric analgesia and anesthesia. *Primary Care, 20,* 705–712.

Fifer, W. P., & Moon, C. M. (1994). The role of mother's voice in the organization of brain function in the newborn. *Acta Paediatrica, 397* (Supplement), 86–93.

Fischer, K. W., & Bidell, T. (1991). Constraining nativist inferences about cognitive capacities. In S. Carey & R. Gelman (Eds.), *The epigenesis of mind: Essays on biology and cognition* (pp. 199–236). Hillsdale, NJ: Erlbaum.

Fiscus, S. A., Adimora, A. A., Schoenbach, V. J., Lim, W., McKinney, R., Rupar, D., Kenny, J., Woods, C., & Wilfert, C. (1996). Perinatal HIV infection and the effect of zidovudine therapy on transmission in rural and urban counties. *Journal of the American Medical Association, 275,* 1483–1488.

Fish, M., Stifter, C. A., & Belsky, J. (1991). Conditions of continuity and discontinuity in infant negative emotionality: Newborn to five months. *Child Development, 62,* 1525–1537.

Flanagan, C. A., & Eccles, J. S. (1993). Changes in parents' work status and adolescents' adjustments at school. *Child Development, 64,* 246–257.

Flannery, D. J., Montemayor, R., & Eberly, M. B. (1994). The influence of parent negative emotional expression on adolescents' perceptions of their relationships with their parents. *Personal Relationships, 1,* 259–274.

Flavell, J. H. (1985). *Cognitive development* (2nd ed.). Englewood Cliffs, NJ: Prentice Hall.

Flavell, J. H. (1986). The development of children's knowledge about the appearance-reality distinction. *American Psychologist, 41,* 418–425.

Flavell, J. H. (1992). Cognitive development: Past, present, and future. *Developmental Psychology, 28,* 998–1005.

Flavell, J. H. (1993). Young children's understanding of thinking and consciousness. *Current Directions in Psychological Science, 2,* 40–43.

Flavell, J. H. (1996). Piaget's legacy. *Psychological Science, 7,* 200–203.

Flavell, J. H., Everett, B. A., Croft, K., & Flavell, E. R. (1981). Young children's knowledge about visual perception: Further evidence for the Level 1–Level 2 distinction. *Developmental Psychology, 17,* 99–103.

Flavell, J. H., Green, F. L., & Flavell, E. R. (1989). Young children's ability to differentiate appearance-reality and Level 2 perspectives in the tactile modality. *Child Development, 60,* 201–213.

Flavell, J. H., Green, F. L., & Flavell, E. R. (1990). Developmental changes in young children's knowledge about the mind. *Cognitive Development, 5,* 1–27.

Flavell, J. H., Green, F. L., Wahl, K. E., & Flavell, E. R. (1987). The effects of question clarification and memory aids on young children's performance on appearance-reality tasks. *Cognitive Development, 2,* 127–144.

Flavell, J. H., Miller, P. H., & Miller, S. A. (1993). *Cognitive development* (3rd ed.). Englewood Cliffs, NJ: Prentice Hall.

Flavell, J. H., Zhang, X.-D., Zou, H., Dong, Q., & Qi, S. (1983). A comparison of the appearance-reality distinction in the People's Republic of China and the United States. *Cognitive Psychology, 15,* 459–466.

Floyd, R. L., Rimer, B. K., Giovino, G. A., Mullen, P. D., & Sullivan, S. E. (1993). A review of smoking in pregnancy: Effects on pregnancy outcomes and cessation efforts. *Annual Review of Public Health, 14,* 379–411.

Folk, K. F., & Yi, Y. (1994). Piecing together child care with multiple arrangements: Crazy quilt or preferred pattern for employed parents of preschool children? *Journal of Marriage and the Family, 56,* 669–680.

Folven, R. J., & Bonvillian, J. D. (1991). The transition from non-referential to referential language in children acquiring American Sign Language. *Developmental Psychology, 27,* 806–816.

Fox, N. A., Kimmerly, N. L., & Schafer, W. D. (1991). Attachment to mother/attachment to father: A meta-analysis. *Child Development, 62,* 210–225.

Francis, E. E., Williams, D., & Yarandi, H. (1993). Anemia as an indicator of nutrition in children enrolled in a Head Start program. *Journal of Pediatric Health Care, 7,* 156–160.

Francis, P. L., Self, P. A., & Horowitz, F. D. (1987). The behavioral assessment of the neonate: An overview. In J. D. Osofsky (Ed.), *Handbook of infant development* (2nd ed.) (pp. 723–779). New York: Wiley-Interscience.

Franco, N., & Levitt, M. J. (1997, April). *Friendship, friendship quality, and friendship networks in middle childhood: The role of peer acceptance in a multicultural sample.* Paper presented at the biennial meetings of the Society for Research in Child Development, Washington, DC.

Fraser, A. M., Brockert, J. E., & Ward, R. H. (1995). Association of young maternal age with adverse reproductive outcomes. *The New England Journal of Medicine, 332,* 1113–1117.

Freedman, D. G. (1979). Ethnic differences in babies. *Human Nature, 2,* 36–43.

Freedman, D. S., Srinivasan, S. R., Valdez, R. A., Williamson, D. F., & Berenson, G. S. (1997). Secular increases in relative weight and adiposity among children over two decades: The Bogalusa Heart Study. *Pediatrics, 99,* 420–426.

Freeman, E. W., & Rickels, K. (1993). *Early childbearing. Perspectives of black adolescents on pregnancy, abortion, and contraception.* Newbury Park, CA: Sage.

Fretts, R. C., Schmittdiel, J., McLean, F. H., Usher, R. H., & Goldman, M. B. (1995). Increased maternal age and the risk of fetal death. *The New England Journal of Medicine, 333,* 953–957.

Freud, S. (1905). *The basic writings of Sigmund Freud* (A. A. Brill, Trans.). New York: Random House.

Freud, S. (1920). *A general introduction to psychoanalysis* (J. Riviere, Trans.). New York: Washington Square Press.

Frey, K. S., & Ruble, D. N. (1992). Gender constancy and the "cost" of sex-typed behavior: A test of the conflict hypothesis. *Developmental Psychology, 28,* 714–721.

Friman, P. C., McPherson, K. M., Warzak, W. J., & Evans, J. (1993). Influence of thumb sucking on peer social acceptance in first-grade children. *Pediatrics, 91,* 784–786.

Fry, A. F., & Hale, S. (1996). Processing speed, working memory, and fluid intelligence. *Psychological Science, 7,* 237–241.

Furman, W. (1995). Parenting siblings. In M. H. Bornstein (Ed.), *Handbook of parenting.* Vol. 1, *Children and parenting* (pp. 143–162). Mahwah, NJ: Erlbaum.

Furrow, D. (1984). Social and private speech at two years. *Child Development, 55,* 355–362.

Furstenberg, F. F., Jr., & Cherlin, A. J. (1991). *Divided families: What happens to children when parents part.* Cambridge, MA: Harvard University Press.

Furstenberg, F. F., Jr., & Hughes, M. E. (1995). Social capital and successful development among at-risk youth. *Journal of Marriage and the Family, 57,* 580–592.

Gallahue, D. L., & Ozmun, J. C. (1995). *Understanding motor development* (3rd ed.). Madison, WI: Brown & Benchmark.

Ganchrow, J. R., Steiner, J. E., & Daher, M. (1983). Neonatal facial expressions in response to different qualities and intensities of gustatory stimuli. *Infant Behavior and Development, 6,* 189–200.

Garbarino, J., Dubrow, N., Kostelny, K., & Pardo, C. (1992). *Children in danger. Coping with the consequences of community violence.* San Francisco: Jossey-Bass.

Garbarino, J., Kostelny, K., & Dubrow, N. (1991). *No place to be a child. Growing up in a war zone.* Lexington, MA: Lexington Books.

Gardner, D., Harris, P. L., Ohmoto, M., & Hamasaki, T. (1988). Japanese children's understanding of the distinction between real and apparent emotion. *International Journal of Behavioral Development, 11,* 203–218.

Gardner, H. (1983). *Frames of mind: The theory of multiple intelligence.* New York: Basic Books.

Garfinkel, P. E. (1995). Classification and diagnosis of eating disorders. In K. D. Brownell & C. G. Fairburn (Eds.), *Eating disorders and obesity: A comprehensive handbook* (pp. 125–134). New York: Guilford Press.

Garland, A. F., & Zigler, E. (1993). Adolescent suicide prevention. Current research and social policy implications. *American Psychologist, 48,* 169–182.

Garmezy, N. (1993). Vulnerability and resilience. In D. C. Funder, R. D. Parke, C. Tomlinson-Keasey, & K. Widaman (Eds.), *Studying lives through time. Personality and development* (pp. 377–398). Washington, DC: American Psychological Association.

Garmezy, N., & Masten, A. S. (1991). The protective role of competence indicators in children at risk. In E. M. Cummings, A. L. Green, & K. H. Karraker (Eds.), *Life-span developmental psychology. Perspectives on stress and coping* (pp. 151–174). Hillsdale, NJ: Erlbaum.

Garmezy, N., & Rutter, M. (Eds.). (1983). *Stress, coping, and development in children.* New York: McGraw-Hill.

Garn, S. M. (1966). Body size and its implications. In L. W. Hoffman & M. L. Hoffman (Eds.), *Review of child development research* (Vol. 2) (pp. 529–561). New York: Russell Sage Foundation.

Garn, S. M. (1980). Continuities and change in maturational timing. In O. G. Brim Jr. & J. Kagan (Eds.), *Constancy and change in human development* (pp. 113–162). Cambridge, MA: Harvard University Press.

Garrick, J. G., & Requa, R. K. (1978). Injuries in high school sports. *Pediatrics, 61,* 465–469.

Gaull, G. E., Testa, C. A., Thomas, P. R., & Weinreich, D. A. (1996). Fortification of the food supply with folic acid to prevent neural tube defects is not yet warranted. *Journal of Nutrition, 126,* 773S–780S.

Ge, X., Conger, R. D., & Elder, G. H., Jr. (1996). Coming of age too early: Pubertal influences on girls' vulnerability to psychological distress. *Child Development, 67,* 3386–3400.

Geary, D. C. (1996). International differences in mathematical achievement: Their nature, causes, and consequences. *Current Directions in Psychological Science, 5,* 133–137.

Geary, D. C., Bow-Thomas, C. C., Liu, F., & Siegler, R. S. (1996). Development of arithmetical competencies in Chinese and American children: Influences of age, language, and schooling. *Child Development, 67,* 2022–2044.

Gecas, V., & Seff, M. A. (1990). Families and adolescents: A review of the 1980s. *Journal of Marriage and the Family, 52,* 941–958.

Gelman, R. (1972). Logical capacity of very young children: Number invariance rules. *Child Development, 43,* 75–90.

Genesee, F. (1993). Bilingual language development in preschool children. In D. Bishop & K. Mogford (Eds.), *Language development in exceptional circumstances* (pp. 62–79). Hove, England: Erlbaum.

Gentner, D. (1982). Why nouns are learned before verbs: Linguistic relativity versus natural partitioning. In S. A. Kuczaj II (Ed.), *Language development.* Vol. 2, *Language, thought, and culture* (pp. 301–334). Hillsdale, NJ: Erlbaum.

Georgieff, M. K. (1994). Nutritional deficiencies as developmental risk factors: Commentary on Pollitt and Gorman. In C. A. Nelson (Ed.), *Minnesota symposia on child development* (Vol. 27) (pp. 145–159). Hillsdale, NJ: Erlbaum.

Gerber, M. M. (1995). Inclusion at the high-water mark? Some thoughts on Zigmond and Baker's case studies of inclusive educational programs. *The Journal of Special Education, 29,* 181–191.

Gerson, R. P., & Damon, W. (1978). Moral understanding and children's conduct. *New Directions for Child Development, 2,* 41–60.

Geschwind, N., & Galaburda, A. M. (1987). *Cerebral lateralization. Biological mechanisms, associations, and pathology.* Cambridge: Massachusetts Institute of Technology Press.

Gesell, A. (1925). *The mental growth of the preschool child.* New York: Macmillan.

Gibson, D. R. (1990). Relation of socioeconomic status to logical and sociomoral judgment of middle-aged men. *Psychology and Aging, 5,* 510–513.

Gibson, E. J., & Walk, R. D. (1960). The "visual cliff." *Scientific American, 202,* 80–92.

Gilligan, C. (1982). *In a different voice: Psychological theory and women's development.* Cambridge, MA: Harvard University Press.

Gilligan, C., & Wiggins, G. (1987). The origins of morality in early childhood relationships. In J. Kagan & S. Lamb (Eds.), *The emergence of morality in young children* (pp. 277–307). Chicago: University of Chicago Press.

Giordano, P. C., Cernkovich, S. A., & DeMaris, A. (1993). The family and peer relations of black adolescents. *Journal of Marriage and the Family, 55,* 277–287.

Gladue, B. A. (1994). The biopsychology of sexual orientation. *Current Directions in Psychological Science, 3,* 150–154.

Gleason, P. M. (1995). Participation in the National School Lunch Program and the School Breakfast Program. *American Journal of Clinical Nutrition, 61,* 213S–220S.

Gleitman, L. R., & Gleitman, H. (1992). A picture is worth a thousand words, but that's the problem: The role of syntax in vocabulary acquisition. *Current Directions in Psychological Science, 1,* 31–35.

Glenn, N. D. (1990). Quantitative research on marital quality in the 1980s: A critical review. *Journal of Marriage and the Family, 52,* 818–831.

Glueck, S., & Glueck, E. (1972). *Identification of pre-delinquents: Validation studies and some suggested uses of the Glueck Table.* New York: Intercontinental Medical Book Corp.

Gnepp, J., & Chilamkurti, C. (1988). Children's use of personality attributions to predict other people's emotional and behavioral reactions. *Child Development, 50,* 743–754.

Goldberg, S. (1972). Infant care and growth in urban Zambia. *Human Development, 15,* 77–89.

Goldberg, W. A. (1990). Marital quality, parental personality, and spousal agreement about perceptions and expectations for children. *Merrill-Palmer Quarterly, 36,* 531–556.

Golden, T. (1996, October 16). In anti-immigrant storm, the pregnant wait. *New York Times,* pp. A1, C24.

Goldenberg, C. (1996). Latin American immigration and U.S. schools. *Social Policy Report, Society for Research in Child Development, X*(1), 1–29.

Goldfield, B. A., & Reznick, J. S. (1990). Early lexical acquisition: Rate, content, and the vocabulary spurt. *Journal of Child Language, 17,* 171–183.

Goldsmith, H. H., Buss, K. A., & Lemery, K. S. (1995, April). *Toddler and childhood temperament: Expanded content, stronger genetic evidence, new evidence for the importance of environment.* Paper presented at the biennial meetings of the Society for Research in Child Development, Indianapolis.

Goldstein, J. H. (Ed.). (1994). *Toys, play, and child development.* Cambridge, England: Cambridge University Press.

Goleman, D. (1995a). *Emotional intelligence.* New York: Bantam Books.

Goleman, D. (1995b, October 4). Eating disorder rates surprise the experts. *New York Times,* p. B7.

Golinkoff, R. M., Mervis, C. B., & Hirsh-Pasek, K. (1994). Early object labels: The case for lexical principles. *Journal of Child Language, 21,* 125–155.

Golombok, S., & Fivush, R. (1994). *Gender development.* Cambridge, England: Cambridge University Press.

Good, T. L., & Weinstein, R. S. (1986). Schools make a difference. Evidence, criticisms, and new directions. *American Psychologist, 41,* 1090–1097.

Goodenough, F. L. (1931). *Anger in young children.* Minneapolis: University of Minnesota Press.

Goodsitt, J. V., Morse, P. A., Ver Hoeve, J. N., & Cowan, N. (1984). Infant speech recognition in multisyllabic contexts. *Child Development, 55,* 903–910.

Gopnik, A., & Astington, J. W. (1988). Children's understanding of representational change and its relation to the understanding of false belief and the appearance-reality distinction. *Child Development, 59,* 26–37.

Gopnik, A., & Meltzoff, A. (1987). The development of categorization in the second year and its relation to other cognitive and linguistic developments. *Child Development, 58,* 1523–1531.

Gopnik, A., & Meltzoff, A. N. (1992). Categorization and naming: Basic-level sorting in eighteen-month-olds and its relation to language. *Child Development, 63,* 1091–1103.

Gopnik, A., & Wellman, H. M. (1994). The theory theory. In L. A. Hirschfeld & S. A. Gelman (Eds.), *Mapping the mind* (pp. 257–293). Cambridge, England: Cambridge University Press.

Gordon, A. R., Devaney, B. L., & Burghardt, J. A. (1995). Dietary effects of the National School Lunch Program and the School Breakfast Program. *American Journal of Clinical Nutrition, 61,* 211S–231S.

Gordon, N. (1995). Apoptosis (programmed cell death) and other reasons for elimination of neurons and axons. *Brain & Development, 17,* 73–77.

Gorter, A. C., Sanchez, G., Pauw, J., Perez, R. M., Sandiford, P., & Smith, G. O. (1995). Childhood diarrhea in rural Nicaragua: Beliefs and traditional health practices. *Boletin de la Oficina Sanitaria Panamericana, 119,* 337–390.

Gortmaker, S. L., Dietz, W. H., Jr., Sobol, A. M., & Wehler, C. A. (1987). Increasing pediatric obesity in the United States. *American Journal of Diseases of Children, 141,* 535–540.

Gortmaker, S. L., Walker, D. K., Weitzman, M., & Sobol, A. M. (1990). Chronic conditions, socioeconomic risks, and behavioral problems in children and adolescents. *Pediatrics, 85,* 267–276.

Gottesman, I. I., & Goldsmith, H. H. (1994). Developmental psychopathology of antisocial behavior: Inserting genes into its ontogenesis and epigenesis. In C. A. Nelson (Ed.), *Minnesota symposia on child psychology* (Vol. 27) (pp. 69–104). Hillsdale, NJ: Erlbaum.

Gottfried, A. W., Gottfried, A. E., Bathurst, K., & Guerin, D. W. (1994). *Gifted IQ. Early developmental aspects.* New York: Plenum Press.

Gottman, J. M. (1986). The world of coordinated play: Same- and cross-sex friendship in young children. In J. M. Gottman & J. G. Parker (Eds.), *Conversations of friends. Speculations on affective development* (pp. 139–191). Cambridge, England: Cambridge University Press.

Graber, J. A., Brooks-Gunn, J., Paikoff, R. L., & Warren, M. P. (1994). Prediction of eating problems: An 8-year study of adolescent girls. *Developmental Psychology, 30,* 823–834.

Gralinski, J. H., & Kopp, C. B. (1993). Everyday rules for behavior: Mothers' requests to young children. *Developmental Psychology, 29,* 573–584.

Gravel, J. S., & Nozza, R. J. (1997). Hearing loss among children with otitis media with effusion. In J. E. Roberts, I. F. Wallace, & F. W. Henderson (Eds.), *Otitis media in young children: Medical, developmental, and educational considerations* (pp. 63–92). Baltimore: Paul H. Brookes.

Greenberg, J., & Kuczaj, S. A., II (1982). Towards a theory of substantive word-meaning acquisition. In S. A. Kuczaj II (Ed.), *Language development.* Vol. 1, *Syntax and semantics* (pp. 275–312). Hillsdale, NJ: Erlbaum.

Greenberg, M. T., Siegel, J. M., & Leitch, C. J. (1983). The nature and importance of attachment relationships to parents and peers during adolescence. *Journal of Youth and Adolescence, 12,* 373–386.

Greenberger, E., & Goldberg, W. A. (1989). Work, parenting, and the socialization of children. *Developmental Psychology, 25,* 22–35.

Greenberger, E., O'Neil, R., & Nagel, S. K. (1994). Linking workplace and homeplace: Relations between the nature of adults' work and their parenting behaviors. *Developmental Psychology, 30,* 990–1002.

Greenberger, E., & Steinberg, L. (1986). *When teenagers work. The psychological and social costs of adolescent employment.* New York: Basic Books.

Greenfield, P. M. (1994). Independence and interdependence as developmental scripts: Implications for theory, research, and practice. In P. M. Greenfield & R. R. Cocking (Eds.), *Cross-cultural roots of minority child development* (pp. 1–37). Hillsdale, NJ: Erlbaum.

Greenfield, P. M., & Cocking, R. R. (Eds.). (1994). *Cross-cultural roots of minority child development.* Hillsdale, NJ: Erlbaum.

Greenough, W. T. (1991). Experience as a component of normal development: Evolutionary considerations. *Developmental Psychology, 27,* 11–27.

Greenough, W. T., Black, J. E., & Wallace, C. S. (1987). Experience and brain development. *Child Development, 58,* 539–559.

Gregg, V., Gibbs, J. C., & Basinger, K. S. (1994). Patterns of developmental delay in moral judgment by male and female delinquents. *Merrill-Palmer Quarterly, 40,* 538–553.

Griffith, D. R., Azuma, S. D., & Chasnoff, I. J. (1994). Three-year outcome of children exposed prenatally to drugs. *Journal of the American Academy of Child and Adolescent Psychiatry, 33,* 20–27.

Grimes, D. A. (1996). Stress, work, and pregnancy complications. *Epidemiology, 7,* 337–338.

Grolnick, W. S., & Slowiaczek, M. L. (1994). Parents' involvement in children's schooling: A multidimensional conceptualization and motivational model. *Child Development, 65,* 237–252.

Grossmann, K., Grossmann, K. E., Spangler, G., Suess, G., & Unzner, L. (1985). Maternal sensitivity and newborns' orientation responses as related to quality of attachment in northern Germany. *Monographs of the Society of Research in Child Development, 50*(1–2, Serial No. 209), 233–256.

Grotevant, H. D., & Cooper, C. R. (1985). Patterns of interaction in family relationships and the development of identity exploration in adolescence. *Child Development, 56,* 415–428.

Group for the Advancement of Psychiatry. (1996). *Adolescent suicide.* Washington, DC: American Psychiatric Press.

Grusec, J. E. (1992). Social learning theory and developmental psychology: The legacies of Robert Sears and Albert Bandura. *Developmental Psychology, 28,* 776–786.

Grusec, J. E., Goodnow, J. J., & Cohen, L. (1996). Household work and the development of concern for others. *Developmental Psychology, 32,* 999–1007.

Grusec, J. E., Saas-Kortsaak, P., & Simutis, Z. M. (1978). The role of example and moral exhortation in the training of altruism. *Child Development, 49,* 920–923.

Guerin, D. W., & Gottfried, A. W. (1994a). Temperamental consequences of infant difficultness. *Infant Behavior and Development, 17,* 413–421.

Guerin, D. W., & Gottfried, A. W. (1994b). Developmental stability and change in parent reports of temperament: A ten-year longitudinal investigation from infancy through preadolescence. *Merrill-Palmer Quarterly, 40,* 334–355.

Gullotta, T. P., Adams, G. R., & Montemayor, R. (Eds.). (1993). *Adolescent sexuality.* Newbury Park, CA: Sage.

Gunnar, M. R. (1994). Psychoendocrine studies of temperament and stress in early childhood: Expanding current models. In J. E. Bates & T. D. Wachs (Eds.), *Temperament. Individual differences at the interface of biology and behavior* (pp. 175–198). Washington, DC: American Psychological Association.

Guns are No. 2 cause of death among the young, data show. (1996, April 9). *New York Times,* p. A8.

Guo, S. F. (1993). Postpartum depression. *Chung-Hua Fu Chan Ko Tsa Chi, 28,* 532–533, 569.

Guralnick, M. J., & Paul-Brown, D. (1984). Communicative adjustments during behavior-request episodes among children at different developmental levels. *Child Development, 55,* 911–919.

Guttentag, R. E., Ornstein, P. A., & Siemens, L. (1987). Children's spontaneous rehearsal: Transitions in strategy acquisition. *Cognitive Development, 2,* 307–326.

Guyer, B., Strobino, D. M., Ventura, S. J., MacDorman, M., & Martin, J. A. (1996). Annual summary of vital statistics—1995. *Pediatrics, 98,* 1007–1019.

Guyer, B., Strobino, D. M., Ventura, S. J., & Singh, G. K. (1995). Annual summary of vital statistics—1994. *Pediatrics, 96,* 1029–1039.

Gzesh, S. M., & Surber, C. F. (1985). Visual perspective-taking skills in children. *Child Development, 56,* 1204–1213.

Haan, N. (1981). Adolescents and young adults as producers of their own development. In R. M. Lerner & N. A. Busch-Rossnagel (Eds.), *Individuals as producers of their own development* (pp. 155–182). New York: Academic Press.

Haan, N. (1985). Processes of moral development: Cognitive or social disequilibrium? *Developmental Psychology, 21,* 996–1006.

Hack, M., Horbar, J.D., Mallow, M. H., Tyson, J. E., Wright, E., & Wright, L. (1991). Very low birthrate and outcomes of the National Institutes of Child Health and Human Development Neonatal Network. *Pediatrics, 87,* 587–597.

Hack, M., Taylor, C. B. H., Klein, N., Eiben, R., Schatschneider, C., & Mercuri-Minich, N. (1994). School-age outcomes in children with birth weights under 750 g. *The New England Journal of Medicine, 331,* 753–759.

Hagay, Z. J., Biran, G., Ornoy, A., & Reece, E. A. (1996). Congenital cytomegalovirus infection: A long-standing problem still seeking a solution. *American Journal of Obstetrics and Gynecology, 174,* 241–245.

Hagerman, R. J. (1996). Growth and development. In W. W. Hay Jr., J. R. Groothuis, A. R. Hayward, & M. J. Levin (Eds.), *Current pediatric diagnosis and treatment, 12th edition* (pp. 65–84). Norwalk, CT: Appleton & Lange.

Hahn, W. K. (1987). Cerebral lateralization of function: From infancy through childhood. *Psychological Bulletin, 101,* 376–392.

Haith, M. M. (1980). *Rules that babies look by.* Hillsdale, NJ: Erlbaum.

Haith, M. M. (1990). Progress in the understanding of sensory and perceptual processes in early infancy. *Merrill-Palmer Quarterly, 36,* 1–26.

Hakuta, K. (1986). *Mirror on language: The debate on bilingualism.* New York: Basic Books.

Hakuta, K., & Garcia, E. E. (1989). Bilingualism and education. *American Psychologist, 44,* 374–379.

Hale, S., Fry, A. F., & Jessie, K. A. (1993). Effects of practice on speed of information processing in children and adults: Age sensitivity and age invariance. *Developmental Psychology, 29,* 880–892.

Halford, G. S., Maybery, M. T., O'Hare, A. W., & Grant, P. (1994). The development of memory and processing capacity. *Child Development, 65,* 1338–1356.

Hall, J. G., Froster-Iskenius, U. G., & Allanson, J. E. (1989). *Handbook of normal physical measurements.* Oxford, England: Oxford University Press.

Halpern, C. T., Udry, J. R., Campbell, B., & Suchindran, C. (1993). Testosterone and pubertal development as predictors of sexual activity: A panel analysis of adolescent males. *Psychosomatic Medicine, 55,* 436–447.

Halpern, D. F. (1986). *Sex differences in cognitive abilities.* Hillsdale, NJ: Erlbaum.

Hämäläinen, M., & Pulkkinen, L. (1996). Problem behavior as a precursor of male criminality. *Development and Psychopathology, 8,* 443–455.

Hamer, D. H., Hu, S., Magnuson, V. L., Hu, N., & Pattatucci, A. M. (1993). A linkage between DNA markers on the X chromosome and male sexual orientation. *Science, 261,* 321–327.

Hamilton, C. E. (1995, April). *Continuity and discontinuity of attachment from infancy through adolescence.* Paper presented at the biennial meetings of the Society for Research in Child Development, Indianapolis.

Hamvas, A., Wise, P. H., Yang, R. K., Wampler, N. S., Noguchi, A., Maurer, M. M., Walentik, C. A., Schramm, W. F., & Cole, F. S. (1996). The influence of the wider use of surfactant therapy on neonatal mortality among blacks and whites. *The New England Journal of Medicine, 334,* 1635–1640.

Hanna, E., & Meltzoff, A. N. (1993). Peer imitation by toddlers in laboratory, home, and day-care contexts: Implications for social learning and memory. *Developmental Psychology, 29,* 701–710.

Hansen, J., & Bowey, J. A. (1994). Phonological analysis skills, verbal working memory, and reading ability in second-grade children. *Child Development, 65,* 938–950.

Hanshaw, J. B. (1995). Cytomegalovirus infections. *Pediatrics in Review, 16,* 43–48.

Harkness, S., & Super, C. M. (1985). The cultural context of gender segregation in children's peer groups. *Child Development, 56,* 219–224.

Harkness, S., & Super, C. M. (1995). Culture and parenting. In M. H. Bornstein (Ed.), *Handbook of parenting. Vol. 2, Biology and ecology of parenting* (pp. 211–234). Mahwah, NJ: Erlbaum.

Harold, G. T., Fincham, F. D., Osborne, L. N., & Conger, R. D. (1997). Mom and Dad are at it again: Adolescent perceptions of marital conflict and adolescent psychological distress. *Developmental Psychology, 33,* 333–350.

Harper, A. E. (1996). Dietary guidelines in perspective. *Journal of Nutrition, 126,* 1042S–1048S.

Harrington, R., Rutter, M., & Fombonne, E. (1996). Developmental pathways in depression: Multiple meanings, antecedents, and endpoints. *Development and Psychopathology, 8,* 601–616.

Harris, B., Lovett, L., Newcombe, R. G., Read, G. F., Walker, R., & Riad-Fahmy, D. (1994). Maternity blues and major endocrine changes: Cardiff puerperal mood and hormone study II. *British Medical Journal, 308,* 949–953.

Harris, M. (1992). *Language experience and early language development: From input to uptake.* Hove, England: Erlbaum.

Harris, P. L. (1989). *Children and emotion. The development of psychological understanding.* Oxford, England: Basil Blackwell.

Hart, B., & Risley, T. R. (1995). *Meaningful differences in the everyday experience of young American children.* Baltimore: Paul H. Brookes.

Harter, S. (1987). The determinations and mediational role of global self-worth in children. In N. Eisenberg (Ed.), *Contemporary topics in developmental psychology* (pp. 219–242). New York: Wiley-Interscience.

Harter, S. (1990). Processes underlying adolescent self-concept formation. In R. Montemayor, G. R. Adams, & T. P. Gullotta (Eds.), *From childhood to adolescence: A transitional period?* (pp. 205–239). Newbury Park, CA: Sage.

Harter, S., & Monsour, A. (1992). Developmental analysis of conflict caused by opposing attributes in the adolescent self-portrait. *Developmental Psychology, 28,* 251–260.

Harter, S., & Pike, R. (1984). The Pictorial Perceived Competence Scale for Young Children. *Child Development, 55,* 1969–1982.

Harter, S., & Whitesell, N. R. (1989). Developmental changes in children's understanding of single, multiple, and blended emotion concepts. In C. Saarni & P. L. Harris (Eds.), *Children's understanding of emotion* (pp. 81–116). Cambridge, England: Cambridge University Press.

Harter, S., & Whitesell, N. R. (1996). Multiple pathways to self-reported depression and psychological adjustment among adolescents. *Development and Psychopathology, 8,* 761–777.

Hartshorn, K., & Rovee-Collier, C. (1997). Infant learning and long-term memory at 6 months: A confirming analysis. *Developmental Psychobiology, 30,* 71–85.

Hartup, W. W. (1974). Aggression in childhood: Developmental perspectives. *American Psychologist, 29,* 336–341.

Hartup, W. W. (1989). Social relationships and their developmental significance. *American Psychologist, 44,* 120–126.

Hartup, W. W. (1992). Peer relations in early and middle childhood. In V. B. Van Hasselt & M. Hersen (Eds.), *Handbook of social development. A lifespan perspective* (pp. 257–281). New York: Plenum Press.

Hartup, W. W. (1996a). The company they keep: Friendships and their developmental significance. *Child Development, 67,* 1–13.

Hartup, W. W. (1996b). Cooperation, close relationships, and cognitive development. In W. M. Bukowski, A. F. Newcomb, & W. W. Hartup (Eds.), *The company they keep: Friendship in childhood and adolescence* (pp. 213–237). Cambridge, England: Cambridge University Press.

Hartup, W. W., Laursen, B., Stewart, M. I., & Eastenson, A. (1988). Conflict and the friendship relations of young children. *Child Development, 59,* 1590–1600.

Hartup, W. W., & Stevens, N. (1997). Friendships and adaptation in the life course. *Psychological Bulletin, 121,* 355–370.

Hartup, W. W., & van Lieshout, C. F. M. (1995). Personality development in social context. *Annual Review of Psychology, 46,* 655–687.

Harvard Education Letter. (1988, September/October). Testing: Is there a right answer? *IV*(5). 1–4.

Harvard Education Letter. (1992, July/August). Youth sports: Kids are the losers. *VIII*(4). 1–3.

Harwood, R. L., Miller, J. G., & Irizarry, N. L. (1995). *Culture and attachment. Perceptions of the child in context.* New York: Guilford Press.

Hashima, P. Y., & Amato, P. R. (1994). Poverty, social support, and parental behavior. *Child Development, 65,* 394–403.

Hatcher, P. J., Hulme, C., & Ellis, A. W. (1994). Ameliorating early reading failure by integrating the teaching of reading and phonological skills: The phonological linkage hypothesis. *Child Development, 65,* 41–57.

Haviland, J. M., & Lelwica, M. (1987). The induced affect response: 10-week-old infants' responses to three emotional expressions. *Developmental Psychology, 23,* 97–104.

Hawley, T. L., & Disney, E. R. (1992). Crack's children: The consequences of maternal cocaine abuse. *Social Policy Report. Society for Research in Child Development, 6*(4), 1–22.

Hayes, C. D., Palmer, J. L., & Zaslow, M. J. (1990). *Who cares for America's children?* Washington, DC: National Academy Press.

Hayne, H., & Rovee-Collier, C. (1995). The organization of reactivated memory in infancy. *Child Development, 66,* 893–906.

Haynes, N. M., Ben-Avie, M., Squires, D. A., Howley, J. P., Negron, E. N., & Corbin, J. N. (1996). It takes a whole village: The SDP school. In J. P. Comer, N. M. Haynes, E. T. Joyner, & M. Ben-Avie (Eds.), *Rallying the whole village. The Comer process for reforming education* (pp. 42–71). New York: Teachers College Press.

Hedegaard, M., Henriksen, T. B., Secher, N. J., Hatch, M. C., & Sabroe, S. (1996). Do stressful life events affect duration of gestation and risk of preterm delivery? *Epidemiology, 7,* 339–345.

Henderson, F. W. (1997). Medical management of otitis media. In J. E. Roberts, I. F. Wallace, & F. W. Henderson (Eds.), *Otitis media in young children: Medical, developmental, and educational considerations* (pp. 219–244). Baltimore: Paul H. Brookes.

Hendry, A. (1996). Math in the social studies curriculum. In D. Schifter (Ed.), *What's happening in math class? Vol. 1, Reshaping practice through teacher narratives* (pp. 9–13). New York: Teachers College Press.

Henker, B., & Whalen, C. K. (1989). Hyperactivity and attention deficits. *American Psychologist, 44,* 216–223.

Henneborn, W. J., & Cogan, R. (1975). The effect of husband participation on reported pain and the probability of medication during labour and birth. *Journal of Psychosomatic Research, 19,* 215–222.

Henriksen, T. B., Hedegaard, M., Secher, N. J., & Wilcox, A. J. (1995). Standing at work and preterm delivery. *British Journal of Obstetrics and Gynecology, 102,* 198–206.

Henshaw, S. K. (1994). *U.S. teenage pregnancy statistics.* New York: Alan Guttmacher Institute.

Heptinstall, E., & Taylor, E. (1996). Sex differences and their significance. In S. Sandberg (Ed.), *Hyperactivity disorders of childhood* (pp. 329–349). Cambridge, England: Cambridge University Press.

Herman-Giddens, M. E., Slora, E. J., Wasserman, R. C., Bourdony, C. J., Bhapkar, M. V., Koch, T. G., & Hasemeier, C. M. (1997). Secondary sexual characteristics and menses in young girls seen in office practice: A study from the Pediatric Research in Office Settings Network. *Pediatrics, 99,* 505–512.

Hernandez, D. J. (1993). *America's Children.* New York: Russell Sage Foundation.

Hernandez, D. J. (1994). Children's changing access to resources: A historical perspective. *Social Policy Report, Society for Research in Child Development, 8*(1), 1–23.

Hernandez, D. J. (1997). Child development and the social demography of childhood. *Child Development, 68*, 149–169.

Herold, E. S., & Marshall, S. K. (1996). Adolescent sexual development. In G. R. Adams, R. Montemayor, & T. P. Gullotta (Eds.), *Psychosocial development during adolescence: Progress in developmental contextualism* (pp. 63–94). Thousand Oaks, CA: Sage.

Herrnstein, R. J., & Murray, C. (1994). *The bell curve. Intelligence and class structure in American life.* New York: Free Press.

Hess, E. H. (1972). "Imprinting" in a natural laboratory. *Scientific American, 227*, 24–31.

Hetherington, E. M. (1989). Coping with family transitions: Winners, losers, and survivors. *Child Development, 60*, 1–14.

Hetherington, E. M., & Clingempeel, W. G. (1992). Coping with marital transitions: A family systems perspective. *Monographs of the Society for Research in Child Development, 57*(2–3, Serial No. 227).

Hetherington, E. M., & Stanley-Hagan, M. M. (1995). Parenting in divorced and remarried families. In M. H. Bornstein (Ed.), *Handbook of parenting.* Vol. 3, *Status and social conditions of parenting* (pp. 233–254). Mahwah, NJ: Erlbaum.

Higgins, A. (1991). The just community approach to moral education: Evolution of the idea and recent findings. In W. M. Kurtines & J. L. Gewirtz (Eds.), *Handbook of moral behavior and development.* Vol. 3, *Application* (pp. 111–141). Hillsdale, NJ: Erlbaum.

Higgins, A., Power, C., & Kohlberg, L. (1984). The relationship of moral atmosphere to judgments of responsibility. In W. M. Kurtines & J. L. Gewirtz (Eds.), *Morality, moral behavior, and moral development* (pp. 74–108). New York: Wiley-Interscience.

Hill, D. J. (1995). The colic debate. *Pediatrics, 96*, 165.

Hilts, P. J. (1995, April 19). Black teenagers are turning away from smoking, but whites puff on. *New York Times*, p. B7.

Hine, J. (1996). What practitioners need to know about folic acid. *Journal of the American Dietetic Association, 96*, 451–452.

Hingson, R., & Howland, J. (1993). Promoting safety in adolescents. In S. G. Millstein, A. C. Petersen, & E. O. Nightingale (Eds.), *Promoting the health of adolescents* (pp. 305–327). New York: Oxford University Press.

Hinshaw, S. P., Lahey, B. B., & Hart, E. L. (1993). Issues of taxonomy and comorbidity in the development of conduct disorder. *Development and Psychopathology, 5*, 31–39.

Hirsch, H. V. B., & Tieman, S. B. (1987). Perceptual development and experience-dependent changes in cat visual cortex. In M. H. Bornstein (Ed.), *Sensitive periods in development: Interdisciplinary perspectives* (pp. 39–80). Hillsdale, NJ: Erlbaum.

Hirschfeld, L. A., & Gelman, S. A. (1994). Toward a topography of mind: An introduction to domain specificity. In L. A. Hirschfeld & S. A. Gelman (Eds.), *Mapping the mind* (pp. 3–35). Cambridge, England: Cambridge University Press.

Hirsh-Pasek, K., Trieman, R., & Schneiderman, M. (1984). Brown and Hanlon revisited: Mothers' sensitivity to ungrammatical forms. *Journal of Child Language, 11*, 81–88.

Hirshberg, L. M., & Svejda, M. (1990). When infants look to their parents: I. Infants' social referencing of mothers compared to fathers. *Child Development, 61*, 1175–1186.

Hodge, K. P., & Tod, D. A. (1993). Ethics of childhood sport. *Sports Medicine, 15*, 291–298.

Hofferth, S. L. (1987a). Teenage pregnancy and its resolution. In S. L. Hofferth & C. D. Hayes (Eds.), *Risking the future. Adolescent sexuality, pregnancy, and childbearing. Working papers* (pp. 78–92). Washington, DC: National Academy Press.

Hofferth, S. L. (1987b). Social and economic consequences of teenage childbearing. In S. L. Hofferth & C. D. Hayes (Eds.), *Risking the future. Adolescent sexuality, pregnancy, and childbearing. Working papers* (pp. 123–144). Washington, DC: National Academy Press.

Hofferth, S. L. (1996). Child care in the United States today. *The Future of Children, 6*(2), 41–61.

Hofferth, S. L., Boisjoly, J., & Duncan, G. (1995, April). *Does children's school attainment benefit from parental access to social capital?* Paper presented at the biennial meetings of the Society for Research in Child Development, Indianapolis.

Hoffman, H. J., & Hillman, L. S. (1992). Epidemiology of the sudden infant death syndrome: Maternal, neonatal, and postneonatal risk factors. *Clinics in Perinatology, 19*(4), 717–737.

Hoffman, L. W., & Manis, J. D. (1978). Influences of children on marital interaction and parental satisfactions and dissatisfactions. In R. M. Lerner & G. B. Spanier (Eds.), *Child influences on marital and family interaction* (pp. 165–213). New York: Academic Press.

Hogue, C. J. R., & Hargraves, M. A. (1993). Class, race, and infant mortality in the United States. *American Journal of Public Health, 83*, 9–12.

Holden, G. W., Coleman, S. M., & Schmidt, K. L. (1995). Why 3-year-old children get spanked: Parent and child determinants as reported by college-educated mothers. *Merrill-Palmer Quarterly, 41*, 431–452.

Holloway, S. D., & Hess, R. D. (1985). Mothers' and teachers' attributions about children's mathematics performance. In I. E. Sigel (Ed.), *Parental belief systems. The psychological consequences for children* (pp. 177–200). Hillsdale, NJ: Erlbaum.

Holmbeck, G. N., & Hill, J. P. (1991). Conflictive engagement, positive affect, and menarche in families with seventh-grade girls. *Child Development, 62*, 1030–1048.

Holmbeck, G. N., Paikoff, R. L., & Brooks-Gunn, J. (1995). Parenting adolescents. In M. H. Bornstein (Ed.), *Handbook of Parenting.* Vol. 1, *Children and parenting* (pp. 91–118). Mahwah, NJ: Erlbaum.

Holmes, S. A. (1996, September 6). Education gap between races closes. *New York Times*, p. A8.

Honzik, M. P. (1986). The role of the family in the development of mental abilities: A 50-year study. In N. Datan, A. L. Greene, & H. W. Reese (Eds.), *Life-span developmental psychology. Intergenerational relations* (pp. 185–210). Hillsdale, NJ: Erlbaum.

Horowitz, F. D. (1987). *Exploring developmental theories: Toward a structural/behavioral model of development.* Hillsdale, NJ: Erlbaum.

Horowitz, F. D. (1990). Developmental models of individual differences. In J. Colombo & J. Fagen (Eds.), *Individual differences in infancy: Reliability, stability, prediction* (pp. 3–18). Hillsdale, NJ: Erlbaum.

Hovell, M., Sipan, C., Blumberg, E., Atkins, C., Hofstetter, C. R., & Kreitner, S. (1994). Family influences on Latino and Anglo adolescents' sexual behavior. *Journal of Marriage and the Family, 56*, 973–986.

Howes, C. (1996). The earliest friendships. In W. M. Bukowski, A. F. Newcomb, & W. W. Hartup (Eds.), *The company they keep. Friendship in childhood and adolescence* (pp. 66–86). Cambridge, England: Cambridge University Press.

Howes, C., & Matheson, C. C. (1992). Sequences in the development of competent play with peers: Social and pretend play. *Developmental Psychology, 28*, 961–974.

Howes, C., Phillips, D. A., & Whitebook, M. (1992). Thresholds of quality: Implications for the social development of children in center-based child care. *Child Development, 63*, 449–460.

Hoyert, D. L. (1996). Fetal mortality by maternal education and prenatal care, 1990. *Vital and Health Statistics, Series 20*(No. 30), 1–7.

Hubbard, F. O. A., & van IJzendoorn, M. H. (1987). Maternal unresponsiveness and infant crying. A critical replication of the Bell & Ainsworth study. In L. W. C. Tavecchio & M. H. van IJzendoorn (Eds.), *Attachment in social networks* (pp. 339–378). Amsterdam: Elsevier/North-Holland.

Huesmann, L. R., Lagerspetz, K., & Eron, L. D. (1984). Intervening variables in the television violence-aggression relation: Evidence from two countries. *Developmental Psychology, 20*, 746–775.

Huntington, L., Hans, S. L., & Zeskind, P. S. (1990). The relations among cry characteristics, demographic variables, and developmental test scores in infants prenatally exposed to methadone. *Infant Behavior and Development, 13*, 533–538.

Hurwitz, E., Gunn, W. J., Pinsky, P. F., & Schonberger, L. B. (1991). Risk of respiratory illness associated with day-care attendance: A nationwide study. *Pediatrics, 87*, 62–69.

Huston, A. C. (1994). Children in poverty: Designing research to affect policy. *Social Policy Report, Society for Research in Child Development, 8*(2), 1–12.

Huston, A. C. (Ed.). (1991). *Children in poverty. Child development and public policy.* Cambridge, England: Cambridge University Press.

Huston, A. C., & Wright, J. C. (1994). Educating children with television: The forms of the medium. In D. Zillmann, J. Bryant, & A. C. Huston (Eds.), *Media, children, and the family. Social scientific, psychodynamic, and clinical perspectives* (pp. 73–84). Hillsdale, NJ: Erlbaum.

Huston, A. C., Wright, J. C., Rice, M. L., Kerkman, D., & St. Peters, M. (1990). Development of television viewing patterns in early childhood: A longitudinal investigation. *Developmental Psychology, 26*, 409–420.

Hutt, S. J., Lenard, H. G., & Prechtl, H. E. R. (1969). Psychophysiological studies in newborn infants. In L. P. Lipsitt & H. W. Reese (Eds.), *Advances in child development and behavior* (Vol. 4) (pp. 128–173). New York: Academic Press.

Huttenlocher, J. (1995, April). *Children's language in relation to input.* Paper presented at the biennial meetings of the Society for Research in Child Development, Indianapolis.

Huttenlocher, P. R. (1994). Synaptogenesis, synapse elimination, and neural plasticity in human cerebral cortex. In C. A. Nelson (Ed.), *The Minnesota symposia on child psychology* (Vol. 27) (pp. 35–54). Hillsdale, NJ: Erlbaum.

Hynd, G. W., Hern, K. L., Novey, E. S., Eliopolus, D., Marshall, R., Gonzalez, J. J., & Voeller, K. K. (1993). Attention deficit-hyperactivity disorder and asymmetry of the daudate nucleus. *Journal of Child Neurology, 8*, 339–347.

Ingram, D. (1981). Early patterns of grammatical development. In R. E. Stark (Ed.), *Language behavior in infancy and early childhood* (pp. 327–358). New York: Elsevier/North-Holland.

Inhelder, B., & Piaget, J. (1958). *The growth of logical thinking from childhood to adolescence.* New York: Basic Books.

Inoff-Germain, G., Arnold, G. S., Nottelmann, E. D., Susman, E. J., Cutler, G. B., Jr., & Chrousos, G. P. (1988). Relations between hormone levels and observational measures of aggressive behavior of young adolescents in family interactions. *Developmental Psychology, 24*, 129–139.

Insabella, G. M. (1995, April). *Varying levels of exposure to marital conflict: Prediction of adolescent adjustment across intact families and stepfamilies.* Paper presented at the biennial meetings of the Society for Research in Child Development, Indianapolis.

Institute for Aerobics Research. (1987). *FitnessGram user's manual.* Dallas, TX: Institute for Aerobics Research.

Isabella, R. A. (1995). The origins of infant-mother attachment: Maternal behavior and infant development. *Annals of Child Development, 10*, 57–81.

Isabella, R. A., Belsky, J., & von Eye, A. (1989). Origins of infant-mother attachment: An examination of interactional synchrony during the infant's first year. *Developmental Psychology, 25*, 12–21.

Istas, A. S., Demmler, G. J., Dobbins, J. G., Stewart, J. A., & The National Congenital Cytomegalovirus Disease Registry Collaborating Group. (1995). Surveillance for congenital cytomegalovirus disease: A report from the National Congenital Cytomegalovirus Disease Registry. *Clinical Infectious Diseases, 20,* 665–670.

Izard, C. E., Fantauzzo, C. A., Castle, J. M., Haynes, O. M., Rayias, M. F., & Putnam, P. H. (1995). The ontogeny and significance of infants' facial expressions in the first 9 months of life. *Developmental Psychology, 31,* 997–1013.

Izard, C. E., & Harris, P. (1995). Emotional development and developmental psychopathology. In D. Cicchetti & D. J. Cohen (Eds.), *Developmental psychopathology.* Vol. 1, *Theory and methods* (pp. 467–503). New York: Wiley.

Izard, C. E., & Malatesta, C. Z. (1987). Perspectives on emotional development I: Differential emotions theory of early emotional development. In J. D. Osofsky (Ed.), *Handbook of infant development* (2nd ed.) (pp. 494–554). New York: Wiley-Interscience.

Jacklin, C. N. (1989). Female and male: Issues of gender. *American Psychologist, 44,* 127–133.

Jackson, E., Campos, J. J., & Fischer, K. W. (1978). The question of decalage between object permanence and person permanence. *Child Development, 14,* 1–10.

Jacobson, S. W., & Frye, K. F. (1991). Effect of maternal social support on attachment: Experimental evidence. *Child Development, 62,* 572–582.

Jadack, R. A., Hyde, J. S., Moore, C. F., & Keller, M. L. (1995). Moral reasoning about sexually transmitted diseases. *Child Development, 66,* 167–177.

Janos, P. M., & Robinson, N. M. (1985). Psychosocial development in intellectually gifted children. In F. D. Horowitz & M. O'Brien (Eds.), *The gifted and talented. Developmental perspectives* (pp. 149–196). Washington, DC: American Psychological Association.

Jenkins, J. M., & Astington, J. W. (1996). Cognitive factors and family structure associated with theory of mind development in young children. *Developmental Psychology, 32,* 70–78.

Jensen, A. R. (1980). *Bias in mental testing.* New York: Free Press.

Jessor, R. (1992). Risk behavior in adolescence: A psychosocial framework for understanding and action. *Developmental Review, 12,* 374–390.

John, O. P., Caspi, A., Robins, R. W., Moffitt, T. E., & Stouthamer-Loeber, M. (1994). The "little five": Exploring the nomological network of the five-factor model of personality in adolescent boys. *Child Development, 65,* 160–178.

Johnson, J. W. C., & Yancey, M. K. (1996). A critique of the new recommendations for weight gain in pregnancy. *American Journal of Obstetrics and Gynecology, 174,* 254–258.

Jones, E. F., Forrest, J. D., Goldman, N., Henshaw, S. K., Lincoln, R., Rosoff, J. L., Westoff, C. F., & Wulf, D. (1986). *Teenage pregnancy in industrialized countries.* New Haven, CT: Yale University Press.

Jones, K. F., Berg, J. H., & Coody, D. (1994). Update in pediatric dentistry. *Pediatric Health Care, 8,* 160–167.

Joshi, M. S., & MacLean, M. (1994). Indian and English children's understanding of the distinction between real and apparent emotion. *Child Development, 65,* 1372–1384.

Kado, S., & Takagi, R. (1996). Biological aspects. In S. Sandberg (Ed.), *Hyperactivity disorders of childhood* (pp. 246–279). Cambridge, England: Cambridge University Press.

Kagan, J. (1994). *Galen's prophecy.* New York: Basic Books.

Kagan, J. (1997). Temperament and the reactions to unfamiliarity. *Child Development, 68,* 139–143.

Kagan, J., Arcus, D., Snidman, N., Feng, W. Y., Hendler, J., & Greene, S. (1994). Reactivity in infants: A cross-national comparison. *Developmental Psychology, 30,* 342–345.

Kagan, J., Kearsley, R., & Zelazo, P. (1978). *Infancy: Its place in human development.* Cambridge, MA: Harvard University Press.

Kagan, J., Reznick, J. S., & Snidman, N. (1990). The temperamental qualities of inhibition and lack of inhibition. In M. Lewis & S. M. Miller (Eds.), *Handbook of developmental psychopathology* (pp. 219–226). New York: Plenum Press.

Kagan, J., Snidman, N., & Arcus, D. (1993). On the temperamental categories of inhibited and uninhibited children. In K. H. Rubin & J. B. Asendorpf (Eds.), *Social withdrawal, inhibition, and shyness in childhood* (pp. 19–28). Hillsdale, NJ: Erlbaum.

Kail, R. (1991). Processing time declines exponentially during childhood and adolescence. *Developmental Psychology, 27,* 259–266.

Kail, R., & Hall, L. K. (1994). Processing speed, naming speed, and reading. *Developmental Psychology, 30,* 949–954.

Kandel, D., Chen, K., Warner, L. A., Kessler, R. C., & Grant, B. (1997). Prevalence and demographic correlates of symptoms of last year dependence on alcohol, nicotine, marijuana and cocaine in the U.S. population. *Drug and Alcohol Dependence, 44,* 11–29.

Kandel, D. B., & Wu, P. (1995). The contributions of mothers and fathers to the intergenerational transmission of cigarette smoking in adolescence. *Journal of Research on Adolescence, 5,* 225–252.

Kann, L., Warren, C. W., Harris, W. A., Collins, J. L., Douglas, K. A., Collins, M. E., Williams, B. I., Ross, J. G., & Kolbe, L. J. (1995). Youth risk behavior surveillance—United States, 1993. *Morbidity and Mortality Weekly Report, 44*(SS 1), 1–55.

Kaplan, R. M. (1985). The controversy related to the use of psychological tests. In B. B. Wolman (Ed.), *Handbook of intelligence. Theories, measurements, and applications* (pp. 465–504). New York: Wiley.

Karen, R. (1994). *Becoming attached.* New York: Warner Books.

Karmiloff-Smith, A. (1991). Beyond modularity: Innate constraints and developmental change. In S. Carey & R. Gelman (Eds.), *The epigenesis of mind: Essays on biology and cognition* (pp. 171–197). Hillsdale, NJ: Erlbaum.

Katz, P. A., & Ksansnak, K. R. (1994). Developmental aspects of gender role flexibility and traditionality in middle childhood and adolescence. *Developmental Psychology, 30*, 272–282.

Kaufman, A. S., & Kaufman, N. L. (1983a). *Kaufman Assessment Battery for Children: Interpretive manual.* Circle Pines, MN: American Guidance Service.

Kaufman, A. S., & Kaufman, N. L. (1983b). *Kaufman Assessment Battery for Children: Administration and scoring manual.* Circle Pines, MN: American Guidance Service.

Kaye, K. L., & Bower, T. G. R. (1994). Learning and intermodal transfer of information in newborns. *Psychological Science, 5,* 286–288.

Keating, D. P. (1980). Thinking processes in adolescence. In J. Adelson (Ed.), *Handbook of adolescent psychology* (pp. 211–246). New York: Wiley.

Keating, D. P., List, J. A., & Merriman, W. E. (1985). Cognitive processing and cognitive ability: Multivariate validity investigation. *Intelligence, 9,* 149–170.

Keeney, T. J., Cannizzo, S. R., & Flavell, J. H. (1967). Spontaneous and induced verbal rehearsal in a recall task. *Child Development, 38,* 935–966.

Kelley, M. L., Sanches-Hucles, J., & Walker, R. R. (1993). Correlates of disciplinary practices in working- to middle-class African-American mothers. *Merrill-Palmer Quarterly, 39,* 252–264.

Kellogg, R. (1970). *Analyzing children's art.* Palo Alto, CA: Mayfield.

Kemper, K. J. (1996). *The wholistic pediatrician.* New York: HarperCollins.

Kendall-Tackett, K. A., Williams, L. M., & Finkelhor, D. (1993). Impact of sexual abuse on children: A review and synthesis of recent empirical studies. *Psychological Bulletin, 113,* 164–180.

Keniston, K. (1970). Youth: A "new" stage in life. *American Scholar, 8*(Autumn), 631–654.

Kennedy, D. M. (1995). Glimpses of a highly gifted child in a heterogeneous classroom. *Roeper Review, 17,* 164–168.

Kennedy, E. T., Ohls, J., Carlson, S., & Fleming, K. (1995). The healthy eating index: Design and applications. *Journal of the American Dietetic Association, 95,* 1103–1108.

Kerns, K. A. (1996). Individual differences in friendship quality: Links to child-mother attachment. In W. M. Bukowski, A. F. Newcomb, & W. W. Hartup (Eds.), *The company they keep: Friendship in childhood and adolescence* (pp. 137–157). Cambridge, England: Cambridge University Press.

Kilborn, P. T. (1996, November 30). Shrinking safety net cradles hearts and hopes of children. *New York Times,* p. 1, 8.

Kilgore, P. E., Holman, R. C., Clarke, M. J., & Glass, R. I. (1995). Trends of diarrheal disease—Associated mortality in US children, 1968 through 1991. *Journal of the American Medical Association, 274,* 1143–1148.

Killen, J. D., Hayward, C., Litt, I., Hammer, L. D., Wilson, D. M., Miner, B., Taylor, B., Varady, A., & Shisslak, C. (1992). Is puberty a risk factor for eating disorders? *American Journal of Diseases of Childhood, 146,* 323–325.

Kilpatrick, S. J., & Laros, R. K. (1989). Characteristics of normal labor. *Obstetrics and Gynecology, 74,* 85–87.

Kim, U., Triandis, H. C., Kâgitçibasi, Ç., Choi, S., & Yoon, G. (Eds.). (1994). *Individualism and collectivism. Theory, method, and applications.* Thousand Oaks, CA: Sage.

Kinney, D. A. (1993). From "nerds" to "normals": Adolescent identity recovery within a changing social system. *Sociology of Education, 66,* 21–40.

Klackenberg, G. (1987). Incidence of parasomnias in children in a general population. In C. Guilleminault (Ed.), *Sleep and its disorders in children* (pp. 99–113). New York: Raven Press.

Klaus, H. M., & Kennell, J. H. (1976). *Maternal-infant bonding.* St. Louis: Mosby.

Klebanov, P. K., Brooks-Gunn, J., Hofferth, S., & Duncan, G. J. (1995, April). *Neighborhood resources, social support and maternal competence.* Paper presented at the biennial meetings of the Society for Research in Child Development, Indianapolis.

Klein, J. O. (1994). Otitis media. *Clinical Infections Diseases, 19,* 823–833.

Klerman, L. V. (1993). The influence of economic factors on health-related behaviors in adolescents. In S. G. Millstein, A. C. Petersen, & E. O. Nightingale (Eds.), *Promoting the health of adolescents* (pp. 38–57). New York: Guilford Press.

Kline, M., Tschann, J. M., Johnston, J. R., & Wallerstein, J. S. (1989). Children's adjustment in joint and sole physical custody families. *Developmental Psychology, 25,* 430–438.

Klonoff-Cohen, H. D., Edelstein, S. L., Lefkowitz, E. S., Srinivasan, I. P., Kaegi, D., Chang, J. C., & Wiley, K. J. (1995). The effect of passive smoking and tobacco exposure through breast milk on sudden infant death syndrome. *Journal of the American Medical Association, 273,* 795–798.

Kochanska, G. (1997). Mutually responsive orientation between mothers and their young children: Implications for early socialization. *Child Development, 68,* 94–112.

Kochenderfer, B. J., & Ladd, G. W. (1996). Peer victimization: Cause or consequence of school maladjustment. *Child Development, 67,* 1305–1317.

Kohlberg, L. (1964). Development of moral character and moral ideology. In M. L. Hoffman & L. W. Hoffman (Eds.), *Review of child development research* (Vol. 1) (pp. 283–332). New York: Russell Sage Foundation.

Kohlberg, L. (1966). A cognitive-developmental analysis of children's sex-role concepts and attitudes. In E. E. Maccoby (Ed.), *The development of sex differences* (pp. 82–172). Stanford, CA: Stanford University Press.

Kohlberg, L. (1973). Continuities in childhood and adult moral development revisited. In P. B. Baltes & K. W. Schaie (Eds.),

Life-span developmental psychology: Personality and socialization (pp. 180–204). New York: Academic Press.

Kohlberg, L. (1975). The cognitive-developmental approach to moral education. *Phi Delta Kappan*, pp. 670–677.

Kohlberg, L. (1976). Moral stages and moralization: The cognitive-developmental approach. In T. Lickona (Ed.), *Moral development and behavior: Theory, research, and social issues* (pp. 31–53). New York: Holt.

Kohlberg, L. (1978). Revisions in the theory and practice of moral development. *New Directions for Child Development, 2*, 83–88.

Kohlberg, L. (1980). *The meaning and measurement of moral development*. Worcester, MA: Clark University Press.

Kohlberg, L. (1981). *Essays on moral development*. Vol. 1, *The philosophy of moral development*. New York: Harper & Row.

Kohlberg, L. (1984). *Essays on moral development*. Vol. 2, *The psychology of moral development*. San Francisco: Harper & Row.

Kohlberg, L., & Candee, D. (1984). The relationship of moral judgment to moral action. In W. M. Kurtines & J. L. Gewirtz (Eds.), *Morality, moral behavior, and moral development* (pp. 52–73). New York: Wiley.

Kohlberg, L., & Elfenbein, D. (1975). The development of moral judgments concerning capital punishment. *American Journal of Orthopsychiatry, 54*, 614–640.

Kohlberg, L., & Higgins, A. (1987). School democracy and social interaction. In W. M. Kurtines & J. L. Gewirtz (Eds.), *Moral development through social interaction* (pp. 102–130). New York: Wiley-Interscience.

Kohlberg, L., Levine, C., & Hewer, A. (1983). *Moral stages: A current formulation and a response to critics*. Basel, Switzerland: S. Karger.

Kohlberg, L., & Ullian, D. Z. (1974). Stages in the development of psychosexual concepts and attitudes. In R. C. Friedman, R. M. Richart, & R. L. Vande Wiele (Eds.), *Sex differences in behavior* (pp. 209–222). New York: Wiley.

Kohn, M. L. (1980). Job complexity and adult personality. In N. J. Smelser & E. H. Erikson (Eds.), *Themes of work and love in adulthood* (pp. 193–212). Cambridge, MA: Harvard University Press.

Kohn, M. L., & Schooler, C. (1983). *Work and personality: An inquiry into the impact of social stratification*. Norwood, NJ: Ablex Press.

Kolata, G. (1992, April 26). A parents' guide to kids' sports. *New York Times Magazine*, pp. 12–15, 40, 44, 46.

Koller, H., Lawson, K., Rose, S. A., Wallace, I., & McCarton, C. (1997). Patterns of cognitive development in very low birth weight children during the first six years of life. *Pediatrics, 99*, 383–389.

Kopp, C. B. (1990). Risks in infancy: Appraising the research. *Merrill-Palmer Quarterly, 36*, 117–140.

Korkman, M., Liikanen, A., & Fellman, V. (1996). Neuropsychological consequences of very low birth weight and asphyxia at term: Follow-up until school-age. *Journal of Clinical and Experimental Neuropsychology, 18*, 220–233.

Korner, A. F., Hutchinson, C. A., Koperski, J. A., Kraemer, H. C., & Schneider, P. A. (1981). Stability of individual differences of neonatal motor and crying patterns. *Child Development, 52*, 83–90.

Kovacs, D. M., Parker, J. G., & Hoffman, L. W. (1996). Behavioral, affective, and social correlates of involvement in cross-sex friendship in elementary school. *Child Development, 67*, 2269–2286.

Kozol, J. (1995). *Amazing grace*. New York: Crown.

Krebs-Smith, S. M., Cook, A., Subar, A. F., Cleveland, L., Friday, J., & Kahle, L. L. (1996). Fruit and vegetable intakes of children and adolescents in the United States. *Archives of Pediatric and Adolescent Medicine, 150*, 81–86.

Kuczaj, S. A., II (1977). The acquisition of regular and irregular past tense forms. *Journal of Verbal Learning and Verbal Behavior, 49*, 319–326.

Kuczaj, S. A., II (1978). Children's judgments of grammatical and ungrammatical irregular past tense verbs. *Child Development, 49*, 319–326.

Kuczynski, L., Kochanska, G., Radke-Yarrow, M., & Girnius-Brown, O. (1987). A developmental interpretation of young children's noncompliance. *Developmental Psychology, 23*, 799–806.

Kuhl, P. K. (1993). Developmental speech perception: Implications for models of language impairment. *Annals of the New York Academy of Sciences, 682*(July 14), 248–263.

Kuhn, D. (1992). Cognitive development. In M. H. Bornstein & M. E. Lamb (Eds.), *Developmental psychology. An advanced textbook* (3rd ed.) (pp. 211–272). Hillsdale, NJ: Erlbaum.

Kuhn, D., Garcia-Mila, M., Zohar, A., & Andersen, C. (1995). Strategies of knowledge acquisition. *Monographs of the Society for Research in Child Development, 60*(Serial No. 245).

Kupersmidt, J. B., Griesler, P. C., DeRosier, M. E., Patterson, C. J., & Davis, P. W. (1995). Childhood aggression and peer relations in the context of family and neighborhood factors. *Child Development, 66*, 360–375.

Kurdek, L. A., & Fine, M. A. (1994). Family acceptance and family control as predictors of adjustment in young adolescents: Linear, curvilinear, or interactive effects? *Child Development, 65*, 1137–1146.

Kurtines, W. M., & Gewirtz, J. L. (Eds.). (1991). *Handbook of moral behavior and development*. Vol. 1, *Theory*, Vol. 2, *Research*, Vol. 3, *Application*. Hillsdale, NJ: Erlbaum.

Kurtz, L., & Tremblay, R. E. (1995, April). *The impact of family transition upon social, sexual, and delinquent behavior in adolescent boys: A nine year longitudinal study*. Paper presented at the biennial meetings of the Society for Research in Child Development, Indianapolis.

La Freniere, P., Strayer, F. F., & Gauthier, R. (1984). The emergence of same-sex affiliative preferences among preschool peers: A developmental/ethological perspective. *Child Development, 55*, 1958–1965.

Lagrew, D. C., Jr., & Morgan, M. A. (1996). Decreasing the cesarean section rate in a private hospital: Success without mandated clinical changes. *American Journal of Obstetrics and Gynecology, 174*, 184–191.

Lamb, M. E., Sternberg, K. J., & Prodromidis, M. (1992). Nonmaternal care and the security of infant-mother attachment: A reanalysis of the data. *Infant Behavior and Development, 15*, 71–83.

Lambert, C. (1993, March–April). The demand side of the health care crisis. *Harvard Magazine,* pp. 30–33.

Lamborn, S. D., Mounts, N. S., Steinberg, L., & Dornbusch, S. M. (1991). Patterns of competence and adjustment among adolescents from authoritative, authoritarian, indulgent, and neglectful families. *Child Development, 62*, 1049–1065.

Lamke, L. K. (1982). Adjustment and sex-role orientation. *Journal of Youth and Adolescence, 11*, 247–259.

Landry, G. L. (1992). Sports injuries in childhood. *Pediatric Annals, 21*, 165–168.

Landry, S. H., Garner, P. W., Swank, P. R., & Baldwin, C. D. (1996). Effects of maternal scaffolding during joint toy play with preterm and full-term infants. *Merrill-Palmer Quarterly, 42*, 177–199.

Langlois, J. H., Kalakanis, L. E., Rubenstein, A. J., Larson, A. D., & Hallam, M. J. (1997, April). *Developmental effects of physical attractiveness: A meta-analytic review.* Paper presented at the biennial meetings of the Society for Research in Child Development, Washington, DC.

Langlois, J. H., Ritter, J. M., Casey, R. J., & Sawin, D. B. (1995). Infant attractiveness predicts maternal behaviors and attitudes. *Developmental Psychology, 31*, 464–472.

Langlois, J. H., Ritter, J. M., Roggman, L. A., & Vaughn, L. S. (1991). Facial diversity and infant preferences for attractive faces. *Developmental Psychology, 27*, 79–84.

Langlois, J. H., & Roggman, L. A. (1990). Attractive faces are only average. *Psychological Science, 1*, 115–121.

Langlois, J. H., Roggman, L. A., Casey, R. J., Ritter, J. M., Rieser-Danner, L. A., & Jenkins, V. Y. (1987). Infant preferences for attractive faces: Rudiments of a stereotype? *Developmental Psychology, 23*, 363–369.

Langlois, J. H., Roggman, L. A., & Musselman, L. (1994). What is average and what is not average about attractive faces? *Psychological Science, 5*, 214–220.

Langlois, J. H., Roggman, L. A., & Rieser-Danner, L. A. (1990). Infants' differential social responses to attractive and unattractive faces. *Developmental Psychology, 26*, 153–159.

La Pine, T. R., Jackson, J. C., & Bennett, F. C. (1995). Outcome of infants weighing less than 800 grams at birth: 15 years' experience. *Pediatrics, 96*, 479–483.

Laub, J. H., & Sampson, R. J. (1995). The long-term effect of punitive discipline. In J. McCord (Ed.), *Coercion and punishment in long-term perspectives* (pp. 247–258). Cambridge, England: Cambridge University Press.

Laumann, E. O., Gagnon, J. H., Michael, R. T., & Michaels, S. (1994). *The social organization of sexuality. Sexual practices in the United States.* Chicago: University of Chicago Press.

Laursen, B. (1995). Conflict and social interaction in adolescent relationships. *Journal of Research on Adolescence, 5*, 55–70.

Leadbeater, B. J., & Dionne, J. (1981). The adolescent's use of formal operational thinking in solving problems related to identity resolution. *Adolescence, 16*, 111–121.

Leaper, C. (1991). Influence and involvement in children's discourse: Age, gender, and partner effects. *Child Development, 62*, 797–811.

Lechky, O. (1994). Epidemic of childhood obesity may cause major public health problems, doctor warns. *Canadian Medical Association Journal, 150*, 78–81.

Lee, I.-M., Hsieh, C., & Paffenbarger, R. S. (1995). Exercise intensity and longevity in men. *Journal of the American Medical Association, 273*, 1179–1184.

Lee, V. E., Burkham, D. T., Zimiles, H., & Ladewski, B. (1994). Family structure and its effect on behavioral and emotional problems in young adolescents. *Journal of Research on Adolescence, 4*, 405–437.

Leichtman, M. D., & Ceci, S. J. (1995, April). The effects of stereotypes and suggestions on preschoolers' reports. *Developmental Psychology, 31*, 568–578.

Lerner, R. M. (1985). Adolescent maturational changes and psychosocial development: A dynamic interactional perspective. *Journal of Youth and Adolescence, 14*, 355–372.

Lerner, R. M. (1986). *Concepts and theories of human development* (2nd ed.). New York: Random House.

Lerner, R. M. (1987). A life-span perspective for early adolescence. In R. M. Lerner & T. T. Foch (Eds.), *Biological-psychosocial interactions in early adolescence* (pp. 9–34). Hillsdale, NJ: Erlbaum.

Lester, B. M. (1987). Prediction of developmental outcome from acoustic cry analysis in term and preterm infants. *Pediatrics, 80*, 529–534.

Lester, B. M., Boukydis, C. F. Z., Garcia-Coll, C. T., Hole, W., & Peucker, M. (1992). Infantile colic: Acoustic cry characteristics, maternal perception of cry, and temperament. *Infant Behavior and Development, 15*, 15–26.

Lester, B. M., & Dreher, M. (1989). Effects of marijuana use during pregnancy on newborn cry. *Child Development, 60*, 765–771.

Lester, B. M., Freier, K., & LaGasse, L. (1995). Prenatal cocaine exposure and child outcome: What do we really know? In M. Lewis & M. Bendersky (Eds.), *Mothers, babies, and cocaine. The role of toxins in development* (pp. 19–39). Hillsdale, NJ: Erlbaum.

LeVay, S. (1991). A difference in hypothalamus structure between heterosexual and homosexual men. *Science, 253*, 1034–1037.

Leve, L. D., & Fagot, B. I. (1995, April). *The influence of attachment style and parenting behavior on children's prosocial behavior with peers.* Paper presented at the biennial meetings of the Society for Research in Child Development, Indianapolis.

Levitt, M. J., Guacci-Franco, N., & Levitt, J. L. (1993). Convoys of social support in childhood and early adolescence: Structure and function. *Developmental Psychology, 29*, 811–818.

Levy, G. D., & Fivush, R. (1993). Scripts and gender: A new approach for examining gender-role development. *Developmental Review, 13*, 126–146.

Lewis, C., Freeman, N. H., Kyriakidou, C., Maridaki-Kassotaki, K., & Berridge, D. M. (1996). Social influences on false belief access: Specific sibling influences or general apprenticeship? *Child Development, 67*, 2930–2947.

Lewis, C. C. (1981). How adolescents approach decisions: Changes over grades seven to twelve and policy implications. *Child Development, 52*, 538–544.

Lewis, C. N., Freeman, N. H., & Maridaki-Kassotaki, K. (1995, April). *The social basis of theory of mind: Influences of siblings and, more importantly, interactions with adult kin.* Paper presented at the biennial meetings of the Society for Research in Child Development, Indianapolis.

Lewis, M. (1990). Social knowledge and social development. *Merrill-Palmer Quarterly, 36*, 93–116.

Lewis, M. (1991). Ways of knowing: Objective self-awareness of consciousness. *Developmental Review, 11*, 231–243.

Lewis, M., & Brooks, J. (1978). Self-knowledge and emotional development. In M. Lewis & L. A. Rosenblum (Eds.), *The development of affect* (pp. 205–226). New York: Plenum Press.

Lewis, M., Sullivan, M. W., Stanger, C., & Weiss, M. (1989). Self development and self-conscious emotions. *Child Development, 60*, 146–156.

Lewis, M. D. (1993). Early socioemotional predictors of cognitive competence at 4 years. *Developmental Psychology, 29*, 1036–1045.

Lewkowicz, D. J. (1994). Limitations on infants' response to rate-based auditory-visual relations. *Developmental Psychology, 30*, 880–892.

Lickona, T. (1978). Moral development and moral education. In J. M. Gallagher & J. J. A. Easley (Eds.), *Knowledge and development* (Vol. 2) (pp. 21–74). New York: Plenum Press.

Lickona, T. (1983). *Raising good children.* Toronto: Bantam Books.

Lieberman, M., Doyle, A., & Markiewicz, D. (1995, April). *Attachment to mother and father: Links to peer relations in children.* Paper presented at the biennial meetings of the Society for Research in Child Development, Indianapolis.

Liebowitz, A. (1996). Child care: Private cost or public responsibility? In V. R. Fuchs (Eds.), *Individual and social responsibility: Child care, education, medical care, and long-term care in America* (pp. 33–54). Chicago: University of Chicago Press.

Lifshitz, F., & Tarim, O. (1996). Considerations about dietary fat restrictions for children. *Journal of Nutrition, 126*, 1031S–1041S.

Lillard, A. S., & Flavell, J. H. (1992). Young children's understanding of different mental states. *Developmental Psychology, 28*, 626–634.

Lin, J., Brown, J. K., & Walsh, E. G. (1996). The maturation of motor dexterity: Or why Johnny can't go any faster. *Developmental Medicine and Child Neurology, 38*, 244–254.

Lindberg, L. D. (1996). Women's decisions about breastfeeding and maternal employment. *Journal of Marriage and the Family, 58*, 239–251.

Linney, J. A., & Seidman, E. (1989). The future of schooling. *American Psychologist, 44*, 336–340.

Lissner, L., Bengtsson, C., Björkelund, C., & Wedel, H. (1996). Physical activity levels and changes in relation to longevity. A prospective study of Swedish women. *American Journal of Epidemiology, 143*, 54–62.

Litt, I. F. (1996). Special health problems during adolescence. In R. E. Behrman, R. M. Kliegman, & A. M. Arvin (Eds.), *Nelson textbook of pediatrics* (15th ed.) (pp. 541–565). Philadelphia: W. B. Saunders.

Livesley, W. J., & Bromley, D. B. (1973). *Person perception in childhood and adolescence.* London: Wiley.

Lo, Y. D., Patel, P., Wainscoat, J. S., Sampietro, M., Gillmer, M. D. G., & Fleming, K. A. (1989). Prenatal sex determination by DNA amplification from maternal peripheral blood. *The Lancet*, 1363–1365.

Loeber, R., Stouthamer-Loeber, M., Van Kammen, W. B., & Farrington, D. P. (1991). Initiation, excalation and desistance in juvenile offending and their correlates. *Journal of Criminal Law and Criminology, 82*, 36–82.

Loeber, R., Tremblay, R. E., Gagnon, C., & Charlebois, P. (1989). Continuity and desistance in disruptive boys' early fighting at school. *Development and Psychopathology, 1*, 39–50.

Loehlin, J. C., Horn, J. M., & Willerman, L. (1994). Differential inheritance of mental abilities in the Texas Adoption Project. *Intelligence, 19*, 325–336.

Loftus, E. F. (1992). When a lie becomes memory's truth: Memory distortion after exposure to misinformation. *Current Directions in Psychological Science, 4*, 121–123.

Lollis, S., Ross, H., & Leroux, L. (1996). An observational study of parents' socialization of moral orientation during sibling conflicts. *Merrill-Palmer Quarterly, 42*, 475–494.

Long, J. V. F., & Vaillant, G. E. (1984). Natural history of male psychological health: Escape from the underclass. *American Journal of Psychiatry, 141*, 341–346.

Looney, M. A., & Plowman, S. A. (1990). Passing rates of American children and youth on the FITNESSGRAM criterion-referenced physical fitness standards. *Research Quarterly for Exercise and Sport, 61,* 215–223.

Lore, R. K., & Schultz, L. A. (1993). Control of human aggression: A comparative perspective. *American Psychologist, 48,* 16–25.

Louhiala, P. J., Jaakkola, N., Ruotsalainen, R., & Jaakkola, J. J. K. (1995). Form of day care and respiratory infections among Finnish children. *American Journal of Public Health, 85,* 1109–1112.

Lozoff, B., Wolf, A. W., & Davis, N. S. (1985). Sleep problems seen in pediatric practice. *Pediatrics, 75,* 477–483.

Lubinski, D., & Benbow, C. P. (1992). Gender differences in abilities and preferences among the gifted: Implications for the math-science pipeline. *Current Directions in Psychological Science, 1,* 61–66.

Lundh, W., & Gyllang, C. (1993). Use of the Edinburgh Postnatal Depression Scale in some Swedish child health care centres. *Scandinavian Journal of Caring Sciences, 7,* 149–154.

Lust, K. D., Brown, J. E., & Thomas, W. (1996). Maternal intake of cruciferous vegetables and other foods and colic symptoms in exclusively breast-fed infants. *Journal of the American Dietetic Association, 96,* 46–48.

Luster, T., Boger, R., & Hannan, K. (1993). Infant affect and home environment. *Journal of Marriage and the Family, 55,* 651–661.

Luster, T., & McAdoo, H. (1996). Family and child influences on educational attainment: A secondary analysis of the High/Scope Perry Preschool data. *Developmental Psychology, 32,* 26–39.

Luster, T., & McAdoo, H. P. (1995). Factors related to self-esteem among African American youths: A secondary analysis of the High/Scope Perry Preschool data. *Journal of Research on Adolescence, 5,* 451–467.

Luthar, S. S., & Zigler, E. (1992). Intelligence and social competence among high-risk adolescents. *Development and Psychopathology, 4,* 287–299.

Lynam, D. R. (1996). Early identification of chronic offenders: Who is the fledgling psychopath? *Psychological Bulletin, 120,* 209–234.

Lynam, D. R., Moffitt, T. E., & Stouthamer-Loeber, M. (1993). Explaining the relation between IQ and delinquency: Class, race, test motivation, school failure, or self-control? *Journal of Abnormal Psychology, 102,* 187–196.

Lyon, T. D., & Flavell, J. H. (1994). Young children's understanding of "remember" and "forget." *Child Development, 65,* 1357–1371.

Lyons, N. P. (1983). Two perspectives: On self, relationships, and morality. *Harvard Educational Review, 53,* 125–145.

Lytton, H., & Romney, D. M. (1991). Parents' differential socialization of boys and girls: A meta-analysis. *Psychological Bulletin, 109,* 267–296.

Maccoby, E. E. (1980). *Social development. Psychological growth and the parent-child relationship.* New York: Harcourt Brace Jovanovich.

Maccoby, E. E. (1984). Middle childhood in the context of the family. In W. A. Collins (Ed.), *Development during middle childhood. The years from six to twelve* (pp. 184–239). Washington, DC: National Academy Press.

Maccoby, E. E. (1988). Gender as a social category. *Developmental Psychology, 24,* 755–765.

Maccoby, E. E. (1990). Gender and relationships: A developmental account. *American Psychologist, 45,* 513–520.

Maccoby, E. E. (1995). The two sexes and their social systems. In P. Moen, G. H. Elder Jr., & K. Lüscher (Eds.), *Examining lives in context. Perspectives on the ecology of human development* (pp. 347–364). Washington, DC: American Psychological Association.

Maccoby, E. E., & Jacklin, C. N. (1987). Gender segregation in childhood. In H. W. Reese (Ed.), *Advances in child development and behavior* (Vol. 20) (pp. 239–288). Orlando, FL: Academic Press.

Maccoby, E. E., & Martin, J. A. (1983). Socialization in the context of the family: Parent-child interaction . In E. M. Hetherington (Ed.), *Handbook of child psychology: Socialization, personality, and social development* (Vol. 4) (pp. 1–102). New York: Wiley.

MacGowan, R. J., MacGowan, C. A., Serdula, M. K., Lane, J. M., Joesoef, R. M., & Cook, F. H. (1991). Breast-feeding among women attending Women, Infants, and Children clinics in Georgia, 1987. *Pediatrics, 87,* 361–366.

Mac Iver, D. J., Reuman, D. A., & Main, S. R. (1995). Social structuring of the school: Studying what is, illuminating what could be. *Annual Review of Psychology, 46,* 375–400.

Mack, V., Urberg, K., Lou, Q., & Tolson, J. (1995, April). *Ethnic, gender and age differences in parent and peer orientation during adolescence.* Paper presented at the biennial meetings of the Society for Research in Child Development, Indianapolis.

MacMillan, D. L., Keogh, B. K., & Jones, R. L. (1986). Special educational research on mildly handicapped learners. In M. C. Wittrock (Ed.), *Handbook of research on teaching* (3rd ed.) (pp. 686–724). New York: Macmillan.

MacMillan, D. L., & Reschly, D. J. (1997). Issues of definition and classification. In W. E. MacLean Jr. (Ed.), *Ellis' Handbook of mental deficiency, psychological theory and research* (pp. 47–74). Mahwah, NJ: Erlbaum.

Maffeis, C., Schutz, Y., Piccoli, R., Gonfiantini, E., & Pinelli, L. (1993). Prevalence of obesity in children in northeast Italy. *International Journal of Obesity, 14,* 287–294.

Maguin, E., Loeber, R., & LeMahieu, G. (1993). Does the relationship between poor reading and delinquency hold for males of different ages and ethnic groups? *Journal of Emotional and Behavioral Disorders, 1,* 88–100.

Mahoney, J. L., & Cairns, R. B. (1997). Do extracurricular activities protect against early school dropout? *Developmental Psychology, 33,* 241–253.

Main, M., & Hesse, E. (1990). Parents' unresolved traumatic experiences are related to infant disorganized attachment status: Is frightened and/or frightening parental behavior the linking mechanism? In M. T. Greenberg, D. Cicchetti, & E. M. Cummings (Eds.), *Attachment in the preschool years. Theory, research, and intervention* (pp. 161–182). Chicago: University of Chicago Press.

Main, M., Kaplan, N., & Cassidy, J. (1985). Security in infancy, childhood, and adulthood: A move to the level of representation. *Monographs of the Society for Research in Child Development, 50*(Serial No. 209), 66–104.

Main, M., & Solomon, J. (1990). Procedures for identifying infants as disorganized/disoriented during the Ainsworth Strange Situation. In M. T. Greenberg, D. Cicchetti, & E. M. Cummings (Eds.), *Attachment in the preschool years. Theory, research, and intervention* (pp. 121–160). Chicago: University of Chicago Press.

Malina, R. M. (1982). Motor development in the early years. In S. G. Moore & C. R. Cooper (Eds.), *The young child. Reviews of research* (Vol. 3) (pp. 211–232). Washington, DC: National Association for the Education of Young Children.

Malina, R. M. (1989). Growth and maturation: Normal variation and effect of training. In C. V. Gisolfi & D. R. Lamb (Eds.), *Perspectives in exercise science and sports medicine.* Vol. 2, *Youth, exercise and sport* (pp. 223–265). Indianapolis: Benchmark Press.

Malina, R. M. (1990). Physical growth and performance during the transition years. In R. Montemayor, G. R. Adams, & T. P. Gullotta (Eds.), *From childhood to adolescence: A transitional period?* (pp. 41–62). Newbury Park, CA: Sage.

Malina, R. M. (1994a). Physical growth and biological maturation of young athletes. In J. O. Holloszy (Ed.), *Exercise and sports sciences reviews* (Vol. 22) (pp. 389–433). Baltimore: Williams & Wilkins.

Malina, R. M. (1994b). Physical activity and training: Effects on stature and the adolescent growth spurt. *Medicine and Science in Sports and Exercise, 26,* 759–766.

Malinosky-Rummell, R., & Hansen, D. J. (1993). Long-term consequences of childhood physical abuse. *Psychological Bulletin, 114,* 68–79.

Malloy, M. H., & Hoffman, H. J. (1995). Prematurity, sudden infant death syndrome, and age of death. *Pediatrics, 96,* 464–471.

Mandelbaum, J. K. (1992). Child survival: What are the issues? *Journal of Pediatric Health Care, 6,* 132–137.

Marcia, J. E. (1966). Development and validation of ego identity status. *Journal of Personality and Social Psychology, 3,* 551–558.

Marcia, J. E. (1980). Identity in adolescence. In J. Adelson (Ed.), *Handbook of adolescent psychology* (pp. 159–187). New York: Wiley.

Marcia, J. E. (1993). The status of the statuses: Research review. In J. E. Marcia, A. S. Waterman, D. R. Matteson, S. L. Archer, & J. L. Orlofsky (Eds.), *Ego identity: A handbook for psychosocial research* (pp. 22–41). New York: Springer-Verlag.

Marcus, G. F., Pinker, S., Ullman, M., Hollander, M., Rosen, T. J., & Fei, X. (1992). Overregularization in language acquisition. *Monographs of the Society for Research in Child Development, 57*(4, Serial No. 228).

Marcus, R. F. (1986). Naturalistic observation of cooperation, helping, and sharing and their association with empathy and affect. In C. Zahn-Waxler, E. M. Cummings, & R. Iannotti (Eds.), *Altruism and aggression. Biological and social origins* (pp. 256–279). Cambridge, England: Cambridge University Press.

Marean, G. C., Werner, L. A., & Kuhl, P. K. (1992). Vowel categorization by very young infants. *Developmental Psychology, 28,* 396–405.

Markman, E. M. (1992). Constraints on word learning: Speculations about their nature, origins, and domain specificity. In M. R. Gunnar & M. Maratsos (Eds.), *Minnesota symposia on child psychology* (Vol. 25) (pp. 59–101). Hillsdale, NJ: Erlbaum.

Martell, C. (1996, September 22). Disordered lives. *Wisconsin State Journal,* pp. 1G, 4G.

Martin, B., & Hoffman, J. A. (1990). Conduct disorders. In M. Lewis & S. M. Miller (Eds.), *Handbook of developmental psychopathology* (pp. 109–118). New York: Plenum Press.

Martin, C. L. (1991). The role of cognition in understanding gender effects. In H. W. Reese (Ed.), *Advances in child development and behavior* (Vol. 23) (pp. 113–150). San Diego: Academic Press.

Martin, C. L. (1993). New directions for investigating children's gender knowledge. *Developmental Review, 13,* 184–204.

Martin, C. L., & Halverson, C. F., Jr. (1981). A schematic processing model of sex typing and stereotyping in children. *Child Development, 52,* 1119–1134.

Martin, C. L., & Halverson, C. F., Jr. (1983). Gender constancy: A methodological and theoretical analysis. *Sex Roles, 9,* 775–790.

Martin, C. L., & Little, J. K. (1990). The relation of gender understanding to children's sex-typed preferences and gender stereotypes. *Child Development, 61,* 1427–1439.

Martin, C. L., Wood, C. H., & Little, J. K. (1990). The development of gender stereotype components. *Child Development, 61,* 1891–1904.

Martin, E. W. (1995). Case studies on inclusion. Worst fears realized. *The Journal of Special Education, 29,* 192–199.

Martin, R. P., Wisenbaker, J., & Huttunen, M. (1994). Review of factor analytic studies of temperament measures based on the Thomas-Chess structural model: Implications for the Big Five. In C. F. Halverson Jr., G. A. Kohnstamm, & R. P. Martin (Eds.), *The developing structure of temperament and person-*

ality from infancy to adulthood (pp. 157–172). Hillsdale, NJ: Erlbaum.

Martorano, S. C. (1977). A developmental analysis of performance on Piaget's formal operations tasks. *Developmental Psychology, 13,* 666–672.

Mascolo, M. F., & Fischer, K. W. (1995). Developmental transformations in appraisals for pride, shame, and guilt. In J. P. Tangney & K. W. Fischer (Eds.), *Self-conscious emotions. The psychology of shame, guilt, embarrassment, and pride* (pp. 64–113). New York: Guilford Press.

Mason, C. A., Cauce, A. M., Gonzales, N., & Hiraga, Y. (1996). Neither too sweet nor too sour: Problem peers, maternal control, and problem behavior in African American adolescents. *Child Development, 67,* 2115–2130.

Mason, C. A., Cauce, A. M., Gonzales, N., Hiraga, Y., & Grove, K. (1994). An ecological model of externalizing behaviors in African-American adolescents: No family is an island. *Journal of Research on Adolescence, 4,* 639–655.

Massad, C. M. (1981). Sex role identity and adjustment during adolescence. *Child Development, 52,* 1290–1298.

Masten, A. S., Best, K. M., & Garmezy, N. (1990). Resilience and development: Contributions from the study of children who overcome adversity. *Development and Psychopathology, 2,* 425–444.

Masten, A. S., & Coatsworth, J. D. (1995). Competence, resilience, and psychopathology. In D. Cicchetti & D. J. Cohen (Eds.), *Developmental psychopathology.* Vol. 2, *Risk, disorder, and adaptation* (pp. 715–752). New York: Wiley-Interscience.

Masur, E. F. (1995). Infants' early verbal imitation and their later lexical development. *Merrill-Palmer Quarterly, 41,* 286–306.

Matas, L., Arend, R. A., & Sroufe, L. A. (1978). Continuity of adaptation in the second year: The relationship between quality of attachment and later competence. *Child Development, 49,* 547–556.

Mather, P. L., & Black, K. N. (1984). Heredity and environmental influences on preschool twins' language skills. *Developmental Psychology, 20,* 303–308.

Mathew, A., & Cook, M. (1990). The control of reaching movements by young infants. *Child Development, 61,* 1238–1257.

Maughan, B., Pickles, A., & Quinton, D. (1995). Parental hostility, childhood behavior, and adult social functioning. In J. McCord (Ed.), *Coercion and punishment in long-term perspectives* (pp. 34–58). Cambridge, England: Cambridge University Press.

Maurer, D., & Maurer, C. (1988). *The world of the newborn.* New York: Basic Books.

McCall, R. B. (1993). Developmental functions for general mental performance. In D. K. Detterman (Ed.), *Current topics in human intelligence.* Vol. 3, *Individual differences and cognition* (pp. 3–30). Norwood, NJ: Ablex.

McClintock, M. K., & Herdt, G. (1996). Rethinking puberty: The development of sexual attraction. *Current Directions in Psychological Science, 5,* 178–183.

McCord, J. (1982). A longitudinal view of the relationship between parental absence and crime. In J. Gunn & D. P. Farrington (Eds.), *Abnormal offenders, delinquency, and the criminal justice system* (pp. 113–128). London: Wiley.

McCrae, R. R. (1996). Social consequences of experiential openness. *Psychological Bulletin, 120,* 323–337.

McCrae, R. R., & Costa, P. T., Jr. (1990). *Personality in adulthood.* New York: Guilford Press.

McCrae, R. R., & John, O. P. (1992). An introduction to the Five-Factor Model and its applications. *Journal of Personality, 60,* 175–215.

McCune, L. (1995). A normative study of representational play at the transition to language. *Developmental Psychology, 31,* 198–206.

McDowell, M. A., Briefel, R. R., Alaimo, K., Bischof, A. M., Cauchman, C. R., Carroll, M. D., Loria, C. M., & Johnson, C. L. (1994). Energy and macronutrient intakes of persons ages 2 months and over in the United States: Third National Health and Nutrition Examination Survey, Phase 1, 1988–91. *Vital and Health Statistics, Centers for Disease Control and Prevention, Advance Data, October 24, 1994(255).*

McFalls, J. A., Jr. (1990). The risks of reproductive impairment in the later years of childbearing. *Annual Review of Sociology, 16,* 491–519.

McGue, M. (1994). Why developmental psychology should find room for behavior genetics. In C. A. Nelson (Ed.), *Minnesota symposia on child development* (Vol. 27) (pp. 105–119). Hillsdale, NJ: Erlbaum.

McGuire, S., Dunn, J., & Plomin, R. (1995). Maternal differential treatment of siblings and children's behavioral problems: A longitudinal study. *Development and Psychopathology, 7,* 515–528.

McGuire, S., McHale, S. M., & Updegraff, K. (1996). Children's perceptions of the sibling relationship in middle childhood: Connections within and between family relationships. *Personal Relationships, 3,* 229–239.

McKusick, V. A. (1994). *Mendelian inheritance in man* (11th ed.). Baltimore: Johns Hopkins University Press.

McLain, L. G., & Reynolds, S. (1989). Sports injuries in high school. *Pediatrics, 84,* 446–450.

McLanahan, S., & Sandefur, G. (1994). *Growing up with a single parent: What hurts, what helps.* Cambridge, MA: Harvard University Press.

McLaughlin, B. (1984). *Second-language acquisition in childhood: Preschool children* (2nd ed.). Hillsdale, NJ: Erlbaum.

McLeskey, J., & Pugach, M. C. (1995). The real sellout: Failing to give inclusion a chance. A response to Roberts and Mather. *Learning Disabilities Research & Practice, 10,* 233–238.

McLoyd, V. (1997, April). *Reducing stressors, increasing supports in the lives of ethnic minority children in America: Research and policy issues*. Paper presented at the biennial meetings of the Society for Research in Child Development, Washington, DC.

McLoyd, V., & Wilson, L. (1991). The strain of living poor: Parenting, social support, and child mental health. In A. C. Huston (Ed.), *Children in poverty. Child development and public policy* (pp. 105–135). Cambridge, England: Cambridge University Press.

McMahon, R. J. (1997, April). *Prevention of antisocial behavior: Initial findings from the Fast Track Project*. Symposium presented at the biennial meetings of the Society for Research in Child Development, Washington, DC.

McManus, I. C. (1991). The inheritance of left-handedness. In *Biological asymmetry and handedness. Ciba Foundation Symposium 162* (pp. 251–281). Chichester: Wiley.

McNemar, Q. (1955). *Psychological Statistics* (2nd ed.). New York: Wiley.

Melby, J. N., & Conger, R. D. (1996). Parental behaviors and adolescent academic performance: A longitudinal analysis. *Journal of Research on Adolescence, 6,* 113–137.

Mellin, L. M., Irwin, C. E., & Scully, S. (1992). Prevalence of disordered eating in girls: A survey of middle-class children. *Journal of the American Dietetic Association, 92,* 851–853.

Melson, G. F., Ladd, G. W., & Hsu, H. (1993). Maternal support networks, maternal cognitions, and young children's social and cognitive development. *Child Development, 64,* 1401–1417.

Meltzoff, A. N. (1988). Infant imitation and memory: Nine-month-olds in immediate and deferred tasks. *Child Development, 59,* 217–225.

Meltzoff, A. N. (1995). Understanding the intentions of others: Re-enactment of intended acts by 18-month-old children. *Developmental Psychology, 31,* 838–850.

Meltzoff, A. N., & Moore, M. K. (1977). Imitation of facial and manual gestures by human neonates. *Science 198,* 75–78.

Menaghan, E. G., & Parcel, T. L. (1995). Social sources of change in children's home environments: The effects of parental occupational experiences and family conditions. *Journal of Marriage and the Family, 57,* 69–84.

Merikangas, K. R., & Angst, J. (1995). The challenge of depressive disorders in adolescence. In M. Rutter (Ed.), *Psychosocial disturbances in young people. Challenges for prevention* (pp. 131–165). Cambridge, England: Cambridge University Press.

Mervis, C. B., & Bertrand, J. (1994). Acquisition of the novel name–nameless category (N3C) principle. *Child Development, 65,* 1646–1662.

Meyer-Bahlburg, H. F. L., Ehrhardt, A. A., Rosen, L. R., Gruen, R. S., Veridiano, N. P., Vann, F. H., & Neuwalder, H. F. (1995). Prenatal estrogens and the development of homosexual orientation. *Developmental Psychology, 31,* 12–21.

Meyers, A., Frank, D. A., Roos, N., Peterson, K. E., Casey, V. A., Cupples, A., & Levenson, S. M. (1995). Housing subsidies and pediatric undernutrition. *Archives of Pediatric and Adolescent Medicine, 149,* 1079–1084.

Meyers, A. F., Sampson, A. E., Weitzman, M., Rogers, B. L., & Kayne, H. (1989). School breakfast program and school performance. *American Journal of Diseases of Children, 143,* 1234–1239.

Miller, B. C., Christopherson, C. R., & King, P. K. (1993). Sexual behavior in adolescence. In T. P. Gullotta, G. R. Adams, & R. Montemayor (Eds.), *Adolescent sexuality* (pp. 57–76). Newbury Park, CA: Sage.

Miller, B. C., & Moore, K. A. (1990). Adolescent sexual behavior, pregnancy, and parenting: Research through the 1980s. *Journal of Marriage and the Family, 52,* 1025–1044.

Miller, K. E., & Pedersen-Randall, P. (1995, April). *Work, farm work, academic achievement and friendship: A comparison of rural and urban 10th, 11th and 12th graders*. Paper presented at the biennial meetings of the Society for Research in Child Development, Indianapolis.

Millstein, S. G., Petersen, A. C., & Nightingale, E. O. (Eds.). (1993). *Promoting the health of adolescents. New directions for the twenty-first century.* New York: Oxford University Press.

Mindell, J. A., & Durand, V. M. (1993). Treatment of childhood sleep disorders: Generalization across disorders and effects on family members. *Journal of Pediatric Psychology, 18,* 731–750.

Mischel, W. (1966). A social learning view of sex differences in behavior. In E. E. Maccoby (Ed.), *The development of sex differences* (pp. 56–81). Stanford, CA: Stanford University Press.

Mischel, W. (1970). Sex typing and socialization. In P. H. Mussen (Ed.), *Carmichael's manual of child psychology* (Vol. 2) (pp. 3–72). New York: Wiley.

Mitchell, J. E. (1995). Medical complications of bulimia nervosa. In K. D. Brownell & C. G. Fairburn (Eds.), *Eating disorders and obesity: A comprehensive handbook* (pp. 271–275). New York: Guilford Press.

Mitchell, P. R., & Kent, R. D. (1990). Phonetic variation in multisyllable babbling. *Journal of Child Language, 17,* 247–265.

Moffitt, T. E. (1990). Juvenile delinquency and attention deficit disorder: Boys' developmental trajectories from age 3 to age 15. *Child Development, 61,* 893–910.

Moffitt, T. E. (1993). Adolescence-limited and life-course-persistent antisocial behavior: A developmental taxonomy. *Psychology Review, 100,* 674–701.

Moffitt, T. E., Caspi, A., Dickson, N., Silva, P., & Stanton, W. (1996). Childhood-onset versus adolescent-onset antisocial conduct problems in males: Natural history from ages 3 to 18. *Development and Psychopathology, 8,* 399–424.

Molfese, D. L., & Molfese, V. J. (1979). Hemisphere and stimulus differences as reflected in the cortical responses of newborn infants to speech stimuli. *Developmental Psychology, 15*, 505–511.

Moll, L. C. (Ed.). (1990). *Vygotsky and education.* Cambridge, England: Cambridge University Press.

Montemayor, R., Adams, G. R., & Gullotta, T. P. (Eds.). (1994). *Personal relationships during adolescence.* Thousand Oaks, CA: Sage.

Montemayor, R., & Eisen, M. (1977). The development of self-conceptions from childhood to adolescence. *Developmental Psychology, 13*, 314–319.

Moon, C., & Fifer, W. P. (1990). Syllables as signals for 2-day-old infants. *Infant Behavior and Development, 13*, 377–390.

Moore, K. A., Myers, D. E., Morrison, D. R., Nord, C. W., Brown, B., & Edmonston, B. (1993). Age at first childbirth and later poverty. *Journal of Research on Adolescence, 3*, 393–422.

Moore, K. L., & Persaud, T. V. N. (1993). *The developing human: Clinically oriented embryology* (5th ed.). Philadelphia: W. B. Saunders.

Morelli, G. A., Rogoff, B., Oppenheim, D., & Goldsmith, D. (1992). Cultural variation in infants' sleeping arrangements: Questions of independence. *Developmental Psychology, 28*, 604–613.

Morgan, J. L. (1994). Converging measures of speech segmentation in preverbal infants. *Infant Behavior and Development, 17*, 389–403.

Morgan, J. L., Bonamo, K. M., & Travis, L. L. (1995). Negative evidence on negative evidence. *Developmental Psychology, 31*, 180–197.

Morrison, D. M. (1985). Adolescent contraceptive behavior: A review. *Psychological Bulletin, 98*, 538–568.

Morrison, D. R., & Cherlin, A. J. (1995). The divorce process and young children's well-being: A prospective analysis. *Journal of Marriage and the Family, 57*, 800–812.

Morrison, F. J., Smith, L., & Dow-Ehrensberger, M. (1995). Education and cognitive development: A natural experiment. *Developmental Psychology, 31*, 789–799.

Morse, P. A., & Cowan, N. (1982). Infant auditory and speech perception. In T. M. Field, A. Houston, H. C. Quay, L. Troll, & G. E. Finley (Eds.), *Review of human development* (pp. 32–61). New York: Wiley.

Mortimer, J. T., & Finch, M. D. (1996). Work, family, and adolescent development. In J. T. Mortimer & M. D. Finch (Eds.), *Adolescents, work, and family: An intergenerational developmental analysis* (pp. 1–24). Thousand Oaks, CA: Sage.

Mortimer, J. T., Finch, M. D., Dennehy, K., Lee, C., & Beebe, T. (1995, April). *Work experience in adolescence.* Paper presented at the biennial meetings of the Society for Research in Child Development, Indianapolis.

Mosteller, F. (1995). The Tennessee study of class size in the early school grades. *The Future of Children, 5*(2, Summer/Fall), 113–127.

Mounts, N. S., & Steinberg, L. (1995). An ecological analysis of peer influence on adolescent grade point average and drug use. *Developmental Psychology, 31*, 915–922.

Muhuri, P. K., Anker, M., & Bryce, J. (1996). Treatment patterns for childhood diarrhoea: Evidence from demographic and health surveys. *Bulletin of the World Health Organization, 74*, 135–146.

Muir-Broaddus, J. E. (1997, April). *The effects of social influence and psychological reactance on children's responses to repeated questions.* Paper presented at the biennial meetings of the Society for Research in Child Development, Washington, DC.

Mumme, D. L., Fernald, A., & Herrera, C. (1996). Infants' responses to facial and vocal emotional signals in a social referencing paradigm. *Child Development, 67*, 3219–3237.

Murphy, S. O. (1993, April). *The family context and the transition to siblinghood: Strategies parents use to influence sibling-infant relationships.* Paper presented at the biennial meetings of the Society for Research in Child Development, New Orleans.

Murray, J. P. (1980). *Television & youth: 25 years of research and controversy.* Stanford, CA: Boys Town Center for the Study of Youth Development.

Muscari, M. E. (1996). Primary care of adolescents with bulimia nervosa. *Journal of Pediatric Health Care, 10*, 17–25.

Musick, J. S. (1994). Capturing the childrearing context. *Society for Research in Child Development Newsletter* (Fall), 1, 6–7.

Myers, B. J. (1987). Mother-infant bonding as a critical period. In M. H. Bornstein (Ed.), *Sensitive periods in development: Interdisciplinary perspectives* (pp. 223–246). Hillsdale, NJ: Erlbaum.

Nachmias, M. (1993, April). *Maternal personality relations with toddler's attachment classification, use of coping strategies, and adrenocortical stress response.* Paper presented at the biennial meetings of the Society for Research in Child Development, New Orleans.

National Center on Child Abuse and Neglect. (1988). *Study findings. Study of national incidence and prevalence of child abuse and neglect: 1988.*

National Center for Health Statistics. (1987). Who drops out of high school? From high school and beyond. Washington, DC: Office of Educational Research and Improvement, U.S. Department of Education.

National Center for Health Statistics. (1996, June). Leading causes of death by age, sex, race, and Hispanic origin: United States, 1992. *Vital and Health Statistics, Series 20*(No. 29).

National Research Council. (1993). *Understanding child abuse and neglect.* Washington, DC: National Academy Press.

Needleman, H. L., Riess, J. A., Tobin, M. J., Biesecker, G. E., & Greenhouse, J. B. (1996). Bone lead levels and delinquent behavior. *Journal of the American Medical Association, 275*, 363–369.

Needlman, R. D. (1996). Growth and development. In R. E. Behrman, R. M. Kliegman, & A. M. Arvin (Eds.), *Nelson Textbook of Pediatrics (15th ed.) (pp. 30–72). Philadelphia: W. B. Saunders.

Needlman, R. D., Frank, D. A., Augustyn, M., & Zuckerman, B. S. (1995). Neurophysiological effects of prenatal cocaine exposure: Comparison of human and animal investigations. In M. Lewis & M. Bendersky (Eds.), *Mothers, babies, and cocaine. The role of toxins in development* (pp. 229–250). Hillsdale, NJ: Erlbaum.

Neimark, E. D. (1982). Adolescent thought: Transition to formal operations. In B. B. Wolman (Eds.), *Handbook of developmental psychology* (pp. 486–502). Englewood Cliffs, NJ: Prentice Hall.

Neisser, U., Boodoo, G., Bouchard, T. J., Jr., Boykin, A. W., Brody, N., Ceci, S. J., Halpern, D. F., Loehlin, J. C., Perloff, R., Sternberg, R. J., & Urbina, S. (1996). Intelligence: Knowns and unknowns. *American Psychologist, 51*, 77–101.

Nelson, C. A. (1987). The recognition of facial expression in the first two years of life: Mechanisms of development. *Child Development, 58*, 889–909.

Nelson, K. (1973). Structure and strategy in learning to talk. *Monographs of the Society for Research in Child Development, 38*(Serial No. 149).

Nelson, K. (1977). Facilitating children's syntax acquisition. *Developmental Psychology, 13*, 101–107.

Newacheck, P. W. (1989). Improving access to health services for adolescents from economically disadvantaged families. *Pediatrics, 84*, 1056–1063.

Newacheck, P. W. (1994). Poverty and childhood chronic illness. *Archives of Pediatric and Adolescent Medicine, 148*, 1143–1149.

Newacheck, P. W., & Stoddard, J. J. (1994). Prevalence and impact of multiple childhood chronic illnesses. *Journal of Pediatrics, 124*, 40–48.

Newcomb, A. F., & Bagwell, C. L. (1995). Children's friendship relations: A meta-analytic review. *Psychological Bulletin, 117*, 306–347.

Newcomb, A. F., & Bagwell, C. L. (1996). The developmental significance of children's friendship relations. In W. M. Bukowski, A. F. Newcomb, & W. W. Hartup (Eds.), *The company they keep: Friendship in childhood and adolescence* (pp. 289–321). Cambridge, England: Cambridge University Press.

Newcomb, A. F., Bukowski, W. M., & Pattee, L. (1993). Children's peer relations: A meta-analytic review of popular, rejected, neglected, controversial, and average sociometric status. *Psychological Bulletin, 113*, 99–128.

Newcombe, N. S., & Baenninger, M. (1989). Biological change and cognitive ability in adolescence. In G. R. Adams, R. Montemayor, & T. P. Gullotta (Eds.), *Biology of adolescent behavior and development* (pp. 168–194). Newbury Park, CA: Sage.

Newell, M., & Peckham, C. (1994). Vertical transmission of HIV infection. *Acta Paediatrica Supplement, 400*, 43–45.

Newman, D. L., Caspi, A., Moffitt, T. E., & Silva, P. A. (1997). Antecedents of adult interpersonal functioning: Effects of individual differences in age 3 temperament. *Developmental Psychology, 33*, 206–217.

NICHD Early Child Care Research Network. (1996a, April 20). Infant child care and attachment security: Results of the NICHD study of early child care. Paper presented at the International Conference on Infant Studies, Providence, RI.

NICHD Early Child Care Research Network. (1996b). Characteristics of infant child care: Factors contributing to positive caregiving. *Early Childhood Research Quarterly, 11*, 269–306.

NICHD Early Child Care Research Network. (1997, April). *Mother-child interaction and cognitive outcomes associated with early child care: Results of the NICHD study.* Paper presented at the biennial meetings of the Society for Research in Child Development, Washington, DC.

NICHD Early Child Care Research Network. (1997). Child care in the first year of life. *Merrill-Palmer Quarterly, 43*, 349–360.

Nichols, M. R. (1993). Paternal perspectives of the childbirth experience. *Maternal-Child Nursing Journal, 21*, 99–108.

Nicklas, T. A. (1995a). Dietary studies of children and young adults (1973–1988): The Bogalusa Heart Study. *American Journal of Medical Science, 310*(Suppl 1), S101–S108.

Nicklas, T. A. (1995b). Dietary studies of children: The Bogalusa Heart Study experience. *Journal of the American Dietetic Association, 95*, 1127–1133.

Nightingale, E. O., & Goodman, M. (1990). *Before birth. Prenatal testing for genetic disease.* Cambridge, MA: Harvard University Press.

Nilsson, L. (1990). *A child is born.* New York: Delacorte Press.

Nolen-Hoeksema, S. (1994). An interactive model for the emergence of gender differences in depression in adolescence. *Journal of Research on Adolescence, 4*, 519–534.

Nolen-Hoeksema, S., & Girgus, J. S. (1994). The emergence of gender differences in depression during adolescence. *Psychological Bulletin, 115*, 424–443.

Nordentoft, M., Lou, H. C., Hansen, D., Nim, J., Pryds, O., Rubin, P., & Hemmingsen, R. (1996). Intrauterine growth retardation and premature delivery: The influence of maternal smoking and psychosocial factors. *American Journal of Public Health, 86*, 347–354.

Nottelmann, E. D., Susman, E. J., Blue, J. H., Inoff-Germain, G., Dorn, L. D., Loriaux, D. L., Cutler, G. B., Jr., & Chrousos, G. P. (1987). Gonadal and adrenal hormone correlates of adjustment in early adolescence. In R. M. Lerner & T. T. Foch (Eds.), *Biological-psychosocial interactions in early adolescence* (pp. 303–324). Hillsdale, NJ: Erlbaum.

Notzon, F. C., Cnattingius, S., Pergsjø, P., Cole, S., Taffel, S., Irgens, L., & Dalveit, A. K. (1994). Cesarean section delivery in the 1980s: International comparison by indication. *American Journal of Obstetrics and Gynecology, 170*, 495–504.

Nowakowski, R. S. (1987). Basic concepts of CNS development. *Child Development, 58,* 568–595.

Nugent, J. K., Lester, B. M., Greene, S. M., Wieczorek-Deering, D., & O'Mahony, P. (1996). The effects of maternal alcohol consumption and cigarette smoking during pregnancy on acoustic cry analysis. *Child Development, 67,* 1806–1815.

Oakley, G. P., Jr., Adams, M. J., & Dickinson, C. M. (1996). More folic acid for everyone, now. *Journal of Nutrition, 126,* 751S–755S.

O'Beirne, H., & Moore, C. (1995, April). *Attachment and sexual behavior in adolescence.* Paper presented at the biennial meetings of the Society for Research in Child Development, Indianapolis.

O'Brien, M. (1992). Gender identity and sex roles. In V. B. Van Hasselt & M. Hersen (Eds.), *Handbook of social development. A lifespan perspective* (pp. 325–345). New York: Plenum Press.

O'Brien, S. F., & Bierman, K. L. (1988). Conceptions and perceived influence of peer groups: Interviews with preadolescents and adolescents. *Child Development, 59,* 1360–1365.

Odom, S. L., & Kaiser, A. P. (1997). Prevention and early intervention during early childhood: Theoretical and empirical bases for practice. In W. E. MacLean Jr. (Ed.), *Ellis' handbook of mental deficiency, psychological theory and research* (pp. 137–172). Mahwah, NJ: Erlbaum.

Offord, D. R., Boyle, M. H., & Racine, Y. A. (1991). The epidemiology of antisocial behavior in childhood and adolescence. In D. J. Pepler & K. H. Rubin (Eds.), *The development and treatment of childhood aggression* (pp. 31–54). Hillsdale, NJ: Erlbaum.

O'Hara, M. W., Schlechte, J. A., Lewis, D. A., & Varner, M. W. (1992). Controlled prospective study of postpartum mood disorders: Psychological, environmental, and hormonal variables. *Journal of Abnormal Psychology, 100,* 63–73.

Olds, D. L., & Henderson, C. R., Jr. (1989). The prevention of maltreatment. In D. Cicchetti & V. Carlson (Eds.), *Child maltreatment* (pp. 722–763). Cambridge, England: Cambridge University Press.

Oller, D. K. (1981). Infant vocalizations: Exploration and reflectivity. In R. E. Stark (Ed.), *Language behavior in infancy and early childhood* (pp. 85–104). New York: Elsevier/North-Holland.

Olson, H. C., Sampson, P. D., Barr, H., Streissguth, A. P., & Bookstein, F. L. (1992). Prenatal exposure to alcohol and school problems in late childhood: A longitudinal prospective study. *Development and Psychopathology, 4,* 341–359.

Olson, R. E. (1995). The dietary recommendations of the American Academy of Pediatrics. *American Journal of Clinical Nutrition, 61,* 271–273.

Olson, S. L., Bates, J. E., & Kaskie, B. (1992). Caregiver-infant interaction antecedents of children's school-age cognitive ability. *Merrill-Palmer Quarterly, 38,* 309–330.

Olweus, D. (1995). Bullying or peer abuse at school: Facts and intervention. *Current Directions in Psychological Science, 4,* 196–200.

O'Neill, D. K., Astington, J. W., & Flavell, J. H. (1992). Young children's understanding of the role that sensory experiences play in knowledge acquisition. *Child Development, 63,* 474–490.

Ornish, D. (1990). *Dr. Dean Ornish's program for reversing heart disease.* New York: Random House.

Osofsky, J. D. (1995). The effects of exposure to violence on young children. *American Psychologist, 50,* 782–788.

Osofsky, J. D., Hann, D. M., & Peebles, C. (1993). Adolescent parenthood: Risks and opportunities for mothers and infants. In C. H. Zeanah Jr. (Ed.), *Handbook of infant mental health* (pp. 106–119). New York: Guilford Press.

Ostoja, E., McCrone, E., Lehn, L., Reed, T., & Sroufe, L. A. (1995, April). *Representations of close relationships in adolescence: Longitudinal antecedents from infancy through childhood.* Paper presented at the biennial meetings of the Society for Research in Child Development, Indianapolis.

Ott, W. J. (1995). Small for gestational age fetus and neonatal outcome: Reevaluation of the relationship. *American Journal of Perinatology, 12,* 396–400.

Overton, W. F., Ward, S. L., Noveck, I. A., Black, J., & O'Brien, D. P. (1987). Form and content in the development of deductive reasoning. *Developmental Psychology, 23,* 22–30.

Page, D. C., Mosher, R., Simpson, E. M., Fisher, E. M. C., Mardon, G., Pollack, J., McGillivray, B., de la Chapelle, A., & Brown, L. G. (1987). The sex-determining region of the human Y chromosome encodes a finger protein. *Cell, 51,* 1091–1104.

Paik, H., & Comstock, G. (1994). The effects of television violence on antisocial behavior: A meta-analysis. *Communication Research, 21,* 516–546.

Paikoff, R. L., & Brooks-Gunn, J. (1990). Physiological processes: What role do they play during the transition to adolescence? In R. Montemayor, G. R. Adams, & T. P. Gullotta (Eds.), *From childhood to adolescence. A transitional period?* (pp. 63–81). Newbury Park, CA: Sage.

Palkovitz, R. (1985). Fathers' birth attendance, early contact, and extended contact with their newborns: A critical review. *Child Development, 56,* 392–406.

Palmérus, K., & Scarr, S. (1995, April). *How parents discipline young children. Cultural comparisons and individual differences.* Paper presented at the biennial meetings of the Society for Research in Child Development, Indianapolis.

Panel on High Risk Youth (1993). *Losing generations. Adolescents in high risk settings. Commission on Behavioral and Social Sciences and Education, National Research Council.* Washington, DC: National Academy Press.

Pannell, D. V. (1995). Why school meals are high in fat and some suggested solutions. *American Journal of Clinical Nutrition, 61,* 245S–246S.

Papousek, H., & Papousek, M. (1991). Innate and cultural guidance of infants' integrative competencies: China, the

United States, and Germany. In M. H. Bornstein (Ed.), *Cultural approaches to parenting* (pp. 23–44). Hillsdale, NJ: Erlbaum.

Paradise, J. L., Rockette, H. E., Colborn, D. K., Bernard, B. S., Smith, C. G., Kurs-Lasky, M., & Janosky, J. E. (1997). Otitis media in 2253 Pittsburgh-area infants: Prevalence and risk factors during the first two years of life. *Pediatrics, 99,* 318–333.

Parcel, T. L., & Menaghan, E. G. (1994). *Parents' jobs and children's lives.* New York: Aldine de Gruyter.

Parke, R. D. (1995). Fathers and families. In M. H. Bornstein (Ed.), *Handbook of parenting.* Vol. 3, *Status and social conditions of parenting* (pp. 27–63). Mahwah, NJ: Erlbaum.

Parke, R. D., & Tinsley, B. R. (1984). Fatherhood: Historical and contemporary perspectives. In K. A. McCluskey & H. W. Reese (Eds.), *Life-span developmental psychology. Historical and generational effects* (pp. 203–248). Orlando, FL: Academic Press.

Parker, J. G., & Herrera, C. (1996). Interpersonal processes in friendship: A comparison of abused and nonabused children's experiences. *Developmental Psychology, 32,* 1025–1038.

Parmelee, A. H., Jr. (1986). Children's illnesses: Their beneficial effects on behavioral development. *Child Development, 57,* 1–10.

Parmelee, A. H., Jr., Wenner, W. H., & Schulz, H. R. (1964). Infant sleep patterns from birth to 16 weeks of age. *Journal of Pediatrics, 65,* 576–582.

Parsons, J. E., Adler, T. F., & Kaczala, C. M. (1982). Socialization of achievement attitudes and beliefs: Parental influences. *Child Development, 53,* 310–321.

Parten, M. B. (1932). Social participation among preschool children. *Journal of Abnormal and Social Psychology, 27,* 243–269.

Passman, R. H., & Longeway, K. P. (1982). The role of vision in maternal attachment: Giving 2-year-olds a photograph of their mother during separation. *Developmental Psychology, 18,* 530–533.

Patterson, G. R. (1980). Mothers: The unacknowledged victims. *Monographs of the Society for Research in Child Development, 45*(Serial No. 186).

Patterson, G. R. (1996). Some characteristics of a developmental theory for early-onset delinquency. In M. F. Lenzenweger & J. J. Haugaard (Eds.), *Frontiers of developmental psychopathology* (pp. 81–124). New York: Oxford University Press.

Patterson, G. R., & Bank, L. (1989). Some amplifying mechanisms for pathological processes in families. In M. R. Gunnar & E. Thelen (Eds.), *Minnesota symposia on child psychology* (Vol. 22) (pp. 167–209). Hillsdale, NJ: Erlbaum.

Patterson, G. R., Capaldi, D., & Bank, L. (1991). An early starter model for predicting delinquency. In D. J. Pepler & K. H. Rubin (Eds.), *The development and treatment of childhood aggression* (pp. 139–168). Hillsdale, NJ: Erlbaum.

Patterson, G. R., DeBarsyshe, B. D., & Ramsey, E. (1989). A developmental perspective on antisocial behavior. *American Psychologist, 44,* 329–335.

Paxton, S. J., Wertheim, E. H., Gibbons, K., Szmukler, G. I., Hillier, L., & Petrovich, J. L. (1991). Body image satisfaction, dieting beliefs, and weight loss behaviors in adolescent girls and boys. *Journal of Youth and Adolescence, 20,* 361–379.

Pear, R. (1996, April 11). Immunization of children up sharply, U.S. reports. *New York Times,* p. A8.

Pederson, D. R., & Moran, G. (1995). A categorical description of infant-mother relationships in the home and its relation to Q-sort measures of infant-mother interaction. *Monographs of the Society for Research in Child Development, 60*(2–3, Serial No. 244), 111–132.

Pederson, D. R., Moran, G., Sitko, C., Campbell, K., Ghesquire, K., & Acton, H. (1990). Maternal sensitivity and the security of infant-mother attachment: A Q-sort study. *Child Development, 61,* 1974–1983.

Pedlow, R., Sanson, A., Prior, M., & Oberklaid, F. (1993). Stability of maternally reported temperament from infancy to 8 years. *Developmental Psychology, 29,* 998–1007.

Pegg, J. E., Werker, J. F., & McLeod, P. J. (1992). Preference for infant-directed over adult-directed speech: Evidence from 7-week-old infants. *Infant Behavior and Development, 15,* 325–345.

Peipert, J. F., & Bracken, M. B. (1993). Maternal age: An independent risk factor for cesarean delivery. *Obstetrics and Gynecology, 81,* 200–205.

Peisner-Feinberg, E. S. (1995, April). *Developmental outcomes and the relationship to quality of child care experiences.* Paper presented at the biennial meetings of the Society for Research in Child Development, Indianapolis.

Peoples, C. E., Fagan, J. F., III, & Drotar, D. (1995). The influence of race on 3-year-old children's performance on the Stanford-Binet: Fourth edition. *Intelligence, 21,* 69–82.

Perelle, I. B., & Ehrman, L. (1994). An international study of human handedness: The data. *Behavior Genetics, 24,* 217–225.

Perez-Escamilla, R. (1994). Breastfeeding in Africa and the Latin American and Caribbean region. The potential role of urbanization. *Journal of Tropical Pediatrics, 40,* 137–143.

Perlman, M., Claris, O., Hao, Y., Pandid, P., Whyte, H., Chipman, M., & Liu, P. (1995). Secular changes in the outcomes to eighteen to twenty-four months of age of extremely low birth weight infants, with adjustment for changes in risk factors and severity of illness. *Journal of Pediatrics, 126,* 75–87.

Perner, J., & Wimmer, H. (1985). "John thinks that Mary thinks that . . .": Attribution of second-order beliefs by 5- to 10-year-old children. *Journal of Experimental Child Psychology, 39,* 437–471.

Perry, C. L., Klep, K.-I., & Sillers, C. (1989). Community-wide strategies for cardiovascular health: The Minnesota Heart

Health Program youth program. *Health Education Research, 4,* 87–101.

Perry, D., Kusel, S. K., & Perry, L. C. (1988). Victims of peer aggression. *Developmental Psychology, 24,* 807–814.

Petersen, A. C. (1987). The nature of biological-psychosocial interactions: The sample case of early adolescence. In R. M. Lerner & T. T. Foch (Eds.), *Biological-psychosocial interactions in early adolescence* (pp. 35–62). Hillsdale, NJ: Erlbaum.

Petersen, A. C., Compas, B. E., Brooks-Gunn, J., Stemmler, M., Ey, S., & Grant, K. E. (1993). Depression in adolescence. *American Psychologist, 48,* 155–168.

Petersen, A. C., Sarigiani, P. A., & Kennedy, R. E. (1991). Adolescent depression: Why more girls? *Journal of Youth and Adolescence, 20,* 247–272.

Petersen, A. C., & Taylor, B. (1980). The biological approach to adolescence. In J. Adelson (Ed.), *Handbook of adolescent psychology* (pp. 117–158). New York: Wiley.

Peterson, C., & Bell, M. (1996). Children's memory for traumatic injury. *Child Development, 67,* 3045–3070.

Peterson, C. C., & Siegal, M. (1995). Deafness, conversation and theory of mind. *Journal of Child Psychology and Psychiatry, 36,* 459–474.

Petitto, L. A. (1988). "Language" in the prelinguistic child. In F. S. Kessell (Ed.), *The development of language and language researchers: Essays in honor of Roger Brown* (pp. 187–222). Hillsdale, NJ: Erlbaum.

Pettit, G. S., Clawson, M. A., Dodge, K. A., & Bates, J. E. (1996). Stability and change in peer-rejected status: The role of child behavior, parenting, and family ecology. *Merrill-Palmer Quarterly, 42,* 295–318.

Phinney, J. S. (1990). Ethnic identity in adolescents and adults: Review of research. *Psychological Bulletin, 108,* 499–514.

Phinney, J. S., & Devich-Navarro, M. (1997). Variations in bicultural identification among African American and Mexican American adolescents. *Journal of Research on Adolescence, 7,* 3–32.

Phinney, J. S., & Rosenthal, D. A. (1992). Ethnic identity in adolescence: Process, context, and outcome. In G. R. Adams, T. P. Gullotta, & R. Montemayor (Eds.), *Adolescent identity formation* (pp. 145–172). Newbury Park, CA: Sage.

Pi-Sunyer, F. X. (1995). Medical complications of obesity. In K. D. Brownell & C. G. Fairburn (Eds.), *Eating disorders and obesity. A comprehensive handbook* (pp. 401–405). New York: Guilford Press.

Piaget, J. (1932). *The moral judgment of the child.* New York: Macmillan.

Piaget, J. (1952). *The origins of intelligence in children.* New York: International Universities Press.

Piaget, J. (1954). *The construction of reality in the child.* New York: Basic Books. (Originally published 1937)

Piaget, J. (1970). Piaget's theory. In P. H. Mussen (Ed.), *Carmichael's manual of child psychology* (3rd ed., Vol. 1) (pp. 703–732). New York: Wiley.

Piaget, J. (1977). *The development of thought. Equilibration of cognitive structures.* New York: Viking Press.

Piaget, J., & Inhelder, B. (1959). *La gènese des structures logiques élémentaires: Classifications et seriations* [The origin of elementary logical structures: Classification and seriation]. Neuchâtel: Delachaux et Niestlé.

Piaget, J., & Inhelder, B. (1969). *The psychology of the child.* New York: Basic Books.

Pianta, R. C., & Egeland, B. (1994). Predictors of instability in children's mental test performance at 24, 48, and 96 months. *Intelligence, 18,* 145–163.

Pianta, R. C., Steinberg, M. S., & Rollins, K. B. (1995). Teacher-child relationships and deflections in children's classroom adjustment. *Development and Psychopathology, 7,* 295–312.

Pickens, J. (1994). Perception of auditory-visual distance relations by 5-month-old infants. *Developmental Psychology, 30,* 537–544.

Pillard, R. C., & Bailey, J. M. (1995). A biologic perspective on sexual orientation. *The Psychiatric Clinics of North America, 18*(1), 71–84.

Pinker, S. (1987). The bootstrapping problem in language acquisition. In B. MacWhinney (Ed.), *Mechanisms of language acquisition* (pp. 399–442). Hillsdale, NJ: Erlbaum.

Pinker, S. (1994). *The language instinct. How the mind creates language.* New York: William Morrow.

Plomin, R. (1995). Genetics and children's experiences in the family. *Journal of Child Psychology and Psychiatry, 36,* 33–68.

Plomin, R., & DeFries, J. C. (1985). *Origins of individual differences in infancy. The Colorado Adoption Project.* Orlando, FL: Academic Press.

Plomin, R., Emde, R. N., Braungart, J. M., Campos, J., Corley, R., Fulker, D. W., Kagan, J., Reznick, J. S., Robinson, J., Zahn-Waxler, C., & DeFries, J. C. (1993). Genetic change and continuity from fourteen to twenty months: The MacArthur longitudinal twin study. *Child Development, 64,* 1354–1376.

Plomin, R., Loehlin, J. C., & DeFries, J. C. (1985). Genetic and environmental components of "environmental" influences. *Developmental Psychology, 21,* 391–402.

Plomin, R., & McClearn, G. E. (Eds.). (1993). *Nature, nurture & psychology.* Washington, DC: American Psychological Association.

Plomin, R., Reiss, D., Hetherington, E. M., & Howe, G. W. (1994). Nature and nurture: Genetic contributions to measures of the family environment. *Developmental Psychology, 30,* 32–43.

Plomin, R., & Rende, R. (1991). Human behavioral genetics. *Annual Review of Psychology, 42,* 161–190.

Polivy, J., & Herman, C. P. (1995). Dieting and its relation to eating disorders. In K. D. Brownell & C. G. Fairburn (Eds.), *Eating disorders and obesity: A comprehensive handbook* (pp. 83–86). New York: Guilford Press.

Polka, L., & Werker, J. F. (1994). Developmental changes in perception of nonnative vowel contrasts. *Journal of Experimental Psychology: Human Perception and Performance, 20*, 421–435.

Pollitt, E. (1995). Does breakfast make a difference in school? *Journal of the American Dietetic Association, 95*, 1134–1139.

Pollitt, E., Golub, M., Gorman, K., Grantham-McGregor, S., Levitsky, D., Schürch, B., Strupp, B., & Wachs, T. (1996). A reconceptualization of the effects of undernutrition on children's biological, psychosocial, and behavioral development. *Social Policy Report, Society for Research in Child Development, X*(5), 1–21.

Pollitt, E., & Gorman, K. S. (1994). Nutritional deficiencies as developmental risk factors. In C. A. Nelson (Ed.), *Minnesota symposia on child development* (Vol. 27) (pp. 121–144). Hillsdale, NJ: Erlbaum.

Ponsonby, A., Dwyer, T., Gibbons, L. E., Cochrane, J. A., & Wang, Y. (1993). Factors potentiating the risk of sudden infant death syndrome associated with the prone position. *The New England Journal of Medicine, 329*, 377–382.

Porter, J. R., & Washington, R. E. (1993). Minority identity and self-esteem. *Annual Review of Sociology, 19*, 139–161.

Posada, G., Gao, Y., Wu, F., Posada, R., Tascon, M., Schöelmerich, A., Sagi, A., Kondo-Ikemura, K., Haaland, W., & Synnevaag, B. (1995). The secure-base phenomenon across cultures: Children's behavior, mother's preferences, and experts' concepts. *Monographs of the Society for Research in Child Development, 60*(2–3, Serial No. 244), 27–48.

Poulson, C. L., Nunes, L. R. D., & Warren, S. F. (1989). Imitation in infancy: A critical review. In H. W. Reese (Ed.), *Advances in child development and behavior* (Vol. 22) (pp. 272–298). San Diego: Academic Press.

Power, C., & Reimer, J. (1978). Moral atmosphere: An educational bridge between moral judgment and action. *New Directions for Child Development, 2*, 105–116.

Powlishta, K. K. (1995). Intergroup processes in childhood: Social categorization and sex role development. *Developmental Psychology, 31*, 781–788.

Powlishta, K. K., Serbin, L. A., Doyle, A., & White, D. R. (1994). Gender, ethnic, and body type biases: The generality of prejudice in childhood. *Developmental Psychology, 30*, 526–536.

Prechtl, H. F. R., & Beintema, D. J. (1964). *The neurological examination of the full-term newborn infant. Clinics in Developmental Medicine, 12*. London: Heinemann.

Prentice, A. (1994). Extended breast-feeding and growth in rural China. *Nutrition Reviews, 52*, 144–146.

Pulkkinen, L. (1982). Self-control and continuity from childhood to late adolescence. In P. Baltes & O. G. Brim Jr.
(Eds.), *Life span development and behavior* (Vol. 4) (pp. 64–107). New York: Academic Press.

Putnam, J. W., Spiegel, A. N., & Bruininks, R. H. (1995). Future directions in education and inclusion of students with disabilities: A Delphi investigation. *Exceptional Children, 61*, 553–576.

Pye, C. (1986). Quiche Mayan speech to children. *Journal of Child Language, 13*, 85–100.

Pynoos, R. S., Steinbert, A. M., & Wraith, R. (1995). A developmental model of childhood traumatic stress. In D. Cicchetti & D. J. Cohen (Eds.), *Developmental psychopathology*. Vol. 2, *Risk, disorder, and adaptation* (pp. 72–95). New York: Wiley.

Quiggle, N. L., Garber, J., Panak, W. F., & Dodge, K. A. (1992). Social information processing in aggressive and depressed children. *Child Development, 63*, 1305–1320.

Raja, S. N., McGee, R., & Stanton, W. R. (1992). Perceived attachments to parents and peers and psychological well-being in adolescence. *Journal of Youth and Adolescence, 21*, 471–485.

Ramey, C. T. (1992). High-risk children and IQ: Altering intergenerational patterns. *Intelligence, 16*, 239–256.

Ramey, C. T. (1993). A rejoinder to Spitz's critique of the Abecedarian experiment. *Intelligence, 17*, 25–30.

Ramey, C. T., & Campbell, F. A. (1987). The Carolina Abecedarian Project. An educational experiment concerning human malleability. In J. J. Gallagher & C. T. Ramey (Eds.), *The malleability of children* (pp. 127–140). Baltimore: Paul H. Brookes.

Redman, S., Booth, P., Smyth, H., & Paul, C. (1992). Preventive health behaviours among parents of infants aged four months. *Australian Journal of Public Health, 16*, 175–181.

Rees, J. M., Lederman, S. A., & Kiely, J. L. (1996). Birth weight associated with lowest neonatal mortality: Infants of adolescent and adult mothers. *Pediatrics, 98*, 1161–1166.

Reinherz, H. Z., Giaconia, R. M., Pakiz, B., Silverman, A. B., Frost, A. K., & Lefkowitz, E. S. (1993). Psychosocial risks for major depression in late adolescence: A longitudinal community study. *Journal of the American Academy of Child and Adolescent Psychiatry, 32*, 1155–1163.

Reisman, J. E. (1987). Touch, motion, and proprioception. In P. Salapatek & L. Cohen (Eds.), *Handbook of infant perception*. Vol. 1, *From sensation to perception* (pp. 265–304). Orlando, FL: Academic Press.

Reissland, N. (1988). Neonatal imitation in the first hour of life: Observations in rural Nepal. *Developmental Psychology, 24*, 464–469.

Remafedi, G. (1987a). Adolescent homosexuality: Psychosocial and medical implications. *Pediatrics, 79*, 331–337.

Remafedi, G. (1987b). Male homosexuality: The adolescent's perspective. *Pediatrics, 79*, 326–330.

Remafedi, G., Farrow, J. A., & Deisher, R. W. (1991). Risk factors for attempted suicide in gay and bisexual youth. *Pediatrics, 87*, 869–875.

Remafedi, G., Resnick, M., Blum, R., & Harris, L. (1992). Demography of sexual orientation in adolescents. *Pediatrics, 89*, 714–721.

Renouf, A. G., & Harter, S. (1990). Low self-worth and anger as components of the depressive experience in young adolescents. *Development and Psychopathology, 2*, 293–310.

Repacholi, B. M., & Gopnik, A. (1997). Early reasoning about desires: Evidence from 14- and 18-month-olds. *Developmental Psychology, 33*, 12–21.

Rest, J. R. (1983). Morality. In J. H. Flavell & E. M. Markman (Eds.), *Handbook of child psychology: Cognitive development* (Vol. 3) (pp. 556–629). New York: Wiley.

Rest, J. R., & Thoma, S. J. (1985). Relation of moral judgment development to formal education. *Developmental Psychology, 21*, 709–714.

Reynolds, A. J., & Bezruczko, N. (1993). School adjustment of children at risk through fourth grade. *Merrill-Palmer Quarterly, 39*, 457–480.

Reynolds, C. R., & Brown, R. T. (1984). *Perspectives on bias in mental testing.* New York: Plenum Press.

Rholes, W. S., & Ruble, D. N. (1984). Children's understanding of dispositional characteristics of others. *Child Development, 55*, 550–560.

Ricci, C. M., Beal, C. R., & Dekle, D. J. (1995, April). *The effect of parent versus unfamiliar interviewers on young witnesses' memory and identification accuracy.* Paper presented at the biennial meetings of the Society for Research in Child Development, Indianapolis.

Ricciuti, H. N. (1993). Nutrition and mental development. *Current Directions in Psychological Science, 2*, 43–46.

Rice, M. L., Huston, A. C., Truglio, R., & Wright, J. (1990). Words from "Sesame Street": Learning vocabulary while viewing. *Developmental Psychology, 26*, 421–428.

Richards, H. C., Bear, G. G., Stewart, A. L., & Norman, A. D. (1992). Moral reasoning and classroom conduct: Evidence of a curvilinear relationship. *Merrill-Palmer Quarterly, 38*, 176–190.

Richardson, G. A., & Day, N. L. (1994). Detrimental effects of prenatal cocaine exposure: Illusion or reality? *Journal of the American Academy of Child and Adolescent Psychiatry, 33*, 28–34.

Rierdan, J., Koff, E., & Stubbs, M. L. (1989). Timing of menarche, preparation, and initial menstrual experience: Replication and further analysis in a prospective study. *Journal of Youth and Adolescence, 18*, 413–426.

Rivara, F. P. (1995). Developmental and behavioral issues in childhood injury prevention. *Developmental and Behavioral Pediatrics, 16*, 362–370.

Roberts, I., & Pless, B. (1995). Social policy as a cause of childhood accidents: The children of lone mothers. *British Medical Journal, 311*, 925–928.

Roberts, J. E., & Wallace, I. F. (1997). Language and otitis media. In J. E. Roberts, I. F. Wallace, & F. W. Henderson (Eds.), *Otitis media in young children: Medical, developmental, and educational considerations* (pp. 133–162). Baltimore: Paul H. Brookes.

Roberts, R., & Mather, N. (1995). The return of students with learning disabilities to regular classrooms: A sellout? *Learning Disabilities Research & Practice, 10*, 46–58.

Roberts, R. E., & Sobhan, M. (1992). Symptoms of depression in adolescence: A comparison of Anglo, African, and Hispanic Americans. *Journal of Youth and Adolescence, 21*, 639–651.

Robins, L. N., & McEvoy, L. (1990). Conduct problems as predictors of substance abuse. In L. N. Robins & M. Rutter (Eds.), *Straight and devious pathways from childhood to adulthood* (pp. 182–204). Cambridge, England: Cambridge University Press.

Robinson, H. B. (1981). The uncommonly bright child. In M. Lewis & L. A. Rosenblum (Eds.), *The uncommon child* (pp. 57–82). New York: Plenum Press.

Roche, A. F. (1979). Secular trends in human growth, maturation, and development. *Monographs of the Society for Research in Child Development, 44*(3–4, Serial No. 179).

Rogers, J. L., Rowe, D. C., & May, K. (1994). DF analysis of NLSY IQ/Achievement data: Nonshared environmental influences. *Intelligence, 19*, 157–177.

Rogers, P. T., Roizen, N. J., & Capone, G. T. (1996). Down syndrome. In A. J. Capute & P. J. Accardo (Eds.), *Developmental disabilities in infancy and childhood* (2nd ed.). Vol II, *The spectrum of developmental disabilities* (pp. 221–243). Baltimore: Paul H. Brookes.

Roggman, L. A., Langlois, J. H., Hubbs-Tait, L., & Rieser-Danner, L. A. (1994). Infant day-care, attachment, and the "file drawer problem." *Child Development, 65*, 1429–1443.

Rogoff, B. (1990). *Apprenticeship in thinking: Cognitive development in social contexts.* New York: Oxford University Press.

Rogol, A. D., & Yesalis, C. E., III (1992). Anabolic-Androgenic steroids and the adolescent. *Pediatric Annals, 21*, 175–188.

Rogosch, F. A., Cicchetti, D., Shields, A., & Toth, S. L. (1995). Parenting dysfunction in child maltreatment. In M. H. Bornstein (Ed.), *Handbook of parenting.* Vol. 4, *Applied and practical parenting* (pp. 127–159). Mahwah, NJ: Erlbaum.

Rohner, R. P., Kean, K. J., & Cournoyer, D. E. (1991). Effects of corporal punishment, perceived caretaker warmth, and cultural beliefs on the psychological adjustment of children in St. Kitts, West Indies. *Journal of Marriage and the Family, 53*, 681–693.

Rooks, J. P., Weatherby, N. L., Ernst, E. K. M., Stapleton, S., Rosen, D., & Rosenfield, A. (1989). Outcomes of care in birth centers. The National Birth Center Study. *The New England Journal of Medicine, 321*, 1804–1811.

Rose, A. J., & Montemayor, R. (1994). The relationship between gender role orientation and perceived self-competence in male and female adolescents. *Sex Roles, 31*, 579–595.

Rose, R. J. (1995). Genes and human behavior. *Annual Review of Psychology, 56,* 625–654.

Rose, S. A., & Feldman, J. F. (1995). Prediction of IQ and specific cognitive abilities at 11 years from infancy measures. *Developmental Psychology, 31,* 685–696.

Rose, S. A., & Ruff, H. A. (1987). Cross-modal abilities in human infants. In J. D. Osofsky (Ed.), *Handbook of infant development* (2nd ed.) (pp. 318–362). New York: Wiley-Interscience.

Rosenbaum, J. E. (1984). *Career mobility in a corporate hierarchy.* New York: Academic Press.

Rosenberg, M. (1986). Self-concept from middle childhood through adolescence. In J. Suls & A. G. Greenwald (Eds.), *Psychological perspectives on the self* (Vol. 3) (pp. 107–136). Hillsdale, NJ: Erlbaum.

Rosenberg, M. D. (1995). Thumbsucking. *Pediatrics in Review, 16,* 73–74.

Rosenblith, J. F. (1992). *In the beginning: Development in the first two years of life* (2nd ed.). Thousand Oaks, CA: Sage.

Rosenthal, R. (1994). Interpersonal expectancy effects: A 30-year perspective. *Current Directions in Psychological Science, 3,* 176–179.

Ross, J. G. (1994). The status of fitness programming in our nation's schools. In R. R. Pate & R. C. Hohn (Eds.), *Health and fitness through physical education* (pp. 21–28). Champaign, IL: Human Kinetics.

Rossell, C., & Baker, K. (1996). The educational effectiveness of bilingual education. *Research in the Teaching of English, 30,* 1–68.

Rothbart, M. K., Derryberry, D., & Posner, M. I. (1994). A psychobiological approach to the development of temperament. In J. E. Bates & T. D. Wachs (Eds.), *Temperament. Individual differences at the interface of biology and behavior* (pp. 83–116). Washington, DC: American Psychological Association.

Rotheram-Borus, M. J., Rosario, M., & Koopman, C. (1991). Minority youths at high risk: Gay males and runaways. In M. E. Colten & S. Gore (Eds.), *Adolescent stress. Causes and consequences* (pp. 181–200). New York: Aldine de Gruyter.

Rothman, K. J., Moore, L. L., Singer, M. R., Nguyen, U. D. T., Mannino, S., & Milunsky, A. (1995). Teratogenicity of high Vitamin A intake. *The New England Journal of Medicine, 333,* 1369–1373.

Rovee-Collier, C. (1986). The rise and fall of infant classical conditioning research: Its promise for the study of early development. In L. P. Lipsitt & C. Rovee-Collier (Eds.), *Advances in infancy research* (Vol. 4) (pp. 139–162). Norwood, NJ: Ablex.

Rovee-Collier, C. (1993). The capacity for long-term memory in infancy. *Current Directions in Psychological Science, 2,* 130–135.

Rovet, J., & Netley, C. (1983). The triple X chromosome syndrome in childhood: Recent empirical findings. *Child Development, 54,* 831–845.

Rowe, D. C. (1994). *The limits of family influence: Genes, experience, and behavior.* New York: Guilford Press.

Rowe, I., & Marcia, J. E. (1980). Ego identity status, formal operations, and moral development. *Journal of Youth and Adolescence, 9,* 87–99.

Rubin, K. H., Fein, G. G., & Vandenbert, B. (1983). Play. In E. M. Hetherington (Ed.), *Handbook of child psychology: Socialization, personality, and social development* (Vol. 4) (pp. 693–774). New York: Wiley.

Rubin, K. H., Hymel, S., Mills, R. S. L., & Rose-Krasnor, L. (1991). Conceptualizing different developmental pathways to and from social isolation in childhood. In D. Cicchetti & S. L. Toth (Eds.), *Internalizing and externalizing expressions of dysfunction: Rochester symposium on developmental psychopathology* (Vol. 2) (pp. 91–122). Hillsdale, NJ: Erlbaum.

Ruble, D. N. (1987). The acquisition of self-knowledge: A self-socialization perspective. In N. Eisenberg (Ed.), *Contemporary topics in developmental psychology* (pp. 243–270). New York: Wiley-Interscience.

Rueter, M. A., & Conger, R. D. (1995). Antecedents to parent-adolescent disagreements. *Journal of Marriage and the Family, 57,* 435–448.

Ruiz, J. C., Mandel, C., & Garabedian, M. (1995). Influence of spontaneous calcium intake and physical exercise on the vertebral and femoral bone mineral density of children and adolescents. *Journal of Bone and Mineral Research, 10,* 675–682.

Russell, J. A. (1989). Culture, scripts, and children's understanding of emotion. In C. Saarni & P. L. Harris (Eds.), *Children's understanding of emotion* (pp. 293–318). Cambridge, England: Cambridge University Press.

Rutter, D. R., & Durkin, K. (1987). Turn-taking in mother-infant interaction: An examination of vocalizations and gaze. *Developmental Psychology, 23,* 54–61.

Rutter, M. (1978). Early sources of security and competence. In J. S. Bruner & A. Garton (Eds.), *Human growth and development* (pp. 33–61). London: Oxford University Press.

Rutter, M. (1983). School effects on pupil progress: Research findings and policy implications. *Child Development, 54,* 1–29.

Rutter, M. (1987). Continuities and discontinuities from infancy. In J. D. Osofsky (Ed.), *Handbook of infant development* (2nd ed.) (pp. 1256–1296). New York: Wiley-Interscience.

Rutter, M. (Ed.). (1995). *Psychosocial disturbances in young people. Challenges for prevention.* Cambridge, England: Cambridge University Press.

Rutter, M., & Garmezy, N. (1983). Developmental psychopathology. In E. M. Hetherington (Ed.), *Handbook of child psychology.* Vol. 4, *Socialization, personality, and social development* (pp. 775–912). New York: Wiley.

Rutter, M., & Rutter, M. (1993). *Developing Minds: Challenge and continuity across the life span.* New York: Basic Books.

Ryan, A. S., Rush, D., Krieger, F. W., & Lewandowski, G. E. (1991). Recent declines in breast-feeding in the United States, 1984 through 1989. *Pediatrics, 88*, 719–727.

Rys, G. S., & Bear, G. G. (1997). Relational aggression and peer relations: Gender and developmental issues. *Merrill-Palmer Quarterly, 43*, 87–106.

Saccuzzo, D. P., Johnson, N. E., & Guertin, T. L. (1994). Information processing in gifted versus nongifted African American, Latino, Filipino, and White children: Speeded versus nonspeeded paradigms. *Intelligence, 19*, 219–243.

Sachs, B. P., Fretts, R. C., Gardner, R., Hellerstein, S., Wampler, N. S., & Wise, P. H. (1995). The impact of extreme prematurity and congenital anomalies on the interpretation of international comparisons of infant mortality. *Obstetrics and Gynecology, 85*, 941–946.

Sadowski, M. (1995). The numbers game yields simplistic answers on the link between spending and outcomes. *The Harvard Education Letter, 11*(2), 1–4.

Sagi, A. (1990). Attachment theory and research from a cross-cultural perspective. *Human Development, 33*, 10–22.

Sagi, A., van IJzendoorn, M. H., & Koren-Karie, N. (1991). Primary appraisal of the strange situation: A cross-cultural analysis of preseparation episodes. *Developmental Psychology, 27*, 587–596.

Saigal, S., Szatmari, P., Rosenbaum, P., Campbell, D., & King, S. (1991). Cognitive abilities and school performance of extremely low birth weight children and matched term control children at age 8 years: A regional study. *Journal of Pediatrics, 118*, 751–760.

St. James-Roberts, I., Bowyer, J., Varghese, S., & Sawdon, J. (1994). Infant crying patterns in Manali and London. *Child: Care, Health and Development, 20*, 323–337.

St. Peters, M., Fitch, M., Huston, A. C., Wright, J. C., & Eakins, D. J. (1991). Television and families: What do young children watch with their parents? *Child Development, 62*, 1409–1423.

Saldanha, L. G. (1995). Fiber in the diet of US children: Results of national surveys. *Pediatrics, 96*, 994–997.

Sale, P., & Carey, D. M. (1995). The sociometric status of students with disabilities in a full-inclusion school. *Exceptional Children, 62*, 6–19.

Sameroff, A., Seifer, R., Barocas, R., Zax, M., & Greenspan, S. (1987). Intelligence quotient scores of 4-year-old children: Social-environmental risk factors. *Pediatrics, 79*, 343–350.

Sampson, R. J. (1997, April). *Child and adolescent development in community context: New findings from a multilevel study of 80 Chicago neighborhoods.* Paper presented at the biennial meetings of the Society for Research in Child Development, Washington, DC.

Sampson, R. J., & Laub, J. H. (1994). Urban poverty and the family context of delinquency: A new look at structure and process in a classic study. *Child Development, 65*, 523–540.

Sandberg, S. (Ed.). (1996). *Hyperactivity disorders of childhood.* Cambridge, England: Cambridge University Press.

Sandberg, S., Day, R., & Gotz, E. T. (1996). Clinical aspects. In S. Sandberg (Ed.), *Hyperactivity disorders of childhood* (pp. 69–106). Cambridge, England: Cambridge University Press.

Sapir, E. (1929). The status of linguistics as a science. *Language, 5*, 207–214.

Saudino, K. J., & Plomin, R. (1997). Cognitive and temperamental mediators of genetic contributions to the home environment during infancy. *Merrill-Palmer Quarterly, 43*, 1–23.

Savin-Williams, R. C. (1994). Verbal and physical abuse as stressors in the lives of lesbian, gay male, and bisexual youths: Associations with school problems, running away, substance abuse, prostitution, and suicide. *Journal of Consulting and Clinical Psychology, 62*, 261–269.

Scarr, S., & Eisenberg, M. (1993). Child care research: Issues, perspectives, and results. *Annual Review of Psychology, 44*, 613–644.

Scarr, S., & Kidd, K. K. (1983). Developmental behavior genetics. In M. M. Haith & J. J. Campos (Eds.), *Handbook of child psychology.* Vol. 2, *Infancy and developmental psychobiology* (pp. 345–434). New York: Wiley.

Scarr, S., & McCartney, K. (1983). How people make their own environments: A theory of genotype → environment effects. *Child Development, 54*, 424–435.

Scarr, S., & Weinberg, R. A. (1983). The Minnesota adoption studies: Genetic differences and malleability. *Child Development, 54*, 260–267.

Scarr, S., Weinberg, R. A., & Waldman, I. D. (1993). IQ correlations in transracial adoptive families. *Intelligence, 17*, 541–555.

Schachar, R., Tannock, R., & Cunningham, C. (1996). Treatment. In S. Sandberg (Ed.), *Hyperactivity disorders of childhood* (pp. 433–476). Cambridge, England: Cambridge University Press.

Schaefli, A., Rest, J. R., & Thoma, S. J. (1985). Does moral education improve moral judgment? A meta-analysis of intervention studies using the Defining Issues Test. *Review of Educational Research, 55*, 319–352.

Schaie, K. W. (1983). What can we learn from the longitudinal study of adult psychological development? In K. W. Schaie (Ed.), *Longitudinal studies of adult psychological development* (pp. 1–19). New York: Guilford Press.

Schaie, K. W. (1994). Developmental designs revisited. In S. H. Cohen & H. W. Reese (Eds.), *Life-span developmental psychology. Methodological contributions* (pp. 45–64). Hillsdale, NJ: Erlbaum.

Schifter, D. (1996). A constructivist perspective on teaching and learning mathematics. In C. T. Fosnot (Ed.), *Constructivism: Theory, perspectives, and practice* (pp. 73–91). New York: Teachers College Press.

Schneider, B., Hieshima, J. A., Lee, S., & Plank, S. (1994). East-Asian academic success in the United States: Family, school, and community explanations. In P. M. Greenfield & R. R. Cocking (Eds.), *Cross-cultural roots of minority child development* (pp. 323–350). Hillsdale, NJ: Erlbaum.

Schneider, M. L. (1992). The effect of mild stress during pregnancy on birthweight and neuromotor maturation in rhesus monkey infants (Macaca mulatta). *Infant Behavior and Development, 15*, 389–403.

Schneider, W., & Bjorklund, D. F. (1992). Expertise, aptitude, and strategic remembering. *Child Development, 63*, 461–473.

Schneider, W., Reimers, P., Roth, E., & Visé, M. (1995, April). *Short- and long-term effects of training phonological awareness in kindergarten: Evidence from two German studies.* Paper presented at the biennial meetings of the Society for Research in Child Development, Indianapolis.

Schoendorf, K. C., Hogue, C. J. R., Kleinman, J. C., & Rowley, D. (1992). Mortality among infants of black as compared with white college-educated parents. *The New England Journal of Medicine, 326*, 1522–1526.

Schoendorf, K. C., & Kiely, J. L. (1992). Relationship of sudden infant death syndrome to maternal smoking during and after pregnancy. *Pediatrics, 90*, 905–908.

Schor, E. L. (1987). Unintentional injuries: Patterns within families. *American Journal of the Diseases of Children, 141*, 1280.

Schramm, W. F., Barnes, D. E., & Bakewell, J. M. (1987). Neonatal mortality in Missouri home births, 1978–84. *American Journal of Public Health, 77*, 930–935.

Schroeder, D. B., Martorell, R., Rivera, J. A., Ruel, M. T., & Habicht, J. (1995). Age differences in the impact of nutritional supplementation on growth. *Journal of Nutrition, 125*, 1051S–1059S.

Schumm, J. S., & Vaughn, S. (1995). Getting ready for inclusion: Is the stage set? *Learning Disabilities Research & Practice, 10*, 169–179.

Schwartz, C. E., Snidman, N., & Kagan, J. (1996). Early childhood temperament as a determinant of externalizing behavior in adolescence. *Development and Psychopathology, 8*, 527–537.

Schwartz, D., Dodge, K. A., & Coie, J. D. (1993). The emergence of chronic peer victimization in boys' play groups. *Child Development, 64*, 1755–1772.

Schwartz, J. (1994). Low-level lead exposure and children's IQ: A meta-analysis and search for a threshold. *Environmental Research, 65*, 42–55.

Schwartz, R. M., Anastasia, M. L., Scanlon, J. W., & Kellogg, R. J. (1994). Effect of surfactant on morbidity, mortality, and resource use in newborn infants weighing 500 to 1500 g. *The New England Journal of Medicine, 330*, 1476–1480.

Seidman, E., Allen, L., Aber, J. L., Mitchell, C., & Feinman, J. (1994). The impact of school transitions in early adolescence on the self-system and perceived social context of poor urban youth. *Child Development, 65*, 507–522.

Seifer, R., Schiller, M., Sameroff, A. J., Resnick, S., & Riordan, K. (1996). Attachment, maternal sensitivity, and infant temperament during the first year of life. *Developmental Psychology, 32*, 12–25.

Seitz, V. (1988). Methodology. In M. H. Bornstein & M. E. Lamb (Eds.), *Developmental psychology: An advanced textbook* (2nd ed.) (pp. 51–84). Hillsdale, NJ: Erlbaum.

Sells, C. W., & Blum, R. W. (1996). Morbidity and mortality among US adolescents: An overview of data and trends. *American Journal of Public Health, 86*, 513–519.

Selman, R. L. (1980). *The growth of interpersonal understanding.* New York: Academic Press.

Serbin, L., Moskowitz, D. S., Schwartzman, A. E., & Ledingham, J. E. (1991). Aggressive, withdrawn, and aggressive/withdrawn children in adolescence: Into the next generation. In D. J. Pepler & K. H. Rubin (Eds.), *The development and treatment of childhood aggression* (pp. 55–70). Hillsdale, NJ: Erlbaum.

Serbin, L. A., Powlishta, K. K., & Gulko, J. (1993). The development of sex typing in middle childhood. *Monographs of the Society for Research in Child Development, 58*(2, Serial No. 232).

Serdula, M. K., Ivery, D., Coates, R. J., Freedman, D. S., Williamson, D. F., & Byers, T. (1993). Do obese children become obese adults? A review of the literature. *Preventive Medicine, 22*, 167–177.

Shaffer, D., Garland, A., Gould, M., Fisher, P., & Trautman, P. (1988). Preventing teenage suicide: A critical review. *Journal of the American Academy of Child and Adolescent Psychiatry, 27*, 675–687.

Shaffer, D., Garland, A., Vieland, V., Underwood, M., & Busner, C. (1991). The impact of curriculum-based suicide prevention programs for teenagers. *Journal of the American Academy of Child and Adolescent Psychiatry, 30*, 588–596.

Shanahan, M., Sayer, A., Davey, A., & Brooks, J. (1997, April). *Pathways of poverty and children's trajectories of psychosocial adjustment.* Paper presented at the biennial meetings of the Society for Research in Child Development, Washington, DC.

Shanon, A., Bashaw, B., Lewis, J., & Feldman, W. (1992). Nonfatal childhood injuries: A survey at the Children's Hospital of Eastern Ontario. *Canadian Medical Association Journal, 146*, 361–365.

Shantz, C. U. (1983). Social cognition. In J. H. Flavell & E. M. Markman (Eds.), *Handbook of child psychology.* Vol. 3, *Cognitive development* (pp. 495–555). New York: Wiley.

Shantz, D. W. (1986). Conflict, aggression, and peer status: An observational study. *Child Development, 57*, 1322–1332.

Shatz, M. (1994). *A toddler's life. Becoming a person.* New York: Oxford University Press.

Shaw, D. S., Kennan, K., & Vondra, J. I. (1994). Developmental precursors of externalizing behavior: Ages 1 to 3. *Developmental Psychology, 30*, 355–364.

Shaw, D. S., Owens, E. B., Vondra, J. I., Keenan, K., & Winslow, E. B. (1996). Early risk factors and pathways in the development of early disruptive behavior problems. *Development and Psychopathology, 8,* 679–700.

Shaw, G. M., Velie, E. M., & Schaffer, D. (1996). Risk of neural tube defect—Affected pregnancies among obese women. *Journal of the American Medical Association, 275,* 1093–1096.

Shore, C. M. (1986). Combinatorial play, conceptual development, and early multiword speech. *Developmental Psychology, 22,* 184–190.

Shore, C. M. (1995). *Individual differences in language development.* Thousand Oaks, CA: Sage.

Shweder, R. A., Mahapatra, M., & Miller, J. G. (1987). Culture and moral development. In J. Kagan & S. Lamb (Eds.), *The emergence of morality in young children* (pp. 1–82). Chicago: University of Chicago Press.

Siegal, M. (1987). Are sons and daughters treated more differently by fathers than by mothers? *Developmental Review, 7,* 183–209.

Siegel, B. (1996). Is the emperor wearing clothes? Social policy and the empirical support for full inclusion of children with disabilities in the preschool and early elementary grades. *Social Policy Report, Society for Research in Child Development, X*(2 & 3), 2–17.

Siegler, R. S. (1992). What do developmental psychologists really want? In M. R. Gunnar & M. Maratsos (Eds.), *Minnesota symposia on child psychology* (Vol. 25) (pp. 221–232). Hillsdale, NJ: Erlbaum.

Siegler, R. S. (1994). Cognitive variability: A key to understanding cognitive development. *Current Directions in Psychological Science, 3,* 1–5.

Siegler, R. S. (1996). *Emerging minds: The process of change in children's thinking.* New York: Oxford University Press.

Siegler, R. S., & Ellis, S. (1996). Piaget on childhood. *Psychological Science, 7,* 211–215.

Sigman, M. (1995). Nutrition and child development: More food for thought. *Current Directions in Psychological Science, 4,* 52–55.

Sigman, M., Neumann, C., Carter, E., Cattle, D. J., D'Souza, S., & Bwibo, N. (1988). Home interactions and the development of Embu toddlers in Kenya. *Child Development, 59,* 1251–1261.

Silbereisen, R. K., & Kracke, B. (1993). Variations in maturational timing and adjustment in adolescence. In S. Jackson & H. Rodrigues-Tomé (Eds.), *Adolescence and its social worlds* (pp. 67–94). Hove, England: Erlbaum.

Silverberg, S. B., & Gondoli, D. M. (1996). Autonomy in adolescence: A contextualized perspective. In G. R. Adams, R. Montemayor, & T. P. Gullotta (Eds.), *Psychosocial development during adolescence: Progress in developmental contextualism* (pp. 12–61). Thousand Oaks, CA: Sage.

Simmons, R. G., Burgeson, R., & Reef, M. J. (1988). Cumulative change at entry to adolescence. In M. R. Gunnar & W. A. Collins (Eds.), *Minnesota symposia on child psychology* (Vol. 21) (pp. 123–150). Hillsdale, NJ: Erlbaum.

Simons, R. L., Robertson, J. F., & Downs, W. R. (1989). The nature of the association between parental rejection and delinquent behavior. *Journal of Youth and Adolescence, 18,* 297–309.

Singh, G. K., & Yu, S. M. (1995). Infant mortality in the United States: Trends, differentials, and projections, 1950 through 2010. *American Journal of Public Health, 85,* 957–964.

Singh, G. K., & Yu, S. M. (1996). US childhood mortality, 1950 through 1993: Trends and socioeconomic differentials. *American Journal of Public Health, 86,* 505–512.

Skinner, B. F. (1953). *Science and human behavior.* New York: Macmillan.

Skinner, B. F. (1957). *Verbal behavior.* New York: Prentice Hall.

Skinner, B. F. (1980). The experimental analysis of operant behavior: A history. In R. W. Riebes & K. Salzinger (Eds.), *Psychology: Theoretical-historical perspectives* New York: Academic Press.

Slaby, R. G., & Frey, K. S. (1975). Development of gender constancy and selective attention to same-sex models. *Child Development, 46,* 849–856.

Slater, A. (1995). Individual differences in infancy and later IQ. *Journal of Child Psychology and Psychiatry, 36,* 69–112.

Slobin, D. I. (1985a). Introduction: Why study acquisition crosslinguistically? In D. I. Slobin (Ed.), *The crosslinguistic study of language acquisition.* Vol. 1, *The data* (pp. 3–24). Hillsdale, NJ: Erlbaum.

Slobin, D. I. (1985b). Crosslinguistic evidence for the language-making capacity. In D. I. Slobin (Ed.), *The crosslinguistic study of language acquisition.* Vol. 2, *Theoretical issues* (pp. 1157–1256). Hillsdale, NJ: Erlbaum.

Small, S. A., & Luster, T. (1994). Adolescent sexual activity: An ecological, risk-factor approach. *Journal of Marriage and the Family, 56,* 181–192.

Smetana, J. G. (1990). Morality and conduct disorders. In M. Lewis & S. M. Miller (Eds.), *Handbook of developmental psychopathology* (pp. 157–180). New York: Plenum Press.

Smetana, J. G., Killen, M., & Turiel, E. (1991). Children's reasoning about interpersonal and moral conflicts. *Child Development, 62,* 629–644.

Smith, D. W. (1978). Prenatal life. In D. W. Smith, E. L. Bierman, & N. M. Robinson (Eds.), *The biologic ages of man* (2nd ed.) (pp. 42–62). Philadelphia: W. B. Saunders.

Smock, P. J. (1993). The economic costs of marital disruption for young women over the past two decades. *Demography, 30,* 353–371.

Smolak, L., & Levine, M. P. (1996). Adolescent transitions and the development of eating problems. In L. Smolak, M. P. Levine, & R. Streigl-Moore (Eds.), *The developmental psychopathology of eating disorders* (pp. 207–233). Mahwah, NJ: Erlbaum.

Smolak, L., Levine, M. P., & Streigel-Moore, R. (Eds.). (1996). *The developmental psychopathology of eating disorders*. Mahwah, NJ: Erlbaum.

Smoll, F. L., & Schutz, R. W. (1990). Quantifying gender differences in physical performance: A developmental perspective. *Developmental Psychology, 26*, 360–369.

Snarey, J. R. (1985). Cross-cultural universality of social-moral development: A critical review of Kohlbergian research. *Psychological Bulletin, 97*, 202–232.

Snarey, J. R., Reimer, J., & Kohlberg, L. (1985). Development of social-moral reasoning among kibbutz adolescents: A longitudinal cross-sectional study. *Developmental Psychology, 21*, 3–17.

Snow, C. E. (1997, April). *Cross-domain connections and social class differences: Two challenges to nonenvironmentalist views of language development*. Paper presented at the biennial meetings of the Society for Research in Child Development, Washington, DC.

Snyder, J. J. (1991). Discipline as a mediator of the impact of maternal stress and mood on child conduct problems. *Development and Psychopathology, 3*, 263–276.

Soken, N. H., & Pick, A. D. (1992). Intermodal perception of happy and angry expressive behaviors by seven-month-old infants. *Child Development, 63*, 787–795.

Sophian, C. (1995). Representation and reasoning in early numerical development: Counting, conservation, and comparisons between sets. *Child Development, 66*, 559–577.

Spector, S. A. (1996). Cytomegalovirus infections. In A. M. Rudolph, J. I. E. Hoffman, & C. D. Rudolph (Eds.), *Rudolph's pediatrics* (pp. 629–633). Stanford, CT: Appleton & Lange.

Spelke, E. S. (1991). Physical knowledge in infancy: Reflections on Piaget's theory. In S. Carey & R. Gelman (Eds.), *The epigenesis of mind. Essays on biology and cognition* (pp. 133–169). Hillsdale, NJ: Erlbaum.

Spelke, E. S., & Owsley, C. J. (1979). Intermodal exploration and knowledge in infancy. *Infant Behavior and Development, 2*, 13–27.

Spence, J. T., & Helmreich, R. L. (1978). *Masculinity and femininity*. Austin: University of Texas Press.

Spencer, M. B., & Dornbusch, S. M. (1990). Challenges in studying minority youth. In S. S. Feldman & G. R. Elliott (Eds.), *At the threshold. The developing adolescent* (pp. 123–146). Cambridge, MA: Harvard University Press.

Spieker, S. J., Bensley, L., McMahon, R. J., Fung, H., & Ossiander, E. (1996). Sexual abuse as a factor in child maltreatment by adolescent mothers of preschool aged children. *Development and Psychopathology, 8*, 497–509.

Spieker, S. J., & Booth, C. L. (1988). Maternal antecedents of attachment quality. In J. Belsky & T. Nezworski (Eds.), *Clinical implications of attachment* (pp. 95–135). Hillsdale, NJ: Erlbaum.

Spock, B., & Rothenberg, M. (1985). *Dr Spock's baby and child care*. New York: Pocket Books.

Sporik, R., & Platts-Mills, T. A. (1992). Epidemiology of dust-mite-related disease. *Experimental and Applied Acarology, 16*, 141–151.

Srivastava, S. P., Sharma, V. K., & Jha, S. P. (1994). Mortality patterns in breast versus artificially fed term babies in early infancy: A longitudinal study. *Indian Pediatrics, 31*, 1393–1396.

Sroufe, L. A. (1988). The role of infant-caregiver attachment in development. In J. Belsky & T. Nezworski (Eds.), *Clinical implications of attachment* (pp. 18–40). Hillsdale, NJ: Erlbaum.

Sroufe, L. A. (1989). Pathways to adaptation and maladaptation: Psychopathology as developmental deviation. In D. Cicchetti (Ed.), *The emergence of a discipline: Rochester symposium on developmental psychopathology* (pp. 13–40). Hillsdale, NJ: Erlbaum.

Sroufe, L. A. (1990). A developmental perspective on day care. In N. Fox & G. G. Fein (Eds.), *Infant day care: The current debate* (pp. 51–60). Norwood, NJ: Ablex.

Sroufe, L. A. (1996). *Emotional development: The organization of emotional life in the early years*. Cambridge, England: Cambridge University Press.

Sroufe, L. A., Carlson, E., & Schulman, S. (1993). Individuals in relationships: Development from infancy through adolescence. In D. C. Funder, R. D. Parke, C. Tomlinson-Keasey, & K. Widaman (Eds.), *Studying lives through time. Personality and development* (pp. 315–342). Washington, DC: American Psychological Association.

Sroufe, L. A., Egeland, B., & Kreutzer, T. (1990). The fate of early experience following developmental change: Longitudinal approaches to individual adaptation in childhood. *Child Development, 61*, 1363–1373.

Stainback, S., & Stainback, W. (1985). The merger of special and regular education: Can it be done? A response to Lieberman and Mesinger. *Exceptional Children, 51*, 517–521.

Starfield, B. (1991). Childhood morbidity: Comparisons, clusters, and trends. *Pediatrics, 88*, 519–526.

Stattin, H., & Klackenberg-Larsson, I. (1993). Early language and intelligence development and their relationship to future criminal behavior. *Journal of Abnormal Psychology, 102*, 369–378.

Stattin, H., & Magnusson, D. (1996). Antisocial development: A holistic approach. *Development and Psychopathology, 8*, 617–646.

Steele, H., Holder, J., & Fonagy, P. (1995, April). *Quality of attachment to mother at one year predicts belief-desire reasoning at five years.* Paper presented at the biennial meetings of the Society for Research in Child Development, Indianapolis.

Stein, Z., Susser, M., Saenger, G., & Morolla, F. (1975). *Famine and human development: The Dutch hunger winter of 1944–1945.* New York: Oxford University Press.

Steinberg, L. (1986). Latchkey children and susceptibility to peer pressure: An ecological analysis. *Developmental Psychology, 22,* 433–439.

Steinberg, L. (1988). Reciprocal relation between parent-child distance and pubertal maturation. *Developmental Psychology, 24,* 122–128.

Steinberg, L. (1990). Autonomy, conflict and harmony in the parent-adolescent relationship. In S. S. Feldman & G. R. Elliott (Eds.), *At the threshold: The developing adolescent* (pp. 255–276). Cambridge, MA: Harvard University Press.

Steinberg, L. (1996). *Beyond the classroom. Why school reform has failed and what parents need to do.* New York: Simon & Schuster.

Steinberg, L., Darling, N. E., Fletcher, A. C., Brown, B. B., & Dornbusch, S. M. (1995). Authoritative parenting and adolescent adjustment: An ecological journey. In P. Moen, G. H. Elder Jr., & K. Lüscher (Eds.), *Examining lives in context. Perspectives on the ecology of human development* (pp. 423–466). Washington, DC: American Psychological Association.

Steinberg, L., & Dornbusch, S. M. (1991). Negative correlates of part-time employment during adolescence: Replication and elaboration. *Developmental Psychology, 27,* 304–313.

Steinberg, L., Elmen, J. D., & Mounts, N. S. (1989). Authoritative parenting, psychosocial maturity, and academic success among adolescents. *Child Development, 60,* 1424–1436.

Steinberg, L., Fegley, S., & Dornbusch, S. M. (1993). Negative impact of part-time work on adolescent adjustment: Evidence from a longitudinal study. *Developmental Psychology, 29,* 171–180.

Steinberg, L., Fletcher, A., & Darling, N. (1994). Parental monitoring and peer influences on adolescent substance use. *Pediatrics, 93,* 1060–1064.

Steinberg, L., Lamborn, S. D., Darling, N., Mounts, N. S., & Dornbusch, S. M. (1994). Over-time changes in adjustment and competence among adolescents from authoritative, authoritarian, indulgent, and neglectful families. *Child Development, 65,* 754–770.

Steinberg, L., Lamborn, S. D., Dornbusch, S. M., & Darling, N. (1992). Impact of parenting practices on adolescent achievement: Authoritative parenting, school involvement, and encouragement to succeed. *Child Development, 63,* 1266–1281.

Steinberg, L., & Levine, A. (1990). *You and your adolescent. A parent's guide for ages 10 to 20.* New York: Harper & Row.

Steinberg, L., Mounts, N. S., Lamborn, S. D., & Dornbusch, S. D. (1991). Authoritative parenting and adolescent adjustment across varied ecological niches. *Journal of Research on Adolescence, 1,* 19–36.

Steiner, J. E. (1979). Human facial expressions in response to taste and smell stimulation. In H. W. Reese & L. P. Lipsitt (Eds.), *Advances in child development and behavior* (Vol. 13) (pp. 257–296). New York: Academic Press.

Stelzl, I., Merz, F., Ehlers, T., & Remer, H. (1995). The effect of schooling on the development of fluid and crystallized intelligence: A quasi-experimental study. *Intelligence, 21,* 279–296.

Stenchever, M. A. (1978). Labor and delivery. In D. W. Smith, E. L. Bierman, & N. M. Robinson (Eds.), *The biologic ages of man* (2nd ed.) (pp. 78–86). Philadelphia: W. B. Saunders.

Sternberg, R. J. (1985). *Beyond IQ: A triarchic theory of human intelligence.* New York: Cambridge University Press.

Sternberg, R. J., & Davidson, J. E. (Eds.). (1986). *Conceptions of giftedness.* Cambridge, England: Cambridge University Press.

Sternberg, R. J., & Wagner, R. K. (1993). The g-ocentric view of intelligence and job performance is wrong. *Current Directions in Psychological Science, 2,* 1–5.

Stevenson, H. W. (1994). Moving away from stereotypes and preconceptions: Students and their education in East Asia and the United States. In P. M. Greenfield & R. R. Cocking (Eds.), *Cross-cultural roots of minority child development* (pp. 315–322). Hillsdale, NJ: Erlbaum.

Stevenson, H. W., & Chen, C. (1989). Schooling and achievement: A study of Peruvian children. *International Journal of Educational Research, 13,* 883–894.

Stevenson, H. W., Chen, C., Lee, S., & Fuligni, A. J. (1991). Schooling, culture, and cognitive development. In L. Okagaki & R. J. Sternberg (Eds.), *Directors of development* (pp. 243–268). Hillsdale, NJ: Erlbaum.

Stevenson, H. W., & Lee, S. (1990). Contexts of achievement: A study of American, Chinese, and Japanese children. *Monographs of the Society for Research in Child Development, 55*(1–2, Serial No. 221).

Stevenson, H. W., Lee, S., Chen, C., Lummis, M., Stigler, J., Fan, L., & Ge, F. (1990). Mathematics achievement of children in China and the United States. *Child Development, 61,* 1053–1066.

Steward, M. S. (1993). Understanding children's memories of medical procedures: "He didn't touch me and it didn't hurt!" In C. A. Nelson (Eds.), *Minnesota symposia on child psychology* (Vol. 26) (pp. 171–225). Hillsdale, NJ: Erlbaum.

Steward, M. S., & Steward, D. S. (1996). Interviewing young children about body touch and handling. *Monographs of the Society for Research in Child Development, 61*(4, Serial No. 248).

Stewart, J. F., Popkin, B. M., Guilkey, D. K., Akin, J. S., Adair, L., & Flieger, W. (1991). Influences on the extent of breast-feeding: A prospective study in the Philippines. *Demography, 28,* 181–199.

Stewart, R. B., Beilfuss, M. L., & Verbrugge, K. M. (1995, April). *That was then, this is now: An empirical typology of adult sibling relationships.* Paper presented at the biennial meetings of the Society for Research in Child Development, Indianapolis.

Stigler, J. W., Lee, S., & Stevenson, H. W. (1987). Mathematics classrooms in Japan, Taiwan, and the United States. *Child Development, 58,* 1272–1285.

Stigler, J. W., & Stevenson, H. W. (1991). How Asian teachers polish each lesson to perfection. *American Educator* (Spring), 12–20, 43–47.

Stipek, D. (1992). The child at school. In M. H. Bornstein & M. E. Lamb (Eds.), *Developmental psychology: An advanced textbook* (3rd ed.) (pp. 579–625). Hillsdale, NJ: Erlbaum.

Stipek, D., & Gralinski, H. (1991). Gender differences in children's achievement-related beliefs and emotional responses to success and failure in math. *Journal of Educational Psychology, 83,* 361–371.

Stocker, C. M. (1995). Differences in mothers' and fathers' relationships with siblings: Links with children's behavior problems. *Development and Psychopathology, 7,* 499–513.

Story, M., Rosenwinkel, K., Himes, J. H., Resnick, M., Harris, L. J., & Blum, R. W. (1991). Demographic and risk factors associated with chronic dieting in adolescents. *American Journal of Diseases of Childhood, 145,* 994–998.

Stoutjesdyk, D., & Jevne, R. (1993). Eating disorders among high performance athletes. *Journal of Youth and Adolescence, 22,* 271–282.

Strassberg, Z., Dodge, K. A., Pettit, G. S., & Bates, J. E. (1994). Spanking in the home and children's subsequent aggression toward kindergarten peers. *Development and Psychopathology, 6,* 445–461.

Straus, M. A. (1991a). Discipline and deviance: Physical punishment of children and violence and other crime in adulthood. *Social Problems, 38,* 133–152.

Straus, M. A. (1991b). New theory and old canards about family violence research. *Social Problems, 38,* 180–194.

Straus, M. A. (1995). Corporal punishment of children and adult depression and suicidal ideation. In J. McCord (Ed.), *Coercion and punishment in long-term perspectives* (pp. 59–77). Cambridge, England: Cambridge University Press.

Straus, M. A., & Donnelly, D. A. (1993). Corporal punishment of adolescents by American parents. *Youth and Society, 24,* 419–442.

Straus, M. A., & Gelles, R. J. (1986). Societal change and change in family violence from 1975 to 1985 as revealed by two national surveys. *Journal of Marriage and the Family, 48,* 465–479.

Strayer, F. F. (1980). Social ecology of the preschool peer group. In A. Collins (Ed.), *Minnesota symposia on child psychology* (Vol. 13) (pp. 165–196). Hillsdale, NJ: Erlbaum.

Streissguth, A. P., Aase, J. M., Clarren, S. K., Randels, S. P., LaDue, R. A., & Smith, D. F. (1991). Fetal alcohol syndrome in adolescents and adults. *Journal of the American Medical Association, 265,* 1961–1967.

Streissguth, A. P., Barr, H. M., & Sampson, P. D. (1990). Moderate prenatal alcohol exposure: Effects on child IQ and learning problems at age $7\frac{1}{2}$ years. *Alcoholism. Clinical and Experimental Research, 14,* 662–669.

Streissguth, A. P., Barr, H. M., Sampson, P. D., Darby, B. L., & Martin, D. C. (1989). IQ at age 4 in relation to maternal alcohol use and smoking during pregnancy. *Developmental Psychology, 25,* 3–11.

Streissguth, A. P., Bookstein, F. L., Sampson, P. D., & Barr, H. M. (1995). Attention: Prenatal alcohol and continuities of vigilance and attentional problems from 4 through 14 years. *Development and Psychopathology, 7,* 419–446.

Streissguth, A. P., Landesman-Dwyer, S., Martin, J. C., & Smith, D. W. (1980). Teratogenic effects of alcohol in humans and laboratory animals. *Science, 209,* 353–361.

Streissguth, A. P., Martin, D. C., Barr, H. M., Sandman, B. M., Kirchner, G. L., & Darby, B. L. (1984). Intrauterine alcohol and nicotine exposure: Attention and reaction time in 4-year-old children. *Developmental Psychology, 20,* 533–541.

Streissguth, A. P., Martin, D. C., Martin, J. C., & Barr, H. M. (1981). The Seattle longitudinal prospective study on alcohol and pregnancy. *Neurobehavioral Toxicology and Teratology, 3,* 223-233.

Stringfield, S., & Teddlie, C. (1991). Observers as predictors of schools' multiyear outlier status on achievement tests. *Elementary School Journal, 91,* 357–376.

Stunkard, A. J., Harris, J. R., Pedersen, N. L., & McClearn, G. E. (1990). The body-mass index of twins who have been reared apart. *The New England Journal of Medicine, 322,* 1483–1487.

Stunkard, A. J., & Sobol, J. (1995). Psychosocial consequences of obesity. In K. D. Brownell & C. G. Fairburn (Eds.), *Eating disorders and obesity. A comprehensive handbook* (pp. 417–421). New York: Guilford Press.

Stunkard, A. J., Sorensen, T. I. A., Hanis, C., Teasdale, T. W., Chakraborty, R., Schull, W. J., & Schulsinger, F. (1986). An adoption study of human obesity. *The New England Journal of Medicine, 314,* 193–198.

Subcommittee on the 10th Edition of the RDAs. (1989). *Recommended dietary allowances* (10th ed.). Washington, DC: National Academy Press.

Sue, S., & Okazaki, S. (1990). Asian-American educational achievements: A phenomenon in search of an explanation. *American Psychologist, 45,* 913–920.

Sullivan, K., Zaitchik, D., & Tager-Flusberg, H. (1994). Preschoolers can attribute second-order beliefs. *Developmental Psychology, 30,* 395–402.

Sulloway, F. (1996). *Born to rebel.* New York: Pantheon Books.

Super, C. M., & Harkness, S. (1982). The infant's niche in rural Kenya and metropolitan America. In L. Adler (Ed.), *Issues in cross-cultural research* (pp. 47–56). New York: Academic Press.

Susman, E. J., Inoff-Germain, G., Nottelmann, E. D., Loriaux, D. L., Cutler, G. B., Jr., & Chrousos, G. P. (1987). Hormones, emotional dispositions, and aggressive attributes in young adolescents. *Child Development, 58,* 1114–1134.

Sutton-Smith, B. (1982). Birth order and sibling status effects. In M. E. Lamb & B. Sutton-Smith (Eds.), *Sibling relationships: Their nature and significance across the lifespan* (pp. 153–165). Hillsdale, NJ: Erlbaum.

Swain, I. U., Zelazo, P. R., & Clifton, R. K. (1993). Newborn infants' memory for speech sounds retained over 24 hours. *Developmental Psychology, 29,* 312–323.

Swayze, V. W., Johnson, V. P., Hanson, J. W., Piven, J., Sato, Y., Geidd, J. N., Mosnik, D., & Andreasen, N. C. (1997). Magnetic resonance imaging of brain anomalies in fetal alcohol syndrome. *Pediatrics, 99,* 232–240.

Swedo, S. E., Rettew, D. C., Kuppenheimer, M., Lum, D., Dolan, S., & Goldberger, E. (1991). Can adolescent suicide attempters be distinguished from at-risk adolescents? *Pediatrics, 88,* 620–629.

Taffel, S. M., Keppel, K. G., & Jones, G. K. (1993). Medical advice on maternal weight gain and actual weight gain. Results from the 1988 National Maternal and Infant Health Survey. *Annals of the New York Academy of Sciences, 678,* 293–305.

Tanner, J. M. (1962). *Growth at adolescence* (2nd ed.). Oxford, England: Blackwell Scientific Publications.

Tanner, J. M. (1978). *Fetus into man. Physical growth from conception to maturity.* Cambridge, MA: Harvard University Press.

Tanner, J. M. (1990). *Foetus into man.* Physical growth from conception to maturity (revised and enlarged ed.). Cambridge, MA: Harvard University Press.

Tanner, J. M., Hughes, P. C. R., & Whitehouse, R. H. (1981). Radiographically determined widths of bone, muscle and fat in the upper arm and calf from 3–18 years. *Annals of Human Biology, 8,* 495–517.

Taylor, E. (1995). Dysfunctions of attention. In D. Cicchetti & D. J. Cohen (Eds.), *Developmental psychopathology.* Vol. 2, *Risk, disorder, and adaptation* (pp. 243–273). New York: Wiley.

Taylor, J. A., & Danderson, M. (1995). A reexamination of the risk factors for the sudden infant death syndrome. *Journal of Pediatrics, 126,* 887–891.

Taylor, J. A., Krieger, J. W., Reay, D. T., Davis, R. L., Harruff, R., & Cheney, L. K. (1996). Prone sleep position and the sudden infant death syndrome in King County, Washington: A case-control study. *Journal of Pediatrics, 128,* 626–630.

Taylor, M., Cartwright, B. S., & Carlson, S. M. (1993). A developmental investigation of children's imaginary companions. *Developmental Psychology, 29,* 276–285.

Taylor, M. G. (1996). The development of children's beliefs about social and biological aspects of gender differences. *Child Development, 67,* 1555–1571.

Taylor, R. D., Casten, R., & Flickinger, S. M. (1993). Influence of kinship social support on the parenting experiences and psychosocial adjustment of African-American adolescents. *Developmental Psychology, 29,* 382–388.

Taylor, R. D., & Roberts, D. (1995). Kinship support and maternal and adolescent well-being in economically disadvantaged African-American families. *Child Development, 66,* 1585–1597.

Terman, L. (1916). *The measurement of intelligence.* Boston: Houghton Mifflin.

Terman, L., & Merrill, M. A. (1937). *Measuring intelligence: A guide to the administration of the new revised Stanford-Binet tests.* Boston: Houghton Mifflin.

Teti, D. M., Gelfand, D. M., Messinger, D. S., & Isabella, R. (1995). Maternal depression and the quality of early attachment: An examination of infants, preschoolers, and their mothers. *Developmental Psychology, 31,* 364–376.

Tew, M. (1985). Place of birth and perinatal mortality. *Journal of the Royal College of General Practitioners, 35,* 390–394.

Thal, D., & Bates, E. (1990). Continuity and variation in early language development. In J. Colombo & J. Fagen (Eds.), *Individual differences in infancy: Reliability, stability, prediction* (pp. 359–385). Hillsdale, NJ: Erlbaum.

Thal, D., Tobias, S., & Morrison, D. (1991). Language and gesture in late talkers: A 1-year follow-up. *Journal of Speech and Hearing Research, 34,* 604–612.

Tharp, R. G., & Gallimore, R. (1988). *Rousing minds to life: Teaching, learning, and schooling in social context.* Cambridge, England: Cambridge University Press.

Thelen, E. (1981). Rhythmical behavior in infancy: An ethological perspective. *Developmental Psychology, 17,* 237–257.

Thelen, E. (1983). Learning to walk is still an "old" problem: A reply to Zelazo. *Journal of Motor Behavior, 15,* 139–161.

Thelen, E. (1989). The (re)discovery of motor development: Learning new things from an old field. *Developmental Psychology, 25,* 946–949.

Thelen, E. (1995). Motor development: A new synthesis. *American Psychologist, 50,* 79–95.

Thelen, E., & Adolph, K. E. (1992). Arnold L. Gesell: The paradox of nature and nurture. *Developmental Psychology, 28,* 368–380.

Thelen, E., & Ulrich, B. D. (1991). Hidden skills: A dynamic systems analysis of treadmill stepping during the first year. *Monographs of the Society for Research in Child Development, 56*(1, Serial No. 223).

Thomas, A., & Chess, S. (1977). *Temperament and development.* New York: Brunner/Mazel.

Thomas, R. M. (1990a). Motor development. In R. M. Thomas (Ed.), *The encyclopedia of human development and education. Theory, research, and studies* (pp. 326–330). Oxford, England: Pergamon Press.

Thomas, R. M. (Ed.). (1990b). *The encyclopedia of human development and education. Theory, research, and studies.* Oxford, England: Pergamon Press.

Thompson, S. K. (1975). Gender labels and early sex role development. *Child Development, 46,* 339–347.

Thorne, B. (1986). Girls and boys together . . . but mostly apart: Gender arrangements in elementary schools. In W. W. Hartup & Z. Rubin (Eds.), *Relationships and development* (pp. 167–184). Hillsdale, NJ: Erlbaum.

Thornton, A. (1990). The courtship process and adolescent sexuality. *Journal of Family Issues, 11,* 239–273.

Timmer, S. G., Eccles, J., & O'Brien, K. (1985). How children use time. In F. T. Juster & F. P. Stafford (Eds.), *Time, goods, and well-being* (pp. 353–369). Ann Arbor: Institute for Social Research, University of Michigan.

Todd, R. D., Swarzenski, B., Rossi, P. G., & Visconti, P. (1995). Structural and functional development of the human brain. In D. Cicchetti & D. J. Cohen (Eds.), *Developmental psychopathology. Vol. 1, Theory and methods* (pp. 161–194). New York: Wiley.

Tomasello, M., & Brooks, P. J. (in press). Early syntactic development: A construction grammar approach. In M. Barrett (Ed.), *The development of language.* London: UCL Press.

Tomasello, M., & Mannle, S. (1985). Pragmatics of sibling speech to one-year-olds. *Child Development, 56,* 911–917.

Tomlinson-Keasey, C., Eisert, D. C., Kahle, L. R., Hardy-Brown, K., & Keasey, B. (1979). The structure of concrete operational thought. *Child Development, 50,* 1153–1163.

Trehub, S. E., & Rabinovitch, M. S. (1972). Auditory-linguistic sensitivity in early infancy. *Developmental Psychology, 6,* 74–77.

Tremblay, R. E., Masse, L. C., Vitaro, F., & Dobkin, P. L. (1995). The impact of friends' deviant behavior on early onset of delinquency: Longitudinal data from 6 to 13 years of age. *Development and Psychopathology, 7,* 649–667.

Troiano, R. P., Flegal, K. M., Kuczmarski, R. J., Campbell, S. M., & Johnson, C. L. (1995). Overweight prevalence and trends for children and adolescents. The National Health and Nutrition Examination Surveys, 1963 to 1991. *Archives of Pediatric and Adolescent Medicine, 149,* 1085–1091.

Tronick, E. Z., Morelli, G. A., & Ivey, P. K. (1992). The Efe forager infant and toddler's pattern of social relationships: Multiple and simultaneous. *Developmental Psychology, 28,* 568–577.

Tschann, J. M., Johnston, J. R., Kline, M., & Wallerstein, J. S. (1989). Family process and children's functioning during divorce. *Journal of Marriage and the Family, 51,* 431–444.

Turiel, E. (1966). An experimental test of the sequentiality of developmental stages in the child's moral judgment. *Journal of Personality and Social Psychology, 3,* 611–618.

Turner, H. A., & Finkelhor, D. (1996). Corporal punishment as a stressor among youth. *Journal of Marriage and the Family, 58,* 155–166.

Udry, J. R., & Campbell, B. C. (1994). Getting started on sexual behavior. In A. S. Rossi (Ed.), *Sexuality across the life course* (pp. 187–208). Chicago: University of Chicago Press.

Umberson, D., & Gove, W. R. (1989). Parenthood and psychological well-being. Theory, measurement, and stage in the family life course. *Journal of Family Issues, 10,* 440–462.

Underwood, M. K., Coie, J. D., & Herbsman, C. R. (1992). Display rules for anger and aggression in school-age children. *Child Development, 63,* 366–380.

Underwood, M. K., Kupersmidt, J. B., & Coie, J. D. (1996). Childhood peer sociometric status and aggression as predictors of adolescent childbearing. *Journal of Research on Adolescence, 6,* 201–224.

Ungerer, J. A., & Sigman, M. (1984). The relation of play and sensorimotor behavior to language in the second year. *Child Development, 55,* 1448–1455.

Upchurch, D. M. (1993). Early schooling and childbearing experiences: Implications for post-secondary school attendance. *Journal of Research on Adolescence, 3,* 423–443.

Urban, J., Carlson, E., Egeland, B., & Sroufe, L. A. (1991). Patterns of individual adaptation across childhood. *Development and Psychopathology, 3,* 445–460.

Urberg, K. A., Degirmencioglu, S. M., Tolson, J. M., & Halliday-Scher, K. (1995). The structure of adolescent peer networks. *Developmental Psychology, 31,* 540–547.

U.S. Bureau of the Census. (1994). *Statistical abstract of the United States: 1994* (114th ed.). Washington, DC: U.S. Government Printing Office.

U.S. Bureau of the Census. (1995). *Statistical abstract of the United States: 1995* (115th ed.). Washington, DC: U.S. Government Printing Office.

U.S. Bureau of the Census. (1996). *Statistical abstract of the United States: 1996* (116th ed.). Washington, DC: U.S. Government Printing Office.

Valdez-Menchaca, M. C., & Whitehurst, G. J. (1992). Accelerating language development through picture book reading: A systematic extension to Mexican day care. *Developmental Psychology, 28,* 1106–1114.

Van de Perre, P., Simonen, A., Msellati, P., Hitimana, D., Vaira, D., Bazebagira, A., Van Goethem, C., Stevens, A., Karita, E., Sondag-Thull, D., Dabis, F., & Lepage, P. (1991). Postnatal transmission of human immunodeficiency virus type 1 from mother to infant. *The New England Journal of Medicine, 325,* 593–598.

Van de Walle, G. A., & Spelke, E. S. (1996). Spatiotemporal integration and object perception in infancy: Perceiving unity versus form. *Child Development, 67,* 2621–2640.

van den Boom, D. C. (1994). The influence of temperament and mothering on attachment and exploration: An experimental manipulation of sensitive responsiveness among lower-class mothers with irritable infants. *Child Development, 65,* 1457–1477.

van den Boom, D. C. (1995). Do first-year intervention effects endure? Follow-up during toddlerhood of a sample of Dutch irritable infants. *Child Development, 66,* 1798–1816.

van IJzendoorn, M. H. (1995). Adult attachment representations, parental responsiveness, and infant attachment: A meta-analysis on the predictive validity of the Adult Attachment Interview. *Psychological Bulletin, 117,* 387–403.

van IJzendoorn, M. H., & Kroonenberg, P. M. (1988). Cross-cultural patterns of attachment: A meta-analysis of the Strange Situation. *Child Development, 59,* 147–156.

van Lieshout, C. F. M., & Haselager, G. J. T. (1994). The big five personality factors in Q-sort descriptions of children and adolescents. In C. F. Halverson Jr., G. A. Kohnstamm, & R. P. Martin (Eds.), *The developing structure of temperament and personality from infancy to adulthood* (pp. 293–318). Hillsdale, NJ: Erlbaum.

van Wel, F. (1994). "I count my parents among my best friends": Youths' bonds with parents and friends in the Netherlands. *Journal of Marriage and the Family, 56,* 835–843.

Vaughn, S., & Schumm, J. S. (1995). Responsible inclusion for students with learning disabilities. *Journal of Learning Disabilities, 28,* 264–270.

Vernon, P. A. (1993). Intelligence and neural efficiency. In D. K. Detterman (Ed.), *Current topics in human intelligence.* Vol. 3, *Individual differences and cognition* (pp. 171–187). Horwood, NJ: Ablex.

Vernon, P. A. (Ed.). (1987). *Speed of information-processing and intelligence.* Norwood, NJ: Ablex.

Vernon, P. A., & Mori, M. (1992). Intelligence, reaction times, and peripheral nerve conduction velocity. *Intelligence, 16,* 273–288.

Vernon-Feagans, L., Manlove, E. E., & Volling, B. L. (1996). Otitis media and the social behavior of day-care-attending children. *Child Development, 67,* 1528–1539.

Victorian Infant Collaborative Study Group. (1991). Eight-year outcome in infants with birth weight of 500–999 grams: Continuing regional study of 1979 and 1980 births. *Journal of Pediatrics, 118,* 761–767.

Vihko, R., & Apter, D. (1980). The role of androgens in adolescent cycles. *Journal of Steroid Biochemistry, 12,* 369–373.

Viinamäki, H., Rastas, S., Tukeva, L., Kuha, S., Niskanen, L., & Saarikoski, S. (1994). Postpartum mental health. *Journal of Psychosomatic Obstetrics and Gynecology, 15,* 141–146.

Vinden, P. G. (1996). Junín Quechua children's understanding of mind. *Child Development, 67,* 1686–1706.

Vorhees, C. F., & Mollnow, E. (1987). Behavioral teratogenesis: Long-term influences on behavior from early exposure to environmental agents. In J. D. Osofsky (Ed.), *Handbook of infant development* (2nd ed.) (pp. 913–971). New York: Wiley-Interscience.

Voyer, D., Voyer, S., & Bryden, M. P. (1995). Magnitude of sex differences in spatial abilities: A meta-analysis and consideration of critical variables. *Psychological Bulletin, 117,* 250–270.

Vuchinich, S., Bank, L., & Patterson, G. R. (1992). Parenting, peers, and the stability of antisocial behavior in preadolescent boys. *Developmental Psychology, 28,* 510–521.

Vygotsky, L. S. (1962). *Thought and language.* New York: Wiley.

Vygotsky, L. S. (1978). *Mind and society: The development of higher mental processes.* Cambridge, MA: Harvard University Press. (Original works published 1930, 1933, and 1935)

Wachs, T. D., Bishry, Z., Sobhy, A., McCabe, G., Galal, O., & Shaheen, F. (1993). Relation of rearing environment to adaptive behavior of Egyptian toddlers. *Child Development, 64,* 586–604.

Wachs, T. D., & Sigman, M. (1995, April). *Chronic mild undernutrition and children's development in Egypt and Kenya.* Paper presented at the biennial meetings of the Society for Research in Child Development, Indianapolis.

Wagner, B. M. (1997). Family risk factors for child and adolescent suicidal behavior. *Psychological Bulletin, 121,* 246–298.

Wahlström, J. (1990). Gene map of mental retardation. *Journal of Mental Deficiency Research, 34,* 11–27.

Wald, N. J., Cuckle, H. S., Densem, J. W., Nanchahal, K., Royston, P., Chard, T., Haddow, J. E., Knight, G. J., Palomaki, G. E., & Canick, J. A. (1988). Maternal serum screening for Down's syndrome in early pregnancy. *British Medical Journal, 297,* 883–887.

Walden, T. A. (1991). Infant social referencing. In J. Garber & K. A. Dodge (Eds.), *The development of emotion regulation and dysregulation* (pp. 69–88). Cambridge, England: Cambridge University Press.

Waldrop, M. F., & Halverson, C. F. (1975). Intensive and extensive peer behavior: Longitudinal and cross-sectional analysis. *Child Development, 46,* 19–26.

Walker, H., Messinger, D., Fogel, A., & Karns, J. (1992). Social and communicative development in infancy. In V. B. Van Hasselt & M. Hersen (Eds.), *Handbook of social development. A lifespan perspective* (pp. 157–181). New York: Plenum Press.

Walker, L. J. (1980). Cognitive and perspective-taking prerequisites for moral development. *Child Development, 51,* 131–139.

Walker, L. J. (1989). A longitudinal study of moral reasoning. *Child Development, 60,* 157–160.

Walker, L. J., de Vries, B., & Trevethan, S. D. (1987). Moral stages and moral orientations in real-life and hypothetical dilemmas. *Child Development, 58,* 842–858.

Walker-Andrews, A. S., & Lennon, E. (1991). Infants' discrimination of vocal expressions: Contributions of auditory and visual information. *Infant Behavior and Development, 14,* 131–142.

Walton, G. E., Bower, N. J. A., & Bower, T. G. R. (1992). Recognition of familiar faces by newborns. *Infant Behavior and Development, 15,* 265–269.

Ward, S. L., & Overton, W. F. (1990). Semantic familiarity, relevance, and the development of deductive reasoning. *Developmental Psychology, 26,* 488–493.

Wartner, U. B., Grossman, K., Fremmer-Bombik, E., & Suess, G. (1994). Attachment patterns at age six in south Germany: Predictability from infancy and implications for preschool behavior. *Child Development, 65,* 1014–1027.

Waterman, A. S. (1985). Identity in the context of adolescent psychology. *New Directions for Child Development, 30,* 5–24.

Waterman, A. S. (1988). Identity status theory and Erikson's theory: Communalities and differences. *Developmental Review, 8,* 185–208.

Waterman, A. S. (1992). Identity as an aspect of optimal psychological functioning. In G. R. Adams, T. P. Gullotta, & R. Montemayor (Eds.), *Adolescent identity formation* (pp. 50–72). Newbury Park, CA: Sage.

Waters, E., Treboux, D., Crowell, J., Merrick, S., & Albersheim, L. (1995, April). *From the Strange Situation to the Adult Attachment Interview: A 20-year longitudinal study of attachment security in infancy and early adulthood.* Paper presented at the biennial meetings of the Society for Research in Child Development, Indianapolis.

Waxman, S. R., & Kosowski, T. D. (1990). Nouns mark category relations: Toddlers' and preschoolers' word-learning biases. *Child Development, 61,* 1461–1473.

Webber, L. S., Wattigney, W. A., Srinivasan, S. R., & Berenson, G. S. (1995). Obesity studies in Bogalusa. *American Journal of Medical Science, 310,* S53–S61.

Webster, M. L., Thompson, J. M., Mitchell, E. A., & Werry, J. S. (1994). Postnatal depression in a community cohort. *Australian & New Zealand Journal of Psychiatry, 28,* 42–49.

Webster-Stratton, C. (1988). Mothers' and fathers' perceptions of child deviance: Roles of parent and child adjustment and child deviance. *Journal of Consulting and Clinical Psychology, 56,* 909–915.

Wechsler, D. (1939). *The measurement of adult intelligence.* Baltimore: Williams & Wilkins.

Wechsler, D. (1974). *Manual for the Wechsler Intelligence Scale for Children–Revised.* New York: Psychological Corp.

Wegman, M. E. (1996). Infant mortality: Some international comparisons. *Pediatrics, 98,* 1020–1027.

Weinberg, R. A. (1989). Intelligence and IQ: Landmark issues and great debates. *American Psychologist, 44,* 98–104.

Weinberg, R. A., Scarr, S., & Waldman, I. D. (1992). The Minnesota transracial adoption study: A follow-up of IQ test performance. *Intelligence, 16,* 117–135.

Weisner, T. S. (1984). Ecocultural niches of middle childhood: A cross-cultural perspective. In W. A. Collins (Ed.), *Development during middle childhood. The years from six to twelve* (pp. 335–369). Washington, DC: National Academy Press.

Weiss, L. H., & Schwarz, J. C. (1996). The relationship between parenting types and older adolescents' personality, academic achievement, adjustment, and substance use. *Child Development, 67,* 2101–2114.

Weiss, M. R., & Hayashi, C. T. (1996). The United States. In P. De Knop, L. Engström, B. Skirstad, & M. R. Weiss (Eds.), *Worldwide trends in youth sport* (pp. 43–57). Champaign, IL: Human Kinetics.

Weitzman, M., Gortmaker, S., & Sobol, A. (1990). Racial, social, and environmental risks for childhood asthma. *American Journal of Diseases of Children, 144,* 1189–1194.

Wellman, H. M. (1982). The foundations of knowledge: Concept development in the young child. In S. G. Moore & C. C. Cooper (Eds.), *The young child. Reviews of research* (Vol. 3) (pp. 115–134). Washington, DC: National Association for the Education of Young Children.

Wentzel, K. R., & Asher, S. R. (1995). The academic lives of neglected, rejected, popular, and controversial children. *Child Development, 66,* 754–763.

Werker, J. F., & Desjardins, R. N. (1995). Listening to speech in the 1st year of life: Experiential influences on phoneme perception. *Current Directions in Psychological Science, 4,* 76–81.

Werker, J. F., Pegg, J. E., & McLeod, P. J. (1994). A cross-language investigation of infant preference for infant-directed communication. *Infant Behavior and Development, 17,* 323–333.

Werker, J. F., & Tees, R. C. (1984). Cross-language speech perception: Evidence for perceptual reorganization during the first year of life. *Infant Behavior and Development, 7,* 49–63.

Werler, M. M., Louik, C., Shapiro, S., & Mitchell, A. A. (1996). Prepregnant weight in relation to risk of neural tube defects. *Journal of the American Medical Association, 275,* 1089–1092.

Werner, E. E. (1986). A longitudinal study of perinatal risk. In D. C. Farran & J. D. McKinney (Eds.), *Risk in intellectual and psychosocial development* (pp. 3–28). Orlando, FL: Academic Press.

Werner, E. E. (1993). Risk, resilience, and recovery: Perspectives from the Kauai Longitudinal Study. *Development and Psychopathology, 5,* 503–515.

Werner, E. E. (1995). Resilience in development. *Current Directions in Psychological Science, 4,* 81–85.

Werner, E. E., & Smith, R. S. (1992). *Overcoming the odds. High risk children from birth to adulthood.* Ithaca, NY: Cornell University Press.

Werner, L. A., & Gillenwater, J. M. (1990). Pure-tone sensitivity of 2- to 5-week-old infants. *Infant Behavior and Development, 13,* 355–375.

Wesch, D., & Lutzker, J. R. (1991). A comprehensive 5-year plan for evaluating Project 12-Ways: An ecobehavioral approach for treating and preventing child abuse and neglect. *Journal of Family Violence, 6,* 17–35.

Whitam, F. L., Diamond, M., & Martin, J. (1993). Homosexual orientation in twins: A report on 61 pairs and three triplet sets. *Archives of Sexual Behavior, 22,* 187–206.

White, K. S., Bruce, S. E., Farrell, A. D., & Kliewer, W. L. (1997, April). *Impact of exposure to community violence on anxiety among urban adolescents: Family social support as a protective factor.* Paper presented at the biennial meetings of the Society for Research in Child Development, Washington, DC.

Whitehurst, G. J. (1995, April). *Levels of reading readiness and predictors of reading success among children from low-income families.* Paper presented at the biennial meetings of the Society for Research in Child Development, Indianapolis.

Whitehurst, G. J., Arnold, D. S., Epstein, J. N., Angell, A. L., Smith, M., & Fischel, J. E. (1994). A picture book reading intervention in day care and home for children from low-income families. *Developmental Psychology, 30,* 679–689.

Whitehurst, G. J., Falco, F. L., Lonigan, C. J., Fischel, J. E., DeBaryshe, B. D., Valdez-Menchaca, M. C., & Caulfield, M. (1988). Accelerating language development through picture book reading. *Developmental Psychology, 24,* 552–559.

Whitehurst, G. J., Fischel, J. E., Crone, D. A., & Nania, O. (1995, April). *First year outcomes of a clinical trial of an emergent literacy intervention in Head Start homes and classrooms.* Paper presented at the biennial meetings of the Society for Research in Child Development, Indianapolis.

Whiting, B. B., & Edwards, C. P. (1988). *Children of different worlds: The formation of social behavior.* Cambridge, MA: Harvard University Press.

Whitney, M. P., & Thoman, E. B. (1994). Sleep in premature and fullterm infants from 24-hour home recordings. *Infant Behavior and Development, 17,* 223–234.

Wiesenfeld, A. R., Malatesta, C. Z., & DeLoach, L. L. (1981). Differential parental response to familiar and unfamiliar infant distress signals. *Infant Behavior and Development, 4,* 281–296.

Wigfield, A., Eccles, J. S., Mac Iver, D., Reuman, D. A., & Midgley, C. (1991). Transitions during early adolescence: Changes in children's domain-specific self-perceptions and general self-esteem across the transition to junior high school. *Developmental Psychology, 27,* 552–565.

Wilcox, A. J., Baird, D. D., Weinberg, C. R., Hornsby, P. P., & Herbst, A. L. (1995). Fertility in men exposed prenatally to diethylstilbestrol. *The New England Journal of Medicine, 332,* 1411–1416.

Wilcox, A. J., Weinberg, C. R., O'Connor, J. F., Baird, D. D., Schlatterer, J. P., Canfield, R. E., Armstrong, E. G., & Nisula, B. C. (1988). Incidence of early loss of pregnancy. *The New England Journal of Medicine, 319,* 189–194.

Wilfley, D. E., & Rodin, J. (1995). Cultural influences on eating disorders. In K. D. Brownell & C. G. Fairburn (Eds.), *Eating disorders and obesity: A comprehensive handbook* (pp. 78–82). New York: Guilford Press.

Wille, S. (1994). Primary nocturnal enuresis in children. *Scandinavian Journal of Urology and Nephrology, 156*(Supplement 156), 6–23.

Williams, J. E., & Best, D. L. (1990). *Measuring sex stereotypes. A multination study* (rev. ed.). Newbury Park, CA: Sage.

Willinger, M., Hoffman, H. J., & Hartford, R. B. (1994). Infant sleep position and risk for sudden infant death syndrome: Report of meeting held January 13 and 14, 1994, National Institutes of Health, Bethesda, MD. *Pediatrics, 93,* 814–819.

Wills, T. A., Blechman, E. A., & McNamara, G. (1996). Family support, coping, and competence. In E. M. Hetherington & E. A. Blechman (Eds.), *Stress, coping, and resilience in children and families* (pp. 107–133). Mahwah, NJ: Erlbaum.

Wills, T. A., & Cleary, S. D. (1997). The validity of self-reports of smoking: Analyses by race/ethnicity in a school sample of urban adolescents. *American Journal of Public Health, 87,* 56–61.

Wilson, W. J. (1995). Jobless ghettos and the social outcome of youngsters. In P. Moen, G. H. Elder Jr., & K. Lüscher (Eds.), *Examining lives in context. Perspectives on the ecology of human development* (pp. 527–543). Washington, DC: American Psychological Association.

Winfield, L. F. (1995). The knowledge base on resilience in African-American adolescents. In L. J. Crockett & A. C. Crouter (Eds.), *Pathways through adolescence* (pp. 87–118). Mahwah, NJ: Erlbaum.

Wolke, D., Gray, P., & Meyer, R. (1994). Excessive infant crying: A controlled study of mothers helping mothers. *Pediatrics, 94,* 322–332.

Wood, D. J., Bruner, J. S., & Ross, G. (1976). The role of tutoring in problem solving. *Journal of Child Psychology and Psychiatry, 17,* 89–100.

World Health Organization. (1982). The prevalence and duration of breastfeeding: A critical review of available information. *World Health Statistics Quarterly, 35,* 92–112.

World Health Organization. (1994). Expanded Programme on Immunization, Global Advisory Group—Part 1. *Weekly Epidemiological Record, 69*(January 28), 21–28.

Wren, C. S. (1996, December 20). Adolescent drug use rose in latest survey from 1995. *New York Times,* p. A8.

Wright, L. (1995, August 7). Double mystery. *The New Yorker,* pp. 45–62.

Wright, P. F. (1995). Global immunization—A medical perspective. *Social Science and Medicine, 41,* 609–616.

Yang, B., Ollendick, T. H., Dong, Q., Xia, Y., & Lin, L. (1995). Only children and children with siblings in the People's Republic of China: Levels of fear, anxiety, and depression. *Child Development, 66,* 1301–1311.

Yonas, A., & Owsley, C. (1987). Development of visual space perception. In P. Salapatek & L. Cohen (Eds.), *Handbook of infant perception*. Vol. 2, *From perception to cognition* (pp. 80–122). Orlando, FL: Academic Press.

Zahn-Waxler, C., & Radke-Yarrow, M. (1982). The development of altruism: Alternative research strategies. In N. Eisenberg (Ed.), *The development of prosocial behavior* (pp. 109–138). New York: Academic Press.

Zahn-Waxler, C., Radke-Yarrow, M., Wagner, E., & Chapman, M. (1992). Development of concern for others. *Developmental Psychology, 28*, 126–136.

Zametkin, A. J., Nordahl, T. E., Gross, M., King, A. C., Semple, W. E., Rumsey, J., Hamburger, S., & Cohen, R. M. (1990). Cerebral glucose metabolism in adults with hyperactivity of childhood onset. *The New England Journal of Medicine, 323*, 1361–1366.

Zani, B. (1993). Dating and interpersonal relationships in adolescence. In S. Jackson & H. Rodrigues-Tomé (Eds.), *Adolescence and its social worlds* (pp. 95–119). Hove, England: Erlbaum.

Zaslow, M. J., & Hayes, C. D. (1986). Sex differences in children's responses to psychosocial stress: Toward a cross-context analysis. In M. E. Lamb, A. L. Brown, & B. Rogoff (Eds.), *Advances in developmental psychology* (Vol. 4) (pp. 285–338). Hillsdale, NJ: Erlbaum.

Zelazo, N. A., Zelazo, P. R., Cohen, K. M., & Zelazo, P. D. (1993). Specificity of practice effects on elementary neuromotor patterns. *Developmental Psychology, 29*, 686–691.

Zelazo, P. R., Zelazo, N. A., & Kolb, S. (1972). "Walking" in the newborn. *Science, 176*, 314–315.

Zigler, E. F., & Gilman, E. (1996). Not just any care: Shaping a coherent child care policy. In E. F. Zigler, S. L. Kagan, & N. W. Hall (Eds.), *Children, families, and government. Preparing for the twenty-first century* (pp. 95–116). Cambridge England: Cambridge University Press.

Zigler, E., & Hodapp, R. M. (1991). Behavioral functioning in individuals with mental retardation. *Annual Review of Psychology, 42*, 29–50.

Zigler, E., & Styfco, S. J. (1993). Using research and theory to justify and inform Head Start expansion. *Social Policy Report, Society for Research in Child Development, VII*(2), 1–21.

Zigler, E. F., & Styfco, S. (1996). Head Start and early childhood intervention: The changing course of social science and social policy. In E. F. Zigler, S. L. Kagan, & N. W. Hall (Eds.), *Children, families, and government* (pp. 132–154). Cambridge, England: Cambridge University Press.

Zill, N., Moore, K. A., Smith, E. W., Stief, T., & Coiro, M. J. (1995). The life circumstances and development of children in welfare families: A profile based on national survey data. In P. L. Chase-Lansdale & J. Brooks-Gunn (Eds.), *Escape from poverty. What makes a difference for children?* (pp. 39–59). Cambridge, England: Cambridge University Press.

Zill, N., & Nord, C. W. (1994). *Running in place: How American families are faring in a changing economy and an individualistic society.* Washington, DC: Child Trends.

Zimmerman, M. A., Copeland, L. A., Shope, J. T., & Dielman, T. E. (in press). A longitudinal study of self-esteem: Implications for adolescent development. *Journal of Youth and Adolescence.*

Zimmerman, M. A., Salem, D. A., & Maton, K. I. (1995). Family structure and psychosocial correlates among urban African-American adolescent males. *Child Development, 66*, 1598–1613.

Zlotkin, S. H. (1996). A review of the Canadian "Nutrition recommendations update: Dietary fat and children." *Journal of Nutrition, 126*, 1022S–1027S.

Zoccolillo, M. (1993). Gender and the development of conduct disorder. *Development and Psychopathology, 5*, 65–78.

Photo Credits

Unless otherwise acknowledged, all photographs are the property of Addison Wesley Educational Publishers, Inc.

Name Index

Subject Index

Note: Page numbers in *italics* indicate material in boxes.

conduct disorder, 399–401
delinquency, 502–505
depression, 501–502
emotional. *See* Emotional problems
learning disabilities, 349–351
mental retardation, 273–274
and resilience, 20–22
vulnerability to, 20–21
Spina bifida, and prenatal folic acid
intake, 94
Sports
choosing sport for child, *344*
participation and health, 342–343
sports injuries, 338–339
Stanford-Binet test, 273
States of consciousness, infants, 119, *120*
Stepfamilies, and adolescents, 493–494
Stereotypes
gender, 304–305
and obesity, 333–334
Steroids, teen use of, 448–449
Stranger anxiety, 188–189
Strange Situation, 31, 190–191
Stress
and asthma attack, 232
and child abuse, 241
and depression, 502
and eating disorders, 447
maternal, and prenatal development, 98
and poverty, 410–411
and preschooler's health, 234–235
and thumb-sucking, 240
Structured immersion, 375
Subcultures, ethnic, 18
Subjects, of research studies, 30–31
Submersion, 375
Sudden infant death syndrome (SIDS), 139
factors related to, 138
Suicide
adolescents, *440–441*
contributing factors, *440*
prevention of, *440–441*
Superego, 42
Superobese, 332
Symbols, preoperational stage, 262–263,
324
Synapse, 82
Synchrony, in attachment development,
185–186
Syphilis, 442
Systematic searching, memory strategy,
364

Tabula rasa concept, 8
Taste, newborn response to, 155
Tay-Sachs disease, 87
Teachers, expectations and achievement,
5, 376–377
Teenage pregnancy, 437–439
future outlook for mothers/children,
438–439
rate of, 438
risk factors, *438*

Teeth
routine of regular care, 238
teething, 129–130
and thumb-sucking, 237, 240
Telegraphic speech, 252–253
Television viewing, 411–416
and aggression, 412–416
and cognitive skills, 412
family viewing patterns, *412*
and obesity, 335–336
positive effects, 411–412
Temperament, 60–62, 198–201
biological basis of, 60–62
consistency over time, 200
dimensions of, 198–199
environmental influences, 200–201
genetic influences, 11
infancy, 198–201
and later problems, 309
meaning of, 198
preschoolers, 309–310
and vulnerability, 309–310
Teratogens, 86–97
AIDS, 87, 89
alcohol use, 91–92
aspirin, 96
cigarette smoking, 91
cocaine, 92
common drugs, 94–95
cytomegalovirus, 89–91
diethylstilbestrol (DES), 96
lead, 96–97
meaning of, 14
rubella, 87
Vitamin A, 96
Terrible twos, 197, 292–293, 491
Tertiary circular reactions, 148, *149*
Testis-determining factor (TDF), 76
Testosterone, 426, 427
and prenatal development of males,
99–100
Texas Adoption Project, 12
Theory of mind, 324
assessment of, *269*
development of, 266–268
Thumb-sucking, 237, 240
breaking habit, 237, 240
problems related to, 237
and stress, 240
Thyroid hormone, 426, 427
Time-lag research design, 26
Toddlers
and day care, 201–207
friendship, 299–300
play, 296
self, sense of, 197–198
terrible twos, 197, 292–293
Tonic neck reflex, 116
Touch, infant sense of, 155–156
Tracking, visual, 154
Transitional objects, and sleep, 224
Triarchic theory, intelligence, *280*
Turner's syndrome, 85, 330

Twins
conception of, 79
dizygotic/monozygotic, 79
Twin studies
example of, 12
intelligence, 278
language development, 272–273
purpose of, 11
temperament, 61

Ultrasound, genetic testing, 88
Umbilical cord, 80
Unconditional stimulus (UCS), 54
Unconditioned responses (UCR), 54
Undifferentiated, sex-role type, 483
Upper respiratory infections, infants, 136
Uterus, 74

Vegetarian diet, and children, 239
Venereal disease. *See* Sexually transmit-
ted disease
Vertical relationships, 290
Very low birth weight infants, 105
Victims, characteristics of, *399*
Visual acuity, meaning of, 154
Visual cliff, depth perception research,
156–157
Visual development, 154–155, 156–161
color vision, 154–155
depth perception, 156–157
early visual strategies, 158–159
face discrimination, 157–160
pattern recognition, 160–161
Visual tracking, meaning of, 154
Vitamin A, and prenatal development, 96
Vitamins, RDAs for children, 237
Vocabulary learning. *See* Language development
Vulnerability
elements of, 21
versus resilience, 20–22, 65
and temperament, 309–310
Vygotsky's theory, 51–52, 271
classroom application of, 52, *363*
contributions of, 53–54
new learning in, 52
zone of proximal development, 52
Walking reflex, 115, 116
Wechsler Intelligence Scales for Children
(WISC-III), 275
Weight
adolescents, 427–428
obesity, 332–336
school-age children, 328
Word meaning, learning of, 254–257
Work, 475–478
pros/cons for adolescents, 476–478

X chromosomes, 75–76, 78

Y chromosomes, 75–76, 78

Zone of proximal development, 52